140.⁰⁰

Twentieth-Century Literary Criticism

Topics Volume

Guide to Gale Literary Criticism Series

For criticism on	Consult these Gale series
Authors now living or who died after December 31, 1959	*CONTEMPORARY LITERARY CRITICISM (CLC)*
Authors who died between 1900 and 1959	*TWENTIETH-CENTURY LITERARY CRITICISM (TCLC)*
Authors who died between 1800 and 1899	*NINETEENTH-CENTURY LITERATURE CRITICISM (NCLC)*
Authors who died between 1400 and 1799	*LITERATURE CRITICISM FROM 1400 TO 1800 (LC)* *SHAKESPEAREAN CRITICISM (SC)*
Authors who died before 1400	*CLASSICAL AND MEDIEVAL LITERATURE CRITICISM (CMLC)*
Black writers of the past two hundred years	*BLACK LITERATURE CRITICISM (BLC)*
Authors of books for children and young adults	*CHILDREN'S LITERATURE REVIEW (CLR)*
Dramatists	*DRAMA CRITICISM (DC)*
Hispanic writers of the late nineteenth and twentieth centuries	*HISPANIC LITERATURE CRITICISM (HLC)*
Native North American writers and orators of the eighteenth, nineteenth, and twentieth centuries	*NATIVE NORTH AMERICAN LITERATURE (NNAL)*
Poets	*POETRY CRITICISM (PC)*
Short story writers	*SHORT STORY CRITICISM (SSC)*
Major authors from the Renaissance to the present	*WORLD LITERATURE CRITICISM, 1500 TO THE PRESENT (WLC)*

ISSN 0276-8178

Volume 70

Twentieth-Century Literary Criticism

Topics Volume

Excerpts from Criticism of Various Topics in Twentieth-Century Literature, including Literary and Critical Movements, Prominent Themes and Genres, Anniversary Celebrations, and Surveys of National Literatures

Scot Peacock
Jennifer Gariepy
Editors

Thomas Ligotti
Associate Editor

GALE

DETROIT · NEW YORK · TORONTO · LONDON

STAFF

Jennifer Gariepy, Scot Peacock, *Editors*

Thomas Ligotti, *Associate Editor*

Susan Trosky, *Permissions Manager*
Kimberly F. Smilay, *Permissions Specialist*
Sarah A. Chesney, *Permissions Associate*
Steve Cusack, Kelly A. Quin, *Permissions Assistants*

Victoria B. Cariappa, *Research Manager*
Michele P. LaMeau, Andrew Guy Malonis, Barbara McNeil, Gary J. Oudersluys, Maureen Richards, *Research Specialists*
Julia C. Daniel, Tamara C. Nott, Tracie A. Richardson, Norma Sawaya, Cheryl L. Warnock, *Research Associates*

Mary Beth Trimper, *Production Director*
Deborah L. Milliken, *Production Assistant*

Gary Leach, *Desktop Publisher*
Randy Bassett, *Image Database Supervisor*
Robert Duncan, Michael Logusz, *Imaging Specialists*
Pamela Reed, *Photography Coordinator*

Library of Congress Catalog Card Number 76-46132
ISBN 0-7876-1170-0
ISSN 0276-8178

Printed in the United States of America
10 9 8 7 6 5 4 3 2 1

Contents

Preface   vii

Acknowledgments   xi

Preface

Since its inception more than fifteen years ago, *Twentieth-Century Literary Criticism* has been purchased and used by nearly 10,000 school, public, and college or university libraries. *TCLC* has covered more than 500 authors, representing 58 nationalities, and over 25,000 titles. No other reference source has surveyed the critical response to twentieth-century authors and literature as thoroughly as *TCLC*. In the words of one reviewer, "there is nothing comparable available." *TCLC* "is a gold mine of information—dates, pseudonyms, biographical information, and criticism from books and periodicals—which many libraries would have difficulty assembling on their own."

Scope of the Series

TCLC is designed to serve as an introduction to authors who died between 1900 and 1960 and to the most significant interpretations of these author's works. The great poets, novelists, short story writers, playwrights, and philosophers of this period are frequently studied in high school and college literature courses. In organizing and excerpting the vast amount of critical material written on these authors, *TCLC* helps students develop valuable insight into literary history, promotes a better understanding of the texts, and sparks ideas for papers and assignments. Each entry in *TCLC* presents a comprehensive survey of an author's career or an individual work of literature and provides the user with a multiplicity of interpretations and assessments. Such variety allows students to pursue their own interests; furthermore, it fosters an awareness that literature is dynamic and responsive to many different opinions.

Every fourth volume of *TCLC* is devoted to literary topics. These topic entries widen the focus of the series from individual authors to such broader subjects as literary movements, prominent themes in twentieth-century literature, literary reaction to political and historical events, significant eras in literary history, prominent literary anniversaries, and the literatures of cultures that are often overlooked by English-speaking readers.

TCLC is designed as a companion series to Gale's *Contemporary Literary Criticism,* which reprints commentary on authors now living or who have died since 1960. Because of the different periods under consideration, there is no duplication of material between *CLC* and *TCLC*. For additional information about *CLC* and Gale's other criticism titles, users should consult the Guide to Gale Literary Criticism Series preceding the title page in this volume.

Coverage

Each volume of *TCLC* is carefully compiled to present:

- criticism of authors, or literary topics, representing a variety of genres and nationalities

- both major and lesser-known writers and literary works of the period

- 6-12 authors or 3-6 topics per volume

- individual entries that survey critical response to each author's work or each topic in literary history, including early criticism to reflect initial reactions; later criticism to represent any rise or decline in reputation; and current retrospective analyses.

Organization of This Book

An author entry consists of the following elements: author heading, biographical and critical introduction, list of principal works, excerpts of criticism (each preceded by an annotation and a bibliographic citation), and a bibliography of further reading.

- The **Author Heading** consists of the name under which the author most commonly wrote, followed by birth and death dates. If an author wrote consistently under a pseudonym, the pseudonym will be listed in the author heading and the real name given in parentheses on the first line of the biographical and critical introduction. Also located at the beginning of the introduction to the author entry are any name variations under which an author wrote, including transliterated forms for authors whose languages use nonroman alphabets.

- The **Biographical and Critical Introduction** outlines the author's life and career, as well as the critical issues surrounding his or her work. References to past volumes of *TCLC* are provided at the beginning of the introduction. Additional sources of information in other biographical and critical reference series published by Gale, including *Short Story Criticism, Children's Literature Review, Contemporary Authors, Dictionary of Literary Biography,* and *Something about the Author,* are listed in a box at the end of the entry.

- Some *TCLC* entries include **Portraits** of the author. Entries also may contain reproductions of materials pertinent to an author's career, including manuscript pages, title pages, dust jackets, letters, and drawings, as well as photographs of important people, places, and events in an author's life.

- The **List of Principal Works** is chronological by date of first book publication and identifies the genre of each work. In the case of foreign authors with both foreign-language publications and English translations, the title and date of the first English-language edition are given in brackets. Unless otherwise indicated, dramas are dated by first performance, not first publication.

- Critical excerpts are prefaced by **Annotations** providing the reader with information about both the critic and the criticism that follows. Included are the critic's reputation, individual approach to literary criticism, and particular expertise in an author's works. Also noted are the relative importance of a work of criticism, the scope of the excerpt, and the growth of critical controversy or changes in critical trends regarding an author. In some cases, these annotations cross-reference excerpts by critics who discuss each other's commentary.

- A complete **Bibliographic Citation** designed to facilitate location of the original essay or book precedes each piece of criticism.

- **Criticism** is arranged chronologically in each author entry to provide a perspective on changes in critical evaluation over the years. All titles of works by the author featured in the entry are printed in boldface type to enable the user to easily locate discussion of particular works. Also for purposes of easier identification, the critic's name and the publication date of the essay are given at the beginning of each piece of criticism. Unsigned criticism is preceded by the title of the journal in which it appeared. Some of the excerpts in *TCLC* also contain translated material. Unless otherwise noted, translations in brackets are by the editors; translations in parentheses or continuous with the text are by the critic. Publication information (such as footnotes or page and line references to specific editions of works) have been deleted at the editor's discretion to provide smoother reading of the text.

- An annotated list of **Further Reading** appearing at the end of each author entry suggests secondary sources on the author. In some cases it includes essays for which the editors could not obtain reprint rights.

Cumulative Indexes

- Each volume of *TCLC* contains a cumulative **Author Index** listing all authors who have appeared in Gale's Literary Criticism Series, along with cross references to such biographical series as *Contemporary Authors* and *Dictionary of Literary Biography*. For readers' convenience, a complete list of Gale titles included appears on the first page of the author index. Useful for locating authors within the various series, this index is particularly valuable for those authors who are identified by a certain period but who, because of their death dates, are placed in another, or for those authors whose careers span two periods. For example, F. Scott Fitzgerald is found in *TCLC*, yet a writer often associated with him, Ernest Hemingway, is found in *CLC*.

- Each *TCLC* volume includes a cumulative **Nationality Index** which lists all authors who have appeared in *TCLC* volumes, arranged alphabetically under their respective nationalities, as well as Topics volume entries devoted to particular national literatures.

- Each new volume in Gale's Literary Criticism Series includes a cumulative **Topic Index**, which lists all literary topics treated in *NCLC, TCLC, LC 1400-1800*, and the *CLC* yearbook.

- Each new volume of *TCLC*, with the exception of the Topics volumes, includes a **Title Index** listing the titles of all literary works discussed in the volume. In response to numerous suggestions from librarians, Gale has also produced a **Special Paperbound Edition** of the *TCLC* title index. This annual cumulation lists all titles discussed in the series since its inception and is issued with the first volume of *TCLC* published each year. Additional copies of the index are available on request. Librarians and patrons will welcome this separate index; it saves shelf space, is easy to use, and is recyclable upon receipt of the following year's cumulation. Titles discussed in the Topics volume entries are not included *TCLC* cumulative index.

Citing *Twentieth-Century Literary Criticism*

When writing papers, students who quote directly from any volume in Gale's literary Criticism Series may use the following general forms to footnote reprinted criticism. The first example pertains to materials drawn from periodicals, the second to material reprinted from books.

[1]William H. Slavick, "Going to School to DuBose Heyward," *The Harlem Renaissance Re-examined*, (AMS Press, 1987); excerpted and reprinted in *Twentieth-Century Literary Criticism*, Vol. 59, ed. Jennifer Gariepy (Detroit: Gale Research, 1995), pp. 94-105.

[2]George Orwell, "Reflections on Gandhi," *Partisan Review*, 6 (Winter 1949), pp. 85-92; excerpted and reprinted in *Twentieth-Century Literary Criticism*, Vol. 59, ed. Jennifer Gariepy (Detroit: Gale Research, 1995), pp. 40-3.

Suggestions Are Welcome

In response to suggestions, several features have been added to *TCLC* since the series began, including annotations to excerpted criticism, a cumulative index to authors in all Gale literary criticism series, entries devoted to criticism on a single work by a major author, more extensive illustrations, and a title index listing all literary works discussed in the series since its inception.

Readers who wish to suggest authors or topics to appear in future volumes, or who have other suggestions, are cordially invited to write the editors.

Acknowledgments

The editors wish to thank the copyright holders of the excerpted criticism included in this volume and the permissions managers of many book and magazine publishing companies for assisting us in securing reproduction rights. We are also grateful to the staffs of the Detroit Public Library, the Library of Congress, the University of Detroit Mercy Library, Wayne State University Purdy/Kresge Library Complex, and the University of Michigan Libraries for making their resources available to us. Following is a list of the copyright holders who have granted us permission to reproduce material in this volume of *TCLC*. Every effort has been made to trace copyright, but if omissions have been made, please let us know.

COPYRIGHTED EXCERPTS IN *TCLC*, VOLUME 70, WERE REPRODUCED FROM THE FOLLOWING PERIODICALS:

The American Poetry Review, v. 19, March-April, 1990, for an interview with Lucien Stryk by Kent Johnson/ v. 4, July-August, 1975, for "Alcohol and Poetry" by Lewis Hyde. Copyright © 1975, 1990 by World Poetry, Inc. Both reproduced by permission of the authors.—*American Quarterly,* v. 39, Spring, 1987. Copyright 1987, American Studies Association. Reproduced by permission of The Johns Hopkins University Press.—*The American Scholar,* v. 57, Spring, 1988. Copyright © 1988 by the United Chapters of the Phi Beta Kappa Society. Reproduced by permission of the publishers.—*The Armchair Detective,* v. 18, Fall, 1985, for "The Longest Goodbye: Raymond Chandler and the Poetry of Alcohol" by J. O. Tate. Copyright © 1985 by The Armchair Detective. Reproduced by permission.—*Black American Literature Forum,* v. 25, Fall, 1991, for "Poetry and Jazz: A Twentieth-Century Wedding" by Barry Wallenstein. Copyright © 1991 Barry Wallenstein. Reprinted by permission of the author.—*boundary 2,* v. 2, Spring, 1974. Copyright © boundary 2, 1974. Reproduced by permission.—*Commentary,* v. 61, March, 1976, for "The Giant Killer: Drink and the American Writer" by Alfred Kazin. Copyright © 1976 by the American Jewish Committee. All rights reserved. Reproduced by permission of the publisher and the author.—*Critical Inquiry,* v. 11, March, 1985. Copyright © 1985 by The University of Chicago. Reproduced by permission.—*Critique: Studies in Contemporary Fiction,* v. 33, Winter, 1992, v. 35, Summer, 1994. Copyright © 1992, 1994 Helen Dwight Reid Educational Foundation. Reproduced with permission of the Helen Dwight Reid Educational Foundation, published by Heldref Publications, 1319 18th Street, NW, Washington, DC 20036-1802.—*Essays in Criticism,* v. 37, April, 1987, for "Modernism and What Happened to It" by Hugh Kenner. Reproduced by permission of the Editors of Essays in Criticism and the author.—*The Georgia Review,* v. 33, Fall, 1979. Copyright 1979 by the University of Georgia. Reproduced by permission.—*The Harvard Journal of Asiatic Studies,* v. 42, June, 1982, for "Beginning with Images in the Nature Poetry of Wang Wei" by Eva Shan Chou. Reproduced by permission.—*The Hudson Review,* v. 31, Spring, 1978. Copyright © 1978 by The Hudson Review, Inc. Reproduced by permission.—*Ideologies and Literature,* v. 2, Fall, 1987. Reproduced by permission.—*Irish Renaissance Annual,* v. IV, 1983. © 1983 by Associated University Presses, Inc. Reproduced by permission.—*Journal of Modern Literature,* v. 6, April, 1977. © Temple University, 1977. Reproduced by permission.—*Journal of Popular Culture,* v. 23, Winter, 1979; v. XIV, Fall, 1980; v. XXI, Winter, 1987; v. XXVI, Spring, 1993. Copyright 1979, 1980, 1987, 1993 by Ray B. Browne. All reproduced by permission.—*Midamerica XIII,* 1986 for "The Oriental Connection: Zen and Representations of the Midwest in the 'Collected Poems' of Lucien Stryk" by Daniel L. Guillory. Copyright 1986 by the Society for the Study of Midwestern Literature. All rights reserved. Reproduced by permission of the publisher and the author.—*The Midwest Quarterly,* v. XXXI, Summer, 1990. Copyright © 1990 by The Midwest Quarterly, Pittsburg State University. Reproduced by permission.—*Modern Fiction Studies,* v. 12, Autumn, 1966. Copyright © 1966 by Purdue Research Foundation, West Lafayette, IN 47907. All rights reserved. Reproduced by permission of The Johns Hopkins University.—*Mosaic: A Journal for the Comparative Study of Literature and Ideas,* v. XI, Fall, 1977. © Mosaic, 1977. Acknowledgment of previous publication is herewith made.—*North Dakota Quarterly,* v. 41, Autumn, 1973. Copyright 1973 by The University of North Dakota. Reproduced by permission.—*Queen's Quarterly,* v. 87, Winter, 1980, for "From High Decadence to High Modernism" by J. Edward Chamberlin. Copyright © 1980 by the author. Reprinted by permission of the author.—*Twentieth Century Literature,* v. 31, Summer-Fall, 1985. Copyright 1985, Hofstra University Press. Reproduced by permission.

Alcohol and Literature

INTRODUCTION

The prominence of alcoholism in American literature, at least in the first half of the twentieth century, is such that the presence of drink in the lives and writings of F. Scott Fitzgerald, Ernest Hemingway, William Faulkner, Eugene O'Neill, and many others has become a literary cliché

And, despite all of the myths surrounding the alcoholism of so many American writers and its relation to their literary talent, the facts remain that any list of American Nobel prize-winning artists would include more than a few heavy drinkers. Critics, and even the writers themselves, have observed, however, that alcohol, rather than inspiring creativity seems to anesthetize the poetic spirit as it deadens the senses. Still the equivocal qualities of alcohol where not lost on the modernists Fitzgerald and Hemingway, who both romanticized and vilified the substance in such works as *Tender Is the Night* (1934) and *The Sun Also Rises* (1926). The modernist affair with alcohol seems to have reached its culmination in 1947 with the publication of Malcolm Lowry's novel *Under the Volcano*. Begun in the late 1930s, Lowry's work, according to some critics, represents a particularly modernist symbolic statement that equates alcoholism with the sterility and paralysis of modern civilization and the malaise of modern man.

By mid-century, however, ideas about alcohol as reflected in literature seem to have been evolving. Although published three years prior to Lowry's novel, Charles Jackson's popular *The Lost Weekend* (1944) treats alcoholism from a less grandiose perspective, as a disease that afflicts an individual and destroys his life. John Cheever, in his short stories and novels such as *Bullet Park* (1969) and *Falconer* (1977), adopts a more light-hearted approach to alcoholism, reminding us that drink has been a mainstay of comic literature since classical antiquity and at least since the time of Shakespeare and Rabelais. Cheever employs alcohol as a means of satirizing upper-middle class America, in addition to presenting some of its more serious consequences for society. The writings of John Berryman, a notorious alcoholic throughout his career, represent a tragic continuation of the place of alcohol in the poetic mind. His *Dream Songs* (1964) and other poetry are informed by the poetics of alcoholism, a disease that critics observe at once defined his verse and destroyed his life. Berryman's attempts to surmount his problem are documented in his novel *Recovery* (1973) left unfinished at the time of his suicide.

REPRESENTATIVE WORKS

Kingsley Amis
  Lucky Jim (novel) 1953
  Ending Up (novel) 1974
  Jake's Thing (novel) 1978
Saul Bellow
  The Victim (novel) 1947
  Humboldt's Gift (novel) 1975
John Berryman
  The Dream Songs (poetry) 1964
  Berryman's Sonnets (poetry) 1967
  Love and Fame (poetry) 1970
  Delusions, Etc. (poetry) 1972
  Recovery (unfinished novel) 1973
  Henry's Fate & Other Poems, 1967-72 (poetry) 1977
Vicente Blasco Ibáñez
  Flor de mayo (novel) 1896
  La barraca (novel) 1898
  Cañas y barro (novel) 1902
Anne Brontë
  The Tenant of Wildfell Hall (novel) 1848
Raymond Carver
  "Drinking While Driving" (short story) 1983
Raymond Chandler
  The Long Goodbye (novel) 1954
John Cheever
  The Wapshot Scandal (novel) 1965
  Bullet Park (novel) 1969
  Falconer (novel) 1977
  The Stories of John Cheever (short stories) 1978
Anton Chekhov
  Tri sestry [*The Three Sisters*] (drama) 1901
Stephen Crane
  Maggie: A Girl of the Streets (novella) 1893
Charles Dickens
  David Copperfield (novel) 1850
Fyodor Dostoevsky
  Prestuplenye i nakazanye [*Crime and Punishment*] (novel) 1866
William Faulkner
  The Sound and the Fury (novel) 1929
F. Scott Fitzgerald
  The Beautiful and the Damned (novel) 1922
  The Great Gatsby (novel) 1925
  Tender Is the Night (novel) 1934
  "The Crack-Up" [published in *The Crack-Up. With Other Uncollected Pieces, Notebooks and Unpublished Letters*] (essay) 1945
  "An Alcoholic Case" [published in *The Stories of F. Scott Fitzgerald: A Selection of 28 Stories*] (short story) 1951

1

Babylon Revisited and Other Stories (short stories) 1960
The Pat Hobby Stories (short stories) 1962
Maxim Gorki
Na dne [*The Lower Depths*] (drama) 1902
Graham Greene
The Power and the Glory (novel) 1940
Thomas Hardy
Jude the Obscure (novel) 1895
Ernest Hemingway
The Sun Also Rises (novel) 1926
A Moveable Feast (memoir) 1964
Charles Jackson
The Lost Weekend (novel) 1944
William Kennedy
Ironweed (novel) 1983
Charles Kingsley
Two Years Ago (novel) 1857
Jack London
John Barleycorn (novel) 1913
Malcolm Lowry
Under the Volcano (novel) 1947
"Lunar Caustic" [published in *Malcolm Lowry: Psalms and Songs*] (poetry) 1975
Carson McCullers
The Heart Is a Lonely Hunter (novel) 1940
Peter Nichols
The National Health (drama) 1969
Frank O'Connor
"The Drunkard" (short story) 1952
Clifford Odets
The Country Girl (drama) 1950
Eugene O'Neill
Ah, Wilderness! (drama) 1933
The Iceman Cometh (drama) 1946
Long Day's Journey into Night (drama) 1956
Walker Percy
Love in the Ruins (novel) 1971
Anthony Trollope
Doctor Thorne (novel) 1858
Evelyn Waugh
Decline and Fall (novel) 1928
A Handful of Dust (novel) 1934
Edmund Campion (novel) 1935
Brideshead Revisited (novel) 1945
Tennessee Williams
Cat on a Hot Tin Roof (drama) 1955
Emile Zola
L'Assommoir (novel) 1879

OVERVIEW

Alfred Kazin

SOURCE: "The Giant Killer: Drink and the American Writer," in *Commentary,* 61, 3, March, 1976, pp. 44-50.

[*In the following essay, Kazin surveys the often close association between alcohol and American writers in the twentieth century.*]

When drunk, I make them pay and pay and pay and pay.

—F. Scott Fitzgerald

America has always been a hard-drinking country despite the many places and times in which alcohol has been forbidden by law. Even in Puritan days Americans were amazingly hard drinkers. It is history that liquor up to the Civil War was cheap as well as plentiful. In the first decades of the 19th century, spirits cost all of 25 cents a gallon domestic, and $1 imported. From 1818 to 1862 there were no taxes whatever on American whiskey, and it took the federal government's need of revenue during the Civil War to change things. The temperance movement, the Prohibitionist movement, the anti-Saloon League were all powerful church-supported bodies, but no more powerful than the "liquor interests" and the freedom and ease that American males acquired for a 4-cents glass of beer in the saloon. America's entry into World War I and the need to conserve grain finally put Prohibition across in 1918. Whereupon the line was marked between what H. L. Mencken called the "booboisie" and the party of sophistication. In the 20's, drinking was the most accessible form of prestige for would-be sophisticates; and this continued to be the case within the professional and wealthy classes as the "tea party" of the 20's became the cocktail party of the 50's (a time when the clientele of Alcoholics Anonymous showed a more representative cross-section of middle-class society than Congress).

But even by these heavy-drinking standards, there is something special about the drinking of so many American writers. Of course there have been famous literary drunks in other countries—Burns, Swinburne, Lionel Johnson, Ernest Dowson, Paul Verlaine, and those two fat boys, Dylan Thomas and Evelyn Waugh. The Russians, famous for knocking themselves out, have produced particularly lurid, despairing, melodramatic poet-drinkers like Sergei Yesenin (the husband of Isadora Duncan) who wrote his suicide note in his own blood. But in 20th-century America the booze has been not just a lifelong "problem" and a killer. It has come to seem a natural accompaniment of the literary life—of its loneliness, its creative aspirations and its frenzies, its "specialness," its hazards in a society where values are constantly put in money terms.

In fact, though no one ever talks about it very much, booze has played as big a role in the lives of modern American writers as talent, money, women, and the longing to be top dog. Of the six American Nobel Prize winners in literature, three—Sinclair Lewis, Eugene O'Neill, William Faulkner—were alcoholics, compulsive drinkers, for great periods of their lives. Two others, Ernest Hemingway and John Steinbeck, were hard drinkers.

Hemingway was also a lover of wine, regularly had champagne with lunch when he lived in Cuba, and (at least in warm climes) drank for pleasure rather than to knock himself out.

The list of American literary drunks is very long. And despite all the fun they must have had, the post-mortem record is full of woe. Scott Fitzgerald (dead at forty-four) and Ring Lardner (dead at forty-eight) were celebrated, dedicated, hopeless alcoholics. Hemingway used to say that a drink was a way of ending a day. But John O'Hara swore off at forty-eight only when he was rushed to a hospital at the point of death from a bleeding ulcer. "A hell of a way for booze to treat me after I've been so kind to it. I used to watch W. C. Fields putting away the martinis at Paramount, and say to myself, 'That's what I want to be when I get big.' Well, I almost made it."

Among the famous suicides, Jack London and John Berryman were alcoholics; Hart Crane had a problem. Poe, the only hard-case alcoholic among the leading 19th-century writers, finally died of drink one election day in Baltimore, 1849, when, already far gone and in total despair, he accepted all the whiskey that was his payment for being voted around the town by the corrupt political machine. Jack London wrote a fascinating account of his alcoholism in *John Barleycorn.* At first, he wrote, liquor seemed an escape from the narrowness of women's influence into "the wide free world of men." A wanderer, making his living from the sea, could always find a home in a saloon. But "suicide, quick or slow, a sudden spill or a gradual oozing away through the years, is the price John Barleycorn exacts. No friend of his ever escapes making the just, due payment."

As a sailor, London was sometimes drunk for three months at a time. Though he could never figure out just why he drank, he hauntingly described his death wish in one extraordinary passage. He had stumbled overboard, and, drunk, was swimming for his life in the Carquinez Strait in the Bay of San Francisco.

> Some wandering fancy of going out with the tide suddenly obsessed me. I had never been morbid. Thoughts of suicide had never entered my head. And now that they entered, I thought it fine, a splendid culmination, a perfect rounding off of my short but exciting career. I who had never known girl's love, nor a woman's love, nor the love of children.... I decided that this was all, that I had seen all, lived all, been all, that was worthwhile, and that now was the time to cease. That was the trick of John Barleycorn, laying me by the heels of my imagination and a drug-dream dragging me to death.

J. P. Marquand, Wallace Stevens, E.E. Cummings, and Edna St. Vincent Millay did not write about their "problem." Edwin Arlington Robinson, Dorothy Parker, Dashiell Hammett, Theodore Roethke, Edmund Wilson did write or talk about theirs. They were all serious drinkers, some more than others, some more openly than others. There is reason to believe that W. H. Auden, a big martini man, voluntarily or involuntarily did himself in by regularly (like Marilyn Monroe) mixing drink with sleeping pills. The Englishman Malcolm Lowry, who understandably felt part of the American scene (for he did his best work in and about North America), died in an acute state of alcoholic distress.

The high point of all-out drinking came in the 20's. Scott Fitzgerald said that he and his generation "drank cocktails before meals like Americans, wines and brandies like Frenchmen, scotch-and-soda like the English. This preposterous melange that was like a gigantic cocktail in a nightmare." Edmund Wilson in a "Lexicon of Prohibition" (1927) solemnly listed over a hundred words for drunkenness "now in common use in the United States. They have been arranged, as far as possible, in order of the degrees of intensity of the conditions which they represent, beginning with the mildest states and progressing to the more disastrous." The list began with *lit, squiffy, oiled,* and concluded with *to have the whoops and jingles* and *to burn with a low blue flame.*

In his notebook of the 20's, Wilson described himself as "daze-minded and daze-eyed" and sobering up only when he read about Sacco and Vanzetti. An editor at *Vanity Fair,* Helen Lawrenson, remembers "hair-raising rides in cars with drivers so pissed they couldn't tell the street from the sidewalk." Robert Benchley was usually so far gone that he no longer went to the plays he reviewed for the old *Life.* A delicious confusion of the senses operated in such key books of the 20's as *The Great Gatsby.* ". . . Everything that happened has a dim, hazy cast over it. . . . Her laughter, her gestures, her assertions became more violently affected moment by moment, and as she expanded the room grew smaller around her, until she seemed to be revolving on a noisy, creaking pivot through the smoky air. . . . "There was blue music from my neighbor's house through the summer nights. In his blue gardens men and girls came and went like moths among the whisperings and the champagne and the stars."

Despite all this gorgeous prose, the background of *The Great Gatsby* is raw alcohol. Gatsby made his pile as a bootlegger and then bought up side-street drugstores in Chicago that sold grain alcohol over the counter. And Fitzgerald's drunkenness, which gave such malicious satisfaction to Hemingway (who, with his overdeveloped competitive sense, knew that stopping in time would give him an advantage over "rummies" like Fitzgerald), was so involved in his need to be picturesque, to ease the money and sexual strains in his life, to keep up with his crazy wife Zelda, that only a writer of such powerful and desperate imagination could have taken it. Destructiveness and charm went hand in hand, all "the good times" and the most heart-sinking depression. A friend said about them: "If you want to get your furniture antiqued up, you want to get the Fitzgeralds in—they'll antique it up in a single night—why they'll put in their own wormholes in the furniture with cigarette ends."

Fitzgerald described his feeling about himself in the weakness of Dr. Dick Diver, the charming psychiatrist in *Tender Is the Night* who sold out and comforted himself more and more by taking two fingers of gin with his coffee. Writers are not the best analysts of their own alcoholism, but psychiatry (a notorious failure in curing *compulsive* drinkers) is not much better about pinpointing *the* reason why. The many thousands of personal confessions recited in AA meetings add up to the fact that the addict to alcohol, like the addict to anything else, believes that he can *will* a change within himself by ingesting some material substance. Like so many of the things we do to ourselves in this pill-happy culture, drinking is a form of technology. People drink for hereditary reasons, nutritional reasons, social reasons. They drink because they are bored, or tired, or restless. People drink for as many reasons as they have for wanting to "feel better." Drinking cuts the connections that keep us anxious. Alcohol works not as a stimulant but as a depressant. But it is exactly this "unwinding," relaxing, slowing-down, this breaking down of so many induced associations and inhibitions, that creates the welcome but temporary freedom from so many restraints, tensions, obligations. Civilization is a tyrant, "hell is other people," and we all need to escape the "ordeal of civility."

But there are periods and occasions when drinking is in the air, even seems to be a moral necessity. The 20's marked the great changeover from the old rural and small-town America. It also marked the triumph in the marketplace of "advanced," wholly "modern" writers and books, ideas, and attitudes. They all entered into the big money and the big time at once. The glamorous, best-selling, restlessly excited Fitzgeralds would never be reconciled to anything less. The Fitzgeralds' drinking began as a perpetual party. Then Zelda went off her rocker, the country went bust, *Tender Is the Night* was not a best-seller, Fitzgerald was writing for Hollywood. When he was doing *Gone with the Wind,* David Selznick fired Fitzgerald for not coming up with "funny" lines for Aunt Pittypat. Gavin Lambert reports that "being taken off the script was a disastrous blow to Fitzgerald's already shaky confidence. He resumed the long on-again-off-again drinking bout that led to his unrequited love affair with the movies. And between the drinking bouts and brief assignments on B pictures, he began *The Last Tycoon.*"

Fitzgerald drunk was pleasanter to be with than Sinclair Lewis, who regularly passed out. One of the most serious drinkers in American history was Eugene O'Neill, who came from a family of serious drinkers. His brother Jamie was a confirmed alcoholic at twenty. His father, the famous actor James O'Neill, regularly had a cocktail before breakfast, and became so possessive about his liquor that he locked it up in the cellar out of the reach of his equally thirsty sons.

During his one stormy year at Princeton O'Neill once finished off a bottle of absinthe in a dormitory room reeking of burning incense. He went berserk, tore up all

the furnishings in his room, and tried to shoot a friend. When the friend escaped and returned with help, they "found the place a shambles and O'Neill, wide-eyed, still on a rampage. It took all four of the other students to subdue him and tie him up." Later, say Barbara and Arthur Gelb in their biography, the slightest upset would send O'Neill to the bottle—and it did not matter what the bottle contained. He once drank a mixture of varnish and water; another time, camphor-flavored alcohol. Louis Sheaffer reports that while still a very young man, worried about his clandestine marriage to Kathleen Jenkins and the imminent birth of an unwanted child, O'Neill hacked up everything in his parents' hotel room in New York. O'Neill's mother (herself a drug addict) "never knew what to expect of him, whether childlike he would turn to her and James for comfort or present the face of a dark brooding stranger impossible to reach." Shortly after this, O'Neill attempted suicide by drinking veronal.

O'Neill claimed that "I never try to write a line when I'm not strictly on the wagon." But he was never able to stay off the booze completely in the crucial twenty years 1913-33, during which he became the most significant playwright America had ever had. It was, however, in the succeeding twenty years (he died in 1953), a dry period by the direst necessity (he had Parkinson's disease), that he wrote his best five plays—*Ah, Wilderness!, A Touch of the Poet, More Stately Mansions, A Moon for the Misbegotten, Long Day's Journey into Night.*

The most boldly determined, all-out, to-hell-with-the-consequences literary soak of the 20's was Ring Lardner. He appears as Abe North in *Tender Is the Night,* a tall, morosely witty, perpetually disoriented creature getting drunk in the Ritz bar in Paris at nine in the morning. Poor Abe, witty yet lost. "Presently he was invited to lunch, but declined. It was almost Briglith, he explained, and there was something he had to do at Briglith. A little later, with the exquisite manners of the alcoholic that are like the manners of a prisoner or a family servant, he said goodbye to an acquaintance, and turning around discovered that the bar's great moment was over as precipitately as it had begun." After an involved fracas in a Paris hotel, Abe says to Dick Diver, "Could I annoy you for a drink?" "There's not a thing up here," Dick lied.

> Resignedly Abe shook hands with Rosemary; he composed his face slowly, holding her hand a long time and forming sentences that did not emerge. She laughed in a well-bred way, as though it were nothing unusual to watch a man walking in a slow dream. Often people display a curious respect for a man drunk, rather like the respect of simple races for the insane. Respect rather than fear. There is something awe-inspiring in one who has lost all inhibitions, who will do anything. Of course we make him pay for his moment of superiority, his moment of impressiveness.

The real Ring Lardner, almost ten years older than Fitzgerald, was much funnier than Abe North. "How do you look when I'm sober?" he once said to a flamboyant actor. But he was just as determined to drink himself to death. And he did. The inoperable final "Why?" haunts us particularly in his case. He came from a sturdy, cultivated Midwest family, was deeply in love with his wife, raised four remarkable sons. It was because Lardner had been "brought up right" that he became fascinated by what illiterate ball players did to the language. Ring Jr. reports his father saying—"Where do they get that stuff about my being a satirist? I just listen." Looking a little like Buster Keaton, sad-faced and quiet except when he had something to say right on target, old-looking enough in his teens to fool saloon keepers, Lardner was from his teens in Niles, Michigan, a citizen of saloon society. There (before Prohibition) a man could be quiet with himself, drink to his heart's content, and listen. Lardner's mother thought Lardner and his brothers (fellow soaks) were putting in extra hours at choir practice.

Lardner was an amazing drinker, a real hard case, even before he was transformed from a journalistic funny man to a literary figure. "I have a reputation—an unfortunate one—for infinite capacity." Living near each other in Great Neck (where Gatsby had his dream house), he and Fitzgerald, easily amused by each other's jokes and each other's alcoholism, would sometimes drink through the night. Ring would not go home on a weekday morning until his sons had left for school. Lardner had greater capacity than Fitzgerald and maintained his physical coordination when drunk for many more years than Fitzgerald did. But Ring Jr., the only living witness, thinks that "Scott may have been fascinated by Ring as the image of his own future; even though he could sleep off a drunk and get back to work with much more ease than his older friend, he must have known that he was heading in the same direction. . . . Even the pattern he came to of setting a specific beginning and ending date for going on the wagon was Ring's."

With a large family to support, Lardner pragmatically set himself a fixed period of abstinence and a fixed quota of work to accomplish in it. Despite the legends of his knocking out a story under the influence of a quart or so, he told his son: "No one, ever, wrote anything as well even after one drink as he would have done without it." But once the allotted work was finished, Lardner just as determinedly went back to the bottle. He had once thought of Prohibition as an enforced solution to his problem, but he soon saw this was an unattainable goal. He told the actress Jean Dixon that if he smelled beer he would drink it and when he drank it he would go on to something else. He went on bats for three months at a time. He knew exactly what he was doing—and could have himself written the decisive "first step" of AA's famous "twelve steps" that an alcoholic must go through in order to recover: "We admitted that we were powerless over alcohol—that our lives had become unmanageable." After Lardner's death in 1933, Fitzgerald wrote: "One is haunted not only by a sense of personal loss but by a conviction that Ring got less percentage of himself on paper than any other American author of the first flight."

Alcoholics, like other prodigies, begin young. Faulkner, always a crazy reckless drinker, came from a family of reckless drinkers. His father and grandfather were known for sprees, and would be taken off at regular intervals to the Keeley Institute, fifteen miles from Memphis, for the "cure." He himself was introduced to liquor by this same grandfather who let him taste the "heeltaps" left over in a glass from toddies. On the famous hunting trips, a necessary retreat for the men, when a drinking bout might go on for three or four days, Faulkner drank the powerful corn liquor made in illegal stills concealed in the hills and pine barrens. At eighteen, Faulkner drank in town with the town drunk. At twenty, he tried to get into World War I by joining the Royal Canadian Flying Corps, but cracked up in a training plane—in which he kept a crock of bourbon. When Prohibition descended upon the land, Faulkner showed ingenuity as well as determination. He drank white mule made by county moonshiners, clear corn liquor in the dice joints, and frequented Memphis brothels because they had a better variety of whiskey. He even did a little bootlegging and "rum-running" in order to make some money. Even when forced to work for a spell in the local post office (he quit because he was at the mercy of "every son of a bitch with a two-cent stamp"), Faulkner was able to console himself with a bottle of "white lightning." He is remembered for saying: "There is no such thing as bad whiskey, some are just better than others."

Faulkner was a social drinker, a private drinker, a convivial drinker, a morose drinker. He drank because it was a habit in the Deep South for men to drink. He drank to ease himself and to knock himself out as a result of the screaming exhaustion—"I feel as though all my nerve ends were exposed"—that came after the tension of writing *The Sound and the Fury*. After finishing this great book, he said to a friend, "Read this. It's a real son of a bitch," and went on a tear for several days without eating. His compulsive drinking regularly led to one or two serious illnesses a year for thirty years. Some of the side experiences were alcoholic exhaustion, DT's, whiskey ulcers, electroshock therapy, the many nicks and gashes in his head, broken ribs, falling down stairs, falls from horses, broken vertebrae, sweats, shakes, organic damage, fibrillation, blackouts.

He sometimes (and probably more and more) drank while writing. When he lived in Greenwich Village at one period, he wrote in small pocket notebooks he bought at Woolworth's for a nickel—occasionally sipping gin as he wrote. Faulkner did not drink in order to *start* writing. He may have been repressed as a man, but certainly not as a writer. "You just keep the words coming," he said. Like so many great novelists, he was productive because his mind kept everything he had seen, heard, lived. As a man he seems to have found existence intolerable from time to time. Who can say just why? But although he could do anything he liked with words, his "drinking habit" inflamed and spoiled his writing as much as it damaged his body.

Of course writing, for Faulkner, was already a form of intoxication. But the insensately long sentences that he went in for suggest the abandon that so often comes to a drinker as the "connections that make up anxiety" are broken off. But it is just connections that make writing— the line-by-line thinking that the writer undergoes so that the reader will see what is in the writer's mind. It was disastrous for Faulkner to lose the thread. After the period 1929-36 in which he composed all his greatest works—*The Sound and the Fury, Light in August, As I Lay Dying, Absalom! Absalom!*—Faulkner wrote windy books like *Intruder in the Dust, Requiem for a Nun, A Fable, The Town.* Donald Newlove has put it more harshly than anyone else:

> Something disastrous happened when Faulkner turned forty-nine; whatever grip he had on his alcoholism faded, and so did the hot focus of his imagination. He wrote for twenty-two years, but his brain was stunned. What we get is the famous mannered diction, senatorial tone, a hallucinated rhetoric of alcohol full of ravishing if empty glory. Dead junk compared to the sunburst pages of *The Sound and the Fury.* . . . Faulkner's ruinous pose as a master of Latinate diction is the direct result of alcoholic hardening of the ego. . . .

After the 20's, later writers like John O'Hara and John Steinbeck did their best to keep up with the careless drinking style they had learned as young men in the 20's. But there was a notable lack of joy. O'Hara as a reporter had been known as a saloon fighter. When he went off the booze, totally, to save his life, he admitted that he still missed scotch and beer. He made up for it by working all through the night, night after night. He wrote so many stories that he virtually ran out of titles, and he made so much money that he boasted that no one anywhere—wanna bet?—had *ever* written short stories as well as John O'Hara. O'Hara sober was just as truculent as O'Hara drunk. Hemingway said that he could beat Tolstoy. O'Hara went after younger writers.

In Algeria during World War II André Gide heard that Steinbeck was in town as a war correspondent and tried to meet him. But Steinbeck was always drunk. Gide told Malcolm Muggeridge that he had tried in the evening, at lunch time, and finally at breakfast, but always with the same result. Dashiell Hammett, whom Lillian Hellman lovingly portrays as a Southern gentleman extraordinarily rational, resourceful, self-possessed, and informed, grimly drank himself into insensibility at regular intervals. Thomas Wolfe amazed Fitzgerald by his ability to keep things in an uproar. One night, when they were having an argument in the street, Wolfe gesticulated so vehemently that he struck a power line support, snapped the wire, and plunged the whole community into darkness. Bernard De Voto, like so many writer-drinkers of the second order, gave the impression of imitating more illustrious writers. He was a martini snob even more tiresome than the usual wine snob. Gancia was the only vermouth to mix with gin; Noilly Prat was too changeable.

Malcolm Lowry would have been shocked by all this twaddle. Lowry, one of the most stupendous drinkers in all recorded history, wrote the greatest novel I know about an alcoholic, *Under the Volcano* (1947). There is nothing like it in modern literature. It is one of the great 20th-century novels in language, form, and in its amazing visionary demonstration of the tie between the alcoholic hero's crumbling life in the 1930's and the disasters about to fall on the Western world. Geoffrey Firmin, a former British consul in Mexico, always called "the Consul," drinks anything, drinks all the time, drinks as a way of life, drinks as a way of living and dying at once. His final collapse and his murder at the hands of fascist thugs take place on a single day in 1939, "The Day of the Dead." The deadly atmosphere that has collected around the helpless Consul finally becomes a signal that the Western world is sliding into war. *Under the Volcano* could have been achieved only by an imagination that already had the qualities of drunkenness. Lowry's imagination was made more itself by drink. Then he died of it, probably feeling that it had all been worth it.

The best-known drinker of my own literary generation was the poet John Berryman (1914-72). Berryman was a natural celebrity. Poets often are, for their personality and their works seem so much of a piece. The language of a good poem is so close to fundamental emotion, to the secrets of the human heart, that the poet is traditionally honored as a prophet among men. Flamboyant poets convinced of their importance make messes in public, delight their humble students, the literary gossips, the jealous psychiatrists (who also deal in the language of emotion, but not so memorably), and get a reputation for genius based on the disorderliness of poets from François Villon to Dylan Thomas. The poet Theodore Roethke wrote a very subdued, miniature poetry about his "lost childhood." But he was an enormous hulking fellow with violent personal emotions and a heavy drinker's gift for asserting himself loudly in public. He regularly put on such a show that it was easier to cheer big Ted Roethke on than to admit that his poems were slight, sometimes inaudible experiments in self-pity.

But of the American poets, it was Berryman who made more literary capital out of his "problem" than anyone since Lowry. Liquor made Berryman more and more special to himself—and famous. He would not have become so famous without it. Berryman was pictured by the caricaturist David Levine with an enormous bottle down his back. It is typical of his celebrity as a boozer that while he was still known mostly to a small literary audience, he was given a big story in *Life* that showed him and his enormous beard convivial in an Irish pub. After he killed himself in the winter of 1972 by jumping from a bridge off Minneapolis onto the frozen Mississippi, his unfinished novel about the "cure," *Recovery,* was published, followed by a novel, *The Maze,* by his ex-wife Eileen Simpson.

Despite his furious drinking, Berryman doggedly pursued his career. He published ten books of poetry and a brilliant critical biography of Stephen Crane. His most famous work, because it is the most personal, is the 308 "Dream Songs"—monologues "about an imaginary character (not the poet, not me) named Henry, a white American in early middle age sometimes in blackface, who has suffered an irreversible loss and talks about himself sometimes in the first person, sometimes in the third, sometimes even in the second; he has a friend, never named, who addresses him as Mr. Bones and variants thereof. . . . *Requiescant in pace.* . . ."

Of course "Henry" is "not the poet, not me"—there were too many Berrymans. What is most striking about these poems is the crossing of so many selves. Only a white man in "blackface" could suggest the layer on layer of disguise and personality that went to make John Berryman! The poems are a fantastic performance in the many voices forever buzzing in John Berryman's mind—the voices of himself as teacher and writer, of his supposed accusers, of the longing to see an end to his self-torturing confabulations with himself, of his dead father and of himself as a father who does not see his own son.

The jauntiness of tone that Berryman brought to his sorrows!

> I'm scared a lonely. Never see my son,
>   easy be not to see anyone,
>
>   . . . . .
>
> I'm scared a only one thing, which is me,
> from othering I don't take nothing, see,
>   for my hound dog's sake
> But this is where I livin, where I rake
> my leaves and cop my promise, this' where we
> cry oursel's awake.

In another "Dream Song" he asks:

> Why drink so, two days running?
> two months, O season, years, two decades run-
>   ning?
> I answer (smiles) my question on the cuff:
> Man, I been thirsty. . . .

Berryman was "authoritative," cocky, even at his lowest. Snooty, heartbreaking, maudlin, clearly written under booze, quick to portray every side of the divided self that emerges under booze, these poems are the human heart's rushed shorthand. They are also in Berryman's most maddeningly allusive style. You have to know a lot about Berryman's friends, girls, most secret worries, and especially his relations with the best poets dead and alive to know what he is referring to more than half the time. The poems are shockingly alive in their emotional distress and in the poet's determination to keep things *looking* good. Disconnected on purpose, disconnected by necessity, abrupt, brilliant at times, and just as often throwaway, the poems are obsessive about the need to move on, to get out of difficulties, to move out of this world if finally necessary. This is what makes Berryman's stuff finally so compelling. The life and the book are one. The

force of his personality (not of the poems in themselves) is overwhelming.

What explains all this excessive, delirious, and often fatal drinking? Hemingway had a theory about it. He called booze "the Giant Killer," and he could have added that the Giant is America itself, or rather the "bitch-goddess" Success which William James said was the great American deity. The history of American writers even in the nineteenth century was already marked by unnatural strain, physical isolation, alienation from the supposedly "sweet and smiling aspects of American life." But it is significant that the only known literary alcoholic of the period was Poe, a magazine writer and editor of genius always desperate for money, who helped to swell the marketplace psychology among American writers. And it was just when that psychology became rampant, as in the 20's the big money and the big time began to seem possible for serious and "advanced" writers, that the really big drinkers emerged.

There were no such "rebels" (in their own eyes) as those in the literary class. They were "different" from "ordinary" Americans because they lived by their wits. They had been around, they knew things. In a "Memoir of the Drinking Life," Pete Hamill shows what an assist to your fantasies of being Hemingway, of knowing things, it can be to drink:

> For a writer, the life was particularly attractive. I learned a lot of things in saloons: about my craft, human beings, about myself. . . . We drank in all the bars of Brooklyn, and later in McSorleys, and the old Cedar Tavern (looking at Franz Kline and Jackson Pollock), and the White Horse (looking for Dylan Thomas), and a lot of other places. . . . Drink was the great loosener, the killer of shyness, the maker of dreams and courage. . . .

But in fact the literary rebels always yearned for success as much as any benighted Babbitt. Only in America have first-class novelists been driven to "prove" their acceptability by *also* becoming bestsellers. Even poetry has to sell, or at least make you famous. Berryman, for example, who worshipped other famous writers in America and knew all about them, was generally disappointed in himself. He wanted fame so badly that he was always hard on himself. He was far from being modest. Of course he had non-literary sorrows. His father was a suicide and probably an alcoholic. Berryman went through all the instability, hysteria, hypochondria, the broken marriages, the "bad sex," the blackouts that are indissolubly the causes *and* effects of excessive drinking. But fundamentally he was driven by competition with other poets and was determined to outdo them.

It was, then, the drive for success of every kind, the hunger for prestige, fame, and money, that drove all these writers to drink: the burden put upon the creative self by so many contradictory pressures was overwhelming and cried out for relief. They drank to escape the hunger; they drank to disguise it from themselves and others; they drank to be different from the unsophisticated "booboisie"; they drank to be the same as the "regular fellers"; they drank to acquire *class*. In one form or another the Giant exacted a final sacrifice—themselves—from the writers who tried to kill their Great Fear over and over again.

FICTION

John W. Crowley

SOURCE: "After the Lost Generation: The Lost Weekend," in *The White Logic: Alcoholism and Gender in American Modernist Fiction*, University of Massachusetts Press, 1994, pp. 135-57.

[*In the following essay, Crowley examines Charles Jackson's* The Lost Weekend *(1944) as indicative of a shift away from the modernist perspective of alcoholism as a sign of the modern distemper and toward the concept of drunkenness as symptomatic of a disease.*]

When *The Lost Weekend* appeared in January 1944, Malcolm Lowry had been toiling for nearly a decade over successive drafts of *Under the Volcano* (1947), the magnum opus on which he had pinned his hopes of literary immortality. For Lowry, the true originality of this work consisted in his use of an alcoholic as a representative man, a symbol of the tragic modern condition. He was understandably devastated by the pre-emptive publication of Charles Jackson's novel, with its unprecedented account of a binge from the drinker's point of view, and envious of its clamorous reception: critical praise, best-seller popularity, a lucrative Hollywood contract. An outstanding film adaptation of *The Lost Weekend* was subsequently honored at the first Cannes Film Festival and awarded Oscars for best picture, best screenplay, best director (Billy Wilder), and best actor (Ray Milland).

Lowry's work was always inseparable from his life, and he inevitably transformed into fiction his resentment of Jackson as a fortunate rival who had stolen his thunder and blighted his dreams of success. Sigbjørn Wilderness in *Dark as the Grave Wherein My Friend Is Laid* is shocked to hear about a hit movie based on a novel called *Drunkard's Rigadoon*. His wife, who has been shielding him from the bad news, attempts to offer consolation: "It's purely a clinical study; it's only a small part of yours. . . . It could be anything else, not drinking. . . . Let him have his little triumph. When there's so much *more* in your book." But Wilderness recognizes that his novel cannot now escape seeming derivative, no matter how much *"more"* it may contain.

> It had meant everything to him, the writing of *The Valley of the Shadow of Death,* the feeling of turning his greatest weakness—he loathed the

phrase—into his greatest strength . . . the feeling that he, who up to that time had been haunted by the suspicion that he would never write anything original, that he was destined to copy all his life, had sunk his teeth into that appalling theme, that he was breaking not merely new ground, but building a terra nova, achieving something that was unique, in a sort of ultima thule of the spirit. And now . . . he would merely be told, as he had already been as much as told by his agent and the two American publishers who had so far rejected it, that—and had they stopped to think they must have known it could not have been so—it was merely a copy of *Drunkard's Rigadoon!*

In a letter to Jonathan Cape, one of the rejecting publishers, Lowry confessed that he regarded *The Lost Weekend* "as a form of punishment," as retribution for sins against his own artistic talent and integrity: "Youth plus booze plus hysterical identifications plus vanity plus self-deception plus no work plus more booze."

Booze eventually destroyed Malcolm Lowry, but in the long run of literary history, *Under the Volcano* has fared much better than *The Lost Weekend*. In retrospect, it seems that Lowry worked himself up over nothing. The very popularity of Jackson's novel should have assured him that it could not pose any threat to the ultimate triumph of his own with readers of discriminating taste—taste molded by the prevailing climate of modernism to favor dense and esoterically symbolic novels like *Under the Volcano* over readable and unpretentiously realistic ones like *The Lost Weekend*. Whereas the former has inspired adulation befitting a literary "terra nova" or an "ultima thule of the spirit," the latter has slipped from view except by association with the classic film. Virtually nothing has been written on Jackson's work since the initial reviews of his four novels and two collections of stories. No biography exists, and little personal information is available.

Born 6 April 1903, in Summit, New Jersey, Charles Reginald Jackson grew up in Newark, New York, a village east of Rochester. His closest companion from childhood onward was his younger brother, Frederick, who was a model for Wick, the alcoholic Don Birnam's brother in *The Lost Weekend*. Another brother and sister were killed in an auto accident when Charles was thirteen; his father left home when he was twelve. After graduating from high school in 1921, Jackson worked as a reporter for the *Newark Courier* and, later, as a bookstore clerk in Chicago and New York. He also attended Syracuse University for two semesters. After the onset of tuberculosis in 1927, he was medically confined for several years. Along with his brother, who too was infected, he sought treatment at the sanatorium in Davos, Switzerland, that had provided Thomas Mann with the setting for *The Magic Mountain* (1924). While a patient there from 1929 to 1931, Jackson developed a drinking problem through the use of alcohol as a painkiller.

Living in New York City during the Depression, Jackson could not find steady work, and his drinking grew unremittingly worse until November 1936, when he checked into Bellevue Hospital. There in the alcoholic ward, where street drunks deposited by the police often served as experimental subjects as they dried out, Jackson's physician was Norman Jolliffe, a physiologist who had undertaken a long-term study of "the etiology of chronic inebriety." After Jackson sobered up, he found a job with the Columbia Broadcasting System, where he wrote radio plays, both originals and adaptations, as well as the daytime serial, "Sweet River." In 1938, he married Rhoda Booth, a staff writer at *Fortune* who, like Helen in *The Lost Weekend,* had been steadfast during the worst of the drinking. The next year he went freelance, continuing to produce successful scripts while teaching radio writing at New York University.

Always a voracious reader, Jackson had conducted his own literary education during his prolonged convalescence, and he had also begun writing fiction—all of which remained unpublished until two of his stories were accepted by the *Partisan Review* in 1939. The same year, he began an autobiographical novel about an alcoholic binge, and he finished the first draft in fourteen months. Four years later, the overnight success of *The Lost Weekend* put Jackson in the limelight. Critics raved; sales boomed; Hollywood beckoned. In April 1944, he began a sixteen-week contract as a screenwriter for Metro Goldwyn Mayer, and his earnings of $1,000 a week allowed him to buy a splendid colonial farmhouse in Orford, New Hampshire, where he lived with his wife and two daughters for the next decade. Jackson's success as a writer carried him through the 1940s. His second novel, *The Fall of Valor* (1946), a frank exploration of homosexuality, was respectfully reviewed and widely circulated by the book clubs; his short stories were selling briskly to mass-market magazines.

Jackson's third novel, *The Outer Edges* (1948), was less favorably received, however, and by 1950, he was running heavily into debt. Although Jackson had quit drinking in 1936, he remained dependent on sedatives (mainly Secanol) to break through writer's block and to keep his inspiration flowing. The strain of revising *The Fall of Valor* led to a spell of mental exhaustion in 1945, and to a jag on drugs early the following year. In July 1947, during another such binge, Jackson started drinking beer as well as taking drugs. Early in 1951, his relapses became more serious and more chronic, as he resumed periodic heavy drinking after fifteen years of nearly complete abstinence. He quickly spiraled downward, and after a suicide attempt in 1952, he was readmitted to Bellevue. Jackson did not recover his stability until he entered a clinic for alcoholism in the summer of 1953 and joined Alcoholics Anonymous upon his release.

Sober again but frozen in a writer's block, Jackson saw his productivity drop off and his celebrity fade. Having ceased to publish much fiction, he sold used cars to make a living. The Jacksons were forced to sell their Orford farm in 1954, and they moved to a rented house in Sandy Hook, Connecticut. In his later years, Jackson again

worked for the broadcasting industry—as a television script editor—and he remained very active in A.A. After a long absence from the literary scene, he attempted a come-back in 1967 with *A Second-Hand Life,* a novel he had started in the early 1950s. The book enjoyed good sales, but it fizzled critically. The following year, his health deteriorating, Jackson ended his own life with an overdose of sleeping pills. At the time of his death, he was writing a sequel to *The Lost Weekend.*

Despite Jackson's present obscurity, *The Lost Weekend* remains a compelling novel fifty years after its first publication. Its title has passed into the American vernacular, and its portrait of the alcoholic has lost none of its psychological acuity. In addition to literary merit, *The Lost Weekend* has historical importance for making a major shift in the representation of alcoholism in American literature. Although the novel owes an obvious debt to *Tender Is the Night*—which Don Birnam considers, despite its failures, to be "the most brilliant and heart-breaking performance . . . in recent fiction"—it neither denies the alcoholism of its protagonist nor elevates him into a culture hero. "We are far from the romantic drinkers of Hemingway and Scott Fitzgerald," as Edmund Wilson says of Birnam. "The man himself is dreary in the extreme."

The man's existence during a five-day bender—the novel was originally titled "The Long Weekend"—is also extremely dreary. As Birnam drinks his way through bottle after bottle, worrying constantly about his supply and borrowing booze money at every turn (but always losing track of it), he inflicts awful damage on himself and those who care about him. An intelligent, charming, and decent man when sober, Don is transmogrified by alcohol into a scheming liar who ruthlessly exploits his well-meaning brother and long-suffering girl friend, a petty thief who cleverly (he thinks) steals a purse but humiliatingly gets caught, and a sodden bar-fly who laments his nonexistent wife's "frigidity" as he angles for a date with the hostess and then forgets about it in a blackout. Having finished off the whiskey on Friday night, he is desperate for a Saturday morning eye-opener, and he rushes out to raise a stake by pawning his typewriter—only to discover, after walking block after block for miles, that he is the butt of a joke "beyond laughter" (p. 109): every pawn shop in New York is closed for Yom Kippur! When Birnam reaches the stumble-drunk stage, he topples down the stairs and wakes up in the hospital with a fractured skull. The next day, as his binge is finally winding down, he must endure the torments of delirium tremens: a horrific hallucination of a bat devouring a mouse.

At the end, Don feels ready nonetheless for another "spell of riot" (p. 3) [All citations from *The Lost Weekend,* Farrar and Rinehart, 1944]. As he hides pint bottles about the apartment, making careful allowance for the loss of those his brother will likely find and confiscate, Don reassures himself that his lost weekend couldn't have been so bad as all that; he has survived it, after all. "God knows why or how but he had come through one more. No telling what might happen the next time but why worry about that? This one was over and nothing had happened at all. Why did they make such a fuss?" (p. 244). Don is trapped by such denial in an alcoholic's vicious circle; his prospects are bleak, his situation seems hopeless.

In its stark realism about what Lowry called "the calamitous suffering drink [can] cause to the drinker," *The Lost Weekend* resembles *Under the Volcano;* but Jackson does not partake, as Lowry does, of the modernist spirit(s) of the White Logic. It is Jackson's refusal to amplify his material—to extrapolate from one drunkard's downfall to a symbolic utterance about the Tragedy of Life or the Decline of the West—that distinguishes *The Lost Weekend* from such grandiose modernist masterpieces as *Under the Volcano.* The force of Lowry's novel is centrifugal; it spins outward from its center (the Consul), traversing the cosmos as it accumulates layer upon layer of Higher Meaning. The force of *The Lost Weekend,* on the contrary, is centripetal; it turns in on itself toward a purposefully reductive focus on drinking, unadorned by any larger significance. Why, Birnam wonders at one point, are there so many kind and faithful women who get themselves mixed up with hopeless drunks?

> But from there you went on to: Why were drunks, almost always, persons of talent, personality, lovable qualities, gifts, brains, assets of all kinds (else why would anyone care?); why were so many brilliant men alcoholic?—And from there, the next one was: Why did you drink?
>
> Like the others, the question was rhetorical, abstract, anything but pragmatic; as vain to ask as his own clever question had been vain. It was far too late to pose such a problem with any reasonable hope for an answer—or, an answer forthcoming, any reasonable hope that it would be worth listening to or prove anything at all. It had long since ceased to matter Why. You were a drunk; that's all there was to it. You drank; period. (pp. 221-22)

With tough-minded pragmatism, *The Lost Weekend* renounces . . . abstract and rhetorical inflation of drunkenness. . . . Jackson, in fact, lampoons this sort of thing in a passage where Birnam the frustrated writer ("the books begun and dropped, the unfinished short stories; the drinking the drinking the drinking" [p. 17]) is inspired with an idea for a modernist masterpiece as he leans on the bar, gazing at himself in the mirror and recalling the literary idols of his childhood ("Poe and Keats, Byron, Dowson, Chatterton—all the gifted miserable and reckless men who had burned themselves out in tragic brilliance early and with finality" [pp. 15-16]). The story of his own miserably drunken life, he suddenly realizes, could be "a classic of form and content" on the artistic order of *Death in Venice* (p. 16). First the perfect title ("In a Glass") leaps to mind, and then the entire book marvelously unfolds before him:

> At this moment, if he were able to write fast enough, he could set it down in all its final

perfection, right down without a change or correction needed later, from the brilliant opening to the last beautiful note of wise and grave irony. . . . Whole sentences sprang to his mind in dazzling succession, perfectly formed, ready to be put down. Where was a pencil, paper? He downed his drink. . . .

> But caution, slow. Good thing there was no paper handy, no chance to begin impulsively what later must be composed—when, tonight maybe, certainly tomorrow—with all the calm and wise control needed for such an undertaking. (pp. 16-17)

Needless to say, Don will be too drunk either tonight or tomorrow for any literary work, if he should even happen to remember what came to him so effortlessly on a bar stool. But the fantasy spins itself out. Already, he can see the pyramidal stacks of copies in the bookshop window; he can hear a puzzled girl in the subway paying him inadvertent but profound tribute by confessing to a friend, "I can't make head or tail of this"; he can savor the bewilderment of his hopelessly ignorant mother, who will regret "the fact that he hadn't published a book she could show the neighbors and why didn't he write something that had 'human interest'" (p. 18). But then a wave of self-disgust crashes over Birnam, and he dismisses "In a Glass" as "so much eyewash": "How could he have been seduced, fooled, into dreaming up such a ridiculous piece; in perpetrating, even in his imagination, anything so pat, so contrived, so cheap, so phoney, so adolescent, so (crowning offense) sentimental!" (p. 18).

But caution, slow! Now the final page appears in Birnam's mind's eye as "clear and true as if he had seen it in print." Yes! Something in the vein of Thomas Mann, but with an ending straight out of Hemingway: with a wise and gravely ironic tag-line worthy of "Isn't it pretty to think so?":

> The hero, after the long procession of motley scenes from his past life (would the line stretch out to th' crack of doom?)—the hero decides to walk out of the bar and somewhere, somehow, that very day— not for himself, of course: for Helen—commit suicide. The tag: "It would give her a lifelong romance." Perfect; but not—oh more perfect still— was the line that came next, the *new* ending: the little simple line set in a paragraph all by itself beneath the other, on the last page:
>
> "But he knew he wouldn't." (p. 18)

Of course, "In a Glass" parodies *The Lost Weekend* itself insofar as it recalls *The Sun Also Rises, Tender Is the Night,* and other modernist drunk narratives. Jackson pointedly calls this genre into question by mocking its bombast and complacency. Later in the novel, once again standing at a bar, Birnam drunkenly wallows in his immense affinity for the White Logic:

> Was there a limit to what he could endure? It seemed not. He was more vulnerable to suffering— and at the same time, paradoxically, he had a

greater capacity for it—than anyone he knew; and this was no idle or egotistic boast, something he merely fancied to be true and was proud of because it set him apart, spoke of a superior sensitivity or sensibility. An occasion or period of suffering in his past which, reckoned now in perspective, was a mere incident, one out of many in a long chain, would have stood out in the average life as a major crisis, perhaps indeed the only one, a moment where the victim had reached a peak or depth from which recovery was a lifelong process. But such moments, such peaks and depths, were his very pattern—natural, it seemed, perhaps even necessary, to his development. Why had he not been destroyed by all that happened to him? How is it he could take it over and over again and yet again? What capacity, vitality, or resilience did he have that others did not? Was it that his imagination laid hold of that suffering and transmuted it to experience, an experience he did not profit from, true, but experience all the same: a realization of who and what he was, a fulfillment of self? Was he trying to find out, in this roundabout descent to destruction, what it was all about; and would he, at the final and ultimate moment, know? (Pp. 201-2)

In a review of *The Lost Weekend,* Edmund Wilson singled out this interior monologue as the novel's "most revealing passage," characterizing it as a "curious perverse meditation in which the hero justifies his drinking to himself as a purposive way of life with a special kind of moral dignity." A special kind of moral dignity? Or a typically alcoholic kind of bloated self-pity? Wilson fails to note that a sober Don Birnam later castigates himself for what he regards as a shameful indulgence in egoism. "Some minor incident of suffering in his past would have stood out in the average life as a major crisis—he had actually thought and said to himself some such thing as that. How true could it be?" (p. 219).

Jackson suggests that truth for Birnam is relative to his sobriety. When he is drunk, Don's imagination heightens minor incidents into calamities, making them "greater in retrospect than they ever were at the time"; and he easily forgets that "what happened to him was no greater or no worse than what happened to everybody else." Other people suffered, "but did their self-centeredness, their self-absorption and preoccupation with self, magnify their troubles or experiences out of all proportion to the actuality and blind them to the fact that trouble was the lot of all?" (p. 219). When Don is sober, however, remorse drives him to the other extreme of self-contempt. Even as he berates himself, he knows that "this chastisement and searching of self" is "all merely part of his present low and depleted state, symptomatic of his physical condition only, and that tomorrow or next week he would bounce right back, all ego again" (pp. 219-20).

Built on a series of such interior monologues, *The Lost Weekend* is, as Roger Forseth remarks [in *Dionysus,* 3 (Spring 1991)], "psychologically exact in remaining largely in the mind of the alcoholic, for that is always where the alcoholic is." In this and other ways, the novel gives "the alcoholic stripped to the essentials" and captures "in amber the clinically defined disease of alcoholism." The oscillation so evident in Birnam between self-absorption and self-contempt, between inflation and deflation of the ego, might be taken as a psychological characteristic of alcoholics. Thus although the novel is not, as Lowry suggested, "purely a clinical study," it does have a didactic dimension that links it to temperance fiction of the nineteenth century. Whether intended by Jackson or not, one effect of *The Lost Weekend,* both as fiction and as film, was to inform the public about "alcoholism" by disclosing the inside story from the perspective of the "alcoholic" himself.

These terms were becoming more and more common in ordinary usage by the time *The Lost Weekend* appeared, mainly through the success of what historians have called the "Alcoholism Movement" in recasting American attitudes toward habitual drunkenness. Between the 1930s and the 1960s, as Bruce H. Johnson observes, a new consensus took shape as "the traditional moralistic interpretations of this form of deviant behavior were abandoned in favor of a 'scientific' or medical point of view according to which the chronic drunkard is the victim of a physiological or psychological aberration." This transformation of public opinion was accomplished, with remarkable efficiency, by a relatively small band of dedicated campaigners associated with a trio of allied institutions with overlapping memberships and interlocking purposes: Alcoholics Anonymous, the National Committee for Education on Alcoholism (later renamed the National Council on Alcoholism), and the Yale Center for Studies of Alcohol (later renamed the Yale Center of Alcohol Studies).

During its first decade (1935 to 1945), Alcoholics Anonymous branched out from its two original groups in New York and Akron, Ohio, to several other cities; and membership rose exponentially from its founding partners (William Griffith Wilson, a.k.a. "Bill W." and Robert Holbrook Smith, a.k.a. "Dr. Bob") to include a few dozen and then about 15,000 persons, nearly all of them white, middle-class men. Thanks in large part to extensive and favorable press coverage, the A.A. fellowship mushroomed to over 100,000 members by 1951. Much of this coverage was generated and orchestrated by Marty Mann, founder of the N.C.E.A., who combined a genius for public relations with an ambition to proselytize for the "disease" concept of alcoholism she had encountered in A.A. (Having first joined in 1939, she became the first female member to remain sober.) Although Mann officially dissociated herself and the N.C.E.A. from A.A., her mission was to develop the grass-roots organization needed to spread the fellowship's message. The academic wing of the Alcoholism Movement, which revolved around the research center created at Yale by Howard W. Haggard and Elvin Morton Jellinek, maintained a dispassionately scientific distance from the more fervent elements of the coalition. But the goal was much the same: to detach the study and perception of habitual drunkenness from the moral frame of reference associated with temperance and Prohibition.

The planks of the Alcoholism Movement's platform, already nailed down by the late 1930s, were that alcoholism is an illness rather than a failure of character and, therefore, a medical rather than a moral issue; that treatment of alcoholism is a public health imperative; and that, fortunately, complete rehabilitation is possible if the alcoholic is placed in competent hands. In one 1938 magazine article, "an eminent physician" was deferentially quoted (in italics, no less) as he put the weight of his medical authority behind the new common sense:

> "Alcoholism," he insists, "is not a vice but a disease. The alcoholic is not a moral weakling. He is tragically ill with a mental malady. If taken in time he can often be cured. The spread of the disease can be stemmed and turned back, but only with the aid of the doctors and the psychologists who have made it their field of research and experiment. To try to do so by sumptuary laws [i.e. Prohibition] is like trying to cure and prevent tuberculosis with a cough-drop."

The visibility and respectability gained by the allied organizations of the Alcoholism Movement reflected one of its major goals: not only to promote a medicalized understanding of alcoholism, but also to create an improved image for the alcoholic—one commensurate with the perception of a post-Prohibition increase of problem drinking within the American middle class. By the 1940s, as ever more such families were affected by habitual drunkenness, the public became receptive to the idea, as Johnson says, that if "well educated, industrious members of the upwardly-mobile middle class could succumb to [the] ravages of habitual drunkenness," then perhaps "problem drinking was not merely a matter of weak will-power and moral degeneracy." Not surprisingly, the temperance stereotype of the drunkard as a skid-row derelict gradually gave way to a far more sympathetic view as the N.C.E.A. disseminated "the image of the alcoholic as a hard-working business executive who was the unfortunate victim of a disease" that strikes indiscriminately at every social level.

As articulated by E. M. Jellinek, the acknowledged spokesman for the Yale Center, the new paradigm of alcoholism posited a sharp distinction between "normal" drinkers and "alcoholics," whose addiction was evinced by an intense craving for drink and a complete loss of control over drinking. Alcohol, that is, was seen to be addictive only for a certain group: those who developed an increased tolerance, who experienced withdrawal symptoms if they tried to quit drinking, and who exhibited bodily deterioration as a result of heavy and habitual consumption. The "disease" of alcoholism was thought to be progressive (it moved from psychological to physiological dependence) and irreversible (the alcoholic could never safely return to normal drinking). The only effective treatment, according to the Alcoholism Movement, was lifelong abstinence.

Except for its absolute distinction between alcoholics and normal drinkers—a distinction that won the praise and support of the liquor industry for locating addiction in the person rather than the substance—the modern disease model offered little that was new. Its major ideas were derived from the Victorian concept of inebriety and a wealth of scientific investigations dating from the late nineteenth century. Jellinek himself first came into prominence through his work of digesting and summarizing all of the old published research on drinking and drunkenness. The new paradigm was, in essence, a triumph of publicity and conceptual packaging. "What was scientific about the disease concept of alcoholism besides its articulation by scientists is . . . not apparent," one historian drily observes. "Neither of its key terms—*alcoholism* and *disease*—was clearly or consistently defined. . . . Nor were any of its key propositions supported by controlled empirical research." Jellinek himself later retreated from his own theories. And by the 1950s, several of the scientists associated with the Alcoholism Movement were troubled by a continuing lack of validation: "In spite of all the propaganda that had been distributed, the scientific evidence supporting the disease concept was extremely tenuous."

Written when the disease concept was still rapidly gaining adherents, Jackson's novel had a symbiotic relationship with the Alcoholism Movement. Early in 1944, according to Ernest Kurtz, a Hollywood producer sought the help of Alcoholics Anonymous in making a feature "that would dramatize A.A.'s understanding of alcoholism." This project became superfluous in view of the 1945 Paramount film of *The Lost Weekend,* for which director Billy Wilder requested A.A. literature "to assist in the movie production." At about the same time, Jackson's publisher, Stanley M. Rinehart, wrote to Bill Wilson, cofounder of Alcoholics Anonymous, to announce the imminent publication of *The Lost Weekend* and to request "A.A.'s help in promoting the book." That Rinehart sought such an endorsement (which was not granted) shows that the novel's success was perceived to depend in part on the favor of A.A. But successful propagation of the disease concept was likewise perceived by the Alcoholism Movement to depend in part on the public's reaction to a story that had potential to transform the common understanding of alcoholism.

After the movie version was released late in November 1945, it was anxiously reviewed in the Yale Center's journal by Selden D. Bacon, a prominent researcher. Because Americans were, in Bacon's judgment, "poorly informed and at the same time easily excited about excessive drinking as a moral problem," the impact of *The Lost Weekend* could be extremely damaging insofar as the film (which was seen to follow the book "quite closely") misled audiences into believing that all alcoholics are like Don Birnam, that anyone who drinks might become like him, that the alcoholic's prognosis is hopeless, and that "hospitals and doctors are not only useless for this condition, but are, in addition, heartless, inefficient and horrendous." What was sorely needed, Bacon insisted, was a "rational solution of the problems of alcohol," a solution based on a sound "medical viewpoint" that had not yet fully crystallized, despite the best efforts of scientific authorities. Unfortunately, the public "does not regard the Don Birnams as ill men engulfed in their habit because of their illness, and needing good medical care, not moral suasion or moral damnation. The serious student of alcoholism has tried earnestly to get public recognition of the fact that the alcoholic is an ill man; *The Lost Weekend* will not further, but will obstruct, this recognition."

In a later issue of the same journal, however, a psychology instructor at New York University reported that the film did *not,* as Bacon had feared, leave audiences with the impression that alcoholism was "hopeless and incurable." On the contrary, in a poll of 116 undergraduate students, a large majority (78%) answered "yes" to the question: "Do you think that 'The Lost Weekend' portrayed the alcoholic as an individual who is ill and requires specialized treatment?" That is, student perceptions of the movie were in accord with the Alcoholism Movement's view that "the alcoholic is ill and needs therapy."

Jackson came by his own knowledge of the disease concept directly. *The Lost Weekend* was based largely on his own textbook case, including his experiences at Bellevue and with private psychiatrists. Although Jackson did not join A.A. until ten years after the novel appeared, he was acquainted with the fellowship while writing it in the early 1940s. *The Lost Weekend* subtly incorporates A.A. ideas, sometimes in echoes or paraphrases of program sayings—as in the scene in which Birnam appears to have "hit bottom" (A.A. lingo for the moment when the alcoholic becomes fully and honestly aware of his powerlessness over alcohol). Don seems at last to be breaking through his denial as he casts aside his excuses for drinking:

> To hell with the causes—absent father, fraternity shock, too much mother, too much money, or the dozen other reasons you fell back on to justify yourself. They counted for nothing in the face of the one fact: you drank and it was killing you. Why? Because alcohol was something you couldn't handle, it had you licked. Why? Because you had reached the point where one drink was too many and a hundred not enough. (p. 222)

The last sentence is a familiar A.A. slogan, and the entire passage expresses the pragmatic spirit of the Alcoholism Movement; its bias toward effects rather than causes, its concern with remedies rather than etiologies.

As an intellectual, Don Birnam can't help being fascinated, however, by psychological theories about drinking—particularly by the psychoanalytic notion that alcoholism and homosexuality are closely related. Birnam recurs several times to his bad experience with "the foolish psychiatrist" who dwelt on Don's homosexual experiences in childhood. He soon discovered that "he knew more about the subject, more about pathology, certainly more about himself and what made him tick, than the doctor" (p.53). But although Birnam rejects psychoanalytic theory as mumbo jumbo, he has nevertheless been

influenced by the doctor's point of view, if only as something to resist.

The Lost Weekend was written when psychoanalysis had its greatest sway in the field of alcoholism studies and treatment. A linkage between "alcoholism" and "homosexuality," both of which terms came into clinical use at the end of the nineteenth century under the aegis of psychiatry, was hypothesized in Karl Abraham's pioneering study of 1908. Abraham claimed that alcohol "stimulates the 'complex' of masculinity" because "respect for prowess in drinking is closely bound up with respect for sexual prowess." The man who does not drink "is accounted a weakling." But alcohol also loosens the mental inhibition of same-sexual libido: "When drinking, men fall on each other's necks and kiss one another: they feel that they are united by peculiarly intimate ties and this moves them to tears and to intimate modes of address." Therefore, he reasoned, "every drinking bout is tinged with homosexuality. The homosexual component-instincts, which education has taught us to repress and sublimate, reappear in no veiled form under the influence of alcohol."

Abraham's standing as Freud's loyal lieutenant gave added weight to his theories; the idea that alcoholics are "latent homosexuals" gained immediate acceptance in psychoanalytic circles and reechoed in the broader medical literature throughout the 1930s. Consider, for example, an important paper by Robert P. Knight, an American psychiatrist of the Freudian persuasion, delivered at the 1936 Congress of the International Psychoanalytic Association. Knight agreed with Abraham that excessive drinking signifies "the regressive acting out of unconscious libidinal and sadistic drives"; that alcoholics exhibit a "strong homosexual conflict," which often results in "a conscious or almost conscious fear of being regarded effeminate"; that alcoholics mask their "spurious masculinity" with alcoholic fellowship, finding that "it is regarded as not grown up, as 'sissyfied', *not* to drink, and that to drink heavily and 'hell around' with the boys is regarded as proof of manliness and potency." From his analysis of ten cases, Knight offered the additional (and tentative) generalization that alcoholics commonly have a family background in which "an over-indulgent, over-protective" mother is combined with a "cold and unaffectionate" father who is alternately severe and indulgent. This parental constellation was often identified by psychoanalysts in the 1930s as characteristic as well of homosexuals.

Two years after Knight's paper, in a book aimed at the general reader, two non-analytic experts acknowledged that "unquestionably, repressed homosexuality may be found at the roots of alcoholic addiction." They also asserted, however, that "our experience does not justify any sweeping statement concerning a basic homosexual trend as the cause of alcoholism." And by the 1940s, even some psychoanalysts were beginning to question the orthodox view. In a clinical study published the same year as *The Lost Weekend* (a study that cited the novel as an informed source), Edmund Bergler reiterated the conventional Freudian wisdom on the regressive nature of excessive drinking: the alcoholic as a fixated "oral" type who acts out sado-masochistic fantasies through the substitution of the bottle for the breast, etc. But in referring to the opinion that "the disease reveals unconscious homosexual tendencies," Bergler saw no necessary linkage. Also in 1944, at the summer seminar on alcoholism sponsored by the Yale Center, Carney Landis drew similar conclusions about the claim that "the psychic reason for alcohol addiction is the incomplete repressed homosexuality which the individual cannot sublimate." Noting recent findings that "the occurrence of overt homosexuality is much more prevalent than was hitherto believed," Landis asserted that "homosexuality is an independent personality factor which is not necessarily associated with other forms of personality disorder, neurosis, psychosis or addiction."

Set in 1936, the year Jackson himself sought treatment for his drinking, *The Lost Weekend* follows the Freudian line on alcoholism he had encountered through his reading and in psychoanalysis. One of Jackson's sources, as the manuscript of the novel reveals, was Karl Menninger's influential book on the modes of human self-destructiveness, *Man Against Himself* (1938), which contains a chapter on "alcohol addiction" as a form of "chronic suicide." Like Robert P. Knight, who was also associated with the Menninger Clinic, Menninger regarded excessive drinking as symptomatic of an underlying neurosis involving psychosexual fixation and latent homosexuality: "It is almost axiomatic that alcoholics in spite of a great show of heterosexual activity, have secretly a great fear of women and of heterosexuality in general, apparently regarding it as fraught with much danger."

Throughout *The Lost Weekend*, Don Birnam is shown to be both wary of heterosexuality and terrified of homosexuality. He recalls a lover once demanding to know, "'Why do you only come to bed with me when you are drunk?'" She had not been mollified by his glib reply: "Because I'm *always* drunk!" (p. 186). As "the foolish psychiatrist" would have insisted, Don's problem lies deeper than that: in his childhood abandonment by his father; in his adolescent fantasies, during masturbation, of his friend's father rather than of Gertrude Hort, a voluptuous girl his own age; in his traumatic experience as a college fraternity pledge, when he developed a "passionate hero-worship" for an upperclassman that "led, like a fatal infatuation, to scandal and public disgrace, because no one had understood or got the story straight" (pp. 48-49). Kicked out of the Kappa U house, Don crept home to nurse psychic wounds that have never completely healed. Years later, when he happens to encounter the man who had filled his abandoned slot in Kappa U, Don is still paralyzed by dread.

This encounter itself, which revives all of Birnam's sexual fear and ambivalence, reads as if Jackson had tailored it to fit the theories of his analysts. Birnam recalls the scene—a Greenwich Village bar—in one of his drunken reveries. A handsome young man had been standing silently beside him; just as Don was about to leave, the man offered to buy him a drink. Don immediately sensed (but did not acknowledge to himself) homoerotic overtones: the hint of a homosexual overture, simultaneously enhanced and veiled by the presence of alcohol and the bar-room practice of treating:

> He looked a little worried; also faintly belligerent; the frown challenged Don not to misunderstand the impulse which prompted the invitation. Don got it at once; and as he recognized, like a veteran before a neophyte, the stage of drinking the other had reached—the confidential, the confiding stage—he began to feel superior, amused, tolerant, generous, and warmly friendly himself. "Why, thank you very much," he said with a smile. "And then perhaps you'll have one with me." . . .
>
> "You probably wonder why I did that," Brad said.
>
> "No I don't, at all." Don smiled to reassure him.
>
> "I'm staying up late tonight and I feel like talking to somebody."
>
> "I understand." Oh, he understood. How many times indeed, under just such circumstances, in just such places, had he been in on conversations of just this sort. That familiar opening line: it was the prelude to who knew what confidences—boring, very likely; nothing to confide about; intimate but unrevealing and finally elusive or even resentful. (Pp. 84-85)

Unlike his erstwhile fraternity brothers, Don understands that man-to-man intimacy, especially the kind inspired by alcohol, need not imply anything unmanly. Brad's familiar opening line is taken as a prelude not to sex, but to talk—and boring talk at that. Don has no more patience for boozy confidences than for homosexuals, such as the pianist at Jack's place—a "fattish baby-faced young man: Dannie or Billy or Jimmie or Hughie somebody," who sings leeringly suggestive lyrics to songs like "The 23rd Street Ferry" and "Peter and the Dyke" in which "*camping, queen, faggot, meat* were words frequently played upon" (p.28). Birnam's homophobic disdain extends even to his taste in bookbinding! He shudders to recall the Elbert Hubbard volumes in his father's library: "the sickeningly limp-leather Roycroft books that almost gave you the creeps to hold" (p. 148).

Don's heterosexual identity depends on his conscious revulsion from homosexuality. But he also conforms to the psychoanalytic profile of the alcoholic; unconsciously attracted to other men, he is "latently homosexual." This hidden truth becomes all-too-painfully clear when Birnam is accosted in the hospital by Bim, the insolently coquettish nurse, who contemptuously struts around the ward, purrs like Marlene Dietrich (p. 129), and makes Don—whom he flirtingly addresses as "Baby"—feel like Pola Negri being mentally undressed by "a lecherous Prussian officer in some ancient film" (p. 134):

Here was the daydream turned inside-out; a projection, in reverse, of the wishful and yearning fancy; the back of the picture, the part always turned to the wall. The flower of the ingrown seed he had in him was here shown in unhealthy bloom, *ad terrorem* and *ad nauseam*. It was aspiration in its raw and naked state, aspiration un-ennobled, a lapse of nature as bizarre and undeniable as the figures of his imagined life were deniable, bizarre, beyond reach. All that he wanted to become and, in his fanciful world, became, was here represented in throwback. He himself stood midway between the ideal and this—as far from the one as from the other. But oh, too—oh, too!—as far from the other as from the one. If he was uncomfortable in Bim's stifling presence, did he not also have reason to be comforted? Or was midway, nothing—nothing at all? (P. 135)

In accordance with psychoanalytic theory, Don understands his own alcoholism to be akin to Bim's homosexuality in the sense that both are atavistic slippages from an evolutionary (Social Darwinian) ideal: outcroppings of a "bizarre" and disgustingly animal nature that falls far short of the spiritual heights; in short, a nightmarish "inversion" of the artist's imaginative daydream. Don takes comfort—comfort that seems also to be a form of denial—in thinking that whatever his kinship to Bim may be, he still holds a higher place on the evolutionary ladder, and he is far more secure in his manliness.

This idea is developed a few pages later, as Don belatedly formulates a response to what Bim whispered to him as he was leaving the hospital: "Listen, baby. . . . I know you" (p. 139):

> He was aware, as Bim was, of the downward path he was on; he knew himself well enough to know and admit that Bim had every reason to say what he said—but only insofar as Bim saw, in him, the potential confederate that was every alcoholic: the fellow bogged down in adolescence; the guy off his track, off his trolley; the man still unable to take, at thirty-three or -six or -nine, the forward step he had missed in his 'teens; the poor devil demoralized and thrown off balance by the very stuff intended to restore his frightened or baffled ego; the gent jarred loose into unsavory bypaths that gave him the shudders to think of but which were his natural habitat and inevitable home so long as drink remained the *modus operandi* of his life. . . . (P. 144)

Yes, Birnam allows, the alcoholic and the homosexual are both cases of arrested development; stuck in adolescence, neither can be fully a man. But "the trouble with homos," Don thinks, is that in their eagerness to embrace their own kind, in their knowing glances of recognition, they smugly assume too much: "They were always so damned anxious to suspect every guy they couldn't make of merely playing hard-to-get; so damned anxious to believe that their own taint was shared by everybody else" (p. 145). Bim, with "the bright eye of his kind," keenly observes the potential "homo" in Don. But what he fails

to see is "that the alcoholic was not himself, able to choose his own path, and therefore the kinship he seemed to reveal was incidental, accidental, transitory at best. If the drunk had been himself he would not be a drunk and potential brother in the first place" (p. 144).

Such passages raise interpretive difficulties, some of which are inherent to Jackson's narrative technique—in which the narrator hovers near Don Birnam, the Jamesian center of consciousness, reporting both his words and his private thoughts (in free indirect discourse), while also keeping some ironic distance from him. But how much distance? How credible or reliable are Don Birnam's opinions meant to be? On the question of psychoanalytic theory, for instance, does *The Lost Weekend* finally affirm or dispute the idea that alcoholics are "latent homosexuals"? How closely may Jackson be identified with a character who is evidently based on himself?

Although Don Birnam's drunken experiences were largely derived from Jackson's, the character lacks his author's sober perspective. Birnam is undercut as a self-deluded alcoholic in the grip of denial. It would seem, then, that the passages quoted above are best read as evidence not of Jackson's sexual insecurities, but rather of Birnam's. Don's thinking is exposed here as a rationalization of his "latent homosexuality," to which he is no more capable of facing up than to his alcoholism. Since Birnam is poised at the novel's end to go off on yet another binge, the reader may reasonably infer that his self-deception will continue. In order for him to stop drinking, the novel implies, Don must accept that the alcoholic *is* himself and that Bim *does* "know" him—because the alcoholic is not only a "potential confederate," but also, as psychoanalysis would insist, a brother to the homosexual.

The Lost Weekend, like *Nightwood*, thus inverts the gender assumptions of those novels in which alcohol is represented as the preservative of manliness and the alcoholic as the polar opposite of the homosexual. Jackson's subversion of the drinking culture of modernism results from the assimilation into his fiction of the concept of "alcoholism" itself, along with its freight of psychoanalytic theory.

During the early decades of the twentieth century, modernism revolutionized the arts in America while Prohibition revolutionized drinking practices. The avant garde reacted against the Victorian idea of inebriation by producing a literature that idealized intoxication as iconoclasm and lionized the drunk as an anti-Puritan rebel. A major element in such texts as *John Barleycorn, The Sun Also Rises, Tender Is the Night, Appointment in Samarra,* and *Nightwood* is the representation of excessive drinking as an inevitable response of the sensitive consciousness to the nightmarish human condition.

The Lost Weekend began to close the book on these drunk narratives by exposing the literariness of their alcoholic despair. "In A Glass," Birnam's hypothetical

Drunkard's Rigadoon, exists only within the claustral confines of a mind soaked in modernist fiction. As Don recognizes, "His very nightmare [the bat hallucination] was synthetic: a dream by Thomas Mann" (p. 215). In his sober moments, he realizes that his existence does not live up to the high romantic tragedy of the sort he admires in *Tender Is the Night,* in which the alcoholic culture hero learns the bitter wisdom of the ages from John Barleycorn. The drunken life is "merely ludicrous—ludicrous but not worth laughing at, something merely to put up with and bear with because there was nothing else to do about it" (p. 216). In its demystification of the White Logic, *The Lost Weekend* inaugurated a new mode of American fiction in which habitual drunkenness was figured less as a sign of The Modern Temper than as the symptom of a disease.

Charles Jackson announced publicly in 1944 that his next book would be "about the regeneration of an alcoholic," a subject which he says he has found more fascinating than that of *The Lost Weekend.* "Farther and Wilder," in which Don Birnam was to reappear, still remained unfinished when Jackson died in 1968; but the "more fascinating" subject of recovery from alcoholism has nevertheless become a flourishing genre.

Once the Alcoholism Movement had reconstructed the framework within which Americans understood excessive drinking, once habitual drunkenness had been medicalized as well as psychologized, then "alcoholic" writers began to become self-conscious of their "alcoholism," and fiction about drinking changed accordingly. Since the 1940s, what might be called the recovery narrative has largely superseded the modernist drunk narrative. American novelists have continued to produce some powerful stories of alcoholic degeneration, such as Natalie Anderson Scott's *The Story of Mrs. Murphy* (1947) or Richard Yates's *Disturbing the Peace* (1975). More common, however, have been fictions about relief from alcohol (and other drugs) that reflect the influence of the Alcoholism Movement in general and of A.A. in particular. Significant examples of this type are Thomas Randall's *The Twelfth Step* (1957), Roger Treat's *The Endless Road* (1960), John Berryman's *Recovery* (1972), Donald Newlove's *The Drunks* (1974), John Cheever's *Falconer* (1977), Ivan Gold's *Sams in a Dry Season* (1990), and David Gates's *Jernigan* (1991).

Numerous Hollywood films, some derived from popular plays or bestselling books, have also dealt explicitly with alcoholism. In several of these, too, A.A. is offered explicitly as the means to "recovery": *Come Fill the Cup* (1950), *Come Back, Little Sheba* (1952), *Something to Live For* (1952), *I'll Cry Tomorrow* (1955), *The Voice in the Mirror* (1958), and *Days of Wine and Roses* (1962).

The proliferation of such works in the immediate postwar period had much to do with the cumulative success of A.A., in which recovery narratives have always played an important part. In A.A. meetings, as in all three editions of the "Big Book," members routinely tell of their personal adventures before and after joining the fellowship and retrace their progress from drunkenness to sobriety. These stories, which constitute a type of spiritual autobiography, have not only been adapted to fiction; they have also created a discourse for the rapidly expanding "recovery" movement of the late twentieth century.

A.A. itself was another creation of the Lost Generation of middle-class Americans who came of age during the early 1920s and who made excessive drinking a hallmark of their youthful rebellion. When this cohort reached middle age at mid-century, it was faced with the resultant drinking problems. (A common pattern in male drinkers is for alcoholism to develop gradually for twenty years or so and then to become acute when they reach their forties.) "The founding of Alcoholics Anonymous in 1935, and its emergence as a national movement around 1940," says Robin Room, "must be seen as the reaction of the initial 'wet generations' to the predicament in which they found themselves." Both the approach and the rhetoric of A.A., moreover, "were carefully attuned to the mind-set of members of the initial 'wet generation' and, in particular, to the men of the generation." The anti-drink discourse of A.A. provided an alternative to the now "discredited invective of the temperance movement."

The blunt and deflationary pragmatism of A.A. also provided an alternative to the seductive grandiosity of The Modern Temper. Donald Newlove recalls how in his drinking days he sought "the just, pure expression of a kind of holy blackness I admired as the richest resource for dark language." Life's gruesome side, which he had often experienced on the job as an ambulance driver, had initiated him, he believed, into the darkest secrets of the White Logic. The deadliest ordeal was having to wrestle with a corpse wedged upside down between a bathtub and toilet:

> [A]s I got down and pried I told myself that if I lived through this, that then I had gone through my Guadalcanal, my Iwo Jima, my Saipan, my Tarawa, my King Lear tree-splitting storm, my Godot, my *No Exit,* my holocaust, my pie-slice of the universal horror and tragedy and that I was now an accredited Twentieth-Century Writer and fully empowered to seek and state the definitive negative statement for my times and to hold a mirror up to the power of blackness, the night within the night, my Dachau, Berlin, Hiroshima, a spiritual desolation that granted me the clear right to drink. I deserved to drink to keep my good cheer and avoid suicide.

Newlove later came to realize that, like Don Birnam, he had been aggrandizing his capacity for suffering: "I still, of course, didn't know I was a drunk or that my bottom was far, far off, and that I was now only groping about in my graveyard period, a merely literary agony."

In contrast to the truly horrific suffering endured at Guadalcanal or Dachau or Hiroshima, the agony of the alcoholic "Twentieth-Century Writer"—agony that was largely self-inflicted through drinking and that served in turn to justify drinking—*was* "merely literary" more often than these writers wished to recognize. When F. Scott Fitzgerald gravely opined, "There are no second acts in American lives," he neglected to mention that he and many other modernists stuck in their "graveyard period" had gotten drunk during the first act and passed out during intermission.

Dale Edmonds

SOURCE: "Mescallusions or the Drinking Man's *Under the Volcano,*" in *Journal of Modern Literature,* 6, 2, April, 1977, pp. 277-88.

[*In the following excerpt, Edmonds recounts the details and blissful qualities of Geoffrey Firmin's drinking binge in Malcolm Lowry's* Under the Volcano.]

My thoughts toward this paper began at the first MLA Malcolm Lowry Seminar in New York in 1974. In the discussion period following delivery of papers David Markson, Lowry's novelist friend and author of the first academic study of *Under the Volcano,* pointed an accusatory finger at me and said, "Obviously you're not a drinking man." After the hysterical outburst on the part of my friends in the audience had died down, Markson took me to task for something I once wrote about the novel. In tracing the mouthful-by-mouthful progress of Geoffrey Firmin, the Consul, through the Day of the Dead (November 2, 1938, the day of the novel's action) I wrote, "The Consul, Yvonne, and Hugh leave [the Consul's house], encounter Jacques, and go to the latter's house. At shortly after 1:30, the Consul downs the four cocktails (whiskey and soda?) Jacques has prepared for the party, then finishes the contents of the cocktail shaker." Now, any drinker worth his salt—and lemon and tequila—knows you do not mix whiskey with soda in a "cocktail shaker." Whiskey-and-soda is not properly a "cocktail" at all, but a "highball" (even if it is served at "cocktail" parties). So, Markson's challenge of my credentials as a drinking man was justified.

Back in New Orleans I imposed upon myself the penance of twenty-four hours of total abstinence, during which time I had ample opportunity for reflection. There was no excuse for my error; I simply blundered. But, I asked myself, why did Malcolm Lowry—and I defy anyone to challenge *his* credentials as a drinking man—use the term "cocktails" for the "despicable repast" Jacques prepares in Chapter VII? [All citations appear from the New American Library edition, 1971]. On virtually every other occasion in the novel when a drink comes up—or goes down—Lowry specifies what it is: Johnny Walker, Burke's Irish, Carta Blanca. Or he refers to the drink by a generic term: whiskey, beer, mescal. Only with the cocktails in Chapter VII does he fail to let us know what the Consul is drinking. So what is in that cocktail shaker? Whiskey sours? Jacques probably wouldn't have bourbon on hand, and I doubt if he would adulterate Scotch with

citrus juice. Manhattans? As I said, probably no bourbon available. Margaritas? I don't think that tequila cocktails were in vogue in the late 1930s. I'll hazard the opinion that the cocktail shaker holds martinis. Purists may cavil that you don't shake martinis. True, but we don't see Jacques shaking them, and you can stir martinis in a shaker.

My pondering of the cocktail business led me to consider the subject of drinks and drinking in *Under the Volcano* in general. Critics have written eloquently and persuasively of the symbolic implications of the Consul's alcoholism, of the reasons buried in his past— or alive and kicking in his present—that drive him to drink, of the pathological nature of his addiction. All well and good. But a consideration of drinking in *Under the Volcano* might begin with some more fundamental matters: what the Consul drinks on the Day of the Dead, how it affects him, and what Lowry wants us to think about it. In an attempt to address myself to these questions, I have compiled . . . a "Record of Geoffrey Firmin's Intake of Alcoholic Beverages, Day of the Dead, 1938, Quauhnahuac, Mexico." I see no need to reiterate here what I cover in [that record], but I would like to make some observations arising from my counting of the Consul's drinks.

First, let me state what is obvious: *Under the Volcano* is a drinker's paradise. References to drinks, drinking, drinking places, and/or drunkenness occur on 252 of the 377 pages of the NAL Plume edition. The longest dry stretch in the novel, which occurs in the midst of Hugh's reverie in Chapter VI, is seven pages in length. To conclude [my record] I list the nine different potations the Consul ingests on the Day of the Dead. But in the course of the novel Lowry mentions virtually every other alcoholic beverage known to man (two notable exceptions: bourbon and vodka).

There is a curious fact about mescal, perhaps the most important drink on the list in terms of *Under the Volcano.* Malcolm Lowry, unquestionably one of the "major adepts in the Great Brotherhood of Alcohol," reveals a serious misconception about this drink (139). He—or the Consul—invests mescal with a potency in relation to tequila which it simply does not have. At the Café Paris in Chapter VII Jacques says of tequila, " . . . If I ever start to drink that stuff, Geoffrey, you'll know I'm done for." The Consul answers, "It's mescal with me. . . . Tequila, no, that is healthful . . . and delightful. . . . Good for you. But if I ever start to drink mescal again, I'm afraid, yes, that would be the end" (216). At the Terminal Cantina El Bosque Señora Gregorio offers to draw the Consul a mescal, but he insists on tequila. Finally, at the Salón Ofélia in Chapter X the consul orders mescal, for "Nothing less than mescal would do" (281). Critics usually see the Consul's decision to drink mescal as the beginning of his end. But, actually, there is no essential difference between mescal and tequila. The relationship of the two is like that of brandy and cognac: as "all cognac is brandy, but not all brandy is cognac," so "all tequila is mescal, but not all mescal is tequila." Mescal is the generic name for a distilled liquor made from a plant belonging to the genus *Agave* or maguey (of which there are reputedly four hundred species). Tequila is a mescal made from the *Agave Tequilana* which grows well only in the State of Jalisco, near the towns of Tapatitlán and Tequila. Mescal, other than the tequila variety, is produced in three wide areas in Mexico: north central (portions of San Luis Potosí, Durango, and Zacatecas), south Pacific Coast (portions of Michoacan, Guerrero, and Oaxaca), and adjacent to the Guatemalan border (primarily Chiapas). The process for making tequila is the same as that for making all other varieties of mescal (and this process has nothing to do with *pulque*). Tequila and other mescals have the same chemical properties and alcoholic content. The only difference is that the maguey from which tequila is made gives it a flavor different from that of other mescals.

Now, after saying this, let me hedge a bit. In Mexico in 1938 barmen, like Diosdado at the Farolito, may have dispensed 110-proof mescal (today this is almost invariably cut to 80-90 proof by addition of distilled water). But I think Malcolm Lowry simply got it in his head that other mescals were stronger, more dangerous, than tequila, and he passed this misconception along to the Consul. This is an understandable error. To anyone accustomed to the pleasant, cactusy tang of tequila, the virtually flavorless but unquestionably potent nature of other mescals does seem sinister. But if the drinking of Mexican distilled liquor is to be the "end" of the Consul, he begins this process about 10:30 a.m. when he has his first pull from the tequila bottle hidden in his garden. The psychological effect of the Consul's drinking of mescal is another matter. If, as seems the case, he is convinced that mescal is more potent than tequila, and that his first drink of mescal will signal the onslaught of his doom, then the intrinsic nature of mescal makes no difference—Orange Crush might have the same effect.

On the Day of the Dead the Consul puts away, by my count, some sixty-one ounces—almost two quarts—of 80-90 proof alcohol (this includes equivalent totals for beer and the like). This is a staggering amount, but is it, as some readers have complained, an incredible one? A man the Consul's size (about 5'9", 170 pounds) metabolizes about an ounce of alcohol per hour through urine, breath, sweat, and action of the liver and other tissues. Thus the Consul in the twelve hours of the novel's action would metabolize about twelve of the sixty-one ounces, leaving forty-nine ounces saturating his bloodstream. For a man the Consul's size five ounces of whiskey will produce a 0.1 per cent blood alcohol level in two hours. The Consul takes in about ten times this amount in the course of the day (not counting the twelve ounces he might metabolize). A level of 0.15 per cent is legally intoxicating; this is achieved by one's drinking 6-8 ounces of whiskey (one ounce per hour will maintain this level). Blood alcohol levels of 0.35-0.4 produce coma and may be lethal. Let us say that the Consul could still function with a blood alcohol level of 0.4 per cent. This means about eighteen ounces of alcohol should make him se-

verely intoxicated, perhaps comatose. Between 7:00 a.m. and noon the Consul drinks about eighteen ounces of alcohol (no telling what he has *before* 7:00 a.m.). But he does space this total over five hours. Between noon and 7:00 p.m. he has somewhat more than forty ounces. Even with metabolic elimination of some of this, I do not see how the Consul could have less than a 0.5 blood alcohol level which, according to the experts, would make him unconscious, if not dead.

In the Consul's—and Lowry's—defense, however, I might mention the following points. The Consul vomits after he drinks some bay rum scalp preparation. This would perhaps clear some of the alcohol from his body (although the greater portion would have been absorbed by his bloodstream long since). He eats half a canapé and perhaps a little of his dinner. Food slows the absorption of alcohol and hence retards the intoxication process. The Consul is extraordinarily active during the day. Hyper-ventilation and/or profuse sweating may intensify the excretion of alcohol. We may assume that both result from the prodigious exercise the Consul gets: he walks from the center of Quauhnahuac to his house; he strides up the Calle Nicaragua (until it rises up to meet him); he rambles about his garden; he plunges up and down the stairs of Jacques' tower; he ambles to the center of Quauhnahuac; he lurches about the square; he rides a carnival machine; he takes a long and arduous bus ride, during which he piles off and back onto the bus; he surges to the Arena Tomalín and climbs to a seat; he strolls to the Salón Ofélia; he runs part way through the forest, then walks the rest of the way to Parián; he copulates with a prostitute; he argues actively with, and finally fights, a number of Mexicans; and, at every stage of the game, he punctuates these activities with exclamation points of elbow-bending. Still, would even this activity ward off the severe intoxication the Consul should be experiencing as a result of what he has drunk?

In apparent contravention of the blood alcohol level figures I have given, Doctors Howard W. Haggard and E. M. Jellinek write: "We do not argue against the fact that occasionally, when on a spree, an abnormal drinker, especially one of large size, may drink a quart or, if spread judiciously over the period, even two quarts of whiskey in one day." The Consul is not "of large size," but he is "strong as a horse" (71), and he is certainly an "abnormal drinker." He spreads his drinks in a surprisingly judicious manner over the twelve-hour period . . . at least until the chaotic last hour at the Farolito. According to Doctors Haggard and Jellinek, then, the Consul could perhaps manage his sixty-one ounces.

But enough flogging of the dead horse (perhaps with "Seagram's 7" branded on its rump) of the Consul's alcoholic consumption on the Day of the Dead. David Markson should have the last word here:

Dear Dale:

Carole Slade [discussion leader of the 1975 Lowry

seminar] just sent me the papers from the Lowry seminar at the MLA shindig, and I wanted to say I enjoyed yours muchly. But it's set me to brooding, and I may have a random thought or two of small value for you if you're pursuing the matter any further.

The problem with contemplating the capabilities of the boozer, it seems to me, is that you can't do it academically and/or get your data out of medical texts. Your doctors who acknowledge that an "abnormal" drinker *could* do a quart or even two a day sound skeptical or grudging about it ("occasionally," etc.). I suppose research here is hard to come by: rummies off skid row ain't reliable, all drinkers lie, etc. But, but, but—would you believe I know people who drink a quart a day, every day of their lives, and *function*? Fact, which throws all that medical speculation out the window. Doctors have to be sober; asking them to comment on drinking capacity is like asking a virgin about fornication.

I think Markson has the right idea. We have all been too sober about this business of drinking in *Under the Volcano.* There has been too much doom-saying about the Consul's "tragedy." Granted, he ends up at the bottom of a barranca, but he has a rollicking good time getting there. As Hugh says, " . . . if a man can hold his liquor as well as that why shouldn't he drink?" (117).

At numerous places in the novel Lowry clearly indicates that the Consul's drinking has a positive—even ecstatic—side. In his unposted letter to Yvonne the Consul writes, " . . . but this is how I drink too, as if I were taking an eternal sacrament" (40). He muses (or Yvonne imagines he does), " . . . what beauty can compare to that of a cantina in the early morning?" (50). The Consul feels " . . . an immense comfort . . . in the mere presence of the whiskey bottle" (69). One of the Consul's familiars tells him that mescal would be "the end though a damned good end" (69-70). The Consul thinks of sobriety as "complete cold ugly" (79); to him nothing in the world is "more terrible" than an empty bottle, unless it is an empty glass (86). At one point he grips a Johnny Walker bottle and murmurs "I love you" (91); shortly thereafter he imagines that clouds say to him, "Drink all morning . . . drink all day. This is life!" (93). As the Consul drinks deeply from a tequila bottle hidden in his garden he thinks, "Ah. Good. God. Christ"; then, "Bliss. Jesus. Sanctuary" (127). Dr. Vigil advises the Consul, "More alcohol is perhaps best" (139). In the picture "Los Borrachones," which the Consul sees in Jacques' room, some of the drunkards plunging downward to their doom reveal on their faces "the most unmistakable relief," and their wives seem to be casting "half-jealous glances" toward them (199). At the Café Paris, after the Consul has a much-needed drink, he feels "the fire of the tequila run down his spine like lightning striking a tree which thereupon, miraculously, blossoms" (215). In Chapter XII, shortly before he is shot, the Consul thinks of the drinks he has taken over the years and concludes, " . . . ah, those burning draughts in loneliness . . . they were perhaps the

happiest things his life had known!" (360). Critics usually see the brilliant passage in Chapter X, in which the Consul imagines the "bottles, bottles, bottles" and "glasses, glasses, glasses" he has piled up over the years, as a litany of despair (292). But could not these bottles and glasses be considered the soaring accomplishments of the dedicated drinker?

The foregoing catalogue could be countered by one of negative references to alcohol. I do not deny this. I want to stress, however, that the Consul's plunge has its moments of bliss and glory and that drink is the Consul's mistress, his muse, his God, no matter what dark fate awaits him. Who is to say that on the Day of the Dead he does not realize his destiny through his long day's drinking? One might ask, what about Yvonne and Hugh, who "love" him? What about his aborted diplomatic career? What about his abandoned book on "Secret Knowledge"? I maintain that the motives of Yvonne and Hugh are basically selfish and that their actions do the Consul more harm than good—he is well rid of them both. As for the Consul's diplomatic job, that is a mere bagatelle; his true career is his drinking. In regard to his book, on the Day of the Dead the Consul conceives in his head several chapters—maybe volumes—of "Secret Knowledge." He may have "no capability for the further tactile effort" of writing this material down, but that is of little consequence, for, as the Consul affirms, "the final frontier of consciousness" lies within (35, 135).

Geoffrey Firmin dies an alcoholic, but he *lives* one too. Lowry spikes his magnum-size stirrup-cup with so much beauty, excitement, wit, and, yes, joy, that I, for one, wouldn't want it to be drained any differently.

Thomas B. Gilmore

SOURCE: "Drinking and Society in the Fiction of John Cheever," in *Equivocal Spirits: Alcoholism and Drinking in Twentieth-Century Literature,* University of North Carolina Press, 1987, pp. 62-80.

[In the following essay Gilmore describes John Cheever's portrayal of alcoholism in his short fiction, both for comic effect and as a social critique of the upper-middle class.]

John Cheever may be the American writer who shows the most thorough and diversified familiarity with drinking in modern American society. At times the familiarity relaxes into comedy. As Cheever sketches the suburban milieu for his novel *Bullet Park,* he introduces the reader to the Wickwires, at first glance an unexceptionably attractive couple but for the arresting fact that "they were always falling downstairs, bumping into sharp-edged furniture and driving their cars into ditches." Their vulnerability to accident is sufficiently explained by an intimate look at the detritus of their Monday mornings. Mr. Wickwire, badly hung over, utters a cry of pain when he sees the empties on the shelf by the sink. They are ranged there like the gods in some pantheon of remorse. Their intent seems to be to force him to his knees and to wring from him some prayer. "Empties, oh empties, most merciful empties have mercy upon me for the sake of Jack Daniels and Seagram Distillers." Their immutable emptiness gives them a look that is cruel and censorious. Their labels— scotch, gin and bourbon—have the ferocity of Chinese demons, but he definitely has the feeling that if he tried to placate them with a genuflection they would be merciless. He drops them into a waste-basket, but this does not dispose of their force.

It is doubtful that a reader can be disturbed by the drinking problem of a man who is so wry and witty about his condition. It is even more doubtful that one would prefer the condition of a doctor, portrayed later in the same novel, who has recently joined Alcoholics Anonymous. In a trenchant parody, Cheever reveals what appears to be first-hand knowledge of two of the least attractive features of some AA parlance: its confessional banalities and the logorrhea of its evangelicalism. Not only the Wickwires' life but even a Rabelaisian abandon to drink would be more fun, at least if one may judge the latter spirit from a scene enacted in another novel by Moses Wapshot and Mrs. Wilston in a room at the Viaduct House, St. Botolphs's hotel. Both are far gone in drink. Moses, attempting to carry his rather too generously pro-portioned inamorata to bed, "weaved to the right, re-couped his balance and weaved to the right again. Then he was going; he was going; he was gone. Thump. The whole Viaduct House reverberated to the crash and then there was an awful stillness. He lay athwart her, his cheek against the carpet. . . . She, still lying in a heap, was the first to speak. She spoke without anger or impatience. She smiled. 'Let's have another drink,' she said."

Although Cheever is capable of using alcohol for nothing more significant than comic shock, as when a character urinates into a sherry decanter and the rector arrives "and sipped piss," or for spinning a kind of grotesque tall tale, as when a woman turns to drunken promiscuity and then commits suicide because her appliances repeatedly break down and she has difficulty getting them repaired, he characteristically goes beyond these relatively easy achievements. Perhaps one reason for his parody of Al-coholics Anonymous in *Bullet Park* is his desire, con-veyed in "A Miscellany of Characters That Will Not Appear," to avoid such clichés as "the alcoholic." The section of this story that deals with the stereotype is in fact an effective satire on it ("X" has a ridiculously ex-aggerated attack of the shakes, for example) and on its potential for sentimental exploitation. X, having been offered a fresh start in Cleveland, is returning home from a trip there. His family, meeting him at the station, is a model of propriety, support, and affection: "His pretty wife, his three children, and the two dogs have all come down to welcome Daddy." Daddy practically flows off the train. Cheever briskly aborts both the scene and the section at this point. It is perhaps not so much that

Cheever objects to sentimentality (he himself is guilty of it on occasion—for instance, in the death of the boy in "An Educated American Woman") as that he objects to the simplicity that enables it. The drunk or alcoholic as such, stripped of every other trait, is neither interesting nor instructive in "the way we live."

When Cheever resorts to stereotyped drinkers, it is usu-ally for some extremely short vignette or some transitory effect. The bibulous Irish maid Nora Quinn, in "The Day the Pig Fell into the Well," briefly parallels the action of the title by tumbling down a flight of stairs. But "The Sorrows of Gin," centering in part on another Irish ser-vant, Rosemary, is complicated by irony and by shifting, largely unreliable perspectives on drinking. We see many of the events and persons through the eyes of a fourth-grade girl, Amy Lawton, who, after looking in on her parents' cocktail party near the beginning of the story, listens at length to their new cook, Rosemary. Unlike her fellow servant and sister, who was repeatedly dismissed from positions for drinking and who died in Bellevue Hospital, Rosemary implicitly eschews alcohol and pro-fesses to find her strength in the Bible. About the drink-ing of Amy's parents she is contradictory: after calling it "all sociable," she counsels Amy quite vehemently to empty her father's "gin bottle into the sink now and then—the filthy stuff!" One irony is that this seemingly respectable domestic, on her first day off, returns from New York totally intoxicated, her coat "spotted with mud and ripped in the back." When Mr. Lawton reprimands her for drinking in front of Amy, Rosemary cries, "I'm lonely. . . . I'm lonely, and I'm afraid, and it's all I've got." Evidently the Bible has deserted her. She is dis-charged at once, and as a result of this object lesson in the ravages of alcohol, Amy pours one of her father's gin bottles down the sink. This act leads the very next day to the discharge of a second newly hired cook, Amy's father angrily assuming that she has drunk the gin and mean-while inveighing against various other servants who have consumed his liquor. Just as he reduces these people to stereotypes, so, in another irony, his daughter reduces him to the level of Rosemary and pours out still more of his gin. This loss produces a third perspective on the father's drinking, one that seems to bear some resem-blance to Amy's and Rosemary's. Having discovered another empty bottle, Mr. Lawton accuses the babysitter, Mrs. Henlein, a member of the suburb's decayed gentil-ity. Her reaction is not only to denounce him as drunk but also to telephone the police with the same disclosure, vociferously urging them to arrest him.

Partly because of the unreliable perspectives, the realities of the Lawtons' drinking are not easy to determine. If the advice of Rosemary and the hysteria of Mrs. Henlein are obviously based on exaggeration, there appears to be an element of truth in their—and Amy's—view of the par-ents. But even Amy's view is not consistent: when not aroused by fears traceable to Rosemary, she seems able to achieve a degree of objectivity. Although Amy detects several changes that alcohol works in her father, most notably a happier mood, she firmly denies to herself any similarity between him and the drunks she has heard about, people who hang on lampposts or fall down. But then she recalls occasions when her father missed a doorway by a foot and once when a cocktail guest, Mrs. Farquarson, missed a chair she went to sit in. Amy concludes that the main difference between clownish drunks and her parents and their friends is that "they were never indecorous." When the other guests and Amy's parents pretend that Mrs. Farquarson did not miss her chair, they imply, for the reader if not for Amy, that such excess is not approved. As if to dispel any lingering possibility that Rosemary or Mrs. Henlein may be right about the Lawtons' drinking, Amy's father, in the final section of the story, awakes "cheered by the swelling light in the sky . . . refreshed by his sleep" and hoping to find some way to teach his daughter, who had tried to run away, "that home sweet home was the best place of all." On these notes, vaguely suggesting that the Lawtons have no serious drinking problem—but perhaps also hinting at paternal repentance and reform—the story closes.

As my concluding remarks on "The Sorrows of Gin" may indicate, Cheever's primary interest in drinking is societal: not so much in enlarging our understanding of alcoholism or in exploring its influence on individuals as in seeing its manifold effects, potential or actual, in marriages, families, or society. This focus is not surprising; it would be hard to think of a modern American writer more concerned with society and less concerned with the introspections of the romantic ego. In a number of Cheever's stories, drinking may be seen in one of three ways, though sometimes in a variety of combinations and permutations: (1) when practiced outside a recognized social form or to excess, drinking usually signals some kind of societal trouble; (2) drinking is occasionally used as a token or an affirmation of a social or familial bond; (3) occasionally, abstemiousness or abstinence is viewed just as dimly as excess, and for much the same reasons—its actual or potential harm either to the abstinent person or to his society. As illustrations of one or more of these approaches to drinking, three stories—"Reunion," "Goodbye, My Brother," and "The Swimmer"—seem the most remarkable for their intensity, their skill, or their complexity. Even more notable, perhaps, because of its transcendence of these approaches and their limitations, is "The Scarlet Moving Van." Finally, in three of Cheever's later stories we shall consider the evidence that Cheever becomes skeptical of society as a satisfactory norm by which to measure and criticize deviation. Instead, these stories suggest, it may be that society is deviant and that heavy drinking, drug abuse, or other forms of behavior traditionally reprehended as deviant are potentially redemptive.

Of the three views of drinking enumerated above, the first is the most common in Cheever's stories. Even extremely brief examples may be memorable and poignant. As the lonely narrator of "The Angel of the Bridge" gazes from his Los Angeles hotel window in the early morning hours, at the entrance of a restaurant across the street there emerges "a drunken woman in a sable cape being led out to a car. She twice nearly fell." Like the images of Blake's "London," this little scene seems only the visible tip of some larger derangement. For what other reason would a woman of means whose companion or husband shows her "solicitude" drink herself into this condition? No explicit answer is provided, but that her condition is either a symptom or a representative cause of social malaise is suggested by another brief scene immediately following, in which the occupants of two cars stopped for a traffic light get out, assault one another brutally, then drive off. Both scenes indicate, whether as cause or effect, a rupture or absence of the social bond. Though escorted, the woman is so isolated by her condition that seeing her can only deepen the narrator's sense of loneliness.

Infidelity, adultery, seduction, or promiscuity is often seen by Cheever as either abetted by or associated with drinking. In "The Five-Forty-Eight," Blake, a married man who is one of the most repugnant characters in Cheever's fiction, makes his move to seduce a newly hired secretary—an accomplishment that proves easy because he takes unconscionable advantage of her gratitude for his hiring her when other prospective employers, learning of her history of mental troubles, would not—by proposing a drink after they have both worked late one night. In "Brimmer," the title character, whose name of course denotes drinking, is portrayed as a master seducer, satyr-like even in appearance, whose natural ally is drink; he is sometimes glassy-eyed and "almost always had a glass in his hand." Although Brimmer arouses a little sympathy when he is later reported to be dying, for the most part the narrator regards his behavior with distaste as a potential source of "carnal anarchy," especially when Brimmer shows no hesitation about seducing a woman he knows to be married. Georgie, the mostly docile and inarticulate husband of "An Educated American Woman," is finally made so unhappy by an increasing awareness of his empty marriage that his wife is awakened one night when he falls, noisily and drunkenly, in their bathroom. Shortly thereafter, more from loneliness than from sexual ardor, Georgie has an affair; as is usual with adultery in Cheever, it is facilitated by drinking. Mrs. Flannagan, the adulteress of "The Brigadier and the Golf Widow," enters an affair with Mr. Pastern for another reason; as he learns to his dismay, it is not love but a key to his bomb shelter that she is after. Again, drinking seems an essential component in initiating the adultery. In "Artemis, the Honest Well Digger," the title character, a canny rustic, discovers that the lust and drinking that excite him in the woman he loves, Maria Petroni, are united with flagrant promiscuity. When she declines his proposal of marriage and he asks whether she wants a younger man, she replies, "Yes, darling, but not one. I want seven, one right after the other. . . . I've done it. This was before I met you. I asked seven of the best-looking men around to come for dinner. . . . I cooked veal scaloppine. There was a lot to drink and then we all got undressed. . . . When they were finished, I didn't feel dirty or depraved or shameful. I didn't feel anything bad at all." Although

Artemis continues to see Maria for a while longer, that account "was about it" for their relationship.

It is, however, "Reunion"—a story of only two and a half pages, the shortest of the sixty-one in Cheever's collected stories—that has the greatest power as a depiction of the devastating effect of excessive drinking on human relations. There are several reasons for this power. One, no doubt, lies precisely in the extreme brevity and concentration; these contrast with a tendency in quite a few of Cheever's stories toward diffuse and multiple effects, authorial or essayistic reflection. "Reunion" is perhaps the most fully dramatized of Cheever's stories. Except for the opening paragraph, which supplies information about the circumstances of the meeting of father and son, nearly everything is carried on by speech or action. Another source of its power may be that the situation it deals with—a boy's profound embarrassment by an inebriated father—draws on some indelibly mortifying experience of Cheever's own boyhood or youth. Judging from the surprising number of times that Cheever has incorporated versions of this experience in other works, though usually in just a few sentences or in short scenes, clearly he is fascinated with it almost to the point of obsession. If these other stories afford only peripheral treatments of this experience, "Reunion," by giving it exclusive attention, also maximizes its force.

A further aspect of the story's artistry is Cheever's tact, what he leaves unsaid. The son, who is also the narrator, at no point refers directly to his discomfort or embarrassment; although our only evidence is his growing insistence that he must leave his father to catch a train, the tacit quality of his feelings renders them all the more affecting. For the most part the narrator-son is only an unobtrusive recorder and the focus is on the behavior of the father. Here too Cheever chooses to underplay: though vivid and loud, the father is by no means grossly obvious about his intoxication; we know that he has been drinking (or that he is a habitual drinker) when he meets his son for lunch only by the observation that the father's smell "was a rich compound of whiskey, after-shave lotion, shoe polish, woolens, and the rankness of a mature male." We know that he is drunk only from one ludicrous slip as he orders drinks ("two Bibson Geefeaters") and from his anger with a waiter for smiling. Probably the father's behavior is only a heightening or extension of his natural personality. For the son, however, this heightening is intolerable. Although he has been living with his divorced mother and has not seen his father for three years, he "was terribly happy to see him again" and to meet him for lunch in New York; he even wants a photograph to commemorate the occasion. But when, at the end of the story, he says that he never saw his father again after this meeting, it is also clear that he never made another attempt. In a mere hour and a half, then, a father's intoxicated behavior ends his relationship with an affectionate son.

The father seems just as eager to demonstrate his love for his son as the son is to have it, but his expression of that love is abysmally misconceived. In slightly different circumstances, his rudeness to waiters in ordering drinks might display a refreshing audacity. The climax of the restaurant scene in the film *Five Easy Pieces,* in which Jack Nicholson sweeps everything off the table and then leaves, evokes gasps of admiration from the audience. Nicholson's rudeness, however, is retaliatory; the waitress fully deserves it. The father's insolence, in contrast, is unprovoked, and, where Nicholson acts deliberately, the father appears simply compulsive. In this characteristic also lies a basic difference between the father and Gee-Gee, the hard drinker of "The Scarlet Moving Van." Not only are his insults less trivial; for the most part Gee-Gee seems to know what he is doing and to be calculatedly indifferent to the consequences. The father is not indifferent to the impression he is making on his son. After they are turned away from four restaurants, either by direct invitation to leave or by refusal of service, the father says to the boy, "I'm sorry, sonny. . . . I'm terribly sorry," though whether he refers to his behavior or their failure to have lunch, or both, is impossible to know. Yet the father then proceeds to treat a news vendor with exactly the abusiveness that he has inflicted on a series of waiters: "Kind sir, will you be good enough to favor me with one of your God-damned, no-good, ten-cent afternoon papers?" The most striking irony of the story is that a man enslaved to drunken compulsiveness seeks to impress his son with his mastery over people. Perhaps not by chance, he resembles the drinker, in one of the most searching parables from the so-called Big Book of Alcoholics Anonymous, who plays at being a kind of cosmic stage manager, with other people merely so many puppets to be manipulated in order to display his power. We can respond with a sense of liberation to Gee-Gee's insults in part because his primary audience is one of adults and equals capable of shrugging him off like the waiters of "Reunion." But the primary if silent auditor of that story is the son; and if his father is as indifferent to the humanity of waiters as Gee-Gee is to that of his fellow suburbanites, we may surmise that, in driving his son away, the father has sentenced himself to a desolating and permanent loneliness.

"Reunion" focuses on the shock of embarrassment, only hinting at a pathos to follow. "The Seaside Houses," though more diffuse and less effective than "Reunion," develops its latent pathos. The narrator, knowing at first only the name, Greenwood, of the owners of a house he is renting for the summer, is saddened and disturbed by his discovery of several empty whiskey bottles around the house and grounds. Cheever, an alcoholic, must have been drawing from fears about his own drinking; his daughter has recorded that "long before I was even aware that he was alcoholic, there were bottles hidden all over the house, and even outside in the privet hedge and the garden shed." The narrator learns from a neighbor that, although the Greenwoods had built a curved staircase for their daughter's wedding, she "was married in the Municipal Building eight months pregnant by a garage mechanic." Then, going to New York on business, the narrator by chance sees Mr. Greenwood in a bar, recognizing him from his photograph: "you could see by the way his hands shook that [his] flush was alcoholic." Cheever captures pathos partly by emphasizing the isolation of such men—Greenwood is one of a "legion" of "prosperous and well-dressed hangers-on who, in spite of the atmosphere of a fraternity" in the bar, "would not think of speaking to one another"—and partly by not characterizing Greenwood extensively. But in his only words, Greenwood exhibits his close kinship to the father of "Reunion": "'Stupid,' he said to the bartender. 'Oh, stupid. Do you think you could find the time to sweeten my drink?'" And in the manner of his daughter's marriage and the words (probably hers) that the narrator has found scrawled on a baseboard of the rented house—"My father is a rat. I repeat. My father is a rat"—"The Seaside Houses" may be regarded as a companion to "Reunion," enlarging on the loneliness and pain stemming from filial affections destroyed by a father's drinking.

Excessive drinking, then, can lead to grievous ruptures of the bonds of domestic affection. But two of Cheever's stories indicate the desirability of moderate or social drinking, in particular as a ritual that affirms or strengthens domestic ties and affections. During summers in the Adirondacks over a period of many years, the Nudd family of "The Day the Pig Fell into the Well," whose primary means of maintaining closeness is its ritual retellings of the story of the unfortunate pig and other events of that day, gathers each evening for drinks. When Russell Young, a local boy once almost a part of the family, is reinstated in its good graces, he is included in this drinking. Joan, who at age forty is the Nudds' problem child, has a temper tantrum at one point but is calmed by a drink and a game of checkers with her father. So drinking has the effect of a ceremony by which the Nudds quietly reassure one another of their acceptance and affection.

Similarly, and even more prominently, the ritual of family drinking has beneficent significance in "Goodbye, My Brother." This is also one of a couple of Cheever stories in which the contrast or conflict between social drinking and apparent or actual abstemiousness is especially important.

Through images, allusive hints, and some well-chosen names, "Goodbye, My Brother" suggests that the tension within the Pommeroy family reflects a larger cultural struggle between freedom and Puritanism. As implied by the names of the narrator's sister and wife, Diana and Helen, most of the family has gained emancipation; and although he reverts to a moment of savagery in smiting his brother Lawrence (an act obviously meant to recall the story of Cain and Abel), the narrator binds Lawrence's wound. The spirit of beauty and liberation is triumphant as the story ends with Helen and Diana emerging naked from the sea after Lawrence has left the family's summer home in Massachusetts. Lawrence is associated with Puritan asceticism; he alone preserves the attitude of his ancestors that "all earthly beauty is lustful and corrupt."

Lawrence's abstemiousness is a major sign of this spirit. He evidently has a long-standing hostility to drinking; he has avoided neighbors for this reason, and he once moved out on a college roommate with whom "he had been very good friends" because "the man drank too much." Reuniting with his family for the first time in four years, he accepts a proffered drink only with indifference and reluctance, thereby indicating his attitude toward the rest of his family, for whom predinner drinks on the evening of his arrival are a rite of inclusion. Ironically, although the family has drunk too much while waiting for Lawrence to appear, it is he who speaks with the effrontery of one with inhibitions lowered by alcohol. Inquiring about a man who comes for his divorced sister Diana after dinner, he asks, "Is that the one she's sleeping with now?" When his mother opens a favorite subject, improvements on their summer home, he asserts that "this house will be in the sea in five years." Though she has had too much to drink, she is at worst indulging in a harmless fantasy, whereas Lawrence is egregiously severe in speaking what he conceives to be the truth. The contrast is not in favor of sobriety.

The story is not simplistically black and white. We see enough of the mother to agree in part with Lawrence's judgment that she is rather frivolous and domineering; and when she becomes definitely drunk late in the evening of his arrival, she shows that she can be cruel as well. Her inebriation on this occasion, however, is a half-conscious contrivance to protect herself against Law-rence's harshness, as is her apparently intentional exclusion of him from an invitation the next day to "have Martinis on the beach." Because the narrator is careful to state that his mother "doesn't get drunk often," Law-rence's charge that she is alcoholic is palpably false. Normally, the family's drinking is moderate; like its shared swimming, tennis, picnics, and backgammon, it is both symbol of and aid to its loyalty and warmth. If Lawrence remains outside this circle, it is by his own choice.

The chief spiritual heir of a forebear "who was eulogized by Cotton Mather for his untiring abjuration of the Devil." Lawrence himself and his narrow abstemiousness are seen as devils that the family must abjure or exorcise in favor of light, beauty, and such innocent, alcohol-inspired fun as diving for balloons off the dock after the boat-club party. At one point the narrator notices that "the wild grapes that grow profusely all over the island made the land wind smell of wine." This touch, appropriate for a family that fosters its solidarity by drinking, is also a fitting portent of the scattering and banishment of puritanical sobriety to the hinterlands, to places such as Kansas, Cleveland, and Albany, where Lawrence has lived.

More complex and problematic than "Goodbye, My Brother," "The Swimmer" also employs a contrast between apparent abstemiousness and drinking. The meanings or values of the two sides of this contrast are in some ways difficult to ascertain, and a reader's responses may undergo major adjustments as the story progresses.

At first the protagonist, Ned or Neddy Merrill, seems largely admirable, like a Ulysses seeking to free himself from the impurities and beguilements of his Circean suburban environment. Its most marked impurity appears to be its dissoluteness. In the opening paragraph, the setting a pleasant summer Sunday afternoon, we hear a litany of complaints about having drunk too much the night before. So although the diminutive, "Neddy," raises some doubts about Merrill's maturity and therefore about his credibility as a hero in the customary sense, we probably approve of his decision to leave the poolside company in which he finds himself as the story opens—a company already drinking again—and to "swim" the eight miles to his home via a series of pools. He fancies that there may be an almost legendary quality about this adventure. If, like his name, this notion may make him seem slightly absurd, the aspiration and energy required for his undertaking at least appear preferable to the torpor and overindulgence of his friends. He is, it seems, becoming a quasi-allegorical figure suddenly set apart from the rest of his society by a destiny or quest, even if this quest is puzzlingly unlike the quests of traditional heroes. Gradually, however, and finally in ways that drastically change these initial impressions of Merrill, we may reach three conclusions: that the difference between him and his society is not nearly as great as he may want to think; that his quest does not represent a clearly preferable alternative; and that the quest itself is seriously compromised by Merrill's confusion about or ignorance of its aims or purposes.

Water, the medium of Merrill's quest, has a number of established associations and symbolic meanings. In addition to its salubrious contrast with the alcohol being consumed by the others, Neddy's repeated immersions in the swimming pools may resemble baptisms; his apparent unconsciousness of any desire to wash away his sins does not necessarily make this meaning illegitimate. Another association, lying closer to Merrill's awareness, seems more plausible in the context of this story: that of water as a preserver or restorer of youth. Merrill is a little like a caricature of the faddish jogger who seems to hope that his exertions will endow him not only with eternal youth but also with a kind of corporeal immortality. A third association of water in the story is with the protection and comfort of the womb; swimming in his first pool of the afternoon, Neddy thinks that "to be embraced and sustained by the light green water was less a pleasure . . . than the resumption of a natural condition, and he would have liked to swim without trunks." This association is an extension of the second one carried to its extreme; to avoid aging, Neddy would apparently go all the way back to a fetal state.

Either of the last two interpretations of water helps to make clear the aptness of the retribution that Neddy experiences for his unworthy, immature longings. In place of youth and its summery weather, in the course of a single afternoon he finds the season becoming autumnal and himself aging. To put the matter another way, Neddy is punished for making a travesty quest. By trying to move away from, rather than toward, the maturity and enlightenment that are the usual goals of a quest, he debases or trivializes it. Perhaps more accurately, Merrill does achieve a type of maturity—but it is a part of his punishment. Instead of culminating in enlightenment, its fruit is the incomprehensibility of Neddy's finding, at the end of his swim, that his house is abandoned and derelict, and evidently has been for some while. By an enormous acceleration, time has taken an apposite if harsh revenge on Neddy for hoping to exempt himself from its vicissitudes and in fact to reverse its flow.

A couple of scenes are especially helpful for seeing not only how Neddy's swim differs from a true quest but also how fundamentally similar he is to the rest of his society. Despite the growing chill of the afternoon, the gathering bleakness of autumn, and Neddy's progressive exhaustion and aging, his pilgrimage is altogether too easy. Unlike the genuine spiritual wayfarer, Neddy ventures into no unknown realms, seeks no real perils or tribulations. The hollowness of his journey is most sharply exposed in scenes reminiscent of but contrasting with the Vanity Fair episode of *Pilgrim's Progress*. Christian and Faithful courageously and unhesitantly reject the snares of Vanity Fair; for this reason and their ability to make converts, they are first smeared with dirt and displayed in a cage, then beaten and put in irons; Faithful is finally burned at the stake. By contrast, during his brief stops at parties of the Grahams and the Bunkers, Neddy is the epitome of temporizing politeness. Although he continues on his swim, he views the practices of these Vanity Fairs not with the aversion of Christian and Faithful but as "hospitable customs and traditions . . . to be handled with diplomacy." He feels "a passing affection . . . a tenderness" for the Bunkers' party, kisses several women, and shakes hands with an equal number of men. Compared to Faithful and Christian, Neddy is practically indistinguishable from the others at the two parties. Unlike Bunyan's figures, who firmly proclaim their destination to be "the Heavenly *Jerusalem*," Neddy just sneaks off from the gatherings—in part, no doubt, because he could not formulate his purposes even to himself.

The thoroughly compromised quality of his quest is also suggested by his drinking. At the outset of his sojourn, in his apparent concern with demonstrating or recapturing a youthful vigor or purity, Neddy seems to reject the dissipation of his drinking friends, but the story as a whole indicates that drinking is no less important to him than to the rest. Although he may only be holding a glass of gin beside the Westerhazys' pool as the story opens, and although he perhaps deliberately refrains from drinking at either the Grahams' or the Bunkers', by the time he reaches the Levys', at nearly the midpoint in his journey, he has had four or five drinks. Later in the afternoon his desire or need for a drink increases; he has one more before his swim is finished, and he tries to get at least three. A pedantically exact count is unnecessary for showing that Neddy's drinking is probably no more moderate than that of his society. There are even a couple of hints (though one is highly ambiguous) that his behavior has violated limits observed by this society. He has had not just a casual suburban flirtation but a mistress, at whose house he pauses in the course of his swim. At another house he overhears the hostess talking about a man who "showed up drunk one Sunday and asked us to loan him five thousand dollars," though she may not be referring to Neddy.

Before the end of the story, Neddy himself seems to regret having left the company of his drinking friends. Whatever their excesses, this is his milieu. Vaguely seeking to transcend it, he has won for his efforts not only a reminder (possibly two) of his past turpitude but the most radical kind of displacement. Moreover, a second look at the opening paragraph may lead to a suspicion that Neddy's quest never had adequate warrant. Cheever's tone, the best indication of his attitude toward the excessive drinkers of suburban society, is one of at least half-amused tolerance, and the refrain of "I *drank* too much last night" conveys a sense of commonality or community that, though far from ideal, is better than the apparently irremediable dislocation of Merrill. As the story ends, he seems to be a kind of aged but infantile Adam, shivering, tearful, and mostly naked, expelled by his own folly from the only Eden he will ever know and with no other world before him.

Gee-Gee, the hard drinker of "The Scarlet Moving Van," achieves a transcendence of society that contrasts completely with Neddy's final misery. In this story, perhaps for the first time, Cheever questions whether society (or its smaller units, couples or the family) offers a valid norm by which to determine or implicitly censure deviations such as heavy drinking. But Gee-Gee's transcendence is difficult to characterize and is made more elusive by the fact that Gee-Gee's wife, his only friend, and Gee-Gee himself evaluate him in ways that are inadequate or unreliable.

Peaches's view of her drunken husband is the most obviously simplistic and unrealistic; she just wants him to return to being the All-American football player, "fine and strong and generous," that he was in college. Fortunately, he is a good deal more interesting than this. But Gee-Gee, too, lacks proper appreciation of his present self. When he manifests any self-awareness, he seems to believe that his role is something like the one Robert C. Elliott has ascribed to the archetypal satirist: that of telling his society such dangerous or mortifying truths that he is often turned into a scapegoat and banished. Although Gee-Gee is driven to move frequently because of his affronts to society and the resulting ostracism (the title of the story may also suggest a branding or stigmatizing like Hawthorne's scarlet letter), Gee-Gee's criticisms of society are extremely rudimentary even for an archetypal satirist. They consist mainly of his repeated declaration "I have to teach them," together with accusations of stuffiness and such outrageous actions as stripping to his undershorts at parties and setting fires in a hostess's wastebaskets. These words and deeds scarcely justify any attention to Gee-Gee as a satirist or critic of society.

Charlie Folkestone, the friend and neighbor at whose house Gee-Gee becomes uproariously drunk on his first night in town, is equally unsuccessful at making a satisfactory appraisal of him. Evidently believing in Gee-Gee's self-professed role of teacher, Charlie at one point attempts to define it: "Gee-Gee was an advocate for the lame, the diseased, the poor, for those who through no fault of their own live out their lives in misery and pain. To the happy and the wellborn and the rich he had this to say—that for all their affection, their comforts, and their privileges, they would not be spared the pangs of anger and lust and the agonies of death." In a way somewhat similar to Gee-Gee's own error of self-judgment, these reflections give him a didactic weight and a moral authority for which there is not nearly enough supporting evidence. How Gee-Gee could be thought to offer any lessons to the wealthy is a mystery that Charlie fails to clarify, and, as a representative of the poor or wretched, Gee-Gee is certainly an odd choice. Though without a visible source of income, he is scarcely one of the poor: his frequent moves must cost a good deal of money and seem always to be from one upper-middle-class suburb to another, and one Christmas he is able to send his wife and children to the Bahamas. If Charlie's reference is not to material want but to loneliness or isolation, a poverty of soul or spirit, Gee-Gee appears to be in circumstances that make this poverty inevitable when Charlie goes to see him one Christmas in another suburb. Gee-Gee is alone; having broken his hip, which is in a huge cast, he can move about only with the aid of a crutch and a child's wagon. His home is in a new subdivision, with most of the surrounding houses still unoccupied and looking, to Charlie, raw and ugly. Oppressed by a sense of dreariness and desolation, Charlie tries to convince himself that these must be Gee-Gee's feelings. In fact, however, Gee-Gee insists that he does not mind being alone, and his heartiness confirms his assertion. To be sure, after returning home Charlie receives a telephone call from a frightened Gee-Gee, who has fallen out of his wagon and beseeches his friend to return. Although Charlie fails to go, we learn at the end of the story that Gee-Gee next called the fire department, one member of which drank "a quart of bourbon every day" with Gee-Gee until Peaches and the children came back from Nassau.

Gee-Gee, then, simply refuses to be victimized by the conventional horrors or disasters of the alcoholic. If he suffers some misfortunes, he recovers with amazing speed and resilience. Nowhere is Charlie quite so wrong as when he associates Gee-Gee with death or dying. He is correct, however, in attributing to Gee-Gee "some tremendous validity" even if he never comes close to defining it. One clue may lie in Gee-Gee's name, which, as his wife explains, is a contraction of "Greek God," a designation given him by admirers in college. Later in the story, when Charlie visits him, he notices Gee-Gee fumbling with some matches and observes to himself that "he might easily burn to death"; a moment later he thinks that "there might be some drunken cunning in his clumsiness, his playing with fire." If the last phrase sounds a little like a reference to Prometheus, Gee-Gee's liver is being consumed neither by vultures nor by liquor. But we are probably not supposed to identify him with a specific god; it is more illuminating simply to see him as an undifferentiated life force or spirit, presided over, as he says, by a guardian angel that Cheever characterizes as "boozy" and "disheveled." We may be further enlightened by remembering that an old name for alcohol is "spirits." Because of his indomitability, his sheer power of survival, Captain Grimes of Evelyn Waugh's *Decline and Fall,* who is also something of a drinker, seems remarkably similar to Gee-Gee even though more fully developed as a novelistic character. If Gee-Gee has a function as social critic, it is conveyed by his spirit rather than by his trivial words or actions. Perhaps Cheever and Waugh suggest that in the almost preternatural vitality of Gee-Gee and Grimes—or in the creative imagination needed to invent them—lies the best hope of surmounting the deadness of society. But the fate of Charlie, who by the end of the story has apparently begun to experience all the alcoholic suffering and degradation that Gee-Gee avoids, may represent Cheever's warning that Gee-Gee's transcendence of society will not always succeed.

In three later works, including the novel *Falconer,* Cheever further utilizes characters whose excesses or aberrations are better than a society that either fails to function as a positive standard or is corrupt. As "The Fourth Alarm" begins, the anonymous narrator sits alone drinking gin at ten o'clock on a Sunday morning. Although he is not yet intoxicated, his isolation seems ripe for excess, and the unnaturalness of the hour and the day for drinking (why is he not in church, or at least innocently playing golf?) may seem to promise the portrait of a man justly expelled from society. But perhaps the chief surprise, in a story of surprises that Cheever handles with unusual adroitness, is that his drinking, even if it should become excessive, seems entirely justifiable as a defense against pain. His wife has virtually abandoned him and their children in order to play a leading part in a nude Broadway show that features simulated copulation and audience participation. The success of the show suggests its eager approval by the rest of the narrator's society. He attends and undresses, as bidden, in an attempt to understand his wife; but when his bourgeois instincts prompt him to carry his valuables on stage, the entire cast jeers him. Although a solitary drinker, the narrator is the only embodiment in the story of the old social decencies and proprieties. His abstemious wife, who now and then will drink a polite glass of Dubonnet, represents the madness of sexual freedom, far more corrupting to society than any conceivable alcoholic excess.

One of the several unconnected stories in Cheever's "The Leaves, the Lion-Fish and the Bear" focuses on a one-night homosexual relationship, with excessive drinking a facilitating agent. Though the story is unconvincing as a look at homosexuality or its causes, the moral implication perhaps fares better. In a society of solitary travel and strange motels (two components in the setting) a homosexual encounter may be a defensible protection and

warmth against otherwise overpowering loneliness. The two men, Stark and Estabrook, are conventional enough that they must get drunk before the encounter in order to lower their inhibitions; but their experience has redeeming social value, for when Estabrook returns home, he is said to find his wife lovelier than ever.

Cheever seems to show some nervousness or uncertainty in his handling of the subject matter of this story. He is a little too insistent on the innocence of Stark and Estabrook. Because Cheever remained uneasy and circumspect about his own homosexuality, which he allowed himself to face and act on only late in his life, he must have had grave misgivings about treating the subject at all in his fiction. *Falconer,* however, is more assured; it is also Cheever's most extended representation of the positive value of alcohol, drugs, and other excesses. Farragut, characterized by his wife as suffering from "clinical alcoholism," is also and more prominently a drug addict; he is in prison for having murdered his brother "while under the influence of dangerous drugs." But in Farragut's several mental returns to the slaying, a reader finds mitigating, perhaps wholly extenuating circumstances, including the brother's odiousness. In this he resembles Lawrence of "Goodbye, My Brother," but, unlike the narrator-brother of that story, who after striking Lawrence a potentially lethal blow saves him from the ocean's undertow and binds his head, Farragut manifests not the slightest compunction about his deed. The novel presents no reasons to condemn his attitude; on the contrary, though Farragut sometimes seems ambitious of little more than shock (as when, in a flashback to his professorial days, he recalls how he and his department head "would shoot up before the big lecture," or when he imagines a priest placing an amphetamine on a communicant's tongue and saying "Take this in memory of me and be grateful"), there is little material in the book to dispute Farragut's claim that "drugs belonged to all exalted experience." Instead, just as in the South Pacific battles of World War II in which Farragut served, so now in the usually less violent but more corrosive conflicts between prisoners and guards, drugs or alcohol seem almost sane, civilizing forces. The alternatives are the sadism of some of the guards or the futile rioting of some prisoners, behavior that simply imitates the barbarity or senselessness of most of the world outside the prison walls, as illustrated by Farragut's wife and brother.

Apart from Farragut, the only heroes of *Falconer* are Jody (his homosexual lover, whose escape foreshadows the ingenuity of Farragut's own) and the first person Farragut meets after escaping. This unnamed stranger, impoverished (though he denies it), crude of speech, physically unattractive, and smelling of whiskey, has just been evicted from his lodging, probably for drunkenness, and is on his way to stay temporarily with a sister whom he hates. Nevertheless, this misfit is Cheever's version of the good Samaritan, paying Farragut's bus fare, inviting him to share his new quarters, even giving Farragut a coat (one of four, he says—but perhaps, like most modern Samaritans, he is embarrassed about his own goodness and therefore minimizes it). When Farragut leaves the bus before he does, the stranger extends his blessing: "Well, that's all right." It is no wonder that at this point, as the novel ends, the thought running through Farragut's mind is "Rejoice . . . rejoice." By the time he wrote *Falconer,* Cheever was a recovering alcoholic and a successful member of AA; so Farragut's benediction at the end of the novel is most of all Cheever's self-forgiveness. But these two characters—the drunken outcast from society and Farragut, murderer, fugitive from justice, and drug and alcohol addict—seem strange occasions for rejoicing when one remembers Cheever's earlier fiction. Although, as Glen M. Johnson points out, Farragut breaks his drug addiction while in prison, he is the hero of *Falconer* even while still an addict. This fact sets him sharply apart from the prosperous New Yorkers or suburbanites for whom heavy drinking was a regrettable departure from desirable social norms in much of Cheever's earlier work.

Paul C. Smith

SOURCE: "The Reliable Determinants: Alcohol in Blasco Ibáñez's Valencian Works," in *Ideologies and Literature*, 2, 2, Fall, 1987, pp. 185-99.

[*In the following essay, Smith examines the means by which Blasco Ibáñez presents alcoholism as a social problem that severely afflicts the poor in his naturalistic novels* Flor de Mayo, La barraca, *and* Cañas y borro.]

Literary naturalism, through emphasis on lower social classes, drew the attention of certain nineteenth-century novelists to the presence of alcohol in the lives of the poor. Foremost among these novelists was Emile Zola (1840-1902), leading theoretician and practitioner of naturalism, who found in the lower classes an ideal subject for his materialistic approach to the study of man. The poor were far less likely than middle-class subjects to conceal their own animal nature (which for Zola constituted man's true nature) beneath a veneer of civilized social behavior. Lower-class protagonists reacted more spontaneously to such basic instincts and passions as sex, hunger, anger, jealousy and revenge. And, as many naturalist authors recorded from observation, it was alcohol that often turned these feelings into impulsive action.

Zola's novels often served as literary models for Vicente Blasco Ibáñez (1867-1928) and a brief commentary on Zola's two celebrated novelistic studies on alcohol provides a logical introduction for my observations on this theme in Blasco's Valencian novels.

In *L'Assommoir* (1879), or "cheap tavern," alcohol's effects on several members of a Paris working-class neighborhood are closely examined. The steady decline and ultimate degradation of the novel's humble heroine, Gervaise Macquart, are traceable largely to her own husband Coupeau. It is he who introduces Gervaise, whose parents had also been drunkards, to hard liquor. The ef-

fect of her newly established pattern of drinking is to weaken her will power and her pride in the small laundry she has established. Zola chronicles how alcohol contributes powerfully to a laziness that proves to be a fatal weakness for Gervaise in the competitive world in which she lives.

Coupeau, a roofer, develops his dependence on alcohol while recuperating from a fall. He dies in a public sanatorium after a final excruciating occurence of *delirium tremens.* Gervaise follows him to the grave several months later, but her death comes more from starvation than from drink.

The alcoholic afflictions of Coupeau and Gervaise weaken them and assure their defeat by an oppressive socio-economic environment that Zola portrays with great detail. Other lives are also affected, for alcohol is omnipresent. Many scenes are set in Colombe's tavern, the "assommoir" of the title, where Coupeau and his friends consume what Zola calls that establishment's "poison." Coupeau's most memorable companion is Mes Bottes, an alcoholic with a pantagruelian capacity for drink. Other pages of the novel describe Bijard, a tenant in Gervaise's tenement building, and a particularly vicious wife-beater when intoxicated. A final example in our quick survey of alcohol in *L'Assommoir* is Bazouges, the undertaker's assistant who drinks in order to get through the travails of each day. It is significant that this long novel ends with Bazouges, drunk as always, lifting into the pauper's box the decaying body of Gervaise.

The action of Zola's other work, *Germinal* (1885), is set above and below ground in a French coal-mining village. This novel of social conflict between labor and capital presents a population that is sexually promiscuous and hard-drinking to a remarkable degree. Drinking establishments abound, since cheap alcohol and sex are the only pleasures available in the brutish lives of most miners. The environmental context of exploitation and economic deprivation in this and in other proletarian novels by Zola establishes drunkenness and alcohol dependence as a natural consequence of such an existence. One major effect of alcohol is to increase the miners' fury when they rise up against the owners of the mines. But *Germinal's* focus is largely on the mining community as a collective or mass protagonist. Consequently, alcohol's effects on individual lives are presented with less variety and specificity than in *L'Assommoir.*

It is clear, then, from these few observations, how Zola establishes alcohol as a significant social reality (rather than a mere background element) in his naturalist novels. Other novelists in France and elsewhere quickly followed his example, reflecting a new awareness of and more careful attention to the potential of alcohol as a destructive force. In this regard such works of American literature as Stephen Crane's *Maggie: A Girl of the Streets* (1893), Frank Norris's *McTeague* (1899), and Theodore Dreiser's *Sister Carrie* (1900) reveal an astonishingly strong debt to Zola. Subsequent American literature, of course, also gives alcohol a prominent role not just in the lives of the lower class, but increasingly in those of other social classes as well.

Before we turn to Blasco Ibáñez's Valencian novels, a few observations are in order about the theme of alcohol in Spanish realist fiction. Especially instructive are the opinions on drunkenness reflected in the writings of Wenceslao Ayguals de Izco (1801-1873). Rubén Benítez, in a revealing and long needed study of Ayguals's life and works, summarizes that popular novelist's views as follows:

> La prostitución es el vicio de la mujer degradada y la embriaguez el del hombre miserable. Ayguals califica el excesivo uso de licores como un criminal olvido de la dignidad humana. Critica a los escritores de talento que describen borracheras sin censurar la conducta de sus personajes. La embriaguez—dice—causa estragos en Francia, Inglaterra y aun en los Estados Unidos: en España se abusa menos de la bebida.

I mention the attitudes of Ayguals (i/n his lifetime an extraordinarily successful popular novelist) not because he influenced Blasco Ibáñez, but because he makes several assumptions and assertions that are central to any discussion of alcohol in the Spanish realist novel.

First, Ayguals takes a moral position in asserting that drunkenness is a personal social vice, controlable by the individual person who, presumably, knows right from wrong. As a kind of pre-capitalist inspired by the ideas of a "humanitarismo filantrópico," Ayguals desired to see the working class move up the ladder of economic success through education, training, hard work, and a virtuous way of life. It is understandable that he would oppose and condemn (as Benítez's summary of his ideas indicates) alcohol abuse as an obstacle to the achievement of that goal. This moral attitude towards the use of alcohol will almost totally disappear with realism and with the naturalist aesthetic of objective observation.

Ayguals also assumes that alcohol abuse constitutes a more widespread problem in certain other countries than in Spain. Further, he implies that it is not a serious problem in Spain, although he concedes that it does exist. If this assumption is correct for Ayguals's lifetime (and for the next three decades, which concern us here), one might indeed expect the question of alcohol to receive relatively little attention in Spanish realist fiction.

In the three decades after Ayguals's death, the period of the realist novel, there was no Spanish novel of the genuinely proletarian kind authored by Zola. There were, however, novels about the rural and urban poor. And even if their socio-economic environments were somehow less dehumanizing (and thus less likely to cause the poor to seek refuge or escape in alcohol) than those shown in Zola's works, some attention to alcohol, as it affected their impoverished lives, might nonetheless be expected to constitute part of that reality.

Obviously, whether or not alcohol abuse was a serious social problem in Spain is not a question to be resolved by students of literature. Only social historians might determine with any statistical accuracy the degree to which chronic or addictive drunkenness constituted a real problem among the poor and other social classes in Spain. But in seeking reflections of such a presence in Spanish realistic fiction (even in these few works seriously influenced by elements of French naturalism, which are precisely the works in which such reflections would more likely occur), one finds the evidence to be sparse. It would be helpful, of course, to have available a catalogue of all significant mentions of alcohol in the works of the major Spanish realists. For the moment, because of limitations of space, I must be content to bring forth a few well known but representative examples of how the theme of alcohol is used by two major Spanish realists other than Blasco Ibáñez.

Overall, however, more extensive reading in Spanish realism convinces me that alcohol, when it appears at all, is almost always part of a background rather than a foreground situation. I also believe that it receives little serious attention or descriptive detail. And I contend that even in those few cases where alcohol is an obvious danger to a character, it tends to be treated with a certain evasiveness or non-seriousness with regard to its constituting a problem of any consequence. I believe the few examples adduced here will prove a foil to Blasco Ibáñez's unusual interest in the question of alcohol in his writings. As I explain later, this difference in treatment reflects both the strong influence of Zola's novels on Blasco and the Valencian's own considerable awareness of and attention to certain of the less happy social realities that are often glossed over or ignored by most of his contemporaries.

I have chosen Pardo Bazán's *La Tribuna* (1882) and *Los Pazos de Ulloa* (1886), and Pérez Galdós's *Fortunata y Jacinta* (1886-87) and *Misericordia* (1897) as novels in which alcohol is mentioned or appears in ways which are representative of the theme's general treatment in Spanish realism.

La Tribuna focuses on the young Galician Amparo Rosendo, whose oratorical skills make her a natural spokesperson for the other women workers at the tobacco factory. Amparo also becomes marginally involved in politics about the time of the Revolution of 1868 and acquires the name of "la tribuna." The extreme poverty of setting and the social inequality portrayed in *La Tribuna,* which is generally conceded to be as close to a proletarian novel in the naturalist mode as any Pardo Bazán ever wrote, would seem to offer a propitious environment for showing some degree of dunkenness or alcohol addiction. In fact, however, nearly the opposite is true. Alcohol is hardly alluded to except for the unexceptional case of Chinto, a teen-age boarder at the Rosendo house. When Amparo's mother detects the smell of wine on Chinto's breath, she reacts angrily: "¡Como otra vez te vea perdido de vino, he de decirle a Rosendo que te arree una tunda con la correa de la caja . . .". Somewhat later, when Chinto is living elsewhere and doing physically demanding work at a factory, he drinks wine as a stimulant on the job. The references to Chinto and alcohol constitute less than a page of text. In general, then, *La Tribuna* portrays a poor working-class community that is characterized by its sobriety, and which drinks in moderation even on festive or social occasions.

In *Los Pazos de Ulloa,* the uncivilizing, brutalizing effect of rural Galician life constitutes a major theme. Indeed, the environment of the "pazos" has a bearing on action by making several of the rural characters regress in behavior into a more primitive, animal-like way of life. But alcohol plays almost no role in bringing this animal behavior to the fore. In fact, it receives little more attention than in *La Tribuna*. As in the earlier work, alcohol is still a background item, rather than an essential factor in exerting influence on plot action or characterization.

The only memorable instance of alcohol abuse in *Los Pazos de Ulloa* is the very brief but celebrated scene (ch. 2) in which Primitivo, the "mayordomo" of the "pazos," bribes his young grandson, who has been drinking wine on his own, to continue drinking until he passes out. The purpose of this incident, however, is not to focus on alcohol or its effects but rather to provide one in a series of episodes that will establish the ruthless character of Primitivo and his tenacity in asserting his will. Almost as important, the scene presents an early sharp contrast between the character of the city priest, the rather delicate Julián Alvarez, and that of his chief antagonist, the tough, wiley Primitivo, who is a product and a symbol of the brutalizing rural environment of the "pazos."

Other brief references to alcohol in this novel have to do with traditional social uses of alcohol and with the physician Máximo Juncal, who relaxes by drinking rum while waiting for the birth of Nucha's child.

Interestingly enough, there are several situations in the novel in which alcohol, in a more fully naturalist novel, might have played a role. The marqués, Don Pedro, physically abuses with a rifle butt his servant-concubine, Sabel, in a fit of jealousy and a rage over her not having dinner prepared on time. Later in the novel there is evidence that he has also physically abused his wife, perhaps out of frustration and anger over her not having received an expected inheritance. In neither case is alcohol mentioned as a catalyst or contributing factor to this physical violence, as is often the case when there are wife-beating scenes in more genuinely naturalist novels.

In the vast, mostly middle-class setting of *Fortunata y Jacinta* Galdós creates several important secondary characters from the lower social classes. One of these serves as the temptress of Fortunata. Mauricia la Dura, with diabolical effectiveness, and at crucial moments, arouses and reinforces Fortunata's natural inclination to return to her lover, Juanito. Mauricia thus effectively helps to in-

sure the failure of all attempts to "redeem" Fortunata. More important for this study, however, is the fact that Mauricia is what we would now classify as a self-destructive alcoholic. Yet when one examines how her dependence on alcohol is treated in the novel, several things stand out. Galdós is uninterested in the origins of her dependence and never describes with any realistic detail the actual circumstances of her drinking. Moreover, as readers of the novel are aware, the tragic dimension of Mauricia's self-destructive alcoholic urge is almost ignored. Aside from her important and brilliantly developed functional role of tempting Fortunata, most of Mauricia's other actions tend to stress her humorous or comic dimension.

A notable example of this is Mauricia's death scene. Galdós does not specifically state that she dies as a result of her addiction, but such an assumption is the only one possible, for he never mentions her having any other affliction. Even in Mauricia's final moments, Galdós extracts humor from the fatal trait around which he has constructed much of Mauricia's characterization. When Doña Guillermina and the attending priest are unable to provoke a response from the moribund Mauricia,

> La santa tuvo una idea feliz. Le dio a beber una copa de jerez, llena hasta los bordes. Mauricia apretaba los dientes; pero al fin debió de darle en la nariz el olorcillo, porque abriendo la bocaza se lo atizó de un trago. ¡Cómo se relamía la infeliz!

A few moments later Mauricia dies, but not before, as the author records,

> Dejó oír una voz que parecía venir, por un tubo, del sótano de la casa. A mí me pareció que dijo: "Más, más . . ." otras personas que allí había aseguran que dijo "Ya." Como quien dice: "Ya veo la gloria y los ángeles." Bobería; no dijo sino *"Más . . ."*, a saber, *más jerez.*

Even Mauricia's internment at the Micaelas convent, where the nuns attempt to reform her, is treated with as much humor as seriousness. Her blasphemous, violent outbursts provide comic contrast to the quiet, disciplined ways of the nuns. Galdós has nonetheless observed the behavior of alcoholics well, for Mauricia's most difficult moments often seem to correspond to a strong craving for liquor and the suffering of withdrawal symptoms produced by lack of the alcohol on which she has become dependent. There is considerable humor in the way Galdós describes the calming effect of the "medicinal cognac" that one of the compassionate nuns shares with Mauricia.

One can scarcely criticize Galdós for not developing a particular character in a different way, especially when that character is as memorable as Mauricia la Dura. But the reader can not but wonder why this alcoholic, who obviously destroys herself through drink, is never examined seriously or realistically in terms of the affliction that largely defines her personality. Nor does Galdós even hint at such mysteries as the social or psychological origins of her affliction, and whether her alcoholism was a result or consequence of her total absence of moral standards. And how are Mauricia's violent outbursts and sudden periods of irritability to be related to her alcohol problem? Interesting, too, would have been some probing into Mauricia's ambiguously feminine psyche to see why perhaps the most memorable of the few alcoholics Galdós creates should be a woman and not a man, as is the case with alcoholics in most other works of Spanish realist fiction.

Finally, as a humorous footnote to this novel, one might mention Olmedo, Maximiliano's pharmacist friend. Olmedo cultivates the image of a bon vivant who 'lo hacía todo tan al vivo y tan con arreglo a programa, que se emborrachaba sin gustarle el vino, cantaba flamenco sin saberlo cantar."

In *Misericordia,* another novel chosen for a setting that would appear to be propitious for scenes of drunkenness, Galdós almost ignores alcohol. Despite an ambient of slum-level poverty in part of the novel and the considerable attention paid to beggars, Galdós limits his references to alcohol to brief mentions of two women companions, both peddlars, who are alcoholics. The first of these is La Pedra, referred to as "Borrachona, sinvergüenzonaza." La Pedra, with whom Almudena shares a cheap room, is shown sleeping off her drunkenness when Almudena and Benina enter the room in search of a small sum of money. Almost nothing else is said regarding Pedra, although Benina's compassionate words of advice provide a clue to her own character:

> a esta pobre desgraciada, cuando despierte, no la pegues, hijo, ¡pobrecita! cada uno, por el aquel de no sufrir, se emborracha con lo que puede: ésta con el aguardentazo, otros con otra cosa. Yo también las cojo; pero no así; las mías son de cosa de más adentro . . . Ya te contaré, ya te contaré.

Later in the novel, when Benina sees La Pedra in the company of a peddlar friend, La Diega, Almudena supplies a few more details about Pedra; she had been left an orphan as a child; Diega had introduced her to alcohol; Pedra, once physically attractive, aged suddenly from drinking brandy; she had been much abused and had slept in the streets. These details are very rapidly given without further elaboration.

In sum, it is no surprise, given the social background of *Misericordia,* that two alcoholics should be fleetingly introduced, if not as genuine characters at least as part of the background. The fact that they are women may be noteworthy, as was the case with Mauricia, but this must remain speculation since Galdós tells us nothing more about them.

Before turning our attention to Blasco Ibáñez's novels, it is important to underscore Blasco's admiration for Zola. Blasco several times visited Zola in France, translated

parts of several novels into Spanish, and published through his own publishing houses Spanish versions of a number of the Frenchman's novels. Approximately 15 long, idolatrous articles written by Blasco and published in his Valencian daily *El Pueblo* from 1897 to 1902 reveal the depth of his firsthand knowledge of Zola's works. These articles also help to explain why Blasco Ibáñez came closer than any other major Spanish novelist to writing naturalist novels on the model of those of Zola.

My focus here will be on Blasco's three Valencian novels of nonurban life: *Flor de Mayo,* (1896), *La barraca* (1898) and *Cañas y barro* (1902). These works exhibit strong thematic unity and depict the lives of the hardworking fishermen and farmers in areas outside the city of Valencia.

A relatively few comments on *Flor de Mayo,* the first and least studied of the three novels, will suffice to show how in this work on Mediterranean fishing life, alcohol is a constant in the lives of the poor. The Retor and his younger brother Tonet are married to Dolores and Rosario, respectively. The plot hinges on the adultery of Tonet with Dolores, and the consequences of the Retor's eventual discovery of this double treachery.

Tonet, from adolescence, is a delinquent and a heavy drinker. As a young adult he frequents the "taberna de las Buenas Costumbres" and the "Café Carabina," often becoming involved in drunken brawls. After he marries, he spends his life avoiding work and is supported by his wife. Occasionally Tonet does help his successful, hardworking brother, the Retor, on his fishing boat, the "Flor de Mayo."

Tonet's lover, the Retor's wife, is herself the daughter of an alcoholic "tartanero," who, while inebriated, fell under the wheels of his own "tartana" and was killed. Tonet, like the alcoholics in many French naturalist novels, is a habitual wife-beater. And like certain other lazy husbands in the other Valencian novels, he allows his wife to exhaust herself working to support them both. The gullible, good natured Retor realizes that his brother is unredeemably lazy, but forgives him because "le dominaba el maldito aguardiente" and because he erroneously believes Tonet married to an intractable woman.

The morning after the night when the Retor finally discovers his brother's infamy, the Retor goes off to a little tavern owned by his mother. The Retor is the first of a series of hardworking, abstemious, and rather ingenuous types who appear in the Valencian novels:

> El, siempre tan sobrio, quería beber, emborracharse, anegar en aguardiente aquel entorpecimiento de idiota que le dominaba. Bebió. . . . , pidió otra copa, ¡y otra después!

Several hours later the Retor resolves to take his fishing boat out into an approaching storm. This decision is tantamount to a death sentence for his entire crew, not just for his brother, whom he now intends to kill at sea. The Retor makes this unfortunate decision while alcohol still clouds his brain, and Blasco describes him already on deck with the "extraño brillo de sus ojos amarillentos, que parecían salirse del rostro rubicundo por el alcohol." A few hours later, with a now cleared head, he realizes how he has criminally exposed the innocent crew to death. His decision to return to port comes late, however, for the boat is destroyed before it can safely enter the port.

In *La barraca,* the best known of the Valencian works, alcohol is essential to the plot, which turns at critical moments on its use and abuse by certain protagonists. Those familiar with the novel will recall that it is structured around a boycott of the farmland owned by the heirs of D. Salvador, who had been killed by Tío Barret, the tenant farmer whom he had evicted. By refusing to lease this land, the farmers of the "huerta" were showing community solidarity and were exerting pressure on other landowners, of whom they were tenants, so they would not raise the rents on their own land. It will also be recalled that Tío Barret, like most of the other hard-working "huertanos," was known for his sobriety. He was a passive man, deeply respectful of the law. But his almost insane rage over his eviction from the "barraca" and the land leads to his violent act of retribution against his usurious oppressor. Significantly, it is alcohol that is responsible for eliminating his inhibitions against violence, thereby preparing him for the vengeful murder of D. Salvador. Although Barret dies in prison for his crime, his act binds the farming community together in its boycott of the land and "barraca" once occupied by Barret.

It is to Copa's tavern, in its way as menacing a presence as Colombe's drink shop in *L'Assommoir,* that Barret goes after his eviction: "Y él, tan sobrio, bebió, uno tras otro, dos vasos de aguardiente, que cayeron como olas de fuego en su estómago desfallecido." An hour later Barret made his way to an orange grove owned by D. Salvador, hoping by chance to encounter his tormentor there. But drunk and exhausted, Barret falls asleep, only to awake a few hours later with an unaccustomed taste in his mouth. Suddenly he sees D. Salvador approaching the grove, and "sintió que toda su sangre le subía de golpe a la cabeza, que reaparecía su borrachera." What follows is the drunken Barret's furious assault on D. Salvador with his razor-sharp sickle.

It is around an attempted violation of the boycott by Batiste Borrull, a poor Aragonese farmer, that the action of the rest of *La barraca* develops. Batiste, an outsider, desperate to feed his large family, accepts the favorable conditions offered by D. Salvador's heirs. He and his family move into the "barraca" and quickly begin to cultivate the surrounding lands. Despite unrelenting opposition in the form of hostile acts and sabotage by the "huertanos," lead by Pimentó, a local bully, Batiste and his family endure. And when Batiste's youngest son dies because of a hostile act by the farmer's children, community regret and guilt over this death cause the "huertanos" to cease their active persecution of Batiste and his fam-

ily. An uneasy truce obtains and the Borrulls are left undisturbed, even though they have defied the boycott. It is a fatal mistake, therefore, when Batiste, more out of curiosity to see the tavern than to have a drink, enters Copa's tavern, the novel's "templo de alcohol," to use the descriptor several times employed by the author. The abstemious Batiste orders a drink and "Sintió gran calor en el estómago y en la cabeza una deliciosa turbación." He becomes part of a crowd that is observing a drinking bout, which is now in its third day, between Pimentó and the two Terrerola brothers. Whoever manages to remain seated longest on his stool after drinking glass upon glass of brandy, will be declared the winner. But as so often happens with characters in Blasco's earlier *Cuentos valencianos* (1893), alcohol has turned a man (here Pimentó), through loss of all inhibitions and rational constraint, into a homicidal animal. When Pimentó observed Batiste among the onlookers, his deep but repressed rancor, his rage against his personal antagonist and violator of the boycott, instantly returns. And his state of brutish intoxication effaces whatever memory remains of the death of Batiste's son. Blasco indicates very clearly, in perfect naturalist style, what has happened to Pimentó:

> . . . se mostró sobrio, y muchos advertieron en él la mirada de través, aquella mirada de homicida que conocían de antiguo en la taverna, como signo indudable de inmediata agresión. Su voz tornóse fosca, como si todo el alcohol que hinchaba su estómago hubiese subido en oleada ardiente a su garganta.

Pimentó's anger grew as he continued to observe Batiste, and he "sintió caer de golpe sobre su cerebro todo el aguardiente bebido en dos días." Sensing the problem that his presence has created, Batiste would have liked to leave the tavern quietly, unobserved. But when Pimentó publicly orders him to leave, Batiste's sense of "hombría," fortified by the unaccustomed effect of alcohol, makes him disobey the order. A bloody confrontation ensues. And although Batiste emerges victorious, his is a pyrrhic victory. For with that one act he has again turned the entire community against him and his family.

The confrontation in the tavern leads to a later attempt by Pimentó to ambush Batiste at dusk, but it is Pimentó, instead, who is mortally wounded. That same night one of the "huertanos," acting for the vengeful community, sets fire to Batiste's "barraca," which is destroyed. Batiste and his family, possessionless, await the dawn before moving on to seek a subsistence living elsewhere.

Blasco, like Zola, presents variety in the kinds of alcohol abuse that he depicts. Nonetheless, one very clear pattern of behavior is discernible. It involves a parasite who is also an alcoholic or heavy drinker. In Blasco's novels this type of character spends most of his time avoiding or even fleeing from physical labor. He contrasts sharply with the majority of hard-working people in the community in which he lives.

In *Flor de Mayo* Tonet exemplifies this pattern of behavior. In *La barraca* the parasite is Pimentó. His anemic wife has ruined her health working dawn to dusk in order to support them both. In the Valencian novels a clear association is made between alcohol consumption and laziness. The philosophy of life of all of these characters is capsulized by Dimoni, an alcoholic flute player in the short story of the same name from *Cuentos valencianos* (1896), when he says: "¿trabajar? . . . Eso para los imbéciles."

Indeed, in *La barraca*, Pimentó is always shown as talking, resting or drinking, whereas his wife never ceases working. In this way, Pimentó is typical of all the Valencian "vagos." However, it is important to observe that Blasco, unlike Zola, does not show drunkenness as a major cause of laziness. In *L'Assommoir,* for instance, both Coupeau and Gervaise initially are steady workers, he a roofer and she a laundress. An unfortunate event, his accident, breaks a pattern of good work habits and modest ambition. It is only then that alcohol, at first merely a momentary escape from problems, becomes an addiction that precipitates an irreversible fall into sloth and degradation.

In the Valencian novels, however, most lazy characters seem to be that way deliberately and consciously in order to avoid the brutal physical labor required to survive in their world of farming and fishing. These characters seem to gravitate towards alcohol as an important element in filling their idle hours, but alcohol dependence is not a fundamental cause of their idleness.

In *Cañas y barro,* where poverty of setting is far deeper and more pervasive than in the two earlier novels, alcohol continues to play an important role. Moreover, a tavern, Cañamel's, on the island town of Palmar in the Albufera, becomes the locale for much of the novel's action. And Tío Paco (Cañamel), unlike Copa, the tavern owner in *La barraca,* is an important character in the novel.

Blasco, rather than using alcohol as a determinant of crucial plot action as he did in *La barraca,* now works with the determinist ideas of heredity and environment to create two vividly drawn characters, an alcoholic father and son, each of whom meets his fate in large part because of drunkenness. The father, Sangonera, drowns in the Albufera when, in a drunken state, he tries to catch a nutria. His son, Sangonereta, is a far more important character and one of the most memorable and appealing of any ever created by Blasco. Those who have read *Cañas y barro* will remember Sangonereta as the boyhood companion of the novel's two protagonists, Neleta and Tonet, and will recall how he grows to adulthood along with them.

Sangonereta is in the tradition of the "vagos" who appear in every Valencian novel and who spend their lives drinking and avoiding work. Like them he is a resourceful parasite, but he is unique because of his gentle nature and his original rationalizations for avoiding work. By necessity and from his father's example, Sangonereta is a moocher from boyhood onward. For a short time he helps a priest at mass, but he is soon dismissed when it is discovered he is stealing wine. Blasco seems to suggest that Sangonereta, an alcoholic from an early age, is addicted because of both environment and heredity. He thereby incorporates into his creation both sides of the naturalist, determinist formula. In showing Sangonereta sleeping in a wretched hut or in some open field, Blasco is describing what is in essence the life of an alcoholic tramp or vagrant whose dependence is satisfied largely with wine rather than hard liquor.

The death of the poetic Sangonereta results from an extraordinary abuse of his body when he consumes enough food for six persons and large amounts of alcohol, ranging from rum to absinthe. His subsequent illness, and the scenes of vomit and filth, have analogues in Zola's *Nana, L' Assommoir* and other novels where drunkenness leads to similar consequences. People who approached the door of Sangonereta's shack "inmediatamente retrocedían heridos por el hedor del lecho de immun-dicias en que se revolvía el enfermo." On the third day of his sickness, this drunkard of the lake died "con el vientre hinchado, la cara crispada, las manos contraídas por el sufrimiento y la boca dilatada de oreja a oreja por las últimas convulsiones."

The theme of alcohol in this novel is presented mostly through the portrayal of Sangonereta, but also through the portrayal of his father. This should not obscure the fact that the protagonist, Tonet, who at times disappears for a week or more on drunken binges with his pals or with Sangonereta through the villages of the Albufera region is what we would today classify as an occasional alcoholic. He is also the lazy, parasitic type seen before and he never works for more than very short periods of time. Tonet is often shown drinking in Cañamel's tavern. And he tends to drink whenever he faces a problem or difficult decision. For instance, after throwing his just born son into the Albulfera to conceal the evidence of his sexual liaison with Neleta, Tonet becomes drunk for several days in a futile attempt to deaden his own awareness of his heinous act. In sum, Tonet is the third alcoholic character depicted in the novel *Cañas y barro.*

I have attempted to demonstrate the major ways in which Blasco incorporates the theme of alcohol into his Valencian novels. My comments, however, are not intended to be exhaustive with regard to these novels nor to imply that the theme is significant only in these works. In fact, from Blasco's most youthful novel *Caerse del cielo* (1889), to several of the works written a few years prior to his death in 1928, the theme remains a novelistic constant.

In nine of the 13 *Cuentos valencianos* (1896), one of which has already been referred to, alcohol also plays a role. Moreover, many situations and characters in these individual stories foreshadow those of the novels. In several of the stories alcohol suddenly and unexpectedly turns people into violent animals who kill for love, revenge, anger, or honor. In others "vagos" drift towards alcohol to fill their empty hours. In the story "La corrección," Groquet is punished "por torpe" and repeatedly jailed for no other reason than to keep the mentally deficient but harmless youth off the streets. Like others in the jail, Groquet was the product of a "fatal herencia de varias generaciones de borrachos y homicidas."

In this paper I have chosen to examine alcohol in three Valencian novels, which artistically are Blasco's finest novels, and which are also his best known novels. The Valencian novels are also Blasco's first recognized works and in them he incorporates almost all the basic situations involving alcohol that are re-elaboratef in subsequent works. Nonetheless, any thoroughgoing examination of the theme in Blasco's fiction would also have to emphasize the social novels: *El intruso* (1903), about mining and industrial life in northern Spain; *La horda* (1905), which concerns the hungry and dispossessed people living in the outskirts of Madrid; and *La bodega* (1905), a depiction of "latifundio" exploitation in the vineyards and "bodegas" of Andalusia. Of all of Blasco's novels, *La bodega* is the one where the question of alcohol production and consumption receives most attention. This is because the novel is built around the thesis asserted by the anarchist prophet Fermín Salvochea that the owners of the "bodegas" are successfully using the rations of alcohol they provide their workers to weaken any desire of rebellion and thus to keep them enslaved.

Blasco, like Zola, creates novelistic worlds in which spiritual satisfactions are, if not impossible, at least very difficult to obtain. It is the satisfaction of basic material needs and instincts that motivates people and explains their actions. Given the nature of the struggle for survival that both authors present, it is natural that alcohol should be shown as a common escape or relaxation from that hard struggle. It is also natural that taverns and drinking establishments should abound and that alcohol consumption should affect a large number of the characters in quite different ways.

Obviously neither Blasco nor Zola anticipates the modern-day perspective on alcohol habituation as a biochemical addiction or even as a medical problem. Their observations suggest that at most they see it as a social problem with serious consequences for behavior. Neither one suggests that addiction is controlable by the individual affected by it.

In the Valencian novels Blasco illustrates, as we have seen, the effects of habitual drunkenness (what we now call alcoholism) in four areas: (1) the physical health of the drinker; (2) his relationship with other persons, especially family members; (3) his self-control and loss of normal inhibitions; (4) the ability to work steadily. In almost all cases, Blasco, like Zola, treats the subject with considerable objectivity, and it is here that the authors' aesthetic of impartial statement is evident. In fact, Blasco rarely even speculates on why certain of the characters he

creates are alcoholics and others are not. He does hint at environmental causes in that the socio-economic environments described will always produce a few habitual drunkards among all the people who drink. Only in rare cases, such as that of Sangonereta, does Balsco suggest any additional hereditary factor in predisposing an individual towards alcoholism.

In Blasco's novels drunkenness is never seen as a woman's affliction (unlike Galdos's works examined earlier). Moreover, it is usually examined as it affects adults, although Sangonereta is an alcoholic from boyhood, as is the delinquent Tonet from adolescence in *Flor de Mayo*. Blasco also shows how individual human capacity for and tolerance to alcohol vary greatly. Some habitual drinkers such as Pimentó have an astonishing capacity for large amounts of liquor, whereas others, such as the Retor, are hypersensitive to even small amounts.

The unusual degree of physical violence that characterizes Blasco's Valencian works and his *Cuentos valencianos* is clearly related to the question of alcohol. Moreover, its depiction is plausible given the character of the simple, passionate, elemental people that Blasco describes.

It was Zola, through is creation of a genuinely proletarian novel, who first opened the eyes of many readers to formerly hidden, often ugly realities in the lives of the poor. One of these realities was alcohol and the condition we now call alcoholism. It was a subject ignored, glossed over, or under-emphasized by most Spanish realists who, when they dealt with the poor in their works often imposed on them a series of spiritual concerns and complexities that reflected the authors' artistic concerns rather than close observation of their subjects' reality.

In summary, Blasco observed and investigated, as did Zola, the society of the poor. Like Zola in France, he found alcohol to be a fundamental part of the existence of that segment of Spanish society he was studying. In presenting that life, he convincingly made alcohol an integral part of a powerful picture of elemental man in his daily struggle for survival. And in Blasco's making this situation a special determinant of action and character, he greatly differed from the practice of his Spanish contemporaries.

J. O. Tate

SOURCE: "The Longest Goodbye: Raymond Chandler and the Poetry of Alcohol," in *Armchair Detective,* 18, 4, Fall, 1985, pp. 392-406.

[*In the following essay. Tate studies the symbolic and autobiographical role of alcohol in Raymond Chandler's novel* The Long Goodbye.]

A host of legends and biographies maneuver us into difficulties about the intentions of writers who were more than familiar with Demon Rum. *The Great Gatsby, The*

Sun Also Rises, and *Sanctuary* are harder to "read" than we would like to admit. Who is not aware of Fitzgerald's love for Keats, and the source of his most evocative title, *Tender Is the Night*? Remembering Fitzgerald's life may lend a certain chill to such warm lines as those of the second stanza of Keat's *Ode to a Nightingale*. The "beaded bubbles winking at the brim" of an imaginary glass of wine are a defining quality of an object of unique poetic totality. But consider the stanza as perceived by an alcoholic, and the bloom is off the rose.

Raymond Chandler's references to drinking are part of the hardboiled ethos parodied by S. J. Perelman and Woody Allen: the hardboiled dick must have his office bottle. But at least once, Chandler followed Fitzgarald in pursuit of a poetic suspension which we may think of as poetic if not Keatsian. And, like Fitzgerald as an artist and possibly as a man, he found bitterness in the dregs. But he would not, could not have come to such knowledge without first exploring the lambent golden greenness—the translucent green goldenness—the chartreuse astringency of a cocktail around which he structured his greatest and most personal work. *The Long Goodbye* (1954) is a ninety-proof revelation of self, an articulated fantasy, and a novel of manners written by a man who resented nothing so much as not being taken seriously as a writer.

John Houseman's well-known memoir "Lost Fortnight" tells perhaps the most dramatic story of Chandler's drinking. An aggrieved Chandler (whom Houseman, himself a veteran of the English public school system, portrays as an inhibited victim of his stay at Dulwich College many years before) demands and receives elaborate secretarial and medical support for a prolonged jag so that he can finish the shooting script of *The Blue Dahlia* (1945)—drunk. When the deal was struck, says Houseman, "We left the studio in Ray's open Packard and drove to Perino's where I watched him down three double martinis before eating a large and carefully selected lunch, followed by three double stingers." Chandler lived on intravenous injections and bourbon and water, and finished the job.

The whole story is illustrative of Chandler's pride, his professionalism (!), and his peculiar relationship with alcohol. But the longer one considers the story, the more one sees: there's a connection demonstrated, in Chandler's mind and behavior, between alcohol and creativity, a "controlled" drunkenness and an ideal of gentle-manliness, which, for Chandler, was somehow specifically *English*. In Chandler's mind, this was, or could be, connected with the work of creation, the craft of writing. Chandler and Houseman were both in Hollywood trying to make a living, but, to Chandler, their English public school background was most important. One cannot imagine such an absurd but serious proposal being made to anyone else—or, perhaps, to any other kind of person. A similar fusion of pride, self-regard, friendship, Anglophile snobbery, and alcohol is the ostensible subject of Chandler's most ambitious, longest novel, *The Long Goodbye*—his last strong work.

Another memoir, Natasha Spender's "His Own Long Goodbye," offers a sophisticated analysis of an older Chandler, alcoholic and suicidally depressed by the death of his wife. Natasha Spender's comments and analysis are the most insightful we have:

> He wrote *The Long Goodbye* as Cissy lay dying, and we who tried to see him through the subsequent "long nightmare" recognize in the book three dis-tinct self-portraits. It may well reflect the interior dialogue between facets of his own personality as he looked back upon their long life together, which he was soon to lose. Afterwards his London con-versations . . . strikingly resembled the dialogue of all three characters in turn. . . .
>
> Like Terry [Lennox], Raymond was a young ex-soldier in the early twenties, battle-scarred and scared, whose pride was that "of a man who had nothing else." [Lennox], when castigated by Philip Marlowe for being a moral defeatist, says that his life is all "an act." Raymond often acknowledged his own tendency to fantasize and play-act. . . .
>
> Like that of Roger Wade, the successful, middle-aged, alcoholic and egocentric writer, Raymond's drunken stream of consciousness could also at bad moments be full of self-hatred, writer's angst, and sarcastic hostility. . . .
>
> Marlowe of course, represents Chandler's ideal self, the conscience which punished the Roger Wade within him though not without commendation for achievement (for Wade in the book is "a bit of a bastard and maybe a bit of a genius too"), and befriended the Terry [Lennox] within, not without censure . . .
>
> All three characters were drinkers, like Raymond himself, two of them disintegrating and despairing, for only the ideal-self Marlowe shows a disposition towards integrity. As aspects of Raymond's own character their dominance veered with his mood, Roger Wade his "bad self," Philip Marlowe his "good self" and Terry [Lennox] his anxious one. These three, often in conflict, were in good times subordinated to a fourth, the genial, generous, and benevolently paternal friend.

Natasha Spender speaks from a knowledge of Chandler the man and from a psychological insight into his work. Her identification of the three leading male characters as a splitting of their creator's personality is a key to the structure and meaning of *The Long Goodbye* which I aspire to employ to unlock further of its secrets. Her specific identification of the fragments of self out of which characters are created has the power to remind us of works of E. T. A. Hoffmann, Poe, Dostoievski, and Conrad. But I wish to emphasize, not the splitting of the selves, but the alcoholic obsession of all three. *The Long Goodbye*, like many if not most fictions, may be a form of wishful thinking; but if so it is uniquely a picture and sublimation of wishful drinking.

Yet Frank MacShane, in his brilliant biography of Chandler, has made it clear that, at the time of the composition of *The Long Goodbye*, Chandler had "mastered his desire for [alcohol]." Yet the novel is at least superficially about drinking. It is what the characters *do*. Drinking is the basis of the relationship of Marlowe and Lennox. Drinking causes the acquaintance of Marlowe and Wade. Marlowe meets Linda Loring (his bride to be) at a bar. Marlowe meets Howard Spencer at a bar, and Mrs. Wade at that same bar. Chandler had mastered his desire for alcohol, at least temporarily; but alcohol was on his mind.

Chandler wrote his first draft worn down by his wife's declining health and his own self-doubt, yet carrying on. He sent the draft to his agent in May 1952. The reaction touched a nerve and led to a break between Chandler and the firm of Brandt and Brandt; the reaction also led to Chandler's revisions, which were interrupted by a trip to England. In a letter to Hamish Hamilton, his English publisher, Chandler declared

> I wrote this as I wanted to because I can do that now. I don't care whether the mystery is fairly obvious, but I cared about the people, about this strange corrupt world we live in, and how any man who tries to be honest looks in the end either sentimental or plain foolish. . . . You write in a style that has been imitated, even plagiarized, to the point where you begin to look as if you were imitating your imitators. So you have to go where they can't follow you.

As MacShane puts it, "There is no doubt that Chandler intended to put all of himself into *The Long Goodbye*." As Natasha Spender suggests, "all of himself" means, in effect, three selves—three drinking selves. But let MacShane advance the story of the composition of Chandler's most ambitious work:

> When Chandler returned to La Jolla in 1952, he announced that he had learned how to drink on the *Mauretania* returning from his first trip to England since 1918. He had discovered the gimlet, a cocktail made with gin and Rose's lime juice. In the evenings before dinner Chandler and his wife would have a single gimlet and that would be all. It was the first time he had done any drinking in his own house for six years. Gradually, as Cissy grew weaker and the situation more obvious, Chandler began to increase the amount he took.

A year after he had first sent out his draft, he was four-fifths of the way through his revision of the novel—and the gimlet was a substantial part of that *re-vision*.

And another year later, after Cissy's death, Patrick Doncaster interviewed Chandler in England for the *Daily Mirror* in a piece that

> was never published because of a newspaper strike. They talked about Hollywood girls, and then Doncaster changed the subject:
>
> "Mrs. Chandler," I said gently.
>
> He put down his gimlet, a gin and lime drink you associate with pukka sahibs and outposts of Empire rather than a Hollywood thriller writer whose chief character swigs Scotch.
>
> "What about Mrs. Chandler?" he said edgily. "She's dead. Died last year." He looked away across the bar. He twitched a little, jumpy. Then something chocked in his throat.
>
> "I've not got over it yet," he said quietly. And a big tear rolled down his cheek.

Doncaster's anecdote sends a chill up the spine because it not only portrays Chandler the suffering man but also gives a glimpse into the imagination of Chandler the haunted artist. We must notice here the association of alcohol with sentiment, even if that sentiment is a deeply felt and genuine grief. In *The Long Goodbye,* it is the gimlet which is the image of a certain sentiment. That potent and noble cocktail is the emotional solvent, the emblem of Marlowe's love for Lennox, and the connection by which Marlowe meets the woman who (in the unfinished *Poodle Springs Story*—1958) was to become his wife. If *The Long Goodbye* is a novel about drinking, then it is a novel about drinking gimlets. But what does drinking gimlets mean? Well—why did Daisy cry about Gatsby's imported English shirts? What do such *shirts* mean? As an image in context, everything. I do not compare Terry Lennox's gimlets—or Jupiter-Jowett—to Gatsby's brilliant collection of various commodities casually.

One measure of the seriousness with which Chandler addressed the composition of *The Long Goodbye* is its sturdy structure. The gimlets mentioned at the beginning, middle, and end of the novel are emblems as firmly placed (though not so meaningful) as the scaffolding/pillory scenes similarly placed in *The Scarlet Letter*. Chandler's firmness of design clarifies for us the unraveling of a tangled skein of action and emotion. The scenes with Lennox at the beginning and end enfold the interior episodes involving Roger Wade; at the end we understand the relationship between the two. Between the Lennox material at the beginning and the introduction of the Wade episodes are a number of lesser actions involving Endicott the lawyer, Morgan the reporter, Peters the private detective, the police, and Menendez and Starr, the gangsters. After Wade's death, these same people and connections are recapitulated before Marlowe finally sees Lennox again. This symmetry, a "geometric structure" or "framing device", strongly resembles the "ring composition" known to classicists.

Chandler's self-consciousness can be appreciated also by his self-inflicted criticism. The taunts of the gangster Menendez, placed about one-fifth of the way into the novel, are not idle street chatter but cunningly devised insults designed to pre-empt the reader. The well-heeled

Menendez sneers at Marlowe's relative poverty and then strikes at the heart of the novel. Saying early what Chandler doesn't want the reader to think later, the criminal tough guy effectively discredits an intelligent position by taking it. He puts his finger on a sentimentality of which Chandler was aware.

> "You got cheap emotions. You're cheap all over. You pal around with a guy, eat a few drinks, talk a few gags, slip him a little dough when he's strapped, and you're sold out to him. Just like some school kid that read *Frank Merriwell*. You got no guts, no brains, no connections, no savvy, so you throw out a phony attitude and expect people to cry over you." (Chapter 11)

Menendez's—that is, Chandler's—citation of Frank Merriwell is an acute piece of literary and even moral analysis. Gilbert Pattern's dime novels (signed by the pseudonymous Burt L. Standish) sold millions of copies from 1896 on. Frank Merriwell, that "wholesome college athlete," was a popular reduction of prep-school fantasy, whose sporting adventures may lie behind Marlowe's reference to a football injury (Chapter 8). Such a connection not only mocks but clarifies Marlowe's, and by extension Chandler's, romantic, even adolescent, code of honor. We may associate this further with Owen Johnson's Dink Stover, or better with a British tradition of boy's books by such writers as Thomas Hughes and R. M. Ballantyne. Chandler, that public school boy, never forgot Dulwich College.

And we must not forget—he never got over it—that Chandler began the career for which he is remembered as a pulpwriter himself, in Joseph R. Shaw's *Black Mask* magazine. Menendez's cutting phrase, "Tarzan on a big red scooter," is not only an effective sneer at Marlowe but a stinging rebuke written by the man whom it hurt most, Chandler himself. Edgar Rice Burrough's Tarzan, the son of a British nobleman, was a popular fantasy-figure of imperial association not as distant from Marlowe as it is comfortable to think. Switching from the vein of prep-school gentility to that of the street-wise tough guy, Marlowe expresses a profound ambivalence between English good manners and an American vernacular, the tension of which drives Chandler's novel. In an unsportsmanlike gesture that indicates a nerve has been touched, Marlowe punches Menendez in the stomach, which action is in effect Chandler lashing out at his own critical sense, setting an example for the reader to suppress the nay-sayer within. Such are the requirements of masculine romance, as written by an elegant and despairing artist of that genre. (The association of public school honor and the composition of "thrillers" is not so dated as it seems, surviving literally and healthily in Gavin Lyall's *Blame the Dead* [1973] and John le Carré's *Tinker, Tailor, Soldier, Spy*.)

Another measure of the seriousness with which Chandler addressed the project (the working title of which was *Summer in Idle Valley*) is its richness of literary allusion and reference. We find Walter Bagehot (Chapter 13), T.

S. Eliot (Chapters 32 and 49), Keats (Chapter 34), Shakespeare (Chapters 26 and 47), Marlowe (Chapter 24) and Robert Frost/Blaise Pascal (Chapter 38), Sir James Frazer (Chapter 35), Flaubert (Chapter 23), Coleridge (Chapter 14), and William Inge (Chapter 23). If Marlowe's name repeats Christopher Marlowe's, it also encapsules Sir Thomas Malory's, for Marlowe was first named Mallory. Similarly, the publisher Howard Spencer conjures Edmund Spenser. But I think that the most important of these references—the most meaningful, the least incidental or decorative—is to F. Scott Fitzgerald, in Chapters 13 and 14.

For Chandler, that sensitive man, critical reader, and professional writer, was well aware of Fitzgerald and, I think, to some extent identified with him. He too labored in the sour vineyards of Hollywood, after Fitzgerald did (and as others such as Faulkner, Hammet, O'Hara, West, and McCoy did). Like Fitzgerald, he wrote a Hollywood novel (*The Little Sister,* 1949), and he had highly developed opinions about Fitzgerald's unfinished *The Last Tycoon*.

One example of Chandler's awareness of Fitzgerald's achievement (in a letter dated May 2, 1949) is stated at the expense of lesser writers:

> But somehow [Marquand's] successful, oh-so-successful soufflés always make me think of little lost books like *Gatsby* and *Miss Lonelyhearts*—books which are not perfect, evasive of the problem often, side-stepping scenes which should have been written (and which Marquand would have written at twice the necessary length) but somehow passing along, crystallized, complete, and as such things go nowadays, eternal, a little pure art—great art or not I wouldn't know, but there is such a strange difference between the real stuff and a whole shelf of Pulhams and Forsytes and Charlie Grays.
>
> Not that I class myself with any of these people . . .

Again, in a letter to Dale Warren of November 13, 1950, while he was working on *The Long Goodbye*, Chandler wrote that

> Fitzgerald is a subject no one has a right to mess up. I think he just missed being a great writer, and the reason is pretty obvious. If the poor guy was already an alcoholic in his college days, it's a marvel that he did as well as he did. He had one of the rarest qualities in all literature, and it's a great shame that the word for it has been thoroughly debased by the cosmetic racketeers, so that one is almost ashamed to use it to describe a real distinction. Nevertheless, the word is charm—charm as Keats would have used it. Who has it today? It's not a matter of pretty writing or clear style. It's a kind of subdued magic, controlled and exquisite, the sort of thing you get from good string quartettes. Yes, where would you find it today?

I think that to a degree Chandler here identifies, in effect, with Fitzgerald: alcoholism, charm, the magic of style, music. The alcoholic identification needs no comment, except to note that alcoholism is associated with both literary accomplishment *and* failure. The word *magic* Chandler used about good writing—and about his own writing. "All good writers have a touch of magic." Or again: "But a writer who hates the actual writing, who gets no joy out of the creation of magic by words, to me is simply not a writer at all . . . How can you hate the magic which makes of a paragraph or a sentence or a line of dialogue or a description something in the nature of a new creation?" Thinking of himself, he wrote that "[A] writer to be happy should be a good second rater. . . . He should definitely not be a mystery writer with a touch of magic and a bad feeling about plots."

In *The Long Goodbye,* the word "charm" is used by Marlowe about Lennox: "[H]e had charm." "Music" he used eloquently and elegiacally about his wife, who had been a fine pianist: "She was the music heard faintly at the edge of sound." At the end of *Playback,* Marlowe has received a long-distance proposal from Linda Loring. The last sentence is: "The air was full of music."

"Charm" and "magic" are directly related. The word *charm* is derived from the Latin *carmen,* meaning song. A charm is a poem or song, an incantation that may ward off evil spirits or bring good luck. By extension, a charm may be a talisman, hence "charm bracelet." This identity of terms—charm, magic, poetry—through the persona of Fitzgerald, or through his legend, is connected by Chandler with alcohol, a distilled magic, a bottled poetry, both the lift of inspiration and the subject of poetry itself. Edward Fitzgerald's arbitrary, antiquarian translations of Omar Khayyám remove us to an ancient world; through the poetry of Callimachus and Anacreon, the tradition reaches further back.

But Chandler and Fitzgerald have a bit more in common than alcohol, charm, and magical writing—which Chandler implies were the same thing, both in Fitzgerald as the other, and in himself as a conscious self. There's the Hollywood connection already mentioned; their membership in the same World War I generation; the profound romanticism that expresses itself variously in both writers as a complex social snobbery, both conscious and unconscious; there's an infatuation with the dialectic of class; an ambivalent "idealization" of woman; a shaky adherence to a prep-school idea of manliness. All of these qualities and themes, rich material for the writer of talent, are present in *The Great Gatsby.* My contention is that *The Long Goodbye* is in part a fond farewell to, a criticism of, an homage to, and a pastiche of *The Great Gatsby.*

Fitzgerald is loudly mentioned in *The Long Goodbye,* through the alcoholic, writerly bitterness of a character Natasha Spender has identified as a projection of Chandler himself: "I do not care to be in love with myself and there is no longer anyone else for me to be in love with. Signed: Robert (F. Scott Fitzgerald) Wade. P.S. This is why I never finished *The Last Tycoon.*" Eileen Wade's comments extend the identifications: "Just attitudinizing. He has always been a great admirer of Scott Fitzgerald! He says Fitzgerald is the best drunken writer since Coleridge, who took dope. Notice the typing, Mr. Marlowe. Clear, even and no mistakes." Marlowe himself suggests that "the Scott Fitzgerald allusion might merely be an off-beat way of saying goodbye." A long goodbye, indeed.

Wade's (and Chandler's) allusion to Keats in Chapter 34 mixes the contemplation of suicide with alcoholism in a blend fixed by the aesthetic mode. "A pretty color whiskey is, isn't it? To drown in a golden flood—that's not so bad. 'To cease upon the midnight with no pain.' How does that go on? Oh, sorry, you wouldn't know. Too literary . . ." Chandler's Keats is filtered through Fitzgerald, and anticipates his own feeble, alcoholic attempt at suicide after *The Long Goodbye* was published and his wife was dead.

I think that Gatsby's seemingly fraudulent "Oxford education," English shirts, Rolls-Royce and pseudo-English diction ("old sport") were latterly reincarnated in Lennox, with his English suitcase and automobile, his British war experience, gangster friends, and mysterious identity. This is a projection of Chandler's self *through* Fitzgerald's lyricism. Chandler served in the Great War in the Canadian Expeditionary Force. Lennox was born in Canada. To further show the connection between Chandler and Fitzgerald, I must also point out that Frank MacShane has demonstrated the imaginative connection between "the girl with the cornflower-blue eyes" from Chandler's poem "Nocturne from Nowhere" (1932) and such later blond incarnations as Eileen Wade in *The Long Goodbye.* In emphasizing the connection with Fitzgerald and *The Great Gatsby,* I do not at all mean to deny the truth of MacShane's assertions but to amplify that truth. In the first place, Chandler's fantasy about the girl was written well after *The Great Gatsby* (1925). When Marlowe meets Mrs. Wade, we have a lush outpouring:

> [A] dream walked in . . . She was slim and quite tall in a white linen tailormade. . . . Her hair was the pale gold of a fairy princess. There was a small hat on it into which the pale gold hair nestled like a bird in its nest. Her eyes were cornflower blue, a rare color, and the lashes were long and almost too pale.

Thereafter, this blonde is called "the golden girl" three times. She has a low voice "like the stuff they used to line summer clouds with." We must be reminded of Fitzgerald's Daisy Fay Buchanan, with her "low, thrilling voice" which is "'full of money.'"

> That was it. I'd never understood before. It was full of money—that was the inexhaustible charm that rose and fell in it, the jingle of it, the cymbals' song of it. . . . High in a white palace the king's daughter, the golden girl.

When Chandler's Eileen pays the waiter at the Ritz-Carlton, "he looked as if he had shaken hands with God."

As for Gatsby: "He knew that when he kissed this girl, and forever wed his unutterable visions to her perishable breath, his mind would never romp again like the mind of God."

Joseph Louzonis has suggested that Philip Marlowe's lengthy digression or disquisition on blondes (Chapter 13)—a polished excursus—is inspired by Semónides of Amórgos's satire *On Women,* written around the middle of the seventh century B.C. Considering Chandler's background in classics, this may be so; but I think that this aria is also indebted to Fitzgerald, and matched by Lennox's set-piece on gimlets.

Ernest Lockridge has written that "Gatsby's dream divides into three basic and related parts: the desire to repeat the past, the desire for money, and the desire for incarnation of 'unutterable visions' in the material earth." Lennox wants to repeat the past by re-marrying Sylvia; in so doing, he seizes wealth. The unutterable vision of *The Long Goodbye* is incarnated in such emblems of wealth as British automobiles, stories of the spoiled rich, and English manners incarnated in the gimlet. Besides: Eileen Wade wants to repeat the past by recovering her first love for Paul Marston; Linda Loring is for Marlowe a sexual lure associated with wealth; the whole novel is a circular gesture of futility less over-reaching, less grand, and less tragic than *The Great Gatsby*.

The Long Goodbye has in common with *The Great Gatsby* the elements of adultery and desire, alcohol in profusion, various forms of violence (including fatal gunfire and violence at cocktail parties), an attempt to recapture the past, Anglophilia, ineffable effusions, a beautiful blonde, an investigative structure, a studied contrast between the low and the high, the squalid and the glamorous, the world of work contrasted with a corrupting and irresponsible wealth, a display of status symbols (automobiles, mansions, etc.), and an inarticulate friendship or male bonding or love or identification or sympathy, the displacement of which excites and explains the writing of both first-person narratives. No more imagination is required to see *The Long Goodbye* as a "lyrical novel" than is required to see *The Great Gatsby* as a detective story.

The world of *The Great Gatsby,* like the world Chandler imagined in *The Long Goodbye,* is both an underworld of the sinister and sleazy and an overworld of glamour and glory. The overworld is chiefly embodied in commercial talismans, advertising emblems, the obvious emblems of status, the thrice-familiar clichés of mass-cult entertainment, the stuff of a thousand B-movies. Both Gatsby and Lennox—and by extension, Nick and Marlowe—are involved with blondes, booze, big bucks, and guns. In context, the underworld and the overworld are hardly distinguishable. *The Great Gatsby* is a *dolcissimo* expostulation, a *legato* apostrophe, and a vulgar tragedy. Both novels are "novels of manners" set in an unmannerly country and a rude century. But *The Long Goodbye* ends not with a bang, but a whimper. Fitzgerald's prophetic, apocalyptic masterpiece still has the power to excite.

Chandler's effort is an elegy to his own lost energy, a plaint for his illusions. Gatsby has two names and dies. Lennox has three. He dies as a man, but is still walking at the end. *The Long Goodbye* is a ponderous farewell to illusion, a laid-back Californian revision of Fitzgerald's fable of East and West. The profoundly shallow elements of these fictions, their superficial depths, are so much a part of the American imagination that it is difficult for us to see them, much less to evaluate them. But Norman Mailer, demonstrating both the power and his knowledge of the power of these cultural symbols, in his underrated *An American Dream,* shuffled a well-worn deck and again dealt us familiar cards—the blonde, the booze (and prohibited marijuana), the bucks, the gun, and so forth. These are (must be?) the stuff of a modern, specifically American melodrama. Not for nothing did Chandler suffuse his mysteries with the imagery of medieval romance so often commented on. His knightly, chess-playing narrator is obsessed with honor, chivalric behavior, the chastity of women and the *gentillesse* of men. When Chandler mounted his greatest production, he made his Anglophile version of good manners and proper behavior the subject of his novel in the most complex way he ever achieved. Marlowe's empathy with Lennox had been foreshadowed, I think, in his sympathy with Moose Malloy in *Farewell, My Lovely* (1940). The opening scene presents Moose staring at the defective neon sign denoting Florian's, where his "little Velma" used to work. This image of irrecoverable romance is highly reminiscent of Gatsby and the green light on Daisy's dock. Like Nick, Marlowe must sympathize with and admire the forlorn, doomed romanticism of such a gesture. Moose is murdered by his dream-girl at the end, as Gatsby was betrayed by Daisy. "Little Velma," who was "cute as lace pants," remakes herself into "Mrs. Lewin Lockridge Grayle" and disastrously ends a career of self-transformation not unlike Gatsby's transmogrification from James Gatz. Like Nick, Marlowe is the narrator-witness who uniquely *knows*.

Farewell, My Lovely also anticipates the "double plot" of *The Long Goodbye,* wherein two seemingly unrelated adventures *are* related in the very unknotting of their covert relationship. In *Farewell, My Lovely,* the Moose Malloy-Velma-Jesse Florian business is revealed to be causally, not casually, related to the Lindsay Marriot-Mrs. Grayle episodes. This is the "mystery" which is solved. Similarly, in *The Long Goodbye,* Marlowe finds that the Lennox matter is causally, not casually, related to the Wade material: he would not have been hired by Mrs. Wade if he had not kept faith with Lennox; but also, Mrs. Wade, as the real murderer, has ulterior motives. The synthesis of the novel is its resolution in the person of Linda Loring, Sylvia Lennox's sister, and Marlowe's attachment to her both in and out of the text of that novel.

For Chandler, the Fitzgerald "magic" and "charm" and "music" required a relaxation into a spontaneity. The poetry of glamour and glory must, in a fallen world, be charged with alcoholic inspiration. Now when I say that *The Long Goodbye* is "about" drinking, I mean what I say—literally, but not exclusively. Perhaps a précis—an alcoholic one—will reinforce the point.

Ch. 1 Marlowe rescues the "plastered" Lennox and takes him home, where there's a half-empty Scotch bottle. The words *drunk* and *booze hound* are used.

Ch. 2. Marlowe rescues Lennox again; the drunk tapers off on beer, and later they sit over "a couple of very mild drinks." Marlowe leaves Lennox alone with a whiskey bottle, which goes untouched.

Ch. 3 Lennox, remarried, takes Marlowe to Victor's for gimlets and talk. The gimlets become a ritual of friendship. They discuss Sylvia's drunk/hung over friends.

Ch. 4 Marlowe and Lennox sit in a bar, drinking, discussing drinking. They exchange words.

Ch. 5. Lennox appears suddenly. He must go to Tijuana. Marlowe serves coffee and Old Grand-Dad. He puts a pint of bourbon in Lennox's suit-case. Lennox refers to Sylvia as "dead drunk."

Ch. 6 Tijuana and back. The cops are waiting. "We had a drink together once in a while."

Ch. 7 Marlowe stands up to two police beatings rather than betray a friend.

Ch. 8. Marlowe behind bars. The drunk tank. Visit from Endicott. Marlowe says, "I'm not here for him, I'm here for me."

Ch. 9. Grenz of the D.A.'s office exhales the smell of whiskey. Marlowe challenges him to "Take another quick one."

Ch. 10. Lonnie Morgan of the *Journal* takes Marlowe home. He refuses Marlowe's offer of a drink.

Ch. 11. Phone call from Endicott. Visit from Menendez. Call from Spencer: "Let's discuss it over a drink." Menendez's war story: Lennox "hit the bottle."

Ch. 12. Letter from Lennox with portrait of Madison (a $5,000 bill): "So forget it and me. But first drink a gimlet for me at Victor's. And the next time you make coffee, pour me a cup and put me some bourbon in it."

Ch. 13. At the Ritz-Beverly bar at 11:00 A.M., Marlowe sees a middle-aged drunk. "There is a sad man like that in every quiet bar in the world." Marlowe has a weak Scotch and water. Enter "the golden girl." Enter Spencer; who orders a gin and orange for himself and one for Marlowe. Spencer broaches the subject of Roger Wade. Marlowe says, "I like liquor and women and chess and a few other things . . ." Spencer tells the story of Wade's wild drinking. A second round of gin and oranges arrives. "The golden girl" introduces herself as

Eileen Wade. Marlowe later has a martini with dinner.

Ch. 14. Coffee with Mrs. Wade reminds Marlowe of coffee with Terry. "A neighbor of ours knew the Lennoxes." Discussion of Wade's drinking problems; mention of Fitzgerald and Coleridge.

Ch. 15. Visit to George Peters at the Carne Organization. Discussion of a "well-heeled alcoholic" at a "sobering-up joint." Mention of Marston: "The guy was drunk all the time . . ."

Ch. 16. Earl and Dr. Verringer. "The guy's a wino."

Ch. 17. Dr. Vukanich. "He lives on the sauce for days on end." "Shoot yourself in the vein, don't you, Doc?"

Ch. 18. Dr. Varley. "Wade, a well-to-do alcoholic . . ."

Ch. 19. "Hooch cases." A whiskey sour at Rudy's Bar-B-Q. Marlowe intervenes and retrieves Wade. "I was foul with strong drink."

Ch. 20. Marlowe takes Wade home. "You the guy that was mixed up with Lennox?" "Aren't you coming in for a drink or something?" Eileen: "Don't you want a drink yourself?"

Ch. 21. Eileen invites Marlowe "for a drink the next evening." Reminded of Terry and the gimlets at Victor's, Marlowe heads there.

Ch. 22. A woman at the bar is drinking a "pale greenish-colored drink." Marlowe orders a gimlet—a double; the bartender mentions Rose's Lime Juice. Discussion of gimlets, England, and Terry. "A couple more of the same . . . in a booth." "A bit of a sentimentalist, aren't you, Mr. Marlowe?" "I reached for my glass and dropped the contents down the hatch." "I need another drink" (third gimlet). Harlan Potter said "Terry was a gentleman twenty-four hours a day instead of for the fifteen minutes between the time the guests arrive and the time they feel their first cocktail." "I came in here to drink a gimlet because a man asked me to." "Three gimlets. Doubles. Perhaps you're drunk." "You had one and a half, Mrs. Loring. Why even that much?" "Maybe I *was* a little drunk." Scene with Agostino. Big Willie Magoon.

Ch. 23. At the Wades': "It was the same old cocktail party . . . everybody talking too loud, nobody listening, everybody hanging on for dear life to a mug of the juice, eyes very bright, cheeks flushed or pale and sweaty according to the amount of alcohol consumed and the capacity of the individual to handle it." Scene-setting mention of the bar, drinks, etc. Marlowe: "I got Lennox killed . . ." Wade: "Let's go get that drink."

Ch. 24. The party is "About two drinks louder." Dr. Loring makes a scene with Wade. Marlowe gets a Scotch. A drunken scene between a man and his wife. Marlowe's thoughts on alcoholism.

Discussion with Mrs. Wade concerning Wade's status. Wade enters with drink in hand and accuses Marlowe. Wade: "Drunks don't educate, my friend. They disintegrate. And part of the process is a lot of fun." Marlowe thinks that "Alcohol was no more than a disguised reaction."

Ch. 25. Wade's emergency phone call. Marlowe takes care of the Wades.

Ch. 26. Candy assists. Wade claims guilt.

Ch. 27. Examination of Wade's drinking leading to fall. Marlowe drinks as he reads Wade's "wild" writing.

Ch. 28. Wade's drunken writing jag: self-loathing, drinking.

Ch. 29. A shot. Fake suicide attempt scorned by Marlowe. Erotic confrontation with Eileen. Marlowe knocks himself out with a bottle of Scotch.

Ch. 30. Scenes with Candy and Eileen.

Ch. 31. Marlowe decides to kill his hangover with "a tall cold one." Meets Mrs. Loring at office. Heads for Potter.

Ch. 32. Potter rings for tea. He calls Wade a "dangerous alcoholic." Mention of gimlets.

Ch. 33. Calls from Wade and Ashterfelt.

Ch. 34. At Wade's, Marlowe "got that look on my face when a drunk asks you to have a drink." Cokes and sandwiches and beer are ordered. Wade calls for a bottle of whiskey.

Ch. 35. Wade has drunk over half the bottle. He gets another bottle. Wade passes out. Speedboat and lake.

Ch. 36. Webley again. Wade a suicide?

Ch. 37. Olds: "Your friends get dead." Mention of demerol. Marlowe home to a couple of cold drinks.

Ch. 38. Candy's accusations. Marlowe has "a stiff one."

Ch. 39. Inquest. At lunch, Marlowe has "a brown Swedish beer that could hit as hard as a martini."

Ch. 40. Calls Endicott and Menendez and Peters. Date at Romanoff's.

Ch. 41. Meets Howard Spencer at the Ritz-Beverley. Spencer orders Amontillado, Marlowe a rye whiskey sour. Spencer quaffs Marlowe's drink when shocked by Marlowe's suspicion of Eileen.

Ch. 42. Spencer: "A writer needs stimulation—and not the kind they bottle." Marlowe contradicts Eileen's story of the pendant. Spencer: "I need a drink badly. . . . Straight Scotch, and plenty of it." Marlowe takes a bourbon on the rocks. "She killed both of them."

Ch. 43. Demerol again. *"La señora es muerta."* Coffee.

Ch. 44. Wade was too soaked with alcohol to have killed himself.

Ch. 45. Eileen's note: Paul Marston (Terry) "an empty shell." Lonnie Morgan and photostat. "Remember the night you drove me home from the City Bastille? You said I had a friend to say goodbye to. I've never really said goodbye to him. If you publish this photostat, that will be all. It's been a long time—a long, long time." Mady and Potter.

Ch. 46. Marlowe returns to Victor's; a gimlet with "two dashes of bitters." He has two. Ohls warns him at home. "I wanted to clear an innocent man."

Ch. 47. Calls from Lonnie and Mrs. Loring, who asks for a drink—in Paris. She warns Marlowe. Menendez.

Ch. 48. Beating. Ohls: "Did the nasty man hurt your facey-wacey?" "In a way cops are all the same. . . . If a guy . . . gets drunk, stop liquor . . . Let's have a drink." Marlowe asks Linda Loring to have a drink. Call to Starr.

Ch. 49. Visit from Linda. Two bottles of Cordon Rouge champagne: "A really auspicious occasion would call for a dozen." "The sting of it brought tears to my eyes." Making love to Linda, Marlowe mentions "that first time I met you in the bar at Victor's. . . . That night belonged to something else." "But liquor is an aphrodisiac up to a point."

Ch. 50. Discussion of marriage. Tears and champagne. "To say goodbye is to die a little."

Ch. 51. Interview with Endicott. Señor Cisco Maioranos turns up with a reference from Starr.

Ch. 52. Maioranos is revealed as Marston/Lennox. "I suppose it's a bit early for a gimlet."

Ch. 53. Lennox takes back the "portrait of Madison." The novel ends bitterly. Lennox says, "Let's go have a drink somewhere where it's cool and quiet. It wouldn't be much risk going to Victor's for that gimlet." "Well, how about that gimlet?"

The gimlets at the beginning, middle and end of *The Long Goodbye* are its symbol and seal. When Terry takes Marlowe to Victor's for the first time, though, the gimlets are not perfected as they will be by the time Marlowe runs into Linda Loring in the same bar:

"They don't know how to make them here. . . . What they call a gimlet is just some lime or lemon juice and gin with a dash of sugar and bitters. A real gimlet is half gin and half Rose's Lime Juice and nothing else. It beats martinis hollow."

Terry's words are more than a recipe; they are deeply felt exactitudes. The emotion he gets into the little speech makes it an aria or soliloquy. He later has another *cri de coeur,* a less specific one about the beauty of drinking, the poetry of alcohol:

> "I like bars just after they open for the evening. When the air inside is still cool and clean and everything is shiny and the barkeep is giving himself that last look in the mirror to see if his tie is straight and his hair is smooth. I like the neat bottles on the bar and the lovely shining glasses and the anticipation. I like to watch the man mix the first one of the evening and put it down on a crisp mat and put the little folded napkin beside it. I like to taste it slowly. The first quiet drink of the evening in a quiet bar—that's wonderful."

I agreed with him.

We also have to agree with Terry: his description rides on its own energy, sweeping our reason before it. But at least part of Terry's love for the ambience of a saloon is Chandler's, and Terry's gimlet lore Chandler picked up on the *Mauretania.* I think it's telling that Terry Lennox's most memorable pronouncements are lyricisms devoted to alcohol, *bel canto* rhetorical swoops that are as moving as they are sincere.

What is a depressant is perceived by the drinker as a stimulant. The special identifying, refined and superior qualities of the gimlet are the property of the gnostic initiated. These qualities exercise connoisseurship. This is the specific image of Marlowe's love for Lennox: the gimlet. That property is "English," a commodity available to any citizen with acceptable clothing and a couple of dollars. Yet the manners—and the charm for Marlowe and Chandler—must go with it, or the magic and the music of love's intoxication are missing. When at the end Marlowe returns for a final gimlet, believing that Lennox is dead, and knowing that Wade is, he is asked by the bartender at Victor's, "You like a dash of bitters in it, don't you?" Marlowe doesn't. He likes the recipe as Terry Lennox gave it. But he says, "Not usually. Just for tonight two dashes of bitters." Two dashes of bitters for the bitter deaths of his two dead Doppel-gängers, his perished shadow-selves. But the next subject mentioned is Marlowe's friend, "the one with the green ice": Linda Loring. Having met through alcohol (gimlets) and loved through more (champagne), Marlowe and Linda will survive as a relationship—though not one that Chandler lived to represent fully.

The history of Rose's Lime Juice, as related in documents sent to me by Mr. John Maher, a vice-president of Cadbury Schweppes, with a letter of April 14, 1983, is perhaps what one would expect. The second Lauchlan Rose (1829-1885), a Scottish descendent of a shipbuilding family from Leith, Edinburgh, founded L. Rose & Co. as "Lemon and Lime Juice Merchants" in 1865. Finding a means of preventing fermentation in the bottle by the use of sulphur dioxide, he was granted in 1867 a patent which made possible the first fruit juice preserved with-

out alcohol. In that same year, the Merchant Shipping Act was passed, dictating that all ocean-going vessels carry sufficient lime juice for a daily issue to ships' companies. Earning the name "Limey" for all Englishmen, the British sailor put scurvy behind him; and the original exporters, outfitting ships, had literally been *Chandlers.*

The business expanded. Headquarters was moved from Scotland to London in 1875. The company purchased the Bath Estate in Dominica, West Indies in 1895. When the company entered the U.S. in 1901, South Africa was its best market. A lime industry was established on the African Gold Coast (now Ghana) in 1924. Suffering in the Blitz, operations were removed from London to St. Alban's in 1940. In 1957, L. Rose & Co. merged with Schweppes and today sells more lime juice than any other company in the world. This history—combining England and Scotland with naval associations—shows Rose's to be an elixir of Empire and Chandler's use of it connected with the themes of adventure, exploration, colonialism, and imperialism as viewed by Martin Green in his *Dreams of Adventure, Deeds of Empire* (Basic Books, 1979), wherein the connections of "adventure tales" and "boy's books" with political and economic developments are firmly drawn.

So a gimlet is a commodity with British associations and provenance and the alcoholic effect, however illusionary, of poetry. Is friendship, affinity, love, magic, or loyalty a commodity which can be condensed and bottled? Symbolically, yes. The fact that a gimlet is a commodity is perhaps most important in *The Long Goodbye;* this fact offers a key to a code of values. These values are perhaps confused, but their entanglements are human; these values are the ones which Chandler worked into the most personal and deliberate of his works.

The bartender at Victor's declares, when Marlowe shows up to memorialize his friend, that he has heard that friend talking; he has obtained a bottle of Rose's Lime Juice. Marlowe orders a double and proceeds to meet Linda Loring.

> "So few people drink them around here," she said. . . . "Gimlets I mean."
>
> "A fellow taught me to like them," I said.
>
> "He must be English."
>
> "Why?"
>
> "The lime juice. It's as English as boiled fish with that awful anchovy sauce that looks as if the cook had bled into it. That's how they got to be called limeys. The English—not the fish."
>
> "I thought it was more a tropical drink, hot weather stuff. Malaya or some place like that."
>
> "You may be right."
>
> The bartender set the drink in front of me. With

the lime juice it has a sort of pale greenish yellowish misty look. I tasted it. It was both sweet and sharp at the same time. The woman in black watched me. Then she lifted her own glass towards me. We both drank. Then I knew hers was the same drink.

The transference of allegiance from Terry to Linda is through the sign of the gimlet, whose disinihibiting alcoholic dispensation is both an identification and an entrée. Later in the novel, Marlowe and Linda spend the night together. At the end of *Playback* (1958), Linda calls from Paris and proposes. When Chandler died, he was attempting to write the story of Marlowe's marriage to the wealthy Linda (*The Poodle Springs Story*).

But it is the first conversation with Linda Loring that gives us our clue to the meaning of the gimlets in the novel. Whether associated with the Home Country of the Empire, it is specifically *English,* a cousin of the pink gin instead of the American martini. The "sweet and sharp" Englishness of the gimlet represents Chandler's powerfully ambivalent feelings about his return to England in 1952 as well as his ambivalence, his equivocation about his own identity as an American of English education. The potency of the gimlet—not to put too fine a point upon it, it is, like a martini, a glassful of cold gin—dissolves these contradictions, the self-aware inhibitions of self, in a unity of feeling and effect. The drinker, not drinking, writes a novel about drinking. The drinkers in the novel discuss drinking, sometimes not drinking, but usually drinking. The narrator/drinker, having lost his drinking friend, goes off to rescue a drinker, who later dies drunk.

If the gimlet is a commodity of magical properties and British associations, it is not alone. Lennox himself, born in Canada and a veteran of the British Army, is a commodity with redeeming good manners. His wife buys him once, disposes of him, and then buys him again. Otherwise, we must note that Marlowe first meets Terry "drunk in a Rolls-Royce Silver Wraith" in the first sentence of the novel. When Terry first takes Marlowe to Victor's for a gimlet, he does so in "a rust-colored Jupiter-Jowett with a flimsy canvas rain top. . . . It had pale leather upholstery and what looked like silver fittings." Another English commodity is Terry's suitcase, which he leaves as a marker in Chapter 2. "The suit case was the damndest thing you ever saw and when new had been a pale cream color. The fittings were gold. It was English made and if you could buy it here at all, it would cost more like eight hundred than two." Eileen Wade's second interview with Marlowe (Chapter 14) ends with her leaving in "a slim gray Jaguar." This automobile is mentioned again in Chapter 42. When Marlowe motors to Idle Valley, (in the first sentence of Chapter 23), he sees another "low-swung Jaguar." Even the sleazy Mendy Menendez claims to own, besides two Cadillacs and a Chrysler station wagon, a Bentley and an MG (Chapter 11). Mrs. Loring drives a humdrum Cadillac, but Roger Wade manages to be killed by an imported British item: a double-action Webley hammerless. George Peters mentions an Upman Thirty

cigar; Marlowe, in a tense moment, talks about the virtues of Huggins-Young coffee—but these brand names aren't English.

Imported British luxury items—or other such items—are distinctive in some way, and expensive. In one sense, it is their expense that makes them distinctive. In another sense, for Chandler such items are totems of his own nostalgia and fantasy, emblems of what is fine and refined. Marlowe, the "shopsoiled Galahad," "Tarzan on a big red scooter," is a *qualified* narrator because he *understands* about Jaguars and gimlets and Webleys. But even more, this understanding is a necessary qualification for Marlowe to be able to perform the two absolutely necessary functions of *The Long Goodbye*—to appreciate Terry Lennox and, in the end, to reject him. Lennox betrayed the code and used Marlowe: he is no longer a gentleman, not even a drunken and irresponsible one. Having broken faith, he is nothing. There will be no more gimlets for Marlowe in *Playback* or *The Poodle Springs Story*.

The Long Goodbye is Chandler's most revealing because it is his most personal work. Chandler's trouble with plots he tried to finesse by replicating types in a shadowy circle leading nowhere. His highly idiosyncratic vision, his own synthesis of conflicting values, is in this text reflected and refracted into a spectrum of tones that register the stresses of his imagination. The unity of style, like the coherence of personality, begins to fray. No wonder Chandler, old and tired, depressed and lonely, could not pull his act together again. He could not balance the forces within. It was the composition of *The Long Goodbye* itself, as well as his wife's death, that marked him.

Unlike Gatsby, Lennox does not turn out "all the right in the end." Although Marlowe thought at one time that Lennox was "worth the whole damn bunch put together," Marlowe ruefully admits that he was wrong. In effect, Chandler killed off one weak version of himself, in the form of Wade, and then dismissed the other, in the form of Lennox. Then Marlowe and Chandler had to grow or die. Chandler tried to push his imagination further on in the years remaining to him. His attempts were weak; they were the best he could do. Chandler had already said goodbye at length to the most emotive and fictionally strategic parts of himself in *The Long Goodbye*.

Anya Taylor

SOURCE: "Ironweed, Alcohol, and Celtic Heroism," in *Critique,* 33, 2, Winter, 1992, pp. 107-20.

[*In the following essay, Taylor locates the importance of alcohol as part of the mythic structure of William Kennedy's novel* Ironweed.]

The hero of William Kennedy's *Ironweed,* Francis Phelan, differs from many other drunks in modern

American fiction—from Don Birnum in *The Lost Weekend,* from Jake, Brett, Mike, and Bill in *The Sun Also Rises,* from Gordon Sterrett and Charlie Wales in Fitzgerald's "May Day" and "Babylon Revisited," and from Julian English in *Appointment in Samarra*—because he is imbued with multicultural myths and stories that glorify his rapture and excess. Layers of legend, folktale, literary allusion, and patterns of the heroic journey reinforce the positive image of his altered consciousness and place him in the ancient tradition of the shaman, magician, voyager to the land of the dead, and culture hero. These carefully constructed layers prevent him from seeming pathological; they reveal him as adept at techniques of ecstasy known since earliest man.

Francis Phelan's shamanism shows in his soul-flights, his crossing into the land of the dead, and his superhuman strength. Shamanism, the subject of study by Mircea Eliade, by Joseph Campbell, and recently by Gloria Flaherty, has distinctive elements that appear in Siberia, in Tibet, in Africa, in North America, and even in early nineteenth-century Germany. The shaman, whether neolithic or literary, desires to transcend the limits of time-bound, space-bound mortality, to imitate the arrow or the bird, to enter the spirit world through a soul-flight. Deprived of food, sleep, shelter, and companionship, sometimes intoxicated by drugs or drink, the shaman is capable of surviving and ignoring hardship. He is lifted by his visions into the surrounding invisible world of the dead, and he speaks their language. The shaman masters the natural living world and the disembodied spirit world by submission to physical suffering and then by power over it. The shaman is athlete, wise man, prophet, poet, and healer, the most intelligent and charismatic man or woman of his group, contemptuous of the elements and filled with extraordinary power.

Shamanic feats are documented in cave drawings as well as in more recent trials of endurance. In *The Way of the Animal Powers,* Joseph Campbell argues that drawings in the Cave of Lascaux represent the temporary death of the shaman's body as his spirit shoots into the spirit world. During the absence of its spirit, the shaman's abandoned body must be protected by fellow tribesmen so that the soul will have a living form to reenter. Many oriental feats of endurance of cold and pain are thought to be related to such techniques of ecstasy, though the exact relation of Zen and other oriental techniques of meditative power to shamanism has not been determined. Mountain climbers sometimes experience isolated moments of shamanic power, which they often claim is accessible in high places. Eliade has suggested [in *Shamanism. Archaic Techniques of Ecstasy,* 1951] that several of the myths of Apollo, Orpheus, and Odin contain vestiges of shamanic experience. In Celtic myth echoes of shamanistic endurance and vision can be heard in the Cuchulain stories or in the stories of Taliesin, the ancient bard who has affinity with the Alaskan angekok.

The shaman, crossing over between the dead and the living, speaking the languages of spirits and of animals, is paralleled in western European culture by the magus, whose aims are similar but whose methods are more recondite. Both figures aim to transcend their mortal limitations, to communicate with spirits of the dead and spirits of universal forces, and to alter quotidian states of consciousness, often to shift their shapes and take on animal forms. But where the shaman experiences physical deprivation in order to achieve freedom from the body, the magus immerses himself in knowledge. Although both sing and chant spells, the magus's spells or charms are more learned and mathematical, drawing on Cabalistic traditions and on medieval and Renaissance systems of numerology and correspondence.

The magus, because of his bookish nature, is more prominent in literature than the shaman. Magus lore is central to Shakespeare's *Tempest,* to Marlowe's, Goethe's, and Mann's expansions of the Faust legend, to Shelley's *Alastor* and *Prometheus Unbound,* and to Malcolm Lowry's *Under the Volcano.* The more physical shaman appears rarely, though elements of shamanic powers to transcend time, to take on shapes, to enter the realm of the dead, or to control other people and animals can be glimpsed in the ecstatic heroes of nineteenth-century Romanticism. By and large, however, Romantic and late-Romantic ecstacies arise from the learned tradition of the Renaissance magus rather than from that of the tribal shaman.

Twentieth-century anthropology has begun to reverse this imbalance, inspiring an emulation of tribal religious and mythical figures and a reawakening sense of kinship with fundamental patterns of tribal belief in a world where all cultures are recognized as creations of human imagination. Jesse L. Weston and Sir J. G. Frazer launched the first wave of anthropologically based literature and art in the period 1910-1930; Eliade and Campbell in recent years have launched another, in which the shaman appears as a cultural hero. Studies have argued that the shamanism described by Eliade and Campbell is a major theme in Margaret Drabble's *Surfacing* and in Ted Hughes's *Crow* poems, not to speak of numerous films that imagine the revival of neolithic cultural patterns after the destruction of the known world. Drawing from Nigerian folktales, Amos Tutuola's novel, *The Palm-Wine Drinkard,* is steeped in the lore of the alcoholically transformed shaman or trickster. Such films as *Quest for Fire, Greystoke,* and *Star Wars* reveal close knowledge of early tribal hero patterns.

Ironweed can best be understood in this context of anthropological and mythological study. In the novel, the last of Kennedy's Albany trilogy (after *Legs* and *Billy Phelan's Greatest Game*), some of the primordial shaman's powers enter a shambling drunk who relives his life in one intense day and forgives himself for it. Beneath the surface of this seemingly naturalistic novel lie many distinctive elements of the shaman's mind-altering experience, which increase the reverberations of the novel: communication with the dead, ghosts, the glorification of violence and power, the keen expansion of consciousness, the deprivation of the body. These shamanic elements can be observed beneath the shabby surface of the hero's presentation.

Francis Phelan is a man drenched in death. A famous third baseman, he participated in an Albany railroad strike of 1901, killed a scab driver with a smooth stone the weight of a baseball, and fled to escape the murder charge. He left town for good when he accidentally dropped his infant son Gerald, wrongly believing that his wife could never forgive him. He roamed America by box car for twenty-two years, abandoning his family and occasionally killing to survive. His guilt for his son's death makes him "a dead man all his life." As his wife tells their surviving children in *Billy Phelan's Greatest Game,* the preceding novel of the trilogy, "when a good man dies it's reason to weep, and he died that day and he wept and he went away and buried himself and he's dead now, dead and can't be resurrected." Phelan is one of the dead ones who returns, in *Ironweed,* like a ghost, a revenu, a messenger from the world of the dead, as Eliade explains the shamanic initiation. Despite his wife's fear, however, he can be resurrected; and in the novel he is wondrously purged and revived.

Ironweed opens in a cemetery. The smells of sweet putrescence from new graves and from the rotting bodies of Phelan himself and his crony Rudy shoveling fresh earth mingle in a mortal stink. This cemetery houses generation after generation of Albany's Irish dead, and Francis wanders into the area of the Phelans, where, miraculously, he can hear his dead mother, father, and son thinking. He hears his mother, a life-denying Irish Catholic, weaving and then eating crosses of dandelion roots with "an insatiable revulsion" (2) [all pages citations are from the Penguin edition, 1984]; he hears her disapprove of his approach and turn in disgust. He smells his father's pipe, senses his curiosity about his son and his amused hostility to his censorious wife; he is addressed by two young Phelan brothers "both skewered by the same whisky bottle in 1884" who read "in Francis's face the familiar scars of alcoholic desolation" (3). Most intensely he feels, without knowing how, the location of his son's grave and, for the first time, dares to approach it, as his own father watches from the underground, and "signalled to his neighbors that an act of regeneration seemed to be in process, and the eyes of the dead, witnesses all to their own historical omissions, their own unbridgeable chasms in life gone, silently rooted for Francis as he walked up the slope toward the box elder" (16-17).

This encounter with his dead son is rich in religious, mythic, and literary allusions. For Gerald, dead at thirteen days, has grown a full head of curls in his grave and learned a radiant wisdom. "Gerald possessed the gift of tongues in death. His ability to communicate and to understand was at a genius level among the dead" (17). Their speech is direct and intimate through the cover of sod. Like a guru, Gerald directs his father's penance and revival and forecasts the tests and trials that will release the hero from the spell that has enthralled him:

Gerald, through an act of silent will, imposed on his father the pressing obligation to perform his final acts of expiation for abandoning his family. You will not know, the child silently said, what these acts are until you have performed them all. And after you have performed them you will not understand that they were expiatory any more than you have understood all the other expiation that has kept you in such prolonged humiliation. Then, when these final acts are complete, you will stop trying to die because of me. (19)

Chapter one ends with this instruction from the grave, the child as father to the man; the subsequent seven chapters accompany Francis on his return to the living world.

On the single day of this novel Francis, like his predecessor on single Irish days, Leopold Bloom of *Ulysses,* inhabits a remarkably multiple consciousness. He not only speaks with the dead in their grave, but also experiences visitations of accusing spirits as he goes through the streets of his town. The present Albany of the novel is doubled or tripled by an overlay of time schemes; and Francis often carries on several conversations at once, to the wonder of living men and women who cannot see or hear his dead interlocutors. The dead sit near him on the bus inquiring about his motives for killing them; they crowd into an invisible stadium in his wife Annie's backyard, scrutinizing his reunion. Harold Allen, the strike breaker killed by Francis's stone, and the horse thief Aldo Compione, whom Francis tried to rescue by gripping his hand out of a moving box car, appear to him in varied ghostly garb, prompting him to recall the exact details of his past. Rowdy Dick Doolen watches him wash his "encrusted orifices" (71) and recalls a night in Chicago under a bridge in 1930 (72) when he tried to axe off Phelan's legs but lost his own life instead.

Significantly for the shamanic and tribal elements of the novel, this day of communicating with the dead is Halloween, "the unruly night when grace is always in short supply, and the old and new dead walk abroad in this land" (29). This day corresponds closely to the day of another alcoholically magical book, *Under the Volcano.* Halloween, the day before All Hallows' Day, or All Saints' Day, and two days before All Souls' Day in the Roman Catholic Church, celebrates the dead and their continued presence among the living. In *Ironweed* we are reminded of the day by children in goblin costumes who scare Francis and the other bums or rob them (60). Nor is this merely the ordinary domesticated Halloween of American customs; the dead return in a more serious way than as disguised trick-or-treaters. *Ironweed*'s Halloween has mythic Celtic overlays of *Samhain,* the celebration, later syncretized with the Christian festival, when the *Side* return from under their mounds to burn cities and castles. The Celtic bonfires that customarily imitated and magically forestalled these attacks are reproduced in *Ironweed* in the numerous references to fires and, cataclysmically, in the finale, when the police torch the "jungle," where bums, drifters, and homeless families huddle in the cardboard shelters of the Depression.

Samhain marks one of the four annual festivals of Celtic ritual, the harvest, which is viewed both as a celebration of the dead and of new beginnings. Sacrificial victims, animal or human, are offered; and "masquerading in the animal's skins, thus assimilating the wearer to the Divine animal, is also found." In the novel, Celtic and Christian traditions of All Hallows are deftly merged, in that Francis Phelan is absolved of his guilt by the dead son he killed, is taught the penance that may finally free him, and is himself reborn when he communicates with the dead.

As the boundaries between the dead and the living are permeable on Halloween, the dead returning and the living imitating them in the disguises of ghosts or skeletons, so Francis Phelan's life is also figuratively underground, the dead more living to him than the living around him. He is the leader of a pack of alcohol-sodden bums, the living dead of the grim streets and vacant lots of the American subculture: "Bodies in alleys, bodies in gutters, bodies anywhere were part of his eternal landscape: a physical litany of the dead" (29). A drunk named Sandra is left by the self-righteous church shelter to freeze and be gnawed by dogs; Rudy, a drunken simpleton, helpless and passive to his accumulating illnesses, clings to Francis for leadership; Helen, an educated singer betrayed by her family, loves Francis and suffers his alcoholism in maudlin but charitable sorrow, which drags her further into destitution; Peewee, "an emotional cripple," Oscar, "another cripple, his ancient, weary eyes revealing to Francis the scars of a blood brother, a man for whom life had been a promise unkept in spite of great success, a promise now and forever unkeepable." (50), Jack and Clara stewing in cloacal sickness (78)—all drop out of the bottom of society, surviving in a primitive starving gang where "fornication [is] standard survival currency" (89).

This group gathers around Francis Phelan, whose power unites them. Rowdy Dick's spirits ask, "Why should any man be so gifted not only with so much pleasurable history but also with a gift of gab that could mesmerize a quintet of bums around a fire under a bridge?" (73-4). Despite his filth, Francis is heroic, articulate, and violent. His is not a world where virtue is rewarded but one where power is revered. Francis as athlete, killer, and drinker stands above the others. He kills by hand like an animal; he hefts Rowdy Dick by the legs and bashes his head on the cement; he throws Big Red around the flophouse; he defends the poor people in the jungle by beating raiding police with boards; he carries the dying Rudy to the hospital on his shoulders. He is possessed of superhuman energy, as well as of superhuman recall and superhuman communication. He is never a victim, he believes, always a warrior (216). Unlike Rudy, he is not beaten, or defenseless, but instead is in free flight.

What is the role of alcohol in creating or releasing these superhuman powers? As a technique for altering consciousness, alcohol is considered easy compared to self-generated meditations. Shamans who resort to it are deca-

dent, having failed at the more difficult, inner techniques. Eliade writes that "narcotics are only a vulgar substitute for 'pure' trance. . . . [T]he use of intoxicants (alcohol, tobacco, etc.) is a recent innovation and points to a decadence in shamanic technique. Narcotic intoxication is called on to provide an imitation of a state that the shaman is no longer capable of attaining otherwise" (401). In Phelan's case penetration into a many-layered time scheme is aided by alcohol, but not exclusively, for his whole life defies ordinary activities and ways of thinking, and his hunger and cold keep him perpetually on the edge. He drinks an enormous amount, in a culture founded on drink, in a subculture of drunks, but, oddly enough, does not attain his visions as a drunk.

The trilogy is drink saturated from the start. *Legs* documents the vicious bootlegging rackets in Sullivan and Green countries south and west of Albany. In *Billy Phelan's Greatest Game*, too, drink is the center of gang life. Though the focus is on Francis's grown son Billy, Francis himself shuffles in, coughing and toothless, to earn money by registering to vote twenty-one times. Even in a drinking culture, Francis's drinking is worthy of note. The reporter Martin Daugherty sees "the bloom of drink in every pore, the flesh ready to bleed through the sheerest of skin." Daugherty and Billy see him in the courthouse: "The tramp dragged his feet, slouched, shuffled on fallen arches, or maybe on stumps with toes frozen or gone." Annie blames wine," and Helen reproaches him, "God, Francis, you were all right till you started on the wine. Wine, wine, wine" (*Ironweed* 84).

Similar descriptions of Francis Phelan's degradation blame his failure on wine, but elsewhere drink is not considered the cause, and sometimes it is even an assertion of freedom. In *Ironweed* he boasts that he "did not need Daddy Big's advice. He did not get sick from alcohol the way Daddy Big had. Francis knew how to drink. He drank all the time and he did not vomit. He drank anything that contained alcohol, anything, and he could always walk, and he could talk as well as any man alive about what was on his mind. Alcohol did put Francis to sleep, finally, but on his own terms. When he'd had enough and everybody else was passed out, he'd just put his head down and curl up like an old dog, then put his hands between his legs to protect what was left of the jewels, and he'd cork off. After a little sleep he'd wake up and go out for more drink" (5-6). Such self-command may be an alcoholic's delusion, but his feats in the jungle suggest that this boast is an accurate assessment, that he is not drinking himself to death like his friend Rudy and that it is not alcohol that has made him a bum. Watching a fellow bum sing, he wonders, "What was it, Oscar, that did you in? Would you like to tell us all about it? Do you know? It wasn't Gerald who did *me*. It wasn't drink and it wasn't baseball and it wasn't *really* mama. What was it that went bust, Oscar, and how come nobody every found out how to fix it for us?" (50). This question, crucial to inquiries about the causes of alcoholism specifically and failure generally, is one of the few moments when Francis views his drinking negatively and indicates that his life might have been better without it.

At the time of the action of *Ironweed,* however, Francis Phelan is not drinking. Because he ran out of money and needed to be sober to register, the graveyard meeting with Gerald signals a day of altered consciousness—altered from alteration—a new cleansed state of mind vibrant with memories of an era, and with possibility of a return. The masterpiece of telescoped memory, visioning his conception of life and death (98), is made possible by this intense state. But the fact that he is not drinking when he is seeing so clearly should not suggest that the novel urges sobriety, for at the end of the novel Francis buys quantities of muscatel and Green River Whiskey (192), hosts a party at the flop house, drinks Rabelaisian amounts, and then joins the "primal scene" in the jungle for the finale in fire and violence.

The question "What was it made us go bust?" is not, after all, a real question because by his own standards Francis Phelan is not bust. He is free. His life is fated to be in flight. Though his views of himself shift, he exalts in his "compulsion to flight," for running was "a condition that was as pleasurable to his being as it was natural: the running of bases after the crack of the bat, the running from accusation, the running from the calumny of men and women, the running from family, from bondage, from destitution of spirit through ritualistic straightenings, the running, finally, in a quest for pure flight as a fulfilling mannerism of the spirit" (75). Like the pure flight from destitution of spirit of his Irish forerunner Stephen Daedalus, escaping the nets of family, church, and nation, Phelan takes the bird as his totem animal and Daedalus as his winged model; he feels himself "in the throes of flight, not outward this time, but upward. He felt feathers growing from his back, knew soon he would soar to regions unimaginable . . ." (163-4). Despite his frequent feelings of worthlessness, he believes himself free (190) and intends to remain that way, to "beat the bastards, survive the mob and that fateful chaos" (207).

Phelan's violence and refusal to submit, his wavering belief in himself as a warrior (216), suggest that Kennedy seeks to place his hero in a different, perhaps pre-Christian, culture, before the Church broke men with guilt and the requirements of goodness. Even though Christian themes of atonement suffuse the trilogy, the novels give as a whole a picture of a Celtic, male, tribal group, whose lives, violent and vengeful, are governed by a code of shame, and whose laws are self-generated. The "Irish-American chieftan" prizes the violence of Celtic story; Phelan follows Cuchulain in his impulsive furies. Displaced from home ground, these Celts reenact the heroism of the Mohawks, the native Americans who ruled the land before them. Pride in the magical power of the dominant male pervades the trilogy. Women appear as goddesses, often in triplicate, as in the threesome of Katrina/Annie/mother in *Ironweed.* Katrina, in addition, is associated with a massive fertile tree, symbol of the energies that run through the globe's center. The bad

women in the novel deny their vitality like Francis's mother; the good ones are forgiving and fiery like Francis's abandoned but waiting wife Annie, or like his girlfriend Helen, who dies singing the "Ode to Joy" and believing that loving Francis was the greatest thing she had done in her life (138). Women are the mediums by which and through which fathers and sons are reunited, as are Martin and Edward Daugherty through Melissa in *Billy Phelan's Greatest Game* or Billy and Francis through Helen, though less carnally. Women are attachments to the core of men; the men ignore as best they can the debilitating values of the Christian overlay—a religion of "self-neutered nuns and self-gelded priest" (*Ironweed* 99)—that would sap their strengths if they would let it. The tribe values the man of power, violence, energy, and memory, especially one who has gone to the land of the dead and returned; it treasures the orally transmitted legends that accrete around him. Such a figure was Legs Diamond, who eschews Christian values entirely, until superstitions overtake him; such a figure also is Francis Phelan, who struggles to free himself from the bondage of Christian guilt and to be the Celtic warrior, the violent Cuchulain, or wise Druid he was fated to be.

In addition to making his hero a tribal figure, a sort of shaman who can speak to the dead and return from the dead, who takes spirit-flights, chooses the bird as his totemic animal, and is endowed with superhuman power, Kennedy also dignifies his drunken bum by allusions to other great literary heroes, whose parallel experiences guide the reader to interpret Francis's experiences in a heroic light. The twenty-two years of Francis's wanderings, for instance, suggest Odysseus's twenty-years' absence. Like Odysseus, Phelan begins his wanderings with violence (here between the workers and the scabs) and is waylaid for nine years by a Circe, here Helen, a fellow bum. Phelan's return home is made possible by the aid of his son Billy, a Telemachus figure who has been left to grow up on his own and survive amid the hostile brawls of Albany's seedy underworld but who nevertheless forgives his father for his abandonment. Just at a time when Billy is shunned by the mob for not betraying a friend (like Telemachus among the hostile suitors), he bails out his father with the last money he has. Like Odysseus, too, Francis returns to a patient wife, loyal to him for twenty-two years, who has held the household together on her own and, despite her store-bought teeth, still stirs his memories of their first kiss on the woodpile (with the woodpile perhaps echoing the massive trunk that forms the platform of Odysseus's and Penelope's bed). The spirit of forgiveness—Annie has never told her children that Francis caused the death of their baby—her silence is one of the wonders that Billy relates that brings Francis back, disguised as a rag man, bearing a propitiatory turkey, just as Odysseus also returned, filthy, disguised as a beggar, and lurked around the doors of his own home to assess the dangers within.

In addition to these and other parallels with the *Odyssey, Ironweed* also makes many allusions to Dante's

Commedia, particularly in conjunction with the two earlier novels in the trilogy. Overt references to Dante include the epigraph to *Ironweed* from the first lines of *Purgatorio*:

> To course o'er better waters now hoists sail the little bark of my wit, leaving behind her a sea so cruel.

Dante's next lines explain his plan for the *Purgatio,* which also becomes the plan for *Ironweed,* submerged in the truncated allusion:

> and what I sing will be that second kingdom, in which the human soul is cleansed of sin, becoming worthy of ascent to heaven.

The epigraph points to the final homing in of Francis Phelan to the high secret attic room in his wife's house where his mementos are cherished and to the release from guilt that she accomplishes for him. A Beatrice to his suffering, truculent, and banished Dante, Annie welcomes the sinner back, absolving him also of guilt for leaving her and the children. She has seen the breaking up of a good man from afar and watches him with compassion.

Though not all trilogies have Dantean elements, many references to hell and to demons suggest that, in rough and inexact correspondence, *Legs* may be the *Inferno, Billy Phelan's Greatest Game,* an *Inferno* with approaches to *Purgatorio* in its themes of parenthood and reconciliation, and *Ironweed* the *Purgatorio* where the purified spirit is toiling upward, nearing completion. *Legs* is a devilish book, and Legs Diamond, the hero admired by Marcus Gorman, Albany lawyer and narrator of the novel, a demonic and daemonic figure. The novel, crammed with facts, depicts in sickening detail Legs' cruelty in a world where the only option is to kill or be killed. Legs kills whatever he wants to. He plays with human beings as he squeezes a canary in his fist and tosses the tiny corpse into his wife's bodice. He turns women into animals (as two women tell him) and draws into his magnetic range the once upstanding lawyer Gorman, who is so mesmerized by his power that he devotes his legal career to getting Legs acquitted for crimes everyone knew he committed. The viciousness of *Legs*—its random shootings in barns; the allure of its unscrupulous hero, whose body heats and trembles with menacing electricity; Legs' seductive power over men and women—indicate its infernal quality. *Billy Phelan's Greatest Game* begins the work of purging the gangland of Albany, in that Billy, a punk and hustler, Martin Daugherty (the son of the playwright and a literary newspaper man), and other young men defy the will of the Irish mob and stand up for individual values. In this purging, the novel is purgatorial, as also in its awakening of love in Billy and many others, including his father. The theme of the novel is less Billy's own personal purgation than the reunion of fathers and sons in several families, Daughertys, Bermans, and Phelans, miracles that bring renewed life.

Along with these references to traditional literary wanderers through the land of death, Kennedy draws on two twentieth-century novels (themselves steeped in the *Odyssey* and the *Inferno*)—Joyce's *Ulysses* and Malcolm Lowry's *Under the Volcano.* Both of these novels take place on a single day inside the multiple consciousness of an observing and remembering hero, who is awaiting a reunion with his more or less Penelopean wife. The affinities between *Ironweed* and *Under the Volcano* point up a deliberate contrast between Phelan and the defiantly failing anti-hero of that novel, Geoffrey Firmin. *Under the Volcano,* written in 1947, and *Ironweed,* in 1983 take place in a single day on Halloween and All Souls' Day, in 1933 and 1938, respectively. In both novels, the Halloween motif emphasizes the presence of death, either within the heroes' wills or in the world pressing on them from without: in *Under the Volcano,* chocolate skeletons, falling bodies, witches, and a dead Indian merge the carnival customs of a Mexican rendition of All Souls' Eve with Firmin's morbid hallucinations; in *Ironweed,* ghosts and costumed goblins berate Phelan, whose hallucinations also summon the dead. The will to die is accomplished in *Under the Volcano,* as Firmin chooses to drink the mescal that he knows will kill him; by contrast, Phelan in *Ironweed* chooses life, even in a small attic room in hiding. In both novels, the heroes prepare for or are surprised by reunions with loving and patient wives. Both wives had been lost through the faults of the drunken heroes, and both women forgive their men their alcoholic betrayals although Yvonne Firmin is less loyal than Annie, who has never taken another man. While both wives are Penelopes, their husbands differ in their treatment of them. Geoffrey, paralyzed by jealousy and impotence, encourages Yvonne to be with Hugh Firmin and Jacques LaRuelle so that he can continue drinking; Francis, by contrast, once he learns that Annie has kept his secret goes in search of her and rejoins her.

Both men are heroic as talkers, entertainers, and drinkers. Geoffrey, a Faustian magus, verbose with knowledge of ancient wisdom, is the model for many of the men in the novel; they borrow his books, his bag, his sneakers, and his wife in order to resemble him. Francis Phelan is also the central figure of his group, admired by all, a legend for his feats. A partial cause of the reckless glory of both men is their stupendous drinking and the wildness and multilayered consciousness that drinking releases in both—wit, violence, rage, defiance, intuition, and memory.

In keeping with the Halloween settings, both novels are lit by firelight: *Ironweed* by the blaze of the jungle, *Under the Volcano* by the blazing rumbles of the volcano looming in the background. Against an even more distant background of political and social upheaval, both novels echo the memory, detail, single day, and reunions of Joyce's *Ulysses.* Both echo the *Inferno: Under the Volcano* full of references to bosques, woods, and the midlife journey in darkness; *Ironweed* similarly depicting a journey among the dead and a resulting purgatorio.

Despite these many similarities the two novels, about alcoholics on Halloween come to quite different conclusions. Firmin's alcoholism leads to his outrage, his courage to speak against his betrayers, his drunken taunting of the authorities, and his eventual death in the *barranca*, tossed in like a dead dog. Phelan's, on the other hand, after a brief week of sobriety, reasserts itself as a wild frenzy of life and strength. Like Geoffrey Firmin, Phelan defies the police; but unlike Geoffrey, Phelan triumphs over them. Firmin's day of death leads to his death, whereas Phelan's, in his warrior culture, leads to new a life.

The literary allusiveness of *Ironweed* is intensified by metafictions within the novel and across the trilogy. The heroes of the first two novels allude to Francis Phelan and his wanderings, as if he existed as a real person cutting in and out of other people's lives. He is also the hero of the imaginary play *The Car Barns,* written by Edward Daugherty, whose son is a major figure in *Billy Phelan's Greatest Game,* and whose wife Katrina introduced the young Francis Phelan into the mysteries of female nakedness. Francis's role as the hero of this play-within-the-novel (and also outside it, because it is referred to in the other novels as an existing fact) increases his guilt for it presents him as the single radical killer of the scab Harold Allen, as a "Divine Warrior" of the Irish, adding another reason for his long exile. Only toward the end of *Ironweed* does Francis Phelan realize that *The Car Barns* is only one version of the story, not the truth, and that other stones were flying that day (206-7). The story-within-a-story indicates that another person's fiction has distorted the hero's view of himself and made him suffer more than necessary. Phelan comes to realize that he must create his own fictions to refute those of others, which either glorify him or, in the case of the fictions of his mother's family vilify him. "If he was ever to survive, it would be with the help not of any socialistic god but with a clear head and a steady eye for the truth; for the guilt he felt was not worth the dying" (207). The fiction led to his escape, and he must free himself from its delusions and write his own script. Curiously, Billy is also elevated by Martin Daugherty's fiction into a magical hero and subsequently dubbed "Magic."

Kennedy affirms this Irish myth-making and magical naming. Both the Daughertys, father and son, are Celtic bards, singing satires and legends to reform the present and keep the past alive. They enforce the values of the warrior code and spurn those of the well-behaved Christian women. The final sentence of *Billy Phelan's Greatest Game* revives the Celtic twilight in the male enclaves of playfulness, as Billy "made a right turn into the warmth of the stairs to Louie's pool room, a place where even serious men sometimes go to seek the meaning of magical webs, mystical coin, golden birds, and other artifacts of the only cosmos in town" (282). The allusion to William Butler Yeats's gold bird in "Sailing to Byzantium" and to its antitheti-cal "dying generations" might also recall the other appropriate Yeats poem, "All Soul's Night," in which Yeats, like Francis Phelan in *Ironweed,* summons up the dead at this significant time. Also imbued with occult powers, Yeats toasts the returning dead with his wine, which the dead need only breathe, their "element is so fine" (224-26). In this Celtic tradition of *Samhain,* both Yeats the poet and Phelan the fictional character drink to the dead whom they recall from underground and bring once again to life in their stories.

Although the relations between fact and fiction are intricate in the novel, there seems to be a truth at the center. Kennedy glorifies the simple, ordinary, ruined man, by connecting him with mythic undercurrents. The more these myths are the hero's own creation, the more powerful and free he is. Francis Phelan is a momentary avatar of shamanistic power and at the same time the single creator of the myths surrounding him that take shape in his remarkably precise memory. In suggesting that this homeless man with shoes tied by string, sleeping under the cold stars, is a hero, Kennedy also suggests, as Joseph Campbell does, that inside each of us glimmers a heroic nature and that each of us momentarily possesses ancient power. Even a criminal vagrant is swathed in dignifying myths if he invents his life in a heroic mode, defying his temporary circumstance.

If we reversed the process and looked at Odysseus as he sat waiting to re-enter Ithaca or at a shaman in a Siberian village starving himself in preparation for his ecstatic lift-off, we would also find a shabby, filthy creature on the lower verge of humankind, secretly filled with power. Such speculation on the hero as avatar is, I suggest, at the heart of *Ironweed,* whose hero is the unlikely embodiment of shamanistic multiple consciousness and, indirectly, the beneficiary of much twentieth-century anthropological work on shamanistic culture.

POETRY AND DRAMA

Lewis Hyde

SOURCE: "Alcohol and Poetry," in *American Poetry Review*, 4, 4, July/August, pp. 7-12.

[*In the following essay concerned with the relationship between alcohol and the poetic mind, Hyde explicates* The Dream Songs *of John Berryman "in terms of the disease of alcoholism."*]

In looking at the relationship between alcohol and poetry I am working out of two of my own experiences. For more than a year now I have been a counselor with alcoholics in the detoxification ward of a city hospital. I am also a writer and, when I was an undergraduate at the University of Minnesota, I knew John Berryman (briefly, not intimately).

Berryman was alcoholic. It is my belief that his disease is evident in his work, particularly in *The Dream Songs*. His last poems and *Recovery,* his unfinished novel, show that by the time of his suicide in January of 1972 he himself was confronting his illness and had already begun to explore its relationship to the poetry. What I want to do here is to continue that work. I want to try to illuminate what the forces are between poetry and alcohol so we can see them and talk about them.

Alcohol has always played a role in American letters. Those of our writers who have tangled with it include Fitzgerald, Hemingway, Malcolm Lowry, Hart Crane, Jack London and Eugene O'Neill, to name a few. Four of the six Americans who have won the Nobel Prize for literature were alcoholic. About half of our alcoholic writers eventually killed themselves.

This essay begins with a short description of alcoholism and then a longer sketch of the ways in which it is entangled in our culture and spiritual life, the two areas where it bears most heavily on poetry. In the second part of the essay I will turn to Berryman and take a close look at *The Dream Songs*.

I

Most of what we know about alcoholism comes from alcoholics themselves, specifically from Alcoholics Anonymous. It is their experience that an alcoholic is someone who cannot control his drinking once he has started. He cannot pick up just one drink ("one is too many, a thousand's not enough," is the saying). Another way of putting this is to say that *if you are alcoholic, you cannot stop drinking on will power*. In this it is like other diseases of the body. It may be hard to believe—and harder for the active alcoholic!—but I have seen enough strong-willed alcoholics to know that good intentions and will power are as useful for recovering from this disease as they are for curing diabetes.

Because of this it seems clear that alcoholism has a biological component. It is common to call this an 'allergy,' that is: alcoholics' bodies react differently to alcohol. Some people may be born with this 'allergy' (it seems to run in families), others may develop it through heavy drinking. Once present in a person, it hooks into his social, mental and spiritual life and it is in these areas that most alcoholics first get hurt. Most have trouble in their family life or with their jobs or end up doing things they don't want to, long before the alcohol destroys their bodies.

Alcoholism cannot be cured. Once a person becomes alcoholic, he can never again drink in safety. However, there is a way to arrest the disease, and that is the program of Alcoholics Anonymous. AA is the 'medicine' and it works. Of those who join a group, get a sponsor, and become active, more than half never drink again and all enjoy some improvement. Those alcoholics who don't manage to find sobriety end up in jail or in mental institutions or dead from cirrhosis, brain damage, suicide or something else related to alcohol.

It is commonly believed that AA is a religious group, but it is more correctly described as a spiritual program. It has no creed. The only requirement for membership is a desire to stop drinking. It does have a series of "12 steps to recovery" and these include the concept of a "higher power." The first three steps read:

> We admitted that were powerless over alcohol— that our lives had become unmanageable.
>
> Came to believe that a Power greater than ourselves could restore us to sanity.
>
> Made a decision to turn our will and lives over to the care of God *as we understood Him.*

They say you can get sober on the First Step alone, but certainly not with the ease of those who find their way to the others. The move from the First to the Second step is a problem for many, but logically it shouldn't be for every active alcoholic already has a higher power at work in his life: the booze.

In AA it is common to refer to alcoholism as a threefold disease: it is physical, mental and spiritual. This wholistic description was first put together in this country in the 1930s and it led immediately to the first recovered alcoholics and the founding of AA. A key insight—that the disease includes the spirit—came indirectly from Carl Jung. The story is interesting and helps me begin to show how alcoholism is tied up with creative life.

Many alcoholics try psychotherapy of one sort or another to deal with their problems. It notoriously fails. They say that alcoholism is "the siren of the psychiatrists." In 1931 an American alcoholic sought out Jung for treatment. Whatever analytic progress they made did not affect his drinking and Jung told him that his only hope was to become the subject of a spiritual experience, a true conversion.

It was Jung's belief, as he explained in a letter 30 years later, that the "craving for alcohol was the equivalent, on a low level, of the spiritual thirst of our being for wholeness . . . , (for) the union with God." He included the line from the 42nd Psalm: "As the hart panteth after the water brooks, so panteth my soul after thee, O God." And he concluded his letter: "You see, 'alcohol' in Latin is *spiritus,* and one uses the same word for the highest religious experience as well as for the most depraving poison. The helpful formula therefore is: *spiritus contra spiritum.*"

What is a 'spirit' in this broad sense? There are several things to say. First, a spirit is something larger than the self and second, it has the power to change you. It alters your Gestalt, your whole mode of perception and action. Both alcohol and the Holy Ghost can do this. But a spirit does more than give you new eyes: it is the mover. This is the sense of spiritual power when St. Paul says "I have planted, Apollos watered, but God gave the increase." A good spirit does not just change you, it is an agent of growth.

Spiritual thirst is the thirst of the self to feel that it is a part of something larger and, in its positive aspect, it is the thirst to grow, to ripen. The self delights in that as a fish delights in water. Cut off from it, it seeks it again. This is a simple and basic human thirst, comparable to the body's need for salt. It is subtle and cannot be extinguished. Once woken, it is very powerful. An animal who has found salt in the forest will return time and again to the spot. It is the same with a taste of spiritual powers.

The disease of alcoholism includes what they call a "mental obsession" with alcohol and a "physical compulsion" for it. Once we have understood this matter of spiritual thirst, we see that this is like saying that the moon has a "compulsion" to orbit the earth, or a whale has an "obsession" with the ocean. Man is compelled to move with powers greater than himself. The compelling forces may be mysterious, but they are not a problem. The problem is why a person would get hooked up with alcohol—which is a power greater than the ego, but not a benevolent one. I do not know why, though by the end of this essay I will make a few guesses.

All the psychotropic drugs—alcohol, the amphetamines, LSD, mescaline and so forth—could be called spirits in the sense I am using. But I would prefer to call them spirit-helpers, first because they are material spirits and seem to be limited to that level, and second because it now seems clear that they are not actually agents of maturation. They do have power: they can show the novice in a crude way the possibility of a different life. I call it crude because it is big-footed and able to bust through the novice's walls. I say 'show' because a spirit-helper does not give you the new life, it merely points.

The amphetamines, for example, can show you that it is possible for huge amounts of energy to flow through your body and leave you in a state of almost hopeless attentiveness. However, this is not you. It affects you, but you do not own it. Properly used, such a spirit-helper makes a demand: Find the path that leads to the place where you can have this experience without the help. Often the path is long and the things the spirit-helper shows you do not actually become yours for 5 or 10 years. The risk, especially in this civilization and without a guide, is that you will get weary, forgo the 5-year walk, and stay with the material spirit. And when you stay with the material spirit you stay at its level, you do not grow. This is why we speak of their effect as 'getting stoned' or 'intoxicated,' rather than 'inspiration.' 'Inspiration' refers to air spirits such as those which come through meditation, or the Holy Ghost, or the power that rises above a group of

people. Air spirits are less crude and they abide. They have power over matter.

Few of these spirits are good or evil of themselves. Their value varies by their use. Alcohol has many uses and all of them change depending on a person's drinking patterns. It is a relaxant and social spirit; it has always been used as a ceremonial spirit; it is a medicinal, a sedative hypnotic and an anaesthetic.

It is also, along with others of the material spirits, a possessing drug: it is addictive. (Withdrawal from alcohol addiction is worse than that from heroin.) As a spirit possesses a person he more and more becomes the spirit itself. In the phrase of AA's First Step—"powerless over alcohol"—is implied the idea that the alcoholic is no longer running his life, the alcohol is. Booze has become his only experience and it makes all of his decisions for him.

If he senses this at all it is as a numbed recognition that he himself is being wiped out. After several years an alcoholic commonly begins to have apocalyptic fears. He stops going out of the house because he is afraid that buildings will fall on him. He won't drive across a bridge because he fears the car will suddenly leap off of it. This is the self realizing it is being forced out, but so blind with the booze that it can't see the true cause, it can only project its death onto everything in the outer world.

I am saying that as a person becomes alcoholic he turns more and more into the drug and its demands. He is like a fossil leaf that mimics the living but is really stone. For him the drug is no longer a spirit in the sense I have used or, if it is, it's a death spirit, pulling him down into itself. He has an ever-increasing problem knowing what 'he' is doing and what the booze is doing. His self-trust collapses. He doesn't even know if his feelings are his own. This state does not require physical addiction. Long after his last drink, the symptoms of the alcoholic's physical addiction linger and recur—sometimes for years—a phenomenon known as the 'dry-drunk.' The drinker becomes alcohol in a human skin, a parasite dressed up in the body of its host.

These issues—spiritual powers, possession, growth, inspiration—clearly have to do with the life of a creative person. But there is a further thing to say about alcohol that connects it even more closely with poetry. Alcohol is described medically as a sedative hypnotic or an anaesthetic. It progressively relaxes and numbs the different centers of sensation, coordination and control, starting with faculties such as judgment and physical grace and progressing (as with other anaesthetics like ether) down through the voluntary nervous system.

'Anaesthetic' does not just mean a thing that reduces sensation. The word means 'without-aesthetic,' that is, without the ability to sense *creatively*. The aesthetic power, which every human has, is the power which forms meaningful configurations out of all we sense and feel.

More than that, it makes configurations which are themselves lively and creative, things which, like art, begin to exist separately from their creator and give meaning and energy back to all of us. If this power were not free and active a human being would die, just as he would die if he lost the power to digest his food.

An anaesthetic is a poet-killer. It is true that some poets have found alcohol a spirit-helper; for some it has broken up static and useless interpretations of the world and allowed them to "see through" and move again. Theodore Roethke appears to be an example. But this doesn't happen for alcoholics. An alcoholic cannot control his drinking and cannot selectively anaesthetize. A poet who has become wholly possessed by alcohol is no longer a poet, for these powers are mutually exclusive. The opposition of these forces is a hidden war in our civilization. On one level it is a social war, for ours is a civilization enamoured of drugs which deaden the poetry-creature. But for many the fight is personal, it has already entered their bodies and become a corporeal war between the powers of creation and the spirit of alcohol.

To conclude the first part of this essay I want to show some of the ways in which alcohol is involved in our culture and civilization. To look at it from this level I want to turn to some ideas developed by Ivan Illich in his new book about health care, *Medical Nemesis*.

One of Illich's main points is that pain asks a question. Discomfort makes an urgent demand on us to find its cause and resolution. He distinguishes between suffering and feeling pain. The latter is passive but it leads to suffering which is the active process, the art, of moving from dis-ease to ease. It turns out that the idea of a 'pain-killer' is a modern one. This phrase appeared in this country only a century ago. In the Middle Ages it was the belief of doctors that if you killed the pain you killed the patient. To the ancients, pain was only one sign of disharmony. It was nice if it went away during the healing process, but this did not mean that the patient was whole. The idea is that if you get rid of pain before you have answered its questions, you get rid of the self along with it. Wholeness comes only when you have passed *through* pain.

Illich's thesis is that "health care and my ability to remain responsible for my behavior in suffering correlate." Relief of this ability, through the use of drugs to separate pain from the performance of suffering, is a cornerstone of which Illich calls "medical technocracy." He writes:

> Pain had formerly given rise to a cultural program whereby individuals could deal with reality, precisely in those situations in which reality was experienced as inimical to the unfolding of their lives. Pain is now being turned into a political issue which gives rise to a snowballing demand on the part of anaesthesia consumers for artificially induced insensibility, unawareness, and even unconsciousness.

A culture in the sense being used here is, by nature, a healing system. Illich speaks of "the health-granting wholeness of culture," and of "medicinal cultures." The native American tribes are a good example: they called their whole system of knowledge and teaching 'the medicine,' not just the things that the shaman might do in an emergency. As a member of the tribe it was your privilege to walk daily inside of the healing air.

A culture faces and interprets pain, deviance and death. It endows them with meaning; it illuminates how they are a part of the whole and thereby makes them tolerable. We do not become trapped in them because the culture continually leads out of pain and death and back into life. Medical civilization reacts in the opposite way: it tries to attack, remove and kill these things. With this the citizen becomes separated from his own healing and interpretive powers and he and the culture begin to pull apart and wither, like plants pulled from the soil until both become dust.

The widespread use of alcohol and other central nervous system anaesthetics is directly linked to a decline in culture. The wider their use, the harder it becomes to preserve, renew and invigorate the wisdom that a culture should hold. This then doubles back and escalates. Alcoholism spreads when a culture is dying, just as rickets appears when there is no Vitamin D. It is a sign that the culture has lost its health-granting cohesion.

The native American tribes would again be an example. Here were cultures rich in spiritual life and healing power. The Indian, cut off from the sources of his own spiritual strength by the European tribes, and unwilling to adopt the gods of his oppressors, was left with an empty spiritual space, and too often the spirit of alcohol moved in to fill it. The Europeans were all too happy at this and often shipped the liquor into the dying Indian villages.

Nobody knows what causes alcoholism. It is one of those things, like a war, whose etiology is so complex that attempts to describe it do not yet help us heal. One of the insights of AA was to quit wondering why a person drinks and just work with the situation at hand. In doing this they figured out how to keep an alcoholic sober after he has stopped drinking. Two chapters in the AA "Big Book" describe how the program works. They list typical situations in which alcoholics who have found sobriety begin to drink again. By looking at these, we can do a sort of backwards etiology of the disease. Here are three examples:

> "Resentment is the 'number one' offender. It destroys more alcoholics than anything else. . . ."

> The alcoholic is "driven by a hundred forms of fear, self-delusion, self-seeking, and self-pity. . . ."

> "The alcoholic is an extreme example of self-will run riot."

In summary, AA has found that the following may lead a sober alcoholic back to drinking: resentment, self-pity, anger, fear, self-will, self-centeredness, managing, trying to do everything yourself, and keeping secret the things that hurt you. There are two categories in this list. An alcoholic will drink again (1) if he sets himself up as self-sufficient and (2) if he gets stuck in the mechanisms that defend this autonomy. *Individualsim and its defences support the disease of alcoholism.* Just one more example: in this civilization we take personal credit for change and accomplishment. But it is AA's experience that if an alcoholic begins to feel personally responsible for his sobriety, or if he tries to take control of the group, or if he breaks his anonymity, he will probably drink.

Getting sober goes against the grain of our civilization. This grain consists of money and technology. For more than a century these have been our dominant models for security and liveliness. I want to show quickly how these models feed 'individualism' and its false sense of human and higher powers. To begin with we have misperceived the nature of machines. First, we have assumed that they run by themselves, that they can be isolated and self-sustaining. Second, we have thought they were our slaves. But it has turned out that the model of life that includes slavery diminishes humans, regardless of whether those slaves are people or machines. And finally, we have forgotten that mechanical power is only one form of power. It is authentic and important, but limited. In the last 50 years it has become so inflated as to impoverish other forms of power. (These points can also be made about money—we have assumed that money could be left alone to 'work' for us and out of this assumption it has become an autonomous and inflated power.)

But neither money nor machines can create. They shuttle tokens of energy, but they do not transform. A civilization based on them puts people out of touch with their creative powers. There is very little a poet can learn from them. Poems are gifts. The poet works them, but they are not his, either in their source or in their destination. The differences between mechanical & monetary power and creative power are not of themselves a problem, but when the former become inflated and dominant, as they have in this century, they are lethal to poetry.

Hart Crane is an example. He was a poet born into a typically mercantile American family. His father invented the life saver and built up the family candy business. Between the time he left home and the time he killed himself, Crane made endless flesh trips back and forth between his creative energies and his father's designs. There was one horrible hot summer when he ended up in Washington D.C. trying to sell the family sweets. You cannot be a poet without some connection to others—to your group or family or class or nation . . . —but all that was offered to Crane was this thing that kills poets. It is not an exaggeration to say that these forces divided him from his own life energies and contributed to his alcoholism and his death.

The link between alcoholism and technical civilization—and the reason they are both antithetical to poetry—is their shared misunderstandings about power and powerlessness. It is a misunderstanding which rises out of the inflation of mechanical power and results in the impoverishment of personal power, the isolation of creative energy, the blindness to higher powers, the limitation of desire to material objects and a perversion of the will.

In a technological civilization one is deprived of authentic expressions of creative energy because contact with the outer world does not lead to real change (transformation). When this happens it becomes impossible to make judgments on the limits and nature of your personal power. You become stupefied, unable to perceive either higher powers or your own. You have a vague longing to feel creative energy, but no wisdom to guide you. Such a person is a sitting duck for alcoholism.

The disease begins and ends with an empty willfulness. The alcoholic fighting his disease has no authentic contact because nothing changes. The revelation that the alcoholic is powerless over his drinking was one of the founding insights of AA. And the admission of this powerlessness is the First Step in arresting the disease. The paradox is that the admission of powerlessness does not lead to slavery or obliteration, but the opposite. It leads to revaluation of personal power which is human, bounded and authentic.

II

Here is a curious quote from Saul Bellow's introduction to John Berryman's unfinished novel, *Recovery*. It refers to the time when Berryman began *The Dream Songs:*

> John had waited a long time for this poet's happiness. He had suffered agonies of delay. Now came the poems. They were killing him. . . . Inspiration contained a death threat. He would, as he wrote the things he had waited and prayed for, fall apart. Drink was a stabilizer. It somewhat reduced the fatal intensity.

What does this mean, "Inspiration contained a death threat"? Bellow is hot on the trail of a half-truth. When one is in-spired, filled with the breath of some other power, many things die. The conscious ego dies, or at least falls back, when the inspiring powers speak. But is this a *threat*? Certainly it is a risk, like any change, but religions and artists have long held that this inspiration is joyful and enlivening, not threatening.

There seem to be two kinds of death: the 'greatful death' that opens outward with release and joy, and the bitter or stone death that tightens down on the self. An alcoholic death is of the second kind. The self collapses, it does not rise. Bellow is right, there was a relationship between this poet's drinking and his inspiration, but he has the structure of it wrong. For an alcoholic, imbibing itself is fatal to inspiration. The poems weren't killing Berryman.

Drink was not the "stabilizer" that "reduced the fatal intensity." Alcohol was itself the "death threat."

It is my thesis here that this war, between alcohol and Berryman's creative powers, is at the root of the Dream Songs. I will show how their mood, tone, structure, style and content can be explicated in terms of alcoholism. Further, that Berryman himself (at the time he wrote the poems) was blind to this. His tactics, aesthetics and epistemology were all wrong and by the end of the book booze had almost wholly taken over. He lost the war. The bulk of the Dream Songs were written by the spirit of alcohol, not John Berryman.

Before I unfold a particular example I want to say a few words related to the tone of the Dream Songs. As I outlined above, in the course of getting sober an alcoholic must deal daily with his own anger, self-pity, willfulness and so on. If he doesn't face these, the booze will latch onto them and keep him drinking. As the "Big Book" says, they "may be the dubious luxury of normal men, but for alcoholics these things are poison."

Self-pity is one of the dominant tones in the Dream Songs. To understand it we must first look at pity. William Blake wrote that "Pity divides the soul." Apparently a part of the soul goes out to a person we pity. A corollary to this is that one cannot grow or change and feel pity at the same time, for growth comes when the soul is whole and in motion. This is old wisdom, common in ancient tales. For example in Apuleius' story "Amor and Psyche" (lately revived by Erich Neumann) Psyche, when she has to journey into the underworld, is warned by a tower that pity is not lawful down there. "As thou crossest the sluggish river, a dead man that is floating on the surface will pray thee, raising his rotting hands, to take him into the boat. But be thou not moved with pity for him, for it is not lawful." Another example: among the Zuni Indians, a gravedigger is supposed to be immune to pity, for if he pities the newly-dead he will be vulnerable to their cries and they will carry him off.

In pity, when a part of the self goes out to the sufferer, the self is not free to move until the sufferer has been relieved of his hurt. So there are two situations in which pity is dangerous. One is that in which the self is in need of all its faculties to survive, as in Psyche's passage through the underworld. The other is the case in which the sufferer cannot be made whole again, as with the truly dead. It seems that death-energy is so strong that if a person identifies with the dying he will be hopelessly sucked in.

This is why Jesus says "Let the dead bury their dead." When Jesus himself took pity on Mary and her tears over Lazarus, his own soul was torn. (St. John says that he "groaned in the spirit.") The interesting thing is that he could not raise the dead in this condition. Before he could act, he had to first address the Father in order to regain his wholeness. You cannot raise the dead if you have pity on them. It is only done with love and love's

wholeness. Pity is directed to the past and present, love is directed toward the future. So Nietzche says "All great love is above pity: for it wants to create what is loved!" It wants the future and pity is a stony place in the present.

Self-pity has the same structure, only it works entirely inside of a person, he needs no outer object. His own soul is divided, to use Blake's image, and self-pity is the mechanism through which the division and its stasis are enforced and solidified. The self casts off its hurt part, sets it up as an object, and broods over it. Resentments work the same way and to a similar end, the maintenance of the status quo. In alcoholism they call it 'the poor-me's' and its metaphysics is "Poor me, poor me, pour me a drink."

In the end, all of the dividing emotions—self-pity, pride, resentments, and so on—become servants of the disease of alcoholism. Like political palliatives, they siphon off healing energy and allow the sickening agent to stay in power. Their tone and mood are part of the voice of booze.

Let us look at a poem, one of the early, solid Dream Songs. When Robert Lowell reviewed the first book of Songs back in 1964 he chose to print Song 29 in full as "one of the best and most unified." It reads:

> There sat down, once, a thing on Henry's heart
> so heavy, if he had a hundred years
> & more, & weeping, sleepless, in all them time
> Henry could not make good.
> Starts again always in Henry's ears
> the little cough somewhere, an odour, a chime.
>
> And there is another thing he has in mind
> like a grave Sienese face a thousand years
> would fail to blur the still profiled reproach of.
>   Ghastly,
> with open eyes, he attends, blind.
> All the bells say: too late. This is not for tears;
> thinking.
> But never did Henry, as he thought he did,
> end anyone and hacks her body up
> and hide the pieces, where they may be found.
> He knows: he went over everyone, & nobody's
>   missing.
> Often he reckons, in the dawn, them up
> Nobody is ever missing.

Though not apparent at first, this poem is deeply connected to alcohol. The last stanza describes what is known as a 'blackout,' a phenomenon of heavy drinking in which the drinker goes through periods of un-remembered activity. In a blackout one is not *passed* out; he goes to parties, drives home, has conversations and so forth, but afterwards he has no memory of what he has done. The next day he may meet someone on the street who thanks him for the loan and returns money or he may find himself in an airport and call home only to discover he has inexplicably taken a plane halfway across the continent. Berryman gives an example in the novel. The main character is a teacher (so close to Berryman that we needn't maintain the fiction) who reports "my chairman told me one day I had telephoned a girl student at midnight threatening to kill her—no recollection, blacked out." This incident may be the actual basis of the last stanza here. (The misogny of the Dream Songs would take another essay to unravel. Suffice it to say here that sexual anger and alcoholism are connected through similar misconceptions of human power. As it has been men who "get into power," men have traditionally outnumbered women alcoholics. This will change to the degree that women mistake feminism for a route to centralized power.)

This poem has one other personal allusion in it. When he was a 12-year old boy, Berryman's father killed himself. (It is implied in the novel that his father may also have been alcoholic.) His suicide is the subject of several of the Dream Songs, especially numbers 76 and 384. In fact it lurks throughout the book. William Meredith reports that Berryman once said of the Dream Songs that "the first 384 are about the death of his father . . . and number 385 is about the illegitimate pregnancy of his daughter." This remark is as much truth as wit. I have no doubt Berryman believed it, certainly when he wrote the Songs and perhaps even when he was writing the novel. Though it is intentionally vague in this poem, if you had asked him what the "thing" was that sat down on Henry's heart, he would have said his father's suicide.

Let us return to Song 29. I take this poem to be about anxiety and I should say a few words about this to make it clear why it is not just the mood of the poem, but the subject. Anxiety differs from fear in that it has no object. This means there is no *action* which will resolve the feeling. The sufferer who does not realize this will search his world for problems to attend to in hopes of relieving his anxiety, only to find that nothing will fill its empty stomach. For example, anxiety is a major symptom of withdrawal from alcohol addiction, in which case it has a cause—the sudden absence of the addicting drug—but still no object. There is still nothing to do to resolve the feeling. If the alcoholic in withdrawal begins to drink again, his anxiety may be relieved but not resolved, it is merely postponed with an anaesthetic glow.

Anxiety is a symptom not just of withdrawal, but of active alcoholism and it even plagues sober alcoholics long after their last drink. The mood in this poem is typical of alcoholic anxiety: it is intense, mysterious and desperate. This is not grief and this is not suffering. It is important to make this clear because both Berryman and his critics have seen the mood here as grief or suffering. But both of these differ from anxiety in that they are active and directed toward an end. The grief we feel when someone dies moves toward its own boundary. The mourning song usually lasts three days and its biological point, as it were, is that it leads out of itself. Grief that lasts much longer than a year does so because it has been blocked in some way. It is then pathologic, just as a blockage in the blood system is pathologic. In fairy tales the person who weeps and cannot stop finally turns into a snake, for unabated grief is not human.

Suffering, like grief, is an activity, a labor, and it ends. There are healthy ways to suffer—that is, ways which move with grace from pain to ease. This is not what happens either in the Dream Songs or in this poem.

Now let us look more closely at the content of Song 29. It is one of the strongest of the Dream Songs precisely because its vagueness is true to anxiety. Throughout the Songs the character Henry is bothered and doesn't know why. The cause of his pain is always abstract, "a thing" here; elsewhere "a departure," (1) [Parenthetical numbers refer to the numbered Dream Songs] "something black somewhere," (92) and so on. Typically an anxious person does not realize this lack of content but projects his mood onto the outer world. Everyone else knows something is being projected because the proportions are all off, as when a dying man begins to worry about his cat. A strength of this poem is that Berryman does not unload his mood directly. However, behind the vagueness there are ghosts.

The first stanza I sense as a description of the recurrent and inescapable memory of his father's suicide. The anxiety is projected backwards. The second stanza has as its main image the "grave Sienese face." The reference is obscure to me but I associate it with art, religion and death ("grave"). It carries Berryman's sense of the future: his hope is that spiritual life and poetry will be the path out of his misery, but he fears he won't make it. (That this was in fact the form of his activity can be shown from other poems. In both Songs 73 and 99, for example, he approaches temples but is unable to make any contact. Song 66 has spiritual wisdom as its background but at the end, "Henry grew hot, got laid, felt bad" and is reproached as he is by the Sienese face here.) The middle stanza of Song 29 is future directed and hopeless. It has in it a premonition, certainly the fear, of his own suicide.

Therefore the structure of the poem is the structure of his anxiety: it is felt as inescapable, it is projected backwards (onto the father's suicide) and forwards (onto his own) and he senses himself, in the blackout stanza, as an alienated field of violence between these two deaths.

We can now return to self-pity which I judge to be the final tone of this song and of the book as a whole. The Dream Songs do not move to a resolution. Berryman told Richard Kostelanetz in 1969: "Henry is so troubled and bothered by his many problems that he never actually comes up with solutions, and from that point of view the poem is a failure." The core mood in the poems is anxiety and dread and when they leave that they do not rise out of it but slide sideways into intellectualizing, pride, boredom, talk, obfuscation, self-pity and resentment. This happens so often that these are the dominant tones of the Dream Songs. Here are a few examples of resentment and self-pity:

God's Henry's enemy. (13)

Life, friends, is boring. (14)

Henry hates the world. What the world to Henry
did will not bear thought.
Feeling no pain,
Henry stabbed his arm and wrote a letter
explaining how bad it had been
in this world. (74)

All this is being scrutinized in the critical literature about
Berryman under the fancy handle of "the epistemology of
loss." But it's really just an alcoholic poet on his pity-
pot. Not having decided if he wants to get well he is
reinforcing his disease with a moan. The poems articulate
the moods and methods of the alcoholic ego. But as the
"Big Book" says, "when harboring such feelings we shut
ourselves off from the sunlight of the Spirit. The insanity
of alcohol returns and we drink again. And with us, to
drink is to die." This means that when approached by an
alcoholic with a magnificient problem, all years a-drip
with complication and sorrow, one's response has to be
"Yes, but do you want to get sober?" To become involved in the pain before the disease has been arrested is
to help the man or woman stay sick.

Berryman's father killed himself more than 40 years before these poems were written. It is a hard judgment, but
inescapable, that the use of the father's death here and
elsewhere in the Dream Songs amounts to self-pity. Certainly there is grief and anger, but in the end the memory
of that death is used as a device in a holding action of the
alcoholic ego. I think Berryman himself saw this before
he died. I presume he is referring to the two books of
Dream Songs (1964 & 1968) when he writes in the novel
of his "self-pity, rage, resentments—a load so great I've
spent two well-known volumes on it."

When making judgements like these the question arises
whether or not Berryman was trapped. If he couldn't
resolve his pain for reasons beyond his control, then his
expressions of it are not self-pity. This is important because this was Berryman's sense of himself. He identified
with the trapped and oppressed: Anne Frank, Bessie
Smith, Victoria Spivey, Job, Jeremiah in the Lamenta-
tions and so on. Can an alcoholic be classified in this
group? In one sense yes, he is trapped: once the booze
has possessed him it also baffles his healing powers so
that demanding he simply quit drinking is a bit like asking a catatonic to snap out of it.

And yet people get sober. AA guarantees a day of sobriety to any who follow their suggestions. So once the alcoholic, like the early Christian, has heard the Word, he
is no longer trapped; it comes down to whether or not he
wants sobriety. And then the real war begins. It is when
the active alcoholic is presented with the option of sobering up that he starts to defend his right to drink, to deny
he is having any trouble with alcohol, to attack AA, and
to hoard his resentments and pain.

In the end Berryman's tone leads me to judge he was not
trapped. The blues don't have that tone. They are not
songs of self-pity. Leadbelly or Billie Holiday have more
resonance than the Dream Songs precisely because they

were not divided against themselves by their oppressor
(as an alcoholic is) and because the enemy is identified
(not vague as in Berryman) and the self is in motion.
Likewise the strength of Anne Frank is that her diary is
direct, not whiny. Berryman was lost and in pain, but not
trapped.

and something can (has) been said for sobriety
but very little. (57)

Why drink so, two days running?
two months, O seasons, years, two decades
    running?
I answer (smiles) my question on the cuff:
Man, I been thirsty. (96)

This voice is to alcohol what the Uncle Tom is to the
racist.

I want to turn now to the structural innovations, the
emotional plot, of the Dream Songs. As a person becomes alcoholic he becomes divided inside and typically
turns into a con-man. The booze-hustler in him will command all of the self's true virtues to maintain its hold. He
has a double voice then: sincerity with a motive.
Berryman's device of having his central figure, Henry, be
a white man in black face is an accurate imitation of this.
Henry has become a con-man and can't figure out why.
His mood is accurate to alcoholism: he is anxious, guilt-
ridden, secretly proud, baffled and driven.

Huffy Henry hid the day
unappeasable Henry sulked. (1)

As Berryman wrote, Henry has "suffered an irreversible
loss." He knows somewhere that he is not responsible for
it and yet he can't escape it either. His sidekick in the
poems, a black man who calls him Mr. Bones, is exactly
like the alcoholic's spouse who keeps saying "You're
suffering, you must be guilty." They conspire in keeping
each other unhappy.

When Berryman says that the book is a "failure" in terms
of finding a solution to Henry's problems, it seems clear
that he would have preferred to work with Henry, to
exorcise him or at least objectify him and his loss. But
this is a disease and not susceptible to such powers. "Will
power is nothing. Morals is nothing. Lord, this is illness,"
he wrote in the novel. That is: when confronted by the
will and the ego, alcohol always wins. James Dickey
noticed that when a Dream Song gets off the ground,
Berryman gets it there "through sheer will and guts."
Some of the poems do work this way, through willpower,
like Song 29. But they are oddly empty, like screams.

The will is a power and a necessary one, but by itself it
is neither creative nor healing. But it is Berryman's tool,
and this is why I said earlier that he loses his fight with
alcohol because his tactics and epistemology are all
wrong. Of course it did not help him that these misunderstandings about power and willfulness are everywhere
imitated in our civilization.

The original design of the Dream Songs has a resonant tension that is lost as the spirit of alcohol (Henry) takes over. This begins in Book III. Berryman's inspiration in Book IV was to kill Henry off. The poems are written from the grave. My guess is that he hoped to cleanse him through a night journey. It fails. Henry leaves the grave in Song 91 and it is the resurrection of a material spirit: the media invoke Henry to rise, he does and immediately calls for a double rum. The last stanza I judge to be Berryman's horror at this, caught in the gut assumption that if the spirit of alcohol won't die, he'll have to:

> A fortnight later, sense a single man
> upon the trampled scene at 2 a.m.
> insomnia-plagued, with a shovel
> digging like mad, Lazarus with a plan
> to get his own back, a plan, a stratagem
> no newsman will unravel.

Berryman always insisted that Henry was "an imaginary character, not the poet, not me." Everyone has disregarded this as a poet's whim, for the two are so clearly connected. When Berryman goes to Ireland, Henry goes; when Berryman is visited by the BBC, Henry is visited, and so forth. So we have said that Henry is only a thin disguise for Berryman. But the opposite is more accurate: during those years, Henry came out of the book and possessed his creator. Berryman was reduced to a shadow. He hardly appears in Book VII at all. Its flatness and silly pride are nothing but booze talking. Nowhere can you find the passion, insight, erudition and music that mark Berryman's earlier poetry. "He went to pieces./ The pieces sat up & wrote." (331)

As a final part of this look at the Dream Songs I want to say a few words about their style. The innovations are fairly well represented by the last stanza of Song 29. They are mostly syntactical oddities: mixed tenses ("never did Henry . . . hacks") and reordered phrases ("he reckons, in the dawn, them up"). It is a deliberately broken speech which is striking when it fills with music and alternates with direct statement. Songs 29 and 1 are both good examples. The voice is reminiscent of and drawn from several sources: black blues & dialect, baby talk, drunk talk, and the broken syntax of extreme anxiety.

Why was Berryman drawn to these sources? The connection is in power relationships. In a power structure, dialect is the verbal equivalent of the slave's shuffle. It is an assertion of self in an otherwise oppressive situation. It says: "I'll speak your language, but on my own terms." Baby talk works the same way. It is the speech equivalent of the child's pout. Both are signs that there is a distance between real personal power and desired personal power. And yet neither of them is a true confrontation of that distance. They reveal that the imbalance has been neither accepted *nor* rejected, for such would lead to direct speech. When the child pouts he doesn't want his parents to leave. When the slave shuffles he has been baffled into the myth that he has no internal power and his only hope is to cajole a piece of the action out of the master. The

cloying voice depends on the audience it hates. it is divided, identifying with a power not its own and hoping to control that power through verbal finesse. This is the style of the con-man.

In a case of real and inescapable oppression, stylized speech might be an assertion of self. But this would be short term; when it becomes a way of life, it is something different. In these poems, written by a grown white male, the voice is a whine. When the child whines he doesn't want the grown-ups to go away and when Berryman writes like this he doesn't want to give up the booze.

The question arises: who is the mean parent/slave driver? At times Berryman thought it must be God himself. He commonly equated Henry with Job, announcing that "God's Henry's enemy." (13) But this won't wash. As before, the tone is the top-off. Job is neither cynical nor ironic. What successfully imitates anxiety in Song 29 deflates into weary irony as it is spread over 385 songs. Irony has only emergency use. Carried over time it is the voice of the trapped who have come to enjoy their cage. This is why it is so tiresome. People who have found a route to power based on their misery—who don't want to give it up though it would free them—they become ironic. This sustained complaint is the tone of active alcoholism.

The stylistic innovations in the Dream Songs are epistemologically wrong—an alcoholic is not a slave—and this is why they are so unsatisfying. The style obscures and mystifies, it does not reveal. Berryman himself knew there was a growing distance between his style and his self. The question is honesty. The more developed the style became, the more he was conning himself, reinforcing the walls of his cage. So in *Recovery* when he tries to write out some self-criticism he reads it over and comments to himself: "No style: good." This is a remarkable sentence for a poet to write.

His last poems, written at the same time as the novel, move away from the old style. They were written in a drying-out place where Berryman had gone for help. Judging from the novel many of his old ploys were falling away as he attended to his disease and, more importantly, as he attended to other people and received their attention. Through other people he began to feel a "personal sense of God's love," which he had not had since his father's suicide. The poems from this period still have syntactic twists, now more like an old nerve tic, but on the whole they are direct and clear, descriptive and loving:

> Jack went it was, on Friday, against the word
> of the staff & our word . . . violent relief
> when Sunday night he & his son, absurd
> in ties & jackets, for a visit brief
>   looked back in, looking good.

I have shown that the Dream Songs can be explicated in terms of the disease of alcoholism. We can hear the booze talking. Its moods are anxiety, guilt and fear. Its tone is a moan that doesn't resolve. Its themes are unjust pain, resentment, self-pity, pride and a desperate desire to run the world. It has the con-man's style and the con-game's plot. It depends for its survival on an arrogance of will, ascendent and dissociated from the whole. These poems are not a contribution to culture. They are artifacts of a dying civilization, like one of those loaves of bread turned to lava at Pompeii.

The way out of self-pity and its related moods is to attend to something other than the self. This can be either the inner or the outer world, either dreams and visions which do not come from the self, or other people and nature. The point is that the self begins to heal automatically when it attends to the non-self. Pablo Neruda is a good example of a poet who did this. He had great trust of the interior world and turned to it automatically when he was otherwise isolated. And when I asked him once what made the melancholy of his early work disappear, he spoke immediately of politics. The Spanish Civil War made him change. "That was my great experience," he said. "It was a defeat but I never considered life a defeat after that. I had faith in human things and in human people."

Berryman found neither of these things. I think his trust was broken early in both the inner and the outer worlds and he was never able to regain it despite his desire. He had no politics except patriotism and nostalgia. He refused to read at the first anti-war readings in Minneapolis. He wrote the only monarchist poem (Song 105) to come out of the sixties. And there is no spiritual energy or dream-consciousness at all in the Dream Songs.

This leads to the question of how Berryman was handled by the rest of us. We did not handle him well. Few of his critics faced the death in these poems. Most were snowed, as he was himself, by Berryman's style and brains, as if they thought rhetoric, intellectualizing and references to famous friends were what poetry is all about. At the end Berryman began to see that his fame was built on his sickness. The character in his novel "really thought, off and on for twenty years, that it was his duty to drink, namely to sacrifice himself. He saw the products as worth it." Berryman felt that "the delusion that . . . my art depended on my drinking . . . could not be attacked directly. Too far down."

This is not true. He could have attacked it. But it would not have been easy. He would have had to leave behind a lot of his own work. He would have had to leave his friends who had helped him live off his pain for twenty years. And the civilization itself, which supported all of that, weighs a great deal. *Life* magazine unerringly made the connection between our civilization and disease and went straight to Berryman as their example of the poet from the sixties. They called the piece "Whiskey and Ink, Whiskey and Ink," and there are the typical photographs of the poet with the wind in his beard and a glass in his hand. Berryman bought into the whole

thing. Like Hemingway, they got him to play the fool and the salesman the last ten years of his life.

I am not saying that the critics could have cured Berryman of his disease. But we could have provided a less sickening atmosphere. In the future it would be nice if it were a little harder for the poet to come to town drunk and have everyone think that it's great fun. You can't control an alcoholic's drinking any more than he can, but the fewer parasites he has to support the better. No one knows why some alcoholics get sober and others don't. They say in AA that it takes a desire to stop drinking and, after that, the grace of God. Here are Berryman's words on this, with which I will close.

> Is escape . . . too difficult? Evidently, for (1) the walls are strong and I am weak, and (2) *I love my walls.* . . . Yet some *have escaped.* . . . With an effort we lift our gaze from the walls upward and ask God to take the walls away. We look back down and they have disappeared. . . . We turn back upward at once with love to the Person who has made us so happy, and desire to serve Him. Our state of mind is that of a bridegroom, that of a bride. We are married, who have been so lonely heretofore.

FURTHER READING

Secondary Sources

"Booze and the Writer." *Writer's Digest* 58, No. 10 (October 1978): 25-33.
    Compilation of responses to a drinking questionnaire sent to a variety of writers, including Norman Mailer, Joyce Carol Oates, Stephen King, and many others.

Donaldson, Scott. "The Crisis of Fitzgerald's 'Crack-Up.'" *Twentieth Century Literature* 26, No. 2 (Summer 1980): 171-88.
    Studies Fitzgerald's autobiographical "Crack-Up" articles for *Esquire*, which note his alcoholic breakdown and other personal problems.

Fabricant, Noah D. "The Medical Profile of F. Scott Fitzgerald." In *13 Famous Patients*, pp. 159-56. Philadelphia: Chilton Company, 1960.
    Recounts Fitzgerald's highly publicized problems with alcohol and numerous other medical infirmities.

Gilmore, Thomas B. *Equivocal Spirits: Alcoholism and Drinking in Twentieth-Century Literature.* Chapel Hill: University of North Carolina Press, 1987, 226 p.
    Observes the importance of alcohol and alcoholism to the work of ten writers, including Malcolm Lowry, Eugene O'Neill, F. Scott Fitzgerald, and John Cheever.

Goodwin, Donald W. "The Alcoholism of F. Scott Fitz-

gerald." *Journal of the American Medical Association* (6 April 1970): 86-90.
> Investigates the relationship between Fitzgerald's writing talent and his alcoholism.

————— . "The Alcoholism of Eugene O'Neill." *Journal of the American Medical Association* (5 April 1971): 99-104.
> Explores the sources of O'Neill's alcoholism and the relation of his drinking to his work as a playwright.

Haffenden, John. "Drink as Disease: John Berryman." *Partisan Review* 44, No. 4 (1977): 565-83.
> Recounts Berryman's alcoholism as reflected in his autobiographical work *Recovery*.

Heyen, William. "John Berryman: A Memoir and an Interview." *The Ohio Review* 15, No. 2 (Winter 1974): 46-65.
> Includes personal observations on Berryman's alcoholism and an interview focused on his poetic career.

Lyons, J. B. "Diseases in *Dubliners*: Tokens of Disaffection." In *Irish Renaissance Annual II*, edited by Zack Bowen, pp.185-94. Newark, N. J.: University of Delaware Press, 1981.
> Mentions the prevalent disease of alcoholism in James Joyce's *Dubliners*, noting that "the city's ambiance is one of inebriation."

Buddhism and Literature

INTRODUCTION

Despite its origins in sixth century India, the religion of Buddhism took hold most strongly in China and Japan after it spread there during the Middle Ages. In general, Buddhism teaches that the phenomenal world is a realm of suffering that may only be transcended through meditation and contemplation. The influence of Buddhism and Buddhist ideas on literature has been enormous, especially in medieval east Asia, where Japanese Zen Buddhism—called Ch'an in China—originated.

Zen propounds the ideals of wholeness, harmony, antirationalism, and the dissolution of the self (called *sunyata*, "emptiness" or "egolessness") as a means of reaching a state of spiritual enlightenment, or *satori*. Among the earliest Ch'an inspired writers was the Chinese poet Wang Wei (701-761). In his landscape poetry scholars have observed a thorough detachment from temporal concerns and a gradual loss of the self into oneness with nature. The seventeenth century Japanese poet Matsuo Basho is largely responsible for the association of 17-syllable haiku verse with Zen Buddhism. In Basho's haiku, critics find brilliant and succinct statements on the nature of Zen enlightenment.

The modern era has witnessed the advent of Buddhist thought in the West, particularly in North America. In the nineteenth century, the American Transcendentalists Ralph Waldo Emerson and Henry David Thoreau absorbed certain aspects of Buddhism into their philosophy—Emerson's Oversoul, for example, resembles somewhat the oneness that the Zen monk seeks to attain by eradicating the boundaries of the self and the other. The modernists also alighted upon certain aspects of Buddhism as part of their eclectic gathering of world myth and spiritualism. Analogies to the Buddhist quest for enlightenment have been observed by critics, for instance, in the poetry of W. B. Yeats and the writings of T. S. Eliot. A less intellectual concern with Buddhism at mid-century can be found in the work of the Beat poets, particularly Jack Kerouac and Allen Ginsberg. Kerouac's *The Dharma Bums* (1958) has done much to popularize the religion and its precepts in the west. In the contemporary era, poets and novelists such as Gary Snyder and Peter Matthiessen have furthered the modern conception of Buddhism in literary form. Meanwhile the American poet and translator Lucien Stryk has helped to strengthen the ties between Eastern and Western Buddhism by translating the Zen writings of the twentieth-century Japanese poet Takahashi Shinkichi for English-speaking audiences.

REPRESENTATIVE WORKS*

Basho Matsuo
  The Narrow Road to the Far North, and Selected Haiku (journal and poetry) 1980
Chomei Kamo
  Ten Foot Square Hut (autobiography) 1970
Di Prima, Diane
  Selected Poems: 1956-1975 (poetry) 1975
  Pieces of a Song: Selected Poems (poetry) 1990
Forster, E. M.
  A Passage to India (novel) 1924
Ginsberg, Allen
  Allen Verbatim: Lectures on Poetry, Politics, Consciousness (lectures) 1974
  Collected Poems 1947-1980 (poetry) 1985
Han Shan
  Poetry of Han Shan: A Complete, Annotated Translation of Cold Mountain (poetry) 1990
Hesse, Hermann
  Siddhartha (novel) 1922
Ikkyu Sojun
  Ikkyu and the Crazy Cloud Anthology: A Zen Poet of Medieval Japan (poetry) 1987
  Crow with Noh Mouth: Ikkyu, 15th Century Zen Master (poetry) 1987
  Wild Ways: Zen Poems of Ikkyu (poetry) 1995
Issa Kobayashi
  Dust Lingers (poetry) 1981
  The Autumn Wind (poetry) 1984
Kazantzakis, Nikos
  Salvatores Dei: AskÂtikÂ [*The Saviors of God: Spiritual Exercises*] (nonfiction) 1927
  Buddha (drama) 1956
Kerouac, Jack
  The Dharma Bums (novel) 1958
  Mexico City Blues (poetry) 1959
Matthiessen, Peter
  Far Tortuga (novel) 1975
  The Snow Leopard (travelogue) 1978
  Nine-Headed Dragon River: Zen Journals, 1969-1982 (journals) 1987
Merton, Thomas
  Mystics and Zen Masters (essays) 1967
  Zen and the Birds of Appetite (essays) 1968
Miyazawa, Kenji
  Milky Way Railroad (poetry) 1996
Myers, L. H.
  The Near and the Far (novel) 1927
Rengetsu
  Lotus Moon: The Poetry of the Buddhist Nun Rengetsu (poetry) 1994

Ryokan
  Between Floating Mists (poetry) 1992
  Ryokan: Zen Monk—Poet of Japan (poetry) 1992
  Dewdrops on a Lotus Leaf (poetry) 1996
Salinger, J. D.
  Franny and Zooey (novellas) 1961
Snyder, Gary
  The Real Work: Interviews & Talks 1964-1979 (inter-
    views) 1980
  No Nature: New & Selected Poems (poetry) 1992
Santoka Tandeda
  Mountain Tasting: Zen Haiku (poetry) 1980
Soseki Natsume
  Zen Haiku: Poems and Letters of Natsume Soseki (po-
    etry) 1994
Suzuki Mitsu
  Temple Dust: Zen Haiku (poetry) 1992
Stryk, Lucien
  Awakening (poetry) 1973
  Selected Poems (poetry) 1976
Takahashi Shinkichi
  Afterimages: Zen Poems (poetry) 1970
  Triumph of the Sparrow (poetry) 1986
Wang Wei
  Laughing Lost in the Mountains (poetry) 1992
Welch, Lew
  Ring of Bone: Collected Poems 1950-1971 (poetry)
    1979
Whalen, Philip
  On Bear's Head (poetry) 1969
Wu Ch'eng-en
  Monkey: A Folk Novel of China (novel) 1958

*Publication dates for works by Chinese and Japanese authors indi-
cate the date of the English-language translation listed.

EASTERN LITERATURE

Lucien Stryk

SOURCE: "Poetry and Zen," in *Encounter with Zen,*
Swallow Press Books, 1981, pp. 51-65.

[*In the following essay, Stryk explores the nature, meanings, dominant moods, and other characteristics of Zen
poetry.*]

I

One spring day in 1912, the German lyric poet Rainer
Maria Rilke had an extraordinary experience, which,
based on the poet's account to her, the Princess Marie
von Thurn und Taxis-Hohenlohe described in the following manner:

> He wandered absent-minded, dreaming, through the
> undergrowth and maze of briars, and suddenly
> found himself next to a huge old olive tree which

he had never noticed before. . . . The next thing
he knew he was leaning back into the tree, standing
on its gnarled roots, his head propped against the
branches. . . . An odd sensation came over him so
that he was fixed to the spot, breathless, his heart
pounding. It was as though he were extended into
another life, a long time before, and that everything
that had ever been lived or loved or suffered here
was coming to him, surrounding him, storming him,
demanding to live again in him. . . . 'Time' ceased
to exist; there was no distinction between what
once was and now had come back, and the dark,
formless present. The entire atmosphere seemed
animated, seemed unearthly to him, thrusting in
on him incessantly. And yet this unknown life
was close to him somehow; he had to take part
in it. . . .

Of course, the princess was suitably impressed and
saw the experience as further proof of the poet's
otherworldliness, romantic disposition. Had Rilke spoken with a Zen master of the event, it would have been
called perhaps by its right name, spiritual awakening. Zen
Buddhism's main purpose is to make such experiences
possible, for their result is liberation.

Because Zen exists as a discipline to make an awakening
possible, and because its adherents are made aware, early
in their training, that all their labors will be fruitless
unless they are enlightened, many have at least simulacra
of the event. If in the West the mystic realization is extremely rare, in the Zen communities of the Far East it is
consciously worked for, induced in a thousand and one
ways. Often the Zenist writes a poem expressing the essence of his awakening, the depth of which is suggested
by the quality of the poem.

Zen is unique as a religion-philosophy of artistic manifestation, the attainments of its practitioners often gauged by
the works of art they make. The disciple is expected to
compose poetry of a very special kind (*toki-no-ge* in
Japanese, or "verse of mutual understanding") on the
occasion of the momentous event which the solving of his
koan, or problem for meditation, always seems to be.
Koans are set to disciples by the masters so as to make
them realize that there are things beyond the reach of
common sense and logic, that the sensible, normal way of
handling things does not always work and that if they
hope to win enlightenment they must break through the
barriers created, in all of us, by "mind." *Satori* poems are
always genuine because only those winning the approval
of the poet's spiritual guide are designated as such: the
poet does not himself refer to a poem as an enlightenment
poem before the fact of his master's approval.

As a consequence of the anciently established practice, a
rather natural process of criticism and selection takes
place: what has passed down as *satori* poetry is, in other
words, the cream—the rest, what in fact was not reproduced, was for some reason found wanting (this is true
only of awakening poetry: "death" poems are written
only by mature and established masters who have earned
the right to be heard at such a time, and "general" poems

written by those masters whose words are considered important enough to preserve). Enlightenment poems rejected by masters are sometimes, as the result of the poet's later eminence, reproduced, as in the case of the Chinese master Chokei, the first of whose following *satori* poems was rejected, the second approved:

> Rolling the bamboo blind, I
> Look out at the world—what change!
> Should someone ask what I've discovered,
> I'll smash this whisk against his mouth.

> . . . . .

> All's harmony, yet everything is separate.
> Once confirmed, mastery is yours.
> Long I hovered on the Middle Way,
> Today the very ice shoots flame.

It would be presumptuous even to try to imagine why the first of these poems was rejected as lacking sufficient insight by Chokei's master (to assume that it was its "arrogance" would be risky, as many true *satori* poems seem even more "arrogant"), but the second is surely an extraordinary poem. Only the master, aware of his disciple's barriers, can determine whether a breakthrough has been made: if it has, the poem will show it. Such judgment, considering the spiritual context, places the highest sort of value on art. The most famous example in Zen history of the manner in which a *satori* poem is written, and the tremendous consequences it can have for the writer, is recounted in one of the most important Zen texts, the *Platform Scripture* of the Sixth Patriarch of Zen in China, Hui-neng:

> One day the Fifth Patriarch, Hung-jen, called all the disciples together and said: "Life and death are serious matters. You are engaged all day in making offerings to the Buddha, going after blessings and rewards only. You make no effort to achieve freedom, your self-nature is obscured. How can blessings save you? Go and examine yourselves—he who is enlightened, let him write a poem, which, if it reveals deep understanding, will earn him the robe and the Law and make him the Sixth Patriarch. Hurry, hurry!" Shen-hsiu, the senior monk, wrote:

> Our body is the tree of Perfect Wisdom,
> And our mind is a bright mirror.
> At all times diligently wipe them,
> So that they will be free from dust.

> Then the humble Hui-neng, who as a mere "rice pounder" was practically unknown in the monastery, wrote in response to Shen-hsiu's poem:

> The tree of Perfect Wisdom is originally no tree,
> Nor has the bright mirror any frame.
> Buddha-nature is forever clear and pure.
> Where is there any dust?

> Which so impressed the Fifth Patriarch that Hui-neng was named his successor, saying: "You are now the Sixth Patriarch. The robe is the testimony of transmission from generation to generation. As to the Law, it is to be transmitted from mind to mind. Let men achieve understanding through their own effort."

Death poems are perhaps the most unusual of the Zen poems: rarely morbid, self-serving, or self-sorrowful, and never euphemistic, they serve a uniquely spiritual end, as inspiration for the master's immediate followers and for the Zen community at large. The tradition of the death poem is very old, and as with many traditions, it perpetuates itself. Expected to write such a poem, the master not only steels himself for the task but for death itself. He is, as a Zenist, expected to face the inevitable stoically, and he does not fail his disciples. There are many anecdotes about the valor, before death, of the masters, the following being well known:

> When a rebel army took over a Korean town, all fled the Zen temple except the Abbot. The rebel general burst into the temple, and was incensed to find that the master refused to greet him, let alone receive him as a conqueror.

> "Don't you know," shouted the general, "that you are looking at one who can run you through without batting an eye?"

> "And you," said the Abbot, "are looking at one who can be run through without batting an eye!"

> The general's scowl turned into a smile. He bowed low and left the temple.

In the Zen communities not only the masters were expected to write death poems. The greatest of the *haiku* writers Matsuo Basho (1644-94) was asked by his friends, when it was clear that he was about to die, for a death poem, but he refused them, claiming that in a sense every poem he had written in the last ten years—by far his most productive period and one of deep Zen involvement—had been done as if a death poem. Yet on the next morning his friends were called by the poet to his bedside and told that during the night he had dreamed, and that on waking a poem had come to him. Then he recited his famous poem:

> Sick on a journey—
> over parched fields
> dreams wander on.

There are perhaps as many ways of dying, or at least of facing death, as there are of living, and though all death poems are compact, deep, intense, they reflect, as might be expected, the many differences to be found among men, including Zen masters. There is, for example, the serenity of Hofuku Seikatsu:

> Don't tell me how difficult the Way.
> The bird's path, winding far, is right
> Before you. Water of the Dokei Gorge,
> You return to the ocean, I to the mountain.

The power of Dogen:

Four and fifty years
I've hung the sky with stars.
Now I leap through—
What shattering!

The self-honesty of Keisen:

The first illusion
Has lasted seventy-six years.
The final barrier?
Three thousand sins!

In the case of enlightenment and death poems, there are certain recognizable norms and standards, and it is possible to compare them for their concision and gravity, whatever the distinction of the poets. The general poems, as might be expected, are less easily judged and cover a multitude of subjects, for in spite of the exigencies of the Zen life, not to speak of the expectations from him of others—to be ignored at peril—the Zen man finds himself moved to poetry by things not ostensibly associated with his discipline (though many general poems are so associated). As some have remarked, Zen art, be it the monochromic inkwash painting (*sumie*) long connected with Zen, or poetry, is best characterized by its celebration of, its wonder at, the intimate relationship of all that exists in the world. Such feeling is, of course, not unknown in the West, and is beautifully expressed by Martin Buber:

> Believe in the simple magic of life, in service in the universe, and the meaning of that waiting, that alertness, that "craning of the neck" in creatures, will dawn upon you. Every word would falsify; but look! round about you beings live their life, and to whatever point you turn you come upon being.

In Zen poetry the phenomenal world is never treated as mere setting for human actions; the drama is there, in nature, of which the human is an active part, in no way separated from his surroundings, neither contending with them, fearing them nor—for that matter—worshiping them. The Zenist is no pantheist: in order to feel at home in nature he does not find it necessary to imagine it as a godly immanence. Many of the general poems, then, express a simple awe at the beauty of the world:

Hearing the Snow

This cold night bamboos stir,
Their sound—now harsh, now soft—
Sweeps through the lattice window.
Though ear's no match for mind,
What need, by lamplight,
Of a single Scripture leaf?
    —Kido

Disciplined by wind and snow,
The Way of Reinan opens.
Look where—moon high, plums a-bloom—
The temple's fixed in stillness.
    —Eun

Though most of the general poems are written in the spirit of celebration, some are clearly meant to instruct or hearten the master's disciples, or as in the case of the following *waka* by Dogen, inspire those among the followers who might in moments of weakness question the purpose of what they are required to do:

Waka on Zen Sitting

Scarecrow in the hillock
Paddy field—
How unaware! How useful!

II

What have all Zen poems, of whatever type, in common and what distinguishes them from poems written by the artistic equals of the masters who work in other traditions, or independently? Zen's aesthetics are well and very subtly defined.

The four traditionally recognized dominant moods of Zen-related art are: *Sabi, Wabi, Aware,* and *Yugen.* Often in large-scale works such as *Noh* plays, as the result of natural modulations, all the moods may be suggested, but in short literary works and in *sumie* painting the mood is clearly apparent. These moods are not consciously created, as in the case of Indian *rasas* (emotional "flavors" so precise that one *rasa,* say of a sitar melody, may "belong" to a particular time of the day and is always deliberately induced): they are experienced as we experience the light of the sky, hardly aware of the delicacy of its gradations.

Sabi may be defined as the feeling of isolation, or rather at a midpoint of the emotion when it is both welcome and unwelcome, source of both ease and unease. This mood, as all strong moods, comes as the result of many things, but clearly associated with *Sabi* is the sense of being detached, as in Honei's poem "Fisherman":

> On wide waters, alone, my boat
> Follows the current, deep/shallow, high/low.
> Moved, I raise my flute to the moon,
> Piercing the autumn sky.

Of importance to the mood of the poem is that in ancient China the fisherman, one of the so-called "four recluses" (the others being the farmer, the woodcutter, and the herdsman), was held in great esteem by Taoists and Zenists. Hakuin, greatest of the Rinzai Zen masters of Japan, significantly titled a remarkable account of his spiritual progress, *Yasenkanna,* which can be rendered as "talk in a boat at night."

Sabi is associated with the period of early monastic training when, if one is to succeed in Zen discipline, a strong detachment must be cultivated. While in training, the fifteenth-century Japanese master Saisho wrote as an interpretation of the *koan* on Joshu's Nothingness a poem the equal of Honei's in its spirit of *Sabi:*

> Earth, mountains, rivers—hidden in this
>   nothingness.
> In this nothingness—earth, mountains, rivers
>   revealed.
> Spring flowers, winter snows:
> There's no being nor non-being, nor denial itself.

Here the feeling of detachment is not only strong, it is identified as an essential precondition of enlightenment. Ch'ing-yuan's well-known words on the importance of *wu-hsin* (no-mind, detachment) will serve to paraphrase Saisho's poem:

> Before I had studied Zen I saw mountains as mountains, waters as waters. When I learned something of Zen, the mountains were no longer mountains, waters no longer waters. But now that I understand Zen, I am at peace with myself, seeing mountains once again as mountains, waters as waters.

Wabi is the spirit of poverty, the poignant appreciation of what most consider the commonplace, and is associated in Zen with one of the principal characteristics, if not ideals, of the sect, antirelativism: what's good? what's bad? what's valuable? valueless? The mood is perhaps most apparent in relation to that quintessential Zen art, the tea ceremony, which—from the utensils employed in the preparation of the tea to the very timber of the tea hut—is a celebration of the humble, the "handmade." The nineteenth-century *haiku* artist Masaoka Shiki writes:

> Thing long forgotten—
> pot where a flower blooms,
> this spring day.

Wabi is not to be found in objects alone. As in the following awakening poem by the sixteenth-century Japanese master Yuishun, it is the feeling of something hitherto ignored suddenly being seen for the precious thing it is (and always has been, though hidden from us by illusion):

> Why, it's but the motion of eyes and brows!
> And here I've been seeking it far and wide.
> Awakened at last, I find the moon
> Above the pines, the river surging high.

One day while practicing *zazen* (formal sitting in meditation) with his followers, the Chinese master Daibai was moved to say aloud for their benefit, "No suppressing arrival, no following departure." Immediately after the words were spoken, the shriek of a weasel pierced through the meditation hall, and Daibai recited this extemporaneous poem:

> I'm at one with this, *this* only.
> You, my disciples,
> Uphold it firmly—
> Now I can breathe my last.

To know what Daibai meant by asking his followers to "uphold" the simple fact of the weasel's shriek is to appreciate the importance of *Wabi* to Zen. How much more real, how much more relevant to the spiritual quest than even the wisest words is Nature's least manifestation, when accepted for the profound thing it is.

Aware is the sadness that comes with the sense of the impermanence of things, the realization that they are lost to us even as they are found. It is so constant a mood in the poetry touched by Buddhism, that as far back as the tenth century, when the Japanese poet Ki no Tsurayuki (died 946) compiled the anthology *Kokinshu,* the first done under Imperial order, he could write:

> When these poets saw the scattered spring blossoms, when they heard leaves falling in the autumn evening, when they saw reflected in their mirrors the snow and the waves of each passing year, when they were stunned into an awareness of the brevity of life by the dew on the grass or foam on the water . . . they were inspired to write poems.

A few centuries later, Kenko Yoshida, a famous poet and court official of his day who became a Buddhist monk in 1324, wrote in his *Essays in Idleness:*

> If we lived forever, if the dews of Adashino never vanished, the crematory smoke on Toribeyama never faded, men would hardly feel the pity of things. The beauty of life is in its impermanence. Man lives the longest of all living things—consider the ephemera, the cicada—, and even one year lived peacefully seems very long. Yet for such as love the world, a thousand years would fade like the dream of one night.

At times the sense of *Aware* is so powerful that the only way of coming to terms with it is to identify with it totally, perhaps retiring from the world and the constant reminders of its limited, conditioned nature. Many of the finest Zen poems, seemingly "escapist," have this spirit of acceptance, of oneness with what *is,* whatever it happens to be. Here is the fourteenth-century Japanese master Jakushitsu:

> Refreshing, the wind against the waterfall
> As the moon hangs, a lantern, on the peak
> And the bamboo window glows. In old age
>   mountains
> Are more beautiful than ever. My resolve:
> That these bones be purified by rocks.

And here the Chinese master Zotan is seen praising a fellow monk, "Shooku" (Woodcutter's Hut), whose retirement very much impressed him:

> Is the live branch better than the dead?
> Cut through each—what difference?
> Back home, desires quelled, you sit by
> The half-closed brushwood door the spring day
>   through.

It is perhaps in *haiku* poetry that *Aware* is most keenly felt, though, because it is so commonly suggested (*Sunt lacrimae rerum*—There are tears for things), it is the spoiler of many otherwise acceptable verses. But by those who care for *haiku*, the sentimental is never mistaken for the poignant, and a piece like the following by Yosa Buson (1715-83), important Nanga-style painter as well as poet, is greatly prized:

> A sudden chill—
> In our room my dead wife's
> comb, underfoot.

Yugen, most difficult of the dominant moods to describe, is the sense of a mysterious depth in all that makes up nature. Often the term is used in almost a purely aesthetic way, as in the theoretical writings on *Noh* theater by the most important figure in its development, Zeami (1363-1443). In his essay, "On Attaining the Stage of Yugen," he speaks of the mood as that which "marks supreme attainment in all the arts and accomplishments" and describes its essence as "true beauty and gentleness," a "realm of tranquility and elegance." Though such may be the effect of *Yugen* on the *Noh* stage, perhaps a better sense of what the mood can represent in Zen is suggested by these words of the contemporary Japanese Soto master Rosen Takashina:

> The true basis of the universe is stillness, its real condition, for out of it comes all activity. The ocean, when the wind ceases, is calm again, as are the trees and grasses. These things return to stillness, their natural way. And this is the principle of meditation. There is night, there is day, when the sun sets there is a hush, and then the dead of night, when all is still. This is the meditation of nature.

Yugen is the sense of the mystic calm in things (in T. S. Eliot's phrase, in "Burnt Norton," "the still point of the turning world"), which is always there, below the surface, but which reveals itself only to the "ready."

Etsuzan, the Chinese master, aware that his time was nearly up, looked into things as never before, and wrote:

> Light dies in the eyes, hearing
> Fades. Once back to the Source,
> There's no special meaning—
> Today, tomorrow.

For him the world had returned to a stillness, its natural condition, and perhaps the realization gave him comfort in his final hour. *Yugen* also suggests the sense of a strong communion with nature, a descent into depths, as in this poem by the seventeenth-century Japanese master Manan:

> Unfettered at last, a traveling monk,
> I pass the old Zen barrier.
> Mine is a traceless stream-and-cloud life.
> Of those mountains, which shall be my home?

And in this poem, one of his most famous, by Dogen:

> This slowly drifting cloud is pitiful;
> What dreamwalkers men become.
> Awakened, I hear the one true thing—
> Black rain on the roof of Fukakusa Temple.

To hear that "black rain" with Dogen, to sense that it—or anything like it, for though intensely particular it is symbolic—is the "one true thing" is to enter the realm of *Yugen*, which as a mood is not of course peculiar to Zen but which, nonetheless, is most commonly felt in its art. Not to hear it, on the other hand, not to know if one hears that one has identified with the Source is to remain a "dreamwalker," blind not only to the beauty of the world but to its reality.

The four dominant moods, however closely associated with Zen art, are not exclusively related to the philosophy, whereas *zenki*, the sense of a spontaneous activity outside the established forms, as if flowing from the formless self, is the constant in its art. Without Zen there could not be *zenki*, just as without *muga* (so close an identification of subject and object that "self" disappears) the goal of Zen, *satori*, could not be realized. There have been occasional attempts to describe in detail the characteristics of Zen art, the most comprehensive being Dr. Hisamatsu's in *Zen and Fine Arts*, which gives as its chief qualities the following (all of which, according to Dr. Hisamatsu, are present harmoniously in every Zen work, whatever the medium): asymmetry, simplicity, freedom, naturalness, profundity, unworldliness, and stillness.

It is perhaps in poetry that these characteristics—subject and theme dictating to what degree, of course—are most apparent, the desired qualities of an aesthetic. The following poems have a common theme, and each in its way might be seen as representing the ideal Zen poem in Japan. This is by the thirteenth-century master Unoku:

> Moving/resting is meaningless.
> Traceless, leaving/coming.
> Across moonlit mountains,
> Howling wind!

And here is one by the fourteenth-century master Getsudo:

> The perfect way out:
> There's no past/present/future.
> Dawn after dawn, the sun!
> Night after night, the moon!

Against the facts of that wind, that sun, that moon, what are concepts such as time? these poems seem to be asking. And as in all genuine Zen art, calm replaces restlessness.

In Zen painting there are only the essential strokes, the space surrounding them being filled in by the mind, which poises itself on (imagines) what it knows best, that which is always tranquil, agreeable. The brush strokes, however few, serve to make the mind aware of the space, suggested not so much by the absence of objects but by the manner in which the objects are absorbed. And in poetry, perhaps the most important things are to be found in the silence following the words, for it is then that the reader or listener becomes conscious of the calm within. It is something felt, not known, and precious in the way that only the spiritual can be.

III

There are distinct types of Zen poetry, and distinguishing qualities, but what makes it unique in world literature is that it is recognized as a mystic Way—to a most difficult truth. Zen has other Ways (*do*) but *Kado*, the Way of poetry, is one that has always held a place of honor in its culture, which has always valued directness, concision, and forcefulness of expression. As Dr. D. T. Suzuki writes in one of his essays, "The Meditation Hall":

> The Zen masters, whenever they could, avoided the technical nomenclature of Buddhist philosophy; not only did they discuss such subjects as appealed to a plain man, but they made use of his everyday language.... Thus Zen literature became a unique repository of ancient wisdom . . . [refusing] to express itself in the worn-out, lifeless language of scholars. . . .

The masters also discouraged the dependence on scriptural writings, and a master like Tokusan could proclaim (in one of the stories of the *Mumonkan* [*Barrier Without Gate*], an early thirteenth-century classic of Chinese Zen): "However deep your knowledge of the scriptures, it is no more than a strand of hair in the vastness of space; however important seeming your worldly experience, it is but a drop of water in a deep ravine." And as the fourteenth-century Japanese master Shutaku wrote:

> Mind set free in the Dharma-realm,
> I sit at the moon-filled window
> Watching the mountains with my ears,
> Hearing the stream with open eyes.
> Each molecule preaches perfect law,
> Each moment chants true sutra:
> The most fleeting thought is timeless,
> A single hair's enough to stir the sea.

While discouraging dependence on scripture (sutra learning), the masters strongly encouraged the cultivation of non-attachment, upheld by all the sects of Buddhism, the ultimate aim of whose discipline was, quoting from Dr. Suzuki again, "to release the spirit from its possible bondage so that it could act freely in accordance with its own principles—that is what is meant by non-attachment."

To give some idea of the manner in which such an important ideal, one with scriptural authority, is dealt with by Zenists, here is the Japanese master Takuan (1573-1645) in a "Letter to the Shogun's Fencing Master":

> If your mind is fixed on a certain spot, it will be seized by that spot and no activities can be performed efficiently. Not to fix your mind anywhere is

essential. Not fixed anywhere, the mind is everywhere. . . . The Original Mind is like water which flows freely . . . whereas the deluded mind is like ice. . . . There is a passage [in the *Diamond Sutra*] that says: "The mind should operate without abiding anywhere."

Presumably dissatisfied with his explanation, Takuan goes on:

> It is like tying a cat with a rope to prevent it from catching a baby sparrow which is tied up nearby. If your mind is tied down by a rope as is the cat, your mind cannot function properly. It is better to train the cat not to harm the sparrow when they are together, so that it can be free to move anywhere. . . . That is the meaning of the passage [in the *Diamond Sutra*]. . . .

How bumbling and obvious when compared with the poem Takuan was to write on the theme some time later:

> Though night after night
> The moon is stream-reflected,
> Try to find where it has touched,
> Point even to a shadow.

Which is perhaps the equal of Dogen's poem on the same passage in the *Diamond Sutra:*

> Coming, going, the waterfowl
> Leaves not a trace,
> Nor does it need a guide.

And resembles the eighteenth-century master Sogyo's:

> Careful! Even moonlit dewdrops,
> If you're lured to watch,
> Are a wall before the truth.

And the contemporary Japanese Zen poet Shinkichi Takahashi's "Fish":

> I hold a newspaper, reading.
> Suddenly my hands become cow ears,
> Then turn into Pusan, the South Korean port.
>
> Lying on a mat
> Spread on the bankside stones,
> I fell asleep.
> But a willow leaf, breeze-stirred,
> Brushed my ear.
> I remained just as I was,
> Near the murmurous water.
>
> When young there was a girl
> Who became a fish for me.
> Whenever I wanted fish
> Broiled in salt, I'd summon her.
> She'd get down on her stomach
> To be sun-cooked on the stones.
> And she was always ready!
>
> Alas, she no longer comes to me.
> An old benighted drake,
> I hobble homeward.

But look, my drake feet become horse hoofs!
Now they drop off
And, stretching marvelously,
Become the tracks of the Tokaido Railway Line.

Thus an important Buddhist principle, first advanced by scripture, often quoted and allegorized by masters (as in Takuan's "Letter . . ." or Hyakujo Ekai's famous injunction, *Fujaku fugu*—No clinging, no seeking), is transmuted into superb poetry by men who not only know truth but feel.

We have examined the nature of the three main types of Zen poetry, its characteristics, and have shown the manner in which it expresses insights afforded by the philosophy. Perhaps from our discussion something like a viewpoint has emerged; namely that if one wishes to "understand" Zen Buddhism, one could do worse than go to its arts, especially the poetry, compared with which the many disquisitions on its meaning are as dust to living earth.

Shan Chou

SOURCE: "Beginning with Images in the Nature Poetry of Wang Wei," in *Harvard Journal of Asiatic Studies,* Vol. 42, No. 1, June, 1982, pp. 117-37.

[*In the following essay, Chou traces natural imagery in the poems of Wang Wei and discusses the possible Buddhist themes implied by these symbols.*]

Wang Wei (701-61) is a poet whose reputation primarily rests on his nature poems. Although in the poems which have survived other themes are well represented—elaborate and perfect poems about the emperor's court, sentimental sketches of bucolic life, poems expressing friendship—it is with the nature poems that his name is universally identified. The prominence given a handful of nature poems reflects both the judgment that they contain the essence of Wang Wei's achievement and an acknowledgment of the position they occupy in the evolution of nature poetry. The sense displayed in these poems of a life lived in harmony with nature marks an important development in the appeal of landscape and nature to the poetic sensibility.

The world of Wang Wei's nature poems is a narrow one of simple and recurring scenes—a brief wind lifts his sash, a slight chill hangs in the air, light fills the mountainside, a bell sounds once. These are small moments intensified, during which nothing much happens. In general, Wang Wei does not draw any conclusions from scenes so presented—and this is the problem. A small area of experience has been sharply delimited, but within this area the reader is not guided to an interpretation. The clarity of the moment distilled seems to bespeak openness, yet the reader who feels that a meaning beyond that moment has been intended finds it concealed and the poems lacking in internal clues. In this Wang

Wei reminds me of Imagist poets, in which the sharpness of the observed details contrasts with the vagueness of the interpretation which has been implied. That a meaning beyond that captured moment has been intended seems a reasonable expectation. Indeed, given Wang Wei's enduring reputation, it seems a necessary one; for it is hardly possible that any nature poetry can continue to hold our attention that does not project a certain amount of significance onto the landscape presented.

The problem of significance—what is there besides descriptions of nature?—has been recognized for a long time. A major response has been concerned with identifying the Buddhist meaning of Wang Wei's poetry. This attempt seems justified in view of the whole of Wang Wei's poetry and also the known facts of his life. Wang Wei began the serious study of Buddhism about the age of thirty, adopted the *tzu* of Mo-chieh (which together with his *ming* Wei formed the Chinese transliteration of the name of the sage Vimalakirti), and began to move in Buddhist circles. In his poetry, his Buddhist interests are reflected in the many poems written to monks, in his appreciative descriptions of their lives, and in the frequent references to Buddhist practices and goals in his own life. These visible effects on his poetry are not disputed, but the most interesting claim of influence is made in a strong form. This is that the Buddhist influence is present in exactly those of the nature poems which show no overt signs of Buddhism, that is, those of Wang Wei's nature poems which I have described as simple and yet elusive. [There is no clear way to divide Wang Wei's poems into categories. I have chosen the ones set in mountains, following the description of landscape as *shan-shui*, and left out those set on the plains, which seem to me more pastoral, *t'ien-yuan*. The core is made up of the twenty poems of the "Wang-ch'uan chi," of poems about returning to Wang-ch'uan, and of those with mountain names or streams in the titles. A peripheral group includes poems about monasteries, whether or not monks are also there.]

The poems meant are such as these:

> In Ching Brook white stones jut out,
> The sky is cold, red leaves thinning.
> On the mountain path, there had been no rain,
> The cloudless blue, clothes are dampened.
>   —"In the mountains"

> All at rest, the cassia flowers fall.
> The night is quiet, the spring mountains empty.
> The moon appears, startling mountain birds,
> Which from time to time cry out from the spring
>   ravine.
>   —"Birdcries Stream"

Of the first poem the Sung-dynasty monk Hui-hung (1071-1128) reports the opinion that it is full of *t'ien-ch'ü* "the essence of nature." Of the second the Ming-dynasty critic Hu Ying-lin (1551-1602) declares that

Wang Wei had entered into the ranks of Ch'an Buddhists. The Ch'ing anthologist Shen Te-ch'ien (1673-1769) says that Wang Wei's poetry does not use Ch'an vocabulary but often attains Ch'an meaning. Such views of the poems are widespread and usually expressed in similarly general terms.

Some modern scholars have therefore recently added various qualifying suggestions to the equation of Wang Wei's nature poems with Buddhist influences. Iritani Sensuke discusses the "Wang-ch'uan chi" in terms of its *Ch'u tz'u* elements, its realism, and its mysticism, but does not bring in Buddhism. Fujiyoshi Masumi emphasizes the limited influence of Buddhism on the T'ang nobility in general and the importance of Taoism in its mediating role between Confucian ideals of service and Buddhist withdrawal. Pauline Yu is at pains to show that Wang Wei's attitude towards retirement from public life was not uncomplicated. None of them denies the pervasiveness of Buddhism in Wang Wei's life and in his works taken as a whole.

I think that ultimately we will have to refer to Buddhism at least in order to appreciate the full context out of which Wang Wei wrote and possibly in order to appreciate the full meaning of the nature poems. However there are aspects of the poems which we can consider before this final appeal that do not deny the possibility of Buddhist influence and yet may make easier the problem of defining this influence. This consideration begins by recognizing the nature of the problems posed by the poems.

I think of the problems as of two kinds. The first is that the literary qualities of the poems are hard to define; hence the persistent fascination with Buddhism as a key to them. Literarily the poems are elusive because they seem to defy further analysis, so simple is the setting, so precise the imagery and unhurried the tone. The stillness and tranquillity seem impossible to explicate further. Discussion would merely intrude paraphrase onto these spare scenes. The poems resist any response other than acceptance; they appear to be the simplest statements about themselves.

The second is that in those poems where Wang Wei does not use Buddhist terms—and these constitute the majority of what I have called nature poems—the Buddhist themes prove elusive to specify. I suggest that we deal with this problem by secularizing it, by looking first to see whether any philosophical viewpoint, rather than a specifically Buddhist one, is expressed in the poems. Then we may ask whether this philosophy can be identified with some aspect of Buddhism. This approach brings us to the more familiar uncertainty that the true meaning or intent of poems might always remain to some degree unverifiable, and especially so in poems, like these and like the Imagist poems, where the reader finds few guides to an interpretation. Differing literary analyses would then stress different themes, not all of which would have

Buddhist analogs, but each of which may nonetheless be literarily acceptable.

I propose in this essay to begin with an analysis of some literary qualities of Wang Wei's nature poems and from this analysis to make a suggestion about the problem of meaning in these poems.

The spareness of a Wang Wei scene is not a reflection of nature but the consequence of careful selection. The images which make up each poem are simple; the elements which make up the images are few. I suggest that it is the physical spacing displayed in the images which provides a key to the remoteness and the uncanny stillness which are their chief impression on the reader.

A central image in the nature poems is the physical isolation of the poet. Not only does he live away from man, but he chooses to live in the mountains, which encircle him on all sides. Furthermore he is often stationed inside an enclosure of some kind:

> I sit alone in a secluded bamboo thicket.
> The bright moon shines among the pines.
> The bright moon shines on me.
> The mountain moon shines on a zither played.

The moon by creating a well of light around the poet emphasizes his placement in a clearing.

Further, the poet is not only isolated, but his existence is not even suspected by others:

> Deep in the forest, no one knows [of me].

He suggests the same isolation for a friend:

> On the wide waters, no one will know [of you].

Again, of monasteries Wang Wei likes to emphasize that to the unsuspecting they do not exist:

> From the city, seen afar, a deserted cloud-capped
>   mountain.

> From the city walls, looking out,
> One would see only white clouds.

The poet lives alone in harmony with nature, but he has not dissolved into nature. As a personality he is self-effacing: there is generally no emotion reaching out to the landscape, no emotion aroused in turn by the landscape. Rather, the continued existence of his ego is expressed by the insistence on an active separation between himself and others. Again, this separation often takes the form of exclusion. One aspect of an experience that he savors is the exclusion of others from it. In poems by Meng Hao-jan (691-740) which describe scenes similar to Wang Wei's, it only gradually becomes apparent to the reader that the poet is alone, for the fact is not stated. Wang Wei, on the other hand, tells us many times and in so many words that no one is around. *Wu jen* ("there is no one") and *pu chien jen* ("I see no one") are used repeatedly. *K'ung* ("empty") is often used of a forest or a mountain to mean that no one is about, save for the poet. This absence of people gives to his solitude a delicious edge:

> The house by the stream is quiet, unpeopled.
> In profusion, [magnolias] blossom and fall.

Where once there had been people living, there is now no one, and the scene is the more piquant. The same sense of specialness can be seen in the poet's being privy to the secrets of the landscape:

> Beautiful spots which only I know of.

Where he walks, no one else seems to have walked:

> Beneath ancient trees, an unused path.

Another type of isolation is often established by the first two characters (the first phrase) of short poems:

> All at rest, the cassia flowers fall.
> The night is still, all movements cease.
> In the empty mountains, after the new rain.

(The second example is twice used as a first line.) Inside the bell jar of quietude defined by the first two characters, the remainder of the poem takes place. Within a poem Wang Wei will often define a space by the silence which pervades it. This silence is then broken by a sound which also emphasizes the space defined:

> The mountains are still, the spring even noisier.
> The valley is still, the spring even noisier.
> The valley is still, the autumn spring noisy.
> The valley is still, only the pines whisper.

Or the sound occurs first, then the space is defined:

> The travellers echo through the empty forest.

The image of isolation explains other types of images that occur, in particular Wang Wei's preference for sound over sight. Again, he can be very insistent, both that he sees nothing, and that he hears only sounds:

> Empty mountains, I see no one,
> But hear the echoes of people's voices.
> The bamboos ring with the returning
>   washerwomen.

The effect is that of a one-way mirror. Through sound images, the poet knows about other people's existence without their guessing his.

Sound has the additional advantage that what the poet hears need not be close by, but can be transmitted over an intervening distance. This distance then acts as an invisible barrier that expresses his isolation:

> From the valley mouth, the sound of a distant bell.
> The fisherman's song enters deep into this

> tributary.
> Deep in the mountains—from where?—a bell.

The last is a refinement, a sound whose source is unknown. The barrier is sometimes made explicit by the use of *ko* ("separated by"):

> At times I hear dogs on the far side of the grove.
> Across the river I ask the woodcutter.
> On the far shore I see homes.

We can compare these examples with a characteristic pose found in Meng Hao-jan's poetry. The figure of Meng's poet is often on a river bank, or by a jetty, from which he can also see the people making the noise. The Meng Hao-jan line "From the mountain temple a bell sounds, day is already dusk" contains elements familiar in Wang Wei too—the temple, the bell, dusk—but in Meng Hao-jan is followed by the cheerful noise of people actually seen ("By the fish dam, at the ferry, the clamor of everyone wanting to cross"). For Wang Wei, on the other hand, the consciousness of humans a distance away and dwindling further makes his solitude the more sweet. It is a solitude that perseveres on the edges of other people's activities and is the consequence not only of the circumstances of composition but of a certain control by imagery of the physical spacing.

It is not hard to find in the work of other poets, especially Meng Hao-jan, lines which are similar to some cited here. The world created in the poem as a whole, however, is almost always different. One much praised line by Wang Wei, for example, in its crucial part can be found in Sung Chih-wen (d. 712):

> Returning rays enter the cliffs and valley.

In Wang Wei:

> Returning rays enter the deep forest.

The returning rays are the afternoon light, which shines in the opposite direction from earlier in the day. In Sung Chih-wen, the line is one of twenty in a poem confiding the poet's hopes and fears during his recovery from an illness. In Wang Wei, it forms part of a pattern of solitude:

> Empty mountains, I see no one,
> But hear the echoes of people's voices.
> Returning rays enter the deep forest,
> Shining once more upon green moss.

The arrangement of sights and sounds, seemingly so artlessly noted as they impinge upon the poet's consciousness, constitute the whole of Wang Wei's world. The exclusion of other concerns is what is meant I think by the common description of Wang Wei's nature poems as the first ones to have been "pure." The subsequent unity of the poet with this world is then effortless, so pared is this world. The poet is able to transcend the world through immersion in nature in part because his natural world already transcends our natural world.

The spacing controlled by the images is physical and literal. I would like to suggest that the same control of spacing has a metaphorical and sometimes symbolic existence on the level of the whole poem. It is possible to interpret the themes of some poems in terms of distance and barriers, and also to offer such an interpretation for other poems which seem to be solely description.

The control of space, for instance, is implicit in one common theme we find, the theme that on the other side of an intervening distance exists a desirable state which I think we may call truth. In one of the ways in which this pattern is worked out, the truth is attained by bridging the distance. This distance is usually bridged only unknowingly: a journey is made which is not deliberately undertaken. At least the goal is not deliberately sought. This is the pattern found in the poem "Visiting Hsiang-chi Monastery":

> I had not known of Hsiang-chi Monastery
> When I was several *li* into the cloudy peak.
> Beneath ancient trees, an unused path,
> Deep in the mountains—from where?—a bell.
> Noise from a spring burbles over sharp rocks,
> The sun's light chills the dark pines.
> At dusk, by the empty curve of the pond,
> Meditation to subdue the poisonous dragon.

The poem begins with the poet isolating himself from men by asserting a limited ordinary knowledge of his world, in this case the existence of Hsiang-chi Monastery. Without saying what he has in mind (for the first couplet constitutes only a denial of a purpose), the poet moves towards and, in the last couplet, reaches the hidden monastery. At this point, in the last line, the image of isolation is repeated at a higher level: the figure in the last line, either a monk or the poet himself, withdraws from his world and from us into meditation.

Real journeys of course often imply a journey of another kind, and not always as subtly as in this poem. In the poems "Green Stream" and "The Shih-men Monastery in the Lan-t'ien Mountains," Wang Wei is explicit about the truth reached at journey's end. In the first, the traveller rounds a bend in the river and sees a spot ideal for living in retirement. In the second, the traveller happens upon five or six hermit monks, living peacefully unbothered by any knowledge of the world outside. It is of course a second Peach Blossom Spring. In both endings, the identification of man and nature is achieved by the fact of his finding an ideal natural end to his journey. Although the moral is obvious, the pattern of the journey is the same as the Hsiang-chi Monastery one. The journeys are made without a purpose, the discoveries are serendipitous, and the distances deceptive. It is just that in these poems Wang Wei depends rather on the charm of such qualities than on the profundity of the meaning. Two couplets from each poem illustrate this:

> To reach Yellow Flowers River,
> One must always follow the waters of Green
>   Stream.

> Hugging the mountains, it makes ten thousand
>   turns,
> The true distance no more than a hundred *li*.

> From afar I had admired the beauty of trees in
>   clouds.
> At first I thought we were on a different course.
> How was I to know the clear stream wound
>   around
> And led to the mountain before us?

Although in the journey poems, the distance is bridged and the truth temporarily seen, in other poems, the stronger theme, and I think the more profound one, is expressed that though the truth lies on the other side of an intervening distance, only across this distance is it knowable. This variant is less obvious than the journey theme and not directly stated. Therefore the tracing of this theme through imagery poses a problem of interpretation. A certain image might be more than an element in the scenery, it might contribute to the poem's meaning, but how much significance we are meant to find in that image is not specified by Wang Wei. Instead we have to bring together hints scattered through many poems to lend some weight to the reading of a single occurrence which might otherwise be a case of over-reading. There is no certainty, however, that in each case the same truth is being so delicately hinted at. These uncertainties do not exist in every poem; Wang Wei can be disconcertingly flat about his meaning. However, where the uncertainties do exist, in Wang Wei it is not enough to consider each occurrence of the image on its own.

The function of the image of white clouds, an image which occurs in about twenty poems, illustrates this problem of interpretation. In many of the poems, the reader feels that the white clouds must be a significant image, but what it is and what is implied in each case is not always specified. I would like to go into this in a little detail.

An example of the unfixed significance of white clouds occurs in the following poem:

> Playing on flutes, we cross to the far shore.
> At day's end, I see off my friends.
> On the lake, I turn back once—
> Around the hill's green are wreathed white clouds.

The poem is the eleventh of the set of twenty quatrains, the "Wang-ch'uan Garland," which Wang Wei wrote about various scenic points on his country estate. This one is entitled "Lake Yi." Is it as simple as it appears to be? The first two lines are purely narration. Are the last two lines more significant? Is it significant that the white clouds are placed last? I will return to this poem later.

In several other poems, the white clouds lie in the unspecified distance, and mark a place towards which some are headed and to which others long to go. It seems to be the ultimate and natural resolution of the scenes of nature described, the home of one's true self. Accordingly, the verb *kuei* ("to go home") is often used of going there. Examples are:

> I am returning to the foot of the Southern
>   Mountains
>
> . . . . .
>
> Where white clouds will never fail.
> My heart has always been in the green hills,
> As though to keep company with the massed white
>   clouds.
> Saddled for going home, beyond the white clouds.

These white clouds exist only in the mind, clearly a symbol for a longed-for place, though, unlike the Peach Blossom Spring, not a readily describable ideal place.

In general, no one is shown as having reached that place, although no difficulties are placed in the way of going. The white clouds are far away, but there is no implication that they are unreachable, or that one needs special qualifications—wisdom, unworldliness, etc.,—to make the journey. It is simply that they are described from a distance. People do live among the white clouds. For example, in lines quoted earlier, monasteries are located within the clouds. But those clouds exist only for the viewer looking upon them from a distance. In poems where one is actually at the monastery, it is only an inhabited monastery and white clouds are not mentioned. There is no line such as "In the midst of white clouds." In a poem about the majestic Chung-shan Mountain, when the poet "turns to look, the white clouds have closed up," but when he "enters it, in the blue mist I see nothing." The image is beautifully apt, for clouds do dissolve into mist when one is in them, so when the poet has covered the distance, he enters to see "nothing."

This double view of the same place depending upon the poet's location and emphasizing the inaccessibility of the place is seen very clearly in the poem "Lament for Yin Yao":

> We escorted your return for burial on Shih-lou
>   Mountain.
> Dark and green, the pines, the cypresses, as the
>   guests turned home.
>
> Your bones are buried under white clouds, for all
>   time.
> Only the flowing stream reaches the human world.

The poet has accompanied his friend's coffin to Shih-lou Mountain and seen his burial (lines 1 and 2). After his return, he visualizes it as the place of the white clouds, remote, its only communication with the world a stream.

The white clouds are most within reach when they can be gazed upon. The two together, the viewer and the clouds, define the boundaries of an ideal world. The poet's content is to sit and gaze:

> I walk to where the waters end

> And sit and watch the clouds begin.
>
> In the past we stopped on our excursions
> When we had come to where the clouds end.

Wang Wei admires a friend's study:

> I envy your refuge here:
> A distant view of white clouds.

Now let us return to the poem "Lake Yi":

> Playing on flutes, we cross to the far shore.
> At day's end, I see off my friends.
> On the lake, I turn back once—
> Around the hill's green are wreathed white clouds.

The poet has made a pleasant excursion out of seeing off his friends, and in line 3 he recrosses the lake to return home. When part way on this crossing he turns to look back, he is looking towards the place, and the day, he has just left: the green hills and white clouds show an untroubled serenity. What is the meaning of this sight? The recrossing of the lake has placed a distance between that day's gaieties and the quiet now. The white clouds confirm that distance; they reveal nothing of what had passed that day and hint at the finality of its pastness. Their presence—their passivity almost—is a comment on the pleasures of the day. That the image can bear the weight of such a firm closural function with some confidence is due not to the poem alone but also to the occurrences of the image in other poems.

It is interesting to see a later evolution in the white clouds image in a poem by Yuan Mei (1716-98). In this poem, "white clouds" has lost its faint capacity to hint at some meaning. The last couplet of a 32-line poem, the clouds nicely end the poet's visit to an unsophisticated village. Naturally the Peach Blossom Spring story is also referred to. I give the first and last couplets:

> I saw in the distance peach orchards in leaf,
> But did not know what village it was.
>
> . . . . .
>
> My one regret is that I must leave it;
> I turn my head; there are only white clouds.

The white clouds, the distance, peach blossoms, and rustic utopia have all blended together in Yuan Mei's easy geniality.

As an image acquires more significance, its vividness in nature begins to fade. The reader begins to discount the literalness of some of the recurring images: the white clouds in a sense had to be there across Lake Yi. The immediacy of the scene gives way before the philosophical meaning that is implied in the recurrence of the images. This is true of the sound of the bell, of the white clouds, and of other images such as the empty mountains or the woodcutters. As the literalness of the images loses force, the questions of the reader about the philosophical meanings grow stronger. As in the case of the white clouds, one could consider all the occurrences together in order to return to an understanding of one poem. Knowing how much to draw upon Buddhist thought as an extra-poetical context would help in these circumstances. We may learn for instance the weight of *pu chih* ("do not know") when it occurs without an object, and of *k'ung* ("empty"), so central a concept in Buddhism. In this paper I have suggested mainly literal readings because I want to emphasize that these words first have a literal function in the poem. The pattern of images I have suggested I hope will prove to hold on several levels and to remain an identifying mark for Wang Wei on the simplest level of the visualizable world he created.

Can poems be explained at a less elaborate length by referring directly to Buddhism? I think that it is a step which follows literary analysis. At this point, for example, we may ask whether the gazing upon clouds can be considered a secular form of contemplation. The unstriving movement towards knowledge I described as a theme is certainly familiar from Buddhism, as is the distance between humans and an enlightened state. I suggest that by fully tracing out a theme, one then knows what kinds of correspondences to seek in Buddhist philosophies. In other words the literary analysis precedes the philosophical one. The theme is after all expressed in literary terms. To say that "Visiting Hsiang-chi Monastery" is Buddhistic because it is a monastery the poet visited rather than because of other qualities in the poem eliminates its literary existence. The problem, however, with this approach—literary analysis preceding philosophical analysis—is that the answers tend to be restricted to a kind of perception of Buddhist influence that is probably too diffuse to satisfy those readers who feel vividly the Buddhist nature of the poems. These answers tend to boil down to the conclusion that certain themes thread through the poems because the consciousness that brought them before us was imbued with Buddhism. Only the themes perceived (and the examples selected) might vary with the analysis. What this approach cannot provide is an answer which states that these poems in their details specifically contain certain Buddhist views of phenomena and truth.

What if we began from the other direction, by considering the possible Buddhist meaning before the literary detail? Of the critics who do give examples of what they mean by the Ch'an nature of Wang Wei's poetry, few also explain how to read the poems that way. Tu Sung-po is one who does, and so I give his reading of the first two poems translated in this essay as an illustration of the direct philosophical approach:

> In Ching Brook white stones jut out,
> The sky is cold, red leaves thinning.
> On the mountain path, there had been no rain,
> The cloudless blue, clothes are dampened.
>
> —"In the mountains"

> All at rest, the cassia flowers fall.
> The night is quiet, the spring mountains empty.
> The moon appears, startling mountain birds,
> Which from time to time cry out from the spring ravine.
>
> —"Birdcries Stream"

Of "In the mountains" Tu Sung-po writes:

> Concealed are principles of Ch'an. The first two lines show that when the visible is exhausted the *tao* manifests itself (*hsiang ch'iung tao hsien*) and that the essential is revealed through its function (*t'i yu yung hsien*). The second couplet shows that the *tao* has no physical form (*tao wu hsing-chih*), but can be responded to and known. If one does not bring to the poem this kind of empathy, then he will see only the technical skill of the polished lines and completely miss what may be called the *t'ien-ch'ü* of the lines.

And of "Birdcries Stream":

> When a person is at rest, all reaches its quietest (*ching chi*). He becomes aware of the falling of the cassia flowers. His mind (*nei hsin*) and his setting (*wai ching*) are as one and thus he becomes aware of the emptiness of the spring mountains. Into this quietness enters a sudden stimulus (*chi*): the moon comes out and the birds cry in alarm. Thus is illustrated the sphere of stimulus (*chi ching*).

One great difference is that this type of interpretation can only be couched in Buddhist terms, for which I have retained the Chinese. Is it possible to arrive at the same explanation of the poems through literary analysis? Yes and no. In the poem "In the mountains," the second couplet has a certain mysteriousness about it (why are his clothes damp? is there a mist? why an empty sky rather than cloudless [for cloudless is my paraphrase]? why *yuan*?). One naturally asks whether the mystery spills over into the other lines and imparts a deeper meaning to the whole poem. For the literary critic, the question is raised by the poem itself in the unexpectedness of the description. I have no explanation for the poem myself, but Tu Sung-po does. Comparing his with the poem, I can see that the mysteriously wet clothes can be accounted for as an image of the nonphysical *tao*, but why involve the first couplet? Literarily the couplets are quite different, but the philosophies Tu attaches to them are of equal weight. If symbolism can be read into the landscape of the first couplet, why not into every landscape described? What are the limits?

The interpretation of "Birdcries Stream" is problematical in a different way. There is no mystery in the poem, and one could give the same description of the poem's development from silence to sudden sound without bringing up Buddhist terminology. The assignment of a technical term, stimulus, to the moon's appearance is the chief addition. What a Buddhist reading misses is that, because of the name of the stream and the title of the poem, the birds' being startled into cries turns the poem on one level into an etymological poem. The literary critic would raise a question about the poem's meaning only because otherwise it seems an inconsequential, though very nice, poem.

Tu Sung-po may well be right in both poems about Wang Wei's intent. There is no way directly to verify it. The Chinese tradition seems to allow an interpretation that parallels the poem without being anchored in it at any point. The oddest example is the way in which love poems from the *Shih ching* were used, according to the *Tso chuan,* in interstate diplomacy with perfect understanding on all sides. (The *Shih ching* poem sung by the envoy substitutes for speech and the poem's scenario is supposed to parallel the situation between the two states.) This is interesting because it is a well-documented instance of the complete confidence and total agreement with which certain poems were at one time understood—and yet from an external source, the discipline of folklore and mythology, we can say with some sureness that theirs was a misunderstanding about the nature of the poems. The question in Wang Wei's case is whether he intended his nature poems to carry a parallel philosophical life as some of the *Shih ching* poems did a political life. Short of external proof, the question is complicated to resolve. The position of the literary critic is conservative in not assuming any intention on the poet's part that cannot be discovered within the poem. Perhaps by this method, however, not enough meaning can be recovered from the poems to do them full justice.

There is overlap and empathy between poetry and Ch'an Buddhism, especially in rhetorical devices. Thus all critics assume that it is Ch'an which permeates Wang Wei's poems, though in fact which sect or sects he held to is not known. In choosing to write poetry, however, Wang Wei displayed no consciousness that language might be unable to express truths, as the Ch'an sect taught. Moreover, although there is empathy between poetry and Ch'an, between poetry and true Buddhist (or Ch'an) poems there is a great difference. In Buddhist poems written to convey a teaching or to voice a truth seen at the moment of enlightenment, the intent of the author is unmistakable: everything in such a poem stands for something else and the whole illustrates a lesson. The appeal is in the beauty of thought. In poetry, there is no such certainty about the creator's intent, and the appeal is in the beauty of language. There is no evidence that, devout as Wang Wei was, he ever attained enlightenment, though such themes hover around his poems.

However much these poems are Buddhistic in premise or inspiration, the level in the poetry that can be paraphrased by reference to Buddhist philosophies is probably not unique to Wang Wei. Poetry, unlike religion, values the language in which a truth is conveyed as much as the truth itself; the paraphrased truth of a poem deprived of the language of which it is composed may be no more than cliché, whereas the truth of religion is abso-

lute, unqualifiable by clumsiness of expression. It is by using the secular tools of language that Wang Wei has preserved for us so much of the beauty of his temporal world and of its eternal principles.

Robert Aitken

SOURCE: "The Old Pond," in *A Zen Wave: Basho's Haiku and Zen,* John Weatherhill, Inc., 1978, pp. 25-29.

[*In the following essay, Aitken analyzes a Buddhist haiku poem by Matsuo Basho.*]

> The old pond;
> A frog jumps in—
> The sound of the water.

Furu ike ya	Old pond!
kawazu tobikomu	frog jumps in
mizu no oto	water of sound

The form *Ya* is a cutting word that separates and yet joins the expressions before and after. It is punctuation that marks a transition—a particle of anticipation.

Though there is a pause in meaning at the end of the first segment, the next two parts have no pause between them. In the original, the words of the second and third parts build steadily to the final word *oto*. This has penetrating impact—"the frog jumps in water's sound." Haiku poets commonly play with their base of three parts, running the meaning past the end of one segment into the next, playing with their form, as all artists do variations on the form they are working with. Actually, the word *haiku* means "play verse."

The Japanese language uses postpositions rather than prepositions, so phrases like the last segment of this haiku should be reversed when translated into English: "water of sound" becomes "sound of water."

COMMENT

This is probably the most famous poem in Japan, and after three hundred years of repetition it has, understandably, become a little stale for Japanese people. Thus as English readers, we may have something of an edge in any effort to see it freshly.

The first line is simply "The old pond." This sets the scene—a large, perhaps overgrown lily pond in a garden somewhere. We may imagine that the edges are quite mossy and probably rather broken down. With the frog as our cue, we guess that it is twilight in late spring.

This setting of time and place needs to be established, but there is more. "Old" is a cue word of another sort. For a poet such as Basho, an evening beside a mossy pond is ancient indeed. Basho presents his own mind as this timeless, endless pond, serene and potent—a condition familiar to mature Zen students.

In one of his first *teisho* (presentations of the Dharma) in Hawaii, Yamada Koun Roshi said: "When your consciousness has become ripe by true zazen—pure like clear water, like a serene mountain lake, not moved by any wind—then anything may serve as a medium for enlightenment."

D. T. Suzuki once said that the condition of the Buddha's mind while he was sitting under the bodhi tree was that of *sagara mudra samadhi* (ocean-seal absorption). In this instance, "mudra" is translated as "seal," as in "notary seal." We seal our zazen with our zazen mudra, left hand over the right, thumbs touching. Our minds are sealed with the serenity and depth of the great ocean in true zazen.

It was in such a condition that the Buddha happened to look up and notice the morning star. As Yamada Roshi has said, any stimulus would do—a sudden breeze with the dawn, the first twittering of birds, the appearance of the sun itself. It just happened to be a star in this case.

In Basho's haiku, a frog appears. To Japanese of sensitivity, frogs are dear little creatures, and Westerners may at least appreciate this animal's energy and immediacy. *Plop!*

"Plop" is onomatopoeic, as is *oto* in this instance. Onomatopoeia is the presentation of an action by its sound, or at least that is its definition in literary criticism. The poet may prefer to say that he himself becomes that sound. Thus the parody by Sengai Gibon is very instructive:

> The old pond!
> Basho jumps in,
> The sound of the water!

Hsiang-yen Chih-hsien became a sound while cleaning the grave of Nan-yang Hui-chung. His broom caught a little stone which sailed through the air and hit a stalk of bamboo. *Tock!* He had been working on the koan "My original face before my parents were born," and with that sound his body and mind fell away completely. There was only that tock. Of course, Hsiang-yen was ready for this experience. He was deep in the samadhi of sweeping leaves and twigs from the grave of an old master, just as Basho is lost in the samadhi of an old pond, and just as the Buddha was deep in the samadhi of the great ocean.

Samadhi means "absorption," but fundamentally it is unity with the whole universe. When you devote yourself to what you are doing, moment by moment—to your koan when on your cushion in zazen, to your work, study, conversation, or whatever in daily life—that is samadhi. Do not suppose that samadhi is exclusively Zen Buddhist. Everything and everybody are in samadhi, even bugs, even people in mental hospitals.

Absorption is not the final step in the way of the Buddha. Hsiang-yen changed with that tock. When he heard that tiny sound, he began a new life. He found himself at last,

and could then greet his master confidently and lay a career of teaching whose effect is still felt today. After this experience, he wrote:

> One stroke has made me forget all my previous
>   knowledge.
> No artificial discipline is at all needed;
>   In every movement I uphold the ancient way
>   And never fall into the rut of mere quietism;
> Wherever I walk no traces are left,
>   And my senses are not fettered by rules of
>   conduct;
> Everywhere those who have attained to the truth
>   All declare this to be of the highest order.

The Buddha changed with noticing the morning star— "Now when I view all beings everywhere," he said, "I see that each of them possesses the wisdom and virtue of the Buddha . . ."—and after a week or so he rose from beneath the tree and began his lifetime of pilgrimage and teaching.

Similarly, Basho changed with that *plop*. The some 650 haiku that he wrote during his remaining eight years point surely and boldly to the fact of essential nature. A before-and-after comparison may be illustrative of this change. For example, let us examine his much-admired "Crow on a Withered Branch."

> On a withered branch
>   A crow is perched:
>   An autumn evening.

Kare eda ni	Withered branch on
karasu no tomari keri	crow of perched:
aki no kure	autumn of evening

Unlike English, Japanese allows use of the past participle (or its equivalent) as a kind of noun, so in this haiku we have the "perchedness" of the crow, an effect that cannot really be duplicated in English.

Basho wrote this haiku six years before he composed "The Old Pond," and some scholars assign to it the milestone position that is more commonly given the later poem. I think, however, that on looking into the heart of "Crow on a Withered Branch" we may see a certain immaturity. Though the poem certainly demonstrates his evocative power, that is not enough. Something is missing. What this haiku shows us, in fact, is quietism, the trap Hsiang-yen and all other great teachers of Zen warn us to avoid. *Sagara mudra samadhi* is not adequate; remaining indefinitely under the bodhi tree will not do; to muse without emerging is to be unfulfilled.

Ch'ang-sha Ching-ts'en made reference to this incompleteness in his criticism of a brother monk who was lost in quietism:

> You who sit on the top of a hundred-foot pole,
> Although you have entered the way, it is not yet
>   genuine.
> Take a step from the top of the pole

And show your whole body in the ten directions.

The student of Zen who is stuck in the vast, serene condition of nondiscrimination must take another step to become mature.

Basho's haiku about the crow would be an expression of the "first principle," essential nature, emptiness all by itself—separated from the world of sights and sounds, coming and going. This is the ageless pond without the frog. It was another six years before Basho took that one step from the top of the pole into the dynamic world of reality, where frogs play freely in the pond and thoughts play freely in the mind.

> The old pond has no walls;
> A frog just jumps in;
> Do you say there is an echo?

Jo Sanders

SOURCE: "Zen Buddhism and the Japanese Haiku," in *Anagogic Qualities of Literature,* edited by Joseph P. Strelka, Pennsylvania State University Press, 1971, pp. 211-17.

[*In the following essay, Sanders examines the importance of Buddhist enlightenment—called* satori—*to haiku poetry.*]

Zen Buddhism, which came from India by way of China to Japan, has had a great influence on Japanese culture in general and Japanese art in particular. Suzuki points out that "the idea that the ultimate truth of life and of things generally is to be intuitively and not conceptually grasped is what Zen has contributed to the cultivation of artistic appreciation among the Japanese people."[1] At this very point we find the closest connection between Zen and haiku poetry, that is, in their intuitive rather than conceptual apprehension of life which is concentrated into one brief, yet atemporal moment. This is *satori* in Zen, or what Yasuda calls "the haiku moment,"[2] the aesthetic experience in haiku. Satori is enlightenment (similar to the concept *wu* in Chinese), a self-awakening, quite similar to the *unio mystica* of Christian mysticism. The haiku poet may also experience an enlightenment, which is seeing reality as it is, seeing "kono-mama" or "sono-mama" (similar to the Sanskrit *thatata*): the suchness, the is-ness of things, with no value judgments as to goodness, badness, or the comparative worth of objects, but accepting everything just as it is. A glimpse into the intrinsic nature of things is afforded by haiku, the seventeen syllable brevity of which allows us one swift image of the world *en soi.*

Haiku is a form of Japanese poetry which is generally characterized by three main elements: first, its form, usually consisting of seventeen syllables divided into the pattern 5-7-5; second, the use of a seasonal word or theme; and third, the restriction of the poem to one scene, experience, or image. The best haiku do not directly express emotions or ideas; a concrete picture is presented

and its interpretation is left to the reader. As Otsuji indicates, "What is expressed in a haiku is a very small aspect of phenomena; yet what the poet experiences is the reality hidden behind what he expresses."[3]

Suzuki states that a haiku puts forward images reflecting intuitions. "These images are not figurative representations made use of by the poetic mind, but they directly point to original intuitions, indeed, they are intuitions themselves. When the latter are attained, the images become transparent and are immediate expressions of the experience. An intuition in itself, being too intimate, too personal, too immediate, cannot be communicated to others; to do this it calls up images by means of which it becomes transferable. But to those who have never had such an experience it is difficult, even impossible, to reach the fact itself merely through images, because in this case images are transformed into ideas or concepts, and the mind then attempts to give them an intellectual interpretation. Such an attempt altogether destroys the inner truth and beauty of haiku."[4]

The roots of haiku reach back to the very beginnings of Japanese poetry. Yasuda indicates that the characteristics typical of haiku: ellipsis, condensation, spontaneity, and nakedness of treatment, are already commonly found in the *katauta* form of poetry around 700 A.D. Related verse forms—sedoka, choka, and tanka—developed into the renga or linked verse, the opening stanza of which was called hokku and was written in the pattern 5-7-5. The hokku fulfilled a function similar to the use of the title in the West: it summarized the theme of the poem. From this hokku the haiku developed into an independent form as early as the fifteenth century.

The haiku has undergone very little change since its origin. The zenith of its evolution was undoubtedly reached in the seventeenth century with the poetry of Basho (d. 1694); since then there have been small peaks in the history of haiku, but the general trend in quality has been downward. In 1957 there were approximately fifty monthly haiku magazines being published in Japan and individual haiku appeared frequently in other periodicals. Henderson estimates that over a million new haiku are published each year, and innumerable others are written privately and enjoyed within a limited circle.[5] These figures would perhaps suggest a haiku renaissance today. There is indeed a renewed interest in haiku, but it must be emphasized that this does not necessarily indicate a spiritual renaissance; many haiku are written by poets who have never experienced satori.

In order to understand where satori is to be found in haiku, we must examine the concept of satori more closely. Unfortunately, the best one can do is hint at its innermost nature because, as in the *unio mystica* of Christian mysticism, one can work all around the essence of the experience verbally without really approaching the heart of the phenomenon. Blyth has referred to satori as a "spiritual orgasm".[6] Suzuki explains it as acquiring a new viewpoint for looking into the essence of things.[7] He tries to define satori by enumerating its most prominent characteristics, and it is striking how similar they are to the features of *unio mystica* reported by Christian mystics. These eight traits are:[8]

1. Irrationality. Satori is not attained by a logical process of ratiocination, and it cannot be explained coherently.

2. Intuitive insight. Another name for satori is *kensho,* which means "to see essence or nature." One perceives the essence of reality; objects become transparent. Satori is the knowledge of an individual object and also of reality which is at the back of it.

3. Authoritativeness. Because the satori experience is direct and personal it cannot be refuted by logic; it is sufficient unto itself.

4. Impersonal tone. Satori is a highly intellectual state, not an emotional one.

5. Feeling of exaltation. One feels a calmness and mild exaltation at the overcoming of the individual being.

6. Affirmation. This is not seeing things in a positive or negative view, but accepting them as they are.

7. Sense of the Beyond. The experience of satori extends beyond the personal level, although it never embraces the concept of a personal God as Western mysticism may do.

8. Momentariness. Satori usually comes abruptly and unexpectedly and is a very brief experience.

Although nearly everyone agrees with some of Suzuki's points, many experts would omit some of his characteristics and add some that he has not mentioned. A briefer listing of traits, yet one which is preferred by some, is the following:[9]

1. Illumination.

2. Thoughtlessness yet awareness. Non-distinction or *jijimuge* is the "unimpeded interdiffusion of all particulars."[10]

3. Elimination of dualism. There is no perceiver, no "perceived," no subject, no object. "The perceiving I is in one sense unaltered," explains Humphreys. "It still sees the morning paper that it knows so well, and the bus to the office remains unaltered, but the perceiver and the perceived have merged into one, and the two-ness of things has gone. The undifferentiated totality of things is, as it were, understood from inside."[11]

4. Stoppage of breathing.

Satori may be either a sudden or a gradual achievement. It may be totally unexpected or it may come after a series of steps or stages designed to lead one up to enlighten-

ment, such as the koans provide. However, even using the gradual stages provided by meditation on the koans, satori comes abruptly and often when one least expects it. Also, there are various degrees of satori, depending on the depth of the experience.

To achieve satori is to overcome the dualistic way of thinking; it is to become conscious of the unconscious. Only the experience which evolves from a person's inner being can be truly his own. His innermost being opens up its deep secrets only when he has passed beyond the realm of conceptual thinking to the sphere of the unconscious, of *mushin,* no-mind, which means "going beyond the dualism of all forms of life and death, good and evil, being and non-being."[12] The mind is empty of thought, as Takuan (d. 1645) demonstrates in this poem:

> To think that I am not going
> To think of you any more
> Is still thinking of you.
> Let me then try not to think
> That I am not going to think of you.[13]

In a state of mushin one may become egoless; the unconscious may go beyond a personal unconscious, or even a collective unconscious, to a sort of cosmic unconscious.[14] Hisamatsu calls satori "recognizing the real noumenon of a person, his original feature . . . [It is becoming] one who is unhinderedly free, released from all chains, one who recognizes himself truly, being no longer attached to the forms of matter and of spirit, one who faces the present world of existence and non-existence, life and death, good and evil, pro and con."[15]

Eugen Herrigel calls satori "jumping into a new dimension."[16] The first characteristic of the new way of seeing, he asserts, is "that all things are of equal importance in its sight. . . . They all seem to have acquired an absolute value." Haiku underscores the basic equality of all things when the body of a dead dog or a "horse pissing" near the poet's ear are not better or worse, no more or less important than Basho's frog or the cherry blossoms at Yoshino. Blyth correctly maintains that in haiku "man has no dignity, nature no majesty."[17] The truth of the universe is expressed in one small intuitive image. Let us look more closely at Basho's famous frog haiku:

> The ancient pond.
> A frog jumps in.
> Plop!

This is not just a serene landscape interrupted by a frog plunging into the water. It is this, but it is also much more: it opened a new perspective of reality for Basho. A Christian would say that Basho saw God in a frog as frog. The sound of the water "was heard by Basho as filling the entire universe. Not only was the totality of the environment absorbed in the sound and vanished into it, but Basho himself was altogether effaced from his consciousness."[18] Basho ceased being the old Basho; he heard the plop of the frog in the water and was enlightened. He saw the suchness, the is-ness of things; he beheld the world with new eyes. Reality became transparent for him in this experience of satori. Basho was not unprepared for this, for he had attained *mushin,* the state of no-mind, having gone beyond consciousness to the cosmic unconscious. In the middle of his selflessness, the sound of the water cut across his tranquility and caused him to perceive reality from a new point of view.

Satori is impersonal in that the Self has been overcome and an unconscious level below the ego has been reached. Haiku, too, must be egoless. The poet must not project his philosophy, ideas, or purposes into the poem; he is merely the person giving expression to the intuition. An example of haiku which is rather poor because it speculates against speculation was written by Basho:

> When the lightning flashes,
> How admirable he who thinks not—
> "Life is fleeting."

Humor is an essential element in Zen Buddhism and may also find a place in haiku, but wittiness certainly does not belong there. In haiku the poet must submerge himself in an object until its intrinsic nature becomes evident. Witty or speculative haiku come from without, not from within; they contain no Zen and certainly are never representative of a poet's satori. There cannot be such a thing as a haiku with a point; this device merely drags the poem down to the level of an epigram. Sokan's haiku does not succeed, in my opinion:

> If to the moon
> One puts a handle—what
> A splendid fan!

In haiku, just as in the Christian *unio mystica* or the Buddhist satori, there is a central point of silence, a *sanctum silencium,* which can never be touched by words. That is why haiku merely points, suggests, indicates; it never explains. In haiku as in most good poetry, the half is better than the whole. Moritake (d. 1549) goes a bit too far in making an obvious comparison:

> A morning-glory!
> And so—today!—may seem
> my own life-story.

The brevity of the haiku poem is by no means an accident. Kenneth Yasuda, Herbert Read, and Igarashi explain it as being the average length of the breath a person draws, and thus the length of the haiku is determined by the number of words one can utter in a normal breath. Yasuda calls this the duration of the state of "ahness."[19] That is, when one is moved by a scene, say the first spring crocus, the duration of one's wonder, as expressed by a drawn-out "ahhhhhhhhh," is the length of a breath. So too the experience works in haiku. This act of perception is explained by Read: "All art originates in an intuition, or vision. . . . This act of vision or intuition is, physically, a state of concentration or tension in the mind. . . . The words which express this vision are arranged or composed in a sequence or rhythm which is

sustained until the mental state of tension in the poet is exhausted or released by this objective equivalence."[20] Blyth agrees with this interpretation of the length of haiku: "The philosophic significance of 5, 7, 5 in Japanese syllables, may be this. Seventeen such syllables are one emission of breath, one exhalation of soul. The division into three gives us the feeling of ascent, attainment and resolution of experience."[21]

Blyth, in his authoritative four-volume work on haiku, sums up the spirit of Zen Buddhism in Japanese haiku: "A haiku is the expression of a temporary enlightenment, in which we see into the life of things. . . . Each thing is preaching the law [Dharma] incessantly, but this law is not something different from the thing itself. Haiku is the revealing of this preaching by presenting us with the thing devoid of all our mental twisting and emotional discoloration; or rather it shows the thing as it exists at one and the same time outside and inside the mind, perfectly subjective, ourselves undivided from the object, the object in its original unity with ourselves. . . . It is a way in which the cold winter rain, the swallows of evening, even the very day in its hotness and the length of the night become truly alive, share in our humanity, speak their own silent and expressive language."[22]

NOTES

[1] D. Suzuki, *Zen and Japanese Culture* (New York, 1959), p. 218.
[2] K. Yasuda, *The Japanese Haiku* (Rutland, Vermont, and Tokyo, 1957), p. 24.
[3] Otsuji, *Otsuji Hairon-shu* (Tokyo, 1947), p. 131.
[4] Suzuki, *Zen and Japanese Culture,* pp. 240-241.
[5] H. Henderson, *An Introduction to Haiku* (Garden City, New York, 1958), pp. 1-2.
[6] R. H. Blyth, *Zen in English Literature and Oriental Classics* (Tokyo, 1942), p. 176.
[7] Suzuki, *Introduction to Zen Buddhism* (Kyoto, 1934), p. 127.
[8] Suzuki, *The Essentials of Zen Buddhism* (New York, 1962), pp. 163-168.
[9] C. C. Chang, *The Practice of Zen* (New York, 1959), pp. 152-3.
[10] C. Humphreys, *Zen Buddhism* (London, 1949), p. 115.
[11] Ibid., p. 116.
[12] Suzuki, *Essentials,* p. 441.
[13] Suzuki, *Zen and Japanese Culture,* p. 112.
[14] Ibid., p. 110.
[15] S. Hisamatsu, "Zen and the Various Acts," *Chicago Review,* vol. 12, no. 2, 1958.
[16] E. Herrigel, *The Method of Zen* (New York, 1960), p. 46.
[17] Blyth, *A History of Haiku* (Tokyo, 1964), vol. 1, p. 28.
[18] Suzuki, *Zen and Japanese Culture,* p. 228.
[19] Yasuda, p. 31.
[20] H. Read, *Form in Modern Poetry* (London, 1953), pp. 44-45.
[21] Blyth, *History of Haiku,* vol. 2, p. 350.
[22] Blyth, *Haiku* (Tokyo, 1947-52), vol. 1, pp. 270-271.

Lucien Stryk with Kent Johnson

SOURCE: "Lucien Stryk: An Interview by Kent Johnson," in *American Poetry Review*, Vol. 19, No. 2, March/April, 1990, pp. 47-55.

[*In the following interview, Stryk, an American poet and translator of Zen poetry, reveals his thoughts on the work of Takahashi Shinkichi, the art of translation, and the nature of Zen in poetry.*]

[Kent Johnson:] *Your work in the past two decades as translator and scholar has been instrumental in bringing Zen literature to the English-speaking world. Your translations of the poems of Shinkichi Takahashi are among the work that has caused the most impact. Sadly, you received a call from Japan a few months ago informing you of his death. I was wondering if you'd be so kind as to reflect today on what his work and friendship have meant to you, both personally and as a poet.*

[Lucien Stryk:] The friendship has meant everything, and I have felt strongly for many years now that he was one of the great poets of the world. This obviously made my sense of him very special. I felt always, in his company, that I was privileged in being with a very great spirit. This led, I suppose, to my taking the greatest possible care with his poetry. The desire at all times was to give the English-speaking reader as full a sense as possible of this man's genius.

So because of the high regard I had for his character and his poetry, the friendship was very special; I would say, in fact, that the feeling was more familiar than such relationships tend to be. It certainly wasn't a literary relationship. I have a very great feeling for his life, not only as a poet, but as a husband and father of two daughters.

I also had a very strong sense of his position in the literary community of Japan. He, of course, benefited, as all would, from his special gift, and was recognized for it. But at the same time he was thought by many as something of an oddball, an outsider—his was a very special kind of position. The feeling, I'll tell you, was very exceptional, and I've never known anyone like him. He set the standard for me. I take it we're going to be talking about the nature of Zen poetry, or of matters along those lines, and perhaps I might say at this time that when I think of Zen poetry written by anyone, wherever in the world, it's always measured against what he accomplished. And this is something that I have become conscious of, if anything, more acutely in recent years, when I have been asked rather often to comment on the work of Zennists—some of the moderns who write what is sometimes termed "Zen poetry." There's always the feeling that he accomplished the very rare feat of expressing his Zen spirit fully through poetry. And this, I think, is very rarely achieved, in Japan or elsewhere. Now when we talk of the older Zen poetry, the sort that I included in books such as *Zen Poetry* and *The Crane's Bill*, well

there, of course, we have great masters and the pure expression of profound insight.

Takahashi's verse is filled with the depth of those older poems. He was of an extraordinary character, as might be expected of an enlightened man, given formal testimonial of his achievement by Shizan Ashikaga, one of the great modern masters. He is, in my judgment, unsurpassed as a poet of our day. What his person, his friendship, have meant to me, is very difficult indeed to put into words.

Judging from comments of his, Takahashi also thought quite a bit of you.

A very remarkable thing, for I had no idea why! What I think he felt was that I made a very great effort to understand him and to render his poetry as it should be in English. Takahashi read English, as you might know, so we worked closely with him through the drafting process. When I say "we," I am speaking, of course, of the late Takashi Ikemoto, my friend and collaborator on so many projects. A very interesting, often complex process . . . Takahashi gave permission in many cases for things in the original to be left out, simply because they did not work well in English. One of the best examples is in the poem "Burning Oneself to Death," one of the best known and most admired of his poems. There was material—about a stanza—that I felt was too discursive. Not in Japanese, perhaps, but no amount of trying could bring it over adequately into English. Hence he agreed, after discussion, that it would be all right to cut that out. This actually happened in a number of cases, and Ikemoto mentions this in his brief account of our translation practice in *Zen Poetry*. So in many cases you have pieces that are greatly compacted, but always with his stamp of approval. The creative element hence became enthralling, because, you see, I was given virtually a free hand in working with the material.

What Takahashi saw as my major qualification was my involvement in Zen thought. It certainly wasn't linguistic, because that work I couldn't have done on my own; I had to work very closely with Ikemoto and Takahashi. There was a sense of exuberance working on texts that were far more than poetry—they were documents, spiritual documents of the most important kind. And when *Afterimages,* the first collection, came out, there were responses that suggested the poems could indeed affect lives in a very profound way.

I remember Jim Harrison's essay in the American Poetry Review.

Yes, his was especially moving—and as you may know Zen is of deep importance to him. The work on the Takahashi poems has always been of that kind, a spiritual exercise, more than just the making of literary translations. Anyhow, these are some of the things I have felt for him.

I was aware that there were a few poems that were "compressed," where things were left out. But it seems some might object, on the basis that the original text was being manipulated.

I think that when the translator is privileged to work with the poet, it's not so much a matter of literalness, because, you see, the poet has made a judgment regarding the nature of what is being done. Takahashi's approval in some instances of deleting material came out of his understanding of the difficulties of bringing certain things into another language. The question of literalness is a central one in translation, of course, but I think in the case of our work with Takashi, we were seeking always to transmit—as "literally" as possible—the spiritual energy of the poem.

Could one say that the more highly charged the "spiritual energy" of a text—such as one tends to find in Zen poetry—the more open to interpretive possibility the translator should be?

Exactly what I have to do as translator of Takahashi is rise to the challenge; rise with passion and tact when that is called for. I've never thought of a translator as someone who should be an apologist, always worried, hat in hand, about the degree of faithfulness to the original. But as someone who when working intensely can spark those magical moments, when in fact he is the equal of the person he is translating—he must be that equal in order to render those poems properly. This is particularly true of Zen literature; an energy level as great as the poet's, a like degree of linguistic inventiveness, simply has to be there, there cannot be a gulf between such things. Otherwise there is only the husk.

When was your last meeting with Takahashi?

Two summers ago. It was when I was in Japan putting together *Triumph of the Sparrow* and also beginning an Issa volume.

Did he give you new poems at that time?

No, he was too ill to be thinking of new poetry. When I was with him that last time he couldn't even stand. You might remember my mentioning that he postponed a visit to the hospital to spend time with me. That touched me very deeply. But he had said the important Zen poems were behind him, and in his last years he was occupied mainly with prose, though far from prolifically. Actually, the poems I've translated were selected from a large group—they represent only that part of his work that I felt capable of dealing with. Other translators, perhaps, will attempt those other poems someday.

So many of the poems still overwhelm me when I think of them: Poems such as "Position of the Sparrow"—I have rarely found any work of poetry which is as compact and full of the deepest philosophical insight and velocity. It's amazing to me how much he was able to get into those verses.

Clearly, then, the work with Takahashi has influenced your own poetry.

I think profoundly. But I must qualify immediately. I don't mean I have hope of ever matching his greatness—far from it!

I think the best things I have done—and some of the poems in my new collection are perhaps among them—may have a trace of his velocity and the impact that comes of the arresting image. In others I'd like to feel I've won through to moments of stillness, though one must not counterpose stillness to energy—and often in Takahashi's work there is an amazing interdependence of the two . . . but it's very difficult to characterize one's own work. You are familiar, I'm sure, with Stephen Berg's book, *Singular Voices.* I'm represented there by my poem "Awakening," and I discuss it at some length. I think that poem shows to what degree there has been from time to time in my work an attempt at that kind of compactness and rigor.

Were you aware of Takahashi when you wrote "Zen: The Rocks of Sesshu"?

I was, though less completely. The thing about that poem to me is that it was, almost by design, an attempt to deal clearly and overtly with Zen principles. Later poems, such as "Awakening" are not ostensibly about Zen, but more personal, maybe take things beyond that stage into areas of further clarity and suggestiveness. Which doesn't mean, incidently, that I would dismiss the earlier poem. I would think of it as one of my lucky moments in poetry. But it so happens that at the time I wrote that I was clearly involved in trying to grapple with and straighten out my attitudes toward Zen at a relatively early stage of my practice. Now I feel that poems written about my immediate world, sitting out in my backyard, here in DeKalb, capture the spirit more fully than anything. There are poems in the last section of my *Collected Poems,* like "Where We Are," which I feel are as deeply grounded in Zen as the earlier, might one say, more "doctrinaire," pieces.

Or "Willows," which is clearly about your practice, yet somehow also a ceremony of place.

Yes, "Willows," and what makes that an important poem for me is that it represents a serious effort to come to terms with problems of discipline, when one lives away from the Zen community for long periods of time. That is, "Where am I?" and "What am I doing?," and "Is it still possible for me to feel that way?" and testing, pushing those questions to their limits. I found, in doing so, what I hope is a productive metaphor.

You used the term "a lucky moment" a few minutes ago to describe writing the "Rocks of Sesshu," and that seems a curious way of referring to a poem that took you two years to compose.

Well, there are "moments" and there are moments! You see, this poem led me to other things, opened up paths I had never suspected, and I speak of this in my essay "Making Poems" in *Encounter With Zen*. Incidentally, I had a very special experience recently in Japan, the time I saw Takahashi for the last time. I visited Joeiji temple where "Zen: The Rocks of Sesshu" was written and made—and I hesitate to use the term, but it certainly felt like it at the time—a spiritual return to the very house in which the poem was done. It was not occupied at the time and I was able to go to the very window and look in where that was experienced, when I stayed up all night, literally, beginning to think in the early afternoon and working until 6:00 the next morning, restructuring and reworking and getting a sense of what I might do with the haiku—like patterning that was emerging so insistently.

I had a powerful sense, looking into that empty room, that I had begun there something that was central to my life. I say "lucky," for in a sense the poem was sparked by my having said something shallow about the rock garden to Tenzan Yasuda, who did not hesitate to dress me down and to challenge me to look at it with fresh eyes. "Willows," I think, was another such moment. It is a poem that deals frankly with the difficulties of practice, and it seems to have struck a chord in others to whom Zen is important: a friend wrote me recently that he's at the "seventh willow"!

As long as we are talking about poems, let me show you this one, which is very recently finished. May I read it to you? (Stryk reads "Translating Zen Poems.")

That's very fine. The image of the vase . . .

It is written in memory of Takashi Ikemoto, of course. This poem was another return to a room—to the one in Yamaguchi where we sat together and worked. The memories of those days are very intense. It is from a new collection, *Of Pen and Ink and Paper Scraps*, which will be published in 1989, and I'd like to feel that it exhibits the kind of thing we've been talking of—where such spirit takes over the work when I'm lucky. Anyhow, I was very fortunate, of course, in having Ikemoto as a friend and collaborator. He was very patient with me, and there was a perfect balance in that he was a very careful scholar, with a deep appreciation of poetry. He knew that I would have to take certain liberties, but never too many, and often he would pull on the reins!

So it was a marvelous thing; we shared in the spirit of the enterprise and in all practical ways. It was a trusting and, really, a loving relationship—a rare thing. All of it a wonderful sense of our doing something important, not only to us, but to others.

This comes back to Takahashi. In his youth Takahashi was influenced by Dada, and his first book is, in fact, titled Poems of Dadaist Shinkichi. *I'm curious about the possible relationship between his intellectual and emotional involvement with Dada and his later Zen, particu-*

larly in regard to his poetry. It seems one could find analogies between the alogical dissociations in Takahashi's Zen imagery and those informing much Dada poetry and art. Are these similarities superficial, or is Dada and its iconoclastic spirit perhaps informed, at a deeper level, by intimations of Zen awareness?

I think in Takahashi's case the *predisposition* was clearly there, the movement away from all things conventional. For Takahashi the literature of 1920s Japan, certainly its poetry, was empty of spirit. And one day he was galvanized by an article on Dadaism which seemed to him absolutely what he was looking for. Well, Takahashi became the central figure of Japanese Dada, publishing a manifesto, his poems, even a novel entitled *Dada*.

He was quite confrontational during this time and was often in trouble with the police. You may remember the story, as I have told it, that he was in prison when his book of Dada poems was published. When he was handed a copy through the bars of his cell, he went into a rage and tore it up. You see, attractive as the feeling was, and as spirited as the work was that came of it, Takahashi realized that he wasn't doing anything for his life. It was that simple.

In Japan it's been a long tradition that when an artist needs help he goes not to an analyst, but to a Zen master. There's a remarkable story, mentioned in my interview with the calendar-maker in *Encounters with Zen*, in which Yukio Mishima sought out Shibayama-Roshi just before his ritual suicide and then canceled the appointment at the last minute. Who knows what might have happened had they met. Mishima was not a Zennist, but clearly there are instances of a Zen-like sensitivity in his work—no artist in Japan, really, can avoid being affected by Zen culture. And one might well find glimmerings of a Zen awareness in those Dada pieces of Takahashi, but—and this must be emphasized—not in any essential way. Perhaps it is useful to speak of the comparison on the level of the individual's psyche: Clearly, the state of spiritual completeness and harmony associated with Zen is quite different from the nihilism so often exhibited by those involved with Dada.

Now Takahashi wanted some advice and guidance and he went to the right man. He went to a man who was a distinguished Zen master, who would not be impressed by his poetry, but would see him as one who might use his poetry as an integral part of a spiritual quest, in handling koans, for example, as in the case of the poem "Collapse."

When he became a Zennist, naturally the poetry he wrote would reflect the kind of freedom Dadaism called for. But it was suddenly anchored in a very special world, with definite principles and clear aspirations, with concerns of a very special sort; the sort, of course, that Dada would never have. Dada had no concerns.

So he brought to his Zen inquiries that same freedom. And one might say he was prepared, as poet, for the kind of freedom that the Zen pursuit requires. But if you look at his poems with their wildness of imagery in mind, you find that when examined properly, they make the most absolute sense in Zen terms. There's nothing "dadaist" about his Zen poems. One thinks, for example, of "Burning Oneself to Death," a poem of profound spiritual and, I might say, political message. Of course, there is also much precedence in Zen literature for the kind of strange vision expressed by Takahashi—in the work of Kiso, Zekkai, Hakuin—and many others.

I'd like to return to the dynamics of form and content in Zen art, but since you mentioned the political implications of one of his poems, I'll pick that up and ask you about Zen's relevance to social issues today. In the Introduction to Afterimages, *Takashi Ikemoto writes of Takahashi: "He had read Marx and Lenin and set out to discover whether Marxism or Zen had the ultimate truth." What seems implied here in the counterposition is that Marxism—and even perhaps the idea of any activist stance towards social reality—decisively lost out to Zen. Could you speak on your views concerning the relationship of Zen art and culture to the social and political issues of today?*

Takahashi discusses his early attraction to Marxism in an essay called "Komu," an autobiographical essay, where he speaks of his youth and of the philosophical issues that preoccupied the young during that time. He was born in 1901, and Marxism was in its heyday—in Japan as elsewhere—during the twenties and thirties. So there was a climate of political excitement sweeping up the young intellectuals of the day, and Takahashi came to feel that too many were allowing themselves to be *too* easily swept up. It is in this sense that his option for Buddhism may be seen as a statement, as the taking of a stand. It was not so much a rejection of the nature of Marxism, as it was an assertion of the essential value of spiritual life. Very difficult point to make, and I'm not sure I'm making it well. But Takahashi was not then and never was "apolitical" or "reactionary."

You see, he could not compromise; the undertaking of Zen study is all-consuming. One cannot have, in Zen, two masters: one that guides and challenges the disciple to revolutionize his or her spirit, and another political or ideological one. But the full commitment to spiritual practice by no means precludes an involvement with social concerns. There is no solipsism in Zen. To the contrary, Zen practice may be seen as a ripening of the subject for a more profound and effective engagement with the world. In fact, this is the disciple's vow, to act compassionately for others. I have never encountered a Zennist who was anything less than hopeful about social progress, and indeed, the Zennists I've known were all strongly progressive in their views.

What is important to recognize is that in the Buddhist worldview, there can be no meaningful social change without an equally radical transformation of spirit. The coupling of these two tasks is, really, an expression of the Zennist's quest to break through the subject/object distinctions that govern our daily consciousness.

You mentioned that training is importantly a preparation to "act compassionately for others." Can "compassion" encompass activist positions that assume ideologically oppositional stances to the social order? One thinks of Gary Snyder, for instance.

Absolutely, and Snyder of course is our most eloquent spokesperson—and example in practice—for that joining of compassionate attitude and full commitment. Hard to measure the extent of his contribution—how the writing, life and political vision are so interwoven . . . an exemplary person, I feel. And of course, we have countless examples of Buddhist monks in Asia who have been visible participants in many movements and causes: against nuclear weapons, for human rights and democracy in various nations, against the war in Southeast Asia. One mustn't deny that there has been, at times, a quietist impulse. Snyder himself has spoken critically of this; certainly Zen has not had throughout its history a hegemonic stance in terms of social action. But, clearly we know that there is no fundamental conflict between Zen spirit and enlightened action. I would say that Buddhism has had, and *must* have, a meaningful role to play in movements for peace and especially in defense of the planet's environment. There is no question that the current disregard for the planet's ecology is a profoundly *spiritual* problem.

I had an interesting experience a number of years back. Let me tell you about it, as it may strike home with the things we are talking about. During the sixties, Alan Watts befriended me. He admired, and was kind enough to say so, the early book of mine, *World of the Buddha.* It was around the time of the '68 election. Watts was invited to give a talk at Purdue University and he suggested that I be invited to be on the panel, which also included Van Meeter Ames and a Japanese Zen Master. I myself had the highest regard for Watts's book, *The Way of Zen,* and found him to be a most generous person. Anyhow, Watts was the keynote speaker and he was very persuasive, because he was a very brilliant man and a thoroughly engaging orator.

There was a huge crowd and the election was very much in the air. McCarthy had spoken at Purdue the day before. During the discussion period someone directed a question at me, asking if my statement that "Zen would guide one's life in all ways," meant also that it would guide one's decisions in an election year. And I said that of course it would, and that it would tell you necessarily for whom to vote, and that if it didn't, questions might be raised about Zen's relevance to modern society. Now Watts did not receive this practical association too kindly, and I found him looking over at me with an expression of—should I say—marked skepticism! But I believed then and I believe even more today that, yes,

Buddhism does guide one in making choices in *all* areas of life.

Watts, then, viewed political involvement as interfering with spiritual life?

He might have explained it that way. But again, if you read carefully the books he was doing in those days, Zen for him was a very personal quest, and if one had personal problems and hang-ups this was a way of getting rid of them. I don't mean to sound critical here. He was a very brilliant man and his writings—especially *The Way of Zen*—will continue to affect lives for a long time to come. But I think there was a sense on his part that one could go too far in bringing Buddhism into the practical arenas; and certainly that concern was legitimate during the spontaneous atmosphere of the sixties. But for me Zen has a vital role to play in the moral and social issues of the day. The people I most respected in Japan—Takahashi and Takayama—expressed this clearly as well.

And yet you recently spoke of Takahashi's personal option for Zen over a practical involvement with the issues of his day. Could you clarify?

It's important that we make a distinction here between the period of formal discipleship, and what may follow a completion of study. One must also distinguish between the responsibilities of the disciple and the lay person with a Zen practice.

You know of the idea of "non-attachment" in Zen. I think that the non-attached state is not only desirable, but absolutely necessary. If one is going to make progress in discipleship, one cannot hope to work properly under the guidance of a master while at the same time attending political rallies and getting excited about things outside the Zen community. In *World of the Buddha,* I have a chapter based on a special sutra in Buddhism that is shocking because it suggests that a disciple should not only be apart from, but be virtually disdainful of all life outside the Zen community. The purpose—and I say as much in my commentary—is to lead to the kind of non-attachment that would make progress in a community possible.

Now this is meant, of course, to be abandoned. And the length of time will vary, from disciple to disciple. That attitude reflected in the sutra is meant to be supplanted by a healthy, positive attitude of commitment to all living things. But in the process of training there can be no divided allegiance. To an outsider, the intense, non-attached spirit of training in the early stages may seem indifferent, cold, lacking in compassion. And that can be a problem, I think, for many.

The assumption, you see, behind the principle of practicing non-attachment, is—and this may seem a paradox—that action is better performed when one is free of those concerns and concepts that will lead to a kind of unsteadiness; so that if one's hands are free to act without

being misdirected by a confused, agonized mind, the action will be all the more perfect. There will be no impulsiveness that might lead to harmful action.

Such as violence?

Zen is uncompromisingly nonviolent.

In relation to this theme of Zen and social commitment, could you comment on one of your better-known poems, "Cherries"?

> Because I sit eating cherries
> which I did not pick
> a girl goes bad under
>
> the elevator tracks, will
> never be whole again.
> Because I want the full bag,
>
> grasping, twenty-five children
> cry for food. Gorging,
> I've none to offer. I want
>
> to care, I mean to, but not
> yet, a dozen cherries
> rattling at the bottom of my bag.
>
> One by one I lift them to
> my mouth, slowly break
> their skin—twelve nations
>
> bleed. Because I love, because
> I need cherries, I
> cannot help them. My happiness,
>
> *bought cheap, must last forever.*

Yes, the poem is an attempt to deal with the suffering of others, not in a self-righteous way, but in the sense of recognizing my own complicity in their suffering. As we luxuriate in our privileges, others suffer; it is not enough to just recognize suffering and injustice. Many of us do indeed "care," and proclaim our opinions, but our lives are so often falsely lived: we go on, taking our pleasures for granted, not thinking that the root of the fruits we enjoy is so often the pain of others. I believe this very strongly, and I think that one might relate that poem to Buddhist Karuna or compassion. I can see it being read very much in that context.

I think we have to examine ourselves constantly. You know this more than most, perhaps, because of your work in Nicaragua; that experience must have helped you more clearly perceive these connections.

The poem works for me as a kind of "ethical koan," if such a thing is possible—a challenge to reevaluate the relationship of one's personal life to one's stated values. It seems that without such self-reflection on deeper motivations and desires, political values will become rigid and self-righteous? You're right that working in Central America opened my eyes to a number of things. It was a rich experience. But frankly, what's interesting to me is how easily upon my return I was pulled back again into the kinds of complicities you deal with in the poem!

I would say that to truly transform one's life—that's the task of Zen. And to be aware of that complicity, to feel that there is something infinitely richer, is a first, difficult step.

On a different theme, but which might bring us back in suggestive ways to some of the questions we've been discussing: Are you familiar with Language poetry?

I'm familiar with the term and I've read some samples of the writing, yes.

Well, as you might know, the Language poets have had a prominent role in the growing interest toward the relationship between politics and poetry here in the U.S. The political "content" of their work is not didactically posed, but rather implicit in the ways the writing itself unsettles conventional constructions of "meaning." I was wondering if you might find any points of convergence between this writing and that of Takahashi, in the sense that he also is involved, insistently, in defamiliarizing conventional ways of seeing and thinking. I've brought along a few poems from Michael Palmer, whose work I admire, and I thought we might use these as a point of reference. Is it possible to see in the ways that both these poets disrupt expected narrative frames, an affinity in attitude toward the relationship of language and world? That conceptual structures are not reflections of reality, but illusions? (Stryk reads "Dearest Reader," "The Night Sky," "Poem in Two Parts," "The Painted Cup" from Palmer's First Figure. *)*

I think the great problem with finding a similarity between such poems as these by Michael Palmer and those of Takahashi is that Takahashi would leave such formal kinds of concerns behind in attacking what Zennists would see as the important issues. I think theme dominates his most important poems, hence you have pieces such as "Position of the Sparrow," "Burning Oneself to Death," "Disclosure," so many others. These poems advance, of course, in very startling, seemingly fragmentary ways, but never lose sight of their central theme. I think the poems I've just read by Palmer would appear to be a denial of theme and reference. I think the poems are impressive on the intellectual level, and I might find, were I to read more, that there are other stimulations, attractions, interesting nuances, but not of the kind I could relate to the Zen poems I most value.

I was wondering if there might be points of contact in the attitude toward the "self." The Language writers are working to an important extent out of post-structuralist theory, and there is an implicit but consistent critique in the work of traditional conceptions of the unitary "I." Clearly, there would seem to be some analogy here to Zen's attitude towards normative perceptions of self. In a related way, it would seem both Palmer and Takahashi might share some affinity in their epistemological stances

towards the "outer world." That is, a strong sense that the narrative continuities we take for granted are not natural, but imposed.

An interesting question, but I would maintain that there is a significant difference. One cannot reduce the intuition of "non-self" to a linguistic or formal matter. And if one adopts the view that language is all pervasive—impenetrable, these poets might say—then one can easily get caught-up in the repetitive exercise of the "imitative fallacy," where "non-self" is mimicked through all sorts of disjunctions and fragments. Takahashi's poems go far beyond being mere critiques of standard ways of perceiving life; they are that, you see, but they are also profoundly assertive of realms beyond the linguistic. They are, we might say, studies of the "non-self," of the oneness of sunyata and tathata (respectively, the Buddhist concepts of "emptiness" and "suchness").

Now I must say that these remarks are given in a cautious spirit, as I do not know the work of the Language writers all that well. I am saying this all rather instinctively, based on the examples you have just shared with me. Certainly, I would be interested in learning more about the views of these poets.

But couldn't that avoidance of "theme" you were talking about in Language writing be valuable in that it might help re-direct our attention toward the fact of language itself, forcing us to pay more heed to the ways in which meanings are constituted? That is, help make us more self-reflexive about the "themes" that structure our assumptions about the world?

It may contribute. But what I would suggest is that fine poems of whatever persuasion or school do that. The fine poem by a Hart Crane, Dylan Thomas, or Wallace Stevens would exhibit all that finesse with language that would ask for the greatest kind of focus on words, the greatest concentration on the manner in which these words mean. I would think that the ideas that inform Language poetry are implicit in many important poems that *also* communicate with—are grounded in—the world outside language.

There are too many urgencies of life, demanding issues which make us constantly aware of our humanity and challenge our spirit. I suppose some would regard my views as conventional, but how can we forget about these things, or counterpose them to the interests of linguistic experimentation? That we must be aware of language, always look at it afresh, why, yes, this is at the heart of the poetic enterprise. But formalism can be taken too far, I think, and method become a substitute for the poet's responsibility to communicate in ways that can make a meaningful difference.

Your comments are interesting and raise, I think, further questions. Again, it is possible, I think, to find significant affinities between deconstructionist critiques of language and the Buddhist views toward self and conceptual thought. Nagarjuna's writings, for example, which are essential to the Zen doctrine of nothingness, posit that the space between the object and its sign is unbridgeable. Wouldn't the questioning of the assumptions we make within *language—an exploration of those linguistic gaps—be a legitimate undertaking from the Zen point of view? In fact, you yourself, in discussing the poems of Takahashi in the Introduction to* Zen Poetry, *quote Pingalaka to illustrate the Mahayana doctrine of interpenetration:*

> *If the cloth had its own fixed, unchangeable self-essence, it could not be made from the thread . . . the cloth comes from the thread and the thread from the flax. . . . It is just like the . . . burning and the burned. They are brought together under certain conditions, and thus there takes place a phenomenon called burning . . . each has no reality of its own. For when one is absent the other is put out of existence. It is so with all things in this world, they are all empty, without self, without absolute existence. They are like the will-o'-the-wisp.*

There are strong suggestions here, it seems to me, to what deconstructionist criticism would term the endless "deferral" of meaning in language.

Let me tell you that Pingalaka's comments are very much the Buddhist view. But as you can see, in order to express it, Pingalaka had to give us very clear images. I think that Language poems might somewhat suggest the *feeling* of non-self, but as with the danger of the "imitative fallacy," they could at the same time be expressing innumerably other things. Pingalaka, like Takahashi and all Buddhists who write of such things, gives us clear, assertive expression. When Takahashi is writing about denying self, or speaking of the disgust he feels with self, that is the *theme*. I don't know quite how to put my complaint, but it's just that the poems—and I take it that these are typical, even distinguished among the Language group—do very little for me, they don't direct my imagination. I would think that they tend to be less effective than surreal poems, which they might, at least superficially, resemble. But in the case of surreal poems, with their force and boldness, there is an assertiveness I think can be engaging. What I suppose I am asking is this: if Language poetry is meant to make us more aware of the ultimate ingredient—the word itself—what makes it so very different from a random selection of words taken from the dictionary, when examined very carefully. What is there about the poem itself apart from what I suppose might be seen as tonal unity—the words seem to be tonally chosen—what is there about these words which call for greater focusing and greater examination than perhaps would the random choice of words from any source? You see, what is so compelling about those words, why not turn to five pages of the dictionary?

Well, this actually brings up another question I had, which is the relationship between Zen and chance. There are American artists and writers—John Cage and Jack-

son MacLow come immediately to mind as artists deeply influenced by Buddhism—who would argue a deep value in chance operations. And actually, a technique employed by some Language writers has been to go to the "dictionary," relying partly on the force of randomness.

Yes, well I'm very much aware of Cage's ideas; I'm very much interested in them. MacLow I know less of, but I'm aware that his name is being increasingly recognized. In the case of the random element in Cage—and here, of course, we are dealing in sound—and I see the parallel and it's a very real one: why not just open your ear to the window, rather than playing Beethoven's Fifth for the five-hundredth time . . . the ear becomes accustomed to the pattern so that it no longer listens with the kind of attention sound deserves. Why not choose from the air, and delight in the pattern—it could be infinitely more exciting than one of those old war-horses thrown at us! There *are* wonderful possibilities in the sounds that come at us spontaneously from the wind, the sound of the cars, the sound of glass against glass, what have you. That I respect very much.

But language is very different, I feel. It doesn't so much come at us as that we go for it. In other words, the randomness is of a very different kind. Who knows if when we look at that page of the dictionary, the randomness is always pure? It seems to me that there are many other factors, pressurings if you will, that direct us, nudge us toward a choice. Of course, this is because words and our relationships to them are always bound up with meaning and the complexities of their signification.

Sound is different. The cry of a creature, and the wind's murmur, let us say, rise out of a pure realm, one that doesn't have its source—as language does—in reflective and conceptual thought.

Again, a personal experience, and one that I speak of in my interview with the aesthetician in *Encounter with Zen,* when we are talking about museum-going, and I say that there have been periods in my life when I had a sense that the movement toward the museum, the walking there, is more visually exciting than anything that happens in the museum. *If* I look as I should look, if I *look* at that face moving toward me on the street—*look* at it, couldn't that experience be more vital than what any painting could give me? The leaf, as I stop to look at it on the branch, or on the pavement, and what Morikawa says to me is, "Well, you can hardly expect me to agree with *that,* I'm an aesthetician!" But, you see, what I'm saying at that moment is very much what Cage is saying: whenever you look at something as it should be looked at, your learned concepts of what is "mundane" and what is "art" begin to collapse.

Yes, well then to go back to my question about the possible affinities between Dada and Zen, couldn't Duchamp's "found objects," for example, be regarded as an expression of—or at least a desire for—"pure seeing" and prereflective awareness?

Hardly. The Dadaists were, I think, searching for odd-ness, very deliberately.

This leads me into a question I had on the relationship between form and content in Zen literature and art. One finds a distinct difference in representation between, for instance, a Ryokan and a Takahashi. Or between the meditative quiet of the T'ang poets who were very close to Buddhism, like Wang Wei, Tu Fu or Li Po on the one hand, and the almost surrealist tone of your translations that appear in The Crane's Bill *and* Zen Poetry. *It seems one could draw similar distinctions between a Sesshu, whose most famous paintings seemed infused with a deli-cate stillness, suggesting at the same time a connection to traditional perspective, and the explosive boldness of a Sengai or Hakuin, whose works have a clear thrust toward abstraction, where the figure's representation is most tenuous. What of the relationship between Zen spirit and form? Are these different styles inscribed in different experiences, or perhaps different levels of en-lightenment, or is there a single source?*

Surely a single source. Now we have to make allowances for very great differences in temperament. We also have to make allowances for the fact that some Zennists, mas-ters included, have been strongly predisposed to the making of powerful poems. Others have been predis-posed to responding in ways that might be seen as more delicate. But one must in no way assume that these dif-ferences reflect a greater or lesser spiritual experience. I think that when you examine some of the Zen death po-ems you must have in mind, you will find differences in temperament—some poems as with Nansen, express a profound stillness; others, such as Dogen's, speak of shattering the very universe. Yes, one must make allow-ances for those differences in temperament that will re-sult in differences in expression.

I think that Takahashi, for instance, would have been seen as genius even had he not gone into Zen. He was, in a sense, the Japanese Rimbaud. But I don't think he would have become as great a human being or as great a poet. Those flashes which distinguish his poetry would still have been there in the formal sense, but of course, we would not have had the powerful resonances that came of his struggle with koans, with those giant issues set before all Zennists: the nature of time, the nature of space, those remarkable insights which derive from his pursuit.

The question is a very interesting one, and I'm sure si-lently asked by many who are drawn to the Zen arts. Why such great differences in expression between people who are part of the same tradition? But I don't think it would be proper to assume that the poem's *form* or its tone is necessarily an indication of the depth of the Zen experience.

To what extent might those differences in temperament and expression take place in a single individual involved with Zen and still reflect an integral spiritual experi-ence?

The feelings of the Zennist will differ according to all sorts of circumstances, but the spiritual feeling of the poems will bear a consistency. I think that each time there is the inclination toward poetic expression, what-ever forces would be generated by that *will,* will come to the surface. In other words, when the poem is triggered, when it is called for, all those predispositions which lead to the poem are funneled toward a determined end.

I ask, partly, because I find that in your own work there is a diversity; in the "Rocks of Sesshu," for example, where there is a terseness and compression, a chiseled quality, which seems to differ markedly from some of your newer work in Bells of Lombardy, *which is clearly more traditional, in a lyrical sense, than your better known "Zen" poems.*

This is a very good question, and I want very much to explain what I think happened. You may remember, from some of the things I have written, the term "man of no title." The Zennist abhors being pigeonholed. When I began *Bells of Lombardy,* I was very much aware that my better known poems had tended toward that terseness, into which I had tried to pack whatever insight and meaning I had received. I was aware of what my "style" was. And now I wished to write a different poem—one through which readers might wander, in the way they do through, say, a Wallace Stevens poem, tak-ing sensory delight in a richness and accumulation of image and phrase. Secondly because I felt I could do it, and wanted to.

So I wanted to see whether it might be possible to sus-tain, using the normal narrative and rhetorical devices, a symbolic structure throughout the range of the poem. And begin to have, through the recurrence of these more "lyrical" resonances, special meaning. Knowing, by the way full well—I think I knew—that I would be returning to a method much more evident in my work up until then. This is very much in the spirit of becoming the "man of no title," of not binding oneself, of remaining open to new challenges and problems.

But your forthcoming collection does represent a return to your more "recognizable" style? That of much of the work beginning with The Pit and Other Poems?

I think so, very much. No, I think *Bells of Lombardy* was a very special book. But I recall delighting at the time in its difference. And I still do.

As you know I'm interested in haiku, and I'd like to ask you a couple of questions on the subject. Here is a quote from your introduction to Zen Poetry:

> *The Zen experience is centripetal, the artist's contemplation of subject sometimes referred to as "mind-pointing." The disciple in an early stage of discipline is asked to point the mind at (meditate upon) an object, say a bowl of water. At first he is quite naturally inclined to metaphorize, expand,*

rise imaginatively from water to lake, sea, clouds, rain. Natural perhaps, but just the kind of "mentalization" Zen masters caution against. The disciple is instructed to continue until it is possible to remain strictly with the object, penetrating more deeply, no longer looking at it but, as the Sixth Patriarch Hui-neng maintained essential, as it.

Yet on the previous page you speak also of the finest haiku having a "range of association that is at times astonishing." Does metaphorization in the art of haiku interfere with or deepen the identification with the object itself? For example, is Basho's "Old Pond," read as symbol of the poet's mind, an obstacle to understanding the poem's transcendent nature, or a signpost pointing the way?

> Old pond,
> leap-splash
> *a frog.*

I think you might remember that in that introduction I draw the comparison between Pound's "In a Station of the Metro,"

> The apparition of these faces in the crowd;
> Petals on a wet, black bough.

and a haiku by Onitsura,

> Autumn wind—
> across the fields,
> faces.

I point out that in the Onitsura piece there is no metaphor, but rather that it stuns with its immediacy. I think that the greatest haiku avoid the kind of symbolization that tends to take place—consciously or not—in most Western poetry. The paragraph you read aloud is as true as anything I've ever written of Zen training or Zen experience. It *is* "centripetal." I have heard Zennists speak constantly of the dangers of mentalization, and they would see the seeking for similes and comparisons as instances of mind-drifting. I think that the most important examples of haiku probably come as a result of that *staying* with the object, exploring *it* for all its worth, finding within *it* the imaginative essence. I'm sure there would be exceptions, but if you take, for example, the great Buson haiku:

> A sudden chill—
> in our room my dead wife's
> comb, underfoot.

Well, there is no metaphor there. And I think there are very few figurative flights in great haiku. The directness, the simplicity, the extraordinary juxtaposition, that in its truest form *cancels* simile.

But what of the "range of association?"

The range of association is precisely the result. For example in the Buson, there is no metaphor to that. The complexity of sentiment that is generated by that act is what I mean by association. It isn't the sort of thing we might mean in speaking of the many different metaphors or images we would be likely to find in a "good" Western poem. There is a very great range of *association* in the Basho poem you mentioned, but not in terms of simile or metaphor.

Very well, but I believe I speak for many in saying that I have read Basho's "Old Pond" on a symbolic level, where the pond is the real pond itself, but also a metaphor for the poet's mind.

That is the way it is often read and quite properly. I think that it might be read on both levels, and why not? That profound symbolism is part of its greatness—and I use "symbolism" here in distinction to metaphor. In Western metaphor an image tends to stand for something beyond itself, and often in a subordinate relation to it. In the kind of "symbolization" we find in the Basho poem, there is a profound dissolution of categories; a pure merging of inside and outside.

I think that one has to know, in order to appreciate the poem as much as it should be appreciated, the circumstances of Basho's conversation with the Master Butcho. It is out of that exchange, and the act of the frog's leaping, that his mind was exploded and enlightenment ensued.

In the way that double reading is made possible, could it be said that haiku collapse the expected hierarchies of symbolization? In other words, that while in our tradition the symbol points to an "other," in the haiku the "suchness" of experience fully encompasses the symbol?

Take, for example, the great poem by Boncho:

> Nightingale—
> my clogs
> stick in the mud

How much that tells us of Boncho's sensibility. We might say the poem is "symbolic," in a narrative sense; we know here that an unusual man has been stopped in his tracks by a bird's song. And we may well imagine many things about the circumstances surrounding the event. And yet the poem simultaneously shatters the narrative connection, exposing the utter strangeness and mystery of the experience. Again, the range of association becomes infinite.

Then the challenge would be to penetrate that narrative level?

Well, I suppose I might say that great haiku ultimately challenge our propensities to make these analytical distinctions! It's curious, I had a meeting with two young poets in Chicago just the other day . . .

Not Language poets, I suppose?

(Laughing) No, though I do hope *they* would understand that my previous comments were made in a modest and non-contentious spirit—perhaps sometime I will have the chance to sit down with one or more of them also, and learn more about their views. But anyway, one of these poets in Chicago was telling me that haiku had influenced his work a great deal and that Issa was his favorite poet in the world. And though his own poetry bears no resemblance whatsoever to the haiku, he spoke to me of how the work startles him and of the way he receives impressive haiku. And he wants, somehow, to bring that spirit into his own work. I mention this, without being more specific, I suppose, because poems by Buson, Issa, Basho, the other great masters, make their impact *through* their method, without recourse to the kinds of elements and practices we seem to feel Western poetry would require. The bareness is the *marrow* of that richness. The Boncho, the Onitsura examples I quoted, make this so clear.

There is a relatively large and vibrant community of haiku poets in the United States and Canada—some of them like Robert Spiess, Marlene Mountain, John Wills, Elizabeth Searle Lamb, to name only a few, important practitioners of the art. But the haiku seems little practiced among "mainstream" poets. In fact, you do not seem to write any yourself! Why?

As for myself, I can only answer with the utmost frankness and risk, I suppose, seeming overly dramatic. Because I have worked now for so many years studying the great haikuists, I find myself powerless, simply not knowing how to begin. I have tried, I have found myself too much concerned, too self-conscious, in a way that I never am with my other writing. I am too aware of the shadow of Issa and Basho, of what this art has brought into being. It's a confession of which I am not proud. But I have tried from time to time, and always have felt the efforts were laughable in comparison. Perhaps those pieces I have come away with might have been seen by others as "publishable." I don't know, because no one except myself has ever seen them! I *do* think I understand the dynamics of haiku, their linguistic structure, their relationship to Zen spirit and principles. But I am afraid I have become too overwhelmed by what has been accomplished to be a true artist in the form. Now, my great hope is that as a translator I am successful in registering the excitement I feel. And I would like to think I have contributed meaningfully in this way.

Another issue is that as a writer of "normal" poems, the world I experience as an American living in Illinois rests, as far as making poems goes, on devices that would have to be seen as more traditional and Western. This is a very odd thing, perhaps. As you know, image and metaphor are very important to my work. The haiku on the other hand, certainly must have affected my work—even if unconsciously—when, for example, I composed "Rocks of Sesshu" or "Awakening." So the feelings here have a strange mixture.

Might that "silence" on your part toward the haiku imply you would consider it the highest expression of written art?

I believe very strongly that the finest haiku are among the most sophisticated expressions of human spirit, yes. No poetry has affected me more profoundly than the haiku of the great masters. But I wanted to return to something you said in your question about haiku not having found an audience among mainstream poets. And I must say that if that has been true, then things would seem to be undergoing a change. Robert Bly, for example, has been deeply affected by the art; Robert Hass, Sam Hamill, I recall, have written well on Basho; and W. S. Merwin, of course, in his fine, recent book *Finding the Islands,* explores the form in interesting ways. So I wonder if we are not seeing a shift toward a new receptiveness.

You have been involved with Zen for many years now, and a number of your poems have dealt frankly with the difficulties and frustrations of spiritual discipline. To return again to "Willows," which closes your Collected Poems*:*

WILLOWS

(for Taigan Takayama, Zen master)

I was walking where the willows
ring the pond, meaning to reflect
on each, as never before, all
twenty-seven, examine twig by twig,
leaf by pointed leaf, those delicate
tents of greens and browns. I'd

tried before, but always wound up
at my leafless bole of spine, dead
ego stick, with its ambitions,
bothers, indignations. Times
I'd reach the fifth tree before
faltering, once the seventeenth.

Then, startled by grinding teeth,
sharp nails in the palm, turn back,
try again. Hoping this time to
focus on each bough, twig, leaf,
cast out all doubts that brought
me to the willows. This time

it would be different, could see
leaves shower from the farthest
tree, crown my head, bless my eyes,
when I awakened to the fact—
mind drifting to the trees ahead.
I was at fault again, stumbling to

the flap of duck, goose, a limping
footstep on the path behind,
sun-flash on the pond. Such excuse,
easy to find, whether by willows
or bristling stations of a life.
Once more, I'm off. This time

all's still. Alone, no one to blame
distractions on but self. Turn in

my tracks, back to the starting point.
Clench, unclench my hands, breathe in,
move off telling the leaves like
rosary-beads, willow to willow. Mind

clear, eye seeing all, and nothing.
By the fifth, leaves open to me,
touch my face. My gaze, in wonderment,
brushes the water. By the seventh,
know I've failed. Weeks now, I've been
practicing on my bushes, over, over again.

You have devoted your life to Zen, and yet speak without
hesitation about being an "unenlightened man." To conclude this interview, I wanted to ask you: How can we be
sure that there really is such a thing as "enlightenment"?

We can be sure by meeting those who have experienced
it. It has been my great privilege to know intimately
people like Taigan Takayama, Shinkichi Takahashi, and
to see how their lives have been affected; to live among
them, to hear them talk, observe their interaction with the
world, to read their work, that is how we can know.

While "Willows" is, on one level, about disappointment,
I want it to be equally seen as a poem of positive values—an expression of an unenlightened man attempting
to better his life, who makes an effort to practice "Zenkan,"
or pure-seeing, so that he might go from one willow to
another, without being turned around constantly by inner
conflicts and problems. It is a mirror poem in the sense that
more than any mirror could show, the trees reveal one
after another the degree of my unenlightenment, the distance I would have to travel in order to find awakening.
And the poem, I suppose, might be seen in its final stanza
as humorous. Maybe it should be! It is in a way amusing
that I must lower my sights by "practicing on my
bushes." But I'm still involved and hopeful, and this is
the most important thing.

And we can be aware of the possibilities of Zen through
practice itself. Zenkan is difficult, but through it we *can*
come to sense, even if we never fully grasp it, that there is
something fathomless of which we are a part. I may never
become enlightened, but I can say that I am not the man I
was when I began. My hope, always, is that the change over
the years has been transmitted through the work.

Makoto Ueda

SOURCE: "Takahashi Shinkichi," in *Modern Japanese
Poets and the Nature of Literature,* Stanford University
Press, 1983, pp. 335-79.

[*In the following essay, Ueda presents an overview of the
literary career of the twentieth-century Japanese poet
Takahashi Shinkichi, in whose writings he observes one
of the few modern Japanese representations of Zen Buddhist poetry.*]

Takahashi Shinkichi (*b.* 1901) is a Zen poet, the only
poet of major stature in modern Japan who can be so

designated. A few other poets have shown an interest in
Zen Buddhism, but none has followed its rigorous discipline with such dedication and persistence. Shinkichi's
connection with Buddhism began in childhood, for his
father's family religion was Zen and his mother had a
profound faith in the teachings of the Shingon sect. When
he was twenty, he spent eight months as an acolyte in a
nearby Shingon temple. Six years later, after meeting
with Master Ashikaga Shizan (1859-1959), he embarked
on a serious training program in Zen. Although he did not
become a Zen monk as he had initially hoped he would,
he continued to attend Zen lectures, participate in Zen
meditation, and study under various Zen masters. By age
51 he had received from Shizan "The Moon-on-the-Wa-
ter Hall," a testimonial certifying completion of the entire
course of Zen training under the master. He himself has
recorded the experience of attaining satori, or enlightenment, more than once. He has read extensively in Buddhist literature and has himself written four books on
Zen. In terms of activities and attainments in Zen, no
other poet in contemporary Japan comes even close to
him.

And yet Shinkichi is a modern poet baptized by Western
civilization. He specializes in free verse, a form imported
from the West; he writes neither haiku nor kanshi, the
two poetic forms traditionally associated with Zen. In
fact, he was considered one of the most daringly experimental poets in the Western style when he made his poetic debut in 1923 with *Dadaist Shinkichi's Poems,*
whose title indicates its indebtedness to Tristan Tzara
and others associated with dadaist movements in Europe
and America. Although notices about dada had appeared in
some newspapers, Shinkichi's book was the first work to
attract much attention to the movement in Japan. If modern
Japanese poetry is an amalgam of East and West, Shinkichi
epitomizes that blend in a highly individual manner.

FROM DADA TO ZEN

Shinkichi first learned of dada through two articles published in a newspaper on August 15, 1920. Under the
headlines "The Latest Art of Hedonism" and "A Glance
at Dada," the articles reported on the current state of
literature and the arts in Europe and America, with a
focus on recent dadaist activities. Although the articles
were largely descriptive and showed no special enthusiasm for dada, they made a profound impression on nine-
teen-year-old Shinkichi. To borrow his expression, he
was hit over the head and knocked out cold. He was
particularly attracted to three comments made in the articles. The first was a citation from Tzara's "Dada Manifesto of 1918": "I proclaim opposition to all cosmic faculties that squirm in the putrid sun. . . . Dada is an
abolition of the future." The second was Walter Serner's
assertion "The world view is a confusion of words." And
the third was the report that dadaists often printed words
horizontally, vertically, and diagonally on the same page.
Shinkichi was not to see the articles again for the next
forty years, but he was to recall these comments over and
over.

For young Shinkichi, then, the appeal of dada lay in the aggressively assertive attitude with which it pointed out and ridiculed the meaninglessness of things. He had been leading a wretched life for several years before his encounter with dada. His first love affair had ended in frustration and sadness when the woman he loved married another man, and in his ensuing depression, he had dropped out of secondary school just before graduation, much to the chagrin of his parents. Leaving his home in Shikoku, he had roamed restlessly from one job to another; then, penniless and undernourished, he contracted typhoid and came close to death. Afterwards, he spent two months in a rehabilitation center in Tokyo as a charity patient, waiting to become well enough to return to Shikoku. The articles on dada, read at this juncture in his life, gave him hope that he might be able to rebound from despair by asserting it to the world. Recalling the significance dada had for him at this time, he wrote, "The word 'Dada' refers to a wooden horse in French; in Rumanian it is equivalent to the French word *oui*. Inherent in Dada, therefore, is a positivism that affirms all after denying and destroying all."

It took some two years—he called it an "incubation period"—for Shinkichi to begin writing dadaist poems. In August 1922, he made his first serious attempt to write free verse. The result was a poem entitled "Dagabaji's Assertion." Since Dagabaji is a corruption of Shinkichi's family name, the poem's title implies an assertion by the poet in thin disguise. "Assertion" here must mean an existentialist assertion by which to turn all negatives to positives or, more precisely, by which to eliminate all distinction between positives and negatives. The poem's two stanzas are:

> DADA asserts and denies all.
> Infinity or nothingness or whatever, it sounds just like
>   a cigarette or petticoat or word.
> All that oozes up in imagination exists in
>   actuality.
> All the past is included in the future of fermented
>   soybeans.
> Things beyond human imagination can be
>   imagined
>   through a stone or a sardine's head—so imagine
>   a
>   ladle, a cat, and everyone else.
> DADA recognizes ego in all.
> It recognizes ego in vibrations of the air, in a
>   germ's
>   hatred, and in the smell of the word "ego."
> All is one and the same. From Buddha's
>   recognition
>   there appears the remark "All is all."
> All is seen in all.
> Assertion is all.
>
> The universe is soap. Soap is trousers.
> Anything is possible.
> To a Christ pasted on a fan, jelly wrote a love
>   letter.
> All this is true.
> How could it be possible for nonsmoking MR.
> GOD to
>   imagine something that cannot be asserted?

Tzara's all-negating manifesto is echoed in such lines as "DADA . . . denies all" and "All the past is included in the future of fermented soybeans." Serner's assertion about words resounds in many nonsensical comparisons, such as those between infinity and a cigarette, between the ego and vibrations of the air, and between the universe and soap. Although Shinkichi did not have the poem's words printed in a drastically unconventional way, the orthography does include some unorthodox deviations. The words "petticoat" and "true" are written in *katakana* syllabary instead of ordinary *hiragana*, for no apparent reason. Roman letters are used for "DADA" and "MR. GOD," the former printed vertically and the latter horizontally. The traits of dada, as understood by Shinkichi, are unmistakably present.

The tone of the poem, however, is surprisingly affirmative. Whereas Tzara proclaimed opposition to all cosmic faculties, Dadaist Shinkichi asserts and denies all in the very first line of the poem and goes on to make more assertions than negations. He accepts infinity, imagination, the past, religion, the ego, the whole universe. His negations, on the other hand, are all eliminations of distinctions. He denies the distinctions between the finite and the infinite, between reality and fiction, between past and future, between self and others, between part and whole. Indeed, he is able to accept all because he denies all distinctions. The remark "All is one and the same" in the eighth line sums up the meaning not only of the first stanza but of the whole poem.

Undoubtedly the positive tone of the poem led Shinkichi to entitle it "Dagabaji's Assertion." The word "assertion" was retained when the title was changed to "Assertion Is Dadaist" upon its re-publication in *Dadaist Shinkichi's Poems* a few months later. The same assertive tone pervades other poems included in the anthology, although in degree it differs from poem to poem. It is less pronounced, for example, in such short pseudolyrics as "Three Dada Poems" and 66 verses collectively called "Poems of 1921," which make use of broken syntax, chance association, and arbitrary lineation. Still, behind the audacious pose and carefree style we sense a poet who believes in the interrelatedness of all things, no matter how disparate they may appear on the surface. The image of this poet becomes clearer in the longer pseudonarratives included in the anthology. "ShinDA Renkichi," for instance, introduces a poet who comes to feel, while watching another poet die, that the past has merged with the future. "Voice-copying Gramophone" portrays a sexologist who has ostensibly destroyed all the old myths about sex but who nevertheless follows a routine, everyday life with his wife and child. "Nosebleed" depicts a destitute Bohemian poet who finds no meaning in life and dreams of draining himself of all his blood, but whose suicide attempt turns out to be a mere dream. In these and other pseudonarrative poems the plot is muddled and the characterization sketchy, yet there always emerges a main character who perseveres in living on, even in a world that he knows is chaotic and hostile.

Shinkichi's concept of poetry during the dadaist phase of his career can be summed up in one statement: poetry is assertion. He had discovered that denouncing can also mean accepting, for through exposure to dada he had learned that a word meaning "a wooden horse" in French can mean "yes" in Rumanian, that things seeming meaningless on the surface can be meaningful in another sphere. Poetry gave him a means of presenting an all-inclusive, all-assertive world in which disparate things coexist, in which disorder becomes order simply by being what it is. To rephrase Serner's dictum, poetry for Shinkichi is a confusion of words that presents a world view.

Dadaist Shinkichi's Poems appeared in February 1923. In July 1924. Shinkichi published a long pseudonarrative entitled *Dada*. But the very next month, from aboard a boat bound for Korea, he threw the book into the sea as a symbolic act indicating his determination to part with dada. Three years later he did just that.

Shinkichi has repeatedly explained why he decided to forsake dada. According to his explanation, it was because he discovered dada to be merely "an imitation of Zen." Even while he was an eager follower of Tzara, he had noticed some similarity between dada and Buddhism. "Dagabaji's Assertion" includes more than one reference to Buddhism; in fact, its thematic statement "All is one and the same" uses a Buddhist idiom. Shinkichi's interest in Buddhism intensified as his fervor for dada cooled, until in 1927 he decided to become an acolyte at a Zen temple. Later he was to recall, "Because I did not know French, my dada was philosophically a Buddhist dada." The comment implies that Shinkichi, unable to read about dada firsthand, tried to interpret it in his own way; inevitably he did so in a Buddhist way.

What were the elements common to both dada and Zen, as seen by Shinkichi? He pointed out several in "Dada and Zen," an essay written more than fifty years after his dadaist phase. They can be summed up as antirationalism, indivisiveness or "oneness," dissolution of the self, absolute spontaneity, and mistrust of language. In Shinkichi's view, Tzara's staunch opposition to abstraction and conceptualization is like Zen, which does not teach a single "law" to its followers. Tzara's realization that "he existed nowhere" seems an echo of what is known as nonself in Zen; his effort to abolish all logical distinctions shares a common goal with the Zen ideal of oneness; his faith in spontaneity has its counterpart in Zen's "now-ness"; and his insistence on "the dislocation of language" appears to echo nonverbalism in Zen, which teaches that five thousand volumes of sutras amount to nothing more than the noisy cries of crows and magpies. The similarities between dada and Zen were not immediately apparent to young Shinkichi; hence his initial enthusiasm for dada. But as they gradually dawned on him, he chose to return to the Buddhist tradition. In Europe dada paved the way for surrealism; for Shinkichi, it cleared the way for Zen.

In October 1928, Shinkichi embarked on his first serious Zen training at a temple in central Japan. At first the rigorous program proved too much even for this young man with a strong physique, and he had to return to his home in Shikoku for several years to recover from physical and mental exhaustion. He had to give up his plan of becoming a Zen priest, too. But he never wavered in his determination to pursue Zen, and that determination has continued. His deep faith in Zen is reflected in most of the books of poetry he has written since his departure from dada—*Gion Festival* (1926), *Words in Jest* (1934), *Solar Eclipse* (1934), *Rain Clouds* (1938), *Kirishima* (1942), *Father and Mother* (1943), *The Body* (1956), *The Bream* (1962), *The Sparrow* (1966), *Afterimages* (1976), and *The Hollow* (1981)—as well as in several editions of *Takahashi Shinkichi's Collected Poems*. Since 1924 he has been a Zen poet, with the exception of a short period during World War II when he wavered between Buddhism and Shintoism. "I don't care how other people may criticize me for this," he once said, "but I know of no way to live except by articulating my cosmic view in poetry. My life would lose its meaning if I were to stop trying to preserve the tradition of Zen."

The cosmos that Shinkichi has endeavored to depict in his later poetry is a world of Zen and all that is held to be meaningful and true in Zen. With him, poetry presents—or represents—less nature than Zen-nature. This assertion, however, contains a basic paradox, for Zen disparages language and favors nonverbal communication, whereas poetry uses words as its medium. Recognizing this contradiction, Shinkichi once asserted, "My poems deny language; they deny poetry." How has Shinkichi resolved the dichotomy?

Shinkichi has addressed this question in several of his essays. In "Modern Japanese Literature and Zen," for instance, he stressed the uselessness of words in capturing the inexpressible essence of Zen and described existing literary works as "rubbish piled on the surface of our society." He did add, however, that at times pure gold was buried under the rubbish, and he concluded, "One might be able to enter Zen by way of literature, although inevitably it is a roundabout way." In an essay entitled "The Unsung Poet," he again disparaged the function of language and criticized poets and philosophers who believe that reality can be expressed in words. He then observed, "Poetry comes closest to truth, but it is not truth." The most direct expression of his view of the relationship between poetry and truth in Zen is found in an essay called "Under the Tower of Babel." Once again he begins his argument by minimizing the value of language, saying, "Words, whatever kind they may be, are forever incapable of expressing truth. We, the human species, who created words arbitrarily in our brains, have put up with expressions that do not exactly correspond to truth. Just as we are content with television, which merely shows images of people and things, we let our brains take care of daily life by using language because it is simpler to do so." He goes on to disparage literature because it is built on words, then reflects on the fact that he is himself a man of letters. The essay almost becomes a soliloquy at this point:

> What, then, do I want to say when I write? I want to transmit truth. I know I have just said truth cannot be expressed in words. Truth is inexpressible. And yet I write because I want to convey that very fact to readers.

> One might tell me that it is also impossible to convey the inexpressibleness of truth. To that remark, I would respond as follows.

> It is impossible to transmit truth to readers, but it is possible to make them verbally understand it. To those readers content with verbal understanding, one is able to present in writing something similar to truth. Because what lies in the presentation is not truth itself, those who try to understand it are wasting their time. The experience, however, may help them some day in some way. It may help them to grasp truth when they have a chance to do so.

From these comments one can gather that Shinkichi considers verse writing a waste of effort from a purely Zen point of view but recognizes in it some pedagogical value.

In brief, Shinkichi believes poetry is a verbal substitute for truth. In his view, truth itself can be grasped only by intuition, after a long period of meditation and other Zen exercises. As he has been fond of pointing out, all Bodhidharma did to attain satori was to sit and meditate facing the wall for nine years. Yet a beginning student of Zen needs advice and direction; consequently a number of books on Zen have been written in China and Japan over the centuries. The Rinzai school, in particular, has long utilized koan, questions to which there are no rational answers, as an important means of inducing trainees to break away from logical patterns of thinking. Shinkichi, whose Zen training was in the Rinzai school, is aware of the merits of koan and once observed that they contain something delicate and indescribable that helps students. Possibly he considers his poetry a kind of koan or a popularized version of koan. Most Japanese seldom have a chance to come in contact with koan today; even when they do, they do not gain much out of the koan because it is written in classical Chinese and intended for the use only of serious Zen trainees. In comparison, poetry has a better chance of being read by the general public. An attempt to approach Zen by way of poetry is, in Shinkichi's words, "a roundabout way," but few people in modern times have the time, motivation, or physical and mental toughness to undergo the rigors of Zen training. Shinkichi thought poetry might fill the gap.

The bulk of Shinkichi's later poetry seems consistent with such a view of verse writing. He does not write poetry with this view in mind; more often, the view comes to permeate his poetry as a natural outcome of his being a Zen Buddhist. Still, by way of poetry he has tried to give a verbal semblance of truth in Zen. His poems deal with such themes as nonself, timelessness, the Zen eye, nonattachment, nondivisiveness, enlightenment, and mistrust of language. They no longer show the explosive energy or the rebellious spirit that dominated his dadaist poems; rather, in a reflective tone and restrained style they try to activate the reader's mind by way of surprise or irony.

One can cite any number of Shinkichi's poems to illustrate those characteristics; a composition entitled "Death," which first appeared in the 1952 edition of *Takahashi Shinkichi's Collected Poems,* will serve the purpose. It consists of just one line:

> Nobody has ever died.

In terms of vocabulary and grammar, few Japanese sentences are simpler than this. But semantically the poem resembles a koan because it defies logical understanding. If there is one sure thing in this unpredictable life, it is death, so how can one say nobody has ever died? Shinkichi puts that question to his reader just as a Zen master would pose a koan to his student. No rational answer is possible, so to respond the reader has to try to go beyond the bounds of intellect. Few readers, if any, will be led to satori by pondering the question, but the experience may help them open their minds some day by some chance.

The implications of the poem "Death" become clearer when it is juxtaposed with the climactic scene of an autobiographical story by Shinkichi called "The Eel." The protagonist of the story is a middle-aged man by the name of Takeha Yasuzo, who all through his life has desperately sought peace with the world and with himself. He has tried Buddhism, Shintoism, and other possible means of salvation, but all in vain; people call him a madman, and indeed he has had more than one mental breakdown. Finally one autumn he visits a Zen temple for week-long *sesshin*—a program of meditation and study under a master. Unexpectedly, he is rewarded with satori. The enlightenment comes one afternoon, just before he faces his teacher in a personal study session. His mind has been especially serene that day, as he sits waiting for his turn outside the teacher's room. When his turn comes he strikes a bell with a mallet twice, following the rule. He cannot believe his ears, for the bell rings out with unearthly beauty, the like of which he has never heard before. In that instant a thought flashes through his mind:

> This is what it means to live. Like a sound, like a cloud.

> There is nobody who is living. We human beings are allowed to live. Like a sound, like a cloud.

> I had read volumes of scriptures and seen the word "nonself" a countless number of times, but I had never understood the true meaning of the word.

We human beings are like that sound. There is no such thing as the self. Only "nonself" exists.

The next moment Yasuzo enters the room and sits down facing the teacher. Later he cannot remember what he said to the teacher, but he does remember what the teacher said to him. "I am no match for you," the master said with a smile. "Go out and have a rest." The strict teacher had never said anything approaching this before, and as he left the room, Yasuzo was filled with incomparable happiness.

The poem "Death" tries to lead the reader to the state of mind attained by Yasuzo in this episode. As Yasuzo came to realize, nobody is living, and therefore nobody has died. To put it this way is nothing more than verbalization, and the reader who understands the truth at this level has understood it merely as a concept. Yet that is all poetry can do.

Shinkichi's longer poems are generally less cryptic and less like koans, but many of them similarly try to awaken the reader to some aspect of Zen truth. They frequently feature an animal: a cat, a mouse, a cow, a groundhog, a rooster, a duck, a pigeon—all are visualized as living in a Zen world. Shinkichi was particularly fond of writing about a sparrow. The poem below, simply called "The Sparrow," is an example:

    when the sparrow
      took a hop

    flowers
      withered away

    the sparrow's
      head feathers are ruffled
        and its chest feathers tremble
          as it crouches there

    the sparrow
      blinks its eyes
        and in that instant
    ten billion years of history pass

It is consistent with Zen that the poem should center on such a plain little bird, for in Zen there is no such thing as profound, esoteric truth; if there is something that comes close to it, it lies in everyday things seen by everyone. The third stanza of the poem, by painting an ordinary image of a sparrow, brings home that point and links other stanzas, which defy our usual ways of conceiving the bird.

Shinkichi's fondness for sparrows seems to have had its roots in a childhood experience:

    It happened when my older sister died and I went to the funeral, which was held at her husband's home deep in the mountains. She was buried in a graveyard in a pine forest located at the edge of a pond.

    As I was trudging toward home, I came upon a dead sparrow lying in the road. I was struck by the thought that the sparrow was my sister.

    I came to believe that my sister had been a sparrow.

    Since then, whenever I see a sparrow, I recall my sister who died young.

Note that the young Shinkichi saw a dead sparrow—not a newborn one—on the day of his sister's funeral. This was not a case of transmigration and rebirth, which is rejected by Zen. Rather, the sight awakened him to the oneness of a sparrow and a human being, and of the past, the present, and the future. His sister died with a physical sparrow but is living in a Zen sparrow that exists outside of time. The bird that appears in "The Sparrow" and many other poems by Shinkichi is such a sparrow, a creature that transcends all divisions and distinctions recognized by the intellect.

In technique "The Sparrow," with its clear imagery and indented layout, looks like an imagist poem. A good many of Shinkichi's Zen poems similarly try to suggest the essence of Zen through images. Others, however, do not. A poem on the nature of the human mind, entitled "The Beginning and the End," is representative of this second type. It also signifies a landmark in Shinkichi's Zen training, for it deeply impressed his teacher, Shizan. Shinkichi has not explained the specific circumstances under which it was written, but he did say something about the kind of problem he was having during his Zen training under Shizan at that time. In a short essay entitled "Blend Your Mind with Your Breathing" he recalled, "Once my teacher said, 'Leave your doubting mind as it is.' I did not understand what he meant. I was naive enough to think that he was referring to the idea that both beautiful and ugly thoughts lay in one and the same mind, that there was no distinction between them. Only recently have I come to learn that man's mind has no right or left because the mind itself does not exist."

No doubt it was after a similar awakening that Shinkichi wrote the poem "The Beginning and the End":

    One cannot say where the mind exists.
    It exists everywhere. The universe is filled with it.
    The mind is beyond being large or small.
    It never vanishes.
    It continues to exist after the body dies. From its
        viewpoint, there is no such thing as dying.
    This mind was present before we were born.
    It is never born.
    Nothing exists outside it.
    All that exists is the mind.
    One cannot say it exists.
    But, clearly, the mind is moving.
    That is the beginning of all.
    The mind always lies in the beginning.
    And it is forever ending.
    Everything is nothing but the mind.
    Between the beginning and the end there is not a
        hair's breadth.

When he sent the poem to Shizan, in return the old Zen master gave him a signed piece of calligraphy that read "I have set your mind at peace." As Shinkichi immediately recognized, the words were those of Bodhidharma's reply to Hui-k'o, a Zen trainee, who had asked, "I have been seeking the mind but cannot get it." The moment Hui-k'o heard his teacher's words he attained satori, and he later became the second patriarch of Zen. Shizan's reply to Shinkichi, then, was intended to do what Bodhidharma's reply did for Hui-k'o; it positively verified Shinkichi's attainment and thereby brought his mind to rest. It also indicated that he had correctly understood the teaching "Leave your doubting mind as it is."

Shinkichi has also written poems that are not ostensibly Zen. Generally these seem to be more popular with the reading public, since they are more lyrical and less abstruse. Yet in them one can still see the pose of a Zen poet, unobtrusive though it may be. Here, for instance, is a short lyric called "Flowering Rose Mallow":

> What is the rose mallow's whiteness?
> Its petals are whiter than snow
> as it opens in the warmth of a summer day.
> White as a distant cloud
> and translucent as tissue paper
> the scentless flower blooms with its head
>   drooping.
> What can it be? White and faintly echoing in the
>   eye,
> the dreamlike flower will vanish at a touch.

The poem has been praised for its lyrical beauty and is among the most popular of Shinkichi's works. Critics have said that it catches the pure, fragile beauty of the rose mallow, a beauty approaching yugen. One can appreciate the poem at that level, and many readers have done so. But another layer of meaning emerges when one remembers Shinkichi's remark "Buddhism is a theory that places nothingness behind matter." By "nothingness" he meant the void that contains all. If one interprets the poem from this angle, one discovers in its poet a Buddhist reaching for that nothingness. When the poet asks about the rose mallow's whiteness, he has started his quest for what lies behind the visible flower. He then notes a series of seeming contradictions: a summer flower whiter than winter snow, a distant cloud right in front of him, a flower that has no scent, and a whiteness that echoes in his eyes. Finally, by transcending these dichotomies he reaches the invisible reality behind visible matter, as physical reality becomes dreamlike and vanishes at a touch.

To conclude, then, Shinkichi's concept of artistic representation is a paradoxical one. In his view, art imitates nature, which is ultimately nothingness. In his younger days he often depended on dadaist means to reduce being to nothingness; in dogmatic assertions he denounced all systems by which people ordered the world. In his mature years he has concentrated on verbalizing various aspects of Zen reality, which transcends and yet includes the physical world. However, the essence of Zen cannot be expressed in words, and this creates a dilemma for the poet. Nevertheless Shinkichi has continued to write poems, believing that they may by chance give a clue to those striving for enlightenment. In a poem entitled "Footnotes" he wrote:

> Is that white thing a rooster?
> All words are imperfect; they are footnotes.

In his view, poetry is a footnote trying, in its imperfect way, to comment on a Zen text that is invisible to common eyes.

LIKE A CLOUD IN THE SKY

The titles of Shinkichi's essays are sometimes deceptive. In a piece called "My Method of Writing Poetry," he merely recalled his early days as a dadaist poet and mourned the alienation of contemporary poets from the general public. In an essay entitled "How to Write and Appreciate Poetry," he did describe how he appreciated three specific modern poems, but he said nothing about methods of writing poetry. His essay "My Poetry and Zen" is largely about the life of a Zen priest who risked his life to save a valuable copy of a Zen classic when his temple burned in a fire. The discrepancy between the titles and the contents of these essays seems due not so much to the author's irresponsibility as to a lack of self-awareness about the creative process. When he wrote down those titles on page one, Shinkichi was quite sincere, yet he simply did not know his own method of writing poetry and therefore could not write about it in the pages that followed. He probably has seldom thought about the art of poetry per se, for abstract speculation is rejected by Zen.

In his voluminous writings, however, there are some passages that touch on the subject in a casual manner and thus shed light on his idea of the verse-writing process. For example, in an essay called "A Talk on Poetry and Zen" he stated:

> In the *Analects* Confucius is reported to have said, "If I am to sum up in one sentence all the 300 poems [in *The Book of Poetry*], I would say they are free of devious thoughts." A composition written with devious thoughts can never be called a poem. In Confucius' view, a piece of writing that contains devious thoughts is nothing more than rubbish, no matter what strenuous effort may have been expended in its making.
>
> One must prize words that come to mind by chance and without premeditation. When my writing is a faithful record of what floated into my mind like a cloud in the sky, I do not have the self-loathing I usually feel whenever I read my own work later.
>
> Some might say that such a natural, spontaneous method of verse writing may be possible for short lyrics but not for epic poems like Homer's. But there are few long pieces in ancient Chinese poetry or in *The Collection of Ten Thousand Leaves* and

The Collection of Ancient and Modern Poems. Confucius' remark on poetry is valid.

The passages point toward three elements of the creative process that Shinkichi held to be important. The first is the need for a specific state of mind, a state free of "devious thoughts." The second is the casual, incidental manner in which inspiration visits the poet. The third is the spontaneous nature of the creative process, which dictates the brevity of the poem produced. All three elements follow along the lines of traditional Japanese poetics, with some noteworthy modifications.

Shinkichi implied that a poet must attain a serene frame of mind, devoid of all impure thoughts, before the verse writing process begins. This, however, is not a Confucian idea, for consciously or unconsciously he misinterpreted the words "devious thoughts." By these words Confucius meant ethically unacceptable thoughts, but Shinkichi used them to designate thoughts that are not natural and spontaneous. Thus Shinkichi's stand is consistent with Zen, which discourages deliberate, willful speculation. As a Zen Buddhist, he wanted to purge all calculated thoughts from the mind of the poet waiting for inspiration. To extend his metaphor, a poet's mind must be as clear as a cloudless sky; when the mind is ready, poetic inspiration will come as naturally as a cloud appears in the sky. Shinkichi once said, "I have written poems as they naturally emerged; there is no other way to make seeds of poetry germinate. One will never be able to produce moving poetry if one uses a method in the same way as one would cultivate flowers in a greenhouse or other man-made environment." Although the metaphor is different, the implications are the same: the beginning of a poem cannot be forced.

In Shinkichi's view, then, a poet is a passive agent who has to wait for the visit of poetic inspiration. He can take no deliberate action to make it come; instead, he must patiently persevere, always ready for the crucial moment. "He must always strive for it, until he finds himself doing so even in his subconscious mind," Shinkichi advised. "When he keeps trying for it, something accumulates within his body without his knowledge, until finally it seeks an outlet and comes pouring forth. Thereupon a seed of poetry germinates." Such poetic inspiration has various ways of manifesting itself, and the poet does not know when or how it will do so. Sometimes it emerges purely by chance in an unexpected place. For instance, one day Shinkichi was waiting for a bus at a bus stop, when suddenly the line "A railway station appeared before my eyes" came to his mind. Inspired by the line, he began composing a poem, which was eventually entitled "The Railway Station." But there are other occasions, too, on which some external stimulus helps trigger an inspiration. As examples of such stimuli, Shinkichi mentioned reading a poem or a book, seeing a movie, and listening to music. He might have added looking at a work of art, for he wrote the poem "Peach Blossoms and a Pigeon Painted by Hui-tsung" after seeing the Chinese painting of that title and "Yakshi" after seeing a statue of an ancient Indian spirit; there are many similar examples. An actual experience can be a stimulus, too. One of his better-known poems, "Dishes," was written while in his youth he worked as a dishwasher in the dining hall of a Tokyo newspaper press. He has also written many travel poems, such as "Mount Fuji," "From Pusan," and "Ruins of Pompeii," all based on actual experiences during his trips in and outside of Japan. In this respect, Shinkichi's theory and practice have been no different from those of most other poets.

Shinkichi's third point about the creative process is more unusual: he feels that a poem should be completed by the force of the initial inspiration and therefore that it has to be short. He believes that not only should the inception of verse writing be natural but the entire process should be spontaneous, too. Referring to the seed of poetry, he said, "Once a seed germinates, the rest is just a matter of waiting for its natural growth." He also explained, "It resembles what a baby goes through in the womb until the time of delivery." Both metaphors stress the naturalness of the creative process and reject a premeditated scheme or correction by afterthought. Shinkichi was more explicit in another comment: "Another method would be to jot down anything and everything as a novelist does and then go about cutting out the unneeded. But I seldom use this 'draft' method." Probably he fears that revision would destroy the spontaneity of the initial inspiration. There are exceptions, but generally he seems to have been faithful to his words in actual practice. Referring to the 1949 edition of *Takahashi Shinkichi's Collected Poems,* he wrote, "I scribbled those poems in the margin of paper scraps or notebook pages whenever they happened to come to mind. I expended no great pains in writing any of them; in no case did I follow a plan or make revisions by afterthought. To draw a comparison with painting, this is like a collection of rough sketches. But that very roughness may have resulted in a kind of artless beauty." He went on to note that most of the poems were necessarily short.

Shinkichi's liking for short, inspirational poetry does not necessarily imply that the verse-writing process, too, is short. Of course some poems may be completed relatively quickly, but in many instances Shinkichi seems to have worked on a poem over a period of time. His metaphors for the creative process, already cited, indicate this: it takes nine months for a baby to be born after its conception, and it takes weeks or months for a plant to flower after its germination. We have noted that *Dadaist Shinkichi's Poems* needed an "incubation period" of some two years after their original inspiration. In Shinkichi's opinion, inspiration can be retained intact in the mind for a long time, especially if it is strong. Of the poem "The Railway Station," he recalled that he wrote nothing for several months after conceiving its first line, but that the initial image was so vivid and powerful that it never disappeared from his mind. Finally he was able to write the second line; after that the words came smoothly, and he was able to complete the poem in several hours.

A couple of examples will clarify Shinkichi's idea of the verse-writing process. The first is a poem called "The Fly":

> I wanted to live for an infinity of time.
> Infinity was in a fly.
>
> At a flick of my hand
> the fly lazily glided away.
> Its leisurely manner
> awakened a friendly feeling in me.
>
> Late at night
> under a bright lamp
> and with the sound of rain outdoors
> I was reading a book.
>
> On the pages of the open book
> a fly
> happened to cast a lonely shadow.
> Like the fly's leg, infinity
> is slender and bent.

Shinkichi explicated the poem in an essay also called "The Fly." As he explained, he was reading a book at home one rainy autumn night when suddenly a fly came out of nowhere and flew over the pages of the open book. He stopped reading and watched the fly for a while. Presently, without being driven away, it flew off with a slow, feeble movement, looking as if its strength were almost gone. The poet never saw the fly again.

This incident inspired Shinkichi to write the poem. He did not say with which line he began to write, but he did mention that the first line expresses something that had been bothering him, perhaps unconsciously preparing his mind for poetic inspiration. "Every human being harbors a desire to live a long life," he said. "Although there are some who kill themselves, most people have occasion to wish that they could live for a thousand or ten thousand years if at all possible. I was no exception; hence I wrote that I had wished for eternal life." But then he had an awakening, after which he no longer wished to live forever. To make that clear, he wrote the second line. This line, he said, is extremely important but difficult to explain. "The more seriously you ponder the line, the more difficult it will become," he speculated. "Even if you spend your whole life studying it, you may not be able to solve the problem. This line demands that much contemplation." In effect, then, the second line is a koan. Shinkichi did not try to interpret it; he just gave some hints, one of which is a line from "Dagabaji's Assertion" that reads "Infinity or nothingness or whatever, it sounds just like a cigarette or . . . word." What he implied is the Zen concept of oneness: there is no difference between the infinite and the finite, whether in a fly, a cigarette, or whatever. To understand the true meaning of infinity one needs to attain satori; hence the difficulty of comprehending the line.

Shinkichi felt that the first two lines of the poem contained everything he wanted to say. But he did not stop writing at this point because he thought some people might want him to show why infinity is in a fly. In the lines that follow, therefore, he tried to describe the relationship between the fly and himself.

The second stanza defines that relationship as "a friendly feeling." No doubt the feeling was awakened in him because he saw an image of himself in the feeble flight of the late autumn fly. He said he considered calling the poem "The Winter Fly," since he was attracted to the lone fly barely surviving the cold autumn days. The words "lazily" and "leisurely" are significant; he saw the fly accepting its destiny with composure, neither fighting against nor hurrying toward death. There is a bit of fiction: in the poem he flicks his hand to drive away the fly, which he did not do in actuality. That change dramatizes his shift of mood from hostility to friendliness.

The third and fourth stanzas mainly describe the physical setting. The lateness of the hour, the sound of the rain, a man reading a book by himself—all enhance the atmosphere of loneliness and prepare for a climax in the last line of the fourth stanza. Explaining that line, Shinkichi said, "It depicts the lonely figure of a fly hovering, but because I myself cut a lonely figure one might say that the fly is my shadow, or perhaps that I am the fly's shadow." In other words, there is no distinction between the poet and the fly, between his life and its life, or between his solitude and its solitude.

Now that the relationship between the poet and the fly has been established and explained to the reader, Shinkichi comes back to recapitulate the poem's main theme in the two concluding lines. These lines echo the previous line "Infinity was in a fly" and elucidate its meaning through a more specific image—a fly's leg. Shinkichi explained, "Here I may sound as though I had a firm grip on infinity, as though no one else understood it better than I did. But I wrote those lines in view of such things as Einstein's theory of relativity, which says that the universe is mathematically finite." By his reference to Einstein, Shinkichi probably means to imply that infinity is itself a relative term. A fly's leg is tiny, fragile, finite—more poignantly so when the season is late autumn. Yet all that seems so because the fly is viewed from the standpoint of the human species, much bigger in size and longer in life span. From the point of view of the universe, man too would seem tiny, fragile, and finite. And the universe itself might seem tiny and finite in relation to some other cosmic system. One can go on and on in this way, infinitely. Shinkichi has demonstrated, then, that infinity is, and is not, in a fly.

At the end of the essay "The Fly," Shinkichi states that he made almost no additions or deletions in wording once he had written the poem. That is consistent with his idea of verse writing. Yet he made some changes later on. The poem was originally published in a newspaper in January 1951. When it was included in the 1952 edition of

Takahashi Shinkichi's Collected Poems, the following version was printed:

> I wanted to live for an infinity of time.
> Infinity was in a fly.
>
> At a flick of my hand
> the fly lazily glided away.
>
> Its leisurely manner awakened a friendly feeling in
>   me.
>
> Late at night under a bright lamp
> and with the sound of rain outdoors, I was reading
>   a book.
>
> On the open book, a fly
> cast a lonely shadow.
>
> Like the fly's leg, infinity
> is slender and bent.

A comparison with the original poem shows that the words "the pages of" and "happened to" have been omitted in this version. The change is a definite improvement, for it tightens the poem. The number of stanzas has been increased from five to six, whereas the number of lines has been reduced from fifteen to eleven. The result is a more proselike poem, creating a greater sense of calm and contemplation. The change, however, has reduced what Shinkichi has called "a kind of artless beauty."

The making of the poem "The Fly" reveals how a trivial incident may strike a chord in the poet's mind and set off the creative process. In the next example, the cause-and-effect relationship is more pronounced. The incident that sparked the creative process occurred shortly after the end of World War II, when Shinkichi was near physical and mental exhaustion in the chaos of war-ravaged Japan. Without wife or child and with hardly any money or other belongings (his apartment had been destroyed in an air raid), he barely managed to keep himself alive. Trying to gather the courage to live on, he began reading the Lotus Sutra, even though he had read it several times before without understanding its meaning. This time, however, he was deeply moved. He felt he understood something of the sutra's profound meaning, and he wanted to record the experience in words. "I was anxious," he recalled, "to sum up my feelings within myself and make a note of them for my later use. So I wrote the poem." The poem, called "Not Home," consisted of just three lines:

> Tell them I am not home.
> Tell them nobody is here.
> I'll be back in five hundred million years.

Shinkichi did not say how long it took him to write this poem or whether he made any changes after its first draft. He probably wrote it in a spontaneous manner because it is short, colloquial, and, to use his word, like a note. It also belongs to the group of poems he said he expended no great pains in writing. Perhaps its "artless beauty" appealed to Japanese readers, since it gained popularity

with the passage of time. The people in his hometown even erected a stone monument with the poem carved on it. Shinkichi is quite fond of the poem himself and once boasted that a poem of this calibre has been rare in modern Japanese poetry since Hagiwara Sakutaro.

Again, the making of "Not Home" is consistent with Shinkichi's idea of the creative process, perhaps more so than the making of "The Fly." He held that poetic inspiration can result from reading a book, and the Lotus Sutra sparked it for him. From the sutra he learned that "our life is not so simple or shallow as to fade away in five hundred million years or one billion years." To most readers, something like this is bookish knowledge. It had been so to Shinkichi, too, each time he read the Lotus Sutra before. But this time the book hit him hard, penetrating through the intellect and reaching the deepest part of his being. What he found in those depths, he did not spell out in the poem. One can surmise, however, that it was similar to a childhood experience he described in an essay called "Nothingness." One day when he was a young boy, he was walking along a path that paralleled a stream when suddenly a thought flashed into his mind:

> I am currently strolling alongside a brook lined by wax trees. Imagine a long string stretching from my present location to a spot in the past several hundred millions of years ago. Then imagine another string that similarly extends into an infinitely remote future. The two strings would be the same length.
>
> I am always at midpoint between the past and the future. If I walk a little over thirty minutes along this embankment, I shall leave the countryside and arrive in a city. But if I try the same experiment again in that city, the lengths of the two strings will remain the same. This is because both the past and the future have the same infinite length. The situation will be unchanged in fifty or sixty years, although I shall be an old man by then.
>
> I am, then, always at the same spot. Minute by minute the time I experience vanishes and is reduced to nothing. Both the time that has passed and the time to come crumble minute by minute, and there always exists nothing but my own self, located at midpoint.

This mystical childhood experience points toward the Zen concepts of timelessness, the void, and nonself. It echoes the words of Master Rinzai (*d.* 867), which Shinkichi was found of quoting: "There is neither Buddha nor the human race. There is neither the past nor the present."

In the end, however, Shinkichi seems to have remained unwavering in his belief that verse writing is a waste of effort from the point of view of Zen, even when it is done in a natural and spontaneous way or provides a record of inspired moments. He was not completely sure until one day he asked his Zen teacher Shizan to write Confucius' words "free of devious thoughts" for him. Apparently he thought to keep the calligraphy by his side as a constant reminder of the proper manner in which to write poetry. Shizan obliged, but on handing over the finished calligraphy he whispered to Shinkichi, "You don't need 'thoughts,' either." Shinkichi did not quite understand the meaning of the teacher's words at the time, but as he reflected on them afterwards he came to know what they meant. As a Zen poet he had believed he should get rid of all deliberate, willful ideas until his mind was filled with nothing but spontaneous thoughts. Yet Zen demanded that he eliminate even those spontaneous thoughts. The mind had to become completely vacant. Could a person with a completely vacant mind ever write a poem? There, again, is the paradox of the Zen poet. . . .

POETIC FORM FOR A MODERN INTELLECTUAL

As we have noted, the literary expression of Zen took two major forms in Japan, kanshi and haiku. The connection between Zen and kanshi goes back to China, where Zen originated. Following the example of Chinese monks, Zen adherents in Japan wrote verse in classical Chinese; this type of poetry reached its peak in the fourteenth and fifteenth centuries with the Zen-inspired poems known as *gozan bungaku* or "literature of the Five Mountains." Then in the seventeenth century haiku became associated with Zen. The most admired master of haiku, Basho, practiced Zen in his youth and incorporated it into his poetry and poetics. For many poets who followed him, writing haiku was a spiritual discipline not unlike Zen. Haiku, in turn, came to be considered a literary form capable of suggesting the essence of Zen.

Why, then, did Shinkichi not write kanshi or haiku? Why did he choose to write in a poetic form that was imported from the West and that, according to Seisensui, embodied a clearly anti-Japanese attitude toward nature?

Shinkichi was born a little too late to obtain the kind of education that would have enabled him to write Chinese with ease. If he had received a good education in nineteenth-century Japan, he might have gained enough proficiency in classical Chinese to compose poems in it. Natsume Soseki, born one generation earlier, could and did write kanshi. Shinkichi was able to read classical Chinese, and by all indications he read a large number of Chinese poems. His admiration for ancient Chinese verse, such as the poems in *The Book of Poetry,* has been mentioned earlier. He also read many Chinese Zen poems, as any Zen trainee is expected to do. But apparently he did not like *gozan bungaku;* to him, the Japanese Zen monks who wrote it seemed too concerned with the art of poetry. "Their works seem worthless in comparison with the verses of Chinese Zen monks," he observed. By reading *gozan bungaku* he undoubtedly learned the futility of trying to write a good poem in a foreign language.

Shinkichi has said why he did not become a haiku poet. He wrote haiku as a young boy, and he even had a haiku name, Makuwauri ("Melon"). Yet in a couple of years he stopped writing in seventeen syllables, for two reasons. First, his interest in writing haiku was vitally connected with a local haiku group of which he and his father were members. When the leader of the group, an employee of a large organization, was transferred to another locale, the group became inactive and Shinkichi lost his motivation for writing haiku. Second, in one of the haiku gatherings he heard an older poet predict the invention of a haiku-producing machine. The prediction shocked young Shinkichi. "I felt," he recalled, "that if a machine could compose every conceivable haiku, there was no sense in racking my brains to write one." Years later he realized that his argument was invalid, but he still could not completely drive misgivings from his mind.

Interestingly enough, Shinkichi has written more tanka, a verse form traditionally less close to Zen, than haiku. He does not know how many tanka he has produced, but he estimates the total to be fewer than three hundred. Below is an example, written one day in 1945 after an air raid had devastated a famous mausoleum in Tokyo:

> Trampling the hot
> roof tiles, I push my way
> through a bombed area:
> lying dead in my path,
> a blue sparrow.

As this example shows, the imagery and diction of many of the tanka have Shinkichi's stamp, yet his tanka are generally more incidental in theme and more lyrical in overtone than his shi. They give the impression of having been written in a more spontaneous manner and with a less serious intent. Except for a few that are tacked onto shi, Shinkichi has not included any of them in his collection of poetry. Apparently, like Takamura Kotaro, he does not regard his tanka as serious poetry.

The main reason Shinkichi has not tried seriously to write tanka or haiku in his mature years appears to lie in their brevity. He is not lacking in respect for these forms; as we have noted, the two poets he admires most are Basho and Shiki. He is also quite appreciative of *The Collection of Ten Thousand Leaves* and has said he recognizes "unparalleled beauty" in those poems. Yet he continued, "I look at them in the same way as I look at antique paintings; I do not feel like composing my own poetry in imitation of them." To his sensibility, tanka and haiku are archaic or are rapidly becoming archaic. "To be competitive with the poetry of the rest of the world, tanka and haiku are too short," he said, and then added, "I suspect tanka and haiku will be absorbed into free verse in the future." On another occasion he was more impatient and declared, "Tanka and haiku are already things of the past."

Shinkichi does not favor short verse forms for modern use, basically because he feels the psychology of a modern man demands a poetic form that is longer, more flexible, and more inclusive—a form that allows more than lyricism. In his view, human life has become considerably more complex than it was in Basho's time or even in Shiki's time, and many problems have emerged that cannot be solved by taking refuge in nature. Shiki's followers tried to modernize tanka and haiku, but they were not entirely successful. As an example, Shinkichi cited the following modern tanka written by a resident of Okinawa. The poem was inspired by an unfortunate incident in which an American soldier stationed in Okinawa shot and killed a local woman:

> A mother
> of three little children
> was shot to death.
> Perish, America!
> Perish, America!

About this tanka, Shinkichi observed:

> In this instance, the mother in the poem may stand for all Okinawans, who share the same ideology, or she may represent the whole Japanese race. But what kind of response did the author expect from the readers by screaming "Perish! Perish!"? I can understand how the author, on hearing about the callous slaying of a mother, was angered by the lawless situation and had to cry out in protest. Yet if that cry amounted to nothing more than this single tanka, it might be taken for the mumbles of a sick man in delirium.

Shinkichi was referring to the complex political and social reality that existed in Okinawa before its reversion to Japan in 1972. There was a great deal of tension between the American occupation forces and local residents; incidents like the one mentioned in the tanka made the issue more emotional. Shinkichi understood the situation and the feelings of people involved, but he was critical when those feelings took a form like this tanka. In his view, a tanka can powerfully express a simple, straightforward emotion but is too short to do justice to the totality of a complex psyche responding to a complex reality. He feels that because of this fact modern tanka poets tend to write rensaku. "But," he has said, "a verse form that requires thirty poems to make a point clear is not a suitable vehicle of expression for a busy poet. Doesn't it save our energy if we write free verse? I may seem to be promoting my own cause, but that is what I think." He said nothing about haiku in this connection, but the same statement can be applied to it as well, or even better, since it is shorter than tanka.

Shinkichi once made the same point from another angle, presenting a free-verse poem of his own that he thought could never be written in tanka or haiku form. It is called "The Turtle":

> The turtle has no basic doubts.
> He is on the side of the status quo.
> When confronted by a principle, he breaks down
>   and shows his belly.
> Look at the turtle paddling slowly in the waters of
>   morality.

> His muddy webs push aside the waves of culture.
> His head looks masochistic, yet it is too short for
>   self- sacrifice.
> His shell resembles a feudal castle.
> That amphibian fellow, always ready to
>   compromise and
>   wait for a chance!

> The turtle sneaked into a yard overgrown with
>   weeds.
> He plucked bashful white flowers, only to throw
>   them away.
> He trampled dark shadows the wilting grass had
>   craved.
> When a flower opens, the turtle spits on its
>   redness.
> He hates the depth of earnest love among the
>   verdant trees.
> He has a savage mouth.
> When he exhales, he does not think of the air he
>   will inhale—
> not in the way the earth thinks of evaporating
>   water when it lets the rain fall.
> With what peace of mind he spends his days, not
> knowing there is no such animal as a turtle!

> One morning the turtle forgot his coat
> at the Dog Star's.

> He must lead an indomitable life.
> Turtle, forsake those petty, loachlike pleasures!

> Would that happen if he denied life by death?
> Death is built on the foundation of life.
> All that is distant from the earth supports the
>   earth.
> If his shell is broken, the turtle will lose his life.

> War is a speed.
> A great speed is needed.
> Where there is no speed, there is death.
> Slowness is not the turtle's virtue.

> Will the turtle fight with the sun?
> Won't he be slain by sunset?

Referring to this poem, Shinkichi said, "In order to go beyond the realm of haiku and tanka (which specialize in nature poetry) and create a new form, I felt a need to write this kind of poem, which is intellectual in expression." One does not need his statement to see the point. "The Turtle" could never be made into a tanka or haiku, for its main theme, an attack on Philistinism, is too complex a subject to be effectively articulated in 17 or 31 syllables. If a haiku (or its comic counterpart, a senryu) were to treat the subject, it would merely smile at people content with the routines of daily life. If a tanka were to do so, it would cry out in protest at their follies as emotionally as did the Okinawan poet. In either case there would not have emerged a reflective, metaphysical poem like "The Turtle." Haiku and tanka are too short to develop a set of images as fully as Shinkichi did in this poem or to probe into a theme as deeply. The poem is longer and more intellectual than the average Shinkichi poem; the theme demanded that. It is a satirical poem, looking at people and society from a transcendental point of view not unlike a Zen Buddhist's. Free verse is a poetic form flexible enough to include all those elements.

Basically, then, Shinkichi has wanted maximum freedom of poetic expression. He rejected fixed verse forms because they seemed too restrictive and favored a verse form that could be long or short, lyrical or intellectual, traditional or radical. His general stand on the question of poetic form is revealed in a short poem entitled "Words":

> Words can be of any kind,
> form can be of any kind, for
> what must be captured is only one;
> it has nothing to do with words or form.

If the poem captures truth, Shinkichi couldn't care less about words or form. Because truth is difficult—ultimately impossible—to capture, he has wanted maximum freedom of choice in his attempts to set it down.

Shinkichi has had very little to say about the form and structure of free verse itself. He chose to write shi precisely because of the freedom of expression it afforded him; he would not want to restrict that freedom by favoring a certain form or structure within free verse. Nevertheless, when one reads his poems and essays one is tempted to make a couple of tentative generalizations. First, he seems to prefer relatively short poems. Second, his lines tend to be more assertive than suggestive, more philosophical than mystical.

In spite of his declared dislike for the brevity of tanka and haiku, his poems, excluding prose poems, are relatively short. In fact, he once observed that "the length of a poem would do best to remain within fifteen or sixteen lines, or twenty lines at most." He mentioned two reasons. First, he had read poems in the *New York Times* and noticed that they were all short. Second, he was too poor to produce a long literary work; he would starve to death if he were to write a long one! Clearly Shinkichi was not completely serious when he made these comments. The main reason his poems are short probably has to do with his high regard for an inspirational creative process. As we have seen, he believes that a poem must be composed by the force of inspiration; he considers a poem to be primarily the spontaneous record of "what floated into my mind like a cloud in the sky." Presumably inspiration, an intuitive insight into truth, is of short duration. Referring to the poems in the 1949 edition of his collected works, Shinkichi himself stated that "the diction is lucid and most of the poems are short." He was right on the last point, at least: of the 134 poems included in the collection, only one has more than twenty lines. Although the ratio of long poems to short is larger in other of his anthologies, most of his poems are shorter than twenty lines, and he has written a sizable number of poems that consist of only one or two lines. A one-line poem called "Death" has been cited; here are two more examples:

The Sun
The sun is shrinking every day.

Potato

In a potato
there are mountains and rivers.

That these are inspirational poetry is evident. The first poem records an inspired moment in which the poet transcended the limits of the ordinary human senses and acquired a cosmic point of view: measured on the astronomical clock, the sun is shrinking visibly every day. In the second poem, he went to the other extreme, viewing things with a microscopic eye. At one inspired moment, he thought he saw the world in a potato.

The poem "The Sun" consists of seventeen syllables; "Death," of twelve syllables; and "Potato," of twenty syllables. As far as syllable count is concerned, they may seem less like free verse than like haiku; certainly they are well within the standard syllable count of free-style haiku as proposed by Seisensui. Yet these short poems by Shinkichi differ from free-style haiku in grammar and syntax. The language of haiku deliberately destroys ordinary relationships between words, so that it can transmit truth that cannot be expressed in logical statements. Shinkichi's short poems do not; by and large they retain the normal grammar and syntax of Japanese prose. Each of the three short poems mentioned above comprises a complete sentence, with all its normal linguistic relationships intact. There is no way to mistake them for free-style haiku. The same applies to Shinkichi's longer poems: his lines usually make grammatically complete sentences. The only major features differentiating the language of his poetry from ordinary prose are frequent line changes and the omission of punctuation. Nevertheless, his lines strike the reader as being poetic because the statements he makes are striking. He shocks his readers by stating, in a grammatically perfect sentence, that the sun is rapidly shrinking or that nobody has ever died. He tosses out an enigmatic idea and hopes it will awaken in readers thoughts to which they have never been exposed before. This is fundamentally different from the method of haiku, which stimulates a reader's imagination by presenting a grammatically incomplete sentence. Shinkichi's method is more intellectual. It appeals to modern Japanese readers, who have been exposed to too much Western literature and philosophy to have complete faith in an anti-intellectual approach to truth. Ultimately, Shinkichi is anti-intellectual; more precisely, he wants to go beyond intellect. But he goes through the intellect to reach for the realm beyond it, and he knows many contemporary readers cannot bypass intellect as some haiku poets seem to do. A lifelong concern with the dichotomy between science and religion also stems from his refusal to underestimate the achievements of intellect in modern times. He wants to write poetry from the perspective of a modern man, a man well aware of the potential of human intellect. The language of his poetry reflects this fact.

The structure of Shinkichi's poems often follows the line of his philosophical speculation, and as a result the poem looks like a philosopher's monologue. The poem's unity is attained through a progression of thoughts expressed in a sequence of complete sentences. Unlike Hagiwara Sakutaro, who tried to verbalize feelings before they became ideas, Shinkichi waits until feelings harden into ideas and then speculates about them. In this respect he is more a philosopher than a poet, and some of his poems indeed look like aphorisms. On the other hand, he is distinctly a poet in relying on images, metaphors, and symbols in giving form to his thoughts. He could be said to be a metaphysical poet, although he has never called himself such.

On the whole, however, no generalizations about Shinkichi's structural method hold true, for it is too diverse. He rejected tanka and haiku because of their formal restrictiveness, and he would not like to be confined to any specific method of unifying a poem. With him, a poem is the outcome of meditation, and its structure and wording must be free to follow the way in which his meditation progresses. The structure can be logical, associational, or narrative, depending on the way his cogitations evolve at the time. He conceives shi to be an all-inclusive verse form freely allowing him to do all these things; that must be part of the reason he thinks free verse will in time absorb both tanka and haiku. The language of his poetry is as flexible as free verse can be.

FOR THOSE WHO DO NOT HEAR THE ROOSTER

A good deal has already been said about Shinkichi's view of the use of poetry. In general, it is not very favorable. At times, when provoked, he has even conceded that poetry is not only useless but harmful. As we have seen, poetry seemed to him nothing more than "rubbish" at one time, "footnotes" at another. Similar derogatory words abound in his writings. The most disparaging of all appear in the essay "The True Nature of the Poet," in which he called poets liars, thieves, and father-killers. Although much of this abuse is rhetorical, there is no doubt that he assigns a secondary importance to poetry in his scheme of things. Of prime importance to him is religion. For a brief period of his life that religion was dada; then it was replaced by Zen Buddhism.

During Shinkichi's dadaist phase, poetry functioned as a vehicle for making assertions and thereby transforming negatives into positives. Believing with Serner that "the world view is a confusion of words," he found poetry useful because it provided explosive power with which to destroy existing systems of thought and reduce them to more primordial, preintellectual matter. Presumably he could have done the same in prose, yet poetry is more pliant in form, more capable of being loaded with intense mental energy. It can express the spirit of rebellion in a freer, more immediate, and therefore more forceful form. As Shinkichi portrayed himself in "ShinDA Renkichi":

> I write with a finger.
> I write with snot.

> I write on a piece of soiled toilet paper.
> For those who drink seminal discharge with a
> tobacco pipe
> my poetry has no use.

His poetry was useless for the genteel middle-class, but served a function for a youthful rebel.

In this concept, poetry is ultimately a means to an end. Young Shinkichi was trying to find a way to come to terms with himself and the world; he thought dada showed him one such way. To him, dada was more a mode of thinking and living than a literary and artistic movement, and unlike many European dadaists, he made almost no effort to propagate dada among his fellow poets and artists. He was content that it help him in his own spiritual quest. Writing poetry provided him with an effective means of making dadaist assertions and thereby striving for the end he sought. Thus it was relatively easy for him to give up being a poet and become a Zen trainee in 1928, because he was first and foremost a seeker for a better spiritual life. He had been a poet only secondarily.

The role of poetry became even less significant in Shinkichi's thought after his serious commitment to Zen. Indeed, his earlier exposure to poetry came to seem a drawback when he began his Zen training. He recalled:

> I continued to write poetry and prose fiction only
> to make a living; my heart was not with literature
> but with Buddhism. I read a great deal of Buddhist
> literature indiscriminately, trying to search out the
> essence of Zen by way of literature. All that was
> a waste of time and energy; many times I stumbled,
> hurt myself, and had to beat a retreat.

He was implying that his orientation as a poet was a disadvantage in his quest for satori. When he was a dadaist, poetry was at least of help in pursuing his goal, but as a Zen student he found literature harmful.

Poetry can be harmful in Zen training because the poet uses words; thus he may be deluded into thinking that he can express truth in words. From a Zen point of view, seeking truth by means of language is as hopeless as trying to complete the Tower of Babel. After all, words are a product of the mind, and the thinking mind represents only one—and a nonessential—part of human life. "I do not believe," Shinkichi said, "that the functions of my mind are related to the whole of my being. I believe my mind is performing its functions on its own within just one part of my being." In his view, there is another, more essential part. That part can be reached, he thinks, only through Zen exercises.

Zen and Buddhism have lost much of their popular appeal in modern times. Since Japan under the Meiji government decided on wholesale Westernization, people have become believers in science instead of religion. "It would not be an exaggeration to say," Shinkichi once observed, "that due to the Meiji government's anti-Buddhist policy, as well as to the invasion of Marxism and Leninism, virtually no Japanese has continued to believe in Buddha or to study Buddhism." His assessment of the situation is basically correct, although he has indeed exaggerated, despite his protestation to the contrary. Buddhism has become only a nominal religion for many Japanese, no longer providing them with a way of coming to grips with their existence.

Here Shinkichi saw a potential use for literature in general and for poetry in particular. Many Japanese have stopped going to temples in search of salvation, but they read novels, short stories, and poems. Shinkichi sees much contemporary literature as nothing more than "rubbish piled on the surface of our society," yet sometimes, he thinks, pure gold may be buried beneath the rubbish. To quote his words again: "One might be able to enter Zen by way of literature, although inevitably it is a roundabout way." It is a roundabout way because literature is dependent on words. But literature has a universal appeal. For the general public, it is more approachable than Zen.

For Shinkichi, then, literature is most useful when it helps readers in their quest for religious truth, even though it can do so only in an indirect way. Literature can be no more than a verbal substitute for truth, but it may serve as a catalyst in their quest some day. Poetry, in particular, is capable of functioning as a Zen koan because of its capacity to be more illogical, more provocative, and more removed from everyday reality than prose. To Shinkichi's way of thinking, poetry is most useful when it acts as a koan—when it plunges the reader's mind into a Zen type of meditation. Shinkichi has written many poems of this kind in his later years. His poem "Death," for instance, tries to open readers' eyes to the eternity of cosmic life. "Flowering Rose Mallow" leads them to see the nothingness hidden behind physical being. "The Fly" makes them begin to contemplate the questions of infinity and relativity. "The Turtle" shocks them by letting them see how meaningless are their daily lives. One can go on and on citing such examples.

It is no wonder that almost all of Shinkichi's later poems feature a Zen Buddhist either as the poem's speaker or as its main character, with or without disguise. Only on rare occasions can one sense the voice of a poet per se. "The Eastern Sky" is one of those few poems. Based on an experience during Shinkichi's Zen training, it will serve as a fitting conclusion to this discussion of his view of poetry:

> Early in the morning a rooster is crowing.
> I want to get a chisel
> and carve that living rooster.
> With the sharp, stainless blade
> I want to gouge its throat.
> The distant crow of a rooster
> is what I want to carve.

The rooster's crow is like the elusive moment of satori. A poet's task is to capture that moment and present it to the uninitiated reader, who is unable to hear the crow by himself. There is a problem in doing so, because the moment dies as soon as it is verbalized; it is like the image of a rooster instead of a live one. Yet the poet keeps trying to capture that precious moment. Even if he fails, he will still present a semblance of the moment or at least a record of his efforts, and his attempt may help the reader in his own spiritual quest. In Shinkichi's view, therein lies the only usefulness poetry can claim.

Ko Won

SOURCE: "Introduction" and "Dada Meets Zen: Tzara and Takahashi," in *Buddhist Elements in Dada: A Comparison of Tristan Tzara, Takahashi Shinkichi, and Their Fellow Poets,* New York University Press, 1977, pp. 1-13, 79-103.

[*In the following excerpt, Won highlights conceptual affinities between Zen Buddhism and the twentieth-century Dada movement, as illuminated by the poetry and thought of Takahashi Skinkichi and Tristan Tzara.*]

It seems important to note that in the past few years of the 1970s at least fifteen full-length literary books devoting either entirely or partly to Dada have been published in the United States—not to mention others elsewhere. Critical studies include *The Poetry of Dada and Surrealism: Aragon, Breton, Tzara, Eluard, and Desnos* by Mary Ann Caws (1970); *Dada* by Kenneth Coutts-Smith (1970); *André Breton* by Mary Ann Caws (1971); *Dada: Paradox, Mystification, and Ambiguity in European Literature* by Manual L. Grossman (1971); *Tristan Tzara: Dada and Surrational Theorist* by Elmer Peterson (1971); *André Breton: Magus of Surrealism* by Anna Balakian (1971); *The Inner Theatre of Recent French Poetry* by Mary Ann Caws (1972); *Dada and Surrealism* by C. W. Bigsby (1972); *Theatre in Dada and Surrealism* by J. H. Matthews (1974); *Memoirs of a Dada Drummer* by Richard Huelsenbeck (1974); *About French Poetry from Dada to "Tel Quel," Text and Theory,* edited by Mary Ann Caws (1975); and *Skyscraper Primitives: Dada and the American Avant-Garde* by Dickran L. Tashjian (1975). Collections of Dada works in translation with critical introductions are *Dadas on Art* by Lucy R. Lippard (1971); *Tristan Tzara: Approximate Man and Other Writings* by Mary Ann Caws (1973); and *Salt Seller: The Writings of Marcel Duchamp* by Michel Sanouillet and Elmer Peterson (1973). In addition, books concentrating more on Dada art published during this period include *Collection of Everything Dada* (1970); *Hans Richter by Hans Richter* (1971); *Marcel Duchamp* (1972); *Arp on Arp* (1972); *Max Ernst* by Sarane Alexandrian (1972); *Homage to Max Ernst* (1972); *Joan Miro: Lithographs,* edited by Michel Leiris and Fernand Mourlot (1972); and *Miro Sculpture* by Jacques Dupin (1972).

The growing attention by scholars and critics appears to reflect the fact that Dada, without being named so (except as "Neo-Dada"), continues to come alive in the streets and parks, in the performing and plastic arts, and in poetry of our time. In this respect, Professor Elmer Peterson, in the Introduction to his *Tristan Tzara,* observes how the influence of Dada has been steady since the spring of 1960, culminating in 1968, in terms of modern man's response to the changing social and political conditions in Europe as well as America. Something similar to this can be found in Asia too. Many people of today in many different places might agree that *"Tout est Dada,"* as Tristan Tzara (pseudonym of Sami Rosenstock, 1896-1963) shouted fifty years ago.

The life of Dada as a poetical and artistic movement was by no means lengthy. Historically speaking, the onset of its group activities, whether they were those of "Pre-Dada" in New York, led by Marcel Duchamp, Francis Picabia, and Man Ray; or of Zurich Dada, whose group including Hugo Ball, Emmy Hennings, Jean (Hans) Arp, Marcel Janco, Tristan Tzara, Richard Huelsenbeck, Walter Serner, and Sophie Täuber, all of whom were to frequent the Cabaret Voltaire as their headquarters, had much to do with these expatriates' or deserters' desperate objections to World War I, which broke out in 1914. As the Dada movement took place roughly between 1914 and 1923, spreading over a large number of European and American countries, its major centers including New York, Zurich, Berlin, Cologne, Hanover, and Paris, some aspects of the movement—especially in Germany—were politically oriented. Strangely enough, however, despite the fact that Zurich was the place of exile for Lenin (who lived close to the Cabaret Voltaire) and other would-be revolutionaries during the war, the Zurich Dadaists, who are said to have sympathized with the Russian Revolution, seem to have hardly been inclined to things like Bolshevism in art.

From a literary-artistic point of view, Dada was, in any case, not necessarily the by-product of war experiences. Well before the structured movement began to develop, the way to Dada was already paved in the realms of poetry, art, and drama as well as philosophy. The Symbolist search for the absolute and belief in universal correspondence, the Impressionist discard of the conventional modes of seeing, breaking up the solidity of objects into a multiplicity of fragments, the Expressionist effort to objectify inner experience, the Futurist objection to nature and glorification of the noise and speed, and the Cubist fragmentation of the elements of an experience and synthetic rearrangement of them, for instance, are all related to Dada in one way or the other.

More specifically, as Professor Grossman examines in detail, Alfred Jarry, Arthur Cravan, and Jacques Vaché may well have been "three of Dada's most radical and most immediate predecessors." Far and near forerunners taken together, common to all is a decisive breakdown of the old conception of external reality, coupled with a revolt against present-day conditions and against the traditional manner of expression, and, in many cases, with the rejection of discursive intelligence. With this background and under the moral impact of World War I, there

followed a general disgust and despair and a particular distrust of all existing values, including those of beauty, form, logic and words, order and system, among the young artists and poets of the mid-1920s. These were also true pacifists, becoming the core of an international movement which happened to be called Dada.

In the history of Western literature and art, Dada, therefore, stands between the trends of Cubism and Futurism and the following movement of Surrealism, which assimilated many aspects of Dada, with André Breton now assuming its leadership. By way of defining the difference between Dada and the former two movements (Cubism and Futurism) from which Dada broke away, let us simply have the then Dada poets, Tzara and Breton, speak for themselves. Tzara said in 1918 that

> Cubism was born from the simple way of looking at the object: Cézanne painted a cup twenty centimeters lower than his eyes, the cubists look at it from above, others complicate its appearance by making one part perpendicular and in putting it nicely on one side. . . . The futurist sees the same cup in movement, a succession of objects one alongside the other embellished maliciously by some lines of force. . . . The new artist protests: he no longer paints (symbolic and illusionistic reproduction) but rather creates directly in stone, wood, iron, tin, rocks, and locomotive organisms that can be turned about on any side by the limpid wind of momentary sensation.

Breton categorized the three trends in the early 1920s as follows: "Cubism was a school of painting, futurism a political movement: DADA is a state of mind. . . . DADA is artistic free-thinking." While admitting that each of these currents differed both regionally and individually within its own scope and according to the period of its development, Dada in general rejected virtually all the Cubist and Futurist "constructive" and modernistic principles. Although Dada shared quite a few methodological aspects of Cubism and Futurism, Dada was definitely against anything decorative and artificial; it was anti*art* and anti*literature;* it never allowed itself to accept the Futurist apotheosis of mechanical and technological civilization. After all, Dada "abolished" everything. At the same time, because of its negative and "destructive" nature, Dada was serious enough to be positive and creative as well. Its accomplishments included the threat to photographic representation, conventional perspective, and syntax in a thoroughgoing manner, replacing all sorts of bourgeois aesthetics with typographical representation, disjointed images, sounds rather than pretentious and limited (inaccurate) words; and the decentralization of logical mind into "nonsensical" humor, paving the way to the movement of the absurd and automatism.

The early phase of Dada became known to the Japanese in 1920, and it served in the following years to change the current mode of Japanese poetry, which now came to see an era of Dada. This new development was far more than accidental. During the 1910s, "modern" Japanese poetry—whose history had started in 1882 with the publication of *Shintaishi-sho* (New style poetry), an anthology of translations of various Western poetry in which the translators introduced the term "new style" as opposed to the traditions of *tanka* and *haiku*—marked an important period of symbolism. Owing a great deal to such anthologies of French and German poetry in Japanese translation as Ueda Bin's *Kaicho-on* (Sound of the tide, 1905); Nagai Kafu's *Sango-shu* (Corals, 1913); Horiguchi Daigaku's *Kino no hana* (Flowers of yesterday, 1918); and to Arthur Symons's *The Symbolist Movement in Literature,* the Japanese translation of which appeared in 1913, most of the Japanese symbolists exhibited at times a fusion of the aspects of European Symbolism and their own Buddhist background. In this Symbolist period, new conventions in Japanese poetry were established: the long-traditional Japanese rhythm pattern of seven-five (also five-seven) syllables was broken to a great extent; the language shifted from a Classic or a Neoclassic literary style (*bungotai*) to a more familiar colloquial style (*kogotai*); poetic vocabularies and metaphorical images were enriched more than ever.

In sharp contrast with this, another aspect of the Japanese poetry of the same period was noted by a tendency toward the popularization of the ideas of democratic and socialistic enlightenments as shown in the so-called *minshushi,* or poetry for the mass. It must be remembered that the end of World War I did not wholly bring about a peaceful and prosperous reign in Japan. Along with the Korean independence movement of 1919, the Siberian intervention of 1918-1922 (which had earlier created the "rice dispute" of 1918 in a Japanese locale) continued, reaching its peak when Japanese troops and civilians were attacked by Siberian partisans at Nikolayevsk, a port of Khabarovsk Territory, in 1920. In the course of "Taisho democracy," a term denoting not so much the democratic accomplishment as the ephemeral experiment of the Taisho era (1912-26), Japan's military activities in Siberia as a whole became the target of criticism in the Diet and the public responded to the expedition with either growing speculation, which caused the rise in the price of rice, or indifference, which was meant to show their disagreement. In a poem by Fukuda Masao, one of the major figures of the "people's poetry school" (*minshushi ha*) of this period, called "A Train and Handkerchiefs," we can visualize the scene:

> Where there passes a train,
> crying out a roar of *banzai,*
> loaded with soldiers on the way to Siberia—
> A mass of handkerchiefs flapping at the windows,
> crowds by the roadside watching them vacantly;
> only an old cartman
> shouted *banzai,* waving his hat.
>
> Soldiers are chosen for death, going off to die.
> What a national tragedy.
>
> I know everything too well to give cheers for you.
> Sorry, but I send you off with my tears instead.

Antimilitarism was also exemplified in such poems as "For Country" by Negishi Masayoshi, a man of the working class; "A Night Chat" by Fukushi Kojiro, a free-verse lyricist; and "War Is Bad" by Mushakoji Saneatsu, the individualistic novelist and the founder of the utopian socialistlike New Village movement. Following are some of Mushakoji's least poetic yet exemplary lines: "Since I hate / to be killed / I oppose murder, / and therefore I oppose war. / Only those who / like to be killed, / those who like to see / one whom they love killed, / only such people / can praise war."

At this time, Japan's reinforcements in Siberia led to her discord with the United States; and the naval expansion of great powers, including Japan, was so competitive that it was eventually limited at the Washington Conference of 1921-22. This limitation, however, did not mean the weakening of the military influence on Japanese politics and society. Edwin O. Reischauer, in his *The United States and Japan,* describes the power structure of the new Japan of the 1920s as consisting of "the highly centralized economic empires of the *zaibatsu* [plutocracy, plutocrats], the huge and omnipresent civil bureaucracy, the all-seeing, all-knowing police, and, worst of all, the closely knit and fanatical corps of army officers." As the trends of democracy and individual liberties kept pace with militarism, so did capitalistic development with postwar financial panic. Thus, the better-organized labor movement began to launch political and legal issues, activities of great impact in 1920 including the Yahata iron-steel workers' strike and May Day rallies in Tokyo and Osaka, which demanded, among other things, the abolition of the oppressive "peace maintenance police" law, an article of which suppressed both labor and tenant disputes. While the nation was still struggling for the adoption of universal manhood suffrage, with demonstrations of the masses and the disturbance in the Diet marking political confusion in 1920, the government retaliated with dictatorial measures. According to Ike Nobutake, branches of the Reservists Association were established in the 1920s even "in factories and mines for the purpose of combatting the growth of labor unions."

In academic and intellectual circles, there was also great controversy. The government's anxiety over radicalism was first evidenced by the suppression of the study of anarchism, the movement of which in Japan had already been confronted with difficulties, such as the execution of Kotoku Shusui and eleven other anarchists in 1911 (i.e., toward the end of the Meiji era, 1868-1912). In January 1920, Morito Tatsuo, an assistant professor at Tokyo Imperial University, was indicted for his article, "Kuropotokin no shakai shiso no kenkyu" (A study of Kropotkin's social thought), published in the same month's issue of *Keizaigaku kenkyu* (Economic studies). His indictment, along with that of Ouchi Hyoe, the editor of the journal, was immediately reported in the daily, *Tokyo asahi shinbun,* which explained the cause as "a result of the government's determination of the assistant professor as a popularizer of anarchism, whose article served to prompt an action of the Society for National

Development (Kokoku Doshikai), a student organization." Accompanied by Morito's suspension from teaching, the charge of his "repugnance to the Japanese constitutional order" became a serious public concern, for, Arima Tatsuo observed, "Morito and Ouchi had on their side the sympathy of interested college students, intellectuals and the major newspapers."

This controversy was followed in the same year by the publication of Peter Kropotkin's *Memoirs of a Revolutionist,* translated by Osugi Sakae, the leading anarchist (murdered immediately following the great Kanto earthquake of 1923), and Volume I of Karl Marx's *Das Kapital,* translated by Takabatake Motoyuki, in a Marxism series. Also established in 1920 were a leftist magazine, *Shakaishugi* (Socialism), and the Japan Socialist Union, followed by the founding of the Japan Communist party in 1922. Anarchism and Marxism were, in fact, the two main streams of thought to which Japanese radicals were allied around this time, although one was in conflict with the other. Except for some political activists, however, the ideological basis of the intellectuals was generally characterized by a sort of radical, liberalistic idealism, which was prevailing among the writers too.

Under these circumstances the works of such "democratic" poets as Walt Whitman, Horace Traubel, and Edward Carpenter were published in translation in the beginning of the 1920s. Their ideas attracted some members of Shiwakai, a poets' association, which came to be dominated around 1921 by the "people's poetry" school. Of the two major literary magazines established in 1921, *Nihon shijin* (Japanese poets) and *Tane maku hito* (The sower), the latter, which was founded by Komaki Chikae who had witnessed World War I in France and was under the influence of Henri Barbusse's *Clarte* movement (a kind of ideological International) on his return from Paris, lured laborers, intellectuals, writers, and thinkers with its motto of cosmopolitanism. In its first issue, a manifesto was published, which reads in part: "Man created God in the past. Man has now killed God. . . . We fight for the truth of modern age. . . . We defend the truth of revolution for the sake of our living. Those who sow the seeds rise here—together with the comrades of the world." At a time when a serious dispute between the anarcho-syndicalists and the Bolsheviks of Japan was going on, *The Sower* devoted its pages to writers inclined to the idea of social revolution and paved the way to an era of proletarian literature.

To sum up the climate of the years from 1920 to 1922, the people did not suffer (unlike those in Europe) directly from the havoc of World War I in which Japan also joined, but they wanted a secure peace after the war. There was a fear of war, and people were against militaristic expansion. Postwar prosperity soon evolved into severe financial panic, which created social problems. The Japanese people began to doubt the established order and the values of the past. They were disenchanted with the aristocracy and disgusted with the growing bureaucracy. Intellectuals were aware of what was wrong and

concerned with what should be done. In the realm of poetry, while the *minshushi,* which also employed the colloquial style, reached its height in the beginning of the 1920s, it could not escape the looseness of expression, because it was little concerned with aesthetics. Naturally, the poets who belonged to this school were confronted with an attack by those who emphasized poetry as a work of art.

Thus, at the turn of the decade, many younger poets became disgusted with the kind of lyricism which was too personal to express the dramatically changing phases of the age, on the one hand, and the prosaic descriptive style which was too plain for the intensity of modern man's thought and feelings, on the other. They wanted a further modernization of Japanese poetry as much as they were eager to revolutionize the political and social systems of Japan. They wanted an aesthetic revolution in style and expression in order to deal with new subject matter and new sentiment in the modern world. Although their war experiences were not as intimate as those of European writers, they were equally interested in reexamining life and society.

At this point, in the beginning of the twenties, a decade which saw an epoch-making development of avant-garde and of proletarian literature in Japanese literary history, the Dada current made its impact felt. Thus the seeds were sown for some of the sophisticated and revolutionary poets to find immediate kinship with Dada. It was Takahashi Shinkichi who became the pioneering poet of the Dada movement in Japan, which flourished during the first half of the 1920s, a movement which exerted influence in a new development of Korean poetry too.

In general, there is a big difference between the West and Japan in the scale and nature of the Dada movements. Western Dada (in both its inception and development) was a truly organized movement in the sense that those poets who shared similar ideas—often in collaboration with artists, and sometimes with musicians—participated together, although places and times varied, in the publication of their manifestative, theoretical, and creative works in journals, many of which were founded for this particular purpose. In addition, their group activities included demonstrations, theatrical events, and the reading of "simultaneous poetry." On the other hand, Dada in Japan was, strictly speaking, seldom organized as a movement. As far as poetic works are concerned, Takahashi was the sole Dada at the outset, aside from Tsuji Jun's moral support. It was only after some of Takahashi's Dada poems had been published in 1921 and 1922 that there appeared other followers of Dada. Personal contact among those who claimed themselves to be Dadaist was very much limited: Takahashi met Tsuji in 1921 for the first time; and as Kikuchi Yasuo points out, Dada in Japan was "permeated" through the friendship between the two writers. It was in 1922 that Takahashi became acquainted with Hirato Renkichi, the Futurist who was also interested in Dada and whose Futurist works attracted the former. The younger Dada poet, Nakahara Chuya, met

Takahashi only in 1927, shortly before Nakahara wrote an essay on Takahashi. Although there were some short-lived little magazines devoted to Dada in the early part of the twenties, they seem to have been least influential. A group of anarchists launched a radical poetry magazine called *Aka to kuro* (Red and black) in 1923, which some of the contemporary Japanese historians tend to associate with the dada movement, but its member poets were, in a strict sense, anarchists who felt certain affinity with Dada rather than Dada adherents. In this respect, Tsuboi Shigeji seems right in observing the following:

> The impact of Dadaism appears to have been felt to a degree where it produced [a special] atmosphere rather than as a theoretical influence. However, even if it was limited to that extent, Dada as a poetic spirit had the power as strong as to set what was moving within each poet's inner world on fire. A characteristic element common to those poets of that time [the early 1920s] who were more or less Dadaistic was the awareness of self-decomposition, and the explosion of energy accompanying this decomposition served as the basis of their poetic spirit.

While the Japanese Dada and semi-Dada poets brought about a revolution in both subject matter and expression, they soon encountered the communists' criticism that Dada was nothing more than intellectual escapism and that it interfered with the social revolution. As the proletarian literary activity grew vigorous in the latter half of 1925, there followed an uncompromising conflict between the leftist- ideology-oriented writers and the other faction. Meanwhile, the year 1925 marked a point of departure for the Surrealist movement in Japan. Aside from Horiguchi Daigaku's new and influential translation of contemporary French poetry, *Gekka no ichigun* (A group under the moon), which included the poems of Philippe Soupault and Ivan Goll, the professor-poet Nishiwaki Junzaburo attracted young Japanese poets of the time with the French Surrealist publications which he had brought with him on his return from Europe in 1925. In the same year, the writings of Louis Aragon, André Breton, and Paul Eluard were published in Japanese translation in a little magazine, *Bungei tambi* (Literary aestheticism), in which also appeared somewhat Surrealistic poems by Japanese. In due course, the Surrealist movement—perhaps the best organized in the history of Japanese literary movements—surfaced in 1927, when a journal called *Bara, majutsu, gakusetsu* (Rose, magic, theory) was published for the Surrealists, alongside an anthology of their writings, *Fukuiku taru kafu yo* (Fragrant stroker!). This trend lasted for a decade or so thereafter.

It is true that none of the Japanese Dada poets has ever been officially associated with the Surrealist movement in Japan. This was unlike the situation in France, where Dada was "taken over" by Surrealism. Although Dada was preceded by Symbolism and followed by Surrealism in the history of Japanese poetry, it seems proper to say that the Symbolist fashion was still going on, Hagiwara

Sakutaro having been an important Symbolist poet, along with Futurism in the Dada period.

Despite the fact that the Dada movement in Japan was short-lived and small-scaled, the Dada works of Takahashi Shinkichi, the author of seventeen books of poetry in addition to ten volumes of essays on art and three collections of literary essays, are significant and important not only because they exerted a remarkable influence on other Japanese poets, both Dadaists and non-Dadaists, an influence which served to mature the modernity of Japanese poetry, but also because they reveal a fascinating blend of Dada and Buddhism, especially Zen. Takahashi, as he has repeatedly emphasized, found in Dada a perfect affinity with Zen. Also, on several occasions the poet has acknowledged, directly or indirectly, the impact of Tristan Tzara on his philosophy and writing. The Japanese Zennist poet even presumed recently that the Rumanian-born cosmopolitan had a profound Buddhist background. All this provides new ground for an examination of Dada, in general, and Tzara's work, in particular, from the viewpoint of Eastern philosophy. A search of the available literature reveals that a careful comparative study of these subjects has never been done either in the East or in the West.

With primary emphasis on the analysis of Takahashi's early poems, various articles (published much later than the poems to be examined), and other related material, this [essay] is intended to probe and prove the following issues:

(1) In both Japanese and Western Dada poetry, the notion of nothingness, the discredit of words and logic, and anticonventionalism are predominant. Underlying these attitudes, at least in part, is Asian thought, particularly Buddhist ideas. There are also some Taoist elements. These aspects are found especially in the works of Takahashi and Tzara.

(2) Not only in their ways of thinking but also in their poetic expression, these two poets (both of whom are interested in art as well) show us, in a number of cases, a close relationship between Dada and Zen in terms of a paradoxical, often totally illogical and sometimes nonverbal, presentation of essence. . . .

I THE PHILOSOPHY OF NOTHING

Takahashi has been a prolific writer of the *zuihitsu* (miscellanies, nontheoretical essays), including several autobiographical sketches; however, he began to write about Dada (in prose) only in 1954, when his commentaries on the three-volume posthumous collections of Tsuji Jun's writings were published. As he states in his short article, "Dada no shusoku" (The end of Dada), published in 1961, on the way to Korea in the summer of 1924, he threw his *Dada* (a novel published in 1924) away into the Korean Straits from the top of the ship, and he has since then severed connections with Dada completely. Since

1961, however, Takahashi has written at least ten articles on Dada, or on those which refer to Dada, and it is in these miscellaneous jottings that one apprehends clearly the nature of his theory of Dada, which basically incorporates Zen ideas.

Of these articles, Takahashi's observations of the works of his fellow-Dadaist Tsuji Jun, who was "fond of the Greek word *panta rei* ('all things' flux')," provide insights into both the similarities and the differences in their ideas and lead us, in fact, to see Takahashi's own Dada viewpoint more clearly. Takahashi says that Buddhism underlies Tsuji's basic thought, and the fact that Tsuji was attracted to Stirner indicates his attempt to liberate himself from the peremptory ethics of Buddhism which had predominated during the Meiji era. Takahashi also points out that Tsuji's interest ranged from Dada to anarchism and Marxism, but his temperament never allowed him to participate in the radicals' destructive activity of his time. Takahashi considers Tsuji "a pure soul" and says that "André Gide recognized Tsuji as an excellent essayist, whereas some Japanese fools still despise Tsuji as a mental bankrupt"; his life was "a rebellion against the common run of people and evil." In these statements, Takahashi reveals his affinity with Tsuji's truly rebellious outlook on reality, which stands against vulgarity and yet is not in accord with activism.

On the other hand, in the following words, Takahashi makes it clear that his Dada is fundamentally different from that of Tsuji: "Tsuji Jun, after his involvement with Dada [between 1922 and 1925], published a magazine called *Kyomu shiso kenkyu* (Studies in nihilist thought). Since I disdained him at that time for having fallen from Dada into the abyss of nihility, I did not contribute any writing to his magazine. My Dadaism is not as plain as what could be explained away by a word like nihilism." Here again he does not regard the Dada essence as nihilism, whereas Tsuji's Dada view is rooted in nihilism and the Stirnerian individualism. In recalling his reading of Stirner's *The Ego and His Own* in Tsuji's translation, Takahashi says that, while the work attracted a large number of young Japanese who were bound to the feudalistic ideas of the time, "I, having had the chance to learn the philosophy of *no-self* through Mahayana scriptures, found a great gulf of contradiction fixed between the two [Stirner's idea and Mahayana Buddhism]."

Takahashi also repeatedly differentiates Dada from anarchism, especially referring to the *Red and Black* group, whose contributing members were generally called "the terrorists of the poetic world." He does not agree with Onchi Terutake and others in their argument that in the 1920s there were two streams of Dada in Japan, anarchistic (or political and social) Dada and nihilistic (or spiritual and Buddhistic) Dada; instead, Takahashi points out that the currents of Dada and anarchism were separate and quite distinct from each other. His disagreement with the idea which associates Dada with anarchism is highlighted in his refutation of Yoshida Seiichi's evaluation of Hagiwara Kyojiro's poetry. Yoshida wrote in 1950 that

> Important as a Dada poet was Hagiwara Kyojiro, who, together with Okamoto . . . in the first manifesto published in the *Red and Black,* negated all the existing being, and cried out for anarchistic destruction for the sake of destruction. . . . Hagiwara's *Shikei senkoku* (Death sentence, 1925) is a book of poetry which deserves attention. . . . What prevails throughout his poetry is—unlike the enervated spirit of decadence which is found in Tsuji and Takahashi—an anarchistic exclamation; it can be called the tumult, noise, and scream of the deadly urban civilization. With very few dilettante elements of Takahashi and Tsuji, there in Hagiwara's poetry swirls directionless anger as well as anxiety and impatience created by despair.

At this point, let us examine some of the characteristics of Hagiwara's poetry. His poem, "Hakabada, hakabada!" (It's graveyard, graveyard!) in the 1925 volume, for example, reveals his negative attitude in such lines as "Hands and feet, all fell apart— / the whereabouts of the body is hardly known—"; "Debts! / money money money money money money money money"; "Dig out yourself and turn it over without reservation!"; "Take your respiratory organs and sexual organs off!"; "Bite, bite! Bite me to death!" Commenting on this poem, Kitagawa Fuyuhiko interprets its theme as "a naive youth's desperate scream caused by the social anxiety toward the end of the Taisho era—after World War I"; and he further implies an "anarchistic, Dadaistic thought" to the expression of "despair, anger, and self-torment." These qualities are also found in another poem, "Arukohoru ni tsuketa shinzo o" (With the heart soaked in alcohol), which reads in part: "As I soak my heart in alcohol / and keep it in a bottle / . . . and when I am about to drink it with a cup, / the red loud laughter, crossing my belly, / turns out to a sorrowful anger." His personal sentiment of this sort often blows up, turning toward social criticism. At the same time, he is fond of the Futurist manner of "bruitism" and typographical methods. . . .

Generally, Hagiwara's *Death Sentence* is characterized by emotional excitement, social consciousness, and tumultuous (noisy) and visual expressions. With Takahashi, he shares vigorous opposition to their older contemporaries' aesthetics of well-balanced beauty, romantic sensibility, and of the symbolic meaning of words. However, the world of Takahashi contrasts with that of Hagiwara, who emphasizes the heat, energy, and speed of "going against a rapid stream, with destruction, revenge, burial, and regeneration set in motion simultaneously."

Appraising Yoshida's analysis cited above, Takahashi argues that the qualities in Hagiwara's poetry which Yoshida interprets as Dada in fact have nothing at all to do with Dada, particularly since the Dada movement in Japan had come to an end by the time Hagiwara's *Death Sentence* was published. Takahashi finds no Dada element in this work except for the formal effect, produced by typographical arrangements, a method already experimented with by the Futurist Hirato Renkichi. One may conclude, then, that Takahashi considers Hagiwara an anarchist poet, one whose methods were under the influence of Futurism and whose poetry therefore lacked the principled understandings of Dada.

While the impact of Dada is, to a certain degree, discernible in the poetry of the *Red and Black* poets like Tshuboi Shigeji and Hagiwara Kyojiro, Takahashi does not regard these as Dadaists at all, largely because of the difference in their notion of destruction and that of negation. Takahashi's opposition to interpreting Dada as being totally anarchic parallels the view of Hans Richter, who, for instance, speaking of the Dada principle of chance, says:

> Compared with all precious "isms," Dada must have seemed hopelessly anarchic. But for us, who lived through it, this was not so. On the contrary, it was something meaningful, necessary and life-giving. The official belief in the infallibility of reason, logic and causality seemed to us senseless— as senseless as the destruction of the world and the systematic elimination of every particle of human feelings. This was the reason why we were forced to look for something which would re-establish our humanity.

Takahashi is closer to Tzara when the latter speaks of the rationale of Dada:

> Dada was born of a moral need, of an implacable will to achieve a moral absolute, of a profound sentiment that man, at the center of all creations of the spirit, must affirm his primacy over notions emptied of all human substance, over dead objects and ill-gotten gains. . . . Dada took the offensive and attacked the social system in its entirety, for it regarded this system as inextricably bound up with human stupidity, the stupidity which culminated in the destruction of his material and spiritual possessions. . . . It is certain that the *tabula rasa* which we made into the guiding principle of our activity, was of value only in so far as *something else* would succeed it. A state of affairs considered noxious and infamous demanded to be changed. This necessary disorder, of which Rimbaud had spoken, implied nostalgia for an order that had been lost or a new order to come.

Although fragmentary and often categorical, the theoretical basis of Takahashi's understanding and practice of Dada is explicitly stated in his articles published in the 1960s and 1970s, such as "Watashi no shisakuho" (My poetic method); "Nihon no dada" (Dada in Japan), "Dada, shururearisumu to sono isan" (a review of William S. Rubin's *Dada, Surrealism, and Their Heritage* in Japanese translation); "Dada no saien" (The revival of Dada), and "Jishin to dada" (The earthquake and Dada), in most of which he refers to Tzara. His discovery of an affinity between Dada and Buddhism is his most relevant point. "Philosophically," he recollects, "my Dada was Buddhistic. As I had read some of the Buddhist scriptures while

I was in a temple near home for about eight months, Buddhism became my Dada's foundation." Takahashi thus declares that "Dada is a universal language and it cherishes the idea of peace common to all men. . . . It is my understanding that Dada is nothing other than a rudimentary version of Zen. Has Dada perished." The Dada movement was finished, but Dadaists are still alive." The Japanese word *aryu,* translated here as "rudimentary version" in this quotation, actually means "a second" or "a follower"; Takahashi seems, then, to interpret Dada as an elementary, embryonic version of Zen Buddhism.

Later in 1970, in another article, "The Revival of Dada," Takahashi refers to Tzara's words from his lecture of 1922: "Dada is not at all modern. It is more in the nature of a return to an almost Buddhist religion of indifference", and he goes on to assert: "Judging from this, it is obvious that Dada was giving off a Buddhist smell." In these statements, one finds an important analogy between the ideas of the two poets. A clue to understanding why Tzara, in his lecture, compares Dada to a "Buddhist religion of indifference" can be found in the following words:

> Dada covers things with an artificial gentleness, a snow of butterflies released from the head of a prestidigitator. Dada is immobility and does not comprehend the passions. You will call this a paradox, since Dada is manifested only in violent acts. Yes, the reactions of individuals contaminated by *destruction* are rather violent, but when these reactions are exhausted, annihilated by the Satanic insistence of a continuous and progressive "What for?" what remains, what dominates is *indifference.* But with the same note of conviction I might maintain the contrary.

In this observation, destruction and indifference seem to be defined as both sides of the same coin, and whichever may come first, one leads to the other. Furthermore, what Tzara is concerned with appears to be the individual, and that individual is examined with a view toward investigating problems relating to "What am I?" (a metaphysical question) rather than "Who am I?" (in terms of corporeal existence). The Buddhist principle of nonattachment, which is to lead up to the point of mind-lessness or will-lessness, comprises the quality of indifference and coldness, a state of great composure which, in turn, demands a crucial destruction of ego.

Tzara's lecture as a whole seems to characterize a Tzara-Dada ("I admit that my friends do not approve this point of view"), which corresponds to a Takahashi-Dada ("my Dada"). Tzara further says that "the *Nothing* can be uttered only as the reflection of an individual. And that is why it will be valid for everyone. . . . Always destroy what you have in you. On random walks. Then you will be able to understand many things." Although we know from his writing that Tzara was aware of Buddhist philosophy, it is uncertain whether he was strongly influenced by it. What is striking is the fact that his views spelled out in the lecture are parallel to Buddhist (especially Zen) ideas. However, no Western studies of Tzara mention any of his Buddhist background. After an exhaustive search of the available literature, it would seem that Takahashi is the only writer who has ever "picked up" this aspect, although his assumption, stated in his miscellaneous articles, does not go into the question in depth.

In addition to Tzara's brief mention of Buddhism in 1922, it is interesting that he also refers to Taoist philosophy in the same lecture: "We are well aware that people in the costumes of the Renaissance were pretty much the same as the people of today, and that Chouang-Dsi was just as Dada as we are. You are mistaken if you take Dada for a modern school, or even for a reaction against the school of today." The Chinese name Chouang-Dsi is no doubt that of Chuang Tzu (i.e., Chuang Chou, c. 369-c. 286 B.C.), whose philosophy idealizes the state of nature or naturalness (*tzu-jên*) in favor of anarchic individualism as opposed to artificiality, conventions, and institutions, the whole idea leading to a denial of the results of "culture," that is, civilization. From the foregoing, it is obvious that Tzara, in his Dada period, knew something of both Buddhism and Taoism, the latter sharing many ideas with the former.

Interestingly, these two ancient Asian philosophies attracted some of the German Dadaists of Tzara's time. For instance, Daimonides, who, in his article, "Zur Theorie des dadaismus," included in *Dada Almanach*, edited by Richard Huelsenbeck and published in 1920, quotes lines from "Laotse, Taoteking," that is, the *Tao-tê-ching* (the book of way and its virtue or effect), attributed to Lao Tzu, the founder of Taoism and a contemporary of Confucius: "—*und er kann wieder umkehren zum Ungewordenen.*" An English version of the lines reads: "And you will again return to being a babe. . . . And you will return to being the uncarved block." R. B. Blakney explains the Taoist key word "the uncarved block" (*p'u* in Chinese) as follows: "A kind of tree and hence a 'virgin block' of wood, untooled, and not artificial; raw material and thence, the natural state of things: substance, plain, simple, sincere. This word is probably an old technical term of the mystics who dwelt long with 'untouched nature' before their views were committed to written words." Walter Mehring, in his essay "Enthüllungen" (also included in *Dada Almanach*), often refers to China and Japan—their places, people, traditional culture, and even "Dada in Japan"; it should be noted that *Dada Almanach* came out in 1920. Also noticeable is his reference to Lao Tzu and Buddha, in addition to "Wedda's," which seems to refer to the ancient Indian sacred (mythological) books, *Vedas*. The word *"Dadayama,"* which Mehring uses extensively in the essay, he defines as follows: *"Dadayama ist vom Bahnhof nur durch ein Doppelsalto zu erreichen. Dadayama hält das Blut in Wallung."* Thus, *"Dadayama"* might be a combination of Dada and Yama, the god of death or underworld in Indian mythology.

Generally, it is not surprising that the young German poets of the early twentieth century were familiar with the cultural heritage of India, because, as the exhaustive study by A. Leslie Willson, *A Mythical Image: The Ideal of India in German Romanticism,* illustrates, Indian myths and philosophies had already exerted a great impact on nineteenth-century German literature. "German readers," Willson points out, "by 1750 had learned much about India." There were, of course, many important Romantic philosophers in eighteenth to nineteenth century Germany, who were either deeply attracted to, or at least partly interested in, ancient Oriental (especially Indian) thought, among them Wilhelm Friedrich Hegel and Arthur Schopenhauer. Also, in French and other European literary and artistic movements of the second half of the nineteenth century, traditional Japanese art and poetry—*japonisme,* or the Japanese taste and vogue—influenced Art Nouveau and Impressionism. Having thus digressed enables us to see the routes that Dada and Buddhism took on the way to their eventual contact in Takahashi's mind.

Returning to the Dada-Buddhism relationship as defined by Takahashi, he quotes a line from Tzara's "Dada Manifesto 1918," "Dada means nothing," which both recollects his own Dada period and observes Tzara as follows:

> [In reading Tzara's manifestoes in Japanese translation], I recalled that, considering Dada the same as Namu Amidabutsu, I used to scream "Namu-Dada." It cannot be doubted that Buddhism was absorbed promptly into the sagacious brain of Tzara, a young Rumanian who studied philosophy. His Buddhist background must have been Zen, because his denial of verbal activity—by saying "thought without words" or "no count on word"—is in common with Zen principle of no-word. . . . Since he was concerned with a quest for meta-physical thought, he seems to have had little time to take interest in social revolution or terrorism.

Namu Amidabutsu (Namo'mitayurbuddhaya in Sanskrit) is a recitation of the name Amitabha Buddha (Amidabutsu in Japanese), worshiped by the Pure Realm sect, *namu* being the Japanese (and Korean) rendering of the Sanskrit word *namas,* a kind of Buddhist mantra, which is used in the sense of "I [we] take refuge in" (the Buddha, the Dharma, and the Sangha). Takahashi's "Namu-Dada" association is expressed in a later poem called "Namu Amidabutsu" (published in 1952, long after the appearance of the *Poems of Dadaist Shinkichi*), which reads:

> *namu amidabutsu mo dada mo hoka no kotoba mo*
> *   onaji*
> *hotoke o shinzuru mono mo shinjinai mono mo*
> *   onaji dearu*

> Namu Amidabutsu and Dada and other words are
>   all the same.
> One who believes in the Buddha and one who
>   doesn't are alike.

In his article cited above ["The Revival of Dada"], Takahashi further says that Dada in Japan was misunderstood by certain communists and anarchists who felt it should have served as a driving force for revolution and slaughter. Takahashi feels the Dada essence is far from that—"one must not overlook Tzara's tolerant Buddhist spirit"; Takahashi then considers the cause of the split between Tzara and the Surrealist Breton coming from the latter's lack of understanding of the Dada essence in this regard. The article concludes with the following argument: "Dada was merely an adherent current [again *aryu*] of Buddhism; Tzara's work like *A haute flamme* [At Full Flame, 1955] is illustrative of his reaching the state of Zen. The reburning of Dada means the restoration of Buddhism." On another occasion, he states:

> Tzara seems to have had a profound knowledge of Buddhism as well, and I think his thought was the same as Zen, which denies the activation of word and attempts the decomposition of word. . . . The fact that Dada spread its flame like wildfire over the ruined mind after destruction signifies that this meaningless word was meant to be a new moral to replace the subverted order of God.

Takahashi, thus concentrating on Tzara as the most important spokesman for Western Dadaists, emphasizes Western culture's disintegration by pointing out that "Dada was antichristianity" (and therefore in closer accord with Eastern religion perhaps); that "it was proclaimed chiefly by Jews" (a startling observation by Takahashi except when one remembers that Christendom represented an irreconcilable schism from its parent religion, so that, in this context, to be antichristian was to be pro-Dada); "and [Takahashi concludes] its philosophy is that which is contained in Buddhism" (a clear statement of the concordance of Dada and Buddhism).

While Tzara, alluding to Buddhism and Chuang Tzu, does not consider Dada a new idea, Takahashi, taking a different tack, attributes the inception of Dada in Japan to the Buddhist background of certain Japanese and not to the chaotic and revolutionary milieu following the earthquake of 1923. It should be noted that when Takahashi speaks of Buddhism, he often looks on the darker side of Japanese society which has generally lost its Buddhist tradition, and he calls for the people's rediscovery of its spirit, which he, himself, found in Dada. The interpretation of Dada as a cultural event, although it flourished in the midst of the great war (an interpretation shared by Tzara and Takahashi), is also analogous to the view of Werner Haftmann, who says:

> [However], the basic impulse of Dada is not despair and protest but a rebellious feeling of joy inspired by new discoveries. . . . Dada's aggressiveness is not the rage of the slave against his chains, but springs from a sensation of total freedom. . . . This very fact would suggest that Dada was not the consequence of political events, but an event in cultural history that would probably have taken place even if there had been no war and no revolutions.

Significantly underlying the ideas of Tzara and Takahashi is the concern here with the concept of nothingness and the illogical yet comprehensive perception of essence. These two facets are, in fact, collateral and interrelated, one being brought vividly to mind by the realization of the other. This is the point where one of the possibilities of linking Dada to Buddhism (particularly Zen) can be ensured.

Throughout Tzara's Dada manifestoes and other writings that reveal his Dada views, a constant and central theme may be drawn from what he says in "Proclamation without Pretension": "We are seeking upright, pure, sober, UNIQUE strength"; "We are seeking NOTHING"; "We affirm the VITALITY of each instant"; "the anti-philosophy of Spontaneous acrobatics." If it is certainly unreasonable to assume that Tzara means, by the second sentence, that we are not seeking anything, then it is most probable that he means, instead, that we are in quest of no-thing. The force which is "upright (direct), pure, sober," and "unique" may then well be one which is able to achieve that search, and that force is obtained by the "vitality" of every "instant," the vitality being illogical (beyond reason, common sense, and preoccupation with erroneous knowledge) and "spontaneous." The "dadaist disgust" (in Tzara's words), despair, and the absurd, all negative qualities, when negated, are to become the personality of the negator.

What is the "nothing" Tzara talks about in his manifestoes and lecture cited above? Tzara does not seem ever to have spelled it out, except as Dada. Is nothing, then, a state of mind, as Dada is often so defined by Tzara and others? Furthermore, how can man "seek" nothing? The means which Tzara seems to provide for this search is the Dada negation of exterior reality.

One wonders again what were the influences on Tzara's thinking. Elmer Peterson, in his study of Tzara as a theorist, points out (rather briefly) the influences of Hegel, Sigmund Freud, C. G. Jung, and Lucien Lévy-Bruhl on Tzara in relation to Tzara's Surrealist and post-Surrealist phases. It is unclear whether these influences were also exerted on the Dadaist Tzara in one way or another, but it is clear that Tzara as a Dadaist deprecates, in his "Dada Manifesto 1918," for instance, dialectic, logic, and psychoanalysis as follows: "Psychoanalysis is a dangerous sickness, lulls the antirealistic tendencies of man and codifies the bourgeoisie. . . . Dialectic is an amusing machine which leads us / in a banal manner / to opinions we would have had anyway. . . . Logic restricted by the senses is an organic sickness." In this same regard, Jack Spector alludes to Tzara's statement with the observation that "the irrepressible iconoclast Tzara felt called upon" to make this statement at the time when the Zurich Dadaists seemed so fascinated with Freud's work.

No matter what and who influenced the young Tzara, a careful reading of his own Dada manifestoes reveals most striking parallels between his ideas and Buddhist (and at times Taoist) doctrine of nothingness. When he pronounces in the 1918 manifesto, for example, the ideas of "no beginning" and "a furious wind" which foreshadows "the great spectacle of disaster, fire, and decomposition," and the "dadaist disgust," protest, and the abolition of everything, including that of logic, memory, the prophets, and the future, he bears in mind the fact that *Mesurée à l'échelle Eternité, toute action est vain"* (Measured by the scale of Eternity, all action is vain). In the same manifesto, he also defines Dada as *"croyance absolue indiscutable dans chaque dieu produit immédiat de la spontanéité"* (absolute and indisputable belief in every god that is the immediate product of spontaneity). Furthermore, when he says, in the concluding "colonial syllogism" of the "Manifesto on feeble love and bitter love," that *"Personne ne peut échapper au sort / Personne ne peut échapper à Dada / Il n'y a que DADA qui puisse vous faire échapper au sort"* (One cannot escape from destiny; One cannot escape from DADA; Only DADA can enable you to escape from destiny), Tzara almost seems to equate Dada with the Buddhist *sunyata* or *nirvana,* or with the Taoist Void, the *Tao.* Therefore, when he cries out, *"Balayer, nettoyer"* (Sweep out, wipe up), this "great destructive and negative task to be accomplished" (which he presents in the 1918 manifesto) seems to imply a deliverence from the cause of suffering on earth—everybody's salvation.

As the negative aspect of Dada has been variously interpreted, so have been *sunyata* and *nirvana.* Nihilism and annihilationism in Western sense have often been applied to these Eastern concepts, and that is misleading. Guy Richard Welbon, in the Preface to his book, *The Buddhist Nirvana and Its Western Interpreters,* aptly introduces an overall view of the Buddhist spirit of negation in conjunction with the notion of man's lot, characterized by *dukkha* (suffering) which is directly linked to ignorance, as follows:

> Most poignant and consequential among the aspects of ignorance, say the Buddhists, is man's failure to comprehend the basic truth about the phenomenal universe: no phenomenon is permanent—nothing abides.... The Way of the Buddha is ... described variously, most commonly as *nirvana (nibbana).* Nirvana is the absence—the destruction—of suffering *(duhkhanirodha).*

It is noteworthy that Edward Conze, in a collection of his selected essays, *Thirty Years of Buddhist Studies,* examines the essential metaphysical thesis of Schopenhauer, who was acknowledgedly influenced by Indian thought and whose impact on Europeans may have been far greater than that of Buddhist specialists, in the light of both the similarity and difference between the German philosopher and Buddhism in the concept of nothingness. In reference to his *The World as Will and Representation* (translated by E. F. J. Payne), Conze points out that "Schopenhauer teaches that the Will is the Thing-in-itself, whereas in Buddhism 'craving' operates within the conditioned and phenomenal world, and the unconditioned noumenon lies in Nirvana." He further argues that it is incomprehensible: (1) "how any cognitive act can ever reach the Thing-in-itself"; (2) "how thought can ever have the strength to stand up against the Will"; (3) "how as a part of the purely illusory phenomenal world it can possibly overcome and effectively 'deny' it"; then he goes on to say that this difficulty was realized by Schopenhauer's immediate successors, Nietzsche and J. Bahsen, "and led them, respectively, into nihilism and a pessimism unrelieved by the hope of escape." In the discussion of the Buddhist Void, Conze also observes the following:

> If the words alone are considered, the emptiness doctrine may be mistaken for one of the forms of European post-Nietzschean nihilism, and the self-naughting of saints is to some extent mimicked by the self-destructive tendencies of German Romantics, like Schlegel, Tieck, Novalis, and so on, who, as a result of vanity, self-reflection and disgust could say that "I feel myself annihilated right in my inmost essence, and destroyed right up to the last depth of my thoughts" [L. Tieck, *William Lovell*]. They, however, also maintained that "the reality behind things destroys us spiritually when we look upon it" [Tieck, *Kritische Scriften*].

If certain aspects of these philosophies were to be called the philosophy of "lay" Buddhists, then Tzara's approach toward nothingness appears closer to the Buddhist view per se. Here again one remembers what Ribemont-Dessaignes said of the Dada principle of purge: "And afterwards? There is no afterwards. Purge yourself forever." In Takahashi's words, "Within death, there isn't even death."

Among the many schools and sects of Buddhism, Takahashi considers Zen "the highest," the essence of which, he says, is inexplicable and inexpressible in words. Although Zen is traditionally conceived of as a self-awakening without words (without explanations), without instruction, and without knowledge, it seems proper for understanding the concept of nothing to refer once again to Hui-nêng, for his teachings (as recorded by his disciple Fa-hai in the *Liu-tsu tan-ching,* [The Platform Scripture of the Sixth Patriarch], along with those of Bodhidharma, are always important to all branches of Ch'an or Zen. Hui-nêng's basic idea was known when he wrote a gatha in response to one which was written by Shen-hsiu, one of the favorite disciples—together with the former—of the Fifth Patriarch, Hung-Jên. Shen-hsiu's gatha on *bodhi* (knowledge, perfect wisdom) reads:

> The body is the tree of Bodhi
> and the mind is like a bright mirror, framed.
> Wipe it always diligently
> and let no dust collect on it.

Hui-nêng responded to it with his own verse:

> Bodhi is originally no tree,
> the bright mirror has no frame either.
> From the first there is not a thing;
> where can the dust collect itself?

In describing the enlightened man, he also spoke of nothingness as follows:

> Peacefully, quietly, he hears and sees nought;
> Poised and balanced, his mind abides nowhere.

Hui-nêng's insight (one might call it theory) of the *recognition* of not-a-thing leads, it would seem, to the definitions of Zen by R. H. Blyth: "Zen, though far from indefinite, is by definition indefinable, because it is the active principle of life itself"; "Zen is not action. Zen is the activity of the mind-body as a total entity (total here meaning universal). Zen is mind-less activity, that is, Mind-ful activity."

In short, "nothing" in Buddhism is theoretically and practically denotative of "everything." This seemingly paradoxical equation is very often similar to Taoism, in which, according to *Tao-tê-ching*, verse I, "the *Tao* [way] that can be spoken of is not the absolute [constant] way; the name that can be given is not the absolute [constant] name"; thus, the secret of life and its manifestations, being the same under different names, are called *hsüan*, meaning "mystery" or "mystic." Interestingly enough, the Chinese word *ch'ung*, used in *Tao-tê-ching*, verse IV, to define the character of the *Tao*, means both "full" and "empty" ("formless"); hence it is possible to render the opening line in two ways: "Tao is all-pervading"; and "The Way is empty." However, it should be noted that the *Tao* is a shapeless and nameless principle or force from which everything comes to being and to which everything returns, whereas the Buddhist *sunyata*, or *nirvana*, has little to do with coming from and going back to. In Buddhism, the sole being is no-thing, which is, unlike *Tao*, even absolutely free from any operative force of the universe. Likewise, the Dada essence tends to lie in not-a-thing.

From the foregoing, it is apparent that to Tzara, Dada is equated with absolute Nothing. Takahashi finds two elements in Dada—Zen and absolute Nothing. He then affirms Dada's equality with Zen. Both Tzara and Takahashi, in extrapolating, find the congruence of absolute Nothing and absolute freedom.

II ILLOGICALITY AND SIMPLICITY

Tzara's views on illogicality, spontaneity, and simplicity in relation to his concepts of word and poetry are often found parallel to those of Takahashi. As the former's ideas have much to do with his (and many other Western Dadaists') preoccupation with childishness, naiveté, and primitivism, those of the latter are grounded in the bare-mindedness (or, to be more accurate, mind-lessness) of Zen.

In this regard, one is led to note an interesting coincidence. While the originator of the arbitrary choice of the word "dada" at the outset of the Dada movement has been controversial (Hugo Ball and Richard Huelsenbeck, or Tzara, for instance), the word has various meanings in European and African languages, many of them being associated with children, as explained in Tzara's "Dada Manifesto 1918" and Huelsenbeck's *En Avant Dada: Eine Geschichte des Dadaismus*; "dada" is, in fact, a Japanese word as well, meaning "peevishness," and it is very much suggestive of certain aspects of Dada essence. In Japanese it is usually used in combination with other word(s): *dadakko* (*dada* + *ko*), meaning "a spoiled [a wayward, an unmanageable] child"; *dada o koneru*, as a phrase, "to be peevish," "to talk peevishly," "to fret [about trifles]," "to sulk," "to cry for the moon"; *dadappiroi* (*dada* + *hiroi*), "unduly wide," "much too roomy." The Japanese word *dame*, meaning—almost like the English word "damned"—"futile" and "no good," also has, when implicated, a hint of Dada.

Takahashi seems to be aware of the Dada implication of childishness ("Dada as babies' prattle" in Huelsenbeck's words) when he describes, in his Dada poem, "Sakurambo" (Cherries), a man (named Ino) reacting to the rabbit's urine passed on the man's knee: *"Ino wa nakimushi ni natte, dadakko no mane o shita"* (Like a cryboy, Ino took off a wayward child). It should be remembered that in another poem, "The Dead Renkichi," he expresses his interpretation of Dada as follows: *"Dada wa kodomo rashisa ni oite seichu mitaida"* (In its childishness, Dada is like a spermatozoon). As to Tzara's concept of naiveté as a Dada quality, Elmer Peterson observes "infantile names" like BleuBleu, CriCri, and Pipi used in the play *La Première Aventure céleste de M. Antipyrine* (1916), and Tzara's use of the image of "a wonderfully naive and imaginative child" which "reflects a cult of childishness which was particularly strong among the dadaists and their precursors." Referring to Tzara's Preface to Henri Rousseau's play, *Une Visite à l'Exposition de 1899*, Peterson also examines the poet's praise of Rousseau's "ability to see things as children and primitives see them."

Alluding to Zurich Dada, Manuel Grossman presents a similar observation of Hugo Ball as follows: "For Ball, Dada symbolized the magical world of the child; a world in which man, having regained his child-like simplicity, could recapture the direct contact with the unconscious that the adult world had lost. Through the power of Dada he thus hoped to create a kind of 'constructive anarchy.'" When Tzara, the philosophical antiphilosopher, who, at one point, claims himself to be "a small, idiotic and insignificant individual," asks a question, "Is simplicity simple or dada?" and gives no answer, which might be "dada," he likewise seems to allude to the world of child-like simplicity, that is, a free world of creativity. This idea is directly coupled with illogicality in that childishness, simplicity, and spontaneity have a common root, which could possibly be the mere fact that they are all mentioned in Dada manifestoes, though not always simultaneously.

In his Dada writings, including manifestoes and the autobiographical novel *Faites vos jeux* (*Place Your Bets*, 1923); essays on primitive art (such as "Note sur l'art nègre" of 1917); and in later works like *Grains et issues*

(*Seeds and Bran*) of 1935, Tzara repeatedly denounces man's dependence on logic and reason. To be sure, this antilogic attitude is true of other Dadaists. Jean (Hans) Arp, for instance, eloquently describes the purpose of Dada in general along this line as follows:

> Dada aimed to destroy the reasonable deceptions of man and recover the natural and unreasonable order. Dada wanted to replace the logical nonsense of the men of today by the illogically senseless. That is why we pounded with all our might on the big drum of Dada and trumpeted the praises of unreason. . . . Dada denounced the infernal ruses of the official vocabulary of wisdom. Dada is for the senseless, which does not mean nonsense. Dada is senseless like nature. Dada is for infinite sense and definite means.

This statement corresponds precisely to what Tzara pronounces in the Dada manifesto of 1918; along with those words already cited, he says that:

> Logic is a complication. Logic is always false. It draws the strings of ideas, words, along their formal exterior, toward illusory extremes and centers. Its chains kill, like an enormous centipede stifling independence. Married to logic, art would live in incest, swallowing, devouring its own tail still attached, fornicating with itself and the personality would become a nightmare tarred with protestantism, a monument, a heap of heavy gray intestines. . . . The rigidity of morality and logic have made us impassive in the presence of policemen—the cause of slavery—putrid rats filling middle-class stomachs and infecting the only bright and clean glass corridors which remained open to artists.

Tzara, in his Dada manifestoes, also makes his negative attitude toward *words* clear: (1) "We seek the central essence, and we are happy if we can hide it"; (2) "You don't build a sensitivity on one word; every construction converges in a boring perfection, the stagnant idea of a gilded swamp, a relative human product"; (3) "Must we cease to believe in words? Since when have they expressed the opposite of what the organ emitting them thinks and wants? Here is the great secret: *The thought is made in the mouth.*"

Opposed to illusive knowledge and "false" logic, and interested in primitive culture and art, especially those of Oceania and Africa, Tzara often employs a special verbal technique in his plays and poetry, a technique in which he prefers the sound and image to the meaning of word. As Peterson says, Tzara, deciding that "his mission was to cure a certain kind of literary impotence, . . . wished to restore magic power to the word by assembling oddly disparate words in poems to create a verbal equivalent of the collage technique used by dadaist artists." One of Dada's antiaesthetic guidelines is thus the "law of chance," which, according to Arp's somewhat Taoist-like definition, "embraces all laws and is unfathomable like the first cause from which all life arises, can only be experienced through complete devotion to the unconscious." As to Tzara's theories of poetry and with

particular reference to language, Mary Ann Caws observes the following:

> poetry is for Tzara the transcendence of language from its tragic incompetence and necessary artifice into the purest demonstration of mental freedom. Tzara describes poetry in *Place Your Bets* as an instrument of life opened at a certain angle under the light, a property like dampness of color. "Poetry starts where the specificity of painting or verse leaves off." In advocating the "predominance of the human over the aesthetic," Dada "made a poetry a way of life more than the accessory manifestation of intelligence and of will. For art was one of the forces, common to all men, of this poetic activity, whose deep roots mingle with the primitive structure of affective life."

While sharing many of Dada's "law of chance" ideas, Takahashi, as a Zennist, always dwells (as he states in his several essays) on the principle of no-words (no-letters)—*furyu monji* (Japanese) in Zen—a principle which is included in the basic teaching methods of Bodhidharma: "A special transmission outside the scriptures; not founded upon words and letters; by pointing directly to man's own mind, it lets him see into his own true nature and thus attain Buddhahood." These are in fact the very self-disciplinary rules of any Ch'an (Zen) sect. As a poet, Takahashi maintains that: "Unless words spring forth from a point where the poet denies words, denies expression, and denies life, what he writes cannot be poetry. . . . One can hardly find the truth in philosophy which is like a rain-leaking film. The fact that human beings came to use words may indicate their degeneration; so does the discovery of science. . . . Only when the poet conceals within himself words that are more intense than atomic energy can he be a true poet." These words, which appear in an article included in his book of 1969, remind us once again of similar ideas stated in Tzara's Dada manifestoes. On another occasion, Takahashi expresses the no-words Zen principle in a more direct manner: "As a follower of the tradition of Zen which is above verbalization, I must confess that I feel ashamed of writing poems or having collections of them published in book form."

Actually, the same ideas can be found in his "Dangen" and other Dada poems: "You can realize a poor poet by the fact that he is rich in the power of imagination"; "A guy who doesn't appreciate mistranslations and misprints is a wretch who only has the occiput developed and nothing else" (both from "To *A Man Who Eats Dreams* and Its Author"); "Death, poetry—even useless for *hors d'oeuvres* to a raw fish dish" ("A Blind Man"); "When you leave a note [will] behind, don't season it" (No. 42). A later poem, "Muimi" (Meaningless), contained in his 1936 volume, *Shinkichi shisho* (Selected poems of Shinkichi), reads in part: "Words are the first of what man does not need."

The Buddhist emphasis on intuitionalism and anti-reasoning, ideas which were in fact those of Gautama Buddha, are enlarged upon characteristically in the Zen practice of *koan* (*kung-an* in Chinese), a series of questions and answers between the master and his student at a private interview called *sanzen*. One of the oldest and the most time-honored Chinese examples of questioning that are still favored by the Zen masters of today would be a question the sixth patriarch (Hui-nêng) addressed to the head monk Ming: "Thinking neither of good nor of evil at this very moment, what had been your original nature [original face] before your parents were born?" Another Chinese example is that Master Chao-chou Ts'ungshên (Joshu Jushin in Japanese, 778-897), when a monk asked him whether the dog had a Buddha nature or not, answered simply *"wu!"* This is, in spite of its literal meaning ("without," "-less," "nothing"), an exclamation which does not allow it to be translated in Zen. An equally famous Japanese example is a phrase of Master Hakuin Ekaku (1686-1769): "Listen to the sound of the single hand clapping!" Many of the deliberately ambiguous, obscure, and even confusing *koan* phrases and the manner in which they are employed might give an impression of a game of paradox, wordplay, joke, or, in the Dada-Surrealist sense, black humor; and yet they have a serious purpose, aiming at *satori* (enlightenment) and self-realization. The use of *koans* is then an art of immersing oneself in the hidden, inner treasures of universal truth, there to commune with the Buddhist state of nothingness in the sublime sense.

Takahashi, who belongs to the Rinzai (Chinese Lin-chi) sect, started practicing the Zen discipline in 1927, and concentrated his writing of poetry on Zen subjects thereafter. However, the Zen qualities prevail in his earlier Dada poems as well, especially in his insistence on the illogical, disconnected, rapidly moving imagery tinged with the flavor of "black humor." In this respect, he resembles Tzara. Mary Ann Caws observes the characteristics of Tzara's early Dada poetry (such as *Twenty-five Poems* of 1918 and *Of Our Birds* of 1923), which, as she says, "at first reading . . . seems to consist of unusual images gratuitously linked to each other in an order invisible to the logical mind and in complete accord with Dada principles of rapidity and vitality," and emphasizes the significance of the Dada joke. "[Yet] one of the primary elements of the Dada joke," says she, "like its parallel, the surrealist game, is its seriousness; its particular type of humor lies precisely there. Tzara always claims for Dada creations an essential interior ordering, a 'constellation' of necessary clarity below the obvious surface." This statement is an excellent description of the fundamental points of Zen in terms of its pursuance of true, "necessary clarity."

Takahashi's admiration of Matsuo Basho, the sixteenth-century haiku poet, for his Zen spirit, on the one hand, and rejection of the haiku-tanka tradition for its conventions regarding diction and formal proportions, on the other, also reveals Takahashi's attitude toward poetry and his approach toward Dada. He tends to direct simplicity toward spontaneity and distinguishes the rhythm of decorum from that of naturalness. This tendency is exemplified in his Dada poetry by his frequent use of

sounds, aside from an arbitrary connection of words, although he has never written the so-called sound-poem per se. He even delights in romanizing repeated sounds. For example, *"PiRi PiRi PiRi/ Goso Goso Goso/ BoRo BoRo BoRo/ JAVA JAVA JAVA"*; *"Piri Piri Piri/ Kori Kori Kori"* ("Cherries"); *"GARA GARA GARA GARA GARA"* (poem No. 23). In addition, onomatopoeia in Japanese transcription is a dominant factor in his Dada volume, such as *"butsubutsu"* (No. 28); *"pun,"* *"hyun,"* *"petpet,"* *"potori"* (No. 34); *"peropero,"* *"pitapita"* (No. 42); *"gatagata"* (No. 43); *"gatsugatsu"* (No. 46). The following lines show the manner in which he associates onomatopoeia with ideas:

> *geta no oto*
> *karakoro*
>   *doko mademo hibiite iku*

> The sound of wooden clogs,
> *karakoro,*
>   echoes without end.
>   —(From No. 32)

> *jinsei ni ison wa nai*
>   *tada shindoi*
>   *pachi*
>   *pichi*
>   *pachi*
> *seitai ni fuman ga aru bakari*

> No craving for life,
>   only sick and tired of it.
>   *pachi*
>   *pichi*
>   *pachi*
> Just discontented with my vocal chords.
>   —(From No. 59)

With the sound *karakoro* in the first poem, Takahashi may have implied "emptiness" (*kara*) in echoes and "tumbling about" (*koro* from the verb *korobu*), depicting life as walking aimlessly, with that sound and "without end." In the second poem, the poet discloses his disappointment with life, fixating on the childlike utterance, *pachi pichi pachi,* and disliking his own voice.

Tzara's early works are also full of sounds and untranslatable exclamations; they are, in many cases, more unusual and more dramatic than those Takahashi uses. To mention only a few examples, in "The Second Celestial Adventure of Mr. Antipyrine" of 1917, Ear shouts *"b.b.b.b. . . . "* (35 *b*'s) and *"boumabarassassa"*; Mrs. Interpretation says *"n.n.j.n.t.h.n.j.h.h.h."*; The Disinterested Brain, *"feeeeeeeeldspaaaaaaaar"* and *"badabà badabà badabà"*; Mr. Antipyrine, *"dadadi dadadi dadadi moumbimba dadadi."* The poem "White Giant Leper of the Countryside" (in *Twenty-five Poems*) contains *"tzantzantza ganga,"* *"bouzdouc zdouc nfounfa mbaah mbaah nfounfa,"* *"gmbababa,"* *"nfoua loua la,"* *"nbaze baze baze,"* *"nfounda nbababa nfounda tata nbababa,"* and so on. A line in the same poem reads: "there are zigzags on his soul and lots of rrrrrrrrrrrrrr," and it is repeated soon after, with seven *r*'s (instead of 14) at the end of a new line. The use of the "zigzag" image, which recurs in another poem, "The Great Lament of My Obscurity Three," bestows, in effect, a weighty significance on the lingual sound *r*.

Peterson and Caws point out that these foreign expressions are African and pseudo-African words. Whatever their origin might be, "his expression," as Peterson observes, "like Beckett's and Ionesco's, is used to 'produce sounds made to re-echo in the void,' the emphasis being on the sound rather than the meaning." Caws, in her careful study of "The Verbal Origin of Tzara's Imagery," examines the changes in the manuscripts and the final printed form, and draws a conclusion about Tzara's aesthetic principle as follows:

> In general, nine out of ten changes made by Tzara in his poetry and poetic prose before 1935 are aesthetically defensible, even if such a criterion as the aesthetic is found unacceptable in itself. Banalities are transformed into unique expressions, the ordinary is transformed into the extraordinary, and the over-sentimental into the majestically simple. The re-markable acuity of Tzara's aural perception bears primary responsibility for the remarkable nature of his poetry.

Tzara's aesthetic can also be found "defensible" when he praises Alfred Jarry, the author of *Ubu Roi* (King Ubu), for having "consciously taken humor away from a certain filthy lowness, by giving it its poetic significance," for being the "Creator also of the *unexpected* and of the *surprise*, [and the] Magnificent handler of the *absurd* and the *arbitrary*." The Dadaist Tzara's method of conveying a poetic message is thus far from a merely negative jest.

When the two antiversifiers Tzara and Takashi are considered together, their preoccupation with simplicity and spontaneity characterized by sounds may be likened to Kandinsky's views on word and poetry. As early as 1912, in discussing Maeterlinck's principal method, he made the following account of the word, which he defines as "an inner sound":

> The apt use of a word (in its poetical sense), its repetition, twice, three times, or even more frequently, according to the need of the poem, will not only tend to intensify the internal structure but also bring out unsuspected spiritual properties in the word itself. Further, frequent repetition of a word (a favorable game of children, forgotten in later life) deprives the word of its external reference. Similarly, the symbolic reference of a designated object tends to be forgotten and only the sound is retained. We hear this pure sound, unconsciously perhaps, in relation to the concrete impression on the soul.

What he calls "pure sound" may echo in such Zen exclamations as *"Ka!"* (or *"Ga!," "Ha!," "Ho!"*—a spontaneous shout made at the moment of enlightenment) and *"Kan!"* (*kuan* in Chinese pronunciation of the same character, literally meaning "barrier," yet a mere sound not to be taken literally, known to have been first uttered by the Chinese monk Yün-mên Wên-yen, 862?-949). To pen-

etrate further into Kandinsky's statement from a Zen point of view, it would appear that the "pure sound" can be heard in Hakuin's "sound of the single hand" which was mentioned earlier in connection with *koan*.

D. T. Suzuki considers that "Zen naturally finds its readiest expression in poetry rather than in philosophy because it has more affinity with feeling than with intellect; its poetic predilection is inevitable." Takahashi, recollecting how he became involved with Dada, says that he preferred poetry to fiction for his launching of the Dada movement in Japan, and he reaffirms that Dada was, at least for him, "merely the modification of Buddhism." Zen and poetry, thus, found their place in Takahashi-Dada, where Dada came to be the purest and clearest unspoken language or the outspoken sound of nothing. For Tzara, "the Dada work is," in Caws's words, "the interior transposition of a highly individual personality, whose language cannot operate under logical exterior norms: so it is at once absurd and nonabsurd, depending on whether one is out or in"; "Dada poetry is not meant to elicit the educated responses of cultured sensitivity, but rather the instant and incoherent primitive reactions of the eye and ear." Therefore, "We can either place our faith," Caws says, "in Tzara's guarantee of an intuitive luminous architecture, or accept his only half-humorous assurance that Dada's obscurity is so dark as to eventually create its own light; or we may, perhaps most wisely, follow his insistent advice that we look at the Dada poem as a simple spectacle, as a creation complete in itself and completely obvious." Although writing about Tzara, Caws's convincing and beautiful testimony to the principles of Dada precisely describes, by implication, those of Zen and Takahashi Shinkichi.

Here again we come to the point where the aesthetic principle of simultaneity coincides with the Zen experience in simultanism. In the words of Roger Shattuck, "The aspiration of simultanism is to grasp the moment in its total significance or, more ambitiously, to manufacture a moment which surpasses our usual perception of time and space." This definition might almost be a precise expression of both Dada's and Zen's sensibilities.

From the foregoing evidence of the accord found in the concepts of nothingness, illogicality, spontaneous simplicity, and simultaneity by Tzara and Takahashi, the Dada worlds in which both poets found expression seem uniquely to concur. Thus, the classical universality of Zen finds its vivid expression in the modern universality of Dada.

WESTERN LITERATURE

R. H. Blyth

SOURCE: "What is Zen?" in *Zen in English Literature and Oriental Classics,* Hokuseido Press, 1942, pp. 1-24.

[*In the following essay, Blyth endeavors to find a definition of Zen by providing examples of the philosophy from English literature.*]

Consider the lives of birds and fishes. Fish never weary of the water; but you do not know the true mind of a fish, for you are not a fish. Birds never tire of the woods; but you do not know their real spirit, for you are not a bird. It is just the same with the religious, the poetical life: if you do not live it, you know nothing about it. . . .

[Zen] is the real religious, poetical life. But, as Mrs. Browning says in *Aurora Leigh,*

> The cygnet finds the water, but the man
> Is born in ignorance of his element.

Dôgen, (1200-1253) founder of the Sôtô Sect of Zen in Japan, expresses this more poetically:

> The water-bird
>   Wanders here and there
>   Leaving no trace,
>   Yet her path
>   She never forgets.

Zen, though far from indefinite, is by definition indefinable, because it is the active principle of life itself.

> The sun passeth through pollutions and itself
>   remains as pure as before,

so Zen passes through all our definings and remains Zen as before. As we think of it, it seems dark, but "dark with excessive light." It is like Alice in The Looking Glass, the more we run after it the farther away we get. Yet we read books on Zen, and more books, hoping to find on some page, in some sentence or other, the key to a door which is only a hallucination. Zen says "Walk in!" Never mind the key or the bolt or the massive-seeming door. Just walk in! Goethe's revised version of the beginning of the Gospel of St. John, comes nearest:

> Im Anfang war die Tat,

for action cannot be defined. In *The Anticipation* Traherne says,

> His name is Now . . .
> His essence is all Act.

Milton describes its unnoticed universality in *Comus:*

> A small unsightly root,
> The leaf was darkish, and had prickles on it,
> But in another country, as he said,
> Bore a bright golden flow'r; but not in this soil;
> Unknown, and like esteem'd, and the dull swain
> Treads on it daily with his clouted shoon.

It is seen selected for our admiration in art, music and poetry. The difference between Zen in actual life and Zen in Art, is that Art is like a photograph (and music like a film), that can be looked at whenever we please. Or, we may say, just as Goethe called architecture frozen music, art is frozen Zen. Truth is everywhere, but is more *apparent* in science. Beauty is in dustbins and butcher's shops as well, but is more visible in the moon and flowers. Religion is in every place, at every moment, but as Johnson says in his *Journey to the Western Islands,*

> That man is little to be envied whose patriotism would not gain force upon the plain of Marathon, or whose piety would not grow warmer among the ruins of Iona.

We need not wait a moment, we need not stir a foot, to see Zen, but it is more evident in *some* acts, *some* works of art, *some* poems. In this [essay] I have chosen examples from those which have a special meaning for me. Emerson says,

> It is as difficult to appropriate the thoughts of others as to invent.

I have tried to appropriate them as far as lay in my power.

Here is an example from *Oliver Twist*. The Artful Dodger, having been arrested, appears in court:

> It was indeed Mr. Dawkins, who, shuffling into the office with the big coat sleeves tucked up as usual, his left hand in his pocket, and his hat in his right hand, preceded the jailer, with a rolling gait altogether indescribable, and, taking his place in the dock, requested in an audible voice to know what he was placed in that 'ere disgraceful sitivation for.

> "Hold your tongue, will you?" said the jailer.

> "I'm an Englishman, ain't I?" rejoined the Dodger. "Where are my priwileges?"

> "You'll get your privileges soon enough," retorted the jailer, "and pepper with 'em."

> "We'll see wot the Secretary of State for the Home Affairs has got to say to the beaks, if I don't," replied Mr Dawkins. "Now then! Wot is this here business? I shall thank the madg'strates to dispose of this here little affair, and not to keep me while they read the paper, for I've got an appointment with a genelman in the City, and as I'm a man of my word, and wery punctual in business matters, he'll go away if I ain't there to my time, and then pr'aps there won't be an action for damage against them as kep me away. Oh no, certainly not!"

> At this point, the Dodger, with a show of being very particular with a view to proceedings to be had thereafter, desired the jailer to communicate "the names of them two files as was on the bench."

(A witness is called who testifies to the Dodger's pickpocketing.)

"Have you anything to ask this witness, boy?" said the magistrate.

"I wouldn't abase myself by descending to hold no conversation with him," replied the Dodger.

"Have you anything to say at all?"

"Do you hear his worship ask if you've anything to say?" inquired the jailer, nudging the silent Dodger with his elbow.

"I beg your pardon," said the Dodger, looking up with an air of abstraction, "Did you redress yourself to me, my man?"

"I never see such an out-and-out young wagabond, your worship," observed the officer with a grin. "Do you mean to say anything, you young shaver?"

"No," replied the Dodger, "not here, for this ain't the shop for justice; besides which, my attorney is a breakfasting with the Wice President of the House of Commons; but I shall have something to say elsewhere, and so will he, and so will a wery numerous and 'spectable circle of acquaintances as 'll make them beaks wish they'd never been born, or that they'd got their footmen to hang 'em up to their own hat-pegs, 'afore they let 'em come out this morning to try it on me. I'll—"

"There! He's fully committed!" interposed the clerk. "Take him away."

"Come on," said the jailer.

"Oh, ah! I'll come on," replied the Dodger, brushing his hat with the palm of his hand. "Ah! (to the Bench) it's no use your looking frightened; I won't show you no mercy, not a ha'porth of it. *You'll* pay for this, my fine fellers. *I wouldn't be you for something! I wouldn't go free, now, if you was to fall down on your knees and ask me. Here, carry me off to prison! Take me away!*"

The Artful Dodger is "the chameleon poet that shocks the virtuous phi'osophers" on the bench. Notice how what seems to be at first mere impudence, rises with influx of energy, into an identification of himself with the whole machinery of the Law. He attains, for moment, to "Buddhahood, in which all the contradictions and disturbances caused by the intellect are entirely harmonised in a unity of higher older." Someone to whom I related the above, said to me, "I suppose the case of Mata Hari, the celebrated woman spy, was similar. When she was being executed she refused to have her eyes bandaged." This is not so. Courage may and does often have Zen associated with it, but Zen is not courage. A thief running away like mad from a ferocious watch-dog may be a splendid example of Zen. Basho gazing at the moon, is an example of Zen; eating one's dinner, yawning—where is the courage in these?

Here is an example, similar to that of Dickens, but taken from real life. I was walking along a lonely mountain road with my wife and we were talking about her elder sister, who had died the year before. She said, "When we were young we would often come back from town at night along this very road. I am a coward, and was always afraid even though we were together, but my sister said, 'I would like to whiten my face and put on a white kimono, and stand over there in the shadow of the pine-trees.'" Once again, it is not the courage, but the willing identification of self, the subject, with the ghost, the object of fear, that has in it the touch of Zen. Here is another example of a different kind, in which there is no trace of ordinary courage; it consists in entire engrossment, conscious and unconscious, in what one is doing. This requires, of course, that one's work at the moment should be thoroughly congenial to one's nature, that is to say, it must be like the swimming of a fish or the flying of a bird. In his *Conversations with Goethe,* under Tuesday, April 22nd, 1830, Eckermann notes the following:

> I was much struck by a Savoyard boy, who turned a hurdygurdy, and led behind him a dog, on which a monkey was riding. He whistled and sang to us, and for a long time tried to make us give him something. We threw him down more than he could have expected, and I thought he would throw us a look of gratitude. However he did nothing of the kind, but pocketed his money, and immediately looked after others to give him more.

What struck Eckermann? Was it the ingratitude of the boy? I think not. It was the complete absorbtion of the boy in the work he was doing to get money. Other people had no existence for him. Three days after, a very similar thing struck Eckermann.

> At dinner, at the table d'hôte, I saw many faces, but few expressive enough to fix my attention. However, the head waiter interested me highly, so that my eyes constantly followed him and all his movements: and indeed he was a remarkable being. The guests who sat at the long table were about two hundred in number, and it seems almost incredible when I say that nearly the whole of the attendance was performed by the head waiter, since he put on and took off all the dishes, while the other waiters only handed them to him and received them from him. During all this proceeding, nothing was spilt, no one was incommoded, but all went off lightly and nimbly, as if by the operation of a spirit. Thus, thousands of plates and dishes flew from his hands upon the table, and again from the table to the hands of the attendants behind him. Quite absorbed in his vocation, the whole man was nothing but eyes and hands, and he merely opened his closed lips for short answers and directions. Then he not only attended to the table but took the orders for wine and the like, and so well remembered everything, that when the meal was over, he knew everybody's score and took the money.

This is a splended example of Zen, which Eckermann calls "comprehensive power, presence of mind and strong memory." We may call it "presence of Mind," or "absence of mind." The memory, as Freud would say, is a matter of the will. We forget because we will (wish) to forget, and remember because we will to remember. "The whole man was nothing but eyes and hands." Turner was nothing but a paint-brush, Michael Angelo nothing but a chisel. There is no greater pleasure in ordinary life, so-called, than to see a bus-conductor, a teacher, anybody, really engrossed in his work, with no thought of its relative or absolute value, with no thought of its interest or profit to himself or others.

A similar example is given in Dickens' *Martin Chuzzlewit.* Mr. Pecksniff and his daughters are dining at Todger's, but the really interesting thing about the hilarious and convivial proceedings is Bailey, the boy who cleans the boots and is temporarily serving at table. He has "life more abundantly," with no self-consciousness or "choosing" or judging or attachment; equal to all circumstances, master of every situation. And be it noted that just as Eckermann's head waiter shows his Zen by doing his work so well, to perfection, so Dickens' boy shows his Zen by doing practically nothing at all, *to perfection,* in similar circumstances.

> Their young friend Bailey sympathised [with the two Miss Pecksniffs] in these feelings to the fullest extent, and abating nothing of his patronage, gave them every encouragement in his power: favouring them, when the general attention was diverted from his proceedings, with many nods and winks and other tokens of recognition, and occasionally touching his nose with a corkscrew, as if to express the Bacchanalian character of the meeting. In truth perhaps even the spirits of the two Miss Pecksniffs, and the hungry watchfulness of Mr. Todgers, were less worthy of note than the proceedings of this remarkable boy, whom nothing disconcerted or put out of his way. If any piece of crockery, a dish or otherwise, chanced to slip through his hands (which happened once or twice) he let it go with perfect good breeding, and never added to the painful emotions of the company by exhibiting the least regret. Nor did he, by hurrying to and fro, disturb the repose of the assembly, as many well-trained servants do; on the contrary, feeling the hopelessness of waiting upon so large a party, he left the gentlemen to help themselves to what they wanted, and seldom stirred from behind Mr. Jenkins's chair: where, with his hands in his pockets, and his legs planted pretty wide apart, he led the laughter, and enjoyed the conversation.

This perfection, which we see always in inanimate things, usually in animals, so seldom in human beings, almost never in ourselves, is what Christ urges us to attain:

> Be ye perfect, as your Father which is in Heaven is perfect.

Many people will no doubt be surprised that Mark Tapley is not used as an example of Zen. His desire "to come out strong" in the most difficult circumstances may seem evidence of this, but actually it is evidence of the opposite. Zen is essentially unconscious, unself-conscious, even unSelfconscious. Notice further that, as Mrs. Lupin says, he is "a good young man." Sad to relate, we can find Zen in Mr. Pecksniff, Mrs. Gamp, Bailey Junior, that is, in hypocrisy, vulgarity, and impudence, more readily than in the conscious unselfishness of Mark Tapley. This is why the latter has something thin, unreal, out-of-joint about him. He is not equal to all circumstances, only to the worst.

There are two fables by Stevenson, *The Sinking Ship,* which shows Zen on its destructive side, and *The Poor Thing,* which illustrates its constructive working. Here is *The Sinking Ship:*

> "Sir," said the first lieutenant, bursting into the Captain's cabin, "the ship is going down."
>
> "Very well, Mr. Spoker," said the Captain; "but that is no reason for going about half-shaved. Exercise your mind a moment, Mr. Spoker, and you will see that to the philosophic eye there is nothing new in our position: the ship (if she is to go down at all) may be said to have been going down since she was launched."
>
> "She is settling fast," said the first lieutenant, as he returned from shaving.
>
> "Fast, Mr. Spoker?" asked the Captain. "The expression is a strange one, for time (if you will think of it) is only relative."
>
> "Sir," said the lieutenant, "I think it is scarcely worth while to embark in such a discussion when we shall all be in Davy Jones's Locker in ten minutes."
>
> "By parity of reasoning," returned the Captain gently, "it would never be worth while to begin any inquiry of importance; the odds are always overwhelming that we must die before we shall have brought it to an end. You have not considered, Mr. Spoker, the situation of man," said the Captain, smiling, and shaking his head.
>
> "I am much more engaged in considering the position of the ship," said Mr. Spoker.
>
> "Spoken like a good officer," replied the Captain, laying his hand on the lieutenant's shoulder.
>
> On deck they found the men had broken into the spirit room, and were fast getting drunk.
>
> "My men," said the Captain, "there is no sense in this. The ship is going down, you will tell me, in ten minutes: well, and what then? To the philosophic eye, there is nothing new in our position. All our lives long, we may have been about to break a blood-vessel or to be struck by lightning, not merely in ten minutes, but in ten seconds; and that has not prevented us from eating dinner, no, nor from putting money in the Savings Bank. I assure you, with my hand on my heart, I fail to comprehend your attitude."

The men were already too far gone to pay much heed.

"This is a very painful sight, Mr. Spoker," said the Captain.

"And yet to the philosophic eye, or whatever it is." replied the first lieutenant, "they may be said to have been getting drunk since they came aboard."

"I do not know if you always follow my thought, Mr. Spoker," returned the Captain gently. "But let us proceed."

In the powder magazine they found an old salt smoking his pipe.

"Good God," cried the Captain, "what are you about?"

"Well, sir," said the old salt, apologetically, "they told me as she were going down."

"And suppose she were?" said the Captain. "To the philosophic eye, there would be nothing new in our position. Life, my old shipmate, life, at any moment and in any view, is as dangerous as a sinking ship; and yet it is man's handsome fashion to carry umbrellas, to wear india-rubber over-shoes, to begin vast works, and to conduct himself in every way as if he might hope to be eternal. And for my own poor part I should despise the man who, even on board a sinking ship, should omit to take a pill or to wind up his watch. That, my friend, would not be the human attitude."

"I beg pardon, sir," said Mr. Spoker. "But what is precisely the difference between shaving in a sinking ship and smoking in a powder magazine?"

"Or doing anything at all in any conceivable circumstances?" cried the Captain. "Perfectly conclusive; give me a cigar!"

Two minutes afterwards the ship blew up with a glorious detonation.

It is very amusing to see how the Captain adopts the absolute position in, "the ship may be said to have been going down since she was launched," and, "time is only relative," and then, descending to the relative in reproving the men for drunkenness, is caught up by the first lieutenant. The "philosophic eye," is the eye of God, which sees shaving in a sinking ship (where the shaving and the sinking have no immediate connection) and smoking in a powder magazine (where the smoking is the cause of the ship's blowing up) as the same. When we have the eye of God we are released from cause and effect ("He that loseth his life shall find it") from space ("If ye shall say unto this mountain, Be thou removed, and be thou cast into the sea; it shall be done,") and from time ("A thousand years in Thy sight are but as yesterday when it is past"). "Doing anything at all in any conceivable circumstances," is the freedom of Zen. A man must be able (that is, willing) to do anything on any occasion whatever. Hundreds of verses in the writings of Zen ex-

press this perfect freedom, which alone allows us to act perfectly. Here are some from the *Zenrinkushu.*

> Stones rise up into the sky;
> Fire burns down in the water.

> Ride your horse along the edge of a sword;
> Hide yourself in the middle of the flames.

> Blossoms of the fruit-tree bloom in the fire;
> The sun rises in the evening.

But the most important word in the fable is "glorious." Glorious means Good, as distinguished from good. The word 'good' is a relative word opposed to 'bad.' The word "Good" is absolute and has no contrary. In the same way we may distinguish, in writing, but not in speaking, 'happy' and 'Happy.' Stephen being stoned to death was Happy; he was certainly not happy. Again, Love is what makes the world go round; love is quite another thing. So as I say, glorious, means Good; we have the Glorious Inferno of Dante, the Glorious deafness of Beethoven, the Glorious sun that Blake saw. The revolt of Lucifer, the career of Nero, the crucifixion of Christ—all these were Glorious, like the detonation that sent hundreds of souls into eternity. "Nothing is Glorious, but thinking makes it so."

Just at this point another fable of Stevenson is relevant perhaps, *The Reader.* Let me insert it here:

"I never read such an impious book," said the reader, throwing it on the floor.

"You need not hurt me," said the book; "You will only get less for me second-hand, and I did not write myself."

"That is true," said the reader, "My quarrel is with your author."

"Ah, well," said the book, "you need not buy his rant."

"That is true," said the reader. "But I thought him such a cheerful writer."

"I find him so," said the book.

"You must be differently made from me," said the reader.

"Let me tell you a fable," said the book. "There were two men wrecked upon a desert island; one of them made believe he was at home, the other admitted . . ."

"Oh, I know your kind of fable," said the reader. "They both died."

"And so they did," said the book. "No doubt of that. And every body else."

"That is true," said the reader. "Push it a little further for this once. And when they were all dead?"

"They were in God's hands, the same as before," said the book.

"Not much to boast of, by your account," cried the reader.

"Who is impious, now?" said the book, and the reader put him on the fire.

The coward crouches from the rod,
And loathes the iron face of God.

Most religious people are impious, far more so than the irreligious. They always tell you, "God wouldn't do that." "The universe couldn't be made like that." "Good is good and bad is bad, and never the twain shall meet." Impiety means ingratitude, not being thankful for what God gives, but wanting, nay, demanding something else, requiring the universe to be different from what it is. Before we are born, all our life, and for all eternity after, we are in God's hands; whether our life continues, or whether it fizzles out, we are to say "Thank God!"

The other fable is *The Poor Thing,* which shows Zen working, as it so often does, in a man of "little lore." This simplicity of mind, which we see and envy in children and idiots, is essential if we would become the real master of our fate, the captain of our soul. Bashô, in his *Oku no Hosomichi* quotes with approval Confucius' saying, that firmness, resoluteness, simplicity and slowness of speech, are not far from virtue, and Theseus, in *A Midsummer Night's Dream,*

Never anything can be amiss
When simpleness and duty tender it.

THE POOR THING

There was a man in the islands who fished for his bare bellyful and took his life in his hands to go forth upon the sea between four planks. But though he had much ado, he was merry of heart; and the gulls heard him laugh when the spray met him. And though he had little lore, he was sound of spirit; and when the fish came to his hook in the mid-waters, he blessed God without weighing. He was bitter poor in goods and bitter ugly of countenance, and he had no wife.

It fell at the time of the fishing that the man awoke in his house about the midst of the afternoon. The fire burned in the midst, and the smoke went up and the sun came down by the chimney. And the man was aware of the likeness of one that warmed his hands at the red peat fire.

"I greet you," said the man, "in the name of God."

"I greet you," said he that warmed his hands, "but not in the name of God, for I am none of His; nor in the name of Hell, for I am not of Hell. For I am

but a bloodless thing, less than wind and lighter than a sound, and the wind goes through me like a net, and I am broken by a sound and shaken by the cold."

"Be plain with me," said the man, "and tell me your name and of your nature."

"My name," quoth the other, "is not yet named, and my nature not yet sure. For I am part of a man; and I was a part of your fathers, and went out to fish and fight with them in the ancient days. But now is my turn not yet come; and I wait until you have a wife, and then shall I be in your son, and a brave part of him, rejoicing manfully to launch the boat into the surf, skilful to direct the helm, and a man of might where the ring closes and the blows are going."

"This is a marvellous thing to hear," said the man; "and if you are indeed to be my son, I fear it will go ill with you; for I am bitter poor in goods and bitter ugly in face, and I shall never get me a wife if I live to the age of eagles."

"All this have I come to remedy, my Father," said the Poor Thing; "for we must go this night to the little isle of sheep, where our fathers lie in the dead-cairn, and tomorrow to the Earl's Hall, and there shall you find a wife by my providing."

So the man rose and put forth his boat at the time of the sunsetting; and the Poor Thing sat in the prow, and the spray blew through his bones like snow, and the wind whistled in his teeth, and the boat dipped not with the weight of him.

"I am fearful to see you, my son," said the man. "For methinks you are no thing of God."

"It is only the wind that whistles in my teeth," said the Poor Thing, "and there is no life in me to keep it out."

So they came to the little isle of sheep, where the surf burst all about it in the midst of the sea, and it was all green with bracken, and all wet with dew, and the moon enlightened it. They ran the boat into a cove, and set foot to land; and the man came heavily behind among the rocks in the deepness of the bracken, but the Poor Thing went before him like a smoke in the light of the moon. So they came to the deadcairn, and they laid their ears to the stones; and the dead complained withinsides like a swarm of bees: "Time was that marrow was in our bones, and strength in our sinews; and the thoughts of our head were clothed upon with acts and the words of men. But now are we broken in sunder, and the bonds of our bones are loosed, and our thoughts lie in the dust."

Then said the Poor Thing: "Charge them that they give you the virtue they withheld."

And the man said: "Bones of my fathers, greeting! for I am sprung of your loins. And now, behold, I break open the piled stones of your cairn, and I let in the noon between your ribs. Count it well done, for it was to be; and give me what I come seeking in the name of blood and in the name of God."

And the spirits of the dead stirred in the cairn like ants; and they spoke: "You have broken the roof of our cairn and let in the moon between our ribs; and you have the strength of the still-living. But what virtue have we? what power? or what jewel here in the dust with us, that any living man should covet or receive it? for we are less than nothing. But we tell you one thing, speaking with many voices like bees, that the way is plain before all like the grooves of launching. Go forth into life and fear not, for so did we all in the ancient ages." And their voices passed away like an eddy in a river.

"Now," said the Poor Thing, "they have told you a lesson, but make them give you a gift. Stoop your hand among the bones without drawback, and you shall find their treasure."

So the man stooped his hand, and the dead laid hold upon it many and faint like ants; but he shook them off, and behold, what he brought up in his hand was the shoe of a horse, and it was rusty.

"It is a thing of no price," quoth the man, "for it is rusty."

"We shall see that," said the Poor Thing; "for in my thought it is a good thing to do what our fathers did, and to keep what they kept without question. And in my thought one thing is as good as another in this world; and a shoe of a horse will do."

Now they got into their boat with the horse-shoe, and when the dawn was come they were aware of the smoke of the Earl's town and the bells of the Kirk that beat. So they set foot to shore; and the man went up to the market among the fishers over against the palace and the Kirk; and he was bitter poor and bitter ugly, and he had never a fish to sell, but only a shoe of a horse in his creel, and it rusty.

"Now," said the Poor Thing," "do so and so, and you shall find a wife and I a mother."

It befell that the Earl's daughter came forth to go into the Kirk upon her prayers; and when she saw the poor man stand in the market with only the shoe of a horse, and it rusty, it came in her mind it should be a thing of price.

"What is that?" quoth she.

"It is a shoe of a horse," said the man.

"And what is the use of it?" quoth the Earl's daughter.

"It is for no use," said the man.

"I may not believe that," said she; "else why should

you carry it?"

"I do so," said he, "because it was so my fathers did in the ancient ages; and I have neither a better reason nor a worse."

Now the Earl's daughter could not find it in her mind to believe him. "Come," quoth she, "sell me this, for I am sure it is a thing of price."

"Nay," said the man, "the thing is not for sale."

"What!" cried the Earl's daughter. "Then what make you here in the town's market, with the thing in your creel and nought beside?"

"I sit here," says the man, "to get me a wife."

"There is no sense in any of these answers," thought the Earl's daughter; "and I could find it in my heart to weep."

By came the Earl upon that; and she called him and told him all. And when he had heard, he was of his daughter's mind that this should be a thing of virtue; and charged the man to set a price upon the thing, or else be hanged upon the gallows; and that was near at hand, so that the man could see it.

"The way of life is straight like the grooves of launching," quoth the man. "And if I am to be hanged let me be hanged."

"Why!" cried the Earl, "will you set your neck against a shoe of a horse, and it rusty?"

"In my thought," said the man, "one thing is as good as another in this world; and a shoe of a horse will do."

"This can never be," thought the Earl; and he stood and looked upon the man, and bit his beard.

And the man looked up at him and smiled. "It was so my fathers did in the ancient ages," quoth he to the Earl, "and I have neither a better reason nor a worse."

"There is no sense in any of this," thought the Earl, "and I must be growing old." So he had his daughter on one side, and says he: "Many suitors have you denied, my child. But here is a very strange matter that a man should cling so to a shoe of a horse, and it rusty; and that he should offer it like a thing on sale, and yet not sell it; and that he should sit there seeking a wife. If I come not to the bottom of this thing, I shall have no more pleasure in bread; and I can see no way, but either I should hang or you should marry him."

"By my troth, but he is bitter ugly," said the Earl's daughter. "How if the gallows be so near at hand?"

"It was not so," said the Earl, "that my fathers did in the ancient ages. I am like the man, and can give you neither a better reason nor a worse. But do you, prithee, speak with him again."

So the Earl's daughter spoke to the man. "If you were not so bitter ugly," quoth she, "my father the Earl would have us marry."

"Bitter ugly am I," said the man, "and you as fair as May. Bitter ugly I am, and what of that? It was so my fathers—"

"In the name of God," said the Earl's daughter, "let your fathers be!"

"If I had done that," said the man, "you had never been chaffering with me here in the market, nor your father the Earl watching with the end of his eye."

"But come," quoth the Earl's daughter, "this is a very strange thing, that you would have me wed for a shoe of a horse, and it rusty."

"In my thought," quoth the man, "one thing is as good—"

"Oh, spare me that," said the Earl's daughter, "and tell me why I should marry."

"Listen and look," said the man.

Now the wind blew through the Poor Thing like an infant crying, so that her heart was melted; and her eyes were unsealed, and she was aware of the thing as it were a babe unmothered, and she took it to her arms, and it melted in her arms like the air.

"Come," said the man, "behold a vision of our children, the busy hearth, and the white heads. And let that suffice, for it is all God offers."

"I have no delight in it," said she; but with that she sighed.

"The ways of life are straight like the grooves of launching," said the man; and he took her by the hand.

"And what shall we do with the horseshoe?" quoth she.

"I will give it to your father," said the man; "and he can make a kirk and a mill of it for me."

It came to pass in time that the Poor Thing was born; but memory of these matters slept within him, and he knew not that which he had done. But he was a part of the eldest son; rejoicing manfully to launch the boat into the surf, skilful to direct the helm, and a man of might where the ring closes and the blows are going.

"Sound of spirit" and "merry of heart,"—to how few is it given to be this. It is a kind of natural Zen. "He blessed God without weighing." Long fish, short fish, fat fish, thin fish, many fish, few fish, no fish—he thanked God for them all. "The way is plain before all like the grooves of launching." In *Inscribed on the Believing Mind,* we have:

The Way is not difficult; but you must avoid
choosing!

("Avoid choosing" means "without weighing,"
"Judge not that ye be not judged.")

Christians and Buddhists alike put their religion in some other place, some other time; but we are all, with or without religion, tarred with the same brush. Like Mrs. Jelleby in *Bleak House,* with her "impossible love of the blackamoors" and indifference to her own husband and children, we think of our religion, our ideals, forgetting (on purpose) that the Way is here and now; in what we are doing, saying, feeling, reading, at this very moment. Confucius says in *The Doctrine of the Mean,*

The Way is not far from man; if we take the Way
as something superhuman, beyond man, this is not
the real Way.

Mencius is even closer to Stevenson:

The Way is near, but men seek it afar. It is in easy
things, but men seek for it in difficult things.

The Way is like a great highroad; there is no
difficulty whatever in recognising it. What is wrong
with us is that we do not really search for it. Just
go home, and plenty of people will point it out to
you.

The *Saikontan* says,

The Zen Sect tells us: When you are hungry, eat
rice; when you are weary, sleep.

That is all religion is; eat when you are hungry, sleep when you are tired. But to do such simple things property is really the most difficult thing in the world. I remember when I began to attend lectures, at a Zen temple, on the *Mumonkan,* I was surprised to find that there were no lofty spiritual truths enunciated at all. Two things stuck in my head, because they were repeated so often, and with such gusto. One of them, emphasised with extreme vigour, was that you must not smoke a cigarette while making water. The other was that when somebody calls you (in Japanese "Oi!") you must answer (Hai!) at once, without hesitation. When we compare this with the usual Christian exhortatory sermon, we cannot help being struck by the difference. I myself heard the "Oi!" "Hai!" so many times I began to wait for it and look on it as a kind of joke, and as soon as I did this, I began to see a light, or "get warm," as the children say. It is like the grooves of launching. Release the blocks and the ship moves. One calls "Oi!" the other says "Hai!" There is nothing between.

"It is a good thing to do what our fathers did, and to keep what they kept without question." This is not a popular doctrine nowadays. Old traditions are forgotten but new ones spring up like mushrooms everywhere. In the Zen temple, together with some unnecessary and old-fashioned customs, there is a vast body of essential religion preserved in the form of rules: regularity of life, celibacy, vegetarianism, poverty, unquestioning obedience, methodical destruction of self-full thinking and acting, complete control of mind and body,—all these systematised into a way of life in which work, we may say, Work, is the grand answer to the question, "What is man's element?"

"And in my thought, one thing is as good as another in this world." This states the absolute value of everything; all things have equal value, for all have infinite value. If you like this kind of mystical truth and can swallow it easily, well and good. If not, it does not matter, because it is only ordinary common sense. The value of a thing is in its use, as Robinson Crusoe found out with regard to the pieces-of-gold on his desert island. It's no good playing the cello to a thirsty man. You can't light a fire with ice-cream. You may protest that things differ at least in their potential value; a drawing by Claude is not equal in value to a grain of sand. It may well be so. The financial, the artistic, the moral values may differ: the point is that the *absolute* value is the same. If you see infinity in a grain of sand and heaven in a wild flower, where is the necessity for anything else? Everything depends on the mind of man;

> There is nothing either good or bad but thinking makes it so.

So when the man was asked what was the use of his rusty horse-shoe, he answered, "It is for no use," This has exactly the same meaning as the 1st Case of the *Mumonkan*.

> A monk said to Joshu, "Has this dog the Buddha-nature or not?" Joshu replied "No!"

Its absolute value is nil. It has the same value as a rusty horse-shoe. Has this rusty horse-shoe the Buddha nature? The answer is, Yes! If you can rise, just for a moment, beyond this No-Yes, you understand that one thing is as good (that is, as Good) as another in this world. "And let that suffice, for it is all God offers." What is happening to me, the writer, in this place, at this moment; to you, the reader, in your place, at the very moment of reading this, what you see and feel, your circumstances internal and external,—It is all that God offers. Do you want to be in some other place, in different circumstances? Take the present ones to your heart, let them suffice, for it is all God offers. If you feel aggrieved with so little, remember that "one thing is as good as another." If your aim is comfort, only some things, some times, some places will do. If your aim is virtue (that is, Goodness, not goodness,) anything, any time, any place will suffice. When Confucius was asked concerning the brothers Haku I and Shuku Sai, who gave up the throne and their lives rather than do wrong,

> "Had they any regrets?"

he answered,

> "They sought for virtue; they got virtue: what was there for them to regret?"

John G. Rudy

SOURCE: Introduction, in *Wordsworth and the Zen Mind: The Poetry of Self-Emptying*, State University of New York Press, 1996, 288 p.

[*In the following essay, Rudy applies several key concepts of Zen Buddhism—wholeness, the state of "no-mind," and the Zen idea of emptiness—to his study of the poetic metaphysics of William Wordsworth.*]

In his Prospectus to *The Recluse* (1814), the work which announces that the chief aim of his poetry is to examine and to celebrate the mind, William Wordsworth writes:

> Not Chaos, not
> The darkest pit of lowest Erebus,
> Nor aught of blinder vacancy, scooped out
> By help of dreams—can breed such fear and awe
> As fall upon us often when we look
> Into our Minds, into the Mind of Man—
> My haunt, and the main region of my song.
> (35-41)

Though it emerges as a potential nightmare realm, the mind appears here as a distinctively human phenomenon accessible to the poetic self committed to exploring it.

In poignant contrast to the image of mind depicted in the Prospectus is that which the poet offers in his "Lines Composed a Few Miles above Tintern Abbey" (*Poetical Works*: 259-63), which he wrote and published in 1798. Describing a moment of deep repose along the banks of the Wye, Wordsworth tells of how he owes to the "beauteous forms" of the harmonious landscape, which includes cottages, orchards, and hedgerows as well as such naturally occurring phenomena as woods, sky, and cliffs,

> sensations sweet,
> Felt in the blood, and felt along the heart;
> And passing even into my purer mind,
> With tranquil restoration. . . .
> (27-30)

Wordsworth does not explain what he means by "my purer mind," and he makes no effort to adumbrate its dimensions. He speaks only of its receiving sensations of the "beauteous forms" of the surrounding environment and of his own subsequent restoration in tranquillity. After mentioning how the "unremembered pleasure" of such experiences contributes to "a good man's life . . . acts / Of kindness and of love" (33-35), he returns to the theme of what he owes to the forms of things, proclaiming finally the emergence of a

> blessed mood
> In which the burthen of the mystery,
> In which the heavy and the weary weight
> Of all this unintelligible world,
> Is lightened:—that serene and blessed mood,
> In which the affections gently lead us on,—
> Until, the breath of this corporeal frame
> And even the motion of our human blood

Almost suspended, we are laid asleep
In body, and become a living soul:
While with an eye made quiet by the power
Of harmony, and the deep power of joy,
We see into the life of things.

(37-49)

Both the Prospectus to *The Recluse* and the lines from "Tintern Abbey" imply that human consciousness must be understood in relation to a deep and abiding spirituality. But the terms of that spirituality are profoundly different in these works and lead to very different perceptions of what Wordsworth means by his reference to the mind of humankind as the "main region" of his "song." The Prospectus depicts the region of mind as a specific place accessible to our understanding through the application of a clearly discernible cultural idiom. The poet's reference to Chaos and Erebus, for example, recalls Milton's portrayal of the fall of Lucifer in the early books of *Paradise Lost*. Though Wordsworth, earlier in the Prospectus, spoke of passing beyond "Jehovah—with his thunder, and the choir / Of shouting Angels, and the empyreal thrones" (33-34), he nevertheless uses Miltonic imagery and the Judeo-Christian culture it evokes to locate himself in relation to the mind he wishes to explore. The effect is two-fold. Firstly, we gather the impression that a journey into mind is a troublesome, possibly a forbidden, undertaking. Secondly, we cannot help but recall Satan's famous claim that "The mind is its own place, and in itself / Can make a Heav'n of Hell, a Hell of Heav'n." The Miltonic references contribute a sense of the mind as a separate realm and suggest, further, that Wordsworth's poetic undertaking is grounded in a culturally rich, dramatic confrontation between human consciousness and the individual self.

Even when the poet abandons his allusions to the mind as a place of fear and awe and as a potential danger to the venturing self, he does not move beyond a dualistic perception of mind as one thing, the world as something else. Later in the Prospectus, for example, Wordsworth evokes the prothelamic metaphor of the healthy mind as existing in a state of marriage with the world. Asserting that "Beauty" is "a living Presence of the earth. . . . An hourly neighbour," while questioning why "Paradise, and groves / Elysian" should be viewed as "A history only of departed things, / Or a mere fiction of what never was" (42-51), he declares confidently that

the discerning intellect of Man,
When wedded to this goodly universe
In love and holy passion, shall find these
A simple produce of the common day.

(52-55)

The marriage Wordsworth here celebrates, however holy its occasion and unitary its effect, preserves nevertheless a distinction between the "discerning intellect of Man" and the world that joins it in the mutual creation of a quotidian paradise of Elysian beauty.

The "purer mind" of "Tintern Abbey," however, is much more difficult to locate and describe. Indistinguishable from its surroundings, it is aligned with a spirituality outside or beyond the idiom of a specific cultural tradition. So far as it can be said to exist at all, the mind to which the poet alludes in "Tintern Abbey" is in a state of disappearance. The "beauteous forms" that attract the poet's consciousness serve not to define it, as in the Prospectus, but to produce first a set of "sensations sweet, / Felt in the blood, and felt along the heart," then feelings that contribute a moral climate of "kindness and of love," and finally a "serene and blessed mood" that suspends "even the motion of our human blood," leaving the percipient "a living soul," adrift in a condition of disembodied, centerless spirituality. The movement of thought and image here, though no less powerful in its effect on him than the soaring expectations of the Prospectus, is downward toward a spiritual ground that hides or obliterates the sense of mind as a distinct intellectual realm. To feel sensations "in the blood" and "along the heart" is to be sensation itself, not a separate being experiencing sensation as impulses different from the self. One cannot locate the mind in a still point or stable perspective outside the moving events that constitute it. The "beauteous forms" that produce the sensations and the "purer mind" that receives them occupy an existential priority, a unitary ground of being in which percipient and perceived emerge as variant aspects of each other.

In the "blessed mood" resulting from this configuration of moving sensations, the poet speaks of seeing into the "life of things." But the "life" into which he sees, like the "purer mind" that perceives, is disembodied, unlocated, a state "In which the heavy and the weary weight" of things "Is lightened." So far as the sensations of things form the very being of the perceiver, the things seen and the act of seeing are extensions of each other. The seeing eye, like the "purer mind," is unsituated, or, if situated, then existing in the motion of the poet's bloodstream; it is moved not, as in the Prospectus, by an impulse to discover something separate from itself but by a "power / Of harmony" that makes it quiet, passive, requiring only that it open simply to what is—literally, to the moving dimensions of its own nature. The result is a mode of seeing in which the weight of things, the density and mass that make things separate and distinguishable, disperses or falls away into a spiritual ground upon which all things, including the observer, appear light, disembodied, free of specific location, lacking not form but substance or essence: having been "laid asleep / In body, and become a living soul . . . We see into the life of things." The light of seeing is coextensive with the lightness of being that comes with the sense of the essential emptiness of all things, their essencelessness.

The cognitive process of these lines, so far as we can employ such terminology, involves a steady renunciation of anything that could stand between the observer and the observed. To be a "living soul" in this sense is to be one with a world in which all things, including the human individual, are in motion and interanimate with all other things, hence disembodied, lightened, continuous with a moving environment. To see into the life of things so construed is to *be* the life of the very things one may perceive initially as "unintelligible" to the separate self. Unlike the visionary state marked out in the Prospectus, the spiritual ground Wordsworth apprehends in "Tintern Abbey" enables him to see not a new paradise, a place construed, so to speak, as the result of a creative engagement with that which is perceived initially as external to himself, but a world of "things" uncolored or unadorned by the imaginative application of a cultural overlay of images extracted from a human spiritual or religious tradition. The intelligibility Wordsworth encounters here, a mode of apprehension that lightens in the sense of both illuminating and disburdening, shifts the grounds of knowing from the individual as a separate observer to a perceptual field in which knowing is a condition of the being of all things. Cognition so conceived is not an act of discovery so much as a surrender to being, a yielding of the separate self to a condition of identity with, rather than apprehension of, "the life of things."

In book 2 of *The Prelude,* the massive poem he devoted to the growth and development of his own mind, Wordsworth describes these early visionary states more specifically and at greater length than in "Tintern Abbey":

> How shall I trace the history? where seek
> The origin of what I then have felt?
> Oft in those moments such a holy calm
> Did overspread my soul, that I forgot
> That I had bodily eyes, and what I saw
> Appeared like something in myself, a dream,
> A prospect in my mind.
>
> (2.365-71)

The question of origin as Wordsworth presents it here is, of course, unanswerable. If indeed all that one apprehends appears like something in oneself, whether viewed as a dream or as a prospect in the mind, the perceiver is for all practical purposes that which he perceives. Her state of consciousness is prior to the question of source and tends to render nugatory all concern with origin. To seek origin as a cause beyond oneself, that is, to seek it outside the dimensions of the mind, is like trying to see the very eye by which one perceives. At the same time, however, the force behind the question, the generative impulse to know, is both pertinent and necessary, for it impels recognition of a profound spirituality, a "holy calm," as Wordsworth calls it, that eliminates all sense of self and other in a condition of radical oneness with the world. To question the origin of one's feelings in the ambient light of such consciousness is to understand that in moments of high unitary vision, we cannot speak of the human as one thing, the natural as something else. Both the human and the natural share the same absence of origin and essence, the same bodilessness, the same lack of density and mass, the same inaccessibility to conventional logic and intellect.

Occasionally, however, Wordsworth's concern with origin, with the desire to know the source of his feelings, becomes a usurpative energy linked to the needs of an insecure, possibly traumatized, self. In the middle portions of "Tintern Abbey," for example, Wordsworth looks back on the visions of his youth with the discerning eye of a suspicious intellectual. Sensitive to the limitations of his present spiritual life, he tells of how he frequently recalls his early visions for solace in his adulthood, amidst "the fretful stir / Unprofitable, and the fever of the world" (52-53). But he is diffident, moved by a sense of their possible vanity, as he implies in line 50, before going on to say:

> And now, with gleams of half-extinguished
>   thought,
> With many recognitions dim and faint,
> And somewhat of a sad perplexity,
> The picture of the mind revives again. . . .
>
> (58-61)

The earlier light is now "dim and faint." What the lines from *The Prelude* offer as a generative question, as an interrogative mood that forwards and enhances the developing sense of mind as a capacious extension of nature, surfaces in "Tintern Abbey" as an admission of limitation. Writing from the perspective of a troubled adulthood, Wordsworth admits that "I cannot paint / What then I was," when nature was "all in all" (75-76). The "picture of the mind" as it emerges for him in the middle portions of "Tintern Abbey" is framed by a "sad perplexity" and distorted by the presence of an alien concern— the compensatory need to derive human lessons from nature and to find for the self a secure, if subdued, place within that which he had earlier experienced as coterminous with his own being:

> For I have learned
> To look on nature, not as in the hour
> Of thoughtless youth; but hearing oftentimes
> The still, sad music of humanity,
> Nor harsh nor grating, though of ample power
> To chasten and subdue.
>
> (88-93)

There is a certain peacefulness here, a marked quietude that bespeaks a mind at rest, but it differs radically from the earlier repose in which the abiding harmony of things rose upon the poet as an innate aspect of his being and as a "power of joy." The quietude Wordsworth now experiences results from learned behavior, from the disciplined submission of a chastened and subdued self. What he had experienced earlier through an efflorescent opening to a realm of disembodied, essenceless forms now comes to him as a teacher, as an otherness bringing with it authority and a poignant sense of the human as somehow distinct from the very nature out of which it comes and to which it is joined in obedient submission. The present learning process is focused in the human dimension and culminates not, as earlier, in a dispersal of the self into a decentralized and disembodied consciousness but in the individual apprehension of a separate coadunate force or power indwelling in things, a kind of *elan vital,* as it were, that yields for all things and all beings a cohesion among, rather than an identity with, each other. In the "sad perplexity" of a troubled adulthood, Wordsworth writes:

> And I have felt
> A presence that disturbs me with the joy
> Of elevated thoughts; a sense sublime
> Of something far more deeply interfused,
> Whose dwelling is the light of setting suns,
> And the round ocean and the living air,
> And the blue sky, and in the mind of man. . . .
>
> (93-99)

The "serene and blessed mood" of lines 37-49 has given way to "a sense sublime / Of something far more deeply interfused." The defining characteristic of the earlier mood is its alignment with spiritual emptiness, with the absence of essence. The later "sense sublime," however, apprehends a "presence," a "something" that is yet separate from the things it inhabits. Moved by this presence, Wordsworth concludes, in lines that parallel the theme of mutual creativity in the Prospectus, that he is yet

> A lover of the meadows and the woods,
> And mountains; and of all that we behold
> From this green earth; of all the mighty world
> Of eye, and ear,—both what they half create,
> And what perceive; well pleased to recognise
> In nature and the language of the sense
> The anchor of my purest thoughts, the nurse,
> The guide, the guardian of my heart, and soul
> Of all my moral being.
>
> (103-11)

If the visionary focus of this passage differs from that of lines 37-49, so also does the sense of pleasure and morality Wordsworth acquires from his experiences in nature. The earlier pleasure, together with the "little, nameless, unremembered, acts / Of kindness and of love" it produced, derived from the visible absence of stability, from a process "In which the affections gently lead us on" until the human is suspended. Wordsworth's experience of pleasure, goodness, and spirituality issued earlier from the happy acceptance of motion. Lines 103-11, however, depict a mood grounded in the need for stability. Wordsworth is now "well pleased" rather than joyous in his acceptance of "nature and the language of the sense" as the "anchor" of his thoughts. He looks now to nature for guidance and protection. The earlier process of opening to the world of things, of blossoming to an acceptance of instability as the ground of his being, of his own being as well as that of other things, has given way to a quest for moral and intellectual anchorage.

It is important for us to understand, however, that the later mood, the "sense sublime / Of something far more deeply interfused," does not replace or in any way negate the earlier state of "serene and blessed" dispersal into centerless consciousness. To his credit, Wordsworth does not reject the visions of his youth as false or vain, nor does he lose the impulse to move somehow beyond the

present selfhood that obscures his earlier experiences of oneness with nature. He turns, instead, to his sister Dorothy, claiming that

> in thy voice I catch
> The language of my former heart, and read
> My former pleasures in the shooting lights
> Of thy wild eyes.
>
> (116-19)

Dorothy retains the "purer mind." Her "wild eyes" have not been dimmed by "the fretful stir / Unprofitable, and the fever of the world." Even in her later years, when the "wild ecstasies" of her youth will have "matured / Into a sober pleasure" (138-39), Dorothy will retain, not a mind that seeks for anything beyond itself, but one that accepts freely, that opens to the impulses of nature—to the shining of the moon, to the play of "misty mountain-winds" (134-36). It is a mind that will persist as a "mansion for all lovely forms" and whose memory will be "as a dwelling-place / For all sweet sounds and harmonies" (140-42). Being the eyes of nature itself, Dorothy reads only what is there and seeks nothing beyond the surface of things.

Structurally, the poem reveals a movement from memories of disembodied spirituality, through a sense of sublimity as inclusive of a chastened but nevertheless persistent selfhood, to a final displacement of the self in the poet's deferral to the spiritual force and authority of his sister. Her acceptance of the mystery of things, her ability to see, hear, and feel without necessarily seeking for an intellectual principle behind things, for a separate logos, as it were, is the measure of her identity with the universe. To the extent that he catches in Dorothy's voice the language of his former heart and in her eyes the quality of his former pleasures, the earlier state is yet alive for the poet. The dimensions of its effect may have altered for him, and the manner of its surfacing may differ from one situation to another, but its power to displace the self is no less persistent. The poem thus celebrates a spirituality grounded in the notion of mind and world as a composite unity manifested through the necessary disappearance of the self as the locus of perception.

But what the poet offers as a vital unity his readers tend for the most part to understand in contexts that emphasize fundamental distinctions among the components of his vision. Influenced more perhaps by the Prospectus to *The Recluse* than by "Tintern Abbey," critical discussions of Wordsworthian unity employ a dualistic idiom that presents mind and nature as complementary, but nevertheless separable, realms. Relying, for example, on the following lines from the Prospectus—

> How exquisitely the individual Mind
> (And the progressive powers perhaps no less
> Of the whole species) to the external World
> Is fitted:—and how exquisitely, too—
> Theme this but little heard of among men—
> The external World is fitted to the Mind
>
> (63-68)

M. H. Abrams claims that the central vision of Words-worth's poetry is the power of the individual mind "as in itself adequate, by consummating a holy marriage with the external universe, to create out of the world of all of us, in a quotidian and recurrent miracle, a new world which is the equivalent of paradise." Kenneth R. Johnston argues similarly that "Wordsworth's great faith is in Nature, the extrinsic, what is 'out there,' and in the *excursive* power of Imagination to go out to meet it." Frederick Garber, also focusing on the marriage metaphor, asserts that "Wordsworth's was a middle way, giving equivalent weight to each partner in the relationship. The high argument in the Preface to *The Excursion* is an exercise in parity, its main point the creative efficiency that comes from interlocking the powers of mind and world." More recently Barbara Schapiro, invoking the principles of modern quantum physics, maintains that "imagination and Nature, or mind and the material world, are mutually reflecting realms for Wordsworth—the order of mind mirrors the order of Nature."

Other readers find in Wordsworth's poetry a radical opposition between the mind and the external world. David Perkins, for example, argues that what is foremost in Wordsworth is "his sense of the gulf between human nature, with all of its greedy demands, its turbulent assertions, its often chaotic passions, and the rest of nature." For Geoffrey Hartman, the central drama in Wordsworth's poetry is an unresolved opposition between imagination and nature, a tension that culminates in a willed, akedah-like binding of the individual mind with the external world. Charles J. Rzepka, extending the work of Robert Langbaum, Frances Ferguson, and David Simpson, sees Wordsworth as struggling to achieve personal and professional identity in a paradoxical dialectic comprising "on the one hand, a solipsistic self-diffusion and mental appropriation of the perceived world as part of the self within, and on the other, a search for right recognition that will give this indefinite, inner self outward form and definition." And John Jones, underscoring Words-worth's high regard for solitude and distinctness, condemns the entire critical involvement with questions of unity in romantic poetry: "The large and lazy assumption that the Romantic poets were all striving to express unity has obscured the structure of distinct but related things which is the world of Wordsworth."

Whether viewed as the poet of nature whose work affirms a vital connection between the individual mind and the external world, or as the complex, problematic, often contradictory poet of a suppressed imagination and a divided identity, Wordsworth evokes for many readers a powerful sense of a separate creative self deeply conscious of, sometimes preoccupied with, its own transforming and organizing energies. The recorded confluence of mind and external world, when it occurs in Wordsworth's poetry, produces critical responses grounded in a dualistic idiom that stresses the notion of unity as a partnership or alliance of deeply related but nevertheless separate items.

The source of the critical tendency to employ a dualistic idiom in discussions of Wordsworthian unity can be traced to the intellectual predisposition of Western culture itself. Western thought is "plagued," as Amalie Enns puts it, with a subject-object dichotomy that "begins with Plato who located truth in the intellect, thereby separating man from his world and the entities in it." This separation, according to Enns, "was intensified by Descartes and continues to preoccupy philosophers to our own day." Though "plagued" is perhaps a little strong, the impulse behind the word conforms to the insights of many thinkers who have looked into the cognitive procedures of Western culture. Winston L. King, for example, remarks that the "Cartesian division of reality into immaterial, invisible, subjective consciousness and material, visible objectivity is the epitome of Western thought, the creator of its cultures and civilization. Out of this climate has arisen the Western dichotomous type of logical assertion that A is *not, ca*nnot be B." Criticism tends naturally to reflect the philosophical milieu which helped to produce the texts readers engage. M. H. Abrams . . . finds Wordsworth's effort to effect a reciprocity of mind and nature representative of "the overall movement of thought in his age." Explaining that Wordsworth represents life "primarily in terms of a transaction between two agencies, his mind and outer nature," Abrams proclaims: "For the great contemporary philosophers in Germany—Fichte, Schelling, Hegel—also represented all human experience as generated by an interaction between two agencies; and what Wordsworth called mind and Nature, they called the self and the other, or subject and object." Readers working within the parameters of Western philosophy, especially as it appears to have influenced romantic poets, employ, imperceptibly perhaps, a critical idiom that reflects such basic dualisms as internal and external, mind and nature, self and not-self. Albert O. Wlecke, for example, understands Wordsworthian consciousness entirely in the dualistic terms of "intentionality" as defined by Franz Brentano: "This characteristic is, quite simply, the fact that consciousness in any of its acts always exhibits 'direction towards an object.' There is never merely consciousness but always consciousness *of*." Wlecke locates consciousness in the percipient. Like Abrams's appeal to a vital reciprocity between mind and nature as the ground of Wordsworthian unity, Wlecke's understanding of consciousness as intentional and directional certainly conforms to the poet's efforts to exalt the generative powers of individual mentalities, but it does not escape the sense of the mind as one thing, the cosmos as something else. Readers influenced by the philosophical authority of such considerations must necessarily employ a dualistic terminology in their analyses of romantic creativity. Thus, Marilyn Gaull, in an overview of the entire romantic epoch, says with considerable confidence that the romantics' "interests were not in external nature itself but in how the mind relates to it" and that their poems "have a common concern: how the poet feels about the external world, how he relates to it, and what it means to him as an occasion, a metaphor, or a symbol."

Much of Wordsworth's poetry, however, labors to hide or to obliterate the felt presence of a separate organizing or opposing self in favor of a prejudgmental, prereflective consciousness so deeply aligned with a perceived matrix of creative forces that it is impossible to say where the world's energies leave off and those of the poet begin. This deeper consciousness, coextensive with the world it illuminates, does not exist apart from, but is rather inclusive of, the mind presented in the Prospectus to *The Recluse*. I would like to explore this inclusive consciousness in the terms offered by Zen thought and art. Combining key elements of Mahayana Buddhism with Chinese Taoism, then carried later to Japan, where it was further refined, Zen is perhaps best understood as neither philosophy nor religion as such but as a spiritual practice that embraces both profound philosophical insight and deep religious experience. So far as we can think of it in philosophical terms at all, we are best served, perhaps, by Masao Abe's definition: "It is a philosophy based on a 'non-thinking' which is beyond both thinking and not thinking, grounded upon 'Self-Awakening', and arising from wisdom and compassion." In like manner, Robert Linssen employs highly qualified terms in viewing Zen as a religion: "If religion means an organization of spiritual aspirations whose aim is to understand and pass beyond the tangible world by freeing ourselves from the impulses attaching us to it, then the various forms of Buddhism could be qualified as religious." Neither a philosophy nor a religion in the conventional sense, Zen offers a perception of mind and world as a vital continuum, as a basic identity or unity beyond or prior to hermeneutic impulses to find meanings, to interpret the world in accordance with the projected needs and wishes of a discerning self and a specific cultural idiom. Tanzen, a nineteenth-century Japanese priest and philosopher who held the chair of Indian Philosophy at Tokyo University and who was later president of the Soto Sect College (now Komazawa University) in Tokyo, defines the Zen mind in terms remarkably similar in spirit to those expressed by Wordsworth in book 2 of *The Prelude*. Asserting that "In other religions and philosophies the so-called mind is looked upon as the governor of the body or the lord of things," a misconception "Which is the outcome of speculation, or stupid reason," Tanzen explains that

> The law of the mind is above human understanding, for the mind is timeless and permeates all. Its function is not merely that of perception and cognition. It is limitless, containing all phenomena— mountains, rivers, the whole universe. A fan can soar skyward, a toad fly, yet never outside the mind.

As in Wordsworth, for whom everything frequently appears like something in himself, an inward prospect, as it were, the mind for Tanzen is essentially subsumptive and combinatory, larger than its own processes and inclusive of the world.

What emerges in Wordsworth's poetry as an inclusive consciousness utterly continuous with the universe appears to Zennists as a state of "no-mind" or "one-mind," a perception that reflects the general Buddhist concept of *'sunyata'*, or "the Void," as it is sometimes called. Buddhist thought is founded on the notion that because all things change, their reality, their suchness (Sanskrit, *tathata*), is not their existential particularity, but a ubiquitous and eternally undivided ground variously called "the Void," "the Buddha-mind," "the Buddha-nature," "the Unborn," or, in Western terms, "the Absolute." The essential nature of this ground, so far as it can be said to have an essential nature, is its emptiness—a state beyond what might ordinarily be conceived as a spatiotemporal dimension. *The Heart of Perfect Wisdom*, a key text extracted from the *Prajñapāramita Sutra* and recited daily in Zen monasteries throughout the world, states the case succinctly: "form is emptiness and the very emptiness is form; emptiness does not differ from form, form does not differ from emptiness; whatever is form, that is emptiness, whatever is emptiness, that is form, the same is true of feelings, perceptions, impulses and consciousness."

The Void or the Emptiness of Buddhist thought is not, however, a mere vacuity or a nihilistic vortex issuing from the perception of universal transience. It is predicated, rather, on the insight that the entire phenomenal world, all that exists, is tied together in a gigantic, interrelated, interanimative web of moving aggregates. Even individual human beings, as Thich Nhat Hanh explains in his commentary on the *Heart Sutra*, are a collection of five elements, called *"Skandhas"* in Sanskrit, which "flow like a river in every one of us." These forms, which are themselves currents of physical, mental, emotional, perceptual, and conscious being, cannot, according to Thich Nhat Hanh, exist individually: "Each can only inter-be with all the others." In the Buddhist view, nothing possesses self-existence. Everything depends on everything else. Nothing remains unchanged. Yet each thing, so far as it comprises eternally moving aggregates, contains, indeed is an expression of, the Absolute. "Form is empty of a separate self," writes Thich Nhat Hanh, "but it is full of everything in the cosmos." Hua-yen Buddhism expresses this sense of interpenetrative fullness in what one philosopher, Steve Odin, calls "the summary formula: 'All is one and one is all.'" Predicated on an acute sense of the dialectical interpenetration of the one and the many, of subject and object, of unity and multiplicity, Hua-yen Buddhism sees the identity of form and emptiness as an eternally shifting spatiotemporal togetherness in which, Odin explains, "the large and small thus interpenetrate without the slightest obstruction" and "every event is virtually present or immanent in every other event."

The oneness Zen thinkers proclaim, however, cannot be apprehended in the dualistic context of self and other, nor can it be ascribed to a separate creative force. Zen unity, according to Masao Abe, "is not a monistic or monotheistic oneness but rather a nondualistic oneness. . . . Monotheistic oneness does not include the element of self-negation and is substantial, whereas nondualistic oneness includes self-negation and is nonsubstantial." There is nowhere to be found in the universe a separately existing logos, a creative center behind or above reality. "In the Buddhist perspective," writes Nolan Pliny Jacobson, "the source of everything is no determinate actuality but a creativity infinitely productive of actualities."

The Zen Buddhist endeavors to experience this creative ground directly, not as a separate habitat, but as the lived and living essence of his own being. Zen master Sasaki Joshu writes: "Absolute being works as complete, perfect emptiness and embraces subject and object. If you want to see God or Buddha, you must manifest yourself as emptiness." This condition of extreme egolessness reveals itself in the disposition to accept all things, to avoid discriminations based on a priori judgments, and to eliminate any thought of a distinction between one's own consciousness and the world one apprehends as seemingly other. Buddhists frequently see this state as a condition of harmony with the Tao or Way, "the origin of the universe and the source of life . . . the undifferentiated, complete reality that existed before Heaven and Earth . . . the life force of all things, animate and inanimate," as Sean Dennison defines the term. Relating this concept of radical harmony to the notion of universal identity Seng-t'san, in his famous treatise "On Believing in Mind," asserts that "In the Mind harmonious [with the Way] we have the principle of identity / In which we find all strivings quieted." This is a place where "All is void, lucid, and self-illuminating" and where "There is neither 'self' nor 'other.'" Eihei Dogen, a thirteenth-century Japanese priest and philosopher generally credited with founding the Soto school of Zen, views the Buddhist understanding of universal identity as resulting from a process of self-forgetting and concurrently as a means by which the universe of myriad things realizes itself through the individual: "To study the buddha way is to study the self. To study the self is to forget the self. To forget the self is to be actualized by myriad things."

For Zen Buddhists throughout the world, freedom from self is identity with all things, a means by which the perceived harmony of life is the actual lived and living center of one's being. "Zen is the essence of Buddhism, freedom is the essence of Zen," writes Thomas Cleary. In a later refinement of this definition, Cleary explains that "Liberation of the human mind from the inhibiting effects of mesmerism by its own creations is the essence of Zen." The freedom that Cleary here remarks is not simply the freedom of the human individual to be and do as he pleases but the freedom of all things to emerge and to illuminate themselves in a field of consciousness at once individual and universal. What Wordsworth describes as seeing without "bodily eyes," to recall book 2 of *The Prelude*, the Zennist understands as a mode of self-illumination in which the seer's identity with that which he

sees is also the means by which, for all practical purposes, things view themselves through the pulse of human perception cleansed of any conceptual frame. A philosophical-religious practice whose deepest insights and experiences issue from a condition of freedom from the very impulses that form the contents of human life, Zen is, then, a way of experiencing life in its deepest ranges without becoming attached to the cultural and psychological conditions that animate and define the moment. Reiho Masunaga, in a summary comment on the spiritual implications of the Buddhist process of self-emptying, remarks simply that "When the self dies, the universe flows in."

Throughout his poetry, Wordsworth chronicles moments of self-forgetting extraordinarily similar in course and profile to the Zen experience of cosmic influx resulting from its formal procedures of self-emptying. As with Zennists, these occasions of self-forgetting form the spiritual basis of his art and the driving force behind his creativity. Wordsworth's poetry issues from a radical spirituality inclusive of, yet beyond, all cultural systems and all modes of self-hood, a spiritual freedom that allows the poet to experience in a condition of profound detachment the very cultural and psychological phenomena that comprise his being at any point in time and space. "I was a Freeman," he tells us early in book 3 of *The Prelude*, "in the purest sense / Was free, and to majestic ends was strong" (89-90). Enlarging upon this condition of radical interior spaciousness, Wordsworth continues:

> I looked for universal things; perused
> The common countenance of earth and heaven;
> And turning the mind in upon itself
> Pored, watched, expected, listened, spread my
>   thoughts
> And spread them with a wider creeping; felt
> Incumbences more awful, visitings
> Of the Upholder, of the tranquil soul,
> Which underneath all passion lives secure
> A steadfast life.
>
> (3.110-18)

As a vital, coherent, yet nonideological, body of thought and experience grounded in the perceived interactive oneness of all beings and things in the universe, Zen offers us an opportunity to understand the "tranquil soul" of Wordsworth's lines, what the poet later calls "the one Presence, and the Life / Of the great whole" (3.130-31), in nonmonotheistic, non-pantheistic terms. A comparison of selected poems in the Wordsworth canon with some of the leading documents in Zen literature and philosophy establishes a less self-conscious, less egotistical strain in Words-worth's art, refines our understanding of the poet's engagement with the *unio mystica*, and creates for his work a less ideological, more universal context than what it has encountered among readers whose understanding of metaphysics is grounded in such traditional Western dualisms as self and other, subject and object, nature and spirit.

Yoshinobu Hakutani

SOURCE: "Emerson, Whitman, and Zen Buddhism," in *Midwest Quarterly,* Vol. XXXI, No. 4, Summer, 1990, pp. 433-48.

[*In the following essay, Hakutani notes similarities and contrasts in the precepts of Zen Buddhism and the American Transcendentalism of Ralph Waldo Emerson and Walt Whitman.*]

Fascinated by the Mysticism of the East, Emerson adapted to his own poetical use many allusions to Eastern religions. From time to time, however, one is surprised to find in his essays an aversion to Buddhism. This "remorseless Buddhism," he writes in his *Journals,* "lies all around, threatening with death and night. . . . Every thought, every enterprise, every sentiment, has its ruin in this horrid Infinite which circles us and awaits our dropping into it." Although such a disparaging remark may betray the young Emerson's unfamiliarity with the religion, as a critic has suggested [Frederick Ives Carpenter, in *Emerson and Asia,* 1930], this passage may also indicate Emerson's aversion to the concept of nirvana. For Emerson, the association of nirvana with an undisciplined state of oblivion to the self and the world is uncongenial to his stoicism and self-reliance.

But, when he declared, "The Buddhist . . . is a Transcendentalist" (*Complete Essays*), he meant that Buddhism, unlike a religion, is a philosophy that emphasizes the primacy of the spiritual and transcendental over the material and empirical. Zen Buddhists, unlike the believers of other sects in Buddhism, are urged to achieve Buddhahood within them, an advice which sounds a great deal like the one given by Emerson, who urges his readers to think not for the sake of accomplishing things, but for the sake of realizing their own world. The achievement of godhead within rather than its discovery elsewhere is echoed in Whitman's poetry as well. In "Song of Myself" Whitman admonishes the reader: "Not I, not any one else can travel that road for you, / You must travel it for yourself" [*Leaves of Grass*]. In "Passage to India," too, Whitman defines God not as the wonder of the world, but as a journey.

In analyzing the mystery of God, Emerson, and Whitman both seem to be emphasizing man's independence from God's power and influence. For them, an individual must achieve enlightenment by himself or herself even at the risk of losing the sight of God, and this is somewhat akin to the doctrine of Zen. Unlike the other sects of Buddhism, Zen is not a religion which teaches the follower to have faith in a monolithic deity. Like American transcendentalism, Zen teaches one a way of life completely different from what one has been conditioned to lead. The instructional tenet inherent in Zen is manifested in a form of colloquy used by a Zen master and his disciple. In some aspects, Zen's method of teaching resembles Whitman's in his poetry and can be compared to the forms of lecture and essay adopted by Emerson.

In Zen, every individual possesses Buddhahood and all he or she must do is to realize it. One must purge one's mind and heart of any materialistic thoughts and feelings, and appreciate the wonder of the world here and now. Zen is a way of self-discipline and self-reliance. Its emphasis on self is derived from the prophetic admonishment Gautama Buddha is said to have given to his disciples: "Seek within, you are the Buddha." Zen's emphasis on self-enlightenment is indeed analogous to American transcendentalism, in which an individual is taught to discipline himself or herself and look within because divinity resides not only in nature but in man.

But there are certain differences between Zen and American transcendentalism. *Satori* in Zen is an enlightenment that transcends time and place, and even the consciousness of self. It is a state of *mu,* nothingness. The state of nothingness is absolutely free of any thought or emotion; it is so completely free that such a consciousness corresponds to that of nature. This state of nothingness, however, is not synonymous with a state of void, but functional. And its function is perceived by the senses. If, for example, the enlightened person sees a tree, he sees the tree through his or her enlightened eye. The tree is no longer an ordinary tree; it now exists with different meaning. The tree contains *satori* only when the viewer is enlightened; Buddha exists in nature only if the follower achieves the Buddha in himself or herself. For Emerson and Whitman, on the contrary, God exists in nature regardless of whether man is capable of such intuition.

Emerson's and Whitman's disenchantment with religion, I submit, can be demonstrated in their poetry. The farther they departed from the religious conceits the deeper they delved into their natural, social, or philosophical concerns. This partly accounts for the facts that Emerson left the pulpit and that Whitman seldom attended church as a worshiper. Just as Zen, an unconventional Buddhistic doctrine, found its aesthetic expression in the arts, American transcendentalism found its expression in poetry.

What Zen and haiku, the quintessence of Japanese poetry, share is a vision of the harmonious relationship man can have with nature. A Zen-inspired haiku, like a Zen painting, scarcely deals with dreams, fantasies, or concepts of heaven; it is strictly concerned with the portrayal of nature—mountains, trees, birds, waterfalls, and the like. For the Zen poet, nature is a mirror of the enlightened self; one must see and hear things as they really are by making one's consciousness pure and clear. What the haiku poet perceives has little to do with true or false, gain or loss, good or evil, war or peace, life or death. Nor does the haiku relate itself with the Buddha or one's ancestry. In short, what is described in it is not the poet's object, but the poet's subject. This principle can be illustrated even by one of the lesser-known haiku by Basho (1644-1694): "How cool it is, / Putting the feet on the wall, / An afternoon nap" (trans. mine). Basho is interested in expressing how his feet, anyone's feet, would feel when placed on the wall on a warm summer afternoon. The subject of the poem is none other than the pure sensation of how the feet feel. The poet does not want to convey any emotion, any thought, any beauty; there remains only poetry, only nature.

One of the reasons for the opposition of Zen poetry to metaphor and symbolism is that figurative language might lessen the intensity and spontaneity of a newly perceived sensation. Such language would not only undermine originality in the poet's sensibility, but resort to intellectualization and what Yone Noguchi (1875-1947) [in *Through the Torii,* 1922] calls "a criticism of life," which traditionally Japanese poetry was not. This poetics can be shown by Basho's famous haiku, "Old Pond": "An Old pond, / A frog plunges, / The sound of water" (trans. mine). Though one may think a frog is an absurd subject for poetry, Basho focuses his attention on the scene of an autumnal desolation. The pond is perhaps situated on the premises of an ancient temple whose silence suddenly is broken by a frog plunging into the deep water. Basho is not suggesting that the tranquillity of the pond means death, or that the frog symbolizes life. He is perceiving the sensation of hearing the sound bursting out of the sound-lessness. This haiku is not a representation of good, truth, or beauty; there is nothing particularly good, true, or beautiful about a frog's jumping into water.

What a Zen poet like Basho tried to express is that man can do enough naturally, enjoy doing it, and achieve peace of mind. This fusion of man and nature is called spontaneity in Zen. The best haiku poems, because of a linguistic limitation (a haiku consists of only seventeen syllables), are inwardly extensive and outwardly infinite. A severe constraint imposed on one aspect of haiku must be balanced by a spontaneous, boundless freedom on the other. From a Zen point of view, such a vision is devoid of any thought or feeling. Ezra Pound, who cherished Eastern poetics in general, called this vision an image. To him an image is nevertheless an intellectual and emotional mode of expression. "It is," Pound writes, "the presentation of such an image which gives that sudden sense of liberation; that sense of freedom from time and space limits; that sense of sudden growth, which we experience in the presence of the greatest works of art" (*Literary Essays*).

In Zen art, nature is the mirror of man. Zen practice calls for the austerity of the mind; one should not allow one's individuality to control action. "Drink tea when you are thirsty," writes Yone Noguchi [in *The Story of Yone Noguchi,* 1914], "eat food in your hunger. Rise with dawn, and sleep when the sun sets. But your trouble will begin when you let desire act freely; you have to soar above all personal desire." This tenet of Zen, which teaches man to emulate nature, was one of the Taoist influences upon Zen. Lao Zse said: "Man takes his law from the earth; the Earth its law from Heaven; Heaven its law from Tao; but the law of Tao in its own spontaneity." The twin deeds of man—naturalness and spontaneity—

are in Zen the means by which man can be connected with the absolute, the achievement of *satori.*

Artists' fascination with and emulation of nature is amply reflected in Zen art. Unlike certain arts in the West, Zen-inspired art abhors sentimentalism, romance, and vulgarity. While Zen art refrains from the negative aspects of life, it seeks a harmony between man and nature. The fusion of man and nature is reflected in a haiku by Kikaku (1661-1707): "Autumn's full moon: / Lo, the shadows of a pine tree / Upon the mats!" The beauty of the moonlight in autumn is not only humanized but intensified by the shadows of a pine tree that fall upon the man-made *tatami* mats. Kikaku's poem constitutes an image of the coexistence of man and nature. The harmony of man and nature has, in effect, resulted in the intensity of beauty that cannot otherwise be enjoyed.

It is this revelatory and emulating relationship nature holds for man that makes Zen akin to American transcendentalism. The basis for such a comparison is the enlightenment one achieves in relating one's spirit to that of nature; Zen calls the enlightenment *satori* while Emerson defines it as one's awareness of the over-soul. In "The Over-Soul," Emerson describes this state of mind as a boundless sphere in which "there is no screen or ceiling between our heads and the infinite heavens." No sooner does the consciousness of self disappear than the over-soul appears on the scene, as Emerson writes, "man, the effect, ceases, and God, the cause, begins." To Emerson, the over-soul is so pervasive "a light" that it "shines through us upon things and makes us aware that we are nothing, but the light is all" (*Complete Essays*). In his essay, "Nature," this light is so powerful that one becomes "a transparent eyeball" which cannot see beyond one's state of mind. In Zen, on the other hand, one is taught to annihilate this eyeball before *satori* is attained. It seems as though Emerson would empower God to conquer the faithful while allowing them to cling to their own individuality.

For Emerson, then, because divinity resides in each and all, individuality has a divine sanction. In his writing the consciousness of self has a corollary to such disciplines as stoicism and self-reliance. "Give All to Love" is an admonition that stoical self-reliance must be kept alive underneath one's passion: "Heartily know / When half-gods go, / The gods arrive" (*Poems*). As long as we rely on others, "half-gods," we cannot reach our enlightenment. In Zen doctrine, however, self-reliance would preclude our attainment of *satori,* for the consciousness of self means that we are not completely free of our thoughts and feelings and have not identified ourselves with the absolute.

Much like Emerson, Whitman inspires the reader to seek enlightenment in self as he says in "Song of Myself" "I am made for it to be in contact with me." The "I" consists of all the senses the person possesses, as well as his emotional and intellectual faculties; the "me" is the essential, real identity, as opposed to the physical, actual

"I." As Emerson calls this identity divine, depicting it as an all-powerful light, Whitman regards it as mystical. While Emerson's divine light permeates each and all in the universe, Whitman's is not so abstruse as Emerson's. What Whitman finds in himself can be found in anyone else. The humanistic and democratic spirit in Whitman rejects the conventional antitheses of man and woman, friend and foe, bride and prostitute. Even though Whitman's means of reaching this state of mind differs from that of Zen, his motto remains similar to what Zen indoctrinates its followers: only by severing oneself from the mundane world of good and evil, love and hate, life and death, can one reach the essential self.

Another striking similarity between Zen and Whitman is that the state of enlightenment is not as "intuitively" realized as it is in Emerson. In the tradition of Zen instruction the attainment of *satori* is as practical as is actual human life. When the young Bassui, who later became a celebrated Zen priest in Japan in the fourteenth century, asked his master, "What's the highway to self-elevation?" The master replied, "It's *never stop*." Failing to understand, Bassui persisted: "Is there some higher place to go on to?" The master finally answered, "It's just underneath your standpoint." The Zen master's pronouncement, *"never stop,"* recalls Whitman's last passage in "Song of Myself," "Failing to fetch me at first keep encouraged, / Missing me one place search another" or the last lines in "Passage to India": "O brave soul! / O farther farther sail! / O daring joy, but safe! are they not all the seas of God? / O farther, farther, farther sail!" Whitman's final statement in "Song of Myself"—"If you want me again look for me under your boot-soles"—echoes the Zen master's: "It's just underneath your standpoint."

Whether man can achieve godhead through intuition as Emerson says, or through deed and discipline as do Whitman and the Zen master, the ultimate goal of man is to discover his or her place in the totality of the universe. Emerson, in a moment of exaltation, can envision a transparent eyeball merging into a divine light, an image of infinity and oneness. "Passage to India" is Whitman's demonstration of monism: the world is one, spirit and matter is one, man and nature is one. In "Crossing Brooklyn Ferry," the people separated by time and space are united in an image of sea-gulls.

This concept of unity and infinity is also the basis for Zen's emphasis on transcending the dualism of life and death. Zen master Dogen (1200-1254), whose work *Shobogenzo* is known in Japan for its practical application rather than his theory of Zen doctrine, observed that since life and death are beyond man's control, there is no need to avoid them. Dogen's teaching is a refutation of the assumption that life and death are entirely separate entities as seasons are. Whitman similarly seeks a reconciliation between life and death: his feat of turning the bereavement in "When Lilacs Last in the Dooryard Bloom'd" into a celebration of death is well known, but less known is his idea of death given in "A Sight in Camp in the Daybreak Gray and Dim." To Whitman, the dead

soldier in this poem appears no less divine than the savior Christ; they both represent the living godhead. Whitman and a Zen Buddhist thus refuse to believe in the dualism of man and God, life and death.

From this comparison of Zen Buddhism and American transcendentalism the justification of their otherwise inexplicable stylistic similarities and differences readily unfolds. Basho's haiku on a frog leaping into the water, quoted earlier, evokes an image of unity and infinity. Basho is said to have awakened to his enlightenment when he heard the sound bursting out of silence; he realized, in Noguchi's words, "life and death were mere change of conditions". [*The Spirit of Japanese Poetry*, 1914]. The Chinese painter Lian Kai's "Sakyamuni Descending from the Mountain of His Awakening" or the Japanese painter Sesshu's "Landscapes of Fall and Winter" also exhibits a Zen artist's view of infinite silence. "In the best 'Noh,'" Ezra Pound notes, "the whole play may consist of one image. I mean it is gathered about one image. Its unity consists in one image, enforced by movement and music" ["Vorticism," *The Fortnightly Review*, 573 (1914)].

In common with Zen art, many of Emerson's poems contain images of tranquillity that suggest not only silence but freedom from agitation of the human spirit. Emerson discovers a fresh rhodora in the woods, "where sea-winds pierced our solitudes" (*Poems*). "Concord Hymn," in its quiet compactness, alludes to death and eternity. In "The Humble-Bee," Emerson leads himself to "gulfs of sweetness without bound / In Indian wilderness found." "Wood-Notes, I" also abounds in images of infinity and death: "When sea and land refuse to feed me, 'T will be time enough to die." Both "Seashore" and "Two Rivers" present symbols of the boundless spirit which, transcending time and space, flows through all things.

In some of Whitman's poems calm imagery dominates their form as well. The "Lilacs" poem, an elegy for Lincoln, abounds in quiet passages and subdued music: the poet's song and the bird's song, as if in a musical recitation, lead one's heart to a sense of infinity and peace, to "Dark mother" and "lovely and soothing death." "On the Beach at Night" shows how a child's awe at the vast universe is mitigated by the idea of immortality and infinity. "A Noiseless Patient Spider" can easily be compared to a haiku, which has a single, concentrated image such as a bird on a withered branch. In Whitman's poem a spider noiselessly spreads his gossamer thread in "measureless oceans of space, / . . . seeking the spheres to connect them, / Till the bridge you will need be form'd, till the ductile anchor hold."

Other poems by Whitman, however, are not entirely conducive to the calmness and liberation found in Zen poetry. "Crossing Brooklyn Ferry" thrives partly on the passages that suggest peace of mind, but the theme of the poem is the mystical unity of the people who have crossed and will cross the East River over the generations. Uniting the people separated in time and space is accompanied by robust passages in contrast with the sub-dued ones that dominate "Lilacs." Actions portrayed in "Crossing Brooklyn Ferry," in particular, are propelled by the scenes that suggest playing the trumpet and the trombone. The music to which such passages allude are the opposite of the kind heard in a noh play or haiku.

The liberation in Zen, moreover, implies one's liberation from man-made laws, rules, and authorities. "America, My Country," in which Emerson airs his disparaging re-marks about England while singling out America's lacks, expresses this spirit of liberation. The argument against his own priesthood in "The Problem" also is buttressed by this spirit of liberation, a desire in him which remains unstated in the course of the argument. For Emerson, lib-eration results from man's desire to adhere to nature's laws: how a woodbird weaves her nest, how a shellfish outbuilds her shell, how a pine-tree adds new needles to her old leaves.

Liberation for Zen also requires that a person liberate self from normality, equilibrium, or perfection. This defini-tion of liberation explains that Zen art shuns full circles, even numbers, balanced squares. The Zen-styled calligra-phy calls for uneven strokes and rugged lines that reflect simplicity, spontaneity, and uncouthness found in nature. In the traditional Chinese and Japanese paintings the only color used is black in various shades, for such coloring reflects the simplicity of nature and the lack of polish. If anything, Zen aesthetics calls for less symmetry, parallel-ism, and fullness. Whitman's poetic form, then, is least reminiscent of Zen's. "Crossing Brooklyn Ferry" is full of round or patterned shapes and figures: "beads," "round masts," "slender serpentine pennants," "the quick tremu-lous whirl of the wheels," "scallop-edg'd waves," "sea-gulls oscillating their bodies."

By contrast, Emerson's poetry is aphoristic in its concep-tion and truncated in its form. Its rhythm, despite the prevailing rhymes, is sometimes uneven. "Days," one of his briefest but richest poems, consists of intriguing im-ages, mysterious events, and sudden movements. Silent and muffled like "Barefoot dervishes," days, daughter of time, look hypocritical and deceptive to man. Marching "single in an endless file," days offer him according to his wish gifts which serve his needs: "diadems," "fagots," "bread," "kingdoms," "stars," "sky." The garden where Emerson watches a day's procession is depicted as "pleached," suggesting disorder and wildness. In the end the Day quickly departs "silent," and Emerson reads her scorn under "her solemn fillet" (*Poems*). In the "Wood-Notes" poem, which I have noted in passing, Emerson encounters nature, puzzles over her workings, and leaves them alone: "Tints that spot the violet's petal, / Why Nature loves *the number five*, / And why *the starform* she repeats:" (italics added). That Emerson accepts nature as it is with all its enigmas is the attitude of Zen. Such an attitude clearly is conveyed in his poems: his lines are often short and cryptic as Whitman's are long and avowed. Emerson's style is markedly in common with what is called in Japanese *yugen*. *Yugen* has all the con-

notations of modesty, concealment, depth, and darkness. In Zen painting, woods and bays, as well as houses and boats, are hidden; hence these objects suggest infinity and profundity. Detail and refinement, which would mean limitation and temporariness of life, destroy the sense of permanence and eternity.

Whitman, on the other hand, expounds the idea of infin-ity in various ways. It appears in "Song of Myself" as a continuous cycle of life and death, for which "grass" and "dirt" figure as a pair of symbols. In "Out of the Cradle Endlessly Rocking" the boy discovers the meaning of life, which is death. In "Passage to India" God is discov-ered within the human soul, defying time and space. In each poem Whitman chooses various symbols in reaching a central idea of his own. While his approach is expan-sive as well as refined, Emerson's is concentrated upon a single scene, a single image, a single object. "The Rhodora" is about a flower found in the American forest in opposition to "the rose" admired in English poetry. Emerson's flower lacks splendor and grandeur because "its leafless blooms" are "in a damp nook" and "the purple petals" are fallen in "the sluggish brook" (*Poems*). Such a scene provides Emerson with a "fresh" picture as a haiku about a lonely crow would lead the reader to the world of infinity.

The vision of infinity and eternity in Zen art also is rep-resented by the imagery of age. Buddha's portrait hung in Zen temples, as Lian Kai's "Sakyamuni" suggests, shows the Buddha as an old man in contrast to the young figure typically shown in other temples. Zen's Buddha looks emaciated, his environment barren: his body, his tattered clothes, the aged tree standing nearby, the pieces of dry wood strewn around, all indicate that they have passed the prime of their life and function. In this kind of paint-ing the old man with thin body is nearer to his soul as the old tree with its skin and leaves fallen is to the very origin and essence of nature.

This aesthetic principle, based upon agedness, leanness, and dimness, can be applied to Emerson's poetry. His use of paradox and irony, evident in such poems as "Brahma" and "Hamstreys," is not entirely characteristic of Zen poetics, but it has an affinity with the Zen artist's predi-lection for the ideas and images that suggest age and maturity. Emerson's use of aphorism and understatement in "Days" and "Grace" betrays a manner of imparting wisdom and restraint to his words. Despite his rhetorical eloquence, which is uncharacteristic of Zen poetry, "Each and All" and "The Problem" both abound in abstractions, suggesting experience and wisdom. Among his poems "Give All to Love" is perhaps the closest to the spirit of Zen in form and content, because the poem resembles the colloquy practiced in Zen Buddhism, in which the master gives his disciples advice, and because Emerson's out-look on life is stoical.

If Emerson's style has the elements of age, leanness, and dimness, Whitman's has a distinct taste for youth, robust-ness, and brightness. As in "Song of Myself," the people depicted in his poetry generate the optimism apparent in his ideas and attitudes. His style mirrors his mood of expansion and exuberance in contrast to Emerson's austerity and stoicism. Those long catalogues, typical of a Whitmanesque poem like "Song of Myself," come from his affinity for the common people and the spirit of freedom and abandonment. Some of Whitman's later poems, however, convey the meaning of the experience and trial in one's life that matures with age. "Prayer of Columbus" is focused on the great admiral stranded on the island of Jamaica, with whom Whitman identifies himself. His hands and limbs growing "nerveless," the poet-speaker declares, "Let the old timbers part, I will not part." "The Dismantled Ship," one of Whitman's last and shortest poems, is an unrhymed five-line poem reminiscent of the *tanka.* Whitman's poem catches a glimpse of "An old, dismasted, gray and battr'd ship . . . rusting, mouldering." The battleship, stripped of its technology and power, is now sunk "In some unused lagoon, some nameless bay / On sluggish, lonesome waters." The admiral and the battleship, whose long careers have met their challenges and accomplished their great deeds, and whose bodies now turn into nature, both provide the poem with concise images of age and experience. As in Zen art, Whitman's fascination with age and fulfillment is expressed with grace and humility.

As a whole, however, Whitman's poetry is far more natural, spontaneous, and expansive than Emerson's. In terms of literary expression, Emerson is least Zen-like in his poetic style if the reader looks for the elements of naturalness. But if one has a taste for the style of age and grace, an Emersonian poem might sound like a noh play or haiku. Similarly, a Whitmanesque verse sounds like a haiku in one way but not in another. Emerson and Whitman are both regarded as transcendentalists, but needless to say they are not cut from the same cloth. The two men share many views about human life, but their poetic styles are poles apart. It is not surprising that Emerson's and Whitman's poems, their reminiscences of Zen philosophy notwithstanding, do differ in their stylistic resemblances to Zen poetry.

American transcendentalism, as epitomized by Emerson and Whitman, and Zen Buddhism seem to have in their teaching similar manifestations about human life. Both philosophies instruct humans how to find peace of mind and happiness on earth. To explain the method of self-reliance Emerson puts it in a form of command: "Insist on yourself; never imitate" (*Complete Essays*). In expounding a theory of happiness Whitman insists in "Song of Myself" that one must reject the conventional dualism of man and woman, friend and foe, good and evil. Zen masters would not disagree with such teachings, for they believe that one's model of life can be found in the world of people and nature rather than in religious dogma.

A Zen Buddhist, Emerson, and Whitman all agree that one's responsibility ultimately rests on self. From Zen's point of view, human beings can be happier by adhering to nature's laws than clinging to theirs. To Emerson,

because God resides in man as well as in nature, man can rely on self to be happy. The Zen discipline, in which woman must sever the self from the human laws, is a severe discipline to anyone just as Emerson's stoicism is a frustrating experience to many. For Whitman, as his exuberant attitude to nature shows, man is inferior to nature where man can achieve godhead more readily. The Zen Buddhist and the American transcendentalist seem to share the belief that one has a capacity to participate fully in real life and that life is what one makes here and now.

Zen Buddhism and the ideas of Emerson and Whitman, however, differ in the means by which woman can attain the state of mind we call peace and happiness. Zen's doctrine of *satori* calls for the follower to annihilate self to reach the state of *mu* so as to liberate self from the habitual way of life. In Zen, one must destroy not only individuality but God, Buddha, Christ, any prophet, or any idol because it is only the self, no one else, that can deliver the person to the state of *mu.* To Emerson and Whitman, on the contrary, one destroys neither God nor individuality; one believes not only in God but in oneself. Emerson's self-reliance, therefore, is opposed to Zen's concept of the state of nothingness. Whitman's denial of dualism in human life, on the other hand, while it resembles Zen's indifference to good and evil, life and death, man and nature, is similar to Emerson's self-reliance. For both Emerson and Whitman, unlike Zen, believe that their vision of life not only emanates from God but derives from humanity's intuition and reason.

Gerald Doherty

SOURCE: "The World that Shines and Sounds: W. B. Yeats and Daisetz Suzuki," in *Irish Renaissance Annual* IV, edited by Zack Bowen, University of Delaware Press, 1983, pp. 57-74.

[*In the following essay, Doherty focuses on several elements of Zen teaching—including the dissolution of antinomies and the violent shock of spiritual enlightenment—in the poetry of W. B. Yeats.*]

Yeats's fascination with Japan and its culture had its origins in his study of the Noh drama under the auspices of Ezra Pound during the winter of 1913-14. Thereafter, references to the "noble plays" of Japan and to Japanese art float casually into his essays, often to highlight some contrast between such plays and the Western predilection for social realism and the intimate personal mode of the theater. From 1927 onwards, however, there is a distinct shift of emphasis; the range of reference widens to include appreciative comments on Zen Buddhism both as a method of meditation and as a dynamic approach to art and life. The source of this new enthusiasm was clearly the first volume of Daisetz Suzuki's *Essays in Zen Buddhism,* which Yeats read shortly after its publication in 1927, and praised as "an admirable and exciting book." Much of the material of the *Essays* appeared simultaneously in the Japanese philosophical journal *The East-*

ern Buddhist, edited by Suzuki himself, copies of which Yeats received regularly. There also Yeats could have read the first translation into English, made by Suzuki, of a text which contains almost all the fundamental tenets of Zen Buddhist teaching, *The Lankavatara Sutra.*

Yeats was much taken not only by the Zen methods of meditation but also by its *mondos,* those abrupt dramatic dialogues between Zen master and disciple. These exchanges vividly portrayed the moment of "enlightenment" (*Satori*) which seemed often to have been precipitated by harsh or even combative encounters. Legends of the Zen monks and their sudden "enlightenment" form part of that remarkable patchwork of meditative reverie and tough comment which goes to make up the substance of the later Yeats essays. The legends themselves are evoked with a deliberate informality and in a number of fairly predictable contexts where the contrast between Eastern and Western modes and attitudes requires it.

Yeats's fine attunement to Zen and his acute penetration to the core of its significance are indeed impressive (this was in sharp contrast to most of his own contemporaries, students of the Japanese scene, who instinctively slotted Zen into a Neoplatonic framework, or who, like Sir George Sansom, mistook it for a cult of "eternal tranquillity," and whom Suzuki had occasion to castigate). Yeats immediately intuited that Zen was not still another manifestation of a religious idealism coupled to a *contemptus mundi,* but a radical vindication of the world *in concreto.* He was also attracted by its rejection of all abstract and systematic formulations in favor of a vital apprehension, life crystallized in a single gesture or action. All of this came as a powerful counterweight to the perpetual lure of the abstract, "the sun-dried skeletons of birds" as he once called it, which haunted his imagination and caused him to turn back "in terror" to the incarnate world and to the beauty of human embodiment. In this sense Zen reinforced the concrete pole of the Yeatsian dialectic. But it was also the portent of a more ultimate hope, that of exploding all antinomies in a sudden and final precipitation of insight, the hope that underscores his own koan-like deathbed comment, "Man can embody truth but he cannot know it." It was an embodiment which he anticipated might be as simple as a glance or a touch.

In this article I should like to explore those aspects of Zen which Yeats appropriated from Suzuki, and more especially Zen's confirmation of that drive towards extreme simplicity and of those electrifying intimations of unified being which characterize the later poems. Much of their violence, barely contained, their rhetorical intensity and gnomic utterance, their aura of frustrated questing, have immediate parallels in Suzuki's presentation of his approaches to *Satori.* We can examine the more general parallels and convergencies first of all.

At its simplest, Suzuki's designation of those qualities of mind most congenial to the flowering of Zen as "aloofness, romanticism, a certain practical temperament" would have attracted Yeats as a flattering mirror-image

of his own disposition. Its rather elitist pretensions as well as its suitability only for those consumed with an exalted energy and purpose, as Suzuki presents it, would have served to intensify the attraction. More specifically, his delineation of Zen as an heroic and neo-Nietzschean drama of the *will,* of the kind of "indomitable will" which the Buddha exemplified, matched one of the more habitual masks of Yeats's later years. Suzuki's Buddha beat upon the wall of truth, then penetrated to the "very basis of creation," the "original abode," and finally proclaimed the wisdom of resolved conflict. Likewise Yeats's "eagle mind" with its protean range of voices aspires to master the ultimate source through the assaults of an exultant energy. As a corollary, Suzuki's emphasis on Zen self-power, the radical "reconstruction of one's entire personality" through one's own efforts, corresponds to the ambitious master-plan and labor of Yeats's old age. Both the Zen and the Yeastian drive is towards an exalted freedom beyond the antinomies of the personal self, towards the transformation of anxiety into celebratory joy. For Zen, this achievement is through the attainment of *Satori,* for Yeats through the expansion power of art to dissolve the boundaries of good and evil, the transvaluation of values through the pure inner act of the agent.

These are suggestions of a convergence of drive and purpose. The challenge of Zen, however, was to Yeats's lifelong predilection for conflict as *the* generator of energy. As Suzuki expansively records it, the path *to Satori* was mined with doubt and internal division, but its attainment marked the dissolution of all dualisms, the cessation of conflict. Yeats was fascinated by Zen's claim to go beyond what seemed to him perhaps the ultimate and irresolvable dualism, that of "the One and the Self with reality" as portrayed in the *Upanishads* and in Patanjali's *Aphorisms of Yoga.* This occurred in a triumphant act of enlightenment in which all such conventional opposites as spirit/matter, sacred/profane, God/creature were resolved and transcended. The consequence was a luminous expansion of the senses in a new coalescence of energies, and the abrupt disclosure of a restored universe in the irruption of supreme joy. This, Zen held out, not as a future attainment or a postponed reward, but as a now-possibility. This was the challenge and the promise for Yeats. Yet the *Last Poems* along with the essays and letters reveal an old man, dedicated to combat and confrontation, deliberately provoking them as a catalyst for the making of poems. Thus each act of creation is, at best, a little *Satori,* a miniature trial of the "unity of being," after which the poet relapses into an excited anticipation of fresh rants and rages. In the context of the poetry, the fascination of Zen for Yeats was primarily in its methods, its precipitation of *Satori* often by sudden shock or violence, that flash of apparent "madness," without which, Suzuki hints, "no great work has ever been accomplished." The parallel with Yeats's own mode of creation is striking, that act of incandescent intensity which completes the "partial mind," after which the poet (unlike the Zen saint who remains permanently whole) fragments into "the bundle of accident and incoherence that sits down to breakfast."

The details of Yeats's appropriation of Zen teaching reveal at once how selective he was, how exclusively indebted to Suzuki, and ultimately how compelled he was by the exigencies of his own quest. Perhaps the single most significant point of attraction for Yeats to Zen was Suzuki's insistence on Zen's "radical empiricism," the apprehension of the world in the state of *Satori* as pulsating and energized matter. This involves no less than the "enlargement of the senses" (Yeats's own phrase) in a vitalized extension of *seeing*. Suzuki characterizes this "empiricism" in a variety of ways: as the celebration of the "concrete and tangible," as salvation through the finite since "there is nothing infinite apart from finite things," as the living of life *in concreto* beyond "concepts" or "images," and as the attunement of the "work of creation" without the corresponding urge to interview the creator. Here the resonances with Yeats's own final philosophical stance, the romantic and passionate empiricism of his old age, are consistent and close. At its simplest, he declares that "the concrete alone is loved." Thus, as he conceives it, the drama of his last years must revolve on the "struggle to exalt and overcome concrete realities perceived not with mind only but as with the roots of my hair." It was an orientation which he felt, had been lost to the Western world, but which was still vibrant in Japan. *There,* he suggests, men still feel the "keen delight in what we have." He discovered an identical orientation in the luminaries of his Irish pantheon, in the Berkeley of the *Commonplace Book,* in the Goldsmith who wrote *The Deserted Village,* in the Burke who savaged "mathematical democracy," and in its newly discovered carriers, the Zen masters of Japan. It was Berkeley, he declares, who envisaged a philosophy so concrete that it would be accessible to all, the revelation of "a world like that of a Zen priest in Japan or in China." It was Berkeley too who, amid the bland indifference of his contemporaries, "was fumbling his way backward to some simple age," an age which already had come to fulfillment in the contemplative activity of the Zen monk and in the "powerful rhythm" of the Zen painter. Most revealing of all is Yeats's identification of Berkeley's "restored world" with that of one of Suzuki's Zen masters who *saw* the world in a new way "when his mental eye was first opened":

> Descartes, Locke, and Newton took away the world and gave us its excrement instead. Berkeley restored the world. I think of the Nirvana Song of the Japanese monk: 'I sit on the mountain side and look up at the little farm—I say to the old farmer: "How many times have you mortgaged your land and paid off the mortgage?" I take pleasure in the sound of the reeds.'

How closely this "radical empiricism" and the restored physicality of the world were associated in Yeats's mind with Zen teaching may be seen by examining one of the short sections of *A Vision*. There in a well-known passage he first of all affirms that all conflict must be ultimately resolved in the revelation of a world which is "concrete, sensuous, bodily," the basic biological cycle of energy whose model is "the living bird . . . (that)

signifies truth when it eats, evacuates, builds its nest. . . ." He immediately reinforces his point by recalling four Zen anecdotes borrowed directly from Suzuki's *Essays,* all of which highlight one or other aspect of Zen "empiricism." The first repeats the "Nirvana Song" of the monk (quoted above); the second portrays a young man who celebrates his attainment of *Satori* with friends and "flute-players"; the third offers a vivid demonstration of Zen's "empirical" methods; and the fourth symbolizes both the suddenness and the radiance of this new mode of perception. The passage, which is rarely quoted, is as follows:

> "No more does the young man come from behind the embroidered curtain amid the sweet clouds of incense; he goes among his friends, he goes among the flute-players; something very nice has happened to the young man, but he can only tell it to his sweetheart." "You ask me what is my religion and I hit you upon the mouth." "Ah! Ah! The lightning crosses the heavens, it passes from end to end of the heavens. Ah! Ah!"

This drive towards a radical empiricism surges through the later poetry, ambiguously rendered, and often with a painful intensity. Paradoxically, however, *there* the concrete world seldom manifests itself in its "shining and sounding," the envied "suchness" of things which was the domain of the Zen masters. Rather from "A Dialogue of Self and Soul" onwards, the concrete is marked down as the extreme antithesis to the state of enlightenment, as a physical embrace violently inflicted and violently endured. Its sole virtue lies in its possession of the kind of resistance and gall which generate poetry. In "A Dialogue," for example, it has nothing of the elegance and fertility of the biological cycle, incarnate in the "living bird," but emerges instead as an image of revolting fecundity, autochthonic aggression, and fruitless human suffering:

> I am content to live it all again
> And yet again, if it be life to pitch
> Into the frog-spawn of a blind man's ditch,
> A blind man battering blind men;
> Or into that most fecund ditch of all,
> The folly that man does
> Or must suffer, if he woos
> A proud woman not kindred of his soul.

Here the concrete is disclosed as the original thrown-ness of existence which must be confronted and purged away with each new incarnation. Throughout the later poems, its keyword is "desolation," whether it be the "desolate source" from which both life and love spring, or the "desolation of reality" which confronts European man (by contrast to the Mount Meru hermits who are contemplatively attuned to ice and snow) when his "ravening, raging, and uprooting" of the world have run their course. It is the lot of "The Wild Old Wicked Man," who, rejecting the "lightning stream" which eradicates suffering (the favorite analogue of the Zen masters for *Satori*), chooses instead a moment of orgasmic oblivion, as brief as it is "second-best":

'That some stream of lightning
From the old man in the skies
Can burn out that suffering
No right-taught man denies.
But a coarse old man am I,
I choose the second-best,
I forget it all awhile
Upon a woman's breast.'

The ultimate instance occurs in "The Circus Animal's Desertion," where in the final stanza, the concrete is disclosed, not in its numinous "suchness," but as the detritus of myth-making, the *dejecta membra* which the lure of dreams and allegories shut out from view:

Those masterful images because complete
Grew in pure mind, but out of what began?
A mound of refuse or the sweepings of a street,
Old kettles, old bottles, and a broken can,
Old iron, old bones, old rags, that raving slut
Who keeps the till. Now that my ladder's gone,
I must lie down where all the ladders start,
In the foul rag-and-bone shop of the heart.

No one knew better than Yeats himself that this was not the "concrete" of Berkeley's aspiration, nor of the Zen masters' attainment. Rather it is the kind of "desolation" which intrudes when the dialectical dream collapses, irretrievably dualistic in form, the gross product of the contradiction between the "painted stage" and the "excrement" of the world which it briefly occludes.

Suzuki consistently stressed the fact that the (Rinzai) Zen route to *Satori* was never gradual, the result, for example, of the meticulous cleansing of the "soul's mirror" through meditative practice. *Satori* was, in fact, an abrupt annunciation, the sudden irruption of hitherto unplumbed energies, a translation of the "whole man" into continuous *seeing,* "Nirvana reached while yet in the flesh." To delineate it, he exploits the traditional range of nature metaphors, the cataclysm, the earthquake, the shattering rocks, the lightning flash, to evoke its intensity. The sudden annunciatory flash which electrifies the whole being is the hallmark of Zen, as the *mondos* which Suzuki records abundantly show. This was an aspect of Zen which lodged in Yeat's memory, and it came as a welcome reinforcement and confirmation of his own aspirations in old age.

As far back as his Golden Dawn days, the metaphorical "lightning flash" had symbolized Yeats's anticipation of a radical access to vision and to ultimate insight. However, it seems that in practice, and as the poetry reveals, these images of transformation "came slowly, there was not that sudden miracle as if the darkness had been cut with a knife." They were types of the hieratic processional figures which appeared to him in trance or in reverie. Zen, by contrast, brought with it the late and revived possibility of the violent precipitation of vision, the lightning strike in the flesh. This, for example, is how Yeats interprets the forehead mark on certain Indian, Chinese, and Japanese images of the Buddha; it is the mark of the

"strike," the physical sign of the opening of the "third eye" in the "mind's direct apprehension of the truth, above all antinomies." Similarly his characterization of the Indian mystic, Bhagwan Shri Hamsa's enlightenment bears a striking resemblance to the enlightenment drama and the "indomitable will" of Suzuki's Buddha: "(Shri Hamsa) strained his heroic will to the utmost, . . . but the Self has brought the event, the supreme drama, out of its freedom, and this revelation, because the work of unlimited power, has been sudden." For Yeats, the Zen masters were to become *the* exemplars, those who raised the method of sudden precipitation to the level of art. He had almost certainly this in mind when he declared that it seemed to him "of late (1934) that the sense of spiritual reality comes whether to the individual or to crowds from some violent shock." This was the abrupt method of enlightenment which, he declares, he had sought for in vain in "encyclopedias and histories," to come upon it at last in "the Scriptures and the legends of Zen Buddhism." By way of illustrating this escape "from all that intellect holds true" through the technique of the violent precipitation "by shock," he recounts one of the most celebrated of Zen instances, known as "Gutei's one-finger Zen." Yeats's version is as follows:

A young monk said to the Abbot, 'I have noticed that when anybody has asked about Nirwana you merely raise your right hand and lower it again, and now when I am asked I answer in the same way.' The Abbot seized his hand and cut off a finger. The young monk ran away screaming, then stopped and looked back. The abbot raised his hand and lowered it, and at that moment the young monk attained the supreme joy.

The *Last Poems* themselves are littered with such moments of violent physical annunciation and transmutation. In the apocalyptic theater of "Lapis Lazuli," for example, Hamlet and Lear experience precisely such an abrupt and unheralded irruption of joy. It is this which transforms them from being creatures of contingency, mere puppets of the apocalypse, into ecstatic and enlightened figures in an extreme drama, transcending the universal and "desolate" reality which threatens to engulf them:

They know that Hamlet and Lear are gay;
Gaiety transfiguring all that dread.
All men have aimed at, found and lost;
Black out; Heaven blazing into the head:
Tragedy wrought to its uttermost.

In "An Acre of Grass," the old man at last confronts the limits of the dialectical quest. Neither the endless projections of "loose imagination" nor the repetitive grapplings of the mind with the empirical world ("its rag and bone") can precipitate the ultimate truth. The alternative which the poem offers—the beating upon the wall of truth, "the reconstruction of one's entire personality," and "the remaking of life itself" in an act of ecstatic enlightenment, whose European exemplars are Timon, Lear, and Blake—is an exact equivalent of the mode of Suzuki's Buddha:

> Grant me an old man's frenzy,
> Myself must I remake
> Till I am Timon and Lear
> Or that William Blake
> Who beat upon the wall
> Till Truth obeyed his call.

The most extreme and dubious instance of such radical transmutations occurs in "Under Ben Bulben." There Yeats promotes Suzuki's suggestion of the incidental and occasional "violence" of Zen and its methods to the status of an ontological dogma. Beyond the limits of language, the poem asserts, every man confronts his destiny, transcends all dualisms and attains the ultimate joy and tranquility through an act of violence:

> Know that when all words are said
> And a man is fighting mad,
> Something drops from eyes long blind,
> He completes his partial mind,
> For an instant stands at ease,
> Laughs aloud, his heart at peace.
> Even the wisest man grows tense
> With some sort of violence
> Before he can accomplish fate,
> Know his work or choose his mate.

The shadow of Nietzsche (whom Yeats reread in 1936-37) rather than that of Suzuki falls darkly across these lines.

Of course, such violence was never gratuitous, a crude display of bad temper. Rather it heralded the trauma which initiated the return to the "original home" (Suzuki), the unification of the man with his archetype (Yeats). Suzuki employs a diversity of Zen metaphors (many of them identical with Yeatsian ones) to encompass this attainment of wholeness: it is your own "original face . . . prior to thy own birth," the unity of dancer and the dance, "pure water poured into pure water," the ultimate act in which actor and action, thinker and thought, the knower and the known are consumed away. Both Yeats and Suzuki agree that these are mere metaphors, shadows of the "formless," imprints of the "deep truth" which is finally "imageless."

The Yeatsian task in old age was to complete his "partial mind," to unite with his own archetype. His earlier enthrallment had been to elaborate symbols and images, often emerging in sleep, and exfoliating into magnificent structures, which threatened to engulf him. *Now* (1932), he declares, the ultimate source is "always an action, never a system of thought." It is this which sets a man free from "a multitude of opinions" and permits him to attend to "the whole drama of life, simplicities, banalities, intoxications." It is precisely this urge to unknow, to reduce his mind to "a single energy" which tempts him "to go to Japan, China, or India for my philosophy" (Balzac alone among Europeans pulls him back to the comic confusion and mess of humanity).

The sole European artist who embarked on an identical quest for unknowing was Goethe. It was he who made his Faust proclaim that "In the beginning was the Act" rather than the orthodox "In the beginning was the Word." And Yeats applauds Gentile, who found "in those words of Faust a conviction that ultimate reality is the Pure Act, the actor and the thing acted upon, the puncher and the punching-ball, consumed away." Yet, Yeats maintains, Goethe failed. Even he lacked the "science or philosophy" that would have precipitated a "different level of consciousness," and so exchanged the "white heat" of enlightenment for the "cold iron" of opinions and of intellectual knowledge. Indeed Yeats declares that it was precisely because there was "no Zen Buddhism, no Yogi practice, no Neo-Platonic discipline" that Europe lost the power to remake itself, and so sank into the toils of "mechanical science." In the same context, and in a remarkable and idiosyncratic historiography, Yeats fabricates a Europe, already devolved through its earlier periods of absorption in Christian myth and of commitment to rational humanism, but now lacking the dynamics of Yoga or Zen which would rescue it from the shipwreck of absolute science. Viewed in this light, the *Last Poems* themselves are trials in the explosive dynamics of art, the last urgent effort by the last romantic to transmute the consciousness of Europe through the assaults of a rhetorical intensity which is now within his control.

There is a noticeable shift in the poetry from the earlier tragic endeavor to create symbols of power and permanence in a destructive world, typical of *The Tower* poems, towards a "joyful" (if sometimes hysterical) drive towards individual wholeness. This strain is already marked in the "Crazy Jane" cycle of poems, those "mad songs" which, as one critic put it, utter "the wisdom of a more radical wholeness than reason, nature, and society combine to permit us." Each short poem pushes towards a single act or gesture, an encounter with the "timeless individuality" shadowed in the sexual archetype, a unity which the dichotomized human lovers struggle to attain. Perhaps the most extreme and memorable version occurs in Poem VI, "Crazy Jane Talks with the Bishop," where the traditional antinomies of sacred and profane, formal courtship and sexual assault, the romantic and the excremental vision are collapsed and transcended in a single savage "rending" out of which wholeness is realized:

> A woman can be proud and stiff
> When on love intent;
> But Love has pitched his mansion in
> The place of excrement;
> For nothing can be sole or whole
> That has not been rent.'

Other love poems also record this quest for individual wholeness under a variety of metaphorical guises. It is crystallized in the young woman's search for her "original face" in "Before the World was Made." It appears as the "single root" of love in "The Three Bushes," as the whole "substance" of love in the Lady's three songs, each of these poems pushing beyond the traditional antinomies of body and soul towards the experience of an energized matter, radiating a sexual vitality, orgasmic and total.

This drive towards wholeness takes on the status of a personal manifesto in "A Prayer for Old Age," where the mind as ceaseless generator of dualisms is rejected in favor of the "marrow-bone" with its connotation of some indivisible substance or material. As an attainment, however, Yeats reserves it exclusively for his Eastern adepts. Thus, in the poetry, only the hermits of Mount Meru and the Chinese ascetics of "Lapis Lazuli" truly embody this wholeness. In so doing, they appear in stark contrast to European man, perpetually roused to frenzy by the power of the archetype, yet doomed in his attempt to subdue it by obsessive thinking and acting (his "ravening, raging, and uprooting") instead of uniting with it in joy. Thus too, even when such wholeness manifests itself in "The Apparitions" as the essence of that embodied joy which floods the aging Yeats, it functions mainly as a defense against those discarnate terrors which *A Vision* so harrowingly portrays:

> When a man grows old his joy
> Grows more deep day after day,
> His empty heart is full at length,
> But he has need of all that strength
> Because of the increasing Night
> That opens her mystery and fright.

Of necessity such single-minded questing for unity of being has direct implications for the process of artistic creation itself. In this area, also, a remarkable convergence is evident between the Zen theory of art, as Suzuki presents it, and Yeats's own final convictions. For Yeats, Suzuki's analysis of the act of artistic creation came as another long-sought-after proof of the existence in Japan of a tradition and of a style of art which had foundered in Europe. The Zen artist puts forth "his whole being" in action, and without reserve. In the act of creation he is possessed by the archetype, by "somebody else." Each brush stroke beats with "the pulsation of a living being." Thus the creative act is neither mimetic nor symbolic. For example, the birds the Zen artist paints are birds of "his own creation," as vital in their justified existence as the living creatures. Thus too, Suzuki claims, the gulf between artist and saint dissolves, the man-artist becoming "divinely human . . . not a manifestation but Reality itself . . . the very thing." The Zen-man transforms "his life into a work of creation" in exactly the same manner as the sculptor chisels a figure out of "inert matter." Ultimately the creative process involves a radical act of evacuation of all that Yeats calls "passion, ambition, desire or phantasy," and the emergence of that spirit of poverty (*wabi*), which implicates the work of art in its loneliness and peace, its final *sunyata* (void-ness). In this sense, the way of the artist is the way of death, the ridding of all that is not attentive to the moment of creation. Thus the fulfillment of art and the bringing of life to its completion in death coincide.

Here was a marvelous reinforcement of Yeats's own intuitions, and soon he wove Suzuki's ideas into the fabric of his final theories about art. In a single paragraph of a late essay, he associates Berkeley's Heaven of "physical pleasure" and Blake's "enlarged and numerous senses" with the Zen monk's *Satori* triggered by "an odour of unknown flowers," and with the Zen painter who gathers "into the same powerful rhythm all those things that in the work of his predecessor stood so solidly as themselves." The climax of art and that of contemplative activity coincides in the "pure indivisible act" of the whole man. He elaborates such correspondences in another late essay where he discusses Patanjali's *Aphorisms of Yoga* and the four stages of deep contemplation (*Samadhi*). The fourth stage is one beyond art where all "objects are lost in complete light"; the third, however, Yeats characterizes as the phase of supernormal sense-perception, where "the man has disappeared as the sculptor in his statue, the musician in his music." And he immediately calls on "the Japanese philosopher" (presumably Suzuki) for confirmation: "One remembers the Japanese philosopher's saying, 'What the artist perceives through a medium, the saint perceives immediately.'" In one of his last letters Yeats indentifies Zen art with "the concordance of achievement and death," that ultimate "poverty" in which the utmost accomplishment in art coincides with the final extinction of the ego. For this reason Zen painters are able to evoke "peace and loneliness by some single object or by a few strokes of the brush."

Yeats also associated this methodological asceticism, this generation of maximum intensity through miminal gesture, with another celebrated aspect of Zen, which Suzuki records. This was the legendary occasion of the transmission of Zen when the Buddha, without speaking, held up a flower to his disciples. Only one of them understood it as the total communication of the "Formless" in a single significant gesture; and he smiled in reply. This, Yeats relates, was also how his friend, Shri Purohit Swami, received his "vision of the formless" by a simple glance from his master. More significantly, however, Yeats links this Zen transmission with the possibility of imprinting the power of the archetype through a sexual glance or a touch. Recalling in a letter the Buddha's holding up of the flower, he continues, "One feels at moments as if one could with a touch convey a vision—that the mystic way and sexual love use the same means—opposed yet parallel existences."

The prototypal instance of such a total transmission in the poetry occurs in "Ribh at the Tomb of Baile and Aillinn." For the dead lovers, now attuned to the ultimate source, communication by touch has modulated into the conflagration of pure vision, the flesh transmuted into mystical orgasmic energy:

> The miracle that gave them such a death
> Transfigured to pure substance what had once
> Been bone and sinew; when such bodies join
> There is no touching here, nor touching there,
> Nor straining joy, but whole is joined to whole;
> For the intercourse of angels is a light
> Where for its moment both seem lost, consumed.

This is a glimpse of transcendent "blessedness" in death. The other versions of that state, which punctuate the prophetic frenzy of the later poetry, are at once more personal and more empirically Zen-like in their contexts.

Here again the Yeatsian and Suzukian versions coincide. For Suzuki, "blessedness" has three connotations: it is the state of joy attendant on the cessation of "seeking" ("when seeking ceases you are blessed"); it involves the opening of "the third eye," the disclosure of the ultimate source; and it is the revelation of the concrete world in its numinous power, the blessedness of life discovered in the living of it. Although for Yeats, transcendent "blessedness" is reserved for those few who attain to the fourth stage of contemplation, that state "beyond generation" described both by Patanjali and *The Mandukya Upanishad,* or for the dead themselves, at last "obedient to the source," nevertheless the poems occasionally offer renderings of humbler epiphanies. These are actualized instances of Berkeley's dream of a concrete and radiant world, or of the Zen manifestation of a universe "that only exists because it shines and sounds."

The poem "Demon and Beast" (written before Yeats had read Suzuki, but whose central experience is thoroughly Zen-like) is built around an unheralded revelation of radical innocence in the natural world. Consequent on the resolution of conflict ("my hatred and desire") comes first of all an upsurge of "aimless joy," followed immediately by the disclosure of the sheer physicality of the "living birds" in St. Stephen's Green park. As the poem subsequently confirms, this is at best a miniature *Satori,* a brief epiphany, which flowers for half a day before fading. The poem "Vacillation (IV)" offers a parallel instance of the "blessedness" of the ordinary. Here the "blazing" out of a usual London shop and street is attendant on a new way of *seeing,* the abrupt enlargement of the physical senses, which heralds the onset of a brief benediction:

> While on the shop and street I gazed
> My body of a sudden blazed;
> And twenty minutes more or less
> It seemed, so great my happiness,
> That I was blessèd and could bless.

Both these epiphanies are "aimless," unprepared for and unsought after. The other type, coincident with the successful penetration of the "source" through self-questioning and final self-mastery, Yeats broaches only on one occasion in the poetry. In "A Dialogue of Self and Soul," "blessedness" is revealed as the outcome of the bitter acceptance and assimilation of the "curse" of existence, and of the blind violence and sexual humiliation which constitute the doom of each incarnation. It is precisely such purging and emptying which ultimately enables the poet and the concrete world to sink in upon one another in an embrace of "blessedness," which "sounds" out in laughter and song:

> I am content to follow to its source
> Every event in action or in thought;

> Measure the lot; forgive myself the lot!
> When such as I cast out remorse
> So great a sweetness flows into the breast
> We must laugh and we must sing,
> We are blest by everything,
> Everything we look upon is blest.

The obsession with "remorse" and "forgiveness" is of course an aspect of Yeats's Western inheritance, and is quite alien to Suzuki's presentation of Zen. Nevertheless the attainment of "blessedness" itself resembles many such instances as portrayed by Suzuki. There too, at the onset of *Satori,* the adept's voice rings out with the kind of laughter and joy, which shorn of all personal nuance, reverberate to the music of the "original source."

Cleo McNelly Kearns

SOURCE: "T. S. Eliot, Buddhism, and the Point of No Return," in *The Placing of T. S. Eliot,* edited by Jewel Spears Brooker, University of Missouri Press, 1991, pp. 128-35.

[*In the following essay, McNelly Kearns contends that T. S. Eliot's study of Buddhism facilitated the development of his critical theory and allowed him to become "the supreme expositor of Buddhist wisdom in our poetic tradition."*]

In a notorious and perhaps exaggerated remark overheard by Stephen Spender, Eliot mentioned once that at the time of writing *The Waste Land* he "almost became" a Buddhist. I suspect that this remark bears about the same relationship to reality as Eliot's other famous pronouncement that he had later become "classicist in literature, royalist in politics and anglo-catholic in religion," though the latter has oddly enough caused far more alarm. Eliot always enjoyed the game of *épater le bourgeois* and these disconcerting declarations of allegiance were in part designed to do just that. In his youth, Eliot said, he had been delighted to find in Buddhism beliefs different from those of his (heavily Unitarian and upper-middle-class) family, and later, I am sure, he delighted in finding in Anglo-Catholicism beliefs different from those of many of his friends.

Nevertheless, we would be wrong to dismiss Eliot's interest in Buddhism as a phenomenon of his youth or simply a reaction against the liberal pieties and false consolations by which he so often felt surrounded. Buddhism was for him, both before and after his conversion to Christian faith, a source of profound contact with truths he deeply believed and sources of poetry he earnestly sought. With its radical critique of human nature, of the concept of deity, and of the illusions of transcendentalist escape, it represented for him both theologically and imaginatively that dimension of otherness and challenge without which thought, sensibility, and religion alike would fall into dereliction and decay.

In what follows I shall attempt first to sketch the basis on which I believe Eliot approached Buddhism and then to indicate the kinds of effects it generated in his poetry. I shall bracket here the question of his sources and indeed the greater question of his definition of Buddhism, which I have treated extensively elsewhere [*T. S. Eliot and India Traditions: A Study in Poetry and Belief,* 1987]. Let me begin then by situating the first part of my discussion within what I take to be an emerging consensus in recent scholarship about the nature of Eliot's philosophical position. As books like those of Harriet Davidson, Sanford Schwartz, William Skaff, and Richard Shusterman have begun to show, Eliot was by no means either the unsystematic *littérateur* or the uncritical devotee of the Absolute he has sometimes appeared to be. Rather, he had a consistent, rigorous and closely reasoned view of texts and the realities to which they purport to refer that amounted to what today we would call a full-scale critical theory.

That theory, however one articulates it, has borne and will, I think, continue to bear comparison with some of the richest textual approaches available to us today, from those of Heidegger and Adorno to Derrida and beyond. It is a theory which, as we have come to understand it better over the last few years, has three main characteristics: (1) an attraction to a realist position in philosophy stemming from Russell and Moore; (2) a radical critique of liberal humanism and of what was known in Eliot's time as "progressive" thought; and (3) a systematic and principled pragmatism, which underlay Eliot's embrace of any particular point of view, whether in philosophy, in religion or in aesthetics.

It is this latter point I wish to stress here, for I think Eliot's pragmatism explains a great deal about his attitude toward Buddhism. The word *pragmatism,* however, may be somewhat misleading. In its nontechnical sense, pragmatism seems to imply something adventitious, something *ad hoc,* something merely prudential in the worldly sense, a license, as it were, to the self-serving kind of thought which ignores rigor, consistency and principle in order to provide rationalizations for willful choice. Nothing could be further from Eliot's views. His pragmatism belongs rather to the extremely principled tradition he inherited from American philosophy in general and from Charles Peirce, William James, and Josiah Royce in particular. It involves the strong conviction that the proof of the pudding is in the eating, or to put it less colloquially, that one is entitled, in choosing a position, to take into account the practice to which it leads and, once embarked on that practice, to revise one's sense of reality in its light. Indeed, Eliot would say, one does this all the time, willy-nilly. To change one's point of view, then, is to change permanently the way one sees the world. Once in a new practice, one cannot simply return to the former state, in part because one can no longer conceive it without qualification.

I raise this issue of pragmatism in the context of Eliot's approach to Buddhism because I think it sheds a certain light not only on his move toward this most pragmatic of religious paths, but, perhaps more important, on his move away from it. In choosing my title for this paper, I was thinking of the furthest point of this trajectory, its extreme margin, where Eliot met the thought of another culture and religious sensibility, recognized its claims, and then chose to meet them only in a highly qualified way. I confess that I was thinking as well of a wonderful proverb by Franz Kafka: "Beyond a certain point there is no return. *This point has to be reached.*" Nowhere is this sense of extremity more necessary to understanding, I think, than in the case of Eliot's apprehension of Buddhism, which demands, or seems to demand, so little of its adherents in terms of dogmatic assent and so much in terms of those "forms of life" that permanently alter the consciousness of those who inhabit them.

Eliot fully realized the magnitude of these claims and realized as well their consonance with much already implicit in his own temperament and thought. He was capable of perceiving even in the most scholastic and complex of Buddhist texts and manuals precisely the same demand for a deliberate and quite clinical transformation of consciousness for which he himself felt the need. He fully understood the Buddha's insistence on the vanity and futility of liberal causes, personal accomplishments, and pious hopes and the necessity for some more basic recognition and eradication of evil than these could encompass. In a review of a history of Indic thought, for instance, Eliot wrote of what seems, in the Buddhist or Buddhist-influenced commentaries on Patanjali's *Yoga-Sutras,* "an arbitrary and fatiguing system of classifications." But Eliot points out that this apparent scholasticism conceals always an "extremely subtle and patient psychology." This psychology aims not to baffle the ignorant with a maze of fine distinctions between mental states, but to transform the perception of the engaged reader who attempts, in practice, to distinguish them.

This very recognition of the demands for change made by Buddhist texts, however, helped to clarify for Eliot where he had to stop in their exploration. Two years, he explained, of studying Sanskrit under Charles Lanman left him in a state of "enlightened mystification." Half the problem lay in trying to "erase" from his mind "all the categories and kinds of distinction common to European philosophy from the time of the Greeks." This, Eliot went on, "for reasons both practical and sentimental," he did not wish to do.

This explanation, made many years later in the weariness of middle age, is more than the dismissal of a philosophy. Like the perception that Henry James, "had a mind so fine that no idea could violate it," it concentrates an important idea. Underneath this passage is the recognition, which many poets in Eliot's own tradition had signally failed to attain, that Buddhism and Hinduism are neither comfortable affirmations of truths we hold to be self-evident nor exotic spices with which we may season an essentially domestic stew. They are highly evolved, historically conditioned, culturally rooted forms of life and religious practice. Those not born to them are by no means debarred from their adoption, but this adoption may well entail forfeiting the entire stock of wisdom which is their more immediate inheritance. There are good reasons—especially for a poet—not to do this (though good reasons *to* do so, too, as the names of Gary Snyder, Nathaniel Tarn, and Janet Rodney might remind us). Eliot perhaps paid Buddhism a higher compliment in recognizing and rejecting its appeal than in ignoring or overriding its demands.

This, then, was Eliot's point of no return, the point at which he fully recognized the claims of Buddhism and yet chose for himself, partly in consequence, another path. This point, however, for Eliot as for Kafka in another sense, *had to be reached,* and its significance was by no means exhausted when he had turned another way. The appeal of Buddhism represented for Eliot one of the many situations in which he was made supremely aware of "The awful daring of a moment's surrender / Which an age of prudence can never retract." It is important to remember that, in this passage from *The Waste Land,* he went on to say:

> By this, and this only, we have existed
> Which is not to be found in our obituaries
> Or in memories draped by the beneficent spider
> Or under seals broken by the lean solicitor
> In our empty rooms.
>
> (ll. 406-10)

It is not recorded in Eliot's obituary that he "became" a Buddhist, nor even that these lines applied specifically to the problem of whether or not he should have done so. Nevertheless, we should recognize here that Buddhism was, for Eliot, the clear and definitive Other, the path not taken, which parallels and gives depth to more apparent commitments and concerns.

For these and many other reasons, I find the most "Buddhist" moments in Eliot's work not always or only the ones where Buddhism is most explicit, but rather those, whatever the official frame of reference, where one senses the presence of a radical, a disturbing, a marginal and yet extremely powerful point of view. One of the problems of dealing with the influence of Buddhism on Eliot's work is that one always seems to be implying a more reductive, more one-on-one relationship than actually exists between the text and its so-called "source." Actually, I think the strongest Buddhist influence on Eliot lies not in local allusions, even very direct ones like those in "The Fire Sermon" section of *The Waste Land,* but in his ever more refined sense of how the mind might actually be modified, in the very categories of its perception, by close, directed attention to experience—including the experience of reading. Such close attention tends, like a child's experimental squint, to render problematic many of the ontological categories that common sense takes for granted, destabilizing, one hopes creatively, our received ideas.

These moments occur throughout Eliot's work, not just in *The Waste Land.* They are characterized, I think, by a specific rhetoric, one marked by three characteristics: (1) a syntax that breaks down or renders ambiguous the classic subject-verb-object pattern by which many languages reinforce their notions of fixed identity and causality; (2) a full exploitation of the possibilities of double entendre and of the random accidents of language which are likely to undercut intentional meanings; and (3) a very subtle exploration of *différance* in the precise Derridean sense. By this I mean the sense in which a gap that is at once frightening and liberating opens up between words or statements that seem clear, self-identical, non-contradictory and / or definitive—even dogmatic—and yet, by their very reiteration, are not quite any of these, or at least not at face value.

I think here of the classic instance of such an effect, the lines in "Little Gidding" (IV) which read "We only live, only suspire / Consumed by either fire or fire." It is the *différance,* the trace, between fire and "fire" that matters here, encoding the whole binary opposition we make between salvation and damnation and then in the next move eliding the distinction between them, which, from another point of view, seems precisely the error that had constituted them in the first place. Or, to cite another instance, there is the vexed line "I do not find / The Hanged Man" (11. 54-55) spoken by Madame Sosostris in *The Waste Land.* From that point on, the absent presence of that card, the Hanged Man, most crucial of cards in the Tarot, hovers over the poem. We are not to seek him, or look for the "key" to his presence, for by such logocentric attempts at determination, the poem warns us, each of us "confirms a prison" (1. 415). And yet if we are not to look, why bring him up in the first place? Just so does Buddhist training treat the quest for some determinate state called enlightenment, a state which is both an enabling goal and, so conceived, an ultimate illusion, to be pursued and bracketed at the same time.

Indeed Buddhist training often has a "do not think of pink elephants" quality which is part of its phenomenology, instilled by such classic koans or questions for meditation as "what was your face before you were born?" Eliot often captures this tantalizing, mind-bending effect in his work. Take the question in the fifth part of *The Waste Land,* "Who is the third who walks always beside you? / When I count, there are only you and I together / But when I took ahead up the white road / There is always another one walking beside you" (ll. 360-63). This question might be said to function precisely as a koan does, to pose a conundrum apparently unanswerable, from which we get relief only by a sharper insight than any provided by its initial terms of reference. In my view, the most remarkable exercise in Buddhist syntax, double entendre, and *différance* in the whole of Eliot's work is the great passage in "Burnt Norton" (I) about the lotus rising from the heart of light:

> So we moved, and they, in a formal pattern,
> Along the empty alley, into the box circle,
> To look down into the drained pool.
> Dry the pool, dry concrete, brown edged,
> And the pool was filled with water out of sunlight,

And the lotos rose, quietly, quietly,
The surface glittered out of heart of light,
And they were behind us, reflected in the pool.
Then a cloud passed, and the pool was empty.

It is difficult to ascertain positively, in a straightforward, declarative, rational, and referential way, whether in the middle of this passage the pool in question is full or empty and whether its fullness or its emptiness is in any case its most meaningful condition. Whatever one's answer to this question, one will, I think, have gone through some mental changes in the process of arriving at it. It is to the significance and effect of these changes that a Buddhist would probably wish to draw attention. He or she might also argue that these lines are perhaps the best rendering we have in English of the experience of *shunyata,* or divine emptiness, an experience which for many lies at the very heart of Buddhism.

These remarks are meant as suggestions and provocations for further study. In exploring them, I myself may already have reached my own "point of no return." Let me conclude, then, in the tradition of Buddhist rhetoric, with a paradox. It was, I think, in recognizing in Buddhism a point of *no* return that Eliot found himself able *to* return, again and again, with a fresh eye, to its fine distinction, its refusal of unmediated affirmations, its suspicion of false consolations, and its corrosive and cleansing power. In relation to Buddhism, his mind was always a "beginner's mind." By never allowing himself the illusion of assimilation, or indeed of its cruder cousin, expertise, Eliot kept his sense of Buddhism alive and allowed it to flow into and modify his essentially Western sensibility and work. His clarity about the limits of his understanding and the economy and restraint with which he approached Buddhist texts actually strengthened, rather than weakened, his insight, so that, again perhaps paradoxically, it was precisely by *not* "becoming a Buddhist" that Eliot became the supreme expositor of Buddhist wisdom in our poetic tradition.

Vasant A. Shahane

SOURCE: "Mrs. Moore's Experience in the Marabar Caves: A Zen Buddhist Reading," in *Twentieth Century Literature,* Vol. 31, Nos. 2-3, Summer-Fall, 1985, pp. 279-85.

[*In the following essay, Shahane describes Mrs. Moore's experience in the Marabar Caves in E. M. Forster's* A Passage to India *as a spiritual encounter with the Zen ideas of non-attachment and the Void.*]

Mrs. Moore's experience in the Marabar Caves, what actually happened in the caves and how it affected her mind, and the implications of this momentous event—these issues are crucial to a deeper understanding of Forster's *A Passage to India* (1924). Although critics seem to agree that the Marabar visit and the temple ceremony are important events, yet their interpretations of what these events signify differ greatly depending on their critical approaches to the novel itself. Whether the

Marabar in *A Passage to India* is a "mystery or a muddle"; whether Mrs. Moore in her mind suffers the "slings and arrows of outrageous fortune" and dares "to take arms against a sea of troubles", or withdraws from the fray by resorting to nullity or negation and drops out "to die, to sleep", a "consummation devoutly to be wished"; or whether, alternatively, she goes under the "pale cast of thought" and has a profoundly disturbing religious experience: these are some of the crucial issues in the novel.

First, the strangeness of the Marabar Caves themselves, their role and function in the narrative, their effect upon the characters, and the placing of their entity, their significance or the lack of it, in the total novel—these are important questions to begin with. What do the caves signify? What do they, in fact, represent? Since they are described as "extraordinary," having uncanny meanings, several problems arise, issuing from the caves' existence, their role, and their effect on the novel's pattern and the way in which they modify or extend the fictional cosmos, the mood and the mind of characters, and the finale of *A Passage to India.*

The Marabar caves are only a fictional name for the Barabar Caves, which are actually situated near Gaya in Bihar, a state in North India. Forster recreates the environment in his own (or Mrs. Moore's) imagination, and the parent Himalayas are described as "older than anything in the world."

> No water has ever covered them, and the sun who has watched them for countless aeons may still discern in their outlines forms that were his before our globe was torn from his bosom. If flesh of the sun's flesh is to be touched anywhere, it is here, among the incredible antiquity of these hills.

Forster skillfully weaves the mountains and the caves into the fabric of his novel, heightening the effect of a recurrent, evergrowing mystery, an expanding elusiveness.

> There is something unspeakable in these outposts. They are like nothing else in the world, and a glimpse of them makes the breath catch. They rise abruptly, insanely, without the proportion that is kept by the wildest hills elsewhere, they bear no relation to anything dreamt or seen. To call them "uncanny" suggests ghosts, and they are older than all spirit.

These caves are admittedly "extraordinary" and beyond the reach of man's grasp and desire for attachment. Do they approximate to the Buddhist or the Hindu way of life symbolised by non-attachment?

> Nothing, nothing attaches to them, and their reputation—for they have one—does not depend upon human speech. It is as if the surrounding plain or the passing birds have taken upon themselves to exclaim "extraordinary", and the word has taken root in the air, and been inhaled by mankind.

Do the caves represent the impersonal cosmic principle emerging out of non-attachment? Or, do they play a dual role? In the primitive state of man, caves functioned, or were used by him, in a dual way; they were his shelter and his tomb; men were born in them and were also buried in their corners. This primordial nature of the caves in relation to man signifies man's attempt to forge unity between the material and the spiritual, the fact of his mortality, a quest for life, and eventual death as a fact of life. The caves thus reinforce one of the principal themes of the novel, the barrier between oneness and separation, matter and essence.

Mrs. Moore's experience in the cave has been interpreted as negative, but in Indian philosophical thought an apparently negative approach (as shown in *Neti-Neti*) is only a prelude to spiritual awareness, a positive outlook to the world of the spirit.

Mrs. Moore had earlier visualised the world as in quest of cosmic unity, the unity of the earth and the moon, the Ganges and the stars. She had seen a beautiful reflection of the moon in the sacred waters of the Ganges, the holy river, and she wished to become one with the universe. But the fists and fingers of the Marabar caves bewildered her, and she experienced an echo which whispered into her ears: "everything exists, nothing has value," and her vision was then overwhelmed by a new nothingness.

This nothingness is at the heart of Mrs. Moore's experience in the Marabar caves and their meaning in the novel's total design.

> But suddenly at the end of her mind, Religion appeared, poor little talkative Christianity, and she knew that all its divine words from "Let there be Light" to "It is finished" only amounted to "boum." Then she was terrified over an area larger than usual; the universe, never comprehensible to her intellect, offered no repose to her soul, the mood of the last two months took definite form at last, and she realised that she didn't want to write to her children, didn't want to communicate with anyone, not even with God.

Mrs. Moore's "Double Vision" emerges out of this particular extraordinary state—the middle state between heroic endeavour and the earthly enterprise. She had come to that state where the horror of the universe and its smallness are both visible at the same time, the twilight of the double vision in which so many elderly people are involved. If this world is not to our taste, well, at all events there is Heaven, Hell, Annihilation, one or other of those large things, that huge scenic background of stars, fires, blue or black air.

> All heroic endeavour and all that is known as art assumes that there is such background, just as all practical endeavour, when the world is to our taste assumes that the world is all. But in the twilight of the double vision, a spiritual muddledom is set up for which no high-sounding words can be found, we can neither act nor refrain from action, we can neither ignore nor respect Infinity.

Everything in the cave produces "boum" signifying a kind of nullity or nothingness.

E. M. Forster had spoken to his interviewers, P. N. Furbank and F. J. H. Haskell, about the caves:

> When I began *A Passage to India* I knew that something important happened in the Marabar caves, and that it would have a central place in the novel—but I didn't know what it would be. . . . The Marabar Caves represented an area in which concentration can take place. A cavity . . . They were something to focus everything up: they were to engender an event like an egg.

The reference to "cavity" is significant and could be related to the concept of the Void or (in Sanskrit) *Sunyata,* which is one of the essential doctrines of Buddhism, more particularly of Zen.

Mrs. Moore's experience is, in part, deeply religious. She has a vision of the vast immensity of the Timeless Absolute which, in a way, the caves themselves signify. In consequence, the inherited values of her Christian faith— "poor little talkative Christianity"—are overwhelmed by this new insight, this new awareness of the Void. Mrs. Moore is up against the true nature of the self, her own self in particular, and the relationship of the self with the world in general. What she experiences in the caves is admittedly a complex issue; however, it seems to me that her experience should be related to what Forster describes as "cavity", or what Buddhism denotes as "Void". To the *Mahayana* (the Greater Vehicle) adherent of Buddhism, the Self is the basic Buddha-nature of which the rest of the world is only a manifestation, and he associates this search for the self with the concept of the Void or *Sunyata.*

"The Buddhist Void," says Nancy Ross, "is far from being a nihilistic doctrine." For a Buddhist, it is claimed as a proper after-death goal, as indeed it seems to be for Mrs. Moore. Nancy Ross continues:

> The Void is not nothingness or annihilation but the very source of all life. In speaking of this theory as taught in the Buddhism of China and Japan (where it has influenced the creation of a very subtle aesthetic) Hajime Nakamura, the Japanese Buddhist scholar says: "Voidness . . . is . . . that which stands right in the middle between affirmation and negation, existence and non- existence. . . . The void is all-inclusive, having no opposite, there is nothing which it excludes or opposes. It is living void, because all forms come out of it, and whoever realises the void is filled with life and power and the love of all beings.

Thus Forster's description of Mrs. Moore's experience in the caves amazingly confirms and reinforces Nakamura's explication of the Void. Mrs. Moore had come to what may be called the "middle state" between heroic endeavour and the earthly endeavour and to a "twilight of the double vision", and this position can be aptly related to the Zen Buddhist void—which "stands right in the middle between affirmation and negation, existence and non-existence." Whoever realises the depth of this void is filled with love for all men. This is precisely what happens in *A Passage to India,* when Professor Narayan Godbole is filled with this overpowering love and when, in his heated state, he imaginatively recreates the image of Mrs. Moore. She "happened to occur among the throng of soliciting images, a tiny splinter, and he impelled her by his spiritual force to that place where completeness can be found. Completeness, not reconstruction. His senses grew thinner, he remembered a wasp seen he forgot where, perhaps on a stone. He loved the wasp equally, he impelled it likewise, he was imitating God."

Mrs. Moore's experience of the cavity in the caves is analogous to the Zen Buddhist experience of the void. Zen art, especially poetry, is deeply concerned with the awakening of the Formless Self. Zen awareness cannot be objectified; it is no longer an object; in fact, it *is* the subject. It is essentially "seeing into one's nature", which is precisely what Mrs. Moore and even Adela Quested attempt to achieve. The Formless Self leads the Zen seeker to an awareness of the void, and thus the void itself becomes a form of linguistic expression.

Forster, while describing Mrs. Moore's experience in the caves, says that "she was terrified over an area larger than usual; the universe, never comprehensible to her intellect, offered no repose to her soul"—and thus she was confronted with a cavity of meaninglessness. In fact, this "meaninglessness" is the essence of Zen; it is the only true Zen. Old Shoju's well-known poem articulates this sense of meaninglessness:

> What "meaningless" Zen?
> Just look—at anything.

Mrs. Moore's mood of resignation to her fate, her disinclination to take any specific action, her loss of worldly interest, her unwillingness even to write to her children are close parallels to the elusive Taoist concept of *Wu-Wei* that is non-action, non-involvement, or non-attachment. Nancy Ross, while explaining this concept, stresses its central idea:

> Taoism emphasized an elusive concept, *wu-wei,* nonaction, or better, noninvolvement, or perhaps more precisely, triumphing over one's insistent ego, letting things "happen" in accordance with their own innate laws instead of attempting to impose one's wishes as if *they* were the very laws of life. "Everything is what it is . . . is all one . . . the Tao," said Lao-tzu. In dwelling on this abstraction, the Tao (which might be compared to the Buddhist Void, or even to Hinduism's Absolute, the indescribable essence of all life, *Brahman*), Lao-tzu wrote: "How unfathomable is Tao—like unto the emptiness of a vessel, yet, as it were, the honored Ancestor of us all. Using it we find it inexhaustible, deep and unfathomable. How pure and still is the

Way! I do not know who generated it. It may appear to have preceded God."

However, it must be said that Zen awakening does not imply total withdrawal from the world. Nor does Mrs. Moore's mood imply total withdrawal from the world or total negation. In fact, her view of life at that moment is affected by non-attachment, which in its essence is not purely negative. On the contrary, it is the first positive step towards realising the true self, to join the human adventure, to spread universal love and harmony as Mrs. Moore actually does in the mind of Professor Godbole when he attempts to recreate her image.

The Marabar Caves and Mrs. Moore's experience in those extraordinary hollows reveal an aspect of the Oneness of the Absolute, the Void in Zen Buddhism, and the impersonal cosmic principle. The Caves are older than all spirit. Their great antiquity, their extraordinary quality affects even the rationalist Miss Adela Quested and for a time she feels that she is up against the inscrutable and that she is encountering an "inverted saucer". This image of the inverted saucer which cannot hold any matter is significant because it is analogous to the Zen Buddhist idea of void, of emptiness, which though apparently negative, is indeed at its depth a very positive doctrine. The great Bodhidharma's famous conversation with the Chinese Emperor unfolds his ideas on this emptiness that is central to Mrs. Moore's experience of the Marabar Caves:

> As for the answer that "Vast Emptiness" was Buddhism's First Principle, he appears here to be simply stressing the doctrine of the nondualistic eternal Void from which all life emerges and which, in Zen terms, must be personally experienced in order to grasp life's true meaning and significance. This idea of emptiness is a receptive rather than a negative concept in Zen. A part of Zen training in its early stage stresses "Empty the mind." Sometimes the aspirant is advised to "take as thought the thought of No-thought".

In fact, this concept of "Emptiness" is the most central part of Zen teaching and it is also pervasively related to Zen art.

> The Zen concept of Emptiness, already touched on in Bodhidharma's rather cheeky bit of dialogue with the Chinese Emperor, is one of the most important points to grasp about Zen teaching. The theme is rehearsed daily in an ancient morning chant of Zen monks that carries a curious suggestion of certain contemporary scientific views. "Form is here emptiness, emptiness is form; form is none other than emptiness; emptiness is none other than form; what is form that is emptiness, what is emptiness that is form." The Zen teaching that Emptiness or the Void is in no way "lacking" but is, indeed, equal to fullness when properly understood has played a significant part in the development of certain important canons of Far Eastern art.

It is interesting to observe, for example, the role and function of "space" in Chinese and Japanese painting. Space is treated as a thing in itself, a positive value and not just a part of a mere arbitrary setting. It is indeed part of the painter's perspective. The vast spaces and immensities of the landscape of the Marabar caves only reinforce the Zen Buddhist concept of space.

Toshimitsu Hasumi's *Zen in Japanese Art,* while elucidating many of these art forms of Zen, attempts to articulate their aesthetic design. Kitaro Nishida, whose work on aesthetics forms the basis of Zen art, emphasises the synthesis of the views of art and experiences of life that endows Zen paintings with deep spiritual meanings. Thomas Merton has perceptively unfolded the basic principle of Zen aesthetics. He writes:

> In particular, it is the function of the beautiful to be, so to speak, *an epiphany of the Absolute and formless Void* which is God. It is an embodiment of the *Absolute* mediated through the personality of the artist, or perhaps better his "spirit" and his contemplative experience.

In attempting to unravel the mysteries of Mrs. Moore's experience in the Marabar caves, Forster is indeed trying to achieve and portray, in words and rhythm, an epiphany of this Absolute and the complex "formless void." The experience is essentially non-verbal, and Forster in *A Passage to India* attempts to encase it in words of a deep evocative quality, which enhances the levels of profundity and complexity in the novel's total design.

Finally, my aim is to show that Mrs. Moore does not merely cave in under the impact of the Marabar Caves (as seems to be the general impression), but her experience touches deeper chords of her spiritual self. Forster attempts to articulate, by use of meaningful words, this essentially inarticulate experience in *A Passage to India.*

Bernice and Sanford Goldstein

SOURCE: "Zen and Salinger," in *Modern Fiction Studies,* Vol. 12, No. 3, Autumn, 1966, pp. 313-24.

[In the following essay, the Goldsteins argue that J. D. Salinger's writings illustrate the Zen theme of effacing and surmounting boundaries between the self and the other as a means of achieving spiritual enlightenment.]

While it is true that Zen has become a glittering catchword as connotative as existentialism and at times as meaningless, the fact remains that Zen does exist and that Salinger has shown a definite partiality towards it. Since Zen recognizes that all boundaries are artificial, Salinger's Western experience is not outside the universe Zen encompasses. The importance of the present moment; the long search and struggle in which reason, logic, cleverness, and intellect prove ineffectual; the inadequacy of judgment and criticism which reinforce and stimulate the artificial boundary between self and other; and some degree of enlighten-

ment which results from the non-rational and spontaneous blending of dualities, an enlightenment which permits experience that is complete and unadulterated and makes the moment and, in effect, life non-phoney—all these aspects of Zen can be found in Salinger's world.

First, what is Zen and what is the participant in Zen experience? An explanation of the latter may help clarify the former. The main actor in the typical Zen drama is besieged by doubt and desire. He is not at all certain what enlightenment is, but is convinced it exists, wants it, and is willing to struggle for it. Believing enlightenment is remote from him yet intensely desiring it, he pursues it only to find it continually eludes him. This peculiar dilemma results from the fact that he believes the search he is making with all his heart and mind, with all his being and self and ego, is for something that is *outside* himself. The Zen master, to whom he has gone for guidance towards the Way, grants him formal interviews with an abundance of ceremony which are probably intended to make him fully cognizant and thoroughly frightened, so the seeker fails in the exercise of the spontaneous answer to the irrational question, for example, "What is the sound of one hand clapping?" When not being questioned by the Zen master, the disciple spends time in the traditional method of sitting, ponders over various *koan* or puzzles like the above, and does various tasks with a minimum of verbal distraction. He is not permitted any of the temporary satisfactions which give his ego an illusion of satisfaction or well-being. These pursuits are not done merely for the sake of subduing or chastising the ego in an attempt to make it deny itself, but rather to expose the ego itself as an artificial entity whose very *searching for enlightenment* is spurious.

A number of Zen poems comment on the state of the universe before the disciple began his search: "The mountains were mountains and the rivers were rivers." During the disciple's search the appearance of the natural world changes, but once enlightenment comes, the mountains are again mountains, the rivers rivers. In the same way in the undifferentiated world of early childhood, the separation between self and the outside world is at a minimum. As Philip Kapleau says in his book *The Three Pillars of Zen:*

> But what the student responds to most keenly is the visible evidence of the roshi's [Venerable Teacher's] liberated mind: his childlike spontaneity and simplicity, his radiance and compassion, his complete identification with his (the student's) aspiration. A novice who watches his seventy-eight-year-old roshi demonstrate a koan with dazzling swiftness and total involvement, and who observes the flowing, effortless grace with which he relates himself to any situation and to all individuals, knows that he is seeing one of the finest products of a unique system of mind and character development, and he is bound to say to himself in his moments of despair: "If through the practice of Zen I can learn to experience life with the same immediacy and awareness, no price will be too high to pay."

Yet for the uninitiated, with the learning of abstractions (language itself being the foremost), self and other are progressively differentiated. Zen's peculiar problem is to bring the self back into a kind of controlled state of infantile non-separation through which it can recognize the arbitrary nature of all the artificial boundaries set up by abstraction and can see the unity in all experience and the existence of ego within that unity. The student seeking enlightenment, therefore, must proceed through his long search and struggle in which reason, logic, cleverness, and intellect prove useless; he must recognize that judgment and criticism reinforce and stimulate the artificial boundary lines of the ego. Finally in the non-rational blending of spurious dualities, he may acquire some degree of enlightenment which will enable him to fully participate in every moment of his day-to-day life. The Zen Master Yasutani-Roshi recites to one of his students the following lines from a famous master: "'When I heard the temple bell ring, suddenly there was no bell and no I, just sound.' In other words, he no longer was aware of a distinction between himself, the bell, the sound, and the universe."

We feel Salinger's main aim is to have his Glass children achieve the liberated moment, that is, experiences fully lived in which there is no separation between self and other. The major conflict in Franny, Zooey, and Buddy concerns the way to achieve this liberated state. Their Zen master is the dead Seymour. The concentrated area in which they will be permitted to act fully, freely, spontaneously, is their chosen métier.

In the same way that a camel will find it easier to pass through the eye of a needle than for a rich man to find his way into heaven, the Glass children have immense barriers that make enlightenment difficult for them, the major being their richly endowed personalities. They are a remarkable breed. Exceptionally bright, they have been raised under the tutelage of Eastern philosophy, but they are equally attune to the external gaiety and tinsel glitter of vaudeville. Thus each member of the Glass family is extroverted yet contemplative, subjectively inclined. The knowledge of languages by certain members of the family (for example, Greek, Latin, Chinese, Japanese, German), the ease with which they sail through ordinary academic pursuits and concentrate on the extraordinary, their wide reading, their use of allusion, their remarkable performance on "It's a Wise Child," all these make the Glass children unique.

Their uniqueness, however, is their Achilles' heel, their burden in the search for enlightenment. Their remarkable endowments hinder them from reaching the pure state of the simple Russian peasant in the pea-green book Franny is so tormented by. In one sense, the Russian peasant is to be envied for his lack of sophistication. Franny, Zooey, and Buddy are all very worldly, all very garrulous, all very academically inclined, all abundantly endowed intellectually and emotionally. Their very genius is their burden, their barrier toward the Way, but they know they must strive for it, for in their midst Seymour,

despite his suicide, stands as the enviable sibling, the seer, guru, poet, master. We are given the impression in *Franny and Zooey* that the enlightenment of the Russian peasant is something out of another time and place when enlightenment was more easily come by than in the twentieth century. Zooey tells Franny that she is not the simple Russian peasant, and earlier Franny had told Lane she wished she had the courage to be a nobody, but she is driven to desire applause, praise, fame, which are, in effect, the results of doing, not the doing itself. In the same way, Buddy, the teacher-writer, wants his stories in print and the praise of his family rather than the doing itself or the teaching itself.

Since Franny, Zooey, and Buddy all desire to reach the state that Seymour had attained, their problem is how to achieve it. What is to be their process toward enlightenment? Salinger, we feel, has in mind a verbal, highly speeded-up version of Zen enlightenment as he conceives it. To take the final step first: the wisdom eventually attained by Franny, Zooey, and Buddy is the wisdom of merging opposites, that is, the cancelling out of supposed opposites, events, objects, ideas, states of feeling, persons, for all dualities are merely arbitrarily drawn lines. Philip Kapleau's comment on Zen *koan* is pertinent here:

> The Chinese Zen masters, those spiritual geniuses who created these paradoxical dialogues, did not hesitate to thumb their noses at logic and common sense in their marvelous creations. By wheedling the intellect into attempting solutions impossible for it, koans reveal to us the inherent limitations of the logical mind as an instrument for realizing ultimate Truth. In the process they pry us loose from our tightly held dogmas and prejudices, strip us of our penchant for discriminating good from bad, and empty us of the false notion of self-and-other, to the end that we may one day perceive that the world of Perfection is in fact no different from that in which we eat and excrete, laugh and weep.

And as the Zen Master Yasutani-Roshi comments to his student:

> Your mind can be compared to a mirror, which reflects everything that appears before it. From the time you begin to think, to feel, and to exert your will, shadows are cast upon your mind which distort its reflections. This condition we call delusion, which is the fundamental sickness of human beings. The most serious effect of this sickness is that it creates a sense of duality, in consequence of which you postulate "I" and "not-I." The truth is that everything is One, and this of course is not a numerical one. Falsely seeing oneself confronted by a world of separate existences, this is what creates antagonism, greed, and, inevitably, suffering. The purpose of Zazen is to wipe away from the mind these shadows or defilements so that we can intimately experience our solidarity with all life. Love and compassion then naturally and spontaneously flow forth.

In *Zooey*, to cite one example of the blending of supposed dualities, Buddy's impetus for finally writing a crucial letter to his brother Zooey comes from meeting a small girl at a supermarket meatcounter. When Buddy asks her the names of her boy friends, she replies Dorothy and Bobby. For Buddy the moment becomes a remarkable one, almost an epiphany. At first sight the reader may not be aware of its significance, but when examined in the light of other events, it can clearly be seen that Salinger has intended the child's statement as profound, the blending of one of the most fundamental of dualities, that of sex.

The girl's statement then reminds Buddy of a haiku Seymour composed on a desk blotter of the hotel where he committed suicide. The haiku is about a girl on an airplane as she turns her doll's head around to look at someone, presumably the poet. Once again the dualities of the so-called real and unreal are resolved. The girl and doll are blended, and both the action of the turning and looking become one and the same in time.

Both of these events, the meatcounter episode and the haiku poem, Buddy recognizes as extremely startling and provoke him to his long-intended letter to Zooey. The result of the letter is to give Zooey the *way*, for the letter contains advice, originally derived from Seymour, concerning what Zooey and, by extension, Buddy and Franny, are to do in this world. Buddy's advice (really Seymour's) is that Zooey should act with all his might. That is his vocation, his mission, his *life* hood. Zooey recognizes the wisdom of the Seymour-Buddy statement and selects acting rather than some other career he had been contemplating up to that time.

The advice given by Buddy to Zooey is again repeated in the advice given by Zooey to his younger sister Franny. Franny's search, according to Zooey, is the kind of search he himself had pursued with little success not too long ago. He suggests that he too had the inclination to follow the way of the Russian pilgrim, but that way was not for him. Zooey tells his sister he will not remove himself from Western experience—that is, he refuses to go Eastward to find what he is looking for. He is determined to stay right where he is. He has no desire to do a motion picture in France even though he thinks the picture may be good. He wants to stay in New York where he was born, where he was run over twice. The key point is that he has chosen acting over another career he has thought seriously about, namely a Ph.D. in Greek or math that would inevitably have led to Academia. The fact that Zooey does choose acting over more theoretical or academic work seems to indicate a need for action. That is, he chooses *to act* rather than to speculate or contemplate. Thus, Zooey has rejected Franny's method in two ways: he has rejected contemplation, theory, speculation, and academic pursuit in favor of acting in the world; on the other hand, he has rejected going Eastward into any other culture or any other point of experience removed from where he is at the present moment. Franny is still searching outside herself, a fruitless pur-

suit since enlightenment is always within the self. In more concrete terms: no pea-green book will bring enlightenment; no solving of a *koan* or intellectual exercise will guarantee the Way; no self-conscious utterance of prayer will advance one toward the higher truth of self.

The advice Zooey gives to Franny is the same Buddy gave to him: act with all your might, for God if you must, but act. The meaning here is not simply the point of Franny's being a good actress, but that Franny, like Zooey himself, must express action to live. Hers is not to be a contemplative existence either, not something removed Eastward in the recital of a prayer that has no special meaning for her or that she misinterprets, confusing, Zooey says, Christ with Heidi's grandfather and Saint Francis. The path toward her salvation is directly in front of her, where she is, within, here. *Here* is where Franny chose to have her nervous breakdown—right at home. And it is right at home that Franny is going to find salvation. Even the homemade chicken soup is consecrated. We feel Salinger's meaning of home is broader than simply the connotative associations of the family abode. It is home within the heart, within the self. It has merely been temporarily lost and needs only to be recaptured.

It is Franny, Buddy, and Zooey's struggle to recapture the state of enlightenment each has temporarily lost. A close examination of Franny's problem will serve to illustrate the same kind of struggle in Buddy and Zooey.

Franny finally becomes somewhat enlightened upon hearing Zooey's advice about acting. To act with all her might is her task in life. And it is her task to act for God, to act as if she were not acting, to act so fully that no point of separation exists between what she is doing and any other conception of herself. Franny's struggle throughout *Franny* is her burdensome ego. Her dilemma is unquestionably the condition of her ego, and unquestionably the burden of the living Glass children is the same. Their trouble is too much ego, which leads us back to the first point we made about their wonderful potential, their magnificent endowments.

Franny is besieged, bedeviled, by the urge to complain, to criticize, to reject, to disapprove. She judges everyone around her, and she judges herself as well (the Glass children are all highly self-critical). She knows she has too much ego. She knows she is overly critical, but she cannot do anything about it. That is, the more she recognizes how critical she is, the more critical she becomes. For a while she may suppress her critical tendencies, but before long these crop up again. She promises Lane that she will stop being destructive, but in the next breath she is again criticizing Lane or something else, someone else. She cannot help herself because she is trying to solve her dilemma through repression, which always implies an opposite. Repression lasts only so long; then the ego reasserts itself with its powerful tendency to judge. Franny is, consequently, separated from all other objects and people around her, including her siblings. She criticizes abundantly people in the educational system, roommates, poets, the main actor in *The Playboy of the Western World,* her coworkers in summer stock, the Wally Campbells of the universe, Lane. She has a personal criticism to make about modern poetry, modern education, modern critics, American tourists, "section men." She has in fact a whole universe of complaint. She has set herself apart and from her high pedestal looks down like some stern lawgiver. She does see herself as one of the phonies, but her way is the way of repression so that the critical faculty is continually functioning.

Her enlightenment comes through Zooey's verbal barrage of identity, identity with self and with the part she is acting, the capacity, in short, to act as if she had no self. And her final point of identity derives ultimately from Seymour's advice that everybody is the Fat Lady. The Glass children, exceptional as they may be, are not exempted. Everybody is the Fat Lady. This image of the Fat Lady is not merely an effusion of love. Salinger is saying something a good deal more explicit than love-thy-neighbor. The major point, we believe, is that Salinger wishes to tell us there *is no difference* between Franny and the Fat Lady, impossible as that is to imagine. Franny and this cancerous Fat Lady with veiny legs rocking in a chair on some unidentified porch—the exceptional Franny and the unpleasant associations of this Fat Lady—are not separate. They are exactly part of the same thing.

Zooey, who gives this advice as Zooey, and who up to this time has been Buddy's spokesman or Buddy himself, has at last succeeded in identifying with Seymour, has in fact become Buddy-Seymour-Zooey. When he is finally recognized by Franny to be Zooey and not Buddy, he gives her the advice about the Fat Lady. We imagine that Salinger at this point intends to have us see Zooey as enlightened by his spontaneous advice, advice communicated to Franny without any separation between them.

The struggle portrayed in *Franny and Zooey* and even in *Seymour* is the same. The essential element in this trilogy is the breaking down of barriers between supposed opposites, artificial barriers created by abstracting and intellectualizing human beings. When the barriers are removed, enlightenment is produced in the form of some positive act. The stories move from conflict toward enlightenment, the conflict centered on the self-contained ego removed from others and other events. That self-contained separate ego leads to actions Salinger recognizes as phoney—that is, actions removed from the experience by judging the experience, criticizing it, dissecting it. Others are removed from the self, and the self is traditionally reenforced as a separate entity continually removed, separated, isolated. Conflict and turmoil, judgment and criticism, all these support a separated ego which Franny in particular and to a lesser extent Zooey and finally Buddy (in *Seymour*) must overcome before they reach some kind of awareness we have called "enlightenment."

It is this removal of self from other that we feel is Salinger's main criticism of the phoney. The three Glass children, far from being part of a cult of self-love, are in a very real sense double-phonies. What places them in a special category of the "phoney class" is the fact that they themselves are aware that they are phonies. Yet in spite of their awareness, of their self-criticism, this awareness does not make them non-phonies. They do not become non-phonies until they reach the critical moment in which they resolve artificial dualities. They are phonies with a difference, though, because they are conscious of their spurious participation in events. Other characters in Salinger's stories are phonies without being aware that they are, such as the famous musician in *Seymour* who complains to the principal about his daughter's music teacher offering "pop" rather than "good, healthy" classical music. Having received a favorable reply from the principal, the father's ego immensely bolstered, he struts home whistling "K-K-K-Katie." But Franny and Buddy and Zooey are double-snarled, for they are phonies aware of their phoniness. That is, they are consciously aware of what they are doing but cannot help doing what they do. Or else they make a remarkable attempt at repression, as in Franny's case, but as we have seen, repression will out. Their awareness of this weakness is another reason why Salinger endowed them so spectacularly so that they would become aware phonies who could search with all their conscious being for something other than what they are.

The phonies in Salinger's world are removed from immediate experience. The eventually partially enlightened Glass trio of Franny, Zooey, and Buddy become enlightened when they cease to isolate themselves as separate egos and so merge with experience that there is not a hair's breadth between will and action. Salinger focuses on the world of immediacy, the here and now, the immersion in the moment, to reintensify his theme of enlightenment which allows full participation in events. What has been called Salinger's verbal diarrhea is exactly this attempt to make concrete everything in sight so that the reader is immersed, say, in the middle of a bathtub or is staring into a medicine cabinet. The wealth of Salinger's descriptive detail helps make the moment concrete. The reader is immersed in the here and now of an event, the character acting in some concrete moment in time.

Salinger is often dating things for us, and Salinger-Buddy bemoans the fact that some writers never tell us what the time is. Buddy gives us the hour and the date and tries to break down the barrier between author and reader. Certainly Salinger's increasingly personal use of first-person narrative gains the added impact of immediacy. Concreteness, the feeling of immediacy, the emphatic immersion in the here and now, the breaking down of barriers between writer and reader by the intimate medium of a character (Buddy or Zooey) who is of course the writer rather than merely the character, all these give us a technical version of a simulated, very immediate experience that we may call part of Salinger's Zen.

Not only do these techniques suggest Salinger's awareness of Zen. He also uses other more direct or allusive Zen references in his stories. The incident of the curbside marbles in *Seymour* is one of the most profound. Salinger undoubtedly derived the inspiration for this scene from Eugene Herrigel's illuminating book *Zen in the Art of Archery* since the comment Seymour makes about marbles is about the same Herrigel makes on archery. Buddy, who was shooting at the marbles, was, according to his brother Seymour, *aiming* at them, and because he was *aiming* with the purpose of hitting another marble or marbles, he was delighted when he succeeded and disappointed when he failed. By being disappointed or delighted with the result of the shot, Buddy, according to Seymour, is indicating the possibility of losing. Here again the desire to win or the fact of winning in itself always brings into play the possibility of losing. The final growth of Buddy in *Seymour* comes when he recognizes the wisdom of his Zen-Master brother. The duality involved in playing marbles is winning and losing, and the state of the self under such conditions, a self that is striving to win, is a troubled self. Buddy has continually told us in *Seymour* that he visualizes everything he writes in eleven-point type. In other words, lines published on a page and success as we imagine it have been to Buddy what he considered important—the result above and beyond the act. The separation of the self which strives after something, in this instance publication and success, the foolishness of such striving, and the non-separated self which does not strive but "writes with all his stars out" is the wisdom Buddy attains from Seymour's advice recalled almost thirty years after the event. What Buddy learns is that he moves from one bit of holy ground to the next, that the act of writing is what is essential, that immersion in one's creation is what is crucial. He can now enter Room 307 of his English composition class with the recognition that it too is holy and that even the terrible "Miss Zabel" is as much his sister as Franny.

That Salinger has had Zen on his mind for a considerable period of time can be illustrated by *The Catcher in the Rye,* the germ of the enlightened or to-be-partially enlightened Glass children present there. We find Holden wandering through a lost week-end in which he himself belongs with the phonies. He proceeds from experience to experience, searching for something but always ending up with phonies of one kind or another. At the end of the story, however, Holden, who has had a nervous breakdown (as Franny has) and is being treated in a psychiatric institution, comes to some kind of awareness, namely that he misses all of the "phonies." Holden finally identifies in some way with the people he has spent so much time criticizing, but always criticizing with some degree of sympathy. He is not going to wander off to the West as a blind man or hobo, nor is he going to follow any of the other romantic visions he has toyed with during the course of the novel. Ultimately he is headed toward home. That, of course, is where he does go when he meets his sister Phoebe, and it is Phoebe and the very concrete image of her in her blue coat on a carrousel that ultimately brings Holden to the awareness that he has to go home. The final words in the novel seem to portend the major theme of the Glass stories. A psychiatrist mistakenly asks Holden what he is going to do in September. Holden says he does not know. How should he know what he is going to be doing at such a removed time as next September? Holden seems to imply that he knows what he is doing only at the exact moment he is doing it, not at some point in some arbitrarily designated future.

Holden foreshadows in a much less explicit way the highly critical Glasses, for he too is very clever, very judgmental, very witty, always striving for something. As Salinger proceeds and matures in his career as a writer, what he suggests Holden was searching for becomes more explicit in the Glass stories. Not only is Holden the Catcher in the Rye, as he explicitly tells us—the catcher who catches children before they fall from the field of rye—but Holden too is caught. He is caught in a way quite similar to Buddy's being caught, and that is by the image of love for a dead brother. Holden's brother Allie is intended to be the wise, sagacious Seymour-type. When Holden needs help, he turns to his dead brother Allie. Holden is caught by love and an awareness of something better in the universe, and he is similarly caught by his younger sister Phoebe when she tells him there is nothing in the world he likes. The stress once more is that Holden is far too critical, his critical tendencies similar to those of the Glass trio of Franny, Buddy, and Zooey. Holden's recognition that he has separated himself from all the people he has been defining as phonies comes in his awareness that he misses all of them.

It is this overly critical tendency in Salinger's characters that we want to stress as a key point in Salinger's Zen, and that tendency to be overly critical says something profound about our modern American life, this very critical time of our own very critical people.

In modern America, various institutions (educational, literary, social, scientific) which at one time or another were regarded as sacred are now no longer seen in that light, but as simply the conscious expression of people in the process of culture-building, society-building. The social sciences have been both a cause and an effect of this recognition. In our highly conscious age, we realize that even God is not beyond the pale of criticism. All of our institutions are now recognized as man-made systems that can be changed, bettered, even made worse. Once the sacred quality of all institutions has been removed, the only thing left is the individual or individuals who make up institutions. But of course even the self has not been untampered with, for psychoanalysis has been busily revising and remodeling it for almost a hundred years.

All institutions and all aspects of culture, therefore, are ultimately derived from human power, but at the same time the forces in the universe which man cannot control seem to grow larger. That is, we recognize that we build political institutions and we build God and we also build atom bombs. On the one hand, the self is endowed with enormous creative power; on the other, the same self is acted upon by even greater powers that make it seem, on the contrary, less powerful than ever before.

From the viewpoint of social critics in the twentieth century, the existing self is a split self, a disconnected self, a separated self, an atomized self—exceedingly powerful as it continues to create, yet acted upon and weakened by the very things it has created. What this cultural determinism means is that various aspects of the culture act upon the self, but ultimately of course these cultural forces that act upon the self are recognized as created by that very self. What results is that gradually, year by year, decade by decade, the area of greater consciousness of self is expanded. Our consciousness has moved from the realm of the divine and the sacred to various aspects of culture or social systems into a very minute consciousness of self. In our atomized world of self and selves, only this component of consciousness remains. That is, every year another system or aspect of the cultural world around us comes into our conscious recognition as having been created by us. We no longer worship, study, create, with the same abandon and spontaneity we once did. Instead, we analyze, dissect, find differences, multiply dichotomies. As a result, all of our increased consciousness becomes endowed to a self that ultimately, after all our critical perspective, stands alone as a unit and decides consciously or self-consciously what it is to do, worship, think, feel, speak. Left with this overabundance of conscious-self, we begin to wonder if we are not at the brink of helplessness.

It is with this overburdened, self-consciously conscious self that Salinger begins his quest. The highly endowed, overburdened, critically conscious Glass children are representative of our time in history. The spectacular Franny and Buddy and Zooey are fully endowed and fully aware and fully self-conscious and quite unhappy. Their self-consciousness is their burden, and they seek to rid themselves of it and to blend it into something else. Salinger's three Glasses manage to attain in their own fashion some freedom from this burdensome self, this critical self, this highly self-conscious self. The solution is the blending of self and other, the removal of abstraction and analysis, the avoidance of criticism, the absorption in the moment.

The most unusual aspect of Salinger's liberated Glasses is that change comes by way of a verbal flow of abstraction. This may be a contradiction-in-terms, for to experience the liberation of Zen by a second-hand conscious verbal overflow is not the usual way of deriving enlightenment. But in Salinger's highly self-conscious world, this is the means by which his characters attain a twentieth century American form of enlightenment. In this enlightened state the Glass children become freed of their critical tendencies, become freed of their highly separate selves, become one with the Fat Lady or the Christ in each that makes for universal empathy. Perhaps Salinger is the keenest social critic of our time. He has, we feel, focused on a major problem in the modern world, on the

last stronghold of the sacred, for an atomized self is disastrous.

Bert Almon

SOURCE: "Buddhism and Energy in the Recent Poetry of Gary Snyder," in *Mosaic: A Journal for the Comparative Study of Literature and Ideas,* Vol. XI, No. 1, fall, 1977, pp. 117-25.

[*In the following essay, Almon investigates the Buddhist metaphysics that inform the poetry of Gary Snyder.*]

For all its attention to the physical world, the poetry of Gary Snyder has always had a metaphysical dimension. He once called poetry "a riprap (cobbled trail) over the slick rock of metaphysics," but metaphysics can also provide a trail over the slick rock of the poetry, providing a path where we might see only a difficult physical terrain. I will put aside the important matter of the influence of American Indian spirituality on Snyder's work and investigate the Buddhist context. Snyder's interest in Zen Buddhism is well-known: he is the poet who spent years in Japan studying it. While much of the material in recent works, such as *Regarding Wave* (1970) and *Turtle Island* (1974), may certainly be clear without a knowledge of Buddhism, some is not, and Snyder's fundamental opposition to industrial civilization can be clarified by understanding the Buddhist influence.

Zen is one of the schools of the Mahayana branch of Buddhism prevalent in Buddhist countries outside of Southeast Asia. It is a very special school, one minimizing philosophy and emphasizing direct experience. Western readers familiar only with the Zen tradition—the Zen master stories, the *koan* exercises—may not be aware of certain basic Mahayana concepts. The Mahayana schools have an ideal of active compassion that extends to all living beings: even the grass should be led to enlightenment by the Bodhisattva, the "enlightenment being" who vows to deliver the whole universe. The Bodhisattva practices *upaya,* "skillful means," stratagems and teachings fitted to the various beings he wishes to deliver. For the enlightened mind, the world is a state of being beyond all conflicts and oppositions. As Snyder puts it in "Four Changes," an important essay in *Turtle Island:* " . . . at the heart of things is some kind of serene and ecstatic process which is beyond qualities and beyond birth-and-death." This state of nirvana is not accessible to most of us, and we experience *samsara,* the world of birth-and-death. On this relative level of being, the universe is conceived of as a dynamic realm of interdependent and transient phenomena. Living beings are temporary groupings of elements of this flux, a conception that Snyder translates into the terms of Western physics: " . . . we are interdependent energy-fields of great potential wisdom and compassion . . ." he says in "Four Changes." He puts it this way in the "Introductory Note" of the same collection: "The poems speak of place, and the energy-pathways that sustain life. Each living being is a swirl in the flow, a formal turbulence, a 'song.'" In Snyder's work, the concept of interdependence is translated into ecological terms, and the conception of the world as flux is rendered in terms of physics: the world is a dynamic field of energy. Modern physics shows no interest in the potential wisdom and compassion of energy fields certainly. Science is an instrument of understanding and altering the world. Archimedes is with us yet, even if he may soon have no world to move. Ecology, on the other hand, is one science that does concern itself with wisdom. The ecologist knows how serious the consequences of acting without foresight and compassion can be. Ecological compassion is not a matter of sentimental humanitarianism, just as Snyder's notion of compassion does not rule out taking life, to sustain life.

But the poems in *Riprap,* and many in *Myths & Texts,* do not convey a world of flux. The poems are often contemplative: meditations set in stable landscapes, even if the poet laments transience and notes the passage of birds. Sherman Paul has said [in *Iowa Review* 1 (Fall 1970)] that "The unity of *Riprap* is essentially one of stillness. . . ." and I must agree with that insight. Zen awareness and Zen detachment permeate the early poems. Often they evoke quiet landscapes and sweeps of geological time. The scenes are *composed,* and composed very skillfully. The art of *sumi* painting comes to mind: vistas of clouds and mountains, a human figure or two almost lost in the mist, birds flying off into limitless space, all done in a few strokes. Not the intricate hum of transient elements in the void. And even the poems in *Myths & Texts,* though they describe logging and hunting, more often deal with contemplation than action.

There are transitional poems in *The Back Country,* but the striking change comes with *Regarding Wave.* Instead of a panoramic view of mountains or valleys, the poems frequently offer a world placed under the microscope. And rather than contemplation, the attitude is involvement. The proper analogy with painting would be the *tanka* art of Tibet, which arouses and transforms psychological energies through a blaze of color: processes instead of scenes. Consider the opening of the first poem ("Wave") in the book:

> Grooving clam shell,
>   streakt through marble,
> sweeping down ponderosa pine bark-scale
>   rip-cut tree grain
>   sand-dunes, lava flow

The dynamism of wave-forms is traced even in static objects. Physics and Mahayana Buddhism would agree that there are no stable objects, merely the illusion of stability. One of the objects of Buddhist meditation is to achieve awareness of impermanence in all aspects of reality, external and internal. The poetry of *Regarding Wave* often deals with what "Wave" calls " . . . the dancing grain of things / of my mind!" The "dancing grain" is a fine metaphor, and the activity of dancing is one of Snyder's favored means of conveying a dynamic world. Running water is another recurrent image used in the

book. And the poet adopts the standard meditation strategy of imagining the physical world permeated with the sounds of the *Dharma* (Buddhist teachings) in several poems. In "Regarding Wave," the *Dharma* is "A shimmering bell / though all," and the slopes of the hills are said to flow. "All the Spirit Powers Went to Their Dancing Place" turns the very landscape into sound: "Hills rising and falling as music, long plains and deserts as slow quiet chanting."

The style of *Regarding Wave* tends toward the break-up of straight-forward description and narration. The lines frequently take the form of image clusters: phrases and single words replacing the extended utterance as the unit of expression. (I say "extended utterance" because Snyder's terseness sometimes led him to avoid the complete sentence in the early poems.) The images themselves often evoke minute particulars, such as seeds, sand grain, thorns, or bark-scales. The world is examined with a close-up lens. Not that the images are always visual. Tactile, auditory, gustatory, olfactory and kinesthetic impressions are prominent and heighten the impression of involvement.

I will return to the matter of involvement in a moment, but I should mention that *Turtle Island* reverses these stylistic trends. We still come upon lines like "Snow-trickle, feldspar, dirt." But the poet is more concerned with narrative, even exposition, and the style is therefore more conventional, less concerned with rendering the flow of process. Social criticism and the desire to come to terms with Western America take precedence over the dancing grain of things. There are poems like "On San Gabriel Ridges" which would easily fit into *Regarding Wave,* but in the later volume Snyder is engrossed with the anecdotal and didactic, and the writing reflects those intentions. The sweep of evolution (300,000,000 years go by in one poem) and the workings of the American political system get more attention than the intricate dynamics of sand grains.

Snyder's Buddhist training has been in the Zen school, but his philosophical position is now influenced by the Vajrayana sect, whose outlook he discusses in *Earth House Hold.* Vajrayana (literally, "The Diamond Vehicle") is a Tantric school, predominant in Tibet before the Chinese invasion of 1959, and still widely practiced in the Himalayan region. Tantra is an approach found in Hinduism as well as Buddhism. The Tantric method is to involve the practitioner with the very reality that most Hindu and Buddhist sects seek detachment from: the world of birth-and-death, the realm of the passions. The key is to transform this reality rather than to escape from it. The attitude toward the emotions in Vajrayana Buddhism is particularly important: passions are aroused and transmuted, not repressed. Anger and desire, for example, can be made instruments of enlightenment. They are changed from poisons into wisdom. Readers who assume that Buddhism is a religion of passivity and kindness may be puzzled by Snyder's ferocity in some of the *Turtle Island* poems. Anger can be a teaching method (consider the Zen master and his stick), and it can also be transmuted into compassion. Better, it is one of the possible forms of compassion, as in the polemics of the ecology movement.

Snyder's "Spel Against Demons" is a good example of the role of wrath in his poetry. The poem originally appeared with "Smokey the Bear Sutra" and "The California Water Plan" in a limited edition entitled *The Fudo Trilogy*. It alone was reprinted in *Turtle Island*. "Fudo" is the Japanese name for a Mahayana deity called "Achala" or "Acala" in Sanskrit. His iconography and the *sadhana* (ritual of worship, visualization and invocation) devoted to him are described in "The California Water Plan." The deity represents the struggle against evil and is sometimes called the Lord of Heat. His imagery is summed up in Alice Getty's *The Gods of Northern Buddhism:* "His appearance is fierce and angry. The sword in his right hand is to smite the guilty and the lasso in his left to catch and bind the wicked." He is associated with fire: "Behind him is a glory of flames, symbolizing the destruction of Evil. . . ." Snyder's Smokey the Bear is fancifully presented as a form of Achala, or Fudo, and the "Smokey the Bear Sutra" is a droll parody of Buddhist scriptures. "Spel Against Demons" is also modeled on a Buddhist literary form, the *dharani*.

A *dharani* is a charm or spell, usually invoking a Buddha or Bodhisattva. Although D. T. Suzuki gives examples of the form in his well-known *Manual of Zen Buddhism*, the *dharani* represents a magical dimension of Buddhism which has received little attention in the West. "Spel Against Demons" attacks "The release of Demonic Energies in the name of / the People" and "The stifling self-indulgence in anger in the name of / Freedom." Mindless terrorism is denounced as " . . . death to clarify / death to compassion." The poem represents anger without rancor: The poem calls upon Achala to bind "demonic killers" with his diamond noose and describes this deity " . . . who turns Wrath to Purified Accomplishment." The poem ends with a Sanskrit *mantra*, a power-formula—the "Spel" of Achala.

It is not, then, contradictory for Snyder to include poems of anger and denunciation ("The Call of the Wild," "Steak," "Control Burn") in the same section of *Turtle Island* that contains the warm family scenes of "The Bath" and the compassionate descriptions of "The Dead by the Side of the Road." The Vajrayana tradition embraces a life-giving exploitation of anger: some of the meditation masters of the Vajarayana were willing to use wrath and even force as teaching tools. The sensuous delight in the flesh that Snyder conveys in "The Bath" is equally respectable. The body is not the "running sore" for Vajrayana that it is for the Southern branch of Buddhism, the Theravada. Mindless craving is condemned, but the power of the senses is power that the spiritual life can harness.

The anger usually has a compassionate thrust. And the outrage Snyder feels often grows out of the abuse of liv-ing creatures that many religions ignore: animals and trees. The theoretical scope of Buddhist compassion is unlimited. The object of compassion is any living being, not just human beings. The Buddhist, like the North American Indian, gives a kind of equality to " . . . the other people—what the Sioux Indians called the creeping people, and the standing people, and the swimming people . . ." (*Turtle Island*, "The Wilderness"). Many of Snyder's "people" are birds, coyotes, whales, insects or even plants. It is easy to dismiss this sympathy as sentimental pantheism but Snyder knows that the ecological crisis grows out of such attitudes. His problem as a poet of the whole range of living beings is to create poems in which animals and plants appear as autonomous presences, not as mere symbols for human feelings or concepts. Naturally, the terms used are anthropomorphic, but anthropomorphism is a problem only for a world view that assumes an absolute gulf between man and other beings. Buddhism provides what Robinson Jeffers would call a transhuman perspective. The aim is not to raise the supposedly lower orders to a human level, but to see all beings as co-citizens in a community of life. Snyder assumes that the artist can imaginatively enter into the lives of other organisms and speak for them. In "The Wilderness," he says: "I wish to be a spokesman for a realm that is not usually represented in intellectual chambers or in the chambers of government." According to Snyder, the way to be such a spokesman is to create paintings, dances or songs to express an interpretation of other beings.

Snyder is perhaps most skilled at interpreting birds: *Myths & Texts* contains some fine descriptions of them, and poems such as "The Wide Mouth" in *Regarding Wave* (depicting a sparrow) and "The Hudsonian Curlew" in *Turtle Island*, are high points in the books. Deer, bears and coyotes get attention also. Plants present the biggest challenge: they are the basis of any ecological system, the "proletariat" on which other living beings feed, directly or indirectly, but they are very static characters, clearly. Snyder managed action in his early poems on plant life by describing forest fires and logging, and in *Regarding Wave* he deals with the dissemination of seeds by wind and water and on the fur of mammals. The distribution of seeds reminds us that plants have an active role in the shifting pattern of life.

Plants form the base of what in "Four Changes" Snyder calls " . . . a vast and delicate pyramid of energy-transformations." Those transformations usually take the form of eating and being eaten. Food is one of Snyder's favorite themes. Many of the poems in his books deal with eating, and sometimes on an Odyssean scale. For example, *The Back Country* ends, not with the mythical splendors of "Through the Smoke Hole," but with "Oysters," a poem about hunting and eating the shellfish. The implied theme of the poem is the abundance of nature. Poems like "Shark Meat" in *Regarding Wave* create an awareness of the interdependence of all phenomena. The shark traveled far to become part of a feast on Suwa-no-se Island.

> Miles of water, Black current,
> Thousands of days
>   re-crossing his own paths
>   to tangle our net
>   to be part of
>   this loom.

And "The Hudsonian Curlew" in *Turtle Island* evokes the complexity of the physical world in which such birds live, then goes on to present the eating of them as an incorporation of their being into the eater: "dense firm flesh, / dark and rich, / gathered news of skies and seas." Eating becomes a reverential act, rather than a brutal necessity. Snyder is probably more indebted to North American Indian attitudes toward hunting and eating in this poems than he is to the Buddhist tradition. Buddhism teaches gratitude toward food—acknowledgement that it represents a loss of life—and that attitude is common among the American Indians, but Buddhism also encourages vegetarianism in order to minimize suffering. It is mindfulness of the interconnections involved in eating which Snyder draws from Buddhism. On the question of vegetarianism he takes the side of the primitive hunter who believes that humility, gratitude and acts of propitiation expiate the blame for eating meat or taking furs. Snyder does see Buddhism and American Indian attitudes as compatible, and both are influences in the poems. In "One Should Not Talk to a Skilled Hunter about What is Forbidden by the Buddha'" (which invokes a Zen master's authority in the title), Snyder describes a Buddhist ceremonial in honor of a gray fox which is to be skinned: chanting the *Shingyo,* or *Heart Sutra,* a text often recited to the dying and at funerals. Another poem in *Turtle Island,* "The Dead by the Side of the Road," presents the use of animals killed by accident. The ceremony described, offering corn meal by the dead body, is North American Indian. The Buddhist tradition that meat not killed by or specifically for one can be eaten without blame, and the conclusion of the poem is an act of mindfulness in the Buddhist sense: it emphasizes that some blame does attach to human beings for building highways across animal trails. The Buddhist and North American Indian elements in Snyder's poems are more likely to reinforce than contradict each other.

Both traditions condemn thoughtless murder of any creature. The poems in *Turtle Island* reject such killing. "Steak" condemns those who eat grain-fattened beef without realizing the cost to the land or acknowledging the suffering of the animals. The poem concludes with an image of the live cattle which are being fattened-up:

> Steaming, stamping,
> long-lashed, slowly thinking
> with the rhythm of their
> breathing,
> frosty—breezy—
> early morning prairie sky.

The key word is "thinking." We prefer not to realize that cattle are sentient beings, capable of suffering.

The greatest anger in *Turtle Island* is reserved for wanton killing for mere gain or comfort, a different matter from eating to sustain life. "The Call of the Wild" is particularly effective, with its acid portrait of the man who has coyotes trapped because they make noise, and its terse, disgusted chronicle of the city hippies who move to the country but sell their cedars because someone tells them that "Trees are full of bugs." The anger is tempered with awareness and compassion that reduce the potential for a self-righteous tone. In "I Went into the Maverick Bar" the speaker disguises himself as a middle American ("My long hair was tucked up under a cap / I'd left the earring in the car.") and observes the mores of his countrymen with some sympathy. I am reminded of the Bodhisattva named Vimalakirti, who was famed for going into brothels and taverns in order to practice compassion. He always appeared to be one of the revelers, but only as a form of *upaya,* skillful means. One of the most interesting poems in *Turtle Island* is "Dusty Braces," in which the poet acknowledges the influence of his wandering, land-destroying ancestors and gives them "nine bows," a traditional form of homage in Buddhism. But acknowledging his *karma*—the formative influences on him—doesn't mean that he accepts the destructive ways of those ancestors.

The indignation recorded in *Turtle Island* reaches a climax in "Mother Earth: Her Whales," a denunciation of the "robots" who " . . . argue how to parcel out our Mother Earth / To last a little longer." This poem, like "Toward Climax" later in the book, strikes me as a good prose essay mysteriously incarnated as a bad poem. "Mother Earth: Her Whales" has too many discordant elements: a manifesto calling for an uprising of "otters, wolves and elk," lyrical passages describing the lives of the whales themselves, rhetorical denunciations of the "robots" at the Stockholm Conference on the Environment, fragments of ballads, and historical sketches. A reader can share the disgust and yet feel that the poem is not successful. Prose might have been a better vehicle for conveying the sense of outrage.

This particular poem does make it clear that the poet wants to take on all exploitative civilizations:

> how can the head-heavy power-hungry politic
>   scientist
> Government two world Capitalist-Imperialist
> Third World Communist paper-shuffling male
>   non-farmer jet-set bureaucrats
> Speak for the green of the leaf? Speak for the soil?

The technological abuses of Western civilization are envied by the non-Western nations: the instrumental approach—pragmatism and exploitation—is shared by many developing as well as developed nations. The energy crisis has shown that this approach is ultimately self-defeating. It breaks down those "energy-pathways" that sustain life. And energy in the narrow sense, mere fuel, can be exhausted.

Technically-advanced societies, and those aspiring to such status, regard energy as a means of controlling, altering and exploiting the natural world. The environment is a mass of raw material to be exploited. For Mahayana Buddhism, the world is a dynamic process to be interpreted through contemplation, or even transmuted (as in Vajrayana)—not cut-down, burned-out, torn-up or strip-mined. In Zen monasteries the ideal is to waste nothing, not even a drop of water. The Buddhist approach is one of gratitude for what one receives, while the industrial approach is to devise ways of getting more. One of Snyder's themes in *Turtle Island* is exploitation and wanton destruction. Much of the wrath can be accounted for by the shameless way in which governments that very slowly awoke to public pressure for environmental protection measures have moved quickly to give up those measures whenever they interfere with the need for energy. A shortage of energy in the limited sense—fuel—justifies further damage to the " . . . vast and delicate pyramid of energy-formations" which makes life possible. The real sources of energy are the sun and the mental energy within the mind. Opposed to these sources is the "Liquid Metal Fast Breeder Reactor," which Snyder sees as "Death himself," a source of contamination likely to heighten the environmental damage already done by conventional approaches to creating industrial energy. The poet insists that "We would live on this Earth / without clothes or tools!" But this is not possible without vast transformations in our way of life, of course, and the prose essays in *Turtle Island* are meant to encourage such changes. His commentary on "As for Poets" declares that " . . . there is another kind of energy, in every living being, close to the sun-source, but in a different way. The power within. Whence? 'Delight.' The delight of being alive while knowing of impermanence and death, acceptance and mastery of this." Such power, he says, " . . . will still be our source when coal and oil are long gone, and atoms are left to spin in peace." He defines "Delight" in terms of Mahayana metaphysics, though he draws the term from William Blake, who said that "Energy is Eternal Delight." It is interesting to note that Herbert V. Guenther, seeking a term for the *Karmamudra* experience of sexual ecstacy in Tantric Buddhism, hit upon Blake's "Eternal Delight" also. For Snyder, Delight grows out of a perception of the world as a luminous, interdependent reality, which can be perceived as serene and joyful when observed without dualistic thinking:

> Delight is the innocent joy arising
> with the perception and realization of
> the wonderful, empty, intricate,
> inter-penetrating,
> mutually-embracing, shining
> single world beyond all discrimination
> or opposites.

In "Charms" (*Turtle Island*), Snyder follows the Tantric tradition in suggesting that "The beauty of naked or half-naked women" evokes this perception of " . . . the Delight / at the heart of creation." There are other ways of evoking Delight, and the celebration of animals, plants and birds is one means of summoning up a joy in the energy of things. The flux of physical reality need not be perceived as a conflict if there is no desire to conquer or

exploit it. And even the passion of anger can be plowed back into "Fearlessness, humor, detachment," genuine forms of power.

Daniel L. Guillory

SOURCE: "The Oriental Connection: Zen and Representations of the Midwest in the Collected Poems of Lucien Stryk," in *Midamerica XIII: The Yearbook of the Society for the Study of Midwestern Literature*, edited by David D. Anderson, Midwestern Press, 1986, pp. 107-15.

[*In the following essay, Guillory examines the Zen-like awareness of the midwestern poems of Lucien Stryk.*]

In 1967 Lucien Stryk edited *Heartland: Poets of the Midwest,* and in his Introduction to that anthology he underscores the aesthetic and poetic possibilities inherent in the Midwestern experience. Although many critics have denigrated the region for being flat and "colorless," Stryk insists that the Midwest can be "rich, complicated, thrilling" (*Heartland* xiv). In the poetry he chooses for that anthology and, more importantly, in his own work, Stryk dramatizes again and again that the Midwest is

> made up of the stuff of poetry. And once those living in it begin to see its details—cornfields, skyscrapers, small-town streets, whatever—with the help of their poets, they will find it not only more possible to live with some measure of contentment among its particulars but even, miraculously, begin to love them and the poems they fill. (*Heartland* xiv)

After this aesthetic manifesto, it is not surprising to discover that the opening poem in Stryk's *Collected Poems, 1953-1983,* is "Farmer," a powerful evocation of the agrarian life that typifies the region. Without rancor or sentimentality, the farmer beholds the landscape purely, observing a world "bound tight as wheat, packed / hard as dirt." His life and even his dwelling place are subsumed by the larger reality of the prairie:

> While night-fields quicken,
> shadows slanting right, then left
> across the moonlit furrows,
> he shelters in the farmhouse
> merged with trees, a skin of wood,
> as much the earth's as his.

In "Old Folks Home," a later and more meditative poem, Stryk imagines such a farmer at the end of his days, useless and unproductive but still tied to the fields by plangent memories and subtleties of perception. From his prison-like cell in the rest home, he follows the "empty path" to "fields pulsing / gold, green under / vapors, rain-fresh / furrows stretching / miles." Then he is overcome by memories of his lost farm and long-dead wife:

> he stands hours, keen
> to the cool scent

of fullness—now
without purpose where
corn-tassels blow.
Returns to the bare
room, high above cedars
gathering gold and green.

The "corn-tassels" are just one of the constituent Midwestern "details" that Stryk invokes in his Introduction to *Heartland;* earlier, in *Notes for a Guidebook* (1965), he refers to the importance of "small particulars," and in a recent interview with this author, Stryk insists on the primacy of the finely perceived detail. He explains that some years ago, after returning from one of his many trips to Japan, he determined "to make a minute inspection of my own world in DeKalb, Illinois . . . You see the smallest things become important as a source of revelation." This emphasis on the "small particulars" is a stylistic hallmark of Lucien Stryk's work. He rarely paints with a broad brush; his method is to focus on single objects, moments, and scenes. In his long poem, "A Sheaf for Chicago'" Stryk reduces Sandburgs comprehensive "city of the big shoulders" to particular scenes. Stryk's own childhood in Chicago is suggested by a catalogue of details, including discarded automobile parts and Christmas trees:

We gathered fenders, axles, blasted hoods
To build Cockaigne and Never-never Land,
Then beat for dragons in the oily weeds.
That cindered lot and twisted auto mound,
That realm to be defended with the blood,
Became, as New Year swung around,
A scene of holocaust, where pile on pile
Of Christmas trees would char the heavens
And robe us demon-wild and genie-tall
To swirl the hell of 63rd Place . . .

Another poem dealing with the theme of childhood is "Rites of Passage," a much later work in which Stryk, the former Chicago street urchin, has become a kind of Wordsworthian man, wandering through a rural corn field with his own son. The poet is even more aware of the importance of details and the intensity of childhood moments, here glimpsed through the eyes of his own son. The poem turns into a kind of incantation in which human language is replaced by the altogether more powerful language of nature itself:

soybeans, corn, cicadas. Stone rings
touch the bank, ripple up my arm.
   In the grass
a worm twists in the webbed air (how things
absorb each other)—on a branch
   a sparrow
tenses, gray. As grass stirs it bursts
from leaves, devouring. I close my book.
   With so much
doing everywhere, words swimming green,
why read? I see and taste silence.

In "Rites of Passage" the words become living entities, as if Stryk short-circuits the linguistic process and returns to an earlier time in pre-history when every word was the actual *name* of a living entity—a development described exhaustively by Ernst Cassirer in his classic work, *Language and Myth.*

Not all Midwestern moments, however, are the basis for transcendent experiences; many characteristic events inspire anxiety or outright terror. The region is visited by every meteorological curse imaginable, including freezing rain, dust storms, ice storms, hail, tornadoes, floods, and earthquakes. These natural disasters occur as background or foreground in many of Lucien Stryk's poems, although he gives each terrifying event a peculiarly personal stamp. In "The Quake," for example, the poet and his wife are thrown out of bed by the mysterious rumbling underground. Their love-making is interrupted by a natural occurrence that shatters their tender interlude of shared intimacy. At first, they view the event as comic:

We laughed when the bed
Heaved twice then threw
Us to the floor. When all
Was calm again, you said
It took an earthquake
To untwine us. Then I
Stopped your shaking
With my mouth.

The "shaking" persists, however, as doubts and fears open in their psyches, fault-lines of a deeper and more sinister kind:

Then why should dream
Return us to that fragile
Shelf of land? And why,
Our bodies twined upon
This couch of stone,
Should we be listening,
Like dead sinners, for the quake?

The most terrifying of all the natural disasters is the tornado—deadly, unmerciful, and always unpredictable. In "Twister" the poet and his family wait out the storm in their basement after the tornado has already "touched down / a county north, leveled a swath / of homes, taking twenty lives." Like countless others, they study the "piled up junk" while wondering "what's ahead":

We listen; ever
silent, for the roar out of the west,
whatever's zeroing in with terror
in its wake. The all clear sounds,
a pop song hits above. Made it
once again. We shove the chairs
against the wall, climb into the light.

Like the earthquake in "Quake," the tornado in "Twister" breaks the numbing routine of ordinary existence and, hence, provides an opportunity for spiritual insight. By placing the poet (and his family) on the edge of death, such disasters force an instantaneous awareness of—and appreciation for—the mysterious and fragile life force. Paradoxically, the poet transforms such potential disasters into positive aesthetic triumphs. Speaking of all the possible setbacks to be encountered in writing poetry about the Midwest, Stryk remarks that "if the poet is worth his salt he is certain to get as much out of it as those who live elsewhere . . ." (*Heartland* xv).

Natural disasters are not the only kinds of setbacks that figure prominently in the poetry of Lucien Stryk; he gives a good deal of attention to the "Babbitry" (*Heartland* xix) that often typifies small-town life in the Midwest. Social disasters seem to occur just as often as natural ones. Every town has its share of malingers and ne'er-do-wells, like the "toughs" and "dropouts" described in "The Park":

> All summer long rednecks,
> high-school dropouts rev
> motorbikes and souped-up
> cars across the isle of
> grass, jeer at cops cruising
> as the horseshoes fly.
> Strollers, joggers, children
> traipsing to the city pool
> flinch at hoots and whistles,
> radio blasts recoiling from
> the trees.

The sociology of prejudice and ostracism is the ugly core at the center of "The Cannery," another poem about malaise in the small midland town. Local residents resent—and fear—the annual influx of migrant workers, especially poor Southern whites and illegal Mexicans who form a cheap labor pool for the local cannery:

> In summer this town is full of rebels
> Come up from Tennessee to shell the peas.
> And wetbacks roam the supermarkets, making
> A Tijuana of the drab main street.
> The Swedes and Poles who work at Wurlitzer,
> And can't stand music, are all dug in:
> Doors are bolted, their pretty children warned,
> Where they wait for the autumnal peace.

Some of the "disasters" may seem minor to someone who has never attempted the supremely difficult task of poetic composition, a process that requires intense powers of concentration. The poet's frustration in "Here and Now" is more than understandable: a poem has been scuttled by the importunate knocking of an Alcoa salesman. The poet's indignation turns on itself again and becomes the catalyst for a poem about not being able to write a poem in peace:

> Hear a knocking
> at the front. No muse,
> a salesman
> from the Alcoa
> Aluminum Company
> inspired by the siding
> of our rented house.

The greatest disaster, perhaps, is to fall victim to the sameness and plainness that, at least on first sight, characterize the Midwestern scene. "And if the poets of the heartland," asks Stryk, "see their territory as often lumi-

nous and wild, are we to conclude that the weary passer-through who views it as a terrible sameness may, in fact, be seeing nothing other than himself" (*Heartland* xix)? In point of fact, seeing things in a new way is one of the primary results of Zen training, and while it is true that good artists acquire this trait in many ways—not merely from Zen—it is also true that Lucien Stryk's work bears an especially strong affinity to Zen. For years he has translated Zen poetry and taught Asian literature; he has actually lived in Japan for a number of years. His most recent books are eloquent examples of his life-long attention to this meditative and aesthetic discipline: *On Love and Barley: Haiku of Basho* (1985) and *Triumph of the Sparrow: Zen Poems of Shinkichi Takahashi* 1986). "I think my life has been profoundly affected by Zen and by meditation, reading, and translating," Stryk observes. "I think about Zen constantly; I believe I'm easier to live with, more able to handle life. And I take joy in reality of a kind that I could not have taken without such Zen training." The kind of joy Stryk means in this remark is well illustrated by the little poem "Constellation," a kind of poetic diary-entry in which the poet records the surprising discovery of beautiful sunflowers in a most unlikely setting:

> Behind the super-
> market where we
> forage for our
> lives, beyond the
> parking lot, crammed
> garbage bins—
> thick heads of
> bee-swarmed
> seed-choked
> sunflowers blaze
> down on me through
> fogged noon air.

Stryk is quite conscious of his unique way of looking at ordinary Midwestern artifacts: he describes himself as "someone whose experiences have all the limitations and, of course, all the possibilities of this particular corner of the universe."

Elm trees, to cite one example, represent one of the many "possibilities" for the poet. Once so numerous that their leafy branches were a trademark of every small town in the Midwest and now virtually extinct because of Dutch elm disease, the elm is a kind of totem for the region. In "Elm" the poet mourns the loss of his elm, a personal favorite destroyed by "beetles smaller than / rice grains." Then the season changed and frost "spiked"

> the twigless air. Soon
> snow filled emptiness
> between the shrubs. I
> fed my elm-logs to the
> fire, sending ghost-
> blossoms to the sky.

Those "ghost blossoms" are an unexpected and wholly Zen-inspired touch, as are the novel ways of seeing clothes hanging on a clothesline in "Words on a Windy Day":

> I watch in wonder
>   As the wind fills
>   Trouserlegs and sweaters,
> Whips them light and dark.
>   In that frayed coat
>   I courted her a year,
>
>   . . . . .
>
>   These mildewed ghosts of love
> That life, for lack of something
>   Simple as a clothespin,
>   Let fall, one by one.

Even more inventive is "Storm," a kind of extended metaphor:

> The green horse of the tree
> bucks in the wind
> as lightning hits beyond.
> We will ride it out together
> Or together fall.

But the poem that best illustrates the Zen method is "Willows," the final selection in *Collected Poems*. Stryk describes the poem as an "embodiment of Zen learning," explaining that it is "based on an old Zen exercise known as 'mind pointing'." Mind pointing involves focusing

> on some everyday scene or object, something you encounter but take for granted. It could be anything . . . there's a stand of willows near the lagoon on the campus of Northern Illinois University, and my self-imposed exercise was to go by the willows, seeing whether in fact I could really look at them without thinking of what happened yesterday, what will happen tomorrow, problems or whatever. And the finished poem is a detailing of that experience.

At one level, "Willows" is a kind of journal of a great experiment that fails, because Stryk never fully succeeds at ridding his mind of distractions. At another level, however, "Willows" is a magnificent accomplishment because it dramatizes the great Zen notion that the search and the thing sought are one and the same. Perhaps the poet does not fully apprehend all twenty-seven of the willows, but he does perceive them in a new way as they become "delicate / tents of greens and browns." Although he once makes it to the seventeenth tree, his trials are marked with various gestures of frustration, wrung hands and clenched teeth. But even his distractions are valuable. Shifting his focus from the nearest tree to the farthest one in the row, he beholds a shower" of leaves. In his passionate attention to the trees, the whole world becomes intense and vivid, and even the distractions are raised to the level of pure comprehension. The poet may not be granted perfect awareness of all twenty-seven trees, but he *does* receive unmediated impressions of reality as if the world around him were suddenly and magically translated into haiku-like imagery:

> the flap of duck, goose, a limping
> footstep on the path behind,
> sun-flash on the pond.

"Willows" concludes with the poet still "practicing" on the trees "over, over again" because in each failure lies the magnificent gift of incidental poetry.

Like Japanese art, the poetry of Lucien Stryk is spare, compressed, and simple—minimalist art at its very best. But Stryk is no Japanese, and his representations of tornadoes, elm trees, willows, and farms revitalize these primary images of midland America. Without them there could be no Midwest; and Stryk deserves the gratitude of his readers for helping to rescue this precious world from oblivion. In "Awakening" Stryk reminds his readers that poetry is the greatest form of awareness; to be fully alive is to participate in the fundamental joy of seeing and, even, of *not* seeing, as in the final moments of every sunset on the prairie:

> and what I love about
> this hour is the way the trees
> are taken, one by one,
> into the great wash of darkness.
> At this hour I am always happy,
> ready to be taken myself
> fully aware.

Rebecca Raglon

SOURCE: "Fact and Fiction: The Development of Ecological Form in Peter Mathiessen's Far Tortuga," in *Critique,* Vol. 35, No. 4, summer, 1994, pp. 245-59.

[*In the following essay, Raglon analyzes and underscores the elements of Zen Buddhism that appear in Peter Matthiessen's ecological novel* Far Tortuga.]

A perception of the interrelatedness of all life underlies the work of any writer with ecological concerns, but no career illustrates this point as clearly as Peter Matthiessen's, and no work as forcefully as his haunting and powerful novel, *Far Tortuga*. However, because this perception of interrelatedness is based upon insights derived from the new science of ecology, a tension is frequently felt between form and meaning in Matthiessen's work. This tension, in part, accounts for the restless shifting between fiction and nonfiction that has occurred throughout his career, as well as for the variety of genres Matthiessen has used in weaving together his most successful narratives. *The Snow Leopard,* for example, has been described as travel literature, spiritual autobiography, philosophy, and nature writing. Matthiessen's *Far Tortuga* has been discussed as a type of pastoral, read as an environmental parable, placed within the tradition of American sea fiction, and viewed as a variation of the Eden story. The sheer variety of approaches suggests the complexity of both books and hints at one of the most intriguing aspects of Matthiessen's work. The problem of form arises because ecological thought, which provides an underpinning of Matthiessen's work, is in itself a critique of older, dualistic ways of constructing the world as a conflict between humanity and nature. Any genre, myth, metaphor, or language that emerges from this milieu is at times bound to provide an uneasy setting for insights based upon wholeness and interrelatedness. The task facing an ecologically sensitive writer, then, is to strive to develop what the poet Gary Snyder has called a "rhetoric of ecological relationships" (*Practice of the Wild*). It is a task Thoreau alluded to when he asked, "where in all the world is the literature which gives expression to Nature?" At best there is tameness and pale imitation; Thoreau was searching for something far more vigorous:

> He would be a poet who could impress the winds and streams into his service, to speak for him; who nailed words to their primitive senses, as farmers drive down stakes in the spring, which the frost has heaved; who derived his words as often as he used them,—transplanted them to his page with earth adhering to their roots; whose words were so true and fresh and natural that they would appear to expand like buds at the approach of spring. . . .

Frequently implicit within ecological thought's critique of dualism is a concomitant dismantling or modification of traditional forms. Pastoralism rather than providing the prototype for an ecological outlook as Leo Marx has argued, might well contain presuppositions that an ecologically minded author must struggle to *overcome* in order to convey a perception of the interrelatedness of life. The pastoral story that characterizes nature as "simple," for example, fails to accommodate ecological revelations that insist upon the complexity of nature. In the same way, pastoral stories that rely on a contrast between sophisticated urban life and the simplicity of nature and that invariably end with the hero's return to "civilization," suggest a mode that ultimately affirms a separation from nature. Annette Kolodny, in a feminist reading of pastoralism, goes even further when she suggests that pastoralism is a metaphor that has contributed to an ecological crisis by creating expectations of abundance and ease that were an entirely inappropriate response to the North American wilderness.

One presupposition of ecological thought, at least in terms of its relationship to literature, is that our language itself is replete with the indications of environmental disaster. Nothing could suggest this more than the word "nature" itself, for deeply rooted in its multifarious uses is an assumption that humans exist apart from "it." The American poet Wendell Berry writes of the implications of such an assumption:

> We have given up the understanding—dropped it out of our language and so out of our thought— that we and our country create one another, depend on one another, are literally part of one another; that our land passes in and out of our bodies just as our bodies pass in and out of our land.

It should not be surprising, given such a lack, that writers struggling to develop an ecological perception turn to other languages, cultures, and religions to discover some way of talking about this missing relationship. One of the suggestive concepts of Zen Buddhism is the existence of a Primary Nature that is often obscured from humanity. D. T. Suzuki writes,

> When we see a mountain, we do not see it in its suchness, but we attach to it all kinds of ideas, sometimes purely intellectual, but frequently charged with emotionality. When these envelop the mountain, it is transformed into something monstrous. This is due to our own indoctrination out of our "scholarly" learning and our vested interests; whether individual, political, social, economic or religious. The picture thus formed is a hideous one. Instead of living in a world presented to the Primary Nature in its nakedness, we live in an artificial, "cultured" one. The pity is that we are not conscious of the fact.

Throughout much of his career Matthiessen has searched for ways to articulate the existence of a Primary Nature, but his ability to do so is intimately linked to his growing involvement with Zen Buddhism. Although *Wildlife in America* (1959) is a landmark volume in American nature writing, Matthiessen discovered, after numerous experiences with traditional societies and with religious thought, that contemporary notions of conservation have a limited value, particularly when compared with the complex links between life and land made in traditional societies. Matthiessen's discovery, however, did not translate into a literary celebration of ritual primitivism (the hunting story, the fishing story, the male bonding-in-the-woods "camping" story). It is not enough to respect nature, or to have an appreciation of nature. It is not enough to partake in rituals that temporarily reunite humans with nature. A perception of interrelatedness must be translated into a way of living or being in the world. Such a perception must come from what the philosopher Thomas Kuhn has called a "paradigm" shift, and what poets and mystics call a transformation of consciousness. Accompanying such a transformation, according to Gary Snyder, is the two-fold obligation to consider what symbolic systems constitute obstacles to ecological awareness, while at the same time attempting to create an awareness of self that includes social and natural environments. The question to ask once such a paradigm shift occurs is how the new perception of the world can be conveyed in terms of literary expression. In other words, what literary form would an ecologically minded author chose to express biocentrism; how would such an author express interrelatedness?

Matthiessen's development as a writer offers insight into these questions. The first period of his career is one of intimations and explorations and begins with Matthiessen's earliest fiction. His first stories, written in the early 1950s and the 1954 novel *Race Rock* deal with humans who are warped and twisted by the uncomfortable knowledge that they do not belong anywhere—familiar enough territory in contemporary American fiction. But this feeling is only a starting point for Matthiessen: he wants not only to describe modern-day dilemmas, but also to find some meaningful response to them. This first period is also one of explorations—a rich and fertile period that includes such diverse works as *Wildlife in America, The Cloud Forest* (1961), *Under the Mountain Wall* (1965), *At Play in the Fields of the Lord* (1965), *Oomingmak* (1967), *The Shorebirds of North America* (1967), and *Sal Si Puedes* (1969).

The second period of Matthiessen's work begins in 1970 and is marked by the author's growing involvement with Zen: rather than a conversion, however, this interest marks an intensification of the concerns and insights that first came to him in his work as a naturalist. In an effort to come to the "one mind" revealed through meditation, Matthiessen begins by imagining himself as a deer or a sapling pine. He writes of his early zazen practice:

> In the midmorning sittings, I become a sapling pine, warmed by the sun, swaying in wind, inhaling wind, water, minerals, exhaling warm, fragrant amber resin. Though roots budge subterranean rock, the trunk expands, sinewy limbs gather in sunlight far above, new needles shining in new sun, new wind, until the great pine is immovable, yet flexible and live, the taproot boring ever deeper into the earth. Then the tree evaporates and there is nothing, and nothing missing, only emptiness and light. (*Nine-Headed Dragon River*)

In addition to the great spiritual intensity of his Zen experiences, his continued interest in the natural world is seen in the publication during this period of *Blue Meridian* (1971), *The Tree Where Man Was Born* (1972), *The Wind Birds* (1973), and *Sand Rivers* (1979). In these years, Matthiessen also experienced his first sesshin "miracle": a sudden, deep insight into the unity of all life. Both *Far Tortuga* (1975) and the better known *Snow Leopard* (1978) were written in this time of intense emotional journeying. Both in their varied ways express the unity of all life and both also take risks in terms of their forms.

Matthiessen once described his nonfiction work as a type of "cabinet work . . . assembled from facts, from research, from observation; it comes from outside, not from within." Although Matthiessen views fiction and nonfiction as two fundamentally different kinds of writing, one could argue that his "cabinet work" is an essential feature of his best fiction. A stubborn respect for "fact" informs the most poetic flights in the lovely "green" novel, *At Play in the Fields of the Lord* (1965), which is closely linked to *The Cloud Forest* (1960), the nonfictional account of a trip to South America. Matthiessen's brilliant sea novel, *Far Tortuga,* germinated from accounts of a trip on a turtling boat written for *The New Yorker.* In both cases the issue, clearly, is why Matthiessen felt the need to go back and reshape his experiences, to express them again through fiction. The answer lies, I think, in what Joseph Campbell has called "creative mythology," that is, in the story teller's ability to make links with the

world through art. Although Thomas Lyon makes it clear that nature writers express a "heresy" in terms of their appreciation of the world, the "appreciator," nevertheless, remains an outsider: an observer of the world. In contrast, mythmaking, which frequently utilizes precise observations of the natural world, has a primary function of reconciling the waking consciousness to the "*mysterium tremendum et fascinans* of this universe as it is" and of rendering an "interpretive total image of the same." Evolution, modified by the insights of ecology, is one of the prevailing myths of our time. As such, it forges links between the human mind and the natural world. The problem is that we have not yet learned to express these insights, and we find ourselves still talking about nature as a separate, uniform "thing." Matthiessen, a writer sensitive to the implications of evolution and ecology, has consistently striven to find ways to express the interrelationships of life. In doing so, he has had to explore fundamental structures in language that have created obstacles to this understanding.

In May 1975, partly on a whim and partly because of a certain unerring accuracy that has brought him constantly into contact with endangered things, Matthiessen found himself walking the still empty beaches of the Grand Cayman island, imagining that he could still sense the presence of the turtles that once made the island their home. After two years Matthiessen was finally able to book passage on one of the remaining turtling boats operating from Grand Cayman. Instead of a fine wind schooner, he found that the boat he had hoped to sail in had disappeared into the jaws of "progress," that the boat's mast had been sawed in half, and that motors had been installed. As he subsequently reported in *The New Yorker,* the disfiguring changes in the boat were emblematic of changes engulfing the entire region:

> The changes in the Wilson, I had discovered, were only a small part of the metamorphoses that was coming fast to Grand Cayman. The first time I had been there, two years before, the tourist had been such an infrequent beast that suntan oil was all but unobtainable. But now there were two supermarkets and a gift shop. . . . There were water skiis and rent-a-cars, and . . . a new night club with its own post office on the premises.

In spite of the technological changes overcoming the area in general, the boat has the air of the decrepit about it, as if it cannot decide whether or not to join the twentieth century. A sense of doom mixed with comedy pervaded the whole enterprise. The boat lacked such primary equipment as

> running lights, horn, fire extinguishers, and life preservers. Captain Cadie had bought himself a radio-telephone to go with his new deckhouse, but it had never worked. I asked him why he hadn't tried it out before he paid for it and he said, "It had ought to work, mahn, or why in hell dey make it?"

In spite of this atmosphere of folly, in spite of the dangers and bad food, Matthiessen found something invigorating in the experience. "On a bright fresh day at sea, the ocean wind against your cheek and the tropical sun on your bare feet can restore childhood's sense of being at the center of time, with no time passing." At one point in the journey, Matthiessen reports that he asked the Wilson's captain why he had not left the boat's spars and sails intact, even if that would have meant running her as a charter for tourists. "He disregarded the tourist trade as something irrelevant to a turtle boat with a long tradition on the banks, and I began to see that he was right." For fishermen, or turtlers, their livelihood is also a complex way of living. Attending to the demands of foreign tourists would begin the long process of alienation from the source of life, from the source of a clarified reality that Matthiessen found aboard the ship and valued so much.

Over the next eight years, Matthiessen worked to reshape his experiences aboard the Wilson into the novel that eventually became *Far Tortuga*. In between the experience on the turtling boat and the publication of the novel, however, Matthiessen became a Zen practitioner, and this, perhaps more than any other influence, would mark the ultimate shape the book would take. In an interview in *Paris Review* Matthiessen stated that he was moved by the stark quality of that Caribbean voyage: "everything worn bare by wind and sea—the reefs, the faded schooner, the turtle men themselves—everything so pared down and so simple that metaphors, stream-of-consciousness, even such ordinary conventions of the novel as he said or he thought, seemed intrusive, even offensive, and a great impediment, besides." Matthiessen seems to suggest here that the prose he had used to convey a nonfiction account of the voyage was in some way limited. What he wanted to do in his book was to examine the experience again, not to "reproduce it," but to find a way to direct the reader to an apprehension of the unblinking heart of reality. To do this, Matthiessen found he had to winnow his prose, to strip *Far Tortuga*, as much as possible, of ordinary conventions, as if in this way he could display to the reader a way to return to the sustaining bedrock of existence.

Through the unusual design of *Far Tortuga*, Matthiessen suggests the existence of a Primary Nature. He used the sea voyage less for its dramatic possibilities than as a chance to reveal a type of life that is in its essence timeless and elemental. Matthiessen suggests that in "Primary Nature" paradise exists. In contrast to this insight, are the wasted possibilities, the sense of change passing through the region, the dreams and fantasies that obscure the reality of a here and now existence. Matthiessen suggests that we fall into a trap of longing that makes it impossible for us fully to live.

The book is designed to draw things out with a clarity that needs no embellishment. Written without indented paragraphs, the novel features single lines as short as "Cock crow" that are isolated, emphasized, and allowed to resonate in the surrounding white space. Throughout the book the time of day is indicated by small circles, empty in full day-light, partially filled to indicate sunrise or sunset, and blackened to indicate night. Sunrise comes to the Cayman graveyard, touches the tombstone of Will Parchment, a crew member aboard the Eden, and lets the reader know at once what the fate of the crew will be. The ship is not described, but mapped; crew members are introduced through the ship's manifest. All these devices introduce the world of fact, stripped of embellishment. In Matthiessen's aesthetics there is no need to draw parallels between the human and nonhuman world, because properly perceived there is no separation between the two. Hence, with two exceptions, the book is bare of similes and metaphors. The basis of Matthiessen's vision is that we are all a part of one inescapable reality, so every aspect of that reality has its own solidness, its own potential to reveal the underlying oneness of existence.

Within this larger reality is set the smaller social world aboard the Eden. Captain Raib Avers, his son, and his crew of seven other men, argue, talk, laugh, and live much as men live anywhere. Generally, however, the close contact aboard the small ship magnifies conflict, though Matthiessen successfully resists the temptation to turn the men into symbols that are larger than life. Rather, he presents life that is elemental, life further intensified by the flickering awareness of death. Raib says to one crew member,

> You hear dat rushin out dere, Byrum? De wind and de sea comin together? Dat de sound of *hell*, boy, dat de sound of *hell*. You way out on de edge, boy, you out on de edge of de world. No mon! Ain't no unions on de turtle banks, I tellin you dat! Ain't no rights out here! Ain't nothin out here but de reefs and de wind and de sea, and de mon who know de bleak ocean de best has got to be coptin, and de men don't listen to de coptin, dey stand a very good chance of losen dere lifes!

Raib's character is both dramatic and complex and is achieved without the need to exaggerate certain monomaniacal or dictatorial tendencies that have become the stock and trade of sea fiction captains from Ahab to Bligh. For instance, Raib's insistence on the need for the captain's absolute control at sea is modified by the dynamics of the crew, by his own sense of humor, and by his being caught inescapably in the net of "modern times."

One of the premises of earlier works concerned with nature is that the hero's retreat to nature was a return to "eternal" values; in *Green Hills of Africa* Ernest Hemingway meditates on the movement of the Gulf stream that has moved since "before man." It is a stream that will flow "as it has flowed, after the Indians, after the Spaniards, after the British, after the American and after all the Cubans and all the systems of governments, the richness, the poverty, the martyrdom, the sacrifice and the venality and the cruelty are all gone." Hemingway goes on to compare civilization to a high-piled scow of garbage, spilling off its load into the blue water.

> The stream with no visible flow takes five loads of this a day when things are going well in La Habana and in ten miles along the coast it is as clear and blue and unimpressed as it was ever before the tug hauled out the scow; and the palm fronds of our victories, the worn light bulbs of our discoveries, and the empty condoms of our great loves float with no significance against one single, lasting thing—the stream.

Nature in this view is not only "eternal"—it is also all absorbing, self-purifying, and self-renewing. In this passive view, nature can "take" whatever humanity chooses to dish out; this is a cherished belief that somehow has managed to survive the onslaught of technology. Although he knows a continent "ages quickly" once Europeans settle it, Hemingway withdraws from the responsibility such an insight demands. Instead he opts for a "new" country, that special place where it is possible to start all over again—in this case, Africa.

In contrast to this more innocent time, it is clearly understood in an age of ecology that there is no escape; there are no more untouched "good countries," and even the wild ocean has not been left untouched. The bad weather that overtakes Raib and his crew is unseasonable, and Raib can't help thinking that "It must be dat atomic trash and shit de Yankees puttin in de sky; man can't even count on de way of de wind no more." The rapaciousness of human technology is in evidence everywhere: huge new shrimp boats are "sucking de last shrimp out of de sea," and Raib says, "Dey killed off de seals just like dey killin' off green turtle, and de crocodiles before dem. De snipes is gone now. Ain't no iguana left up at Northwest. Mahogany, logwood, fustic—all dat gone now! Dey cutten it all away." If there is any evidence of "eternal nature" anymore, it exists only in the heavens, as Raib points out to his son Buddy:

> See, Buddy? Dat de north star. Goes very bright, and den she fades again, every four days. Dat is one thing you can count on. Everything else in dis goddom world chagin so fast dat a mon cannot keep up no more, but de north star is always dere, boy, de cold eye of it, watching de seasons come and go.

Raib belongs to the "back time": he has old-fashioned notions and values that form the basis of his life, but that also hinder him in terms of trying to survive in what another crew member calls "modern time, mon." Raib's attempts to modernize his boat, for example, are disastrous. The Lillas Eden, formerly a wind schooner, has had its mast shortened, engines installed, and a new deck house built that resembles an outhouse. The boat's wheel, remaining in its old position at the stern, is, according to one crew member, "a hell of an arrangement. . . . De mon at de helm cannot even see where de ship *goin*." He has all the necessary navigational skills to guide the vessel but is undone by his own equipment; his watch doesn't keep proper time, and as a result, Raib loses the boat's position, endangering everyone aboard. Not having the money to complete the job of modernization means the crew start their voyage with a bent shift in the engine and a leaking cat boat; later it is learned that Raib would need $3,000 just to make the boat seaworthy. To compensate, Raib falls back on the mystique of the captain, emphasizing to his crew his years of experience, his skill, and knowledge. His failures to provide certain necessities in terms of basic equipment (light, fire equipment, life jackets) are overlooked, and he continually blames his crew for not being good enough to be turtlemen.

Raib is described as having lines of merriment that seam his face, but his eyes also have a "mean squint." This combination of toughness, even meanness, with humor and gentleness is seen throughout in flashes. As he baits hooks with strips of flying fish, for example, "his thick hard lumpy fisherman's hands move gently, and though it is dead, he talks softly to the wild-eyed fish as if to calm it." When he sees four porpoises rolling along the hull of the Eden, he plays with them, tossing a pole at them; the "creatures return to be tagged over and over." When Raib, Speedy, and Vemon go ashore in Nicaragua to report to customs, they get bogged down in the muddy channels of the Coco River, but irritation is overcome, briefly, with laughter. Yet he is hard with his own boy, and the crew's mutters, reported in smaller print throughout the book, hint at a dark past.

One of his duties, Raib feels, is to instruct his crew in the importance of seamanship. In part this is to emphasize his own importance and legitimize his status. But in part, too, he is passing on a tradition, telling his crew that he knows every rock on the banks. "It were Copm Andrew Avers dat taught me, and come to pilotin he were de island's best." Over and over again he tells his crew to keep their eyes and ears open so that they can learn from the ocean.

Throughout his difficulties, Raib's pride sustains him; pride, however, also interferes with his ability to survive. Part of the reason Raib gets bogged down in the Coco River is because he will not listen to Byrum, a crew member who had been on the river since the last time his captain had been there. Raib, characteristically, turns on Byrum, "You sayin I don't know my way on de Miskita Coast? By God, Byrum, I never thought I hear *dat!*" Raib is proud of the turtling tradition of which he is a part, but his idealism and his hubris, expressed in his conviction that he knows all there is to know about the turtling grounds, ultimately interfere with his responsibility as a captain.

Captain Raib is no hero, for as Joseph Meeker points out, an ecological drama has no heroes, only successful survivors:

> Comedy is careless of morality, goodness, truth, beauty, heroism, and all such abstract values men say they live by. Its only concern is to affirm man's

capacity for survival and to celebrate the continuity of life itself, despite all moralities. Comedy is a celebration, a ritual renewal of biological welfare as it persists in spite of any reasons there may be for feeling metaphysical despair.

Tragic heroes suffer and die for some great ideal that is more important than life itself; comic survivors muddle through, according to Meeker.

Yet Raib is clearly a finer man than his half brother, Desmond Eden. Unlike Raib, with his sense of pride and tradition, Desmond is an opportunist, on the surface a successful survivor but also a man who in many ways is already soul dead. Desmond scours the sea in a boat taken from Cuban refugees: to Raib it looks like a whorehouse and the very name given the boat connotes frivolity and lack of respect, "A mon dat would call a vessel *Davy Jones,* funnin with de bleak ocean in dat manner, dat mon can't learn nothin from de sea!"

Desmond fits the sickness of "modern time"; he represents that time's worst, just as Raib represents some of the best of the "back times." Desmond has no respect for anything: not for himself, for his occupation, for other people, for the ocean, or the life in the ocean. His yacht is "decrepit" and littered with refuse. The turtles he has caught are left out on the main deck "unprotected from the sun," and he spends a morning rigging up a loggerhead turtle so he can slit its throat for his own amusement. (Raib, on the other hand, throws a loggerhead overboard, refusing to slit its throat, because as he explains, "Don't like de way it lookin' at me, darlin'. Don't like foolin' with dem log'reds—dey looks too scornful." Raib exists in a world composed of other subjects: Desmond lives in a world composed of things.

When Raib goes to confront Desmond on Bobel Cay, he finds a shabbiness found only in the exploited poverty of "modern times"—a litter of tin and broken glass, the smell of human excrement. "Eternal nature" is the hawksbill turtle, but it is seen pushing aside "torn purslane and trash to dig her nest." On the beach, where Desmond has gone for "rum and pussy," Raib finds a man and a pregnant woman copulating, another man stabbed. In the shallow water on the lee side of the cay "wavelets lift melted labels, floating feces, a pale plastic bottle. In the offal is the bobbing head of a green turtle, its shell and guts are scattered on the sand. Another turtle lies upright on the beach, facing inland. Its flippers are bound, and its great weight, unsupported, slowly smothers it."

In a few tense words Matthiessen catches the devastation and waste of a time that places little value on life. Desmond's entire way of being in the world is profligate and wasteful; Raib's two small actions on the cay underline the differences between the men, while at the same time draw parallels between the misery in all forms of life. When the woman reaches for the bottle her companion clutches, it falls, and its liquid drains out in the sand. Raib rights the bottle. The woman, briefly conscious of the man's action. "raises her hand as if to brush sand

from her eyes but does not complete the gesture. The hand falls back. She lowers both forearms to the sand and rests her cheek upon her hands, her mouth forced into odd disfigurement." Raib's second action is to turn the turtle that is smothering under its own weight on its back; "it blinks, gasping its ancient sea sound and sand grains falling from its lids stick in the fluids from its eyes."

Misery is pervasive, yet even here Matthiessen insists on the links between human life and all other forms of life. Human misery has consequences, and the consequences reverberate in the misery and desecration of the entire world. The supposed "purity" of nature can no longer act as a comfort or antidote for the impurity of human life because the two are inseparably related. All that Raib treasures is assaulted in this scene: his sense of tradition, his pride, his need for order. Further, what has been desecrated is not simply inert, a useless, empty cay. The one measurement of value of "modern time" is economic value, but Matthiessen makes the point that deeper values pervade every aspect of creation because everthing in the world is alive: the world itself is a living being. As Raib stands transfixed, everything around him moves; a bleeding-tooth snail, a ghost crab, a white feather, a purple morning glory. Above all there is the presence of "the sea, breathing." Wounds can be inflicted not only on the human body and human psyche but in the body and spirit of the living world as well.

Raib is aware of the changes affecting his ability to make a livelihood; still he clings fiercely to the foolish human belief that while things are bad everywhere else, on Grand Cayman, at least, people still have certain values. But Raib is existing partially in fantasy, in the "back time," and so cannot accommodate the changes in an area where boatloads of refugees are floating out in the ocean, where once-deserted coastal forests are being cleared and burnt, and where old turtling areas are destroyed by gangs of poverty-stricken Jamaicans. According to Raib,

> Used to be dat in Caymans a mon respect hisself.
> He don his job, took care of his family, all of dat.
> He had his land and his own provision ground; he
> built his own catboat and hung his own nets. Things
> like dat.

Contrasted to this bucolic vision of the "back times" is another crew member's depiction of "modern times" when uncontrolled population growth has created a Malthusian state of shortages. According to Speedy, Raib is able to cling to his idea that somehow there are fundamental differences between humans only because there is plenty of water between "you and de world. But you just wait a while, you gone to see. Modern time, mon—dey ain't no place to hide."

Raib, in fact, seems to know that he is no longer able to function properly in the world, and weariness begins to descend on him:

> Dis mornin sea tryin to tell me something, Speedy.
> It so *old,* mon. Make me wonder what I doin way

out here on dese reefs, all de days of my life.
(sighs) Life has got away from me, some way—I
just goin through de motions.

Raib's weariness and withdrawal from the world as he
finds it are a constant contrast to Speedy's energy and
immersion in the modern time. When all the other turtling
grounds fail him, Raib charts a course for Mistoriosa
Reef, a reef so isolated it is not even noted on the maps.
Raib dreams of building a little shack out on Far Tortuga,
an island in the reef:

> Dat island is a very nice place. A *very* nice place.
> And dere good shelter in de lee, cause it high
> enough so it got trees—grape trees and jennifer
> trees, and den logwood and mongrove: got a little
> water dere if you know how to dig for it. Plenty
> birds. I thinkin one day I might build a little shack
> out dere on Far Tortuga. Dass my dream.

Speedy, however, replies that he has no dream: Speedy is
still part of the world, living with day-to-day contingen-
cies, satisfied with reality. "Got no dream, mon. I got
fifty-five acres, mon, and cows. I go along everyday, do
what I got to do, and den I lays down to my rest." Speedy
exemplifies not only the type of comic survivor Meeker
claims as a prototype for any ecologically sensitive art
but also a type of enlightened Buddhist, somewhat like
Tukten, one of the sherpas Matthiessen admired as a true
bodhisattva in *The Snow Leopard*. Like Tukten, Speedy
is bright, quick, and cheerful, a man interested in doing
his work well, and ready to learn without being servile.
He has an innate courtesy that is found in every one of
his actions; in his duties as cook he goes out of his way
to make "crude doughnuts" for the rest of the crew. "I
hear on de radio about hot doughnuts and coffee makin
people hoppy, Mist' Will, so dat is what you eatin dere,
hot doughnuts." When Raib hectors his son Buddy,
Speedy tries to mediate. "Dat boy seasick again, goddom
it." "Well, dat wind *cuttin,* Copm Raib, it plenty rough.
My first trip, I was so green." When Raib complains that
Buddy lacks nerve and is always staring at him, Speedy
replies, "Maybe he stand dere lookin at you cause he
hopin dat one day you look at *him.*"

Speedy also shows a type of impersonal sympathy for
everyone aboard the Eden, all those caught in the helplessness of "damnable need," the "pit of longing" that is
the common human plight (*Nine-Headed Dragon River*).
All the crew members are suspicious of "Brownie," the
Spanish man who seems to be from nowhere in particular
and who has nothing but a shady past. He is sullen,
touchy, and violent, and the other crew members, with
the exception of Speedy, give him wide berth. When they
return, drunk, from shore leave, Brownie ranting violently about the whore that laughed at him, Speedy comforts Brown, lifting the man's head into his lap.

The reef Raib sets sail for, that last "good place" of the
imagination, is no longer paradise; a group of Jamaican
bird-egg hunters have arrived ahead of the turtlers. The
paradise Raib has been seeking is, in fact, hell. With
this confrontation, it is suddenly clear that the only
paradise in the book has been aboard the aptly named
Eden. For all the quarreling and complaining, for all
the accusations and wounded egos, it is still in the
heart of life, whatever its complexities, that paradise
exists. For all the diversity of the crew, in terms of
race, language, background, and character—Vemon is
a drunk, Brown an outlaw, Buddy a studious boy,
Wodie a type of mystic, and Speedy a black man from
Honduras—they have come together on the boat, amidst
life in the ocean, to form a crew, a whole. They are
unified in their work and in their pursuit; and on a
broader level, they are unified with the sea and the sky
and with all the creatures that touch their lives. One of
the most shocking events is when Raib strands Vemon;
the crew talks about the incident in the dark. "Feel bad
about Vemon. He ain't much, but he our shipmate."
"Never do *dat* in de back time. Maroon a shipmate on
de Sponnish coast!"

Life for the Jamaican "pan heads," in contrast, consists of
nothing more than a degraded sexuality and rum. There is
no sense of community, no sense of paradise, no home
called Eden. The Jamaicans have been stranded for
weeks on the island by Desmond, and are running short
of food and water. Afraid that they will return and com-
mandeer the boat, Raib attempts to bring the vessel out of
Far Tortuga's reef by night. For a moment Raib is exalted, sure he has brought her through the darkness into
clear water; the next moment the ship strikes a submerged rock.

One of the principles of Zen is that to gain satori, or
insight into the nature of reality, one must be able to
abandon fear of death. That is, one must give up clinging
to life. In a discussion of Zen-swordsmanship D. T.
Suzuki writes that

> We carry on all kinds of imagination in regard to
> life and death. And is it really this imagination, or
> strictly speaking, this delusion, and not the actuality
> of things as they are, that creates in us every
> occasion for worries, fears, harrowing anti-
> cipations? When this delusion is wiped away,
> would not life itself look after its own welfare
> as it deems best?

Suzuki also comments on the success that comes to the
swordsman able to put the thought of death from his
mind. According to Suzuki this is the state of "emptiness" or egolessness that Buddhist philosophers call
sunyata.

> When there is the slightest feeling of fear of death or
> of attachment to life, the mind loses its "fluidity."
> The fluidity is nonhindrance. Have the mind devoid
> of all fear, free from all forms of attachment, and
> it is master of itself, it knows no hindrances, no
> inhibitions, no stoppages, no cloggings. It then
> follows its own course like water.

Speedy, alone of all the crew, survives because he is not driven by desperation or "harrowing anticipations." Speedy is able to act, without the hesitation and intellectual and emotional machinations that restrain true endeavor. As a survivor adrift in a catboat with two other crew members, Byrum and Wodie, Speedy takes over the task of doling out the remaining water fairly. Byrum, however, soon argues that the water shouldn't be "wasted" on Wodie who is dying. Speedy and Byrum "gauge each other, red-eyed, dry lips parted"; then Speedy says, "Maybe two more days of no wind and dis heat you find a reason to take my water too. Ain't hard to find a reason when you thirsty." Unlike Byrum, Speedy offers no justification for his actions. His knife, "wet with sea dew," lies next to him in the boat, and Speedy is able to use it like a trained samua when Byrum once again threatens the others in the catboat. Here, too, Speedy seems to exemplify the qualities of a Zen master because in his determination he is able to handle his larger, stronger opponent.

Unifying the novel is the presence of the green turtle, constantly felt, much as is the presence of the sun and stars and wind. The green turtle is the purpose for the voyage. It is a mysterious and beautiful creature that all the men aboard the Eden respect and love. Stories are told about the incredible navigational skills of the turtle and about its amazing natural history. The men are excited when they spot their first turtle of the voyage, "inset in the green sea." There is an affection for this ancient creature: the men admire its mysterious nature, that it is quiet and gentle, clean, and pretty. On board ship, in captivity, the turtles sigh and gasp, in ways that echo the sighs and gasps of the crew, again underlining interrelationships that compose the world.

In the Cayman's early history, the turtles were sought because they could be kept alive on board a ship, and so provide fresh meat for the crews. When the *Eden* sinks, a turtle is placed in each catboat as insurance of survival. Speedy, ultimately the sole human survivor; never reaches the point where he feels he can eat raw turtle meat, and so his final action when he sees land is to set the green turtle free. "Don't cry, girl. Swim. Das very very fine." Speedy celebrates his survival by extending survival to a fellow creature. This is a type of sacrament, a "useless" action in economic terms, but one that briefly suggests a communication between living things that celebrates the survival and homecoming of all.

For Matthiessen, Zen provides a way of looking at the world that heals the pervasive sense of separation between "man" and "nature" within his own cultural heritage. Matthiessen once wrote that if a native American spiritual teacher were available to him, he might have chosen that path of study. What is important for Matthiessen is finding a way to bridge the gap between humans and nature—that terrible gap that turns the rest of the world into a wasteland, a blank place, a thing incapable of speaking to the human heart. His search for a way to close that gap is an underlying motif in all his books, but nowhere more profoundly than in *Far Tortuga*.

FURTHER READING

Anthologies

Kamens, Edward. *The Buddhist Poetry of the Great Kamo Priestess: Daisaiin Senshi and 'Hosshin Wakashñ.'* Ann Arbor: The University of Michigan Center for Japanese Studies, 1990, 170 p.
    Offers Buddhist readings of the poetry of Daisaiin Senshi, a Japanese writer of the late tenth and early eleventh centuries.

Master Sheng-yen. *The Poetry of Enlightenment: Poems by Ancient Ch'an Masters*. Elmhurst, N. Y.: Dharma Drum Publications, 1987, 103 p.
    Translated collection of Chinese Buddhist poems designed "to describe the ineffable experience of Ch'an" (Chinese Zen).

Pollack, David, ed. *Zen Poems of the Five Mountains*. Decatur, GA: Scholars Press, 1985, 166 p.
    Anthology of medieval Japanese Zen poetry.

Stryk, Lucien and Ikemoto Takashi, trans. *Zen: Poems, Prayers, Sermons, Anecdotes, Interviews*. Second Edition. Athens: Ohio University Press, 1981, 160 p.
    Includes translations of Zen Buddhist poems of enlightenment and interviews with the Masters of Yamaguchi.

Tonkinson, Carole, ed. *Big Sky Mind: Buddhism and the Beat Generation*. New York: Riverhead Books, 1995, 387 p.
    Anthology of writings by and about beat generation authors whose works in some way relate to Buddhism.

Ury, Marian. *Poems of the Five Mountains: An Introduction to the Literature of the Zen Monasteries*. Tokyo: Mushinsha Limited, 1977, 137 p.
    Selection of translated poetry—originally written in classical Chinese—by Japanese Zen monks.

Bibliographies

Gardner, James L. "Zen and Asian Literature" and "Zen and Western Literature." In *Zen Buddhism: A Classified Bibliography of Western-Language Publications through 1990*, pp. 241-60. Salt Lake City, Utah: Wings of Fire Press, 1991.
    Bibliographies of Zen influence on a range of writers in Asia and the west.

Reynolds, Frank E. with John Holt and John Strong. "Popular Beliefs and Literature." In *Guide to Buddhist Religion*, pp. 137-51. Boston: G. K. Hall, 1981.

Annotated bibliography of Buddhism and the literature associated with it in the Far East.

Yoo, Yushin. *Books on Buddhism: An Annotated Subject Guide*. Metuchen, N. J.: The Scarecrow Press, Inc., 1978, 251 p.
    Compilation of subjects related to Buddhism, including sections on Buddhist fiction, history, philosophy, and poetry.

Secondary Sources

Andu, Shuei. *Zen and American Transcendentalism—An Investigation of One's Self*. Tokyo: The Hokuseido Press, 1970, 218 p.
    Comparative study of Zen and the nineteenth-century Transcendentalism movement as realized in its main proponents, Ralph Waldo Emerson, Henry David Thoreau, and Walt Whitman.

Bien, Peter. "*Buddha*: Kazantzakis' Most Ambitious and Most Neglected Play." *Comparative Drama* 11, No. 3 (Fall 1977): 252-72.
    Analyzes Nikos Kazantzakis's comprehensive and tragic play, *Buddha*.

Bishop, Peter. "The Geography of Hope and Despair: Peter Matthiessen's *The Snow Leopard*." *Critique: Studies in Modern Fiction* XXVI, No. 4 (Summer 1985): 203-16.
    Notes Buddhist tendencies—including several mini-essays on the subject—in Matthiessen's unconventional travel book, *The Snow Leopard*.

Dauenhauer, Richard. "Some Notes on Zen Buddhist Tendencies in Modern Finnish Poetry." In *Snow in May: An Anthology of Finnish Writing 1945-1972*, edited by Richard Dauenhauer and Philip Binham, pp. 60-66. Cranbury, N. J.: Associated University Presses, Inc., 1978.
    Observes the existence of Zen qualities—alongside "the 'objectivist' tendency . . . of the dichotomizing intellect of Western tradition"—in the poetry of Finland.

Hare, Thomas Blenman. "Reading Kamo no Chumei." *Harvard Journal of Asian Studies* 49, No. 1 (1989): 173-228.
    Discusses the works of the twelfth and thirteenth century Japanese writer Kamo no Chumei, especially his *Hosshinshn*, a collection of 102 tales.

Hart, John E. "Future Hero in Paradise: Kerouac's *The Dharma Bums*." *Critique: Studies in Modern Fiction* XIV, No. 3 (1973): 52-62.
    Decribes the classical structure of Jack Kerouac's confessional novel of spiritual awakening, *The Dharma Bums*.

LaFleur, William R. *The Karma of Words: Buddhism and the Literary Arts in Medieval Japan*. Berkeley: University of California Press, 1983, 204 p.
    Contains eight essays on medieval Japanese Buddhism, including studies of such topics as symbolism, cosmology, and satire.

Mather, Richard. "The Landscape Buddhism of the Fifth-Century Poet Hsieh Ling-yòn." *Journal of Asian Studies* XVIII, No. 1 (November 1958): 67-80.
    Analyzes the nature poetry of a lesser-known Chinese Buddhist poet.

Matthiessen, Peter. *Nine-Headed Dragon River: Zen Journals 1969-1985*. Boston: Shambhala Publications, 1986, 288 p.
    Contains personal thoughts on Zen by the well-known western novelist and travel writer.

Murphy, Patrick D. "Mythic and Fantastic: Gary Snyder's 'Mountains and Rivers without End.'" *Extrapolation* 26, No. 4 (Winter 1985): 290-99.
    Mentions Snyder's emphasis on Buddhist *satori* (enlightenment) in his poetry inspired by myth and fantasy.

Poulakidas, Andreas K. "Kazantzakis' Spiritual Exercises and Buddhism." *Comparative Literature* 27 (Summer 1975): 208-17.
    Studies affinities between the theology of Nikos Kazantzakis in his *The Saviors of God: Spiritual Exercises* and the precepts of Buddhism.

Rodrigues, Eusebio L. "Out of Season for Nirvana: Henry Adams and Buddhism." In *Indian Essays in American Literature*, edited by Sujit Mukherjee and D. V. K. Raghavacharyulu, pp. 179-94. Bombay: Popular Prakashan, 1968.
    Recounts Henry Adams's interest in Buddhism, particularly as demonstrated by his 1891 poem "Buddhism and Brahma."

Sanford, James H., William R. LaFleur, and Masatoshi Nagatomi, eds. *Flowing Traces: Buddhism in the Literary and Visual Arts of Japan*. Princeton, N. J.: Princeton University Press, 1992, 275 p.
    Includes several essays on Japanese Buddhist aesthetics.

Sri, P. S. *T. S. Eliot, Vedanta and Buddhism*. Vancouver: University of British Columbia Press, 1985, 154 p.
    Traces the "influence of the Indian philosophical systems of Vedanta and Buddhism on the poetry and drama of T. S. Eliot."

Stryk, Lucien. *Encounter with Zen: Writings on Poetry and Zen*. Athens: Ohio University Press, 1981, 259 p.
    Comprises essays and anecdotes by the Zen-influenced American poet.

Williams, Richard A. "Buddhism and the Structure of *The Blind Owl*." In *Hedayat's 'The Blind Owl' Forty Years After*, edited by Michael C. Hillmann, pp. 99-107. Austin, Tex.: Center for Middle Eastern Studies, 1978.
    Maintains that Buddhism is "chief among the major influences said to constitute the framework and content of *The Blind Owl*" by Iranian writer Sadeq Hedayat.

Modernism

INTRODUCTION

Modernism was the most influential literary movement in England and America during the first half of the twentieth century. It encompassed such works as *The Waste Land* (1922), by T. S. Eliot, *Ulysses* (1922), by James Joyce, and *The Great Gatsby* (1925), by F. Scott Fitzgerald. Representing an unequivocal rejection of Victorian aesthetic standards, moral precepts, and literary techniques, Modernism was initiated during the opening decade of the century, a time of extensive experimentation in the arts. Writers of the movement embraced the psychological theories of Sigmund Freud and Carl Jung and the anthropological relativism espoused by Sir James Frazer, and in their works the Modernists emphasized the psychological state of a character through the use of such devices as the interior monologue, or stream-of-consciousness narrative.

In English literature, manifestations of the modernist aesthetic in fiction range from the sexual explicitness of D. H. Lawrence to the formal experimentation of Virginia Woolf and the myth-based narrative of James Joyce. The disorienting effects of the era of modern warfare that began with the First World War gave rise to such American expressions of modernist concerns as the novels of John Dos Passos, whose *Manhattan Transfer* (1925) utilized montage-like effects to depict the chaos of modern urban life, and Ernest Hemingway, whose *The Sun Also Rises* (1926) portrayed the aimlessness of the "lost generation" of American expatriates in Europe during the postwar era. Similarly, *The Great Gatsby* is seen to epitomize the demoralization of American society and the end of innocence in American thought.

While sharing the novelists' preoccupation with themes of alienation and ambivalence, Modernist poetry is chiefly known for its dependence on concrete imagery and its rejection of traditional prosody. Considered a transitional figure in the development of modern poetry, W. B. Yeats rejected the rhetorical poetry that had gained prominence at the height of the Victorian era, favoring a personal aesthetic, natural rhythms, and spare style. American expatriate Ezra Pound, who with Richard Aldington and Hilda Dolittle founded the Imagist movement in poetry in 1910, favored concise language and free rhythms, and became a champion of avant-garde experimentalists of the era. The thematic preoccupations and technical innovations of Modernist poetry are seen to culminate in *The Waste Land,* Eliot's complex, erudite expression of modern malaise and disillusionment.

REPRESENTATIVE WORKS

Anderson, Sherwood
  Winesburg, Ohio (short stories) 1919
Crane, Hart
  The Bridge (poetry) 1930
Dos Passos, John
  Manhattan Transfer (novel) 1925
  U.S.A. (novels) 1930-36
Eliot, T. S.
  "The Love Song of J. Alfred Prufrock" (poetry) 1917
  "Tradition and the Individual Talent" (prose) 1919
  The Waste Land (poetry) 1922
  Murder in the Cathedral (drama) 1935
  Four Quartets (poetry) 1943
Faulkner, William
  The Sound and the Fury (novel) 1929
Fitzgerald, F. Scott
  The Great Gatsby (novel) 1925
Ford, Ford Madox
  The Good Soldier (novel) 1915
Hemingway, Ernest
  The Sun Also Rises (novel) 1926
Isherwood, Christopher
  The Berlin Stories (short stories) 1935-49
Joyce, James
  A Portrait of the Artist as a Young Man (novel) 1916
  Ulysses (novel) 1922
  Finnegans Wake (novel) 1939
Lawrence, D. H.
  Sons and Lovers (novel) 1913
  The Rainbow (novel) 1915
  Women in Love (novel) 1920
  Lady Chatterley's Lover (novel) 1928
Pound, Ezra
  The Cantos (poetry) 1925
Richardson, Dorothy
  Pilgrimage (novel) 1915-38
Stein, Gertrude
  The Autobiography of Alice B. Toklas (memoir) 1933
Stevens, Wallace
  "Sunday Morning" (poetry) 1923
Woolf, Virginia
  Mrs. Dalloway (novel) 1925
  To the Lighthouse (novel) 1927
  The Waves (novel) 1931
Yeats, William Butler
  "Easter 1916" (poetry) 1916
  "The Second Coming" (poetry) 1920
  "Sailing to Byzantium" (poetry) 1928
  Purgatory (drama) 1938

DEFINITIONS

Anna Balakian

SOURCE: "Problems of Modernism," in *The Snowflake on the Belfry: Dogma and Disquietude in the Critical Arena,* Indiana University Press, 1994, pp. 24-43.

[In the following essay, Balakian considers the variety of meanings and manifestations of Modernism.]

Each generation of writers had the habit of reacting against the past by declaring itself "modern." The quarrel of the Ancients and the Moderns used to be a cyclical phenomenon. "New" is in itself empty of meaning, a connective word between what was and what is to come. In early uses the word had a pejorative meaning, implying that what was new and modern could not be as good as what had the prestige of approval over a period of time.

Baudelaire as both poet and critic was one of the first to splice the meaning of "modern" in a modest article relating to his viewing of the art of his time. In his piece called "La Modernité" he first gives the image of a little man running around searching for the modern and expresses the normally accepted derogatory meaning: "the transitory, the fugitive, the contingent," but then adds "that which is capable of drawing the eternal from the transitory."

Since the middle of the nineteenth century critics as well as artists in the broader sense of the word have compounded ambiguities on "modern" by using it in both senses. Succeeding generations have been calling themselves modern and allowing the word to lose gradually its defensive tone and instead assume an attitude of contestation and even arrogance. It has become in many cases a cry of rebellion, and sometimes what the late Renato Poggioli called agonism, no longer apologetic but rather challenging. Others have claimed the label "modern" in the Baudelairian sense that while reflecting the passing climate of the time, what is modern has caught "the eternal and the immutable." Critic-readers have learned to distinguish between these two definitions by calling the protesters avant-garde and have retained for the latter the label "modern" and even "high modern" cast in solid gold.

In both cases there has emerged an added aspect of the confusion. There has developed a tradition of the anti-traditional, and the label of "modern" has been retained for works of the past. Let me explain. With the passage of time each era claiming the advantage of a little distance used to delimit what had passed with a more precise label and claim for its own rebellion or renewal in the arts its own modernity. Ours is the first era on record in which succeeding waves of moderns carry on their backs the memorabilia of their ancestors and sustain the myth that modernism, proclaimed and acknowledged at a moment in time for a group of works, forever retains that label in reference to those works, that it survives in a cumulative form, generation after generation, and that avant-gardes as well as golden-seal moderns can follow each other without a posteriori appraisal, which might result in a more permanent label than the temporal one of "modern."

Seen from the Anglo-American perspective, Joyce, Proust, Ezra Pound, D. H. Lawrence, Virginia Woolf, all so different from each other, remain under the label of "modern" on the basis of their capability of retrieval of the eternal from the transitory, and writers as different from each other as Henry Miller, Gertrude Stein, André Breton remain "modern" from the avant-garde angle of protest and rebellion. The French, more pedagogical in their classifications, have adhered to Baudelaire's definition in one sense but, unable to define their own modernism, have virtually abandoned the label itself and created newer "ism" labels. The Spanish still cling to "modernismo" with its special reference to Rubén Darío and his particular brand of Symbolism. They complicate the chronological problem by following up with "postmodernismo," which is not of the vintage of the Anglo-American postmodernism. The Germans associate modern with Expressionism and Dada, the Russians hang on to Futurism as the ultimate modern before the curtain came down on any further movement in the arts. The common agreement among all of them is to call a certain moment in time modern and surrender the word to it for eternity. In calling the past modern the commentators would let their elders retain the label and in amazing timidity would relegate to their own era the rank of rear-garde, paradoxically labeling the contemporary scene "postmodern." Then the sometime literary critic, sometime philosopher Jean-François Lyotard comes along to usher us into the post-postmodern in his book entitled *The Postmodern Condition.* Has there ever been such ancestor worship recorded on the part of writers and artists themselves or of critics and literary historians? In terms of literary criticism the ambiguity simply tells us that out of the plethora of books on the market on "modernism" or "the avant-garde" there is very little chance that they are discussing the same artists or writers or the same period in literary history.

Jean Weisgerber, in structuring his two volumes on modernism in the twentieth century for the monumental project of the *Comparative History of Literature in European Languages,* tried to eliminate the problem by using the collective title *Les Avant-gardes littéraires.* But thereby he raised a new problem; in borrowing a term metaphorically from military terminology one expects the garde itself after the avant-garde. For more than two decades in the course of various communications I have been asking, "Where is the garde of the avant-garde?" I have heard no answers. Instead we observe in studies of theories of the avant-garde such terms as "old avant-garde," "the return of the avant-garde," "post-avant-garde" (although I can't quite see how you can be out front and at the tail end simultaneously), "academy of the first avant-garde," "other avant-garde," "the twilight of the avant-garde," and most recently "the neo-avant-garde." The implications of these two labels, the meaningful and meaningless one of "modern" and the uncomfortable one of "avant-garde," suggest the inability of the current moderns to provide self-determination or in retrospect attribute to past "moderns" more precise and discrete qualifications. It is no solution to suggest, as Ihab Hassan has in relation to Surrealism, that "these movements have all but vanished now, Modernism has proved more stable." Existentialism and Minimalism, the two most recent efforts at group classification, have already outlived their recentness. The end of the century that has had in its existence so many ruptures with the past has not yet had the vision and the courage to proclaim the past moderns as *pre-something* that would define changes in literature and art in our era reflecting our society and at the same time preserving those of its qualities that may have resilience and permanence.

The reason that one sometimes denigrates a phenomenon or task is the realization that one cannot cope with it. That is perhaps why literary history is a bad term these days and the practice of analysis has priority over attempts at synthesis. We have dwelt on the most comfortable assumption that ruptures in the realm of arts can be paralleled with political revolutions, but in doing so we may be overlooking the fundamental cohesions that existed beneath the many "isms" of the first half of our century, alternately called modern and avant-garde.

My perspective tells me that there is something else that is understressed: throughout the century all literature and art that could be termed modern in its time and that laid the foundations of what exists today as "the arts" and qualifies as our modernity is related to radical concepts, not politically radical but scientifically so, that have altered our philosophy of existence and thereby reshaped our notions of aesthetics, mimesis, representation, and creativity. Such are the drastic changes in concepts of reality, time, nature, causality and chaos, indeterminacy, and above all, in terms of all the arts, the notion of communication and reception.

As the spectrum of reality enlarges, replacing the old opposition between real and supernal, a progressive distinction is perceived between mimesis and more sophisticated representations of the relative notion of reality. And we have gradually understood that the unconscious is not simply the opposite of the conscious but part of a continuum within the totality of human experience. The old and sage dichotomies between the real and the unreal, the conscious and the unconscious, simply no longer hold, and the dialectics involving them have been run into the ground. The famous phrase of the early decades of the century, "the juxtaposition of distant realities," so often cited as the basis of daring associations created in poetry and paintings by the still so-called moderns and a governing principle of so many works of art and poetry, has lost much of the meaning it had at its inception because we know now that distance exists only in the eye of

the beholder, and that if the creative artist has brought two entities together, it is because on some level of sensorial lucidity a connection was made.

In the same way, disordinate perceptions—such as what Rimbaud called the reasoned disorder of the senses—and their representation reflect disorder only if the natural world is perceived as a network of determinable and tested physical laws producing predictable results. But we have discovered that every law of physics does not have a Newtonian regularity or if it does it is not yet within our capacity to grasp, and we have also learned that there are phenomena which cripple at least temporarily our perception of a logical, precise universe. And in accepting these facts we, as a society, have had to develop the ability to express with mathematical precision the indeterminacies of the material world. Because this ambiguity or presumed randomness is part of our reality, it can be said that the writers or painters who once were considered avant-grade because they performed in an unrealistic or irrational way are from a more educated view no longer avant-grade because they are still holding the mirror up to nature when they represent this indeterminacy: it is not that the mirror is distorted but that nature is discovered to have parameters beyond those previously known and areas of the unknown but not unknowable realities. In other words, the perceived disorder is part of the system of laws whose supposed randomness may be only an appearance manifested in our partial knowledge of the totality.

Early in the twentieth century, Guillaume Apollinaire, whose voice was more European than French, said in his essay *Les Peinters cubistes:* "Great poets and great artists have the social function to renew unceasingly the appearance that nature assumes in the eyes of humans." Obviously even then he did not consider nature a constant but an ever changeable factor.

From hard ground to soft terrain, the writer moves with the scientists, stunned by his own ignorance, which he characterizes as indeterminacy, replacing previous attitudes of positivism and determinism. In his isolation and sense of loss of control, he drifts into a nonanthropocentric universe. And whereas most observers of the strong element of alienation in the literature of our century may continue to attribute it to psychological disturbances and social maladjustments, the alienation may more correctly be explained by cosmic causes.

The sense of dispersion emphasized by neophilosophers such as Derrida and Foucault is not new to modernism. All self-named moderns have had it. An early avant-gardist, Hugo Ball, often too exclusively associated with Dada but closer in reality to Rimbaud, described the condition of the modern man of his time in an article on Kandinsky in 1917 during a devastating war. Curiously, his apocalyptic fresco is not politically inspired but reflects a metaphysical anxiety: "The world showed itself to be a blind juxtaposition and opposing of uncontrolled forces. Man lost his divine countenance, became matter, chance, an aggregate. He became a particle of nature . . . no more interesting than a stone: he vanished into nature . . . a world of abstract demons swallowed the individual . . . psychology became chatter."

If, in responding to the effect of this condition on the arts, Ortega y Gasset coined the phrase "dehumanization of the arts," "dehumanization" means something quite different today from what it meant in the early part of the century. We can each select a cast of characters to reflect this dehumanization from the annals of literary and art history of the seventy-five years since Hugo Ball's statement and Ortega y Gasset's definition: from Marcel Duchamp's mockery of art in his ready-mades to the latest involutions of abstract art, from the boldness of collage to the whimperings detected in the techniques of fragmentation in all the arts, from the suddenly meaning-stripped world of Sartre's then modern, now classic character Roquentin in *La Nausée* to the nameless soldier in Alain Robbe-Grillet's *In the Labyrinth,* from destruction of time-perspective in John Hawkes's novels to the randomness of images in William Burroughs's writings. All were "modern" in a moment in time, and all can be said to hold the mirror up to nature as nature was perceived at that moment in time. In that sense, in each case the classical dictum of a Boileau or a Pope was applicable to his aesthetics and in that sense his forms of representation are from our vantage point mimetic. If his expression of nature is being called antirealistic by some contemporary critics it is so only in terms of previous definitions of reality and nature. The minute one considers our changed perception of reality, such writings and art expressions fit the changed definitions of reality. The disparity between the perception of the critics and the artists is due to the fact that critics are clinging to the older notions of reality and nature, and they are not as agile in grasping the ontological changes. They are bridging the gap between their superannuated notion and the artist's more updated one with the convenient use of the label "modern."

One of the most important transitions—oh so gradual but so irreversible once it is made—in the changing characterization of "modern" is the manner in which the "modern" artists are reacting to the passing of a centrality of purpose and of a supernal presence. Instead of mourning they are accepting the plurality of the universe, of which their predecessors had been warned three centuries earlier but had not seriously implemented, that changes their art forms. There was to be a giant difference between the Nietzschean proclamation that God was dead and the proposition that God never existed. As the poet-artist Jean (or Hans) Arp observed, "Dada was the revolt of the nonbelievers against the disbelievers." The concept was there, but not many practitioners in the arts were implementing that view. It had not yet been ingrained. The revolution in the arts that I would call a postapocalyptic posture is a more radical one than reactions to the kind of sociopolitical events that are generally attributed to avant-garde manifestations and their reflections on the arts. I would suggest that modernism today, responding primarily to passing political winds and ideologies, is

modern only in terms of the first part of Baudelaire's definition, "transitory, fugitive, contingent," or in my own words I would call them contemporary works dependent on circumstantial events, reserving the label "modern" for those which anchor their vision on phenomena relating to decentralization and decontrol in what is perceived to be an indifferent universe.

Among those who share these deeper disquietudes there are some who reject the continuity more generally perceived between themselves and earlier moderns; instead they sense grave schisms separating them from their predecessors. Nathalie Sarraute has expressed this distance with some irony: "The works of Joyce and Proust already loom in the distance like witnesses of a closed era. It will not be long before we shall be taking guided tours of these historic monuments in the company of schoolchildren in silent respect and in somewhat mournful admiration." By habit and respect, Joyce, Yeats, Thomas Mann, Proust, and others of their generation may still be called modern, particularly from the Anglo-American perspective because neither England nor the United States had an early-century onslaught of "isms." But the fact is that in terms of their works, the signifier "modern," still applied to them, has subsequently acquired another set of signifieds. These great writers of the recent past are indeed part of what Mallarmé called an interregnum; they are waiting for literary historians to give them a more permanent classification than the temporary and provisional "modern" can sustain, and if such a designation does not come forth they will simply join the ranks of the classics without any special label of their own.

Even if we isolate the writers and artists who gave form as well as expression to their sense of the decentralization and instability of the dimensions of reality and apply to them the label of "modern" in our time, we will find great disparities in the ways they reject or represent their adjusted vision of human and physical nature according to Freud and according to Einstein (just to mention two of the many shakers of our reality).

From this angle it is now possible to view as premodern some of those who are still being called modern in literary history and in books on modernism. Such are the makers of Symbolism and Dada and other refugees into language. Of the Symbolists, an early twentieth-century critic, Raoul Hausman, denigrated their resistance to a drastically changing world; he called their act a "naive nostalgia to see the world through human will as if it was imagined by man." The symbolist nihilism, and in some countries it was called aestheticism, was quiet and introverted. In man's quicksand entrapment, the literary icon was able to create an artificial world to serve as the vitalizing power of the writer's slipping individuality. The second mode of the premodern was a direct attack on the growing notion of a nonanthropocentric world. It was a much more hostile and sometimes teasing reaction in verbal terms. It was flamboyantly represented as we know by Dada: "Dada wants nothing, it is a sure thing that they will achieve nothing, nothing, signed by Francis

Picabia who knows nothing, nothing." This was a modernism of rupture, asserting that the assumption of a meaning-free cosmos reduces the perceiver to an equally meaning-free status. Simultaneous with a rejection of language expressed in such structures as phonetic poems was the development of a language of rejection. This rejection was paralleled in the plastic arts with a challenge of the objects to which aesthetic qualities had been attributed.

If the rejection of language developed a language of rejection, it is also true that in the reality of language others sought their sole comfort and strength, a replacement of the divine Logos by a new confidence in language which would equate naming with the act of creation. Stephen Hawking, an eminent popularizer of science, suggests in *A Brief History of Time* that neophytes viewing the changes catalyzed by recent scientific activities take the advice of the philosopher-mathematician Wittgenstein and in their perplexities seek refuge in language. Earlier poets had done that in a premodern era. Vicente Huidobro, Pierre Reverdy, James Joyce, the early surrealists had perceived language as an armor and a staff in the resistance to chaos. To quote Hugo Ball again, "You may laugh, language will one day reward us for our zeal, even if it does not achieve any directly visible results. We have loaded the word with strengths and energies that helped us to rediscover the evangelical concept of the word (logos) as a magical complex image." And a number of years later, Octavio Paz: "Against silence and noise I invent the Word, freedom that invents itself and invents me every day." To this day language has had a main hold both on poets and in major areas of philosophy.

But I see three other modes directly confronting the decentralized universe, modes in which language is not an end in itself but a means of making responses to the cosmos. They are the modernisms dealing with identification, representation, and revision, all responding to the expanded definition of nature.

Identification (or imitation) with the decontrolled universe is expressed by simulation of it, signaling direct involvement with it. This form of mimesis is demonstrated in the random spirit of collage, in happenings theatrically staged, connective structures suggesting sequence replaced by gaps suggestive of dark holes in thought, action, or human perception of time, in the fragmentation of language or object in text or canvas or celluloid to suggest correspondences between the dislocated narrator and his incohesive surroundings, wherein anger and indifference are personalized not in pathos but through irony and complacency, as if the joke were not on man but on the universe. If life is a travesty, let art be a game! In adopting an amorphous structure and discarding even the elementary codes of art, it is as if the writer or artist were confirming that nothing short of the negation of art can be the symbol of a terminal era. It is this involvement of the perceiver with the perceived chaos,

using irony as the only weapon against total dissolution and silence, that has become the literary fortune of Dada among those modernists of today, self-identified as postmodern.

If indeed there are many evidences of authors and painters who identify with flotsam and chaos through their subjective and lately minimalist response, there is also in evidence the *representation* of human dispersion in the form of personas who are *not identified* with the narrator but are his cast of characters in a dramatic narrative, creating a distance that protects the narrator from pathos and self-entrapment. I view as such the works of Samuel Beckett, Marguerite Duras, John Hawkes, Günter Grass, Alain Robbe-Grillet, and many so-called neorealists or antirealists in British, Italian, and South American literature. When Molloy, and not Beckett, says "I listen and the voice is of a world collapsing endlessly, a frozen world under a faint and untroubled sky," we, the readers, are joining the author in the act of observing his characters struggling with a redefined notion of reality, and in sharing the detachment of the author we are immune to the element of the tragic. (The voice is not necessarily that of the author; why do critics assume that every somber utterance must necessarily represent the author's attitude?)

It is significant that some of the most prominent writers who have taken the decontrolled, decentralized universe in their stride use the myth of the labyrinth.

Molloy searches for the lost center in the metaphor of the return to the Mother. Robbe-Grillet's nameless, faceless character searches out his memory-stripped consciousness in a void. In neither case is there an Ariadne in sight. These new Theseuses are engaged in what Robbe-Grillet calls "an interminable walk through the night," going nowhere, dying everywhere. A situation of impasse is very structurally staged, the decor is selected, landmarks on the journey are consciously chosen; the central character pirouetting has no recourse to human support, or reliance on a benevolent nature or outside force. There is no possibility of battle or an act of courage at the end; because no single danger can be identified, there is no opportunity for risk and no need to manifest resistance.

Robbe-Grillet's unidentified protagonist copes with the ambiguities not only of space but also of time. We have the excellent example here of architectonic form without a content of supplied meanings. There is the structure of allegory, explicit in the title and implemented in the geometric engineering of the composite events, but the author warns us that there is no allegory of values implied; if no interpretation is invited, then all meaning is exterior and polysemous. If human memory is emblematically present in a box that the protagonist carries around in an eternally present moment, there are no questions as to where or why. The loss of identity is spelled out in a series of maneuvers, compounding each other, and yet the character never says "I am lost." This is not an imitation of the randomness perceived in nature or a thrusting of the author into the whirlpool of nothingness but *a staging of it*.

Similarly, in Claude Simon's *The Grass* the author tackles the age-old theme of the devastations caused by the passage of time; the metaphor of the grass is used as the emblem for the imperceptibility of the passage of time, as a measure of growth whether on a physical or a psychological basis. To demonstrate the difference between Proust's handling of time and the newer manipulations of the time dimension, let us presume that Proust views the past as a contained package of memories that he can retrieve according to the power of the faculty of remembering: voluntary memory, involuntary flashback, association memory, etc. The newer novelists represent not so much hindsight as the degree of clarity of their troubled eyes, which are not at all sure that anything remains; they believe only in the centrality of the moment. In describing the precarious quality of the moment, man's meager and sole possession, Octavio Paz sees it as a form of instantaneous eternity in his meditative essay "The Dialectics of Solitude," included in *The Labyrinth of Solitude*.

Previous novelists, modern in their time, have presented alienated heroes. Famous among them are Kafka's protagonists, Dostoevsky's underground man, and Sartre's nauseated Roquentin. But it is important to note that in the case of Kafka and Dostoevsky the social rather than the ontological factor underlies the alienation; in the case of Sartre's hero, there is strong author identification rather than objective representation of character, and at the end there is a therapeutic solution to the malaise with autobiographical overtones.

Characters not judged, time deprived of continuity, space used circularly, objects distanced from their functional associations, characters unidentifiable with their creators, acceptance of inconsistencies in personality attributed to the normal interplay of degrees of consciousness, use of verbal and phenomenal chance as acceptable factors of life as of art: these features prevalent in recent modernist writings separate them from earlier concepts of the modern and necessitate newer classification for *past* moderns.

I have referred to identification and representation. The other mode, that of modernism, of revision, is the mode of those who, instead of representing a changed perception of the universe, take artistic control of it. André Breton's most important contribution of the groundwork of the literature of modernism as it is shaping up today was his earlier adjustment to the new factors in a way to make literature and art and their need for determined absolute values viable in a relativist world. He called upon a moral rather than an aesthetic motivation to free the various forms of art from engulfment in the unreliable. The so-called moral value of such willed revision would make both writer and painter, as well as reader and beholder, better able to cope with daily life, as he thought. Such an objective contains a philosophy directed to a concrete and pragmatic achievement rather than to abstract levels of dialogue.

Viewing surrealism in the context of realism—a correction Breton made in his definition as he proceeded from the First Manifesto to *Surrealism and Painting*—he explained that there can exist a process of transformation of the real into the artifact. The primary function he demanded of himself and of his fellow surrealists was to recuperate the random and the senseless, the automatic and the fortuitous, and to submit them to the control of the artist. The artistic universe need not be decontrolled to match a decontrolled universe. Beauty, for instance, can survive the demolished canon of an art representative of an orderly world only if it is made to correspond to an unpredictable universe: it has to be convulsive in order to suggest that convulsive nature the poet or artist accepts; but here we have a process neither of imitation nor of representation; instead the surrealists resort to subterfuges of controls to recreate the turbulence on their own terms: not through breaks in grammar or ruptures of syntax but through self-referential associations opening up limitless meanings and interpretations, not the destruction of familiar objects but their dislocation or recycling. It is not an attempt to represent the indeterminacy of nature but a creation of indeterminacies in those very aspects of nature that are presumed to have remained constants. But expecting neither sympathy nor meaning in nature, the poet or painter began to project his own countenance onto the world around him.

The poets and painters acted according to consorted theories that brought about great understanding of each other's work. But the painters' manifestations, as it turned out, can be more graphically perceived: the defiances of the laws of gravity painstakingly manifested in the paintings of René Magritte; the dislocations of familiar objects, their change of function in Dali and his imitators; the annihilation of the barriers between the kingdoms of the animal, vegetable, and mineral in the spectacular amalgams of Max Ernst; the efforts to create new objects and new horizons in the case of Yves Tanguy; the surrealist signets such as the Minotaur and the Mandragora that suggest a correction of nature's separation of man and animal. All these manifestations can be summarized as the poet-painter's effort to engender purpose where we can outwardly perceive none. The ultimate question proposed to modernisms of the future is whether human desire can give direction to objective chance. In their self-referential structures the best of surrealists appeared to think so.

The prophetic Apollinaire had foreseen two kinds of artists in modern time. One instinctively and intuitively lets the representation of modern humanity seep through him into the work of art; in that respect the postmoderns are justified in claiming that there is a touch of everyman in the so-called work of art and that it is therefore a collective possession. The other category, in which Apollinaire named Picasso as the original force, recreates a universal model, an aggregate of stylized projection to what might be called a cosmic scale of naturalism. Picasso has been much more recognized of course than his counterpart in literature, Breton. But even in Picasso's case, I wonder whether that admiration has been sufficiently focused on that moment of epiphany when he slipped out of his blue period into the stream of light coming from the depths and the edges of night.

A fundamental argument emerges among moderns concerning the destiny of the metaphor. Robbe-Grillet declared some twenty-five years ago that in view of the absence of human meaning in the universe, the practitioners of the arts should eliminate analogy in their works and thereby suppress the metaphor. But the neosurrealists, particularly the poets of Hispano-America, have increasingly sharpened the image as the sole device to guard what Breton had recognized as the creative spirit in its efforts to overcome what would otherwise be a solipsistic existence "when the primordial connections have been broken." The aim would then be to readjust and conciliate the apparatus of the poetic analogy to the new materialistic data. To quote Breton again: "For me the only *evidence* in the world is controlled by the spontaneous relationship, extra-lucid, and insolent, which becomes established under certain conditions, between such and such things which common sense would avoid confronting. . . . I am hopelessly in love with all that adventurously breaks the thread of discursive thought, takes off suddenly into a stream of light, illuminating a life of extremely fertile relationships." In fact Breton and those who have followed him into today's modernism are compelled to inquire into the nature of nature, which is the ultimate subject of modern inquiry.

As we know, the element of rebellion, which is an essential feature of any and all modernism, can be expressed—and indeed was spectacularly expressed early in this century—by deconstructions in perceptions of aesthetics and in sociopolitical activisms. But the rebellion involved in the moral concerns of any serious artist penetrates a deeper level of the art of expression.

Apollinaire described the evolution of Picasso as the calm after the frenzy; "calm" in that context means mastery of process as an answer to unilateral, belligerent attitudes toward the conditions of life in the twentieth century. What Apollinaire perceived in the development of the art of Picasso is the transformation of circumstantial rebellion into the multitiered image of subversion in painting, in poetry, in film, whereas frenzy is the overt exercise of uncontrolled, unsparing movement. One of the great changes in subsequent manifestations of modernism is the channeling of these energies of rebellion so that they are no longer the outer garment of the artist but assume through shocking analogies the double-edged meaning of reconstruction, constructing while deconstructing, espousing no single issue but catalytic of any issue.

It is too early to take inventory of all the avant-gardes that constitute the self-perpetuating modernism of the twentieth century. What matters for the moment is to proceed beyond the attempt to understand motivations, beyond tolerance of each and every one, because indeed

to love the avant-garde has become as popular and trendy as it previously was to shun it. Instead it may well be time to go beyond tolerance to critical discrimination. The distinctions between modes should be helpful in discerning the degree of craftsmanship in any such modes. If there emerges what appears to be sloppy composition, is it because the artist wants to represent a sloppy state of existence or is it simply a sloppy state of composition for lack of technical and aesthetic expertise? If the plot dissolves, if character remains flat, is the structure an intentionally reductive form of art, an act of artistic minimalism, or is it due to a lack of imaginative resourcefulness or a unilateral desire to shock and nothing more? If there is no ending, is it because the author believes that the elimination of a sense of ending suggests the quagmire in which humanity is engulfed or does it betray on his part a lack of inventiveness or a weakness in the mastery of the particular art? When does the excremental image lose its power of analogy to return to its original signification of waste? When does erotic language and its objectification lose its luxurious quality to become standard pornography? Are awkwardly shaped figures on a canvas or tedious repetitions of geometric lines a statement about the destruction of human form or a sign of haphazard bluff? Is it time to ask at what point even the most flamboyant avant-garde artist gets repetitious, tired, boring? Or, on the other hand, when do minimal linguistic discourse and gaps of total silence, hailed as achievements of the most recent examples of modernism, become merely indicative of clinical aphasia or verbal deficiencies?

One of the greatest powers of the modernisms of the past has been the overtone of sincerity and commitment; how far can the ironic element of author distancing from reality be carried out without bringing about reader-spectator distancing as well from the work declared as art?

The time has come, I think, when answers to this type of questioning may have to replace the more current, simplistic responses to the avant-garde—which have consisted either of rejecting it totally and in principle or accepting it and embracing it totally and without reservation and without even recognizing that in a single writer or artist there are better and lesser degrees of achievement. I bought some time ago at a book fair the latest work of a very personable playwright whose fame as a "neo-avant-garde" is fast rising. The title was "Burn This," and after reading it I had the feeling that the title was very appropriate. But this piece of trash received acclaim and an award. Audiences used to be too resistant to the avant-garde; now either they have become pushovers if the work is overt or they run away if it is a bit subtle—and the artists are becoming too eager to please.

Renato Poggioli, whose *Theory of the Avant-Garde* has become a universal reference in any serious discussion of the question of modernism in spite of the availability of many books subsequently written on the subject, thought that it was too early to evaluate. He therefore made his classifications according to the sociological factors involved. But his book is of 1950 vintage. It is hard to believe that we are designating moderns in the same way more than forty years later. Political protest and social negativism are still being rated as the basic elements of modernism and it is no longer too early to begin evaluation. It is time to look empirically at achievements rather than intentions. There is good and bad avant-garde no matter what standards of evaluation we use. A torso on canvas hanging on the wall may shock the viewer. Maybe it is a protest against violence and as such it is perhaps a sociological document, but it has to fulfill certain other criteria to be classified as art, and to be judged as modern it has to have a quality that extracts out of the transient something of the eternal. I have suggested certain categories of the modern. My distinctions are arbitrary and have to do with my own reading lists and philosophy of art. My intention is not to impose them on anyone else but to indicate that it is time to establish values, or at least guidelines, whereby we can regroup the moderns of the past with a good triage in the bargain, and gauge what to expect in current and even future moderns as eventually viable classics. With the ever-changing political and social scene, it is time to minimize the element of protest as a signal of the modern and to ask, what else is there? It is time to scrutinize the various powers of construction rather than be overwhelmed by the destructive intensity of the work. It no longer matters who shouted loudest, who shocked most widely. The question now is who shaped a permanent ticker tape of pleasure behind the instant notoriety, who went beyond talk about the unconscious to really give verbal approximation of unconscious or dream discourse, who conveyed the power of reality in the midst of concurrent processes of awareness and unawareness, whose work nourished the works of others instead of cloning itself endlessly?

Underlying the great variety of forms and attitudes loosely grouped and retained under the provisional title of "modernism" there emerge new encodings in search of new classifications. Writers and artists have had to make choices between identifying with new challenges to new notions of time, space, chance, consciousness, and reality and distancing their art from these factors, revising the parameters of the arts accordingly. The transitory label of "modern" must be passed along to new editions of modernism while the great work of separating the chaff from the wheat is carried out as we weigh the viability and degree of meaning and change of meaning of previous modernisms.

I am concerned as I read from the pen of scholars with solid reputations such subservient remarks as "from Lacan we know," "from Foucault we learn," "Derrida tells us." Academic scholars acquiesce too much and thereby plant in their disciples dangerous seeds of docility. Has it occurred to some that Lacan, Foucault, and Derrida could learn a few things from those of us who have been reading literature rather than psychology, archaeology, and philosophy?

As the post, post, post accumulate they seem to announce the ultimate end. Whereas some commentators on our era are eager to proclaim the death of literature, others obsessed with the prefix "post" are laboring under the assumption that we are witnessing the inevitable afterglow of a setting sun. How discouraging this attitude must be both to young writers and to their prospective critics! The paradox is that with the radical changes in the meaning of meaning, the broadening of the channels of communication, and the multiplication of the inner and outer aspects of nature, there has never been such an auspicious moment for the creator as well as the receiver to discover the imminent modern.

Malcolm Bradbury

SOURCE: "The Nonhomemade World: European and American Modernism," in *American Quarterly,* Vol. 39, Spring, 1987, pp. 27-36.

[*In the following essay, Bradbury focuses on the divergent origins and development of Modernism among American and European writers.*]

At the beginning of *A Homemade World: The American Modernist Writers* (1975), Hugh Kenner performs an elegant act of metaphorical magic by yoking violently together two items in the history of modernity separately much celebrated, but not usually associated. One is the flight of the Wright brothers at Kitty Hawk in 1903, the first serious proof of powered flight, and a clear triumph of American technological inventiveness. The other is a work of fiction started the next year in which the image of the artist as modern flyer has a striking place. That fiction, of course, is Joyce's *A Portrait of the Artist as a Young Man,* where Stephen Dedalus's flight into the unknown arts provides us with a figure for the rising spirit of artistic modernism. Metaphorically juxtaposing the one with the other, Kenner can now link two powers, those of American modernity and those of European modernism. As he says of the Wrights: "Their Dedalian deed on the North Carolina shore may be accounted the first American input into the great imaginative enterprise on which artists were to collaborate for half a century." The cunning connection gives him his book. American flyers came to the First World War, and also to the not much less embattled bohemias of Paris and London, where the new arts were being forged. At this stage American technological dominance and European forms were separate. To most Americans, Modernism was foreign; but since it was modern they wanted it, but made in a homemade way. Poets like William Carlos Williams and Wallace Stevens, and many American novelists, musicians, and painters obliged, becoming Modernist without even going to Europe, exploring the new preoccupations as an aspect of the problems of the American language, the needs of American perception and American consciousness, American plenitude and American emptiness. This Kenner explains: "That doctrine of perception, like general semantics, seems peculiarly adapted to the American weather, which fact helps explain why, from Pound's early days until now, modern poetry in whatever country has borne so unmistakably American an impress."

I have done little justice to Kenner's cunning book; but I start with it because it serves as an example of a familiar historiographical process, providing as it does both a narrative of an American act of artistic appropriation and a skillful critical mechanism for reinforcing it. It is a way of telling Modernism's story largely by dislodging the venturesome modern spirit in the arts from a European soil, in which it appears unrooted, to modern American soil, where it prospers and fertilizes, grows with the American grain, and then, an abundant crop, returns to the world market, rather like Frank Norris's nirvanic wheat. Modernism bears the American impress, even outside America, it and American modernity being natural kin. Such narratives are, of course, not new, but they have flourished powerfully since the 1940s when, with F. O. Matthiessen's *American Renaissance* (1941), the modern history of American literature began to be seriously written, and the idea of the native grain, of an encompassing and modern American tradition based on American vision and American mythology, enlarged. Matthiessen's brilliant book, the first truly convincing exploration of the way the American writers of the Transcendentalist pre-Civil War period constructed a new art that seemed to pass beyond inherited forms, constructing itself anew, released a fresh idea of the relation between the American imagination and American culture. In the same year, Alfred Kazin, in *On Native Grounds,* made a similar case for American Naturalism, which might well have been thought to owe much to European ventures of the same kind; after all Frank Norris had studied art in Paris and was seen around the Berkeley campus with a volume of Zola in his hand, and the European Naturalists were much in vogue among the young American writers. But Kazin seeks to establish a difference: where in Europe Naturalism had the force of a literary doctrine, in America it "just came, . . . grew out of the bewilderment, and fed on the simple grimness of a generation brought face to face with the pervasive materialism of American capitalism"—and it "had no center, no unifying principle, no philosophy, no joy in its coming, no climate of experiment." It was the art of an American process, of industrialization and modernization; and all done on native grounds.

This sense of the power of native soil, the guiding texture of the American grain, stimulated a splendid new generation of critical studies which have shaped all our thinking. In Richard Chase's fine *The American Novel and Its Tradition* (1957) the novel-form comes to the United States in rather the same way, countermanding the European tradition of the social and moral novel and generating its own neo-mythic form, the romance. This was a season for nativizing literature, valuably giving the modern American arts a tradition, a sense of a usable past. American mythographies arising from American beliefs and motifs, ideologies and theologies, American institutions and landscapes, American notions of election, mission and destiny powerfully illuminated a literature that,

while it might run curiously in parallel with the arts of Europe, and assimilate much from them, had self-creating powers in the homemade world. And this notion was reinforced by another—that the American arts had from the beginning a special relation to the modern itself. That view owed as much to the European Enlightenment as America itself, and its notions of the course of empire—according to which, as Bishop Berkeley reminded Americans, history moved ever westward, and brought the new arts in its train. When the Revolution brought into being the First New Nation, itself a startling appropriation of modern history, the motif intensified, supplementing the Calvinist sense of mission that came with settlement with the diachronic notion of rising modernity that came with continental spread and intensive development of industry and resources. As Hegel famously said, America was "the land of the future where, in the ages that lie before us, the burden of the world's history shall reveal itself" (we sometimes forget that he saw that revelation taking the form of a conflict between North and South America). Such ideas had a natural appeal to Americans, and applied alike to society and the arts. As Melville declared in *Pierre,* the Americans were history's own *avant-garde,* a people advancing into the wilderness of untried things. In Whitman the message grew clearer, modernity in society and experience leading to modernity of form in the arts. "One main contrast of the ideas behind every page of my verses, compared with establish'd poems, is their different relative attitude towards God, towards the objective universe, and still more (by reflection, confessional, assumption, &c.), the quite changed attitude of the ego, the one chanting or talking towards himself and towards his fellow-humanity," he wrote in *A Backward Glance,* going on to add that the material, inventive, and war-produced revolutions of the times, but above all the *moral* one, had produced what he called a change of army-front through the whole civilized world. And this meant modern form: "For all these new and evolutionary facts, meanings, purposes, new poetic new forms and expressions, are inevitable."

This sense of alliance—between America's modern history and modernity of form—Gertrude Stein took with her when, with the twentieth century in her blood (she meant, she said, to be historical, from almost a baby on, and was there "to kill what was not dead, the nineteenth century which was so sure of evolution and prayers"), she went in 1903 to settle in bohemian Paris, where among the *refusés* the spirit of twentieth-century modernism was in process of birth. "So the twentieth century had come it began with 1901," she wrote in *Paris France.* The new century was widely summoned in the United States as "the American century" and Stein shared the view, saying that the twentieth century came in America even though it had to go to France to happen. England was consciously refusing the new era, "knowing full well that they had gloriously created the nineteenth century and perhaps the twentieth was going to be one too many for them," while France took it all in its stride, since "what is was and what was is, was their point of view of which they were not very conscious." They were soon made conscious, in part by the Americans who came to Montparnasse, collecting, hunting the new, purchasing modern art on an extraordinary scale which can best be tested by inspecting the collections of the major American galleries and their dates of purchase, and stirring modernity into action. It had to be admitted that the novelties had a European source, and that the United States was puritanical and unartistic—"a half-savage country, out of date," said Ezra Pound, who played a somewhat similar role in motivating and stimulating London with American energies at around the same time—and so, argued Stein, Americans needed Paris because they could not be artists, they could be dentists at home. But she carried with her the familiar American conviction, that the United States was a nation with a special disposition toward progress, and with its technological advance, democratic social order and distinctive space-time continuum it required the "new composition." By this interpretation Modernism was a progressive movement of the arts aptly suited to a progressive nation, and we can see how powerful this kind of account of Modernist evolution has been in the development of the new arts in America.

It needs hardly be said that these ideas have been held in Europe also, both by those seeking to fund the modernity of Modernism and those attempting to expel it and all its works. Al Alvarez said for English-language writing, Modernism "has been a predominantly American concern"; Philip Larkin was happy to hand over to Americans "the two principal themes of modernism, mystification and outrage," and stay near the line of Hardy, and sanity. European Modernists often acknowledged their connection with the American spirit, Picasso observing that if Modernism was born in France it was the product of Spaniards and Americans. The images of rapidity and synchronicity that came from American culture, the beat of American popular music, the rhythms of jazz and the American dances, had great appeal to those artists in Paris who were moving toward both spontaneous primitivism and a new abstraction. The American motif was widespread, in Picabia, Duchamp, Cocteau and many more. Mondrian explained that "True Booogie-Woogie I conceive as homogenous in intention with mine in painting." Mayakovsky saw the skyscraper American city as the heart of the modern, and read the implications of Brooklyn Bridge with the same radical intensity as Hart Crane. The motif has lasted, in Sartre, Butor, Robbe-Grillet, and has much to do with the engagement of many European critics with American literature and culture. The "modern" image of America which so strongly affected Russian and Italian Futurism, and German Expressionism even made its mark in Britain. Indeed, D. H. Lawrence's *Studies in Classic American Literature* (1923) recovered, in a remarkable and visionary way, from the little-read classic American tradition the same sense of modernity: "Two bodies of modern literature seem to me to come to the real verge: the Russian and the American. . . . The furtherest frenzies of French modernism or futurism have not yet reached the pitch of extreme consciousness that Poe, Melville, Hawthorne, Whitman reached. The Europeans were all *trying* to be extreme. The great Americans I mention just were it. Which is why the world has funked them, and funks them today."

. . . . .

Yet if Modernism was to become, as Alvarez said, "a predominantly American concern," it hardly started as such. It began in Europe, and took a long time to cross the Atlantic; indeed the American writers from the 1890s to the War were largely preoccupying themselves with a Zola-esque Naturalism that in Europe was mostly considered exhausted. Indeed the full impact of the Modernist tendency came in America at least a generation later than it did in Europe; we normally date it from the ferments around 1912, when Freud and Cubism, the abstract art of the Armory Show and the new poetry that Pound sought to press upon *Poetry,* Harriet Monroe's magazine, begin to implant in American soil. This is no place, with no space, to expatiate at length on what we mean by Modernism, a contentious matter now as it always was, in part because on detailed inspection it dissolves into a plurality of different, often substantially conflicting, movements or tendencies, with many different sources, many different philosophies and culture-readings, many different versions of the modern, and the deliverances required of the modern arts. The complex problems of definition I and James McFarlane sought to address are discussed at length in the "Introduction" to *Modernism: 1890-1930,* where we note the heterodoxy of ideas that have gone into most of the attempted definitions. But let me here suggest that for many Western writers and thinkers a nineteenth-century synthesis seems to dissolve or come to crisis in the 1880s and 1890s—when positivism struggles with intuitionalism, sociology with psychology, naturalism with aestheticism, when there is a deep sense of perceptual crisis which throws attention onto consciousness, when world-views pluralize, and dusks and dawns both in the arts and civilization are much thought of. The result in ideas and forms is a period of remarkable intellectual and aesthetic innovation, a general upheaval manifest also in science and philosophy; this all has some prophetic or precursory relation both to the dislocation of the Great War and the postwar synthesis. These changes and disorientations are strongly manifested in the arts, displacing the role of artists, privatizing and specializing them, in some sense dislocating them from the familiar or the homemade. All this has social roots in the processes of late nineteenth-century change, the political upheavals of growing democratization and radical if not revolutionary feeling. It was an international affair, and if any thing distinguishes modernism it is surely its international interfusion—which is to say that whether through simultaneous generation or traceable flows of ideas and influence related artistic phenomena occur right across the Western nations, from Oslo to Rome, Moscow to Chicago. One then should add that they do not occur at quite the same time, in the same order, with the same aims or underlying philosophies, with the same degrees of hope, or despair, or the same historical expectations.

And since the familiar perspective in much English language-centered theory of Modernism sees it largely as an affair of Paris, London and New York, let us consider how wide a matter it was, and how enormous was the thought-flow passing through the European cities, making some capitals and some provinces at different times. Ibsenite Naturalism started in Scandinavia, went to Germany to happen, and turned with late Ibsen and Strindberg toward Expressionism. In France Zola-esque Naturalism turned toward aestheticism, symbolism and the art of the soul and the senses; both of these traditions seemed to cross over in German Expressionism in the immediately prewar years. Paris gave London much of its 1890s Naturalism and its aestheticism, but Germany won some attention, especially via Nietzsche and Ibsen, and D. H. Lawrence of course was drawn by Frieda toward Expressionism. In Russia another version of Symbolism moved toward Futurism; in Vienna another compound evolved which linked modern music, psychology, and new linguistic theory. In Paris, Marinetti was inventing and disseminating Italian futurism, though there were many other crucial movements, including Unanimisme, to the point where Pound, constantly visiting, felt that movements were just what London needed to stir the pot. Imagism in London derived in part from French symbolism, in part from the German art historian Wilhelm Worringer, and to some not very great degree from Whitman, with whom Pound contracted a painfully slow pact. It did have a significant American constituent, though Pound denied America as the main source of its ideas, and credited, amongst others, Selwyn Image, T. E. Hulme, and F. S. Flint, as well as the Chinese ideogram. Vorticism, on the other hand, was both borrowed from Worringer and the Futurists and was in revolt against them, and suitably one of its founding figures, Wyndham Lewis, was born on a ship at sea. Dada came in a wartime Zurich that, as Tom Stoppard shows, contained the odd synthesis of Tristan Tzara, Lenin, and Joyce. The war over, it took off in two directions—to Berlin and to Paris, where it interacted with French surrealism, which inherited from earlier symbolism, the impact of Cubism, and generated the Revolution of the Word, which brought together, or apart, contingents from France, Germany, England, Ireland, Romania and the States, to name but a few.

What we can say is that Modernism was an affair of many movements, of a common *avant-gardizing* tendency, with international origins and a massive and constant change of personnel, and considerable capacity for transit. It was also an affair centered in certain cosmopolitanizing cities capable of concentrating the flow of art-news and sustaining a large bohemian population of polyglot character. And one of the marks of Modernism was that it seemed to have no home. That flight Stephen takes in *Portrait of the Artist* into the unknown arts is a voyage of broken ties, fracturing the bonds of kinship, religion and country as he goes off to Paris, certainly to forge the uncreated conscience of my race, but from an anxious expatriate distance which set over Joyce's tales of Dublin, the paralyzed city, a modern pluralism and polyglotism. Homelessness was part of the

story. As George Steiner says, it was largely an art unhoused, an art of "extra-territoriality," and it was no accident that multilinguists have been the major artists of our age. Indeed, he says, of Nabokov, so clearly a part of this tradition, "It seems proper that those who create art in a civilization of quasi-barbarism in which so many are made homeless, which has torn up tongues and peoples by the root, should themselves be poets unhoused and wanderers across language." That wandering of language, that separation of the signifier from the signified which Saussure was intuiting in the immediately prewar climate, that "defamiliarization" of which the Russian formalist critics began to speak at much the same time, indeed seems near to the heart of Modernism. Thus what Kenner domesticates, and makes friendly with modern society and modern change, Steiner deracinates, and associates with modern anxiety and historical suffering. There are indeed many versions of Modernism.

In this Americans, essentially the expatriate ones, played their part from the early stages, a part which intensified in quantity and influence as time went on: James and Henry Harland, Pound, Eliot, Robert Frost and John Gould Fletcher in London; Gertrude and Leo Stein in Paris, to be followed by the expatriate wave of the 1920s, and so on. But support funds at home were not great, as Pound discovered when he tried to transmit European news back to Harriet Monroe. When Pound explained that American bards had to study Remy de Gourmont, Henri de Regnier, Francis Jammes and Tristan Corbiere, her magazine waved its homemade banner in behalf of its version of Modernism: "Mr [Vachel] Lindsay did not go to France for *The Congo* or *General William Booth Enters Into Heaven*. He did not even stay on the eastern side of the Alleghanies. . . . " It was the midwestern "moderns" like Lindsay, Masters and Sandburg that the magazine took pride in, while the great modern epic Monroe was looking for was not "Prufrock," which Pound sent her and which she tried to edit down, but a nativist epic celebrating the Panama Canal. Much of what Pound was saying was in fact an embarrassment. Nonetheless a "home-made" school did evolve, with Williams, Wallace Stevens, Marianne Moore and others, who may not have headed for Europe but who took much of their funding from Pound, Imagism and French symbolism. Williams may have felt that *The Waste Land* set back poetry by twenty years, but his Imagist debts are clear. Stevens for some time impersonated a French symbolist poet, and submitted poems under the dandy-name of "Peter Parasol," taking many of his titles from French poetry and paintings. American writing itself bred many modernisms, from the cultural despair of Eliot and Pound to the contrary affirmation and surer nativism of Stein or Williams. Indeed an assimilation took place, so that we see the American arts as modern not simply because they explore the cultural experience of an advanced or futuristic society, but because they have incorporated into that culture the lore of the modern art forms.

Not all saw the elegant equation of American modernity and European modernism as virtue. Stein's tactics of takeover, representing Cubism as an art that, though invented by Frenchmen and Spaniards, was really American, fitting prairie space, skyscraper cities, and filmic speed, were not universally accepted. Braque, in the famous *transition* testimony against Gertrude Stein, said: "Miss Stein obviously saw everything from the outside and never the real struggle we were engaged in. For one who poses as an authority on the epoch it is safe to say that she never went beyond the stage of a tourist." Certainly she perceived in terms of abstract, detachable styles justified by broad reference to twentieth-century needs, and never touched the deeper historical and perceptual anguish behind much modernism. Yet in her way she was right. Americans had a taste for stylistic radicalism, for forms that suggested a modern version of life, for new structures. American modern style did assimilate much from modernist style, in architecture and art. Indeed modernism seemed to pull together the apparently lonely and eccentric history of American artistic endeavor right through the nineteenth century. By the middle twenties, Americans seemed in one fashion or another major participants, and a modernism of sorts settled as an acceptable American style, along with Freud and Jung, Picabia and Picasso, the skyscraper and the futurist lines of the motor car, the radical spontaneity of jazz. And when in the 1930s the rise of Hitler and Mussolini reversed the tide of intellectual and artistic migrations, the alliance between Modernism and modern America seemed secured. Mann and Brecht, Auden and Isherwood, along with many of the intellectual supporters and major figures of theater, and architecture, found themselves on American soil, and in the American grain. In 1939, the year of new war, Joyce published *Finnegans Wake,* that summative and polyglot myth; a year later he died, displaced back to Zurich, and around the same date so did Virginia Woolf, a clear casualty of war. Of the two great American expatriate figures who had so much to do with the transaction, Pound, staying in Italy, ended with threatened charges of treason, and Stein, remaining in France, just survived the war, still asserting that America was her country and Paris was her home town. In America modernism seemed settled, and Bauhaus became not so much our house as the American corporate office building. Stein's prophecy for the century seemed fulfilled. Modernism had become the twentieth-century American style, the language of its progressivism, pluralism, cultural convergence; its commerce, its aesthetic drive, its modernity.

Thus, we seem to agree now, Modernism both endured and ended, fractured by the war but leaving its overwhelming trace on the Modern. Its demise left us with a problem, at least of nomenclature, for what comes after the modern, what follows the future, what happens when now turns suddenly into then, is not easy to define. But after the war there came, as Sartre said, a "third generation" of writers, called by the historical fracture and the collapse of entire social orders to new responsibilities. Modernism was now historicized, something came after, and we have come to talk of Postmodernism. No one has been more helpful and thoughtful than Ihab Hassan in trying to interpret the transition and gloss the term, and I quote him in paracritical flight: "If we can arbitrarily state that literary Modernism includes certain work between Jarry's *Ubu Roi* (1896) and Joyce's *Finnegans Wake* (1939), where will we arbitrarily state that Postmodernism begins? A year earlier than the *Wake?* With Sartre's *La Nausee* (1938) or Beckett's *Murphy* (1938)? In any case, Postmodernism includes works by writers as different as *B*arth, arthelme, ecker, eckett, ense, lanchot, orges, urroughs, utor. . . ." The list, you will notice, is provisional, capacious and international, with a large European contingent. So is that in another fine and undernoticed book on the same matter, Christopher Butler's *After the Wake: An Essay on the Contemporary Avant Garde* (1980), which also takes the wake as a break, the break as a wake, but sees a distinctive new phase of style developing after Existentialism, during the 1950s, with the *nouveau roman,* the *nouvelle vague* in cinema, a new music and a new painting. "For better or worse," he says, identifying this Postmodern time, "this is the age of Beckett and Robbe-Grillet, of Cage, Messiaen, Boulez, of Pollock, Rothko, Stella, and Rauschenberg." Butler not only emphasizes the internationality of the matter but draws less than usual on contemporary literary theory, concentrating on the statements of artists themselves. And I would suppose that most Europeans (and even the British now call themselves European, or certainly when it is in their interest to do so) would recognize some such history, seeing the after-modern or postmodern tendency or aesthetic equation as owing much to the postwar evolution of Existentialism, with its struggle between the humanistic and the absurd, and the subsequent challenges to it in successor arts and philosophies, the reassimilation of some aspects of Modernism, the rejection of others, the pervasive sense of the "imaginary museum" of plenitude and emptiness that passed through so many Western arts, the spirit of what Nathalie Sarraute calls "the ear of suspicion," when, as Robbe-Grillet puts it, in an era beyond humanism and tragedy art lives with "the smooth, meaningless, amoral surface of the world."

What is clear is that Postmodernism does have a larger American constituent, reflecting in part the fortunes of Modernism, and the dominance of America as modern art patron, high stylistic consumer, and *émigré* haven. It is surely equally clear that its great marking figures include Beckett, an Irishman writing in Paris in French; Nabokov, a Russian refugee writing in his native language, German, French, and latterly English; and Borges, an Argentinian writing in Spanish and with a Latin American, Iberian, French and Anglophile background. Thus it draws on a tradition that had moved through Modernism and the Absurd toward a new minimalism, a tradition based in a latter-day adaptation of early Russian symbolism, and a South American tradition which relates the fantastic to historical realism. Its present centers certainly include South America, Paris, Italy, Germany, to some degree Britain, and to some further degree the Indian subcontinent, Australasia and Canada. Its intellectual sources appear to be, amongst other things, Russian formalism, Saussurian linguistics, later Surrealism, Existentialist philosophy, and what has followed it, that Deconstructionist revolution that spread throughout the entire Gallic World (as I believe Yale University is sometimes called). It includes, I would say virtually by definition, an eclectic principle of multiple quotation, stylistic pluralism, creative misprision. There has indeed been a strong American contingent, which Saul Bellow, who has made clear his resistance to the tendency, has distinguished from the *nouveaux romanciers* and European writers "whose novels and plays are derived from definite theories which make a historical reckoning of the human condition and are particularly responsive to new physical, psychological, and philosophical theories." In this matter, he says, American writers are again the modern primitives, writing in the same spirit but "seldom encumbered by such intellectual baggage, and this fact pleases their European contemporaries, who find in them a natural, that is, a brutal or violent acceptance of the new universal truth by minds free from intellectual preconceptions." If this is not entirely true, some part of American Postmodernism having a clear intellectual face related to those European philosophies, it does seem that there is a Postmodernism of the homemade world.

Today the tendency indeed seems to have been domesticated within the cultural heterodoxy of American culture, and become a convention. As Alan Wilde ways with some irony in *Horizons of Assent: Modernism, Postmodernism, and the Ironic Imagination* (1980), "postmodernism is an essentially American affair." The term has been generalized to apply to the broad eclecticism of forms and referents in contemporary American writing, architecture and art, a way of speaking of an art that appears "self-creating" *and* "in the American grain." Indeed this is the form of modern writing that has grown particularly exemplary, so literary that Post-modernism often seems to mean innovative American fiction read—or rather misread—with the methods and slippages of French Deconstructionist criticism. It is, in effect, the art of the "homemade world," a consequence of American stylistic abundance, provisional form, intermedia arts, futurism and, often, optimism. So, says one American critic, James Rother, "to be American is, quite simply, to be postmodern, and to be postmodern entails nothing more than knowing (in the full light of a communally held fiction) that one is."

I have suggested here that for a sufficient account of Modernism we need many Modernisms, and a far more challenging and international perception of the relation between American and broader international culture. By necessary logic the same would apply to Postmodernism, which has inherited, certainly, the pluarlity and multiple signification of Modernism and a good part of its philosophical, linguistic and formal skepticism. If the term means anything, it surely means an art of stylistic plurality and cultural synchronicity, rebarbative plenitude and decultured emptiness, formal enquiry and parodic self-reference, random signification and infinite quotation, that marks much of world-culture in our multimedia,

high-noise, wide-traveling internationalist age. To attend to it we need a capacious attention, if we are to construct not only a sufficient historiography of the immediate past of our arts but of their present. For we live, after all, in the age of Marquez, Calvino, Handke, Eco, Fowles, Pinter, Stoppard, Wittig, Coetzee, and many many more, and there is a major international literature of extraordinary power which needs drawing into any cogent mapping of the late twentieth century arts that both succeed to and react to the overwhelming Modernist inheritance. The arts of Postmodernism, like those of Modernism, are of no single and unidirectional kind; they are a contention, a quarrel, seeded in many places, often floating free of them in a large extraterritoriality, and funded by polyglot and multistylistic sources. It is almost forty years after the wake, as indeed the wake was just around forty years after *Ubu Roi*. The task of charting this is immense, and hardly begun in terms of a conceptual historiography. But as we begin to assimilate theoretically the arts of our own long time, we will find almost certainly that in our age of cultural melting-pot and extraordinary global interfusion they are hardly the arts of a homemade world.

Lawrence B. Gamache

SOURCE: "Toward a Definition of 'Modernism,'" *The Modernists: Studies in a Literary Phenomenon,* Associated University Presses, 1987, pp. 32-44.

[In the following essay, Gamache illuminates the origins and meaning of the term "Modernism" in both literary and nonliterary contexts.]

Because the ambition to define modernism completely would be almost Miltonic, I will begin this study with an explanation of its limitations. By considering the history of the words *modern* and *modernism* and by adumbrating the cultural context that defines their literary usage, I intend to suggest several essential constituents of both literary and nonliterary modernism and to provide several examples of modernists whose lives and works manifest those constituents.

My initial intent was to clarify the uses of *modernism* and *modernist* to describe some twentieth-century writers and their works. I considered referring to four major figures—Eliot, Yeats, Joyce, and Lawrence—to represent what I think are the constituents of a cultural phenomenon that reaches back at least several centuries in its genesis. This I found difficult: much clarification was needed before the examples could be discussed.

The word *modernism,* given its complex range of uses, has all the traps of others like it, for example, *romanticism;* it presents even greater difficulty just now because of the proximity in time of the phenomena it pretends to identify. My revised ambition has not been overreaching, I think, but it has, nevertheless, led to a very cumbersome project. Previous studies have dealt with rather limited literary and artistic applications of the word, and have discussed points of specific agreement and disagreement about the phenomena it usually refers to; but little has been done to relate nonliterary uses of the word, especially its earliest uses, to descriptions of the larger cultural context that frames recent literary history. A larger study might seem more appropriate than this attempt to outline a difficult subject, but in the context of the series of essays to which it will relate, what I have undertaken is apropos. The apparently disparate cultural phenomena referred to in a number of contexts by uses of *modern,* or many of the modifications of that word current in theological and religious, scientific and technical, linguistic, philosophical, and psychological study, in social, economic, and political practice as well as ideology, make an unequivocal usage impossible. Studies of the literature and art from origins other than Anglo-American, French, German, and Italian (most often treated as the mainstream sources of the "modernist tradition") and of its nonliterary uses can help to identify what is basic to the phenomena the word refers to. My final intent has been to clarify the literary meaning of this term by identifying its earliest usages, in particular the religious, the first context in which it gained currency, and to suggest parallels between appropriate literary and nonliterary figures who illustrate essential modernism.

It is the core of the meaning of modernism, then, for which I will suggest an explanation. I think there is a felt sense of crisis in human existence reflected in many late nineteenth- and twentieth-century cultural products to which the following constituents of modernism can be attributed: (1) a preoccupation with the present, usually urban and technical rather than rural and agricultural in its sense of place and time, is related to the loss of a meaningful context derived from the past, from its forms, styles, and traditions; (2) this sense of loss gives rise to a search for a new context—cosmopolitan, not provincial, in scope—and for new techniques to evolve an acceptable perception of reality, often, paradoxically, in the form of an attempt to rediscover roots in the depths of the past; (3) but this search tends to an increasingly relativistic, inward, often disillusioned vision and a compulsive need to develop techniques to embody it. As Monroe K. Spears suggests, however, the modernist may also react to modern cultural changes "as emancipation, a joyful release from the dead hand of convention, from stale pieties and restrictions." The culmination for many modernists is the rejection of the present in favor of the values of the past (Eliot), a singular vision of the future (Lawrence), a substitute reality (Yeats), or the diminishing conviction that there is any stable external reality to which that inward search relates (Joyce). For a writer to be a modernist, each of these constituent elements should to a noticeable degree be not just arguable but evident preoccupations; someone may be modernistic in some ways without being a modernist, as is true of George Bernard Shaw, the early Yeats, Robert Frost (at least in much of his work), and the later Eliot.

My proposed description of modernism is really a fairly basic reduction to a common ground of what most commentaries on modernism state as defining constituents. What has been most revealing during the study of this common ground is the extent to which it applies to the wide range of phenomena in our culture referred to above, that is, to our struggles as artists, scientists, philosophers, even technologists, to deal with that sense of crisis in our evolution that has increasingly pervaded human life through at least the last two centuries. Although a specifically modernist period, analogous to the romantic period of the late eighteenth and early nineteenth centuries, can be argued to have existed in the late nineteenth and early twentieth centuries, based on the prevalence to a significant extent of its defining characteristics in the rhetorical and poetical products of writers, be they artists, philosophers, or scientists, the word itself must be allowed to function descriptively, unfettered by temporal constraints, as are *romanticism* or *classicism.* Certain ancient authors, therefore, might be legitimately said to manifest modernist attitudes or responses, without the assertion being considered absurd. For example, Euripides, for some critics, at times reflects very modernist reactions to certain human quandaries. In 1938, Robert L. Calhoun argued this point as he defined the meaning of *humanitarian modernism* in contrast to traditional Christian religious views. He applied his definition to several sociocultural contexts without limiting himself to a purely twentieth-century frame of reference. He said that "its key note is active, conscious preoccupation with the present" and that "the obstinate, urgent past embodied in living tradition is disparaged." Confidence in a "new critical insight," which may issue in "rationalism, in positivism, or in skepticism," he attributes to the modernists' cutting away of "spiritual bonds which else would hold present and future to the past." While I would qualify Calhoun's sense of the modernists' perfectabilitarian optimism and decisiveness in divesting themselves of the past and a pride and confidence about themselves and their programs, his awareness that the phenomenon is not a "school of thought" and is a "particular recurrent mood of temper, which in essence is very old, which during the past two hundred years has become more widespread," are insights uncharacteristic of early considerations of the meaning of "modernism," especially in a religious context.

It is very difficult to discuss any examples of modernism in isolation, and, for that reason, I will preface my examples of a prototypical form of modernism with a consideration of the word as such and with what I hope will be sufficient acknowledgment of the appropriate larger context necessary for a coherent discussion of representative patterns of moral, religious, and existential crises drawn by the examples I will cite. According to the *OED, modern* was first used in the sixth century A.D. by analogy with the modification of *hodie* to *hodiernus; modo* became *modernus,* meaning "just now." It would seem both by virtue of analogy and etymology that a preoccupation with "just now," rather than with the past or the future, is fundamental to what *modern* suggests, in particular when it is modifying statements of attitudes or states of mind, not simply designating what is coeval. In

England, from the seventeenth to the nineteenth centuries, it usually referred to qualities of thought, style, or workmanship that were current rather than classical in sympathy or affinity, often with pejorative connotation.

This long history of usage is, in part, the source of some of the confusion in the use of *modernism* (that is, one that assumes apparently differing significations in differing contexts while, at the same time, retaining a core of meaning). When the suffixes *-ism* and *-ist* are added to *modern,* an irresistible and fascinating challenge to the ingenuity of lexicographers and semioticians develops. Defining it for use as a descriptive term in literary-cultural history is no less challenging. The addition of *-ism* and *-ist* to a word can make it refer to a set of tenets, an attitude or complex of attitudes held in common by a more or less identifiable group. Individuals, and the phenomena related to them for which the word is also used as a modifier, must in some significant measure adhere to those tenets or manifest those attitudes. The danger is to reduce complex human phenomena to the *-ism,* making it a vague tag, rather than to have it point at a perceivable propensity whose identification clarifies a complex idea; it can help us to be aware of an underlying coherence amid confusing diversity. Any definition of such a term that comes to grips with the fundamental problem—the relationship of the literary to the larger context of cultural influences that, in the final analysis, define it—will necessarily have to be relative: flexible, yet have the precision to suggest more than a meaningless set of ambiguities or, worse, a distorting category.

Some evidence of the scope of a study of Western intellectual traditions affected by modernism is provided by Richard Ellmann and Charles Feidelson in *The Modern Tradition,* a seminal anthology of source materials that goes as far back as the eighteenth-century roots of twentieth-century thought for evidence. Their collection of bits and pieces suggests the range and richness of a modern tradition for which no single concept, no matter how complex its explanation, seems appropriate. Considering the multitude of *-isms* and *-ologies* they touch on (for example, in philosophy, Kantianism, Hegelianism, Marxism; in the arts, impressionism, surrealism; in psychology, Freudianism, Jungianism; in socioeconomic theory, socialism, liberalism), it might appear that this tradition is nothing more than an amorphous slagheap of ideologies that volcanizes out of the heat of human evolution. The tradition is, however, far more real and has, in its reality, touched individual lives far more powerfully than such a conception would allow for; such a conception admits no distinction between the living heat of the volcanic eruption and its residue.

The longstanding practice of identifying the time span from the early Renaissance to the present as "the modern period" (the source of much ambiguity in its current usages) to distinguish it from the medieval, was based on an awareness of a shifting focus of attention from a medieval God-centered to a man-centered vision of this world. In this context, the so-called modernist span, considered most broadly to begin in the last third of the nineteenth century, peaking between 1900 and 1930, and continuing to about World War II or shortly thereafter, is the period of the failure of Renaissance and post-Renaissance aspirations; but between the sixteenth and nineteenth centuries the center had shifted from man to nature—seen at first abstractly and analytically, then more imaginatively and emotionally by some and more empirically by others—in reaction to the incompleteness of the optimistic programs, for example, of the Baconians and Cartesians.

Valuable studies done earlier in the century by such scholars as Arthur O. Lovejoy, Erich Auerbach, Joseph Warren Beach, Basil Willey, Paul Oscar Kristeller, and Meyer H. Abrams have helped to clarify this pattern: there has been a progression from the optimistic attempt to discover the real world, studied confidently as the proper object of philosophy and science and as the artist's guide, to man reduced to skepticism and to his own subjectivity. The individual, considered to be full of potential (as in the Renaissance), was gradually replaced by mass consciousness and individual subconsciousness or unconsciousness. Nature has changed from an object to know and control to a noumenal universe beyond our minds' direct grasp, and Nietzsche's "death of God" has been succeeded and completed by Michel Foucault's "death of man." The process of this succession constitutes the history of the modernist era.

The effects of these shifts on efforts to understand fundamental reality are primary indicants of the modernist temperament; by looking into the earliest attempts to embody these effects in the forms of our culture, especially in its religious forms, we can clarify them somewhat and apply them to literature by more precise use of analogy than is usual. The majority of studies of modernism thus far tend to isolate the object matter of the study—be it art, literature, philosophy, or religion—from the other areas of human activity that manifest the incursion of the modernist spirit, thereby rendering our perception of that phenomenon piecemeal and our understanding fragmentary. I have chosen to use the development of modernism in Roman Catholicism to exemplify what I think are its major constituents because religion touches most directly on those facets of human thought and feeling affected by modernism and because, historically, Roman Catholic intellectuals were the first to pursue consciously and deliberately the modernist enterprise as I am defining it.

Evidence of the spirit, the motivations, and the genesis of modernism can be studied in particular in the careers and thoughts of two exemplary figures from the history of the Roman Catholic modernist controversy, that is, in the personal and religious development of Alfred Loisy and George Tyrrell. Each of these men is considered the founder of Catholic modernism in his own country, France and England respectively; their lives suggest the terms of a crisis indicative of not only what religious modernism was at the turn of the century, but also of what it cost, and why it, too, is identified by those defining constituents mentioned above. These men were concerned with their own times, with the moral and intellectual issues they themselves felt and also saw others troubled by, both Catholic and not Catholic, in their own countries and beyond. They were aware of a loss of belief in the efficacy of religious traditions, in form and in content; they turned to new methods to discover new foundations for spirituality, but, in the case of Loisy in particular, became increasingly relativistic and disillusioned. Characteristic of the scholarly endeavors of each of these men was an awareness of the intellectual pursuits, in their own and in other fields, of colleagues in other countries. This cosmopolitanism was, in fact, the source of some of their difficulties with their more provincially-minded and ultramontane superiors. Each of these qualities contributed to Roman Catholic modernism and to the controversy surrounding it.

Pope Pius X, in his encyclical *Pascendi* (1907), identified a complex of attitudes and theories, especially certain avant-garde approaches to biblical study and to doctrine, as embodying the "modernist heresy." According to J. J. Heaney, a Catholic spokesman, "[*Pascendi*] condemned theories on dogma and Biblical criticism which had agnostic, immanentist-evolutionary and anti-intellectualist bases." He also claims that "immanentism, neo-Hegelianism, and agnosticism were the terminal point rather than the *point de depart*" for some modernists only. This judgment would apply to Loisy, but not to Tyrrell.

From such a point of view, *Pascendi* focused on the negative influence of current, often conflicting, varieties of epistemological phenomenalisms like those of Mill, Spencer, Pierce, and Comte; of philosophical idealisms like Bradley's, Hegel's, Bergson's or Croce's; of forms of scientific and historical determinism as preached by Thomas Henry Huxley or Hippolyte Taine; and of the religious historicism of such scholars of religion as Schleiermacher, Ritschl, von Harnack, and Renan. The views of these last supported, in varying measure, and paradoxically, scientific historicism in biblical and doctrinal studies—a relativistic development in matters of faith, and subjectivism, that is, feeling, as the basis for a commitment to religious belief in the absence of intellectual certitude. It is the force of intellectual currents such as these, in particular those that affected twentieth-century man's confidence in his knowledge of the world outside his mind, and, for that matter, the worlds of his mind as well, that have influenced modernists in literature from Joyce, the rational technician, to Lawrence, the intuitive man of feeling.

According to Leighton Parks, an early twentieth-century Protestant modernist, what was "somewhat contemptuously" condemned by Pius X was more than a series of explicit, highly formulated positions; it was, rather, a complex of "certain social, philosophical, and historical movements in the Roman Catholic Church" that the Pope stigmatized as heretical. To Parks, modernism "is not a body of doctrine. It is a state of mind. It is an attempt to 'justify the ways of God to man,' that is, to man in the

twentieth century." To many, both inside and outside the Catholic Church, it was that "state of mind" the Pope condemned. The examples of Loisy and Tyrrell support Parks: they did not uphold the same theses; they were involved in different ways, as scholars and as idiosyncratic minds, with different areas. Yet they did share common attitudes, those I have cited above as specifically constituting the modernist spirit.

Alfred Loisy has often been called the father of Roman Catholic modernism. He was born in 1857 in Ambrières, Marne, and began studying for the priesthood at the age of seventeen. He was ordained five years later. He became a student and, later, Professor of Hebrew and Biblical Exegesis at the Institut Catholique in Paris, between 1881 and 1893; he was dismissed in 1893 as a result of an article on the Bible and inspiration. He served as Chaplain to the Dominican Sisters at Neuilly, Seine, from 1893 to 1899. In 1900 he was Biblical Lecturer at the Ecole Pratique des Hautes Etudes in Paris but had to retire in 1904 because of his controversy with Rome; a number of his books were placed on the Index by Pius X in 1903. He was finally excommunicated in 1908.

In 1909 he became Professor of the History of Religions at the Collège de France. He abandoned Catholicism and eventually Christianity in any traditional sense, but continued to publish studies of the Bible and other religious subjects until his death in 1940. His career spanned the modernist era, but his earlier years are the most important.

In 1913, Loisy revealed his earlier torments while a student of theology:

> Just in the degree to which certain objects of faith had impressed me when employed as sources of religious emotion, to that same degree their Scholastic exposition in terms of naked intellect filled my mind with an ill-defined disquiet. Now that I was required to think all these things rationally, and not merely to feel them, I was thrown into a state of prolonged disturbance. For my intelligence could find no satisfaction, and with my whole timid, immature consciousness I trembled before the query that oppressed, in spite of myself, every hour of the day: Is there any reality which corresponds to these doctrines?

The conflict felt by Loisy as a sickly, delicate young seminarian might be used, *mutatis mutandis,* to describe James Joyce during his adolescence.

Loisy was but eleven years old when the doctrine of papal infallibility was declared during Vatican Council I (1869-70); but the sources of tension within and outside the Catholic Church that led to that declaration lie behind Loisy's declared "four years of mental and moral torture," during which he was introduced to the study of Roman Catholic theology. Joseph Ernest Renan (1823-92), an agnostic and author of the highly controversial *Vie de Jésus* (1863), had used textual-historical critical tools in treating the New Testament story of Christ as a romance, reducing Christ to a purely human historical figure; David Friedrich Strauss (1808-74), a German theologian, had mythologized the Christ figure. These uses of "modern" textual-critical approaches, compounding the effects of current archaeological discoveries in the Middle East and the unsettling effects of popular Darwinianism, deeply disturbed many of Loisy's contemporaries. It was as a response to such influences that Rome declared infallibility and that Leo XIII published his encyclical *Aeterni Patris* (1879) in support of neo-scholasticism for an approved method in philosophical and theological studies.

In his late adolescence, Loisy entered religious studies in a milieu of heated controversy and a deeply-rooted historical division between "liberal" and "fundamentalist" Catholicism. Those who stood on a middle ground or who, like the Baron von Hügel and Giovanni Genocchi (both contributors to religious studies associated with Loisy during his controversy with Rome), attempted to mediate the "modernist" cause with traditionalists, were caught, often painfully, between two irreconcilable extremes. As Loisy developed in his studies of scripture, he became the spokesman of the "modernist" extreme. It was in his mid-twenties, after he took his degree in theology, that he embarked on his career as a modernist student of the Bible. By 1882, he expressed his awareness of the conflict that would eventually lead him to break with Roman Catholicism and, in the long run, with any traditional notion of Christianity:

> On the one hand [is] routine calling itself tradition; on the other, novelty calling itself truth. . . . These two attitudes are in conflict as to the Bible, and I wonder if anyone in the world is able to hold the scales even between faith and science.

That same year, he became a student of Renan at the Collège de France.

By 1890, when he published his first piece of biblical scholarship, the way before him was becoming clearer and his direction was being set. In 1893 he lost his position at the Institut Catholique in Paris. In 1900 he criticized the notion of inspiration in Leo XIII's *Providentissimus Deus* (1893). Loisy's claim that theologians "are as able as others to write . . . free criticism, because in the field of biblical history, *as in every other subject* [emphasis added], faith directs scientific investigations" was, paradoxically, the source, according to Genocchi, of his pronouncements that contradicted traditional teaching. Genocchi warned Loisy against the inevitable conflict he would engender between biblical textual history and philosophical and theological analysis. To Genocchi there was a fundamental difference between historical-critical and philosophical methods: they must not be confused or reduced the one to the other. Loisy began to treat purely philosophical and theological questions, "though protesting that he wished to write a purely historical work." The philosophical and theological methods to which Genocchi referred were neo-scholastic, more

specifically neo-Thomist. Genocchi was a declared devotee of Thomas Aquinas from his earliest years of study. Loisy sought in these years to apply new, *nonscholastic* methods to biblical studies as an apologist; he in fact referred to his work concluded in 1899 as an "apologetic." The final section, according to Francesco Turvasi, served as the rough draft for chapters on the historical Jesus and on Christian dogma and worship in *L'Evangile et l'Eglise* and *Autour d'un petit livre* (1903), two works that seriously disturbed many of his confrères, and evidently caused a number of young clerics to question their religious convictions. This work was originally entitled *La crise de la foi dans le temps présent: essais d'histoire et de philosophie religieuses;* he clearly saw himself in the vanguard of a new approach to religious studies.

Loisy believed he was being maligned, not because of his audacity in implying radically different theological and philosophical (particularly implicitly epistemological) positions, but because of his accusers' ignorance of the true nature of the crisis and of the methods of modern study that might resolve that crisis. This seems, at least, to have been his sense of the conflict at the turn of the century. He was moving consistently toward an evolutionist view of church teaching, and an immanentist (anti-transcendent) view of God's relationship to the world and man, and toward a "Catholic" agnosticism in his view of the person of God and of Christ's divinity: he evidently wanted to remain *in* the Church while, at the same time, teaching views inconsistent with its traditions in theology. In 1913, he acknowledged the impossibility of maintaining these two positions.

Loisy's "ill-defined disquiet," his intense sense of a mission, felt early in his intellectual development, to find new techniques for dealing with the issues of faith he recognized as increasingly troublesome for his contemporaries, and his desire to open his quest to the discovery of new, rational grounds for a new kind of religious faith offered by research outside the strict confines of traditional religious study, are the areas I think suggestive of analogies to be drawn to the urgency shared by literary and visual artists contemporary with him in their thematic preoccupations, and in their search for new techniques to embody those themes (whether products of thought or of feeling or, in Pound's words, of an "intellectual and emotional complex [experienced] in an instant of time." Loisy's gradual movement away from the given heritage of his religious ancestry toward an agnostic, relativistic approach to biblical and doctrinal interpretations presages similar developments in other, equally sensitive products of late nineteenth- and early twentieth-century cultural evolution.

George Tyrrell and Alfred Loisy have often been linked in studies of Roman Catholic modernism as the leading lights of the movement, because both were excommunicated after *Pascendi* was promulgated and because both resisted the attempt to stop their endeavors to change basic conceptions of Catholic teaching; however, these two men could hardly have differed from each other more completely in their backgrounds and personalities. Loisy was born into a peasant farm family, very traditionally French Catholic, was destined very early in life for the priesthood, and was educated from his earliest years wholly in Church schools; Tyrrell was born in Dublin, in 1861, into a Protestant Irish family, made fatherless just before his birth, and was constantly moved about (eighteen times by the age of eighteen). He was exposed "to a variety of religious traditions, including Methodism, Calvinism, and Evangelicalism." His older brother, a very important influence during his formative years, was an agnostic. Between the ages of ten and fourteen, George Tyrrell claimed he did not believe: "It was simply my first self-chosen attitude in regard to religion; I did not cease to be a believer, but, from a non-believer, I became an unbeliever at about the age of ten." His family were believers, except for his brother Willie, but they were not aware of his attitudes. A childhood friend later wrote, "for Tyrrell, his change of religion was a necessary precondition to his gaining of his soul spiritually or intellectually."

Tyrrell found his direction toward religious faith in his fourteenth year; he discovered Grangegorman, an Anglican High Church in Dublin. Of this experience, he said he "felt instinctively what I, long afterwards, understood clearly, namely: that the difference between an altar and a communion table was infinite." Ellen Leonard describes Tyrrell's progress toward Catholicism by contrasting it with that of Newman, a figure of importance in Tyrrell's early modernist thought: "Whereas Newman began with a belief in God's presence in the voice of conscience, which led him ultimately to a belief in Catholicism, Tyrrell began with Catholicism, which led him to Christianity and then to Theism." He became a Roman Catholic after having moved to London in 1879, and almost immediately he decided to become a Jesuit priest.

Tyrrell's "spiritual odyssey," according to Leonard, was the result of his "strong 'wish to believe'"; it was an urgent search for a conception of order that would provide meaning for people living in a modern, not medieval, world. He was guided by a "strong sense of mission, a conviction that his search was not for himself alone. . . . His concern was for others who were experiencing the same darkness through which he had come." The introduction, during his seminary studies, to neo-scholastic methods had a long-lasting influence on him; he felt St. Thomas Aquinas gave him the intellectual instruments to pursue his quest:

> Whatever order or method there is in my thought . . . I owe . . . to St. Thomas. He first started me on the inevitable, impossible, and yet not all-fruitless quest of a complete and harmonious system of thought.

It is ironic that his condemnation was, in part, for not acquiescing to the authority of neo-scholasticism in the teaching of Church doctrine.

Tyrrell's acceptance of the Jesuit discipline was based on a conviction "that the originality of Ignatius [founder of the Jesuits] lay in his willingness to adapt new means to meet the needs of his time." It was to revive this Ignatian spirit, that is, to seek again the means, suitable to the realities of the turn-of-the-century, to speak to the people of a modern world, that he dedicated himself. He gradually came to believe that what he called Jesuitism had become "the maintainer of the *status quo,* rather than an innovative force within the Church." He felt it contributed to an exaggerated sense of Church authority that stultified attempts to accommodate Church teachings to the research of modern science and scientific criticism. It became his hope to "historicize" St. Thomas, who "represents a far less developed theology than that of the later Schoolmen. . . . I would study Aquinas as I would study Dante, in order that knowing the mind of another age we might know the mind of our own more intelligently." Tyrrell here sounds much closer to a Gadamer than to any neo-scholastic of his own time. His attempts to use this critical approach to Thomas as a teacher of philosophy at Stonyhurst, between 1894 and 1895, led to his removal from teaching and to his early difficulties within the Society. At this point he began to search for alternative ways of understanding and interpreting Catholicism. John Henry Newman seemed to offer such an alternative.

From Newman, Tyrrell adapted the conception of Christianity as developmental, that is, that the teachings of the Church in any age are the articulation of Christ's revelation for that age—that the Church itself evolved and is evolving continuously. He said that Newman recognized "the fluctuating character of science and religion" and that Newman wanted "to make the preambles of faith in some sort independent of, and indifferent to, those very fluctuations." Tyrrell wanted to establish the critical bases of faith upon which subsequent studies, such as Loisy's adaptation of German criticism in his work on the Bible, could rest without need or fear of authoritative censure from Church officialdom. His was the position of mediator: "The Church may neither identify herself with 'progress' nor isolate herself from it. Her attitude must always be the difficult and uncomfortable one of partial disagreement and partial assent."

At the close of the century, Tyrrell published an article on the dogma of Hell; in the course of his statement, rejecting the scholastic position, he remarked:

> In a saner spiritual philosophy born of a revolt against materialism—the last and lowest form of rationalism [e.g., scholasticism]—a basis is found for a certain temperate agnosticism, which is one of the essential prerequisites of intelligent faith; . . . the essential incapacity of finite mind to seize the absolute and which governs and moves everything towards itself, the natural necessity of seeming contradictions and perplexities in our estimate of God's thoughts and ways are accepted as inevitable.

This article led to the conflict with the authorities of his Society and of the Church in Rome that culminated eight years later (22 October 1907) in his excommunication, a little more than a month after *Pascendi* was promulgated.

Tyrrell's way of dealing with this conflict—without denying his basic acceptance of Catholicism, on the one hand, or of acquiescing to the pressures of authority, on the other—was to see himself as one who "will stand on the doorstep and knock and ring and make myself a nuisance in every possible way." He had a sense of his own faith that echoes Newman's of *A Grammar of Assent* (1870), in rejecting "extravagant claims for what reason can prove about God. We have assents based . . . on the total response of the whole person to a concrete fact." He also had to deal with uncertainty:

> As to faith, it is my hope that there is a solution yet to be discovered; and that not very far hence. I think there are crises in human thought comparable to those in evolution when life, sense and reason first come on the scene; and that after such crises there are seasons of great confusion pending readjustment; . . . How far away even Newman seems to one now! How little he seems to have penetrated the darkness of our day!

His answer to the darkness, and his urgent reason for knocking at the door of the Church rather than retiring, is contained in his conception of the proper relationship between Catholicism and the modern world:

> If a religion is to influence and leaven our civilization and culture it must be recognized as a part of it, as organically one with it; not as a foreign body thrust down from above, but as having grown up with it from the same root in the spirit of humanity.

Death did not come to Tyrrell suddenly; he had expected to die even sooner than he did, but the spectre did not deter him from his convictions or his chosen course of action. Up to 1909, when the effects of Bright's disease and, undoubtedly, the strain of the conflict he was in took their toll, he continued to adhere, within himself, to his Catholicism, hoping that he might contribute to making it adapt more coherently to the ways of the modern world.

Earlier in the nineteenth century, Tennyson had expressed his fears of the image of nature being proffered by biological science *(In Memoriam)* and technology ("Locksley Hall Sixty Years After"), but he did not grasp the challenge to his most basic perception of reality that would evolve by the time of Tyrrell and Loisy. And Arnold's "darkling plain" in "Dover Beach" was perhaps his most extreme expression of human prospects after the withdrawal of the "Sea of Faith." On the whole, Victorians saw the direction of coeval developments in human knowledge positively or, at worst, fearfully; but the fearful did not realize the radical effect on their sense of the past and of the present about to invade their basically stable perceptions of the right order of things. The apparent darkness of modern human horizons became evident to religious searchers sooner than it did to most of their contemporaries, and their perception of that darkness—unlike, for example, a Hardy's—was framed by a modernist's sense of place and time and of the general human condition in a modernized world. The careers of both Tyrrell and Loisy echo the mind and world of a Stephen Dedalus or a Paul Morel far more than they do a Michael Henchard, or any of the Forsyths for that matter.

The patterns of the modern novel described by Frank Kermode in *The Sense of an Ending* or Alan Friedman in *The Turn of the Novel,* that is, their open-endedness and apocalyptic, urgent struggles for an intellectual and emotional vision to give a meaningful context of belief in which to act out human life, are more applicable to Loisy's and Tyrrell's biographies than they would be to their mentors' life stories, such as, for example, Renan's or Newman's. The descriptions of literary modernism presented by such commentators as Spears, who acknowledges the importance of religious modernism in his *Dionysus and the City,* or Bradbury and McFarlane, who never allude to it in their collection of essays entitled *Modernism: 1890-1930,* are clearly relevant to a study of religious modernism; and a knowledge of religious modernism does make clearer and more vividly real the intensity and nature of the human conflict the growth of modernism in our culture represents. I have attempted to sketch, briefly, the outlines of that conflict, in particular as it is represented by the lives of two of its most famous and most painfully intense figures.

In discussing the attempts of modern artists to produce their works, William Graham Cole offers the following description of modernists:

> Many modern artists have portrayed the predicament of twentieth-century man with jarring expressiveness. . . . In [all the arts], the creative mind has found the old forms hollow and mute. They no longer communicate; they have ceased to contain or convey. The search for new media, new symbols, new techniques is everywhere painfully apparent. . . . Those who peer at the present age, penetrate its mask and probe into . . . themselves no less than [into] the world outside . . . : for [modern artists] there was a chaotic breakdown of all traditional forms of communication. Impressionism, Expressionism, Fauvism, Cubism, Surealism [*sic*], Dadaism are all late nineteenth-century and twentieth-century efforts to understand and to express what is happening to modern man and his world, they are exercises in the attempt to bring order out of disorder, to manage the unmanageable, to express the ineffable.

Cole's remarks can be used to comment almost as well on the motivations and actions of Loisy and Tyrrell. It is his reference to the "painfully apparent" search of the artists for the means to voice their sense of the breakdown of meaning that is particularly apt in describing the religious quest of the two priests. It is, perhaps, the sense that the pain is no longer so acutely apparent in many works of writers and artists of more recent years that suggests the passing of the dominance of modernism. It is as though we have gotten used to a sore and are no longer quite so sharply conscious of its continued presence.

MODERNISM AND EARLIER MOVEMENTS

Gabriel Josipovici

SOURCE: "Modernism and Romanticism," in *The World and the Book: A Study of Modern Fiction,* Macmillan Press, 1979, pp. 179-99.

[*In the following excerpt, Josipovici studies the relationship between Modernism and the earlier artistic movement of Romanticism.*]

[The] years between 1885 and 1914 saw the birth of the modern movement in the arts. What are the specific features of that movement and how are we to account for its emergence?

Two points need to be made before we start. First of all we must be clear that in one sense our inquiry is absurd. There is no physical entity called 'modernism' which we can extract from the variety of individual works of art and hold up for inspection. Every modern artist of any worth has achieved what he has precisely because he has found his own individual voice and because this voice is distinct from those around him. Yet it cannot be denied that something *did* happen to art, to all the arts, some time around the turn of the century, and that Proust, Joyce, Picasso, Klee, Schoenberg and Stravinsky, for all their manifest differences, do have something in common.

The second point is more in the nature of a reminder of a historical fact which, if rightly interpreted, should serve as a guide and a warning throughout this investigation. Although the First World War effectively marks the break between the world of the nineteenth century and our own, both in the minds of those who lived through it and for those of us who only read about it in the history books, the modern revolution in the arts did not take place during the war, or immediately after it, as one might have expected, but a decade or so *before* it. This should make us wary of too facile an identification of art with the culture and the society out of which it springs.

The modern movement in the arts cannot be understood in isolation. It must be seen as a reaction to the decadent Romanticism which was prevalent in Europe at the turn of the century. Some of the apologists of modernism, such as T. E. Hulme, tried to argue that the movement was nothing other than a wholesale rejection of Romanticism and all that that stood for, and a return to a new classicism. Looking back at those pre-war decades from our vantage point in the mid-century, however, we can now see that the situation was a good deal more complex than Hulme suggests; that it was more a question of redefining Romanticism, of stressing some of those aspects of it which the nineteenth century had neglected and discarding some of those it had most strongly emphasised, rather than rejecting it outright. If we are to understand what the founders of modern art were doing it will be necessary to try and grasp the premises and implications of Romanticism itself.

Romanticism was first and foremost a movement of liberation—liberation from religious tradition, from political absolutism, from a hierarchical social system and from a universe conceived on the model of the exact sciences. Reason and scientific laws, the Romantics felt, might allow man to control his environment, but they formed a sieve through which the living breathing individual slipped, leaving behind only the dead matter of generality. What man had in common with other men, what this landscape had in common with other landscapes, was the least important thing about them. What was important was the uniqueness of men and the uniqueness of each object in the world around us, be it a leaf, a sparrow or a mountain range. There were moments, they felt, when man is far from the distractions of the city and of society, and when the reasoning, conceptualising mind is still, when life seems suddenly to reveal itself in all its mystery and terror. In such moments man felt himself restored to his true self, able to grasp the meaning of life and of his own existence. It is to experience and express such moments, both in our lives and in our art, that we should perpetually strive, for these are the moments when we throw off the shackles of generality and are restored to our unique selves.

The function of art thus becomes that of exploring those areas of the mind and of the universe which lie beyond the confines of rational thought and of ordinary consciousness, and the hero of Romantic art becomes none other than the artist himself, who is both the explorer of this unknown realm and the priestly mediator between it and his audience. Something of this is suggested by August Wilhelm Schlegel, who was probably responsible for the introduction of the word 'Romantic' as a description of the age, when, in his lectures on dramatic art and literature of 1808-9, he made the following comparison:

> Ancient poetry and art is a rhythmical *nomos,* a harmonious promulgation of the eternal legislation of a beautifully ordered world mirroring the eternal Ideas of things. Romantic poetry, on the other hand, is the expression of a secret longing for the chaos . . . which lies hidden in the very womb of orderly creation. . . . [Greek art] is simpler, cleaner, more like nature in the independent perfection of its separate works; [Romantic art], in spite of its fragmentary appearance, is nearer to the mystery of the universe.

Schlegel, it is true, is not here talking only of the nineteenth century; he is contrasting the whole 'modern' or Christian era with the classical age of Greece and Rome. But his stress on the transcending impulse of Romanticism, on the aspiration towards the mystery of the universe, is taken up by Baudelaire several decades later when, in a discussion of the 'Salon' of 1846, he writes: 'Romanticism means modern art—that is to say, intimateness, spirituality, colour, aspiration towards the infinite, expressed by every means known to art.' And yet already here a curious contradiction begins to emerge, a contradiction which lies at the heart of the whole Romantic endeavour, and whose nature was to determine its future course. Two quotations, the first from Rousseau and the second from Schleiermacher, will bring it out into the open. In his *Rêveries du promeneur solitaire* Rousseau tells how he came to after a minor accident to find himself lying in the middle of the countryside:

> Night was falling. I perceived the sky, a few stars, and a little verdure. This first sensation was a wonderful moment; I could still only feel myself through it. In that instant I was born to life, and it seemed to me that I filled with my frail existence all the objects I perceived. Entirely within the present, I remembered nothing; I had no distinct notion of my individuality, not the least idea of what had just happened to me; I knew neither who nor where I was: I felt neither hurt, nor fear, nor anxiety.

And Schleiermacher, in his *Speeches on Religion:*

> I am lying in the bosom of the infinite universe, I am at this moment its soul, because I feel all its force and its infinite life as my own. It is at this moment my own body, because I penetrate all its limbs as if they were my own, and its innermost nerves move like my own. . . . Try out of love for the universe to give up your own life. Strive already here to destroy your own individuality and to live in the One and in the All . . . fused with the Universe. . . .

Romanticism had begun as a movement of rebellion against the arbitrary authorities of the eighteenth century and its abstract laws, a rebellion undertaken in the name of the freedom of the individual. But this freedom, which of course involves the suppression of the tyrannical intellect, in fact turns out to be synonymous with the loss of individuality. 'In that instant I was born to life', writes Rousseau. The world around him soaks into his body, he becomes one with it and in so doing gains a sense of his own uniqueness, while Schleiermacher too feels the universe as if it were his own body. But this feeling is also one of the loss of self—'I did not know who I was', 'Strive already here to destroy your own individuality . . .'. The paradox is there: the ultimate freedom, according to the Romantic logic, can only be death.

Where consciousness itself is felt to be an imprisoning factor, keeping man from his true self, freedom must lie in the transcending of consciousness. Yet the only time we escape from it for more than a brief moment is in sleep, or under the influence of alcohol or drugs, or else in madness. And the only total escape is death. Hence the key place accorded by Romanticism to dreams, to various forms of addiction, to madness, and to the death-wish. And in all these cases the result is, of course, ambiguous. The freedom from consciousness and from the bonds of society may result in deeper insight, but it results also in rendering the individual more vulnerable, more prone to destruction from outside as well as from within. Hence the general tone of Romantic art and literature is one of melancholy gloom, for there seems to be no way of resolving the paradox.

This tension between freedom and annihilation is even easier to discern in the forms of art than in its contents. The task of the poet, as the Romantics saw it, was to communicate those moments of visionary intensity which he experienced, moments in which the meaning and value of life seemed to emerge. But the poet's only means of expression is language, and language belongs by definition to the realm of consciousness and social intercourse. For language, as Plato had already noted, only exists at a certain degree of abstraction and universality; it takes for granted that there is some sort of social agreement among the users of a language. But if you feel that what is important is the uniqueness of this tree or that man or this experience—then how are words going to help you to convey this uniqueness? This of course has always been one of the problems of art, but with the Romantics it comes right into the foreground of their consciousness. The Romantic poet finds himself struggling to express by means of language precisely that which it lies beyond the power of language to express. He becomes a man desperately striving to escape from his own shadow.

Only one poet in the nineteenth century was fully aware of the implications of the Romantic endeavour and was also prepared to accept and overcome them. In Rimbaud's famous letter to Paul Demeny of 15 May 1871 we can see that he had fully understood the problem and had decided on a radical solution:

> Thus the poet is truly a stealer of fire.
>
> He is the spokesman of humanity, even of the animals; he will have to make men feel, touch, hear his creations. If what he brings back from *down there* has form, he will bring forth form; if it is formless, he will bring forth formlessness. A language has to be found—for that matter, every word being an idea, the time of the universal language will come! One has to be an academician—deader than a fossil—to compile a dictionary in any language. Weak-minded men, starting by *thinking about* the first letter of the alphabet, would soon be overtaken by madness!
>
> This [new] language will be of the soul, for the soul, summing up everything, smells, sounds, colours; thought latching on to thought and pulling. The poet would define the quantity of the unknown awakening in the universal soul in his time: he would produce more than the formulation of his thought, the measurement *of his march towards Progress!* An enormity who has become normal, absorbed by everyone, he would really be *a multiplier of progress!*

The failure of this ideal can be traced through the poems themselves, and it forms the explicit subject-matter of *Une Saison en enfer.* And, indeed, how could Rimbaud succeed? What he desires is not communication but communion, the direct and total contact of one person with another through a language so charged that it will act without needing to pass by way of the interpreting mind at all; in other words, a language that is not conventional but natural. But, as we have seen, such a wish can never be more than a Utopian dream, since to give words the meanings I want them to have regardless of their dictionary definitions is tantamount to abolishing language altogether. When Rimbaud recognised this, with admirable logic he gave up writing altogether.

But just because he was so ready to push the premises of Romanticism to their ultimate conclusion, Rimbaud remains one of the key figures of the nineteenth century, marking forever one of the two poles within which modern art is to move. His contemporaries, both in England and in France (Mallarmé excepted), chose a somewhat less arduous and therefore less interesting path. They tried to solve the problem by making their verse approximate as closely as possible to their conception of music, since music seemed to them to be the ideal artistic language, with none of the disadvantages of speech. To this end they made their verse as mellifluous as possible, stressing its incantatory qualities, smoothing out all harshness of diction, minimising its referential content, and rigidly excluding all forms of wit and humour for fear these would break their fragile spell. The result was aptly described by Eliot in his essay on Swinburne:

> Language in a healthy state presents the object, is so close to the object that the two are identified. They are identified in the verse of Swinburne solely because the object has ceased to exist, because the meaning is merely the hallucination of meaning, because language, uprooted, has adapted itself to an independent life of atmospheric nourishment.

As with Rimbaud, the normal function of language is denied and words take on an independent meaning. But here the meaning is not just independent of general usage, it is no longer under the poet's control at all. The result is not revelation but empty cliché, not the articulation of what lies beyond the confines of consciousness and rationality but simple reflex, the verbal equivalent of the canine dribble:

> Before the beginning of years
>   There came to the making of man
> Time with a gift of tears;
>   Grief with a glass that ran. . . .

Or:

> O Prêtresse élevant sous le laurier verdâtre
> Une eau d'antique pleurs dans le creux de tes
>   mains,
> Tes yeux sacrés feront resplendir mes chemins,
> Tes mains couronneront de cedre un jeune
>   prêtre. . . .

For language, as we have seen, has a way of getting its own back on those who try to step over it in this manner.

Just as the Romantic dreamer found that he escaped from the bonds of the intellect only at the cost of his sanity or his life, so the Romantic poet, trying to escape from the bonds of language, found himself its prisoner, uttering platitudes in the voice of a prophet.

But if the poets dreamt of living in a world freed from the stifling restrictions of language, and looked with envy at the composers, these, had the poets but known it, were in the same plight as themselves. For if language is not natural, if, that is, words are not inherently expressive, as Rimbaud had imagined, then the same is true of the language of music. Although E. T. A. Hoffmann wrote enthusiastically about the inherent qualities of the chord of A flat minor, the truth of the matter is that music is nearly as conventional a form of expression as speech. We find it difficult to grasp music which is distant from us in space or time (Indian or Japanese music, or Gregorian chant, for instance), to know when it is being 'cheerful', when 'sad'. Musical instruments too have different and highly specialised functions in other societies, and so are associated with different things; it is only through frequent hearings, through a familiarisation with its language that we can come to appreciate Indian music or the music of Bali. The composer, no less than the poet, works in a language which is largely the product of convention, and according to rules to which he voluntarily submits in order to create a meaningful work. Thus, when the initial heroic impetus of Romanticism starts to peter out, we find a development in music parallel to that which we traced in poetry: a slackening of formal control, a loosening of harmonic texture, and the emergence of a soulful, cliché-ridden style which strives to lull the listener into a state of trance while the music struggles to express the world of the infinite which Baudelaire had urged the artist to seek with every means at his disposal. Naturally enough the piano, instrument of the half-echo, the suggestive, the indefinite, becomes the favourite of composer and public alike. And in music, as in poetry, the attempt to express *everything,* the totality of experience, unfettered by the rules and limitations of conventions and consciousness, leads to self-destruction. More than any of the other arts, Romantic music is imbued with the melancholy which stems from the knowledge that to achieve its goal is to expire.

Wagner's operas, as all his contemporaries realised, form the apotheosis of Romantic art. These vast music-dramas seemed to them to be the perfect answer to Baudelaire's plea for a work of art that would make use of all the resources of all the arts, lifting the spectator into the realm of the infinite, into the very heart of the mystery of the universe. We are fortunate in possessing a critique of Wagner by one of the few men who really understood the implications of Romanticism because he was so much of a Romantic himself—Friedrich Nietzsche. Nietzsche's analysis of the 'decadent' style sums up many of the points we have already noted:

> What is common to both Wagner and 'the others' consists in this: the decline of all organising power;

the abuse of traditional means, without the capacity or the aim that would justify this. The counterfeit imitation of grand forms . . . excessive vitality in small details; passion at all costs; refinement as an expression of impoverished life, ever more nerves in the place of muscle.

This is extraordinarily perceptive. Nietzsche has put his finger on one of the main characteristics of expressionism: the richness of sensual detail, of the feel of things, allied to the poverty of overall form. And how could it be otherwise, once the dichotomy expressed by Thomas Hooker is accepted? We are left with either meaningless sensation (the traveller) or knowledge devoid of feeling (the historian, map-maker). Thus it becomes easy to trace even a historical connection between Luther, the Puritans, the German Romantics, the German expressionists, and a film-maker like Bergman. This has little to do with innate German or northern characteristics or geography and a great deal to do with cultural tradition.

But Nietzsche is not content with a simple catalogue of Wagner's characteristics; he wants to understand what lies behind them and to try and account for Wagner's enormous popularity. He sees first of all that for Wagner music is only a means to an end: 'As a matter of fact, his whole life long, he did nothing but repeat one proposition: that his music did not mean music alone! But something more! Something immeasurably more! . . . *"Not music alone"—no* musician would speak in this way.' And he explains what this 'more' is: 'Wagner pondered over nothing so deeply as over salvation: his opera is the opera of salvation.' And this, thinks Nietzsche, is the source of Wagner's power and popularity: what he offered was nothing less than the hope of personal salvation to a Europe—and especially a Germany—bewildered by the rapid social and technological changes of the previous half-century. 'How intimately related must Wagner be to the entire decadence of Europe for her not to have felt that he was decadent,' he writes in the same essay. And again: 'People actually kiss that which plunges them more quickly into the abyss.' We remember that Schlegel had already talked about a 'secret longing for the chaos . . . which lies hidden in the very womb of orderly creation', and that this longing was nothing other than the Romantic desire for an absolute freedom. Nietzsche's suggestion that with Wagner this longing spills out of the realm of art into that of politics allows us to glimpse the connection between decadent Romanticism and mass hysteria. The cataclysmic events of the first half of the present century would have occasioned him little surprise.

What Nietzsche particularly objects to in Wagner is precisely the fact that by trying to turn his music into a religion he debases both music and religion; by trying to turn the entire world into a music-drama, drawing the audience up into the music until they shed their dull everyday lives and enter the heart of the mystery, he dangerously distorts both the life of everyday and the true nature of art. By blurring the outlines between life and art he turns art into a tool and life into an aesthetic phenom-

enon—that is, into something which is to be judged entirely by aesthetic criteria and where the rules of morality therefore no longer apply.

Only one other thinker in the nineteenth century had seen as clearly as Nietzsche where the assumptions of Romanticism were leading, and that was Kierkegaard. In *Either/Or*, written in 1843, he set out to analyse what he calls the aesthetic attitude to life, and from then on the category of the aesthetic or the 'interesting' occupied a key place in his writing. He noted that the point about a work of art is that we are not in any way committed to it. We can pick up a book and put it down again, turn from one picture to another in a gallery. We are surrounded by a growing number of works of art and we can move among them at will, sampling here or there according to our whim. Art makes no claims on us, and surely an attitude of disinterested contemplation is the correct one when we face a work of art. It so happens, however, that people carry this attitude over into their lives. A man will take up with one woman, for instance, because she 'interests' him, and when she begins to bore him he will turn to another. The philanderer, Don Juan, is the archetype of the aesthetic attitude to life, an attitude which depends on a complete surrender to the moment, the immediate, the sensual, and which for that reason is wholly amoral. That is why music is the most perfect medium for the aesthetic mode, and why, Kierkegaard argues, Mozart's *Don Giovanni* is the greatest work in that mode. But when we transfer this attitude from art to life its immediate implication is that no choices are binding. The person who lives in the category of the aesthetic never thinks in terms of 'either/or', but always of 'and/and'. Yet life, Kierkegaard argues, does not consist of a series of aesthetic moments. Choices are essential in life, and a genuine choice implies a genuine renunciation. That man is a creature who must make choices is evinced by his awareness of *time*. The aesthetic category does not know the meaning of time, but man is a creature of time, as can be seen from the fact that no absolute repetition is possible in life although it is perfectly possible in art. Repetition in life always implies change and difference, and so always forces us to recognise the fact that we do not exist in the category of the aesthetic.

The extension of the term 'aesthetic' to imply an attitude to life as well as to works of art allows Kierkegaard to show how much the European bourgeoisie of the nineteenth century had in common with the Romantic artists, just as Nietzsche had noted the close links between Wagner's art and the mentality of his patrons. But Kierkegaard was able to extend his insight into a critique of the prevalent philosophy of the time, Hegelianism. For Hegel, as he saw, was the supreme philosopher of aestheticism. He it was who had undertaken to show that all history should be contemplated as a work of art, the product of one great Mind, moving inevitably forward towards the completion of its pattern. But this view of history, though tempting, is also subtly distorting, as Kierkegaard noted. Luther or Cromwell or Napoleon, when confronted with a choice between one action and another, did not have the benefit of Hegel's vision of the totality of history to guide them. For them the future was open, their choice fraught with consequences they could not foretell. It is only by virtue of hindsight that a pattern emerges, and each of us lives life forwards rather than backwards. Hegel sees history as akin to the plot of some great novel, sees it, in fact, as an aesthetic object, to be contemplated and understood; whereas in fact history—and our own life—can almost be defined by the fact that it is *not* a book.

Kierkegaard's attacks on Hegel and on the 'aestheticism' of the society in which he lived were of course made in the name of his own particular brand of Christianity. But he felt that it was essential that he make them, if only to reveal to his readers the impossibility of his task. For how is he to convey the difference between life lived according to the religious or the ethical category and life lived according to the aesthetic category, when all he has at his command is his pen, an instrument good only for the creation of aesthetic objects? How can he bring home to each reader the uniqueness of his life and the irreversibility of his choices through the generalising medium of language and of philosophical discourse? The answer is of course that he can't, except by the roundabout way of drawing the reader's attention to the problem in the first place. That is why reading Kierkegaard and Nietzsche is such an uncomfortable activity, for they introduce us not to some foreign realm of experience, but to ourselves.

Kierkegaard's problems, and some of his solutions, are the problems and solutions of modernism. For even as Wagnerism swept through Europe and Nietzsche sank into his final madness, the reaction to Romantic decadence had begun. This did not take the form of a movement in the sense that, say, surrealism, was a movement, with polemical manifestos and self-appointed leaders and spokesmen; it was not even a movement of men who thought alike on such general topics as human freedom and the role of the artist in society, as Romanticism had been in its early stages. Proust and Joyce met once and did not take to each other; Schoenberg loathed Stravinsky; Eliot was more interested in Donne than in Mallarmé or Mann; Kafka ignored and was ignored by all the rest. Yet it is easy for us today to see that all these men were united by one common attitude, albeit a negative one: they all insisted on the *limitations* of art. More than that, they all stressed, in their art itself, that what they were creating were artifacts and not to be confused with life: that painting was first of all a series of brushstrokes on a flat canvas; music certain notes played by certain combinations of instruments; poetry the grouping of words on a page.

The Romantics had regarded art as simply a means to a transcendental end, and they therefore tended to see all art as more or less interchangeable—it didn't matter what train you caught since they all arrived at the same destination. The insistence on the part of the moderns that their work was art and not something else, their stress on the particular *medium* in which they were working, was

not meant to be a denial of the importance of art. On the contrary, it was a reassertion of art's vital function. Art, they argued, was not a means of piercing the sensible veil of the universe, of getting at the 'unknown', as Rimbaud and others had claimed, for there was nothing *beyond* the world we see all around us. The whole mystery is there, in front of our eyes—only most of us are too blind or lazy to see it. What most of us tend to do in the face of the world, of ourselves, of works of art even, is to neutralise what is there in front of us by referring it to something we already know. Thus we are forever shut up inside our preconceived ideas, reacting only to that which makes no demands on us to see. As Giacometti wittily remarked:

> Where do we find the greatest number of people? In front of the *Sacre de Napoléon*. Why do people look in particular at this painting? Because they imagine themselves to be present at the scene, participating in it. They become 'little Napoleons.' At the same time the spectacle becomes the equivalent of the reading of a novel.

In other words, it becomes an excuse for daydreaming. The modern artist, on the other hand, holds that the work of art is meaningful precisely because it reveals to us the 'otherness' of the world—it shocks us out of our natural sloth and the force of habit, and makes us see for the first time what we had looked at a hundred times but never seen. Art is not the key to the universe, as the Romantics had believed; it is merely a pair of spectacles. Valéry, echoing Proust's Elstir, points out:

> In general we guess or anticipate more than we see, and the impressions that strike the eye are signs for us rather than *singular presences,* prior to all the patterns, the short cuts, the immediate substitutions, which a primary education has instilled in us.

> Just as the thinker tries to defend himself against *words* and those ready-made expressions which protect people against any feeling of shock and thus make possible everyday practical activities, so the artist may, through the study of objects with a unique form [a lump of coal which is like no other, a handkerchief thrown anyhow onto a table, and so on], try to rediscover his own uniqueness.

Art, then, does not feed us information and it does not provide us with a passport to some higher realm of existence. What it does is to open our eyes by removing the film of habit which we normally carry around with us. The work of art does this by shocking us into awareness through its insistence on itself as an object in its own right, an irreducible *singular presence*. The cubist picture, for instance, teases the eye as we follow shape after shape on the canvas, always on the verge of understanding it, yet never quite allowed to do so. For understanding would mean fitting the picture into our preconceived world, in other words denying its uniqueness. And because we cannot step back and say: 'Ah yes, a mandolin, a glass of wine, a table . . .', we go on looking at the canvas and in time learn to accept its own reality instead of reducing it to our unthinking notion of what a mandolin or a glass of wine looks like. Thus Braque can say: 'The painting is finished when the idea has disappeared', and Valéry, elsewhere in the essay on Degas: 'To look means to forget the names of the things one is seeing.' Proust's whole novel, of course, can be seen as the attempt to substitute the object for the name, to render the uniqueness of existence by relentlessly destroying all the names by which we explain it to ourselves.

An art of this kind makes the spectator work. It does not, like Wagnerian opera, claim to hand him the key to salvation, or, like the 'Sacre de Napoléon', allow him simply to indulge his day-dreams. What it claims to do is to *recreate* within the willing listener or spectator the liberating experience of the artist himself as he makes the object. When Picasso said of his famous sculpture of the bull's head made out of the seat and handlebars of a bicycle that the whole point would be lost if the viewer, through excessive familiarity with it, were to see *only* a bull's head, he neatly illustrated this aspect of modern art. What is important is not the finished product, but the process. Picasso wants us to be aware of the fact that what is in front of us is not a bull's head but a man-made object. The product is not there to be contemplated for its own sake but to make the viewer re-enact the creative discovery for himself. What is important is to see the bull's head in the handlebars, and handlebars in every bull's head. It is the play of wit which turns a universe we had taken for granted into a source of infinite possibilities, and therefore wakes us up to the miraculous nature of everything that *is*. The object—the head/handlebars—is necessary, for wit is always the result of the transformation of what is given, never the creation of something totally new; but Picasso is not interested in bicycles or bulls as such, he does not want us to say: 'Now I understand what a bull is really like,' but, if anything: 'Now I understand that a bull is.' We must not rest with the object, but with the object-as-created-by-wit. In much the same way *A la Recherche du temps perdu* does not so much tell *a* story as create within the reader the possibility of telling the story Marcel is about to set down as the work ends. In this way the artist's acceptance of limitation, his open acknowledgment of the medium in which he is working, leads to the creation of an art that strikes more directly at the life of the reader or viewer than any art since the Middle Ages.

The modern revolution in the arts was a reaction to decadent Romanticism, but this reaction, we can now see, entailed a break with four centuries of the Western artistic tradition. Shifts in taste and in the forms of expression had of course occurred at regular intervals throughout these four centuries, but they were adjustments and alterations of emphasis within a fixed framework. Romanticism, by trying to give full and unfettered expression to the individual, burst this framework and so made it possible for the moderns to step out of the wreckage and discover that the frame only enclosed a small fraction of the universe. Or perhaps a more accurate way of describing the change would be to say that what the artists of the previous four centuries had taken for *the* universe was now seen to be nothing else than the universe as seen through the spectacles of Renaissance norms. It is not by chance that the birth of the modern coincides with the discovery or rediscovery of Japanese graphics, Balinese music, African sculpture, Romanesque painting and the poetry of the troubadours. This is not simply a widening of the cultural horizons; it is the discovery of the *relativity* of artistic norms. Perspective and harmony, far from being a datum of experience, are suddenly seen to be as much the product of convention as the sonnet form, though, unlike the latter, they were clearly the product of certain metaphysical assumptions which began to emerge in the West in the years between 1350 and 1700.

All art, since the Renaissance, had been based on the twin concepts of expression and imitation. In some of the previous chapters I tried to suggest why the two should always go hand in hand and why they should have emerged as the primary criteria of art at a time when medieval notions of analogy were no longer acceptable. The Romantics, by stressing expression at the expense of imitation, helped to bring the hidden assumptions of both out into the open. Baudelaire, writing about the 'Salon' of 1846, quotes at some length from Hoffmann's *Kreisleriana*. The passage is central not only to Baudelaire's own aesthetic, but to that of Romanticism in general:

> It is not only in dreams, or in that mild delirium which precedes sleep, but it is even awakened when I hear music—that perception of an analogy and an intimate connexion between colours, sounds and perfumes. It seems to me that all these things were created by one and the same ray of light, and that their combination must result in a wonderful concert of harmony. The smell of red and brown marigolds above all produces a magical effect on my being. It makes me fall into a deep reverie, in which I seem to hear the solemn, deep tones of the oboe in the distance.

The implicit belief behind this passage is that individual sights, sounds, smells and tastes touch each one of us in the same way and are themselves interchangeable. There is an analogy here, but it is not between two sets of events, two orders of reality, but between the different senses. And this correspondence can find an echo in each one of us because the senses speak a natural language. The poet has simply to reach down into himself and express what he feels and it will immediately enter the soul of the reader. We have seen how this mistaken view of the poetic process led to the breakdown of art into a series of utterances so private that they no longer made sense, or turned into the banal expression not of vision but of cliché. This failure made it clear to the moderns that art is not the expression of inner feeling but the creation of a structure that will allow us to understand what it means to perceive, and will thus, in a sense, give us back the world. Already at the start of the Romantic movement, as though to spite the historian of ideas with his clear notions of historical change and development, Lichtenberg had written: 'To see something new we must make something new.' And this explains the insistence on the part of the moderns on the impersonality of the poet, that distinction between the man and the artist which forms the basis of the work of Proust, Valéry, Rilke and Eliot. For the artist, *qua* man, is no different from other men; the only difference lies in the fact that he is a craftsman, a man who makes objects which will refract reality in a way the tired eyes of habit never do. Thus St. Beuve's biographical method is not only useless as a critical tool, but misleading, since the artist has, if anything, a less interesting life than other men, since so much of it is given up to the making of artifacts. Robbe-Grillet expresses the extreme position with wit and elegance: 'The artist is a man with nothing to say.'

The Romantic artist claimed in some way to be a magician. Words and sounds, he implied, hid within themselves certain magical properties over which he alone had power. Through this power he could confer salvation on the rest of mankind; the reader or listener (I am thinking of Rimbaud and Wagner, different though they are in so many respects) had simply to submit to the words or sounds in order to shed the pains and frustrations of his daily life and to emerge into a free world where there was no conflict between desire and fulfilment, imagination and reality. The consequences of this view were quickly seen by Nietzsche, and the modern reaction to this notion of art as magic was to stress the idea of art as game. The work of art, said the moderns, does not offer permanent salvation to anyone. Its function is to increase the reader's powers of imagination, to make him see the world again cleansed of its stiff and stubborn man-locked set. This requires active participation rather than passive submission, and a willingness to play according to the rules laid down by the artist. At the same time the modern rediscovery of the hieratic and stylised arts of other periods went hand in hand with the rehabilitation of forms of art which had not been considered serious enough to form part of the mainstream of post-Renaissance art in Europe: the puppet play, the shadow-play, children's games, street games and ballads were all used by Jarry, Stravinsky, Picasso and Eliot, and all helped them to forge their own individual styles. In these archaic and popular forms of art there is no pretence at illusion. Art is a game and its creation involves making something that will be of pleasure to others.

This is a very different view of art from that held by the Romantics. But it is not perhaps all that far removed from art as it was known from the time of Homer down to the Renaissance. The acceptance by artist and audience of the rules of genre and rhetoric shows that there was always an implicit awareness of the fact that for art to be true it must not pretend to be other than it is, a made thing, an object put together according to the rules of tradition and convention in order to satisfy. It is in fact only with the painting and the fiction which emerged from the Renaissance revolution in thought that the extraordinary belief grew up that art could do without rules altogether, that it could simply imitate external reality and tell the whole truth starting not from axioms but from observable facts.

But we have seen that the imitation of the external world, however detailed, does not really answer the questions: Why this bit of the world rather than that? Why should the artist paint *this* subject, include *this* detail, why should the novelist tell *this* story, recount *this* incident? Is it enough to say: Because he feels like it? Will he feel like it tomorrow? If there is no answer to these questions then the freedom of the artist to do what he likes is a meaningless freedom. The hero of Kafka's last novel, standing in the snow outside the inn, recognises the force of this paradox only too well:

> It seemed to K. as if at last those people had broken off all relations with him, and as if now in reality he were freer than he had ever been, and at liberty to wait here in this place usually forbidden to him as long as he desired, and had won a freedom such as hardly anybody else had ever succeeded in winning, and as if nobody would dare to touch him or drive him away, or even speak to him; but—this conviction was at least equally strong—as if at the same time there was nothing more senseless, nothing more hopeless, than this freedom, this waiting, this inviolability.

The problem had already haunted the Romantics and we find it everywhere in their poetry. But so long as they held to an expressive theory of art they could never resolve it. We see them trying to blur the outlines of their fictions, their music, their painting, until the artifact almost merges with the surrounding world—but of course it never does completely or it would cease to be an artifact, and until it does so they are bound to remain unsatisfied. In music they try to slow down the forward thrust of their art so that it ceases to unfold in time according to the premises laid down at the start and spreads instead like a sluggish river in marshy country. This is particularly evident in the work of Bruckner and Mahler, but again, it is not till the entire nature of the medium is reconsidered that they can escape the inner contradictions of their art. Schönberg undertakes such a reconsideration, introducing a new, non-linear principle of composition to replace the subjective and time-bound principles of the sonata form, and in Webern we find the tradition reaching its logical conclusion, since in a three-minute work he can present us with the means of generating a hundred Mahler symphonies (just as a five-page work by Borges is capable of generating a hundred three-decker novels). In painting the decisive break comes with Cézanne, and his phrase 'Je pars neutre' is the key to this aspect of modernism. What he means by this is that in his painting he wishes to eliminate the personal slant in the choice of both subject-matter and treatment, and to seek instead to discover the general laws of light and space present in the scene before him—as in every other. Thus it is not so much that the artist refines himself out of existence as that he tries to establish the laws of perception and of the process of art itself. In a similar way Wittgenstein was to argue that he wished to develop not a new *area* of philosophical inquiry, but an investigation of the nature of that inquiry. This has led to the charge that his work is concerned with trivialities, since it is not concerned with 'life', a charge familiar enough to the ears of modern artists who are accused of wilfully shutting their eyes to the world by writing books on the writing of books and painting pictures whose subject-matter is the painting of pictures. Proust, whose design is similar to Cézanne's, comes back to this point again and again in *Le Temps Retrouvé:* he is not interested in imitating a flat reality, in writing one more book which tells one more story; what he wants to do is to draw out the laws inherent in love, in speech, in perception, in art. And, thinking perhaps of a Cézanne, and comparing it to one of those society portraits so popular at the time, he writes:

> If, in the realm of painting, one portrait makes manifest certain truths concerning volume, light, movement, does that mean that it is necessarily inferior to another completely different portrait of the same person, in which a thousand details omitted in the first are minutely transcribed, from which second portrait one would conclude that the model was ravishingly beautiful while from the first one would have thought him or her ugly, a fact which may be of documentary, even of historical importance, but is not necessarily an artistic truth?

It might be thought that such an art, an art of total potentiality, of laws rather than subject-matter, would result in a dry abstraction. Many modern works certainly display this characteristic, though different people would have different works in mind as they made that statement. There is of course no legislation for art or for criticism, and membership of a school, whether it be Imagist or Nouveau Roman, does not confer automatic value. We are not really concerned with the countless imitations of the great modern masters, imitations no better or worse than those of the great classics. What is important is that such an art need be neither solemn nor cold. On the contrary, there has never been an art more joyous, or one that brings joy back to our response to older art, than that of Stravinsky, Picasso and Eliot. For the interest of these artists in the tradition is of course bound up with their search for laws rather than new subject-matter. Stravinsky has called *Pulcinella* 'the epiphany through which the whole of my late work became possible. It was a backward look, of course—the first of many love affairs in that direction—but it was a look in the mirror, too.' Such a love affair was Picasso's with Velasquez when, by producing dozens of imitations of 'Las Meninas', he made us see that picture anew by revealing the necessity of its particular being. Had 'Las Meninas' not been reworked by him we would have taken it for granted and thus in a sense failed to see it. By showing us all the things it *might* have been Picasso as it were freed it from the realm of the 'given' and revealed to us how all its elements were both chosen *and* necessary. And in a precisely similar way the greatest modern art, concentrating as it does on laws rather than on subject-matter, para-

doxically gives us back the world we had lost through force of habit. Picasso, in conversation with his friend the photographer George Brassai, sums up the spirit of modernism as I have tried to sketch it in this chapter:

> I always aim at the resemblance. An artist should observe nature but never confuse it with painting. It is only translatable into painting by signs. . . . But such signs are not invented. To arrive at the sign you have to concentrate hard on the resemblance. To me surreality is nothing and never has been anything but this profound resemblance, something deeper than the forms and colours in which objects present themselves.

J. Edward Chamberlain

SOURCE: "From High Decadence to High Modernism," in *Queen's Quarterly,* Vol. 87, No. 4, Winter, 1980, pp. 591-610.

[*In the following essay, Chamberlain links Modernism to the late nineteenth-century Decadent movement.*]

"Sympathy with suffering," suggested Oscar Wilde, "is the joy of one leper meeting another leper on the road." Misery likes company; but as well as company decadence needs an audience. Indeed, the one thing which the celebrated decadents of the nineteenth century needed more than their absinthe, their indolence or their sometimes picturesque debauchery was a large middle class to be offended, a phalanx of bourgeois outrage. "To bewilder the middle class" might be, as Arthur Symons suggested, itself a thinly disguised middle-class occupation; but it was, as well, an appealing obligation for those who thrived on the deliciously self-righteous pleasures it afforded.

Wilde, more than anyone of his age, advertised the conspicuous consumption of decadent pleasures. He did not walk down a country lane with a lily in his hand, but down Picadilly, where he would be seen; and he wore his notorious green carnations in the buttonholes of his morning coat or his evening jacket, not of his dressing gown—unless, of course, he might be wearing a dressing gown to the theater. He set as one of his early ambitions to live up to the beauty of his blue and white china, but he certainly intended to do so in public. In more general terms, for which Wilde also provided a glossary, the virtues of clarity and openness were transformed by decadent instincts into the habits of confession and display.

Of course, decadence meant other things than floral decoration and fine porcelain. It meant a precious over-refinement in all things, an obsessive concentration on apparently useless detail, a preferring of the hot-house to the open air; it meant a cavalier refusal to take the broad and balanced view, and a corresponding susceptibility to a dog's breakfast of neuroses; it meant a nervous fascination with the forms of decay, a morbid interest in disease and death, a quixotic celebration of the unnatural and the artificial, a deliberate dalliance with the perverse. But most of all, decadence meant a flaunting of the conditions under which art and life become confused. Thus, ease or leisure, the *otium* that Virgil associated with the achievement of art, is transformed into the companion of life—into easeful death, idle tears, or foolish indolence, Baudelaire's "luxe, calme et volupté." Or the artistic instinct to embellish and decorate is transposed into an emphasis on style instead of substance, a cherishing of the human importance of display. The tactful notion that what is on the surface is not necessarily superficial was thereby taken to its extreme, and what is on the surface accepted as perhaps the only thing which is profound, or at the very least permanent. "One should so live that one becomes a form of fiction," Wilde advised. "To be a fact is to be a failure." To succeed in the way he hoped, it was necessary to extend the logic, and to celebrate the more general conditions under which the imagination competes with reality, or fancy with fact; the conditions under which form is detached from its function, and ethics dissociated from the appreciation of art. Writing of Thomas Chatterton, Wilde noted that "he did not have the moral conscience which is truth to fact [he was of course a forger, among other things] but had the artistic conscience which is truth to beauty." And Wilde would not let that paradox rest, insisting elsewhere that even in life "being natural is simply a pose, and one of the most irritating poses I know."

One of Wilde's provoking critical remarks, that Life imitates Art far more than Art imitates Life, gives witty form to this pattern of confusions.

> Where, if not from the Impressionists, do we get those wonderful brown fogs that come creeping down our street, blurring the gas-lamps and changing the houses into monstrous shadows? To whom, if not to them and their master, do we owe the lovely silver mists that brood over our river, and turn to faint forms of fading grace curved bridge and swaying barge? The extraordinary change that has taken place in the climate of London during the last ten years is entirely due to a particular school of Art . . . At present, people see fogs, not because there are fogs, but because poets and painters have taught them the mysterious loveliness of such effects. There may have been fogs for centuries in London. I dare say there were. But no one saw them, and so we do not know anything about them. They did not exist till Art had invented them. Now, it must be admitted, fogs are carried to excess. They have become the mere mannerism of a clique, and the exaggerated realism of their method gives dull people bronchitis. Where the cultured catch an effect, the uncultured catch cold.

The critical argument that Wilde is making, that all perception is informed by the imagination—that the perceiver intends the perceived—this needs the exaggerated flourish that he provides if it is to hit its mark. For its aim is not exactly logical assent. Though he is declaring that nature imitates art, Wilde is not advising us to look to the pages of the newest journal of the arts for the last words

on Arctic cold fronts or atmospheric inversions. Nor is he saying, as a scientist such as Darwin essentially did, that phenomena such as natural selection imitate, or at least are recognizable only following our familiarity with, such ingenious artifice as that practised by the selective domestic breeder. Instead, Wilde is after a conspiratorial complicity, a sense of brotherly blasphemy. We need to feel slightly wicked as we smile at Wilde's outrageous statement; for which feeling of course we need a sense of its outrageousness as well as of its truth. Wilde is much more anxious that we be initiated into a complex and subversive understanding than that we be convinced. We must know what it is to be silly before we can know what it is that we know. We must laugh with, or more precisely be serious with, Aubrey Beardsley, explaining that he caught a cold because he went out that morning and left the tassel off his cane. "One should spend one's days in saying what is incredible," Wilde advised, adding the less comfortable advice that we spend the evening doing the improbable.

But we pay the price for such silliness, for soon other people stop taking us seriously. So if we want to be taken seriously, we need to do more than amuse or bewilder, we need to give offence, to turn the screw, as it were, and be not only foolish but outrageous, and not only outrageous but perverse. Folly and vice are, the good people tell us, phases of a spiritual disease, something like (the same people tell us) marijuana and cocaine. Therefore, if we are concerned about the life of the spirit, as Wilde most certainly was; and if we are told that the self-satisfied mediocrity and pernicious puritanism that we see around us are manifestations of health, then we might well choose disease as the only salvation for our spirit, and follow its increasingly pathological or hysterical phases. Wilde's eccentric version of this logic was to assert that not goodness but sin is the essential element of progress.

One of the standard complaints about the literature and art of Wilde's generation was that it was "unhealthy," and the crowd feared that the disease might be contagious. As Dionysus moved from the country to the town, this was certainly a reasonable concern; and just as certainly, it was the hope of the afflicted. For if, like Wilde, we are instinctive evangelists, as so many in the nineteenth century seemed to be, then we want converts; and so we want our outrageousness to be taken seriously, we want the contagion to spread. There is nothing quite like adversity to strengthen our resolve to hold to our principles, which are by now outrageous only to the uninitiated, diseased only to those who have not succumbed. Panic afflicts only those who have not already embraced the goat god. Furthermore, a combination of ignorance and belligerence on the part of the uninitiated or the disdainful makes us feel positively chosen to take a stand. "The capacity of finding temptations is the test of the culture of one's nation," Wilde proposed. "The capacity of yielding to temptation is the test of the strength of one's character." So the continuum from the foolish to the vicious offered a natural recourse to those who felt called to match complacency with effrontery, propriety with abandon, realism with artifice—especially if they could show that reality was most truly apprehended by the imagination, that an ennobling decorum could only be achieved by setting aside inhibitions, and that a bold confrontation with the mundane held more promise than a bland acceptance of it. Decadence was the obligation of the independent-minded, the open-hearted and the free-spirited; and since, as Wilde insisted, it is much more difficult to talk about a thing than to do it—anybody can make history; it takes a great man to write it, he argued—most of Wilde's contemporaries chose the hard way, and talked and talked and talked about it. And they all, being quite genuinely silly, were confident that they knew what they were talking about. Some, such as Wilde, also knew that the game was anything but trivial. "Everything is a poison," he wrote. "But there are two kinds of poisons. There are the poisons that kill, and the poisons that keep alive. The last are the more terrible."

The decadence of the last decades of the nineteenth century clarified the conditions, and determined the limits, of the modernism of the first few decades of the twentieth. There was a sense of refined complicity about the literature and art of the period, a sense that they *knew,* or that *they* knew, what was going on; and that the conspiratorial nod, the furtive understanding, was all that was needed to carry the day. For the decadent artists, it was the secrecy of the secret that was crucial, the unexpressed and inexpressible agreement that it all mattered. They were like connoisseurs, assuming a shared sense that the wine cork needs to be sniffed. And they were up against those who liked to drink Cold Duck. With this connoisseurship went a certain egotistical detachment, and a corresponding inability to sympathize with different conditions. Dealings with others tended to be either conspiratorial or coercive; dealings with oneself tended to be relentlessly and paralyzingly candid. The possibilities of either engagement or transcendence became negligible, replaced by the high probability of "sterile introspection, infinite delay."

Nowhere was the issue joined more directly than in aesthetic matters. From the middle of the century, the idea had been about that art was an autonomous activity, independent of normal categories of experience (as well as of moral censure), and appealing to our aesthetic sense or sense of beauty alone. Théophile Gautier, who first elaborated this notion of art for art's sake, argued the case in his Preface to his novel *Mademoiselle de Maupin* (1835), itself variously called "the Bible of the decadence" (because of the perverse sexual confusions upon which its story depends) and "the holy writ of beauty" (because, following an Aristotelian logic, it inspired the soul (in Swinburne's words) to "burn as an altar-fire/To the unknown God of unachieved desire"). That this desire was profane rather than sacred merely added to its exquisite charm.

Gautier insisted that "there is nothing really beautiful save what is of no possible use. Everything useful is ugly, for it expresses a need, and man's needs are low and disgusting, like his own poor, wretched nature. The most useful place in a house is the water-closet." The next step might be to insist that anything even as useful (and as mundane) as a water closet can by the imagination be rendered useless, and be transformed into a work of art. This step was taken by Marcel Duchamp, who in 1917 submitted a urinal (entitled "Fountain") to the exhibition of the Society of Independent Artists in New York.

By the time Duchamp submitted his urinal, both painting and poetry had accepted the radical redefinition of the idea of beauty which had begun almost a century earlier. Cubism in its disintegrated manner eliminated the traditional aesthetic values attached to the subject matter of painting, and along with abstract art defined a new attitude to beauty which was not easily reconciled with either classical or romantic verities. In poetry, Ford Madox Ford was affirming that poetry must be as well written as prose, must be also objective, clear, factual, contemporaneous. On another tack, Wallace Stevens was writing poems preferring crows "anointing the statues with their dirt" to the more conventional (and incidentally Yeatsian) swans. Hart Crane was talking about "making a grail of laughter of an empty ash can," while T. S. Eliot rejected the heroic prettiness of some of his contemporaries for a description of twilight as a patient etherized upon a table. The notion of beauty, obviously, had undergone more than a sea change, and this change had been part and parcel of the decadent ambition to confront propriety on its own ground. The trouble was that, whereas in former times it could be assumed that only the few might appreciate true beauty, English and European romanticism (and American transcendentalism) created the illusion in many minds that theirs, too, was an appreciation capable of apprehending the beautiful. Indeed, the apostles of beauty (of which Wilde for a time was chief) who took up the Pre-Raphaelite banner in the 1870s and 1880s operated from this assumption, but it was never a very comfortable campaign. Like most apostles, they soon concentrated on who to keep out of their circle, rather than how to get in. Beauty was becoming popular, "decreed in the marketplace" (as Ezra Pound put it), and this clearly would not do. So the increasingly decadent custodians of the central beauty bank simply withdrew some of the supply, to combat such tedious inflation. Decadence, in ways, became simply the signature of a new elite. To pick up our earlier figure, as soon as everyone claimed to be sick, then one needed to redefine disease. Even the ostentatiously unorthodox beauty which found a form in the grotesque had become much too comfortably domestic to be accepted by the decadent camp, in part because of Ruskin's enthusiastic and moralistic celebration of the savage and the grotesque as central to the honest appeal of Gothic architecture, the embodiment of the true north strong and free.

Two things happened. First of all, beauty (and truth, its counterpart) became individual and relative, so that Wilde could say that "a truth ceases to be true when more than one person believes in it," and Walter Pater could emphasize that "in aesthetic criticism the first step toward seeing the object as it really is [which is what Matthew Arnold had defined as the function of criticism] is to know one's own impression as it really is, to discriminate it, to realize it distinctly"; and he also spoke of how "every one of those impressions is the impression of the individual in his isolation, each mind keeping as a solitary prisoner its own dream of a world." Second, the conventionally beautiful or even the ruggedly grotesque were rejected in favor not just of the idiosyncratic but of the dangerously fantastic and the sinister grotesque, which were the most obvious sources of wonder in an age that had been raised on Gothic melodrama and Byronic romance, and in which the highest praise was of the sort that Victor Hugo had for Baudelaire's *Les Fleurs du Mal,* that its author had "invented a new shudder."

Those who had a fondness for the old ways were not amused. Richard LeGallienne, a sometime friend, wrote of Wilde that "his face grew strangely sweet—As when a toad smiles. He dreamed of a new sin." Novelty as an instrument of revolt; sin as an element of progress. It was all nicely circular. Decadence, in short, appropriated the Johnsonian virtue of invention in art, often under the perennially dubious guise of novelty, but nonetheless with an emphasis on the demonstration of individuality that would become the modern hallmark of authenticity; as when F. R. Leavis took for one of the new bearings of English poetry "the need [for the poet] to communicate something of his own"—a new truth incorporated in a new beauty. "Make it new," announced Ezra Pound and William Carlos Williams to each other. Or in decadent terms, seek "new perfumes, larger flowers, untried pleasures" (in words from Gustave Flaubert's *La tentation de Saint Antoine* [1874], words which were intensely admired by Des Esseintes, the hero of J.-K. Huysmans' novel *A Rebours* [1884], the model for the book which "poisoned" the soul of Wilde's Dorian Gray).

The difficulty of achieving this new and decadent kind of beauty in art was no greater than achieving beauty in art had ever been, and just as much subject to superficiality, but it was to a much more obviously initiated group that such art appealed. Part of the pleasure in being thrilled by what Yeats referred to as the "visionary beauty" of Beardsley's hauntingly grotesque drawing of "Salome with the Head of John the Baptist" was that one knew there was something dangerous about its compelling forms, its insinuations of sinister desire, and that most who saw it would be merely repulsed by the perversity of the content as well as the form. Beardsley commented to Yeats that such "beauty is the most difficult of things"; those who admired such beauty would recognize its rare charms, and feel as fortunate to be party to the rarity as to the charm. Ezra Pound gave an account of the process of realizing one's impression of a Beardsley grotesque, in one of his later Cantos (LXXX):

> La beauté, "Beauty is difficult, Yeats" said
> Aubrey Beardsley

> when Yeats asked why he drew horrors
> or at least not Burne-Jones
> and Beardsley knew he was dying and had to
> make his hit quickly

> hence no more B-J in his product

> So very difficult, Yeats, beauty so difficult

> "I am the torch" wrote Arthur "she saith"

"Arthur" was Arthur Symons, whose poem "Modern Beauty" began: "I am the torch, she saith, and what to me/If the moth die of me?" This is clearly a different beauty from "that fair lamp from whose celestial ray/That light proceeds which kindleth lover's fire," the beauty of which Edmund Spenser wrote and to which Ruskin referred in his central discussion of beauty in *Modern Painters.*

Beauty is difficult, certainly; but the beauty which appealed to the decadent artists is also dangerous, with its difficulty and its danger together constituting much of its appeal. It is a beauty, as Wallace Stevens insisted in one of his early poems ("Sunday Morning"), whose mother is death; and it may well need its own aesthetic, an "esthétique du mal" for the beautiful flowers of evil. Edgar Allan Poe had made a strong argument, which especially appealed to the French writers who were at the center of the nineteenth-century interest in symbolism, that beauty is the sole province of poetry, and that its most intense manifestation is through sorrow and melancholy. Furthermore, in Poe's view, such a melancholic tone is most exquisite when heightened by what he called "the human thirst of self-torture," by which he meant the delicious anguish of despair, of asking the raven more and more desperate questions about when one's beloved will return, questions to which one knows that the answer will always be "nevermore."

The paradoxical conjunction of beauty and despair, of joy and sorrow, is one which poetry has always employed, and it became a particular darling of the romantic poets. But the artists of the nineteenth century that were called decadent intensified this juxtaposition to a dangerous pitch, to the point that it became unclear whether the pleasure that one felt was in the beauty evoked or in the deliberate and often suicidal despair that accompanied its evocation. This confusion was compounded by the tendency to separate what was said or represented from the way in which it was presented, so that language approached incantation, and forms became abstract or decorative—in either case, relatively safe from the mediation of the moralist or the realist. As a result, the effect of the aesthetic forms—the language and its rhythms, in this case—was independent of and uncompromised (which in many cases could mean uncomforted) by a rational perspective. This attracted a generation that was becoming more and more suspicious of the tendency of language to distort, to establish irrelevant structures of meaning or intention. It was increasingly suspected that the only defence against such a tendency was to detach language from its syntactical forms and the compromised structures of meaning to which it refers, and to focus more upon its pure sounds, and upon the capacity of the carefully selected and detached word or phrase or image alone to capture the momentary sensation, the symbolic meaning. The plastic arts moved in a similar direction, towards abstraction. So when Mallarmé wrote in the early 1880s a sonnet on "The Tomb of Edgar Poe," he referred to Poe's attempt "donner un sens plus pur aux mots de la tribu"—to give a purer meaning to the words of the tribe. Most of us are more familiar with this phrase from Eliot's remark in "Little Gidding" that "since our concern was speech . . . speech impelled us/To purify the dialect of the tribe."

Here, we touch once again on one of the central paradoxes linking decadence and modernism. Both, in ways that are congruent, were informed by an almost puritan zeal to maintain standards appropriate to what were received as the sacred values of art, and to protect these values against compromise. Just as one defense against large institutionalized religion was to break into small, decentralized groups of fellow worshippers, so a defence against the futile institutionalizing of language and other forms of communication was to break them down into their smaller constituent elements—images, words, sounds, and so forth. Decorative and other similarly abstract forms of art were in a way a defence of this sort against the perversions of representative art; just as symbolism, with its isolation of the elements of a numinous reality, was (in Arthur Symons' view) a defence against materialism. Art for art's sake was in some respects therefore not so much a preciously decadent affectation, and an indication of the loss of a sense of probity and responsibility by the artists who advocated it, as it was an element of the constant negotiation that took place in the late nineteenth and early twentieth centuries between the prerogatives of the poem or painting and those of its ostensible subject. Artists who worked on behalf of one side or the other were reviled as advocating a lively decadence or a deadly realism, and both were told by the custodians of the *via media* (which was to say, of the middle-class culture) to "drive their pigs to some other market."

All of this, in its indication of the intentions and expectations associated with uses of language in particular, has a surprisingly modern tone to it, as anthropologists of a certain bent argue that the structures of language underlie cultural and other social arrangements. On a more mundane level, writers—the most apparent users and abusers of language—are often identified as responsible for the maintaining of certain civilized values. One needs only attend to the ubiquitous and perennial rage displayed in letters to the editors of newspapers about shoddy uses of language, usually associated with a slipping of the standards that made the Empire, or whatever, what it was and could be again, if only people could learn not to split their infinitives.

And so we are back to the origins of decadence in the nineteenth century, to what Gautier referred to as the style of decadence, which is an

ingenious complicated style, full of shades and of research, constantly pushing back the boundaries of speech, borrowing from all the technical vocabularies, taking colour from all palettes and notes from all keyboards, struggling to render what is most inexpressible in thought, what is vague and most elusive in the outlines of form, listening to translate the subtle confidence of neurosis, the dying confessions of passion grown depraved, and the strange hallucinations of the obsession which is turning to madness. The style of decadence is the ultimate utterance of the Word.

It was the sense of disintegration which most of all fascinated the stylists, as they employed analogies from science. (In this following case, the passage is from an essay by Havelock Ellis, in which he quotes the French critic Paul Bourget.)

> If the energy of the cells becomes independent, the lesser organisms will likewise cease to subordinate their energy to the total energy and the anarchy which is established constitutes the decadence of the whole . . . A similar law governs the development and decadence of that other organism we call language. A style of decadence is one in which the unity of the book is decomposed to give place to the independence of the page, in which the page is decomposed to give place to the independence of the phrase, and the phrase to give place to the independence of the word.

In a broader perspective, Roland Barthes defined (in *Writing Degree Zero*) "modern poetry" (written after the revolutionary year of 1848) as

> distinguished from classical poetry and from any type of prose [in that it] destroys the spontaneously functional nature of language, and leaves standing only its lexical basis. It retains only the outward shape of relationships, their music, but not their reality. The Word shines forth above a line of relationships emptied of their content, grammar is bereft of its purpose, it becomes prosody and is no longer anything but an inflexion which lasts only to present the Word.

The decadent style, then, apparently like the modern style, is one in which the classical subordination of the individual parts to the unity and harmony of the whole is broken, in favor of a celebration of the constituent parts, an obsession with the part that in one sense may embody the whole and yet in another remain part of it—an obsession, that is to say, with the symbol. Those who understood such matters, those who were part of the conspiracy, if you wish, felt themselves to be part of a cabal. Thus, the separation of text from context becomes a special mission, which joins together the proponents of collage and cubism, of the new modern criticism, and of the gem-like flame which Pater argued that the momentary experience might afford. And when Symons associated the style of Mallarmé with "the kind of deprivation undergone by the Latin language in its decadence," and suggested that this deprivation was necessary to the kind of "exact noting of sensation" to which Mallarmé and his contemporaries aspired, he was also inviting Mallarmé's readers to fancy themselves ripe with the indulgence of Rome in its decline, in which any act is freed of its association with a motive, and instead attaches itself to an effect.

The disunity, the separateness, the disintegration, that seemed to define decadence both fascinated and bothered the artists who moved from decadence to modernism, and few escaped the ambivalence. Ezra Pound's pitiful (and representative) lament in the (late) Canto CXVI

> I have brought the great ball of crystal;
> who can lift it?
> Can you enter the great acorn of light?
> But the beauty is not the madness
> Tho' my errors and wrecks lie about me.
> And I am not a demigod,
> I cannot make it cohere

has to be set in the context of a poetic career dedicated to splendidly rhyming patterns of incoherence. In the same way, Eliot's poetic celebration of a desperate state of mind which "can connect nothing with nothing" is the expression of a sensibility which delighted in shoring up the fragmentary with a very ambivalent expression of disdain.

There is a curious element in all of this, which it is easy to miss. From scientific analogies which were provided in the nineteenth century, there developed a recognition of some axioms in the study of biological (and by extension social and cultural) phenomena derived from direct observation: specifically, the axioms that there are "higher" and "lower" species, that the progression from lower to higher corresponds to a progression from less to more complex, and that there is an increase of complexity in the development of the heterogeneous from the homogeneous. That is, increased complexity constituted progress or development, the way forward. No one in the nineteenth century needed to be told that the alternative direction to forward was backward. So when Pater criticized Wilde's novel *The Picture of Dorian Gray,* he did so on these terms: "To lose the moral sense therefore, for instance, the sense of sin and righteousness, as Mr Wilde's heroes are bent on doing as speedily, as completely as they can, is to lose, or lower, organization, to become less complex, to pass from a higher to a lower degree of development." Many forms of decadent behavior, in particular, were subjected to this type of analysis. Certain kinds of insanity were commonly understood to be the product of arrested development, as were various forms of sexual deviance and criminal behavior. And when Freud subtitled *Totem and Taboo* (1913) "some points of agreement between the mental life of savages and neurotics," he was specifically applying the theory of developmental arrests to support his theory of neuroses.

This leads to one of the most unsettling paradoxes associated with decadence, the notion that it is a mark both of progress and of decline, and can be taken to justify both optimism and pessimism. Wilde's remarks about sin being an element of progress were specifically intended to focus this paradox with a typically decadent flourish. The pessimistic line was straightforward enough, drawn by such encouraging figures as Schopenhauer and Max Nordau; the optimism, however, had two aspects. One view, which was really a kind of latter-day romanticism, perceived in the perversity of much decadent art an indication of the ungovernable (and thereby exhilarating) character of man's spirit. The other (and eventually more common) view was apocalyptic, and followed anything similar to Carlyle's dictum (from *Past and Present* [1843]) that "the eternal lights shine out again, as soon as it is dark *enough.*" Yeats celebrated this most dramatically, but it had some specific origins in the nineteenth century, and in a broad tradition of western millennial speculation. And one cannot but think, for example, that anyone who listened to Colonel Maud'huy in France in 1912, addressing his assembled regiment (he later became commander of the Tenth Army in Artois during the Great War), must have expected or hoped that the limit of the intensely decadent inane had finally been reached, and that such obsession with form and style might best lead to some apocalyptic transformation of the ideas of utility and beauty: "Many men salute correctly, very rare are those who salute beautifully; those latter are necessarily the ones who have achieved complete suppleness and received a thorough physical and moral instruction; they are the elite. One could say that the salute is the hallmark of education."

Ambivalence, then, was central to decadence. Wilde, in particular, celebrated the unnervingly ambiguous character of decadence, a character which abounds in modernism, as (for example) we accept the expression and embodiment of violence in art with an uneasy sense that our response is therapeutically vicarious and defensively detached at the same time—that is, that we both enjoy and abhor the violence, that it gives us both pain and pleasure. Writing of the style of the "poisonous book" that Dorian Gray read, for which the prototype was *A Rebours,* Wilde noted its

> curious jewelled style, vivid and obscure at once, full of *argot* and of archaisms, of technical expressions and of elaborate paraphrases, that characterizes the work of some of the finest artists of the French school of *Symbolistes.* There were in it metaphors as monstrous as orchids, and as subtle in colour. The life of the senses was described in the terms of mystical philosophy. One hardly knew whether one was reading the spiritual ecstacies of some medieval saint or the morbid confessions of a modern sinner.

When Oscar Wilde went to trial in 1895, he defended himself from the accusations of homosexual debauchery that were made against him by referring to "the Love that dare not speak its name"—a love which, he reflected, the mediocre bourgeois mind of his contemporaries would be quite unable to understand. *Punch* magazine quickly picked up the phrase, and remarked that apparently the art which Wilde championed also "has a mission that may not be named/With scarlet sins to ennervate the age." As so often, *Punch* had an unerring instinct. Wilde and his cohorts—and here I do not refer to Wilde's lovers but to the literary and artistic circle of which he was part—acted in an almost comically conspiratorial manner, deploying a flurry of passwords, catch phrases and esoteric references which would make Tom Sawyer dizzy, and acting as though they belonged to subversive urban guerrilla cells, separate in their organization but mysteriously united in a high-minded purpose too pure and ideal (and too easily distorted) to set down in words. They had a sacred mission, they had their "scarlet sins," and they posed as an ennervated and ennervating lot, determined in their ennervation to subvert the virtues of industry and thrift which the age espoused, and to keep art away from utilitarian and moral ambitions.

The arts have often relied upon this sort of mystery and intrigue in a functional way, of course. The gothic tradition in the novel depended upon secret knowledge which was slowly and nervously disclosed; while one of the ancient sources of poetry is the riddle, and the riddling character of metaphor provides one of its central charms. The oracular inheritance of the poet is one to which poetry often refers with pride, especially when misunderstood (and it even invites misunderstanding in order to refer to this inheritance); and the image of the riddling Sphinx confirms this kind of fascination in its wide and consistent appeal in western art and literature. When Wilde returned from his tour of America in 1883, he went to Paris to do some writing. He was always very ambitious, and had obviously decided that the volume of poems he published a couple of years earlier, though it gave him some additional notoriety, had not made his literary mark. (He may have felt, however, that despite its derivative and imitative character, the volume marked him as a "bad influence"—just the sort of mark he might wish to embellish. The publication of *Poems* in 1881 precipitated at least one serious dispute of a personal nature, with Rev R. H. W. Miles, the father of Frank Miles, with whom Oscar had been living since his arrival in London from Oxford in 1879. Wilde and Rev Miles, who was a thoughtful and not especially narrow-minded man, had been on very good and familiar terms. Miles now insisted that Wilde should stay away from his son.) In any case, Wilde now set himself to write a play (*The Duchess of Padua*) because plays were *the* thing to get one's name in the lights; and he determined to write a poem of note. Poe's *The Raven* had been a staggering success, of which Wilde had been made particularly aware on his tour, and he decided to try a longish poem of a similar sort, which he called *The Sphinx,* and which would also play on the fascination with the mysteries of Egypt that such writers as Flaubert had developed. Though it was not published until a decade later, with as frontispiece the figure of Melancholy, and illustrated and designed by Charles Ricketts, it is a model of decadent motifs for the age, emphasizing pleasure in pain, beauty in the grotesque, the sinister in the sensuous, the erotic in the religious. Several reviewers said that it embodied the "new humour," a grim conjunction of incompatibles. One

correspondent wrote to Wilde from Turkey asking what the new humor was, that he had not heard of it in Smyrna, from the regions of which it presumably derived something of its inspiration.

The juxtapositions are deliberately perverse—the Christ child and the boy Antinous, darling of the Emperor Hadrian, for example—and the images are nightmarish, or as one wag remarked, positively asphynxiating. Finally, the poem relied upon a sense of the universal immediacy of arcane mysteries and sacred truths, which might in their startling and ineffable power replace the tatty methodistical conventions to which the middle class seemed bound. This appeal was carried on into the twentieth century by Yeats, with apocalyptic images of sphinxes slouching towards Bethlehem, or gyroscopic visions of human destiny; by Pound, with his fascination with eastern religion and Renaissance power and his compulsion to codify that fascination into his own kind of oriental ideogram; by Eliot, chanting "da, daya, dayadvham" and "shantih, shantih, shantih" at the end of a poem so incomprehensible in many of its details as to force our assent to the chant even if, as is almost certain on first reading, we have no idea what is going on, and at best can view the poem as (in Eliot's own words) "just a piece of rhythmical grumbling." The words have been freed from their meanings, we have been freed from our petty expectations (of propriety, perhaps, or coherence, or meanings in words), and the art has been freed from its limitations. It takes a special knowledge to know this; not a knowledge *of* anything exactly, but a knowledge of the ways in which we must suspend our ignorant curiosity, detach ourselves from conventional notions of morality, utility, meaning, and wallow in wise unknowing, in graceful irrationality—a knowledge of the questions not to ask.

This is the signature both of modern art and of the kind of decadence for which Wilde at his best provided a focus. Art (and the life which imitates it) thereby becomes something illicit, something whispered in secret, something only the initiate understands—though its forbidden character must for greater effect be announced from the rooftops. Wilde's importance is in part because he performed that office in a spectacular way during his trial and conviction. His is, if you will, the version from life of bringing John the Baptist's head out on a platter in a work of art. Beheading in private is butchery; in public, it becomes ritual, however decadent or perverse. The initiates to this kind of ritual are those in whom the aesthetic temperament is alive, and who recognize that art appeals to that temperament alone—not to the rational, moral or utilitarian instinct in us. Wilde used to emphasize that all art has its rites of initiation; tragedy, for example, has the Aristotelian process of catharsis, by which we are purged of our emotions of pity and terror, and consequently (and very oddly) can enjoy watching Othello smother Desdemona with a pillow. Decadent art went to the limit on this, and created conditions in which we might enjoy images of the most harrowing and depraved of human experiences. In going to this limit, it deliberately tested the character and conditions of aesthetic appeal—tested, furthermore, the basis of art, and its relationship to life, which is why the practices of the decadent artists so appealed to artists of the twentieth century.

It was much more than the fact that the decadent novelties of one age became the revolutionary traditions of the next. There was something about the sense of forbidden pleasure or illicit charm, something about shared secrets and inexpressible understandings, something about a siege mentality or a doomsday state of mind—something in all of these things which were part of the decadent spirit—that art found to its liking. Certainly, there was always the deliberate secrecy which paradox flaunted, or the conspiratorial energies of apolcalyptic vision, to feed the perennial appetite for that which is either hidden away or revealed only to a few, through the agency of the kind of "economy" which John Henry Newman had earlier defended with such success. And science had its intrigues, as Freud was just beginning to titillate the fancy with his distinctions between the manifest and the latent content of dreams.

Most pervasive of all, perhaps, was the shared and profoundly affecting secret that there was sorrow and sadness at the heart of life, and that we are at best (which is to say, at our most entertaining) "the zanies of sorrow, clowns whose hearts are broken," as Wilde said from his prison cell. It was little wonder that the mask of Pierrot was adopted by so many, with his sobbing quite audible behind his clowning. And nothing less than a deep sense of imaginative complicity could account for the extraordinary popularity and influence among late nineteenth-century writers and artists and musicians of such pantomimic charades as the "Pierrot assassin de sa femme" (1881) of Paul Margueritte, Mallarmé's nephew, in which a "subtle neurotic, cruel and ingenuous Pierrot, uniting in himself all contrasts, a veritable psychical Proteus" makes his wife die from laughing by tickling the soles of her feet.

Religion usually claims something of a corner on the trade in secrets, as well as on the bizarre, and in nineteenth-century England Roman Catholicism on the one hand and various occult movements on the other provided the most stodgy as well as the most discriminating with an arcane feast from which some choice yet awful truth, heretofore hidden from view, might be selected. But religion had no more monopoly on the truths which art was now revealing than it did on those of science. Wilde himself, in company with many of his adolescent contemporaries in the 1870s and 1880s, oscillated between the masonic temple and the scarlet woman, to be sure, but he also flitted between a number of other cabals, at the most trivial moving from the family secrets of the upper classes to the coterie secrets of the cafe, eventually (and typically for his time) inventing instead his own order to which only the true aesthete and the confirmed decadent might belong. Yeats a decade or so later wandered somewhere between the Celtic Twilight and the

Golden Dawn trying to find a wearable cloak to mask the secrets which he intimated in the world around and beyond him. Once again, the arts provided the only durable form in which secrets could be shared, and perhaps it was inevitable that there would be a kind of surreptitious conspiracy about those who participated in its rituals.

In their turn, the arts of the early twentieth century either depended upon or referred to such a conspiratorial conspiracy. "So much depends upon a red wheelbarrow," says William Carlos Williams, and we nod our heads with the same kind of furtive agreement that we might display in a church, the rituals of which we do not quite understand, but feel we should admire intensely. T. S. Eliot's earliest success in "The Love Song of J. Alfred Prufrock" depends in large part on our sense of knowing, even if we could not say, the overwhelming question which he insistently evades, as well as on our sense of sharing a secret knowledge of depravity with some evil figures now suffering in Dante's Inferno, or in Eliot's London. Eliot's later embellishments in "Gerontion" rang the changes on this, as the suspicious mysteries of Easter are vaguely associated with Dionysian spring sacrifices, and with an unnervingly sinister communion involving Mr Silvero with the caressing hands, Hakagawa bowing among the Titians, Madame de Tornquist and Fräulein von Kulp, and the reader. Pound writes of the image which he celebrated that its precise definition "does not concern the public and would provoke useless discussion"; and as we read his haiku poems we feel sure that we do not need the definition anyway, and useless (or indeed any) discussion of "the apparition of these faces in a crowd;/Petals on a wet, black bough" was not at all on our minds. And so it goes—we are either in or out, and once in, we must only whisper. "Is there any secret in skulls,/The cattle skulls in the woods?/Do the drummers in black hoods/Rumble anything out of their drums?" asks Wallace Stevens in "The Pleasures of Merely Circulating," forcing us to deal with that challenge in the next breath from reading about how "the clouds flew round and the clouds flew round/And the clouds flew round with the clouds." Clearly, we are in particular company here.

Now all art requires a sense of complicity, whether it is Alexander Pope taking ostentatiously for granted the urbane understanding we share with him, or Wordsworth matter-of-factly assuming we know the sensation of the rural manic depressive, of dropping from the heights of joy to the depths of despair in the plash of a rabbit's foot, and just in time to greet the old leech-gatherer. Some romantic poets took this further, however, by developing a sense of complicity in inexpressible motives (such as the Ancient Mariner's) and unnamable (usually intimated as incestuous) acts (such as that of Byron's Manfred). The notion of the poem as an encounter is replaced by that of the poem as a nudge. With these refinements on the unspeakable, love and hate became incorrigibly intertwined, and the artists of the nineteenth century delighted in this unsettling confusion. This sense of entanglement easily slips into a fascination with the affiliations between saint and sinner, or between virtue and vice—particularly, between unnatural virtue and unnatural vice—affiliations with which Wilde certainly dallied, and which found one form in his play *Salome.*

The images of androgyny, the ubiquitous story of Tannhauser, the legend of Narcissus, the fascination with the dance, the Dionysian energies, the attractions of the *femme fatale,* the complex confusion of fear and desire—all of these are important to Wilde's play, and it is little wonder that Salome's strangely murderous passion for John the Baptist provided one of the most compelling motifs for the generation of artists following Wilde. Once again, there is a nice sense that only the initiated can understand such debauchery, such a disturbing fusion of the religious and the erotic. When Wilde sent Beardsley a copy of the Paris edition of *Salome* in 1893, he inscribed it: "For Aubrey: for the only artist, who, besides myself, knows what the dance of the seven veils is, and can see that invisible dance." "He who knows the power of the dance," wrote Hugo von Hofmannsthal several years later, "knows that love kills." And unless we are incorrigibly mundane, we say "yes, we know that power"; and we watch Salome's dance with appropriately perverse fascination, unable to avoid a shivery sense that *Salome* embodies something to which we are mysteriously vulnerable, something like the inseparability of Beauty from Decay and Death. And we develop a set of strategies for maintaining ourselves in a kind of delicious moral and rational suspension in the face of this mystery. Paradoxically enough, Remy de Gourmont's expression about a "dissociation of sensibility" was intended to provide just such a strategy, though Eliot later employed the phrase in quite a different way.

All in all, there was an appropriate focus for much of this in the complex fusion of joy and sorrow, or (as Yeats would have it) the bitter and the gay, which informed both the life and the art of this period. The exquisitely anguished exhilaration which this created found an artistic form in structures of often precarious ambivalence, as the nineteenth-century artist (and his successors in the twentieth) shifted between the majestic and the maudlin, between the models of psychodrama and those of the melodrama, between introspection and evasion, between the literature of inscape and that of escape. As the line between art and life was deliberately (and in this case necessarily) obscured, we have once again the sense of an initiation into a new kind of knowledge. At worst, what resulted was the embodiment of convivial despair or mindless aspiration. At best, it produced a celebration of the word becoming flesh and dying. "In the actual life of man," Wilde argued, "sorrow is a passage to a lesser perfection. But the sorrow with which Art fills us both purifies and initiates." In modern art, Wilde affirmed, one hears the cry of Marsyas more clearly than the song of Apollo.

There were two related directions which late nineteenth-century art took to find a suitable form for the desperation that it sought to embody. One was an escape into images of blatantly trivial entertainments—such as the circus; or the amusements of cosmetics, costume and fancy dress, Eliot's realm of "strange, synthetic perfumes." From Baudelaire to Beerbohm, the nineteenth century relished the extremes of artifice, and flirted with the limits of art, suggesting that fine lace represented the ultimate spiritualization of the material, or that the rapid, elliptical effects of the circus and the music-hall provided specific analogies for the frenetic urban life which more and more people were experiencing. And so, with the advent of modernism, we have Wallace Stevens assuming the "complacencies of the peignoir" while Robert Coady, in his magazine *The Soil* (to which Stevens contributed), celebrates Toto, the Italian clown, as "the most creative artist that has visited [American] shores in many a day. He is a clown at the Hippodrome who has invented a bow which has given pleasure to thousands"—all of this contemporary with Duchamp's urinal and part of the American collaboration between Dada and the *avant-garde,* the modern apotheosis of high decadence. In fact, there are complex affinities between decadence and *avant-garde,* especially in an age when the idea of transition has a considerable appeal. And if decadence is characterized, as the Russian poet Vyacheslav Ivanov suggested in the early 1920s, by "the feeling, at once oppressive and exalting, of being the last in a series," then it fits nicely into a notion of the *avant-garde* as having a mission to prepare the way for or indeed inaugurate a new series, opening up new possibilities to excite an exhausted sensibility.

The other direction which art took to celebrate its despair involved a retreat into the self, eventually into a labyrinth of indolent gestures, psychic dead ends, emotional impasses—a world of dead souls, as Gogol had suggested. Pierrot, the laconic haunted fool out of Commedia del'Arte and Paris street theater by way of Gautier, Verlaine and Laforgue, provided one image which combined these elements, linking the lame reflectiveness of the would-be Hamlets of the time to figures from popular entertainment—circus performers, dancers, singers, actors, magicians. Fantasy and the fantastic, especially when juxtaposed with a failure of the will and a loss of a center of belief and meaning, offered to Wilde's contemporaries a sort of secular sublimity to replace that which had degenerated when beauty declined into syrupy prettiness and earnest realism. Under such conditions, as Wilde suggested, "the first duty in life is to be as artificial as possible. What the second duty is no one has yet discovered." This notion arose in an age which was cultivating a fashionable pessimism to match the fashionable boredom it had inherited. Of course, there were always those, such as Carlyle and Ruskin and one's schoolmaster, who counselled that work was the answer to boredom, pessimism, the dangers of enchantment, and unnatural (or indeed natural) desires. But how dreary. No—anyone with a soul had to turn elsewhere for salvation. One had to stop listening to conventional pieties, and pick up Wilde's advice that the folly of youth contains more wisdom than the conviction of age. When life, as Strindberg said, is "like the tuning of an orchestra which never begins to play," then one is sorely tempted, perhaps even obliged, to take up an instrument oneself, to turn to art, to a world of illusion and artifice. As for living: as Yeats noted (taking a line from Villiers de L'Isle Adam), "our servants will do that for us." When F. R. Leavis quoted this in the 1930s in *New Bearings in English Poetry,* it was to castigate it as a futile, and not entirely genuine, gesture unworthy of the poet who would find his authentic voice in "the actual, waking world." Art as (in Pater's words) "a sort of cloistered refuge from a certain vulgarity in the actual world"; and the specific image of the poet in his ivory tower (which comes from a passage in a poem written by Charles Augustin Sainte-Beuve in 1837 about Alfred de Vigny)—these were the hallmarks of decadence to some.

The arts responded to the challenge which the dreariness and the desolation of life presented, and artists tried to achieve in their art what Wallace Stevens called its "essential gaudiness." And so we get perverse but entertaining exaggeration and excess, art on the verge, the counterpart to the trapeze artist's daring, the dancer's leap, the singer's high note, the magician's disappearance, the actor's final flourish—a kind of transcendence achieved by the flagrantly contrived, the final paradox of modernism. And we get the Crazy Janes and Emperors of Ice Cream and Sweeneys Erect of Yeats and Stevens and Eliot, Pound's Mauberley and Hart Crane's Charlie Chaplin—or, indeed, Charlie Chaplin's Charlie Chaplin. Or we get Pozzo and Lucky in Beckett's *Waiting for Godot;* or the compleat circus, Lawrence Ferlinghetti's *Coney Island of the Mind.* The world that these artists created was a world of what Paul Klee, who was much influenced, called "visible laughter and invisible tears," a world of nervous extremes, of ambiguous emotion, of covert feelings which floats apart from any specific individual or event, a world of anxious ecstasy and desperate exhibitionism, a world in which Dadaism found a home. It was a world of gallows humor and witty perversity, but also of zealous disenchantment and earnestly egotistical alienation. One of its manifestations was the dandy, the ultimate conjunction of art and life, a figure who had been on the scene for most of the nineteenth century. We meet him as Platon Mihailovitch Platonov in Gogol's *Dead Souls,* and as Alfred Mountchesney in Disraeli's novel *Sibyl.* "Nothing does me any good," says Alfred at the beginning of Disraeli's story. "I should be quite content if something could do me harm"; and he spends his time mourning the "extinction of excitement," and trying to revive the coals. The Monchenseys of T. S. Eliot's play *The Family Reunion* are his descendants, watching the final disintegration of Wishwood, the family seat—a genteel version of Poe, a kind of Fall of the House of Monchensey. The only way out, as Alfred surmises, is to find something that does one harm, and this way involves both an escape from and a return to or isolation of the self.

A Faustian pattern of escape into forbidden and dangerous knowledge was modulated throughout the nineteenth century into a pattern of encounter within the self, an exploration of the ways in which the self becomes divided, and a delineation of its double. The artificiality of this kind of enterprise gave a paradoxically appropriate accent to its naturalness, as Wilde discovered in *The Picture of Dorian Gray.* And so, the ambivalence that attached to the natural and the artificial transformed the standard melodramatic oppositions between the good and the evil into a more subtle succession of decadent juxtapositions: between rebellious sin and repentant yearning, the sphinx and the crucifix, beauty and decay, the masculine and the feminine. Even Wilde's play *The Importance of Being Earnest* displays a milder but still disconcerting array of oppositions, between the spirit and the flesh, the country and the town, the real and the imagined, truth and falsehood, and seriousness and triviality. Wilde's genius here was to focus on the language itself, magical and fatal at the same time, both to mask and reveal the secrets which intrigue the audience. But the play, like much decadent and much more modern art, develops around the difficulty of distinguishing between the important and the unimportant, of deciding whether cucumber sandwiches or the trivialities of Paterson or the discontinuous fragments shored against our ruin are to bear the burden of our spirit and sensitivity.

Wilde used to say that the Creeds are believed, not because they are rational, but because they are repeated. Just so, the rituals to which one gives indolent allegiance become the rationale for one's life, as marrying for love or money belongs beside marrying the name Earnest. Nothing is sacred, or everything may be; and whatever the case, our instincts are by now to look upon everything as possibly replete with secret meaning. Ernest Newman, one of Wilde's contemporaries and a biographer of Richard Wagner, remarked in an essay on Wilde written in 1895 that "the function of a paradox is really the same as the function of religion—not to be believed." The paradoxes embodied in decadence, like those of modernism, have a similar function, as well as an opposite one.

STYLISTIC AND THEMATIC TRAITS

James Sloan Allen

SOURCE: "Self-Consciousness and the Modernist Temper," in *Georgia Review,* Vol. 33, No. 3, Fall, 1979, pp. 601-20.

[*In the following essay, Allen considers self-consciousness as a defining trait of the Modernist temperament.*]

If there is one undisputed attribute of the modernist temper, it is self-consciousness. Even quarrels over the merits of that temper fall into agreement here: self-consciousness—in such guises as the mirror, shadow, multiple selves, self-reflecting thought, an anxious pause between sensation and expression, shuffling feet, or quickly averted eyes—marks every work of the modernist imagination.

Critics who find fault with that temper often locate the fault in self-consciousness. A generation ago, Jacques Barzun, observing that "the first striking trait of the modern ego is self-consciousness," belabored this trait for subverting the "willingness to take risks" and thereby working "to the detriment of happiness . . . and of art." W. H. Auden agreed. Although Auden believed self-awareness could enhance imagination, he saw modernist writers usually crushed by it; and he concluded that the modernist temper tested itself upon one question alone: "How shall the self-conscious man be saved?" Robert Langbaum, surveying quests for psychological identity in modern literature, is less ambiguous. "Modern self-consciousness," he says, "produces the emotional and moral blankness" that constitutes the modernist's "hell"—as nowhere more grimly portrayed than in the early poetry of Eliot. Eliot himself made his loathing explicit in images of disease: he called self-consciousness "the cancer that eats away at the self"—just as Robert Musil held it largely responsible for the disintegrated "human type that our time has produced"—and found it the besetting malady of the age. Lionel Trilling became disquieted by the odd effect this malady had on his students in the 1950's: instead of being disturbed by the torturous "self-consciousness and self-pity" of modernist fiction, as he had been in the 1930's, they blithely accepted it all as the natural mood and manner of modern life. Finally, both the cult of self-consciousness and the criticism of it found ironic culmination in John Barth's story, "Title," where Barth sighs, "Oh God comma I abhor self-consciousness."

If critics of self-consciousness assail it for weakening the will and imagination, others praise self-consciousness for enabling the mind to pierce the disguises of appearance and seize truth. Such praise was implicit in works of the French *moralistes* from Montaigne onwards. And Diderot's *Rameau's Nephew* carried that praise toward enthusiasm. But that enthusiasm became full-blown first among Romanticists—as we shall see—and again later in the nineteenth century with the likes of Dostoyevsky's Underground Man, who aspires to what he calls "higher consciousness" (that is, full self-knowledge achieved only by abandoning all objective self-control and "rational self-interest" and by steeping himself in "humiliation" and anguished introspection). Around the turn of the twentieth century, in both literature and social theory, the exploration of a consumingly reflective "higher consciousness" sparked a far-reaching intellectual revolution. The historian of that revolution, H. Stuart Hughes, explains how thinkers and imaginative writers alike "found themselves inserting between the external data and the final intellectual product an immediate stage of reflection on their own awareness of these data. The result was an enormous heightening of intellectual self-consciousness—a wholesale re-examination of the presuppositions of social thought itself." This interpretation—like Dostoyevsky's and akin to ideas advanced in the 1930's

by Edmund Wilson, David Daiches, and Talcott Parsons—finds the deepest insights of modern social thought to have been born of the discomforts and dangers of self-consciousness. But it should be added that sociologists of modernization, such as Daniel Lerner, Alex Inkeles, and David H. Smith, have shown that the self-consciousness typical of modern societies—by contrast to the "naïve" personality type common to traditional societies—breeds confidence in people that they can control their lives rather than increasing their discomfort: here again, the merits of self-consciousness are disputed but not the influence of self-consciousness upon the modern mind.

. . . . .

This sampling of opinion from literature, criticism, and social theory plainly illustrates the prevalence of, and debate surrounding, self-consciousness in modern culture, but it also discloses diverse meanings of self-consciousness. The state of mind disapproved by Jacques Barzun or T. S. Eliot, for example, is not the same as that praised by H. Stuart Hughes; and that of the social theorists is something else still. This diversity only hints at the confusion that muddles debate and conceals the unique character of *modernist* self-consciousness.

The confusion derives in part from a cloudy history: self-consciousness has seemingly had as many cultural births as, say, Romanticism or modernity. And these births may plausibly be assigned to every age. The Enlightenment may be seen as the fount of that intellectual self-awareness that dissolves naïve certainties, as evidenced by Hume's agonizing scrutiny of knowing, Rousseau's and Kant's demand for moral self-determination, and the rise of an aesthetic sensitivity which, in W. J. Bate's words, introduced "a self-consciousness unparalleled in degree at any time before." Yet the seventeenth century has impressive claims to priority in self-consciousness with the birth of modern philosophy in Descartes' self-reflecting *cogito;* the unabashed critical psychology of La Rochefoucauld and La Bruyère; and the conflict between "moderns" and "ancients" in the Battle of the Books. But then no student of the sixteenth century could fail to assert that modern self-consciousness had its origins in the subjectivity of that age: aesthetic Mannerism and Montaigne's self-searching; the Protestant Reformation and the revival of Pyrrhonian skepticism; the perfection of the mirror and the emergence of autobiography and the self-portrait; Cervantes' invention of what Robert Alter calls "the self-conscious novel" and Shakespeare's self-absorbed heroes; the cult of sincerity and the rise of the role-playing self. Nor could students of the Italian Renaissance resist placing the source of self-consciousness in the Quattrocento's high valuation of man, new assertive ego, and cultivation of secular intellectual and artistic pursuits.

Yet even before the modern individualism of the Renaissance, the reforms of Gregory VII had given life to a type of man who was, in the words of the great historian Marc Bloch, "more self-conscious" than any Christian before him and whose "self-consciousness indeed extended beyond the solitary human being to society," where it stimulated the art and thought of the High Middle Ages. But Christianity itself may also be credited with introducing into Western culture a self-reflectiveness unknown to ancient times through its psychological definition of sin—as formulated in The Sermon on the Mount and Paul's Epistles and reflected in the spiritual autobiographies and confessional day books of believers. But no sooner has the novelty of Christian self-awareness been recognized than classical antiquity asserts new priorities with the metaphysical self-consciousness of Plotinus; the critical, secular spirit of Latin literature; and beyond these the rise of philosophical skepticism and heterodoxy among Hellenistic philosophers and of an educated cosmopolitan personality in the Hellenistic cities. Even earlier still, there are manifestations of self-consciousness in Aristotle's ideal of self-contemplating intellect, Plato's intuitive rationalism, Socrates' irony, and—unavoidably—the motto at Delphi: Know Thyself. In fact, no search for the historical origins of self-consciousness could stop before that awakening of human self-knowledge in the Garden of Eden when Adam and Eve lost not only moral purity and hallowed sanctuary but psychological innocence: they clutched at fig leaves, having become painfully conscious of themselves.

Of course, no quest for the historical origins of ideas can fix either an idea's first appearance or its meaning. Such a quest, like Arthur Lovejoy's well-known essay, "On the Discrimination of Romanticisms," more nearly justifies dismissing an idea altogether than using it. To discriminate the self-consciousness of modernists from that of others requires more than an analysis of ideas; it demands an inquiry into the manners and the psychological underpinnings of this attribute of the modernist temper. And that means, first, to scrutinize some of the relations between modernism and its principal forebear, Romanticism.

. . . . .

It is commonly said that at the end of the eighteenth century a new self entered the cultural life. This self had among its attributes a large appetite for feeling and fantasy, abundant restless energy, and a marked preoccupation with itself. This preoccupation not only heightened the self-awareness already much developed in Western culture but prompted the study and exploitation of it. The new personality was conscious of its self-consciousness.

This intensely reflexive self emerged first in Germany among Goethe's generation, when many young men withdrew from society into themselves, where, as Werther said, they could "find a world" of perfect freedom. The German Romanticists who followed Goethe began to depend on self-absorption to satisfy every desire, whether for emotional release, psychological and metaphysical certainty, or artistic expression. Hence Ludwig Tieck wrote plays within plays within plays. Chamisso recorded a man's search for his shadow. E. T. A. Hoffmann told

the bizarre adventures of divided selves. Jean Paul Richter invented the literary *Doppelgänger* after discovering himself to be both the subject and object of consciousness ("Never shall I forget," he wrote, "when I was present at the birth of my own self-consciousness. Suddenly the internal vision 'I am I' passed before me like a lightning flash from heaven . . . my 'I' had seen itself for the first time and forever."). Fichte constructed a metaphysics around a discovery like Jean Paul's, concluding that the objective world depends for its existence on human consciousness (and he taught this theory by asking students to contemplate the wall in front of them and then to contemplate the thing that had contemplated the wall; but, as one student recorded, "It was curious how confusion and embarrassment ensued; many of the listeners seemed not to be able to discover anywhere the thing which had thought of the wall"). Hegel skirted these dizzying flights into subjectivity, without diminishing the importance of the theme, by identifying self-consciousness with the unfolding of objective Spirit in history: for Hegel, self-consciousness (*Selbstbewusstsein*) means wholeness and strong self-possession not deep introspection.

Outside of Germany, Kierkegaard adopted and modified Hegel's usage in his influential existentialist version of the human self. "Generally speaking," he said, "consciousness, i.e., consciousness of self, is the decisive criterion of the self. The more consciousness, the more self; the more consciousness, the more will, and the more will, the more self. A man who has no will is no self; the more will he has, the more consciousness of self." But unlike Hegel, Kierkegaard was ambivalent toward this kind of self-consciousness; and Kierkegaard's ambivalence, as we shall see, points directly towards the modernist temper. I should note that such an ambivalence, as experienced by poets, had already been suggested in Schiller's great essay, "On Naïve and Sentimental Poetry," which contrasts spontaneous, natural, unreflective poetry with poetry that is halting, subjective, self-aware. Schiller saw virtues in both but believed the modern poet more likely to create the sentimental kind, and critics have since agreed—W. J. Bate and Harold Bloom, for example, having explained how modern poets, from Romanticism onward, could be nothing but "sentimental," burdened as they are by the awareness of their predecessors and the accumulating expectations of art.

These examples—mainly German—of Romanticist self-consciousness illustrate a deliberate mental exercise intended to advance self-realization or self-discovery. And this exercise, with the ambivalences it aroused, lay at the source of two of the major themes of European Romanticism. The first was a fear of being consumed by self-consciousness or regressing uncontrollably into the self—"Romantic anti-self-consciousness," as Geoffrey Hartman has called it. Expressed by poets like Byron and Keats as the desire to flee from the demon of consciousness into art, this fear could also erupt in the unpoetic despondency of John Stuart Mill, who believed himself the "most self-conscious person alive" in a world where anguished self-consciousness afflicts all geniuses. The second was the probing of psychological and aesthetic ambiguity known as Romantic irony and manifested, for example, in the entanglements of truth and illusion, the ideal and the real in F. Schlegel's *Lucinde;* in the interplay of sublime and ridiculous modes of love in Gautier's *Mademoiselle de Maupin;* and in Stendhal's mockery of social pretense and self-deception from behind a protective front of pseudonyms, masks, and lies. It may be that these themes and styles of Romantic self-consciousness had their homes in different nations—the English Romanticists inclined to lyrical anguish, the Germans to psychological and metaphysical adventures, and the French to heartfelt discord between their public and private selves. Yet no European of the early nineteenth century could deny that self-consciousness flourished everywhere. Like Goethe, they might have said that so subjective a culture cannot be a healthy one, but they would have agreed with Carlyle that "Never since the beginning of Time was there, that we hear or read of, so intensely self-conscious a society."

. . . . .

Romanticist self-consciousness became the parent of the modernist self-consciousness. But like all passages between generations, this one saw an inheritance enfolded in new needs and appearances. The Romanticists' bold quest for self-realization and self-discovery, even at the expense of emotional disquiet and intellectual bafflement, gave rise among modernists to a confused longing for such positive ends overlaid by pervasive anxiety about experience. This anxiety manifests itself in a variety of moods and manners—e.g., ill ease, embarrassment, discomfiture, affectation, histrionic stances, disillusion, resentment, self-contempt, nihilism—none of them the sign of a willed and exploring self-awareness (can we imagine Kafka ingenuously announcing the birth of his self-consciousness, like Jean Paul?) but of a self-awareness that has impaired the will, the ego, and the self.

Upon wondering what caused the modernist temper to lose the strength of its Romanticist forebear, we discover, for one thing, that the Romantic inheritance of self-awareness was absorbed into that spirit of criticism which induced self-criticism. Schiller hinted at this consequence in his idea of "sentimental" poetry; but Gautier was correct to mark the intrusion of criticism into the act of artistic creation with Baudelaire: "His is a very subtle mind," Gautier wrote, "highly refined, most paradoxical, and one which makes criticism play a part in inspiration." This statement "could serve as a shorthand definition of our modernism," says Jacques Barzun; and Peter Gay puts the idea more sharply still: "Modernism is the creature of criticism." Thomas Mann's Doctor Faustus found this hegemony of criticism detrimental to art, and to escape it sold his soul to the devil in exchange for uncritical spontaneity, pure "unreflectiveness," in musical composition. But criticism may have achieved its final conquest of un-self-conscious art with the influential works of Harold Bloom which attribute the highest accomplish-

ments of modern poetry to the critical imagination that enables "strong poets" to "misread" and vanquish their predecessors.

Whether approved or not, criticism (a manifestation of self-consciousness) shapes the modernist temper. But this criticism is not only a rational appraisal of art and life; it is also an irrational or even unconscious hostility, which is often directed against the self as well as others. Nathaniel Hawthorne devised a graphic image of this nonrational self-criticism (associated for him with conscience): the "bosom snake" that bites its victim from within and free of his control. This self-criticism beyond the critic's control gives the modernist self-consciousness its nasty, often mocking mood and manners.

Self-criticism grew organically with other forms of self-consciousness during the social and intellectual revolutions of the nineteenth century. As early as Goethe's generation, deepening subjectivity had induced self-contempt: once Werther let his aspirations soar beyond the constraints of objective reality, his failure to realize those aspirations in art, love, and action bred in him hostility toward the world and himself; his suicide only dramatized his sense of self-defeat, and in doing so prefigured the alliance of self-inflicted torment and performance characteristic of the modernist temper. But the cutting edge of self-criticism began its most injurious work only after Waterloo, when the young in France equated the defeat of Napoleon with the death of heroism and the loss of life's meaning. Alfred de Musset correctly saw that they had in truth translated their own incapacities and ennui into an "affectation of despair" and denounced everything, when actually they suffered only from being "idle and tired." The victims of a failed idealism and its resulting self-contempt, they relished the display of despair.

After the abortive revolutions of 1848, this floundering, self-destructive, and histrionic rage redoubled, with Baudelaire as its exemplar. In the poem "Au Lecteur," which became the Prologue to *Les Fleurs du Mal,* he tells of the ennui that "makes no grand gestures or cries," but "would willingly reduce the earth to ruin, and swallow the world in one gaping yawn." In the closing lines, he names this ennui as the common horror of humanity and takes a taunting swipe at himself and everyone: "You know that fastidious monster—O hypocritical reader— my fellow man—my brother!"

. . . . .

In Baudelaire, the modern artist steps forward to act out his hostility toward himself and others. This performance fulfills the same self-justifying intentions as had led Werther to his private but theatrical suicide and recalls Musset's suspicion that his contemporaries' cries of despair were self-serving acts motivated by ennui. And in this marriage of criticism and performance lies the soul of the modernist self-consciousness. Yet it is a soul whose character and needs disclose themselves but darkly. This darkness results in part from the psychological tricks played by the critical or aggressive desires and by the unconscious defenses against them—the resistances, repressions, sublimations, and so on. But it also arises from the conscious urge to satisfy affirming appetites for recognition, self-assurance, self-realization, psychological coherence, and the like, which make role-players of us all, in life and art. All human actions and creations being therefore searches for a fitting self—as the sociologist Erving Goffman and the critic Richard Poirier have made it their business to explain—the critical and histrionic works and manners of the modernists are complex searches indeed.

Baudelaire illustrates this complexity when he first directs his hostility toward others—*hypocrite lecteur*—in order to exalt himself at their expense, and then turns this hostility on himself—*mon semblable, mom frère*—to convey proud possession of intimate and embarrassing truths about everyone. Both gestures grant him privileged status while seeming to demean him—although neither Baudelaire nor any other modernist could confess this without lapsing into an endless series of self-maskings and unmaskings.

Baudelaire's performances of hostile criticism, like the symptoms of ennui, betray a social-psychological malaise of the kind Durkheim called anomie—the loss of respect for goals or norms or for the capacity of one's actions to attain goals or fulfill norms (Durkheim referred appropriately to Musset's writings). A person suffering anomie aches with a sense of impotence or disregards accepted behavior, resulting in socially destructive actions, like suicide or crime. Baudelaire's life and works played upon this theme continually: failed hopes and splenetic impotence lead to self-denigrating or antisocial acts or ideas. Baudelaire was no Romanticist plagued only by the discomforts of introspection, self-awareness, and the ambiguities of truth and illusion; he was more the modernist driven to act out his hostilities toward himself and the world by a sense of social and psychological weakness. The myth he invented of the martyred artist sanctioned his performance: Baudelaire was the archetypal Pierrot, enchanted by the mood and performance of loneliness and pained clowning—a persona he portrayed in *Le Vieux Saltimbanque.* Or, to use his own word, Baudelaire was *L'Héautontimorouménos,* the self-tormentor, who played the role of victim very well:

> I am the wound and the knife!
> I am the slap and the cheek!
> I am the limbs and the rack,
> The victim and the torturer!
> I am the vampire of my own heart
> —One of the great abandoned
> Condemned to eternal laughter,
> Who can never smile again!

A clue to Baudelaire's and the modernists' anguished and histrionic anomie lies in a commonplace of the sociology of the avant-garde: the economic dependence of the artist on a public he deplores. Troubled in his relations with

both family and public, Baudelaire turned his sense of isolation and impotence into an entire mythology of the modern poet. The poet, he wrote, must avoid places where "the rich and joyous congregate" and remain with the "feeble, destitute, and forlorn," for only there can he preserve his inspiration; and yet this requires removing himself from the very society that could sustain him. Baudelaire, to be sure, followed this rule only when his improvident expenditures and foolish debts left him no alternative. But this duplicity only intensified his sense of being an artist who desires a life he cannot have and resents the failure. To mythologize and embody this conflict was to be Baudelaire's historic role, as Jules Laforgue knew when he attributed to Baudelaire the motto: "I am damned on account of the public—Good—The public is not admitted."

Baudelaire's histrionic defiance and self-pity did not in any way strengthen his will, but they did strengthen his conviction that powerlessness is the inspiration of art. Unable to make the public heed even his greatest achievements, which he believed to be his lyrical poems, he cultivated worldly impotence and pursued artistic potency in alcohol, opium, and aestheticism (his "artificial paradises"); and he praised uselessness while abandoning himself to the urban crowds, crying fatalistically: "It is the devil who pulls the strings that make us dance."

Through these social and artistic performances of despair and self-effacement, Baudelaire established many of the gestures and the mood of the modernist self-consciousness. In Laforgue's words again, Baudelaire "is the first who is not triumphant, but accuses himself, reveals his wounds, his laziness, his bored uselessness in the midst of this hardworking, devoted century." And both the wounds and the uselessness were largely of his own making in a society whose comforts he wanted but not at the cost of vulgar, bourgeois labor.

Baudelaire thus gives the modernist self-consciousness its drama, mask, and public face: the histrionic criticism of self and others. But there is a private face, too, and this is not a mask donned, consciously or unconsciously, and believed in as one's public self. It is rather the expression of an anguish more painful and a conflict more deeply unconscious than the discontents of ennui. This private face is guilt. The seeds and forms of guilt can be detected in Baudelaire—say, in his harsh ambivalence toward his mother and his treatment of her. But the rise of guilt and its place in the modernist temper is better illumined by writers who knew guilt as a constant haunting or an open obsession.

. . . . .

There is no written history of guilt—and we will probably never have one—for guilt is a psychological drama enacted amid abundant confusions and concealments. The actors in this drama are barely conscious of their roles and wholly unconscious of those roles' origins; yet what those actors do and say carries such force that guilt is charged with the power to wound. And that power signals the nature of guilt: guilt is an injury, a wounding of the heart—or the ego—by a weapon inside the victim acting in response to commands beyond his control. Little can be known of this drama in ages long past because the intimate human relations that form and energize the deeply unconscious self-criticism of guilt lie hidden. But no better illustrations of the rise of this self-criticism can be found than the lives and works of the two most guilt-ridden writers of the nineteenth century: Nathaniel Hawthorne and Søren Kierkegaard.

These may seem unlikely choices here since both men preceded modernism and both were deeply religious—Hawthorne a captive of New England Puritanism, and Kierkegaard of Lutheran conscience and existential anguish. But both foreshadowed the modernists with a guilt ungoverned by religion: they demonstrate that religion may manipulate and even strengthen guilt, but cannot create it; and that the modernist temper can be at once unencumbered by religion and steeped in guilt. The clue to guilt, as given by Hawthorne and Kierkegaard, lies not in a harsh Protestantism but in lives and writings marked by painful insecurity, neurotic self-criticism and self-contempt, and by a preoccupation with the psychological and philosophical nature of guilt.

Hawthorne's self-critical temper was nourished mainly by his reclusive and moralistic mother, who worshipped at the shrine of her deceased husband and fed her memories and devotion to her son throughout the prolonged illness and dependency that confined him to home. "I scarcely had human intercourse outside my own family," he wrote; and his sister later remarked that although he had wanted to be among the "multitude," he was too "conscious of being utterly unlike everyone else" and "began to withdraw into himself." Just before leaving for Bowdoin College, Hawthorne admitted to her: "The happiest days of my life are gone. Why was I not a girl, that I might have been pinned all my life to my mother's apron."

This self-absorbed and timid temper doubtless arose in part from the limited physical activity allowed Hawthorne as the result of a severe leg injury. But his feelings of inadequacy reached deeper than physical weakness, for he was persistently driven into self-contempt by what he considered the overpowering demands of maturity and his own aspirations. Even after achieving some prominence as a writer and establishing a family of his own, he denigrated himself for his uncertain financial circumstances and erratic periods of creativity. Disregarding his accomplishments, he remained tormented by "that same dream of a life hopelessly a failure." This is guilt without religion—severe irrational self-criticism.

Hawthorne drew upon this spirit in portraying guilt in fiction. Harry Levin correctly observes that Hawthorne's literary preoccupation with guilt derived not from misconduct but inhibition: Hawthorne knew little of active sin but much of weakness. Hence, Hawthorne's renderings of guilt concern sins of consciousness not action. In "Fancy's Shadow Box," for example, he calls guilt "a stain upon the soul," concluding that it comes not from actual misdeeds but from those contemplated: even "in a church, while the body is kneeling, the soul may pollute itself." Then, when the evil wish is recognized, conscience "strikes a dagger to the heart"; yet, this pang of conscience is not caused by the sinner: like the viper in the breast of another tale, "The Bosom Snake," it strikes with a will of its own. Thus do inhibition, self-awareness, and unconscious self-criticism join to injure the ego independent of both the claims of religion and rational self-punishment.

No one can read Hawthorne's parables of guilt without noting, with Quentin Anderson, that this guilt gains its power from the strength of the social bond. Hawthorne tells of individuals inseparably tied to others through shared beliefs and the common conscience which speaks for those beliefs. So pervasive and domineering can this common conscience be that it induces Dr. Grimshawe, in Hawthorne's last, uncompleted tale, to experience moral reproach in an empty room; and it causes Dimmesdale, in *The Scarlet Letter,* to suffer a self-critical remorse suggestive of Kierkegaard's "sickness unto death." Here Hawthorne's tales of psychological impotence, moral anxiety, and self-contempt escape their Puritan settings and enter the modern world of self-conscious, Kierkegaardian despair.

Upon turning from Hawthorne to Kierkegaard, it must be said that the "sickness unto death" of Kierkegaard's essay by that name (published two years before *The Scarlet Letter*) does not truly represent Dimmesdale's remorse. For Kierkegaard meant a thoroughgoing "sickness of the self" that arouses a desire for extinction, whereas Hawthorne has Dimmesdale actually die in the fullness of repentence, presumably to the joyous redemption of his soul. Yet Kierkegaard would have found Dimmesdale's self-lacerating guilt exemplary of the moral type he explained, because it enabled Dimmesdale to reach a higher stage of self-awareness.

I have previously cited Kierkegaard's belief that the self exists only through self-awareness. Now this awareness discloses itself as guilt. Remove all worldly manners, Kierkegaard says, and "the only thing remaining is the individual himself, the single individual, placed in his God-relationship under the rubric: Guilty/Not Guilty?" And this means that the highest state of the self is not, as it was for Hegel, a state of potency and wholeness but one of anxiety and despair over that self's insufficiency before God, its powerlessness to deny existence, its ambivalence before freedom and sin, and its inescapable, guilt-ridden burden of responsibility.

Although Kierkegaard conceived of guilt more metaphysically than did Hawthorne, there were ample reasons in his life, too, for defining human nature through guilt. Even more than Hawthorne, Kierkegaard as a youth was isolated from the public world and dominated by a morally obsessed parent. His widower father taught him a fearsome Christianity, with the crucifixion as its central image. But more important in fostering Kierkegaard's sense of guilt was his father's demand that Kierkegaard, even as a child, accept full responsibility for his actions. Kierkegaard's childhood was thus more an exercise in self-criticism than in religious devotion; and his earliest memories of school record a nearly compulsive will to do what was expected of him:

> To me it was as if heaven and earth might collapse if I did not learn my lesson; and on the other hand, as though even if heaven and earth were to collapse, this would not exempt me from doing the task assigned to me, from learning my lesson. . . . I had only one duty, that of learning my lesson, and yet I can trace my whole ethical view of life to this impression.

Nor did this obsession originate in fear of explicit punishment. Kierkegaard's father neither threatened nor cajoled him into accepting his secular obligations; he merely mantled them with the cloak of moral imperative. When he handed his son new books for the next level of the boy's education, for instance, he added these words: "When the month is up you are the third in your class." No more was said or needed saying. "I was exempted from parental twaddle," Kierkegaard remembered; "he never asked me about my lessons, never heard me recite them, never looked at my exercise book, never reminded me that now it was time to read, now time to leave off. . . . I was left entirely to my own responsibility." And in consequence, Kierkegaard concludes, "I got a thoroughly deep impression of the fact that there was something called duty and that it had eternal validity."

Even the rules of Latin grammar assumed for Kierkegaard the authority of moral injunction. Viewing their regular order with "unconditioned respect" and "reverence," he "looked down upon the miserable life the [grammatical] exception led" with "righteous contempt." Understandably, he identified these regular rules with his father: "When under this influence I regarded my father, he appeared to me the incarnation of the rule; what came from any other source was the exception, in so far as it was not in agreement with his commandment."

In the light of this exalted moral idealism, it comes as no surprise that Kierkegaard's discovery of his father's human fallibility left him devastated—"The Great Earthquake," he named it, although he left in doubt whether the cause was an indiscretion of spirit or flesh. But this disillusion did not lead Kierkegaard to abandon his moral idealism; rather, it made him simply repudiate instead of emulate the source of that idealism—namely, his father. Hence, relations with his father were never completely restored, and, although he led a dissolute life for a time, he always experienced aching guilt for violating any obligation to others, as, for example, when he broke his engagement to be married. And he later elevated this consuming private conscience to serve as the judge of

modern Christianity and of the existential responsibilities of the modern self.

. . . . .

These details of Kierkegaard's and Hawthorne's lives and ideas disclose the private face of modern self-criticism, just as Baudelaire disclosed its public face. When the two are joined, the bitter, mocking, anguished temper of modernism is formed: unconscious self-punishment, or guilt, energizing the feelings of impotence, ill ease, and hostility that are acted out in art, ideas, and life. The full measure of this modernist self-consciousness does not find embodiment in all modernists, of course, but its elements and their pattern are discernible.

The modernist who most exemplifies the private sufferings of self-criticism and the literary performance of them is Kafka. He knew better than any other, as he said, the "pressures of anxiety, of weakness, or self-contempt," and the "boundless sense of guilt" that lives beyond all reason. Kafka was so like Kierkegaard in temperament and childhood experience that they might have been brothers. Both were overwhelmingly dominated by their fathers; neither could bring himself to marry, although both were engaged and seemingly in love; and both were victims of exalted idealism, extravagant disillusion, and obsessive guilt.

Kafka's *Letter to His Father*, written when he was thirty-nine, recalls the agonizing forming of his temper. His first childhood memory is exemplary. At about the age of three, Kafka had once complained in the night of thirst and been threatened by his father with punishment if he persisted. When he continued to complain, his father, without speaking, took him from his bed to the outside of the house and made him stay there for the rest of the night. Kafka interprets this episode as a primary cause of his feelings of self-contempt: "I dare say I was quite obedient afterwards," he remembered, "but it did me inner harm," for his father's action "meant I was a mere nothing to him," and this bred the persistent "feeling of nothingness that often overwhelms me."

Kafka goes on to say that such silent, psychological punishment typified his father's relations with him: "You hardly ever really hit me," he wrote, rather "you put special trust in bringing up children by means of irony." And this assertion of his father's psychological authority led Kafka, like Kierkegaard, to idealize his father's moral stature: "everything you called out at me was a heavenly commandment, I never forgot it, it remained for me the most important means of forming a judgment of the world." And, also like Kierkegaard, he suffered a shattering disillusionment over an unexpected act of his father. Kafka's filial disillusion was provoked by a seemingly trivial incident. During adolescence, Kafka had once boasted of his knowledge and curiosity in matters of sex, while in the company of his parents and in a moment of boyish self-dramatization. He anticipated reproach, but instead his father only told him "how I could go in for these things without danger." The moral disappointment caused "the whole future world to come tumbling down"—although, unlike Kierkegaard, it made Kafka feel that his father "became still purer, rose still higher," while he became more worthless than before: "the purity of the world came to an end with you," he said, "and by virtue of your advice, the filth began with me." Here Kafka turned his moral idealism upon himself rather than his father because he was himself all too completely "seized in my innermost being" by "the weakness, the lack of self-confidence, the sense of guilt" that "your method of upbringing" fostered. And this weakness and guilt then inspired his distinctive art.

Kafka so thoroughly embodies the private, unconscious sufferings of self-criticism that he is exceptional. But consider some other modernists. There is Gide, whose self-assertiveness and labored candor emerged, as he confesses, to compensate for his "lack of self-confidence," feelings of ugliness and inferiority, weak "sense of reality," and aching guilt. The biographer of Gide's early years, Jean Delay, attributes these feelings to the influence of his mother's Protestantism and, even more, to an innate "psychological weakness in energy or in the nervous structure." This latter suspicion is unprovable, but there is no doubt that Gide was trained in youth, like Kafka and other modernists, to be exceedingly critically self-conscious—that is, to govern himself according to ideal standards and to punish himself for his lapses. Gide's famed displays of self-awareness, with all their histrionics of sincerity, derived from self-criticism implanted in him by others and beyond his control.

T. S. Eliot enjoyed—or suffered—a childhood like Gide's. His mother ruled him unyieldingly, in part because she feared that his congenital physical weakness would worsen if his activities were not limited, and in part because her Unitarian moral impulse demanded self-denial and intellectual achievement. Eliot learned the necessity of work and self-control, but also-in the words of his sensitive biographer, Lyndall Gordon—a "self-destructive introspection" and a "self-disgust" that "was in a class of its own" among modernist poets, so entirely lacking was it in the tenderness that touched even Baudelaire. It was this spirit, Gordon observes, that gave Eliot his "central persona—a performer fixed in his silly role, unable to take command of his real self which is socially unacceptable, outcast, or elusive." Eliot was at home in the company of his characters: Prufrock, Sweeney, the Hollow Men, and Edward Chamberlayne, who speaks for them all in "The Cocktail Party": "I am obsessed by the thought of my own insignificance"; they are all ruined from within.

Pirandello is another steeped in the critical self-consciousness that dissolves confidence. He also came to literature through a highly dependent adolescence and parentally inspired idealism. And when his own idealism collapsed, first through the foibles of his father, then the failings of the clergy, he extended his disillusion to the whole of human nature and penned the nihilistic literature

of psychic confusion for which he is famous. Victimized by that "voice of others within us," which he knew to be conscience without God and represented as such in the novel *L'Esclusa* (1893) and the play *Ciascuno a suo modo* (1924), Pirandello found the most powerful expression of his critical self-consciousness in the theatre, where confusions of identity between people and within the self made ingenious, even spellbinding, drama.

Jean-Paul Sartre exemplifies this same profoundly self-conscious temper despite his belief that he had no conscience, or super-ego, as a result of growing up without a father. In fact, his childhood ideally illustrates the formation of conscience, for, although fatherless, he was raised by his maternal grandfather, who cherished him and demanded perfect social performance of him. Sartre therefore idealized his own image of himself—and he confesses experiencing guilt over even so slight an imperfection as catching a cold! It may be, as Victor Brombert has said, that such a "sense of guilt" afflicted Sartre's entire generation of middle-class Frenchmen: "an all-pervasive, generic, subjective, largely unaccountable feeling of culpability presenting the symptoms of a new *mal du siècle*." Yet Sartre carried this guilt beyond morality into the imagination: he demonstrated how this acutely self-critical temper can give rise to intellectual *nausea*. Like guilt, the nausea of Sartre's hero Roquentin occurs in moments of psychic impotence. At these times, self-awareness overwhelms the mind, preventing it from spontaneously and objectively organizing experience. The consequence is chaos—sensations become things, words fly about, and the head grows dizzy. Sartre calls this chaos the brute realm of "existence," pervaded by nausea and bereft of cognitive meaning: the existentialist here becomes almost psychotically self-conscious.

These instances of uncontrollable self-criticism suggest what Freud, during the heyday of modernism, denoted the super-ego. Perceiving that such self-criticism involves numerous psychic actions—such as the acquiring of ideals, criticizing oneself and others, disillusion and punishment, the mental disorientation or self-contempt that issues from persistent failure, and so on—Freud came to believe that this network of actions, collectively known as the super-ego, was responsible for many psychological maladies, among them, narcissism, melancholy, anxiety, and, of course, neurotic guilt. And he became convinced that these maladies were forms of self-punishment, which he found to be the epidemic emotional malaise of the twentieth century—as psychoanalysts still do, although nowadays they associate it especially with narcissism.

Freud's metaphor of self-punishment as disease recalls and may seem to justify the criticism of self-consciousness as disease cited in the early pages of this essay. But like many psychoanalytic metaphors, this one misleads by attributing substantive malignancy to psychological states. And although it is a theme of this essay that those who suffer from self-criticism are to some extent ignorant of its cause and helpless to effect its cure, it is also a theme that these sufferers often choose to dramatize their discomforts as substantive and irremediable: the modernist delights in playing the afflicted and unhealable heart. This desire to act out his pains leads the modernist to all of his agonizingly self-conscious manners, gestures, themes, literary devices, and ideas—e.g., embarrassment, nervous laughter, debunkery, defensiveness, affectation, inhibition, self-pity, vexation at the burdens of history, society, and art, and the images of helpless people, insects, puppets, rodents, crustaceans, and the like. To say these manners and images are histrionic is not to say they are false or hypocritical, for the self-criticism that thrusts them forward is genuine; nevertheless, dramatizing affliction is as important to the modernist temper as the affliction itself. As Baudelaire knew: the performance of symptoms dignifies the disease; but as he did not know, it may also make the disease suspect.

The psychological uses of performance do not, of course, belong exclusively to the modernists. Nietzsche viewed most of cultural life as unwitting performance: strong people, he said, impose style on their lives and thereby behave according to their highest natures; lesser people mask their weaknesses in self-justifying ideologies, like religion, socialism, decadence, and pessimism, and allow their masks to become reality for them. Alfred de Musset had observed this self-deception among his generation in the 1830's: they cultivated an "affectation of despair" to hide the dull fact of their ennui. In this light, the manners and nihilism of modernists appear as masks of inadequacy: modernists act tough or nervous or knowing to disguise the weakness caused by obsessive self-consciousness.

Yet, besides concealing or dignifying this weakness, the histrionics of modernist self-consciousness also provide an actual identity—in Gide's words, a "fabricated personality"—to the performer. Hence, the modernist's self-conscious performance is a form of idealization which is likely to be more anguished, awkward, defensive, and disquieted than the actual emotions; he may praise and seem to achieve authenticity, but even this belongs to his performance: the persona of Pierrot is never lost, for, in many ways, the modernist *is* Pierrot.

This constancy of performance helps to explain the puzzling disjunction between the cheerfulness observed in Kafka, Sartre, Eliot, and others by their friends and the bleak despair and nihilism that dominate their works. And it illumines the progress of many modernists from dramatic pessimism to political, religious, or moral commitment. Such a disjunction has typified all self-conscious writers since Goethe, who explained to Eckermann that his own youthful anguish had been mainly a melodrama of restless subjectivity. Like Goethe, Sartre looked back to discover and confess the embarrassing secrets of his youthful passions: "Fake to the marrow of my bones and hoodwinked," he admitted, "I joyfully wrote about our unhappy state" and about "the bitter unjustified existence of my fellow men." And why had he done it? To acquire a persona, a social-psychological identity that fit. "The object of my mission, the springboard of my glory," he said, was to decry the "impossibility" of everything

human. "I was," he concluded, "a prisoner of that obvious contradiction, but I did not see it, I saw the world through it" and "regarded anxiety as the guarantee of my security; I was happy" and "exonerated."

This remarkable confession is, of course, another performance, as any reader of that artful venture in self-revelation, *Les mots,* knows. But it perfectly describes how the modernist self-consciousness, even at its most philosophical, as in Sartre's early existentialism, is a quest for personality through public performance; a quest made the more necessary by the sting of internal self-criticism.

. . . . .

Once the modernist self-consciousness is seen to be an interplay of unconscious self-criticism and histrionic self-seeking, the appearances of modernism take on a new character. The debunking manners, social nervousness, cultural hostilities, and the vision of an arid and brutish world lose their objectivity to become ideological stances. Uncertain of himself, the modernist dramatizes his uncertainty with the hope of gaining security and stature, always perceiving his experiences through the lens of his self-consciousness.

This ideological distortion has been suspected by critics of the modernist temper for a long time. Lionel Trilling said this suspicion finally led him to "the view that art does not always tell the truth or the best kind of truth and does not always point out the right way, that it can even generate falsehood and habituate us to it, and that, on frequent occasions, it might well be subject, in the interests of autonomy, to the scrutiny of the rational intellect." But I hasten to repeat that the modernist's "distortions" are not strictly false. For internal self-criticism is painfully real; hence the view of life it promotes is subjectively true. If the modernist temper often displays itself, as Hugh Kenner says, in an "orgy of self-depreciation, each man confronting in his own way his own bankruptcy," that bankruptcy of the self is neither more nor less than the psychic wound inflicted by unconscious self-criticism; and the "orgy of self-depreciation" is but one of the performances that the self-conscious modernist gives in seeking his own ego's satisfaction. And here is the clue to modernism: the subjective sufferings of a wounded ego and their dramatization have shaped both a temper and a culture.

Hugh Kenner

SOURCE: "Modernism and What Happened to It," in *Essays in Criticism,* Vol. 37, No. 2, April, 1987, pp. 97-109.

[*In the following essay, which was originally delivered as a lecture in 1987, Kenner considers the linguistic complexity of Modernist works.*]

To commence with good news: the Last Modernist is well in Paris where he lives under the name of Beckett. He has a typewriter and an unlisted phone, but is so much the man of some *ancien régime* that he grants no interviews and never did. He writes by preference in a language he can remember learning at Portora Royal School in the north of Ireland, and one of his plays contains (in English paraphrase) the following exchange:

> —Have your seeds sprouted yet?
>
> —No, they have not sprouted. If they were going to sprout they would have sprouted by now. Now they will never sprout.

In the French in which he originally wrote it, that takes the verb *germir* through some recondite aspects of its conjugation, remembering the classroom where artificial problems are posed. 'If they were going to sprout they would have sprouted by now': an unlikely thing to be said in French, unless on an examination paper. A language, it seems, is a game played by intricate rules. One can learn the rules, but switching to a different language means learning new ones.

That is a particularly cold eye to cast on Language, which by convention is something we cannot remember learning. Your mother tongue, runs the idiom; which means you likely learned it from your mother, and what were the first words you learned from her you cannot say. For you did not learn 'words'. You learned a habit of discourse which you later learned to analyse into words. Since novelists used to specialize in growing awareness we might have expected them to depict the process, but by and large they were indifferent to it.

Not even the author of *Frankenstein* rose to the challenge. Soon after her monster divines that human sounds denote things (and seemingly that's all there is to language—names) we find him deep in Plutarch's *Lives* and *Paradise Lost*. Or, if Mary Shelley's book isn't really a novel—a frenzied visionary parable perhaps—*David Copperfield* seems a fair instance. It commences with the chapter-heading 'I Am Born'; after which there's a fascinating elision, since the next thing we know he is reading from a book.

> Peggoty and I were sitting by the parlour fire, alone. I had been reading to Peggoty about crocodiles. I must have read very perspicuously, or the poor soul must have been deeply interested, for I remember she had a cloudy impression, after I had done, that they were a sort of vegetable. . . .

Three paragraphs earlier David was already gleaning such words as 'Mr. Bodgers late of this parish' from tablets on the church wall, and his ability to do that passes without remark. In short, neither Dickens nor any reader of Dickens was impressed by the miracle of language or its acquisition, let alone the acquisition of its written signs. It seems agreed that reading comes like breathing. That was 1850. But by 1914 *A Portrait of the Artist As a Young Man* is commencing,

> Once upon a time and a very good time it was there was a moocow coming down along the road and this moocow that was coming down along the road met a nicens little boy named Baby Tuckoo. . . .
>
> His father told him that story: his father looked at him through a glass: he had a hairy face.
>
> He was Baby Tuckoo. The moocow came down along the road where Betty Byrne lived. She sold lemon platt. . . .

I submit that page as the beginning of Modernism, indeed as its proclamation, not least because it recognizes autonomous Language, something alien to a small child. Language—the Mother Tongue—is second only in strangeness to the cold air that smites a neonate. 'Once upon a time'—what can that expression mean? We may imagine Baby Tuckoo wondering. 'And a very good time it was': that conveys his father's questionable judgment that the word 'time' in the mysterious 'Once upon a time' can be interchanged with the word 'time' in a phrase such as 'Those were good times'. But 'to have a good time', a phrase Joyce skirts but implies: what does 'time' mean there, when it's something you can *have?*

The *OED* tells us that 'to have a good time' was idiomatic in England from c. 1520 to c. 1688; after that it lingered in America, whence England re-introduced it in the 19th century. Tracing such lore so exactly is a hallmark of the great dictionary's epoch. As for 'Once upon a time', the *OED* is strangely incurious; I don't find the phrase anywhere in the 16 columns it devotes to **Time,** though perfunctory mention does get made under **Once.**

Well, a novel that can send you to the *OED* is not your ordinary 19th century novel, the working convention of which was to keep you altogether unaware of language except when a character was being idiosyncratic, as by dropping aitches or by recycling a pet expression. But James Joyce was born the year the publication of Skeat's *Etymological Dictionary* was completed, and the first fascicle of the *OED* (**A-Ant**) appeared before he was two. As a student, we are told, he read in Skeat 'by the hour,' and his dealings with the *OED*, which was up to the S's and T's by the time he commenced *Ulysses,* have been noted by James Atherton and other scholars. One thing that was modern when Modernism was new was awareness of Language as a mode of human behaviour virtually unexplored. It was not, as it had been for Dickens, simply *there;* it required devoted attention. Mysterious, it could screen off as much as it conveyed. It is not too much to say of Joyce that he was fascinated throughout his career by the fact that a reader of a printed page, unguided by a speaker's intonations and gestures, has a hope of understanding anything at all. Common words in particular have so many senses; by rough estimate, the *OED* entry for **Set,** on which Murray rightly commended his chief deputy, runs to two-thirds the length of *Paradise Lost*. To any specific appearance of the word nearly all of this is irrelevant; how on earth have we such skill at excluding so much?

That is a Modernist question, cognate with the Modernist custom of paring words from a text, the better to isolate what is left behind and let small words bend the energies of their neighbours. 'And then went down to the ship . . .': how much weight 'And' carries, and what tension in the studied deferral of a subject for 'went'! We read that line as we'd read it were it all that survived of the poem, and at century's turn Greek scholars were attending to poetry quite as exiguously present; seven words of Sappho, say, salvaged by someone who wanted to exemplify a meter.

Ezra Pound, analogously, was attentive in classrooms where the 19th century's philological adventure was being particularized, and was held by the romance of much of Europe speaking dialects of Latin: Latin as it had mutated below and above the Alps, below and above the Pyrenees. The Dante he revered was the author of the *Commedia* but also of a treatise on language, the *De Vulgari Eloquentia;* that had not been routinely esteemed as a major work of Dante's, and Pound is a man of his time in citing it often. He came to the Provençal poets of his early enthusiasm by way of the scholarly editions that were still appearing when he was an undergraduate; one thing plain from those was the difficulty of retrieving, from a chaos of manuscripts, anything close to the sound in the poet's mind. Canto XX tells us of his walk from Milan to Freiburg to ask the lexicographer Emil Levy about one doubtful word, a word Levy had brilliantly solved, thereby making sense of a whole stanza of Arnaut Daniel. And Professor Fred Robinson has recently shown how dubieties in Pound's 1911 English *Seafarer* reflect, not the ignorance that used to be imputed, but much pondering of textual notes in the Sweet edition, which in turn condense the effort of many scholars to comb a coherence out of manuscript static: the way, nowadays, we patiently coax an image out of satellite transmissions from nigh the planet Jupiter. It's noteworthy how the *Cantos,* as Pound's control faltered in his extreme old age, tend to unravel into celebrations of single words.

So that was one strain of Modernism, a generation's alertness to a problematic of words.

> April is the cruellest month, breeding
> Lilacs out of the dead land, mixing
> Memory and desire, stirring
> Dull roots with spring rain.

—That *exhibits* its participles, 'breeding', 'mixing', 'stirring'; places on exhibition too the word 'April', inviting us to remember the opening of *The Canturbury Tales;* whereas Shakespeare's

> daffodils
> That come before the swallow dares, and take
> The winds of March with beauty

do not urge us to search out old contexts for 'March'.

And if the great Modernist wrtiers inherited the century-long concern which the *OED* epitomizes, they encountered also something the *OED* had no obligation to anticipate, the modern city, a city turned into a machine. Modernism, it is important to recall, was a phenomenon localized in large European cities; we should recall how its practitioners encountered the modern big city as a sudden novelty, not having been, like the city's native inhabitants, immersed unaware in piecemeal change. As Ovid had come to Rome from the Abruzzi, Virgil from marshy Mantua, Catullus from near Verona, so Eliot came to London from St. Louis and genteel Boston, Pound and H.D. to London from a Philadelphia suburb, and Joyce, always the exception, to Zurich and Paris from a Dublin that boasted when he left it the most extensive tram system in Europe. The systems of transportation deserve stressing; when Pound arrived in London in 1909, then Eliot in 1914, the tracks and trains were in place whereby people could be moved by the thousand and the hundred thousand underground in from suburbs to a place of work, thence out again to 'home', there to clear the breakfast, light the stove, and lay out food in tins. Rapid transit had not previously been part of human experience; it underlies the 'episodic' structure of *Ulysses,* where on turning a page we are suddenly somewhere else, and the quick-cutting of *The Waste Land,* where one moment we watch eyes and back turn upward from a desk (a line which, in asking to be read literally, conveys Picassoesque distortion) and the next moment the remains of an early morning's breakfast being cleared in a dreary flat as the sun goes down. The poem works like a stripped and crisp machine.

Urban syncopation of the rhythms of life; also an underbeat of distraction, of attention given and withdrawn: of such is the warp and woof of many High Modernist texts. The reader, moreover, is drawn into close collaboration, of the kind we expect a work of learning like *Paradise Lost* to exact. Yet what the modernist text concerns itself with is precisely what has grown familiar, and in fusing the customary with the difficult it asserts its philological origins. Let me offer an intricate instance from fairly early in *Ulysses.* Mr Bloom has emerged from Westland Row postoffice with a letter he is itching to read; he's encountered an acquaintance he has no wish to dally with; the small talk he's trying to abridge is about a funeral.

—I must try to get out there, McCoy said. Eleven, is it?

I only heard it last night. Who was telling me?

Holohan. You know Hoppy?

—I know

Mr Bloom gazed across the road at the outsider drawn up before the door of the Grosvenor. . . .

The Gosvenor is a hotel across the street; but 'outsider'? Though Joyce could have written 'carriage', 'outsider' would be Bloom's natural word, in the *OED*'s sense 3, 'an outside jaunting-car', listed without further explanation. Referring next to 'Outside [adj.]', we locate with some effort a cross-reference to 'jaunting-car', where the term is finally explained. 'A light, two-wheeled vehicle, popular in Ireland, now carrying four persons seated two on each side, either back to back (*outside jaunting-car*) or facing each other (*inside jaunting-car*).' With that much effort we might expect to resolve a minor crux in Dante, and what we've gained is that we know what to visualize. The passage proceeds:

> The porter hoisted the valise up on the well. [We'll not pause over 'well'.] She stood still, waiting . . . [Note how abruptly a 'she' has come into Bloom's field of attention] while the man, husband, brother, like her, searched his pockets for change. [Note the subtext of speculation: is she married? Mr. Bloom is preparing to fantasize.] Stylish kind of coat with that roll collar, warm for a day like this, looks like blanketcloth. Careless stand of her with her hands in those patch pockets. Like that haughty creature at the polo match. [Now we're following Bloom's thoughts, which are suddenly disrupted by the intrusive voice of McCoy:]
>
> —I was with Bob Doran, he's on one of his periodical bends, and what do you call him Bantam Lyons. Just down there in Conway's we were.
>
> Doran Lyons in Conway's. [Bloom registering this talk with semi-attention.] She raised a gloved hand to her hair. In came Hoppy. [The voice of McCoy again.] Drawing back his head and gazing far from beneath his vailed eyelids he saw the bright fawn skin shine in the glare, the braided drums. Clearly I can see today. Moisture about gives long sight perhaps. Talking of one thing or another. Lady's hand. Which side will she get up?

And we have our reward for tracking down 'outsider'; since the passagers face outside, then if she gets up on *this* side, Bloom may expect a titillating glimpse of ankles. Those 'vailed eyelids', by the way—'vailed' with an *a*—are 'lowered or drooped'; the *OED* calls the word both rare and obsolete. It wasn't too rare for Shakespeare, and Joyce likely found it in *Hamlet;* by using it here he effects an odd tang of detached pedantry, shifting the viewpoint momentarily to outside of Bloom. As for 'braided drums', the *OED* has no help to offer; it's been conjecturally explained as a tightly-coiled hairstyle, in fashion just too late for editors who'd finished with the letter D by mid-1897.

> . . . Which side will she get up?
>
> —And he said: *Sad thing about our poor friend Paddy! What Paddy?* I said. *Poor little Paddy Dignam,* he said.
>
> Off to the country: Broadstone probably. High brown boots with laces dangling. Wellturned foot. [At a time when ladies' feet were considered so provocative they were frequently trimmed out of

photographs, Bloom's eye knows where to rest.] What is he foostering over that change for? Sees me looking. Eye out for the other fellow always. . . .

> —*Why?* I said. *What's wrong with him?* I said.
>
> Proud: rich: silk stockings.
>
> —Yes, Mr Bloom said.
>
> He moved a little to the side of McCoy's talking head. Getting up in a minute.

By this time the narrative planes are multiple. Bloom has his mind on the woman and no more than a safe fraction of his attention on McCoy. McCoy meanwhile is not only talking, but is reciting verbatim a conversation that occurred in Conway's public house the previous night. To keep his recall and his narrative separate our text is having recourse to italics. Meanwhile an odd rare word— 'vailed eyelids'—breaks into the immediacy to apprise us of a narrative vocabulary that could dazzle us if it chose with a show of resources surpassing those of anyone here. We find, too, that uncommon words like 'vailed' and once-common words like 'outsider' are laying an equal tax on our attention.

> —*What's wrong with him?* he said. *He's dead,* he said. And faith, he filled up. [What does that mean? Did Hoppy's eyes fill, or his glass?] *Is it Paddy Dignam?* I said. I couldn't believe it when I heard it. I was with him no later than Friday last or Thursday was it in the Arch. *Yes,* he said. *He's gone. He died on Monday, poor fellow.*
>
> Watch! Watch! Silk flash rich stockings white. Watch!
>
> A heavy tramcar honking its gong slewed between.
>
> Lost it. Curse your noisy pugnose. Feels locked out of it. Paradise and the peri. Always happening like that. The very moment. Girl in Eustace Street hallway was it Monday settling her garter. Her friend covering the display of. *Esprit de corps.* Well, what are you gaping at?
>
> —Yes, yes, Mr Bloom said after a dull sigh. Another gone.
>
> —One of the best, McCoy said.
>
> The tram passed. They drove off toward the Loop Line bridge, her rich gloved hand on the steel grip. Flicker, flicker: the laceflare of her hat in the sun: flicker, flick.
>
> —Wife well, I suppose? McCoy's changed voice said.
>
> —O, yes, Mr Bloom said. Tiptop, thanks.

In often interrupting this narrative I've been faithful to its spirit, an orchestration of distractions and interruptions, and, once absorbed, an amazing technical achievement, whether we regard its wit, its economy, or its mimetic precision. Some themes I began by stating are surely evident: the foregrounding of language, both colloquial and narrative; the multifaceted urban order of experience mimed; and the demand for our intense participation, as we both construct the scene and safeguard a chief source of our pleasure, a certain textual obduracy, never quite subduable. We're not allowed to forget how it's words, words, words we're coping with: exactly what Hamlet famously said he was reading. By attention to words, since Alexandrian times, we have read Homer. Lexicons of the Homeric Dialect exist; a *Ulysses* lexicon is quite conceivable, with 'Outsider' for one entry and 'Drums' for another.

Let us next confront the Easy Book, a genre with which Milton was unacquainted. In a time when the production of reading matter (remarkable phrase) was first being commercialized on a large scale, the reading public was also being enlarged to include a great many who possessed, often with facility, the technical skill of reading although it was impossible to be certain *what* they had read already. It was natural for Milton to assume that anyone who knew how to read had some familiarity with texts one could enumerate. Thus the Bible could be taken for granted. So, probably, could certain Latin works, for instance Caesar and parts of the *Aeneid.* That meant that, while allusiveness could reach far—

> Blind *Thamyris* and blind *Maeonides,*
> And *Tiresias* and *Phineus* Prophets old

(where 'Maeonides' is a sidelong way to say 'Homer' and Thamyris and Phineus summon a scholar), still there was a core you could safely allude to. 'That warning voice, that he who saw th' *Apocalyps,* heard cry in Heaven aloud . . . *Wo to the inhabitants on Earth!'* would not have been obscure to anyone literate. But what can Defoe assume his readers have read, save pages as referentially circumspect as his own? By Victoria's century the Easy Book was the norm; about all that Dickens can assume is that readers of his novels have read other novels, and while we've heard him use words like 'perspicuously' we don't find him presupposing easy acquaintance with Homer. Reading Matter, consisting almost wholly of Easy Books, was the principal mass-produced artifact of the late 19th century. Poetry too had become Easy; thus Everyman's Library assimilated Adelaide A. Proctor, author of 'The Lost Chord', well before it got around to Donne or even Dryden. A. E. Housman, though a classicist, was an Easy poet. George Meredith, by contrast, was thought a Difficult novelist, though less because he presupposed prior reading than because he drew on so big a dictionary.

'Everyman', wrote the series' long-time editor Ernest Rhys, 'is distinctly proverbial in his tastes. He likes best an old author who has worn well or a comparatively new author who has gained something like newspaper notoriety.' That meant, people either bought Scott or Dickens, who had worn well, or else some best-seller or other (a guaranteed Easy Book). 'As one reads it for the first, or re-reads it for the fifth time', affirmed Rhys, *Ivanhoe* is 'one of the best of all story-books. . . . It carries into its far time that immense humanity and tireless heartiness which were part of Sir Walter Scott's character.' 'Heartiness' is a word to be alerted by. Rhys is telling us that *Ivanhoe* is an Easy Book, like—oh, mutatis mutandis, like Michael Arlen's long-forgotten *The Green Hat,* a great '20's best-seller.

I'm affirming what it would take a volume to demonstrate, that by the early 20th century the Easy Book was an unexamined norm. You might read it once and discard it, like *The Green Hat,* or re-read it for the fifth time, like *Ivanhoe,* but reading it would never be an exacting experience: in particular, would require no special awareness of the words it used. Now Modernist works came packaged exactly like Easy Books, and that was a great affront. *Ulysses* for instance looked like a long novel. *The Waste Land* on the page looked rather like *Maud.* Later, if you went to see *Waiting for Godot,* the curtain rose on what looked like the set of a proletarian play, though a play which after a while didn't seem to be getting anywhere. (True, its first words give fair warning: 'Nothing to be done'.)

What was happening, in each case, was the turning back on itself of a public convention; a novel and a poem part of the subject of which was the normal inattention exacted by novels and poems; a play part of the subject of which was the essential unreality of expecting, in the mirror held up to nature, some neatness of stark *events.* Exactly because they defamiliarized the familiar, such works were widely and vociferously denounced. The *TLS* condescended to *The Waste Land,* and did not so much as take notice of *Ulysses.*

Criticism has its sociology, a subject I want to evade. We might spend an hour or so on early reviews, learning little save that lazy journalists and a docile public were locked in an embrace of mutual trust. (The 'parodies' in *The Waste Land* were judged 'inferior', and someone disliked its 'erudition-traps'; the skewed expectations there would be fun to anatomize.) But I want to stress instead how the very nature of the Modernist enterprise entailed return to a time before the Easy Book. Joyce was never more the contemporary of Dante and Milton than when he spoke quite casually of making no demand of his reader save a lifetime's attention. Dante would have understood that. Likewise Eliot's valuation of Donne requires no stressing, nor Pound's of the troubadour Dante valued most, that most 'difficult' of troubadours, Arnaut Daniel. (But when the troubadour texts were being recovered, Jaufre Rudel seemed among the best because he resembled Tennyson, and you'll still see that judgment repeated.)

Dante assumed he was bequeathing us a book we'd not wear out in a lifetime; assumed, too, that we'd be expecting no less. That went with a rarity of books; you expected one to last you. But it went, too, with a shared valuing of the intellectual pleasure of discovery; also with the notion of a *community* of readers, letting one another know what they had found. The Commentary is one way such a community shares knowledge. It was the Easy Book that taught us to say 'pedantic' and 'academic'. Not that pedantry is recent, or ever other than boring, though if we keep our eyes from glazing over, the pedant, even, can often tell us something.

One thing Joyce and Pound and Eliot and Beckett share—and W. B. Yeats too, a part-time modernist—is a veneration for Dante; it's perhaps *the* one thing, by the time we've included Beckett. And all of them save Yeats read him in the Italian. Modernism for that matter was notoriously polyglot, and Philip Larkin perhaps announced the end of it when he denied that foreign languages were of any value. 'I don't see how one can ever know a foreign language well enough to make reading poems in it worthwhile', he told a Paris Review interviewer. Larkin even affirmed a naive word/thing identity: 'If that glass over there is a window then it isn't a *Fenster* or *fenêtre* or whatever'.

'It seems to me,' he ruminated, 'that up to this century literature used language in the way we all use it', a proposition rich with implications about the street-talk of Milton's contemporaries. As for what Larkin read, he read 'Novels I've read before. Detective stories: Gladys Mitchell, Michael Innes, Dick Francis. . . . Nothing difficult'.

Even if, as may be suggested, Larkin was trailing his coat, there are implications to the sympathy he was fishing for and the outrage he was counting on. What he's saying, you see, is that it was all a fraud: that no one ever really *understood* a foreign poem, that the French lines in *The Waste Land* are impostures, that it's really the easy books that we reread, to renew their easy sensations, and that poring over Modernist texts is a highbrow game. He implies, by the way, that Oxford is a fraud, likewise such a journal as *Essays in Criticism*. Matthew Arnold, to whom the journal's title does homage, is the man we might like to hear from at this juncture. That Larkin was mentioned as a possible Poet Laureate is what the author of *Culture and Anarchy* would have known how to make much of. He'd have made something, too, of Sir John Betjemen's accession.

So the ghost of Arnold beckons me from the shades. I borrow the trope from Eliot, who felt beckoned by the sad ghost of Coleridge at the end of a series of lectures in which he proposed a strategy: taking a popular form and making of it something rich and strange. He was speaking of drama, remembering perhaps his aborted *Sweeney Agonistes*, but also describing the great Modernist enterprise in which he played so signal a part. For it coopted popular forms, to submit them to irradiation; and it fell afoul of the guardians of those forms. To revive, in the heyday of the Easy Book, the learned book that yields its satisfactions slowly, was to presuppose, and venture to recreate, a vanished readership, feasible now only in universities. What Milton deemed prerequi-

sites are now nearly post-requisites. Students read a translated *Odyssey*, for the first time, because *Ulysses* exacts it. I've known a few who felt driven to the study of Greek; that would have pleased James Joyce, whose Greek was scant. I think of another man who undertook, and pretty well mastered, five foreign languages at the behest of the *Cantos;* Pound would have welcomed a fellow-learner.

Modernism came to pass because a few men of genius seized a precarious moment's opportunity. As much because genius is rare as because the moment passed, the movement had no hope of lasting. But its major texts last, the thorny admonitory artifacts of our era. If there's any Greek left at the other side of the democratic divide, or any recollection of the tale of Odysseus, of the etymologies of Give, Sympathize, Control, or the sound of Provencal, of rumours of a Europe when the Munich Hofgarten was more than a coffee-house, it will be thanks to a few books from an age the phrase 'post-modern' is assuring us we're well clear of.

James W. Tuttleton

SOURCE: "The Vexations of Modernism: Edmund Wilson's Axel's Castle," in *American Scholar*, Vol. 57, No. 2, Spring, 1988, pp. 263-72.

[*In the following essay, Tuttleton focuses on conflict between the radically experimental stylistic innovations of Modernist literature and the conservative, often reactionary, attitudes of Modernist authors.*]

In "Catching Up with the Avant-Garde," a recent essay in the *New York Review,* Roger Shattuck—after taking up some eight new books that attempt to define "Modernism"—throws in the lexicographer's towel. At present the task of definition seems beyond us: "There is as much disagreement about the dating and the essential features of modernism as about the existence and nature of a fundamental particle in physics." "Modernism," Shattuck concludes, is "no more than an umbrella or bucket word" that has to do its service for movements as diverse as Impressionism, Aestheticism, Bohemianism, Symbolism, Surrealism, Dadaism, Vorticism, Futurism, the Avant-Garde, and so on. His is a problem we all share, for criticism has not yet accomplished an essential task—that of reformulating the chronology and characteristics of Modernism, putting the movement in context, and renaming it (and its successor "Post-Modernism") so as to reserve the term *modern* for what participates truly in the here and now.

I want here to explore one aspect of the problem of Modernism—the complex relationship between radical aesthetic experimentalism and the conservative cultural ideology that often accompanied it. The paradox of this relationship has been a source of consternation to radical critics from the era of the *New Masses* to that of the *Partisan Review* and beyond. Even liberals express dismay at the apparent aversion of the Modernists to the agenda of the Left. I cite merely one instance—from Lionel Trilling's recently published notebooks for 1945:

> In three-four decades, the liberal progressive has not produced a single writer that it itself respects and reads with interest. A list of writers of our time shows that liberal-progressivism was a matter of contempt or indifference to every writer of large mind—Proust, Joyce, Lawrence, Eliot, Mann (early), Kafka, Yeats, Gide, Shaw—probably there is not a name to be associated with a love of liberal democracy or a hope for it.

In exploring this paradox, my method will be to return us to a decisive moment when these tensions between radical technique and conservative attitude, as a characteristic of Modernism, received their first important expression. That moment occurred in 1931 with the publication of Edmund Wilson's *Axel's Castle: A Study of Imaginative Literature, 1870-1930.*

Wilson is a useful point of departure because, in *Axel's Castle,* in the treatment of Yeats, Valéry, Eliot, Proust, Joyce, and Gertrude Stein, he brought into focus a wide range of experimental writings that constitute at least some of the central texts of Modernism. So acutely intelligent and instructive was his account of the aims and intentions of these writers that he taught virtually a whole generation how to read their work. At the same time, however, Wilson's virtual repression of his political attitudes while writing *Axel's Castle* produced a good deal of confusion in readers as to his exact relationship to the movement, with which he is often identified as an unqualified supporter. This view of Wilson as the champion of Modernism needs, I believe, to be reconsidered in the light of the recent publication of his *Letters on Literature and Politics* and his diaries—*The Twenties, The Thirties, The Forties,* and *The Fifties.*

By way of a brief propaedeutic on Wilson's relation to Modernism, it will be useful to keep in mind his education in the classics at the Hill School; his studies in modern French literature at Princeton; his relationship there and thereafter with his mentor Christian Gauss; the shock of recognition when he discovered the Modernists, virtually simultaneously with some of their finest achievements; his editorial work in the 1920s at *Vanity Fair* and the *New Republic,* which put him in direct touch with some of them; and his response to the changing domestic political situation in that decade (particularly to the trial of Sacco and Vanzetti and the stock market crash). All of these experiences—especially Wilson's growing political radicalism—were decisive, I believe, in the composition of *Axel's Castle* (1931), the first book to make plain to readers interested in the avant-garde the aims, intentions, and methods of the Modernist writers. These experiences were equally decisive in turning him against the Modernists' most cherished beliefs and against some of their most brilliant and representative techniques. All this, in my view, calls into question the relation of Edmund Wilson to the Modernist movement,

about which he is widely but wrongly regarded as a major sympathetic spokesman.

I

Let me begin with Wilson's letter to his Princeton classmate, the poet John Peale Bishop, dated August 1, 1922. Wilson was twenty-seven and the managing editor of *Vanity Fair.* Bishop had just married and sailed for Europe when Wilson wrote him this letter:

> I was much impressed by the furious storm which burst upon the city just at the minute of your sailing and abated as suddenly about half an hour afterwards. Ominous and heroic thunders resounded across the city and one felt in the voice of the elements something fateful and definitive, as if an epoch had been ended, a drama brought to its close—or as if it signaled some august periphery in the ardors of a god. . . .
>
> Since then, though a brightness be gone from the day, everything has gone on much the same. I discovered the key to the modern movement the other day, but will not disclose it to you here because I am on the point of writing a tremendous article about it.

The young man who had "discovered the key to the modern movement" had been educated at the Hill School and Princeton, two extremely traditional schools. While his mastery of French had prepared him to read Mallarmé, Verlaine, Remy de Gourmont, and Rimbaud in the original, I emphasize here Wilson's training in the classics and the early development in him of a combative rationalist temperament. This temperament was manifest in Wilson's hostility to religion, to the supernatural, to mystery, to feeling as a source of value, and to nineteenth-century Romanticism as the corrupting site of expressivist literary phenomena.

The evidence of his letters and diaries suggests that Wilson's love of the classics and of the classical values of reason, order, balance, and lucidity made his discovery of programmatic irrationalism in the French decadents, Symbolists, Surrealists, and Dadaists a problem for rational comprehension. Nothing in his formal education had adequately prepared Wilson for the willed repudiation of the cognitive in these forms of Modernism, which he conceived to be a latter-day manifestation of Romanticism. To a man of Wilson's classical and rationalist temperament, the literature of the Symbolists and Modernists resisted his intelligence, withheld its meaning, cloaked itself in mystifications, seemed a willed obscurantism. Yeats, Valéry, Joyce, Eliot, Proust, and Stein can only be understood, Wilson tells us in *Axel's Castle,* as having founded their work on a revolution effected in the previous generation in France, a revolution largely unknown to the Anglo-American mind.

The critical method by which Wilson will account for French Symbolism in *Axel's Castle* is predicated on an analytic procedure defined in his dedication of the book to Christian Gauss. Criticism, in Wilson's view, should provide "a history of man's ideas and imaginings in the setting of the conditions which have shaped them." This formulation, by the time Wilson comes to develop it fully, implies a historical-critical method that owes a great deal to the shaping influence of Voltaire, Descartes, Vico, Herder, Renan, Vigny, Anatole France, Hippolyte Taine, Shaw, Wells, Bennett, and Marx, as well as to the scientists Darwin, Einstein, and Freud. All of these influences were either fundamentally oriented toward history as providing the key to interpretation or were rationalist, scientific, and skeptical in temperament. Many were both. In any case, as an amalgam of such influences, Wilson's method leads him to interpret the French Symbolism of Mallarmé, Rimbaud, Verlaine, and Adam as a second wave of early nineteenth-century Romanticism, indeed as a degeneration of it.

The revolution that preoccupied Wilson in *Axel* manifested itself in a set of specific characteristics that made literary Symbolism exceptionally difficult for the curious rationalist to read and understand. He stresses Symbolism's destruction of the formal rules of literary art, its synesthesia, or "confusion between the perceptions of the different senses," their attempt "to make the effects of poetry approximate to those of music," and "the confusion between the imaginary and the real, between our sensations and fancies, on the one hand, and what we actually do and see, on the other." Wilson's Symbolists present a further problem to understanding in that they turn away from the objective world of bourgeois men and affairs and make the content of poetry subjective with the effect "of making poetry so much a private concern of the poet's that it turned out to be incommunicable to the reader."

The art of the incommunicable, such as we find in Mallarmé, Rimbaud, and the others, is antithetical to the *lumen siccum,* the luminous intelligence, the precision of order in the classical mind—at least as the handbooks at Hill and Princeton had then defined it. At the very moment when Wilson launches his investigation into the modern movement, he confesses to John Peale Bishop on September 5, 1922, his need for relief from the self-involvement of this kind of subjective art: "My great ambition now is to buy a little house in the country whither I can retreat and derive strength from contact with the classics and the uninterrupted contemplation of my own thoughts." The next year he reports, "I have been reading, as you will readily guess, Virgil and would commend him to your attention. He was really one of the very great poets of Europe but has been spoiled for most people by being taught in school." The *Eclogues* are praised as the inspiration to Dante; and Wilson celebrates Virgil's classical virtues—his "rigorous artistic conscience, his careful fitting of the manner to the matter, and his lifelong devotion to his craft."

Steeped in the classics, then, Wilson found it difficult to grasp why the French Symbolists were averse to rational,

discursive statement and to the non-linguistic, actual world. Their preoccupation with oneiric visions; with altered states of consciousness induced by opium and morphine; and with what Wilson calls (apropos of Rimbaud) the "long, immense and reasoned *derangement of all the senses*" struck him as antithetical to common sense. He found the Symbolists' work marked by a desire "to intimate things rather than to state them plainly," an intimation presented in a "complicated association of ideas represented by a medley of metaphors" intended merely "to communicate unique personal feelings."

It is the nature of the rational mind to ask why the French writers should have done this. Wilson accounts for these literary developments by invoking the revolution in scientific thought, as described by Alfred North Whitehead. Whitehead had presented modern science as having subverted any real dualism between external nature and the mind and feelings, seeing them as "interdependent and developing together in some fashion of which our traditional notions of cause and effect, of dualities of mind and matter or of body and soul, can give us no true idea." To articulate the new understanding of the scientific view of man and nature, the Symbolist poets had thus had "to find, to invent, the special language" that would alone be capable of expressing the personality and feelings of the artist. "Such a language," Wilson wrote, "must make use of symbols: what is so special, so fleeting and so vague cannot be conveyed by direct statement or description, but only by a succession of words, of images which will serve to suggest it to the reader."

II

Having grasped the nature of these older French experiments and the conclusions of science on which they were grounded, Wilson then turns in *Axel's Castle* to his Modernist contemporaries. The intent of the individual chapters on Yeats, Valéry, Eliot, Proust, Joyce, and Stein is to show how the extension of Symbolist techniques into the work of these writers produced the modern movement. The result is a wonderfully ambivalent act of criticism. Wilson explicates Yeats's interest in the fairies, the motif of seclusion in the tower, the aestheticist influence of Pater's *Renaissance,* Yeats's experiments with automatic writing, theosophy, clairvoyants, astrology, and magic. Wilson understands that he is in the presence of a lyric master, but he is impatient with Yeats's devised identities, and he is critical of the mystical-metaphysical system of *A Vision* with its daimons, tinctures, cones, gyres, husks, and passionate bodies. Who can believe in this nonsense? Even Yeats doesn't believe in it. What right has he then to impose it on us? Wilson is critical of Yeats for "rejecting the methods of modern science" and so cutting "himself off in a curious way from the general enlightened thought of his time."

Wilson contrasts Yeats's visionary style with that of George Bernard Shaw's "Guide to Socialism and Capitalism" in order to show that Shaw's style is admirably figurative without being murky; indeed, all good writing (not just the Symbolist-Modernist style) operates by suggestion. The implication is that Shaw's style in presenting socialist ideology is superior to Yeats's visionary self-indulgence. Yeats is a poet, Wilson tells us, who wants "to stand apart from the common life and live only in the imagination." And Wilson is obliged to warn us of the effects of living for beauty alone, of living only in the imagination: "We shall be thrown fatally out of key with reality—we shall incur penalties which are not to be taken lightly." These penalties, however, are not specified, although his correspondence, to which I shall turn in a moment, makes the danger plain.

In respect to Valéry, Wilson finds it absurd that the poet asserts "that prose deals exclusively in 'sense' as distinguished from suggestion, and that one has no right to expect from poetry, as Valéry says in another passage, 'any definite notion at all.'" Valéry's equation of poetry and mathematics as inapplicable to reality as such, his insistence on form and form alone, is contrasted with the solid sense of Anatole France, a writer who was lucid and voluminous in all genres and who genuinely communicated with his audience on the plane of intelligence and ideas. (Anatole France, even more than Dr. Johnson, is the paradigm of Wilson's whole career in letters.)

Wilson resists vigorously "the real effect of Eliot's as of Valéry's literary criticism," namely: "to impose on us a conception of poetry as some sort of pure and rare aesthetic essence with no relation to any of the practical human uses for which, for some reason never explained, only the technique of prose is appropriate." He finds their position to be "an impossible attempt to make aesthetic values independent of all the other values. Who will agree with Eliot, for example, that a poet cannot be an original thinker and that it is not possible for a poet to be a completely successful artist and yet persuade us to accept his ideas at the same time?"

Wilson treats Proust as the first Modernist exemplar of Symbolist fiction in that he imports into the novel Bergsonian metaphysics—namely, a subjectivization of time. Wilson understands that memory is celebrated in Proust because it nullifies time. The timeless character of memory, transfixed in the novel, transforms art into a transcendental experience itself outside of time. This anti-historical bias in Proust is so defiant to common sense that Wilson seeks an explanation in the medical pathology of his author: Proust's ideas—like his physical and psychological illnesses (such as his asthma, his seclusion in the cork-lined room, his homosexuality)—are so abnormal and distinctive to him that they cannot be of general use to us.

With respect to Joyce's *Ulysses,* the technical devices that establish the mythic method (which most readers since Eliot have regarded as the chief originality of the book) are criticized in *Axel's Castle* as an interruption of the story line, interpolations that Wilson finds himself skipping "in order to find out what has happened." Stein's rhythmic experiments with the sentence are "car-ried to such immoderate lengths as finally to suggest some technique of mesmerism." What she has written in the twenties, Wilson writes, "must apparently remain absolutely unintelligible even to a sympathetic reader. She has outdistanced any of the Symbolists in using words for pure purposes of suggestion—she has gone so far that she no longer even suggests."

Having indicated Wilson's irritation with the Modernists, let us pause here at the curious break that occurs in the process of writing *Axel's Castle,* a break that has its source in Wilson's increasing political radicalism in the 1920s. (Malcolm Cowley recognized the break in *Exile's Return,* but could not adequately account for its causes). Wilson's use of *Symbolism* shifts in meaning from the deployment of *literary techniques,* techniques of suggestive implication, to *a view of life,* a conception of the writer's relation to reality. *Symbolism,* for Wilson, comes to mean that aversion to reality, that cultivation of the self, that religion of art, that he finds aptly symbolized in Villiers de l'Isle-Adam's poem "Axel," with its Castle of Art as a refuge from the longueurs of actuality. This poem does indeed give Wilson's book its title and point of departure; but what truly bothers him is the persistence of this aestheticism in his own time.

We ought not to forget that the ultimate manifestation, for Wilson, of this Symbolist and Modernist deficiency—the departure from communication, from lucidity, from intelligibility, from serious engagement with the world of men and affairs—was the work of his contemporary, Tristan Tzara, whose "Memoirs of Dadaism" Wilson had reprinted in *Vanity Fair,* while he was managing editor there. This bizarre document forms the final appendix to *Axel's Castle* and was a vade mecum for Village Dadaists like Matthew Josephson and Malcolm Cowley in their zanier moments. Though Wilson reprints it without comment, Tzara's "Memoirs" stands as the ultimate absurdity of degenerate Modernist Romanticism.

III

Thus far I have isolated those moments in *Axel's Castle* where Wilson's classical values and rationalist temper recoil in distaste from the values and methods of his Modernist authors. This procedure seems to put Wilson out of all sympathy with his contemporaries. But since he is so widely regarded as the spokesman for Modernism, the method is essential to establish how alienated Wilson indeed was from the characteristic techniques and attitudes of these writers. It is now time to rectify the imbalance this method has produced. This necessary adjustment of the balance is compelled by the example of Wilson himself, for one of the features of what I have called the classical temper of Edmund Wilson is the desire to avoid extremes of critical judgment.

However distasteful his view of the Modernist disavowal of historical time and social responsibility, a Wilsonian sense of justice to his authors lifts him above the plane of any merely tendentious ideologue. If he is critical of

Yeats's fairies and automatic writing, he finds a ground to applaud Yeats for entering the Irish Senate and devoting himself to national affairs. Yeats is now "much occupied with politics and society, with general reflections on human life—but with the wisdom of the experience of a lifetime, he is passionate even in age. And he writes poems which charge now with the emotion of a great lyric poet that profound and subtle criticism of life of which I have spoken in connection with his prose."

Eliot is saluted for having left upon English poetry, in a mere ten years, "a mark more unmistakable than that of any other poet writing English." *The Waste Land* is brilliant in its "new technique, at once laconic, quick, and precise, for representing the transmutations of thought, the interplay of perception and reflection." Eliot is in fact "a complete literary personality." Proust, though regarded as a candidate for psychoanalysis, is recovered for didactic purpose when Wilson locates a passage in which Proust commends "the reality of those obligations, culminating in the obligation of the writer to do his work as it ought to be done, which seems to be derived from some other world, 'based on goodness, scrupulousness, sacrifice. . . .'"

The very classical demand for balanced judgment, then, obliged Wilson to acknowledge the Modernists' greatness. He explains the ground of his judgment to Maxwell Perkins, in a letter in 1928:

> Now I consider three of these writers—Yeats, Proust, and Joyce—among the greatest in modern literature, and even now, not half enough appreciated. And I consider the others—even Gertrude Stein, in her early fiction—very fine. And I believe that there is a good deal of justice in their criticism of the group before them—I believe that such a reaction was inevitable.

He told Perkins that he wanted "to give popular accounts of them which will convince people of their importance and persuade people to read them."

But the balance, with Wilson, fails of equipoise, because his politics overpowered him as writing the book dragged on toward 1931. Even though he acknowledges the Modernists' power, Wilson was really intellectually allied with the previous generation of Renan, Taine, Anatole France, Bennett, Shaw, and Wells, and with a literature more focused upon the social issues of the 1920s. Wilson wrote Perkins that

> the difference between these two generations—Shaw and France on the one hand, and Yeats and Valéry on the other—is, as I have suggested, that the earlier group were deeply influenced by the materialistic and mechanistic ideas of science, and that, partly as a consequence of this, they occupied themselves with public affairs in a way that their successors scorn. The generation since the war go in for introspection: they study themselves, not other people: all the treasures, from their point of view, are to be found in solitary contemplation,

not in any effort to grapple with the problems of the general life.

However much Wilson appreciated his Romantic and Modernist contemporaries, then, he could not help constructing *Axel's Castle* in such a way as to bring their work under severe criticism. To Perkins he observes:

> In every one of them, the emphasis on contemplation, on the study of the individual soul . . . has led to a kind of resignationism in regard to the world at large, in fact, to that discouragement of the will of which Yeats is always talking (I mean that he actually advocates discouraging the will in order to cultivate the fruits of lonely meditation). The heroes of these writers never act on their fellows, their thoughts never pass into action.

Instead of resignation, passivity, inaction, Wilson wanted a literature of social engagement, reflecting the will to power, manifest in action and politics. The Modernist aversion to grappling with the problems of the general life was spectacularly illustrated for him by E. E. Cummings, whom he visited in the summer of 1929. To Allen Tate, Wilson wrote:

> I have just been up to see Cummings. . . . He certainly has the most extraordinary point of view. It is 100 percent romantic. The individual is the only thing that matters, and only the gifted individual—in fact, only the poet and artist. The rest of the world is of no importance and has to take the consequences. He keeps protesting his lack of interest in anything outside the world of his own sensations and emotions. . . . I don't know whether the type of pure romantic can survive much longer, though perhaps I think this merely because the romantic in myself has recently been giving up the ghost.

The Romantic figure—such as Cummings, the visionary Yeats, the hallucinated Eliot, the neurotic Proust—was to be understood as a reaction to the events of World War I that had produced a general disgust with the terms and conditions of the modern world. Their subjective impressionism had political implications, and Wilson promised Max Perkins that he would touch upon this fact.

But in *Axel's Castle* Wilson's politics are latent and never very obtrusive, although he does preposterously reduce Proust, in *A la recherche du temps perdu*, to "the last great historian of the loves, the society, the intelligence, the diplomacy, the literature and the art of the Heartbreak House of capitalist culture. . . . " He wrote to Perkins, in criticism of the Romantic strain of Modernism:

> I believe that any literary movement which tends so to paralyze the will, to discourage literature from entering into action, has a very serious weakness; and I think that the time has now come for a reaction against it. The disillusion and resignationism of contemporary European literature is principally the result of the exhaustion which

has followed the war; and we in America, in taking from Europe . . . our literary standards and technique, have taken also . . . a sea of attitudes and ideas (I mean that the literary people have) which have absolutely nothing to do with the present realities of American life and which are largely inappropriate for us.

Wilson wanted an end to the paralysis of the will in Modernist literature, and he hoped that it would be initiated in the United States. Taking a cue from Van Wyck Brooks's *Letters and Leadership* (1918), Wilson claimed to detect "certain signs of it: in another generation or two, we may be leading the world intellectually. I feel that Europe is coming now to look to us for leaders while we are still respectfully accepting whatever they send us." But, in fact, *Axel's Castle* does not explicitly lay out Wilson's radical politics, nor does it so evidently reject the modern masters as reflections of a European mentality no longer of value to American art and its social conditions.

IV

For Wilson, the Modernist era had ended and would soon be replaced by a literature directed outward to the social and political realities of American life. I have called this view a recoil from the subjective impressionism of Modernist literature. When Christian Gauss suggested to him in 1929 that he write the confessions of a child of the century, Wilson replied:

> As for a *confession d'un enfant du siecle,* I fear that I shall never write one. That kind of thing is really repugnant to me, and I expect to become more and more objective instead of more and more personal. Incidentally, the diet of Symbolism, early and recent, which I have lately been consuming, has had the effect in the long run of wearying and almost disgusting me with this kind of subjective literature. I have a feeling that it has about run its course, and hope to see its discoveries in psychology and language taken over by some different tendency.

The different tendency was of course a literature of political engagement. It was already taking shape in his mind. Long before 1931 when *Axel's Castle* finally appeared, Wilson's interests were shifting to what he perceived to be the exploitation of the working class. The Sacco-Vanzetti case, which dragged on between 1920 and 1927, helped to radicalize Wilson's politics, and he and Herbert Croly at the *New Republic* quarreled over whether or not the case was a manifestation of class conflict. Wilson later remarked to Arthur Schlesinger, Jr., that "it was from this moment that I realized that [Croly] and I could not really agree about such matters (I had always had at the back of my mind the *Fabian Essays* and the Russian Revolution) and that I began to gravitate toward the socialist left." By May of 1930, Wilson was telling Allen Tate, "Politically I am going further and further to the left all the time and have moments of trying to become converted to American Communism. . . ."

Communism, he opined, was theoretically sound and practically right for Russia, but he naturally had trouble figuring out how the theory could be domesticated in America. In the year that *Axel's Castle* came out, he remarked to R. P. Blackmur: "As for politics, I wish that I knew of some promising movement or program for action, but I don't, and all that we write in *The New Republic* is still almost as much in the domain of pure literature as the productions of the Symbolist poets." What he wanted was the wedding of literature to political power, in the service of radical socio-economic change. Marxist action was necessary to contain big business (which he detested), to redistribute income, and to repress bourgeois liberalism. The Crash in 1929 seemed to pose the imminent possibility of political revolution.

For the next decade, Wilson's politics were avowedly Marxist, and, for a short while, he found his political program in the Communist party, which he wanted to be seized by native radicals like himself and thoroughly Americanized. Wilson's leftist position was manifest in his call in 1932 for the election of the Communist party candidate for the presidency, William Z. Foster; in signing various appeals and open letters; in joining the National Committee for the Defense of Political Prisoners and the American Committee for the Defense of Leon Trotsky; in reporting on labor disputes in America and political conditions in the Soviet Union, which he visited in 1935; and in publishing his polemics in such periodicals as the *New Masses,* the *Modern Monthly,* and *Partisan Review.* Wilson's Marxist phase subsides after *To the Finland Station* (1940), by which time he has had the good sense to become disillusioned with the Soviet Union's totalitarian purges and with American Stalinists at home.

I have leaped ahead from *Axel's Castle* in order to suggest how Wilson's growing radicalism in the twenties came to separate him from the Modernist movement to which he had at first been sympathetically drawn. Between 1930 and 1950 or thereabouts, left-wing radicals continued to lay claim to the Modernists whom Wilson had celebrated, even though, like him, they could not square their admiration with the cultural conservatism of these writers, whom they came to regard as an "anti-democratic intelligentsia." Wilson's tack was somewhat different. During these decades, much like the youthful radical Van Wyck Brooks, Wilson withdrew from the Modernists because they had proved themselves uncongenial to the left-wing politics he had developed. Lawrence, Yeats, Pound, Eliot, Cummings, Wyndham Lewis, and other conservative writers seemed to Wilson to have swept the field. Hence he retreated into the past. In *A Piece of My Mind* (1956) Wilson characterized himself as

> more or less in the eighteenth century—or, at any rate, not much later than the early nineteenth. I do not want any more to be bothered with the kind of contemporary conflicts that I used to go out to explore. I make no attempt to keep up with the

younger American writers; and I only hope to have the time to get through some of the classics I have never read. Old fogeyism is comfortably closing in.

Of course it would be a mistake to take the last remark at face value, as some of Wilson's critics did. But his aversion to Modernism and his longing for the ordered world and the polished classicism of the ancients are indeed hallmarks of his later work.

V

The ambivalence in Wilson's view of Modernism, as indicated in his letters and journals, makes it possible now to bring his limitations into clearer focus and to assess his place among the early students of the modern movement. First, Wilson's combative atheism, his naive faith in science, his hostility to religion, and his reduction of the inner life to a question of psychology (if not psychopathology) prevented him from fully engaging with the spiritual claims of some of these Modernists, such as Yeats and Eliot. These claims did not follow the direction in which Wilson's own secular rationalism invariably led. The very historical method that Wilson brought to bear upon his subjects could not adequately account for their representations of spiritual experience.

Second, their preoccupation with the inner life in lyric verse seems to have turned Wilson away from poetry itself toward a preoccupation with social novels, which he believed to reflect more directly the outward historical conditions then making a claim upon his attention. Wilson as a critic of poetry has always stirred controversy, but it is in *Axel's Castle* that he first commits the fatuity that verse is a dying technique and that the iambic line is no longer applicable to modern conditions. For this he was taken sharply to task. As Delmore Schwartz wrote in "The Criticism of Edmund Wilson":

> [W]hen it becomes a point of describing the technical working, the craftsmanship and the unique forms, which are an essential part of Symbolism, and the authors who were greatly influenced by the Symbolists, Wilson is impatient and hurried. He is not actually interested in the formal working which delivers the subject-matter to the reader. . . . It is for him the wrapping-paper which covers the gift; it is necessary to spend some time taking off the wrapping-paper and undoing the difficult knots of the cord tied about it, but the main thing is the gift inside, the subject matter.

Third, Wilson's criticism of subjectivist impressionism assumes—improperly, I think—that this literature has little relevance to external reality. But Wilson's view discounts the alterations in the consciousness of readers that such a literature may effect, with political consequences. His own reaction is exemplary in this respect.

Fourth, Wilson's treatment of Modernism failed of balance by the very inflexibility of his functionalist view of literature. His thought is of course consistent with the classical view of the purpose of literature—that it should please and instruct, and especially instruct by means of the inducement to aesthetic pleasure. But Wilson's position is taken virtually in defiance of that nineteenth-century revolution in aesthetic theory that—serving as a timely corrective to Victorian utilitarianism in art—argued for the relative to absolute autonomy of the artwork itself, a position that grounded in some measure the emerging New Criticism of the twenties, which rationalized the modern movement.

While defending himself in correspondence with Allen Tate, Wilson reformulated, more explicitly, the position that underlay his treatment of the Modernists in *Axel's Castle:*

> The point that I am trying to make when I talk in this vein is that art and science both are merely aids to getting by in the world. They harmonize or explain limited fields of experience and so comfort and reassure us and also, in proportion as they are original and profound, actually make it easier for humanity to live and improve itself. The end is not art or science but the survival and improvement of humanity. So that it seems likely that the time will come eventually when the artistic and scientific masterpiece will be not a theory or a book but human life itself.

Such a view of human perfectability is of course wildly visionary and reflects a utopian belief in the "New Man" to be created by the advent of Communism. But Wilson—who believed in the false claim of Marxism to be an objective science—could not see that his utopian view of human nature was a manifestation of the ghost of his own Romanticism. He told Tate that he had dramatized this idea in his novel *I Thought of Daisy,* where "the hero, seeing science and art as techniques for getting by, . . . embraces art as a useful trade like carpentry."

In a revealingly coarse redefinition, Wilson told Tate, "Symbolism was the atmospheric or arty side of art and naturalism the factual side," and, the two having become divorced, a reintegration of them needed to take place again. Wilson contrasted himself to Tate by pointing out that he was older enough than Tate

> to have been brought up on a literature which did mix these two elements in better proportions than the literature of after the war, which was what you were reading when you were in college and which seems to you the normal thing. It seems abnormal to me and that is the reason I take the point of view I do in *Axel's Castle;* I'm looking back to Shaw, Wells, Bennett, France, Flaubert, Dostoevsky, Ibsen, Renan, et al. You call some of these people propagandists, but I don't see how you could if you had read them— which I bet you haven't—if by propaganda you mean the kind of thing which is put out by governments, political parties, etc. If by propaganda you mean, on the other hand, merely attempts to persuade people of one's point of view or particular way of seeing things, every writer is a propagandist.

Wilson's position here reduces art to the rhetoric of persuasion, defining it functionally as a mere instrument, or technique, like science, for explaining experience, comforting and reassuring us, didactically helping us to survive, and effecting social progress. While this view is founded on the classical function of art as didactic, Wilson's notion that art is persuasive (if generalized) propaganda and the view that it is a "useful trade," like any other, reveal an unfortunate philistinism reminiscent of Shaw, Wells, France, and the other socially oriented anti-Symbolists with whom Wilson so unmistakably allied himself.

Art ultimately does, I believe, reveal a didactic horizon, but this horizon comes into view only after the immediate effect of the work of art—on feeling, on emotion, on sensibility—has been brought into the mind with its capacity for reflective thought. Wilson's chief deficiency as a critic of Modernism is that he had no vocabulary for the effect on sensibility of the ineffable, the mystical, or the transcendental. But this is a vocabulary that we need, for it is the language that poets use—and not always in ways that imply a vulgar religious superstition. As valuable as Wilson's Apollonian perspective may be, there is a Dionysian energy in art, an energy that may be terrible in its revelations, that gives to art a life—inseparably intertwined with its form—that we find humanly compelling. We see this most clearly in the dance, in music, in styles of painting like abstract expressionism where a direct and unmediated experience of this pre-rational, this primordial energy is sought for or expressed. It is a feature of art that is beyond cognition and rational analysis. Analysis may, in fact, in trying to explain art, end up in explaining art away. Wilson has a momentary intuition of this danger—the danger of transposing the irrational into the rational—in his comment on Valéry in *Axel's Castle:* "In trying to clear up his meaning, one clears it up too much." On the whole, however, Wilson was unwilling to concede the reality of the inexplicable as such or to admit that the revelation of the tragic and terrible in art may not "help" us in any tidy, cheerful way.

Wilson's was thus an agenda for what Denis Donoghue has called, in another context, *The Arts Without Mystery.* As Donoghue has observed, the arts do contain a mystery. This mystery, this energy, this life in art that eludes rational explanation, is transcendental, but its ineffability is not to be confused with the religious experience. Art is not religion and can never be a substitute for religion or for an ethics properly founded on religious belief. Donoghue is absolutely on target when he remarks, "If you wanted to neutralise the arts and remove their mystery, the best strategy would be to reduce them to psychology and politics."

In *Axel's Castle,* Wilson undertook to tame the Modernist writers by invoking the canons of a naturalistic psychology and a left-wing politics. Yeats's claim for a visionary experience, Proust's notation of a timeless dimension of consciousness, Joyce's location of the present within the cycle of the mythic return, Eliot's timeless moments of epiphanic revelation—all of these are neutralized by Wilson's reductionist historicism (in the manner of Taine, Renan, and Marx) to matters of psychology and politics. Yet if Wilson was not the perfect reader, he was, in his grasp of trends, movements, and typologies of literature, of immense value in his time; and his skeptical response to his major contemporaries made him a very lucid (though ultimately reductive) analyst of their work. At the very least, in *Axel's Castle* he formulated the problem that has continued to vex radical critics in their relation to the great conservative Modernist masters.

Barry Wallenstein

SOURCE: "Poetry and Jazz: A Twentieth-Century Wedding," in *Black American Literature Forum*, Vol. 25, No. 3, Fall, 1991, pp. 595-620.

[*In the following essay, Wallenstein discusses the influence of jazz on poetry as an exemplary artistic phenomenon of the twentieth century.*]

I

In a manner of speaking, poetry has always craved the company of music. Tone, rhythm and cadence, and lyricism, too, are the property of both. It is the music inside the poet's head that determines the meter and often the mood of the words as they fall to the page. So there is nothing odd about poets joining with musicians in the performance of their work. Minstrels, the troubadours and trouvères of Provence, and, in more recent times, poets have collaborated with musicians and composers in the creation of opera, lieder, tone poems, choral works, songs of all kinds, and jazz.

There are, it seems to me, three plausible ways to approach the jazz-poetry connection. The first is to search out traditional poetic definitions and values in jazz lyrics. Any number of songs have the effect of poetry, and one of the ways people often express deep affection for a lyric is to say, "That's poetry!" One especially good example is Billie Holiday's much admired recording of "Strange Fruit," originally a poem by Lewis Allen.

Since the performance of jazz is not unlike the performing language of poetry, one could also study the structure of a jazz composition and note how improvised solos break away from the original harmonic and melodic structure. Similarly, in much of modern poetry, especially free verse, the range of improvisatory gesture is immense. One could observe how a traditional-sounding first line will not necessarily be followed by a regular meter, rhyme, or rhythm.

The poet Hayden Carruth, in *Sitting In: Selected Writings on Jazz, Blues, and Related Topics,* talks at length about the juxtaposition of jazz and poetry. "The great contribution of the twentieth century to art," he says, whether it be jazz, poetry, or other types, "is the idea of spontaneous improvisation within a determined style, a style comprising equally or inseparably both conventional and personal elements. . . . Today," as one could easily say about jazz, "the open-ended, random, improvised, indeterminate poem, whatever its length, concluding usually with inconclusion, is our norm."

Throughout his book Carruth speaks of poetry and jazz in the same breath. "Those who burn out young . . . like John Keats or Charlie Parker," he says in one such example, "do not give us the solidity of achievement that we have from those who stay the course, like William Shakespeare and Coleman Hawkins." Charles Simic has made a similar linkage:

> The poet is really not much different from the tenor player who gets up in the half-empty, smoke-filled dive at two in the morning to play the millionth rendition of "Body and Soul." Which is to say that one plays with the weight of all that tradition but also to entertain the customers and to please oneself. One is both bound and free. One improvises but there are constraints, forms to obey. It's the same old thing which is always significantly different.

Still another approach to the jazz-poetry relationship, really an outgrowth of the first, is to observe the effects of jazz on twentieth-century poetry, including jazz-influenced diction and a recognition of jazz's place in American culture. In "Who Cares, Long as It's B-Flat," the first half of which appears below, Hayden Carruth combines his interest in jazz personalities with an ambiguous reclamation of Western poetry's *ubi sunt* ('where are they?') theme, which dates back to the twelfth century. This poem doesn't merely enumerate jazz names and places, but incorporates humor with frequent references to jazz expressions:

> Floyd O'Brien, Teagardens Charlie & Jack
>   where are the snowbirds of yesteryear?
>
> Boyce Brown, Rod Cless, Floyd Bean
>   Jimmy McPartland, Danny Polo
> Hank Isaacs, Davy Tough, Jim Lannigan
>   where are you, Jim Lannigan?
>
> Jesus but you were awful musicians
>   Pee Wee, Abby, and you Faz
> awful awful. Can you please
>   tell me the way to Friar's Point?
>
> "Aw, Jess." "Shake it, Miss Chippie, but don't
>   break it."
> "Listen at that dirty Mezz!" Can you
>   tell me please
> the way to White City? Where
>   can I find
> the Wolverines, Teschemacher?

Frank O'Hara's elegy to Billie Holiday, "The Day Lady Died," like all fine elegies, allows the mourned figure to inform and color all observations. The whole poem can be compared to an improvised performance around a set theme, in which the personality of the poet (or musician) sets the mood:

> It is 12:20 in New York a Friday
> three days after Bastille day, yes
> it is 1959 and I go get a shoeshine
> because I will get off the 4:19 in Easthampton
> at 7:15 and then go straight to dinner
> and I don't know the people who will feed me
>
> I walk up the muggy street beginning to sun
> and have a hamburger and a malted and buy
> an ugly NEW WORLD WRITING to see what the
>   poets
> in Ghana are doing these days
> ace to after days I go on to the bank
> and Miss Stillwagon (first name Linda I once
>   heard)
> doesn't even look up my balance for once in her
>   life
> and in the GOLDEN GRIFFIN I get a little
>   Verlaine
> for Patsy with drawings by Bonnard although I do
> think of Hesiod, trans. Richmond Lattimore or
> Brendan Behan's new play of *Le Balcon* or *Les
>   Nègres*
> of Genet, but I don't, I stick with Verlaine
> after practically going to sleep with quandariness
>
> and for Mike I just stroll into the PARK LANE
> Liquor Store and ask for a bottle of Strega and
> then I go back where I came from to 6th Avenue
> and the tobacconist in the Ziegfeld Theatre and
> casually ask for a carton of Gauloises and a carton
> of Picayunes, and a NEW YORK POST with her
>   face on it.
>
> and I am sweating a lot by now and thinking of
> leaning on the john door in the 5 SPOT
> while she whispered a song along the keyboard
> to Mal Waldron and everyone and I stopped
>   breathing

Similarly, Michael Harper, in his book *Dear John, Dear Coltrane*, pays tribute to the saxophonist and to Coltrane's album *A Love Supreme* (1964), as the following excerpt from "Brother John" suggests:

> Trane, Coltrane; John Coltrane;
> It's tranetime; chase the Trane;
> It's a slow dance;
>
> It's the Trane
> In Alabama; acknowledgement,
> *a love supreme,*
>
> It's black Trane; black;
> I'm a black man; I'm black;
> I am; I'm a black man—

Besides the common bond of improvisation in performance, poetry and jazz seek out fresh expression, as in these lines by Sonia Sanchez from "A Chant for Young / Brothas & Sistuhs": "yall / out there. looooken so coool / in yo / highs. / yeah yall / rat there / listen to me / screeaamen this song." Jazz historian Neil Leonard has written about "the incapacity of ordinary language to express extraordinary feelings. Unable to convey his deepest emotions in the received idiom, the jazzman invented terms of his own . . . prob[ing] the unknown or unexpressed with metaphor, oxymoron, and synecdoche in ways puzzling to unattuned ears." Likewise, the poet, unable to tell the deepest truths directly, often employs oblique references to emotions and events.

Both poetry and jazz-with-lyrics are arts of indirection, often extremely ironic constructs, sad and funny at the same time. Poets, like jazz artists, have traditionally been on the other side of the approved culture's speech and attitudes. This might explain the attraction many poets feel toward the music and language of jazz—especially African-American poets, for whom the jazz influence has been most profound.

Such are two faces of the jazz-poetry interaction: the poetry embedded in jazz lyrics, and the jazz influence so deeply felt and executed in the poetry of our time. But a third type, perhaps the most unusual, occurs when the two arts physically combine, when poets, collaborating with music in performance on stage or on record, merge language and music into a highly personalized synergism.

II

Jazz with poetic elements actually has origins in the church services of plantation blacks, where the preacher was one of the community who had a way with words. Like the poet/priests of ancient times, these preachers were said to have received the "call" from heaven. Their sermons moved emotionally and fluidly from speech to poetry: "to song to dance to moaning and back again," as one ex-slave has said. In the 1930s, recordings were made reenacting portions of these services, in which the preacher is calling out the gospel and the congregation is singing in response. The voices of the congregants reveal a fast, uptempo response to each call, combining the intensity of religion with the feel of poetry.

Some of the early recorded jazz talks or raps are ironic, humorous dialogues; siblings, one might say, of the give-and-take practice of the preacher-congregation "performance," without the religious element. In Louis Armstrong's 1927 recording of "That's When I'll Come Back to You," for example, the words are half-sung, with the man's response overwhelmingly nasty after the self-effacing plea of the woman:

> Woman: Now Daddy, I'll treat you right
> Promise never to fight
> If only you'll come back to me.
> You can knock me down, treat me rough
> And even kick me
> Black both my eyes, but Daddy,
> Please don't quit me.
>
> Man: Now Mama, when the rain turn to snow
> And it's ninety below—oh!
> That's when I'll come back to you.
> When I have nothing to eat
> No shoes for my little feet

> Then I will think what you been through.
> (But I know that's a lie.) (Armstrong)

Cab Calloway's first jazz raps—those recorded between 1930 and 1934, such as *Minnie the Moocher, Hotcha Razz-Ma-Tazz,* and *Kickin' the Gong Around*—are certainly humorous, but offer a marked departure from the dialogue tradition. Instead, they are monologues with coded language: words used as "covers" for subjects such as sex, drugs, anger, and sorrow not discussed "on the outside." Calloway's liner notes to a reissue of his early recordings show his penchant for this kind of language:

> Whether you're a queen—or even a cool V-8—or merely a jack, may we invite you to bust your conk to place this platter on your record deck at once. When you do, you'll hear these Calloway cats beat out the grooviest sounds. 'Cos when they play, the joint is jumpin'. The music is kopasetic! You'll blow your wig. And if you wanna lay some iron . . . well, do it, Jack—you don't have to be a rug-cutter. You don't have to wear your finest drapes to make this scene—a yarddog, with nothin' more than a dreamer can still make it. But if it's Mantovani or Mott The Hoople you're into, then it's gotta be neighho, Pops . . .

As Neil Leonard has pointed out, "Jazz talk has been highly eclectic, combining black English with the jargons of gambling, prostitution, larceny, music, and dance. Successive versions of this rapidly changing parlance started as semi-secret codes, vocational idioms which were proud symbols of the jazz community's identity and separateness." Another way to view the black jazzman's hip lingo may be as a bold manifestation of Whitman's maxim that American poetry be the language of the ordinary man. One kind of jazz talk—certain "mumbles" by Clark Terry that satirize the sometimes unintelligible "language" of downhome blues singers—is the furthest extension of this tendency.

Scat singing, an essential ingredient of the jazz singer's performing language, is akin to Terry's imaginative word play. "In the scat idiom," Leonard contends,

> are all of the characteristics of extreme, verbal ritual: special styles and registers, fast delivery, high pitches, broken rhythms, grunts, anomalous mumbo jumbo words, and prosaically pleasing repetitions. We can hear a good deal of this in the reet-a-voutee routines of Slim Gaillard and the bop utterances of Dizzy Gillespie in songs like "Oop-Bop-Sh'Bam." And the same qualities are evident in the early singing of Louis Armstrong, most notably in "Heebie Jeebies," which inaugurated the scat craze of the twenties.

Dizzy Gillespie's vocal antics, in particular, express a freewheeling exuberance, an irreverence, a feeling for nonsense—all with a style built on poetic phrasing and a keen sensitivity to word music. The jazz instrumental "Salt Peanuts," for example, is punctuated by the briefest of lyrics—the title recited in the same rhythmic durations of one of the tune's dominant phrases. Gillespie's "Oop-Bop-Sh'Bam," a group of nonsense words that act as a kind of scat chant, has no meaning even in the underground vocabulary of the bebopper. They are nonetheless funny, rhyming, rhythmic words that take on the essence of poetry. They are not merely filler, but central to the tune's energy and character.

Other novelty numbers that rely on talking raps, minimal language, or some other language device occur in the performances (to mention only a sampling) of Louis Jordan, Jon Hendricks, and Slim (Gaillard) and Slam (Stewart). One particularly engaging tune of Slim and Slam's—about playing the numbers—includes a rap in the place where a jazz improvisation often occurs:

> A tip on a number from the sly old fox
> You can play it straight or in the box
> On a Monday it's 284
> If you hit that day you gonna play some more.
> On a Tuesday 825
> If that comes out, good gracious alive!

Another Gillespie tune, truly the light verse of jazz-poetry performance, is his tongue-in-cheek version of the Negro spiritual "Swing Low, Sweet Chariot." Gillespie's rendition begins with a parody of call-and-response chant, which is then followed by this revision:

> Swing low, sweet Cadillac
> coming for to carry me home.
> I looked over Jordan and what did I see
> coming for to carry me home
> An Eldorado coming after me
> coming for to carry me home.
>
> *(Ebullient)*

As has often occurred with pioneers who are breaking new ground, the inventions of Gillespie and Charlie Parker were strongly criticized by the arts establishment in the 1940s. Even jazz patriarch Louis Armstrong, who incorporated talking, humorous narratives, and nonsense scatting in his own performances, joined those discontented with bebop's break with basic requirements, particularly that of making much sense.

Two recordings that presumably rankled jazz conservatives actually enlarge our understanding of how poetry/talk joins with jazz performance. The first is "Manhattan Fable" by Babs Gonzales, from his recording *Tales of Manhattan*. The narrative, for which Gonzales provides a glossary, is a spoken rap in front of music by Kenny Burrell and Roy Haynes. It is a fable about hipsters in the city, and behaves like poetry with its rhymes, strong rhythms, and indirection:

> Well about a deuce of long blacks and whites ago
> A guy from the lowlands came to the Apple
> He copped him a haine on Edison Blvd.
> Payin' those delivery dues
> Everything was fine as wine until he ran into
> Miss Hollywood eyes. . . .

Such entertaining verbal invention rounds out the lyric, affording a teasing glimpse into meanings that would suffer from more direct expression.

The second example is from Charles Mingus's *A Modern Jazz Symposium of Music and Poetry,* on which the one cut of poetry, Lonnie Elders' "Scenes in the City" (written with the assistance of Langston Hughes), is narrated by Melvin Stewart. This is a long composition, more serious than Gonzales's rap, more textured with frequent changes in tempo. The issues are similar—poverty and jazz—and in both cases the words would be fairly uninteresting without the musical accompaniment; but, as unified compositions, they engage lyrically as well as musically. Mingus's arco bass provides a sad fabric for Elders' words: "Well, here I am / right back where I was yesterday / the day before—the day before that / sittin' on a high bar stool / holding my dreams up to the sound of jazz music."

The same year Mingus recorded "Scenes in the City," his album *The Clown* was released. Even before the recording date, Mingus had conceived the story of a sensitive soul for the title cut. The "hip radio commentator" (Jean Shepherd) felt free during the recording session to embellish his narration with an improvised rap. As Mingus biographer Brian Priestley notes, "The verbal content of this piece was a collaboration between author and improviser in exactly the same way that Mingus's music had become."

Another jazz artist who utilized poetry in his work, especially in his longer compositions, is Duke Ellington. An early innovator of verse drama, Ellington orchestrated spoken poetry into songs and instrumental sections in *A Drum Is a Woman* (1957). Ellington's musical *My People,* staged in Washington in 1963, uses Negro spirituals and the blues to enhance its spiritual and civil rights message; and his religious works, such as the *Second Sacred Concert,* along with earlier compositions concerned with black consciousness, pointed the way for a generation of black poet/musicians who used music to transmit their own poetic language and cultural identification.

An example of this is "The Sojourner," the title cut from a 1974 album by Ensemble Al Salaam. As in Ellington's works, the vocal part of "The Sojourner" is primarily chanted and sung poetry with a religious orientation. Al Salaam's musical style is part-Eastern, part-African, and the poetry is stretched onto the voice, which (as in Ellington's case) is used as an instrument. Another example of black consciousness poetry is Juno Lewis's "I Juno," which comprises the entire first side of John Coltrane's album *Kulu Sé Mama* (1966). This work, a vocal and percussion feature dedicated to Lewis's mother, is chanted in an Afro-Creole dialect known as Entobes. It has both the ancient quality of an extended chant and a Whitmanesque openness and concern to define the self:

> I JUNO
> a drummer born. American.
> My father

a tuxedo drummer,
"Once a tuxedo drummer, always
    tuxedo drummer."
My mother's father was a captain's
    drummer,
F Company, 84th Regiment, Union Army
    during the Civil War, 1863-6.
For the past 12 years I have been a
    maker, designer,
    a son . . . . of drums.

Most of the poetry discussed in this section was conceived as part of a musical composition. As with the performance of song, these compositions of Gillespie, Ellington, Coltrane, and others are so well integrated that the term *collaboration* fails to define the degree to which the music and poetry are unified.

III

Langston Hughes, who recorded some of his poetry with Red Allen, Charles Mingus, and other jazz musicians, blazed the trail for jazz poets who would follow. All of his verse expresses the influence of the American music that was growing up simultaneously with him. Born in 1902, Hughes began performing his poetry with music in the 1920s and continued to do so throughout his career, with artists such as Randy Weston and Thelonious Monk. His poems, like his songs (which, by the way, outnumber the poems), are rich in allusion. Hughes's commentary is generally understated, and references to the source of his narrators' pain are oblique, as if the cool, detached tone could perhaps influence a change in fortune. Hughes's "Maybe" is subtle in this way:

I asked you baby,
If you understood—
You told me that you didn't
But that you thought you would.

One of Hughes's most anthologized poems is "Harlem," from the 1951 collection *Montage of a Dream Deferred.* "What happens," the narrator asks, "to a dream deferred?" Questions follow that are not meant to be answered but to provoke the auditor. The poem's rhetorical control—its movement from "dry up" to "fester" to "stink" to "*explode*"—is extraordinary. Another short poem in *Montage* is "Dream Boogie," in part reminiscent of Dizzy Gillespie's raps:

Good morning, daddy!
Ain't you heard
The boogie-woogie rumble
Of a dream deferred?

Listen closely:
You'll hear their feet
Beating out and beating out—

*You think
It's a happy beat?*

Listen to it closely:
Ain't you heard
something underneath
like a—

What did I say?

Sure,
I'm happy!
Take it away!

*Hey, pop!
Re-bop!
Mop!
Y-e-a-h!*

Later in *Montage* is "Flatted Fifths," a title that describes an important musical characteristic of modern jazz. It is as fine an example as possible of pure musical energy in a jazz poem:

Little cullud boys with beards
re-bop be-bop mop and stop.

Little cullud boys with fears,
frantic, kick their draftee years
into flatted fifths and flatter beers
that at a sudden change become
sparkling Oriental wines
rich and strange . . .

Little cullud boys in berets
    oop pop-a-da
horse a fantasy of days
    ool ya koo
and dig all plays.

Hughes was quite conscious of the impact of his work in performance. He remarks in *I Wonder as I Wander* that he "had worked out a public routine of reading [his] poetry that almost never failed to provoke, after each poem, some sort of audible response—laughter, applause, a grunt, a groan, a sigh, or an 'Amen' ." His strategy was first to offer jazz poems for humor and relaxation, then political poems and those with social messages for serious consideration. Like the jazz entertainer, Hughes needed to gauge audience response and sense that his poems were part of the audience's language.

IV

The conscious collaboration between formal poetry and jazz flowered in the 1950s, reflecting the gradual and ongoing twentieth-century adventure between poetry and other art forms, and contributing to the evolution of the poetic language built into jazz from its earliest days. Looking back on the 1950s, the two figures who stand out most clearly in the jazz-poetry field are two Kenneths: Patchen and Rexroth. By the fifties, bebop had entered the sensibilities of many poets; its jargon was a potent force, a magical language, particularly for these two rebels. Patchen and Rexroth were among the many poets who, stylistically opposed to the allusive, intellectualized work of the Pound/Eliot school, naturally gravitated toward jazz rhythms and jazz language. While Langston Hughes was actually transmitting that language into his verse, thus preserving an ethnic tradition, Patchen, Rexroth, and the entire school of beat poets developed a separate and distinct poetry—a poetry less derived from folk tradition than from the ego, but still within the tradition Hughes defines so clearly.

Hughes, Patchen, and Rexroth came of age in the 1930s— the "years of protest" in the arts and politics—, and they sympathized with the leftist thinking of the proletarian movement. Hughes brought ethnic consciousness to the general awakening of the white intelligentsia; Patchen was a writer of social consciousness; and Rexroth, also an anti-establishment figure, became known as an elder statesman to the beat movement in San Francisco.

In 1958 Rexroth published an appreciative essay on Patchen's work in which, verbalizing a common theme of the fifties literati, he remarked that "there is no place for a poet in American society." Nevertheless, "the bobby soxers do have [Patchen]. Against a conspiracy of silence of the whole of literary America, Patchen has become the laureate of the doomed youth of the Third World War. He is the most widely read younger poet in the country." Rexroth felt that Patchen's idiosyncratic language, along with his "integrity" and "earnestness," placed him in a line of independent voices that stretched loosely from Whitman through Vachel Lindsay and Carl Sandburg. But more than these poets, and even more than Rexroth, Patchen stands with such mavericks as Henry Miller and William Burroughs, who worked mostly apart from literary trends and movements.

Patchen's first recording of jazz and poetry appeared about the time of Rexroth's essay about him. (Either Rexroth hadn't yet heard the record or chose not to comment on it.) The poet recites or half-sings a wide range of his work, all of which appears in the third edition of his *Selected Poems*. The music on the record, performed by Allyn Ferguson and his Chamber Jazz Sextet, often sounds like a swing band, though there is also the suggestion of Miles Davis's 1950s ensemble sound. In the liner notes, Ferguson explains the "pact" between himself and Patchen:

> When first discussing the possibility of setting poetry to jazz, Kenneth and I agreed that the usual procedure of setting text to music would have to be abandoned. The final product, we felt, should be conceived in terms of the *poet's interpretation* of the text. It seemed evident, however, that the music would be quite unnecessary were there no attempt to bring about a meaningful union between the two mediums. We decided, therefore, to tape record the readings and underscore them. This procedure would have the double value of retaining the spontaneity of original reading while still allowing freedom for the creation of a significant musical entity. The music, then, was composed to the poet's readings—and designed to fortify the emotional content of the poetry.

The first poem on the record is "The Murder of Two Men by a Young Kid Wearing Lemon-Colored Gloves," which consists of the word *Wait* stated fifteen times, followed by the word *NOW*. On the record, Patchen shifts his intonation of each utterance of "Wait" to build up drama.

Wit and finesse, though, are only part of the story. That Patchen is a most musical poet may be gleaned from the page alone. Consider "And with the Sorrows of This Joyousness," which is made up entirely of transformations ("O apple into ant and beard / Into barn, clock into cake and dust," and so forth). The recorded version of the poem begins with a jolly, thirties-type swing introduction of some length. The series of metamorphoses builds in intensity, supported by the musical accompaniment, and, ultimately, the music crescendos with the ecstatic " . . . and years / Into yieldings . . O zeals of these unspeaking / And forever unsayable zones!"

Patchen's second poem on the record, "The Lute in the Attic," is set to a sixteenth-century tune by Thomas Campion. Many spaces are left open in the recitation for the music to establish a mood. The poem has a most lyrical ending:

> Come you and lie here at the side of your
>   brother . . .
>   I can tell you exactly how many times
>   these seven lean ducks have gone
>   fiercely round the rock of Santa Maura—
> And show you worse things than your father sees
> And show you things far worse than your father
>   sees, Willy.

Considering that Willy's "father's gone daft," the implications of such terrors make an exquisite contrast to the Elizabethan melody.

Next Patchen strings together a number of short poems and juxtaposes them against an unbroken jazz improvisation. Surreal and biting, the joyous music barely disguises a bitterness that is at the center of Patchen's vision:

> There was a man two inches shorter than himself
> Who always kept getting stuck in the sidewalk;
> And when the curious townsmen came
> To yank his arms and crush his hat,
> He'd spit in the eye of the lean,
> And steal the wallets off the fat.

The last poem of the series strikes a different tone—sad and wistful—and is close to song both in its lyrical refrain and in the way it rides the music:

> I Went to the City
>
> And there I did weep,
> Men a-crowin' like asses,
> And livin' like sheep.
> *Oh, can't hold the han' of my love!*
> *Can't hold her little white han'!*
> Yes, I went to the city,

And there I did bitterly cry.
Men out of touch with the earth,
And with never a glance at the sky.
Oh, can't hold the han' of my love!
Can't hold her pure little han'!

Patchen's second jazz album, released in 1959, was recorded with the Alan Neil Quartet. As occurred with the Ferguson band, the musicians here aimed for spontaneity and avoided literal interpretations. Alan Neil comments in the liner notes that the "feeling the poet releases through his reading must be met by the jazz guys with the same type of honest paralleling in their own speech, in the idiom of jazz." One poem that Patchen had recorded on his first LP ("Lonesome Boy Blues," *Selected Poems*) is reinterpreted on the second. In the first version, the poem is set to a mellow, downhearted blues. Patchen's voice is low and deadpan, his delivery slow, and there are significant breaks in which the musicians can solo. The recording with the Neil ensemble, however, emphasizes other possibilities. Patchen races through the poem, with the music of Charlie Parker propelling him. The words are more accented—with a swing feeling that the beat generation poets were in the process of imitating and developing.

Generally speaking, Patchen's voice on the second album is more involved with lyrical phrasing, through which he attempts to approximate the drama of a singing style. One particularly arresting segment consists of four song poems (with music composed by George Wallington) held aloft on a continuous, undulating melodic line that occasionally verges on schmaltz. These call attention to Patchen's unabashedly romantic side. His exalted, almost religious feeling, reminiscent of seventeenth-century love poetry, is heightened by numerous nature images that are brought down to earth by the music—sometimes soaring to coincide with the most emotional phrases, but always highlighting the most high-flown passages.

Kenneth Rexroth also recorded with jazz. Like Patchen's, Rexroth's collected poems contain tendentious elements (e.g., the money lords are strangling us, to hell with middle-class politics, and so forth), and, like Patchen, he was anti-establishment long after the thirties were over. A comparison between Rexroth's and Patchen's performances on record is irresistible, for both had similar styles. As with Patchen, Rexroth's voice veers toward song occasionally, and both are given to the romantic image ("The summer of your hair," intones Rexroth, a phrase that could as easily have been spoken by Patchen). Patchen's delivery contains more variety of phrasing, intensity, and tone. Rexroth's approach is frequently to pronounce short lines staccato, with an upswing at the end. Each of these lines is emphatic, to the point of making many of them sound like first lines.

Rexroth's poetic voice is generally more formal and stylized than colloquial or idiomatic. It is his delivery, as well as his immersion in the jazz world, that brands him a jazz poet. Rexroth's recordings are testimony to the

fact that it isn't necessary to use hip phrases and jazz talk to work well with jazz. He recites sixteenth-century English poetry to a jazz background—Edmund Waller's "Go Lovely Rose" is one example—, and it fits as well as his own!

Whitney Balliett, in an essay on Rexroth, calls him "the Daddy-O of the jazz poetry movement" and cites the poet speaking about jazz-poetry and his work as a jazz poet:

> "A good many people . . . think of jazz poetry at first as something only a weedhead would do. Not long ago, I worked with a symphony bassist, and he told me afterward . . . '[it was] one of the greatest experiences of [his] life.' I didn't start this thing. Renegade monks were doing it in the Middle Ages. Charles Cros, a nineteenth-century poet read his stuff . . . to *bal-musette* bands. There have been countless talking-blues singers in the South. Maxwell Bodenheim did it in the twenties and Langston Hughes in the thirties, and even I did it in the twenties, at the Green Mask, in Chicago, with Frank Melrose, a K.C. pianist. I've been reading poetry to jazz for years now, starting in The Cellar, in San Francisco, with a quintet. Since then, I've done all of the West Coast, St. Louis, Chicago, Minneapolis. . . . Modern jazz has outgrown everything. The audience can't get into the music without verbal contact. The poetry gives you that, and the jazz gets the poetry out of those seminars taught by aging poets for budding poets in cornbelt colleges. I plan a good deal of the musical accompaniment, which isn't all jazz by any means. I use bits of Satie, Webern, Boccherini. Each musician has a copy of what I'm reciting, with cues and musical notations on it."

Balliett's essay was first published in the late 1950s, at the height of the jazz-poetry revival. Around the same time, Rexroth's essay "Some Thoughts on Jazz as Music, as Revolt, as Mystique" was published in *New World Writing*. Rexroth's article was inspired by his 1958 jazz-poetry performance with the Pepper Adams Quintet at the Five Spot Café in New York, where a number of literary critics—"highbrow men-about-town," Rexroth calls them—were put off by the jazz accompaniment. In his apologia Rexroth says, among other things, that in jazz, "melody, rhythm, dynamics, ornamentation, tone color, sonority—all owe a great deal to imitation of the human voice." By extension, we may then think of poetry with jazz as actually reading jazz or speaking in jazz.

"We think that good poetry gives jazz words that match its own importance," Rexroth wrote in the liner notes to his album recorded live at the Blackhawk in San Francisco. "Then, too, the combination of poetry and jazz, with the poet reciting, gives the poet a new kind of audience. Not necessarily a bigger one, but a more normal one—ordinary people out for the evening, looking for civilized entertainment. It takes the poet out of the bookish academic world and forces him to compete with 'acrobats, trained dogs, and Singer's Midgets' as they used to say in the days of vaudeville." For his live recording,

Rexroth chose poems "which are simple enough so that they can be put across to the average audience in a jazz room" (*Poetry and Jazz*). He did not try to match his words to musical notes—utter them, say, in unison with the melody—but aimed for a spontaneous, free mutuality between the words and music. Nevertheless, the material was carefully prepared: Standard tunes, for example, were chosen for certain poems and were well-rehearsed.

The first poem on the album, "Married Blues," is presented in mock dramatic style. The poet leaves lots of room between stanzas for up-tempo blues improvisation:

> I didn't want it, you wanted it.
> Now you've got it you don't like it.
> You can't get out of it now.
>
> Pork and beans, diapers to wash,
> Too poor for the movies, too tired to love.
> There's nothing we can do.
>
> Hot stenographers on the subway.
> The grocery boy's got a big one.
> We can't do anything about it.
>
> You're only young once.
> You've got to go when your time comes.
> That's how it is. Nobody can change it.
>
> Guys in big cars whistle.
> Freight trains moan in the night.
> We can't get away with it.
>
> That's the way life is.
> Everybody's in the same fix.
> It will never be any different.

Rexroth's true poetic commitment, however, is to the graceful, romantic lyric. "Quietly" is one such work. On the recording, its first four lines are intoned in silence. Then a trumpet provides a steady melodic line behind Rexroth's gentle voice:

> Lying here quietly beside you,
> My cheek against your firm, quiet thighs,
> The calm music of Boccherini
> Washing over us in the quiet,
> As the sun leaves the housetops and goes
> Out over the Pacific, quiet—
> So quiet the sun moves beyond us,
> So quiet as the sun always goes,
> So quiet, our bodies, worn with the
> Times and penances of love, our
> Brains curled, quiet in their shells, dormant,
> Our hearts slow, quiet, reliable
> In their interlocked rhythms, the pulse
> In your thigh caressing my cheek. Quiet.

Despite his sway upon and affection for the poets of the fifties, Rexroth was opposed to their fostering a jazz mystique. The "influence of jazz on modern poets, particularly people who, like man, dig the beat scene, like, has been most unfortunate," Rexroth wrote in his liner notes to *Poetry Readings in the Cellar*. "Nothing is more lamentable than a poetaster in a beard reciting what he considers hip poetry." In "Some Thoughts on Jazz," he asks, "Does the hipster with his green beret, black glasses, and embouchure whiskers, . . . dirty feet in Jesus sandals, the amateur dope fiends with their adulterated marijuana, the Beat Generation, do these people represent 'jazz as a way of life'? God forbid!" Rexroth shared with the beat poets what may be called an autobiographical strain, but he regarded them as overly self-promotional. In the final analysis, however, it was because of the beat movement that poets got together with musicians in a visible effort to get that audience Rexroth realized was so essential to his art.

Jack Kerouac, with his love for jazz and his own expansive style of composition, was a fine jazz poet—much better, I think, with the music than on the page—, though his novels, especially the early ones, did much to promulgate the jazz mystique. *On the Road,* the book which more than any other defined the beat generation, is full of scenes at jazz joints where the hipster heroes groove on the music:

> Out we jumped into the warm, mad night, hearing
>   a wild tenorman
> bawling horn across the way, going "EE-YAH!
>   EE-YAH! EE-YAH!"
> and hands clapping to the beat and folks yelling,
>   "Go, go, go!" Dean was
> already racing across the street with his thumb in
>   the air, yelling,
> "Blow, man, blow!"

The jazz of the beats was bebop, and among their heroes were Charlie Parker, Dizzy Gillespie, and Thelonious Monk. As bebop expanded jazz's possibilities, it also provided the model of spontaneous composition that Kerouac and his circle followed. Kerouac made two recordings with jazz in the late fifties. One features Steve Allen on piano, the other Al Cohn and Zoot Sims on saxophones. The first, *Poetry for the Beat Generation* (1959), begins with Kerouac's friend Neal Cassady, the hero of *On the Road,* improvising a rap in front of the barely audible band. Steve Allen, using popular melodies such as "How High the Moon" to set the theme, plays an old-style, honky-tonk piano behind several of Kerouac's readings. The overall execution is rarely exciting, however, since Kerouac's emphatic, always intense voice is asserted over an unobtrusive musical background, preventing a fully unified effect. Nevertheless, Steve Allen's piano work is perfect for reinforcing the humor in Kerouac's poem "104th Chorus":

> I'd rather be thin than famous.
> I dont wanta be fat,
> And a woman throws me outa bed
> Callin me Gordo, & everytime
>   I bend
>   to pickup
>   my suspenders
>   from the davenport
>   floor I explode
>   loud huge grunt-o
>   and disgust

    every one
    in the familio

    I'd rather be thin than famous
    But I'm fat

    Paste that in yr. Broadway Show

Kerouac's sense of street language is always complemented by his detached wit.

The connection of voice to music is handled differently on *Blues and Haikus,* Kerouac's record with Zoot Sims and Al Cohn. In keeping with the call-and-response tradition, the saxophonists answer each line of poetry with a line of music. The integration of music and voice is awkward, however, as if the horns were playing the poem just recited. Whatever preciosity might be felt on the page by "No Telegram today / only more leaves fell," and similar turns of phrase, is successfully masked by Kerouac's forceful delivery on record. Still, Kerouac is able to introduce and make acceptable a so-called feminine sensibility in his identification with nature images: "Bee, are you staring at me? / I'm not a flower. / Why are you staring at me?" is one example.

Allen Ginsberg shares much of Kerouac's excitement for jazz and, like his friend, has incorporated it in his poetry. Though he doesn't carry on about jazz in his poetry as Kerouac did in his fiction, Ginsberg has acknowledged its influence. In his "Note Written on Finally Recording 'HOWL,'" Ginsberg observes that "by 1955 I wrote poetry . . . arranged by phrasing or breath groups into little short line patterns . . . [and] long saxophonelike chorus lines I knew Kerouac would hear the *sound* of . . ." (*Howl, and Other Poems*). Over the past few years Ginsberg has recorded *First Blues,* a collection of blues poems, and *The Lion for Real,* with Beaver Harris, Bill Frisell, and other jazz musicians.

A major irony of the beat movement, which has not been unnoticed, is that, despite its emulation of black culture, its practitioners were almost exclusively white. Anthologists of the period have had to search far in order to include a few black poets, such as LeRoi Jones (Amiri Baraka) and Ted Joans. Both performed with jazz in the fifties and are still largely associated with jazz-poetry today. Baraka has recorded several of his poems with jazz musicians. "Black Dada Nihilismus," a brutal, didactic, apocalyptic work that can be heard on the 1965 record *New York Art Quartet,* is probably the most compelling. Here is a brief excerpt:

    . . . Come up, black dada

    nihilismus. Rape the white girls. Rape
    their fathers. Cut the mothers' throats.
    Black dada nihilismus, choke my friends

    in their bedrooms with their drinks spilling
    and restless for tilting hips or dark liver
    lips sucking splinters from the master's thigh.

The strong imagistic sense, the overwhelming rhythms, and the sophistication throughout somewhat free this rant from its hard message and separate it from lesser works of angry social protest. Baraka's book *The Dead Lecturer* and the recording of this poem from it, more than any other single effort, seem to give license to rage.

In 1981 Baraka recorded an album with David Murray (tenor sax) and Steve McCall (drums) called *New Music—New Poetry.* In the liner notes, Baraka remarks that "poetry, 1st of all, was and still must be a musical form. It is speech musicked. It, to be most powerful, must reach to where speech begins, as sound, and bring the sound into full focus as highly rhythmic communication. High speech. The poetry I want to write is oral by tradition, mass aimed as its fundamental functional motive." Near the end of his notes, he adds that "we wanted the music and the words to extend each other, be parts of the same expression, different pieces of a whole. And the work to produce this product seemed effortless—it was a pleasure, a beautiful experience." Maybe, but the poetry on this album is mainly instructive verse and didactically political. There is little of the inventiveness for which Baraka is justifiably famous. The titles alone tell the story: "The Last Revolutionary," "Against Bourgeois Art," "Class Struggle in Music." This kind of poetry rarely reaches beyond sloganeering and could easily be mistaken for self-parody.

A few years earlier, however, on July 2, 1978, at The Public Theater in New York, Baraka recited (chanted, shouted, sang) his early poem "Rhythm and Blues (for Robert Williams in Exile, 1962)." Though this performance has not been commercially released, a tape I've heard of that evening's program stands for me as a high point in the collaboration of jazz and poetry. This modernistic piece—fragmentary, imagistic, with its narrative threaded beneath clusters of words—is no less political than Baraka's later work, but it is far more textured and personal than the material he recorded in 1981. The predominant musical theme—Simon and Garfunkel's "Home"—provides a lyricism to match the words. And as imagery and Baraka's tone of voice shift, the music keeps pace, becoming, finally, wonderfully discordant.

Many insights into Baraka's life in jazz and his views towards jazz-poetry can be found in his *Autobiography.* Here is a sampling:

    [A] poet I heard [who] had a great influence on
       me [was] Amus Mor (once
    David Moore) from Chicago. I heard him read in
       Chi his masterwork,
    "We Are the Hip Men." The way Amus put the
       music directly into the
    poem, scatting and being a hip dude walking
       down the street letting the
    sounds flow out of his mouth—putting all that
       into the poetry—really
    turned me on. We wanted to bring black life into
       the poem directly. Its
    rhythms, its language, its history and struggle. It

was meant to be a
poetry we copped from the people and gave them
   right back, open and
direct and moving. . . . [We] were drenched in
   black music and wanted
our poetry to *be* black music. Not only that, we
   wanted that poetry to be
armed with the spirit of black revolution.

V

Throughout the '70s and '80s, jazz-poetry on record has been dominated by black poets speaking directly and musically of their racial experience. As Amiri Baraka observes in his liner notes to *New Music—New Poetry,* "Black poetry in the main, from its premise . . . means to show its musical origins and resolve as a given. Just as Blues is, on one level, a verse form, so Black poetry begins as music running into words. . . . Poets like Larry Neal, Yusuf Rahman, The Last Poets, Askia Touré, Jayne Cortez write a poetry that brings the words into music and the music into words, reflecting the most contemporary of both expressions, made one."

The Last Poets is a performing group with shifting personnel. Their one album of poetry and percussion includes performances by the poets Ablodun Oyewold, Alafia Rudim, and Omar Ben Hassen. The titles—"Run Nigger," "New York, New York," "When the Revolution Comes"—indicate the subject and emotional content. Rage is more controlled and filtered through popular rhetoric here than in Baraka's poetry, and the language is more street poetry than anything else.

Another jazz poet is Eugene Redmond, who has performed his work with the jazz trio of Jimmy Daniels on guitar, Ed Jefferson on percussion, and Ike Paggett on soprano sax. Redmond's record *Blood Links and Sacred Places* (1973) contains political poems such as "Angel of Mercy," for Angela Davis. The record is most memorable, however, for its infusion of street poetry—nonpolitical this time. "Invasion of the Nose" is one such work, an original folk poem about a ghetto super-hero. Redmond produced his album, one of a growing number of independent productions of jazz-poetry that so far have been condemned to limited availability.

In 1974, Strata-East, a small jazz label, released two very different jazz-poetry albums. *Winter in America,* by poet/musician Gil Scott-Heron, was something of a hit, probably due to the Leon Thomas-style singing and lyrics. "H2O-Gate Blues," a spoken poem on the record, exhibits an excellent wedding of music and voice, in addition to being a clever and satirical protest poem. Strata-East's other poetry record, *Celebrations and Solitudes,* is by poet Jayne Cortez, whose voice is the perfect instrument for jazz: flexible, warm, hard-edged, and swinging. Cortez's recitation style suggests song and is set off beautifully by the inventive bass playing of Richard Davis.

Cortez's second album, *Unsubmissive Blues,* has a more assertive race consciousness and a greater presence of African rhythms and references. These qualities are augmented on two subsequent albums, *There It Is: Jayne Cortez and the Firespitters* and *Maintain Control,* which feature Denardo Coleman, Charles Moffett, Jr., and, on the more recent album, Ornette Coleman. *Maintain Control* features a heavy, electrified back beat, and Cortez's own version of dub poetry. There is much variety here, from James Brown riffs to church music to marching band harmonies. Cortez's poetry is no less political than Baraka's, and her delivery is just as rhythmic and powerful.

Because of commercial marketing practices and a long history of seeing poetry as a nonprofit venture, Jayne Cortez and others are forced to distribute their work at readings and concerts. Yet in the cafés of large cities, in the jazz lofts, and at college campuses, jazz-poetry is being performed. Patti Smith, though her fame rests on rock music rather than jazz, and Tom Waits are both poets who successfully present their verse to large audiences. Jeanne Lee is a jazz vocalist who sings and recites her own poetry. Bill Zavatsky is a poet who sometimes accompanies himself with piano. Boruk, who recorded the album *Black Hole Boogie* in 1974, combines his poetry with music and slide shows. Doug Hammond, a pianist and percussionist, included poetry on his album *Ellipse* (1977). Harry Lewis frequently performs with jazz artists such as David Murray and Fred Hopkins, and Archie Shepp has been known to recite his poetry at gigs.

And while today's rap music is hardly jazz and the language of rap is often something other than poetry, there are nonetheless examples that may somehow enlarge the ongoing collaboration between poetry and jazz. *The Breaks,* by Kurtis Blow with Tito Puente (1980); Grand Master Flash's *The Message* (1982); *Suicide,* by Busy Bee (1987); Kool Moe Dee's *How Ya Like Me Now* (1987); and K.R.S.l's *Stop the Violence* (1988) are all interesting for their amalgamation of music and verbal pyrotechnics.

The poetry read with jazz music takes particular risks in its duality. It is necessarily rooted in black culture and is also transcendent and aspiring. With one foot in the street and the other in the skies, only the best blends are satisfying.

POETRY AND DRAMA

Philip Hobsbaum

SOURCE: "The Growth of English Modernism," in *Tradition and Experiment in English Poetry,* Rowman and Littlefield, 1979, pp. 289-307.

[*In the following excerpt, Hobsbaum examines Modernism in English poetry.*]

A conventional account of the rise of modern poetry would, I suppose, run something like this. The Georgians of Sir Edward Marsh's anthologies represented the last lap of Victorianism; sheltered subjects and literary diction. English poetry was shocked out of such torpor by the Imagists; insistence on experiment, free verse. The resistance to 'modernism', so called, was overcome by the mature work of T. S. Eliot in *The Waste Land* and of Ezra Pound in *Hugh Selwyn Mauberley*. But their work has never been satisfactorily implemented in English poetry. Hence the thin poetic haul of the last thirty years.

There is a lot in this that one can agree with. Yet it seems to me far from the whole truth. And, indeed, a certain amount of dissatisfaction with this account has been shown already. In a broadcast of 1961, George MacBeth clearly showed that the Georgians were not so whimsy-whamsy as popular accounts, and popular anthologies, have suggested. He maintained that the links between the Georgians, such as Lascelles Abercrombie, and the modernists, such as Eliot, were closer than had been suspected. In Mr MacBeth's opinion, the true division was in terms of subject matter—whether, for example, the poet was committed to violence as a mode of purgation or whether he was himself half in love with it.

But this, again, may be only part of the truth. It is one thing to show that both Eliot and Rupert Brooke were influenced by the Metaphysicals. It is quite another to demonstrate that they made comparable use of that influence. One may suggest, too, that Pound's attitude towards the First World War was a very different matter from that of his fellow non-combatant Lascelles Abercrombie.

There is a third account of the rise of modernism which has become rather fashionable. It can be located in the critical work of academics who are also practising poets. Examples that come to mind are John Holloway (*The Colours of Clarity,* 1964) and Graham Hough (*Image and Experience,* 1960). Their account of modernism would suggest that it was interesting while it lasted, and even salutary, but that its impetus is now spent. For them, this is an age of consolidation rather than experiment. From this view, it is only a step to regarding Eliot and Pound as eccentric side issues. Yet, in a sense, they are— at least, as far as English poetry is concerned.

It is not often enough remembered that Eliot was an American by birth and upbringing. Of course, he lived in England for many years, was a naturalised citizen and had associated himself with a number of characteristically English institutions. Even his intonation was impeccably English—and, in its way, this was a disadvantage. One could say, for example, that Eliot's urbane reading of his own verse rather muffled its colloquial, experimental and, I would add, very much American qualities.

For one thing, Eliot characteristically wrote in free verse. This form has never sat very happily on the English lan-

guage, as the nineteenth-century attempts of Southey, Arnold and Henley show. Yet Eliot brings it off. How?

Again, Eliot's work exhibits the characteristic American qualities of free association or phanopoeia and autobiographical content. English verse, however, has been at its best as fiction: an arrangement of what is external to the poet to convey the tension or release within. Yet Eliot's work succeeds. Why?

Associated with the problem of Eliot is that of Ezra Pound. This poet has a name for being erudite, cosmopolitan. Yet even in his most polyglot cantos he is most himself in colloquial American speech. For instance, in Canto XCVI (*ante* 1959) Pound describes Justinian's law reforms in the tones of the Idaho of his boyhood.

It may well be that both Eliot and Pound have been read with too English an accent. To my ear, the rhythms of 'Sweeney Agonistes' (1924-7) are akin not only to those of demotic American speech but also to the attempt of the Beat poets to write a genuinely popular poetry. And doesn't such a lyric as 'My little island girl' very much anticipate the innovations of 'Poetry and Jazz'?

To go further than this: one could say that the experiments of Eliot and Pound have not fallen on stony ground in the United States. R. P. Blackmur (*Language as Gesture,* 1952) has demonstrated the influence of the *Four Quartets* (1936-42) on Wallace Stevens's 'Notes toward a Supreme Fiction' (1941-2). The grinding personal verse of Pound, in *Mauberley* (1920) as in the Pisan Cantos (1948), seems to me, raised to the nth power of concentration, to be right behind Lowell's *Life Studies* (1959). But, of course, American poets have always excelled in the public presentation of the minutely personal. One thinks of Whitman, who wrote in what has always been agreed to be a distinctively American language. I would never deny that Eliot and Pound, who derive so much from Whitman, are fine poets. But is it not time to insist that they are fine *American* poets? And that therefore the influence they may be expected to have on English poets is limited?

Certainly it is true to say that the influence of Eliot and Pound on English poetry has, so far, been damaging. The American language lends itself peculiarly to the assemblage of images in an emotional rather than a logical connection. Whitman's catalogues (and, indeed, those of F. Scott Fitzgerald) would convey next to nothing if compiled by an Englishman—or even an Irishman, as so many dead pages in Joyce's *Ulysses* only go to show. Yet free association in free verse was what was recommended to a rising generation of poets in the 1930s by that most astringent critic of modern poetry, F. R. Leavis.

New Bearings in English Poetry (1932) is a model of approach to the modern poets with which it deals—in many respects. But it was written at a chaotic period in English literature. That we are now able to challenge some of Leavis's formulations is, in no small part, due to the efficacy of his work as a critic. He must, however, be held responsible for the view that English poets could do nothing better than to learn from the experimentalism of the modernists; by which he particularly meant Eliot and Pound. And, although he has deprecated the talent and influence of W. H. Auden, Leavis must be seen as part of the same movement—a movement which sought to graft Eliot's essentially American experimentalism on to English poetry.

And so we have Auden writing long poems such as 'Easter, 1929' with a distinctively *Waste Land* mood and landscape; Louis MacNeice, closest of all the 1930s poets to Eliot technically, trying to produce a spiritual diary (1938) in the mode of *Four Quartets;* and the weakest of them, Day Lewis and Spender, sticking odd Eliot properties on to a characteristically Georgian nostalgia, traditionalism—even patriotism. The 1930s poets adapted Eliot's vatic utterance to their own leftish brand of doom; but they all grew out of it.

Stephen Spender and Cecil Day Lewis—how did their reputations come about? More important, how did they, along with Louis MacNeice, come to be joined with W. H. Auden, a poet of really considerable talent? Most important of all, how did the work of these four come to be acclaimed as a renaissance in English poetry?

The renaissance, it is now plain, was stillborn. A revaluation of the 1930s would establish William Empson, Robert Graves, Norman Cameron and perhaps John Betjeman as the most interesting new poets then writing; that is, apart from Auden himself. And the whole does not amount to more than an orbit of rather minor satellites. What is most immediately noticeable is that they lack any sort of a sun.

Auden himself was incapable of supplying the necessary energy. For one thing, he himself was poorly chanced for survival. Some of his early poems are at once synthetic and impenetrable:

> Between attention and attention
> The first and last decision
> Is mortal distraction
> Of earth and air,
> Further and nearer,
> The vague wants
> Of days and nights,
> And personal error. . . .
>
>   ('Easy Knowledge', 1930)

The tone is, in cant phrase, 'significant'—but significant of what? Do all these abstractions really refer to anything beyond themselves? And this riddling nicety—'Between attention and attention'—is it really making any sort of valid distinction? It is easy enough to see where it all derives from:

> Between the idea
> And the reality
> Between the motion
> And the act

> Falls the Shadow
>   —*For Thine is the Kingdom.* . . .

Eliot's 'Hollow Men' (1924-5), no less. And Eliot's hollow men were what the poets of the renaissance were to become.

For, if we look at the periodicals of the time, we shall find singularly few of the rave notices that literary historians have led us to expect. On the contrary, it seems as though the editor of *The Criterion* had a busy private line to Oxford and Cambridge—spying the coming man before he had come, as A. S. J. Tessimond, a neglected poet of the time, was to write.

Auden's play *Paid on Both Sides,* dedicated to Cecil Day Lewis, appeared in *The Criterion* in January, 1930; 'Four Poems' by Stephen Spender, dedicated to W. H. Auden, appeared in October, and were followed by three more a year later. Meanwhile reviews by the coming men began to appear: Auden on psychology, Spender on belles lettres. It was not a revolution in the palace so much as a tacit capitulation. The Editor of *The Criterion,* of course, was T. S. Eliot.

Not all the new young men were untalented. The reviews by Empson and James Smith are still worth looking up, and *Paid on Both Sides* has a sustained brilliance that Auden never was to achieve again. What one objects to is the way these reputations were made: there is about it all a distinct air of *fait accompli.* Whatever F. S. Flint or Peter Quennell said in *The Criterion*'s poetry chronicles, Auden had come to stay. And with him came a good deal else.

Because, it's no good pretending, a great deal of bad verse was published, and not so much held up to acclamation as passed by default. There it was, the new writing, and that was all there was to say about it. Even the more traditionalist *London Mercury* had an article solemnly discussing the young poets in terms of a new range of emotion: 'the reader's receptive faculties, then, have to be sharpened'. But what one may question is the whole mode of reading involved.

There is no doubt that Eliot did a great deal to disrupt English poetry, as distinct from that of the Americans. He claims descent from the Jacobean playwrights and Laforgue, but the most evident ancestor is Walt Whitman. Whitman's abstractions and random collocations have a raw life of their own, a form even through their formlessness; and this has remained highly characteristic of American poetry ever since. *The Waste Land* (1922) is, indeed, a heap of broken images: this is its meaning, and, to some extent, its distinction. But that kind of writing has never worked well in England. And so Eliot's revolution seems nowadays not so much modernistic as alien.

This is borne out by a look at English poetry written before his influence became a *sine qua non* for young poets. Who wrote this, for example?:

Sixty odd years of poaching and drink
And rain-sodden waggons with scarcely a friend,
Chained to this life; rust fractures a link,
    So the end. . . .

(c. 1923)

Hardy? Edward Thomas? In fact, it is the earliest
Auden—Auden before the influence of Eliot. And I do
not think that it is accidental that this gifted poet showed
himself at the very first in the direct line of Hardy and the
war poets; that is to say, in the mainstream of English
poetry. But in the absence of any strong direction—
Hardy was very old and the war poets had not survived—
English poetry became Americanised, and the result was
the brilliant obscurity of Auden's first (1930) volume.

Auden himself came out of it all rather well, which only
goes to show how difficult it is to extinguish an original
talent. Many of his 1930s poems have a warmth of moral
indignation that irradiates the distorted language in which
he felt constrained to write. There are moving passages in
'Easter, 1929', in *The Orators* (1932), even in *The Dog
Beneath the Skin* (1935). He is seen at his best in an
interim selection, *Some Poems* (1940). And it seems to
me that Auden's reputation will have to rest mainly upon
the poems which exist as finished wholes. Many of these
are to be found in his sequences, 'In Time of War'
(1938) and 'The Quest' (1940). Not surprisingly, they are
couched in the unEliotesque—and very unAmerican—
form of the sonnet.

Other poets were not so lucky: at least in their achievement—for their success, of course, was assured. The
earliest Spender reads like Eliot's 'Preludes' sucked in
and spat out again:

Moving through the silent crowd
Who stand behind dull cigarettes . . .
The promise hangs, this swarm of stars and
    flowers,
And then there comes the shutting of a door. . . .

(1933)

But Auden soon replaced Eliot in his work, and it gained
a new—but suspiciously general—exaltation:

oh young men oh young comrades
it is too late now to stay in those houses
your fathers built where they built you to build to
    breed
money on money it is too late. . . .

(1933)

This is shrill, and the sense is governed by the sound, as
witness the functionless outbreak of alliteration in the
third line quoted. Compare it with the Auden poem from
which it obviously derives:

Seekers after happiness, all who follow
The convolutions of your simple wish,
It is later than you think. . . .

('Consider', 1930)

One would have thought that such a comparison would
have stamped Spender as a second-rate derivative, but
nothing of the sort. The resemblance assured him of a
currency among those who wanted to know what, in poetry, was the latest thing. Even his anthology pieces do
not very much transcend the sort of verse I have quoted.
Image after image defies visualisation, and offers little to
any other kind of reading. The end of 'I think continually' is characteristic in its evasive rhetoric:

Born of the sun they travelled a short while
    towards the sun,
And left the vivid air signed with their honour.

(1933)

The reputation of Cecil Day Lewis seems to have grown
less rapidly, though it is interesting to see that the *London Mercury* backed him most heavily of all the new
young poets. Perhaps this was an involuntary tribute to
his Georgian temperament: the modernism of his work
never seems more than a superficial overlay. *Transitional
Poem* (1929) came out with the usual *Waste Land* sort of
notes, but, in spite of its pretensions, was quite evidently
a collection of harmless lyrics:

It is becoming now to declare my allegiance,
To dig some reservoir for my springtime's pain,
Bewilderment and pride, before their insurgence
Is all sopped up in this dry regimen. . . .

The allegiance is most immediately, of course, to Auden;
but the quatrains and rhymes take us back to a world
before Eliot. Day Lewis mentions charabancs as well as
hedgerows, but then so did Sir John Squire, and it is open
to doubt whether either of them realised that there were
more subtle ways of being modern. Later on, Day Lewis
was to coarsen the fabric of his verse and produce this
sort of claptrap:

Look west, Wystan, lone flyer, birdman, my bully
    boy!
Plague of locusts, creeping barrage, has left earth
    bare:
Suckling and centenarian are up in air,
No wing-room for Wystan, no joke for kestrel
    joy. . . .

(*The Magnetic Mountain,* 1933)

But, towards the end, Day Lewis gave up what must always have been an unequal battle. Those who thought
him one of the new modernists lived to see him read and
remembered for poems such as his later 'Sheep Dog Trials in Hyde Park' and 'View from a Window' (1961):
gentle, discursive, countrified in that urban way beloved
of Squire and the *London Mercury*.

Louis MacNeice is something of a different proposition.
Unlike his two contemporaries, he seems to have been
able to go direct to Eliot. Just as early Auden sometimes
reads like Edgell Rickword's parodies of Eliot, so early
MacNeice often looks like those of Henry Reed:

But I, Banquo, had looked into the mirror,
Had seen my Karma, my existences
Been and to be, a phoenix diorama,
Fountain agape to drink itself for ever
Till the sun dries it. . . .
                              (*Blind Fireworks*, 1929)

However, to do MacNeice justice, he seldom in his later work takes himself as solemnly as this. His last volume, *The Burning Perch* (1963), is a craftsmanlike collection. One reason why even his work of the 1930s has worn better than that of his contemporaries is because he is, on the whole, unsentimental and often genuinely witty:

The country gentry cannot change, they will die in
   their shoes
From angry circumstances and moral self-abuse,
Dying with a paltry fizzle they will prove their
   lives to be
An ever-diluted drug, a spiritual tautology. . . .
                       ('An Eclogue for Christmas', 1933)

But, one's tempted to remark, Auden did this sort of thing much better; and this brings us to the crux of the whole problem.

The renaissance of the 1930s rested largely on the shoulders of one man: W. H. Auden. And, as we have seen, he himself had ignored his earliest influences and embarked upon a misdirected course. His consequent idiosyncrasies were therefore erected into a style for modern poetry, and one has only to look at the Preface to Michael Roberts's *Faber Book of Modern Verse* (1936) to see how rooted the misconception became. Modern poetry was to be obscure, condensed, fantastic in diction, freed from logic. The result was that a lot of minor talents, such as Kenneth Allott and Charles Madge, wrote themselves out for want, among other things, of a viable tradition; and the revolution ended in Dylan Thomas and the New Apocalypse, when poetry in England ceased to mean anything even to an educated reader.

The conventional account of the last fifty years would suggest that the social realism of the 1930s was succeeded by the romanticism of Dylan Thomas, George Barker and the New Apocalypse. In fact, of course, the resemblance between these two 'schools' is obvious. Both indulged in longish autobiographical poems full of private allusion, usually in free verse, often of considerable obscurity, indulging in a scolding rhetoric unparalleled since the best days of Shelley. Pound could get away with this; in the Usura Canto (*ante* 1937), for example, or in 'Pull down thy vanity' (Canto LXXXI, *ante* 1948). And Eliot could admit his reader to his inner vision in 'Burnt Norton' (1935) and not for a moment seem posturing or rhetorical. But then Eliot and Pound are Americans; and their 'modernism' is only suited to an American language. In English poetry of the 1940s, obscurity grew so fast and rhythms broke down to such an extent that the whole attempt at modernism collapsed in the nerveless verse and chaotic imagery of the New Apocalypse. Hence, of course, what came to be known as the Movement.

This was largely academic in origin—an attempt by several poets who were also critics to consolidate English verse. In comparison with Dylan Thomas, or even with early Auden and Spender, the poems of the Movement were self-contained, formal, and sought to be unrhetorical. Like most schools of poetry, the Movement proved too constricting for its more talented members. Philip Larkin, Kingsley Amis, Donald Davie and Thom Gunn wrote in the 1960s better than they ever did before, but not in a Movement style. That style, abstract and gnomic, produced little of real value. But the Movement was a necessary spring-cleaning whose real achievement may have been to arouse interest in a number of poets of the 1930s who had been unjustly neglected. The most impressive of these is probably William Empson. His verse represents a concern for form, and this is an integral quality in the best English poetry. Without it, it turns into something very like prose.

This concern for form is a characteristic of a development in our poetry which has not, I think, been separately recognised. Perhaps it is best called English modernism—as opposed to the American brand of Eliot, Pound, Stevens and Lowell.

The chief heroes of English modernism died sixty years ago, in the First World War. I am thinking particularly of Edward Thomas, Wilfred Owen and Isaac Rosenberg. They seem to me quite distinct from the Georgians, on the one hand, and the modernists, on the other. Their deaths were probably as great a set-back as those of the young Romantics, Shelley, Keats and Byron, even though, it is true, their achievement is less. And their deaths were a set-back for much the same reason. Their uncompleted work was not sufficient to prevent the tradition of which they were the latest development from falling into misunderstanding and neglect.

Only a superficial classification would relate Edward Thomas to the Georgians. His poems certainly belong to an English tradition. But it was one that had been much misunderstood, as was shown by the cool reception of Hardy's *Wessex Poems* in 1898. This tradition was as much one of prose as of verse: the tradition of Cobbett and Jefferies—on whom, as a critic, Thomas had written most eloquently. Indeed, it was Thomas's own prose that led his friend, Robert Frost, to suggest that he should try his hand at poetry. Thomas never actually followed Frost's advice to write up his nature studies into free verse. But there is no doubt that much of Thomas's strength is that he has no time for the merely 'poetic'. His poetry really is 'a valley of this restless mind'. He objectifies his inner emotions in terms of landscape, or even fiction. That is to say, Thomas will often act out his feelings in terms of story, scene and character, rather than state it in his own person. And this brings him close to the writings of the finest poetic realists—Wordsworth, for example, whose best work is in narrative form, and is akin to the great nineteenth-century novelists, themselves the heirs of Shakespeare. This inclination towards fiction rather than autobiography or lyric is characteristic of much good English poetry.

Palgrave's attempt to exclude all but lyric from the canon of English verse gave us a singularly denuded *Golden Treasury* (1861). Hardy, who had grown up in the age of Palgrave, was concerned to point out rather deprecatingly—in his introduction to *Wessex Poems*—the fictional element in his own verse. And perhaps it was this element of fiction in Thomas's work, as well, that disturbed the Georgians. It is notable that the lyric 'Adlestrop', rather a conventional production, was for years Thomas's prime anthology piece, as 'The Darkling Thrush' was Hardy's. There is nothing so decisively great in Thomas's output as Hardy's cycle 'Veteris vestigia flammae' (1912-13). But no more than for Hardy does the countryside represent for Thomas an escape. Thomas has been much admired for his powers of observation and presentation of particulars. And they are remarkable. But more remarkable still is Thomas's placing of war as a senseless evil against the life-giving rhythms of the countryside. This can be seen in his poem entitled 'As the Team's Head-brass' (1916). Here, the certainty of the ploughman's coming and going is contrasted with the delays and uncertainties of the war. The lovers going into the wood, the ploughman harrowing the clods, are an assertion of life against maiming and death. And the war's encroachment on these rhythms is symbolised by the fallen tree that, if the ploughman's mate had returned from France, would have been moved long ago. The relationship with Hardy's war poems is clear enough. One thinks most immediately of 'In Time of "The Breaking of Nations"' (1915)—where there is also a pair of lovers and a ploughman.

The difference between Thomas and even the better Georgians is that his work is an advance on that of the poetry of a previous generation. His is a genuinely modern sensibility. His view of life has none of the heroics easily assumed by those who never saw action, or who joined the army in a spirit of public-school patriotism. But Thomas had little chance to produce trench poetry. His best work was written before leaving for France, while training as an officer. He had time to contrast the English countryside he was forsaking with the Front—known only by hearsay and implication—to which he was going. And he was killed soon after reaching it.

There were Georgians who saw more action than Thomas; most notably Siegfried Sassoon. And Sassoon's poems certainly include much first-hand reaction to experience. But I am not so sure that his technique is equal to his sensibility. In 'Break of Day' (1918) he presents an escape from battle into the memory of a happy day's hunting. Here we have the detailed realism for which Sassoon was to become famous. No doubt this is a strong poem if compared with the early, and now suppressed, war poems of Graves. Graves is prone to smother his action in whimsy and allusion. But, if we think of Edward Thomas, Sassoon's tone seems over-insistent; and perhaps the most telling comparison is with Wilfred Owen.

It cannot be too often stressed that Owen's technique is not just a matter of half-rhyme. Half-rhyme had been used before in English; though not, it is true, so systematically. Owen's genius can be localised in the actual function of the play of the vowels. They mute those overconfident metres which Owen, in common with other war poets, inherited from the previous, more peaceful, generation. He makes them as exploratory and tentative as his feelings about war. In comparison, Sassoon's verse seems too assured for its content. It is impossible to feel that "Strange Meeting", for example, will ever date.

Owen's verse, like Thomas's, is akin to fiction rather than lyric. He will adopt a persona, as in 'Strange Meeting' (1918), where he acts as interlocutor; or he will don the mask of narration or of dramatic monologue. Even when he seems to be speaking more directly, as in his poem 'Exposure' (1917), he will use the first person plural rather than singular. So that he seems to be speaking for all the soldiers of the war, not just himself. His details are never merely descriptive. In 'Exposure', they are selected to create an atmosphere and a human attitude—the cold, and the soldiers waiting. It is rather too simple to regard Owen as the poet who hated war. His verse has a distinctively modern ambivalence. In 'Exposure', as well as a grim endurance on the part of the troops, there is a desire for action—a desire which is mocked by the way in which the weather is presented in this poem through a metaphor of war: dawn massing in the east her melancholy army.

Owen recognises with startling modernity that death can be as certain out of battle as in it, and dispiritingly inglorious. His poems are the defeat of lyric; anything but a subjective cry of pain. We are not asked to take an interest in something just because it was happening to Wilfred Owen. A point is made, through the evocation of a war, about war itself. Owen's landscape has all the conviction of Sassoon's with a dramatic quality which Sassoon never achieved. Not one death is expressed in Owen's work, but many:

> Tonight, His frost will fasten on this mud and us,
> Shrivelling many hands, puckering foreheads
>   crisp.
> The burying-party, picks and shovels in their
>   shaking
>   grasp,
> Pause over half-known faces. All their eyes are
>   ice,
>   But nothing happens.
>
>   ('Exposure')

Like Owen, Isaac Rosenberg characteristically uses the plural first person. But he appears to use words, as D. W. Harding remarked (*Scrutiny*, 1935), without any of the usual couplings—as though the poetry were formed at a subconscious pre-verbal level. Although as authentic as Owen's stretcher-party, that of Rosenberg is alarmingly unexpected:

> A man's brains splattered on
> A stretcher-bearer's face;

His shook shoulders slipped their load,
But when they bent to look again
The drowning soul was sunk too deep
For human tenderness. . . .
('Dead Man's Dump', 1918)

One can see why Gordon Bottomley, Rosenberg's first editor, was so hesitant about publishing this poetry. And why, even when it was published, it took so long to make its way. Even the iambic metres have been abandoned in this plasm of verse.

Rosenberg's technical innovations cannot be so readily discussed in terms of a past norm as those of his fellows. One can hear in the lines of Owen's 'Strange Meeting' the rhythms of the Induction to 'The Fall of Hyperion' (1819); but muted down, made tentative by the half-rhyme. The poem gains much of its strength through adapting familiar material to an utterly new situation. Keats's goddesses occur, too, in Rosenberg's 'Daughters of War'. But that is as far as resemblance goes. The myth is created in strikingly individual terms—a kind of sprung verse, for example, developed quite independently of Hopkins. To find Rosenberg's antecedents, one has to look at the juvenilia, as one does with Hopkins's surprisingly Keats-like fragments (c. 1866). The mature poems resemble nothing but themselves—though there are signs that gifted poets of our own time, such as Ted Hughes and Peter Redgrove, have learned from them. It would be absurd, then, to call Rosenberg a traditionalist, except in the sense that he is in the tradition of Keats and Shakespeare. His sprung verse, use of myth, are wholly unlike anything produced by the 'traditional' Georgians. It is as though an overmastering experience had blasted out a new form:

The old bark burnt with iron wars
They blow to a live flame
To char the young green days
And reach the occult soul; they have no softer
    lure—
No softer lure than the savage ways of death. . . .
('Daughters of War', 1918)

Nobody could call this traditional in manner or content. Yet it is certainly not modernist, if by modernist one thinks of a play of images, a montage in free verse. If Rosenberg's verse has affinities, it is not with Eliot or Pound but with the apocalyptic prose of Lawrence. Not, indeed, with Lawrence's verse, which seems to go more diffuse as it gets further from Hardy and nearer to Whitman. Rosenberg, unlike the modernists, does not go in for phanopoeia or free association. His poems exist through images, but never for them. And the poems are not autobiographical, though they may be a projection of his inner feelings, in terms of myth. Rosenberg projects outwards. As in 'Daughters of War', he creates a fiction in which feelings are acted out. Like Thomas and Owen, he conveys his emotion through poems about something other than himself.

These poets used forms and, at the same time, changed them. Thomas used Wordsworthian blank verse that had also learned from nineteenth-century novelists, and could absorb further narrative and symbolic properties. Owen muted the rhythms of the Romantics by the use of pararhyme, and applied the Romantic sensuousness to a new and grimmer end. Rosenberg manipulated events even more resourcefully than the others, and revitalised dramatic blank verse into a sprung rhythm that has not been fully exploited even now. They all marked an advance not only in technique but in sensibility. The world of 1911 must have seemed very remote in 1915. A glance at the newspapers of the time would establish the difference in terms of an increased sense of strain, a wedge driven between the generations, criticism of hitherto accepted values by the young. But it was only the exceptional writers who could get much of this into their verse. In the last analysis, the success of Thomas, Owen and Rosenberg as poets could be attributed to their recognition of the need to adapt the old forms to express new experience.

This should differentiate them on the one hand from the American modernists, who broke forms down, and, on the other, from the Georgians, who relied on them even when they proved inapplicable to modern experience. But Thomas, Owen and Rosenberg died young, and, after the war in which they died, a debate broke out about which was the right path for poetry. The alternatives offered were American modernism, as represented by Eliot, Pound and the Imagists, and traditionalism, as represented by Abercrombie and Squire. As Mr MacBeth has reminded us, this debate was quite irrelevant to the facts. This, indeed, was seen at the time by that most penetrating reviewer, John Middleton Murry. In reviewing two volumes, one from each of the opposed schools (*Athenaeum,* 1919), Murry said that there was no distinction between them, and the only distinction he himself would be prepared to recognise was one of quality. Such quality was found in the only good poem in either of the volumes: it was Owen's 'Strange Meeting'.

But this distinction was not made by Leavis in *New Bearings* or Michael Roberts in the influential anthology *The Faber Book of Modern Verse.* Leavis and Roberts got rather taken in, it seems to me, not by Eliot's poetry, but by his position *vis à vis* tradition. They thought that Eliot would be more of a healthy influence than he could possibly be, at least on Englishmen. Leavis and Roberts were examples of progressive opinion at the time. Other *loci classici* are the contemporary undergraduate magazines, such as Cambridge's *Experiment* (c. 1929), edited by Empson and Bronowski. And this, in its turn, led to the misapplication of the talent of many young poets, notably the so-called Auden group. Out of this came the misunderstanding of the stream of consciousness which eventually led to the confused writings of the 1940s; when it became the fashion for writers, even some of undeniable talent, to switch off their intellect before they started composing.

Poets of Auden's generation could have saved themselves by learning less from Eliot and Pound and more from

Thomas, Owen and, perhaps especially, Rosenberg. But history was against them. My main thesis, I suppose, is that English poetry in the twentieth century has had four atrocious strokes of luck. They are worth enumerating. First of all, that the wrong emphasis should have been placed on the work of one great Victorian who could have had a useful influence—I mean Hardy. Secondly, that the Georgians, for the most part, should have chosen to regard tradition as a resting-place rather than a launching-pad. Thirdly, that three of the poets who *were* developing an essentially English modernity should have been killed in the war—their publication, too, was delayed and incomplete. And, lastly, that Eliot and Pound should have chosen to start an essentially American revolution in verse technique over here rather than in the United States, and so filled the gap which the death of the war poets left with an alien product whose influence has been a bad one.

But, over the period since the First World War, some talented poets stuck out against this. John Betjeman ignored Eliot and did what no Georgian ever really managed: married a modern sensibility to a Victorian verse technique. Andrew Young carried on the Georgian mood, but with a first-hand reaction to experience and a metaphysical wit most of the Georgians lacked. Of these poets, Norman Cameron now seems to be one of the most valuable. But his hard economical verse excludes so much of life that he hardly seems to be a man of our own time. And what I have said of Cameron would do very well for Robert Graves too. There has been a tendency to erect Graves into a great modern poet. But he does not seem to me to have done much more than refine the Georgian techniques. Much of what Mr MacBeth finds to admire in the Georgians at their best will be found in the work of Graves. His place is with Sassoon and Blunden rather than with Owen and Rosenberg. What one misses in Graves is a real sense of the world we live in. His keen eye is directed inwards. His verse represents, for all its formal toughness, a retreat from a concern with man as a social animal into a species of pastoralism. Though more skilled than Cameron, he seems to me inferior in sensibility.

Auden could have saved himself by learning more from Owen and less from Eliot. But William Empson is a different case entirely. His imitators in the Movement laid stress on all the wrong aspects of his verse—the tedious refrains, the occasional stiffness of form. Empson's better poems are probably his early ones: for example, 'To an Old Lady', and 'Part of Mandevil's Travels' (c. 1928). His best later poems are those like 'Let it Go' and 'Success' (c. 1935) which were not imitable by the technical means at the disposal of most of the Movement writers. Empson is not a straightforward traditionalist. As Owen did, he uses forms in such a way as to make them new. With all this, his subject matter is restricted and his *oeuvre,* though intense, is narrow.

Neither those who passively imitated Eliot nor those who explicitly reacted against him have produced a very rich crop of poetry. But Empson, who did neither, is an example for the poet of today in more ways than the obvious one. The work of a gifted poet who owes little directly to him, Philip Larkin, shows many of the qualities one finds in Empson's work and in the sonnet sequences of Auden. Larkin is a formalist in so far as he uses rhymes and writes in regular metres. But his rhyme is not the clanging full rhyme which suited the self-confidence of a Swinburne rather more than the self-doubt of a Francis Thompson, let alone of an Elroy Flecker. Larkin uses mainly pararhyme in his poem 'Church Going' (c. 1951), creating, in the varying degrees of rhyme he utilises, the unease in church, not of a worshipper, but of an agnostic.

This is done even more subtly by a rather younger poet, Peter Porter. He uses degrees of pararhyme to secure different degrees of emphasis. Here is an example, from his poem "Metamorphosis' (1959):

> This new Daks suit, greeny-brown,
> Oyster-coloured buttons, single vent, tapered
> Trousers, no waistcoat, hairy tweed—my own:
> A suit to show responsibility, to show
> Return to life—easily got for ten pounds down
> Paid off in six months—the first stage in the
>   change.
> I am only the image I can force upon the town.
>
> The town will have me: I stalk in glass,
> A thin reflection in the windows, best
> In jewellers' velvet backgrounds—I don't pass,
> I stop. . . .

Notice the pattern of pararhyme here. In the remainder of the stanza, 'glass' rhymes with 'mask' and 'last'—mocking the assurance of his attitude, 'I am myself at last'. In the same way, the vowel of the 'town' echoes throughout the first stanza before it comes clanging in on the keyline, 'I am only the image I can force upon the town'. The rhyme here is made all the more blatant by alternating with unrhymed lines. The rhythms, too, are flexible. The basic unit is a five-stress line, but there is no syllable count. The first line of the first stanza, 'This new Daks suit, greeny-brown', has only seven syllables for its five stresses, while the last line, 'I am only the image I can force upon the town', has fourteen—from diffidence to brash self-confidence, one might say.

There is a poem by another contemporary, Peter Redgrove, called 'Bedtime Story for my Son' (1955), which chases a rhyme through many kinds of assonance and half-rhyme, just as the couple in the poem chase the ghost of a child, and catches up with it only in the last two lines, as the couple do:

> Love pines loudly to go out to where
> It need not spend itself on fancy, and the empty air.

Of course, it is cruel to isolate metre and rhyme in this way, particularly when one is sure the poet himself did not. But it is a way of bringing home a point: that what is best in English poetry generally and in the present generation of English poets is this vigour within the discipline of shape—freedom through reshaping a form rather than breaking it down. Inevitably, there are poets such as Charles Tomlinson who are trying to carry on the technique of the American modernists, just as there are poets, like David Holbrook, who have pushed traditionalism further than ever the Georgians did. But they seem to me to be fighting against the genius of the time and the language. D. J. Enright, Philip Larkin, Ted Hughes, Peter Porter and Peter Redgrove—to name only five of our best contemporary poets—did not get together in a huddle to find out which form they ought to write in. Their feeling and experience come out in the way I have described, a way that is neither modernism nor traditionalism—perhaps because it is the only way it can come out in English poetry at present. It is a way that relates back to Owen, master of the half-rhyme, and through him back to the Keats of the 'Fall of Hyperion' and back to Shakespeare. Another line could be traced through Redgrove and Hughes through Thomas and Rosenberg to the blank-verse fictions of the Romantics, Shakespeare and even back to the medieval poets. Either way, it is the central line of English poetry. And I cannot see much good work being done far away from it. Like any tradition, however, it is alive only as long as it can be re-created. But I am not being optimistic when I say that it seems to be in process of re-creation, after a long quiescence, at the present time.

Martin Esslin

SOURCE: "Modernity and Drama," in *Modernism: Challenges and Perspectives,* edited by Monique Chefdor, Ricardo Quinones, and Albert Wachtel, University of Illinois Press, 1986, pp. 54-65.

[*In the following essay, Esslin provides an overview of the sources and characteristics of Modernist drama.*]

Concepts, it must be said at the outset, like modernity, modernism, and the avant-garde fill me with apprehension and doubt. They are, after all, concepts of relation rather than fact. To ask, "What is the avant-garde? What is modern?" is rather like asking: "How long is a piece of string?" In relation to yesterday's art, today's art is modern, or avant-garde. As the great illuminator Oderisi tells Dante in the eleventh canto of the *Purgatorio:*

> Credette Cimabue nella pittura
> tener lo campo, ed ora ha Giotto il grido,
> sì che la fama di colui è scura.
>
> Così ha tolto l'uno a l'altro Guido
> la gloria de la lingua; e forse è nato
> chi l'uno e l'altro caccerà del nido.

(Once Cimabue held sway in painting, but now does Giotto have the cry, so that the fame of the former is obscured. Similarly has the one Guido taken from the other the glory of the language, and perhaps one has been born who will chase both from the nest.)

"Modern," after all, only means "le dernier cri." In German it can even mean no more than "fashionable." The term, I suppose, entered discourse about art and literature with the Renaissance, when there were disputes as to the relative merit of works produced in Greek and Roman antiquity as against those of the period; Swift later dramatized this conflict in his *Battle of the Books.*

And yet, in the course of the nineteenth century the concept of modernity *did* acquire a special significance, at least for the people then experiencing what to them seemed a truly epochal change of lifestyle and thinking. With the coming of the industrial revolution, the introduction of the steam engine, powerlooms, railways, the telegraph, and photography, and the new uses of electricity, together with the rise of new ideologies (Darwinism, Marxism, positivism) and the decline of belief in revealed religions, it must have seemed to these people that an age had truly come to an end. As it happens—and this is particularly true of the drama—there had previously been a longish period during which academicism, i.e., a fairly rigid adherence to what seemed immutable standards of excellence and technique in the writing and performance of plays, was prevalent, so that it really seemed that these orthodoxies were destined to undergo the fate of all the others that were being swept away. In fact, of course, this was merely an optical illusion: the rigid standards of the French Academy or the English Augustans were themselves fairly recent phenomena and by no means immovably fixed as absolutes, as then appeared.

Seen from this angle, the beginnings of Modernism, in our present sense, in drama dates from the rise of the romantic movement, or, in Germany, from the *Sturm und Drang.* As such, initially, it was a revolt against *formal* restraints, the tyranny of the three unities, and the rigid rules of seemliness that governed the art of acting, the restraints on what could and what could not be shown on the stage.

When absolutes are dethroned, everything becomes *relative;* and the beginnings of Modernism in this sense are intimately linked with the growth of a sense of the differences between cultures synchronically and between historical epochs diachronically. Different standards of ethics, different values of beauty are suddenly perceived as possible. With the rapid technological changes of the nineteenth century the historical sense became dominant. As Nietzsche put it in *Jenseits von Gut und Böse* (1886):

> Der historische Sinn . . . auf welchen wir Europäer als auf unsre Besonderheit Anspruch machen, ist uns im Gefolge der bezaubernden und tollen Halbbarbarei gekommen, in welche Europa durch die demokratische Vermengung der Stände und Rassen gestürzt worden ist—erst das neunzehnte Jahrhundert kennt diesen Sinn, als seinen sechsten Sinn. Die Vergangenheit von jeder Form und Lebensweise, von Kulturen, die früher hart nebeneinander, übereinander lagen, strömt dank jener Mischung in uns "moderne Seelen" aus, unsre

Instinkte laufen nunmehr überallhin zurück; wir selbst sind eine Art Chaos. . . . Durch unsre Halbbarbarei in Leib und Begierde haben wir geheime Zugänge überallhin.

(The historical sense . . . which we Europeans claim as our specialty, has come to us as a consequence of the enchanting and mad semi-barbarism into which Europe has been plunged by the democratic commingling of social classes and races—the nineteenth century is the first to know this sense, as its own sixth sense. The past of every form and way of life, of cultures, that previously had lain in hard distinction side by side, or one above the other, now, thanks to that commingling streams into us "modern" souls, our instincts now run back to everywhere; we, ourselves, are a kind of chaos. . . . Through our semibarbarism, in body and in desire, we have secret access everywhere.)

And, significantly, among the examples Nietzsche quotes for this semibarbarity, caused by the newly acquired historical sense, is the renewed vogue of Shakespeare, whose drama he calls an

erstaunliche spanisch-maurisch-sächsischen Geschmacks-Synthesis, über welchen sich ein Altathener aus der Freundschaft des Äschylos halbtot gelacht oder geärgert haben würde: aber wir—nehmen gerade diese wilde Buntheit, dies Durcheinander des Zartesten, Gröbsten und Künstlichsten, mit einer geheimen Vertraulichkeit und Herzlichkeit an, wir geniessen ihn als das gerade uns aufgesparte Raffinement der Kunst und lassen uns dabei von den widrigen Dämpfen und der Nähe des englischen Pöbels, in welcher Shakespeares Kunst und Geschmack lebt, so wenig stören als etwas auf der Chiaja Neapels: wo wir mit allen unsren Sinnen, bezaubert und willig, unsres Wegs gehn, wie sehr auch die Kloaken der Pöbel-Quartiere in der Luft sind.

(astonishing Spanish-Moorish-Saxon synthesis of tastes, about which an ancient Athenian from among the friends of Aeschylus would have almost died of laughter or anger: but we—we accept this very wild proliferation of colors, this mixture of the most tender with the most coarse and artificial, with a secret connivance and heartiness, we savor him as the highest refinement of art that has been specially vouchsafed to *us;* and in doing so we are as little disturbed by the noxious exhalations, and the proximity, of the English mob, in which Shakespeare's art is at home, as we are when walking down the Chiaia in Naples: where we go on our way, enchanted and willing with all our senses, however much the cloacas of the slums are in the air.)

And to complete this analysis Nietzsche—who, while obviously deploring what he describes, yet must reckon himself one of the semibarbarians of the modern age, with its sense of history—adds:

Das *Mass* ist uns fremd, gestehn wir es uns; unser Kitzel ist gerade der Kitzel des Unendlichen, Ungemessnen. Gleich dem Reiter auf vorwärts-

schnaubendem Rosse lassen wir vor dem Unendlichen die Zügel fallen, wir modernen Menschen, wir Halbbarbaren—und sind erst dort *in unsrer* Seligkeit, wo wir auch am meisten—*in Gefahr sind.*

(Let us admit it: we are strangers to the concept of *measure;* what tickles us is precisely the tickle of the infinite, the unmeasured. Like a rider on a horse that is bolting we drop our reins, confronted with the infinite, we modern human beings, we semi-barbarians—and we are in our greatest ecstasy where we also are most—*in danger.*)

I have quoted this passage of Nietzsche's at such length because I believe that he more than anyone else was the true prophet of modernity, whose wild, extravagant thought perceived and penetrated the nature of the epochal change that the nineteenth century brought to human history, and predicted with astonishing insight many of the terrible and cataclysmic events that inevitably followed from that change of human destiny. It is ironic that Nietzsche is just now being discovered by the currently fashionable intellectual gurus in France, for already in his own time he was very much perceived, even by the popular imagination, as the embodiment of all that was dangerous in modernity. I remember how as a child I got hold of some pious piece of popular fiction—alas, I have forgotten its author and title—published in Germany around the turn of the century. When its heroine confessed to her parents that she had fallen in love with a young man, her father sternly said, "I hope he is not one of those who reads Ibsen and Nietzsche."

And indeed, Ibsen and Nietzsche have much in common. It is sometimes as though Ibsen, outwardly the sober, well-regulated bourgeois, embodied basic traits of Nietzsche in his characters; Nietzsche, for example, wrote the passages I have just quoted in the highest village of the Swiss Alps, Sils-Maria, at the foot of a glacier, shortly before madness engulfed him—as though he was living out the destiny that Ibsen had given Brand; and Ibsen's Stockmann rages against the rule of the mob as much as Nietzsche ever did. Above all, Ibsen, like Nietzsche, denounced the false morality of a dying world. This, to my mind, is the essence of Modernism in the sense in which we are discussing it here: the "revaluation of all values" of which Nietzsche spoke, the quest for a new morality beyond the old concepts of Good and Evil; and the rejection of the philosophical and religious, metaphysical, basis of those beliefs. If Ibsen, in *The Lady from the Sea,* created the first truly, and consciously, existential heroine in drama, who can make her choice only after she has been given total freedom to make it (and whether Ibsen got this existentialism from Kierkegaard or not is as yet a matter of dispute), Nietzsche also clearly prefigured the drama of existential choice:

Wenn ich den Vorgang zerlege, der in dem Satz "ich denke" ausgedrückt ist, so bekomme ich eine Reihe von verwegnen Behauptungen, deren Begründung schwer, vielleicht unmöglich ist,—zum Beispiel, dass *ich* es bin, der denkt, dass überhaupt ein Etwas es sein muss, das denkt, dass Denken eine Tätigkeit und Wirkung seitens eines Wesens ist, welches als Ursache gedacht wird, dass es ein "Ich" gibt, endlich, dass es bereits feststeht, was mit Denken zu bezeichnen ist—dass ich *weiss,* was Denken ist.

(If I dismantle [perhaps today we should translate "deconstruct"] what happens that is expressed in the phrase "I think," I'll get a series of daring assertions, that are difficult, perhaps impossible, to prove: for example that it is *I* who is thinking; that, indeed, it must be something that is thinking: that thinking is an activity and an effect on the part of an entity that can be regarded as a cause; that, finally, there is such a thing as I; and that it is already established what it is that can be called thinking—that I *know* what thinking is.

Much of Beckett is prefigured in these ideas, as it is, even more clearly, in this passage in which Nietzsche deals with the concept of the soul:

Man muss zunächst auch jener andern und ver-hängnisvolleren Atomistik den Garaus machen, welche das Christentum am besten und längsten gelehrt hat, der *Seelen-Atomistik.* Mit diesem Wort sei es erlaubt, jenen Glauben zu bezeichnen, der die Seele als etwas Unvertilgbares, Ewiges, Unt-eilbares, als eine Monade, als ein *Atomon* nimmt: *diesen* Glauben soll man aus der Wissenschaft hinausschaffen! Es ist unter uns gesagt, ganz und gar nicht nötig, "die Seele" selbst dabei loszu-werden und auf eine der ältesten und ehrwürdigsten Hypothesen Verzicht zu leisten: wie es dem Unge-schick der Naturalisten zu begegnen pflegt, welche, kaum dass sie an "die Seele" rühren, sie auch verlieren. Aber der Weg zu neuen Fassungen und Verfeinerungen der Seelen-Hypothese steht offen: und Begriffe wie "sterbliche Seele" und "Seele als Subjekts-Vielheit" und "Seele als Gesellschaftsbau der Triebe und Affekte" wollen fürderhin in der Wissenschaft Bürgerrecht haben.

(We must give a *coup de grâce* to that other and even more fatal atomism that Christianity has been teaching best and longest, the *atomism of the soul.* Let us be permitted to use that term to denote the belief that regards the soul as something ineradicable, eternal, indivisible, as a monad, an *atomon:* that belief must be thrown out of science. It is, let it be said among ourselves, quite unnecessary to get rid of the soul itself in doing so . . . as happens through the clumsiness of those naturalists who, hardly have they touched the soul, immediately lose it altogether. But the way to new versions and refinements of the hypothesis of the soul is open: and concepts like "a mortal soul" or "the soul as the multiplicity of the subject" and "the soul as the social edifice of drives and emotions" should in future have their right of citizenship without science.)

If the little play by Yevreinov, *The Theater of the Soul,* which was produced at the Claremont Colleges Comparative Literature Conference on Modernism, is almost a word-for-word translation of this passage from Nietzsche's *Jenseits von Gut und Böse* into theatrical terms, how much more so is the whole mighty *oeuvre* of Samuel Beckett, who never ceases to dismantle and deconstruct the Cartesian "cogito ergo sum." And, if we turn to another giant among the creators of Modernism in drama, Antonin Artaud, we find that he, too, in his own way, followed on a path that Nietzsche, as the first thinker to gain an insight into the meaning of what was happening in his time, had opened up and prescribed:

Man soll über die Grausamkeit umlernen und die Augen aufmachen; man soll endlich Ungeduld lernen, damit nicht länger solche unbescheidne dicke Irrtümer tugendhaft und dreist herumwandeln, wie sie zum Beispiel in betreff der Tragödie von alten und neuen Philosophen aufgefüttert worden sind. Fast alles, was wir "höhere Kultur" nenne, beruht auf der Vergeistigung und Vertiefung der *Grausamkeit*—dies ist mein Satz; jenes "wilde Tier" ist gar nicht abgetötet worden, es lebt, es blüht, es hat sich nur—vergöttlicht. Was die schmerzliche Wollust der Tragödie ausmacht, ist Grausamkeit; was im sogenannten tragischen Mit-leiden, im Grunde sogar in allem Erhabnen bis hinauf zu den höchsten und zartesten Schaudern der Metaphysik, angenehm wirkt, bekommt seine Süssigkeit allein von der eingemischten Ingredienz der Grausamkeit.

(We have to revise our notions of cruelty and open our eyes; we should at last be eager to prevent such immodest and gross mistakes to run about virtuously and impertinently, as, for example, those that have been bred up by ancient and new philosophers about tragedy. Almost everything that we call "higher culture" is based on the spiritualization and deepening of *cruelty*—that is my verdict; that "wild beast" has not been deadened, it lives, it flourishes, it has even been made divine. What determines the sorrowful lust of tragedy is cruelty; what is felt as pleasurable in the so-called tragic pity and essentially even in everything sublime right up to the highest and most tender tremors of metaphysics, gets its sweetness solely from the ingredient of cruelty that is mixed up with it.)

I apologize for quoting Nietzsche so copiously, but I feel that his diagnosis of the nature and consequences of the sea-change that European culture had undergone in his time is a profound help in understanding the quality of that change. And, of course, Nietzsche has an intimate connection with drama, not only because he started on his career as a brilliant and original interpreter of the nature of Greek tragedy, but also because he was intimately associated with another of the great creators of the modern theater, Richard Wagner. Wagner, I believe, is as important as Ibsen and Strindberg in the genesis of the Modernist drama. It is no coincidence that the man who did most to naturalize the concept of Modernist drama in the English-speaking world, George Bernard Shaw, was an Ibsenite as well as a Wagnerian, and, of course, philosophically decidedly a Nietzschean. What is Shaw's life force but an English version of Nietzsche's vitalism, his will to power? Shaw's love of paradox is comparable to Nietzsche's revaluation of all values with the addition of an Anglo-Irish sense of humor. (If we wanted to bring Strindberg into the Nietzschean orbit we would only have to mention Nietzsche's insane anti-feminism, so religiously echoed by Strindberg. But, of course, Strindberg's de-atomization of the human soul and his take-off into introspective expressionism also echo Nietzsche's insights about the ultimate consequences of the abandonment of the Christian concept of the immortal soul, one and indivisible.)

But to go back to the beginnings: the revolt of the romantics and their precursors against the classical ideal and the tyranny of the unities and the Alexandrine was initially a revolt against worn-out forms. That the whole movement ultimately arose from an endeavor to reinstate Shakespeare as the model of great drama shows not only the modernity of Shakespeare but that ultimately the "Modernist" movement was a return to the roots of drama *before* the academicism of the seventeenth and eighteenth centuries seemed to have put a stop to all development by decreeing a perfect model to be followed (and in painting and sculpture as much as in drama).

But once the formal bounds had been broken, new subject matter, new substance, could stream into the drama. And it must not be forgotten that of all forms of art the drama is most closely linked with technology, back to the *deus ex machina,* the God who appeared by courtesy of a machine in ancient Greece. Throughout history drama has been highly technological. In fourteenth- and fifteenth-century Florence elaborate machines enabled the angels in mystery plays to fly high above the worshippers in some of the great churches of the city. The baroque age luxuriated in machinery for transformation scenes, flying clouds inhabited by Gods, and other spectacular effects. The coming of gas and then electric light, hydraulically operated stage machinery, and the cinema and other means for mechanically reproducing and electronically distributing drama have put drama into the very center of a whole series of industrial revolutions. And each of these innovations and technological advances has, in turn, opened the floodgates for the new contents, the new things that drama could say, that Nietzsche had so brilliantly discerned.

If romanticism was the initial revolt, naturalism seems to me the actual root of all our Modernist drama. As Otto Brahm, the German apostle of Ibsen, put it in one of the earliest manifestos of his *Freie Bühne:*

> Der Bannerspruch der neuen Kunst, mit goldenen Lettern aufgezeichnet . . . ist das eine Wort: Wahrheit; and Wahrheit, Wahrheit auf jedem Lebenspfade ist es, die auch wir erstreben und fordern. Nicht die objektive Wahrheit, die dem Kämpfenden entgeht, sondern die individuelle Wahrheit, welche aus der innersten Überzeugung frei geschöpft ist und frei ausgesprochen: die Wahrheit des unabhängigen Geistes, der nichts

zu beschönigen und nichts zu vertuschen hat. Und der darum nur einen Gegner kennt, seinen Erbfeind und Todfeind: die Lüge in jeglicher Gestalt. . . .

> . . . Die moderne Kunst, wo sie ihre lebensvollsten Triebe ansetzt, hat auf dem Boden des Naturalismus Wurzel geschlagen. Sie hat, einem tiefinnern Zuge dieser Zeit gehorchend, sich auf die Erkenntnis der natürlichen Daseinsmächte gerichtet und zeigt uns mit rücksichtslosem Wahrheitstriebe die Welt wie sie ist. Dem Naturalismus Freund, wollen wir eine gute Strecke Weges mit ihm schreiten, allein es soll uns nicht erstaunen, wenn im Verlauf der Wanderschaft, an einem Punkt, den wir heute noch nicht überschauen, die Strasse plötzlich sich biegt und überraschende neue Blicke in Kunst und Leben sich auftun. Denn an keine Formel, auch an die jüngste nicht, ist die unendliche Entwickelung menschlicher Kultur gebunden; und in dieser Zuversicht, im Glauben an das ewig Werdende, haben wir eine freie Bühne aufgeschlagen, für das moderne Leben.

> (The slogan that the new art carries in golden letters on its flag . . . is one word: truth; and truth, truth on every path of our life is what we strive for and demand. Not objective truth, which escapes anyone engaged in a fight, but individual truth, which is freely arrived at from deepest convictions and freely uttered: the truth of the independent spirit who has nothing to embellish or conceal. And who, therefore, has only one opponent: his hereditary and mortal enemy: the lie in any form whatever. . . .

> . . . Modern art, where it is developing its most vital shoots, has put its roots into the soil of naturalism. It has, obeying a deep inner feature of our time, directed its attention to gaining knowledge of the powers of nature and it shows us the world as it is, with ruthless truthfulness. Friends as we are of naturalism we want to travel a good deal of the road with it, but it should not surprise us if, in the course of our wanderings, at a point we cannot as yet see, the road should suddenly bend and unexpectedly disclose new vistas in art and life. For the infinite development of human culture is not bound to any formula, not even the most recent; and in this hope in continuous growth we have established a free stage for modern life.)

This openness of the naturalists, indeed, their eagerness to branch out into an infinity of new, as yet undiscovered paths, is often overlooked by those whose own ideas originated in a rejection of the original, primitive forms of naturalism as a photographic reproduction of reality, as life in a room without its fourth wall. In fact, just as, in the novel, it was a consequent application of the desire for the truth, the whole truth, and nothing but the truth that led Dujardin, Schnitzler, and Joyce into the realms of the internal monologue, so in the case of Strindberg and the expressionists it was introspection and the desire to represent the world as it was perceived by an individual (this being the only verifiable experience of reality available to anyone) that led to the dramatization of dreams, hallucinations, fantasies, and nightmares.

"Der mittelpunkt den Welt ist in jedem ich" (The center of the world is inside each ego), said Theodor Däubler in one of the early manifestos of German expressionism, which contains what I find to be one of the pithiest definitions of that style:

> Der Volksmund sagt: wenn einer gehängt wird, so erlebt er im letzten Augenblick sein ganzes Leben nochmals. Das kann nur Expressionismus sein!

> (Popular belief has it: when someone is being hanged he relives his whole life in his last moment. And that can only be Expressionism!)

That is how realism turned into surrealism; it was Apollinaire who coined the term in his preface to *Les Mamelles de Tirésias*. He felt that the reality, the truth, of walking was best expressed in the invention of the wheel, which did not look like walking legs but performed the same action more efficiently and therefore more truly. Yvan Goll, the bilingual French and German poet, formulated the same thought when he said, in his preface to one of his *Überdramen* (superdramas) in 1922:

> Überrealismus ist die stärkste Negierung des Realismus. Die Wirklichkeit des Scheins wird entlarvt, zugunsten der Wahrheit des Seins. "Masken," grob, grotesk, wie die Gefühle, deren Ausdruck sie sind. Nicht mehr "Helden," sondern Menschen, nicht Charaktere mehr, sondern die nackten Instinkte. Ganz nackt.

> Der Dramatiker ist ein Forscher, ein Politiker und ein Gesetzgeber. Als Überrealist statuiert er Dinge aus einem fernen Reich der Wahrheit, die er erhorchte, als er das Ohr an die verschlossenen Wände der Welt legte.

> Alogik ist heute der geistige Humor, also die beste Waffe gegen die Phrasen, die das ganze Leben beherrschen. Der Mensch redet in seinem. Alltag fast immer nur, um die Zunge, nicht um den Geist in Bewegung zu setzen. Wozu soviel reden, und das alles so ernst nehmen!

> (Surrealism is the strongest negation of realism. The reality of appearance is unmasked in favor of the truth of being. "Masks," coarse, grotesque, like the feelings of which they are the expression. No longer "heroes" but human beings, no longer "characters" but naked instincts. Totally naked.

> The playwright is an explorer, a politician and a legislator. As a surrealist he decrees things that come from a distant realm of truth, that he has overheard when he laid his ear against the closed walls of the world.

> Nonsense [Goll calls it "Alogik"] is today the humor of the spirit, and thus the best weapon against the clichés that rule all of our lives. Human beings in their everyday existence almost always merely talk to move their tongues, not their intellects. Why should one talk so much and take everything seriously!)

So here too the argument for surrealism, for what we later came to call "the absurd," is derived from the same search for the *truth* that animated the early naturalists, who had rejected the concept of *beauty,* or *seemliness, measure,* and *control.* Thus had the scientific spirit turned a somersault into the absurd.

How then does that other self-proclaimed scientific impulse, that of Marxism, which lies behind the work of Brecht and the Brechtians—another important sector of Modernist drama—fit into this picture? Well, surely Marxism, out of Hegel, is a blatant case of the historicism, that sense of history, that Nietzsche had diagnosed as the essential characteristic, the sixth sense, of the modern world. And what is more: Brecht's theory of epic theater and the *Verfremdungseffekt,* his rejection of introspective psychology in favor of a behavioristic model of man as the product of his social environment, is another variant of Nietzsche's rejection of the soul as a monad, of character as an indivisible whole. If the introspection of the expressionists, surrealists, and absurdists dissolves that unity of the soul from the *inside,* Brecht's insistence that all that matters is what is observable on the *outside* dissolves it from the opposite end of the spectrum. There is no such thing as one individual human character, Brecht claimed, there is only one human being in social contact with another; the same person will be utterly different when confronted with his boss from what he is when confronted with a social inferior. Human character, Brecht once said, is *not* like a grease stain that you can't get out of a garment however much you rub it.

The point I am trying to make is simply this: behind the vast diversity, the proliferation of forms and -isms, the seemingly diametrical opposition between the different strands of contemporary drama, there still lies that one single impulse, born of the nineteenth century's rejection of the traditional world system that had seemed to contain and explain the ways of the world and to justify the ways of God to Man. The impulse behind all this modernity to this day is thus essentially a negative one—a rejection of any closed worldviews, any closed world systems. Hence the curious paradox, for example, that totalitarian countries, whether Marxist or fascist, reject Modernist art, because they *need* to constitute a closed system, however simplistic and primitive it might be. Hence Brecht's Marxist dramatic theory and practice had to struggle against the totalitarian orthodoxies of the Stalinist aesthetics and prevailed in the end in that world only after it had been rigidified into a lifeless exhibit in a museum of prestigious artifacts.

The original negative impulse of Modernism, however, that rejection of formal rules that arose with the romantics and broke through with naturalism, has by no means exhausted itself: the contemporary avant-garde in drama, whether political or aesthetic, environmental or street-theatrical, whether in performance art or Grotowskian intensity, is still nourished by that impulse.

Where will it end? Have we not reached the limits, the point at which even the definition of what drama, what theater, *is* has been almost totally dissolved by the tearing down of the distinction between actor and spectator, audience and participant-in-the-action? Are we not reaching an area of total negation, total anarchy?

I must confess that I do not know the answer to these questions. What is undoubtedly the case, however, is that the proliferation of new forms and theories (that all, ultimately, go back to the same root concept) has not obliterated all previous forms; we still have classical drama, well performed today, perhaps better than at any previous time; and we still have, in the mass media, an almost obscene profusion of the most old-fashioned premodernist comedy and melodrama. All that is still drama, and indeed we have today more old-fashioned, premodernist drama than at any time in human history: it has become omnipresent. The revenge of the philistines, of the fathers who did not want their sons to find their own ways, is all around us. Perhaps in light of this fact, the cavortings of the heirs to the Modernist impulse, those knights in shining armor who see themselves as the advance guard of a new and better humanity, are reduced to their true proportion and their true function: to continue hammering at the fossilized rules of form and seemliness that spread a simplistic and primitive worldview and thus carry an obtuse and outmoded content into the consciousness of the people of a homogenized mass culture and an atomized society.

Or is it that it was the destruction of those old formal structures that has created the present state of affairs? It is at least possible that this is the case, and it *would* be the ultimate irony.

What, to my mind, is essential is that in the area of serious endeavor at the frontiers of the art of drama there should be a powerful desire to maintain the highest standards of quality. In fields where new soil is being broken, where rules have been overthrown and new conventions are being sought, it is inevitable that there should be much that is pretentious, silly, stupid, and untalented. That is inevitable and will always remain so; it lies in the very nature of things. All the more important then has the function of the critic become; all the more crucial is it that his or her endeavors should be pursued without pretentiousness, censoriousness, or pedantry, but with insight, humility, openness of mind, rejection of all prejudice, and above all with the maximum of intelligent self-awareness and self-criticism.

REDEFINING MODERNISM

Harry Levin

SOURCE: "What Was Modernism?" in *Varieties of Literary Experience: Eighteen Essays in World Literature*, edited by Stanley Burnshaw, New York University Press, 1962, pp. 307-29.

[*In the following essay, Levin reflects on the distinguishing traits and cultural significance of the Modernist era in literature.*]

A new apartment building in New York City, according to a recent announcement, has been named The Picasso. Though I have not had the pleasure of seeing it, I would suggest that it ought to be hailed as a landmark, indicating that we Americans have smoothly rounded some sort of cultural corner. Heretofore it has been more customary to christen our apartments after the landed estates or the rural counties of England, as if by verbal association to compensate for the rootless transience of metropolitan living. A few years ago the name of Picasso, as household god, would have conjured up notions of a jerrybuilt structure and a Bohemian ambience. Prospective tenants, in their perennial quest for comfort and security, would have been put off by a vision of collapsible stairways, rooms without floors, trapezoidal kitchenettes, or neighbors with double faces and blue-green complexions. But in the meanwhile the signature has brought untold wealth and unquestioned prestige to its signer, and now it becomes a warrant of domestic respectability. If this is not an arrival, no painter can ever be said to have arrived. But where? At the latest and strangest phase of a restless career, where previous arrivals have always been points of departure.

We must admit that our eponymous hero has met with more appropriate recognitions, notably the retrospective gathering of Picasso's works, exhibited in several cities on the occasion of his seventy-fifth birthday. That was indeed a retrospect: not only of the productivity wherewith a single man could fill a museum, but of the versatility that enabled him to master such varied styles and numerous media. To follow his progression from room to room and period to period—from drawing and painting to sculpture and ceramics, or from Romanticism and Impressionism to Cubism and Primitivism—was to recapitulate the history of art. Above the labels of the catalogue loomed the dynamic personality of the artist, not merely a school in himself but a whole succession of schools, seeking to outrival his own work at every subsequent stage as well as the work of so many earlier artists. If there was any text he was born to illustrate, it was Ovid's *Metamorphoses*. The conceiving eye that could turn a broken mechanical toy into a monstrous ape or a sacrificial goat, the shaping hand that could transform a terra-cotta pitcher into an archaic goddess of love, such are the faculties that Marcel Proust must have had in mind when he described the impact of great painters as *"une métamorphose des choses."* Emerson, a favorite writer of Proust's, had described the poetic process as "a metamorphosis of things."

Pablo Picasso, who will be eighty next year, is unique in his field, but not in his artistic eminence. In the sister art of music, we think at once of the protean achievement of Igor Stravinsky, his junior by one year. There, with due allowance for technical differences, we seem to note a similar tendency, which some bewildered cataloguers might have labelled Ultraism. This is the will to change, in other words that metamorphic impetus, that systematic deformation, that reshaping spirit which must continually transpose its material and outdistance itself in a dazzling sequence of newer and newest manners. Picasso was asked by a conventional person who admired his classical illustrations, "Since you can draw so beautifully, why do you spend your time making those queer things?" He answered succinctly, "That's why." He might have countered with another question: why retrace familiar lines? Similarly Stravinsky might have replied, to hearers aware that his departures were firmly grounded upon past mastery of his craft: why go on repeating the recognized chords? There are other possible modalities, though they may sound discordant the first time you hear them. The original composer is he who must try them, in the interests of further discovery.

Since more and more combinations have been tried, more and more possibilities have been exhausted, and the problems of experimentation have become harder and harder. The public, of course, is shocked; it prefers the accustomed harmonies to the neoteric experiments, and it finds cubist projections unrecognizable. However, the development of the arts is registered through a series of shocks to the public—which, after all, in buying cars or clothes, accepts the principle of planned obsolescence. At its own pace, it too is animated by "the need for a constant refreshment," as has been pointed out by James Johnson Sweeney, who as Director of the Guggenheim Museum has done so much to supply that need. The shift of taste fits in with a dialectical pattern of revolution and alternating reaction, as the breaking of outmoded images gives way to the making of fresh ones. Hence the successful iconoclast frequently ends as an image-maker. Witness T. S. Eliot, whose career has been a literary parallel to Stravinsky's or Picasso's. Since his conversion to the Anglican Church and his naturalization as a British subject, we have come to view him as a living embodiment of tradition. Yet he emerged as an experimentalist, whose problematic endeavors startled and puzzled his early readers.

This realignment corresponds with the usual transition from the *enfant terrible,* who is naturally radical, to the elder statesman, who is normally conservative. But it does not explain why such grand old men as Bernard Shaw and André Gide, several years after their respective deaths, still seem so alive and so much younger than their survivors. It does not account for the patricidal attacks, launched against Modernism in general and Mr. Eliot in particular, by angry middle-aged men such as Karl Shapiro, whose rallying cry is *In Defence of Ignorance.* It throws no light on the charlatanical fame that has accrued to Picasso's younger compatriot, Salvador Dalí, for turning back his limp and dripping watches. Yet one of the spokesmen for a resurgent conservatism, Peter Viereck, throws out a meaningful hint, when he speaks of "the revolt against revolt." And the Institute of Modern Art at Boston has officially marked the mid-century transition by changing its name to the Institute of Contempo-

rary Art. Now, we are all contemporaries; about that we have no option, so long as we stay alive. But we may choose whether or not we wish to be modern, and the present drift seems to be toward the negative choice and away from the hazards of controversial involvement.

"An intellectual deliverance is the peculiar demand of those ages which are called modern." So Matthew Arnold had declared in his inaugural lecture "On the Modern Element in Literature." But though that lecture was delivered at Oxford in 1857—the year that inaugurated French modernism by dragging both *Madame Bovary* and *Les Fleurs du Mal* through the lawcourts—it was not much more than another of Arnold's pleas for classicism. By recourse to his criteria, which were those of high civilization, Sophocles and Lucretius could be ranked among the moderns. It remained for the late Edwin Muir to work out the implications of this relativistic conception, applying it also to the Renaissance and to such nineteenth-century prophets as Nietzsche. Muir's sharply pointed paragraphs in *The New Age,* collected under a pseudonym as *We Moderns* in 1918, were republished in the United States two years later with a polemical introduction by H. L. Mencken. Modernity, they argued, does not necessarily mean the very latest thing; rather it is a program of cultural emancipation, "a principle of life itself" which can only be maintained by "constantly struggling." The struggle of the moment was against such reactionaries as Chesterton and such derivatives as Galsworthy. The long-range conflict would meet those forces which, recognizing the challenge of modernism, damn it as heresy in every sphere.

Today we live in what has been categorized—by whom but Arnold Toynbee?—as the Post-Modern Period. Looking back toward the Moderns, we may feel as Dryden did when he looked back from the Restoration to the Elizabethans, contrasting earlier strength with later refinement. "Theirs was the giant race before the Flood. . . . The Second Temple was not like the First." But, we may console ourselves by reflecting, there are times of change and times that seek stability; a time for exploring and innovating may well lead into a time for assimilating and consolidating. We may well count ourselves fortunate in that we can so effortlessly enjoy those gains secured by the pangs of our forerunners. Lacking the courage of their convictions, much in our arts and letters simply exploits and diffuses, on a large scale and at a popular level, the results of their experimentalism. F. Scott Fitzgerald, because he managed to catch some of the glamor that finally caught him, has himself been sentimentalized as a hero of biography, fiction, and drama. Compare his own reckless hero of the Twenties, the great and flamboyant Gatsby, with a typical protagonist of the Fifties—the decent, judicious, respectable Arthur Winner in James Gould Cozzens' *By Love Possessed*—and you can measure how far we have advanced into the middle age of the Twentieth Century.

Compare a militant novel of the Thirties—let us say John Steinbeck's *Grapes of Wrath*—with a penitent novel of the Forties, Lionel Trilling's *Middle of the Journey,* and you can locate the turn that came *nel mezzo del cammin.* World War II was the Flood; but the Temple had been crumbling and the giant race disappearing through what W. H. Auden, retrospectively and rather too severely, called "a low dishonest decade." Some of the talents were prematurely sacrificed: Guillaume Apollinaire, García Lorca. Others survived without honor in their own countries, as Ezra Pound and Boris Pasternak did for such different reasons. Many of their amiable juniors were led astray by those "enemies of promise" which Cyril Connolly demurred at but did little to resist. The query "Who killed Dylan Thomas?" has prompted some maudlin accusations. The poignant fact about James Agee's writing, much of it published posthumously, is his uneasiness about not living up to his genuine promise. The gifted J. D. Salinger, who writes so movingly of adolescent confusions, has yet to free himself from them. Our colleges are full of writers in residence, who offer courses in "creative" writing, and publish embittered novels whose principal source of interest is the noncoincidental resemblance between their colleagues and their characters.

Though our Miltons may not be glorious, they are both vocal and pampered. Poetry has become a caucus-race, where there are prizes for all the participants and where there are virtually no spectators. The little magazines that "died to make verse free," as people used to say, have been resurrected on the campuses, where they specialize in the stricter Provençal forms. Joyce's books, which were burned and censored during his lifetime, have become a happy hunting ground for doctoral candidates; while his dishevelled disciple, Samuel Beckett, is the subject of an article in a current issue of *PMLA.* One of my intermittent nightmares is based on two tons of Thomas Wolfe's manuscripts now reposing in a vault of the Houghton Library, and the thought that future scholars will gain reputations by putting back what the editors cut out. It is significant that Lawrence Durrell's tetralogy, one of the very few ambitious novels to appear in Britain latterly, takes place in the self-consciously decadent city of Alexandria. "Art," as Thomas Mann announced and illustrated in *Doktor Faustus,* "is becoming criticism." In the same vein John Crowe Ransom, who turned from poet to critic some thirty years ago, lately announced that literature has been moving from an age of creation into an age of criticism.

Mr. Ransom, interviewed on his retirement from his influential chair as teacher and editor at Kenyon College, stressed the happier aspects of the prevailing situation: the necessity for thoughtful rereading, the opportunities for self-cultivation and renewed understanding of the existent classics. An instance might be the revival of Henry James, far more dominant now than he ever was in his day. These are valid and absorbing pursuits, and I am too ingrained an academic myself to deplore the amenities of the Academy. Then too, it must be conceded, there are positive advantages to living in an epoch which technology has enriched with esthetic appliances, so that our acquaintance with music and with the fine arts is vastly augmented by long-playing records and photographic reproductions. But this is reproduction, not production; we are mainly consumers rather than producers of art. We are readers of reprints and connoisseurs of High Fidelity, even as we are gourmets by virtue of the expense account and the credit card. For our wide diffusion of culture is geared to the standardizations of our economy, and is peculiarly susceptible to inflationary trends. The independence of our practitioners, when they are not domesticated by institutions of learning, is compromised more insidiously by the circumstances that make art a business.

The prosperous and the established, *The Just and the Unjust,* find their mirror in the novels of Mr. Cozzens, as opposed to that concern for the underprivileged which novelists used to profess. Genius, more understanding than misunderstood, rises to worldly success in the shrewd fiction of C. P. Snow, where science and scholarships provide the means for "the new men" to enter "the corridors of power." From England we hear of young men who are angry, presumably at the various conformities which they sum up in their conception of an Establishment. It is not quite so clear what is beating our so-called "beat generation"; they seem to be rebels without a cause, born too late in a world too old. Jack Kerouac, in *On the Road,* has produced a document which fills some of us with the wistful feeling that experience must somehow have passed us by. Yet his friends, for all their violent whims, do not seem to be having nearly so good a time as Hemingway's playboys in *The Sun Also Rises.* The school associated with San Francisco, for whatever a personal impression may or may not be worth, looks very much like Greenwich Village transported across the continent long after its heyday. It exemplifies the cultural lag rather than the advance-guard.

As it happens, I have been somewhat associated with the publishing firm known as New Directions, which was founded in the late Nineteen-Thirties by my college friend, James Laughlin. In spite of its vanguard title, it has been primarily engaged in fighting a rear-guard action. The leading innovators on its list have been Ezra Pound and William Carlos Williams, both of whom are advanced septuagenarians nowadays. The other day I noticed a reference to the annual miscellany, *New Directions,* which was characterized as "the accepted place for off-beat publication." Here is an interesting contradiction in terms, which reveals a deeper contradiction in our standards. Whether it expresses the nonconformist's yearning for conformity or the conformist's urge toward nonconformity, it gives with one hand what it takes away with the other. It weighs the notion of acceptance against the compound, "off-beat," which is so characteristic an expression of the mid-century. The noun "beat" accords with the terminology of jazz; as an ungrammatical participle, the same word carries certain sado-masochistic overtones, e.g. "beat-up." Rounded off by a Slavic suffix, which may be either affectionate or contemptuous, and which must have been reinforced by the Sputnik, it has become an epithet for the fashion of being flagrantly unfashionable, "beatnik."

However, its underlying connotation seems to derive from the cop who is off his beat, the man in uniform who has gone off duty and strayed into unfamiliar territory. Thus it subserves the ambivalent curiosity of the denizens of a well-grooved society about whatever may lie beyond its beaten paths. It represents an ineffectual effort to vary the cliché, and probably owes its currency to those whose own beat is Madison Avenue. A cognate phrase, "off-Broadway," is more concrete in specifying the relationship between that main thoroughfare, the precinct of uniformity, and its bypaths, where novelty may perchance be encountered. Legitimate drama, all but superseded on Broadway by musical comedy, has had to improvise its theaters in devious lofts and makeshift basements. Shaw's *Pygmalion,* in its Broadwayized version of Covent Garden, *My Fair Lady,* is the soaring index of this trend. Like those bland composites to which Hollywood reduces imported ideas, it is an entrepreneurial accomplishment, another by-product of the middleman's pragmatic philosophy as stated by Pope:

> Be not the first by whom the new are tried,
> Nor yet the last to lay the old aside.

That sentiment is reversed paradoxically when an advertisement for *Esquire,* the haberdashery magazine, salutes its clientèle as "the aware moderns who are the first to embrace a new idea and speed it upon its way to becoming the popular fashion." Well, we Post-Moderns like to eat our cake and keep it, to take a chance on a sure thing. We tipsters want to call the long shot while hogging the inside track, to take credit for originality without risking unpopularity. Hence we congratulate ourselves upon our broad-mindedness because *Lady Chatterley's Lover* is now a best-seller after thirty years of suppression.

Thirty years constitute nature's round number for the span from infancy through maturity, and consequently a kind of basic rhythm for reckoning the progresses and regressions of mankind. Thirty years is just about the age-difference between a playboy and an academician: consider the case history of Jean Cocteau. What is generally regarded as the Irish Renascence began in 1892 with Yeats's *Countess Cathleen* and terminated in 1922 with Joyce's *Ulysses.* Broader movements, succeeding one another, are comparable in their periodicity. Thus, if we start with Wordsworth's manifesto of 1800, we observe that the continental triumph of Romanticism dates from 1830. Shortly before the end of another cycle, this gives way to the countertendencies toward Positivism, Realism, and Naturalism; whereas, when we move from the Sixties to the Nineties, the latest watchwords are Symbolism, Estheticism, and Decadence. It will be seen that a revolutionary generation tends to be succeeded by a reactionary one; to put it less politically and more psychologically, there seems to be a cyclic oscillation between tough and tender minds. That would help to explain the phenomenon of the hard-boiled Nineteen-Twenties, recoiling as it were from the softness of the *fin du siècle.* It might also set the acknowledged weaknesses of the Fifties into clarifying perspective.

But nostalgia for the vigorous youth of our century is a weakness in which we need not indulge ourselves; nor would it serve any purpose to draw invidious comparisons between our immediate contemporaries and our elders. The average life is privileged to span two generations, and we live at least in the afterglow of the Moderns. Insofar as they were ahead of their time, we can even claim to be nearer to them. Furthermore, each generation has three decades, in which either to gather momentum after a wavering start, or else to subside from a powerful beginning. Accordingly, the manic Twenties declined into the depressive Thirties, which yielded in turn to the war-interrupted Forties. If the countermovement of the Fifties seems to have begun unpromisingly, we may take comfort in expecting the Sixties to proceed on a rising plane, looking toward the next watershed in the Nineteen-Eighties. There George Orwell's object-lesson gives us pause, and we shift with relief to a backward glance and a less complex set of variables. We can examine the material factors, chart the framing conditions, and project the hypothetical curves of artistic activity. Yet we have no means of predicting how the human sensibilities, in their most individualized manifestations, will respond.

The best we can do is recognize when those responses have occurred with a special resonance. But that point cannot be established by generalizations; let me particularize instead, with a handful of titles and names and dates. Among the latter, 1922 stands out as the year of Proust's death, of the publication of his central volume, *Sodome et Gomorrhe,* and the first appearance of his work in England. English letters had likewise to absorb the twofold shock of *Ulysses* and *The Waste Land.* And if this was not enough for the reviewers, D. H. Lawrence offered them *Aaron's Rod,* Virginia Woolf *Jacob's Room,* and Katherine Mansfield *The Garden Party.* Readers of poetry faced not merely the Georgian anthology but Hardy's *Late Lyrics and Earlier,* Yeats's *Later Poems,* and Housman's *Last Poems*—it sounded rather autumnal, but the harvest grew with reaping. Lytton Strachey's *Books and Characters* was more narrowly *de l'époque,* while Max Beerbohm's *Rossetti and his Circle* was an antiquarian curio. Among the highlights of the season in France were *Charmes,* Valéry's collection of verse, and the first installment of Martin du Gard's *Les Thibault.* Germany saw Bertolt Brecht's first play, *Baal,* and *Die Sonette an Orpheus* by Rainer Maria Rilke. Americans were reading Sinclair Lewis' *Babbitt* and being scandalized by Eugene O'Neill's *Anna Christie.*

Though I have been highly selective, the list is sufficient to justify an *annus mirabilis*—or would be, if there were not others comparably brilliant. Let us therefore sample another year, jumping arbitrarily to 1924, when Franz Kafka died, scarcely known, since his novels would only be published during the next three years. The greatest event for the critics was Thomas Mann's masterwork, *Der Zauberberg.* The noisiest, perhaps, was the Surrealist Manifesto, which proved to be something of an anticlimax; but Valéry counterbalanced it with his first collection of critical prose, *Variété;* while Gide braved scandal by signing *Corydon*. America witnessed Sherwood Anderson's autobiography, *A Story-Teller's Story,* Marianne Moore's salient volume of poetic *Observations,* and William Faulkner's first book, also in verse, *The Marble Faun*. In Britain, George Moore waxed more reminiscent than ever with *Conversations in Ebury Street;* T. E. Hulme's posthumous *Speculations* were to have continuing influence on criticism and poetry; each of the three Sitwells contributed to the ebullition by bringing out a book; and Bernard Shaw was inspired to touch his heights by the theme of *Saint Joan*. E. M. Forster's *Passage to India* may have been an omen as well as a milestone; for it was his most important novel to date, and it is the last that Mr. Forster has given us.

Everyone can multiply for himself these modern instances; while students of Russian or Spanish literature can point to additional flowerings which were either transplanted or nipped in the bud. Futurism, as Joyce foresaw, had no future; Marinetti fell in line behind Mussolini; and Hitler was to proscribe Modernism as degenerate art or *Kulturbolschewismus*. We hardly need to underline the pressures or constraints that limited the epoch so poignantly, *entre deux guerres,* to Mr. Forster's "long week-end," 1918-1939. Nor could we blame the generation confronted with the task of continuing to write, if they found it hard to forgive such knowledge. Yet at this distance we can perceive, with increasing clarity, that the modernistic movement comprises one of the most remarkable constellations of genius in the history of the West. And while some of its lights are still among us, before they have all been extinguished, we should ask ourselves why they have burned with such pyrotechnic distinction. What, if anything, have such figures in common, each of them vowed to idiosyncracy, practising a divergent medium, formed in a disparate background? Above all, the elementary circumstance that they happen to be coeval, more or less; that they are all, or would have been, in their eighth decade today. But what, if we are not to beg the question, was the *Zeitgeist* they shared? What was there in the air they breathed that differed from the intellectual climate of their successors or predecessors?

All of them grew up in the late Nineteenth Century and matured in the early Twentieth, reaching their prime in the period between the wars. The Nineteenth was not so well organized as the Eighteenth, nor so deeply speculative as the Seventeenth, nor so richly magniloquent as the Renaissance. But, as the apogee of middle-class liberalism, it permitted a maximum of leeway for the emergence of individuality; it educated individuals thoroughly; it collected art and fostered science; it cultivated human relationships; it developed temperament and talent. Into its world the Modernists were born, and yet they were not quite shaped by it. To it they often hark back, with that acute sensibility which they have reserved for their own impressions of adolescence. Had they been born any earlier, they might have felt—with Henry Adams—that they had missed a still earlier boat. Had they been Mid-Victorians, they might have poured their creative energies into

causes that they now could take for granted. If they had reached maturity in the Nineties, their views would have inevitably been colored by the outlook of the Decadents. But they took the *fin du siècle* in youthful stride; for them, it was not so much the end of one century as it was the beginning of another.

One of the determining characteristics of modern man, which influences the role he plays and relates him to pre-existing phenomena, is the awareness of chronology. We who are children of the Twentieth Century never experienced the excitement of welcoming it. Our casual habit of predating centuries makes us insensitive to the West's first realization that its second millennium was now in sight. The bliss that Wordsworth inhaled at the dawning of the French Revolution had been a disillusioning adumbration. "Years of the modern! years of the unperform'd!" Such had been Whitman's prologue to a performance which he anticipated all the more keenly because, as he chanted, "No one knows what will happen next." At all events, things would be happening; and those whose existence falls within the limits of a single century may well envy those who cross temporal boundaries and have a chance to inscribe their names on history's blank pages. How terribly much it must have meant to James Joyce, as an eighteen-year-old university student, to have set his ambitions down on paper and dated them "1900!" Here was the brave new world that had been heralded by his mentor Ibsen, by Nietzsche whose death came that very year, by Tolstoy and those other Proto-Moderns who had been breaking the images that had stood in its way.

One of the assumptions about World War I was that it had settled history. Its sequel was to teach T. S. Eliot that "History is now and England." But the interval thought of itself in the present tense, separating modernity from history. The past was over; the present was happily more comfortable—though unhappily less colorful, as Miniver Cheevy and other time-snobs lamented. Ernest Hemingway's first book of stories was aptly entitled *In Our Time,* and its grasp of immediacy was heightened by its reminiscences of battle. His intensive concentration on the instant, which imparts a film-like quality to his fiction, is pinpointed in "The Snows of Kilimanjaro," when a polyglot series of synonyms runs through the mind of a dying writer: "Now, *ahora, maintenant, heute. . . .*" Whatever the language, the meaning is imminence; and that "nowness" is a precondition of the search for newness, for what Whitman had termed "the unperform'd." To perform the unperformed! *La nouvelle revue française!* "The Great English Vortex!" The sense of novelty, of potentialities being opened up, does not seem any less eager because it is juxtaposed to the inherited sense of the past and the pleasures of retrospection. Everyman, in his more thoughtful moods, is conscious of his overwhelming patrimony as heir of all the ages; and his relation to them takes the guise of an endless stroll among the masterpieces of their invisible museum.

Time was of the essence, not only for the metaphysician Bergson, but for the innumerable poets, novelists, painters, and scientists who worked in the dimension he formulated. Vainly did Wyndham Lewis assail the time-consciousness of his contemporaries. As the Gracehoper retorted to the Ondt, in Joyce's fable, "Why can't you beat time?" The lifework of Proust was precisely such an attempt, the attempt of an aging dilettante to make up for lost time by recapturing the past, repudiating its ephemeral concerns and crystallizing its highest moments through an appeal to the timelessness of art. Yeats pursued the same objective symbolically, when he pictured himself abandoning the earthbound sphere of nature and setting sail for the timeless art-city, Byzantium. His poet, Michael Robartes, had desired to remember forgotten beauty. The feeling of belatedness has the habitual effect of stimulating the act of memory, along with the stylistic consequence of sounding echoes, evoking reverberations, and playing with *pastiche*. When Pound advised disciples to "make it new," he was repeating a maxim as old as Confucius, and was well aware of the irony; for his studies in the Renaissance had won him insights into the processes of cultural renewal, and shown him how renovation could be innovation.

What I have ventured to call the metamorphic impetus seems to have resulted from this paradoxical state of feeling belated and up-to-date simultaneously, and of working experimental transformations into traditional continuities. But there are other preconditions of Modernism, geographical as well as historical. Joyce and Picasso, Eliot and Stravinsky have another trait in common—alas, too common among the uncommon artists of our time. How few of them have lived out their careers in the lands of their origin! To be sure, migration is a civilizing force, and sojourn abroad has been a classic step in the artistic *curriculum vitae*. Unfortunately we have had to learn, through dint of wars, revolutions, and political persecutions, the distinction between expatriation and exile. The hyphenated German-Jewish Czech, Kafka, though he did not live to share it, clairvoyantly sketched the plight of the Displaced Person. Mann, who was destined to become a Transatlantic nomad, had situated his magic mountain in neutral Switzerland. There, in the International Sanitorium Berghof, his Teutonic hero undergoes successive exposure to a Swiss physician, an Italian poet, a Polish priest, a Dutch businessman, and a Russian mistress. Then, having gained an education while regaining his health, he is lost in combat with the Allies.

The catchphrase employed by continental architects, "The International Style," might be very appropriately extended to other works of the Twenties. Many of them were composed in Paris, the capital of between-the-wars cosmopolitanism. "The School of Paris"—a topographical designation for unacademic painting—was presided over by our expatriate Spaniard, Picasso, who now has his monument in New York. Paris was the inevitable headquarters for those Russian dancers, designers, and choreographers who staged Stravinsky's ballets. It was where a famous generation of Americans got temporarily lost, under the Sybilline tutelage of Gertrude Stein. Meanwhile, in an apartment near the Etoile, the self-ex-

iled Irishman Joyce was carefully elaborating the most minute and comprehensive account that any city has ever received from literature—his account of his native Dublin. *Ulysses* is of its time, in endeavoring to arrest the eighteen hours of time it exhaustively chronicles. Nineteenth-century novelists, especially Balzac, had set forth the complexities of the metropolis, but through a sequence of loosely connected novels where more or less conventional narrative was filled in with sharply detailed observation. Joyce's unexampled contribution was a gigantic yet rigorously experimental design, which controlled the accumulating details as they fell into place.

It is the metamorphic impetus that provides this controlling device: the transmutation of Dublin citizens into mythical archetypes out of the *Odyssey*. In the novel, as Naturalism had left it, the environment came dangerously close to swamping the personages. That was not the fault of the Naturalists, but of the situations with which they dealt. The dehumanization of art, if I may build upon a useful phrase from Ortega y Gasset, mirrors the dehumanization of life. Joyce, by resorting to metamorphosis and even to mock-apotheosis, was trying to rehumanize his characters; and he succeeded in giving them contour, if not stature. Journalistic novelists like John Dos Passos and Jean-Paul Sartre, seeking a panoramic or kaleidoscopic approach to the urban scene, have imitated Joyce's structural methods. But the problem, to which the French *Unanimistes* and the German proponents of the *Gesamtkunstwerk* have also addressed themselves, goes beyond—or else within—the matter of structure. If the object is unity, that must bear an organic connection to the multiplicity; its collective pattern must be revealed and confirmed through individual lives; its outward view of social interaction must be combined with an inner focus on psychological motivation.

Hence the old-fashioned type of rounded fictional character, standing between the narrator and the reader, seems to dissolve in the stream of consciousness, which directly and transparently conveys a flow of impression and sensation from the external world. Though the novelist need not utilize the internal monologue, increasingly he approximates to the voice and the viewpoint of his protagonist. The very completeness of the ensuing intimacy forces him to fall back upon the raw materials of his own autobiography, refining them into self-portraiture of the artist. The intensity of Proust's introspection pushed him to the point where he disclosed an abyss between the *moi* and everything else. Gide, by writing his novel about a novelist writing a novel, *Les Faux-monnayeurs,* including his novelist's journal, and then publishing the journal he kept while writing that novel, *Le Journal des Faux-monnayeurs,* demonstrated that first-person narrative may become a double mirror reflecting infinity. Fiction was spurred to such feats of self-consciousness by the revelations of psychoanalysis: the Freudian probing for unconscious motives, the Jungian search for universal patterns. It may be an exaggeration to argue that human nature changed in 1910, but Virginia Woolf was bold enough to do so, though probably unaware that the International Psychoanalytical Association had been founded in that year.

That argument was a measured overstatement, put forward in defending the new Georgian novelists against such Edwardians as Arnold Bennett. Mrs. Woolf knew that it would have just about as much validity as the assertion that sunsets have changed since Monet and the Impressionists undertook to paint them. It was true, in the sense that characterization had changed, that people too were being visualized through the eyes of other people, and that another metamorphosis was thereby being effected. The author of *Orlando* understood that permutations so subtle and subjective might have a circumscribing effect on the novel. Most flexible of genres, it readily focuses either upon the recesses of the self or the expanses of society; and the Twenties took it to both extremes, sometimes at once, with their mental analyses and their monumental constructs. Here is where Ultraism may have attained its *ne plus ultra*. Joyce himself could go no farther than *Finnegans Wake;* few others could get that far; and later novelists have understandably made no attempt to press beyond *Ulysses*. This has stirred some critics to announce that the novel is an obsolete or dying form. One cannot deny that it seems to be regressing toward the plane of documentary realism, where at best it may be indistinguishable from reportage or good journalism.

But fiction is doomed to failure in its competition with fact. What it possesses that non-fiction lacks is fantasy—that is to say, the projective power of the imagination, which confers value and significance on the stuff of our everyday apprehension by rearranging and transmuting it. Thus the apparent sordidness and purposelessness of our day with Leopold Bloom in Dublin are transmuted into a symbolic reënactment of Homer's epic. Some of those cross-references seem far-fetched, and others grimly ironic; yet, as a whole, they interpret for us data which would otherwise be meaningless. Joyce's use of myth makes the past a key to the present. More than that, wrote T. S. Eliot in his review of *Ulysses*, "It has the importance of a scientific discovery." Future writers would take advantage of it, as he predicted; and even then he had just finished his *Waste Land,* which abounded in flashbacks and parallels. In that least heroic and most fragmentary of epics, he exorcized the blight of contemporaneous London by tracing through it the outline of a quest for the Holy Grail. A timeless ritual, a timely critique, I. A. Richards commented that it completed the severance between poetry and belief. But, in the long run, it proved to be a station on Mr. Eliot's pilgrimage toward faith.

It is not surprising that Modernism, the product of cities, should be so impelled to recreate the image of cities. One of the greatest Modernists, in this respect, is Charlie Chaplin, who has so brilliantly rendered the metropolis in all its frustrations and incongruities. For T. S. Eliot, London is "unreal"; but its apparition is that of Vienna, Athens, Jerusalem, or Alexandria; and his elegiac vision becomes prophetic when he imagines "falling towers."

The prophecy was apocalyptically fulfilled by the bombings of the next war, which Mr. Eliot—combining his own observation as air-raid warden with a reminiscence from Dante's *Inferno*—has powerfully invoked in the last of his *Four Quartets*. That he should proceed by musical analogy, finding his inspiration in the austere but imposing string quartets of the later Beethoven, is still another trait of his generation. Poets' poets and novelists' novelists, painters' painters and musicians' musicians, they were profoundly versed in their own particular crafts, and so whole-heartedly devoted to craftsmanship that they attempted to transfer it from one art to another. Writers borrowed thematic techniques from Wagner, who himself had aimed at a synesthesia, to be induced by music in conjunction with other arts. Poetry encompassed painting and music, when Wallace Stevens presented—after Picasso—his *Man with a Blue Guitar.*

The thought that a man of letters should consider himself a practitioner of the fine arts, or that he should be designated professionally as an artist, is a legacy from Flaubert's generation which is not likely to outlast Joyce's by long. The cult of intransigent artistry, which both men practised as devoutly as if it were their religious vocation, is embodied in and elucidated by the latter's *Portrait of the Artist as a Young Man,* where the archetypal figure is Daedalus, the fabulous Greek artificer, and the epigraph is a line about him from Ovid's *Metamorphoses: "Et ignotas animum dimittit in artes."* Joyce was clearly inviting the application to himself: "And so he turned his mind to unknown arts." Paul Valéry discerned a historical prototype in the artist-engineer of the Italian Renaissance, and paid his homage in two essays upon the method of Leonardo da Vinci. He made his own apologia through the personage of M. Teste (M. Tête, Mr. Head), whose cerebral soliloquies begin with the unabashed admission: *"La bêtise n'est pas mon fort."* Stupidity has decidedly not been the forte of the Modernists; they have left that virtue to their Post-Modern attackers, who can now write in defence of ignorance. If M. Teste seems arrogant, let them make the most of that last infirmity. He was just as firm, in refusing to suffer fools, as they are weak in appealing to philistines.

Though recent literature prides itself upon its outspokenness, there remains one organ of the body which it is almost taboo to mention, and that is the brain. What may seem a sin, on the part of the Moderns, is that they were preoccupied with the minds of their characters, and—what is worse—that they make serious demands upon the minds of their readers. This cannot be lightly forgiven by an era whose culture-heroes are persistently mindless—whether they be the good-hearted goons of John Steinbeck, the epicene slobs of Tennessee Williams, or the analphabetic gladiators of the later Hemingway. But popularity was excluded, by definition, from the aims of the writers I have been discussing; their names did not figure upon the best-seller lists of their day; many others did, which are now forgotten. The aura of obscurity or unintelligibility which may still occasionally tinge these intellectuals, in some degree, emanates from their refusal to advertise themselves or to talk down to their audience in the hope of enlarging it. That, for them, would indeed have been a treason of the clerks. Their ultimate quality, which pervades their work to the very marrow, is its uncompromising intellectuality. Like the intelligentsia of old Russia or the class of Mandarins in China, they looked upon letters as a way of life.

But this may have presupposed, along with their own dedication, other conditions which may no longer be possible. The extraordinary spread of higher learning has lowered it, and introduced a large amount of dilution. The highbrows and the lowbrows have intermarried, and their children are—exactly what Virginia Woolf dreaded most—all middlebrows. Instead of a tension between the uncomprehending majority and the saving remnant—or, if you will, between sensible citizens and longhaired coteries—there has been a *détente,* a relaxation, and a collaboration for mutual profit between the formerly intractable artist and the no longer hostile bourgeoisie. Out of it there seems to be emerging a middlebrow synthesis, the moderated expression of our mid-century. But that is a subject notoriously better appreciated by professors of sociology and experts on mass communication than it is by old-fashioned scholars or modernist critics. Nor do I wish to imply that all of our talents, responding to technological pressure and economic attraction, have become mere purveyors of entertainment. On the contrary, many of them profess an engagement of the sincerest kind to the responsibilities of common welfare. The Modernists did not have to make such commitments, because they were not threatened by such urgencies. Hence they could strive for artistic perfection in single-minded detachment.

Alfred North Whitehead was strongly convinced that the early Twentieth Century was one of the greatest epochs in the march of intellect. Though he was thinking basically of mathematics and physics, he held a lively belief in the interplay between the sciences and the humanities. He concurred with the opinion that Wordsworth, writing from the opposite vantagepoint, had expressed in the opening year of the Nineteenth Century:

> If the labours of Men of science should ever create any material revolution, direct or indirect, in our condition, and in the impressions which we habitually receive, the Poet will sleep then no more than at present; he will be ready to follow the steps of the Man of science, not only in those general indirect effects, but he will be at his side, carrying sensation into the midst of the objects of the science itself.

Certainly such a material revolution has taken place; the arts have struggled to adapt themselves to it; and we gain a fuller comprehension of the modern artist, if we envision him—in Wordsworth's terms—at the side of the scientist. The partnership, however uneasy, has intensified his curiosity and sharpened his preoccupation with his own technique. He has been encouraged to experiment, not by blindly accepting hypotheses as Zola did in

his *roman expérimental,* but rather as Valéry did in transferring to poetry the lessons he had learned from geometry, or in taking for his motto *"ars non stagnat."* Successful experiment involves trial and error and incidental waste, as scientists know. This is a necessary function performed, upon the fringes of the arts, by that continued ferment of willed eccentricity whose products we can usually dismiss. But "the two cultures," as Sir Charles Snow has lately reminded us, are still too far apart. What should draw them together, more than anything else, is the shared recognition that conjointly they cover an area which man has set aside for the free play of painstaking intelligence.

Science no longer underprops our world view with rationalistic or positivistic reassurances. It has undergone a modernist phase of its own, and seen its solid premises subverted by such concepts as relativity and indeterminacy. Where, then, can we turn for illumination? Can we come to no more helpful conclusion than the message that E. M. Forster discerned in the Marabar Caves of India? "Everything exists; nothing has value." Critics of the Moderns have accused them of being deficient in a sense of values, of believing in nothing beyond that negativistic credo. However, to reread Eliot's "Fire Sermon," or Kafka's "Parable of the Law," or Mann's farewell to his soldier-hero, or Proust's commemoration of a great writer's death, or Joyce's hallucinating encounter between a sonless father and a fatherless son, is to feel the glow of ethical insight. A younger and more plain-spoken writer whom we have lost much too soon, Albert Camus, received the Nobel Prize three years ago for having "illuminated the problems of the human conscience in our time." That citation recalls the warning of an earlier French moralist, Rabelais, at the very dawn of modernity, that *"science sans conscience"* would bring ruin to the soul. Joyce's young artist, Stephen Dedalus, pledged himself to create the "uncreated conscience" of his people. Has it not been the endeavor of his generation to have created a conscience for a scientific age?

Robert Martin Adams

SOURCE: "What Was Modernism?" in *Hudson Review,* Vol. 31, No. 1, Spring, 1978, pp. 19-33.

[*In the following essay, Adams enumerates reasons for the inadequacy of "Modernism" as a critical-historical term.*]

> "The past serves only as a means of knowing the present. But the present eludes me. *What, after all, is the present?*"
> —Henri Foçillon, quoted by
> George Kubler: *The Shape of Time*

Since the ironic reservations and self-questioning cautions that surround the topic of "the modern" are potentially infinite, it's best to start with a blunt and vigorous citation from Mrs. Woolf, who tells us flatly that on or about December, 1910, human nature changed radically. I think she's right. Within five years either way of that date a great sequence of new and different works appeared in Western culture, striking the tonic chords of modernism. Ten years before that fulcrum of December, 1910, modernism is not yet; ten years after it is already. The "human nature" that changed is not the substructure and component systems of the animal, but his way of seeing himself as expressed in works of art, literature, music. Naming the great works that inaugurated this period, and thinking, however loosely, about their quality, may lead to the rudiments of a definition.

Specifically, then, Picasso began working on the "Demoiselles d'Avignon," that idyll of a Barcelona whorehouse, in 1906-07; Stravinsky's "Sacre du Printemps" had its riotous premiere in 1913. The first book by Ezra Pound to bear the title *Personae* came out in 1909; J. Alfred Prufrock made his debut (in Chicago, of all places) in 1915. In 1914, Joyce had just finished the *Portrait* and was turning his full attention to *Ulysses*. In 1914 Wyndham Lewis published *Tarr*. Roger Fry's Post-Impressionist show at the Grafton Galleries (November 1910 to January 1911) was followed in 1913 by the New York Armory show, which introduced Post-Impressionist art to America. D. H. Lawrence took his first steps as a poet and novelist in the years around 1910. From 1910 onwards, F. T. Marinetti was lecturing explosively around Europe on an ill-defined but violent esthetic program that he called "Futurism." It would gain adherents in France, England, and Russia, as well as Italy; the adherents soon faded or wandered, but the movement, despite Marinetti's frequent silliness, had wide repercussions. It was more than a sideshow.

This list could be extended to include names like Bartok, Braque, Musil, Modigliani, Epstein, Kafka, Klee, Kandinsky, and so on almost indefinitely, but already it has given us grounds to talk about modernism's concrete character. Doubtless there was some new spirit in the air, around December of 1910, and very likely it was connected with world-events like the miserable World War that was just around the corner or the unhappy Boer War that was just over the horizon. But these amorphous spirits in the air are very hard to pin down, and it's better to start by noting some specific things that modernism as a style was and wasn't. For example, Marinetti's futurism was loudly and explicitly hostile to the past as such: it wanted works of art as dynamic, efficient, and mechanical as automobiles or airplanes, and furiously repudiated all sorts of nineteenth-century historicism, humanitarianism, and softness. Except perhaps for the art of music, where it produced only a few laughable and sterile cacophonies, futurism had significant reverberations throughout the arts. Brancusi the sculptor was touched by this idea of stripped energy; so, more importantly, was Le Corbusier the architect; and if the movement didn't strongly influence Cubist painting, that was because the Cubists had already embarked on a very similar program of their own. Blok and Mayakovsky in Russia wrote Futurist poetry; Wyndham Lewis in the several issues of

Blast and in his first novel *Tarr,* produced Vorticist prose which was closely allied to Futurist work in its bold discords, its stark and simplified syntax. Pound's version of Imagism is first cousin to Vorticism, and so in the same family group as Futurism; but here we run suddenly into confusion, because Pound, quite as much as his master Browning, was always fascinated by the past, and among his many styles wrote in a number of deliberately archaic forms and manners.

And this deliberate cultivation of the past seems, as we look around, rather more characteristic of modernism than the direct and violent assault mounted by the Futurists on what they delighted to call *passéisme*. Two root inspirations of Picasso's first and most famous Cubist painting, "Les Demoiselles d'Avignon," were a big Paris exhibit of prehistoric Iberian sculpture and an equally comprehensive exhibit of primitive African masks. Stravinsky's "Sacre du Printemps" is based on and expressive of the vegetation rites and barbaric dances of ancient Russia. Both works were not only the last word in avant-garde style (for their day); they were more deeply rooted in primitivism than anything Europe had seen for a long time. And so with Eliot and Pound. They were "modern" poets from the beginning, and before long they were to be almost the touchstones of modernism; but all their work was deeply rooted in consciousness of the past. "The Waste Land" revolves around a priest-poet-prophet whose various incarnations include the Cumaean sybil and the ancient blind sexologist from Thebes, Tiresias. Pound's voyages in the *Cantos* took him through a series of events buried far in the past (the classical, the medieval, the Renaissance, the Chinese, the American past). One way or another, they all rhymed or were supposed to rhyme on events of the present; but the sheer volume of them made the *Cantos* look like an historical lumber-room. For Joyce, another of the great modernists, the Dublin episodes of June 16, 1904 were—among other things—but "a spume that played / Upon a ghostly paradigm of things." That paradigm was as old as any literary origin in the Western world; it was Homer's *Odyssey*. Far from repudiating and rejecting the past, as the Futurists demanded, modernism under one major aspect explored and exploited it.

The style of exploitation was new, the materials being exploited very old. The new primitivism sought a more remote past than people had been used to, and made very different applications of it. The polite, polished, Olympian side of the classic past was not what intrigued the modernists, rather it was the primitive, the barbaric, the mystery-side of the ancient world. Evidently they picked up a lot of these materials from the work of anthropologically-minded mythographers like Herr Max Muller, from the so-called "Cambridge anthropologists" led by Frazer, and from the work on archetypes done in the name of psychoanalysis by Jung and his followers—men like Ferenczi and Otto Rank. When Eliot went back to the Grail legend to structure his "Waste Land," he read it as something even more primitive than the medieval legend, he saw it as a vegetation ceremony out of prehistory.

Prokofieff filled his "Scythian Suite" with barbaric clangor; the "Classical Symphony" is a twittering joke on Haydn.

What their materials were and where they got them were clearly less important than what the modernists did with them. The nineteenth century had crammed itself on classical and medieval pastiches, where the modern poet or painter used myth as a familiar container into which to pour highminded contemporary sentiments. We don't need a better word for this sort of thing than "kitsch." Everyone can think of his favorite example—whether it's Bouguereau or Sir Lawrence Alma-Tadema, Lord Leighton or Robert Bridges, Bulwer-Lytton or Arnold Böcklin. But when Pound and Eliot, Stravinsky and Picasso took in hand the antique, they did so in a spirit at once deeper and more ironic than that of traditional neo-classicism. They used the past structurally, not for decorative ends; they incorporated fragments from the past in a structure stridently of the present; they emphasized grotesque disparities as much as harmonies; instead of a smooth surface, either antique or modern, they produced a broken one, which was both. Pound made Sextus Propertius talk of Wordsworth and frigidaires; Eliot's bowler-hatted, brolly-carrying clerk wandered the City streets anxiously inquiring about corpses buried in backyard gardens; Bloom put out the glaring eye of Cyclops by lighting a cigar instead of downing a John Jameson. Behind this change was a new sense of time as cyclical and repetitive, not sequential and developmental. The past wasn't a series of incremental stages on the road to the present, it was a single pattern replicated pointlessly and potentially to infinity. History became a series of all-but-identical arabesques traced on sheets of transparent plastic and lined up behind one another, so that only a slight shift of perspective could transpose any particular story into the Homeric age, the medieval era, the Renaissance, or the "present." Whatever its momentary embodiment, the configuration would always be much the same. A hard and jagged style of disparate elements juxtaposed without nexus or comment, an a-chronological patterning of correspondent themes (like a shape in space, not a sequence in time), these were techniques that admirably suited the translucent vision. This was the first major distinctive style of modernism, and not even one whose first interest is letters can fail to notice how closely it corresponded with the fractured surfaces of cubism, the broken, syncopated rhythms of Schoenberg and Stravinsky, the montage method of the movies.

The Futurist element of modernism was not only (by contrast with what preceded it) abstract and non-representational, perhaps in line with Worringer's thesis that abstract art represents fear, rather than acceptance, of the exterior world: it was, to borrow a word from José Ortega y Gasset, increasingly "dehumanized." The marks of this quality are everywhere, and one needn't labor the point. Fictional heroes, for example, could no longer be interesting because they embodied or exemplified "human nature": they were verbal patterns at second, third, or 26th hand, and they advertised the fact, as in Giraudoux's thirty-eighth retelling of the Amphitryon story. They were passive as beanbags, and they were also transparent—passive as in Kafka, transparent as in Gide. Bloom, by the end of the book which is so largely his, has been flattened as thin as a piece of strudel-dough; he is Everyman and Noman, a mountain-range, a heavenly body wandering beyond all astronomical waifs and strays, to the extreme boundary of space, and then returning, not once, but again and again, forever, in eternity, as best our imagination can reach that term. And Humphrey Chimpden Earwicker in the next and greatest book is explicitly described as a "human pest cycling (pist!) and recycling (past!) about the sledgy streets, here he was (pust!) again." "The Waste Land" has often been described as a miniaturized epic, and so it is; what's been left out is simply the epic hero and his story. Finally, one doesn't find much of the human form divine in Arp or Mondrian or in the Cubist works from which they derive. Modern painting, the greater part of it, doesn't represent human beings or the nature they inhabit; in fact, it doesn't generally represent at all. "Black on Black" or "Untitled No. 6" are characteristic labels, and they conjure up before us pictures on whose merits we may not agree, but which certainly don't have much use for the greasy commonplaces of flesh and blood.

Yet there was from the beginning an exception to modernism's dehumanization; and that was the ancient, inescapable commonplace of sex. Not love, not by any manner of means: not love in the reconciling and humane sense familiar to novel-readers and occasionally to people—nor yet the doomed passion of Wagnerian lovers, though one can't fail to note the remarkable survival-value of *Liebestod* as a literary theme. Maeterlinck and D'Annunzio were replicating it well into the new century; even Proust can be seen in this line, and so can our late contemporary Nabokov, for whom the grand consuming passion was still possible. Yet in most modernist documents it's sex, not love, that predominates. Sexual pathology was an important ingredient of both *Ulysses* and "The Waste Land"; the hero of consciousness was also a hero of inhibition, and the so-called stream of consciousness flowed to most interesting effect when it was turbid or even choked. After Joyce the medium of that stream was assumed to be sex, one major interest lay in its failure or frustration, and we can see the theme being used by Hemingway, Faulkner, and lesser imitators beyond number. Even when the symptom of his condition was called alcoholism, writer's block, or what Auden named "the liar's quinsy," the afflicted hero was characteristic, and his disease involved sterility or impotence.

Complementary, not contradictory, is the kind of therapy accomplished by the priapic heroes of D. H. Lawrence, who find a cure for the brittle, mechanical superficiality of modern life, not merely in sex, but in the dark, primitive impulses of the blood. Sex, for Lawrence, is a kind of cognition, a necessary filling out of the human form and figure. The work of literary art that embodies his feeling throbs with the rhythms and repetitions, the enthusiastic vocabulary of sensuality. Whether sex can convincingly sustain all the psychic burdens that Lawrence and the Lawrentians loaded on that wholly delightful activity may discreetly be doubted. In effect, Lawrence, Miller, and Durrell made a religion of the genitalia to replace other religions (including that of art), which had apparently lost their stimulating effect. The point isn't that the religion of sex amounted to a big operation; as a piece of social pathology, indeed, the less it amounted to, the more significant it is.

For this variety of sex-and-sensuality modernism grows out of the "dehumanization" view of modern art, even while protesting as vigorously as possible against it. Because modern society seems to consist of cutouts and robots going through predetermined mechanical routines, Lawrence proposes that we get under the hard carapace to a vital and tender existence that's available to us all in the life of the instincts, the dark river of the subconscious. And here he chimes on the thought of that very different and apparently much more crustacean man, James Joyce. For Joyce too, there's a vital giant buried within each of us; that's why his title includes as one of its many potentials an imperative—Finnegans, wake up! Within each of us a giant Finn lies buried under mountains of psychic detritus, cultural habit, social conditioning, acquired guilt. As we accept this load, we sleep or die; but if we throw it off, we can be reborn to the life that has always been there inside us. What Joyce and Lawrence, from rather different perspectives, join in seeing as the great enslaver, the brutal jailer of the human animal, is the conscious, rational mind. Even Stephen Dedalus knows this much before the end of *Ulysses*: "In here it is," he says, tapping his forehead and echoing Blake, "in here it is I must kill the priest and the king."

As one might anticipate, this anti-intellectualism isn't a simple phenomenon, and it hasn't yet found its historian or even its analyst. Quite obviously the trend owes something to those giant enemies of ideology, Marx and Freud; just as obviously, it includes elements deriving from neither, including an amorphous kind of culture-weariness and nostalgia for barbaric vitality that became very prevalent in the nineties of the last century and continued into this. The Futurists, with their fondness for fistfights and nonsense-syllables chanted at the top of their lungs, manifested this mood as well as anyone. Whether rationally or not, the weight of war, empire, and technology (all of which the Futurists in fact welcomed), the pressures of mass civilization, the exhaustion of religions, and the accumulated inhibitions of artistic artifice, all got mixed together in some minds as hostile to instinctual being. The mood was more anti-civilization than actively primitivist. Somebody like D'Annunzio, who stood up to his knees in esthetic decadence, yet promoted the swashbuckling, blood-and-iron side of fascism, spans much of the gamut. But there are ultra-violet bands beyond D'Annunzio, where hostility to the mind and its works spreads into hostility toward esthetic elitism and the category of art, hostility toward the mental reservation and bad faith implicit in artistic arrangement, hostility toward the

very codes of equivalence which constrain our ultimate yawping, fecal Yahoo-sincerity.

But here we pause on the shore of a wide sea of modern irrationalist, anti-rationalist, and absurdist movements to note a couple of curious, half-way phenomena among some of the modernists. There's been a lot of talk about the fact that men like Pound and Eliot, Wyndham Lewis, Céline, and Lawrence all had a special weakness, more or less overt, for authoritarian if not fascist governments. This needn't be put down to irrationalism as such. In some cases at least, these men had an abiding devotion to what they called rationalism, which they thought required an authoritarian and elitist group to embody and defend it. "Reason" in these cases isn't like a quiet room that you can walk into or out of; it's an area that men fight to control, from which you can be dispossessed despite your best intentions. Céline and Lawrence really lived some part of the time in a deliberately cultivated delirium; not so, or at least not so completely, Eliot and Wyndham Lewis. A key document for some of the early modernists, those whom Mr. Kermode slyly calls palaeo-modernists, was Julien Benda's *Trahison des clercs*. For all that it included a broad streak of anti-intellectualism, modernism was in many respects a learned, a clerkly phenomenon. And this isn't altogether an absurd concatenation: who, after all, has a better right to be anti-intellectual than a clerk?

A related ambiguity of literary modernism that hasn't been much explored is its attitude toward "surfaces," which has amounted to calling into question what we mean by that strangely elusive word. Works that consist of a series of receding congruent outlines obviously don't have any fixed, primary surface; they are deliberately polysemous literature, to be experienced now at this level, now at that, or at all at once, according to the reader's elasticity of mind. Relatively familiar is the trick with literary surfaces that involves fragmenting them and inviting the reader to construct constellations of significant shape across the vacant gaps between them—a kind of structure that defines the strongest areas of work's surface as those where nothing is expressed. Many modernist works destroy trust in a specious surface by filling it with deliberate anomalies and absurdities; or they modulate the narration of an ostensible event into another mode, possibly the tale of the narrative's own generation; or they work into the texture of an ostensible narration subliminal patterns of correspondence that can be seen (by a retrospective rearrangement) to constitute a counter-narration. Still more frequent is the use of unreliable (absurd or contradictory) and therefore unsettling narrators, from whose faltering indications the reader must construct whatever consecutive and coherent shape he can. One of the easiest ways to define a façade as "genuine" is to take another façade away from in front of it; given an antagonist relation, one can play off a fake into a double-fake just as easily as into a counter-fake. All these tricks with surface (and many more in common use) imply an equivocal attitude, at best, toward the reader and his impulse to "understand." In effect, the artist works with and against the reader's logical inertia. What we mean by understanding is simply identifying on some level a surface sustained and consistent enough to support a general idea that has formed in our minds. And modernist works from Pirandello to Beckett are concerned to delay, confuse, and impede, as much as to assist, the reader's definition of such an appropriate surface.

Game-playing is fun, but a very crude consideration of raw materials may tell us more about the real character of modernism. In architecture, it's particularly clear that modernism brought to the fore new materials used in distinctive new ways, just as the Futurists had proposed. Plate glass, stainless steel, reinforced concrete, even erector-set framing techniques, all came into prominence pretty abruptly, and with results ranging from Taliessin West at one end of the scale to the typical ungainly, shamefaced academic box at the other. In music, modernism brought about increased use, not only of discords and syncopation (particularly as the old distinction between "high" and "low" art faded toward insignificance), but of actual noise as a musical element. When Honneger imitated a locomotive, and Antheil mounted an airplane engine on the concert platform, we were well on our way to John Cage's famous "Four Minutes and Thirty Three Seconds," where random noise is not only incorporated in the performance, but constitutes the whole thing. For painting and sculpture the case is even more apparent. The first effect of modernism was to widen the palette and increase enormously the range of materials that the artist could use. The revival of collage and the importation into painting of sand, cigarette butts, linoleum, hair, straw, mud, or anything else that came to hand—this development is as familiar from jokes as from actual experience. Whatever could be seen in an esthetic way was potentially a work of art. And finally, I think the same sort of thing happened in the verbal arts as well: the range of literary language widened extraordinarily. I'm not thinking simply of the dirty words which crept in modestly with *Lady Chatterley's Lover,* expanded through Henry Miller's trilogy, and became a kind of buried speech-norm in *Last Exit to Brooklyn.* More interesting than this change is the increasing use for literary purposes of contaminated language—clichés and quotations, formulas and phrases out of the linguistic garbage-midden, sufficient to make up an independent, semi-private language of its own.

Radical linguistic innovation naturally came as a particular shock in a country like France, where the standards of literary correctness had long been strict. Anatole France, whose terminal date is 1924, refused to learn any foreign tongue, lest he corrupt the purity of his French idiom; but on the same principle, he might well have refused to learn French itself, since the way Frenchmen really talk is a couple of light-years away from the style in which Anatole France prided himself on writing. When Céline and Vian began writing French of the sort that the truck-driver and the scow-skipper use, they created real shock-waves. Americans and Englishmen had to do more than

that to ripple the pond, but in fact they widened enormously, not just the vocabulary, but the general verbal resources of the tongue. To cast a novel in the form of an index or a catechism, to investigate the resources of absolute asininity or even idiocy, to cross-breed English with a dozen other tongues, to represent complex synthetic states of mind and the full multiplicity of our emotional subcurrents—all this involved a kind of verbal explosion, to parallel which we have to reach back to the age of Shakespeare and Montaigne. Explosions aren't, to be sure, necessarily great literary events in themselves: classical French drama emerged when the French vocabulary was contracting, not expanding, and is all the better for that. Still, the age of palaeo-modernism was one of expansion, invention, updating, radical refurbishing—down to the roots of the vocabulary. Following an age of avowed decadence, and often describing itself (maybe a bit wishfully) as an age of retrenchment and restraint, the palaeo-modernist era was in fact one of explosive and revolutionary change. Indeed, the difference between palaeo-modernism and neo-modernism may prove in the end too great to be bridged by a couple of half-comic prefixes. Maybe palaeo-modernism will prove to have been the only real modernism, while what succeeded it will prove to have been merely (and momentarily) contemporary.

At any rate, if modernism represented a change at all, that change was worked by palaeo-modernism; and from a short perspective at least, it seems real enough. One odd if forceful proof of its reality is that we've so far been unable to write a coherent history of modern English literature. The old survey-title took us, one writer after another, in decent chronological order, from *Beowulf* to Thomas Hardy; and there's a clear line to be traced there. But to get from Hardy to Eliot we have to go back to Laforgue and Donne. To reach Pound we must consult Lao Tze and Peire Vidal: and in order to get a background for Joyce we have to combine Swift, Flaubert, and Ibsen with a dash of Dante. In cosmic terms, nothing is new under the sun; but modernism gives us a sense of an entire cultural heritage being ploughed up and turned over.

It's much easier, however, to say where and how modernism started than where it ended, or if it has: the central and hardest problem is always the closest, the problem of *now.* We seem neither to have pushed beyond the innovations of modernism nor to have rejected them decisively. Primitivism no longer seems like a spacious new dimension of art, sex as a theme offers no larger perspectives than leit-motifs and montage as techniques. A lot of play continues to be made with varieties of illusionism, including the manipulation and disintegration of surfaces: in that sense and perhaps a few others, modernism can be thought of as pushing forward, though its heroic days are certainly over.

Whether we need a new term for the period that has succeeded modernism depends in fact on where we imagine ourselves to be standing—a *locus standi* being exactly what's hardest to achieve in considering the *now*. On the customary loose accounting the middle ages lasted for a thousand gigantic years after the death of Boethius, from 500 to 1500. If we take a perspective anything like that long, the entire subject of modernism disappears from view. What happened in 1910 wasn't a new definition of human nature, and modernism never happened. It was just a tertiary wrinkle or ripple in a movement loosely labelled romanticism that began around 1750 or so. If we think of ourselves as still working through romanticism (protesting against it like all the other romantics before us), then we only have to go back a few years before romanticism to get to the renaissance, of which romanticism as a whole can very well be seen as a stage. Then we have three handsome periods in the history of the west—the classical age (800 B.C. to 500 A.D.), the middle ages (500-1500), and the renaissance, which, as it began about 1500, can reasonably be expected to peter out about 2500, give or take a couple of centuries. At that time we may be ready for the new Dark Ages, of which some romantic pessimists already profess to see multiplying signs.

Should I be sent on a Fulbright to some remote galaxy, this or something like this might be a good first perspective on the history of western culture. It's neat, it's symmetrical, and it divides the subject into three parts, which is always reassuring. For us, however, being who, where, and when we are, it has the slight disadvantage of being altogether useless. All these distinctions of schools and movements over the last century or two are doubtless trivial in the long run—if you run long enough. Futurist and modernist, symbolist and Parnassian, pre-Raphaelite and surrealist, expressionist and impressionist, realist and naturalist and so forth and so on—no doubt they will all iron out with the passage of time, and schoolchildren will be taught exquisitely simple generalities about the first machine age (1750-2400) or something like that. But if only for mnemonic purposes (and I'm sceptical enough to think those the only real purposes of cultural categories), we do need some scale calculated for the here and now, not for hypothetical inhabitants of Sirius and Betelgeuse.

So modernism we've got, its waves and reverberations have filled our lives, ephemeral as they are, and at the moment, though they've been damped, flattened, attenuated and subjected to frequent counterpressure, I see no sign that they've been supplanted by any other major unit of cultural energy. That, after all, is the only conclusive event that can write "finis" to a cultural era—the arrival, in thunder, of a new cultural era. I haven't heard any rumors of such an event. It would seem that, like ancient geographers, we have here a blank spot on our cultural map, to be filled with amorphous, nondescript creatures. Yet if we can't specify any cultural earthshakers over the past fifty years (since palaeo-modernism started fading into eclectic, harlequin neo-modernism), we may still remark some characteristic strains and pressures of what we may yet someday call "the age of undertow."

For one thing, where modernism has simply pushed ahead, it has exaggerated tendencies which were in it from the beginning, by making symptomatic jokes out of them. Hostility to artifice continues to make itself felt, along with violent dislike of that placatory packaging which makes art as easy to take as placebo pills. Artforms that consist of holes and trenches dug in the desert, or a twenty-mile canvas fence to the sea, are a way of thumbing one's nose at 59th street and Madison Avenue. One young man has distinguished himself as an arranger of excelsior in piles—the admirer is challenged, as it were, to buy *that,* take it home, and put it in his living room. Akin to this impulse is another which disclaims, so far as possible, any participation of the artist in the arrangement of his materials. Minimalist art and aleatory art (which introduce a deliberate element but undeliberate quantity of disorder and chaos into the art work) are ways of repudiating the artist's role of God over his own creation. One can see this as a natural development from pop art, which deliberately accepted the forms of vulgar life, resizing them or reduplicating them, but often doing as little to them as possible. Andy Warhol, tired of imitating Brillo boxes, soon began acquiring real Brillo boxes, signing his name to them, and sending them to the galleries. Robert Rauschenberg, finding to hand a drawing by De Kooning, erased it, signed the paper, and listed it among his works as an "Erased De Kooning" by Rauschenberg.

Simultaneously, books are being written which consist entirely of the love-hate romance of the story with the story-teller—in which every ostensible story collapses into the story of the story-teller, and no surface exists which is not potentially and ultimately a phantom of his mind. The self-conscious novel is the mirror image, as it were, of minimalist art: in the one, the artist is nowhere, in the other he is everywhere. And both varieties of elusive game-playing (pretending as they do to delude us on a point where common sense is not to be deluded) bespeak a kind of radical tension between the craftsman and his craft. I think this tension could be traced widely, through Beckett's explicit efforts to murder prose fiction, through parodists and self-parodists, through joky nihilists beyond number. And there seem perfectly sufficient reasons for this state of affairs. By and large, our artistic forms do have long histories: they are mature forms. Yet the pressure on artists to produce something new is unremitting. The new mass audiences with their new leisure time gulp cultural artifacts at a staggering rate. To take a single instance, movies and television, though simply extensions of the drama, have multiplied a thousandfold the appetite for narrative, and so hastened a thousandfold the wearing-out of dramatic and narrative clichés. Even before the contemporary deluge broke, the pressures of mass society were creating in a few a nostalgia for the void, a fascination with the dark unknown, and thus a hatred of culture and its forms. By now, one of the few formulas for artistic distinction seems to be the repudiation of artistic distinction as a category.

And when even this extreme position has become hackneyed, where do we go? We fracture, we eclect. Some fall back, declining the gambit entirely; a few push ahead faster and faster. In recent painting particularly, phases and stages and fads and manners seem to succeed one another so fast, that even the competitors are hard put to keep up. I don't think it's just an illusion that artistic periods not only get shorter as we approach the modern era, but cultural classifications get continually hazier and looser. History is moving faster; eclecticism offers us ever-wider fields of choice for parody, pastiche, or imitation; the big alternatives have already been used. So categories multiply as the reasons for having them languish. Of all the empty and meaningless categories, hardly any is inherently as empty and meaningless as "the modern." Like "youth," it is a self-destroying concept; unlike "youth," it has a million and one potential meanings. Nothing is so dated as yesterday's modern, and nothing, however dated in itself, fails to qualify as "modern" so long as it enjoys the exquisite privilege of having been created yesterday. Collections of so-called modern art thus fall between two stools: I've walked through some that seemed to me absolutely petrified—as dead as a collection of dodo-skeletons—and through others that were so determined to be up-to-the-minute, that they were simply trendy. What's new isn't to be defined just chronologically. A lot of work pretending to be new is the old stuff covered with a glossy varnish of artificial novelty; a lot of innovation proceeds lockstep down the corridors of prescribed nonconformist conformity; and a lot of apparent novelty is new simply because previous workers in the vineyard had enough sense to see that that particular path wasn't worth following. Separating what's really modern from what's simply contemporary is an exacting speculation, and language doesn't help with the distinction. More than anywhere else in criticism, we need a rich if not indeed a rational vocabulary to discuss our own times: though we're poor everywhere, we're poorest of all here.

In one sense, then, we can say that the "modernist" period has never ended and never will end, though as a perceptible piece of time it has ceased to exist. If "modern" means no more than "born yesterday," the modern age won't cease till there are no more todays. So modernism will never end, it will just attenuate and diffuse itself more and more. In *The Shape of Time*, George Kubler says, neatly, "Every new form limits the succeeding innovations in the same series. Every such form is itself one of a finite number of possibilities open in any temporal situation. Hence every innovation reduces the duration of its class." This is true, and very sharply put, but it presupposes a clearly defined class. If your class is infinitely elastic, as "modernism" may become if we don't tack it down here and there, it may well achieve total comprehensiveness at the cost of total meaninglessness.

According to some of my colleagues, we are already into the postmodernist age—a formula that flatters one with the sense of being an amazingly up-to-date fellow, but also implies an awful degree of terminological desperation. Doesn't the heedless fellow who dreamed up this formula anticipate the day when we'll have worked our way into forms like post-post-post-modernist and its in-

evitable, infinite sequels? The more such patches one sticks on "modernist," the more obvious its inadequacy as a descriptive term in the first place.

So in answer to the question of my title, "What was modernism?" I'd like to propose a pretty restrictive response. Modernism was an inaccurate and misleading term, applied to a cultural trend most clearly discernible between 1905 and 1925. When it is understood to refer to distinct structural features that some artistic works of this period have in common, it has a real meaning, though it still isn't a very good term. As it departs from that specific meaning, it gets fuzzier and fuzzier, and sometimes it doesn't mean much of anything at all. Still, it has been a prevalent and widely accepted stopgap term, with a loose, emotive tone, and one of the ways to get better terminology is to pick it apart, and see how many different things it has been used to cover. Then perhaps we can get better names for them.

Richard Poirier

SOURCE: "The Difficulties of Modernism and the Modernism of Difficulty," in *Images and Ideas in American Culture: The Functions of Criticism,* edited by Arthur Edelstein, Brandeis University Press, 1979, pp. 124-40.

[*In the following essay, Poirier confronts the problematic nature of Modernism as it has been variously designated by literary critics and historians.*]

On every side, these days, there is talk of modernism— what was it? what is it? when did it happen?—and partly because these questions have been voluminously but not satisfactorily answered, the modernist period threatens to stretch into a century, or, for some people, into two. Literary history has never allowed such longevity, and the prospect raises a number of embarrassing questions. During this whole time, has there been so little change in the cultural and social conditions which supposedly begat modernism that there has been no occasion for a radical change in literary consciousness? Or could it be said that poets and novelists have either been unresponsive to upheavals in the culture or that they have been able to respond only by modifications of Joyce, Eliot, and Pound—or, stretching it a bit, of Hawthorne, Melville, and James? Or perhaps we should ask if there has been a wholly uncharacteristic failure on the part of literary historians to make those discriminations of periods which keep them busy. They have proposed subdivisions like neomodernism, paleomodernism, or postmodernism, which only serve to illustrate the problem.

In fact, modernism in literature has become so amorphous that it is possible to be half persuaded by Harold Bloom when he says that "modernism has not passed; rather it is exposed as never having been there." While this seems in no way a satisfactory solution, it is generated by a healthy and beneficial contempt for the kind of thinking that has encumbered attempts to locate the specific cultural anxiety we call modernism. For it is not cultural anxiety itself, scarcely the sole privilege of the twentieth century, but a peculiar form of it that needs to be diagnosed. We can begin simply by noting that modernism is associated with being unhappy. It is associated with being burdened by the very materials, the beliefs, institutions, and forms of language, that are also our source of support as we labor under the burden. To be happy in the twentieth century is to see no burden *in* these supports; it is to be trivial. Modernism carries a very learned but always a very long face. I recall in college hearing an unusually beautiful and vibrant young woman from Smith murmur to herself in the middle of a party, "I have measured out my life in coffee spoons." Obviously, at eighteen or nineteen, she was boasting. Nowadays she would probably say, "Keep cool, but care," and while this might register an advance in social amiability, it would not be an advance for literary criticism, which has found it more or less impossible not to take everything in modernist texts seriously. Or perhaps seriously is the wrong word. It finds it impossible not to take everything solemnly.

The phenomenon of grim reading—that is what I would like to offer as my initial definition of modernism. Modernism happened when reading got to be grim. I locate modernism, that is, in a kind of reading habit or reading necessity. I am concerned with the degree to which modernist texts—and it should be remembered that in the annals of twentieth-century literature these texts are by no means in the majority—mostly prevent our asking questions about any spontaneous act of reading, even when it is accompanied by a high degree of learned competence. Modernism in literature can be measured by the degree of textual intimidation felt in the act of reading. That act can become, especially in the classroom, a frightened and unhappy experience in which we are made to feel not only inferior to the author but, in the face of constant reminders that he is himself dissatisfied with what he has just managed to put before us, totally uncritical. There are almost no critical as distinguished from interpretive readers of the twentieth-century classics. Speaking only of English and American literature, but knowing of a similar but more politicized argument made by Leo Bersani with respect to French literature as exemplified in Malarmé, it can be said that modernism is to be located not in ideas about cultural institutions or about the structures of life in or outside literary texts. It is to be found, rather, in two related and historically verifiable developments: first, in the promotion, by a particular faction of writers, of the virtues and necessities of difficulty and, second, in the complicity by a faction of readers who assent to the proposition that the act of reading should entail difficulties analogous to those registered in the act of writing.

Modernism is an attempt to perpetuate the power of literature as a privileged form of discourse. By its difficulty it tries, paradoxically, to reinvoke the connections, severed more or less by the growth of mass culture, between the artist and the audience. Since this special connection

is no longer based on inherited class, as it was up to the Restoration, and since there is no provision for a Spenser, a Milton, a Marvell—great writers who were also members of a governing class for whom they wrote—a corresponding community of writer and reader has to be created. To this end they are asked to participate in a shared text from which others are to be excluded. This may sound as if modernism were a snob's game. It certainly was and is just that, despite all the middle-class keys and guides to the club. It was and is, of course, much more. Significantly, modernism in English literature is nearly exclusively the result of American and Irish—Pound, Eliot, Joyce, Yeats—rather than of English writers and, as I have argued elsewhere, Melville and Hawthorne are, in what they require of the reader, modernist in theory and practice. (It took the inculcation of "difficulty-as-a-virtue" in this century before either of these writers began to be read properly.) Obviously involved here is a colonialist protest on the part of these writers against the shapes the language had assumed as it came forth from England, the seat of cultural and political authority. More importantly, the protest occurred when English literature had itself begun, in the novel and in the great popular poets of the nineteenth century, to cater to the ethos of the so-called common man or common reader. It was to escape incorporation in the ethos that modernist writers turned to the City, with its sharpened social and cultural discriminations, to ancient myth and its hierarchies, to the coteries of French literature, and to English literature of the seventeenth century, a literature of privilege. It is consistent with all this that the two great twentieth-century writers who often seem comparatively easy, Lawrence and Frost, were charged by their modernist contemporaries with being relatively deficient in the sophistications of culture as embodied in the university and the modern city.

Modernism can be thought of as a period when, more than in any other, readers were induced to think of literary texts as necessarily and rewardingly complicated. It represents a demand made upon readers not by anything called twentieth-century literature but by a few peculiarly demanding texts which were promoted as central during this century. In most cases the authors were also remarkably persuasive as literary critics, both in their poems and novels and also in critical writing itself. They rewrote literary history from the retrospect of their own preeminence, expected or achieved. So successful were they in doing this that only in about the past fifteen years has it become possible to bring to vividness on the map of English literature those areas left rather dingy since the advent of modernism as a *critical* fashion. If, through the preeminence of Eliot early in the century, it became necessary to give prominence to Donne and Marvell, it is because of the later eminence of Stevens that Wordsworth has recently been seen for an ever more strange and wonderful poet, just as it is thanks to Frost and Stevens together that the extraordinary importance of Emerson has still to be coped with.

Literary history is to so great an extent the product of such tactical moves and thrusts for power that I cannot agree with the argument offered by Robert Adams in his essay "What Was Modernism." Of the term itself, Adams writes that "one odd if forceful proof of its reality is that we've so far been unable to write a coherent history of modern English literature." No one can argue with this proposition, but it is possible to take it as a case for celebration rather than bewilderment, and certainly not as an occasion for holding one's breath. A major achievement of recent criticism has been the effort to break down the coherencies that have passed for literary history and to invalidate the principles on which that coherency has traditionally depended. It is possible now to see that the very cult of modernism is in itself a demonstration of the arbitrariness and impertinence by which literary history gets made and remade. Fortunately there is no longer a "coherent history" of English poetry to replace the one which could claim coherence only by reading Shelley out of the line of succession and by trying to dislodge Milton from it. Nor is there a coherent history of American literature, since it has in the past been so often only a history of the Northeast. The coherencies that may ultimately be found will have less to do with chronology, or with periods, or so I hope and expect, than with habits of reading, and related fashions in classroom pedagogy.

Modernism, then, is not an idea or a social condition. The ideas usually associated with it are in themselves not unique to any historical period. It is, rather, the proffered experience which, in its intensity, is unique to this century. Thus, some of the ideas ascribed to Eliot or Joyce or Faulkner belong just as much to Matthew Arnold or to Diderot; they can be extrapolated from Shakespeare, especially from *Troilus and Cressida,* or from the tragedies of Seneca. But none of these is a modernist writer. No one of them has written a book that asks to be read with the kind of attention—unique in the history of literature—required by Eliot or Joyce or Faulkner. It is through Joyce and Eliot especially, and the works published roughly between 1914 and 1925, that most people have learned about modernism, learned to think of it as a phenomenon of the first half of this century, and learned also that it is supposed to entail great difficulties, both for the writer and for the reader.

The peculiar and contradictory nature of that difficulty is the subject to which I can now turn. The necessity of difficulty was put in an unabashedly intimidating way by Eliot in an essay of 1921, "The Metaphysical Poets." "We can only say," he writes, "that it appears likely that poets in our civilization, as it exists at present, must be *difficult.* Our civilization comprehends great variety and complexity, and this variety and complexity, playing upon a refined sensibility, must produce various and complex results. The poet must become more and more comprehensive, more allusive, more indirect, in order to force, to dislocate if necessary, language into his meaning." There is a most unappealing quality in Eliot's prose when he is in this particular mood, a Brahmin indirection, as of a fastidious gentility reluctantly, but no less arrogantly, taking on the whole of the twentieth century. "We

can only say that it appears likely that poets in our civilization, as it exists at present . . ."

But Eliot's statement is only arrogant on the face of it. His explanation of why modern poetry is of necessity "difficult" is in fact a self-protective, reductive, and defensive apology for "difficulty." The passage translates difficulty into social and historical causes which in themselves were not at all as peculiar to "our civilization" as he makes them out to be. It is an attempt, that is, actually to vulgarize the necessity for "difficulty," and it might make us wonder how much of his difficulty derived from causes more intimately personal and sexual. Self-serving or not, the representative importance of this insistence on the necessary difficulty of poetry and prose in the twentieth century—Eliot makes even more pointed remarks on the subject in his essay on *Ulysses*—ought to be apparent. It became the bedrock of literary criticism and the study of literature from about 1930 onward. No one can object to difficulty or to any effort to cope with it. At issue are the implications that the difficulty was something only the poet could confront *for* us, and that the reader should be selfless and humble and thankful for the poet's having done this.

It has been said that modernist texts have been misread in the interests of making them more available, more rationally organized, more socially and historically referential than they truly are, and that instead of demystifying these texts, criticism ought to protect their inherent mysteriousness and their irreducible power to baffle. But can it not also be claimed that one reason for the kind of reductive misreadings and interpretations that modernist texts have received lies *in* the works and the writers themselves? Modernist texts make grim readers of us all, that is, by the claim that most people are inadequate to them. We are met with inducements to tidy things up, to locate principles of order and structure beneath a fragmentary surface. We work very hard at it. And then we are told that in fact we have been acting in a witless and heavy-handed fashion, embarrassingly deficient of aristocratic ease. We should have let things be, problematic and unresolved, the meanings perpetually in abeyance. This may seem like a contradiction, but in fact there is not even a choice. We are left precisely within the alternatives, and honestly to recognize this situation as our own allows us, at last, to recognize the writer as being in a situation not very different. It encourages us to humanize the work, the industry of modernist writing, to locate a self and a personality in it. Against Eliot's dictum, it is time to insist that the man who writes is also the man who suffers. In this view, the modernist writer is working within the same contradictions as the reader. The text becomes a drama wherein the culturally or biologically determined human taste for structure or for structuring is continually being excited into activity, and just as continually being frustrated. Each thrust toward order proves no more than another example of the urgency to achieve it.

Modernist literature is tough going, and there is no point in deluding ourselves, and especially our students, with talk, too slowly going out of fashion, of "an erotics of reading," or an escapade of reading, for claims for the sheer fun that awaits us in the pages of Pound or Pynchon. In an engaging book on Ezra Pound, for example, Donald Davie proposes that the best way to read the *Cantos* is to read them "many at a time and fast":

> This indeed is what irritates so many readers and fascinates an elect few—that the *Cantos*, erudite though they are, consistently frustrate the sort of reading that is synonymous with "study," reading such as goes on in the seminar room or the discussion group. It is hopeless to get at them cannily, not moving on to line three until one is sure of line two. They must be taken in big gulps or not at all. Does this mean reading without comprehension? Yes, if by comprehension we mean a set of propositions that can be laid end to end. . . . Which is not to deny that some teasing out of quite short excerpts, even some hunting up of sources and allusions, is profitable at some stage. For the *Cantos* are a poem to be lived with, over years. Yet after many years, each new reading—if it is reading of many pages at a time, as it should be—is a new bewilderment. So it should be, for so it was meant to be. After all, some kinds of bewilderment are fruitful. To one such kind we give the name "awe"—not awe at the poet's accomplishment, his energy, or his erudition but awe at the energies, some human and some non-human, which interact, climb, spiral, reverse themselves, and disperse, in the forming and reforming spectacles which the poet's art presents to us or reminds us of.

This is a charming prescription with which I am anxious to agree, and it is impossible to live up to. It is impossible because Pound has made it so, just as have Eliot and Joyce, Beckett and Pynchon.

These writers lent themselves to and *encouraged* a programmed and widespread misreading. For reasons to be argued later, the notion that every reading is a misreading seems to me theoretically acceptable if you wish to quibble but wrong and misleading when it gets down to specific cases. The misreading in question—with its emphasis on order and design—is demonstrably less synchronized with the "work" than are misreadings that like to play fast and loose. That most readers were led away from the nerve centers of these books by the stimulations of merely external design cannot be explained by claims that for historical reasons literature "must be difficult" in this century. There has been instead, on the part of the writers themselves, a curious *will* to reduce and impoverish what the texts potentially offer. The kinds of clues supplied by Eliot's famous *Notes*, Joyce's handouts, Yeats's system, Faulkner's Christian symbolism—all tended to nullify a reading experience which was in itself meant to mock the efficacy of such clues. As a result, there have been for most readers at least two texts of works like *The Waste Land* or *Ulysses*. One is full of marginalia by which the work is translated into something orderly, fit for class discussion, lectures and articles; while the other is remembered with fondness for all sorts of fragmentary pleasures. There has been almost no critical acknowledgement that these works are a sort of battleground: the flow of material wars against a technology which, however determined, is inadequate to the task of controlling the material. This imbalance is, of course, a contrived one, meant to demonstrate the breakdown of any technique or technology in the face of contemporary life, and it received its most articulate expression first, I think, not in Henry Adams but in Henry James, when in *The American Scene*, he remarks that "The reflecting surfaces, of the ironic, of the epic order, suspended in the New York atmosphere, have yet to show symptoms of shining out, and the monstrous phenomena themselves, meanwhile, strike me as having, with their intense momentum, got the start, got ahead of . . . any possibility of poetic, of dramatic capture."

Pynchon is a remarkable instance of a writer who uses literary technique as an analogue to all other kinds of technology, and does so in order to show that where technique or technology work, it is always at the expense of the material it processes. He seems to call for a labor of exegesis and to encourage the illusion that he will be best understood by those who bone up on entropy or quantum theory or theories of paranoic closure. In fact, his works can best be appreciated by those who can, like Davie's supposititious reader, take his arcane knowledge for granted and be in no way confused by the elaborateness of his "plotting," treating it not as a puzzle to be solved but as a literary symptom of social, historical, economic plotting, an image of the so-called network. But, again, no such reader exists, and it is of no practical use to badger ourselves into thinking that we might become wholly adequate to a text like *Gravity's Rainbow*. It is absurd to posit ideal readers—a favorite exercise of literary criticism—in instances where there cannot be one. But this is where our reverential concessions to literary difficulty have led us. No one *can* be the right kind of reader for books of this sort—open, excited, titillated, knowing, taking all the curves without a map. Some of the exhortations to do this in critical writing smack of high cultural fantasy, the aristocratic pretension that one can be at the same time casual and encyclopedic.

Let us try to tell the truth: writers as well as readers of twentieth-century classics have to do more book work than writers or readers have ever had to do before in history. Why is this the case, even for people from educated households? And why have so many assented to its being necessarily the case? At issue is not the basic difficulty of gaining the competence to read almost anything that is fully aware of the resources of its own language—Shakespeare or Spenser, Milton or Marvell, Wordsworth or Frost. For all the learning and allusiveness in such writers, they only infrequently exhibit the particular kinds of difficulty encountered in what I would call modernist literature. Granting Eliot's proposition—that "our civilization at present" requires a "difficult" kind of writing—why need that difficulty register itself as at once compendiously learned and disjointed, at once schematic in its disposal of allusions and blurred in the uses to which it puts them?

There is a clue, curiously enough, in that plainest of all modernists, Hemingway. Hemingway is not a difficult writer; to read him requires no special knowledge and a familiarity with only a limited repertoire of vocal tones, of sentence sounds. So the connection is made with the proviso that only after the difficult bookishness of Joyce or Eliot has been mastered, if it ever can be, can the reader then fully appreciate their sensuous and rhythmic pleasures. Ideally, that is, the apparatus of Eliot or Joyce functions the way bull fighting or boxing functions metaphorically in Hemingway, and the apparatus therefore probably deserves, though still on the other side of a bookishness Hemingway does not require, the same kind of response from the reader. The learning, the cultural displays, the mechanics of structuring, are forms of partial discipline, of willful signification in a situation where it is being admitted that acts of signification refer themselves to no authority other than the will. They offer an opportunity for making a kind of form which is effective precisely because it is temporary, satisfying only because it is allowed to remain local and finite. It is appropriate to invoke the great William James here, and to use, rather freely, a passage from his "Humanism and Truth." We might say that form in modernist literature is imagined as "the advancing front of experience." And as James so beautifully puts it

> Why may not the advancing front of experience, carrying its immanent satisfactions and dissatisfactions, cut against the black inane as the luminous orb of the moon cuts a caerulean abyss? Why should anywhere in the world be absolutely fixed and finished? And if reality genuinely grows, why may it not grow in these very determinations which here and now are made?

Any "form," in a memorable phrase of Robert Frost, our most William Jamesian poet, is no more than "a momentary stay against confusion." And how momentary some of these can be is evidenced in Eliot's *Notes* where he is not giving the reader much of anything except an example of how he can cheer himself up with bits and pieces: "The interior of St. Magnus Martyr is to my mind one of the finest of Wren's interiors. See *The Proposed Demolition among Nineteen City Churches:* (P. S. King & Son, Ltd.)." Thus also the relish of Joyce in lists, parodies, schemes. The best way to read such persistent schematization is an *act,* an action, something a writer is *doing* in a posited situation; and the posited situation, conceived by Joyce and Eliot as being more unique to their historical moment than either William James or Frost would have allowed, is one in which all more encompassing orders have become as arbitrary and as subject to deterioration as any they are themselves proposing. It is not, to repeat, so much the substance as the act of allusiveness or of schematization which should occupy the reader. In general it can be said that middle-class anxieties about culture and about some possibly terminal and encompassing acts of interpretation, both fostered by

the mythologies of general education, were only further increased by the often trivial or boned-up cultural erudition of the middle class "great" writers of the twentieth century, with their religious and cultural nostalgias.

Eliot and Joyce are not romantic writers; they are not classical writers either. In Eliot's telling phrase about Joyce, they are "classical in tendency." "Tendency"—they are what they are *in* an action, and by virtue of a kind of self-monitoring by which a writer interprets the forms he has just offered up for interpretation. It is said, with no embarrassment about being obvious, that the reader helps in the creation of the text and therefore functions, in his reading, like a poet. It can be said, less obviously, that Eliot and Joyce must be classified as readers of the text they are writing. Critical reading, that is, is simultaneously a part of the performance of writing, and to some degree it always has been. At the outset of "Tradition and the Individual Talent" Eliot remarks that "criticism is as inevitable as breathing, and that we should be none the worse for articulating what passes in our minds as we read a book and feel an emotion about it, for criticising our own minds in their work of criticism." This is precisely what he does in his poems.

In thus suggesting the kinetic, the volatile nature of both the reading and the writing, Eliot calls our attention to an active authorial presence even while forswearing it. That presence is supposed to be notoriously hard to find, according to him; it does not have a "voice" even in the great varieties of style displayed in modernist writing. But it can be found, if not in any of the styles, then in the mode of variations among them. It is to be found not in any place, despite all the formal placements made available, but in the acts of *dis*placement by which one form is relinquished for another. Recall how Faulkner described the reading-writing experience that gave us *The Sound and the Fury.* He wanted to tell a story that occurred to him when he saw a girl with dirty panties in a tree. He told it from a point of view that proved inadequate. So he told it again from another point of view, and on reading the second version he found that it, too, was inadequate; so he told it a third time from yet another, and when that did not satisfy him, he told it in more or less his own voice. That, too, was unsatisfactory, but the whole thing, the four versions, constituted the novel as we have it, a novel made from Faulkner's having read what he had written as a source of what he would then write. Apropos of this is an offhand remark by Gore Vidal which is altogether more useful than his considered and therefore superstitious observations on contemporary fiction: "In a way I have nothing to say but a great deal to add."

Eliot is so much a poet of probing additions, additions seeking a destination, that he could easily accept most deletions and abridgments made by Pound in *The Waste Land.* The penultimate admission in "Preludes" that "I am moved by fancies that are curled / Around these images, and cling: / The notion of some infinitely gentle / Infinitely suffering thing" comes from a poet for whom narrativity—with a destination—would have been an act of presumption. He can never take anything in stride; he moves, falteringly, toward the formation of images and concepts which dissolve as soon as he has reached them. The indecisiveness was as pronounced after as it was before his religious conversion. In the later poetry of *The Quartets,* as Leavis shows, the reader is not invited to translate abstract concepts about "time present and time past" but rather to witness and participate in the intensity of Eliot's personal engagement as he tries to arrive at some security, never actually achieved, about such abstractions and the feelings engendered by his use of them. Eliot became a poet precisely because he embraced those conditions which prevent others from becoming one—of being "moved" by something even while not knowing what to make of it. Writing for him was more or less indistinguishable from a critical reading that was all but crippling.

For Eliot's use of images that remain at once evocative and random there are well documented poetic precedents in Laforgue and others. But the images do not refer only to other images; they refer us also to a man named T. S. Eliot and to a feeling in him—we are allowed only faintly to sense it—that is close to an envy of natures more masculine, or should we say more operatically masculine, than his own. It is as if he imagines that for some other man the images in a poem like "La Filia ché Piange" would not remain transient and painful. They would instead initiate and sustain a plot. Eliot is someone—man as well as poet—incapable of initiating a plot within which the images could be secured and pacified.

Joyce exhibits, flamboyantly, altogether more psychological, sexual assurance. It is a commonplace that the Joycean hero is customarily on the fringe of activities—a game, a dance, a family dinner, a boisterous conversation. Other people can take pleasure in these activities unconscious or careless of what the hero knows about them: that they are bound by sometimes deadening rules and clichés, that the activities are programmed and encoded without consultation with the participants. Privileged consciousness, as Poulet would have it, is not at the center but on the circumference of the area of inhabited space, and it is ready to move still further out into abstractions, as at the end of "The Dead." But Stephen is no more his hero than Gabriel is, and no one can read him with a deserved relish without feeling that the true hero of Joyce's writing has been identified by those who say it is Joyce himself. He took a kind of pleasure—to call it sadomasochistic is to be obvious—in the fact that a Stephen or a Gabriel is forced to confront, to be intimidated by, the power, the exuberance, the virtuosity, however prefabricated, that is emplanted *in* the programmed or encoded life, in codes which only a genius can release onto the page. Joyce exulted in the evidence that he was master of the codes, master of the techniques, the revelry of forms. All writers are cold and calculating, but no one more brazenly celebrates his own arbitrariness. He is unlike Eliot in the delight he takes in *not* feeling put upon or anguished by what he has just written. Joyce is the quintessential celebrant of literary technology.

All literature is to some extent aware of itself as a technology. But literary modernism thrusts this awareness upon us, and to an unprecedented degree asks us to experience the enormous difficulties of mastering a technology. It is this matter of degree which allows us to distinguish literary modernism from the sort of literary self-consciousness which may be exhibited by any text in any period. Modernism manifests itself whenever a text chooses to demonstrate that one of its primary purposes is to expose the factitiousness of its own local procedures. In order to do this, it must make the experience of reading in some way almost directly analagous to the experience of writing. It can be said that modernist texts are about the corrosive effect of reading, by author and reader, upon what has just been shaped by the writing.

Modernist writers, to put it too simply, keep on with the writing of a text because in reading what they are writing they find only the provocation to alternatives. "To begin to begin again," as Gertrude Stein once said. If the texts are mimetic in that they simulate simultaneously the reading/writing activity, then *that* is the meaning of the text. The meaning resides in the performance of writing and reading, of reading in the act of writing. This is emphatically the reverse of saying, as part of a rear-guard perpetuation of humanism, that these texts are subject to multiple interpretations. Rather, their capacity to mean different things, to take different shapes, is in itself their meaning.

It is important to insist on this as against the fashion that imposes an infinite variety of possible readings. In that proposition is one evidence of a kind of ahistoricism in contemporary theory importantly different from the kind with which this essay might be charged. Modernist texts are of enormous historical consequence as *texts.* They are of consequence to the extent that their meaning resides in an induced habit of reading, using that word in the broadest sense, a habit finally of analysis that can be exercised outside the literary text on social and economic structures.

Modernist texts are important less for any commentary they offer on contemporary life than for the degree that they empower us, by the strenuous demands made upon our capacities for attention, to make our own commentaries.

To say that modernist poetry and fiction exists also and simultaneously as works of literary criticism is therefore to say that literary criticism can be a unique schooling in the workings of structures, techniques, codes, stylizations that shape the structured world around us.

Of course it could be argued that the plays of Shakespeare or the poetry of Wordsworth also exist as works of literary criticism. And where Shakespeare in *Troilus and Cressida* or Wordsworth in his shapings and reshapings of *The Prelude* reveal an extraordinary degree of self-consciousness about being critics of their own creation, they too are modernists. But it is well to remember that they become available to us *as* such only by virtue of what we have learned about the strains and difficulties of literature from Eliot, Joyce, and the like.

Modernism exists predominantly in the twentieth century only because it is predominantly there that we have been forced to become what I have called "grim readers." Modernism does not occur, that is, whenever a work addresses itself to literary traditions, the genres or tropes or topics which it shares with other poems and novels. Modernist texts include such allusiveness but are also consciously occupied with the nature of reading and writing then and there going on and with the relation between these two acts.

Modernism enters history not with a mirror, not even with a lamp, but with instruments by which to measure the hidden structure of things and the tactics of their movement. It enters history as a mode of experience, a way of reading, a way of being with great difficulty conscious of structures, techniques, codes, and stylizations. In modernist works the revealed inadequacy of forms or structures or styles to the life they propose to explain or include is meant in itself to be a matter of historical importance, regardless of whether the material is historically accredited. Our training in this could begin as easily with Melville as with Joyce. Modernist texts teach us to *face* the failure of technology in that version of it which we call literary technique—the failure significantly to account for all that we think technology should account for. In that sense, the reader of these works is made conscious, in Hawthorne's phrase, of "what prisoners we are," and this could be a discovery of great spiritual as well as cultural importance.

Robert Conquest

SOURCE: "But What Good Came of It at Last? An Inquest on Modernism," in *Essays by Divers Hands,* edited by Michael Holroyd, Boydell Press, 1982, pp. 61-77.

[*In the following essay, which was originally delivered as a lecture before the Royal Society of Literature in 1979, Conquest questions the ultimate artistic and cultural value of Modernism.*]

You will not expect—indeed you will probably be delighted not to have to listen to—a full conspectus of the modernist movement, tracing all the schools through cubism and vorticism and expressionism, through suprematism and constructivism and De Stijl, through Valery and Kafka and Gertrude Stein, through *Merz* and *Blast* and *Transition,* describing the interactions, the sectarian strife, the manifestos, the denunciations. And you will not, I hope, expect me to deal with modernism in every field—for instance in music or in architecture (though much of that, unfortunately, seems to be more lasting than bronze). I should, before this society, restrict myself largely to literature. Yet one cannot avoid some broader references. For, of course, all the arts were deeply af-

fected; and it is even the case that painters like Picasso, for example, wrote a number of 'poems'. Moreover, the condition of painting may sometimes illuminate that of the other arts. For painting is, in its very nature, more dependent than the written word on the apparatus of culture-pushers—patrons, galleries and so on. Again, it is probably easier to inflict a striped rectangle on the consumer, who only has to give it a look occasionally, than to make the same consumer read a damned thick book or even a fourteen-line poem. And this is apart from the perhaps partisan estimate made by Auden, that

> those who feel most like a sewer
> Belong to painting not to literature.

More broadly, in dealing with modernism, any approach is bound to be a reflection of the reading, viewing and experience of the writer: yet I do not think that any other selection of experience would lead to general conclusions different from what I suggest.

But first let us consider our terms. When one speaks of movements, of modernism, one is using great general words. In practice there are individual books, written by men with their own characters and idiosyncrasies, not mere ectoplasm of the Zeitgeist. But I take it that I will not be held to any precise definition of modernism; in this sort of sphere above all we are surely entitled to rely on Aristotle's dictum that words should be used with the precision or generality suitable to the field. With that in mind, we may start by defining modernism in an illustrative rather than a formal way: modernism is what makes the Tate Gallery buy and exhibit a pile of bricks.

Now, when some supposed novelty of this sort is criticized, one finds to this day the rhetoric put forward that the critic is evidently a shocked and uncomprehending fuddy-duddy faced with something beyond his ken. But of course this is, generally speaking, nonsense. Modernism has been with us for some seventy years. In 1913, to take an example from poetry, Marinetti published the following lines of a type which has long since become so tediously familiar that none of us would be surprised to see them today in a state-subsidized 'little magazine':

> plombs + lave + 300 puanteurs + 50 parfums
> pave matelas detritus crottin charognes
> flic-flac entassement chameaux bourricots
> tohubohu cloaque.

No, the critic of modernism is criticising a tradition which has been established now for generations, which has been the ambience of all of us since childhood. It long ago received the seal of academic approval, which Housman calls 'the second death'; its lumpish sculpture has been taken to the heart of the most establishmentarian corporations and government departments; its half-dimensional stripes and squares masquerade as paintings on the mantelpieces of New York stockbrokers. It is a paradox unique to our time that a traditionalism which has long lost its energies and spirits should yet contrive to be 'new', so that we still have to insist that it is a postmodernist rather than a pre-modernist generation which now points out its deficiencies. It is the younger and fresher writers in the architectural journals who are now insisting that American Victorian architecture is better than the post-Gropius stuff. It is Tom Wolfe, from the heart of the New York art world, who (in his *The Painted Word*) familiarly and devastatingly destroys the pretensions of the cycle of schools of pseudo-art which followed the—already bad enough—American neo-expressionists.

And so it is with literature. I should perhaps add that you can check my own case by looking at the *Penguin Book of Surrealist Verse* where a poem of mine written in my teens is displayed, I fear, for all to see. Indeed, while in this confessional mood, I will go further and admit that the earliest of my manuscripts that I can find is not only surrealist prose but aggravates the offence by actually being in French . . .

Modernism does not appear to be a literary movement in the older sense. The relation between it and the sensibility of the age seems quite different from anything that has preceded it. A special disjunction has taken place. But at what point does this occur?

I think we can, if only roughly, set up a criterion. First, by asking ourselves whether the changes in scope as seen in the novels of Proust, James, Lawrence, Svevo and the early Joyce were broader and more radical, or even as broad and as radical, as those of the novels of Dostoevsky and Tolstoy as compared with *their* predecessors. We must surely answer no. So let me first of all distinguish between the 'modern', naturally different from the art of previous periods, in reflecting a different sensibility, and the 'modernist'—something, in principle, total and revolutionary, which in prose one may associate with *Finnegans Wake* and Gertrude Stein. In painting, I would place it at Kandinsky and Picasso, at the point they had reached in 1914, (when they were so nominated by Pound)—or, possibly a little earlier, with Braque's first formulation of the idea of painting without content, around 1910.

In poetry . . . but first let us remember the deplorable state of English poetry in the first decade of this century. While the freshest prose reading, or seeing, of the man of cultural fashion was Wells and Bennett, Ibsen and Nietzsche and Shaw, in our poetry the leading names were—William Watson and Stephen Phillips.

The point at which, among other reactions against this sub-Victorian stuff, a specific modernism set in may be taken as the conscious setting up of Imagism around 1913, and the imported impact of Futurism, founded around 1907, but reaching Britain in 1912—containing all the ideas which were to infest poetic modernism for generations—above all, what Wordsworth speaks of as a 'degrading thirst after outrageous stimulation'.

Thus, from all these dates, it will be seen that modernism was *not* the product of a violent period, but of a peaceful period seeking violence.

So much for its birth. What about its life and, I would argue, its recent death. But, you will say, is it yet time to have an inquest? Modernism is more pervasive than ever among a huge semi-educated class. At the Tate, in the English Departments, its momentum is not yet spent. Yet it is dead, or nearly dead, as a live idea inspiring worthwhile work. So that when, for example, one reads Philip Toynbee enthusing over Mr John Berger in *The Observer* (June 3, 1979) it is as though one was listening, in the reign of Queen Anne, to an elderly Shaker praising the zeal of some veteran Fifth Monarchy Man. And the temperament involved does indeed seem to be that which seeks a final revelation in fields where no such revelation is possible.

Modernism is sometimes distinguished from other movements in literature by its greater programmatic self-consciousness. This might be disputed: one could put forward such documents as the Introduction to the *Lyrical Ballads,* to say nothing of the poetic manifestoes of French and other schools long preceding Mallarmé and Rimbaud. We may feel, rather, that it is not so much the existence as the totality, the omnipresence of the programmatic side of modernism that makes the difference.

In Ortega y Gasset's extraordinary essay 'The Dehumanization of Art' he takes the line that the urge behind the modernist visual art was to deny the public any pleasure but the purely aesthetic. But once such over-conscious ploys are adhered to, a great change has taken place. Neither Cézanne nor Van Gogh painted according to theory. It was the complex unarticulated directions given them by their own psyches which formed their work, rather than any programme.

With their successors, the role of the explanation of the painting became more and more important. The aim in the first place was to stop painting having any 'literary' appeal. First, of course, story and situation were removed; then human beings; then any physical object whatever. And so on, until in the world of neo-expressionism it was thought that some colours were more sentimental than others so only harsh shades were permitted; then it was felt that the texture still gave a sentimental result—so only smooth brush strokes of a single uninteresting colour were permitted. As Tom Wolfe says, these paintings gradually became nothing more than illustrations of verbal instruction—in fact, paradoxically, 'literary' to an infinite degree.

This implies a knowledge of the way in which art works on us. We do not in fact have that knowledge. It follows that theory must base itself on what we do know, which is to say on comparatively superficial aspects of the subject, or on ignorant fantasy.

Readers of poetry too often seemed by long training to have suppressed their direct responses and replaced them by an unnatural set of automatisms drawn from such critical theory. However, no critical machinery has yet been devised which can take over from the intelligent sensibility the job of deciding what poems are good—are readable, moving and felicitious. If you go on wearing a straitjacket long enough you lose the use of your arms.

At any rate, theory became the main driving force. Critics abounded. (That ours is an age of criticism and at the same time of frigid inventiveness is surely no coincidence. It was true to an important degree of ancient Alexandria.)

One new phenomenon of our time was the establishment of English schools and departments in the universities at about the same time as modernism arose. For the first time we had a specific and separate group guaranteed exceptionally qualified to judge literature, as against that larger, more heterogeneous set of people constituting the cultural community.

Academic critics claimed to be the only people competent to discuss poetry properly and indeed to prescribe its forms, methods, and contents. This is as if a claim should be put forth that cricket should only be discussed by professors of ballistics. The American poet Karl Shapiro remarks that though he has known scores of poets he has almost never heard from them the adulation of Eliot that is found in the text-books.

To quote from a recent book of mine:

> In the old days no one paid much attention to the low-level critics. They knew their place: Grub Street. But in the first decades of this century the foundation of English schools and departments in the universities suddenly gave them status. Alf Shagpen, wheedling the price of a pint of porter from the editor of Blackwood's, became Doctor A. Shagpen, D. Litt., author of *Texture and Tension in Thomas Traherne*. The increase in sophistication was not accompanied by any improvement in taste, and the greater systematization of his delusions was far from representing an improvement in sanity, but the fellow was now an Authority.

> Soon he found himself envying the other "disciplines". Perhaps he too could be a scientist and achieve rigour. Perhaps he too could imitate the philosophers and speak for the ultimate springs of human life. The trouble was, that he was trained in neither the scientific nor the philosophical disciplines.

We may thus feel that a central fault in all the various attitudes of modernism lay in pursuing an aesthetic half-truth, or quarter-truth, to extremes. As a result, Philip Larkin pointed out some twenty years ago, poetry 'lost its old audience, and gained a new one. This has been caused by the consequences of a cunning merger between poet, literary critic and academic critic (three classes now notoriously indistinguishable): it is hardly an exaggeration to say that the poet has gained the happy position wherein he can praise his own poetry in the press and explain it in the classroom, and the reader has been bullied into giving up the consumer's power to say I don't like this, bring me something different . . . if the medium is in fact to be rescued from among our duties and re-stored to our pleasures, I can only think that a large-scale revulsion has got to set in against present notions.'

One great delusion which has added to our troubles is that every country and every period now believes itself entitled to its share of great poets, authors, painters, and so forth. This is obviously untrue. There have been important periods in important countries which have produced nothing worthwhile. The rationing of talent is grossly unfair. Two great poets and one pretty good one in a century in the tiny Duchy of Ferrara and nothing to match them in the whole of Italy put together over the next two or three centuries is a typical story. Today the USA in particular feels entitled to its share of Great Creativity, so we get Jackson Pollock and de Kooning—and I say nothing of the painters that followed them—treated as though they were Rembrandt and Cézanne.

A further point is the mere proliferation of 'artists'. There are now, for example, more professional painters in the West than have existed in the whole world throughout previous history. None unfortunately is up to an apprentice of an assistant of Fra Lippo Lippi. When it comes to poets . . .

By about 1920, modernism had become *fashionable:* as Osbert Lancaster put it, 'art came once more to roost among the duchesses.' Modernism in the visual arts was overwhelmingly institutionalized by 1929—that is exactly half a century ago—when the New York Museum of Modern Art was founded in John D. Rockefeller's living room, as Tom Wolfe puts it, 'with Goodyears, Blisses, and Crowninshields in attendance.' Soon (and recognize the parallel in England with Shell advertisements) the Container Corporation of America was commissioning Léger and Henry Moore, and then undertook a long-running advertising campaign in which (as Wolfe says) 'it would run a Great Idea by a noted savant at the top of the page, one of them being 'Hitch your wagon to a star'—Ralph Waldo Emerson. Underneath would be a picture of a Cubist horse strangling on a banana.'

We finally reached the absurdity of alienation being rewarded by the establishment: of Picasso, the Lord Leighton of the period, approved by academics and patrons alike; of big-time Bohemianism; of knighthoods accepted by anarchists and surrealists—Sir Herbert Read, Sir Ronald Penrose.

At first it had been only the academics and the duchesses who admired the new art. Ortega y Gasset remarked, 'Modern art . . . will always have the masses against it. It is essentially unpopular; moreover, it is antipopular. He went on to say that its works automatically divided the general public into two groups: one very small, formed by those who are favorably inclined towards it; another very large—the hostile majority. (Let us ignore that ambiguous fauna—the snobs.)'

But this description is no longer recognisable or alternatively the 'snobs' have proliferated to an inordinate degree. Starting about twenty-five years ago came a second phase of modernism. Surrealism found a new audience, this time not in an elite innovative group, but as a mass-culture phenomenon. It need hardly be said that its quality catastrophically declined in the process . . . But it dominated, or at least deeply affected, the fashionable young, the fashionable media.

A. E. Housman decries the soul which 'commands no outlook upon the past or future, but believes that the fashion of the present, unlike all fashions heretofore, will endure perpetually, and that its own flimsy tabernacle of second-hand opinions is a habitation for everlasting.' Nor should we imagine that even the most impressive-looking Kulturtraeger are exempt from the appeal of mere fashion. As ever, they are the product of their time and their experience. If they can go wrong even more spectacularly than their predecessors, it is because modernism, and in particular modernist pseudo-aesthetics, opens up such a wide range of pointless or meaningless effort.

The crux, the main and major disjunction in all fields, was when the artist took the decision to abandon the laity.

It may be argued that artistic alienation had been around for a century, ever since the 'superfluous man' of Lermontov, the Byron of continental imagination, the romantic idea of the mad or maddish poet, grandly isolated from the rest of mankind. As W. H. Auden puts it,

> Chimeras mauled them, they wasted away with the
>   spleen,
>   Suicide picked them off; sunk off Cape
>   Consumption,
> Lost on the Tosspot Seas, wrecked on the
>   Gibbering Isles
>   Or trapped in the ice of despair at the Soul's
>   Pole. . . .

With this notion of artistic alienation came the similar, but logically distinct element of the existential human in his condition; and with the 20th century, though deriving from earlier thought, came Angst.

It has often been said that the decline of religion led to the idea that art could undertake, in some obscure way, the salvation of mankind. This is an idea which preceded modernism, and which was not in this form generally accepted by modernists. Nevertheless, they did regard their work as in some sense transcending any other. And this could not but add to their self-importance.

At a less pretentious level, it is natural that an artist gets bored with doing what he can do, and goes on to try to do what he can't do, or what can't be done at all. But the writer and artist pressed his autonomy too far, into the direction of almost total independence from an audience.

In poetry, surely, the first true modernist is Mallarmé. And indeed, modernist verse has always been much affected by its French origins. But the whole circumstances for French verse were different from English. Loose metres have been permissible here since Tudor times. Mixed images have been natural to us for centuries:

Pity, like a naked new-born babe/Striding the blast. This would have been impossible in French. In fact, French translation even of Shakespeare was unable to cope until quite recently—with Yves Bonnefoy. Earlier attempts, for example, at

> She that is Queen of Tunis, she that dwells
> Ten leagues beyond man's life

always came out something like:

> . . . dix lieux par delà la distance un
> homme pourrait atteindre en voyageant pendant
>   toute da vie

Thus, it was a theory originally produced in France to give the French poets some of the liberties already enjoyed by their English colleagues, which was supererogarorily brought to England early this century.

Even if its proponents did not say that all obscurity is profound—and they came near to saying that—they certainly said that all profundity is obscure. But a muddy puddle may pretend to any depth: a clear pool cannot. Coleridge writes somewhere that he read one of Dante's shorter poems every year for ten years, always finding more in it. This did not mean that it lacked comprehensibility at first reading; merely that in this comprehensibility there were resonances which did not immediately declare themselves.

Mallarmé's own poems are not 'difficult' as to meaning. They have no meaning, in any ordinary sense, beyond what is there, given, in their words. They have, it is true, other *effects,* but these are effects which are also seen, in addition to, or fused with, ordinary meaning in poems of all types. His poetry is, in fact, ordinary poetry with one of its components omitted. This is not, in itself, to say that it is inferior. And the Mallarméan argument would of course admit the point, claiming that its poetry is 'pure'—claiming, that is, that the extra content of ordinary verse constitutes a dilution.

Even on this argument, it cannot be said that his poetry has some extra level of meaning, as against an omissive technique which may or may not give some different illumination. 'Symbolism' is a misleading word. Something like Penumbrism, or Obliquism, should have been selected.

The point in favour of these procedures is that a different and possibly rewarding effect may be gained by looking from a different angle, at the object of one's attention. The counter argument is obvious—do both.

Mallarmé provided velleity, but further development of the principles which the next generation drew from his work led to Marinetti and worse, to poets of whom it could be complained, in Housman's words, 'you treat us as Nebuchadnezzar did the Chaldeans, and expect us to find out the dream as well as the interpretation.'

Modernism often got by on the simple argument that people had (or so modernists said) laughed at Beethoven. There is of course a logical fallacy involved. But more to the point is the fact that people with the highest reputation as innovators at a given period—Klopstock for example—are equally often regarded with horrified boredom by posterity.

But it is also relevant that the 'controversial' side of a 'new' artist often has little to do with any real quality he may exhibit. Indeed, when the novelty is little more than novelty pure and simple, reputations die with astonishing speed. An example is of Epstein whose immensely famous 'Genesis' is, I believe, lying in a rubbish heap in one of the keepers' compounds in Battersea Park. Quite recently, such superficial attention was briefly secured in poetry by the most extravagant soul-and-body airing by writers in the recent confessional mode, such as Anne Sexton . . .

When the English modernist mode began the most visible talker and writer was Ezra Pound. In examining his supposed novelty we find two main components. First, verse which is apparently 'free' but is usually in effect a sort of resolved Whitmanesque hexameter: (and right through his career we find his allegedly 'new' artifacts crammed with 'thou' and 'didst' and all that). On the other hand (leaving aside economic and other nonsense), the main run of the more admired portions of the *Cantos* is little more than that Imagism which Hilda Doolittle and others developed from their notion of Japanese verse. The original conception was clearly limited to fairly short and fairly unified lyrics, and would have been better if it had been left there.

As to free verse, once it had established itself in the 1920's, in England it became pervasive. The school magazines of expensive girl's schools—always keener on 'creativity' than boy's schools—were full of vague pieces of chopped up prose with vaguely emotional content by the thirties, perhaps earlier. Which may remind us that one notoriously bad effect of 'free' verse is that large numbers of people educated during the last half century no longer understand the structure of real verse.

W. H. Auden was to remark in his later years

> I cannot settle which is worse
> The anti-novel or free verse . . .

The truly astonishing discovery made by free versifier and anti-novelist alike was how much they could get away with. People have taken seriously, in recent times, novels consisting of loose pages in a box which the reader is invited to shuffle in any order he likes. It was of such things, and the many worse ones which will be familiar to all of you, that Philip Larkin writes: 'The

adjective "modern", when applied to any branch of art, means "designed to evoke incomprehension, anger, boredom or laughter"' and defines modernism as 'tending towards the silly, the disagreeable and the frigid'.

In a fuller context the same writer tells us:

> I dislike such things not because they are new, but because they are irresponsible exploitations of technique in contradiction of human life as we know it. This is my essential criticism of modernism, whether perpetrated by Parker, Pound or Picasso: it helps us neither to enjoy nor endure. It will divert us as long as we are prepared to be mystified or outraged, but maintains its hold only by being more mystifying and more outrageous: it has no lasting power.

No account of modernism can be complete without some reference to Freud. The extent to which Freudianism was taken as the last word on the human mind, the huge influence of the psychoanalytic myth, may surprise us nowadays. Yet it is worth remembering how fresh—and indeed shockingly so—was the Freudian concentration on sexuality. In particular every 'advanced' young man and woman was able to point to what were still thought as disreputable motives in all the actions of their elders or rivals. The idea of the Unconscious as a major—in fact senior—partner in the personality led directly, of course, to surrealism. But it also led in a less doctrinaire way to a treatment of images, in verse and prose, on a far more self-conscious basis that had yet been seen.

And then there was Marxism, which purported to give more or less final and definite answers to all matters of human society and behaviour. To this attraction was added the fact that (like Freudianism) its mechanisms were so flexible that anything whatever could be fitted in somehow.

Is there then a connection between political radicalism and the aesthetic radicalism we call 'modernism'?

The appeal of Marxism and in general of theories implying that history could now about to be brought to its final conclusion in the form of a perfect order, exhibited a certain parallel with the views taken by sponsors of modernist aesthetics—that an entirely new form of liberated art was now available, and that there would be no looking back. In both cases the predictions were false, and false for similar psychological reasons—a taste for novelty raised almost to a metaphysic, and a failure to consider that the intellectual fashions of any period, including one's own, eventually give way to something else.

Except for satire in its narrowest sense, there is remarkably little good political poetry in English. Even really good causes, far from being productive of good poetry, seem to have been sources of bathos, and this is true even of our greatest poets. As J. C. Furnas remarks in his scholarly and sensitive study of slavery, *The Road to Harpers Ferry,* 'When touching on slavery, Cowper,

Blake, Wordsworth and Southey produced drivel'. Less good, or at any rate less straightforward causes, handled by greatly inferior poets, are more characteristic of our own time.

Few English poets have much *experience* of the political. They have generous impulses, no doubt, and concern for humanity. These can be expressed in various ways and are not sufficient for a poem involving facts. On political issues it is extremely rare for the facts to be so clear, and the human involvement so direct and simple, as to approach the immediacy and undeniability of experience.

Not that even those few poets with some political knowledge and experience find it easy to produce political poems. Lawrence Durrell, one of those few, has dealt directly with political events in prose, in *Bitter Lemons*. But in the poem which concludes this book, as soon as he approaches the subject he had the modesty, a sense of the subject's intractibility, to write: 'Better leave the rest unsaid'. Excellent advice, for several reasons.

The Mexican painters like Rivera well illustrate one aspect of political modernism. And it is clear that an important part of the impact and the effect of their 'new' art was due far more to the political type of content than to the quasi-cubism involved in the forms chosen, In the palace at Chapultepec, one may see romantic revolutionary paintings of a century ago, showing liberators like Juarez and Diaz crushing venimous foes, etc., to the applause and enthusiasm of romantically conceived peasants and of 'The People' in general. The difference between these and the more modern Mexican paintings is not great: and indeed the later generation owes a good deal not merely to this political inheritance but also to an element of primitivism already to be seen in their predecessors.

In fact art with a 'revolutionary' component of the political sort is very much a traditionalist form. The only exception I have come across, where a genuine new impulse seems visible, is in the strange statuary of Kemalist Turkey with its earthy New Turks pushing up out of the soil. Here, perhaps, novelty may be due to a total previous lack of representational art.

One should also note a sentiment not exactly political but strongly tied up with attitudes to politics: the attraction avant-garde art had for those among the rich and privileged who felt guilty about their status. Just as with supporting or appeasing enemies of the bourgeoisie from Lenin to the Viet-Cong, there was (as Tom Woolfe puts it) 'a peculiarly modern reward that the avant-garde artist can give his benefactor: namely, the feeling that he, like his mate the artist, is separate from and aloof from the bourgeoisie, the middle class'—(though as I quote this I have to add that many unaffected by radical chic in politics were susceptible to its manifestations in the arts; that the right-wing *National Review* for example, is still a bastion of Poundism and so forth.)

This enmity of artists to 'capitalism' and the 'bourgeoisie' is a sign: precisely of this radical *temperament*—. Of course, the notion that 'capitalism' is hostile to art is in itself absurd. In fact, capitalist or bourgeois patronage has often marked a great flowering of art: the Medicis; Venice and Holland; or, to go further back, the great merchant-republic of Athens.

In the first and second decades of this century there was an immense ferment of revolutionary-sounding attitudes and these attracted precisely some of the aesthetically radical—Marinetti into Fascism, Mayakovsky into Bolshevism. Lenin, indeed disliked the futurists, and referred to Mayakovsky's views as 'hooligan communism', but his cultural Commissar Lunacharsky supported them. It is hard to remember now that political posters by Chagal were plastered on the trams in Vitebsk after the revolution. And outside Russia, a typical enough figure of time was Ernst Toller, modernist playwright and revolutionary prisoner.

The revolutionary temperament emerged vis-à-vis a prerevolutionary society, and this involved sharp and continual criticism of everything. But when a revolution comes, the ruling party is committed to a single truth, and thus to the destruction of the hitherto powerful critical faculty within its own ranks. So it was of course wholly misleading when the Nazis denounced modernism as Kulturbolschewismus: official Soviet art, by the mid-20's, had become clearly Victorianised. Even so, some Soviet attraction remained.

Surrealism, of course was, in its origins, a highly doctrinaire and tight little movement, and one with a political commitment to communism. Andre Bréton, as its chief theorist, took this into a more Trotskyite, anti-Soviet direction. But many of its adherents turned to Stalinism, in particular Louis Aragon but also to some degree Eluard.

And, even though orthodox Communism repudiated modernist principles, there were plenty of 'modernists' from Picasso to Neruda, who happily went along with it even in its most Stalinist phase.

And on this issue, Brecht, whose intense artistic commitment to extremes of honesty is spoken of in the most lachrymose fashion in the drama departments of universities around the west, was totally dishonest at every level when it came to politics. No one, not even Sartre, has such a despicable record: and yet, politics formed a decisive element in his aesthetics. There is a certain paradox in the comparison between the subtlety and complexity sought by such writers in the structure of their prose and verse, and the complete crudity of the politics they embraced.

And what good did come of it at last? When we look back we can, surely, say that the great revolution which the modernists thought they were bringing about simply failed.

But that is not the whole story. First of all, even if they were not as world-shaking as they imagined, they may still have left us some valuable, if peripheral, work. Such a modest contribution, after all, is all that Mallarmé claimed: 'Pour moi, le vers classique—que j'appellerai *le vers officiel*—est la grande nef de cette basilique 'la Poesie française'; le vers libre, lui, edifie les bas-côtes pleins d'attirance, de mystère, de somptuosités rares.'

It is a remarkable fact that despite the opposition of well-established academics, (a real priesthood of modernism), the more recent works which have against these odds forced themselves on the educated mind as the best writing of the last two or three decades are almost entirely 'non-modernist'. In Britain the novels of Anthony Powell and Graham Greene have little resemblance to *Finnegans Wake* or *To the Lighthouse*. The poetry of Auden and Larkin is almost ostentatiously 'unmodern' and mostly in traditional forms. But is there something of value that these writers of our generation have after all inherited from modernism.

I think there is.

Our rhythms have been loosened; our rhyme and assonance scheme has broadened; obliqueness—in verse or prose—is available on those occasions where it seems to work.

Such things as the attempt, in painting, to disentangle pattern from content may have its point in providing some sort of partial insight into why a great painting of the Quattrocento produced its effects, even if as a prescription for present work it failed. (It is a curious thought that even today, of our two most successful playwrights, one presents more or less emotional plays with a minimum of rationality; the other rationality carried to the point of lecturing.)

The inventiveness sometimes produced charming or interesting results as with a 'poem' of Arp's consisting of a square or oblong with, instead of pictorial detail, the words describing each part of a presumed painting, nicely phrased.

There was, also an element, and often a very attractive one, of joking in the early avant garde. Dada showed this to a very high degree. But the Dadaists mostly went on to Surrealism. And although the latter contained an element of rather heavy-handed wit, this came largely a matter of ageing charlatans like Salvador Dali, embraced by, instead of shocking the bourgeois taste. On the whole, surrealism and its derivatives were merely solemn. As Auden writes:

> With what conviction the young man spoke
> When he thought his nonsense rather a joke;
> Now, when he doesn't doubt any more,
> No-one believes the booming old bore.

Still one finds the saving note of the comic not only in E. E. Cummings, but also in Dylan Thomas for example—even at his most portentous he seems to fit Lautreamont's

description of Byron: 'L'hippotame des jungles infernales': more sympathetic, even as a monster, than the tyrannosaurs then infesting the continental countries.

Then, we are (of course) much freer on sexual themes, and even in the use of obscene words—which are to be found even in such works as *A Dance to the Music of Time*. But it is hard to believe that the uptightness which came into its own round the end of the last century and went on in publishing circles for another 30-40 years, would not have anyhow given way to a more liberal view as previously puritanical episodes have always done. In fact the 'modernist' contribution proper, whether associated with Freud, with radical anti-bourgeois notions, or with verbal theory, seems if anything to have been comparatively harmful—in that a gross excess of obscenity was thrust upon us in such things as the works of William Burroughs.

When it comes to a general consideration of modernism, was there another way open, back in the years following the turn of the century? Perhaps not. The arts were, it seems, driven in new directions in part at least by the mere exhaustion of the old at that particular time.

I think we should recognize the freshness, the excitement, which affected the young as they came for the first time in contact with these new works which their elders found shockingly incomprehensible. In my teens, I will recall the first surrealists, the first copies of *New Verse* and *Twentieth Century Verse*. (It is true that one found almost equal excitement in science fiction and jazz, both of which reached one through more ordinary channels: Wells and Verne preceding *Astounding Stories*, ragtime preceding swing.)

Of our reading of the time, what has survived? First of all, I think one should say that the victory of modernism in the minds of the young was never that total, that totalitarian sweep envisaged by its true believers. We (and Auden and Eliot too) continued to read Housman and Kipling.

But who would we regard as a 'modernist' poet in English? To us, today, Eliot, Yeats, Auden appear traditionalists. With Dylan Thomas one may perhaps think that something wholly novel has been achieved. His poems, or many of them, are indeed the declamatory output of images scarcely connected at any conscious seeming level. Still, there is nothing new in this idea of merely incantatory poetry, with little obviously 'rational' content. It was no less a product of classicism than Gibbon himself who spoke of the alternative aims of poetry being to 'satisfy or silence our reason'. Moreover, incomprehensibility and pointlessness are not the same thing. There is nothing 'incomprehensible' about a pile of bricks or a 'concrete' poem . . .

What I am suggesting is that many writers claimed as modernist were merely modern. Which is not to say that they were not affected by modernism, or experimentalism, proper, to various degrees. Thomas can properly be regarded, surely, as at least heavily charged with modernism: and we can add that it is his more 'modernist' verse ('altar-wise by owl-light') which fades most quickly from our view—together to be fair, with some of his slacker and later poems. Yet much remains—as can also be said of that true surrealist Kenneth Allott, though it may be noted that in both these cases disjunction of sense is matched by considerable rigour of form.

We have indeed been enriched by modernism: though, as I have suggested, the damage its attitudes have done in deadening both audience and mass sensibility by mere excess remains with us still.

In 1960 Pasternak, himself a modernist of the Russian Silver Age, said that

> . . . all this writing of the Twenties has terribly aged . . . our works were dictated by the times. They lacked universality . . . I have never understood those dreams of a new language, of a completely original form of expression. Because of this dream much of the work of the Twenties which was stylistic experimentation has ceased to exist. The most extraordinary discoveries are made when the artist is overwhelmed by what he has to say. Then he uses the old language in his urgency and the old language is transformed from within.

That seems a very good summing up. Modernism was above all an attempt to create something which was not merely new in the sense that previous movements have been new, but rather a commitment to total and endless modernising and remodernising, a Permanent Revolution.

When this led to the pointless and the meaningless, it became the main mission of the modernist type of mind less to produce or even procure this rubbish, than to explicate endlessly on its supposed value.

Having said all this, let me nevertheless quote a recent poem of that arch-anti-modernist Philip Larkin:

> Mussels, limpets
> Husband their tenacity,
> In the freezing slither.

We may agree that such lines could hardly have been written but for the modernist interlude and its effect on the language.

To justify the destructive side of it is another matter. Above all, modernism as such has failed heavily in its claim to be fresh, new, lively. The expression 'The Lively Arts', if in a decadent and degraded way, represents the essential claim made. On them, at least, we may suggest an epitaph.

> Their constant cry
> Was *Never say die,*
> Which they're dead
> Without having said.

William A. Johnsen

SOURCE: "Toward a Redefinition of Modernism," in *Boundary* 2, Vol. 2, No. 3, Spring, 1974, pp. 539-54.

[*In the following essay, Johnsen suggests a new definition of Modernism based on the rejection of such "binary oppositions" as order and chaos.*]

> Deux dangers ne cessent
> de menacer le monde:
> l'ordre et le desordre.
>
> —P. Valéry

Students of modern literature of whatever period have always justly admired the emerging artist's compulsion to be modern, to make it new. Western civilization's obsessive use of the adjectives "modern" and "new" to describe its current cultural artifacts has never been more prevalent than in what we call, appropriately, the Modern Century. Yet these adjectives also create a climate of relentless avantgardism that makes heavy demands on both emerging and pre-existing art. If our task as modern scholars is to do more than merchandize the newest sensibilities, we must investigate that compulsion to be modern as well as its latest manifestation. In fact, we cannot adequately define our period style until we understand the dynamics of modernism, for every attempt to finish off Modernism becomes another Modernism.

With few exceptions, discussions of the Modern period of Yeats, Eliot, and Joyce are based on Eliot's formulation of the "mythical method." The Moderns faced a world devoid of order; fearing entropy, they intuited, primarily through the potentialities of metaphor and myth, an order behind, within, or above the chaos of modern experience. Yeats' gyres, Eliot's Classicism, Joyce's system of allusion and cyclical history are descriptions of this order released through assuming masks, personae, or other modes of impersonality.

The general movement to define, even circumscribe, the sensibility of the Modern period is complex—generated at times by the feeling that we cannot sustain the special intensity of Modernism, at times by a sense that we have fashioned or must fashion for ourselves a new sensibility different from or in opposition to the canonical Moderns, perhaps, in some cases, by a resigned admission that if we are to get on with the business of describing historical periods we must somewhat regretfully close the door on further specimens.

Harry Levin's 1960 essay "What Was Modernism" is a representative attempt to distinguish Modernism from a postmodern sensibility. Levin feels a kinship with Dryden looking back from the Restoration to the Elizabethans, contrasting earlier strength with later refinement. Levin's gentle farewell to Modernism allows for the new sensibility only the task of consolidating and assimilating the fruits of Modernism, but his intuition that it is time to distinguish the modern from the new sensibility is shared by other students of Modernism with a more energetic sense of what the new sensibility must do.

Charles Olson sought to extend the musical quality of verse reclaimed by Pound and the Imagists to include the breath making the music. At first glance, Olson's 1950 essay "Projective Verse" merely consolidates and assimilates Imagist principles and, in particular, Pound's later conception of the poem as a high energy construct but, in fact, Olson's extension of Modernism subtly but effectively alters the Modernist relation of poet to audience. "What we have suffered from, is manuscript, press, the removal of verse from its producer and its reproducer, the voice, a removal by one, by two removes from its place of origin *and* its destination. For the breath has a double meaning which latin had not yet lost." Olson extends Imagist esthetics to suggest what the reader is to do with that energy Pound would transfer via the poem. In Modernist esthetics, a poem contains a quantum of energy gotten from somewhere, transferred by an impersonalized or masked poet to an unseen audience. Olson's poet uses the typewriter to program an oral performance of the poem that reproduces, reincarnates his *spiritus* through the reader's own voice. Robert Duncan's "An Owl Is An Only Bird Of Poetry" provides a nearly perfect example of Projectivist esthetics. Next to Figure 2, a drawing of the interlocking fingergrip necessary to reproduce the hoot of an owl, *mouthpiece pointed towards the reader,* are the lines

> The consonants are a church of
> hands interlocking, stops
> and measures of fingerings
> that confine the spirit to
> articulations of space and time.

The hands, like the poem, urge the spirit to a sacrament of immanence: articulations of space and time. The reader is invited to put his mouth to the poem, take a deep breath necessary to play the poet's fingering, thus drawing in the poet's spirit that he will reproduce with his own breath. The implications of this revisioning must be left for another time, but we can note at least how far we have moved from Stephen Dedalus' notion of dramatic art—projectivist esthetics is closer to Longinian ecstasis than Aristotelian catharsis. Contemporary poetry as a whole, in so far as it can be described as more personal than dramatic, attempts to achieve that Longinian relation of poet to audience which Northrop Frye describes as an "ideal union in which poet, poem, and reader participate."

William Spanos has distinguished the modern from the postmodern imagination by their attitude towards time. For Spanos, the moving spirit behind Imagism, Stephen Dedalus' esthetics, Yeats' artifice of eternity, and New Criticism has its

> specific source in the obsessive effort of the modern literary imagination to escape the destructive impact of time and change, of which a disintegrating cosmic order has made it acutely and painfully

> conscious, by way of achieving the timeless eternity of the esthetic moment or, rather, of "spatial form."

Thus, argues Spanos, the Moderns' interest in Worringer's theory of abstraction and empathy: man, at home in the world, imitates its natural forms; at odds with a dreadful world, he prefers a geometric art. The choice between empathy with a hospitable world and transcendence of a hostile world avoids the third possibility of encountering a dreadful world that the postmodern imagination is now and should continue to explore through an art that confronts rather than flees from time.

Iris Murdoch, in "The Sublime and the Beautiful Revisited," diagnoses Modern literature as suffering from the pervasive influence of Symbolists like Eliot, Hulme, and Richards who believed that art had been erroneously conceived in human terms. What they wanted, she argues, were small, clean, resonant, self-contained things of which the image or the symbol was the type: art, including literature, should be the creation of such unique self-contained things. The motive for this purity is a fear of contingency, a yearning to pierce through the messy phenomenal world to some perfect and necessary form and order. The self-contained art work is an analogon for the good man, the self-contained individual. Modern literature presents us with the triumph of myth as a solipsistic form. Modern Man is Totalitarian Man, alone, intolerant toward the messiness of experience and complex, contingent other selves. For the Modern novel, a tightly wrought Symbolist pseudo-poem which extends the author's thinly disguised fantasies and obsessions for private contemplation, Murdoch would substitute a novel open to the undramatic messiness of existence, and complex, contingent other selves that are not mere reflections of the author's troubled psyche. Jake Donaghue, the first person narrator (conventionalized author) of *Under the Net,* Miss Murdoch's first novel, discovers that his compulsion to see himself as the center of a vast symbolic drama has obscured his perception of others. He learns that he must stop projecting his own plot onto other lives if he is to see them at all. He gives up self-definition for vulnerability, sensitivity, and a sense of wonder towards others.

Richard Wasson has used Murdoch, Robbe-Grillet, John Barth, and Thomas Pynchon to characterize the new sensibility of the late fifties and early sixties as "antimyth and antimetaphor."

> Contemporary literature reacts against the literature we call modern, the literature represented in English by Yeats, Eliot, and Joyce, in French by Proust, in German by Hesse. Contemporary writers are skeptical of modernist notions of metaphor as a species of supra-rational truth that unifies paradoxical opposites and modernist conceptions of myth which makes it a principle of order for art and of discipline for the subjective self.

Unification, order, discipline, keep the self isolated from an alien world. The Contemporaries would exchange the totalitarian esthetic of the Moderns for an openness to the undramatic relationships between the subjective self, and the world of other men and things. The new sensibility represents an epistemological break with the canonical Moderns, but on a deeper level it is another symptom of our compulsion to be new: postmodernism, out-moderning the moderns.

The Contemporary strategies of antimyth, antimetaphor, being against interpretation, and postmodernism, have a deceptively obvious theoretical similarity; all define themselves by rejecting earlier modes of thought, especially modes peculiar to the Moderns of the early twentieth century. The negative prefix often defines the newest sensibility; Beckett emphasizes that his work is not Joycean, Murdoch calls for a novel opposed to the Modernist delight in order and myth, Robbe-Grillet calls metaphor into question, Susan Sontag is against interpretation, William Hamilton says that the new optimism was born the day T.S. Eliot died.

The new sensibility consistently defines itself by characterizing pre-existing works as old, repressive, and neurotic, then rejecting these works for new works which will provide or make possible what the pre-existing works repressed. A classic Oedipal drama: the tyrannical father and rebellious son fight to save culture from outrage.

The work of anthropologists, literary critics, and linguists, within the structuralist movement, suggests that the opposition of postmoderns to Moderns contains one of the most typical gestures of the human mind. Many structuralists theorize that man compulsively orders his world by means of differentiation and binary opposition. Edmund Leach has suggested the color spectrum as a useful pedagogical model for explaining these two terms. Man differentiates seven primary colors by ignoring the way each color blends insensibly into the next color. These differentiated colors are further opposed for the sake of further order: red/green, black/white. Structuralists who see this technique as the primary strategy of the human mind have sought the binary opposites common to most cultures, such as hot and cold, raw and cooked. The presence of common underlying structures reveals that opposites such as black and white are inverted mirror images of each other, mutually dependent, ordered by a common point of view (the absence or presence of light).

Contemporaries reject Modernist use of metaphor, history, and myth to support a totalitarian obsession with order, by embracing the freedom of disorder. Their interest in contingency and disorder reveals their attempt to become truly new, to escape what the structuralists see as the common element of all thought: structure, order, and myth. Edward Said, reviewing Lévi-Strauss' *The Savage Mind,* calls this compulsion for order that structuralism formulates and perpetuates "totalitarianism of mind":

> the structure's impulse to totalization derives from
> the logical observation of the rule of the excluded

middle: if there is order and meaning, it must be everywhere. Conversely, if there is *no* order, there can be no order at all. There is no third possibility. The mind elects the first alternative, perhaps because it cannot tolerate "the blank stare" of a "virgin landscape . . . so monotonous as to deprive [even] its wildness of all meaning."

Said's description of Lévi-Strauss' system helps us to recognize the underlying principles of the compulsion to be modern. The postmodern sensibility defines itself by differentiating itself from its immediate ancestors, and placing itself in opposition to them. The postmodern conception of Modernism parallels the first alternative Said describes; the order and meaning created or perceived by the poet is expanded over the world. The new sensibility sees itself as exploring the second possibility mentioned above; the lack of personal order is expanded to suggest there is no order at all. Structuralism reveals that these two choices of order or disorder are binary opposites. The Contemporaries are still participating in the closed systems of structure, order, and myth. Their definitions of the new sensibility depend on the old sensibility the way a prefix depends on a noun or verb: disorder, antimetaphor, antimyth. The new is incomprehensible without the old; the new is the old turned upside down or profaned.

A more rewarding approach for modern scholars, especially those with new sensibilities, is not to reject Modernism, but to reread the canonical Moderns through the sensibilities of the Contemporaries. A Contemporary reader, distrustful of the uses of history, metaphor, and myth, finds that same mistrust in Modern writers—finds, in fact, the image of man in Modern Literature confronted by the same polarized alternatives of order or disorder, knowledge or experience, Aristotle or Longinus, Classicism or Romanticism, art or life, speech or silence, faced by the Contemporaries before they choose the second of these opposed terms.

By studying the compulsion to be modern, as well as the latest manifestation of Modernism, we begin to perceive some underlying connections between Moderns and Contemporaries necessary to start writing the literary history of the Modern Century. If one avowed purpose of a modern work is to escape its predecessors, another effect of Modernism is to liberate unperceived insights into pre-existing works: the Contemporaries' aversion to the totalitarian esthetic, sharpened by the insights of structuralism, gives us a new look at the Modern period itself. Newly sensitized to the Moderns' own mistrust of myth and metaphor, we find, allowing for individual permutations, Moderns such as James Joyce, W. B. Yeats, T. S. Eliot, and D. H. Lawrence articulating a common, threefold pattern of experience: (1) Man suffers the frustrating disparity between a fallen outer world of disorder and a more perfect inner world; he exchanges the soft, wet outer world of disorder, contingency and chaos for the hard, dry inner world of metaphor, myth, and history. This is the process that Ortega y Gasset called dehumanization, and Worringer the urge to abstraction, the withdrawal from the natural world towards geometric form. This is the movement in Yeats towards Byzantium, Stephen Dedalus' flight into the world of myth in Joyce, the quest for nonhuman order in Eliot, and the impulse to theorize in Lawrence: 'you are Gothic,' Paul Morel tells Miriam, 'but I am Norman.' (2) Man realizes both the falsification of reality that order irrevocably produces, and his loss of immediate contact with humans and things; confronted with a world becoming ethereal and narcissistic, he returns to re-examine the real, the natural, the unordered. These two movements are represented in Joyce by Stephen's flight from and return to Ireland in *Ulysses* ("Dublin I have much to learn"). In Yeats, by the waxing and the waning of the moon in "The Phases of the Moon" ("Before the full/It sought itself and afterwards the world"). In Eliot, by the recognition of narcissistic withdrawal in "Ash Wednesday" ("And I pray that I may forget/These matters that with myself I too much discuss") that activates a return to the world. In Lawrence, by a return to sensuality after a surfeit of self-indulgent theory: Paul with Clara, Birkin with Ursula, Kate with Don Cipriano. (3) Facing again two polarized choices, man tries to envision an excluded middle when he comes to understand what the structuralists understand: opposed choices are inverted mirror images of each other, mutually dependent, ordered by a common point of view. Existing between polarities, the excluded middle or third possibility cannot be grasped with the same sureness as the first two stages, but it is glimpsed in Yeats' ability to view the polarities of Nature and Byzantium from some middle ground; in Joyce, the excluded middle is coincidence, the third possibility between order and disorder; in Eliot, sitting still at the still point of the turning world; in Lawrence, the impulse of some protagonists like Paul Morel and Birkin to move beyond the tyranny of polarities set at the end of the novel, of others, like Kate, a vague dissatisfaction with a set of polarized or closed possibilities.

Thus a Contemporary rereading of the Moderns suggests the coherency of the early Modern period and, better still, the Moderns offer to both the Contemporaries and pre-Moderns a glimpse of a third possibility won from their own confrontation with the totalitarian esthetic of differentiation and binary opposition. Now I shall suggest a Contemporary rereading of Joyce's Stephen Dedalus that reveals more completely the three-fold experiential pattern of Modernism and suggest, in concluding, how the reread Moderns return the favor, making possible new perceptions of Contemporary art.

Clongowes Wood College clearly represents for Stephen the soft, wet outer world of disorder, contingency, and chaos. While Stephen stands apart from the football game, watching the flight of the "greasy leather orb," his senses still register yesterday's dunking in the square ditch. Wells has caused Stephen to experience what Norman O. Brown would call an excremental vision; Stephen sees Clongowes, as he will later see Ireland, through the turfcoloured bogwater of the square ditch. He

feverishly dreams of escaping this world of queer, unreasoning aggression.

> Sitting in the study hall he opened the lid of his desk and changed the number pasted up inside from seventyseven to seventysix. But the Christmas vacation was very far away: but one time it would come because the earth moved round always.

Stephen is consoled when he remembers the world inevitably turns, days pass. He finds relief from a sordid, disordered world by imaginatively removing himself beyond the world until earth, not the cosmos, appears to be rotating.

Imaginatively still in outer space, Stephen continues to experiment with a cosmic view. He looks down at the picture of earth on the first page of his geography book, "a big ball in the middle of clouds." Down the flyleaf he reads his cosmic address, "Stephen Dedalus/ Class of Elements/Clongowes Wood College/Sallins/ County Kildare/Ireland/Europe/The World/The Universe." Fleming, for a cod, had written a matching entry on the facing page:

> Stephen Dedalus is my name,
> Ireland is my nation.
> Clongowes is my dwellingplace
> And heaven my expectation.

Fleming has shrewdly noted the significance of Stephen's entry and parodied his aspirations. Stephen's heavenward flight is mocked by his earthly companions throughout *Portrait*.

Stephen's extended musings on his own flyleaf entry become his characteristic attitude towards earth. Stephen reads the list downward, voyaging from the Class of Elements to The Universe, trying to imagine what was after the universe. Attempting to understand the space that encloses all space, Stephen arrives logically at the being that comprehends all space—God, the first entelechy, form of forms. Although there are different names for God, God is the same God and his real name is God. "It made him very tired to think that way. It made him feel his head very big. He turned over the flyleaf and looked wearily at the green round earth in the middle of the maroon clouds. Stephen looks down upon the earth he has left, weary from thinking like God while still inextricably fixed in his earthly position. This weary contemplative pose compromised by earthly existence grows into a scrupulous disdain for commonness and is perfected in a Flaubertian esthetic.

The trip to Cork with his father further aggravates Stephen's hypersensitivity to the commonplace sordidness about him by documenting the decay of the Dedalus fortunes. Stephen's imagination desublimates the idealized forms of Catholic Ireland to reveal their sordid excremental base. Yet Stephen is also frightened by the interstellar spaces that separate him from his own father.

He heard the sob pass loudly down his father's throat and opened his eyes with a nervous impulse. The sunlight breaking suddenly on his sight turned the sky and clouds into a fantastic world of sombre masses with lakelike spaces of dark rosy light. His very brain was sick and powerless. He could scarcely interpret the letters of the signboards of the shops. By his monstrous way of life he seemed to have put himself beyond the limits of reality. Nothing moved him or spoke to him from the real world unless he heard in it an echo of the infuriated cries within him. He could respond to no earthly or human appeal, dumb and insensible to the call of summer and gladness and companionship, wearied and dejected by his father's voice.

We have already seen how a cosmic view wearies Stephen, but detachment is now felt as a terrifying separation from human contact. Stephen now feels beyond humanity, beyond earth—an outcast from life's feast.

How strange to think of him passing out of existence in such a way, not by death, but by fading out in the sun or by being lost and forgotten somewhere in the universe! It was strange to see his small body appear again for a moment: a little boy in a grey belted suit. His hands were in his side pockets and his trousers were tucked in at the knees by elastic bands.

The dunking made Stephen allergic to the mold of Irish decay; the resulting fever burnt out his capacity to live on earth. Stephen envisions this process as myth. The effect of the sunlight breaking suddenly on Stephen's sight recalls the fate of Icarus: Daedalus, trying to save his son (here: "when you kick out for yourself, Stephen"), unwittingly prepares his destruction. But the image of the boy that fades in the sun is Stephen's creation; Stephen has assumed the role of Daedalus, father and creator, as well as Icarus. Stephen becomes his own father; by creating, extending, then contemplating an image of himself he recreates the father-son relationship in his imagination. He purifies an earthly existence made troublesome by an incapacity to love and accept love from his father, then recreates a more vivid past self by regarding himself in the third person: an impalpable, imperishable, impersonalized portrait of himself. Earlier in Chapter II, Stephen resolved his distance from Emma by purging their nocturnal encounter of its commonness, transforming it into a poem, and rewriting, strengthening their parts. Stephen replaces erotic and familial relations unfulfilled in the real world with more perfect relations conceived, consummated, and contemplated in his imagination.

Finally, Stephen's cosmic perspective is raised to the level of esthetics.

The personality of the artist, at first a cry or a cadence or a mood and then a fluid and lambent narrative, finally refines itself out of existence, impersonalizes itself, so to speak. The esthetic image in the dramatic form is life purified in and reprojected from the human imagination. The mystery of esthetic like that of material creation is accomplished. The artist, like the God of the creation, remains within or behind or beyond or above his handiwork, invisible, refined out of existence, indifferent, paring his fingernails.

Once again, Stephen has removed himself to a God-like position by refining himself out of earthly existence. The reasons for the rewriting of Stephen Daedalus into Stephen Dedalus must be left for another time and place, but the distinction between the formulation of the artist's role in *Stephen Hero* and *Portrait* represents a more critical understanding of the totalitarian mind. In *Stephen Hero,* the artist must adjust his spiritual eye to the exact focus to perceive an object or human situation reveal its *quidditas.* Life reveals itself to the scrupulous observer; the artist records these epiphanies for the enlightenment and moral elevation of the public. But in *Portrait* the esthetic image is life *purified in and reprojected from* the imagination. The artist confronts not imitations of reality, but extensions of his own imagination that have replaced the world of humans and things.

Ireland does not willingly submit to this purification; Stephen's God-like role is still compromised by earthly existence. An esthetic grounded in Flaubertian scrupulousness and clerical severity ends with "Lady" Boyle's idiosyncrasy of nail paring; a fervent, ritualistic villanelle is interrupted by the memory of the physics hall gibe about ellipsoidal balls; the identification of Cranly as St. John the Precursor is blocked by the memory of Cranly's dark womanish eyes. Stephen can preserve the private world of cosmic significance created by esthetics from the perverting effect of the earthly world of humans and things only by leaving Ireland.

Stephen's return to Dublin in *Ulysses,* on the strength of his father's request ("Mother dying come home father") acknowledges family ties. Stephen is fulfilling his mother's wish in *Portrait* that he learn "away from home and friends what the heart is and what it feels," initially in Paris, but more completely at home. Stephen's remorse of conscience over his failure to be a better son to his mother is "pain, that was not *yet* the pain of love" (Italics mine). In *Ulysses,* Stephen has given up exile to renew contact with men and things: he patiently exposes himself to the law of matter in the Proteus episode, the social graces of urban camaraderie in the Aeolus episode ("Dublin, I have much to learn"), even the treachery of Mulligan and the brutality of Private Carr in the Circe episode as deliberately as he once rejected the material world, trivial conversation, and another's will to shape their relationship. Stephen now dismisses history as a nightmare, a purifying of human experience to generate a few cryptic sentences: the corpsestrewn plain of Tarentum epiphanized into "another victory like that and we are done for." Stephen now argues for the presence, not the absence of the artist's humanity in his work, in the Scylla and Charybdis episode, and persistently mocks the orders made possible by esthetics, myth, and history.

Stephen is the incarnation of the figure of man in the literature of the Modern period I sketched earlier: (1) He first removed himself from earthly existence because he found it chaotic and obscene; his imagination created a better world by inverting the world he rejected. If earthly existence is soft, moist, and chaotic, Stephen will retreat to a hard, dry, orderly world in his imagination populated with appropriate symbolic companions. (2) He returned to earthly life when he found himself separated from men and things; in *Ulysses* he submits himself indiscriminately to dear dirty Dublin. *Ulysses* develops towards the revelation of Stephen's initial withdrawal from reality in *Portrait* (stage 1), and his subsequent immersion in reality in *Ulysses* (stage 2), as binary opposites in a closed system. Stephen can't escape reality, yet he can't seem to get any closer to it either. The task of *Ulysses* is to suggest a third alternative to these two opposed choices.

Stephen expresses his commitment to earthly existence and disaffection for myth, history, and transcendental esthetics in the Library and, such are the ironies of *Ulysses,* the Brothel. His theory of the artist's relation to his work is the binary opposite of A.E. Russell's position, which has similarities to Stephen's earlier theory in *Portrait.* A.E. stirs the whirlpool of narcissistic, purifying contemplation of formless spiritual essences. Stephen bases the artist's creations on the rock of experiential knowledge. Yet his philosophical dialogue on the primacy of earthly experience does not, as he had hoped, bring him closer to the humanity before him: "What have I learned? Of them? Of me?" He is still in a closed system, where opposed positions are interchangeable. When Mulligan enters the Library, Stephen's position, apparently the opposite of Russell's, is now identified with it. Stephen now represents the whirlpool of all esthetic and philosophical speculation, whether transcendental or experiential, while Mulligan is the rock of sense experience itself. The only constant is his isolation: "My will: his will that confronts me. Seas between." Significantly, if ambiguously, Bloom, like Odysseus, marks out a middle course between Stephen and Mulligan at the end of the chapter, passing out of the Library between them.

The underlying similarity of Stephen's new commitment to and earlier disdain for earthly existence is re-emphasized in the Circe episode. As in *Portrait,* Stephen must pour his ideas into the skeptical ears of Lynch. On the surface, Stephen is renouncing his earlier belief in esthetics and myth for interpreting the world; Stephen now claims that interpretation is particular and limited, not universal. The psalms that Stephen chants to Lynch are "susceptible of nodes or modes as far apart as hypophrygian and mixolydian and of texts so divergent as priests haihooping round David's that is Circe's or what am I saying Cere's altar and David's tip from the stable to his chief bassoonist about his almightiness." Stephen's miscue substantiates his theory; the drunken interpolation of Circe's name is quite appropriate to his situation thus changing, for a while, the meaning of the psalm. This is the rationale behind the dialectics of the Library. Each reader creates his own Shakespeare: Jew, Irishman, homosexual, shrewridden.

But Stephen's whetstone (Lynch's cap) perceives the underlying principles of binary opposition below his promiscuous theorizing. "(*With saturnine spleen.*) Bah. It is because it is. Woman's reason. Jewgreek is greekjew. Extremes meet. Death is the highest form of life. Bah!" Challenged, Stephen looses another dagger definition—his theory of the relation of experience to selfhood.

> What went forth to the ends of the world to traverse not itself. God, the sun, Shakespeare, a commercial traveller, having itself traversed in reality itself, becomes that self. Wait a moment. Damn that fellow's noise in the street. Self which itself was ineluctibly preconditioned to become. *Ecco!*

Indiscriminate submission to experience will confirm the self potentially present in the imagination: "If Socrates leave his house today he will find the sage seated on his doorsteps. If Judas go forth tonight it is to Judas his steps will tend." Stephen will encounter the world like Mallarme's Hamlet, "lisant au livre de lui-meme." Stephen has divided the world of human experience into self (Stephen's) and not-self. In a closed system of binary opposition, opposed terms are inversions of each other, and interchangeable: notself can become self, God can become dog.

The special character of the totalitarian imagination is to expand its own private experience and perception into an assumed general condition. In *Portrait,* Stephen's totalitarian imagination expanded his personal sense of violation until all Ireland played a part in his drama of heroic rebellion, betrayal, and exile. In *Ulysses,* Stephen apparently gives up perceiving order in or imposing his own order upon the world for the sake of encountering it, but he is still totalizing his own experience of the intractability of the world to interpretation as a general condition. Further, Stephen isolates himself once more by dramatizing the perceived separateness of self and other as an agon of the self intuiting itself by encountering the notself.

Stephen's failure to encounter reality leaves him as weary and oversensitive as his failure to escape reality left him, at the beginning of *Ulysses.* In the Cabman shelter, Stephen turns aside Bloom's symbolic victory over the Citizen: "*Ex quibus,* Stephen mumbled in a noncommittal accent, their two or four eyes conversing, *Christus* or Bloom his name is, or after all, any other, *secundem carnem.*" Tolerance for the particularity and perceptions of others has slackened to a feeling that earthly existence makes any symbolic identification gratuitous. Stephen is still unhappy, alone, unable to live apart from or in the world. Yet by the end of *Ulysses,* Stephen's illtemper and weariness have been assuaged by that good Samaritan, Leopold Bloom.

If Bloom and Stephen first speak at cross purposes, they eventually establish a mode of conversation that allows easy commerce of their differing opinions. "Was the guest conscious of and did he acknowledge these marks of hospitality? His attention was directed to them by his host jocosely and he accepted them seriously as they drank in jocoserious silence Epp's massproduct the creature cocoa." Bloom and Stephen establish an ambience that makes gestures of affection and graceful acceptance of those gestures possible. By mocking the seriousness of his gesture to disarm it, Bloom makes it possible for Stephen to accept it seriously; together, jocoseriously, they drink their cocoa. Whatever its importance in an elaborate symbolic pattern, Stephen's quiet conversation with Bloom in the kitchen tells us something about Stephen's development as a human being. Molly draws the correct conclusion: "I hope hes not that stuck up university student sort no otherwise he wouldn't go sitting down in the kitchen with him taking Eppss cocoa."

Yet if Stephen can find companionship with Bloom, he also recognizes that Bloom, like Myles Crawford, Mulligan, Haines, and his mother, have asked him to play a prescribed role in a plot designed to order or reorder their lives. Bloom's plot, perceptively unravelled by Stanley Sultan in *The Argument of Ulysses,* is to get Molly interested in Stephen so that she will drop Boylan, and to catch Stephen for Milly by letting Molly seduce him.

Stephen does not accept Bloom's entire proposal. He considers teaching Molly Italian in return for singing lessons, and participating in intellectual dialogues with Bloom. But the offer of a room in the Bloom household was "promptly, inexplicably, with amicality, gratefully . . . declined." Stephen does not give himself up indiscriminately to Bloom precisely because he recognizes Bloom as a human being with his own aspirations and problems. Bloom can never be only a symbol of paternal affection, raw experience, or Hebraism in Stephen's plot because he himself is generating symbols and plots.

Stephen shrewdly decides to live elsewhere; to avoid being tyrannized by Bloom's imagination, Stephen must find new forms for their discourse. The counterproposals to Bloom's offer of sanctuary "were alternately advanced, accepted, modified, declined, restated in other terms, reaccepted, ratified, reconfirmed." Stephen accepts Bloom provisionally, but he will create new forms of companionship as the human situation requires. It is Stephen's decision to negotiate, rather than control or be controlled by Bloom, that offers a way out of binary opposition.

Stephen has achieved the state of mind necessary for liberation from the totalitarian frame: disintegration of obsession. Stephen now has the freedom to move among pockets of order and disorder, companionship and betrayal, without obsessively totalizing these experiences. Bloom offers companionship, advice, shelter, and enslavement; Stephen must recognize these various and conflicting possibilities, separate in Bloom what he wants from what he doesn't want, redeem whatever is worth redeeming, and let the rest go. Similarly, Stephen's growing awareness of his mother's love for him leads him to accept, after much agony, the tyranny of her influence. When Stephen leaves Bloom, they hear the bells of St.

George's Church. For Stephen, the bells assume a special significance. "Liliata rutilantium. Turma circumdet./ jubilantium te virginum. Chorus excipiat." By making the association of bells, death agony, and the special prayer for the dying, Stephen is at least considering, and perhaps belatedly fulfilling, his mother's last wish that he pray for her. Stephen has resigned himself to the form in which his mother's affection can assert itself. Remorse is the only way Stephen can begin to feel his love for his mother. This tyranny may be painful, but it is the pain of love.

If each character in *Ulysses* takes part in an elaborate plot based on *The Odyssey,* as Stuart Gilbert, following Joyce's lead, first showed us, if much of the book seems unordered, as many sceptics since Carl Jung have suggested, another mode of human possibilities in *Ulysses* is coincidence—the hundreds of parallels in dreams, idle thoughts, gestures, encounters, and acquaintances that, once recognized, proliferate the novel. Coincidence is the excluded middle between order and chaos. Coincidence allows one to recognize a partial, temporary order without totalizing or tyrannizing human experience as orderly or, when the order disappears, chaotic. Coincidence prepares many of the significant human encounters in *Ulysses*.

This line of reasoning would suggest an adjustment of critical opinion on *Ulysses.* Much criticism on Joyce has been totalitarian: in *Ulysses,* jewgreek meets greekjew. The novel is chaotic or orderly, the Homeric parallels ennoble or mock the characters, incidents of plot, character, and narration are primarily surface or symbol. *Ulysses* must now be approached with a third alternative that recognizes the three modes of human possibility: order, disorder, and coincidence—the partial orders with ragged edges, achieved through juxtaposition, whose spirit defies totalization. Richard Ellmann, in *James Joyce,* repeatedly emphasizes Joyce's own delight in coincidence. When we accept the possibilities of coincidence we need no longer identify James A. Jackson (Robert M. Adams' nutshell example of surface mistakenly read as symbol) as either surface or symbol, not even as at once surface and symbol, but as another quality of significance that passes beyond surface and symbol. James A. Jackson as a cryptic reference to Joyce (Jack Joyce's son), or a Dublin bicycle racer who lived circa 1904, is less interesting than the name as a fortunate coincidence. When we argue that Stephen is reconciled to the Father in Bloom as Shakespeare, Odysseus, Noah, or that Stephen (or Bloom) is ignorant of the real significance of their encounter, we lose the resonance *Ulysses* achieves by moving beyond these two opposed choices. Bloom can, and can't be Stephen's Father, but this is paradoxical only for someone who believes Bloom can be only one or the other, or, even, only both.

It is here that I would, belatedly, recognize the fine rereadings of early Modernism suggested by postmodern critics as I try to clarify by contrast the redefinition of modernism I am suggesting. Richard Poirier has established continuities between Modernism and postmodern attitudes by distinguishing Modernism from the interpretative criticism it usually receives.

> The literary organizations they adumbrate only to mimic, the schematizations they propose only to show the irrelevance of them to the actualities of experience—these have been extracted by commentators from the contexts that erode them and have been imposed back on the material in the form of designs or meanings.

The climate of compulsive avantgardism that encourages new artists to set themselves in binary opposition to their antecedents generates, in critics sensitive to their own times, a sympathetic rereading of the literature the avante garde would supersede. The best postmodern critics stand in polar opposition to earlier criticism of and during the Modern period, not the Moderns themselves. However grateful we are to critics like Poirier, Spanos, and Wasson, for rescuing Moderns like T. S. Eliot from the charge of Fascist esthetics, and making apparent the value of Modernism for a postmodern sensibility, our rereadings of Modernism must ultimately come to terms with the original contexts of these works to keep from subsuming Modernism under our own postmodern mythology. The attitude of "self parody" (Poirier's term) towards totalitarian esthetic and philosophical structures in the monuments of Modernism must be squared with the undeniable compulsion for order exhibited by Joyce and other moderns and perceived by New Criticism.

I have suggested that we can see both the quest for order and an attempt to escape order in Modernism because the Moderns, intuiting the insidious relationship between two apparently opposed choices, were feeling their way towards an understanding of, and escape from, the techniques of binary opposition which characterize the totalitarian mind. It is clear that criticism must now escape the tyranny of binary opposition. Postmodern critics, released from merely contemplating extensions of themselves by seeing their preoccupations within the context of Modernism, can return to their Contemporaries with new eyes and, possessed of a fuller conception of the Modern Century, they can go back to Milton and Homer, find and then lose themselves once again.

Let me sketch quickly what a reentry into postmodernism from a rereading of Modernism might look like. Newly educated in the possibility of the excluded middle between order and chaos in Joyce, the sign of postmodern esthetics is no longer contingency, antimyth, and antimetaphor, but coincidence. Here Carl Jung's essay "On Synchronicity" and Borges' whole corpus inherit the center of a redefined postmodernism, ranging from a metaphysical attitude towards coincidence in Kesey and Burroughs, towards urbane acceptance in Burgess and Barth. Then, our understanding of and potential liberation from the techniques of binary opposition that characterize the totalitarian mind (gained from a study of the literature of the Modern Century) might discover Milton threading his

way between the narcissistic contemplation of one's own creations inherent in both Metaphysical wit and Spenserian copiousness, or Odysseus escaping Achilles' enslavement to the opposed choices of a short glorious life and a long uneventful life, by steering a middle course, being both father and son, patrician and warrior, and much else besides, *polutropos*. Again, we must not give up the worthy task of retrieving, as best we can, the galaxy of conditions that allows Homer to happen only once, for an indiscriminant modernism. Only when we recognize the Greek's Homer is fulfilled, but not completed, in our Homer, just as the Greek's Homer keeps our Homer from becoming a narcissistic extension of ourselves, do we move beyond the binary opposition of synchrony and diachrony—works frozen in a timeless presence, or condemned to die because they once lived.

FURTHER READING

Anthologies

Ellmann, Richard, and Feidelson, Charles, Jr., eds. *The Modern Tradition: Backgrounds of Modern Literature.* New York: Oxford University Press, 1965, 953 p.
> Presents thematic arrangement of writings by novelists, dramatists, poets, artists, and philosophers.

Bibliographies

Davies, Alistair. *An Annotated Critical Bibliography of Modernism.* Totowa, N.J.: Barnes & Noble Books, 1982, 261 p.
> Includes books and essays discussing the origins, development, techniques, and cultural context of literary Modernism, and provides comprehensive individual bibliographies on such figures as W. B. Yeats, Wyndham Lewis, D. H. Lawrence, and T. S. Eliot.

Secondary Sources

Bergonzi, Bernard. "The Advent of Modernism, 1900-1920." In *The Twentieth Century,* edited by Bernard Bergonzi, pp. 17-45. London: Barrie and Jenkins, 1970.
> Traces the origins and delineates prominent traits of Modernism in English literature.

Craig, David. "Loneliness and Anarchy: Aspects of Modernism." In *The Real Foundations: Literature and Social Change,* pp. 171-94. London: Oxford University Press, 1973.
> Craig decries expressions of loneliness and anarchy in Modernist literature.

Dettmar, Kevin J. H., ed. *Rereading the New: A Backward Glance at Modernism.* Ann Arbor: University of Michigan Press, 1992, 385 p.

Contains thematically arranged essays that consider the origins of Modernism, Modernist aesthetics, and the relationship of Modernism to popular culture, and offers postmodern assessments of such significant Modernist texts as *Ulysses, Heart of Darkness,* and *To the Lighthouse.*

Eysteinsson, Astradur. *The Concept of Modernism.* Ithaca, N.Y.: Cornell University Press, 1990, 265 p.
Examines several theories of literary Modernism, traces Modernism in literary history, and views Modernism in the context of postmodernism and avant-garde aesthetics.

Faulkner, Peter. *Modernism.* London: Methuen & Co., 1977, 86 p.
Outlines the development of Modernism and focuses on its flourishing from 1910 to 1930 through specific examinations of T. S. Eliot, Virginia Woolf, Ezra Pound, James Joyce, and D. H. Lawrence.

Fraser, John. "Leavis, Winters, and 'Tradition'." *Southern Review* 7, No. 4 (Fall 1971): 963-85.
Defends the critical positions of F. R. Leavis and Yvor Winters who rejected modernist writings that disavowed traditional beliefs and ideas.

Garvin, Harry R., ed. *Bucknell Review, Special Issue: Romanticism, Modernism, Postmodernism.* Lewisburg, Pa.: Bucknell University Press, 1980, 193 p.
Contains "Virginia Woolf and Romantic Prometheanism," an essay by L. J. Swingle discussing Virginia Woolf's concept of gaining freedom through artistic creation, and "Defamiliarization, Reflexive Reference, and Modernism," by Donald R. Riccomini.

Giles, Steve, ed. *Theorizing Modernism: Essays in Critical Theory.* London: Routledge, 1993, 190 p.
Reconsiders Modernism in the context of current critical theory and the dominance of postmodernism in contemporary literature. Contributors to the volume include Richard Sheppard, Bernard McGuirk, David Wragg, Mike Johnson, and Steve Giles.

Hamilton, Alastair. "England." In his *The Appeal of Fascism: A Study of Intellectuals and Fascism, 1919-1945,* pp. 257-90. New York: Macmillan, 1971.
Documents the responses of British writers and intellectuals to the rise of Fascism in Europe during the 1930s.

Head, Dominic. *The Modernist Short Story: A Study in Theory and Practice.* New York: Cambridge University Press, 1992, 241 p.
Identifies the short story as "a quintessentially modernist form" through an examination of works by James Joyce, Virginia Woolf, Katherine Mansfield, Wyndham Lewis, and Malcolm Lowry.

Hoffman, Michael J., and Murphy, Patrick D., eds. *Critical Essays on American Modernism.* New York: G. K. Hall & Co., 1992, 274 p.

Includes manifestos, theoretical statements, and critical assessments by practitioners of literary Modernism and their contemporaries as well as retrospective analyses of the movement by modern academic critics.

Howe, Irving. "The Culture of Modernism." In his *Decline of the New,* pp. 3-33. New York: Victor Gollancz, 1971.
Howe identifies major characteristics and underlying principles of Modernism and observes how these relate more generally to modern culture.

Kenner, Hugh. *A Homemade World: The American Modernist Writers.* New York: Alfred A. Knopf, 1975, 221 p.
Discusses the impact of modernist experimentation on American novels and poetry.

Kiely, Robert, ed. *Modernism Reconsidered.* Cambridge, Mass.: Harvard University Press, 1983, 264 p.
Contains essays focusing on authors outside the front ranks of Modernism and on the lesser known works of major writers of the movement.

Levenson, Michael H. *A Genealogy of Modernism: A Study of English Literary Doctrine, 1908-1922.* New York: Cambridge University Press, 1984, 250 p.
Traces the development of modernist literary doctrine in England from the time Ezra Pound arrived in London in 1908 to 1922, when T. S. Eliot's *The Waste Land,* James Joyce's *Ulysses,* and W. B. Yeats's *Later Poems* were published.

Lukács, Georg. "The Ideology of Modernism." In his *The Meaning of Contemporary Realism,* translated by John and Necke Mander, pp. 17-46. London: Merlin Press, 1963.
Marxist indictment of Modernism, concluding that "modernism leads not only to the destruction of traditional literary forms; it leads to the destruction of literature as such."

Mellard, James M. *The Exploded Form: The Modernist Novel in America.* Urbana and Chicago: University of Illinois Press, 1980, 206 p.
Identifies three developmental phases of the modern novel in American literature: *naive*—exemplified by William Faulkner's *The Sound and the Fury, critical*—represented by Joseph Heller's *Catch-22,* and *sophisticated*—epitomized by Richard Brautigan's *Trout Fishing in America.*

Mitchell, Roger. "Modernism Comes to American Poetry: 1908-1920." In *Twentieth-Century American Poetry,* pp. 25-53. Carbondale: Southern Illinois University Press, 1991.
Studies the introduction of Modernist themes and techniques into American poetry.

Raleigh, John Henry. "Victorian Morals and the Modern Novel." In his *Time, Place, and Idea: Essays on the Novel,* pp. 137-63. Carbondale and Edwardsville: Southern

Illinois University Press, 1968.
  Discusses the disparity between the strict moral code of the Victorian middle-class with the liberal social standards of the high and low classes of the time and traces two separate traditions that developed out of the great Victorian novel: the Butler-Forster-Lawrence line, emerging from the extremes and the Eliot-James-Conrad-Woolf-Joyce line, representing middle-class consciousness.

Ryan, Judith. *The Vanishing Subject: Early Psychology and Literary Modernism.* Chicago: University of Chicago Press, 1991, 267 p.
  Examines the importance of pre-Freudian psychology on the development of literary Modernism.

Sherry, Vincent. *Ezra Pound, Wyndham Lewis, and Radical Modernism.* New York: Oxford University Press, 1993, 228 p.
  Attempts to reconcile the avant-garde aesthetics of such literary modernists as Ezra Pound and Wyndham Lewis with their reactionary social ideologies.

Spears, Monroe K. *Dionysus and the City: Modernism in Twentieth-Century Poetry.* New York: Oxford University Press, 1970, 278 p.
  Traces the development of Modernism in poetry from W. B. Yeats, Ezra Pound, and T. S. Eliot, through the Fugitive poets and the development of New Criticism, to Robert Lowell, Ted Hughes, and James Dickey in the 1950s.

Spender, Stephen. *The Struggle of the Modern.* Berkeley and Los Angeles: University of California Press, 1963, 266 p.
  Defines fundamental qualities of Modernism in art and literature, distinguishes modernists from contemporary writers who did not pursue modernist aims in their works, and provides a context for Modernism within the development of literature since the Romantics.

Stead, C. K. *The New Poetic: Yeats to Eliot.* New York: Harper Torchbooks, 1966, 198 p.
  Focuses on the origins and development of English modernist poetry, offering both general discussion of British poetry from 1909 to 1916 and individual investigation of the works of W. B. Yeats and T. S. Eliot.

Trilling, Lionel. "On the Teaching of Modern Literature." In his *Beyond Culture: Essays on Literature and Learning,* pp. 3-27. New York: Harcourt, Brace, Jovanovich, 1965.
  Calls attention to "a particular theme of modern literature which appears so frequently and with so much authority that it may be said to constitute one of the shaping and controlling ideas of our epoch. . . . the disenchantment of our culture with culture itself."

Weiss, Theodore. "The Many-Sidedness of Modernism." In his *The Man from Porlock: Engagements, 1944-1981,* pp. 131-44. Princeton: Princeton University Press, 1982.
  Favorable review of M. L. Rosenthal's *Sailing into the Unknown: Yeats, Pound, and Eliot* that first appeared in the *Times Literary Supplement* in February 1980.

Popular Literature

INTRODUCTION

Long neglected as a topic of scholarly interest, popular culture has in recent years attracted the close and sustained attention of critics. Novels and stories of various genres, including detective fiction, mysteries, thrillers, romances, westerns, fantasies, science fiction, and the like—works rapidly consumed by a huge reading public in the United States, Europe, and around the world since the debut of the paperback in the late 1930s—have been increasingly scrutinized by academics using the tools and techniques of literary criticism. As a result, scholars have produced studies on the works of such popular authors as detective novelists Raymond Chandler and Dashiell Hammett, citing the merit of their "hard-boiled" writings as literature and as cultural documents. While many critics still denigrate works of this type as simple entertainment, "escapist" fiction, marred by formulaic narratives, superficiality, and sensationalism, some adherents of modern literary theory have challenged the accepted notions of what constitutes serious literature. In addition, there are scholars who have opted to dismantle the barriers between elite and popular culture in order to understand both more fully. Thus, new strategies are being formulated to draw all modes of literature, from the canonical works of Shakespeare to something as seemingly ephemeral as advertising copy or paperback fiction, together in the study of cultural history, both in the past and in its most contemporary manifestations.

REPRESENTATIVE WORKS

Alcott, Louisa May
  Little Women (novel) 1868-69
Allen, Hervey
  Anthony Adverse (novel) 1933
Andrews, V. C.
  Flowers in the Attic (novel) 1979
Asimov, Isaac
  Foundation (novel) 1951
Barrie, J. M.
  Peter Pan (novel) 1904
Bradbury, Ray
  Fahrenheit 451 (novel) 1953
Burroughs, Edgar Rice
  Tarzan of the Apes (novel) 1914
Cain, James M.
  The Postman Always Rings Twice (novel) 1934
Carroll, Lewis
  Alice's Adventures in Wonderland (novel) 1865
  Through the Looking Glass (novel) 1871

Cartland, Barbara
  Jig-Saw (novel) 1925
Chandler, Raymond
  The Big Sleep (novel) 1939
  The Long Goodbye (novel) 1953
Christie, Agatha
  The Mysterious Affair at Styles (novel) 1920
  The Murder of Roger Ackroyd (novel) 1926
  The Murder at the Vicarage (novel) 1930
Clarke, Arthur C.
  2001: A Space Odyssey (novel) 1968
Doyle, Arthur Conan
  A Study in Scarlet (novel) 1888
  The Adventures of Sherlock Holmes (short stories) 1892
  The Hound of the Baskervilles (novel) 1902
Du Maurier, Daphne
  Jamaica Inn (novel) 1936
  Rebecca (novel) 1938
Fast, Howard
  Spartacus (novel) 1951
Fleming, Ian
  Casino Royale (novel) 1955
  Doctor No (novel) 1958
  Goldfinger (novel) 1959
Haggard, H. Rider
  King Solomon's Mines (novel) 1885
  She (novel) 1887
Hammett, Dashiell
  The Maltese Falcon (novel) 1930
  The Thin Man (novel) 1934
Heinlein, Robert A.
  Stranger in a Strange Land (novel) 1961
Herbert, Frank
  Dune (novel) 1965
Hilton, James
  Goodbye, Mr. Chips (novel) 1957
Grahame, Kenneth
  The Wind in the Willows (novel) 1908
Grey, Zane
  Riders of the Purple Sage (novel) 1913
Hunter, Evan
  The Blackboard Jungle (novel) 1950
King, Stephen
  The Shining (novel) 1978
Koontz, Dean
  Phantoms (novel) 1983
Le Carré, John
  The Spy Who Came in from the Cold (novel) 1963
Leonard, Elmore
  Hombre (novel) 1961
Lewis, C. S.
  The Chronicles of Narnia. 7 vols. (novels) 1950-56

Michener, James
　Tales of the South Pacific　(novel)　1947
Mitchell, Margaret
　Gone with the Wind　(novel)　1936
Radcliffe, Ann
　The Mysteries of Udolpho　(novel)　1794
Rice, Anne
　Interview with the Vampire　(novel)　1976
Robbins, Harold
　Never Love a Stranger　(novel)　1948
Rohmer, Sax
　The Hand of Fu Manchu　(novel)　1917
Salinger, J. D.
　The Catcher in the Rye　(novel)　1953
Sheldon, Sidney
　The Other Side of Midnight　(novel)　1974
Shelley, Mary
　Frankenstein　(novel)　1818
Steele, Danielle
　Changes　(novel)　1984
Stevenson, Robert Louis
　Treasure Island　(novel)　1883
Stoker, Bram
　Dracula　(novel)　1897
Stone, Irving
　Lust for Life　(novel)　1934
Tolkein, J. R. R.
　The Hobbit　(novel)　1936
Wallace, Irving
　The Chapman Report　(novel)　1962
Wallace, Lew
　Ben-Hur　(novel)　1880
Walpole, Horace
　The Castle of Otranto　(novel)　1764
Winsor, Kathleen
　Forever Amber　(novel)　1950
Yerby, Frank
　Foxes of Harrow　(novel)　1946
Wister, Owen
　The Virginian　(novel) 1902

OVERVIEWS

Morris Dickstein

SOURCE: "Popular Fiction and Critical Values: The Novel as a Challenge to Literary History," in *Reconstructing American Literary History,* edited by Sacvan Bercovitch, Cambridge, Mass.: Harvard University Press, 1986, pp. 29-66.

[*In the following essay, Dickstein examines attitudes toward the popular novel.*]

The growth of academic criticism in the twentieth century has come partly at the expense of other kinds of writing about literature, including literary journalism, belles lettres, and literary history. Great changes have occurred, for example, in biographical writing. In the nineteenth century a grandiose "life and letters" was often entrusted as a pious duty to either a family member—Scott's son-in-law, Macaulay's nephew, Hawthorne's son—or trusted protégé like Forster or Froude. (Later Thomas Hardy would exploit this moribund tradition by writing his own biography under the name of his second wife.) The mockery and brevity of Lytton Strachey put an end to these family affairs; in the hands of a new breed of glib popular writers, biography became a branch of narrative history, as smooth and digestible as a novel—or as a novel used to be. But the coming of an Age of Criticism, along with the general decline of popular interest in writers' lives, made this kind of confection anomalous. Literary biography passed from the professional biographers, innocent of all critical insight, to the verbose academic scholars, innocent of the ability to shape dramatic scenes, select vivid details, and tell a gripping story. With some significant exceptions like Ellmann's *Joyce,* literary biographies became overlong critical studies bulked out with a mass of chronological information about writers' day-by-day lives, or guided by some pet psychological theory about the writer's development. Criticism and psychoanalysis have given biographers new tools toward a deeper understanding of their subjects, but they have bloated the biographies themselves, which turn static or break down under the pressure of so much analytical argument and organized evidence.

The spirit of criticism has also altered the nature of literary history. As omnivorous antiquarian scholars like Saintsbury gave way to severely judgmental critics like Leavis, a hierarchical canon of great writers came to dominate the landscape of literary history, giving enormous priority to imaginative writing over discursive writing and leaving most writers as mere footnotes to a small band of acknowledged geniuses in each age. In C. H. Herford's once-standard handbook *The Age of Wordsworth* (first edition, 1897), the staggering range of writers who appear in less than 300 pages marks the book as a product of its time. Herford includes French and German Romantics, political philosophers like Godwin and Bentham, religious thinkers and historical writers, essayists, novelists, and dramatists, to say nothing of minor poets like Bowles, Crabbe, Hogg, and Landor, all in addition to the major writers. A typical work of our own period, Harold Bloom's *The Visionary Company* (1961), devotes more than 400 pages to poem-by-poem readings of the six major Romantic poets, followed by brief chapters on three minor poets. Informed by a revisionist view of the place of the Romantics in English literature, it treats literary history of the old kind as an irrelevance. It tells us that literary history inheres in the poems themselves and in their imaginative dialogue with other great poems from the Renaissance to the modern period, not in the circumstances of their composition, or in biographical relationships, or political and intellectual "backgrounds." Though Bloom sets out to overturn nearly all the judgments of the New Critics, he implicitly ratifies their emphasis on close reading and canon-formation. Behind his approach, like theirs, is an almost religious affinity for great poetry as secular scripture, and a sense of minor poetry and discursive writing as spiritually deficient, faulty in their worldliness. For Herford literary history is a branch of history; for Bloom it is a branch of criticism, or of the spiritual history to which critical reading gives us access.

An even more drastic reshaping of literary history along critical lines has taken place within American literature. When I was in high school in the 1950s, the line of American poetry still enshrined in our textbooks ran from Bryant, Longfellow, Whittier, and Lowell in the nineteenth century to Stephen Vincent Benet, Carl Sandburg, Robert Frost, and Edna Millay. Of these figures not even Frost can be said to survive today: the Frost who now bestrides the canon like a latter-day Wordsworth is quite different from the harmless, avuncular gaffer we were forced to read. In those textbooks, Whitman and Dickinson were treated like quirky, eccentric individualists, outside the main line, like Hopkins in England. Eliot and Pound were a distant rumor, Stevens and Hart Crane not even a rumor. For new figures like Robert Lowell you had to read *Partisan Review,* no staple in my high school.

In prose the upheaval has probably been less great, except for the rediscovery of Melville in the 1920s, but Emerson and Thoreau were renovated almost as sweepingly as Robert Frost. As the influence of modernism spread with the critical techniques which it spawned, nearly every older writer's work took on a new coloring, and methods of interpretation were soon translated into canons of taste, judgment, and critical discrimination. Fresh from a study of T. S. Eliot, F. O. Matthiessen helped create the canon of the American Renaissance, and this was inevitably reflected in Spiller's *Literary History of the United States,* to which Matthiessen contributed. The first edition of this work came out in 1948, the same year as Leavis's rigorously selective study of the English novel, *The Great Tradition.* As a collective work of scholarship the Spiller volume was hardly a book in the same class as the Leavis, but in its own terms it was in every way a work more discriminating and less catholic than *its* predecessor, *The Cambridge History of American Literature* (1917-1921). The Cambridge volumes, relatively speaking, are precanonical, premodern history as C. H. Herford might have written it. The Cambridge scholars deal with every kind of writing from discursive and religious tracts to imaginative writing, from dialect writers to newspaper and magazine writers to children's authors. The last chapters include studies of economists, scholars, patriotic songs and hymns, oral literature, popular bibles (like *The Book of Mormon* and *Science and Health*), book publishers, the English language itself, writings in German, French, and Yiddish, as well as native American myths and folktales ("Aboriginal").

From a later point of view, no doubt, there was something slightly monstrous—or at least deplorably miscella-

neous—about the inclusion of all these matters in a literary history: a blinding nationalism and a default of critical judgment, if not some kind of obtuse ignorance about the very word "literature" enshrined in the title. Or so it must have seemed to the more advanced authors of the *Literary History of the United States,* who included some of these items, along with a good deal of political and intellectual history, as background or interchapters in a work that centers on major authors from Jonathan Edwards and Benjamin Franklin to Edwin Arlington Robinson, Theodore Dreiser, and Eugene O'Neill. In the closing section of this work, "A World Literature," the cosmopolitan modernism of Eliot and his school gets its due; it jostles for primacy with the remnants of the left-wing literary culture of the 1930s. But although the contributors include leading leftist critics like Malcolm Cowley, Matthiessen, and Maxwell Geismar, the accounts of individual authors tend to float free of any cultural context. Thanks to the new spirit of criticism, literary history is reduced to a succession of the great and near-great. Background chapters which begin each section are frequently entrusted directly to historians like Allan Nevins and Henry Steele Commager, as if to acknowledge that critics no longer feel equipped to write literary history.

In the second edition of 1953 this split is formally recognized, as the new preface indicates: "In the listing of chapters, the titles of those which were designed to supply information about the history of thought and the instruments of culture have now been distinguished from those which deal more directly with literature by being set in italics. The master plan of the work may thus be seen more clearly, it is hoped, as a literary history of the United States rather than as a history of American literature." But the goal of seeing literature in relation to culture is seriously undercut by such an arbitrary mechanical division.

Since the individual critics seem unable to develop an intrinsic cultural perspective, the enlightened sentences that follow seem like an attempt to disarm objections and compensate for felt deficiencies: "The view of literature as the aesthetic expression of the general culture of a people in a given time and place was, from the start, an axiom in the thinking of the editors and their associates. Rejecting the theory that history of any kind is merely a chronological record of objective facts, they adopted an organic view of literature as the record of human experience." Discarding the fact-bound positivism of the old history, the editors appeal implicitly to a new "organic" history that descends from Hegel and Coleridge to Croce and the New Criticism. Unfortunately, there is a deep contradiction between the historicism of Hegel and the ahistorical organicism of the New Critics. In Hegel, culture and history are part of the foreground, crystallized in the work itself; but to the New Critic the "well wrought urn" is a unique artifact, detached from history, the "foster child of silence and slow time," occupying its own imaginative space and pursuing its own formal and rhetorical strategies.

The conflict helps account for the slippery use of words like "literature" and "aesthetic expression" in this interesting preface. Is literature seen as "the aesthetic expression of the general culture" and a "record of human experience," or is it to be confined to the critic's choice of the best poems, plays, novels, and autobiographies, as in the actual body of this work? Interpretive insight and critical discrimination are things to be valued in any consideration of the arts, including literary history. Evaluation is as instinctive and inevitable as breathing. But the more vigorous the discrimination, the more limited the canon of accepted works is likely to be, and the more skewed the literary history may become. Critics in recent years have repeatedly drawn attention to exclusions based on ethnocentrism or on gender and class. "In the twenties," writes Paul Lauter, "processes were set in motion that virtually eliminated black, white female, and all working-class writers from the canon." Less attention has been paid to the exclusion of popular culture and of borderline works on the margin between high and popular art. By resolutely refusing to fit, these works bring into question the hierarchical basis of the canon itself. When scholars venture into film history, there is no question that whatever has been made is potentially part of the subject, not just the accepted masterpieces. There is no workable definition of "film" that ignores the mass of existing movies, as there *are* definitions of "literature"— and histories of literature—that exclude most of the novels, poems, and plays ever written.

A great many of them, of course, are of little interest to anyone. My concern here is not with what is ignored, rightly or wrongly, but with what is categorically excluded or devalued because of critical preconceptions. Here judgments of quality, themselves very variable, are never the sole determinant. Continuous innovation is a key feature of artistic activity since the middle of the eighteenth century. This is partly the result of the commodification process, the shift from a conservative patronage system to the needs of the marketplace, where artists are forced to differentiate their products from those of other artists, and even from the things they themselves have already produced. But innovation can also arise from a rejection of the marketplace by a Wordsworth or Coleridge who is revolted by the popular taste and following his own star. In either case, the marketplace creates a demand for criticism that can mediate between the growing number of artists and the expanding middle-class audience, uncertain of its bearings in the brave new world of culture.

This system works better in theory than in practice. At times a whole new body of criticism may arise to serve and interpret a new movement in the arts, as it did during the modernist period. At other times the artists themselves will move to create the criticism they are not receiving from their contemporaries, as Wordsworth and Coleridge did, as Poe and James did after them, as Eliot and Pound did in the twentieth century. Art as we know it is inherently dynamic and unstable, while criticism seems intrinsically synthetic and retrospective. Like the

French general staff, criticism is always fighting the previous battle, the last war; its standards are inevitably drawn from an earlier phase of creative activity, from which it codifies the rules that artists feel almost obliged to violate.

Sometimes this balance of innovation is reversed. For reasons that also relate to the marketplace, popular art is often more conservative than vanguard art, wary of drastic innovation, given to repeating formulas which have worked in the past. Faced by the crowd-pleasing formulas of mass culture, sometimes combined with advances in technology that seem to threaten the existing arts, the critic falls back on originality and high seriousness as the sine qua non of all genuine art. He relegates popular culture to the history of taste and turns it over willingly to the sociologist and the historian. A work like the *Literary History of the United States* resembles a topographical map with all peaks and no valleys, not even the most lush and verdant ones. For example, nearly a quarter of all the new novels published in the 1930s were detective stories, rising from 12 in 1914 to 97 in 1925 to 217 by the last year of the thirties. Dashiell Hammett was certainly one of the best writers who worked in this form, and he was at the height of his fame by 1948, after a series of films and radio programs based on his characters; yet we search the *Literary History of the United States* in vain for any substantive discussion of what he wrote. Instead, in a chapter on fiction, we find a parenthetical reference to "the talented mystery writer Dashiell Hammett" (though the context actually refers to his politics), along with three more references in a concluding chapter on American books abroad, where Hammett's literary quality was better recognized than at home. Popular culture in general gets short shrift in Spiller's capacious volume, though it does include literary discussions of major writers like Cooper and Poe who happened at some point to be popular. (We never learn how they accomplished this paradoxical feat.)

Some of the serious gaps in the *Literary History of the United States* are filled when we turn to indispensable works like James D. Hart's *The Popular Book: A History of America's Literary Taste* (1950) and Russel Nye's *The Unembarrassed Muse: The Popular Arts in America* (1970). Each contains materials that would never belong in any literary history. Hart includes both foreign books that were popular here and nonliterary works like Bruce Barton's biography of Jesus as an American-style huckster, *The Man Nobody Knows,* and Dale Carnegie's manual on *How To Win Friends and Influence People.* Nye aptly brings in everything from dime novels and popular music to film and television. Yet these books are also mirror images of academic literary histories. They offer essential missing links and highlight all that is shadowy or absent in the official literary canon. Just as Tom Stoppard cleverly looked at Hamlet from the point of view of Rosencrantz and Guildenstern, Hart and Nye see Hawthorne and Melville from the tilted angle of the "mob of scribbling women" who—so they felt—stood between them and their rightful readership. [Hart, *The Popular*

Book] No history of our literary culture is complete without some account of these writings.

Hart and Nye are not simply drawing attention to the popular or forgotten works. For them the whole social history of reading, writing, and publishing are an intrinsic part of any history of literature. Thus Nye writes about changes in the marketplace, the growth of the reading public, the vast increase in the number of newspapers and magazines in the early nineteenth century, and the "succession of technological innovations in the mechanics of printing" that enabled publishers to produce "the acres of print demanded by this huge audience." [Nye, *The Unembarrassed Muse: The Popular Arts in America*] For the Spiller group, however, such matters are peripheral at best. Literary history is a record of the imaginative heights scaled by talent and genius, with little regard for the conditions under which they worked, the cultural factors that helped determine how their work was conceived and received, and the different kinds of talent and intensity that could operate in the popular arts.

The artificial separation of the "literary" and the "popular," and the parallel split between the "critical" approach and the "cultural" one, is especially vexing when we are dealing with fiction. Most modern critical techniques were developed to deal with the more self-contained artifacts of lyric poetry. The novel, with its looser weave, was the child of the marketplace. It was born only after the old patronage system gave way before the spread of literacy and leisure within the new middle-class audience. No form better illustrates the time lag between creative practice and critical acceptance. As Leslie Fiedler has written,

> From any traditional point of view, then, from the standpoint of those still pledged in the eighteenth century to writing epics in verse, the novel already seemed anti-literature, even post-literature . . . In the jargon of our own day, the novel represents the beginning of popular culture, of that machine-made, mass-produced, mass-distributed *ersatz* which, unlike either traditional high art or folk art, *does not know its place;* since, while pretending to meet the formal standards of literature, it is actually engaged in smuggling into the republic of letters extra-literary satisfactions. ["The End of the Novel" in *Perspectives on Fiction,* edited by James L. Calderwood and Harold E. Toliver]

While Fiedler is certainly accurate about the resistance to the novel among the upholders of high culture in the eighteenth century, the way he poses the issue ratifies the presumed gap between the literary and the popular by defending popular culture against its detractors, then and now. In what sense was the novel *"pretending* to meet the formal standards of literature"? It invented new formal standards that were also literary, besides being instantly understood by nearly all readers. In what sense did the novel illicitly provide "extra-literary satisfactions"? That can only be so if we limit our definition of the literary as strictly as any elitist critic might wish. Fiedler's wild-man

stance is his way of thumbing his nose at the critic he once was.

Even in the heyday of modernism, the novel never entirely lost its roots in popular storytelling. Publishers today may find it convenient to distinguish between popular and literary fiction, but this refers to the size of the audience, not to any absolute formal differences. Most fiction continues to occupy the large middle ground between self-conscious experimentation and the predictable formulas of the best-seller list. The formal qualities of the novel were established early on by Defoe, Richardson, and Fielding, who each felt in different ways that he was creating "a new species of writing," quite distinct from epic and romance. [Quoted by Lennard J. Davis, *Factual Fictions: The Origins of the English Novel.*] The narrative devices they used were so quickly understood and accepted that they could be manipulated with impunity by Fielding, wildly parodied by Sterne, and turned into self-conscious play by Sterne's French follower, Diderot. Despite these formal elements, a grey area blurs the line between fiction and romance and between fiction and nonfiction. A good measure of looseness and ambiguity distinguishes all fiction from the beginnings of the eighteenth century to the present. As John J. Richetti writes of the forgotten books he surveys in *Popular Fiction Before Richardson,* "many narratives of the period, presented as fact and accepted as such by many, were sheer fabrications. Many 'novels' were only thinly disguised romans à clef, gross mixtures of slander and scandal. It is, in short, extremely difficult to separate fact from fiction in a great many of the prose narratives of the period that are customarily called fiction."

It would be wrong to attribute this ambiguity solely to the immaturity of pre-Richardsonian fiction. Even the major writers hid behind a screen of truthfulness, posing as the mere editors of their material. In other words, they used a blatantly fictive device to ward off charges of lying and creative invention. But even after this fiction was discarded, the course of the novel right up to the present has continued to rely on some confusion between art and life. In his notes for an autobiographical lecture, Lionel Trilling described the novel as "the genre which was traditionally the least devoted to the ideals of *form* and to the consciousness of formal consideration . . . of all genres the most indifferent to manifest shapeliness and decorum, and the most devoted to substance, which it presumes to say is actuality itself." The novel as a genre "presumes to say" this, Trilling hints, though we ourselves, with our heightened formal awareness, are confident that we know better. Trilling is as conscious as we are of the fictive character of all human constructions. Yet he continues to stand with the great apologists for the novel, D. H. Lawrence and Henry James, when he describes it as "the literary form which most directly reveals to us the complexity, the difficulty, and the interest of life in society, and which best instructs us in our human variety and contradiction." [Trilling, "Art, Will, and Necessity" in *The Last Decade*]

In a famous passage in his essay "Why the Novel Matters," Lawrence had boasted that "being a novelist, I consider myself superior to the saint, the scientist, the philosopher, and the poet, who are all great masters of different bits of man alive, but never get the whole hog."

> The novel is the one bright book of life. Books are not life. They are only tremulations on the ether. But the novel as a tremulation can make the whole man alive tremble. Which is more than poetry, philosophy, science, and any other book-tremulation can do.
>
> The novel is the book of life. In this sense, the Bible is a great confused novel.

From Aristotle to Wordsworth and Matthew Arnold, critics and poets had used this argument to defend poetry and to proclaim its universality against the more factual claims of history and science. Lawrence directs the same argument against poetry itself, in the name of a form whose dignity and truth were still in question as he was writing. "The crown of literature is poetry," wrote Matthew Arnold in 1887, after taking due note of the creative ferment in French, English, and Russian fiction. Here, at the end of his life, Arnold ruefully acknowledged that fiction was "the form of imaginative literature which in our day is the most popular and the most possible," but this was further evidence to him that literature had fallen on hard times. Arnold's conservatism exemplifies the time lag between creative achievement and critical recognition. The popular character of fiction, for him, was an argument against it.

This was the very period when Flaubert and Henry James were bidding to elevate fiction from popular culture into art by holding it to an unheard-of standard of formal control. This can be observed in the exacting craftsmanship of their novels and stories, but also in Flaubert's letters and James's reviews, essays, and prefaces—documents in their struggle to achieve a precision of language and a consistency of narrative viewpoint that were alien to the early novelists. Yet the novels of both men, like later "serious" fiction, include generous helpings of romance and melodrama, those indispensable staples of popular fiction. Henry James's legacy to later criticism and fiction was especially ambiguous. In the hands of Percy Lubbock and the academic critics who came after him, James's critical prefaces were turned into rules of craft that made "creative writing" less creative and more teachable, rules that the best novelists had usually felt free to ignore. Lawrence, one of the writers who broke those rules most flagrantly, wrote that "a character in a novel has got to live, or it is nothing." James's general view of the novel is really not very different from Lawrence's.

The revival of Henry James in the 1940s and 1950s coincided with a certain academic deadness and tame respectability that invaded the novel. Yet the key terms in Henry James's essays on the novel, such as "The Art of Fiction," are not "form" or "point of view" but "experi-

ence" and "freedom." Like Lawrence he stresses "life" rather than "art," sincerity, vitality, accuracy, and variety rather than mere consistency of design. The novel, says James in his preface to *The Portrait of a Lady,* has not only the power to deal with an immense range of individual experience, but also "positively to appear more true to its character in proportion as it strains, or tends to burst, with a latent extravagance, its mould."

> The house of fiction has in short not one window, but a million—a number of possible windows not be reckoned, rather; every one of which has been pierced, or is still pierceable, in its vast front, by the need of the individual vision and by the pressure of the individual will.

James feared the moral censorship of his age more than any deficiency of craft; he saw how preconceived ideas could blind a writer to the variety of life and to his own wealth of experience. In a letter to the students at the Deerfield summer school, he wrote:

> There are no tendencies worth anything but to see the actual or the imaginative, which is just as visible, and to paint it. I have only two little words for the matter remotely approaching to rule or doctrine; one is life and the other freedom. Tell the ladies and gentlemen, the ingenious inquirers, to consider life directly and closely, and not to be put off with mean and puerile falsities, and to be conscientious about it. It is infinitely large, various, and comprehensive. Every sort of mind will find what it looks for in it, whereby the novel becomes truly multifarious and illustrative. That is what I mean by liberty; give it its head, and let it range. If it is in a bad way, and the English novel is, I think, nothing but absolute freedom can refresh it and restore its self-respect.

This is the real significance of point of view in James: not a limiting rule of craft, as it is applied mechanically in writing courses, but an individual aperture from the house of fiction onto the plenitude of life. There is almost a Paterian emphasis in James's insistence that "a novel is in its broadest definition a personal, a direct impression of life: that, to begin with, constitutes its value, which is greater or less according to the intensity of the impression . . . The form, it seems to me, is to be appreciated after the fact." Later on in this essay, "The Art of Fiction," James tries to define the impressions and intuitions that constitute novelistic "experience":

> The power to guess the unseen from the seen, to trace the implications of things, to judge the whole piece by the pattern, the condition of feeling life in general so completely that you are well on your way to knowing any particular corner of it—this cluster of gifts may almost be said to constitute experience . . . Therefore, if I should certainly say to a novice, "Write from experience and experience only," I should feel that this was rather a tantalising monition if I were not careful immediately to add, "Try to be one of the people on whom nothing is lost!"

Far from laying down a set of rules for the novel, "The Art of Fiction" is directed against the mechanical prescriptions of another writer, Walter Besant, who, in a misguided way, was trying to have fiction recognized belatedly as one of the fine arts. When Besant advises the aspiring writer to carry a notebook and jot down what he observes, James comments that "his case would be easier, and the rule would be more exact, if Mr. Besant had been able to tell him what notes to take. But this, I fear, he can never learn in any manual; it is the business of his life." Henry James would dearly love to have the imaginative potential of the novel acknowledged and to have its cultural status secured. But he refuses to do so by codifying its techniques into a practical routine, which was just what some later critics would extract from his own novels and essays. The seemingly modest shift from James's *art* of fiction to Percy Lubbock's *craft* of fiction is really an ominous devolution toward an academic model.

Trilling once described this questionable process as a way of bolstering the superego of the novel. Lawrence and James see the dead hand of formal rigor as a contrivance of classifying critics and cultural watchdogs, not as a true understanding of what fiction is. "The only classification of the novel that I can understand," writes James,

> is into that which has life and that which has it not. The novel and the romance, the novel of incident and that of character—these clumsy separations appear to me to have been made by critics and readers for their own convenience, and to help them out of their occasional queer predicaments, but to have little reality or interest for the producer, from whose point of view it is of course that we are attempting to consider the art of fiction.

I have gone into James's view in such detail because he is usually taken as the leading defender of the novel as an art form, and as the point of origin of the formal and academic study of fiction and its techniques. Yet James himself is eager to deter such pedantry, which has increased immeasurably since his time. But since reality itself is unstable, the language of fiction, so long as it was to remain responsive to the real world, could hardly remain unchanged. This was the wrinkle that complicated the realist program of later James and other modern writers. According to Frank Kermode, the split between advanced and traditional fiction became critical during the Edwardian period, with James, Conrad, and Ford Madox Ford leagued against Wells, Galsworthy, and Arnold Bennett. "Much of the history of the novel in the present century," Kermode writes, "is dominated by the notion that technical changes of a radical kind are necessary to preserve a living relation between the book and the world." [Kermode, *The Art of Telling*] Kermode views the split entirely from the vantage point of the incipient modernism, yet he justifies technical innovation in terms of fidelity to life, as James does, not simply as experiments in language. From this point of view, Molly Bloom's stream-of-consciousness monologue in *Ulysses* is the last word in fictional realism, however much it may

have widened the new chasm between vanguard fiction and the popular audience. This was a separation that James himself regretted and deplored, unlike the critics who followed his wake.

Even in its many experimental adventures and deformations, the novel remained the wild child of literature, the natural son that could never be fully legitimated. While making the case for realism, craftsmanship, and imagination in fiction, James confirms its essential character as an open and indeterminate form, oriented toward life rather than self-referential. "Many people speak of it as a factitious, artificial form, a product of ingenuity," James writes, only to insist that the contrary is true: "Catching the very note and trick, the strange irregular rhythm of life, that is the attempt whose strenuous force keeps Fiction upon her feet."

This openness toward life is one of the key features of Mikhail Bakhtin's theory of the novel, the only modern theory that does full justice to the novel as a mixed and indeterminate genre, an uncompleted genre constantly in process of formation. Bakhtin's view helps account for the fierce resistance to fiction by the upholders of culture, for he sees the novel not as a genre like epic and tragedy but as a parodic, destabilizing force which renovates older genres but also "infects them with its spirit of process and inconclusiveness." [Bakhtin, *The Dialogic Imagination*] Even in ancient times, he argues, the spirit of the novel was one of contemporaneity, a spirit which undermined the classical vision of "a world projected into the past, on to the distanced plane of memory, but not into a real, relative past tied to the present by uninterrupted temporal transitions; it was projected rather into a valorized past of beginnings and peak times." In Bakhtin's theory, epic and tragedy are completed genres in which the "past is distanced, finished and closed like a circle." The novel, on the other hand, with its deflationary immediacy, its self-consciousness about genre, and its awe before the mystery of individual behavior, embodies the spirit of modernity that resists the closure of genre and recreates the open weave of life itself.

This carefully created illusion that fiction gives us life "*without* rearrangement," without artifice, is deeply ingrained in the early history of the novel. It helps explain why the novel was so long ignored or viewed with suspicion by critics and aestheticians. In its transparency and popularity it remained a challenge to literary history, and it violated classical decorum in both its style and subject. Arguing against those who hoped to see fiction *elevated* into art, purified of its gross realism (especially the French kind), James wrote that "art is essentially selection, but it is a selection whose main care is to be typical, to be inclusive." If Defoe was our first novelist, it was partly because he seemed so artless and unselective, so rooted in matter-of-fact. In *Factual Fictions* Lennard J. Davis has written a convincing study of the origins of fiction in the journalism of the eighteenth century. Davis's starting points are the many assertions of documentary veracity that distinguished early novelists from writers of romance, who trafficked in the marvelous, the exotic, and the improbable. Thus Lord Chesterfield described a romance as "twelve volumes, all filled with insipid love, nonsense, and the most incredible adventures." According to Dr. Johnson, "Why this wild strain of imagination found reception so long, in polite and learned ages, it is not easy to conceive." The novel, on the other hand, in the words of Clara Reeve, "gives us a familiar relation of such things, as pass everyday before our eyes, such as may happen to our friend, or to ourselves and we are affected by the joys or distresses of the person in the story, as if they were our own." If the novelists of the period, says Davis, "refused to concede that they were writing fiction, perhaps it was because fiction was too limiting a concept for them; they were in their own sense of themselves still writing news—only, in this case, news stripped of its reference to immediate public events."

Daniel Defoe is the crucial case, the prototype of the journalist-turned-novelist who did not even take up fiction until he was nearly sixty. In his own time he was known almost exclusively as a prolific journalist and political pamphleteer. "Defoe the great novelist is an invention of the nineteenth century," says Pat Rogers. "In his own day . . . he was thought of as a controversialist." [Rogers, *Defoe: The Critical Heritage*] After his death he was forgotten for decades. Yet *Robinson Crusoe* stood apart from his other work to become perhaps the most famous book of the eighteenth century, as widely read and frequently imitated on the continent as in England and America. *Robinson Crusoe*'s position in the history of the novel is likely never to be fully pinned down, for some of the very qualities that make Defoe a novelist also separate him from most of his successors. The flatness of his prose is part of his remarkable realism of circumstantial detail, yet it carries over into a flatness of emotional tone that limits the subjective element so important to fictional realism. Though Defoe's novels are cast as autobiographical narratives, his protagonists are too engrossed in the struggle for existence to waste much time on feeling or sensibility. The psychological novel begins with Richardson rather than Defoe or Fielding.

Robinson Crusoe creates special difficulties for the historian of fiction. Though it is often described as the first English novel, its isolated setting and lonely hero belong more to the exotic realm of travel writing, adventure, and romance than to the social world of the novel. Davis is only the most recent of many critics who express uneasiness with the accepted place of Defoe's novel at the head of the fictional line: "*Robinson Crusoe,* in many ways, seems like the wrong locus—the exquisitely wrong place—to begin a consideration of the origins of the novel. *Crusoe* is such an atypical work, so devoid of society, of human interaction, so full of lists and micro-observations." [Davis, *Factual Fictions*]

He goes on to suggest that perhaps it is precisely their artlessness, their intermediate status between fact and fiction, that accounts for the paradoxical centrality of

Defoe's novels within the fictional tradition. If it is true that his novels have "no dazzling plots, not much in the way of form—just a kind of dogged attention to the cumulative details, to getting the story down on record," then this is peculiarly consistent with James's remark that "the air of reality (solidity of specification) seems to me to be the supreme virtue of the novel—the merit on which all its other merits . . . helplessly and submissively depend" (p. 53). This is a good explanation of Defoe's importance, as well as his ambiguous status, but it doesn't account for the special fame of *Robinson Crusoe,* which was universally known and read long before Defoe's other novels began to be rediscovered. The oddity of *Crusoe*'s position dissolves when we see it as a landmark in popular culture, not just as the first English novel.

Though fiction itself, as we have argued, is prototypical of the popular arts, there are fictional genres and individual novels that have achieved a special hold on the popular imagination. Often these works compensate for their literary deficiencies—clumsiness of plot, shallow characterization, merely workmanlike style—by their strength as parables or archetypes, their mythic force, or their psychological reverberations. Typically, the characters and their stories transcend the works themselves; they go into orbit as proverbial lore and get translated repeatedly into other media—into puppet shows, plays, comic books, and films, where they become known to many who have not read the originals, to many who can not even read. One of the marks of popular art, as Leslie Fiedler has argued, is that it depends so little on its original form, as if its author has accidentally tapped into a psyche much larger than his own, and made himself irrelevant in the process. The power of such works seems capable of surviving an infinite range of adaptation, simplification, even betrayal. Many critics and literary historians see these novels as merely crude and deficient, or worse still, pandering to mass taste, even when they themselves have helped create that taste. In the standard histories of literature these works are often peripheral or missing entirely, but when included they are consigned to a twilight zone, a no-man's land between art and the popular imagination. If they come from the pen of major authors—I'm thinking of *Crusoe* here, or Cooper's Leatherstocking Tales, Poe's detective and horror stories, and Hawthorne's and H. G. Wells's prototypes of science fiction—they slip in under the *auteur* theory, or as significant items for cultural history or the study of genres. Other enduring works like Bram Stoker's *Dracula* or Owen Wister's *The Virginian* are rarely admitted, despite their importance to the popular myths and genres that flow from them like irresistible undercurrents in literary history.

Though not strictly original themselves, these books initiate vigorous, almost unkillable popular traditions. The mutations of Gothic can be traced from Walpole's *Castle of Otranto* to the most recent horror films. *Robinson Crusoe* gave rise to hundreds of adventure novels, though Paul Zweig has argued that its hero, cautious, calculating, and methodical, is anything but an adventurer himself. Its influence is most obvious in boys' novels and children's literature, but it can be found more subtly in every variety of masculine action story, with its emphasis on plot, its paucity of inwardness and complex emotion, and its concentration on risk, physical action, individual fortitude, and survival. I have already mentioned other genres and their progenitors—Poe and the detective story, Cooper and the Western, Wells and science fiction. These are also works which engendered indestructible myths—*Frankenstein, Dracula, Tarzan of the Apes*. These and other novels could be discussed as anomalous popular fiction that tests the boundaries of the canon, confounds traditional criticism, and stymies literary history. For the remainder of this essay, however, I'll confine myself to the strand of action and adventure that descends from *Crusoe* and the strain of lurid sentiment and sensuality that is an important element of Gothic. As a prototype for Gothic I'll use not the frigid, cerebral *Castle of Otranto* but Matthew G. Lewis's genuinely terrifying and lubricious novel *The Monk* (1796), one of the wildest excesses of Gothic fiction—an immensely popular and scandalous work in its period. Between these two dialectical poles I hope to cover a broad spectrum of popular fiction: masculine and feminine, natural and supernatural, behavioral and psychological, asexual and hypersexual, action-oriented and feeling-bound.

In one sense these popular novels seem to violate the prescriptions of Lawrence and James: they are elaborately formal, highly patterned works. Lawrence writes that "in the novel, the characters can do nothing but *live*. If they keep on being good, according to pattern, or bad, according to pattern, or even volatile, according to pattern, they cease to live, and the novel falls dead." [Lawrence, "Why the Novel Matters"] But when Lawrence set out to confront the classics of American literature, he was quick to grasp the mythic and psychological patterns in Cooper, Poe, Hawthorne, and Melville. Though many of their books were far from popular when they first came out, the quasi-mythic patterns of American romance are closer to popular fiction than to the European novel of social realism. This didn't mean that the romance writer was free of the need to be concrete and credible, within the limits of his *donnée* or objective. "I can think of no obligation to which the 'romancer' would not be held equally with the novelist," wrote Henry James. "The standard of execution is equally high for each." In his famous comparison of *Treasure Island*—one of *Robinson Crusoe*'s best-known descendants—with a novel by Edmond de Goncourt about "a little French girl," James wrote that "one of these productions strikes me as exactly as much of a novel as the other, and as having a 'story' quite as much. The moral consciousness of a child is as much a part of life as the islands of the Spanish Main." James here is insisting on the eventfulness of his own fiction of "moral consciousness" but his point is broader and cuts both ways.

Popular fiction generally combines a realism of detail with a premise that is mythical, exotic, or formulaic. As Robert Warshow says of popular film genres like the gangster film and the Western, "one goes to any individual example of the type with very definite expectations." In another essay he writes, "the proper function of realism in a Western movie can only be to deepen the lines of that pattern." [Warshow, *The Immediate Experience*] This may put too strict an emphasis on formula, not enough on the realism that makes the formula fresh and credible. The closer a piece of writing comes to the fantastic and the surreal, the more it depends on vivid details to make the fantasy believable. This was one of the lessons of Kafka's style that was lost on most of his imitators.

All fiction requires a degree of projection and identification on the reader's part, but popular works appeal more directly to the reader's (or viewer's) fantasy life and less to his sense of verisimilitude, his recognition of lived reality. Soap operas and pornographic works are extreme examples of stories that obey their own laws, with only occasional resemblances to the real world. They appeal to their audience's fantasy lives directly, within a self-enclosed setting. In a work like *Robinson Crusoe,* the enclosed setting is minutely realized, just as Kafka methodically constructs Gregor Samsa's life as an insect (in a story in which only the first sentence, the premise, stretches the laws of nature: everything else flows naturally from it). Thus Robinson Crusoe makes himself and his own life the object of almost scientific observation. This is Defoe's conception of the novelist's craft as well as Crusoe's character. After describing some of his own reactions to things, Crusoe writes: "Let the naturalists explain these things, and the reason and manner of them; all I can say to them is to describe the fact, which was even surprising to me when I found it."

Within the popular novel, as in the traditions of the American romance, the relationship to nature is often more important than social relationships. *Robinson Crusoe* is a prototypical story of isolated man and the quest for survival apart from the props of social life. Crusoe is presented at the outset as an unskilled man who must learn all the crafts and skills on which human survival was founded, from making clothes and hunting to boatbuilding, agriculture, and the raising of domestic animals. (John J. Richetti has written of "Crusoe's informal recapitulation of the history of civilization." [Richetti, *Defoe's Narratives: Situations and Structures*]) The book has been imitated in other stories about survival influenced by Freud's account of the conflict between biological man and social man, such as William Golding's *Lord of the Flies* and Bernard Malamud's recent *Crusoe* imitation, *God's Grace*. The latter work, like other recent social fables, portrays a postnuclear devastation in which the social structure has disappeared, leaving unaccommodated man to act out the logic of his own nature.

In the eighteenth century, this Freudian questioning of the imperatives of civilization—or of a particular social order—was a major theme of travel literature and its fictional imitations, such as *Crusoe, Gulliver's Travels,*

Montesquieu's *Persian Letters,* Voltaire's *Candide,* and Diderot's *Supplement to Bougainville's "Voyage".* The descendants of these works in the nineteenth century were in the literature of adventure and the novel of imperialism, such as Conrad's *Heart of Darkness,* where a jungle of inner and outer horror takes the place of the seraglio of Montesquieu and the island paradise of Diderot. This is a kind of test-tube literature, a set of controlled experiments on human nature, and its findings have darkened with the passage of time. In the twentieth century this fundamental moral probing gives a serious dimension to popular culture; each genre in its own way tries to define the fringes and limits of civilization. Science fiction is one obvious example, but Westerns and hard-boiled detective novels also pursue this theme.

In the frontier setting of the Western, the rule of law and the norms of society have either been suspended or are scarcely in place. Like Crusoe on his island, the Western hero is an isolated man who imposes his own kind of order in a world of moral chaos and physical danger. But Crusoe is less a hero than a survivor, a cunning and resourceful man. He is like the ordinary Englishman raised to the highest power, nursing his fears, building barriers against the unknown, accumulating, defending, and domesticating everything around him. Yet for all his homely virtues, his wanderlust was his original sin; his hankering for adventure and fortune made it impossible for him to follow the tepid, prudent advice of his father. Quiet times are anathema to him and lead him into spectacular errors of judgment; only danger brings out his skill, fortitude, and practical sharpness.

The hero of the Western is a transitional figure for a transitional stage of culture. When he creates at least a minimum of order out of a situation of lawless violence he renders himself irrelevant. Once evil has been expelled, as at the end of *High Noon,* he can remove his badge and fade away into the peaceful sunset of love and marriage, or, like John Wayne at the end of *Stagecoach,* to a ranch in Mexico where he will be "saved from the blessings of civilization." But in the detective novels of Dashiell Hammett, James M. Cain, Raymond Chandler, and Ross Macdonald, evil is not something that can simply be expelled by solving a crime or closing a case. The desert island and the wild frontier give way to the urban jungle whose mean streets reflect a corruption that seems implacable and ineradicable. Though these stories are set in populated towns and cities, the men charged with bringing order are as solitary as Crusoe and his man Friday, and as terse as the tight-lipped Man of the West.

Very few serious modern novels allow their characters to claim any real mastery over the world they live in, or even over their own inner lives. Only in popular culture do we find a remnant of the old heroes of epic, imperfect men who are now often implicated in the corruption of their environment. "Down these mean streets a man must go who is not himself mean, who is neither tarnished nor afraid," wrote Raymond Chandler in his famous tribute to the hard-boiled detective created by Dashiell Hammett

and the *Black Mask* writers of the 1920s. Yet in the same essay in which he romanticizes this hero, he praises Hammett and the genre he created for their realism, at least in comparison to the cerebral and abstract puzzle-mysteries that preceded them: "Hammett gave murder back to the kind of people that commit it for reasons, not just to provide a corpse; and with the means at hand, not with hand-wrought dueling pistols, curare and tropical fish. He put these people down on paper as they were, and he made them talk and think in the language they customarily used for these purposes." [Chandler, *The Simple Art of Murder*]

Though Hammett's plots could be baroque and his style a little purple, in some ways he did to the murder mystery what Defoe had done to the literature of travel and adventure: he brought to it a new realism of detail and simplicity of style. At the same time he personalized it around the experiences of memorable and authentic characters. Perhaps under the influence of Hemingway as well as his own laconic personality, Hammett was a great believer in clean, simple, and direct writing. His biographer, Diane Johnson, has unearthed a miniature essay on style which he wrote for an advertising magazine in 1926. It attacks florid and gaudy writing not for being too literary but as "not sufficiently literary." The plain style, with the shortest sentences, he argues, is the hardest thing in the world for literature to achieve, and the last place we would find it is in a transcription of actual conversation:

> There are writers who do try it, but they seldom see print. Even such a specialist in the vernacular as Ring Lardner gets his effect of naturalness by skillfully editing, distorting, simplifying, coloring the national tongue, and not by reporting it verbatim.

> Simplicity and clarity are not to be got from the man in the street. They are the most elusive and difficult of literary accomplishments, and a high degree of skill is necessary to any writer who would win them.

But Hammett not only knew his craft—he described himself in a letter, in a rare spasm of immodesty, as one of the few people interested in making "literature" of the detective story—he also knew his subject. How much Hammett had learned from observation, and from his experience as a Pinkerton agent, is clear enough from his fiction but also from another essay dug up by Johnson, this one on being a private detective, from the *Saturday Review.* With his usual brevity and understatement, Hammett itemizes twenty-four nuts-and-bolts details about weapons, wounds, corpses, fingerprints, and even criminal argot—all things that ignorant or indifferent detective-story writers usually get wrong. (These sometimes remind me of Blake's "Proverbs of Hell.")

> 6. When you are knocked unconscious you do not feel the blow that does it.

Others emerge jokingly from the trained ear of a writer who listens:

18. "Youse" is the plural of "you."

Still others have the patient, pedantic simplicity of a manual:

19. A trained detective shadowing a subject does not ordinarily leap from doorway to doorway and does not hide behind trees and poles. He knows no harm is done if his subject sees him now and then.

21. Fingerprints are fragile affairs. Wrapping a pistol or other small object up in a handkerchief is much more likely to obliterate than to preserve any prints it may have.

Despite this emphasis on realistic detail, Hammett's wildly complicated plots are as far-fetched as his slangy dialogue is dated. Just as the brisk, busy action of *Robinson Crusoe* is framed by a religious allegory that resembles *Pilgrim's Progress,* the gang wars and innumerable murders in *Red Harvest,* Hammett's first novel, form a parable of corruption that touches even the detective himself. The Bunyanesque name of the town, Personville, has become "Poisonville"—toxic to all who pass through it, including the detective, who says: "I've arranged a killing or two in my time, when they were necessary. But this is the first time I've ever got the fever. It's this damned burg. You can't go straight here." Later he adds: "Poisonville is right. It's poisoned me." At one point he suspects himself of having murdered the one person there who means anything to him—a woman who is also the all-purpose traitor in a town in which anyone will sell anything and betrayal is a way of life. The detective cleans up the town in an unorthodox way, by setting the rival gangs up against each other. But he's upset to find he's begun to enjoy it: "I've got hard skin all over what's left of my soul, and after twenty years of messing around with crime I can look at any sort of a murder without seeing anything in it but my bread and butter, the day's work. But this getting a rear out of planning deaths is not natural to me. It's what this place has done to me."

The tough skin of the hard-boiled hero is like the defensive shell Crusoe develops to survive on his desert island. He too rarely lets moral qualms stand in his way. There are few moments in the book when Crusoe's motivation doesn't seem entirely secular, expedient, and self-interested. This leaves room for many readers to ignore or doubt the importance of the religious framework of the novel. Martin Green does not even bother to argue that "the spiritual autobiography aspect of the book is unimportant," because "everything that is vivid and exciting in the book is independent of that framework." [Green, *Dreams of Adventure, Deeds of Empire*] The best evidence for Green's position is that very few readers even noticed this framework until scholars like G. A. Starr and J. Paul Hunter made an issue of it in the 1960s. Crusoe has neither the depth nor the vocation for a protagonist of spiritual autobiography. Yet this motif recurs frequently enough in the novel to dispel any hint of insincerity on Defoe's part. Still, Crusoe's recurring bouts of self-accu-

sation have so little connection to his practical skills and worldly motives that they call to mind the rhetoric of sin, damnation, and redemption that sometimes frames works of pornography. There too we sometimes find puritanical authors deeply immersed in all they condemn; there too it can be said that "everything that is vivid and exciting is independent of that framework." There too, as in a great deal of popular culture, there may be unresolved conflicts of values rather than a deliberate cynicism. Or else a moral framework may be a defense mechanism against the kind of social censorship that is quick to condemn popular fantasies and to insist on strict poetic justice.

Crime and detective stories are among the last outposts of the kind of individualism that enters fiction with *Robinson Crusoe:* the belief in the power of the individual to solve problems, to correct wrongs, and to control his own destiny. The classic detectives like Dupin and Holmes express a nineteenth-century faith in the power of mind to create order out of a welter of mean motives and jealous passions. In the twentieth century this kind of mastery survives *only* in popular culture, as a fantasy which compensates for the widespread feeling that larger, more impersonal forces now dominate the destiny of individuals. Heroism becomes a beleaguered and questionable idea. The hard-boiled detective is very close to the moral chaos of his opponents, skirting the edge of the law in a world where law itself has been bought and corrupted. His individualism has been reduced from a belief in an ordered, rational society only temporarily out of balance to a mere personal code, a stubborn, irrational insistence on some kind of individual honor among grasping people in an insane and arbitrary world. "You'll never understand me, but I'll try once more and then we'll give it up," says Sam Spade to Brigid O'Shaughnessy at the end of *The Maltese Falcon,* as he's about to send her up. "Listen. When a man's partner is killed he's supposed to do something about it. It doesn't make any difference what you thought of him. He was your partner and you're supposed to do something about it." But he also has other, less honorable motives. Though he loves the treacherous Brigid, again and again he says, "I'm not going to play the sap for you." Later he adds, "Don't be too sure I'm as crooked as I'm supposed to be." Even some of the killers in Hammett's world have the same stoical virtues. Of one of them at the end of *Red Harvest* we're told, "He meant to die as he had lived, inside the same tough shell." This was the way Hammett himself died, some thirty years later.

The moral chaos we find in hard-boiled fiction can also be found in the Gothic novel going back to the eighteenth century. If *Robinson Crusoe* comes at the beginning of a whole line of masculine adventure stories, full of laconic, purposeful, unemotional heroes, the Gothic novel sets in motion a feminine line of popular fiction—elusive, lubricious, impassioned, and centered around female vulnerability rather than male mastery. This is the most Freudian of all literary modes, built on dreams, fears, and sexual fantasies to an amazing degree, and often hedged about by a teasing moralistic framework. These episodic works resemble modern serials and soap operas. J. M. S. Tompkins sums up the usual plot of an Ann Radcliffe romance in the following way:

> They play, for the most part, in glamorous southern lands and belong to a past which, although it is sometimes dated, would not be recognized by an historian. In all of them a beautiful and solitary girl is persecuted in picturesque surroundings, and, after many fluctuations of fortune, during which she seems again and again on the point of reaching safety, only to be thrust back into the midst of perils, is restored to her friends and marries the man of her choice. [Tompkins, *The Popular Novel in England, 1770-1800*]

In M. G. Lewis's *The Monk* there are no neat resolutions and happy endings. Instead of picturesque surroundings we find grim convents and monasteries which sit atop secret passages and charnel-like catacombs where women are sadistically tormented and sexually abused under the guise of religious severity. The lawless isolation of the Gothic convent or castle is like a nocturnal phantasmagoria of Crusoe's solitude on his desert island. Both are northern, Protestant visions, one of industry, sublimation, and salvation through good works, the other of Mediterranean Catholic decadence, self-indulgence, and immorality.

The violent settings of Gothic novels go back to the Spanish and Italian locale of Elizabethan revenge tragedies and gory Jacobean dramas of lust, incest, fratricide, and religious hypocrisy. To this the writers add touches of the Restoration rake, Clarissa Harlowe's interminable, operatic defense of her innocence, and the new taste for medieval ballads, supernatural tales, German romances, graveyard poetry, and sublunar Romantic melancholy. The claptrap of Gothic exists on two levels, a mumbo-jumbo of trite supersition and cumbersome machinery and a deeper psychological penetration of the kind we meet in Ambrosio, the diabolical, depraved monk of Lewis's scabrous novel. When we first meet Ambrosio he is like Shakespeare's Angelo in *Measure for Measure,* a man so repressed and severe that he "scarce confesses / That his blood flows." [From the epigraph to chapter 1 of Lewis, *The Monk*] We hear it said that "too great severity" may be his "only fault", making him as harsh on others as he is on himself. But these rigid spirits are the first to fall, especially in a world so repressed, yet so saturated with desire, that even a glimpse of skin can evoke murderous, all-consuming passions. The core of *The Monk* is the same sex and violence that have been the mainstays of popular culture ever since. The moral and religious framework is a mere container for garish fantasies of sin and violation, sex and damnation. We are meant to identify with both the seducer Ambrosio and the virgins he despoils; the book plays on our fantasies of both omnipotence and vulnerability, violence and violation.

Significantly, Ambrosio's own tutor in evil is an androgynous woman—really an agent of the devil—who has disguised herself as a boy to get close to him. In male action stories men flee from women, ignore them, or use and discard them. Robinson Crusoe does not even seem to be sublimating, as Gulliver does, for sex and women mean little or nothing to him. He lives in a daylight world of doing rather than feeling, surviving and accumulating rather than desiring. But the equally self-enclosed world of the Gothic novel belongs to the night-side of consciousness, full of irrational needs and sexual symptoms. Women are demonic goddesses in this world, figures of irresistible innocence or unfathomable deviousness setting up a fatal field of attraction in a secret world cut off from our norms of law and morality. The most lucid and consistent exponent of Gothic is the Marquis de Sade, who performs experiments on the parts of human nature Defoe leaves out.

One striking feature of *The Monk* that is still with us in recent horror films is the association of sex with terror, putrescence, and decay. The novel's two heroines, the innocent virgin, Antonia, and the pure but fallen woman, Agnes, end up imprisoned in dungeons beneath the holy convent. There Antonia is finally ravished and later stabbed by the lustful monk (actually her long-lost brother), who has been coveting her tender flesh through most of the novel, and Agnes actually gives birth to a baby, who eventually dies and decays under her very eyes. ("It soon became a mass of putridity, and to every eye was a loathsome and disgusting object, to every eye but a mother's".) Most of the novel is not quite this ghoulish, but when Agnes, who survives, tells her story, this is the kind of thing we hear:

> My slumbers were constantly interrupted by some obnoxious insect crawling over me. Sometimes I felt the bloated toad, hideous and pampered with the poisonous vapour of the dungeon, dragging his loathsome length along my bosom. Sometimes the quick cold lizard roused me, leaving his slimy track upon my face, and entangling itself in the tresses of my wild and matted hair. Often have I at waking found my fingers ringed with the long worms which bred in the corrupted flesh of my infant. At such times I shrieked with terror and disgust; and, while I shook off the reptile, trembled with all a woman's weakness.

This reads like an unintentional parody of Edmund Burke's recent definition of the sublime as a form to beauty founded on terror, a catharsis of pain and fear. It could only have been written when religious ideas of heaven and hell had begun to lose their following and to migrate into pop mythology. Like some of the work of the Marquis de Sade, *The Monk* is a genuine product of that revolutionary decade, the 1790s, when the Enlightenment both came to fulfillment and turned into the Terror, with its dreams of reason transformed into the nightmares of unreason.

Gothic novels, like detective stories and tales of adventure, are among the bastard children of literature, naked and artless in their emotional appeal yet artificial and formulaic in their literary strategies. They are stories in which the machinery of plot and atmosphere overshadows individual characters, yet this machinery and the people caught in it can reach us with surprising power, as they do in the last pages of *The Monk,* where the gruesome fate of Ambrosio takes on some of the fierce coloring of the downfall of Milton's Satan, and becomes a link to the Byronic criminal-heroes of the nineteenth century. Donald Fanger has shown how a significant strain of the Gothic and the grotesque runs through the great European realists like Balzac, Dickens, and Dostoevsky, and helps account for the heightened and intense effects they achieve. The importance of the Gothic line in American fiction, from Brockden Brown, Poe, and George Lippard to Faulkner, Carson McCullers, and other Southern writers, has been discussed too frequently to need further comment here. Richard Chase explains this by arguing that

> melodrama is suitable to writers who do not have a firm sense of living in a culture. The American novelists tend to ideology and psychology; they are adept at depicting the largest public abstractions and the smallest and most elusive turn of the inner mind. But they do not have a firm sense of a social arena where ideology and psychology find a concrete representation and are seen in their fullest human significance. [Chase, *The American Novel and Its Tradition*].

This is well formulated but also very much of its time, the 1950s, for it implies an aesthetic hierarchy in which social realism is the norm and melodrama the mutation, the despised variant, not fully formed, unevenly developed. This becomes clear when he remarks wittily that melodrama is "tragedy in a vacuum," or that "the American novel abounds in striking but rather flatly conceived *figures*" but "has been poor in notable and fully rounded *characters*." But tragedy, canonical as it is, has been available to writers at only a few periods of Western cultural history, and "fully rounded characters" may not be what an author most needs to express the world as he imagines it.

Chase's remarks may help explain why Gothic has played such an important part in another branch of literary history: in women's writing. Ellen Moers devotes two important chapters in *Literary Women* to what she calls Female Gothic. This includes her famous interpretation of Mary Shelley's *Frankenstein* as a birth fantasy, built around "the revulsion against newborn life, and the drama of guilt, dread, and flight surrounding birth and its consequences." But comments like this may be too literal-minded to be of much use, as when Moers adds that "most of the novel, roughly two of its three volumes, can be said to deal with the retribution visited upon monster and creator for deficient infant care. Perhaps a broader view of Female Gothic may be adapted from Chase's assertion that "melodrama is suitable to writers who do not have a firm sense of living in a culture." This is more true of women writers, deprived of any role in public life, barred from most economic activity outside the home, than it is for American writers in general. The themes of enclosure, imprisonment, and victimization which are central to Gothic have a quite realistic relation to women's lives in the eighteenth and nineteenth centuries, however exotically they appear in the novels. Melodrama abstracts women from a social space where their behavior is constricted, into a realm of exaggerated feeling which is all the more intense for reflecting an essential powerlessness. Male critics in turn have marked down Gothic as second-rate literature or subliterature, having helped create the social vacuum and psychological maelstrom which defines the limits of the genre.

The surprising thing about the dismissal of Gothic from the domain of literature is that, because of its hothouse atmosphere, its artificiality, the form is intensely literary. We have a stereotype of popular fiction as something transparent, artless, and essentially unwritten. This is far from true of most Gothic writing, which tends often to be literary in the wrong sense: as decorated or ornate as the architectural style to which it is distantly indebted. The temptation for Gothic writers—or for neo-Gothic filmmakers like Brian De Palma—is to turn their work into exercises in style, leaving a good deal of human reality behind. But the Gothic novel is also literary in a more serious sense, in its elaborate structural complexities. The interminable subplot of *The Monk* is a negative example, interestingly parallel to the main plot but only tenuously and clumsily interwoven with it. Important characters, including the protagonist Ambrosio, disappear for more than a hundred pages at a time, suspended in mid-gesture while the reader seems to have fallen into a different novel. But this eccentric architecture reflects the labyrinthine vision of the novels.

Works like Mary Shelley's *Frankenstein* and Bram Stoker's *Dracula,* which have come down to us in simplified film versions, are prodigies of internal complexity; their stories, told in an arch and elevated style, reach us by way of a hall of mirrors of multiple narrators: fragments, confessions, letters, diaries, with third-person accounts alternating with first-person accounts, as if the essential reality were far too terrible to be approached directly, as if the heart of the novel were a conundrum rather than explanation. The morbid and shadowy mysteries of Gothic make the simpler mysteries of most detective stories seem like child's play rather than a truly problematic vision of the nature of things. "This secret is nothing at all," Edmund Wilson complained. [Wilson, "Who Cares Who Killed Roger Ackroyd?" in *Detective Fiction*] "A good writer," adds Geoffrey Hartman, "will make us feel the gap between a mystery and its laying to rest . . . Most popular mysteries are devoted to solving rather than examining the problem. Their reasonings put reason to sleep, abolish darkness by elucidation, and bury the corpse for good." [Hartman, "Literature High and Low: The Case of the Mystery Story," in *The Fate of Reading and Other Essays*] But all the creaky conventions of Gothic cannot conceal a more truly frightening depiction of human irrationality and vulnerability.

When these conventions are refreshed by a first-rate writer, like Melville and Hawthorne, or like Emily Brontë in *Wuthering Heights,* the wheels-within-wheels of Gothic narrative take on exceptional and mysterious power. *Moby-Dick,* with its heightened, claustral environment and baroque language, with Queequeg's coffin and the deformed Ahab's obsessive pursuit of revenge, can be seen as a specimen of shipboard Gothic—a weird cross between Gothic and adventure. Reading *Wuthering Heights,* like reading *Frankenstein* and *Dracula,* is like peeling away the layers of the onion or opening a series of Chinese boxes. The various narrators refract the tales through their own partial perceptions, giving us fragments of the past while amplifying what is terrible and strange about it. Realistic fiction, by contrast, aims at transparency, a world in which the social surface is continuous with the human reality. Thus Erich Auerbach in *Mimesis* stresses "the complementary relation between persons and milieu" in Balzac, as in Madame Vauquer's boarding house in *Le père Goriot,* where "sa personne explique la pension, comme la pension implique sa personne." But Gothic novels, like many mystery stories, insist on the difference between surface and substance, between the clarity of outward forms and the shadowy reality of inner motives and intentions.

Why have Gothic and other forms of genre fiction been ignored or rejected by critics and literary historians, just as the novel in general was long excluded from serious literature, just as movies were consistently belittled as commercial entertainment when the greatest directors in film history had already done their best work? There's probably no higher a proportion of pure trash in popular culture than of mediocre, derivative works in high culture, yet we judge poetry and drama by their deepest reaches, not by their mean product. In the case of Gothic, there's probably something in the outlook of the genre that specially offends the critical mind, a lurid, garish vision of life that sets our orderly procedures and rational assumptions at nought. (Classical British detective stories may be the only kind of genre fiction that doesn't do outrage to the academic mind; that must be why so many dons dashed them off on the side.)

Classically trained critics in the eighteenth and nineteenth centuries condescended to fiction because, like its middle-class audience, it lacked pedigree, decorum, and elevation of manner. Its cast of characters was neither tragic nor dignified; its realist aesthetic was antiformal; it blurred the lines between art and life and broke sharply with the respected genres of ancient writing. But with the triumph of literary realism and the arrival of a new breed of middle-class critic, the same animus was directed against genre fiction—for being *too* formal, *too* generic. Now *its* audience became the rabble who trampled on standards and knew nothing about art, who abused their newly gained literacy with trashy, mass-produced fantasies. The coming of modernism sharpened the split between high and popular fiction by emphasizing originality, difficulty, and experimentation and devaluing the formulaic, stereotypical elements which modern mass culture shares with the folk cultures of the past. It also led to a distrust of storytelling—the vital core of all

narrative, from folklore and epic through nineteenth-century fiction. But the writers themselves rarely heeded this split, and always borrowed freely from every part of the cultural spectrum. Only the critics, sociologists, and literary historians drew sharp boundaries, routinizing the imaginative.

Well, we live in an age of Affirmative Action, even in cultural history. The academic establishment has grown so large that it's always hungry for new subjects, and since the 1960s a new generation has done much to enlarge the canon and to recuperate excluded works for critical study. We forget that in its own time even *The Great Tradition* was a work of recuperation, designed not to limit the English novel to five writers but to gain a more respectful hearing, within a slack and genteel literary culture, for the novel of controlled moral realism. In more recent years, the excluded traditions of blacks and women have been given rooms of their own in the academic structure—in critical studies, anthologies, and course assignments. We can see the beginnings of the same redress in popular culture as well, as the eclectic, antihierarchical spirit of the 1960s inspires a reshaping of the literary canon. Books like Paul Zweig's *The Adventurer,* John G. Cawelti's *Adventure, Mystery, and Romance,* Martin Green's *Dreams of Adventure, Deeds of Empire,* and Leslie Fiedler's *What Was Literature?* apply the same kind of critical attention to popular genres that has already been directed at such excluded categories as the bourgeois novel, the classic film genres, and the writings of blacks and women.

Some of these books on popular writers, like Green's and Fiedler's, have a distinct autobiographical tinge; they read like specimens of conversion literature by critics once committed exclusively to high culture. This gives their writings, especially Fiedler's, a proselytizing edge: a misplaced zeal for popular forms and a polemical bias against something called the "art novel," which evidently includes some of the best fiction ever written. The effect is to confirm the split between high and popular art by inverting it, and to keep popular culture in a gilded ghetto instead of integrating it into a broader, more pluralistic version of literary history. Like fiction as a whole, popular fiction since *Robinson Crusoe* has been created by new kinds of artists for audiences which had never existed before. Not all popular culture is art, but no conception of how art and culture have interacted over the last two and a half centuries can be complete without understanding the role it has played, the needs it satisfies, and the antipathies it arouses among conservative and nostalgic guardians of the old order.

Kenneth C. Davis

SOURCE: "Two-Bit Culture: The Great Contradiction," in *Two-Bit Culture,* Houghton Mifflin Company, 1984, pp. 145-215

[*In the following essay, Davis discusses mass-market paperbacks as a prevailing form of popular literature, describing the development of the paperback book while detailing the competition among publishers.*]

During the first ten years of its existence, the mass market paperback had been the subject of frequent arguments and controversy, but most of the discussion took place within the publishing industry. Trade publishers either liked or didn't like what the paperback houses produced and treated them accordingly. Some trade houses still refused to sell rights to the reprinters. Among the others who did, there were those who handled the reprinters gingerly, like dead fish, at arm's length. Often they assigned a secretary the task of carrying out reprint arrangements. (Ironically, that strategy placed many women in key roles just as subsidiary rights flowered in importance to hardcover publishers.) However, the option of ignoring the paperback grew less viable as the reprint was increasingly viewed as a source of income. Reprint royalties were once thought of as icing on the cake of regular trade and book-club sales. But this income was beginning to mount as paperback sales grew, more titles were reprinted, and prices, led by Mentors and Dr. Spock, crept up to thirty-five cents. By the fifties, some hardcover publishers had already turned to the practice of lining up paperback guarantees before signing contracts with the author for a book. Economically at least, the paperback had come of age.

Soon the rest of the world was sitting up and taking notice of this precocious ten-year-old. To be sure, much of the discussion centered on those (gasp! ugh!) covers. And a great deal of the press coverage accorded to paperbacks treated them as a sort of novelty, a late-1940s version of the Hula-Hoop or Pac-Man. With the coming of the fifties, there was a fundamental change in attitude. Previously, all talk of a Paperback Revolution had been limited to Publishers' Row. But as the sales figures climbed at a seemingly geometric rate, the serious journals, pulse takers, and opinion makers realized it was time to turn this flat rock over and see what crawled out. In the process, they would decide exactly what it all meant for the Republic. Some liked what they found; others thought they had uncovered evidence of the decline of Western civilization. Predictably, there was little agreement. It was the dawn of the great debate over paperback books.

One of the first critics to take a serious look at paperbacks and what they meant was Harvey Swados. Writing in the *Nation* in 1951, Swados outlined the essence of the disaccord that lay ahead:

> Last year, the stupefying total of 214,000,000 paper-bound books was published in this country, as compared with 3,000,000 in 1939. Most of them were sold and the probability is that a larger proportion of them was read than of hard-cover books, many of which are bought as unwanted gifts or as book-club prestige items for the coffee table. Whether this revolution in the reading habits of the American public means that we are being inundated by a flood of trash which will debase farther the popular taste, or that we shall now have available cheap editions of an ever-increasing list of classics, is a question of basic importance to our social and cultural development.

The business that Swados was examining with such gravity was in a state of flux, a rapidly changing period of transition from new-born industry to one in healthy adolescence, complete with growing pains, as new companies seemed to come and go almost overnight. Paperback sales were moving forward, and each year after 1946 brought increases in production and sales. As 1950 began, *The Publishers' Weekly* reported that a large increase in paperback production was planned for the year, and it told of caution and concern among the reprinters who recalled the overproduction and devastating returns of 1946. Nevertheless, most paperback publishers were reporting steady sales gains that went as high as 40 percent over previous years. By year's end, a survey of the industry estimated 1950 paperback sales at 200 million copies (compared with 147 million in 1948 and 184 million in 1949), with some eight hundred titles issued, worth about $46 million in revenue. A breakdown of production by individual firm gave an indication of Pocket Books' size and relative strength: Pocket, 50 million books; Bantam, 38 million; New American Library, 30 million; Dell, 25 million; Avon, 15 million; Popular Library, 15 million.

Another indication of the changing face of the paperback business was the upward movement in cover prices. For ten years, twenty-five cents had been an inviolable barrier, with two exceptions: Penguin had pushed the price of the nonfiction Pelicans (later NAL's Mentors) to thirty-five cents, and Pocket Books had done likewise with *The Pocket Book of Baby and Child Care,* which had already become the company's fastest and best-selling book. But fiction was still universally priced at twenty-five cents in paperback. Then, in June 1950, New American Library shook the industry by announcing its plans to publish longer novels at thirty-five and fifty cents. In order to get customers to shell out the extra dime, NAL called the thirty-five cent books Signet Giants. (Allen Lane had already used a similar strategy in England with Penguin Giants.)

The first book in the thirty-five-cent series was Richard Wright's *Native Son.* Wright was born outside Natchez, Mississippi, in 1908, the son of a sharecropper who deserted the family when Wright was five. After a childhood of roving from one foster home to the next, he ended up in Chicago in 1927, living on odd jobs and going on relief when the Depression hit. He joined the Communist party in 1934 and turned his talent to writing Marxist publications, later working for the Federal Writers' Project. In 1936, after moving to New York, he wrote the *WPA Guide to Harlem,* and in 1938 he won a prize from *Story* magazine for his novelette "Uncle Tom's Children," which became the title story in a collection published that same year. Living in Brooklyn on a Guggenheim Fellowship, he wrote his first novel, *Na-*

tive Son (1940). It was a brutally violent story of a young black man in Chicago whose frustrated circumstances force him to commit murder. Highly naturalistic, the novel established Wright as a major talent. A stage version followed and then a film in which Wright himself played the lead. In 1945, he added *Black Boy,* an autobiographical account of his first seventeen years, to his accomplishments. It became a best seller that year, a rather extraordinary achievement for a black writer in a still overwhelmingly racist society.

When NAL published *Native Son* in 1950, the company had established itself as the only mass market reprinter willing to consistently handle serious work by black writers or about blacks. In addition to Wright's work, NAL (Penguin before it) had published Chester Himes's *If He Hollers, Let Him Go* and Lillian Smith's *Strange Fruit,* a 1944 best seller about racial relations in the South that had been banned in Boston in a notorious First Amendment case. Later NAL would publish Wright's *Black Boy* and Ralph Ellison's *Invisible Man.*

The company's plan for fifty-cent books required a subtle deception, and it is unlikely that anyone was actually fooled by it. Kurt Enoch devised what he called a double spine, printed in two colors on which the book's title appeared twice, giving the appearance of two books in one. The first of the Signet Double Volumes were Willard Motley's *Knock on Any Door,* Kathleen Winsor's *Forever Amber,* Irwin Shaw's *The Young Lions,* and Norman Mailer's *The Naked and the Dead.* The increase in cover price was more than simply a way to make more money. The rise was unavoidable because of two factors. With a twenty-five-cent ceiling, longer books could not be profitably published without abridgments or condensations. This kept many major writers and books from being reprinted. More significant was the fact that the new cover prices reflected an increasing intensity in the competition for desirable reprint properties. The success of Pocket Books' rivals, specifically NAL and Bantam, meant that jockeying for rights to major novels was becoming more fierce.

The system of acquiring paperback reprints had evolved out of the formula established by the dollar hardcover reprinters like Grosset & Dunlap during the 1930s. The paperback publisher licensed for a limited time the right to issue a paperbound edition of a book at a certain price in English and to sell it in certain specified parts of the world. The paperback publisher guaranteed a stated amount of money (the advance), whether the book earned back the money or not. In the early years, this royalty rate was one cent on the first 150,000 copies and one and a half cents on sales thereafter; if the retail price was higher, the royalty was proportionately increased. The paperback royalties were then split fifty-fifty between author and original hardcover publisher.

The method of acquiring reprint rights involved a simple sealed-bid auction. The winner was the publisher who offered the largest advance without knowledge of what his competitors were proposing. Such modern paperback auction techniques as "floors" (minimums), "topping privileges," and round-robin auctions in which successive bids are solicited by the auctioneer were all creatures of the future. But the auction was where explosive changes were already beginning to transform the paperback and upset the traditional balance of publishing power. By 1952, Doc Lewis of Pocket Books cautioned, "Increasingly, the amount of money required to secure a reprint contract is reaching a level above the amount which is being earned by sales. I would estimate that of the 'big bid' books of the past two years, that is, titles which were acquired by guarantees of *$15,000 or more* [Emphasis added], less than five will ever earn out their minimum guarantees." [Freeman Lewis, *Paperbound Books 17 America*]

The "big bid" books to which Lewis referred undoubtedly included the four titles NAL had issued as Double Volumes. Victor Weybright, in a sort of mad shopping spree, purchased all four books in one week in February 1950, paying $30,000 for *Forever Amber,* $30,000 for *The Naked and the Dead,* $25,000 for *The Young Lions,* and $25,000 for *Knock on Any Door.* With the exception of Willard Motley's *Knock on Any Door,* each book had been a best seller a few years earlier. Mailer's novel had almost reached 200,000 combined bookstore—book-club sales in 1948 and *The Young Lions* had sold around 75,000 copies. Kathleen Winsor's *Forever Amber* was a historical romance with an emphasis on the bawdy, set during the Restoration period. It became the number-four fiction best seller in 1944, was banned in Boston, and then became the number-one seller in 1945, selling 868,630 copies that year alone. Miss Winsor, very photogenic and highly publicized by her hardcover publisher, might have fit in nicely on the television talk show circuit if one had existed in 1945. She looked pretty, could draw a crowd, and yet had little to say. On a promotional tour for Victory bonds during the war, Winsor traveled with Bennett Cerf, MacKinlay Kantor, and Carl Van Doren. Cerf later said of her, "Kathleen Winsor was an amateur speaker at the time and she never learned her speech by heart. She'd come out on stage and fish in her bag, which had everything in it but a live seal, and she'd finally come up with a piece of paper, which she'd carefully unfold. She then read in a colorless monotone." [Bennett Cerf, *At Random*]

For New American Library, Miss Winsor and the other Double Volume gambles paid off, at least temporarily disproving Lewis's dire prediction of the failure to meet guarantees. Appearing on the newsstands in August 1950, *Knock on Any Door* sold out its first printing of 250,000 copies in two weeks. *Forever Amber,* spiced with the "Banned in Boston" imprimatur, sold out its 410,000-copy initial printing in less than a month after it appeared in September, as did the first printing of *The Young Lions.* But of those first four, *The Naked and the Dead* was destined for the greatest success in paperback. The book had been greeted with great fervor when it was initially published. It was also obviously very controversial, presenting a view of the American boy in combat totally at odds with the widely accepted notions that Hollywood had fostered in countless wartime propaganda films starring the likes of Errol Flynn and John Wayne. Mailer, the new enfant terrible of American letters, launched his career amid controversy and mixed critical appraisal. Though the hardcover had been a success, the paperback edition, released in January 1951, had sold one million copies by the following October.

The next two Double Volumes were Kathleen Winsor's *Star Money,* a novel about a successful young writer that had little of the impact of its predecessor, and Louis Bromfield's novel of India, *The Rains Came.* When the plan for Double Volumes at fifty cents had been announced, most other publishers were skeptical, if not convinced that it was doomed. The assumption was that the public was too conditioned by "quarter books" and would balk at the 100 percent price increase. But the Double Volumes were soon outstripping the sales of the regular Signet editions. NAL had taken a key step in breaking down the barrier of price resistance, an ill-defined psychic roadblock that publishers still argue over the way judges used to deal with obscenity: they couldn't say exactly what it was, but they knew it when they saw it. In the wake of NAL's success, other paperback houses naturally followed suit with their own thirty-five- and fifty-cent editions. Bantam countered with Bantam Giants at thirty-five cents and Bantam Fifties. Pocket Books produced Cardinal Books at thirty-five cents and Cardinal Giants at fifty cents. In the meantime, NAL went a step further in 1952 with seventy-five-cent Signet Triples, the first of these being Ayn Rand's *The Fountainhead;* then came James Jones's *From Here to Eternity,* which set a new advance record when Weybright paid $102,000 in one of the first competitive auctions.

The heightened competition for reprints and the surging advances it created, along with the doubling of cover prices and the proliferation of new houses, indicated that the industry was on the move. Before 1950, two more houses that were to survive more than a year were launched. Pyramid Books was the creation of Matthew Huttner and Alfred R. Plaine. In 1949, their first list of mysteries and love stories also included an abridged edition of Wilkie Collins's *The Moonstone.* In that same year, Doubleday launched a hybrid of the hardcover and paperback called Permabooks, rack-sized books bound in laminated board covers. In 1951, Permabooks were shifted over to true paperback covers. At first, Permabooks were mostly anthologies and light nonfiction of the type popularized by Pocket Books, including how-to, self-help, and inspirational books, such as the company's best-selling *The Greatest Story Ever Told* by Fulton Oursler. As the list grew, fiction was later added.

A third new paperback house, launched in 1950, represented a much more portentous branching-out for the paperback business—into the area of original paperbacks. The concept was the child of the Fawcett family and was called Gold Medal Books. Like several of the

paperback imprints that preceded it, Gold Medal had its roots planted firmly in the magazine business. When Pocket Books turned to independent distribution in 1941 to get its paperbacks into the mass market, the magazine world quickly exploited this potential new profit maker. Among the magazine publishers, the Fawcett family was prospering during the heyday of the American magazine—the days before radio, television, and cut-rate subscriptions when magazines were sold almost exclusively on the newsstands. The company's story was a classic rags-to-riches success cut from the Horatio Alger mold. After World War I, Wilford H. "Captain Billy" Fawcett returned to his home in Minnesota where he began producing a small bulletin of barracks humor and chatter for disabled servicemen in a veterans' hospital. A local wholesaler eventually started putting copies of the little magazine in hotel lobbies and drugstores. From this came *Captain Billy's Whiz Bang.* Although the sexual innuendo of the title was intentional, the name came from a notorious World War I artillery shell.

Within a short time, the magazine was circulating half a million copies per month and the company flourished. So did the Fawcett clan. In addition to Captain Billy, there was a brother, Roscoe (who died in 1946), and four sons, Wilford, Jr., Roger, Roscoe, and Gordon, who ran the business following Captain Billy's death in 1940 after the company had been brought east to Greenwich, Connecticut. Though perhaps not an influential giant like Luce's Time, Inc., empire or the powerful Curtis-published *Saturday Evening Post,* Fawcett built a large, successful magazine line with *True, Cavalier,* and *Mechanix Illustrated* for the male market and *True Confessions* and *Motion Picture* for women and teenage girls. The jewel in the family crown, *Woman's Day,* was added in 1948.

While Avon, Dell, and Popular Library had used their magazine experience and the power of the American News Company to join Pocket Books and Penguin before the war, the Fawcetts did not gain their toehold in the paperback industry until 1945 when Ian Ballantine left Penguin to set up Bantam, taking Curtis Circulating with him. Kurt Enoch turned to the Fawcetts as Penguin's national distributor to the independent magazine wholesalers, and two years later, when Weybright and Enoch formed New American Library, Fawcett came along as distributor of the new line.

Encouraged by NAL's seemingly easy success and the apparent license to print money called paperbacks, the Fawcetts soon decided that they wanted a piece of the pie. However, under their contract with NAL, they were forbidden to compete for reprints. So they settled for the next bext thing: an all-original paperback line. Following test runs with *The Best of True Magazine* and *What Today's Woman Should Know About Marriage and Sex*—both adapted from Fawcett magazines—the company launched its Gold Medal line in January 1950. Overseeing the company's editorial direction was Ralph Daigh, who had worked for Captain Billy since 1925. The first editor of the books was Jim Bishop, a *Collier's* magazine editor who later became known for his best sellers *The Day Lincoln Was Shot, The Day Christ Died,* and *The Day Kennedy Was Shot.* Bishop departed after a year and was replaced by William Lengle, a veteran editor at Fawcett magazines. Also to pass through Gold Medal's doors was a Radcliffe graduate named Rona Jaffe, who joined the company in 1952 and left in 1955 to pursue a writing career after being described by *Good Housekeeping* as "Miss Brilliant Promise of the Year." She turned her Fawcett experiences to good use in her first novel, *The Best of Everything* (1958), an "insider's" account of working girls at a large magazine and paperback publishing company obviously modeled on Fawcett.

With initial print runs of two hundred thousand copies, the Gold Medal Books were primarily "category" originals in the Western, mystery, and thriller genres aimed at the male adventure reader. Authors were paid $2000 per book, advances that were based not on sales but on print runs. When the initial printings were increased to three hundred thousand copies, the advance rose to $3000. That was not a bad piece of change for a writer in 1950. If Gold Medal's literary achievements fell short of candidacy for the Pulitzer, the company could lay claim to introducing into paperback two of the giants of the mass market field. John D. MacDonald, chronicler of the corrupt in golden Florida with his Travis McGee mysteries, made his debut with *The Brass Cupcake* (1950). Louis L'Amour, successor to Max Brand as the best-selling Western writer, wrote *Hondo* (1953), which was released in conjunction with the John Wayne film of the same title. The company was also producing original novels by established writers like Sax Rohmer and MacKinlay Kantor, along with works by John (William's brother) Faulkner and Howard Hunt (who later came to fame for his role in Watergate). One of the company's biggest and most notorious best sellers was written by a woman—or so it seemed. *Women's Barracks,* an account of a group of French women soldiers stationed in England during the Occupation, had strong lesbian undertones and a cover showing women in a locker room as they stripped down. The book was ostensibly written by Tereska Torres, but Ralph Daigh later revealed it had been translated by Meyer Levin, not yet known as a best-selling writer. Levin was also Tereska Torres's husband.

A congressional committee damned them, censors yanked them from newsstand racks, and critics sniffed lightly and quickly passed them off as trash—not an unfair assessment in the main. But Gold Medal Books sold. By November 1951, the firm had produced more than nine million books, going back to press with most of the titles and reissuing several of them as many as three or four times.

Although Gold Medal had started the trend toward original publishing in 1950 and the company created a stir over the implications of paperback originals for the industry, the line did not cause the industrywide fear and trembling that accompanied the announcement of still another new firm in early 1952. The plan behind this new

company called for a daring concept that went beyond simple original paperback publishing. It was the brain child of Ian Ballantine, with twelve years of experience now an old-timer in the paperback business. Ballantine proposed publishing simultaneous hardcover-paperback editions of new books in cooperation with regular trade houses, thereby circumventing the established reprinting system and turning the industry on its collective ear. Although the idea has become increasingly common practice in contemporary publishing (in 1982, for instance, it was done with *Pinball* by Jerzy Kosinski and Thomas McGuane's *Nobody's Angel*), it was not the case in 1952. In fact, it was downright subversive, like advocating Communism before the House Un-American Activities Committee.

But Ballantine had proven himself no stranger to controversy and conflict. In fact, they seemed to follow him. He had lived through one great upheaval when he split away from Penguin Books to form Bantam in 1945. The end of his days at Bantam proved to be no less stormy, and he left the company early in 1952. Although he had proven himself an astute student of the art and science of paperback publishing, Ballantine had less facility for the ins and outs of boardroom politics and bottom-line management. He was also thought to be headstrong and unbending. But the board of directors at Bantam was no trifling bunch. The heavy hitters from the publishers who owned Grosset & Dunlap—which in turn owned half of Bantam—were joined by their man John O'Connor, Grosset's president and Ballantine's immediate superior, as well as the men from Curtis Circulating. In other words, it was a formidable line-up. If nothing else, Ballantine prided himself as an innovator, an experimenter. Businessmen often have little truck with such types. Ballantine wanted to do things other paperback houses were not doing. But he was under tremendous pressure from the directors, who wanted to do just that, direct. They also didn't want to tamper with a sure thing. Theater and film critic Stanley Kauffmann, who joined Bantam in 1949 as an editor, was watching from the sidelines as Ballantine took the field. "There was a struggle between Ian Ballantine and the ownership. He had ambitions to seriousness that they didn't share. They had a goose that was pouring out golden eggs. They didn't want to monkey with it. There was a power struggle and he lost."

One of the first battles in this struggle came over book prices. Like others in the paperback field, Ballantine saw the necessity for higher prices because twenty-five cents was a constraint on the reprinter. There was simply no way to introduce longer novels and serious nonfiction without raising prices or making condensations and abridgments (which many reprinters did without qualms). In this, Ballantine was opposed by his superiors. The first battle came over Ballantine's desire to reprint a book called *Roosevelt and Hopkins: An Intimate History* by Robert E. Sherwood, a major work about FDR and his most trusted and powerful lieutenant, Harry Hopkins. Originally published in 1948 by Harper & Brothers, the book had been a nonfiction best seller that year. In April

1950, Harper reissued the book in a revised edition. In July, Bantam announced that it would publish the book on an experimental basis, in two volumes at thirty-five cents each. In addition, the book would be available for only 120 days. At the time of the paperback's release, Ballantine said of the plan, "A low cost edition published at the right time can create tremendous word-of-mouth recommendations for the right book through hundreds of thousands of new readers. . . . Because *Roosevelt and Hopkins* is one of the most interesting and most important books of the last ten years, we believe that the reading public will prove that this technique of publishing a limited edition, at the lowest possible price, will shape a new pattern and a greater market for fine books."

Ballantine believed that the book had passed the peak of its hardcover performance and that a paperback edition could successfully revive it. In other words, his interest went beyond profiting from the sale of a reprint and into creating new life cycles for books deserving a wider market and a longer life. This penchant for toying with the accepted relationship between one edition of a book and another was to become a driving force in Ballantine's long career in publishing. Sometimes they were a great notion; in other cases, they fell by the wayside. Unfortunately, the latter was the case with *Roosevelt and Hopkins*. Although Ballantine asserts that the book was a success, the record is less certain. Walter Pitkin, then Bantam's editor in chief, called it "a dismal failure" and later commented, "Ian did succeed in publishing through enthusiasm. *Roosevelt and Hopkins* was a case of that. It involved enormous difficulties because of the amount of the investment and the judgment that it was likely to turn out to be a 'dog,' as the Curtis people would say. It was a very complex and unhappy kind of thing, really over the protests of the directors. Ian, being the publisher, finally insisted, 'I want to do this,' and we did it."

While the book's failure might have proved, first, that two-volume paperbacks were dead before they left the warehouse and, second, that *Roosevelt and Hopkins* was not the right title for the mass market, the thirty-five-cent cover price was not held to blame. NAL had already gone ahead with its plan for thirty-five-cent Giants and fifty-cent Double Volumes. Bantam and Pocket Books also made plans to launch thirty-five-cent books. For Bantam, the first of these was Taylor Caldwell's *This Side of Innocence*.

The second of Ballantine's battles was far more serious and ended in his departure from Bantam. In 1951, Ballantine had set his sights on expanding into the British market and established a British subsidiary, Transworld, to publish paperbacks in England under the Corgi imprint for the British Commonwealth markets. Contractual agreements kept American books from being exported directly into these markets. Without the approval of the executive committee of the board of directors, Ballantine lent Transworld some much-needed cash. The board members were either outraged by this relatively minor offense or saw in it a way to rid themselves of a boat rocker. In his memoirs, Bennett Cerf commented on the affair:

> He was forced out of the business he had brought to us. I think this was shameful, but the others overruled me. Ballantine was a very difficult fellow to handle. He didn't know what diplomacy meant and he didn't realize he was dealing with some very successful gentlemen who liked their prerogatives respected. . . . They forced him to resign. I was outraged and demanded another hearing. Ian had been foolish enough to confront these strong publishing men without a lawyer. They made up their minds even before he could plead his case. [*At Random*]

After the close of business on February 5, 1952, Ballantine was gone.

It did not take him long to resurface. In May 1952, *PW* carried news of Ballantine's plan for a new company that would simultaneously publish hardcover and paperback editions of selected books. The idea set the world of publishing abuzz. Simply, the Ballantine notion was to publish a hardcover edition for the bookstore trade that would also gain review attention while a paperback edition would reach the mass market. Theoretically, the advantage of this system meant the hardcover house could undercut existing cover prices from the average of $3 down to $1.50 or $2 through shared plant costs and other production efficiencies while gaining review attention as well as the widest possible distribution. As Ballantine pointed out, his plan was not meant for well-known, best-selling authors who would not necessarily benefit from such a strategy but for lesser-known writers who needed exposure. A key element of the scheme was the increase in the author's royalty to 8 percent, with the entire paperback royalty going to the author instead of being split with the publisher.

The concept of simultaneous editions was not without precedent. Ballantine had himself used it at Penguin during the war, with *Iwo Jima* and *Tank Fighter Team*, two Fighting Forces Specials published in conjunction with Dial Press and *Infantry Journal;* in 1943, Simon & Schuster had published Wendell Willkie's *One World,* an extremely influential book that sold millions of copies that year through newsstands and drugstores in a large-sized paperback edition as well as several thousand copies in hardcover through bookstores; Pocket Books had done the same with Dr. Spock, turning the hardcover edition over to Duell, Sloan & Pearce; and NAL had done some co-publishing with a number of publishers on illustrated books about wildflowers and birds.

At the heart of the plan was Ballantine's contention that the paperback was the best way to reach the mass audience. Not only would the paperback edition sell by itself, but Ballantine believed that the word of mouth generated by the paperback would spur greater interest in the hardcover, thereby creating a mutually beneficial relationship. The plan was also tacit recognition of the immense power wielded by the distributors in editorial matters. At Bantam, Ballantine had witnessed this firsthand with the Curtis organization. He saw his idea as a means of balancing the magazine distributor's voice with that of the trade publisher, who might otherwise lose all influence over what was being produced for the paperback market. In theory, the plan meant a smaller percentage of profit for the publisher. But to Ballantine that was as it should be. He was saying that the author should be profiting from his book, a subversive idea if ever one was spoken by a publisher.

This was the most controversial aspect of the Ballantine concept because it represented a new alignment in the hardened relationship between authors and publishers, radically altering the traditional roles played by each. For all its supposed liberalism, the publishing industry was extremely resistant to change. Nowhere were attitudes more rock-solid among publishers than in matters relating to writers. Ballantine took his case before such writers groups as the Authors' Guild, the Authors' League, and the Mystery Writers of America. The reaction was somewhat mixed; to the writers it sounded too good. Where was the catch? Why did a publisher want to give them more? Nonetheless, the leaders of the Guild endorsed the plan.

By September, Ballantine Books announced its staff and first titles. In addition to Ballantine and his wife, Betty, who served as corporate secretary and was also growing in stature as an editor, the editorial staff included Bernard Shir-Cliff, a young Columbia graduate who had been hired by Ballantine while he was still at Bantam, and Stanley Kauffmann, then a novelist of some note. The firm's first office was Ballantine's apartment in London Terrace off West Twenty-fourth Street in Manhattan, though it was soon moved to 404 Fifth Avenue. As a national distributor to the magazine wholesalers, Ballantine enlisted the Hearst Corporation's International Circulation Distributors. Two hardcover publishers, Houghton Mifflin and Farrar, Straus & Young, announced their interest in the concept and planned to participate on a title-by-title basis. The first book on the list was *Executive Suite*, a first novel by Cameron Hawley, a businessman who had written short stories for the *Saturday Evening Post*. Along with it were *The Golden Spike*, a novel of juvenile delinquency by Hal Ellson, whose earlier books in this genre were the very successful *Duke* and *Tomboy; All My Enemies*, a novel by Stanley Baron about a Communist agent on a secret mission in America; and *Saddle by Starlight*, a Luke Short Western published in hardcover by Houghton Mifflin. For books not published by another trade house, Ballantine set up his own hardcover operation; *The Golden Spike* was the first of these.

By the end of 1953, the results of Ballantine's first year of operation were encouraging. *Executive Suite*, the first title, which had been released in hardcover by Houghton Mifflin, had been well reviewed by the media. A story of corporate boardroom intrigues, it even won a favorable nod from the dean of reviewers, Orville Prescott of the *New York Times*. In eight months, the hardcover had sold a respectable 22,000 copies and the simultaneous paperback went over the 475,000 mark. The book was also sold to MGM and was made into a film with William Holden, Barbara Stanwyck, Walter Pidgeon, and other big names. Luke Short's Western sold more than 200,000 copies in paper without damaging sales of the $1.50 hardcover. Ironically, Houghton Mifflin's Lovell Thompson, the man who had earlier berated "low-price publishing," talked about the advantage of the Ballantine plan. He cited the example of Ruth Park, an Australian novelist who, despite excellent sales abroad and fine reviews, had not sold well in the United States and was passed over by reprinters. Houghton Mifflin "simul-published" her third book, *Witch's Thorn*, to considerable success in both editions. Another critical success was the original publication of *The City of Anger*, a novel of political corruption and the numbers game and the first work of fiction by William Manchester, then known for his biography of Mencken. The biggest commercial success was *The Burl Ives Song Book*, which Ballantine published in both editions. A color-illustrated songbook, it sold tens of thousands of copies as a popular Christmas gift just as the folk music craze was beginning to gather force.

In addition to Westerns, mysteries, war books (which followed Ballantine from Penguin to Bantam and then to Ballantine Books) and other novels, Ballantine soon began to publish books that stood outside the existing categories. Just as the entire Ballantine Books concept was unconventional, the Ballantine list began to acquire an offbeat appeal. One new category was a type of nonfiction different from the academic-oriented Mentors or the how-to Pocket Books. It was a brand of contemporary reportage best exemplified by the work of reporter John Bartlow Martin, a well-known journalist, in such books as *Why Did They Kill?*—a predecessor of sorts to *In Cold Blood*—and *Break Down the Walls*, a serious inquiry into the American penal system. The genre later took a more political tone when Ballantine began to publish the controversial writings of C. Wright Mills. Far less distinguished was a brand of sensationalist nonfiction, often historical in nature, such as *Those About to Die* by Daniel Mannix, a book about the excesses of the Roman circuses.

Another much more successful new area was offbeat humor. Until that point, paperback humor books had been limited to borrowings from the *Saturday Evening Post*, joke books, and Bennett Cerf's anecdotes. But in 1954, Ballantine published *The Mad Reader* by Harvey Kurtzman, the first in a series of enormously popular *Mad* paperbacks. Taken from the fledgling *Mad* magazine, which was just beginning to style its own form of unconventional humor and exaggerated illustration—as well as its 1950s archetype, Alfred E. "What Me Worry" Neuman—the typical *Mad* humor was, if not subversive, at least nonconformist. Parents found it sick; but it appealed to kids unlike anything appearing in mainstream comics. It was irreverent, anti-authoritarian, and iconoclastic. It spoke to a younger generation that would, in a few years, be taking over the campuses. In fact, the initial printing of *The Mad Reader* even contained an attack on Senator Joseph McCarthy; Ballantine later said that around the time of the eighteenth printing, it was time to drop that feature because kids no longer had any idea who McCarthy was. *The Mad Reader* was brought in to Ballantine by Bernard Shir-Cliff, who was given the magazines by one of the Ballantine salesmen whose son was a *Mad* fanatic. While Ballantine was still at Bantam, his uncle Saxe Commins called to say that he had a very good student in his publishing course at Columbia University and that Ballantine should make a job for him. Bernard Shir-Cliff came to Bantam in a make-work position of gathering statistics about paperback books. He eventually was made a junior editor, and when Ballantine left Bantam, Shir-Cliff went along with him as a full-fledged editor at Ballantine Books.

The *Mad* books provided the groundwork on which Ballantine built a collection of irreverent humor books that poked a stick in the eye of contemporary styles and shibboleths, such as *The Power of Negative Thinking*, a Shir-Cliff-inspired riposte to Norman Vincent Peale. Another notorious example came a few years later when Ballantine published *I, Libertine* in response to a hoax. Late-night radio host Jean Shepherd, famed for his program on WOR and its audience of "Night People," enlisted his listeners in a conspiracy against the smug, conservative "Day People" by creating demand for a product that did not exist—a book called *I, Libertine*. Advertisements for the nonexistent book were taken out, an entry for the book was placed into the Philadelphia Public Library's card catalog, an airline pilot urged his colleagues to harass bookshops across the country for the book, and another disc jockey produced an interview with the "author," Frederick Ewing. Ballantine soon heard that booksellers were frantically asking for a book that did not exist. So he commissioned the book. Tracking Shepherd down, he signed him to write it in collaboration with Theodore Sturgeon, the science fiction writer. The result was a send-up of the eighteenth-century historical novel popularized by *Forever Amber*. The copy touted the book as "Turbulent! Turgid! Tempestuous!"—and according to Ballantine, the cover was also a trick, containing twenty-four visual errors such as light coming from the wrong direction. The book prompted an editorial in *Life* and was soon the most widely publicized book of the day. Ballantine published a modest 180,000-copy printing, and Shepherd and Sturgeon did full-blast publicity events in keeping with the spirit of the book. They held an autographing party in a Liggett drugstore in Times Square, a favorite spot for the "Night People," after Shepherd initially requested that the party be held in a remainder bookstore in order to "eliminate the middleman."

While Ballantine Books employed this type of humor to good publicity effect, it was not the core of the company's program. Very quickly, the genre that became almost synonymous with Ballantine Books was science fiction. Until this point, science fiction had no significant place in paperback publishing. In fact, it barely existed in book form at all. It was viewed by publishers as a sort of fringe genre that they knew or cared little about. The field belonged principally to the magazine and pulp publishers who flourished from the 1920s through the 1940s, and from which writers like Heinlein, Asimov, Bradbury, and del Rey drew their sustenance. With the exception of novels by Jules Verne and H. G. Wells and Shelley's *Frankenstein*—which were considered "classics" rather than science fiction—and more recent works like C. S. Lewis's trilogy commencing with *Out of the Silent Planet* (1939)—actually religious allegory—or Huxley's *Brave New World* (1932) and Orwell's *1984* (1949)—political and social allegories in a science fiction guise—book form science fiction before 1950 was limited to a few anthologies of magazine short fiction.

In 1943, for instance, Pocket Books had published the first science fiction paperback, *The Pocket Book of Science Fiction,* an anthology edited by Donald A. Wollheim, a veteran editor of science fiction magazines and later a dominant figure in paperback science fiction publishing. The following year, Penguin produced an anthology called *Out of This World,* edited by Julius Fast, brother of Howard and later the author of successful pop psychology books including *Body Language*. In 1950, Bantam also published a collection called *A Shot in the Dark,* science fiction stories thinly disguised as mysteries. However, before 1952, no paperback publisher could lay claim to what can be called a science fiction program.

Ballantine radically changed that. On the company's early lists were not only collections of science fiction from the magazines but an impressive line-up of full-length novels that became classics of the genre and books that ultimately transcended the category. The first full-fledged science fiction novel on the list was a collaboration between Fred Pohl and C. M. Kornbluth, a first novel by a pair of veterans who had collaborated previously on short fiction. Serialized in *Galaxy* magazine as "Gravy Planet," the completed novel was retitled *The Space Merchants* by its editor, Stanley Kauffmann. Not a simple story of rockets, robots, and cosmic damsels in distress—the recycled elements of the Western in futuristic garb known as the "space opera"—*The Space Merchants,* if not high art, was a social satire. In the story, an overcrowded future Earth is controlled by advertising agencies, and Congress consists of representatives of large corporations (as in the "Honorable Senator from Yummy Cola"). The plot involves an ad agency's plan to control Venus by luring "consumers"—as average people are called—to join the first colony there. In the background, a subversive group called "Consies," short for conservationists, fights as outlaws to prevent the destruction of natural resources. This satirization of contemporary culture in futuristic guise had its predecessors—*Gulliver's Travels* is arguably a tale of science fiction—but it became typical of the style in science fiction pioneered by Ballantine Books. Ian Ballantine called the books he published "adult science fiction." "Adult" not in the sense of "For Adults Only" movies, but in their thematic seriousness, relative sophistication, and literary ambitions.

An even greater example of this style came through in another Ballantine Book brought in by Kauffmann. As he recalled, "The idea of Ballantine's methods struck a chord in Don Congdon, Ray Bradbury's agent, and he relayed it to Bradbury. We got a manuscript and I did some work on it. Then he got the galleys and wouldn't let go of them. He was fussing with them. So I had to fly out to California and work with him for a week out there." The finished novel, an extension of a *Galaxy* story called "The Fireman," appeared in 1953 as Ballantine Book No. 41, *Fahrenheit 451*—the "temperature at which book paper catches fire and burns."

The historical context in which Bradbury's book appeared is more than a little significant. The House investigations into un-American activities and Senator Joseph McCarthy were on the rampage. Communist writers were being suppressed. Paperback books were under fire by local censors, and late in 1952, the Gathings committee—a congressional investigation into the paperback business—was empowered. In other words, Bardbury's jeremiad about a future dystopia in which books are burned and the people anesthetized by a vacuous, omnipresent television soap opera was no fantasist's vision. In 1953, in a famous speech at Dartmouth College, President Eisenhower had warned, "Don't join the book burners," a rebuke aimed at McCarthyism. *Fahrenheit 451* was informed and shaped by the culture that Bradbury was observing, including the growing threat of a nuclear cataclysm, an event with which the book ends, unlike the pale Truffaut film version. Other memorable science fiction novels from the early Ballantine period include the Arthur C. Clarke classic *Childhood's End,* John Wyndham's *The Midwich Cuckoos,* and other works by Pohl, Kornbluth, and Sturgeon. All of these received the unique stamp of illustration by Richard G. Powers, surrealistic Dali-esque imagery and geometric abstractions that were in marked contrast to the pulpish semiclad space maidens with metallic cones on their breasts who were always in the clutches of an invading monster. Ballantine's unique science fiction cover treatment even extended to Gore Vidal's novel *Messiah.* Although it seems unlikely, the packaging of a Gore Vidal novel as science fiction was not a misunderstanding of Vidal but a measure of the seriousness with which the category was viewed. The recurrent themes in Ballantine science fiction—serious over-crowding of the earth, dread of nuclear catastrophe, a dwindling food supply, ecological insanity, excessive government control—were all part of a pattern of concerns that later emerged on the Ballantine list in the form of serious nonfiction, including the work of C. Wright Mills, Paul Ehrlich's *The Population Bomb, Diet for a Small Planet,* or the nature books published in association with the Sierra Club and Friends of the Earth.

The fact that science fiction had arrived as a potential category for paperback publishers was underscored later in 1952 with the arrival of another paperback house that became known primarily for its publishing in the science fiction field. Ace Books was the creation of Aaron A. Wynn, who had been in the confessional magazine business for seventeen years when, in 1945, he started a book line called Current Books. In 1946, he acquired the L. B. Fischer Publishing Corporation, which had been started by two German refugees, Gottfried Berman-Fischer and Fritz Landshoff. Wynn merged these two operations into A. A. Wynn, Inc. His paperback operation had a gimmick conceived by Walter Zacharius; it would publish two paperback novels bound back to back and call them Double Novels, priced at thirty-five cents. The appeal to the reader was obvious. They were getting two novels for a little more than the price of one. In fact, the two "novels" were often novelettes or long short stories rather than full-length novels. But the plan appealed to readers and the sight of the Ace Double Novels, with the back cover "upside-down" in the racks, became a familiar one.

Generally the two books printed together were of the same category, principally, at the outset, two mysteries or Westerns. The first mystery package included *The Grinning Gringo* by Samuel W. Taylor, a reprint of a book originally published by A. A. Wynn, Inc., and *Too Hot for Hell* by Keith Vining, an original. The first Western duo was *Bad Man's Return* by William Colt MacDonald, a reprint, coupled with *Bloody Hoofs,* an original by Edward J. Leithead. Without a doubt the most famous of the Ace Double Novels was Ace D 15, the combination of *Narcotics Agent,* a typical genre thriller by Maurice Helbrant, with *Junkie,* "Confessions of an Unredeemed Drug Addict," by "William Lee" who in fact was William S. Burroughs. Ace felt it necessary to include a glossary, in a vain bid to make Burroughs comprehensible. Ace came by the book through Wynn's nephew Carl Solomon, who worked for his uncle as an editor but happened to have been a poet and Allen Ginsberg's compatriot in a psychiatric hospital. Ginsberg passed *Junkie* to Solomon, who gave it to Wynn, and it was published by Ace.

One feature of the Ace Double Novel was that it allowed Ace to combine an unknown (cheaper) writer's work with that of a better-known author. This strategy was put to good effect by the series editor, Donald A. Wollheim, who was the leading promoter of the genre and a guru to the growing legions of science fiction fans. Wollheim got good mileage out of the Double Novels as he launched new writers in the format, moving Ace more heavily toward that genre until it pulled alongside Ballantine and the two companies began to dominate the field. By 1954, Ace had also branched out into the business of twenty-five-cent editions of single novels in paperback. In order to concentrate on Ace paperbacks, Wynn sold off his hardcover operation in 1956 to two of his executives, Lawrence Hill and Arthur W. Wang, who formed Hill & Wang.

The introduction of Ballantine and Ace was only a part of the growth spurt that made 1952 something of a momentous year in the paperback's development. Another major surge was under way at Dell Books. After its strong beginnings in 1942, Dell had slipped out of contention as a meaningful competitor to Pocket Books when Bantam and New American Library vaulted ahead on the basis of more imaginative, diversified editorial programs featuring best-selling books and noteworthy fiction. Fawcett's Gold Medal had also been an instant success, and Dell was soon floundering at the bottom of the heap with Avon and Popular Library. The principal reason for their situation was that Dell was still essentially oriented toward comic books and magazines. Books were an afterthought at Dell, and no one in the Dell hierarchy had developed into a competent book publisher. The Dell list was composed almost entirely of category fiction, an editorial policy dictated by the demands of the American News Company. Western Printing in Racine, Wisconsin, was responsible for selecting and producing the books for Dell, but there was no strong central editorial figure there either. In 1952, however, the company's status took a sharp upward turn with the overhaul of the Western editorial staff. That year Western hired Frank Taylor to oversee Dell's reprints, and having seen Gold Medal reap impressive rewards, George Delacorte brought in Knox Burger to establish a series of originals called Dell First Editions.

The addition of these two editors marked a major turning point in Dell's fortunes. Taylor was a literary man, through and through. He had worked in advertising sales at *Saturday Review* before joining the young but, in Taylor's words, "terribly exciting" firm of Reynal and Hitchcock in 1941. He soon rose to editor and vice president there, bringing into the firm Lillian Smith's *Strange Fruit* in 1944 and after the war heading for England, where he signed on Stephen Spender, V. S. Pritchett, and other prominent British writers. When Reynal and Hitchcock dissolved in 1947 after Curtice Hitchcock's death, Taylor moved on to Random House as a roving editor and was responsible for initiating the publication of Ralph Ellison's *Invisible Man*. He left Random House for three years to work as a producer in Hollywood but returned to New York unhappy with West Coast movie life. He asked Bennett Cerf, his former boss, what he might do. Taylor recalled, "Bennett told me the Paperback Revolution had occurred in my absence and said, 'My advice to you is get in it.' I was very snobby about it because for years I had been the discoverer and finder—there is excitement in finding new writers. The idea of reprinting was not appealing to me." Nonetheless, Taylor took the job of overseeing the Dell reprints at Western. He found that Dell Books came in three flavors—romance, Western, and mystery. The endpapers of the romances were printed with hearts, the Westerns with steer horns, and the mysteries with skull and crossbones. He also learned that a large part of his job involved "educating," as he put it, the Dell organization about books.

Taylor also found some assets when he arrived. The most important of these was a young editor named Allan Barnard, a holdover from the previous Western staff. As Taylor put it, "Allan had tentacles and enormous sensitiv

ity to what sells." The other boon was the fact that there was no shortage of funds at either Dell or Western, which were both cash rich. Taylor immediately set out to employ these funds. He took Allan Barnard off the tether and encouraged him to follow his instincts. Taylor himself set about charting a fresh editorial direction for the company. One of his first exercises was to go through lists of authors and see who was not being reprinted. His initial find was Evelyn Waugh, and Taylor spent a rather hefty $41,000 to acquire all nine of Waugh's novels from Little, Brown. He also discovered Mary McCarthy just "kicking around," and added her to the Dell list.

At the same time that Taylor was revitalizing the Dell reprint list, Knox Burger was preparing to put together an all-originals program. Burger came to Dell from *Collier's* magazine, where he had developed a solid reputation as a young fiction editor. His contacts with writers from *Collier's* were powerful, and he would bring many of these writers to First Editions, including John D. MacDonald and Kurt Vonnegut. He also started to beef up his own editorial department. As his second in command, Burger brought in Donald Fine, formerly with Doubleday, and hired as a receptionist/reader Arlene Donovan, who had been a baby sitter for Burger's children and who quickly rose to an editor's position.

Dell First Editions established itself by aggressively acquiring books, although still staying close to the mystery, suspense, and adventure vein that Gold Medal had successfully mined. The emphasis was on bringing in good writers. Burger published some John D. MacDonald, who had already done several of his Travis McGee mysteries for Gold Medal. Fine discovered the Australian novelist Morris West, then a radio announcer, whose first American book was Dell's *Kundu,* a story of lycanthropy set in New Guinea. West later wrote for Dell First Editions under the pseudonym Michael East. When Dell turned down one of West's mysteries set in Rome, the writer took it to William Morrow, which published it in hardcover. The next book after that was *The Devil's Advocate.* Fine later said about Dell First Editions, "We conducted business like a fine, traditional hardcover publishing house. Tremendous time was lavished on editing and back and forth with authors. We wouldn't publish anything unless we were terribly pleased with it. That's what we cared about." It was commonly acknowledged that a rivalry existed between the two divisions, reprints and originals; Arlene Donovan later called it a "polite cold war." But with Burger, Fine, and Donovan on one side and Taylor and Barnard on the other, Dell now had an editorial staff that combined commercial instincts with literary sensibilities, and a strong "hands-on" editorial expertise. It was a team that compared favorably with any in the industry, reprint or hardcover.

Perhaps because paperbacks could supply economic incentives greater than those at hardcover houses, the paperback business was increasingly drawing editorial talent that would be welcome in any trade house. At NAL, Victor Weybright had supplemented his staff with Arabel

Porter and Marc Jaffe, who came from *Argosy* magazine and was as at home with Westerns and mysteries as he was with William Styron or Peter Mathiessen, both of whom he encountered in Paris while scouting around Europe. At Pocket Books, Doc Lewis's staff had grown to include Herbert Alexander, a former advertising man who knew what sold, and Lawrence Hughes, later the head of William Morrow. Ballantine could boast of Stanley Kauffmann and Bernard Shir-Cliff. At Bantam, Saul David and Grace Bechtold were establishing themselves. Though hardcover publishers still behaved condescendingly or patronizingly toward the paperback houses that were increasingly buttering their bread, it was clear that the paperback publishers' marketing strength was now being buttressed by solid editorial expertise. These editors, who all surely could have found places in trade publishing, were going to push the paperback in new and more interesting directions.

It was also becoming clear that the paperback was a growing force on the American cultural scene. The surging growth in sales, the proliferation of new companies and imprints, the phenomenon of paperback originals, the flurry of controversy over Ballantine's plan, and the rising advances and cover prices all heightened the paperback's visibility in literary and intellectual circles. Among writers and critics, the paperback had its cheerleaders, who believed that inexpensive paperback books were democratizing American literature, taking it out of the hands of the select few and putting it before the masses. On the other hand were the critics who said trash in any guise still smells like trash; and the paperback was trash. Others worried that the paperback meant the death of the hardcover and wondered what it would mean for writers. At the extreme were those people who saw paperbacks as nothing but a pox on the land, a plot to subvert American morality and fit only to be wiped clean from the newsstands and drugstore racks.

This emerging debate underlined the growing schizophrenia of the paperback industry. It was the Great Contradiction between the lowest of lowbrow fiction on one end of the scale and serious nonfiction and literature on the other. *New York Times Book Review* editor David Dempsey, writing in the *Atlantic Monthly* in January 1953, characterized this duality.

> There are today about twenty paperback houses in the field. Seven of these account for approximately 85 per cent of the total business. Their product is a highly competitive melange of serious literature and trash, of self-help and pseudo-science, of sex and inspiration. Never before has American publishing put forth such a nicely homogenized product, with the cream of letters so palatably disseminated in the total output. This explains why Edith Hamilton's *The Greek Way* and the novels of Kathleen Winsor can be sold bust by jowl on drug counters. It accounts for the fact that Faulkner's *The Wild Palms* has been made available, if not necessarily comprehensible, to a million rank-and-file buyers. It has suddenly made the books of

Flaubert, Hawthorne, and D. H. Lawrence contemporary with Steinbeck. If the reprints have done nothing else, they have taken the classics away from the protective custody of the pedants.

While writers and critics like Professor Eduard C. Lindeman and Malcolm Cowley were taking sides in such magazines as the *New Republic, Harper's,* and *Saturday Review*—and as Ashley Montagu put forward the suggestion that paperbacks should be the "standard book while all other books remain the luxuries they have become"—the debate over the paperback's rightful place in America's cultural hierarchy came to a head in 1954. Kurt Enoch wrote an extensive essay about the paperback for the *Library Quarterly* in June 1954. In it he related the history and workings of the paperback business and then turned his sights on the social role of the paperback. Characterizing the paperback as part of the mass media, Enoch explained that paperbound books were different because they were free from the pressures of government or advertisers. Stated Enoch, "There has been a sort of law: the wider the audience, the less provocative or disturbing to established ideas and taboos the medium has to be. The fundamental problem . . . is thus to achieve a mass audience while preserving the special virtues of books. . . . We offer predominantly contemporary American literature, without neglecting to make available a good cross-section of the best or most important foreign writing. Informative or scholarly nonfiction is steadily increasing. . . . " In Enoch's eyes, the paperback was fulfilling a specific—and uniquely American—function by achieving, "in matters of the mind and arts, as we have already achieved in the economic area, the broad and general distribution of goods that are a vital factor in the dynamic expansion of a free society."

Shortly afterward, from his spot in "The Easy Chair" at *Harper's* magazine, Bernard DeVoto wrote "Culture at Two Bits," an acerbic rejoinder to Enoch's article and the sentiments it expressed, which DeVoto called "a mossy stone." His criticism centered on the fact that while "important" books—many of which Enoch had listed—were being reprinted, they were rarely available. "If you are quick on your feet, you can get or could have got Machiavelli, Benvenuto Cellini, Crane Brinton, Aaron Copland, George Kennan and much more substantial stuff at the corner newsstand." But DeVoto told of walking into every cigar stand, drugstore, and newsstand he could find, looking for the products of the cultural revolution, without any luck. "Tripe," he wrote, "always has been the basis of the publishing business, and in the two bit book it is performing the functions of all popular literature in all ages. At worst it is preventing boredom, assisting digestion and peristalsis, feeding people's appetites for daydreams, giving the imagination something to work on and taking the reader out of a momentarily unsatisfactory life into a momentarily more enjoyable one. At best, or so the theory of revolution holds, it is plowing, harrowing and seeding the soil." DeVoto completed his critique by suggesting that unless more good books were published alongside the awful ones, "the tripe merchants" should stop talking about their cultural service to a "dynamically expanding free society."

It was fitting that Kurt Enoch should be the object of DeVoto's scorn. No firm was more clearly a symbol of the Janus-faced paperback industry than Enoch and Weybright's New American Library. The home of Mentor Books—the only line of paperbacks besides Pocket Books that had developed any brand-name recognition—and the publisher of Faulkner, Caldwell, Silone, Moravia, Farrell, Joyce, Tennessee Williams, Lawrence, Woolf, Ralph Ellison, and a host of the other leading contemporary novelists, NAL claimed as its best-selling writer Mickey Spillane.

Frank Morrison Spillane was born on March 9, 1918, in Brooklyn and raised, as he later said, "in a very tough neighborhood in Elizabeth, New Jersey." If he had a motto as a writer, it might well have been, "You can keep all your awards. All I want is a fat check."

For Spillane, fat checks were never a problem. In 1947, E. P. Dutton published his first book, *I, the Jury*. It sold a modest few thousand copies but was picked up for reprint by Victor Weybright, and in January 1948 New American Library published it at twenty-five cents. In a little more than two years, paperback sales of *I, the Jury* had surpassed 2 million copies. In the meantime, Spillane had written three more books, all published by Dutton in 7500-copy first printings and reprinted by NAL. By the end of 1951, NAL had sold more than 5 million of Spillane's Mike Hammer thrillers. In December 1951, the company issued a 2.5-million-copy first printing—the largest one at that point in paperback history—of his fifth book, *The Big Kill*. After *I, the Jury* Spillane wrote six more Mike Hammer novels: *Vengeance Is Mine* (1950), *My Gun Is Quick* (1950), *One Lonely Night* (1951), *The Big Kill* (1951), *The Long Wait* (1951), and *Kiss Me, Deadly* (1952). Spillane was estimated to be earning about $80,000 per book in that early period. By 1953, Spillane's first six novels had topped 17 million copies sold, and Mike Hammer's creator had pulled past Erskine Caldwell and was now in second place as the best-selling author behind Erle Stanley Gardner. Yet in 1952, at the peak of his sales and without explanation, Spillane stopped writing and took a nine-year break. Although he returned in 1961, popularity undiminished, Spillane is best known for those early titles.

Mickey Spillane broke into the business by writing for the comic books, and the techniques of that genre informed his literary style. Spillane had to be taken as seriously as Superman. His characters were one-dimensional grotesques yanked from the garish pages of the popular comic books of the period. Leading the parade was Mike Hammer, the two-fisted, craggy-faced (not handsome; that was an effeminate trait) private dick with a crew cut; his voluptuous secretary, Velda, always trying to get Mike to tie the knot; and Pat Chambers, the beleaguered homicide detective and pal of Hammer's who vainly tries to keep the private eye from taking the law

into his own hands. Spillane surely did not take himself seriously. His tough-guy act before the press and cameras, right down to his own regulation skinhead haircut, was all bluff, a play to the grandstands. The sublime contradiction in Spillane was his devout religious conviction following a 1952 conversion to the Jehovah's Witnesses. He handed out tracts and participated in baptisms by immersion. Victor Weybright once told of arranging a meeting between Spillane and some Catholic priests, among his most vociferous critics. The expected confrontation over Spillane's books never materialized because the meeting turned into a theological discussion of the precepts of the Jehovah's Witnesses. There was also the suggestion that Spillane's nine-year sabbatical was the result of his conversion, although later, in typically tough-guy fashion, he laughed that off, asserting he had come back to make some more money—the only reason he ever wrote anything.

By stretching things a bit, Spillane's Jehovah could be seen as the active principle in his books. Mike Hammer—the Hammer of God?—was his fictional avatar, an angel of death incarnate, wreaking almighty vengeance upon the immoral, corrupt, criminal, and godless. If Dashiell Hammett had created the hard-boiled private eye, Spillane perverted him. In many ways, Sam Spade was the model for Hammer. But Mike Hammer was a Frankenstein, Sam Spade gone haywire. (Often Spade seemed more than just a model. In a scene in *Kiss Me, Deadly,* Hammer disarms a would-be assassin the same way Spade handles Wilmer Cook, the "gunsel" who has been following him in *The Maltese Falcon*.) But it would be difficult to find two writers more diametrically opposed: Hammett, the leftist whose heroes were no heroes at all but lonely, somewhat seedy men who asked more questions than they answered; Spillane, the anti-Communist crusader whose comic book hero Mike Hammer shot first and asked questions later.

Spillane's books were the obvious products of their times. He took his plots from the headlines. In 1951, these included the investigations into organized crime launched by Senator Estes Kefauver of Tennessee. Kefauver's hearings went public, and mobster Frank Costello was grilled on live television, outdrawing the World Series in those days of television's infancy. The Kefauver hearings put organized crime on the front pages. (Not coincidentally, Kefauver was readying for a run at the Democratic presidential nomination.) Organized crime thus became the chief bugaboo in several Spillane plots. Tales of call-girl rings, the narcotics trade, and murder rings—now out in the open—became grist for Spillane's mill. When Senator McCarthy emerged, Spillane found himself a new model and a new villain. Mike Hammer switched to fighting Communists (*One Lonely Night* was Spillane's first anti-Communist book) and became the ultimate cold warrior, an *Übermensch* for frightened Americans who had heard tales of baby-eating Stalinists. Hammer's methods went beyond loyalty oaths, smears, and blacklisting. The evil of the Communists was battled with the only weapons Hammer possessed: a blast from his forty-five, a kick that shattered bone on impact, strangulation by Hammer's meaty hands.

Spillane's Hammer was a creature of his times. But was he more? Was Mike Hammer an archetype, a metaphor for a darkly violent animus within the millions who bought the books? If Spillane was laughing in his cuff, did his readers take him seriously? There was more than simply sex and violence in his novels. Hammer embodied many perverse notions that seemed to represent the male Zeitgeist of the fifties. The first of the Hammer books, *I, the Jury*—the all-time best seller of the group—was typical of the series; it contained the rage that was seething beneath the supposed civility of American life in the early 1950s. The book introduced war veteran Mike Hammer as a private investigator who chose his profession over police work because the cops are tied down by the rules and regulations imposed by a "pansy" bureaucracy. Hammer sets himself above the law because of the "right-ness" of what he does. The law and order cant of modern conservatives in 1950 was no different than it is today. When Hammer's war buddy is murdered by a heroin ring, Hammer vows vengeance; he will become cop, judge, jury, and executioner. Not even the state's worst threat—hanging or "frying"—is justice enough for Hammer; he must exact an eye for an eye.

In the course of his search, Hammer encounters the beautiful psychiatrist Charlotte Manning, who like all women is overcome by Hammer's sheer maleness. She quickly accepts Hammer's marriage proposal, sacrificing her career without hesitation. He will not, of course, even consider the possibility that his wife will hold a job. All women in Hammer's world are purely sexual objects, and most of them are criminals as well. Sex is primitively animal; Hammer doesn't make love—he ruts. Yet though he is constantly brought to the peak of arousal by Charlotte, Hammer will not succumb because she is to be his bride, a streak of perverse Victorian chasteness within Spillane. Of course, Charlotte turns out to be the leader of a heroin ring run from her psychiatry practice. Charlotte is a woman, an intellectual, a criminal. Ergo she must die and does at the hands of Hammer on the last page, as do so many women in Spillane's books.

Hammer stood for, in no special order, sexism, racism (blacks are either shuffling genetic defectives or pimps and pushers), anti-intellectualism, homophobia, and a brand of jackbooted fascist vigilantism in the guise of preserving order. Though he is a war veteran, Mike Hammer evidences no vitriol toward the Nazis. Indeed, a beautiful woman is often described as a Nordic or a Viking. His disdain is reserved for women, professionals, homosexuals or "pansies" (lesbians are twice cursed), and the criminal class—often ethnics. If Spillane was diagramming the psyche of the American male circa 1952, the picture was a disturbing one. Or was he merely playing out a fantasy and, in doing so, defusing the furies that Mike Hammer represented? Was Hammer simply Walter Mitty with two fists and a .45? In their book *The Fifties,* Douglas Miller and Marion Nowak comment,

"Hammer was popular because he enacted a daydream. He catered to the politically disarmed and sexually insecure, the ambiguous American who needed a powerful dose of artifice and reassurance."

Other contemporary critics did not look upon Spillane with much delight. In their view, he was not only a bad writer but a bad habit for Americans. And more, he stood for the threat that paperback books presented. Critic Dwight Macdonald wrote:

> The kind of detective fiction which might be called the "classic style" . . . has been overshadowed by the rank noxious growth of works in the sensational style . . . enormously stepped up in voltage by Mickey Spillane. . . . The sensationalists use what for the classicists was the point—the uncovering of a criminal—as a mere excuse for the minute description of scenes of bloodshed, brutality and alcoholism. . . . A decade ago, the late George Orwell showed how the brutalization of the genre mirrors the general degeneration from the 19th century standards. What he would have written had Mickey Spillane's works then been in existence, I find it hard to imagine. ["A Theory of Mass Culture" in *Mass Culture in America,* edited by Bernard Rosenberg and David Manning White]

Inveighing against both Spillane and the publishers who brought him forth to the masses, critic Bernard Rosenberg commented, "What makes mass culture so tantalizing is the implication of effortlessness. Shakespeare is dumped on the market along with Mickey Spillane and publishers are rightly confident that their audience will not feel obliged to make any greater preparation for the master of world literature than for the latest lickspittle."

Spillane found a somewhat less harsh critic in Charles Rolo, who at Victor Weybright's behest wrote an article comparing Spillane to Georges Simenon, the French novelist who was then Europe's best-selling writer and the master of using the mystery to explore the psychology of character. While glorifying neither Spillane's technique nor the sophistication of his plots, Rolo found something in Spillane and Simenon—in fact, in most modern mysteries—that previous commentators had passed over. Rolo declared that the mystery was the twentieth-century version of the Passion play. The murderer is Everyman; the murder, the imperfection in all mankind. Wrote Rolo, "They allow us to play, vicariously, the role of different kinds of Savior." ["Simenon and Spillane" in *New World Writing: First Meator Selection*]

While Rolo's metaphysical musings seemed to wander pretty far afield—did Spillane really see Hammer as a "parfit gentile knight"?—his essay served as a counterpoint to critics of the reprinters, who asked, "Can anything good come out of the paperback?" Spillane, because of his extraordinary successes and excesses, had become a lightning rod for criticism of paperbacks. In him, all of the sins of the paperback reprinters were gathered. But the adventures of Mike Hammer were far from the only example of how low the paperback could sink. Many of the Gold Medal originals, for instance, were drawing the ire of censors who found the covers pornographic and the contents immoral. Ace, Avon, and Dell were not far behind, and a score of lesser reprints that came and went stuck to the low road. After Spillane, however, perhaps the most infamous group of paperbacks was the surge of urban gang novels that emerged in the late forties and early fifties. Juvenile delinquency was increasing at the beginning of the 1950s—or at least it was getting more attention. "More discipline" was already being preached from the pulpits. Ennui, the beginnings of affluence, and the atmosphere of fear and repression that characterized the American fifties probably all played their part. Perhaps it was the beginning of the restlessness that found full expression in the Beat Generation and their flower children successors. Parents and preachers began to link their children's unruly behavior with the rude new music called rock and roll, so wild and frenzied compared with the gentler tones of Liberace, Patti Page, Perry Como, and Pat Boone. Whatever the cause, the unsettling specter of an angry young generation began to appear in movies and books.

In an attempt to "expose" the craziness of the young, Hollywood produced the generation's first cult gods in *Rebel Without a Cause* (1955), with James Dean, and *The Wild One* (1954), with Marlon Brando. ("Whatcha rebelling against, Johnny?" "Whaddya got?") The trend was also visible in novels like Irving Shulman's *The Amboy Dukes* (Avon), which sold more than four million copies, and Hal Ellson's *Duke* (Popular Library), *Tomboy* (Bantam), and *The Golden Spike* (simultaneous Ballantine hardcover/paperback). Another of the most famous of this teen gang genre—one of the first books to be passed around by kids who "indexed" the good pages—was *The Blackboard Jungle* (1954), Evan Hunter's first novel. The book was especially well thumbed for two reasons: the scene in which a teacher is assaulted and an early appearance in paperback of the word *fuck* (until that time, it had been deleted, bowdlerized, or printed as "f—k"). Bud Egbert, then a Pocket Books salesman who had joined the home office at the time the book was released, later recalled, "A wholesaler sent a wire to our office and said under no circumstances would he put this book out, and if we had any questions, see page so-and-so. That sent all our little secretaries dashing to find the book. And there it was." Although it was successful in paperback, *The Blackboard Jungle* had an even greater impact as a film. In the screen version, Bill Haley and the Comets sang "Rock Around the Clock," and rock and roll was here to stay. Parents now had irrefutable evidence that rock and roll and juvenile delinquency went hand in hand.

While Mickey Spillane and the teen gangs seemed to be taking control of the paperback racks in the heartland, their domination was not complete. Like a wildflower struggling up through the ash heap, better books were pushing through to the marketplace and surviving. Despite DeVoto's contention that good books in paperback were impossible to find, quality—as subjective a term as any—was finding its way through the cracks. The promise of the Paperback Revolution was that all books would find their audience, given the opportunity. If the reprinters were guilty of bringing forth the worst that the mass culture in the 1950s was capable of producing, they were also responsible for some of its finer moments. At its best the paperback could offer, as NAL's slogan neatly put it, "Good Reading for the Millions," and this was the Great Contradiction, echoed in the comment of critic David Dempsey. "As for the horrendous Spillane—perhaps he is the price we must pay in a democratic culture, for being able to buy *A Passage to India* for 25 cents. As bargains go, it is not so bad."

KEY PAPERBACKS: 1950-1955

1950

This Side of Innocence
Taylor Caldwell (Bantam; first 35¢ Giant)

Laura
Vera Caspary (Popular Library; movie tie-in)

Knight's Gambit
William Faulkner (Signet)

The Revolt of the Masses
José Ortega y Gasset (Mentor)

The First Lady Chatterley
D. H. Lawrence (Avon)

Reflections in a Golden Eye
Carson McCullers (Bantam)

Sex and Temperament
Margaret Mead (Mentor)

Focus
Arthur Miller (Popular Library)

The Young Lions
Irwin Shaw (Signet Double)

Forever Amber
Kathleen Winsor (Signet Double)

How to Survive an Atomic Bomb
Adapted from the government's "The Effect of Atomic Weapons" (Bantam)

1951

The Man with the Golden Arm
Nelson Algren (Pocket)

Judgment Day
James T. Farrell (Signet)

Tender Is the Night
F. Scott Fitzgerald (Bantam Giant)

The Man Who Sold the Moon
Robert Heinlein (Signet)

For Whom the Bell Tolls
Ernest Hemingway (Bantam Giant)

The Naked and the Dead
Norman Mailer (Signet Double)

1984
George Orwell (Signet)

A Rage to Live
John O'Hara (Bantam Fifty)

All Quiet on the Western Front
Erich Maria Remarque (Lion)

The Snow Was Black
Georges Simenon (Signet)

A Streetcar Named Desire
Tennessee Williams (Signet)

1952

When Worlds Collide
Edwin Balmer and Philip Wylie (Dell)

What to Listen for in Music
Aaron Copland (Mentor)

The 42nd Parallel
John Dos Passos (Pocket)

The Story of Philosophy
Will Durant (Pocket)

A General Introduction to Psychoanalysis
Sigmund Freud (Perma Special)

The Way West
A. B. Guthrie (Pocket)

Brave New World
Aldous Huxley (Bantam)

A Documentary History of the United States
Richard D. Heffner (Mentor original)

Buddenbrooks
Thomas Mann (Pocket)

The Greatest Story Ever Told
Fulton Oursler (Perma)

Burmese Days
George Orwell (Popular Library)

Fountainhead
Ayn Rand (Signet; first Triple Volume, 75¢)

Lie Down in Darkness
William Styron (Signet Double)

Only the Dead Know Brooklyn
Thomas Wolfe (Signet)

New World Writing, No. 1
(Mentor)

1953

Fahrenheit 451
Ray Bradbury (Ballantine simultaneous original)

The Shaping of the Modern Mind
Crane Brinton (Mentor)

Out of My Life and Thought
Albert Einstein (Mentor)

Invisible Man
Ralph Ellison (Signet Double)

Mosquitoes
William Faulkner (Dell)

Sartoris
William Faulkner (Signet)

The Diary of a Young Girl
Anne Frank (Pocket)

Mythology
Edith Hamilton (Mentor)

Kon Tiki
Thor Heyerdahl (Perma)

New Poems by American Poets
Rolf Humphries, ed. (Ballantine original)

The Night Has a Thousand Eyes
William Irish (pseudonym of Cornell Woolrich) (Dell First Edition)

From Here to Eternity
James Jones (Signet Triple Volume)

The Imitation of Christ
Thomas à Kempis (Pocket)

Studies in Classic American Literature
D. H. Lawrence (Anchor)

Growing Up in New Guinea
Margaret Mead (Mentor)

The Lonely Crowd (abridged edition)
David Riesman (Anchor)

A Stone for Danny Fisher
Harold Robbins (Pocket)

The Catcher in the Rye
J. D. Salinger (Signet)

The Day of the Locust
Nathanael West (Bantam)

I Thought of Daisy
Edmund Wilson (Ballantine; reissue of a 25-year-old novel with negligible original sale)

The Theory of the Leisure Class
Thorstein Veblen (Mentor)

Discovery, No. 1
Vance Bourjaily and John W. Aldridge, eds. (Pocket)

New Voices: American Writing Today
(Perma)

7 Arts (reprinted arts criticism)
(Perma)

Junkie
William Lee (William S. Burroughs) (Ace)

Lady Chatterley's Lover (abridged)
D. H. Lawrence (Signet)

Sons and Lovers
D. H. Lawrence (Signet)

1954

Go Tell It on the Mountain
James Baldwin (Signet)

The Sea Around Us
Rachel Carson (Mentor)

The Long Goodbye
Raymond Chandler (Pocket)

The Body Snatchers
Jack Finney (Dell First Edition original)

An Analysis of the Kinsey Reports on Sexual Behavior
Donald Geddes, ed. (Mentor)

The Wall
John Hersey (Pocket/Cardinal Giant)

The Song of God: The Bhagavad-Gita
Christopher Isherwood, translator (Mentor original)

Daisy Miller and *The Turn of the Screw*
Henry James (Dell)

The Mad Reader
Harvey Kurtzman (Ballantine original)

Philosophy in a New Key
Susanne Langer (Mentor)

Down and Out in Paris and London
George Orwell (Perma)

The Meaning of the Glorious Koran
Marmaduke Pickthall, translator (Mentor simultaneous original)

Never Leave Me
Harold Robbins (Avon original)

Nine Stories
J. D. Salinger (Signet)

East of Eden
John Steinbeck (Bantam)

Messiah
Gore Vidal (Ballantine)

Utopia-14 (Player Piano)
Kurt Vonnegut (Bantam)

The Outsider
Richard Wright (Signet)

1955

The Age of Enlightenment
Isaiah Berlin (Mentor original)

You Asked for It (Casino Royale)
Ian Fleming (Popular Library)

The Age of Belief
Anne Freemantle (Mentor original)

The Blackboard Jungle
Evan Hunter (Pocket/Cardinal)

The Fires of Spring
James Michener (Bantam)

Sayonara
James Michener (Bantam)

The Red Pony
John Steinbeck (Bantam)

Just as the much-vilified Spillane was gaining his full stride in the paperback market, New American Library was diverting some of its profits toward a project so at odds with everything that Mickey Spillane's novels represented that NAL's involvement in both undertakings seemed implausible. Victor Weybright's once-strong relationship with Allen Lane had soured after their bitter separation in 1947, but Weybright still looked to Lane and Penguin as the model paperback operation in many respects. And it was Weybright's translation of Penguin ideas into New American Library actions that inspired a cultural high-water mark for the paperback book during the 1950s in the *New World Writing* series. As Weybright wrote in the introduction to the first issue, "By publishing new work in these pages, we hope to give aspiring authors a respected position in a sort of literary salon amongst the eminent. . . . If our publication can expedite the flow of international literature, it will fulfill its most important purpose."

The statement was bold, if not audacious—as well as somewhat pompous. Particularly coming, as it did, from a paperback publisher, Mickey Spillane's publisher, no less. But having announced such lofty goals, the editors of *New World Writing* spent seven years in the pursuit of literary excellence. From 1952, the year in which New American Library launched the series, until 1959, when the fifteenth and final NAL issue was released, *New World Writing* represented the best and brightest in American letters ever published by an American paperback house. To a large degree, Weybright's ambitious designs were fulfilled. Among its achievements, *NWW* could count the first appearance of a segment from a biting antiwar novel then titled *Catch-18* by unknown Joseph Heller; one of the first American appearances of an obscure Irishman named Beckett, living in Paris and writing in French, and the first excerpt from an unpublished novel by another unknown named Kerouac.

The concept behind the project was simple: to combine the literary excellence and avant-gardism of small magazines like the *Kenyon Review* and *Story* with the mass market distribution machinery of the paperback book. If the experiment worked, it would attest to the existence of a large, unacknowledged American audience for serious fiction, poetry, drama, and belles-lettres. At the same time, it would prove to a disdainful literary community that the paperback wasn't all trash. It was not an idea without precedent, and Weybright readily credited the influential *Penguin New Writing* as the model. Launched in November 1940, at the nadir of Britain's war fortunes, *Penguin New Writing* had been the result of an unlikely collaboration between Allen Lane, the mastermind behind Penguin but never an intellectual or even at home with the literary elite, and John Lehmann, a Brahmin in that same elite and a partner in the Hogarth Press with Virginia and Leonard Woolf. J. E. Morpurgo later said of the project, "*Penguin New Writing* was dedicated to two gods: Literary excellence and anti-Fascism. Allen was prepared to offer devotion to both deities." [*Allen Lane: King Penguin*]

Throughout the war years and after, *Penguin New Writing* served as home to some of the finest British writers of the period, including Graham Greene and George Orwell. At *New Writing*'s peak, each issue sold more than a hundred thousand copies. Wrote Morpurgo, "*Penguin New Writing* must be numbered amongst the most significant of all Penguin ventures, the voice of a literature at war, a platform for distinguished writers of the middle generation, a source of hope to their neophyte juniors and a link between writers and their dispersed audience."

For Weybright and Enoch of New American Library, the link to Penguin and *New Writing* was more than inspirational. New American Library had developed out of the New York office of Penguin, and while still associated with Allen Lane, the American operation had imported the series into the United States along with other Penguin books. To Weybright, the demise of *Penguin New Writing* in 1950 offered the opportunity to plant NAL's flag in new literary territory. In a confidential memo to Rudolf Littauer, NAL's attorney and, like Kurt Enoch, a German émigré, Weybright outlined the rationale behind *New World Writing*. "The proposed journal would identify NAL at once with the important writers of the future; it would win their respect and good will; it would be an investment in our future list." In addition, Weybright said, such a project would build morale and summon up the creativity of the staff, and "it will give us a standing among critics, writers and teachers. It would establish NAL as the intangible salon of literature in New York."

Less than one year later, in April 1952, after months of extensive contacts with agents, writers, and other publishers, the first issue was ready. With an initial print run of one hundred thousand copies, the book had been designed by the prominent book designer Ernst Reichl, perhaps most famous for his work on the Random House edition of *Ulysses*. The issue also introduced the fifty-cent cover price to the Mentor series, up from thirty-five cents. On the front cover, *New World Writing: The First Mentor Selection* was billed as "An Important Cross Section of Literature and Criticism."

In an introductory note, Weybright wrote:

> It is intended to be more than just a sprightly anthology which at first glance it may appear to be. It is a Mentor Book. As a Mentor, it will benefit from widespread distribution, at home and abroad, to thousands of newsstands and bookshops no existing literary or scholarly publication reaches. . . . The intention of *New World Writing* is to provide a friendly medium through which promising, genuine and vigorous talent may be communicated to a wide and receptive audience, and also to provide an instrument for serious letters and criticism. . . .

The cover of the first issue offered evidence that the editors had gone a long way toward reaching their goal. The line-up was, as promised, a mingling of the established with the newcomers. Isherwood, Williams, Auchincloss, Vidal, and Merton were familiar to both the literary community and a wider audience. Isherwood's

Berlin Stories had already made him something of a cause célèbre. Williams was internationally famous for *A Streetcar Named Desire.* Auchincloss and Vidal were both young darlings of the literati. Merton's *Seven Storey Mountain* had been a hardcover best seller in 1949. But among the other names—some of which later gained fame—were some newcomers whose published works had been limited to the small magazines. Flannery O'Connor had published only in the *Sewanee Review* and the *Partisan Review,* although *Wise Blood,* her first novel, from which her contribution was excerpted, was about to be published. Shelby Foote had written three books, and the excerpt that appeared was from his concurrently published Civil War novel, *Shiloh;* his piece reads with as much power and immediacy thirty years later as when it first appeared. William Gaddis—whose selection was the most avant-garde piece in the first collection—was at the time unpublished, his novel *The Recognition* not yet complete. Giuseppe Berto, whose novels had been published by New Directions, was a young Italian writer-journalist who began to write while a prisoner of war in Texas during World War II, and his contribution was set in a prison camp.

Upon publication, *New World Writing* garnered an enthusiastic reception. Calling it a "consciously high-brow but eclectic anthology of avant-garde writing," George Mayberry of the *New York Times* wrote, "The overall worth of the volume certainly outweighs the inadequacy and ineptitude of a good many of the writers included. [He liked Isherwood, Locke, Foote, Morris, Macauley, and Seide; he disliked Gaddis, Williams, and Alice Dennis.] It is salutary that, at a time when the paperback book field is largely dominated by private eyes and cowboys, the publishers of Mickey Spillane have seen fit to bring this experiment, and frequently exciting volumes, to the newspaper stands and railway terminals." Critic Carlos Baker wrote to Weybright, "It strikes me as a superior piece of sampling of the present new writing." Publisher William Targ commented, "The best 50 cents worth of reading in this or any other year." Northrop Frye said in a letter to Weybright, "It seems to me not only an excellent selection in itself but an ingenious and admirable publishing idea. I have often thought that something like this was the only way of getting good new writing across, as bound volumes don't sell and little magazines fold." However, not all the responses came from the literary world. A reader in Brookline, Massachusetts, wrote to NAL, "I read with keen interest the first volumes in your *NWW* series and I am moved to express my admiration for you for publishing them. It is refreshing to find a publisher who does not share the views of Hollywood producers, Broadway producers and most magazine publishers and who believes that intelligence and creativity are not incompatible with wide circulation. The trend which you have started may well be the beginning of a sweeping change of attitude among the businessmen who are engaged in presenting the arts to the people in this country." And from a housewife in Alexandria, Virginia: "Your *NWW* is a joy to me. It is lonesome to be a 36 year old housewife living on love, PTA, seed catalogues and

a lousy library. The little book gives me a lot of new thought—new names to look for—new things to see. I hope you continue the selection."

Though the series was helpful to careers and boosted morale among the contributors, it did not make any of them rich. The payment rate was two and a half cents per word, whether you were unknown William Gaddis or celebrated Tennessee Williams (except in cases where pieces were specially commissioned). For the first issue, for instance, Louis Auchincloss received $142.43 on the first printing and an additional $16.09 when the issue went back to press. Flannery O'Connor got $83.08 plus $9.38. Wright Morris earned a total of $76.34. Poetry was even less profitable for the writer. James Schuyler received $7.50; Howard Moss, $11.53; Howard Nemerov, $22.50. The smallest payment, for the shortest poem, went to James Laughlin for his whimsical contribution:

> "The Egotrori"
>
> I think is what those science
> fellows should develop next.

NAL's executive editor, Arabel Porter, was given the job of overseeing the editorial composition of the series, coordinating submissions, commissioning articles, and contacting writers. However, it was apparent that *New World Writing* would demand the attention of the rest of the editorial staff, and the other editors as well as Weybright were pressed into service as readers. All submissions were read by the staff and selection by consensus rapidly developed. Most of the material that made it into the magazine, which was scheduled twice yearly, came from agents, by direct solicitation from writers, or from other publishers eager to place material from forthcoming novels because they realized that an appearance in *NWW* was an influential platform for their writers. However, unsolicited manuscripts came pouring in over the proverbial transom. Arabel Porter once estimated that at least fifteen hundred original manuscripts were read for each issue of *New World Writing.* While the reading alone constituted a herculean task, there were also problems of legal questions, rights clearances, and the awesome job of designing and typesetting such a wide variety of materials in an aesthetically pleasing format—a challenge further complicated when the series grew to include original artwork and photography.

A key member of NAL's editorial staff during this period was Marc Jaffe, a Harvard graduate and a Marine during the Second World War who had worked for *Argosy* magazine before joining NAL. Although he was nominally the mystery and Western editor at NAL, Jaffe became an important contributor to *New World Writing's* editorial development. On vacation in Europe in 1952, for instance, Jaffe also did some scouting for NAL. Writing to Arabel Porter from Paris, Jaffe suggested that NAL publish something of Jean Genet's, and a portion of *The Thief's Journal* appeared in the second issue. Jaffe also wrote of having dinner there with William Styron, whose

Lie Down in Darkness NAL published, and Peter Mathiessen, at that time organizing *The Paris Review,* who was a contributor to *New World Writing* No. 3. Jaffe also wrote, "Have you heard about Samuel Beckett, an Irishman (not young) writing in French?" That was the beginning of *New World Writing*'s courtship of the future Nobel Prize winner. Some time after his return to New York, Jaffe wrote in a memo to Porter, "I have been following developments on this author ever since my return from Europe and now we are actively interested in getting some of his work in the next *NWW.* I have been in continuous contact with his American publishers-to-be, the Grove Press, and his agent Marion Saunders. The Grove Press intends to publish his play, *En Attendant Godot,* next spring. I thought it might be advisable to get an extract from the play, but it seems that this is inadvisable due to the structure and style of the work."

Weybright's interest in Beckett was sparked, and he wrote to Porter, "What would you think of having Niall Montgomery undertake an article on Beckett? I think we could do a great turn for modern literature by an article on Beckett that described his life as well as his work and attempted to interpret his significance." Certain that *Godot* was not right for *NWW,* Jaffe instead proposed an excerpt from the novel *Molloy.* "I think it would be quite a coup to publish the *Molloy* translation. Whatever the significance of Beckett, I think we want to get him into the next *NWW* before any of our competing publications publish any of him." An excerpt from *Molloy* did indeed appear—along with an essay, "No Symbol Where None Intended" by Niall Montgomery, a vain attempt at Beckett-explicating—in *New World Writing* No. 5 (April 1954), netting Beckett $100. A second piece, "Yellow," a short story, was published in No. 10 (November 1956), for which Beckett received $128.

Jaffe's concerns about "competing publications" were legitimate. Although *New World Writing* was first out of the gate with the idea of a "mass market small magazine," Pocket Books was readying a similar project, and in February 1953 *discovery* No. 1 was published. Unlike *New World Writing,* which was conceived and edited inside NAL, *discovery* was the child of two outsiders who brought their idea to Pocket Books: Vance Bourjaily, who had published a first novel to little success and no paperback reprint, and John Aldridge, who had written admiringly of Bourjaily in his essay "After the Lost Generation." The two met as a result of that article, and the idea for *discovery* was hatched. Bourjaily was familiar with *Penguin New Writing,* which he had read while stationed in Cairo and Beirut during the war. Like Weybright, Bourjaily cited *New Writing* as the inspiration for a similar American publication. Aldridge and Bourjaily took the idea to Pocket Books, where they got a receptive hearing from Herbert Alexander, Pocket Books' vice president and editorial director. Doc Lewis was less enthusiastic. As Bourjaily recalled, "He took the view that paperbacks were, and always would be, an adjunct to hardcover publishing. He may have changed later. But the idea that a paperback should be a reprint

was being challenged at NAL by Victor Weybright. Doc never doubted that he was right, but he was willing to hedge his bets. He felt that within two years he would know who would prevail." With the prodding of Herbert Alexander, who realized that the project meant Pocket Books' editors would gain experience in handling writers, contacts with authors and agents, and advance word about books in progress, Pocket Books went ahead with the series, launching it under its thirty-five-cent Cardinal imprint.

Given an office and a borrowed secretary, Aldridge and Bourjaily edited the first issue. In their preface, they wrote, "In planning *discovery,* we began by rejecting the cynical portrait of the American reader as a juvenile oaf. We rejected the timorous assumption that pressure groups can put an honest magazine out of business. We rejected the kind of practicality which dictates that the contents of a large-circulation magazine must be inoffensively general, meeting the romantic needs of the pablum set at both ends of the human life span and leaving nothing of merit for the adults in the middle."

The magazine was dedicated to the principle of no principles. No "school" was encouraged, no trends promoted, no style rejected as unstylish. It was, as the editors said, "for its writers rather than its readers in the firm conviction that the role of literature in human history is to lead and not to follow." There were only a few unwritten general guidelines. All material was appearing for the first time; at least one new writer was introduced in each issue; a novella was published in each issue; and in marked contrast to *New World Writing,* all the contributors were to be American.

If the whole affair had the ring of "The Hardy Boys Start a Literary Revolution," the youthful enthusiasm was not misspent. In the first issue, with its Paul Klee-ish cover, were stories by Norman Mailer, Stanley Baron, Hortense Calisher, Herbert Gold, and the first appearance of William Styron's *The Long March.* Having collected all the work, Bourjaily discovered there was no nonfiction, so he wrote "Confessions of an American Marijuana Smoker" under the pseudonym U.S.D. Quincy. It was an account of seven disappointing experiences with "hemp." Bourjaily later learned of a graffiti exchange that took place in a Greenwich Village bar known for its marijuana smokers, where someone wrote "U.S.D. Quincy is a fink." Underneath was added, "U.S.D. Quincy is the editor of *discovery.*" Bourjaily later commented about the essay, "That piece was important to me. It formed the core of my novel *Confessions of a Spent Youth.*"

After two issues, Aldridge departed amicably and Bourjaily received more assistance from Pocket Books personnel. Future novelist Anne Bernays became his assistant, and Robert Pack took on the poetry editing. Pocket Books editors Bob Kotlowitz and Larry Hughes also had a hand in the selection, and the publisher set up Bourjaily in an office at 20 West Forty-seventh Street from which he could edit the series. Pocket Books was rewarded when *discovery* used an Evan Hunter story, later published in hardcover by Simon & Schuster as *The Blackboard Jungle* and reprinted by Pocket Books to strong success.

A healthy rivalry between *discovery* and *New World Writing* soon developed. As Bourjaily put it: "My feeling was that there were two camps, *discovery* fans and *New World Writing* fans. There were distinctions between us. It's fair to say they weren't redundant. We did different things. We weren't pros; we thought of ourselves as writers. These were the emerging group of postwar American writers, rather than an eclectic selection of world literature." Although they competed for manuscripts, Bourjaily and Arabel Porter met and became friendly, with Porter occasionally tipping off Bourjaily to something *New World Writing* did not use. Saul Bellow's "The Gonzaga Manuscripts," which appeared in *discovery* No. 6, had been rejected by *New World Writing*. Victor Weybright was not interested in reciprocation. Bourjaily reported that Weybright said, "We won't do *discovery* rejects."

By the time the sixth issue of *discovery* rolled around, Bourjaily was already moving on, returning to his own writing. He had never intended to make *discovery* a permanent position for himself—he was a writer, not an editor—but he expected the project would continue after his departure. He was mistaken. As Bourjaily put it, "They wouldn't have missed me, but my leaving provided the occasion for Doc to say, 'If Vance isn't going to be the editor, perhaps we should discontinue.'" In addition, although *discovery* was paying for itself, it was making no "contribution to overhead." The sixth *discovery* was the last. In the meantime, others had tried similarly to make a go of it. Avon published *Modern Writing* and *New Voices* taken from the *Partisan Review,* and Permabooks put out *New Writers* and *7 Arts.* (All of these reprinted material from magazines rather than publishing original work.) But after brief life spans, these too disappeared, leaving *New World Writing* to carry the banner for mass market paperback publishers in the little-magazine area.

Through seven years and fifteen issues, it more or less succeeded. The pressures of a two-a-year schedule meant occasional unevenness in the quality, but in the main, *New World Writing*'s track record was dazzling. Not only had the most interesting emerging writers of the fifties been published—those on the cutting edge of new trends in fiction of the period—but Weybright had fulfilled his promise of internationalism by offering the contemporary work of Irish, Dutch, Japanese, Arabic, South Korean, Brazilian, Ghanaian, and Icelandic poets.

But it was for short fiction that the series was best known. Few major writers of the period were not represented. Norman Mailer, Nelson Algren, James Baldwin (an excerpt from *Go Tell It on the Mountain*), Heinrich Böll, Jorge Luis Borges, Ralph Ellison, James T. Farrell, Nadine Gordimer (a chapter from her unpublished first novel), Eugene Ionesco (*The Bald Soprano,* with illustra-

tions by Saul Steinberg), James Jones, Nikos Kazantzakis, Seán O'Faoláin, Boris Pasternak, Ignazio Silone, Glendon Swarthout, and Dylan Thomas (*Adventures in the Skin Trade* was excerpted before publication) all appeared one or more times. There were also essays by Margaret Mead ("Sex and Censorship in Contemporary Society," commissioned by Weybright in response to the Gathings committee's investigation into obscene paperbacks); a section from Louis Armstrong's autobiography, "Storyville Days and Nights"; Erskine Caldwell's "How to Live Like an Author"; Malcolm Cowley's "The Time of the Rhetoricians"; André Gide's "On Literary Influence"; and Dan Wakefield's discussion of J. D. Salinger.

There were also the famous newcomers such as Joseph Heller, whose "Catch-18" was the first chapter of a novel in progress. When it was received from Heller's agent, one of NAL's editors, Walter Freeman, told Porter, "Of all the recommended pieces lately, this stands out. It seems like a part of a really exciting, amusing novel." Victor Weybright called it the "funniest thing we have ever had for *NWW.*" The other editors agreed, and "Catch-18" was accepted. Heller received $125 for the excerpt. He wrote to Arabel Porter, "I should like to tell you at this time that it was with great delight and pride that I received news that you were interested in publishing a section of *Catch-18;* and I should like to express my thanks for the recognition implicit in your decision and the encouragement I have received from it." After the first excerpt was published, another, called "Hungry Joe," was rejected, but Arabel Porter asked Heller's agent, "Has he finished the novel? And if so, may we see it?" Unfortunately for NAL, the publication of Heller's excerpt did not give them the inside track on the novel, which was published by Simon & Schuster as *Catch-22* and reprinted by Dell.

One of the over-the-transom submissions that made the pages of *NWW* was from unknown Thomas Berger. In her comments to the other editors, Porter wrote, "I think this is an extraordinary piece of writing, a good muscular style and considerable irony. I think we should buy it." Porter asked Berger for a more arresting title than the one he had submitted, "The Advocate." He wrote back suggesting "Confession of a Giant." Published in *NWW* No. 8, the story was a piece of Berger's unfinished first novel, *Crazy in Berlin.* He was paid $217, and the story led to the novel's publication. (The money came in handy. At the time, Berger was struggling and also took on some freelance copyreading chores from Porter to help make ends meet.) *New World Writing* also launched Shirley Ann Grau ("White Girl, Fine Girl" in *NWW* No. 4 and "Isle aux Chiens" in *NWW* No. 10) and published in *NWW* No. 10 Anatole Broyard's "For He's a Jolly Good Fellow," a story that Broyard had submitted himself after earlier work had been published in *discovery.*

The other great "find" of *New World Writing* came by way of Malcolm Cowley, who suggested a manuscript recently rejected by Viking, where he was an editorial consultant. "It's a very long autobiographical novel by John Kerouac. It's about the present generation of wild boys on their travels between New York, San Francisco and Mexico City. . . . Of all the beat generation crowd, Kerouac is the only one who *can* write and the only one who doesn't get published." "Jazz of the Beat Generation" was published in *NWW* No. 7 under the pseudonym "Jean-Louis"; Kerouac received $120 for the excerpt from what came to be *On the Road.*

Despite its critical successes, *New World Writing* was barely paying its bills. The first several issues had gone to press more than once, raising unrealistic expectations that were gradually brought down to earth as print runs went up to 135,000 copies and then fell back down to 100,000 for the later issues. Although the series was covering its own expenses, it was creating an enormous drain on the editorial staff, and by 1959, after fifteen issues, New American Library was ready to call it quits. The total sales for the series had been over one million copies, but its influence on readers and writers and the contemporary literary scene far outweighed simple numbers. In the supposedly uneventful fifties, *New World Writing,* along with *discovery,* had stood for the new, the challenging—the assault on the status quo. Even if the series did not always succeed, it was not for lack of enthusiasm. At the time of its demise, Victor Weybright said, "The silver lining in the dark cloud over *NWW* is that Lippincott will carry on with the project henceforth. [It was dropped after three issues.] It has been financially successful [not so], but we are encountering arrears of energy, so I hand the torch to others so our editors can get on with the many projects facing us. Besides, we don't need *NWW* to demonstrate—as seemed important in 1952—that paperback books are not a vulgar juggernaut."

The liveliness of these "small magazines" was testimony to the fact that this period of the 1950s was not just a stretch of eight years when Eisenhower slept. The social novelists of the 1930s—Farrell, Caldwell, O'Hara—and the reportorial novelists of the 1940s—Hersey, Michener, Wouk—were giving way to a literature of alienation in the 1950s, represented by Styron in *Lie Down in Darkness,* Ellison's *Invisible Man,* Mailer's essay "The White Negro," and later by Saul Bellow. It was a sense of disaffection peculiar to America's youth, and while some paperback publishers had exploited this disaffection with violent gang fiction, other writers were treating it more seriously. To a large extent, they were writers who appealed to the growing ranks of younger paperback readers who were discovering their deepening estrangement from mainstream, grey flannel America. It was an unease voiced by Mailer, Malamud, and Styron, and in the non-fiction of C. Wright Mills. But two novelists seemed to capture this growing separation between the old generation and the new better than anyone else. Both were published in paperback by NAL, as were Styron, Mailer, and Ellison. They were J. D. Salinger and Jack Kerouac, and they became two of the first authors deserving of a label coined years later, the "paperback literati." Although

Salinger's and Kerouac's disgust with society was mutual, it took the two in opposite directions.

J. D. Salinger was born in New York City in 1919, attended public schools, a military academy, and three colleges; he served in the army from 1942 to 1946. Salinger had been writing stories since he was fifteen and was already familiar to *New Yorker* readers when *The Catcher in the Rye* was published by Little, Brown in 1951 and became a Book-of-the-Month Club selection. After winning wide—not unanimous—critical acclaim, the novel made it to the best-seller list in *The Publishers' Weekly* and stayed there for five months, although not selling well enough to make it as one of the year's ten top-selling novels. (On the best-seller list along with Salinger's novel were Herman Wouk's *The Caine Mutiny,* Nicholas Monsarrat's *The Cruel Sea,* James Jones's *From Here to Eternity,* and William Styron's *Lie Down in Darkness.*) New American Library had purchased paperback rights in advance of publication, as Victor Weybright later recounted:

> One Friday afternoon I had received an advance copy of J. D. Salinger's *Catcher in the Rye.* I read it that evening and went into a cold sweat lest the reprint rights should be seized by a competitor if I waited until Monday morning. I tracked [Little, Brown publisher] Arthur Thornhill down on the telephone, made a deal and discovered later that we had beaten the field, most of whom did not receive their advance copies until [the] Monday or Tuesday following." [The Making of a Publisher]

Having propelled Weybright into such a fevered paroxysm, the slim volume about sixteen-year-old Holden Caulfield and his forty-eight-hour quixotic revolt against "phoniness" appeared in a twenty-five-cent Signet edition with a first printing of 350,000 copies in April 1953. A box on the cover read, "This unusual book may shock you, will make you laugh, and may break your heart—but *you will never forget it.*" For Signet and thirty years of readers to come, that statement was largely true. Few people were disappointed or unhappy about the book. Save one: J. D. Salinger.

Marc Jaffe (still an NAL editor at this point), who had been in communication with Salinger, recalled that the writer came to NAL's offices to discuss the book prior to its paperback appearance. "He said he would be much happier if the book had no illustrated cover at all. In fact, he would be happier if the book was distributed in mimeographed form. Of course, he had no control over the cover." Kurt Enoch, who was then responsible for covers, assigned NAL's star artist, James Avati, to paint the cover for *The Catcher in the Rye.* Avati produced a simple but effective illustration that showed Holden, wearing his famous red hunting hat turned backward and carrying his Gladstone bag, walking along a city street. He was passing in front of a nightclub that had some posters of semidressed women out front and Avati was asked to dress them up a bit, even though they were in the background. It was a most inoffensive cover, yet

Salinger was dismayed by it. As Jaffe explained, "The book went on to tremendous success, but even knowing Salinger was unhappy, NAL never changed that cover. When the license came up for renewal, I was at Bantam and it became known he was unhappy." Oscar Dystel, by then the head of Bantam, recalled that Little, Brown's Arthur Thornhill (who was on the Bantam board of directors) called to tell him of Salinger's difficulties with NAL. "He asked me if I might be interested in discussing Salinger. I said, 'I'll be on the next airplane.' I dropped everything, went to Boston, and asked Arthur what he wanted. We shook hands on a two-cent-per-book royalty and Arthur then told me that Salinger had to approve the cover. I said, 'Anything he wants. We'll do it on plain brown paper.' Salinger actually sent us a swatch to show us the color he wanted. He even selected the typeface. The *J* and the *D* were set in different types. Bantam still uses that cover."

Though writing out of a similar sense of alienation, Jack Kerouac couldn't have been more different from J. D. Salinger. In temperament, public visibility, and literary styles—the beats had only disdain for anyone who wrote for the "slick" *New Yorker*—Salinger and the high priest of the beats were in different universes. Yet they spoke to the same audience. Twenty-five years after *On the Road*, Jack Kerouac and his cohorts have attained near-mythic heights, like some beat Knights of the Round Table. Biographies, memoirs, and reconsiderations of Kerouac and the beats are churned out yearly, either adding to the myth or attempting to demystify this wild bunch who were sainted by the next generation when it also took to the road.

Jack Kerouac was born in 1922 in Lowell, Massachusetts, the third and last son of French-Canadian parents. The son of a printer, Kerouac earned local fame as a high school halfback good enough to win a scholarship to Columbia University, provided he take a year of college prep at the Horace Mann School. During the Second World War, he joined the merchant marines and wrote an unpublished novel, *The Sea Is My Brother*. He returned to the city, pulled by some force of culture or circumstance to the people he came to call the beats—Allen Ginsberg, William S. Burroughs, Herbert Huncke (who introduced Kerouac to speed), John Clellon Holmes, and, finally, the low-life drifter Neal Cassady, prototype for Dean Moriarty in *On the Road*. In 1950, Kerouac published his first book, *The Town and the City*, an autobiographical novel edited by Robert Giroux and published by Harcourt, Brace. While the book was in preparation, Kerouac was on the cross-country odyssey with Cassady that inspired *On the Road*. In 1951, he wrote *On the Road* in twenty days, a furiously typed, 120,000-word paragraph written on a single roll of taped-together art paper. Giroux rejected it. Through Allen Ginsberg and Carl Solomon, whose uncle was A. A. Wynn of Ace Books, Kerouac had gotten a contract with Ace, but Ace also turned down *On the Road*. It finally reached Malcolm Cowley at Viking, now in regular typescript, but there was no enthusiasm there besides Cowley's. The critic-editor nonetheless placed an excerpt with the *Paris Review* and another with Arabel Porter in *New* World Writing No. 7. The section that appeared in April 1955, "Jazz of the Beat Generation," was set in a San Francisco jazz club, an extended meditation on bop, written in a frenzied outpouring, a seemingly speed-induced paean to Lester Young and Charlie Parker. Kerouac insisted on using a pseudonym because he feared that his ex-wife would want the fee for child support of a daughter he claimed was not his.

On the Road, still with the support of Cowley, gained another sponsor at Viking, and they published the novel in 1957. Kerouac found a champion in Gilbert Milstein, daily book reviewer of the *New York Times,* who praised the novel to the skies, calling its publication a "historic occasion" and concluding, "*On the Road* is a major novel." The book made the *New York Times* best-seller list. Kerouac attained instant celebrity. In 1958, Signet issued the novel in a fifty-cent edition, to long-lasting success. (Kerouac's agent sold two other novels, *Maggie Cassidy* and *Tristessa,* to Avon as paper-back originals, published respectively in 1959 and 1960.)

Although Viking accepted Kerouac's *The Dharma Bums,* written in 1957 and published in 1958, it rejected his other work. However, he had found a new patron in Barney Rosset of Grove Press, who published *The Subterraneans* in 1953. Barney Rosset had emerged out of the early 1950s as the most enthusiastic publishing advocate of the avant-garde. The son of a wealthy Jewish banker and an Irish Catholic mother, Rosset attended Swarthmore and discovered Henry Miller, about whom he wrote a college paper. On a trip to New York he purchased a sub-rosa copy of *Tropic of Cancer*—printed in Mexico—from Frances Steloff in the legendary Gotham Book Mart. Finding Swarthmore restrictive, he transferred to the University of Chicago. A stint in the army followed. Rosset was an admirer of the books being published by New Directions, an avant-garde house famous for its annual review. While he was studying literature at the New School after his army service, someone suggested he buy a publishing company that had put out three books but was about to fold. So, almost on a whim, he bought Grove Press. The three books were Melville's *The Confidence Man, The Selected Writings of the Ingenious Aphra Behn,* and *The Verse in English of Richard Crashaw.* Hardly a daring beginning for the man who was to be almost single-handedly responsible for the rewriting of censorship laws in this country. Rosset proved his publishing inexperience by taking the three books, which had been paperbound, and issuing them in hardcover. It was 1952. Rosset was doing the exact opposite of what several other trade houses were about to try: converting out-of-print and academic titles into inexpensive paperback editions. It was the initiation of the next major stage of the Paperback Revolution, the "quality" paperback.

The idea of the trade paperback—which is sold mainly to the bookstore trade rather than through the mass market racks serviced by the magazine wholesalers—was not a new one in 1952. Many other experiments, including the Modern Age and Boni books of the 1930s, had been tried earlier in the century. But none of them seemed to fire the imagination of booksellers, who undoubtedly saw paperback books as a threat to their sales of hardcover books. Even the success of the mass market paperbacks had done little to dent their disdain. However, Mentor Books, because of their superior quality and higher price, began to gain a toehold in university classroom adoptions and eventually in regular bookstores.

The idea of direct paperback sales to bookstores gained more currency when Allen Lane of Penguin dispatched Harry Paroissien to the United States to pick up the pieces of Penguin Books, Inc., after the split with Enoch and Weybright. Relocating the operation in Baltimore, an East Coast port city that was cheaper to do business in than New York, Paroissien, at Lane's direction, moved the Penguins away from the mass market. Working from the strength of its rich backlist of literary classics, history, and other academically oriented titles, Paroissien aimed at the growing university and college market. As an indication of its principal interest in the educational market, Penguin made an agreement for distribution with the D. C. Heath Company, one of the country's largest textbook publishers. Clinging to this specialized market, Penguin sold some six hundred thousand books in America during 1951. Its profits were important to the home office, but the U.S. Penguin fulfilled another important function by providing a convenient overflow valve for its parent, which could set larger print orders back in England with the assurance of a certain level of American sales. Although the Penguins eventually flourished in this somewhat rarefied atmosphere and the Penguin name acquired a certain cachet among the literary, the company never gained in the United States the full measure of power and influence that the name Penguin conferred elsewhere in the world.

At about the same time that Paroissien was transplanting Penguin to Baltimore, a neophyte publisher named Hayward Cirker was building a company in Lower Manhattan out of scholarly titles that had been remaindered or lay dormant and out of print. In 1951, Cirker took three of the books from his Dover list of scientific, scholarly, technical, and art books and turned them out in paper covers. The books were Unamuno's *Tragic Sense of Life,* Planck's *Thermodynamics,* and *The Handbook of Designs and Devices.* Principally known as a mail-order house, Dover did have some penetration into the bookstore trade.

However, neither Penguin nor Dover had the astonishing impact that accompanied the appearance in 1952 of Doubleday's Anchor Books. Doubleday had already attempted mass market publishing with its Permabooks line, launched in 1948 with laminated board covers—more permanent than laminated paper covers, hence Permabooks—but had switched the series into paper covers in 1951 for reasons of economy. Doubleday apparently did not have the mass market touch, and by 1952 Permabooks was on the endangered species list. But Doubleday owned presses for the Permabook line and wanted to keep those presses rolling. Enter Jason Epstein, a young Columbia University graduate who proposed reissuing out-of-print hardcover titles, specifically tailored for the needs of colleges, as paperbacks that would be more expensive and better produced than the mass market books. The break-even point for the books was set at twenty-seven thousand copies. Could Doubleday really sell twenty-seven thousand copies of *The Lonely Crowd* or *Lafcadio's Adventures?* Or *The Idea of a Theater?* Epstein reportedly said, "I don't know how many people want to read it. But I'm sure that there are at least twenty-seven thousand who *think* they want to read it." [Martin Mayer, "Spock, Sex and Schopenhauer" in *Esquire*]

The books were rack-sized, as the Permabooks had been, many with covers by Edward Gorey, the noted and eccentric illustrator. The prices ranged from eighty-five cents up to $1.25, which was comparatively expensive even though a few mass market books had reached seventy-five cents by this time. And although they were aimed at graduate and post-graduate students, Anchor Books soon exceeded that circumscribed audience in an extraordinary fashion. In a few weeks, ten thousand copies of the first four titles had been sold. By 1954, sales were over six hundred thousand copies for the year. The reach of the books had gone beyond the university, into the bookstores and beyond. One element of this success was the fact that Anchor Books—as well as later trade paperbacks—offered a full "trade discount" of 40 percent to the bookstores instead of the 20 percent offered by mass market houses. Doubleday could also back Anchor with one of the largest and best-established groups of salesmen in the publishing business.

Aaron Asher, an editor who moved through a series of different trade paperback imprints during a distinguished career in publishing, recalled his first contact with Anchor. "I was serving in the army, stationed in Alabama between 1953 and 1955. I remember going into a stationery store in this strange southern town where they had a few newspapers and magazines. If you wanted a bookstore you had to go to Atlanta. But I was immediately struck by the first list of Anchor Books, and I was astonished to see them there. They were around ninety-five cents, which was startling then; it was still the day of the twenty-five-cent mass market book. But their covers were different and the books were completely different in nature."

By the time the Anchor series was off and running, Alfred A. Knopf soon joined in and issued its series of Vintage Books (Knopf himself is a great oenophile, and these books were the best from his "private stock"), all priced at ninety-five cents, published in rack size, and drawn from the estimable Knopf backlist, which included many of the finest writers of the preceding fifty years. Among the first Vintage titles were *The Art of Teaching* by Gilbert Highet, *The Stranger* by Albert Camus, *Death in Venice and Seven Other Stories* by Thomas Mann, and a two-volume edition of Tocqueville's *Democracy in America.*

The existence of the two new lines was unspoken testimony to the irrefutable fact that the paperback now occupied a central position in the publishing world. Anchor, Vintage, and their successors were another step in the continuum that had begun with Robert de Graff in 1939. While the mass market paperback that de Graff had brought forth helped to create a paperback readership, it had not always given that readership what it wanted. Anchor and Vintage quickly maneuvered to fill that void. As Epstein later explained, "When Anchor Books and Vintage began they tried to occupy some ground which was free at the time; that is, the mass market houses were publishing mainly books through magazine distributors while Anchor and Vintage and the other trade paperback lines that came later found that they could distribute profitably through direct accounts. We were trying to reach a much smaller and more specific audience, mainly academic, literary, highbrow—specialized in these and other ways."

The immediate widespread acceptance and success achieved by the two lines quickly inspired others to do the same. Beacon Press paperbacks, an offshoot of a Boston-based publisher, were originated by Sol Stein, and Meridian Books was launched by Arthur Cohen, co-founder with Cecil Hemley of Noonday Press; both Beacon and Meridian were among the first houses to go to a large-sized format, thus prompting the phrase "oversized paperback." Because they, like Vintage and Anchor, were primarily publishing serious nonfiction and classics and they all exhibited major improvements in design and production values over the mass market paperbacks, these books were soon christened quality paperbacks, a name that stuck for years to come. This was to the great displeasure of Enoch and Weybright at New American Library, who were properly peeved because they believed they had been publishing quality books since 1947. Another popular name for the trade paperbacks then was "egghead paperbacks," because of their intellectual qualities as well as the national prominence of "egghead" Adlai Stevenson, two-time loser to Eisenhower. Whatever they were called, by 1957 there were many more of them. R. R. Bowker, publisher of reference materials for the library and book market as well as of *The Publishers' Weekly,* began to produce a catalogue called *Paperbound Books in Print* in 1956 as a supplement to its annual *Books in Print.* The 1957 edition listed more than ninety firms issuing paperback books at that time, including the dozen or so mass market houses. (Those early issues of *Paperbound Books in Print* listed about 6000 titles, were bound in paper, and cost $2 per issue or $3 for a year's subscription to two volumes. The current edition comes in three volumes, bound in cloth, each the size of the Manhattan phone directory; it lists more than 220,000 titles and costs $69.50.)

Among this new wave of paperback publishers was Barney Rosset of Grove Press, who quickly saw the error

of his ways in binding his three books in hard covers. At considerable expense, he had the bindings cut off, and the three original Grove books were once again paperbacks, the first in the Evergreen line that was launched in 1954. It took much of Rosset's considerable personal fortune to keep Grove afloat in the early days as he published such titles as a bilingual edition of *Mid-Century French Poets,* Erich Fromm's *The Forgotten Language,* and Henry James's *The Sacred Fount.* But his reputation was shaped after a 1953 trip to Paris during which he saw *En Attendant Godot* and made the acquaintance of Samuel Beckett. Rosset brought the play back to the United States and published it in English in a hardcover edition that sold about three hundred copies at about the same time that the Broadway production with Bert Lahr mystified New York theatergoers and closed after some fifty performances. Rosset had already published some of Beckett's prose in Evergreen editions, and *Waiting for Godot* joined the list. (Rosset saved No. 33, his school football number, for *Godot.*) Although it didn't set any records, the paperback edition caught on as Beckett began to be considered more carefully in the United States. (The Evergreen edition of *Waiting for Godot,* so familiar to a generation of college students, has sold more than a million copies.) After Beckett, Rosset added the plays of Ionesco and Brecht. He was acquiring more visibility among the ranks of avant-gardists, particularly after the introduction of the *Evergreen Review,* a twice-a-year paperback magazine that was a showcase for the most experimental poets and novelists of the period, including Beckett, Burroughs, Ferlinghetti, Ginsberg, Robbe-Grillet, Camus, Henry Miller, and Günter Grass. In addition, Rosset underwrote Kerouac after Viking turned down his earlier work, and *The Subterraneans* (Evergreen 99) and *Doctor Sax* (Evergreen 160) were followed by later Kerouac work.

It was in 1959, however, that Rosset firmly fixed for himself and Grove a place in publishing and literary history. It also marked the beginning of a (somewhat) unfair image of Barney Rosset as "the dirty book man." (Writer Seymour Krim said of Rosset, "He was criticized in later years for making bucks out of porn when it was just that he was fascinated by sex in every conceivable shape and form.") Rosset, an ardent believer in the freedom to publish, decided that America was ready to read one of the great novels by one of the great novelists, *Lady Chatterley's Lover* by D. H. Lawrence. "It was part of my publishing philosophy to be against censorship," Rosset later remarked. "It was a perfect vehicle to fight censorship." With the approval of Lawrence's widow, Grove prepared an unexpurgated edition of the novel, which had been published in the United States only in an expurgated edition (in hardcover by Knopf and in paperback by NAL) because of a Post Office Department ban. To improve his case as a publisher of seriousness, Rosset enlisted the critic Mark Schorer to write an introduction, and the poet Archibald MacLeish, then Librarian of Congress, contributed a preface. Rosset's deliberate act of nose-thumbing was a signal that the sexual revolution and the massive social loosening of the 1960s were about to begin and censorship and the age of repression were on their way out.

KEY PAPERBACKS: 1956-1959

1956

Malone Dies
Samuel Beckett (Evergreen)

Waiting for Godot
Samuel Beckett (Evergreen)

Nerves
Lester del Rey (Ballantine original)

I, Libertine
"Frederick Ewing" (pseudonym of Jean Shepherd and Theodore Sturgeon) (Ballantine original)

Why Johnny Can't Read
Rudolf Flesch (Popular Library)

The Dead Sea Scriptures
Theodore H. Gaster, translator (Anchor original)

Child Behavior
Gesell Institute (Dell)

Existentialism from Dostoevsky
Walter Kaufmann (Meridian to Sartre original)

Out of the Silent Planet
C. S. Lewis (Avon)

Listen! The Wind
Anne Morrow Lindbergh (Dell)

A Night to Remember
Walter Lord (Bantam)

The Deer Park
Norman Mailer (Signet Double)

White Collar
C. Wright Mills (Oxford/Galaxy)

A Good Man Is Hard to Find
Flannery O'Connor (Signet)

79 Park Avenue
Harold Robbins (Pocket)

Bonjour Tristesse
Françoise Sagan (Dell)

God Is My Co-Pilot
Col. Robert L. Scott (Ballantine original)

Zen Buddhism
D. T. Suzuki (Anchor original)

Best Television Plays
Gore Vidal, ed. (Ballantine original)

The Man in the Gray Flannel Suit
Sloan Wilson (Pocket)

1957

Notes of a Native Son
James Baldwin (Meridian)

James Dean: A Biography
William Bast (Ballantine original)

The Quare Fellow
Brendan Behan (Evergreen original)

The Hedgehog and the Fox
Isaiah Berlin (Mentor)

The Bridge Over the River Kwai
Pierre Boulle (Bantam)

The Anatomy of Revolution
Crane Brinton (Vintage)

Naked and Tender
R. V. Cassil (Avon original)

Tales from the White Hart
Arthur C. Clarke (Ballantine original)

The Marquis de Sade
Simone de Beauvoir (Evergreen)

The Ginger Man
J. P. Donleavy (Evergreen)

On Life and Sex
Havelock Ellis (Mentor)

The Quiet American
Graham Greene (Bantam)

Death Be Not Proud
John Gunther (Pyramid)

Goodbye, Mr. Chips
James Hilton (Bantam)

The Journey to the East
Hermann Hesse (Noonday)

Siddhartha
Hermann Hesse (New Directions)

Andersonville
MacKinlay Kantor (Signet)

Profiles in Courage
John F. Kennedy (Pocket/Cardinal)

Perelandra
C. S. Lewis (Avon)

Gift from the Sea
Anne Morrow Lindbergh (Mentor)

Tales of the South Pacific
James Michener (Pocket)

Peyton Place
Grace Metalious (Dell)

The Cruel Sea
Nicholas Monsarrat (Pocket)

The Last Hurrah
Edwin O'Connor (Bantam)

Ten North Frederick
John O'Hara (Bantam)

Life of Christ
Giovanni Papini (Dell)

Evergreen Review
Barney Rosset and Donald Allen, eds. (Evergreen original)

Lectures in America
Gertrude Stein (Beacon)

Realm of the Incas
Victor W. Von Hagen (Mentor original)

The Day of the Locust
Nathanael West (Bantam)

The Organization Man
William H. Whyte (Anchor)

Marjorie Morningstar
Herman Wouk (NAL)

1958

After the Lost Generation
John Aldridge (Noonday)

The Second Foundation
Isaac Asimov (Avon)

Giovanni's Room
James Baldwin (Signet)

Flowers of Evil
Charles Baudelaire (New Directions)

Endgame
Samuel Beckett (Evergreen original)

The Wapshot Chronicle
John Cheever (Bantam)

A Coney Island of the Mind
Lawrence Ferlinghetti (New Directions)

Civilization and its Discontents
Sigmund Freud (Anchor)

From Russia with Love
Ian Fleming (NAL)

The Confidential Agent
Graham Greene (Bantam)

Dubliners
James Joyce (Viking/Compass)

On the Road
Jack Kerouac (Signet)

The Subterraneans
Jack Kerouac (Evergreen)

Compulsion
Meyer Levin (Pocket)

A Charmed Life
Mary McCarthy (Dell)

Mandingo
Kyle Onstott (Fawcett/Crest)

The Hidden Persuaders
Vance Packard (Pocket)

On the Beach
Nevil Shute (NAL)

1959

The James Beard Cook Book
James Beard (Dell original)

Watt
Samuel Beckett (Evergreen original)

Seize the Day
Saul Bellow (Popular Library)

The Martian Chronicles
Ray Bradbury (Bantam)

The October Country
Ray Bradbury (Ballantine original)

The Myth of Sisyphus and Other Essays
Albert Camus (Vintage)

The Edge of the Sea
Rachel Carson (Mentor)

Childhood's End
Arthur C. Clarke (Ballantine original)

By Love Possessed
James Gould Cozzens (Fawcett/Crest)

The Presentation of Self in Everyday Life
Erving Goffman (Anchor)

Lord of the Flies
William Golding (Capricorn)

Our Man in Havana
Graham Greene (Bantam)

The Worldly Philosophers
Robert Heilbroner (Simon & Schuster)

The Burl Ives Song Book
Burl Ives (Ballantine original)

Finnegans Wake
James Joyce (Viking/Compass)

Zorba the Greek
Nikos Kazantzakis (Simon & Schuster)

The Dharma Bums
Jack Kerouac (Signet)

Maggie Cassidy
Jack Kerouac (Avon original)

Please Don't Eat the Daisies
Jean Kerr (Fawcett/Crest)

The White Negro
Norman Mailer (City Lights)

The Intimate Henry Miller
Henry Miller (Signet original)

The Causes of World War Three
C. Wright Mills (Oxford/Galaxy)

The Power Elite
C. Wright Mills (Simon & Schuster)

Atlas Shrugged
Ayn Rand (Signet)

Jealousy
Alain Robbe-Grillet (Evergreen original)

Exodus
Leon Uris (Bantam)

The Sirens of Titan
Kurt Vonnegut (Dell original)

Lady Chatterley's Lover
D. H. Lawrence (Grove)

Leslie Fiedler

SOURCE: "Towards a Definition of Popular Literature," in *Superculture: American Popular Culture and Europe,* edited by C. W. E. Bigsby, Bowling Green University Popular Press, 1975, pp. 28-42.

[*In the following essay, Fiedler argues that popular literature deserves a higher regard from those critics who, despite having never read a particular mass-market work, will automatically "ghettoize" it according to genre.*]

Any essay in definition which begins with a term in common use courts disaster, since it seems initially to encourage certain expectations which it must finally frustrate. Let me say at the start, therefore, that by 'popular' I do not mean necessarily or primarily what is most widely read, much less what is read by 'everybody'; and by 'literature' I do not mean what is customarily 'studied' in classes in literature, certainly not university classes in English Literature or American Literature or Comparative Literature. Indeed, I use the term 'Popular Literature' only because the misapprehensions occasioned by each of the two words cancel each other out, because it is a contradiction in terms. What I shall be discussing are the kinds of songs and stories which have tended, since the invention of moveable type, to be 'ghettoized', which is to say, excluded from classes in 'literature', and endured only as long as they clearly know their own place. Such a description of my subject matter is, however, already a rough or preliminary definition. When I have rendered it as clear and patent as any commonplace, I will be done.

I reserve the term 'Folk Literature' for orally transmitted song and story before the time of Gutenberg which must be discussed in a quite different historical and cultural context. I do not, however, restrict the term 'Popular Literature' to what is transmitted by print, applying it also to lyrics and narratives transmitted orally by post-print electronic devices: using it, in short, for everything in the realm of 'mass-communications'. But this means everything deemed unworthy, whatever its medium, by the critical establishment created since the Gutenberg era, of being ranked with those 'classics' (Epic, Verse Tragedy, etc.), originally preserved by the painful process of manuscript copying in a time of quite limited literacy. Such 'unworthy' works could not, of course, be denied publication, at first in book form, then as movies, radio or TV plays; because Gutenberg and post-Gutenberg technology, which began by making the publication of anything and everything possible, ended by making it compulsory. As everyone is aware by now, book-publishing and the mass media tend to become even more voracious, demanding an unending supply of raw materials to be transformed into culture-commodities. If

the mother of popular literature is mass-production technology, the midwife which gives it birth, and the wet-
nurse which suckles it is the 'free enterprise' marketplace. But such fostering is not disinterested; since
books, movies and TV shows make large profits for the
few who 'own' them, even as they put bread and milk
into the mouths of many who work for them—including,
of course, authors.

What cannot be banned from the market-place, however,
which is to say, from wide circulation and, sometimes,
financial success, by a self-perpetuating body of reviewers and critics, could, it turned out, be excluded from
libraries and classrooms at all school levels. It could, in
short, be denied the quasi-immortality bestowed by such
critics on the 'Classics', and a small number of Modern
works which are in their opinion of equal merit. Sometimes, indeed, it seems as if the self-appointed guardians
of culture demand that works which attain market success
pay for that good luck by being thus banned. Or to put it
more circumspectly, institutionalized criticism has sought
to identify the 'popularity' it cannot hamper with aesthetic or formal inadequacy, which, presumably, it alone
can judge. The touchstones of such judgment have come
to be called 'standards': presumably universal or at least
long-term values, which prove more often than not the
prejudices of a particular class at a particular historical
moment. At its worst, therefore, which is to say, at its
most shamelessly elitist, such criticism has moved toward
the theory that there is an inverse relationship between
literary merit and market-place success.

To be sure, certain Romantic, Populist, Democratic and
Socialist critics have found it embarrassing to sustain the
view that the art-forms preferred by the majority of the
people are the least admirable, the least worthy. And to
salve their consciences, they have invented the paranoic
theory of the corruption of the Innocent Masses by the
Degenerate Masters of the Media—agents, presumably,
of the ruling economic classes. In fact, however, such
'masters' spend their professional lives in vain pursuit of
popular taste, which they not only do not make, but do
not even understand—and surely (as anyone who has
watched their efforts at first-hand can attest) cannot predict. There is also a condescending corollary to the
theory of the Seduction of the Innocent: a corollary
which maintains that it is possible through education to
purify the taste of the betrayed masses, to deliver them
from their bondage to horror, porn and sentimentality, by
showing them the 'truth'. In practice, this view amounts
to the belief that the people can and should be
unbrainwashed, or rather re-brainwashed by enlightened
schoolmasters, or the rulers of enlightened states, or their
cultural lackeys, into recognizing what is really, *really*
good for them—which of course such schoolmasters, rulers and lackeys, have known all along.

It is hard to say who deserves credit for having invented
this theory and its corollary, which come to us primarily
as nineteenth century products though they somehow
persisted until nearly the end of the twentieth, growing

ever more untenable and palpably absurd. It is tempting,
in a way, to give the credit to Matthew Arnold, re-read-
ing whom recently I decided—son of Israel that I am—
to enlist in the ranks of Philistia for the rest of my writing
life. But Karl Marx had staked a claim early on in *The
Holy Family,* which includes an enraged elitist attack on
one of the greatest popular writers of the mid-nineteenth
century: a novelist who managed to reach a large working
class audience with a hectic mixture of hardcore violence, soft-core pornography, flagrant sentimentality and
Utopian Socialism. I am referring, of course, to Eugène
Sue, particularly the Sue of the *Mysteries of Paris,* not
yet informed by the followers of Fourier that he was a
'friend of the people'. In his later *Mysteries of the
People,* he becomes too explicit, too doctrinaire; but in
his early work, he is one with the masses in their inchoate
erotic-terrific dreams of liberation.

But if Sue was falsified in his own self-consciousness by
the theorizing of the *Phalange;* in the consciousness of
his contemporaries and ours, he was even more drastically falsified by Marx, who taught us first to regard him,
and all like him, as purveyors of junk, panderers to the
misled masses. What I am trying to say, is that popular
literature is not, as a category, a type, a sub-genre, the
invention of the authors of the books which we have been
taught to believe 'belong' to it, but of certain theorizers
after the fact. It exists generically in the perception of
elitist critics—or better, perhaps, in their mis-perception,
their—usually tendentious, sometimes even deliberate—
misapprehension. It will, therefore, cease to exist as a
category when we cease to regard it in the way we have
been misled into doing. Clearly, what we consider 'serious novels' or 'art novels': works, say, by Henry James
or Marcel Proust, Thomas Mann or James Joyce, are
indistinguishable, *before the critical act,* from 'best-sellers' or 'popular novels' by Jacqueline Susanne or John
D. MacDonald, Conan Doyle or Bram Stoker. Despite
peripheral attempts to sort them out before the fact by
invidious binding or labelling, by and large, they are
bound in the same boards and paper; edited, printed,
distributed, advertised and peddled in quite the same
way.

Moreover, even if the fashion were to change and universal ghettoization were to be instituted *ab ovo,* they would
remain *finally* the same; since they can happen to us,
become a part of our consciousness, our vicarious experience, in one way only. We do not have different processes for ingesting works which transmit image, idea
and feeling via print or the post-print media, depending
on their critical status. We may think back on them differently, but we absorb them in quite the same fashion.
How then did we ever come to distinguish one from the
other? And more importantly, why did we once (some of
us, at least, are now through with all that) ever want to
separate out, to classify and rank, not merely what is
more skillfully executed from what is less, i.e., the better
from the worse; but also what has the loftiest of ambitions from what is humbler in intent, i.e., the high from
the low? How finally have we come to believe that 'lit-

erature' is divided not just in terms of quality but of kind, which is to say, in terms of status and audience?

Initially, men of goodwill, at least, read or listened to all song and story before thus classifying it. But we have reached a point at which some among us aspire to ghettoize certain writers, certain books, certain whole sub-genres of the novel before reading them. Indeed, in a world where division of labour and delegation of responsibility have been carried to absurd extremes, certain professionals and sub-professionals have been trained to do that job for the rest of us. In the United States, for instance, and elsewhere I suspect, librarians have learned to relegate some books, as they arrive on the order desk to ghettostacks as 'Juveniles', 'Teen-Age Fiction', 'Detective Stories', 'Westerns', 'Science Fiction'—or to a super-Ghetto, locked and guarded, as 'Pornography'. Moreover, judges for our major Fiction Awards, the Pulitzer Prize, for instance, and the National Book awards, are preconditioned to assume, sight unseen, that 'Juveniles' and 'Science Fiction' are simply not to be considered for the major prizes. And, I have been told, the jobbers and wholesalers of books tend to sort out certain disreputable kinds of novels, including Science Fiction, which are not to be sent to 'serious' bookstores: the major distributors and sellers of books. Finally, there are more marginal fictions which do not make it to this level of discrimination, being excluded from even temporary storage and discriminatory display by most American libraries. This ultimately untouchable category includes 'paperback originals' of all kinds, and most notably comic books; though the latter, among children and young adults at least, are probably the most widely read of all narrative forms.

Such generic pre-censorship—or, if that be too strong a term, pejorative pre-classification—provides an easy way out for relatively unsophisticated and fundamentally insecure librarians or bookstore clerks. And who can blame them, trapped as they are in an unworkable system; since even the 'experts', highly educated and well-read critics, find it difficult to indicate the cut-off points on the Gutenberg continuum which separate High from Low or, as certain more ambitious graders of literature were fond of trying to do a decade or two ago (*mea culpa!*)—High from Middle from Low. In the light of all this, it pays to remember that the novel as such was considered by many formalist critics, in the years just after its emergence as a major genre, Pop *per se*—quite like Comic Books or Soap Operas now. And since the promotion of the genre to the ranks of accepted literature, despite the fact that it is quite clearly more closely related to the movies, TV serials and comic books than Poetic Epic or Tragedy, critics have been forced to play ridiculous sorting-out games: distinguishing 'serious novelists' from 'mere entertainers', and 'Best Sellers' from 'Art Novels'.

Such attempts have been compromised by the fact that over and over there have been cases of borderline writers, embarrassingly like what their own times have defined as 'Pop', but endowed with energy and skill, inven-

tion and mythopoeic power which will not let them be confined to the limits of any critical ghetto. I am thinking of such stubbornly unclassifiable 'geniuses' (the term itself is an evasion) as Dickens and Twain, Cooper and Balzac, perhaps even Samuel Richardson, father of them all. For the sake of such writers, élitist 'standards' have been bent a little, shame-facedly adjusted or hypocritically ignored, by critics unwilling to abandon either those standards or the writers who challenge them. To have one's cake and eat it too is the choice always of the cowardly or the confused. But some of the critics involved, Samuel Johnson, for instance, that embattled formalist who boldly indulged his perhaps inconsistent taste for Richardson, cannot be so easily dismissed.

Why were they, then, so reluctant to give up categories so clearly unviable? And why, even more distressingly, are some of our critical contemporaries, admirable in other respects, unwilling to do so? The answer lies not in the closed circle of 'aesthetics', but in a larger historical and social overview, which begins by investigating the moment at which modern criticism came into being. If we look hard at the mid-eighteenth century, when it all properly began, it becomes clear to us that the notion of literary standards, along with the emergence of the critic-pedagogues as their official 'enforcers', is a product of the cultural insecurity of the rich merchants and nascent industrialists, who were just then taking over control of society in the Western World. Wielding first economic and then political power seemed to them not quite enough to satisfy hungers bread during their long cultural exclusion. They wanted also to dominate literary culture, as had the ruling classes whom they superseded. They demanded, therefore, first and foremost to be the chief consumers (delegating this function to their wives and daughters) and sustainers (this function they reserved for their male selves) of song and story, which for them had become almost exclusively identified with print and the 'book'. But they desired also to be its judges, the guardians of the 'values' which it embodied and re-enforced.

But this they proved incapable, either in their own right or by delegation to the distaff side, of doing—certainly not with the insouciant self-assurance of the feudal aristocracies who had imposed their taste in this area, at first despite, and later even on and through an established clergy which theoretically despised all 'literature'. Unlike their predecessors, the new ruling classes were born with a sense of insecurity which has since grown indurated rather than being mitigated by time and the habit of command.

They were even, perhaps especially, insecure about the Pop forms which first assumed a central importance with their political rise. The earliest and most notable of these, is of course, the novel itself, which reflected in its archetypal plots the communal dreams of the New Class; and embodied in its very shape and substance, those dreams made paper and ink and boards, a commodity, in short, to be hefted and bought and sold. The incarnate myths of the bourgeoisie are commodities, even as the marketplace and technology are its collective unconscious. Yet they did not, could not in the nature of the case, understand on the level of full consciousness the significance of the technology which they controlled, or the new methods of production and distribution which such technology made possible. Yet these were to replace the handcrafted *objets d'art* of the aristocracy with mass-produced and mass-distributed goods; and to transform the economy of culture from one of scarcity to one of plenty.

If the printing-press was, indeed, the first mass-production machine invented by Western society, the modern or bourgeois novel was the first literary genre invented to be produced and reproduced on it. Earlier forms, whether the products of a high minority culture, like Epic, Tragedy and the Lyric, or of folk culture, like fairy tales or ballads, came to lead a second life in print. But the novel was born with and for Gutenberg technology. It has, therefore, changed not superficially but essentially, with every technological change in that area, as well as with every new development in marketing: the invention of stereotyping, the perfection of techniques for making cheap paper, the creation of libraries, private and public. Even the displacement of stagecoach travel by the railroad made a substantial difference in fiction, as men grew accustomed to moving from place to place in an environment which made reading easy, and the Railroad bookstall was developed to satisfy the new need for disposable travel literature. It seems possible at this moment that even as print-technology created the novel, post-print technologies may destroy it; and so Marshall McLuhan, among others, has been insisting. Although his most dire prophecies are clearly not being fulfilled, since even boys and girls continue to read books, sometimes in front of the television screen itself, clearly the novel is being challenged at least, forced to accommodate and adjust by new media which tell tales with greater speed and efficiency to a wider audience than can (apparently) ever learn to read print with real ease. Even among those with Gutenberg skills, their prestige and glamour have been undercut by the electronic media, which transmit speech directly into the ear and images to the eye without the intervention of printed words.

All this, however, was unsuspected by the emergent bourgeoisie, who remained for a long time unaware that insofar as they controlled the technology of print, the machines which reproduced the works of literary culture, they controlled that culture, too. Nor did they suspect that the market-place, which was also in their hands, determined which works of art would persist and be remembered, by winnowing not the 'good' from the 'bad', perhaps, but certainly the more popular from the less. The bourgeoisie were blinded by obsolescent mythologies of Art, which envisaged 'poetry' as the creation of a lonely genius and his Muse, rather than the product of technological man and his machines. Consequently, they thought of literary 'survival', or as they insisted on calling it still, 'immortality', as the result of critical consensus rather than the workings of the market-place. Believing in the division of labour in all fields, they appointed

'experts' to prepare themselves by the study of the Classics, and to tell them (to 'brief' them, we would say these days) whether novels were O.K. in general; and if so, which were more O.K. than others.

Obviously, they did not always take the good advice they sought. Quite often, in fact, they continued to read what their critical mentors had taught them to regard as 'trash'—defiantly in the case of sentimental-pious 'trash', shamefacedly and secretly in the case of pornographic 'trash'. But they did snatch such work from the hands of their children, especially their daughters, when they caught them reading it. In the light of this, it is clear that the function of modern critics and schoolmasters whose subject is literature was from the start rather like that performed by the writers of Etiquette Books, Dictionaries and Grammars. Like the latter, the former responded to the cultural insecurity of the eighteenth century middle classes by providing 'rules' or 'standards' or guides to 'good behaviour'. The new rich wanted to know which fork to pick up; how to spell things 'right'; when, if at all, it was proper to say 'ain't'; and also what books to buy for display in their libraries or on their coffee tables.

At first, the critics had to compete in establishing 'values' or 'standards' in the field of literature with the clergy, who were also assigned by their uncertain masters the task of guiding them right. It was unclear on both sides, and doubly unclear to those caught in the middle, into whose territory literature properly fell, the schoolmaster's or the parson's. Indeed, as long as the critics themselves continued to maintain—borrowing the notion from their pre-Gutenberg predecessors—that literature must 'instruct' as well as 'delight', it proved impossible to separate the domain of Art, in which critics were the 'experts', from that of Prudence, in which the clergy had the final word. And who, in any case, was to mediate between aesthetics and ethics: the critic or the pulpit-moralist?

Since in the hierarchal value system of the bourgeoisie the ethical ranked higher than the aesthetic, it was more than a century before any critic dared confront the power of the church head-on, by asserting the creed of 'art for art's sake'. More typically, critics and pedagogues alike tried instead to beat the moralists at their own game, by dividing all of art along essentially Christian lines into what was Serious, Elevating, Uplifting and of High Moral Purpose, on the one hand; and what was trivial, debasing, vulgar and of no redeeming value, on the other. But such ethical distinctions turned out, to no one's surprise, merely to reinforce distinctions made on presumably aesthetic and formalist grounds, i.e., in the name of Greece and Rome rather than Jerusalem and Galilee. Finally, however, the literary experience confounds moral distinctions, even as it does those based on formal elegance, beauty of structure, precision of language, control of tone, avoidance of sentimentality and cliché or whatever criteria are currently chic. Think of the writers presumably to be excluded from the Canon on ethical grounds who have been smuggled into respectability by bending or adjusting moral 'standards', or simply by lying to oneself or the political guardians of morality, or both. And think especially of how in recent days duplicity has become the rule in courtrooms, where the most eminent literary critics rise to defend banned works ranging from the *Kama Sutra* to *Justine* to *Deep Throat*, by claiming for them underlying moral qualities.

Having just seen Shakespeare's *Titus Andronicus* in public performance, and having noted the amoral, indeed anti-social responses in myself and those who sat beside me, I would head the list of such smuggled ethically subversive writers with the name of Shakespeare. But the 'Bard', as his more pious apologists love to call him, has been so successfully 'kidnapped' by the forces of respectability that I will pass him by; urging the reader interested in prudential questions in the realm of art to reflect instead on still unredeemed and perhaps unredeemable figures like the Marquis de Sade, Sacher-Masoch, Cleland, De la Clos, Jean Genet and Hubert Selby, Jr. Such a tack would make clear that the key to the whole question lies in pornography, especially that Porn which treats centrally, sometimes even obsessively, deviant or sado-masochistic sex; the official name of the latter coming of course from two of our selected list of subversive writers. Such works represent the very pole of Pop—Pop at its most disreputable, disturbing, and unredeemable.

To them I shall return in conclusion; but first I must explore a little a profound difference between our own age and that in which criticism was born; the well-advertised Death of God and the slow erosion of Christian morality, which has debouched in the even better advertised New Sexual Morality of the dying twentieth century. Oddly enough (and this unpredictable event casts real light on the subject) those developments have not served to mitigate the conflict between Art and Prudence, or to undercut the distinction between Belles Lettres and Pop. On the contrary, in their initial stages at least, they tended rather to exacerbate the former and to reinforce the latter, as is exemplified very clearly by the line which runs from Matthew Arnold to Henry James and D.H. Lawrence to F.R. Leavis. They are, despite their disagreements on other fronts, crypto-Puritans all of them: convinced that with the death of traditional religion, Art in general and Literature in particular had to become the Scriptures of a New Faith, the Culture Religion. And to do so, they taught each in his own way, it had to subscribe to 'High Seriousness' and to be measured by rigorous 'Standards'.

Such standards were entrusted to a priestly brotherhood of critics, who feeling themselves the sole legitimate heirs of both the lay and clerical taste-makers of the past, sought to establish a New Canon, which would exclude philistine, vulgar, trivial or otherwise heretical stuff, even when, or rather especially when it was enjoyed by the unwary many. What won their supreme contempt, however, was the counter-Canon sponsored by a naive counter-Clergy, unaware that their orthodox God was dead, and the ethics of bourgeois sentimental Christianity along with him. Only through the exponents of the Higher Morality of Art did the true apostolic succession descend. Only they could loose and bind under the New Dispensation.

In America, the Arnoldian line was even more unabashedly élitist and genteel; for it represented, in a land which had boasted no other aristocracies before it, an attempt to define one based solely on being at ease in the world of High Culture. And it found itself from the start confronting a less accommodating bourgeoisie in the form of its own literal as well as metaphorical fathers: ministers or Senators or merchants. I am alluding, of course, to the line of descent which runs from Arnold through Paul Elmore More to T.S. Eliot to Cleanth Brooks and other genteel Fascists of Southern origin. Furthermore, their epigones of the second and third generation, who have not been exposed from birth to the reactionary mythology of the South—by and large Eastern and urban in origin, the sons or grandsons of European working class or petty-bourgeois Jews, who have made it or failed trying—such epigones sought to achieve on the level of culture the sort of success their immediate forebears had yearned for in the economic and social arena. Such culture-climbers found the University a congenial place in which to establish themselves, by their ability to distinguish between Art and pseudo-Art, Belles Lettres and junk, Serious Literature and the crap their fathers and mothers continued to read. Moving to ever higher levels of exclusivism, they devoted their lives to the explication of notably obscure works in terms even less available to the mass audience than those texts themselves. It was at this point that obscurity, or at least high density and opacity tended to become—along with symbolism, irony and the rest—the accepted hallmarks of High Art: touchstones for judging the works of the past, and guides for producing new works worthy of classroom exposition in the future.

With the second and third generation of 'New Critics', at any rate, élitist criticism was almost totally academicized in the United States; which is to say, the University had become the chief, almost the sole guardian of 'taste' and 'Standards'. This meant the establishment, *de facto* at least, of a new definition of both High and Popular Literature. The term 'literature' came to be used exclusively for proper or serious books, others being condescendingly labelled 'para-literature', as if they were abortive or failed attempts at achieving a status to which often they clearly did not aspire. But there was a certain destructive circularity in the new definition of 'literature' as what was taught in University classes in Literature; since what was taught in those classes was, presumably, 'literature' to begin with, i.e., what had been taught in earlier classes on the subject. But how did it all start, and when will it end?

Even after the recent loss of prestige by the old 'New Criticism', our Universities, especially in their Departments of Literature, continue to function as the last bastions of élitism; finding newer, more fashionable versions of formalism to justify the hierarchal ranking of books. What has seemed particularly attractive has been the latest embodiment of French Neo-Classicism called 'Structuralism', which flourishes even in the publicly supported institution of Mass Higher Education in America, both in the politically Rightist form it has assumed passing through Johns Hopkins—and in the Leftist version, which comes to us directly from Vincennes and the Collège de France. It seemed quite proper that critical élitism and nostalgic Southern Agrarianism be linked. But it is more than a little disconcerting to find hierarchal formalism allied to Marxism in currently chic *gauchiste* forms.

Yet from the start, as I have already indicated, Marxism proved to be profoundly, essentially élitist in the realm of art. Indeed, all ideologies which presume man to be a rational animal, whether actually or potentially, end up in such a trap; for to such ideologies art seems to play an ambiguous, if not a downright disruptive role in the state. It is all art which they fear, and, indeed, at an earlier stage of things, they concentrated their fire on 'Highbrow' or 'Avant-Garde' or 'Experimental' art, i.e., élitist art in its modernist phase. More recently however, as Modernism has been tamed, the attack has shifted (think of the war against 'pornography' in the United States, and that against 'Science Fiction' in the Soviet Union) to the more vulnerable and unredeemably subversive popular arts; which is to say, art untamed, uncastrated, unpurified—anarchic and dionysiac, vulgar, obscene and blasphemous; To all 'rational' believers in Law and Order, whether 'Red' or 'White', 'East' or 'West', the enemy is no longer *Ulysses* or the *Wasteland* but *Deep Throat* and *Beyond the Valley of the Dolls*; no longer surreal chain poems or *The Andalusian Dog,* but comic books, soap-operas and TV commercials.

The need to distinguish between High Literature and Low, and to denigrate or ban the latter persists beyond the historical moment which gave it birth, because it is based on a human response which existed before that moment, and which may cease only with the disappearance of man. Superficially it may seem the creation of an age characterized by the dominance of the bourgeoisie and the development of mass-production, mass-distribution and mass-communications. But essentially it represents, in a new form, the ancient distrust, fear, even hatred of the arts in general and literature in particular. That feeling has, in all ages since the invention of speech, plagued men who are ill at ease with their animal inheritance, the impulsive or irrational aspects of their own psyches; and it has assumed special virulence ever since the Gutenberg Revolution. For a while, however, it looked as if a compromise had been reached between haters of literature and its writers. Even mad, bad poetry, which, as utopian reformers and rationalists have been telling us ever since Plato, 'waters the emotions', seemed under control at last. First in Ancient Greece, and then again in post-Medieval Europe, poets—instructed by philosophy and theology—paid lip service at least to the principle of Law and Order, to which their craft is essentially antithetical. Like 'good niggers', they had 'learned

their place': their proper function in the large polity, which is, of course, to instruct and delight; and especially to instruct delightfully those not yet mature enough for grimmer forms of mental discipline.

Since nothing is forbidden to poetry, it remains free, of course, to instruct and delight *among other things*. And sometimes it seems, in fact, to perform primarily these two socially desirable tasks, though not always as decorously as schoolmasters and critics are deceived into believing. Behind the obsequious smile of the 'good nigger' so patiently striving to please 'ole massa', that is to say, lies the subversive grin of the mocker. Certainly, instruction and delight are not the exclusive or essential functions of literature, as even some dissenting élitist artists have been driven to insist. When, however, high art in pursuit of other ends, goes Dada, it is forced to learn from the popular arts: Krazy Kat or Charlie Chaplin, the Marx Brothers or the makers of soup-can labels. Indeed, it is the so-called 'weaknesses' of Pop which make for its strength in this area; since it is essentially unable either to instruct or delight: being, on the one hand, notably weak in *ethos* and *dianoia,* and on the other, not very strong in *architektonike.* Even in the realm of Aristotelian *mimesis,* it is likely to be less than adequate; since it prefers fantasy to the representation of our shared human lot, either as it is or as it ideally should be.

Yet Popular Literature moves us all the same, both those of us who also respond to High Literature and those of us who subsist entirely on it. Indeed it may, by this very token, move us all the more, touching levels of response deeper and more archaic than those which abide distinctions between instruction and delight, much less the division into High and Low. If we are interested in *how* it moves us—and how, presumably, *all* literature moves us beyond or beside or below the level of social utility—it will repay us to look briefly at three forms: genres or sub-genres of Popular Literature, of which élitist critics remain distrustful or downright contemptuous, though they have traditionally been favourites of the mass audience. These are:

1. Sentimental Literature, particularly as it has developed from novels written by the first women imitators of Samuel Richardson, down through such late nineteenth century bestsellers as *The Lamplighter* and *The Wide, Wide World,* to present-day 'soaps', the daytime serials on television;

2. Horror Literature from, say, M.G. Lewis's *The Monk,* down through *Varney, The Vampire, Frankenstein, Dr Jekyll and Mr Hyde* and *Dracula,* to the Horror Comics and *The Rocky Horror Show* of this moment;

3. Classic Pornography from Cleland and the Marquis de Sade, to Frank Harris, *The Story of O* and *Fritz the Cat.*

It is possible, of course, to combine all three, as they are combined in the Kung Fu movies starring Bruce Lee;

such a film, for instance, as *Fist of Fury,* in which the single erotic scene is clearly a last-minute addition to make sure that the whole range of popular taste is satisfied. Moreover, there is a real sense in which all three of these forms can be regarded as varieties of pornography or titillation-literature: handkerchiefly or female-oriented porn, erotic or male-oriented porn, and sado-masochistic, or universally appealing porn. The last can also be thought of as juvenile-oriented porn; but this amounts perhaps to saying 'universal', since almost everyone is willing to indulge the child in himself, while many are wary about giving rein to what persists of the other sex in their male or female bodies. Terror, indeed, seems sometimes the only form capable of crossing all conventional role boundaries: not only generational and sexual, but ethnic as well (I have seen black and white kids, along with adults of all hues and genders, responding to Bruce Lee movies), and class lines, too. But some types of erotica seem limited in appeal not just because they represent, say, the fantasies of men rather than women; but because they appeal only to readers of a certain social status and educational level—like limericks, for instance, which are apparently an exclusively bourgeois form.

In any case, the pornographic classification seems appropriate in the light of the fact that all three sub-genres aim at 'watering the emotions', rather than purifying or purging them by way of the famous Aristotelian process of 'catharsis'. Indeed, the whole baffling and unsatisfactory theory of catharsis seems to me at this point a pious fraud perpetrated by the dutiful son of a doctor; drawing on the terminology of his father's socially acceptable craft, in order to justify his own shameful taste for what seemed to more serious thinkers of his time exactly what pop literature seems to their opposite numbers in ours. Greek Tragedy, as a matter of fact, aimed at evoking precisely the responses stirred by Sentimental and Horror Porn in all ages, responses which Aristotle called honorifically 'pity and terror'; though Athens of the Golden Age banned the portrayal of sexually exciting scenes from the stage—presumably because they could not be ethically neutralized, like those which stir shudders or tears, even in a ritual setting.

For the sake of the popular drama which he loved as I love soap-operas, Aristotle found it strategic to pretend that the thrill of tragedy and the release of comedy could be subsumed under the rubric of instruction and delight. In our era, however, it seems advisable to readjust the balance by insisting that the plays of Sophocles and Euripides, quite like the three forms of pornography I am considering, at their most effective, cause the audience to get out of control, 'out of their heads', as the modern phrase has it. If such works teach us anything it is *not* to be wise; and if they provide us with pleasure by making us blubber, shiver or sustain an erection, it is a pleasure on the verge of pain. We need, therefore, another term than catharsis to say how we are moved, a term less anal and more erotic; for whatever Aristotle may have urged in his age of genital repression, metaphors of a child on the potty (or even at the mirror) will not do for us. We

need to redefine literature in terms of images based on the aspiration of the soul for the divine and the body for other bodies.

Such images are to be found in the single surviving work of one we call 'Longinus', though that is not his name: in an essay we call 'On the Sublime', though the last word is a misleading translation, which allowed 'Longinus' to be co-opted and compromised by eighteenth century formalists. That perhaps-Christian critic used the word *ekstasis* to describe the effect not of popular or debased art alone; but of all art at its peak moments—from the tag 'Let there be light and there was light' in the Scriptures of the barbarous Hebrews, to the most precious poetry of the enlightened Greeks. And what is incumbent on us now, it seems to me as I reach the end of definition and move on to advocacy, is to take a cue from Longinus by creating an approach to literature which will if not quite abandon, at least drastically downgrade both Ethics and Aesthetics in favour of 'Ecstatics'.

Once we have made *ekstasis* rather than instruction and delight the center of critical analysis and evaluation, we will find ourselves speaking less of theme and purport, structure and texture, ideology and significance, irony and symbolism, and more of myth, fable, archetype, fantasy, magic, and wonder. And certainly, when we have granted that the essential function of story and song is to release us temporarily from the limits of rationality, the boundaries of the ego and the burden of consciousness, by creating a moment of privileged insanity, compatible with waking awareness as the analogous experience of dreaming or 'tripping out' are not, we will be out of the trap; delivered at long last from the indignity of having to condescend publicly to works we privately relish; and relieved of the obligation to define, as I began by doing in this essay, distinctions which were from the start delusive and unreal.

"FORMULA" FICTION

Cynthia S. Hamilton

SOURCE: "Formula and the Marketplace," in *Western and Hard-Boiled Detective Fiction in America: From High Noon to Midnight,* Macmillan Press, 1987, pp. 50-67.

[*In the following essay, Hamilton defines the term "formula literature" and traces its role in the mass production and selling of books.*]

Writers, editors, readers and critics all talk about formula, but it would be unwise to assume that all agree on the nature of the beast. For critics, formula is a necessary tool, a part of their taxonomy of literature; it allows them to classify works and to talk about the dynamics of the elements within any given work. A reader's notion of formula helps him to select works in accordance with his interests; it may also involve him in judgements about whether the author is 'playing fair' within the rules of the game. Advertisers see formula as a marketing-tool. And editors see it as a set of editorial guidelines. But what of the writer himself? Is formula merely a matter of substituting new elements for old over and over again, as is often assumed by critics and readers?

At first glance, formula writers talking about the tricks of their trade seem to have just such a ready-made pattern in mind: 'if you go after the mechanics of Western stories as such you'll find that it's a simple group of rules by which one may cut the pattern of any number of yarns', Frederick Faust admonished. 'And your bank account need never fail it you follow the rules, and clip carefully along the marked lines. And not so carefully at that. . . . '

Frank Gruber, another pulp writer, and one who, like Faust, wrote both Westerns and detective stories, mulled over the problem of a fool-proof formula for writing detective yarns. After two years he came up with his eleven-point mystery-plot formula. 'To this day I claim that this plot formula is foolproof', Gruber writes. 'You can write a perfectly salable mystery story with perhaps only seven or eight of these elements, but get them all into a story and you cannot miss.'

On closer scrutiny, the cut-and-paste version of formula writing which Gruber and Faust seem to espouse looks rather different. When Faust was asked how he managed to find so many stories, he replied.

> Perhaps the best way to go about it is to ask one's self what there is about a theme that invites the writer. How much is background and how much is character, how much is action? Then you should ask yourself what kind of action develops the character most perfectly. There is a certain logic in the working out of stories, a sort of mathematical necessity in the operation of order to get the right answers, and I think you can surrender to the nature and the kind of emotion with which you are dealing. It will lead you to the right denouements.

Alan R. Bosworth, who wrote Westerns for the Street and Smith publications under a variety of pseudonyms, echoes Faust's advice. The secret of writing salable pulp fiction, he says, was to use a 'narrative hook' which 'could be adapted to fit any pulp magazine, Western or otherwise'. The result of this insight was his 'All-Purpose Little Jim Dandy opening': he 'crammed a character, a setting and a situation into one packed paragraph, and after that the plot and its unfolding took care of themselves.'

And when Gruber begins listing his eleven elements it becomes clear that his check-list is not at all restrictive. His list runs:

1. Colorful hero
2. Theme
3. Villain
4. Background
5. Murder method
6. Motive
7. Clue
8. Trick
9. Action
10. Climax
11. Emotion

Gruber goes on to elaborate, but his comments do not transform his list into a kind of algebraic prescription where one adds a to b, puts in a dash of c at a given point, then rounds off with e. On Background, for example, he says,

> BACKGROUND. The story must be played against a colorful or unusual background. The streets of a big city are not necessarily colorful. If they're not, make them so.

His discussion of Theme merely explicates his meaning. Theme is 'what the story is about in addition to, over and above, the ACTUAL MYSTERY Plot.' So, for example, *The Lock and the Key* is about locksmiths, and *The Nine Tailors* is about bell-ringing:

These devices indicate that authors such as Gruber and Faust are using formula to generate plot line. For them, formula is a skeleton on which to flesh out a story rather than a die with which to stamp out preconceived patterns from new material. However, the finished body is also dressed to suit other people's preconceptions of the formula.

Editorial preconceptions and prejudices were undoubtedly a major influence. Stories which did not conform to an editor's conception of his readers' tastes were not published. Faust was well acquainted with his editor's preferences:

> This is the sort of yarn that Blackwell laps up: A Western tale of action, without Mexicans, without women whose virtue is endangered, and concerning anything from sheepherding to lumber or mining or trapping, but preferable [*sic*] something about the old Western ranch house and a taint of cowdung early in the story. Action, action, action, is the thing. . . . There has to be a woman, but not much of one.

Blackwell, the editor of *Western Story Magazine,* had once informed Faust that there were 'only two kinds of plots, "pursuit and capture", and "delayed revelation,"' and that 'delayed revelatio n' was merely a variant of 'pursuit and capture.' 'In the delayed revelation situation,' Blackwell added, 'the opening of the story should take place a little farther along in the course of action.'

Captain Joseph Shaw, the most famous of the *Black Mask* editors, also had strong ideas about the kind of writing he wanted for his magazine: 'We felt obliged to stipulate our boundaries. We wanted simplicity for the sake of clarity, plausibility, and belief. We wanted action, but we held that action is meaningless unless it involves recognisable human character in three-dimensional form.' Frank Gruber complained of the rigours of Shaw's editorship:

> He asked you to submit stories, he suggested lengthy, detailed revisions, *urged* you to make them and you found yourself rewriting and rewriting . . . and in the end you got the most wonderful rejection. No printed rejection slip. His arm around your shoulder, his warm enthusiasm, his vast regret that this one didn't quite make it, but please, please try another one—and soon!

Editorial dictates could affect a number of aspects of a writer's craft: type of story, quality of writing, and what was deemed extraneous, what crucial. Chandler complained bitterly about editorial blue-pencilling:

> A long time ago when I was writing for the pulps I put into a story a line like 'He got out of the car and walked across the sun-drenched sidewalk until the shadow of the awning over the entrance fell across his face like the touch of cool water.' They took it out when they published the story. Their readers didn't appreciate this sort of thing—just held up the action.

Chandler was certain that the editors were mistaken in their assessment.

Characteristically, Hammett was more circumspect in his rebellion. He derived great amusement from using the argot collected during his years with Pinkerton's, especially as the editors of *Black Mask,* who often did not know the exact meaning of these terms, but who had a strict policy against language which might be considered of questionable taste, sometimes eliminated the wrong ones.

There are tales, which may or may not be apocryphal, of much more extreme acts of editorial intervention. From the slightly earlier time of the Nickel Weeklies, there survives the story of an editorial edict that the hero of the Nick Carter stories must remain a bachelor. A tug of war between writer and editor ensued. Nick's engagement was announced, but editorial policy necessitated the demise of his fiancée in the next installment. Finally, in defiance, Fred Dey described his hero's wedding:

> Now it happened that week that the editors did not read his copy. It arrived late, and was sent directly to the linotype room. Suddenly a printer's devil came bounding upstairs with the news that Nick Carter was married. The office seethed like an angry sea. . . . Messengers were dispatched to all parts of the city in search of Fred Dey. When he appeared, he was pushed into a chair and compelled to describe the bitter death of the bride, while his own tears blotted the page.

Clearly intervention on this scale required tame or very hungry authors, and it is unlikely that it was widespread.

Editorial intervention was often justified not on aesthetic grounds, but in terms of 'giving the reader what he wanted'. The editor had a number of ways of gauging readership response, sales being the most important. When Carroll John Daly's tough hero Race Williams was featured on the cover of *Black Mask,* for example, sales jumped dramatically. *Western Story Magazine* climbed in circulation quickly from its first issue in 12 July, 1919. By November 1920 it had become a weekly with a circulation of 300,000. The next year Faust's stories began appearing, and circulation climbed even higher.

Readership polls were also used to determine favourite authors. The progress of one such poll by *Black Mask* was reported in the February 1930 issue: Dashiell Hammett, Carroll John Daly and Erle Stanley Gardner were top favourites.

Letters sent to editors also gave some indication of readers' enthusiasms: 'Boss of the Round-Up and Folks: Just a few lines to tell you how much I like Max Brand's story, "Pleasant Jim." I couldn't think of going to bed before finishing it. What? After waiting all week fer it— "fer" as Grizzly Gallager says.' Another letter in the same issue of *Western Story Magazine* complained, 'George Owen Baxter left Thunder Moon not a bit nicely, and I think he aims to finish that later.' Ironically, both writers were Frederick Faust.

Despite editorial edicts and readership preferences, the range of stories published by editors shows that considerable scope remained for the author to manoeuvre. Lacking the direct feedback editors received from the readership of their magazines, and the self-confidence and open-mindedness this must have encouraged, critics have taken editorial pronouncements at face value. They have focused on the assessment of readership as a kind of key, but have ignored the actual readership of the magazines, instead substituting their own preconceptions about appeal. Cawelti, for example, assumes a certain readership for the Western when he discusses its appeal in terms of the Oedipus conflict:

> For blue-collar and white-collar workers at the lower echelons of the large industrial organization, or for independent farmers facing the increasing competition of large industrial organization, the corporation plays somewhat the same psychological role as the father does for the adolescent boy. . . . Couple this with the fact that the culture of working-class groups had traditionally placed a strong emphasis on masculine dominance, and it is not hard to see how the Western might fill an important psychological function for these groups.

No attempt is made to match this against the actual readership of the Western. Had he done so, Cawelti would have been forced to wonder at the serialisation of Zane Grey's Westerns in a number of leading women's magazines. Even *Western Story* had a faithful female following: 'I want to tell you-all I have been reading WESTERN STORY for two years, and I think it is one wonderful magazine', wrote a lady from Philadelphia. Pronouncements on the restrictiveness of writing for a specific readership based on critical preconceptions are nonsense.

The inability of critics to look beyond their own preconceptions and their failure to heed contradictory evidence have encouraged a restrictive view of formula. To understand this myopia one must look at the pressures and trends within the publishing-industry at the time the American adventure formula was being shaped by and for mass-marketing. These forces shaped critical preconceptions and have since helped to perpetuate them.

Formula literature developed during a specific phase in publishing-history. The industry was expanding as population and readership increased: the population of the United States was growing rapidly, from 50,155,783 in 1880 to 105,710,620 in 1920, and illiteracy was declining dramatically from 17 per cent in 1880 to 6 per cent in 1920. Increasing urbanisation made the distribution and sale of magazines easier and more economical, while the lowering of postal rates in 1885 and the introduction of rural free delivery after 1897 made it possible for publishers to penetrate more sparsely populated areas. In an effort to court readership, publishers began to lower their prices. In 1893 general readership magazines such as *Harper's Monthly, Scribners'* and *Century* all cost 35¢ an issue. In July of that same year *McClure's* was introduced, priced at 15¢; in the same month *Cosmopolitan* came out for 12½¢; and *Munsey's* started publication in October at 10¢ a copy. Within two years all had dropped to 10¢. 'There never was anything deader in this world than the old idea of big profits and small volume', Munsey commented in 1898. 'Small profits and big volume have driven this antiquated theory to the wall'.

Munsey set the pace in other ways as well; it was he who introduced the first pulp magazine, *Argosy,* in 1896, printed on rough wood-pulp paper in order to save on both production costs and postal charges. It took a while for the impact of this innovation to be felt, but, when it came, the expansion of pulp publishing was explosive. Barely two dozen pulps were being published at the close of the First World War, but by the middle years of the Depression over 200 pulp magazines reached 25 million readers. Outside the pulp field, expansion was also taking place; both the number of magazines and their aggregate circulation increased through 1929.

The book-publishing industry was undergoing a more modest expansion, keeping pace with the growing population, but declining as a percentage of manufactured wealth in the economy as a whole. The number of book publishers had doubled between 1859 and 1914 to number 819 by the end of the period. Book sales were also on the increase. Before 1890 a book that sold 25,000 copies was considered successful, but after the mid 1890s sales of 100,000 were common and best-sellers could top a million. Between 1901 and 1915, nineteen books surpassed the million mark.

The expanding periodical market and book trade stimulated, indeed demanded, the increased production of fiction. The 1891 copyright law, which outlawed the use of pirated British texts, further increased demand. The pulps alone consumed 200 million words a year at the height of their popularity. The prodigious output of many formula writers, with Frederick Faust as an outstanding example, is an indication of the vast appetite of the fiction industry. Complaints such as those made by Florence Kelly in a 1916 article in *The Bookman* expressed common fears: 'Quantity rather than quality seems to be the feature most admired and striven for in American fiction. The more novels an author puts out in one year and the less time he spends upon each one the surer he can be of his publisher's staunch support and the consequent winning of readers and dollars'.

More indirectly, the expanding market may be judged by the appearance during the 1880s and 1890s of a number of periodicals intended to assist the beginning writer. Among these was *Writer,* founded by the director of a correspondence school. Other aids were also marketed. Frank Gruber remembers two he purchased, *Plotto* and *Plot Genie,* both designed to help generate usable story lines. Neither worked for him.

The expanding market, both potential and realised, provided tremendous opportunities for both writers and publishers. It also placed certain pressures on both. Book publishers constantly complained of shrinking profit margins as they were squeezed on the one side by increasing royalty and promotional costs, and on the other by price-cutting. They complained too of the public's lack of attentiveness and its tendency to squander expendable income on bicycles and other forms of recreational activities instead of buying books.

Writers had to cope with the pressures imposed by calls for increased productivity, while serialisation imposed its own demanding schedule on writers. These pressures became more widespread, though both had been felt for decades in some segments of the industry. Multiple authorship was one tried and tested way of coping. Such popular heroes as Buffalo Bill, Old Captain Collier and Nick Carter were serviced by a succession of authors. Conversely, publishers could stretch the talents of a single prolific writer to provide a bevy of salable names. *Western Story* often published more than one contribution of Faust's. Indeed, on twenty occasions, three differently attributed Faust pieces appeared in a single issue.

The forces of the marketplace influenced the way fiction was written, and ultimately shaped the literature itself. None the less, this shaping-process was not as uniformly deleterious nor as irresistible as is sometimes assumed. The pressures which encouraged writers to produce quickly, fluently, and without revision allowed them to escape the rigours of careful craftmanship, but did not prevent careful artistry. *Gunman's Gold,* one of Faust's Westerns, bears the hallmarks of hasty, sloppy execution. The reader can almost sense the line at which Faust decides he must shift the portrayal of a character to accommodate the developing story line. At the other end of the scale we have Hammett's tight, brilliant plots.

The nature of the standard pricing-policy, payment by the word, discouraged writers from trimming excess verbage from their stories. Erle Stanley Gardner, writing Westerns at 3¢ a word, was once asked by an editor why his crack shots took all six cartridges to get their man. He replied, 'If you think I'm going to have the gun battle over while my hero has got fifteen cents worth of unexploded ammunition in the cylinders of his gun, you're nuts.' However, not all formula writers can be accused of deliberate wordiness.

Advertising and the new marketing-mentality brought new kinds of pressures to bear, shaping the fiction and the perception of the fiction in new ways. Though advertising had been around for many years, national advertising was new. It required national distribution of both advertising and the products it helped to sell, and these circumstances did not exist until near the end of the nineteenth century. Advertising began its concerted assault on the American consumer during these years. Revenues from both newspaper and magazine advertising rose 80 per cent during the 1880s, slowed down to a growth rate of about a third in the 1890s, then increased by more than 50 per cent in the first five years of the twentieth century. Advertising-jingles and catchphrases began to insinuate themselves into the cultural consciousness: 'It floats', 'Have you a little Fairy in your home?'

The explosion in advertising had a direct impact on the marketing of literature. 'The quack-novel is a thing which looks like a book, and which is compounded, advertised, and marketed in precisely the same fashion as Castoria . . . and other patent medicines, harmful and harmless', complained Owen Wister. Advertising-expenditures in the book trade skyrocketed despite scepticism over returns. By 1900 it was not uncommon for large publishing-houses to spend $50,000 a year on promotion. One house is reputed to have spent $250,000 in 1905, or 17 per cent of its gross proceeds; by the eve of the First World War, 10 per cent was considered an acceptable promotions budget.

The increasing preoccupation with promotion was reflected in ways other than the increasing budgets allowed for the purpose. *Publishers' Weekly,* the most influential of the trade papers, began running a 'Hints to Salesmen' column in 1891. In this and other related columns, *Publishers' Weekly* would discuss the dos and don'ts of successful marketing-practice, from the proper arrangement of shops to the making of eye-catching window displays and the design of advertising-copy and layout.

It was during this period that interest in the best-seller as a phenomenon began to agitate the industry. Best-seller lists began appearing in crude form in the *Bookman* in 1895, though the term itself was not introduced intil 1911, in *Publishers' Weekly.* The accuracy and influence

of these lists were much debated, despite improvements in the sampling-technique used. In his *Economic Survey of the Book Industry, 1930-1931,* O. H. Cheney voiced his scepticism:

> Like all trade evils, the practice has developed insidiously. A bookseller, asked to report on sales, begins by trying to remember or he asks the friendly traveler what he thinks is the best-seller, Or else he sees a stack of a title which has been decreasing—and at the next step he sees a stack which he wishes would disappear—and then he remembers a title on which he ordered too many. The title becomes one of his best-sellers.

Despite his scepticism over the methods used, Cheney felt the lists were influential. He agreed with such critics as Johan J. Smertenko and Frederick Lewis Allen that they stimulated the 'herd instinct' crucial to the making of a big best-seller.

There was much speculation regarding the essential components of a best-seller. Conjectures relied heavily on hindsight: Frederick Lewis Allen's 1935 article looked for trends in the best-selling books of the preceding thirty-five years. George Stevens derided the humbug element in pronouncements on the making of a best-seller and suggested that no formula could be isolated. If such distillation were possible, it would be a simple matter of combining elements in order really to hit the marketing jackpot. Hence the tongue-in-cheek suggestion for a best-seller about 'Lincoln's Doctor's Dog'.

The intense interest in the best-seller phenomenon and the use of the term in advertising carried a much deeper significance. Marketing books as best-sellers was one way of circumventing a central problem for the book industry. The difficulty was that of supplying the public with a uniform product identified by a brand name such as the advertisers of soap, baking-powder or sewing-machines enjoyed. Turn-of-the-century book-advertising exhibits a fumbling search for an effective marketing-strategy. The advertisements are often cramped, indigestible lists without white space. Increasingly, attempts were made to highlight the most salable aspect of a book. In the aftermath of the Spanish-American War, for example, war books were given prominence, and any war connection was emphasised.

Authors' names were often used to sell books. In advertisements, they were emphasised by using large, bold type. Later, the sales potential of popular authors was more blatantly exploited: 'When They Write Books— You Make Money' announced one advertisement to the trade in *Publishers' Weekly* in 1933. Not surprisingly, Grey was one of the authors featured. In its advertising, the Book of the Month Club gave prominence to photographs of popular authors.

Genre-oriented marketing was another way of providing the potential book-buyer with a reliable 'brand name': formula fiction came as close to providing uniformity of product as it was possible to get in the publishing-business. Ploys designed to highlight the generic identity of mysteries were quickly developed and used. An advertisement in the *New York Times* in late 1910 called *The Paternoster Ruby* by Charles Edmonds Walk 'The best mystery yarn this fall. . . . ' By the mid twenties, genre advertising for mystery stories was extensive and self-conscious. In 1928, Doubleday set up a special subsidiary, the Crime Club, to issue large numbers of mystery and detective stories. Its logo was a man with a gun. Harpers ran huge double-page advertisements in the *Saturday Review of Literature* for its Harper Sealed Mysteries, while Dutton marketed Dutton Clue Mysteries.

Advertisers did not handle the Western with such ease. They often seemed somewhat confused about the nature of the genre. According to the *Oxford English Dictionary,* the first recorded use of 'Western' as a self-sufficient noun is as late as February 1930, when it appeared in an advertisement in *Publishers' Weekly.* Actually, my research shows that the term was used rather earlier. An advertisement in the 15 October 1927 edition of the *Saturday Review of Literature* describes George M. Johnson's *The Gun-Slinger* as 'A Western with the kick of a .45.' It took a while for the new term to catch on; a sense of improvisation lingered: 'Sell this popular new "WESTERN"', urged an advertisement for Ernest Haycox's *Whispering Range* in December 1930, fencing off the new term with quotation marks, and using upper-case letters to add emphasis. After 1930 advertisers began using the new label with relish: 'A Grub-stake market for prospecting and established booksellers' announced one double-page advertisement in *Publishers' Weekly* in late 1933, 'And when you feature the Morrow "brand", you're rounding up plus sales with Westerns written for intelligent men and women. . . .'

Even before the genre was labelled so handily, advertisers attempted to draw attention to a family resemblance. Line drawings of cowboys on horseback with cattle in the background often featured prominently, an appropriate counterpart to the ominous shadows often used in mystery advertisements. The 1910 advertisement for Dane Coolidge's *Hidden Water* in the *New York Times* used just such a drawing. The accompanying blurb compared the book to Wister's *The Virginian.* 'Western' was sometimes used as an adjective, as when B. M. Bower's *Skyrider* was presented to the public in 1918. 'Ever since B. M. Bower's "Chip of the Flying U", the western novels from this author's fertile pen have been increasing in popularity.'

None the less, the treatment given to Zane Grey's work reflects the advertiser's confusion over the generic identity of Western fiction. In 1910, *The Heritage of the Desert* was marketed as a love story. Ten years later, *The Man of the Forest* was pushed as a 'best seller': 'More then half a million people (not counting those who have read library copies) have read this romance of a man and a girl and a hidden paradise. . . . ' Even as late as 1930, Grey's *Sunset Pass* was advertised as 'A New Novel of

the Old West'. The blurb called it 'A thrilling story of two men who fought to the death for the love of a girl when the old Southwest was frontier country.' By 1933, the advertisements had changed course. A huge advertisement in *Publishers' Weekly* for *The Hash Knife Outfit* called Grey 'America's favorite author—the ace western writer of them all.' The accompanying blurb was also different in tone: 'A galloping, breathless story of hard living and fast shooting founded upon a bloody episode in Arizona history.'

By 1934, the *Saturday Review of Literature* felt confident enough of genre awareness to use a grid system for reviews. 'The Criminal Record—The Saturday Review's Guide to Detective Fiction' used a four-column summary giving title and author; crime, place and sleuth; summing-up; and verdict. That year Hammett's *The Thin Man* was reviewed in this fashion. Crime, place and sleuth were reported as: 'Eccentric inventor vanishes, his secretary is murdered, his ex-wife calls in ex-tec Nick Charles and hell pops.' The book was summarised with the remark, 'It's the telling more than the tale that counts here, and both are even better than earlier Hammetts.' The verdict was 'extra swell'. A similar grid system was used for 'Over the Counter—The Saturday Review's Guide to Romance and Adventure'. Here the columns were headed 'Trademark', 'Label', 'Contents' and 'Flavor'. Max Brand's *The Outlaw* is labelled 'western'; its contents are described as 'Love 10%, Courage 111%, Compassion 1%; the flavour is dismissed as 'usual'.

In the magazine field, the rapid development of genre pulps from general fiction magazines, and their large and faithful following are indicative of the perspicacity of publishers and editors. *Western Story Magazine, Black Mask, Love Story Magazine,* and the later *Astounding Stories* and *Amazing Stories* were each aimed as a specific sector of the public, and all flourished. *Western Story* had an estimated average weekly circulation of 350,000 during the 1920s. Within a year of its launch, *Black Mask* had acquired a regular purchasing readership of 250,000. The circulation of *Lover Story* built up to 600,000 by 1932, and within months of its founding in April 1926 *Amazing Stories* had achieved a following of over 100,000.

Editors tried to make their readers feel that they belonged to a club of like-minded fellows. *Black Mask* published a column called 'Our Readers' Private Corner: Inside Dope from Authors' in which Hammett figured prominently for a while. A letters column in *Western Story Magazine* announced, 'Miss Helen Rivers, who conducts this department, will see to it that you will be able to make friends with other readers, though thousands of miles may separate you.' Badges were offered for sale at 25¢. *Detective Story* featured a column to which handwriting could be submitted for analysis, if accompanied by the printed coupon. A puzzles column with a printed honour roll also made regular appearances.

Though each magazine had its own slant and became identified with a particular genre, a wide range of stories were published. Donald R. Arbuckle's accusation that special-interest pulps rigidified formula is therefore of questionable validity. *Western Story* was not above bowing to seasonal interests by publishing such Christmas stories as 'The Providential Tree', a tale of the remarkable survival of a homesteader and his son who moved house to have a Christmas tree, then returned to find the location of their old homestead devastated by a tornado. 'The Gray Leader', published in the 22 November 1930 issue, stretches the 'Western' labelling in different ways. The story, set in a city, deals with a gang of thugs. It is not until the end that the hero and his girl head for open country, riding off toward the North-west wrapped in furs. The accompanying illustration is of a man wearing a Canadian Mountie hat staring in the window of a pet shop at a Husky puppy; a flapper looks on.

The range of stories published by *Black Mask* was even more varied. Indeed, it was first billed as a 'Magazine of Mystery, Romance and Adventure'. By the February 1926 edition, the emphasis had clearly changed, and the subtitle read, 'Mystery, DETECTIVE and Adventure stories'. Only 'DETECTIVE' is in bold red capitals; the other words are in black, with only the first letter capitalised. None the less, even as late as October 1930, the cover could feature a two-fisted gun-slinger promoting a Carroll John Daly detective story: Race Williams, it turns out, is 'out of town on a gun job'. The subtitle had changed yet again by this time, to claim, 'Western, Detective, and Adventure Stories'.

Besides using genre-oriented sales tactics, pulp-publishers pushed their 'brand name' authors through the use of cover advertising and announcements of coming stories. The appearance of Race Williams on the cover described above undoubtedly boosted circulation. It has been said that covers announcing new Race Williams stories could raise sales by as much as 20 per cent. Dashiell Hammett and Erle Stanley Gardner were also heralded as sales-boosters.

The marketing-strategies of both magazine and book-publishers have had a profound effect on the critical reception of formula literature. It might even be argued that the marketplace has exerted a more profound and deleterious effect on critics than it has on the formula writers or on the literature itself. Critics have taken over market-defined categories as though these are possessed of objective reality. What is more, they have rigidified these categories with mindless fervour. The critical treatment of the hard-boiled detective formula offers an interesting case study of the use of inappropriate categories by critics suffering from a mass-marketed variety of functional fixedness.

Hard-boiled detective novels have long been marketed as mysteries, bracketing them with works in the puzzle tradition. One Knopf advertisement for *The Maltese Falcon* used excerpts from a review by Ted Shane which compared Hammett's work directly with a contemporary mystery-writer in the classical tradition: 'Even S. S. Van Dine must lower his monocle. . . . It is everything you want.'

There were good reasons for the hard-boiled detective novel to be marketed as a mystery. It featured a detective and a crime, as did the classical variety. The firmly established generic distinctiveness of the mystery was certainly another factor. This labelling provided a handier marketing-tool than the Western with its long-amorphous generic identity. In fact, vitually anything that resembled a mystery was marketed as such; even Eric Ambler's *A Coffin for Dimitrios* (1939) was sold as 'a mystery masterpiece'.

Once the hard-boiled detective became associated with the classical mystery it was almost inevitable that any deep links with the Western would be overlooked. The perceived distance between the mystery tradition and that of the Western was too great to encourage the recognition of generic ties. Indeed, a cartoon which appeared in the *Saturday Review* in March 1940 underscored the extent of separation. Two men are being introduced by a third. The gentleman making the introduction is attired in an ordinary business suit, as is one of the others. The third is wearing a bowler, neat vest and jacket, but also a six-gun, woolly chaps and cowboy boots. 'Mr Shipley writes both detective and western stories', reads the caption.

One can see this division reproduced in the critical treatment afforded to the hard-boiled detective story. It is alleged that this subgenre started as a reaction against the more staid puzzle-type of mystery story. Advertising of the late twenties, when both Carroll John Daly and Dashiell Hammett had their first books published, would certainly seem to support this notion. The advertisements of the period were conspicuously dominated by classical mysteries. This conveyed the impression that the hard-boiled formula was a new variant of the puzzle stories appearing in such abundance. Unfortunately, this misguided idea has been bolstered further by the impressive credentials of those supporting it. In his seminal essay 'The Simple Art of Murder' (1944), Raymond Chandler contrasts the 'traditional or classic or straight-deductive or logic-and-deduction novel of detection' with the work of Dashiell Hammett. This essay probably helped to cement the notion of the revolt of the hard-boiled writers. Joseph T. Shaw's claim, in the Introduction to *The Hard-Boiled Omnibus* (1946), that he worked with Hammett to 'create a new type of detective story differing from . . . the deductive type' carried weight because of Shaw's position as editor of *Black Mask*. By the time Shaw took over the editorship of *Black Mask* in November 1926, however, the formula was already well developed, though Hammett's best work was yet to come. Julian Symons's important history *Bloody Murder: From the Detective Story to the Crime Novel: A History* (1972) also treats the hard-boiled novel as a rebellion against the classical pattern.

The validity of this classification is highly questionable from the standpoint of historical development, however. The adventure detective tradition had been around in the dime novels and early pulps since the time whan Allan Pinkerton began publishing accounts of the exploits of his operatives in such books as *The Expressman and the*

Detective (1875) and *The Molly Maquires and the Detectives* (1877). A number of detective heroes peopled the dime novels and early pulps. Old Sleuth was one of the most popular, inspiring imitation which resulted in a highly publicised court case. He was first introduced in *The Fireside Companion* in 1872. One of his competitors was Old Captain Collier, whose detective series began running in the early 1880s with such titles as 'Old Cap Collier; or "Piping" the New Haven Mystery' (1883). By 1898 a series of novels based on this hero's exploits numbered more than 700 titles.

The adventure-detective story is a very different breed from the classical detective yarn. It is part of a tradition which grew up along side the puzzle type of story. One can see the two traditions side by side in Arthur Conan Doyle's *The Valley of Fear* (1915). The first part of the book is a classical-type Holmes story, where deduction is uppermost. The second half relates the story of an adventure detective, drawing heavily on Allan Pinkerton's *The Molly Maquires and the Detectives*. The differences between the two traditions are so great that the book effectively splits in the middle, leaving critics to complain of its 'broken-backed' character.

Mary Noel distinguishes the Old Sleuth type of story from those needing mental detective work: "Violence rather than thought was Old Sleuth's method. He was extraordinarily handy, not so much at tracing the clues of a previous crime, as at snatching the brandished knife from the villain's own hand'. She also suggests two reasons for Old Sleuth's popularity. The first is the urban setting, the second the unusual style, featuring slang-ridden dialogue. Edmund Pearson quotes the beginning of 'Old Electricity: The Lightning Detective' by Old Sleuth (1885) in this regard:

'Don't wink your peepers, Larry.'

'What's up, cull?'

'That's what's up. Keep your eyelids raised for strangers.'

'Oh, stash it! and throw in your light, chummie. What's the "peep" now?'

This slang-ridden dialogue is the forerunner of the colloquial style of the hard-boiled detective formula.

The adventure-detective story, then, has a history that goes back to the 1880s, when it merges into other adventure-story patterns. Marry Noel has argued that the early detective stories 'made no fundamental change in either characterization or plot'. She claims that these stories simply substituted a detective for a hero of another occupation. The story of Western adventure provided ample scope for such variations and it was one of the staples of the dime novel. It is not at all certain, therefore, that, when Carroll John Daly and Dashiell Hammett began to work towards a new, and highly successful, formulation of the adventurer-detective story, they were rebelling against the inadequacies of the classical pattern. Even if

they were, it seems likely that the shaping of the hard-boiled formula was more positively influenced by the adventurer-detective type than it was by any negation of the classical formula.

Critical examinations of the hard-boiled detective formula which rely on the classical formula to provide a definitive framework are therefore hopelessly inadequate. John G. Cawelti's treatment of the hard-boiled formula in *Adventure, Mystery, and Romance* provides a case in point. Cawelti identifies the major elements of the hard-boiled detective formula as 'the detective', 'the crime', 'the criminal' and 'the pattern of action'. He therefore gives primacy to the plot; his formulaic elements are all defined in terms of their plot function. For Cawelti the pattern of action 'moves from the introduction of the detective and the presentation of the crime, through the investigation, to a solution and apprehension of the criminal'. This, as Cawelti points out, is the same basic pattern of action as found in the classical mystery story. And yet, as he also points out, 'Most significantly, the creation of the hard-boiled pattern involved a shift in the underlying archetype of the detective story from the pattern of mystery to that of heroic adventure'. As a result, he is forced to use a pattern that never really fits properly, leaving him with the compulsion continually to contrast the hard-boiled treatment of elements with the treatment given them in the classical mystery.

When one finds a critic who has written as much pioneering work as Cawelti lumbering with the burden of misinformed critical tradition, explanations must be sought. To uncover these, and to understand the misguided treatment given to formula literature generally, one must look to the impact of the marketplace. Formula literature was sold as a 'brand-name product', a sales technique which activated certain kinds of expectations and prejudices. These ranged from assumptions about the appeal of particular genre to judgements of the inherent quality limitations of work produced for mass consumption. Critics have always tended to do things backwards. Too often they make ill-founded assumptions concerning readership. Their conjectures about the artistic limitations of formula are used to create broad critical categories which have all the surgical potential of a bludgeon. It is hardly surprising that the marketing-categories for formula fiction were usurped by critics and treated as though endowed with objective reality, or that, once made, the mistake was ossified into a critical tradition.

Patrick D. Morrow

SOURCE: "The Concept of Formula," in *The Popular and the Serious in Select Twentieth-Century American Novels,* The Edwin Mellen Press, 1992, pp. 29-41.

[In the following essay, Morrow distinguishes the differences between "formula" and "complex" fiction through the analysis of two poems, "Trees" by Joyce Kilmer and "Approach of Autumn" by Stanley Kunitz.]

It is the premise of this study that formula fiction is different in kind, not degree, from complex fiction. If we abandon the term *popular* and start using *formula,* we can see how this premise can have some value. By the same token, it is also true that the whole issue exists on a kind of paradoxical continuum. If one drew a long line and, on the extreme left put a Barbara Cartland novel, and on the extreme right put James Joyce's *Finnegan's Wake,* we would get a sense of the range that is possible in all literature. Without question, at certain places, essentially in the middle of this continuum, there is a blending of formula fiction and complex fiction. Nonetheless, we need to consider these two terms as very definitely in opposition, different in kind much more so than in degree.

let us now move to some definitions. What is complex fiction? Complex fiction is what we study in standard English department literary courses. Complex fiction is a statement from the consciousness of an individual writer. Complex fiction deals principally with invention, stressing invention rather than convention. Complex fiction is a virtuoso performance of language, and often with language in complex fiction, there are intricate patterns of metaphors, thematic issues, all inextricably bound with developing motifs. Also in complex fiction, narrative point of view becomes truly crucial. Innovation is dominant here. In complex fiction, there may be switches in point of view, a use of stream of consciousness, and a blurring of external consciousness with internal reality. Complex fiction moves to an involved milieu. Certainly with Proust or Faulkner or Joyce, we can see that serious fiction is an act of intricate language. In complex fiction, there is an artistic and moral vision that dominates the novel. Complex fiction has a great interest in the ambiguous and the thoughtful. A modern novel that is complex can show us new ways, new procedures, and new insights, and is certainly into challenging our beliefs, rather than reinforcing what we may already believe.

Modern complex fiction tends to ask questions instead of presenting answers. The thrust in the complex novel is to be provocative, to try to get at, frequently through the use of mimesis, what existence is really like. This is one of the reasons why a writer such as Virginia Woolf is never going to have widespread popular appeal: Woolf deals so much with perception, in such novels as *To the Lighthouse* and *Mrs. Dalloway,* and perception does not per se translate very well into formula fiction. Furthermore, complex literature of all sorts is typically critical and typically evaluative, attempting to portray what is genuine and what is spurious. One of the functions of serious art of any sort is to separate and to make judgments about what is unreal and what is real. In modern complex fiction, there is a distinct criticism of the modern world, and of modern society.

Whereas *Airport* by Arthur Hailey, clearly a formula work, is quite supportive of modern systems and technology, there is hardly a complex novel of today that can be found which supports the modern world. This is frequently a shock to readers of modern serious literature. The modern novelist is typically quite critical of the world in which she or he lives. In the modern complex novel, characterization is multidimensional. Almost always, with the lead characters, we cannot tell the good characters from the bad characters. There are again multiple possibilities, with a good deal of ambiguity.

Frequently, the modern complex novel will have a particular approach or slant, but it also frequently contains a sort of counter slant, so that the modern novel frequently runs on a basis of antagonistic forces. Again, as in such a work as Joan Didion's *Play It As It Lays,* we see the conflict, but questions are raised rather than answers given. The complex novel is pridefully notorious for its lack of plot. Plot is secondary in the complex novel. Rather than being so preachy, the modern complex novel is interested in what conditions and situations feel like. Frequently, as developed in the American complex novels of the 1920s, this centers around frustration, which is why so many American novelists from Hemingway to Faulkner to Fitzgerald concentrate on the Hippolytus myth in one form or another. This complexity in complex fiction leads to an important distinction between theme and message. Complex art seems to have three themes: love, death, and art. But a theme is an issue, a sort of domain wherein the action and the ambiguity will be centered. Thus, the word *theme* means an area of interest, a concern. What frustration could feel like could be a theme. What initiation feels like could be another theme.

The word "message" should *not* be used with complex fiction. A message is a reduction, and it is part and parcel of formula fiction. Messages are like clichés. Here we need to encounter Morrow's Law of Clichés: For every cliché, there is an equal and opposite cliché. There are numerous examples, but one should suffice. Absence makes the heart grow fonder; or, out of sight, out of mind. Messages work in a similar kind of way, and to talk about a message in complex fiction is to distort the thematic and complex component of a novel. A message would be something such as: true love will triumph; or perhaps, in the more recent formula and anti-formula works, there would be a message such as: everything is screwed up.

Moving to formula fiction, we find some distinct differences when we compare formula novels with complex novels. Formula fiction deals in conventions, rather than in inventions. The purpose of these conventions is to reinforce and reaffirm, not to attack or to challenge values. This is one of the reasons that formula fiction is frequently called escape literature. But, for most middle-class readers, who are the bulk, the profitable bulk, of the reading public, there is no escape, but rather there is intensification. If standard middle-class readers wished to escape for a while, then they would study Urdu or Differential Calculus.

If we take a novel *cum* screenplay, such as the James Bond film *Moonraker,* we can see that, although this is planned for a lively afternoon's entertainment, it is not escape for anybody who lives in the electronic, technological world of today, but rather is an intensification of that world. Bond, too much bound by this our physical earth, and largely tongue-in-cheek, goes to outer space.

In formula fiction, there is generally a kind of patina of realism, but behind this realism lies what John Cawelti in *Adventure, Mystery. and Romance* calls a moral fantasy. This is a mythic approach, at times a kind of wish fulfillment, but frequently, at other times, a subversive knowledge and thrust. The moral fantasy is an important component of all types of formula literature. In terms of plot and characterization, formula fiction works in exactly the opposite way of serious fiction. What formula fiction attempts is to present a series of stereotyped characters. Stereotyped characters are not inadequate in terms of how formula fiction actually works. While complex fiction sometimes uses stereotyped characters for subordinate roles, stereotyped characters are used for all the main roles in formula fiction. What happens in formula fiction is that these stereotyped characters work out and through, frequently in a predictable fashion, a series of crises. It is for this reason that formula fiction is so strong in plot, while plot is one of the weaker areas of complex fiction.

In American formula fiction, the messages delivered by the novels tend to have some element of what critic Max Westbrook calls the sacred or "sacrality." Formula novels, very popular in the nineteenth century, tend to stress, with no tongue-in-cheek aspect whatsoever, no sense of doubt at all, a kind of game plan for Christian messages positively working. The twentieth-century anti-formula works, such as *Little Big Man* or *McCabe and Mrs. Miller* or Nathaniel West's *The Dream Life of Belso Snell,* take the sacred issue and run it in reverse, thus creating an anti-formula story that is totally profane rather than totally uplifting and sacred.

Paradoxically, I believe that we can discern the difference between the concept of formula and the concept of complex literature by looking at two poems. Let me pick two twelve-line poems about nature. One of them is the much-celebrated "Trees" by Joyce Kilmer; the other, "Approach of Autumn" by Stanley Kunitz, a poem that probably only those who are seriously interested in modern poetry have ever heard of or seen.

TREES
by Joyce Kilmer

I think that I shall never see
A poem lovely as a tree.
A tree whose hungry mouth is pressed
Against the earth's sweet flowing breast.
A tree that looks to God all day
And lifts her leafy arms to pray.
A tree that may in summer wear
A nest of robins in her hair.
Upon whose bosom snow has lain
Who intimately lives with rain.
Poems are made by fools like me
But only God can make a tree.

APPROACH OF AUTUMN
by Stanley Kunitz

The early violets we saw together
Lifting their delicate swift heads
As if to dip them in water, now wither
Arching no more like thoroughbreds.

Slender and pale, they flee the rime
Of Death: the ghosts of violets
Are running in a dream. Heart-flowering time
Decays, green goes, and the eye forgets.

Forgets? But what spring-blooded stock
Sprouts deathless violets in the skull
That, pawing on the hard and bitter rock
Of reason, make thinking beautiful?

In the seminal volume which transported the concept of New Criticism from theory or critical practice into classroom teaching, *Understanding Poetry* by Brooks and Warren, "Trees" is established as the quintessence of a hideous, "bad" poem. It is difficult to disagree with Brooks and Warren. They talk about the obsessive iambic tetrameter rhythm, the idea that each line rushes at the ending with the exact couplet rhyme of aabbccdd, etc., as though there was a sense of closure, a sense of completion and order. Brooks and Warren also talk about the literal meaning of the poem in terms of the description of the tree. They create a truly grotesque vision, since Kilmer after all created a grotesque version, and what happens in the poem is clearly extra-artistic. It is this dimension of the poem that has managed to keep said poem alive, at least in the junior high mentality of Mid-America.

It is a great shock sometimes to young students of poetry to realize that Joyce Kilmer was not a Kansas schoolmarm with marvelously powdered white hair and a tear in her eye, but was actually a World War I soldier, strapping and strong, who was killed in the trenches. Kilmer comes out of that early portion of the twentieth century when strong men would weep. This is the *"invictus"* era, an era which also produced Owen Wister and certainly Theodore Roosevelt. For our purposes, the importance of "Trees" is how it works as a popular culture artifact. One of the most intriguing features of the poem is its obsession with topic sentences and couplets. The poem is written in couplets, rhyming exactly aabb, etc., in case one misses the point, but each couplet works as a topic sentence that is never, throughout the course of the poem, fulfilled. So what happens is that Kilmer blurts two lines and then moves on to another blurting of two lines.

A poem is a collection of words, and this makes Kilmer very nervous apparently. Therefore, he wishes to rush through the words. He runs into serious trouble with elegant variation, line 4, "against the earth's sweet flowing breast," and this concept shows up again later with the connotation/denotation of the line "Upon whose bosom snow has lain." So, what Kilmer has done in terms of the actual words is created a sort of Hugh Hefner, 1950s version of the notorious popular American breast fixation. However, the poem has not ended with this particular image. Indeed, like every other couplet in the poem, the ideas, the words, are abandoned. What Kilmer does is to realize the inadequacy of the poem that he has produced—indeed, no one was more shocked at the poem's almost immediate popularity than Joyce Kilmer. He shouldn't have been: a key feature of the poem is that it is easy. Anybody can understand it, at least apparently. After all, the word-recognition level is at about the fourth grade.

What happens at the poem's conclusion, however, is probably the most important. After going through a series of ten incompetent lines, a mutilation of images, and a lot of language which is neither innovative nor powerful, Kilmer gives up. Throwing himself on, so to speak, the bosom of the audience, pleading clemency for writing such an atrocious poem, Kilmer says that final famous couplet. Think about the implications of the couplet. Kilmer agrees that he, as a poet, is terrible, that "poems are made by fools like me." What he has done here, especially with the famous last line, is to acknowledge, by throwing himself down, his inadequacy. After all, it is only God who can make a tree. The issue that a modern poet would likely raise is "So what? Maybe God can make a tree, but has He ever made a great poem?" This Kilmer does not consider.

What we have in this poem, then, is something that is a little bit different from what serious readers of poetry are likely to think of as quality poetry. The poem has existed for so long not because of what is says, but because of the tone that it emanates. Here we have a contradiction between the tone of the poem and what the actual words say. This, in itself, is quite an accomplishment, although it is not an accomplishment that any serious poet would wish to have. The tone of the poem is one of sacrality, one of the recognition that God ruleth all, and that the poet is subservient to God. In a century where the poet as a complex writer seriously gets into the idea of virtuosity and creativity, this poem is well recognized and well appreciated by those who would like poets to realize their place.

If we take a look at Stanley Kunitz's "Approach of Autumn," we can see a real live poem that readers of complex literature would perceive as a serious work of art. "Trees" is nonverbal, perhaps antiverbal, and Kilmer can generate a tone again, really in counterpoint, to what the words are actually saying, and this is an accomplishment, dubious though it may be. Kunitz's "Approach of Autumn" is a totally different kettle of fish. This is a serious, difficult poem. It begins with a throw-away line which is quite characteristic in contemporary poetry, the misleading line. "The early violets we saw together" sounds like a line from a greeting card, not quite up to the quality of Hallmark, but this is simply the beginning, because quickly in the first quatrain, Kunitz establishes a conceit. He is comparing violets with thoroughbreds. Also, we notice his formal component. He uses a slant

rhyme which creates immediately a sense of dissonance with the rhyme scheme in line one, together with the rhyme scheme in line three, "now wither."

That harsh dissonance is not unlike hitting a minor second of C and C sharp on a piano, a characteristic of modern poetry which suggests its disaffiliation and disaffection with the modern world. The conceit comparing violets and thoroughbreds begins in the first stanza and continues. We notice that the lines run on, in Kunitz's poem, whereas Kilmer has an absolute demand that the end of the line is the end of the statement, as though lines of poetry were sentences, and for Kilmer every other line shows up with a period. What Kunitz does is try to set up a counterpoint between the form and the content so that the lines run on. Also, Kunitz uses a measured quantitative verse. This type of verse, caricatured by Robert Frost with his comment that free verse is like playing tennis with the net down, impacts images and metaphors to stress the potency and the power of language, quite different from Joyce Kilmer's "Trees."

In the second stanza, we move from the basic comparison of violets and thoroughbreds as similar, with their attitude towards arching in terms of water, to the idea that "Slender and pale, they flee the rime," and with this word "rime," Kunitz does not so much make a pun as he makes a rich use of this concept. A rime is a barb of ice, the beginning of fall. Rime is seen in most parts of the United States, usually on trees. But the word *rime* also indicates a kind of continuity or cycle. The poem is about approaching autumn, and what Kunitz is discussing is death. He moves, after the colon, into an alternate dimension. The poem leaves the rigid, external world of "Trees," and moves inside into perception: "the ghosts of violets / Are running in a dream." What Kunitz attempts to do here is to impact images, to make the poem as intense and as compact as possible. His description of autumn, for instance, is only two words, but the description shows that Kunitz understands what autumn is all about: "green goes." Line by line, the poem gets more difficult.

In this poem, Kunitz makes each stanza more difficult and demanding on the reader than the last. In contrast, "Trees" demands a passive, receptive audience. Kunitz's modern complex poem demands an active, critical, inquiring audience. The last stanza of Kunitz's "Approach of Autumn" consists of two questions. "Forgets?" begins the stanza; then in a flurry of virtuoso words, Kunitz moves to set up and imply an answer. We notice his intense use of sibilant sounds. There is, for all of this intellectual inquiry, a good bit of drama. Kunitz also, starting with the second stanza, moves into the question of the relationship between the present tense and memory. The answer to Kunitz's question is implied, but not overtly stated. What Kunitz is probably talking about at the conclusion of "Approach of Autumn" is a subject that few readers of formula literature care at all about, that is, the subject of writing itself, in this particular case, poetry.

We can see that it is poetry that is the spring-blooded stock that sprouts deathless, meaning eternal, violets (beauty) in the skull. We attend to that in our minds: "That, pawing on the hard and bitter rock / Of reason." Anyone who has ever written anything of any substance knows what such means, and all of this makes thinking beautiful. Poetry is often called a making of thinking beautiful. I am not suggesting that this is any message of "Approach of Autumn"; indeed there *is* no message to "Approach of Autumn." There is, however, a thematic component. As we have discussed previously, the themes of art tend to be love, death, and art. Here is a poem that is about art. Kunitz searches for mimesis, intensification, and feeling—Kunitz does not search for eternal truths. As is typical of modern complex poetry, his range is much more narrow, but it is also much more deep than formula writing.

Having seen, then, the same basic principle that works in formula fiction working in poetry (sometimes poetry is easier because there is not so much length, and there is a lot of compressed intensity), we are ready now to encounter the basic concept of formula fiction. For our study of formula fiction, we need to turn to John Cawelti's insightful study of the typology of formula in a book called *Adventure, Mystery, and Romance*. Cawelti's approach is principally neo-Aristotelian in the sense of describing a phenomenon, rather than leading with a kind of critical judgment or evaluation. It is Cawelti who says that formulas all have a moral fantasy, who says that formula relies on convention rather than innovation, and who perceives the moral fantasy in different types of formulas.

With one exception that I will get to in a moment, I agree with the basic categories that Cawelti divides formula fiction into. But my perception of how the formulae work is somewhat different from Professor Cawelti's. The first example he sees is the formula fiction of adventure. This is principally male-oriented, and the moral fantasy of this male story is the triumph over death. In an adventure story, the hero, involved in a considerable amount of heroic action, goes forth in time and space, and triumphs over adversity in the form of a crisis. Frequently the hero takes on a plan of revenge or a cause that is justified. The hero usually picks up some kind of sidekick or foil, and perhaps the most memorable caricature version of this sidekick is Gabby Hayes, the foil to Gene Autry. Women in the adventure formula are fringe benefits. The male hero, being successful, gets to enjoy these fringe benefits, and James Bond is the most outrageous example of a character who reaps fringe benefits. But said benefits never interrupt his mission, his cause.

Lately, popular television has taken the adventure story and featured a female. The most overt, caricaturish, and obvious example of this is *Wonder Woman*. Wonder Woman's boss, the bland but gorgeous Lyle Waggoner, happens to be her sidekick. Wonder Woman, much like Superman, has two identities. In one identity, Wonder Woman is a bland, nice, bespectacled secretary, and in the other, the turnabout role, Wonder Woman triumphs over virtually everything. Other groups too, besides feminists, have appropriated the adventure formula. Shaft, for example, is a black detective who works for black identity and follows, in the Shaft stories, the basic road map of formula adventure stories. Whereas the action in the adventure story, as Cawelti perceives it, is basically out, forward in time and space, the adventure can run in reverse. Such is true, for example, with the adventure components in *Gone With the Wind*. What happens is that the crisis comes toward the characters. The crisis must be dealt with in terms of an oppressive, tremendous force heading towards the characters, wishing to destroy them, or at least to control them. What an adventure hero like Bond does is to move out in time and space towards a crisis.

Whereas the adventure paradigm has been set up for males, the romance paradigm has been established for traditional female audiences. The romance is typically much more cloistered, and generally centers on female/male entanglements. Generally, what happens is that there will be one female and two or more males. Frequently the crisis consists of having to make a decision, a life-long decision in favor of one or the other. Usually the males are divided into Mr. Safe, who is dull, predictable, and reliable, the kind of male that one's parents would be likely to approve and Mr. Excitement, who frequently is from a slightly different ethnic stock, and who is much more of a speculator than Mr. Safe, who is an investor. Mr. Excitement has a great deal of allure. Generally, however, in the romance, Mr. Safe wins out over Mr. Excitement. Thus, as noted, despite whatever uproar and excitement the sexual arena of a romance delves into, there is a strong and powerful moral ending.

While the adventure story deals in caricaturish stereotypes of females, the romance deals with caricaturish stereotypes of the males. *The Thorn Birds,* a celebrated novel and later, television movie, by Colleen McCullough, serves as a useful example. Although *The Thorn Birds* is set in Australia, with McCullough spending a good deal of time describing the desolation and the loneliness of the Australian Outback, it is clear that McCullough has learned a considerable amount from Western films. *The Thorn Birds* is one of the most powerful validations for female suffering ever written. The novel centers around Meghan Cleary, who is the heroine, and the stereotyped characters are an advanced version of Mr. Safe versus Mr. Excitement. What we have here is Mr. Brutal versus Mr. Impossible. Mr. Brutal is a character named Luke who is as nasty an Australian "yob" as one could possibly imagine. He clearly would prefer to cut sugar cane with his "mates" rather than be with Meghan. The audience immediately turns against him, and this antagonism deepens towards Luke as he appears not so much to use Meghan as to ignore her. The final scene between Luke and Meghan must have created a good deal of applause when shown in the television movie, because Meghan uses the one dependable weapon that she has, language and her tongue, to absolutely turn Luke into flaccidity.

The Mr. Impossible in *The Thorn Birds* should be called Father Impossible. This is Father Ralph de Bricasault, who is a master of the serious modern device of the unconfirmed gesture. What Father Ralph does is to try to create Meghan, to dangle himself over her, and then, as soon as she, as a small child, says such things as "I'll marry you when I grow up," he withdraws. Clearly the situation is totally impossible. Luke is oppressive, almost beyond belief, and Father Ralph is available to Meghan only during the moral holidays that he periodically takes, or when he is dying. Whereas Meghan has a marvelous scene of eloquency against Luke, Father Ralph has a final scene with Meghan in which he says that he was wrong, he should have married her, it was ambition that drove him, and he realizes now that he made a terrible, catastrophic mistake. Since Father Ralph at least realizes that he has made Meghan suffer, her life is in essence validated.

A third form of formula fiction that Professor Cawelti perceives is the detective story. Detective stories are divided into two types. One, the simpler type, works this way: the story begins with a scene wherein we perceive a crime. The criminal is unusually stereotyped here. On television, he shows up typically with a Hawaiian shirt and two days' worth of beard. The atrocity is committed, we know the situation, and then it is up to the detective to find out whodunit. This is the standard situation with a television series such as *Barnaby Jones,* and frequently with some of the simpler Mike Hammer detective stories. What is at issue here is the cleverness of the detective, and point by point, we see how the detective, like Poe's C. Auguste Dupin, solves the situation and the mystery.

One of the most intriguing features of this kind of detective story is its use of logic. Logic appears to be the method of the detective, but in point of fact, the detective gives the audience (or readers) several different contradictory, ambiguous [equivocal?] options. The detective possesses an almost unerring sense of immediately perceiving the right choice or the right clue for identifying the criminal. Detective novels, even Agatha Christie's work, run on the basis of the detective as a hero going through a moral maze or labyrinth, solving problems, and taking very few wrong turns. This simple type of detective story relies even more on conventions than the second type of detective story, which we will encounter in a moment. Consider, for example, the *reduction ad absurdum* of this type of detective story—*Hawaii Five-O* on prime-time television. At the end of most episodes of *Hawaii Five-O,* Steve McGarrett, always dressed in a suit, always conscious of the fact that he is, in point of fact, a "howlie," says, with the apprehended criminal, to his lead associate, James MacArthur, "Book him, Dan-O. Murder One." How different this series would have been if instead of this final clincher that wraps up, without any sense of questioning at all, the episode, McGarrett had said, "Wait, Dan-O. Can we convict a criminal for what in essence is his enforced depravity by society? Are we not all, in a way, responsible for the actions of this man?" As in the one-dimensional detective story, such an am-

biguous and convention-breaking stance would no doubt short-circuit the audience.

The second and more complex type of detective story is the one where we know who the hero is, in that the hero is the detective, but we are not entirely sure of what exactly the crime is, and we certainly do not know who is guilty. This is an intriguing form of fiction, and is close enough, sometimes even verbal enough, to complex fiction, so that readers of complex fiction will also be readers of this type of detective fiction. Naturally, advanced readers do not take this kind of fiction seriously; nonetheless, they may indulge in it and even give the occasional compliment to such fiction. An example of this type of detective fiction can be seen in Dashiell Hammett's *The Maltese Falcon.*

A fourth type of formula fiction that Professor Cawelti sees is the "Mysterious Stranger" story. This he typically associates with science fiction, but the mysterious stranger can show up in all sorts of other forms of fiction as Roy R. Male, in his important book *Enter Mysterious Stranger,* explains to us. Male perceives that there are two types of American fictional stories, one the journey, and the other the story set in some kind of enclosed area—or what Male calls a cloister. Perhaps the most celebrated recent mysterious stranger story is the Oscar-winning movie *E.T., the Extraterrestrial.* But science fiction from early on deals a lot with the mysterious stranger. After all, that's what *Frankenstein* (1818) and *Dracula* (1896) are really about. The mysterious stranger has considerable power. The mysterious stranger comes into a situation and may change it for the better, or may change the situation, as in Mark Twain's *The Mysterious Stranger,* for the worse.

Cawelti also sees a fifth type of formula which he calls "social melodrama." Here I strongly disagree with Professor Cawelti, because it seems to me that melodrama is a mode that all forms of formula fiction use. Thus, I do not consider this a type of formula fiction, but a method employed in formula fiction.

READERS OF POPULAR LITERATURE

Peter J. Rabinowitz

SOURCE: "The Turn of the Glass Key: Popular Fiction as Reading Strategy," in *Critical Inquiry,* Vol. 11, No. 3, March, 1985, pp. 418-31.

[*In the following essay, Rabinowitz investigates the assumptions readers make when they delve into genre fiction.*]

1. INTRODUCTION

Even among critics not particularly concerned with detective fiction, Dashiell Hammett's fourth novel, *The Glass Key* (1931), is famous for carrying the so-called objective method to almost obsessive lengths: we are never told what the characters are thinking, only what they do and look like. Anyone's decisions about anyone else's intentions (which, in this underworld of ward politics, often have life-and-death consequences) are *interpretive* decisions, dependent on correct presuppositions—on having the right interpretive key. The novel's title, in part, refers to this kind of key. Ned Beaumont, the protagonist, has to decide how to govern his relationship with Janet Henry; one of his major clues to her mind is a dream that she tells him, a dream that climaxes in an attempt to lock a door against an onslaught of snakes. Dream interpretation is difficult enough to begin with, and Janet Henry compounds that difficulty by telling the dream twice. In the first version, the attempt to lock the door succeeds; in the second, the key turns out to be made of glass and it shatters. Ned Beaumont, in deciding which dream to use as his key, chooses the second (as do most readers)—but it is a choice based on an intuitive mix of experience and faith, knowledge and hunch.

A reader often faces the same difficulties that Ned Beaumont does. Reading a book, too, requires us to make a choice about what key to use to unlock it, and that choice must often be based on an intuitive mix of experience and faith, knowledge and hunch. For example, as I shall show, the experience of reading certain texts—not all, but a significant number of them—is problematic because it depends in part on whether the reader has chosen, before picking them up, to approach them as popular or serious. My argument hinges on two prior claims. First, I contend that one way (but not the only way) of defining genres is to consider them as bundles of operations which readers perform in order to recover the meanings of texts rather than as sets of features found in the texts themselves. To put this crudely but more modishly, genres can be viewed as strategies that readers use to process texts. Second, I argue that popular literature and serious literature can be viewed as broad genre categories.

Before discussing each of these points in detail, I would like to offer a limitation and a definition. When I address the distinction between popular and serious literature, I limit myself to American and British novels from the 1920s to the 1960s. Although I suspect that parallel arguments would hold for other countries and other periods, I am sure that many of my more specific claims would have to be altered. When I discuss interpretation and appropriate questions, I'm talking in the context of what I define as "authorial reading," the attempt to recover the author's intended meaning. My purpose in so doing is not to deny the problems that reader-response critics and post-structuralists raise about the priority of such author-centered meaning but rather to make my task manageable in a short essay by focusing on a single type of reading. In other words, I am not claiming, as F. D. Hirsch does,

that we have a moral injunction to read in this way. All I am claiming here is that authorial reading is *one* way of approaching a text. It is certainly significant enough to justify close scrutiny—for two reasons.

First, a lot of people actually do read (or attempt to read) this way a great deal of the time. The critical revolutions of the past few years may have blinded us, but it is hardly likely that the millions who turned to Len Deighton's *SS-GB* or Judith Krantz's *Scruples* were interested either in deconstructing texts or in discovering their underlying semiotic codes. In fact, even among the most jaded readers—academics—authorial reading is still the most prevalent form of literary interpretation, as is clear if you consider the sum total of academic production and not just the journals devoted particularly to literary theory. I suspect that it is more common still in the classroom, where the pressure to be original is less intense.

Second, authorial reading provides the substructure for most (although not all) other kinds of reading. True, some ways of approaching a text seem to skip over the author entirely: certain kinds of structuralist or stylistic studies, for instance, or the kind of subjective reading proposed by David Bleich in *Readings and Feelings,* a reading validated by community concerns rather than authorial intention. But then again, many types of reading depend for their power on a prior understanding of the authorial meaning. The manifest/latent distinction of certain Freudian studies, for instance, collapses if we do not have a manifest meaning to begin with; Georg Lukács' analysis of Honoré de Balzac depends on the distinction between what Balzac wanted to see and what he really did see. Most important—if critical importance has any connection to the degree to which criticism can make us recognize the world with fresh eyes—we see the same dependence on authorial intention in much feminist criticism. Judith Fetterley's resisting reader can only come into being if there is something to resist.

Let me turn now to my three claims.

2. GENRES AS READING STRATEGIES

Genres can be viewed as strategies for reading. In other words, genres can be seen not only in the traditional way, as patterns or models that writers follow in constructing texts, but also from the other direction, as different bundles of rules that readers apply in construing texts. There are three parts to this assertion.

First, a reader is not a tabula rasa. Even before we pick up a book, we need to know, among other things, certain reading conventions—using the term to refer not to plot formulas but rather to rules that regulate the reader's operations on the text. These conventions, part of what Jonathan Culler calls "literary competence," go well beyond the linguistic.

Second, not only must we learn a vast number of implicit conventions of reading before we can understand anything as complex as a novel, more significant, we must learn different "rules" for processing different books. Indeed, if any analogy holds between literary and linguistic systems, we must view *Life with Father* and *The Sound and the Fury* not only as different utterances but also as manifestations of the equivalent of different languages. Although we may not frame it in these terms, the principle that there are different ways of reading is fundamental to the ways we think about teaching. When we complain that students don't know "how" to read, we mean that they do not know how to read in the "right" way. The same notion informs our critical discourse as well. Everyone who has worked on *The Turn of the Screw* has confronted the question of whether or not it should be read "as" a ghost story; no one is apt to think it eccentric when a critic like Fernando Ferrara says "Just as one can study *A Midsummer Night's Dream* as document, one can also study *Das Kapital* as fiction."

To a large extent, then, our actual practice as teachers and critics confirms that "reading" is always "reading as." It is significant for my argument that the terms used to describe various modes of reading are often genre terms: *The Turn of the Screw* can be read *as* a ghost story. For this brings me to the third part of my first claim: not only is reading a process of applying rules, not only do different books call for different operations, but, furthermore, rules tend to come in generic packages. Even though each text, examined in detail, calls into operation a specific collection of rules, on a more general level of analysis each work *shares* a large number of rules with other works of the same genre. We often know to apply rule d to a certain text because that is usually the case in texts where we have already applied rules A, B, and C.

So far, I have talked about rules of reading in the most abstract way. What kind of rules *are* these rules A, B, and C? How, specifically, do the operations that readers perform differ from work to work or from genre to genre? There are a number of ways of putting it. For instance, different questions are appropriate to different genres—using the word "appropriate," as I have said, in the context of the search for the author's intended meaning. It is appropriate to ask about the metaphorical implications of William Faulkner's title *Sanctuary* in a way that it is not appropriate to ask about the metaphorical implications of Agatha Christie's title *The Mystery of the Blue Train;* it is appropriate to ask what will happen to Janet Henry and Ned Beaumont after the end of *The Glass Key* in a way that it is not appropriate to ask what happens to the happy lovers after the end of Philip Barry's *Holiday.* Similarly, we approach different genres with different sets of expectations. The ending of Raymond Chandler's *Big Sleep* has the impact it does only because, given our assumptions about what sort of text it is and given our knowledge of how that sort of text is "supposed" to wind up, we falsely expect some kind of justice at the end. The same kind of presupposition can be seen in our experience of Anton Chekhov's *Cherry Orchard*: the perennial question of why it is called a comedy is usually answered in terms of the text per se. But we can also see it as a question about the reader's experience—especially about what sorts of desires and expectations are aroused by the explicit signal to read it as a comedy.

Our understanding of the conventions of reading may become clearer still once put into some kind of order. There are numerous ways of classifying them, but I'd like to suggest now a four-part system which, while neither exhaustive nor privileged (for instance, it complements, rather than replaces, the typology suggested by Steven Mailloux), is at least useful for a rough sorting out of an extremely thorny area.

First, there are what I call "rules of notice." Despite repeated claims by critics that, in literature, "everything counts," we know from experience that there are always more details in a text—particularly a novel—than we can ever hope to keep track of, much less account for. We have learned to tame this multiplicity with a number of implicit rules, shared by readers and writers alike, that give priority to certain kinds of details and that thus help us sort out figures from ground by establishing a hierarchy of importance. Some of these rules of notice seem to cover a wide spectrum of texts: for instance, the simple rule that titles are privileged. This may seem trivial, but it's a tremendous help, for instance, for the first-time viewer of *Hamlet*: in the opening scenes, there are so many characters that we would not know where to focus our attention if we did not have the title to provide a core around which other details could crystallize. Similarly, the first and last sentences (like the first and last chapters) of most texts are privileged: that is, any interpretation of a text that can't account for those sentences is generally deemed more defective than a reading that cannot account for some random sentence in the middle. Other rules of notice apply specifically to smaller groups of texts. For instance, when we are given some apparently obscure detail about a character's grandmother in a novel by Faulkner or Ross Macdonald, we are supposed to pay more attention to it than we would in a novel by Fyodor Dostoevsky.

Second, "rules of signification" tell us how to recast or symbolize or draw the significance from the elements that the first set of rules has brought to our attention. Included here are rules for determining symbolic meaning (the rules that tell us when to invoke the religious connotations of words, for instance); rules for distinguishing degrees of realism in fiction (the rules that allow us to discriminate, for instance, among the degrees and types of realism in the various representations of Napoleon in *War and Peace, Napoleon Symphony,* and *Love and Death*); the rule that allows us, in fiction, to assume that post hoc *is* propter hoc; rules that permit us to draw conclusions about the psychology of characters from their actions.

Third, there are "rules of configuration," which enable us both to develop expectations and to experience a sense of completion. Certain clumps of literary features tend to occur together; our familiarity with such groupings prompts us to assemble disparate elements in order to make patterns emerge. Our ability to perceive form—in Kenneth Burke's sense of the creation and satisfaction of appetites—involves applying rules of configuration; as the work of Barbara Herrnstein Smith demonstrates, so does our ability to experience closure; so does our recognition of the plot patterns and formulas so often illuminated in traditional genre studies. We need not get much further than the opening scenes of *Holiday* to know how it is going to end. That is not, however, because it signals its own unique form. Rather, it is because we know how to put together a few elements—a charming man, a rigid fiancée, an attractively zany fiancée's sister—and see an emerging pattern.

Finally, there are "rules of coherence." The most general rule here states that we should read a text in such a way that it becomes the "best" text possible. From this follow more specific rules dealing with textual disjunctures, rules that permit us to repair apparent inconsistencies by transforming them into metaphors, subtleties, and ironies—or, in the case of deconstructive criticism, that allow us to tear apart the text, revealing the abyss behind it. The relationship between rules of configuration and rules of coherence is roughly analogous to that between rules of notice and rules of signification. Rules of configuration alert us to particular patterns and tell us what to expect; rules of coherence permit us to take the details of the text (including those patterns) and extrapolate to larger meanings. Thus, it is rules of configuration that lead us to expect justice at the end of *The Big Sleep*; it is rules of coherence—which demand that the work fit together as a whole—that require us to interpret our frustration at the novel's irresolution in terms of Chandler's overall political message.

While there is a certain logical order to any discussion of these sets of rules, I am not suggesting that we read a text by applying them one after another. Reading is a far more complex, holistic process in which various rules interact in ways that we may never understand (the old hermeneutic circle again), although we seem to have little difficulty in putting them into practice intuitively. Thus, for instance, rules of notice would seem to precede rules of configuration, since we cannot notice a pattern until we notice the elements. But one of the ways that elements become visible is by forming parts of a familiar pattern. Thus, in *Dombey and Son,* Charles Dickens heightens our awareness of the traditional pattern of the manipulative underling by giving Mr. Carker even, white teeth. But we tend to notice his teeth in part because they are an element in that larger pattern.

Nevertheless, even if this classification of conventions does not reflect the order of our mental operations, it is still a useful analytic device. For, by allowing us to view texts as sets of strategies performed by readers rather than as sets of concrete verbal features, this approach makes explicit some of the normally unrecognized as-

sumptions involved in the act of reading. Specifically, it reminds us that literary works "work" only because the reader comes to them with a fairly detailed understanding of what he or she is getting into beforehand. I am not denying that every work of fiction creates its own world, but I am saying that it can do so only because it assumes that the reader will have certain skills to begin with. Every literary theoretician these days needs a governing metaphor about texts: text as mirror, text as body, text as system. I suppose that my metaphor would have to be "text as unassembled bunk bed from Sears." It is a concrete thing, but you have to assemble it; it comes with rudimentary directions, but you have to know how to perform basic tasks and must have certain tools at hand; most important, the directions are virtually meaningless unless you know beforehand just what sort of object you are aiming at. If you have never seen a bunk bed before, your chances of sleeping comfortably are slight.

3. POPULAR FICTION AS A GENRE

Once we map out some of the parameters of reading in this way, we can see that the pop/serious distinction has many of the characteristics of a genre distinction. Genre categories, of course, vary in their specificity, from such broad classes as the epic through such smaller groupings as the classic locked-room mystery, and Tzvetan Todorov's "fantastic," on to more and more precise categories. And needless to say, the pop/serious distinction is the broadest possible. The rules that apply, therefore, are both extremely general and subject to numerous exceptions. Still, we can say that, as a genre, popular literature seems to differ from serious fiction in two ways.

First, popular fiction emphasizes a different *category* of reading rules, Roland Barthes has made a similar claim, in different terms, when distinguishing popular tales from the psychological novel—one of the epitomes of serious fiction in the period I am discussing. "Some narratives," he claims, "are predominantly functional (such as popular tales), while some others are predominantly indicial (such as 'psychological' novels)." In Barthes' own vocabulary, popular tales tend to be more metonymic, while psychological novels are more metaphoric; translated into traditional genre terms, this means that popular tales are more plot oriented, psychological novels more character oriented. Recast in my terminology, his remarks suggest that when we read popular fiction, we tend to stress operations of configuration, while in reading psychological novels, we tend to emphasize operations of signification.

Pop and serious fiction differ not only according to which type of rule their readers put into effect more often but also with respect to the particular rules that readers are asked to apply within each category. First, rules of notice: what we attend to in a text is greatly influenced by two factors—the speed with which we read, and the other works we have in the background of our minds and against which the text is read. Particular details stand out as surprising, significant, climactic, or strange only in the context of a particular intertextual grid—a particular set of other works of art. And we not only read pop fiction more quickly, with less intensity, but we also tend to read it against a different background. Whether or not we pay particular attention to the name "Marlow" that Eric Ambler gives his hero in *Cause for Alarm* (1939) will depend on whether it is read "against" other popular spy novels or against the tradition that includes the works of Joseph Conrad. And while one is apt to be on the lookout for ciphers and anagrams in serious post-Joycean fiction (without such predisposition, the climax of Vladimir Nabokov's "Vane Sisters" would be missed completely), we are not apt to do so in a popular spy novel—even one that, like Robert Littell's *Amateur,* concerns a code breaker who has discovered, encoded in *The Tempest,* proof that Francis Bacon wrote Shakespeare's plays.

Even when what is noticed is the same in popular and high art (for instance, a title), there is often a difference in the rules of signification applied to it. Titles in serious novels during the period under discussion are supposed to be treated largely metaphorically or symbolically. Thus, when a college teacher is at a loss for an exam question about a serious novel, he or she can always ask, Why is the book called *Sanctuary?*—or *For Whom the Bell Tolls* or *Edna His Wife?* But in reading popular titles, we are supposed to treat them, on the whole, as broadly descriptive (they give clues about genre and general content) and discriminatory (they help distinguish one book from another so that we will know whether or not we have read it already). You could not reasonably ask students to write for an hour on Why is this book called *The Case of the Sleepwalker's Niece?* because the function of Erle Stanley Gardner's title is less rich. The reader is merely supposed to determine from it that it is a mystery story and that it is a different book from *The Case of the Howling Dog;* the title is not supposed to provide a springboard for metaphoric association.

Rules of configuration, as well, differ for the two types of literature. As I have already suggested, popular art tends on the whole to encourage activities of configuration rather than activities of signification anyway. But in addition—as I will demonstrate in detail in the last part of this essay—the particular configurations you impose on or expect in a book depend, in part, on the books you are reading it against.

Finally, in high art, we demand—and seek out—greater and more elaborate forms of coherence. We are, for instance, more apt to look at apparent inconsistencies as examples of irony or undercutting, whereas in popular art we are apt to ignore them or treat them simply as flaws. This, too, has something to do with the speed of reading—as well as with the reader's tendency, in serious fiction, to reread, to refine interpretations, and to exercise ingenuity.

4. THE AMBIGUITIES OF READING

It would be a pleasure to stop theorizing at this point and move on to the task of listing the differences in the rules

for the two genres in more specific detail. But the argument sketched out so far leads into some theoretical problems that cannot be ignored. The rules I am talking about, remember, do not exist in the text but rather are rules applied by a reader. Furthermore, their application is conventional, not logical. That is, there is no way to determine by reason alone what rules apply in a particular case. When we read Christie's *Mystery of the Blue Train,* we should expect that the culprit will be an unlikely suspect. That is not because there is any logical imperative to do so but instead because we live in a community where it is usual to apply that rule in novels that present themselves as Christie's does. Thus, not only do readers, as free beings with subjective concerns, have the power to apply them in a personal or eccentric fashion; more important, even readers aiming at the recovery of the author's intended meaning will often find themselves faced with alternatives that are hard, if not impossible, to decide among. And the experiences that result from applying these alternative processes may be quite different.

In other words, there are always a variety of sets of rules that one can apply to a text; and while some texts are more or less resistant to certain kinds of misreadings, it is the case—more often than those of us committed to the notion of "better" and "worse" readings would like to believe—that a work will leave considerable leeway and that several different sets of rules will apply to it equally well. I am not here taking the fashionable position that all books are, by their very nature, inherently ambiguous. Quite often, a text will give fairly precise signals as to how the author intended it to be read. For instance, Gardner's title *The Case of the Sleepwalker's Niece* nudges us into a pop strategy of reading by blocking a metaphorical interpretation, just as the title *The Sound and the Fury,* by forcing us both into metaphor and into Shakespeare, steers us into the serious mode. The recurring religious imagery of Nathanael West's *Miss Lonelyhearts*—which begins with Shrike's poem in the very first paragraph—makes it nearly impossible for an experienced reader to infer that the author wanted us to treat the novel as a popular tale; the play-within-a-play format and the exaggerated stylization of the opening of Tom Stoppard's *Real Inspector Hound* signals the reader that he or she should take the work not as an imitation of a detective story but rather as a parody of one; the flat, unresonant prose of most paperback romances discourages us from the kind of attentive reading we usually apply to high art.

Other works are more confusing—even a work as apparently straightforward as Mickey Spillane's *Vengeance Is Mine.* Its title can be read as a pop title, a marker to distinguish it from yet relate it to *I, the Jury.* But it can also be interpreted as a serious title, as a call to read the novel in the context of Leo Tolstoy's *Anna Karenina* (which starts with the same biblical citation), to notice its ironic religious implications, and to take a critical attitude toward the arrogant hero who takes God's work on himself.

Now good reading is a process of matching presuppositions against text and revising strategies as the text moves in unanticipated directions. And it would be comforting to believe that the reader who assumed that *Vengeance Is Mine* was the title of a serious ironic novel would soon find his or her reading corrected by other elements in the text. But as we have all seen in the variety of readings put forth by our journals—and as we have seen argued theoretically by critics such as Stanley Fish—it is not easy for a text to win over a reader who is committed to finding in it values that do not belong there, particularly when that reader is a sincere one. Given the numerous references to hell and damnation, to playing God, to "making" people; given the antagonist's name, Juno, and the frequent references to Olympus; given what can be interpreted as its *Sarrasine* references (references especially noticeable in a critical climate greatly influenced by Barthes' *S/Z*)—it would not be hard to read Spillane ironically.

I am not claiming that such an ironic reading would be a good one. Rather, I am saying something quite different: bad as it is, it would not necessarily run against stumbling blocks in the text. In other words, the *success* of any genre placement—that is, the success of any particular reading strategy—is no guarantee of its correctness. The ironic reading of Spillane, whatever its textual grounds, would be wrong as an interpretation of the author's intentions, just as I suspect that Samuel Rosenberg's ingenious reading of Sherlock Holmes, however successful, is wrong when it concludes that Arthur Conan Doyle had Friedrich Nietzsche in mind when he invented Moriarty. In neither case, though, does the text itself dictate conclusively what rules ought to be applied. Whether you hit upon the right reading will often depend simply on what you think it likely to be before you begin.

This brings us back to *The Glass Key*. As I noted at the beginning of my essay, the novel itself raises the issue of how presuppositions influence interpretation. In analyzing the dream scenes as a metaphor for reading, though, I had already made a decision to treat the novel as serious rather than as popular. But the book is nowhere near as clear as I pretended it was; in fact, it really holds itself open for placement in either broad genre.

Take the opening sentence: "Green dice rolled across the green table, struck the rim together, and bounced back." In either genre it is a privileged position, and in either it raises questions for the reader. But the questions—that is, the expectations that it nourishes, the way it is experienced—are quite different for each genre. If it is a pop detective story, we will ask configurational questions: Who is playing? Did he or she win or lose? How will that trigger future actions? If it is a serious novel, we will stress questions of signification: What is the role of chance in this novel? Why the symbol "bouncing back"? In either case, the book follows through: the dice game does generate much of the early action, but the images of chance and resiliency are also central to the novel's metaphoric structure.

One might legitimately argue that the good reader can take both of these approaches at once and read the novel in both classes simultaneously—although I suspect only academics actually read in that way. Be that as it may, there are other consequences of genre placement that demand an either/or decision about reading strategy. Take configuration: If we construe the book as a popular novel, subgenre "detective story," we will be on the lookout for a particular configuration—a problem, a false solution (often stemming from a false confession) about three-quarters of the way through, a correct solution about ten pages from the end, and a postclimax wrap-up of secondary importance. If we look for that pattern, we will find it. As a consequence, we will not for a moment believe Paul's "confession," and we will concentrate more on the solution than on the wrap-up. The book will not, even in this reading, be a particularly jolly one, but its despair will be muted by the reader's privileging of Ned Beaumont's investigation. But if we read it as a serious novel, subgenre "personal discovery novel" under the spell of Proust, Conrad, and Faulkner, we will be alerted to another potential configuration. The correct solution will come earlier than it would in a detective story but will be followed by something even more important—an examination of its psychological and philosophical ramifications. If we are on the lookout for this configuration, we will find it, too, with a bit of a twist: we are more likely to believe Paul's confession and be surprised by the real solution, but, in any case, we will be more interested in the consequences of the truth than in the facts of the murder itself. In this reading, we will give less attention to the solution, and we will stress the novel's final image more strongly: Ned Beaumont staring at an empty doorway, a doorway we will immediately begin to tie metaphorically to the door in the dream and all the other doors and entryways into mysterious psychological blanks that give this book much of its character when it is construed as a serious novel. Intellectually, perhaps, we can have it both ways and call the novel some kind of hybrid. But for the actual act of reading, we must choose one genre or the other (or some discrete third): we cannot both emphasize and de-emphasize the solution. And our genre choice will substantially color our entire reading experience.

As I have said earlier, of course, the pop/serious distinction is a genre distinction on the broadest level of analysis. When we read, we think also in terms of far smaller groups: detective story, spy novel . . . or even classic British detective story, cynical they're-all-bastards spy novel. But the principles enunciated here are just as applicable to those genres as well. Even though I have raised the issue in the most general terms, I hope that my analysis still does at least serve as a reminder of something about which we need to think more: the ways in which and the extent to which a reader's initial assumptions about genre determine the route that a reading experience follows, and the difficulties that a novelist may face in trying to force his or her readers to make the right turns.

Thomas J. Roberts

SOURCE: "A Variety of Readers," in *An Aesthetics of Junk Fiction,* The University of Georgia Press, 1990, pp. 71-86.

[In the following essay, Roberts groups the readers of genre fiction into distinct types based on their relationships to the material.]

We often speak of readers of popular fiction as though they were simpler and more predictable than they are. Carelessly, we speak as though one discrete group of readers always chooses westerns and nothing but westerns and as though a different group reads only detective stories, a third only fantasies, and so forth. We would say, I suppose, that the groups overlap thinly at their edges, but we probably feel that they remain fundamentally distinct. We would be willing to grant that individual readers look now and then into the stories other groups admire and that one genre occasionally does win readers from another genre; for we would grant that there must be some mechanism that permits readers to abandon one genre and take up another; but we are not likely to be much interested in this.

And we seem to be assuming that the relations between a genre and the people who read in it are equally simple. That is, we think (or at least we speak as though we think) that even readers who display excellent critical judgment when reading outside the paperback traditions lose their critical standards while reading inside one of the popular genres.

Whether we individually credit it or not, it is this image that determines which questions we shall ask and whether we shall accept the answers people give us. We ask, what kind of person reads the romance? what kind reads the western? science fiction? the detective story? And we expect that the answers to these questions will be different, that the people who read the romance and the people who read the western will appear on different pages of a national census of readers and, additionally, that they are different in character and situation and in the rewards they are getting from their genres.

Sometimes we need simple images if we are to get anything done, but this image of discrete readerships, of single-genre loyalties would be difficult to validate. People who read most often in one genre usually follow other traditions too; they dip into still other genres with moderate frequency; they manifest strong though temporary enthusiasms for something they have just discovered; they develop fierce genre antipathies.

Here I set that familiar one-genre/one-readership image aside to look more closely at the relationships readers have with the genres they know. The following, I suggest, is a minimal set of distinctions, the smallest number needed to make sense of the variety of reader-to-genre relationships that we find among readers of the paper-backs: the exclusivists, the users (who include certain odd forms of the reading addict), the fans, the occasional readers, and the allergics.

EXCLUSIVISTS

Exclusivism is enthusiasm at its highest pitch. For exclusivists, a certain genre is not just the preferred, it is the only acceptable source of fiction. Donald A. Wollheim, the science-fiction editor, spoke of enthusiasms and exclusivisms.

> The phases of being a science-fiction reader can be traced and charted. So many read it for one year, so many for two, so many for life. For instance, reading it exclusively can be as compulsive as a narcotic for a period of an intelligent teenager's life. The length of time as I see it—and I have seen and talked with and corresponded with hundreds and hundreds of such readers in my lifetime—is about four or five years of the most intense reading—usually exclusive, all other literature being shoved aside. After that a falling off, rather rapid (often due to college entry or military life or the hard stuff of getting a job for the first time). There is, I suspect, something like an 80 per cent turnover in the mass of readers of science fiction every five years.

There has been so little interest in the reading of fiction outside literature that I find nothing in print on patterns of exclusivism among adult readers. Wollheim himself may have been a lifelong exclusivist for science fiction, and most of the romance readers Janice Radway located and studied were still exclusivists. My impression, nevertheless, is that adult genre exclusivists are less common than we suppose, that single-focused reading enthusiasms are short-lived. There are exceptions, but the old rule is sound: the people who read anything read everything.

Exclusivism, which readers themselves think of as a temporary aberration, would not be worth our attention if it were not that a certain kind of inquiry into popular fiction is predicated on that default assumption that the typical reader of popular fiction is an exclusivist. The results, too often, are essays and books that bibliographers if they were not so polite would lump together under the label *Thunderings.* The thunderers want to show us how ugly, or how violent, or how mindless modern culture has become; and so they use the comic book or a television series or pornography or the stories of Mickey Spillane to create for us an image of Calibans of both sexes created by and living under the exclusive governance of these materials. (A better-than-average example of this sort of thing is William Ruehlmann's *Saint with a Gun,* an essay on the origins and significance of private-eye fiction that sets out to demonstrate, with crushing contempt, that Spillane, his characters, and his simple-minded readers are all dangerously psychotic.) The weakness in the thunderers' presentation, as we have seen, is their unlikely assumption that anyone who reads pornography or watches television or reads comic books, or westerns, or science fiction, or detective stories or anything else, reads that and nothing else. To show that a culture is unhealthy by citing the deficiencies of one popular genre or one successful writer is like demonstrating that all America will soon be toothless because one of the popular soft drinks lacks five essential vitamins. The exclusivist reader is a fiction convenient for the thunderers; but while we can find isolated instances of the exclusivist reader and while most of us have at one time or another (sometimes, many times) briefly been exclusivist in our reading, no genre, and certainly no writer, could survive for long if it had to depend wholly on exclusivistic enthusiasm. The exclusivist is not a significant presence for popular fiction. There are only people who also read science fiction or who also read westerns, and so on. That, of course, is something entirely different.

USERS

To readers outside a genre, users are indistinguishable from exclusivists, but the two are never in doubt about their differences. If, as we have seen, an exclusivist's motto is, say, "*X* only!" (that is, "The romance only!" or "The western only!"), the user's motto is "*X* also." Most of Wollheim's 20 percent of science fiction's readers who retain a lifelong interest in the genre are users, not exclusivists. Though users are not so visible as exclusivists in the many activities that buzz around the various genres (the publication of fan magazines, the organization of conventions, and the like) there is evidence enough even in the fan magazines that readers of any one genre are deeply interested in others as well. In an article in *The Armchair Detective*, Richard Meyers interrupted a survey of mysteries on television to write angrily about television's misunderstanding of science fiction. *Locus: The Newspaper of the Science Fiction Field* regularly surveys its readers, and each year they report that they are interested in more than science fiction. The 1985 survey shows that 74 percent of them are interested in movies, 44 percent in mysteries, 32 percent in historical fiction, and 23 percent in the comics, for instance ("Locus Survey Results,"). *Zimri*, an excellent British fanzine of a few years ago, was not at all atypical in combining an interest in science fiction with an interest in poetry.

It is its users, not its exclusivists, who keep each vernacular genre alive, and each of those users has several reading interests. The romance readers that Janice Radway studied were exclusivists, but we would suppose that the more characteristic romance reader is not exclusivistic, that she does not read romances only. She may read two or three dozen each year—an average of three per month, say. Eight or ten weeks may pass without her having any interest at all in the romance, but she will one day find herself standing before a shelf of romances in a drugstore, idly poring over the titles, the cover illustrations, the back-cover blurbs. An experienced reader, she also studies the title pages, since she knows that paperback publishers do clever things with titles. (Frank Herbert's first science-fiction novel has appeared as *Under Pres-*

sure, as *Dragon in the Sea*, and as *21st Century Sub*. Forrest Carter's *Outlaw Josey Wales*, a fine western, first appeared as *The Rebel Outlaw: Josey Wales* and was then reprinted as *Gone to Texas*.)

If our romance reader is like many of the rest of us, she may find herself standing outside the store a few minutes later with a sales slip in one hand and books in the other. She may feel that she is afflicted with an innocent form of kleptomania, as though she unconsciously steals books but then unconsciously pays for them. It is of course one of her reading addictions that is governing her.

She will feel momentarily foolish, but she will read those romances—perhaps in one glorious weekend binge. When whatever drew her to those stories in the first place has been satisfied, she will stop reading. She cannot predict when she will stop, but, of course, the better the stories the longer the binge. She will put the romance completely out of her mind. Two weeks later, however, she may find herself standing in front of some shelves in a library, looking through the detective fiction: the start of a new but different binge.

Plainly, we are dealing in cases like this with addictions, no less addictions for being multiple and discontinuous. We readers dislike it when others say we are "compulsive" and "addictive," but these terms do seem to describe some of our behavior. So much has been said about popular fiction being an opiate, however, that we should also insist that these reading dependencies are found not only among readers of paperbacks. That devout Christian who cannot let a day pass without reading a chapter in the Bible is an addicted reader, as are those among us who cannot go for more than a few days without reading in Shakespeare or in Karl Marx or in history.

The taxonomies of readers that we would find most useful in the study of the vernacular genres have yet to be designed. These would identify readers not by reference to their favorite genres alone but by reference to their addiction clusters: that, say, one group that reads westerns also reads eighteenth-century fiction and Proust, but that another group that reads westerns reads nineteenth-century poetry and James Joyce. The mysteries of taste lie hidden in curious, overlapping patterns of superficially contradictory addictions that defy easy explanation. It is an indication of the inadequacy of older explanations that the people who do read in one of the vernacular genres always feel that the explanations describe other readers, not them.

We can lump exclusivists and users together as *enthusiasts*. Most—not all—of the next group are enthusiasts, too.

FANS

In "Paradise Charted," a good history of pulp science fiction, Algis Budrys explains the importance to the genre of its fandom.

While tens or perhaps hundreds of thousands of "science fiction" readers have never heard of it, everyone who publishes, edits, writes, or illustrates in the field must take its articulations into account. It is the repository of the amorphous oral tradition; almost all professionals who are now adults were imbued with its preconceptions as children.

. . . ."Science fiction" has hundreds, perhaps thousands, of amateur publications; at least one convention of some size nearly every weekend, culminating in an annual world convention with attendance approaching five thousand; innumerable subgroups founded on special interests within the special interest, particularly heroic fantasy; art shows; costume balls; its own repertoire of folk ("filk") songs; a well-developed jargon sufficient for good communication without more than passing reference to English.

Its development of its own special vocabulary in its amateur magazines is a sign that fandom is a special world that knows it is a special world. Budrys offers the following sample: "'I used to look at things in a fiawol way, you know. I was really into crifanac. Then I sent this poctsard to all the smofs about my idea for marketing filksongs. Well, it turned out four of them had gafiated, and three of them were just letterhacks. So, I don't know, man. I feel this fijagh attitude coming on'". The playfulness of the language suggests something of the feelings of the fans about the stories that are at the putative center of interest. The jargon, like most jargons, amounts to a few hundred new nouns, verbs, and adjectives firmly embedded in English syntax: *Crifanac* is "critical fan activity"; a *poctsard* is a postcard about science fiction; *smofs* are the sardonically termed "secret masters of fandom"; to *gafiate* is to "get away from it all"; a *letterhack* is a fan whose only fannish activity is the writing of letters to the *fanzines,* the magazines the fans publish for one another. The acronyms *fiawol* and *fijagh* advance the opposed opinions that "fandom is a way of life" and that "fandom is just a goddamned hobby." The nontechnical *gafiate,* to "get away from it all," that is, to withdraw temporarily from social activity, may eventually find a wider use; but the jargon seems designed chiefly to serve as a barrier between fans and others. It is interesting—significant, I should say—that the jargon seems to have little analytic value for students of the genre. Fandom is a quasi-orgy, an erotics of reading, not a scientific assault on a genre.

While everyday usage names any reader of any genre a fan of that genre, the more careful use of the term identifies fans as those readers of a genre who correspond with one another. Very few of any genre's readers know that a fandom exists, and few who do learn of it have any interest in becoming a part of it. (When Radway questioned romance readers, she learned that as enthusiastic as they were about the stories they were reading they had no interest in keeping in touch with others like themselves.) The modal genre reader, in the statistical sense, is the isolated user.

Genre fans are a tiny minority; but, as Budrys suggests, they are of special importance both to the genre itself and to anyone who is trying to understand it. Fans can easily be located, are very cooperative, and every year are writing thousands of pages of comment on the stories, the genre, its writers, and its readers. Even if their sociability as readers makes them atypical, they are invaluable as sources of information for students and readers of any of the vernacular genres.

It is with the fanzines that we would begin. One definition of the amateur fan magazine is that its editor pays no one for anything he or she prints and that it appears at least four times a year. Its readers contribute most of the text and art; the editor puts it all together and mails it out to his readers. The fanzines come and go so quickly that any list of purely amateur fanzines is quickly out of date, and any attempt at quick characterization is doomed. They come, for instance, in many forms: in 1984, a fanzine calling itself *FSFNET: BITNET Fantasy-Science Fiction Fanzine* began to be sent out from the University of Maine via a computer network (BITNET) to readers at other universities. Some of the fanzines I have enjoyed were Ed Cagle's *Kwalhioqua,* a zany publication that became too popular for its editor's wallet; Harry O. Morris's *Nyctalops,* which dealt intelligently with fantasy; Richard E. Geis's *Science Fiction Review;* Edward C. Connor's *SF Echo,* which came in the shape of a hand-made paperback; Dave and Mardee Jenrette's wide-ranging and inimitable *Tabebuian;* Otto Penzler's prozine *The Armchair Detective;* the lighthearted obeisance to sword and sorcery, *Amra,* which came to us from the Terminus, Owlswick and Ft. Mudge Electrick St Railway Gazette. I have been reading Bill Danner's *Stefantasy* with pleasure for years, and I remember with a special regard J. J. Pierce and Paul Walker's argumentative *T.A.D. (Tension, Apprehension, and Dissension),* which insisted upon taking science fiction seriously. Some twenty to fifty of the hundred and more fanzines I have read were as interesting as the stories they discussed.

In 1973, Fredric Wertham published his *World of Fanzines: A Special Form of Communication,* which, though hasty and inadequate, at least identified the cultural significance of the fanzine. Through fanzines, any group can create its own network of literary criticism, can give the books that interest it adequate review (they are mostly overlooked elsewhere), can publish its readings of those books, can query its writers (and have them answer), can award prizes, and can publish its own first, shy efforts in the writing of genre fiction.

Students of popular fiction who do not search out and study the fanzines and fandom associated with it put themselves at great disadvantage. The fanzines are easy to locate. Some of them announce themselves in the professional magazines, and their editors read and talk about one another all the time. A single LOC (letter of comment) to one of them puts one's address on display to all, and one is soon receiving issues from strange places. At least in the case of science fiction, readers who write letters of comment to the fanzines can find themselves receiving fifty different magazines within a few months of getting their first. Some fanzines are worth reading in their own right: some of the fanzines devoted to the art of the comic book (*Witzend,* for instance) have been better than most of the comics they discuss.

In the fanzines the readership of a genre becomes conscious, and if the silliest and most naive remarks on any genre are found in its fanzines, there too appear the shrewdest, the best-informed, and the most imaginative criticism.

These users and exclusivists, some of them fans, are a genre's readers. Beyond their number are other readers and nonreaders who contribute to the floating mass of misinformation about any genre that we all accept as a part of general knowledge. Among the nonreaders are people who, though they do not read, are sure they understand the western novel or the detective story, say, because of the films they have seen. I will not look at all the sources of sincere inaccuracy, but I will examine the people who read stories in a genre now and then but not often enough or widely enough to get an intuition into the life of the tradition. I will then complete this minimal survey with a consideration of the people who detest certain genres, who will read anything except the stories that come out of these genres.

OCCASIONAL READERS

All readers are users of more than one reading category and only occasionally a reader of many others, by which I mean that we are all willing to read now and then in some area we favor less—in this author, in that genre—but that we never become interested enough to stay with it. That reader who loses control of herself in a bookstore or a library every few weeks is a user of romances and detective stories; we can imagine that she is an occasional reader of spy stories, ready to read Eric Ambler's *Mask of Dimitrios* if strongly urged to and even to enjoy it but won by neither Ambler nor the espionage tradition to read more. Against the exclusivists' "*X* only!" and the users' "*X* also," occasional readers would hoist aloft that mildest of all reading mottoes, "*X* sometimes."

As occasional readers we come in different forms, each producing a characteristic misunderstanding. In some cases we were enthusiastic readers of a genre when younger and are now returning to it as adults, anticipating a misremembered simplicity. We had last read the John Buchan style of spy thriller, something like *The Thirty-Nine Steps,* or the E. E. Smith type of science-fiction novel, *Skylark Three,* say, and now pick up John Le Carré's *Tinker, Tailor, Soldier, Spy,* a story in which our spies are just as bad as theirs, or Ian Watson's *Embedding,* a novel about the human incapacity to accept multiply embedded linguistic structures, and we become annoyed. We were looking for a nice little daydream but are being asked to think. If we are not careful, we may find ourselves speaking of a Golden Age of this or that genre

and complaining that a once-delightful tradition has become self-conscious and pretentious. The probable truth is that we had then known only adolescent versions of the genre's stories or had read adult stories with an adolescent eye, quite naturally and properly overlooking those features that would catch our attention later. We certainly had not thought the stories mindless while we were reading them.

There are other varieties of the misinformation-generating occasional reader: for instance, the one-book expert. Every now and then, a popular genre will produce a book that sells hugely, as did A. B. Guthrie's *Big Sky,* a western; Walter Miller's *Canticle for Leibowitz,* a science-fiction novel; Frederick Forsyth's *Day of the Jackal,* a crime thriller; and John Le Carré's *Spy Who Came in from the Cold.* These books are widely read and discussed and they produce a blossoming in us of one-book expertise. Our opinions are the stronger and more powerfully advanced because they have the virtue of extreme simplicity. When we do look into other stories in that tradition, we are disappointed. We had expected a certain characterology, the thematics we find in the reading categories we do use, or at least that solidity of specification that so often distinguishes best-sellers. We do not find any of this, and we feel we have been misled—that, contrary to the implied promise of that book, only a few writers (the kinds of writers who specialize in the genres we favor, of course) can do anything with the tradition. Readers of Aldous Huxley's *Brave New World,* an interesting novel which is from, but not in, the science-fiction tradition (for one thing, it is shot through with Huxley's curiously obsessive hatred of "vulgarity"), typically feel that way when they try to read Robert Heinlein's novels or one of science fiction's short-story anthologies.

We are one step closer to understanding a genre than we were as one-book experts when we become one-writer experts. There are many one-writer experts among us, for it seems to be the case that when we occasional readers visit another genre more than once we go usually to the same writer. Those of us who read no more than two or three detective stories a year may know only the works of Agatha Christie. For us, to read the mystery means little more than reading an Agatha Christie novel; reading the western, reading a novel by Louis L'Amour; reading science fiction, reading something by Isaac Asimov; and reading the spy thriller, reading one of Ian Fleming's stories. The writers of choice differ from one reader to the next, of course, and with each generation; once the best-known writers in their genres would have been Conan Doyle, Zane Grey, Jules Verne, and E. Phillips Oppenheim. Against this identification of the genre with a single writer, the users of that genre protest in vain. We occasional readers are surprised to learn, if we ever do, that none of those names has nearly so high a reputation with the genre's regular readers as we outsiders suppose.

We are occasional readers when we pick up a story in a new genre out of curiosity or while we are still learning how to read a genre that is beginning to interest us.

Neither the curious reader nor the novice reader is likely to issue ex cathedra statements about the genre, however. Other occasional readers are not always careful: most notoriously, those angry journalists who read one detective story or horrific fantasy randomly chosen and then bemoan (and in themselves reveal) the death of mind in Western civilization. Academic scholars who assign themselves the task of discovering the appeal of some genre or subgenre they do not read themselves—historical romances, sword and sorcery, the caper novel—and who solemnly read and annotate some six or twenty of the novels are handicapped by the ignorance of the occasional reader, though they cannot afford to allow their readers, or themselves, to recognize this. The misunderstandings they foster do more mischief, for their descriptions are supported with massive citations and are snugly embedded in method.

It would of course be impossible to say at what instant an occasional reader has become a user. The one-book reader who evolves into a two- or three-writer reader may soon be a genre user and no longer an occasional visitor.

When we are genre allergics, of course, no one who listens to us is in any doubt about that.

ALLERGICS

In the course of her research for *Reading the Romance,* Janice Radway discovered that the suburban readers she was studying detest the pornographic romance.

> The reactions of the Smithton women to books they are not enjoying are indicative of the intensity of their need to avoid offensive material and the feelings it typically evokes. Indeed, twenty-three (55 percent) reported that when they find themselves in the middle of a bad book, they put it down immediately and refuse to finish it. Some even make the symbolic gesture of discarding the book in the garbage, particularly if it has offended them seriously. This was the universal fate suffered by Lolah Burford's *Alyx* (1977), a book cited repeatedly as a perfect example of the pornographic trash distributed by publishers under the guise of the romance.

When we feel like this, we find it difficult to read the stories, as though we were trying to eat spoiled or taboo food. We do not think of ourselves as having an allergic reaction, of course, but as truth seeing: this or that sort of story *is* obscenely violent, or viciously snobbish, or stupid, or grossly ignorant, and those who read it are themselves violent, brutish, stupid. Our reading motto then replaces the words "only," "also," and "sometimes" with "never": "X? Never!"—that is, "The detective story? Never!" or "Science fiction? Never!"

Readers of any genre learn to live quietly—if possible, anonymously—with that genre's allergics. As allergics we are just as abrasive, and so fierce and simple in our dislikes that our voices have an influence out of proportion to our numbers. The occasional readers, the nonallergic avoiders, and the inexperienced will always hear our voices of hatred more clearly than the milder approval of the users.

Reading allergies have indirect consequences when not recognized for what they are. Even if we are expert in fiction and in the theory of fiction, when we look into a genre or writer to which we are allergic we will not be able to read enough of the stories to make sense of them: Mickey Spillane has suffered grievously from the hit-and-miss reading that is all that allergics can manage. An allergic historian refuses to acknowledge, even to see, that a book worth admiring comes from the hated tradition, as when the science-fiction allergic insists that Hawthorne's "Artist of the Beautiful" and Twain's *Connecticut Yankee in the Court of King Arthur* are not science fiction, not even nineteenth-century proto-science fiction, and when readers allergic to westerns deny that James Fenimore Cooper's Leatherstocking Tales are westerns. Sometimes it is useful to think of proposals for censorship of this or that kind of book as the consequence of unadmitted reading allergies.

No one has taken the trouble to study reading allergies, though they are interesting in their own right. Walker Gibson offered one (partial) explanation for our dislike of some reading materials. He suggested that each book elicits from its readers a personality appropriate to it. A story that is intelligent, or nasty, or comic creates in its real human reader a mock reader who is intelligent, or nasty, or amused. Mark Twain asks us to be one person; Henry James, another. When we find that a story is making us into someone we do not want to be, Gibson continued, we throw it down and say it is a bad story.

I am not persuaded that this alone accounts for the Smithton rejection of pornographic romances, but it does help us understand some of our more passionate dislikes. Readers who pass up the British, country-house tale of detection, as I do, are perhaps suffering from a mild allergic reaction. Those of us with other social origins and loyalties feel that the British style of detective story asks us to give full approval to the preoccupations of the middle class—to its love of gossip, for instance. In the course of the inquiries, the detective uncovers precisely the kinds of secret about each of the suspects that would send delighted shivers through a middle-class dinner party: this woman has been having an affair with her husband's brother, that man has embezzled, a third proved a coward while serving in Northern India, that woman has had an illegitimate child, that man has gone broke. Only one of these people is a murderer, but the gossip-hunting season is declared open on anyone unlucky enough to be named a suspect. It all seems definitively "tribal," and some of us are not sure we want to join the dance of social excommunication. Other readers, some of them our friends, feel a similar reluctance to participate in the ceremonies shadowed forth by the genres we favor.

The people who read paperbacks are not the simple souls their critics make them out to be. They read across genre boundaries. They manifest intricate patterns of reading addictions, reading preferences, reading avoidances, and reading allergies.

They are not easy to understand even when they are speaking about a single, favored genre. Few of the enthusiasts can even agree as to what is and what is not science fiction, say, or what is and what is not a detective story. They politely overlook their differences when they meet, but the differences are not trivial.

Suppose that we want to know what a detective story is to its admirers and so turn to Barzun and Taylor's *Catalogue of Crime,* which is described on its dust jacket as a "Reader's Guide to the Literature of Mystery, Detection, and Related Genres." This is a fine collection of notes on hundreds of stories, and when we have learned to compensate for its biases it makes an excellent guide and companion to our reading. Barzun and Taylor tell us about (*a*) tales of detection and (*b*) ghost stories, but they do not tell us about (*c*) spy stories. That is one ostensive definition of *the detective story*.

We might turn instead, and with equal assurance, to Julian Symon's *Mortal Consequences: A History—From the Detective Story to the Crime Novel.* This is not a reading companion; as its title tells us, it is a history of *the detective story,* but it will also serve as an excellent reading guide. Symon's history does not cover (*b*) ghost stories, however, but *does* cover (*c*) spy stories. For people who are interested in the two volumes only for their help in finding a good read, these differences are only mildly amusing. When we are trying to understand what *the detective story* is to the people who read it, however, they are unsettling. Ghost stories and spy stories are not at all alike. What is the detective story to its readers, we ask, if some of them think of it as the tale of detection plus the ghost story and others think of it as the tale of detection plus the spy story?

There are other differences, differences in topography between the two genrescapes these readers map for us. The tale of detection—the sort of story that Conan Doyle made famous with his tales of Sherlock Holmes—looms large in Barzun and Taylor's *Catalogue of Crime.* For them, the later "crime novel"—the study that focuses on motivation rather than detection—is a decline from the Olympian heights of an earlier, golden age of the detective story. In the genrescape that Julian Symons describes in *Mortal Consequences,* however, the tale of detection that Barzun and Taylor love is snobbish, silly, adolescent—merely a stage the tradition had to go through if it was to mature into the crime novel. What is the detective story to its readers if some of them think that we shall find its center in those tales of detection and others think we shall find it in the contemporary crime novel? Nor are these the only images of that detective story we encounter when we listen to its readers. Neither of those two volumes is greatly impressed with the American style of

detective story that descended from the *Black Mask* school of writers and included such honored names as Dashiell Hammett and Raymond Chandler—a school of writing that other, equally expert readers value above all others. "What *can* readers be finding in the detective story?" its critics ask. Which readers? we ask. Which detective story? "What can readers be finding in the romance?" Which readers? Which romance?

It would be difficult enough to identify the "typical reader" and the "typical science-fiction story" if we had only exclusivists to consider—people who read nothing but science fiction or the detective story or the romance. Few readers are so simple of focus, and most of those who are will be shifting to something else later.

Within every reader there lies an intricate pattern of addictions, preferences, random interests, avoidances, and allergies which is never quite the same as the pattern in any other reader. We can easily imagine two friends who exchange detective stories. One of them, though comfortable with that genre, is uncomfortable with the ghost story, is only occasionally a reader of a western, is indifferent to science fiction, violently allergic to romances. The other, also a user of the detective story, enjoys ghost stories too, however, but is allergic to westerns, uncomfortable with science fiction, and merely indifferent to the romance. What, other than the detective story, do these two readers have in common? As often as not, the reader of paperbacks is a user of many genres who becomes exclusivist only briefly. It is easier to study the long-term exclusivists; they have an attractive, laboratory-like purity about them; surely we will not be satisfied until we understand the multigenre users, however. It is the exclusivists who are atypical.

There are some other standards we can set for ourselves in our slow progress toward a better understanding of some very subtle matters: for instance, that when we set out to investigate any of the genres we first determine our own relationships to that genre—that is, whether we ourselves are exclusivists, users, fans, or occasional readers—and that when we start giving explanations, we decide whether we are addressing our remarks to users, to occasional readers, or to nonreaders. While it is not always easy to know whether we are still operating under the handicaps of the occasional reader or have through some creative leap of reading insight grasped the logic and potentiality of a genre, we should be able to tell when we are allergic, at least, or when our information about a genre comes from stories in the same tradition but in another medium—from television programs or from feature films, for instance.

We shall also want to be wary when we read the explanations that others give. We should not entirely trust either praise from exclusivists or blame from allergics, of course. We should recognize that the observations of occasional readers, though well meant, are astigmatic: occasional readers just do not know enough. A still unexploited resource, as we have seen, is the body of readers who have become fans. The men and women who write for such fanzines as *The Armchair Detective* and *The Science Fiction Review* know more about those two genres than do academic sociologists, ethnologists, and literary scholars. Further, they are intelligent, and they too want to know whether, how, and why they are different from others.

Their explanations, too, are governed by tradition, however, and we can be confident that some of them will enthusiastically assure us that reading thrillers or romances or science fiction is "fun" and that it provides "escape" and that the writers are providing them with "surrogate daydreams." One of these explanations is worth looking into, but the other two should have been thrown out long ago.

Gry Heggli

SOURCE: "Talking with Readers: An Alternative Approach to Popular Literature," in *Journal of Popular Culture,* Vol. XXVI, No. 4, Spring, 1993, pp. 11-17.

[*In the following essay, Heggli utilizes discussions with a sampling of female readers to explain the popularity of weekly family magazines in Norway.*]

In the many-sided world of popular culture, weekly magazines stand out as products of some significance. The 4.2 million inhabitants of Norway constitute a relatively limited market, but the Norwegian weeklies boast a circulation of 1.6 million, half of which is contributed by three major family magazines. According to recent market research, though, their actual audience verges on a staggering 2.8 million.

The Norwegian family magazines are marketed as reading for the entire family—grandparents, mothers, fathers and children alike. The tables of contents includes serials, short stories, true confessions, interviews and articles covering ordinary people who have done remarkable things, Norwegian celebrities and European royalty, quizzes, recipes and letters to various columnists.

The weekly magazines are labeled as popular literature and have been subject to numerous studies that have focused on their texts while leaving readers standing on the sidelines. Traditional studies of popular literature have primarily been preoccupied with assessing the magazines from an ideological point of view, and they generally conclude that the weeklies represent inferior reading. The lack of "literary" qualities is said to have negative effects on the readers; the magazines blur causal relations and power structures and distort reality.

How do the users relate to the magazines? There seemed to be a conflict between the weeklies' vast number of readers and their bad reputation. As a folklorist I was interested in finding another reality, invisible in public debate, but in which readers feel at home. I was curious

as to how readers use their magazines, what they read, how they read it, and how they relate to their own reading. As a consequence, I carried out in-depth interviews with a group of female readers with highly varied backgrounds, all of whom had been reading one or more family magazines regularly over a period of up to 30 years. By closing in on these women, I hoped to understand more about their motivation, preferences, interpretations and involvement in relation to the magazines. I wanted the readers to voice the pleasure that they found in reading, and based on their accounts I hoped to come up with an answer to the overwhelming popularity of the weekly magazines, an answer that was richer in detail than previous studies.

In spite of the fact that they are being marketed as reading for the entire family, the family magazines are clearly written for, and are read by, women and must therefore be regarded as part of female culture. In order to understand the femininity of these weeklies, I found that recent American reader-response criticism would be a useful instrument of thought, because its theories cover issues such as the implication of gender on reading. Studies have shown that men and women approach texts differently. Whereas men tend to establish a certain distance to the text, women easily identify with persons in the story, even with emotions and situations, and they often go through a range of social emotions while reading (Flynn and Schweickart).

The magazines offer problem-oriented reading as well as idealizing stories, but both kinds of text stimulate the inclusive, compassionate attitude that values attentiveness and identification. Whether it was the readers' demand that fictional characters recognize the need for close relations, as shown by their partiality to articles that emphasize compassion and helpfulness, or the congenial activities that they were encouraged to by the practical pages, the readers' interpretations clearly showed that they related themselves to the text with understanding and involvement.

THE READERS AND THE SERIALS

The serials are popular and are usually one of the first columns to be read. However, my interviews clearly showed that the readers were selective; certain criteria had to be met for the stories to please them. Key concepts were credibility and compassion, credibility being a prerequisite for identification. The texts had to describe a known world that the reader knew how to relate to. Reading involves confirmation of identity and construction of a reality in which the events must be probable from the reader's point of view. One of the women I talked to mentioned a story that failed to meet this criterion, and that she consequently rejected. She was unaware of what was bothering her about it before we started talking. Then she gradually realized that the principal character's passivity was the cause of her annoyance:

> Unni: I think I'm bothered about the whole thing,
> that she doesn't tell the police how crazy her

husband is, for instance, that's probably what it is, that's what's so bloody annoying.

Gry: You've been thinking about that?

Unni: Yes, she can't go on like that, you know, it's dangerous, isn't it? He's a bastard and a criminal and should have been reported ages ago. She keeps putting things off all the time. I think that's probably what annoys me.

Gry: That you think she acts kind of stupid?

Unni: Yeah . . .

Because Unni cannot vouch for the principal character's passivity, the lingering conflict fills her with dismay, and consequently the story fails to provide the prerequisite for identification. Earlier Unni described how she was able to ignore everything else when reading a catchy story, and when she was asked to pick the serial that she liked the most, her arguments were based on the quality of the feelings they aroused in her.

One of the most popular serials proved to be a story called "The Gipsy Boy." The principal characters are a grown man who suffers from cancer and a ten-year-old gipsy boy. The story tells us about their friendship and how the child brings the man to new awareness during the last stage of his life. One of my interviewees described the story's qualities like this:

> Else: It was just fabulous, 'cause you'd have thought that you'd want that man to go on living, right? But it was all about this boy and how he used his intuition and feelings to understand what that guy needed and what he was thinking before he actually said it, right? He made the last part of that man's life a wonder, and he sort of realized that he'd been living all his life without really realizing what it was all about, the animals and nature and all. So he sort of calmed down and got some peace of mind. Harmony, you know. Yeah, it sure was a fabulous story.

The Gipsy Boy must have given the readers special cause for involvement. The gipsy is not just any child, he belongs to a commonly stereotyped people. The story emphasizes that the boy is a "child of nature," that his intuition is unspoiled and that his capability of identification surpasses that of ours which has been weakened by "civilization."

By using a gipsy child instead of a woman in the caring role, the story strengthens its message. The fundamental values that form the basis of a full life stand out more clearly; we have to take care of each other and free ourselves from the chase for physical comforts.

The story describes the last stage of the principal character's life in a way that grants the female readers closeness to a man's inner thoughts and feelings in a critical situation. In her article "Rhythms of Reception," Tania Modleski writes about the frequent use of close-ups in soap operas: "Close-ups provide the spectator with training in reading other people, in being sensitive to their (unspoken) feelings at any given moment".

The emotional effect is strengthened by the fact that the dying person is a man. His strength and masculinity crack, and he realizes that his previous priorities were not the right ones; he has underrated the importance of values such as intimacy, simplicity, care and love. The female readers have their choice of values confirmed; living for and with others, is a prerequisite for satisfaction.

As follows from the readers' liking for stories that create the right atmosphere of compassion and care, they dislike stories in which the characters are "evil." One of my informants told me how she distinguishes between serials that are marked by "compassion and love" and serials whose characters "bug each others to death." Some of them used words like "brutal," "mean" and "unpleasant" when asked to say what was wrong about a certain story, whereas others found it "annoying" when heroes were up against adversities, and felt "disturbed when things turned out bad." However, behind all of these statements we find the same disheartened state of mind.

This does not imply that popular serials lack dramatic events that give cause to suffering. The readers accept great portions of war, disease and death, as long as the misery can be claimed to be caused by fate, or reasons beyond the characters' control. Once the characters become aggressive and violent, however, the readers lose interest.

THE SOCIAL ACT OF READING

The social act of reading is another aspect of women's reading habits. What do they signal to the people around them when they sit down with their magazines?

Reading calls for concentration—it is difficult to do other things at the same time. It is an activity that makes interaction with other people impossible; there is room for nothing but the reader and the text. This means that when a woman sits down to read, she deliberately chooses to indulge in her private pleasure for a little while.

Through the years my informants had developed rigid reading habits. They usually read their magazine in the evenings, and they often pick it up while sitting in the living room after they are through with the chores of the day. Nevertheless, most of them prefer to read in bed, as this is the place that provides them with the peace and quiet they need to concentrate.

The family magazines are all published on Tuesdays, and normally my informants read them on Tuesdays, Wednesdays and Thursdays. In other words, reading is a weekday pastime. In her article "TV and Ritualization of Everyday Life," the Norwegian folklorist Torunn Selberg points out how we assign meaning and content to the hours of the day and the days of the week based on their position in a pattern, its distance from the weekend is an important criterion for the emotional content of a certain weekday. We find the same qualitative difference between weekday leisure and weekend leisure. Our expectations differ according to whether it is a weekday or a day of the weekend—Saturdays and Sundays are assumed to be spent in the company of others. Weekends offer the best opportunity for social contact.

"Weekend" is commonly understood to be the time between Friday afternoon and Monday morning. It is defined by the work week that most of us have to conform to. Weekends are supposed to be spent on recreation and rest, and family life is supposed to receive top priority in order to create a meaningful feeling of community with partners and children.

Women take on the responsibility for protecting their families' common leisure. They are to set up strategies so that they can provide for the welfare of other people, primarily children and husbands, no matter the inconvenience to themselves. The magazines are part of women's weekdays and are not supposed to be read during weekends. This is in line with the policy that is advocated by the magazines; women should spend their weekends on strengthening family ties. The family magazine deals with every aspect of family life; during weekdays women spend their spare time reading about how to care for their families during the weekend.

My informants' reading habits show that they refrain from reading the magazine until they are given the chance to indulge in it. One of them puts it like this:

> Gry: So the magazine usually lies on the bedside table, then?
>
> Randi: Yes, but I keep it down here in the kitchen, so that I can pick it up whenever, except it's impossible to concentrate then, you really need some peace and quiet.

The way these women make their priorities shows that they rarely or never let their own urge to read stand before others' call for attention.

The weekly magazine is a flexible product; its composition offers a varied mix of texts, which makes it well suited for browsing during short breaks. Those of my informants who were housewives used to pick up the magazine every now and then in between various chores. Constant interruptions and multiple concurrent tasks are part of their normal workdays:

> . . . she must be prepared to drop what she is doing in order to cope with various conflicts and problems the moment they arise. Unlike most workers in the labor force, the housewife must be beware of concentrating her energies on one task—otherwise her dinner could burn, or the baby could crack its skull. (Modleski)

This is how Unni described the day of the week when she used to buy the magazine:

> Unni: Well, it used to be Tuesdays, you know, when we were living in the city center. I put the little one to bed, and Lisa sat down with her bricks, and then I picked up the magazine.
>
> Gry: So you were looking forward to it?
>
> Unni: Yeah, sure, it was great. Couldn't sit for that long, though, they kept interrupting me all the time, but it was kind of nice, yeah . . .

The way the magazine is composed, then, makes it satisfy two different needs: that for intensive, concentrated reading as well as that for superficial browsing.

Some of the women described situations in which they picked up the magazine in order to dissociate themselves from the people around them, their message being "leave me alone for a while." They had been using their energies for associating with their families and needed to withdraw for a while to collect themselves and to gather strength to join the family again.

> Unni: Well, it's in the evenings now, after I've put the kids to bed. "Now I'm gonna sit down"—sort of, 'cause then I know I won't be interrupted, that's probably why I'm doing it. I'm kind of tired then, you see, and I need to relax. That's when I sit down with things like that, and a little snack perhaps, and a cup of tea.
>
> Gry: What happens if someone interrupts you?
>
> Unni: The first 30 minutes I get real cross and grumpy, 'cause then I really want some peace and quiet. I always demand that half-hour, and if my husband has been waiting for me to join him for some reason, then those first 30 minutes are banned. He's not allowed to say anything. He has to wait, no matter what. (She gives a little laugh). I've been nagging for a couple of hours then, you see, to make this work . . .

In Janice Radway's study, *Reading the Romance*, she interprets the act of reading as a deliberate choice to attend to one's personal needs rather than to those of others:

> In picking up a book, they refuse temporarily their family's otherwise constant demand that they attend to the wants of others even as they act deliberately to do something for their own private pleasure.

Reading becomes a refuge where women feel unattached from the duties that they normally fully accept as their own.

The reader of family weeklies has part of her female identity confirmed by her reading. The magazine tells her that feminine values related to care and reproduction are central and important, and that the intimacy and intensity that she wishes to have in relation to other people are ideals that are worth fighting for. The aim is to gain male recognition, and ultimately, that men should also recognise their feelings towards their fellow human beings and their needs to be intimate.

Traditionally, the weekly magazines have been considered ideologically confirmative and suppressive. However, once we change our perspective, another view seems compelling: that women's reading of magazines is a tacit protest against the underrating that women's care for others has been subject to. Women are not merited for the work that they do in this area of society, financially or status-wise, and there are few places for them to find encouragement and confirmation that certain central feminine values are in fact valuable. Having read their magazines, women return to their domestic duties with renewed inspiration, convinced that their priorities are right when they choose to put all their effort into caring for the common good of their families.

THE WEEKLY MAGAZINES AND THE FOLK NARRATIVE

In an essay from 1958, Herman Bausinger, the German folklorist, describes how the time of the classical genres has past, but that their themes survive in different forms. The tales of magic, the legend and the joke were parts of world that was small and surveyable, but in which inexplicable supernatural phenomena were important elements. The tales of magic voiced the dreams and the fantasies, the longings that were sought beyond the limits of this restricted world. The legends discussed the borderline between the known and the unknown. The world we live in today has become big and chaotic, and what used to be supernatural has become natural. Today's narratives draw their content from the factual world that we all have to relate to, and are there to tell us about the various revelations of the "real" world. In Bausinger's opinion, the basic structures of the classical genres can now be found in our preference for telling about and listening to happy events, crazy incidents and merry situations (Bausinger).

If the family magazines are read with this in mind, we will see that the happy events of the magic tales are reflected in the descriptions of weddings, child births, reunions and remarkable cures found in serials, true confessions and articles. The legend's discussion of the frightening and the strange is primarily found in true confessions and in the many readers' letters that discuss personal experiences and problems. Bausinger's third genre, the joke, is practically non-existent in the family magazines, but it is well covered e.g. in men's magazines.

We have seen that readers wish for realistic serials, as credibility is an important criterion for identification. Corresponding tendencies can be found if we examine folk tales. The novella with its emphasis on realism used to be more popular among women than men (Hodne). Early folklorists reflected on the differences between men's and women's relation to the narrative. Several re-

searchers have described the intensity with which women narrate. Moltke Moe, who was Norway's first Professor of Folklore, characterized women's narratives in a essay from 1894 as "rounded and communicative, somewhat gentler and smoother". In 1939, the German folklorist Merkelbach-Pinck experienced that "Frauen erzählen innerlicher, sie erzählen mit dem Herzen". In 1962 Linda Degh, the folklorist, characterized the stories told by female narrators in her thesis, *Folktale and Society:* "(. . .) feeling, finesse, tenderness and sentiment are prevalent in the tales of the female narrators". Both Moltke Moe and Linda Degh emphasize the fact that women base their stories on personal experience; events and feelings that concern them are woven into their narratives. "They can never remain as factual as male narrators" (Degh). This indicates that the features that characterize women's reading can be found in their narrative style as well. They enter into the experience offered by the story and easily involve themselves with persons and situations.

EVOLUTION OF POPULAR LITERATURE

Harriet E. Hudson

SOURCE: "Toward a Theory of Popular Literature: The Case of the Middle English Romances," in *Journal of Popular Culture,* Vol. 23, No. 3, Winter, 1979, pp. 31-47.

[*In the following essay, Hudson reconsiders the notion of "popular" as it applies to English romances of the Middle Ages.*]

Among modern forms of popular literature, romance is unique in its continuity with the Middle Ages. Even before the advent of popular romance as we know it, medieval romances were referred to as "popular antiquities" by early scholars such as Bishop Percy and Joseph Warton. In spite of this long standing identification of romance with popular literature and the frequent use of the word "popular" to describe certain Middle English romances, the designation "Middle English popular romance" remains problematic. It presents a number of difficulties: the word popular itself has several meanings, many of the conditions usually associated with popular literature did not exist in the Middle Ages, and the romances written in medieval England are a diverse lot. This paper examines current theories of popular culture and literature in light of what we know about the romances themselves and offers a dialogue between medievalists and scholars of popular culture from which we may draw a clearer and more satisfactory analysis of the romances' popularity.

Although popular literature has been with us for a long time, the study of it is relatively new and often deals with modern materials. Thus, as sociologist Zev Barbu says, there has been a "tendency to confine the phenomenon of popular culture to its most recent version, namely popular culture in advanced industrial society, and to apply to it models and analytical tools relevant for this and for no other type of study." In this way "popular culture" has become associated with mass production and consumption, and a largely middle class audience; "popular literature" suggests widespread literacy. Yet, in medieval England, members of the middle classes made up only a small portion of the population and it was not until the Renaissance that they produced a literature of their own. Actually, as Derek Brewer explains, "the nineteenth—century idea of upper, middle and lower classes did not exist in England at the time the romances were composed and cannot be applied to the society of that day." Though literacy gradually became more common, D. W. Robertson says there was "nothing like the large homogeneous audience available for writers today." Despite the efforts of medieval bookshops with their standardized operations, volume production of reading matter—to say nothing of mass production—was not possible until the introduction of the printing press. While it is not necessary to equate popular culture with mass culture, Robertson's assessment of the matter seems accurate: "It is probably fair to say that there was no popular literature in the modern sense in late medieval England and except for certain religious beliefs held in common, it lacked a 'mass culture.'" Bruce Rosenberg concludes that "popular culture contributed little to medieval life." Recent studies of romances have questioned the usefulness of the term popular as applied to these narratives. Susan Crane's study of indigenous insular romances, and Carol Meale's comparison of the three versions of *Ipomedon* find much in these narratives that runs counter to our expectations of popular literature and received notions about the romances.

The Middle English romances themselves are so diverse that one can not easily make generalizations about them. Some statement of this difficulty has become almost conventional in discussions of these works. There are more than one hundred narratives, composed over a period of 275 years (from approximately 1225 to 1500). Most, however, were composed between 1350 and 1450. A few are unique in English, the rest have French sources. The romances range in length from 500 to 20,000 lines and come in various forms of verse, and in prose. Some are frankly fictional entertainments, others have the authority of history; some are folktales, others read like psychological novels. There are religious epics (the Charlemagne romances, *Titus and Vespatian*), homeletic tales of chivalry (*Ami and Amiloun, Isumbras, Florence of Rome*) tales of romance (*Floris and Blancheflur, Sir Launfal*), exploits of English heroes (*Guy of Warwick, Richard Cour de Lyon*), stories belonging to the Great Matters of Greece and Rome, France, and England (romances of Arthur, Tristran, Gawain, Roland, Alexander and Troy). The themes, style and provenance of the romances are as varied as their subjects.

In spite of all this variety, "popular" can be a useful word for describing certain Middle English romances. It is also an important consideration at this time of cultural study. I have sought to address both sides of the question: what does the word "popular" mean and what are the romances like? The object of the present essay is to enhance our understanding of the romances and to test our theories of popular literature. What we need is a working definition of popular that will help us better understand the cultural dynamic of the romances. Or, as Paul Strohm succinctly puts it, to better study generes and "how they live in history."

The meaning of a term is conditioned by its semantic context. In part, "popular" must be understood in the context of other cultural terms it may be distinguished from—"folk" and "elite." Folklorist Jan Harold Brunvand describes elite culture as academic, progressive and institutionalized; popular culture as mainstream, normative, mass; folk culture as conservative, traditional, and largely oral. He calls these "levels" of culture, in the sense of strata, but other scholars understand them as a continuum with folk and elite forming the ends of the spectrum. Still other scholars, among them Joseph Arpad, understand elite and folk cultural artefacts in terms of opposites (such as oral-written, official-unofficial) and see popular culture as a kind of anomalous mediator between folk and elite. The limitations of the designations "folk," "popular" and "elite" are apparent, though. As Rosenburg notes, they are arbitrary lables, not analytic categories. They are based upon extrinsic rather than intrinsic features. Such conceptions tend to suggest that popular, folk and elite are mutually exclusive categories, and that literary artefacts like the romances can be classified according to these categories. In fact, any individual romance is a blend of various cultural elements. The Middle English romances incorporate many elements found in folktales. Their plots can be analyzed according to the Tale Types of folklore and their details can be identified with motifs in the folklore motif indexes. Rosenburg devotes most of his essay on the folkloric sources of medieval popular literature to the romances' and their similarities to *marchen*. Yet the genre romance originated in the courts and it is to these elite origins that Middle English narratives owe their noble characters and concern for chivalry. If artefacts can be, in a sense, multicultural, members of their audiences can be too. Though social stratification was greater and mobility more limited in the Middle Ages than in modern times, it was still quite possible for an individual to participate in more than one kind of culture.

An image of the relationships between cultural kinds of literature must be multi—dimensional and dynamic. Such a model has been proposed by Donald Dunlop and others who seek to understand folk, popular, and elite literature in terms of the dynamic relationship between author, artefact and audience. The elements of the triad are mediated by formulas, media and middlemen. The artist shapes the artefact according to a formula and the material is imbued with a certain aesthetic. The material comes to its audience through a particular medium and various middlemen bring the author's work to its audience. Though one factor may dominate the interaction of two elements, the other factors are always engaged. Thus the audience responds to the artefact according to its formula or aesthetic. The medium the artist uses also shapes his material. Middlemen bring the artefact to the audience and sometimes have a hand in shaping it. An author's choices of material and aesthetic usually reflect the audience's interests and tastes. The complex interrelationship of the author, material and audience lies at the heart of a work's cultural dynamic.

There do seem to be characteristic dynamics of author, audience and artefact which distinguish folk, popular and elite literature. Both folk and elite audiences constitute a close, or high context group. The elite audiences of the medieval courts constituted a close group based on noble birth or membership in the noble household. The court of Marie de Champagne, for which Chretien de Troyes composed his romances, would be a case in point. Its literature, especially the romances, required an appreciation of chivalric conduct—the nobility's self—styled *raison d'etre* and its high context. Georges Duby's studies of this chivalrous society and his comments on the romances show their audiences to have been a close as well as closed group. Crane refers to twelfth century French romance as a kind of *"récit clos"* in that it sought to be exclusive rather than accessible. If elite and folk literatures are high context, popular literature is low context. Hinds proposes that only artefacts which find "adoption/consumption by more than one regional culture and by more than one narrow socio—economic group" be considered popular. To appeal to a large, diverse audience, the work must not rely on media and materials available only to particular groups.

A further implication of popular cultures's low context can be seen in statements such as Northrop Frye's that popular literature is accessible with minimal formal training or education. This is not to say that only the minimally educated appreciate popular literature, but formal education does provide much of the high context for elite literature. Historical studies of literacy and education in late medieval England contribute greatly to our understanding of the dynamics of literary genres in the period. It has been assumed that the earlier English romances were intended for native speakers with minimal education because those with more education would have used French.

That the romances are written in English is sometimes taken as *de facto* evidence of their popularity and middle class audience. By the Fourteenth century, English was the most widely accessible language in England. The composer of *Arthour and Merlin* took note of this fact in his introduction, and similar sentiments are expressed in similar language elsewhere.

> Right is that Inglishe vnderstond,
> That was born in Inglond;
> Freynsche vse this gentilman,
> Ac euerich Inglishe can.
> Mani noble ich haue yseize
> That no Freynsche couthe seye.

Estimates suggest that fifty percent of London lay males were literate in English. Even at court, many who knew French knew English as well. Chaucer was the first major poet to compose for the royal court in English; his early career was devoted to the translation of works in French such as the *Roman de La Rose*. If English was finding acceptance among the aristocracy, French was being used by the bourgeoise in the fourteenth century. Sylvia Thrupp, describing the books owned by middle class Londoners of the time, notes that many of their romances were in French. Thus it is not possible to distinguish the audience of English romances from that of French romances on the basis of language alone. A few romances survive in manuscripts that are bi-, or even tri-lingual. The fact that the romances are in English is significant not because English was the language of the lower classes, but because it was the most widely accessible literary language.

Whatever else the word popular may mean, it always carries the sense of widely known and well liked. Thus some quantitative measure of the audience or the artefacts is relevant to their status as popular culture. However, quantitative information about the romances is very incomplete and conjectural. Any interpretations of the data that we do have must recognize the limitations of medieval book production and of our information about minstrel performances of romances. By various estimates, about 120 Middle English romances have come down to us, and there were others of which no text survives. Few of the romances exist in many manuscript copies. *Titus and Vespatian* has the most, 11, *Robert of Sicily* 10, *Isumbras* 9, *The Sege of Jerusalem* 7, *Richard Cour de Lyon* and *Bevis of Hampton* 7, *Partenope of Blois* 6, *Guy of Warwick, Degaré, Libeaus Desconus* 5, *Amis and Amiloun, Eglamour of Artois, Seege of Troy, Earl of Toulous* and *Arthor and Merlin* 4 (though these are not all identical versions). Most romances survive in only one or two texts, but, of course, many copies have been lost. D. S. Brewer computes that for each remaining copy, there were once at least five more ("Introduction" x). For comparison we might mention the English works which survive in the most manuscripts—*The Prick of Conscience* in over one hundred, *The Canterbury Tales* in ninety, *Piers Plowman* and *The South English Legendary* in more than fifty, *Troilus and Criseyde* in twenty. Since most book production was in the hands of the church or the court and literacy was more common in these mileux, it is to be expected that learned and aristocratic works would survive in many copies. It is also not surprising that didactic works of religious instruction would have reached a large audience. If individual romances do not survive in really large numbers of manuscripts, the size of the corpus suggests that the genre had significant appeal. The many catalogues of romance heroes in romances themselves and in other kinds of works indicate that their names were well known and associated with a certain type of story.

Besides reaching a large audience, popular literature is assumed to reach a varied audience, particularly members of the middle classes. Many would agree with Derek

Pearsall that, with the exceptions of Chaucer's and the alliterative poems, the verse romances in Middle English were popular literature since they were composed for "lower or lower-middle-class audiences who wanted to read what they thought their social betters read." The most conclusive evidence we have about the romances' audience is what we know about the owners of the manuscripts containing romances. Unfortunately, though, the number of volumes whose owners can be identified is small. Nor are the manuscripts' owners the original audiences for whom the romances were composed; most romances survive in texts made fifty to one hundred years after their composition. A number of important literary anthologies were owned by members of the gentry class. Robert Thornton, a Yorkshire knight of a locally prominent family, copied out two large manuscripts containing a variety of romances, including our only surviving copy of the Allitertive *Morte Arthur*. The Findern manuscript contains several works by Chaucer, as well as the romance *Sir Degrevant,* and was the property of the Findern family, members of the Derbyshire gentry. The Auchinleck manuscript, a product of a London bookshop, was designed for commercial if not mass distribution. It is thought to have been owned by London civil servants. MS Harley 2252 is the commonplace book of John Colyns, a prominent London merchant, into which were copied *Ipomedon* and our one extant text of the Stanzaic *Morte Arthur*. Another version of *Ipomedon* survives in a fine illuminated copy associated with Richard III.

Chaucer, who assigned tales to his Canterbury pilgrims with an eye to their social status, gives romances to the Knight, Franklin, Wife of Bath and himself. The tales are quite various. Only his own burlesque, *Sir Thopas,* and the Wife's fairy tale have ties to other Middle English romances. It would not do to take these assignments as a simple reflection of cultural reality. Chaucer was also following literary decorum which associated elevated (or at least idealistic) genres with the higher classes and comic, realistic stories with the lower—only his lower class pilgrims tell fabliaux, and the bourgeois Wife's tale is a fabliau in romance guise. The Franklin and the Knight are members of the gentry, and Chaucer's descendents were such. While in practice literary genre and social status were not so simply related, it is significant that Chaucer's contemporaries felt the tales were socially appropriate to the tellers. The evidence suggests, then, that the romances appealed to the country gentry and to prominent merchants and city bureaucrats, among others. These are not members of the lower classes, though they are also not members of the court elite. Really, what strikes one is the diversity of the audience implied by these examples and difficulty of making correspondences between the manuscript owners' social status and the types of romances they read. If the romances are popular literature, it is not because they were favored by the lower classes, but because they reached a varied audience and were attractive to more than a single socio-economic group.

Since the gentry class will be important to later discussions, we should take a moment to describe it here. According to Thrupp, the gentry included those belonging to the four military ranks of knight, banneret, esquire and man-at-arms, those who held senior posts in the estate and household service of the great barons (though the rank was associated with the post, not the person who held it), and those who performed high services in municipalities or in the administration of the crown. Rodney Hilton further describes the country gentry as those who had incomes of fifty pounds a year and held half a dozen manors. These people witnessed local charters, stood on grand assize juries and performed tasks imposed by sheriffs or the central government. To fill out our picture of the gentry, we might note with M. T. Clanchy that the great merchant dynasties took on the coloring of landed gentry rather than forming a distinct bourgeoise. Thrupp enumerates the distinguishing marks of the gentry as birth, money and a distaste for manual labor. Usually three or more generations passed before members of a family of lower origins, for example, merchants or lawyers, could be considered truly gentle.

In part because popular audiences do not constitute a high context group, they are less likely than elite or folk audiences to have direct relationships with the authors whose works they read or hear. The relationship between author and audience may be characterized by degree of closeness or distance. Artistic expressions of both elite and folk culture come to being in direct, relatively unmediated relationships of author and audience. Rosenberg and Schroeder note the similarity, suggesting that the presence of middlemen is more characteristic of popular literature. This is certainly true of modern popular literature with its mass production and mass marketing, but even in the Middle Ages there were scribes, bookshops and scriptoria, and minstrels who acted as middlemen.

The roles of mediators vary according to whether the material is popular or popularized. As distinguished by Barbu, popular literature is widespread owing to an intrinsic condition, while popularized works profliferate as a result of organized social action. One is widespread naturally, the other is made to be widespread. Instances of medieval popularized literature would be exempla and saint's legends, which were widely disseminated by the Church through the sermons of the friars and other orders whose main function was to preach to the general populace. Not only did these narratives circulate orally, but ecclesiastical scriptoria and clerks produced many texts as well. In medieval England, the closest thing to mass literature was this popularized literature of religious instruction. Manuscripts and early prints indicate that such items were the most widely circulated. Religion would seem to be the driving force of popular literature before and after printing. Few Middle English romances can be said to be popularized in Barbu's sense. Indeed, they were officially regarded with suspicion by the Church, the only institution capable of a program of popularization. At times, however, the church seems to have appropriated the intrinsically popular form for its own purposes, as in the case of the Charlemagne romances. Albert Baugh has proposed a theory that these, and other romances, were composed in writing by clerics for oral dissemination to lay (unlettered) audience by minstrels. There are relatively few romances relating to Charlemagne in English—the attempt to popularize them seems not to have succeeded. Some romances do incorporate features of popularized genres like saints' legends—*Guy of Warwick, Ami and Amiloun, Isumbras* and *Florence of Rome* are cases in point.

These terms, "popular" and "popularized," may also be used to distinguish between what A. C. Gibbs calls

> a sophisticated aristocratic romance which has been simplified, or even debased to suit the needs and understanding of a popular audience and a poem which has been deliberately put together out of the tastes and attitudes of such an audience and borrows the form of romance for reasons of convenience and literary prestige.

A number of romances are popularized in the sense that they are transformations of narratives originally composed for elite audiences. But we must, I think, reject the assumption that popularized romance is somehow romance *manqu'e* and that popular romance is really something else dressed up as romance. There are Middle English romances which could be called simplified, even debased versions of the original stories; *Sir Tristrem* would be a case in point. But there are numerous others which do not fit this description. *Sir Launfal,* based on *Lanval* by Marie de France, has a more complex narrative than its source and none the worse for it. *Yvain and Gawain* is in some ways simpler than Chretien's *Yvain,* but has virtues not found in its source. The impoverishment of *Sir Tristrem* should be attributed to the author's modest literary ability as much as to the audience's intellectual and artistic perceptivity. The question of literary sophistication and social status of the romances' audiences is rather complex, as we have seen in our earlier discussions. The questions of aesthetics and of the relationship of form to content raised here will be considered in later sections. The English romances mentioned above, and many others, all demonstrate that the stories of the courtly French works were adapted for an audience with different interests and literary expectations. While still elitist, the narratives are less exclusive than their sources, in their broadened accessibility. The Middle English romances are potentially popular literature. Mediators made them more accessible—in this sense the stories have been popularized. But because the romances were not popularized in the sense of created in order to be widespread, they did not necessarily reach a large audience. They were not the product of a large, organized, well supported program of dissemination as were popularized religious works. The notable feature of the mediation of popularized romances is that the mediators fundamentally alter the material of their source before passing it on, and have contacts with different social groups within the culture.

There is one other point that should be made about the distance between author and audience and the manner of the artefact's mediation. This pertains to the artefact's medium. In the case of a Middle English romance, that medium could be either writing or voice, and if oral, the story could be sung or spoken, recited from memory, improvised or read aloud. Of course, in the Middle Ages, society was less literate and more dependant on oral communication in all areas of life than is modern. Most medieval literature was written to be read aloud. The oral/written distinction which applies to certain forms of folk and elite literatures is less clear when we deal with medieval romances. They do display a number of oral traits. Certain romances contain evidence of oral formulas (as compositional units in the classic sense described by Lord and Parry), and some employ an oral style of narration which gives the effect of a minstrel performance. However, most were based on stories already written in French and were probably not composed orally, or performed by minstrels after the middle of the fourteenth century.

If the Middle English romances are not, primarily, oral literature, in some ways they behave like oral literature. They exist in variants, as oral tales do, thus there is no fixed text and no single correct version. Reliance on a fixed text, whether in writing or in perfect memorizations of oral literature, seems characteristic of elite, official cultures. Modern scholarship, a part of elite culture, has often confirmed this reliance as when H. S. Bennett, in writing about the romances, comments on "the gradual degeneration which is inseparable from oral transmission." (Folklorists and others would object.) Concern for textual integrity is a mark of the elite artist—see Chaucer's envoy to Scoggan, his erring scribe, and Chretien's warnings about those who would add lies to his stories. To some extent, reliance on a written text may come about in elite literatures because, as Franz Bauml has found in his studies of medieval literacy, without a fixed text it is difficult for an author to establish an individual voice, and elite audiences value this. Hans Jauss, in discussing the alterity of the Middle Ages, reminds us of "the great extent to which our modern understanding of literature is formed by the written character of tradition, the singularity of authorship, and the autonomy of the text understood as a work." These biases may distort our understanding of medieval popular literature by leading us to identify as elite literature only those works conforming to the tastes of modern cultural elites and to overlook what orality, convention and textual plurality have contributed to the development of literature.

In part, the dynamic character of medieval texts, so troubling to modern editors, may be related to the way medieval authors understood their role as artists. Like folk artists, they often functioned as mediators or passers-on of traditional materials. Medieval theories of art cast the author as a mediator between the audience and stories already in existence. Literary decorum required that they at least appear to play this role. Medieval rhetorics and works on the art of poetry were primarily concerned with enumerating devices for the amplification or diminution of material. Such topoi and colors of rhetoric would be useful to an artist working with received material. The authors of the Middle English romances were indeed mediators of pre-existing stories. The story recounted in any individual text had a life outside that text, in other versions mediated by other composers.

Bauml's remark about the importance of the fixed text to authorial individuality indicates another source of aesthetic alterity—the modern predeliction for novelty and originality. For us, heirs of the Romantics, works which reflect the individuality and creativity of the author are most significant. This emphasis on novelty may be a function of cultural change. When cultures change and become more heterogeneous, Cawelti says, intellectual elites place more emphasis on invention, "out of a sense that rapid cultural changes require continually new perceptions of the world." But it does not follow that elite literature is that which is original while popular literature is derivative and conventional, and folk is traditional literature. Again, the writings of Jauss suggest a corrective. He contrasts the modern reader who admires that in a work "which makes it stand out against the received tradition" with the medieval reader who "found texts enjoyable because they told him what he already knew, and because it satisfied him deeply to find each thing in its correct place in the world model." Such an appeal is often associated with popular literature. Many theories of popular aesthetics are based on the pleasure of fulfilled expectations and an appreciation of the familiar. Cawelti's studies of formula fiction show how the formulas function as "conventional materials for structuring cultural models: favorite plots, stereotyped characters, common metaphors." These are found in the Middle English romances and in romances and medieval narrative generally.

Aesthetics are among the most important factors in the cultural dynamic of author, audience, and artefact. They play a part in the relationship between author and artefact, for authors shape their material in accordance with an aesthetic. Aesthetics also enter into the relationship between material and audience, for the audience anticipates a certain kind of presentation, a certain kind of experience. Scholars still have not arrived at an accepted aesthetic of popular literature. The aesthetics of the Middle English have always been problematic.

Toelken defines fine art as that "based on the study of objects that are related to an ever-developing intellectual sense of proportion, design and individual creativity held by and judged by people of educated and sophisticated taste." High literature tends to be academic, exclusive and formal, judged by the standards of a small intellectual elite. Another study of cultural aesthetics, by Arpad, touches on several other points we have noted before. High literature is characterized by complex expression, reliance on the permanence of the written record, individual creativity, innovative outlook, self-conscious design and selection of materials. On the other hand, popular literature may be said to be characterized by direct expression, pragmatic outlook, conventional design, the

use of received materials and non—exclusiveness. David Madden says that the audience for high literature judges the achievements of artists by how well they are able to transform their inherited material through their imaginative conceptions. Popular artists are judged by their skill in manipulating the conventions and formulas of the genre for a calculated effect. Popular aesthetics are based on receptivity and familiarity, affirming accepted values and encouraging the individual to identify with a picture of the world as he would have it be—a moral fantasy. Such literature reaffirms, in an intense form, values and attitudes already known; it reassures. Its design is conventional because such works are said to be derived from a limited repertoire of elements which are combined in stereotyped, formulaic ways.

Some would stress the fact that all genres go through their own cycle of innovation and conventionlization. Others have noted that some innovation is essential to the success of popular literature. Winfred Fluck suggests that it is not so much the fulfillment of expectations which accounts for a particular popular work's appeal, since other formulaic works would fulfill the same expectations. What matters is the way in which it threatens (but only threatens) not to fulfill them—the test and trial of convention through a fictional process of disturbance followed by reintegration.

Such generalizations must be tempered in light of the features of medieval literature we have noted above. Most medieval audiences enjoyed that which was familiar, and did not privilege originality or individual creativity as we do. Nor did most medieval authors strive for these. Per Nykrog, writing of twelfth century French romances, comments on the practices of medieval narrative artists. Most, he says, "selected (modified, develped) a certain number of thematic elements found in literary tradition and/or in . . . [their] . . . own experience as a historical person, and combined them into a story." It appears that many composers of medieval romances behaved in ways we would associate with popular artists today. Only an atypical few sought originality for its own sake. The Middle English romances and popular literature in general have suffered in some discussions of aesthetics, as the earlier quotes from Gibbs and others suggest. "Popular" implies an artist with inferior abilities and an audience with inferior tastes. In particular, the Middle English romances have been criticized for being conventional and poetically inept. A classic statement of this point is Laura Hibbard Loomis' in her study of the Auchinleck manuscript. She refers to romances'

> "patter" of well-worn cliches, the same stereotyped formulas of expression, the same stock phrases, the same stock rhymes, which Chaucer was to parody in such masterly fashion in *Sir Thopas*.

Advances in scholarship—theories of oral-formulaic composition and stucturalist analysis as well as studies of formula fiction—have given us more insight into the formulaic nature of romance. Susan Wittig's analysis of the romances shows that their repetitive style is not a function of the authors' lack of talent but a conscious choice of narrative technique integral to the stories' meanings. Forms of popular culture have their own aesthetics; they are not simply denegrated or naive forms of the fine arts.

There is a question as to whether an aesthetics of popular literature can be evaluative. Richard Peterson objects to an aesthetic basis for a theory of popular culture because, he says, "aesthetic value inheres in the acts of evaluation and not in the object of evaluation, *per se.*" This is to say that the aesthetic values are those of the audience rather than the artefact itself. But artefacts are embued by their authors with their aesthetics, so aesthetics do have some bearing on the nature of popular literature. Hinds objects to a value based aesthetic because the value of a popular artefact is determined by the number of people who adopt or consume it. He further suggests that there is no bad popular literature, because a bad work would be a failure and so not attract many readers. Roger Rollin, talking about modern culture, says "the only evaluation which counts is the strictly quantitative one . . ." As we have seen, quantitative information about the Middle English romances is limited, so such an approach is not very fruitful. One can distinguish popular literature which is artful from that which is not, just as one can distinguish masterpieces from lesser works of elite literature. An evaluation of the romances' artistry does not determine their status as popular artefacts, though the nature of the artistry into which they aspire is relevant to this status. Aesthetics are more than a matter of evaluation—they are also a matter of function; how a work seeks to engage the audience and shape its response.

All art has a double aspect: it is both a model for life and a model of life. It is not only that art imitates life and life imitates art, but that both processes are essential to the generation of meaning. Anthropologist Clifford Geertz elaborates on this observation. "cultural expressions. . . give meaning, i.e. objective conceptual form, to social and psychological reality both by shaping themselves to it and by shaping it to themselves." He further explains that through its art, a culture expresses its ethos (its "tone, character and quality of life, its moral and aesthetic style and mood") and presents its worldview (its picture "of the way things in sheer actuality are," its "most comprehensive ideas of order." Any particular work of art offers, then, a synthesis of ethos and world view; the nature of that synthesis is determined by the kind of aesthetic the work employs. One aesthetic attempts to create a unique synthesis that is complete and conventional, affirming accepted values and attitudes. Another aesthetic privileges unique synthesis of ethos and worldview and works which challenge audiences to construct their own.

For an example of how ethos and world view, life and art interact in the romances, we may observe the narratives of twelfth century France and those of fifteenth century England. The fact that rapid cultural change may stimulate intellectual elites to demand a literature of new per-

ceptions, which we noted earlier, is particularly relevant to the synthesis of ethos and world view. It would seem that at times of rapid change, ethos and worldview are not in accord and therefore require revision or reinterpretation. The twelfth century was a time of such change, and though there is not yet consensus as to its processes and details, its general nature is well understood. Among the most important changes, for the romances, was the development of chivalry and the formation of a rigidly hereditary aristocracy which consolidated family holdings by primogeniture. Much has been written on these complex topics, but historian Georges Duby's description of the chivalric society makes clear the cultural significance of the early French romances' blend of idealism, realism, fantasy and ironic self-consciousness. These features, among others, distinguish these romances from earlier related narratives such as the *chansons des gestes.* The development of romance was partly a literary response to the new experiences brought about by the changes in the way people lived.

Eric Auerbach has said that the purpose of twelfth-century French romances was the "self-portrayal of the ideals and mores of the feudal knightly class." This statement neatly encompasses both aspects of these romances-they present models for life in ideals, but also models of life in self-portraiture. Basic to this class's conception of itself was the idea that its members were superior to non-nobles not just in degree, but in kind. This superiority manifested itself in chivalric behavior of which only the nobility were thought to be capable. The idealistic ethos of the courtly romances came about because, Auerbach says, the aristocracy held that nobility, greatness and intrinsic value had nothing in common with anything ordinary.

The concept of chivalry, developed during the twelfth century remained an important cultural pattern throughout the later Middle Ages in Western Europe. In one of the better known cases of life imitating art, those who felt themselves to be members of the chivalrous society of fifteenth century England (and Europe as well) modeled their activities and attitudes upon those of the characters in earlier romances. What had been a kind of fiction objectifying its audience's experience in an idealized chivalric past came to be regarded as akin to history, a record of practice and a model for emulation. Chretien and other writers of the twelfth century were creating the patterns, the world view of their romances. By the fifteenth century this view had become traditional. However, the social realities of fifteenth century Englishmen were rather different from those of their predecessors.

Interestingly, though England in the later Middle Ages was undergoing changes as profound and accelerated as those of Chretien's time, the cultural elite was essentially conservative and continued to insist upon the relevance of older forms. This is clearly demonstrated in Caxton's programme for translating and publishing romances of the Nine Worthies and chivalric treatises from the libraries of the Dukes of Burgundy. By the fourteenth century, the function of romances had changed as the relationship between art and reality changed. If, in parts of France during the twelfth century, the upper classes became a hereditary hierarchy, in England during the fourteenth and fifteenth centuries the upper class became stratified as social mobility increased. As K. B. McFarlane explains,

> a nobility of a type peculiar to England, having little in common with the French *noblesse*, first came into existence. . . . The essential changes had already occurred by 1485; they had hardly begun in 1300. In the reign of Edward I a dozen earls, the dwindling survivors of a seemingly obsolescent baronage, shared their nobility with an undifferentiated mass of some three thousand landowners, each of whose holdings were said to be worth £20 a year or over. . . . By the second half of the fifteenth century the lords were sharply distinguished from those without the fold. Nobility had parted company with gentility, the quality with which those rejected were still permitted to be endowed. The gentry, that is to say, did not so much rise (though some did) during the later middle ages as fall from the nobility which their antecessors had enjoyed in common with all landowners from a great earl to the lord of an estate worth £20 a year.

A similar dynamic is suggested by Crane's discussion of the romances. Unlike French romances of the twelfth century whose exclusivity asserts their audience's noble status, "English romances facilitate the Barony's claim to status by their very openness, by advertising the naturalness and imitability of their new courtly love and chivlary." Susan Wittig shows that the non-cyclic romances are structured on the pattern of the male Cinderella, a formula which bridges two classes within the society by offering the possibility of upward mobility to worthy man of low station through marriage to a noble woman. At the same time, the formaula "endorses the upper-class belief that worth and birth are synonymous, that only a noble man can be nobleman." To quote Katheryn Hume's discussion of medieval English romance and modern science fiction, both "justify an elite in its possession of power," but must balance the contradiction that this justification and self-idealization are made popular and even palatable to an audience partly composed of those outside the power group.

The process of social stratification described by McFarlane was expressed culturally by the withdrawal of the greatest folk from the communal dinners and entertainments of the hall. This practice was one of the many signs of degeneration lamented by Langland in *Piers Plowman*. Romances were part of these communal entertainments, but the great folk took them with them as they withdrew to the privacy of their chambers. We find numerous references to the reading of romances in such settings. Social stratification of culture and life increased as medieval civilization was transmuted into what might be called early modern Europe. Peter Burke says that not until the Renaissance did the aristocracy withdraw from the common popular culture which had until then been part of its cultural tradition along with courtly culture. This was accompanied by the development, among the middle classes, of a distinctive culture and literature which expressed their concerns.

We have already seen that several important collections of Middle English romances belonged to gentry families in the fifteenth century. It is easy to see how members of this class would have found the more open form of romance appealing—would have felt it necessary to create a more open form of romance—since their gentility entitled them to gentry status. Though they were no longer among the power elite, their ancestors had held nobility in common with the ancestors of that elite. Those gentry who did rise to this status would have identified with those rising heroes whose innate gentility entitles them to marriage into the upper classes. However, even in the stories of Havelok, Octavian, and the Squire of Low Degree—all variations of the male Cinderella story—we court reductionism if read in the romances only their putative audiences' supposed social anxieties. They have meaning in other areas of experience as well. Also, as I have shown, most romances reached a varied audience over a period of time during which the structure of society changed, so it would not do to associate particular narratives with a single, narrowly defined class. Some scholars would question the existence of a chivalric class, in Duby's sense, and this is an important reservation to the argument that I have been following in regard to the origins of romance. Crane's association of the barony with Anglo-Norman romances and their English versions, and my own emphasis upon the Middle English romances' connections with the gentry need to be corroborated by more detailed studies of the social structures in medieval England and the audiences of romances.

There can be little question, though, that social status is significant to the meaning of the romances. The early romances had their origins in a particular social milieu and rather directly express their audience's preoccupation with class. The characters in romances all belong to the chivalric class. Literary convention associated the reading of romances with characters of the social elite.

What points can we make, then, about the popularity of English romances and the nature of popular literature? It would seem that the Middle English popular romances did not originate among a lower class of social aspirants. They owe their existence not to the appropriation of a form by an outside group, but to a development from within. In their formulaic aesthetic they accord with the predominant elite aesthetic of their time, which was intensified by the heightened conservatism of late medieval elites. Theories of popular literature, even when corrected for the lack of mass culture in the Middle Ages and the small scale of popular literature in medieval England, must acknowledge the biases of Romantic and Post-Romantic literary theory, as well as the medieval proclivity for authority and convention which influenced the role of the author and the audiences' expectations.

Theories of popular culture, insofar as they take social class to be a determinant in the creation of cultural artefacts, should be based on historical studies and recognize the fluidity of social systems. Further studies of individual romances and their cultural and bibliographic contexts are needed to reveal the cultural dynamics of the genre.

The following will serve as a concluding illustration of this dynamic. Per Nykrog notes that the early French romances (particularly Chretien's) are unique in their cultural and psychological realism—two elements which contributed greatly to the exclusivity, novelty and difficulty of these works, and to their appeal for modern scholars. Middle English versions tend to downplay such matters, as in *Yvain and Gawain,* thereby reducing the tension between realism and the idealized chivalric world. Of the English romances, only those by Chaucer, Malory and the Gawain Poet employ a realism akin to the early narratives'. Robert Jordan, recognizing this, argues somewhat facetiously that these are decadent works, reversions to an earlier state of the genre. This formulation runs counter to the usual observation—that the English romances are generally decadent and only works by these great authors make contributions to the form. In fact, by easing the tension between realistic and idealistic elements in romance, the anonymous English composers made it more accessible and created a more enduring form. Paradoxically, they, not the elite authors, could be considered the important innovators.

Phyllis R. Klotman

SOURCE: "The Slave and the Western: Popular Literature of the Nineteenth Century," in *North Dakota Quarterly,* Vol. 41, No. 4, Autumn, 1973, pp. 40-54.

[*In the following essay, Klotman compares two forms of popular fiction from the nineteenth century—the western, by such authors as James Fenimore Cooper, and the fugitive slave account, a precursor to the "running man" stories found in later American fiction.*]

The American colonies were peopled by running men, fugitives from another continent, fugitives from justice as well as injustice. Some were high-minded, moral and religious men; others were cutpurses or cut-throats. Some came to settle, others to exploit. These men were non-heroes, as often as they were men of heroic proportions, bent on adding gold and glory to the coffers and reputation of an acquisitive monarch. There were, of course, the persecuted, those attempting to escape religious or political oppression abroad. These were men who, thinking to escape tyranny, often brought it with them secreted in their own souls. Hawthorne has peopled American literature with the most memorable of these running men, those whose psyches solidified into the immutable Puritan consciousness. Much of the growth and stability of America comes from these once mobile antecedents who, having put down their roots in a new country, stubbornly refused to shake themselves free of the soil again. The

majority of emigrés to America in every season have been settlers of this kind: those who came to stay, the pioneers of one frontier. Langston Hughes has the settler speak in his own voice:

> O, I'm the man who sailed those early seas In search of what I meant to be my home—For I'm the one who left dark Ireland's shore, And Poland's plain, and England's grassy lea, And torn from Black Africa's strand I came To build a "homeland of the free." ["Let America Be America Again," *The American Writer and the Great Depression*]

Yet America in fact and in fiction has also produced a perennial Running Man who has moved by foot or vehicle, restlessly picking his way across the country, sometimes pursued, sometimes in pursuit of some real or imagined goal. Spiritually he is akin to the fugitive slave, that Running Man whose desperate need was escape to freedom in or beyond the "homeland of the free."

Running, according to a character in Ossie Davis' *Purlie Victorious,* has saved more Negroes' lives than the Emancipation Proclamation; in fact, according to the slaves' own narratives, running had saved hundreds of lives prior to January 1, 1863. In the slave narrative the Running Man is in flight from bondage to freedom. A more positive goal for him is difficult to envision. He is running toward freedom and identity, in pursuit of a humanity denied him, in search of a state of being. All of these aspirations are clearly and specifically developed by later writers: James Baldwin and identity; John A. Williams and the state of being; Richard Wright and the question of humanity. At the same time these later writers attest that the goal of the black protagonist never again has the simplistic purity of that of the runaway slave whose experiences were narrated by himself, told to others, or set down in fictionalized form over a period of a hundred years. Before we examine his narrative, however, we have first to consider briefly his genesis in America.

In 1526 the first black slaves were brought to North America by the Spanish. With about 100 blacks from Hispaniola in the West Indies, these colonizers landed on the coast of what is now South Carolina for the purpose of setting up sugar cane plantations. But disease, to which the Indians and the Negroes were apparently immune, ravaged the Spaniards. There was, in addition, another element, which neither the Spaniards nor other slaveholders have ever been able to eschew—that disease symptomatic of all enslaved men—the ineluctable desire to be free. As soon as these sixteenth-century slaves found that the Indians were friendly and could guide them to freedom, they began to escape in significant numbers. Torture was, of course, used to dissuade those recaptured from again attempting such folly, but the flight to freedom continued and the colony was doomed to failure. "The Negro slaves who escaped were Americans, seventy-five years before the first settlement in Virginia." [Nicholas Halasz, *The Rattling Chains; Slave Unrest and Revolt in the Antebellum South*]

What happened in 1526 was the beginning of an inevitable series of painful yet amazing events which precipitated the schismatic development of the United States, a country founded on a great unspoken dichotomy: Freedom—for some. The desire for freedom produced the first black Running Man in America and he subsequently produced his own biography. His impulse to flee developed as a matter of course out of the very fact of his enslavement, for nothing deters a man from attempting to secure his freedom, not even the threat of brutality or loss of life. This was clearly recognized by Judge St. George Tucker of Virginia in a letter written by him in 1800, the year of Gabriel Prosser's conspiracy:

> The love of freedom is an inborn sentiment, which the God of nature has planted deep in the heart. Long may it be kept under by the arbitrary institutions of society; but, at the first favorable moment, it springs forth with a power which defies all check. This celestial spark which fires the breast of the savage, which glows in that of the philosopher, is not extinguished in the bosom of the slave. It may be buried in the embers, but it *still lives,* and the breath of knowledge kindles it into a flame. Thus we find there never have been slaves in any country, who have not seized the first favorable opportunity to revolt. These, our hewers of wood and drawers of water, possess the power of doing us mischief, and are prompted to it by *motives which self-love dictates, which reason justifies.* Our sole security, then, consists in their ignorance of this power, and their means of using it—a security which we have lately found is not to be relied on, and which, small as it is, every day diminishes. [*An Account of Some of the Principal Slave Insurrections,* edited by Joshua Coffin]

The consternation of Judge Tucker was well founded and his caveat, that the tenuous security of the slave-holder was founded on the slave's continued ignorance of his potential power, was heeded by the slave-holder but not by the slave. A cursory glance at the number of slave rebellions recorded between 1728 and 1831 attests to that fact. Before the colonies rebelled against England, there were slave uprisings in Georgia in 1728 (Savannah), in Virginia (Williamsburg) and South Carolina (1730), in Rhode Island aboard a slave ship (1731); three in South Carolina (1739); in New York (1741); in Rhode Island (1747); in Charleston (1754), and another contemplated in 1759. The sizable conspiracies were those planned by Zamba in New Orleans in 1730; Gabriel Prosser in Richmond, Virginia, in September 1800; Denmark Vesey in Charleston, South Carolina, in 1822; and Nat Turner in Southhampton County, Virginia, 1831.

One thing that these major rebellions had in common was the annihilation of the whites. Both Vesey and Turner, for example, refused to contemplate exceptions, citing the Scriptures for their rationale. Vesey insisted that "on the precedent of San Domingo, Negroes could not sustain power while 'one white skin' remained intact." Whether the conspirator was a freedman, as in the case of Vesey, or the slave of a good *or* vicious master, the element of revenge as well as that of escape was always at the heart of the plan. Only Denmark Vesey, however, had predetermined and apparently negotiated a plan with the government of Haiti to "receive and protect" the victorious rebels. Unfortunately we have no narrative written by any of these determined and skillful conspirators. All that is extant is the "told-to" narrative, *The Confessions of Nat Turner* by Thomas R. Gray published in Richmond in 1832. The avenge-and-run narrative for obvious reasons did not achieve the popularity in the nineteenth century that it has in the twentieth, and it should be considered as a variant of the major type.

The period of ex-slave literature then extends from 1760 (Briton Hammon's *Narrative*) to 1861 (Harriet Jacob's *Incidents in the Life of a Slave Girl*). The great period of the flowering and fulfillment of the slave narrative, however, coincides with the abolitionist campaign (1830-1861). The abolitionists were, of course, accused of breeding the form and writing the narratives for their own propaganda purposes. And there is some evidence to support this accusation. Because James Williams could neither read nor write, he dictated his autobiography to John Greenleaf Whittier, whose integrity we would find difficult to impugn, but which the editor of *The Alabama Beacon* did not. He insisted that Whittier had been "hoodwinked," that there was no such plantation in Alabama, although ex-slaves often used fictitious names and places in order to avoid recapture. *The Narrative of James Williams, an American Slave Who Was for Several Years a Driver on a Cotton Plantation in Alabama* was, therefore, suppressed by the Antislavery Society which had published it in 1838 because even a hint of fraud would do their cause no good. For it was quite true that the experiences of fugitive slaves did help immeasurably in influencing the uncommitted to join the fight against the execrable system of slavery. Works of doubtful authenticity do exist, among which Arna Bontemps includes Charles Ball's *Slavery in the United States,* 1836. That account apparently contains some "fictionized" truth, while others, "like Emily Pierson's *The Fugitive* and Mattie Griffith's *Autobiography of a Female Slave,* are out-and-out fiction." [Arna Bontemps, "The Negro Contribution to American Letters," *American Negro Reference Book*] "Genuine slave narratives, however, authentic autobiographies recalling the bondage and freedom of gifted black men and mulattoes who happened to be born under the peculiar institution, are the ones that give significance to this body of writing and justify its place in American literary and cultural history." [Bontemps, "The Negro Contribution to American Letters"]

There were a sufficient number of authentically documented narratives and live, articulate ex-slaves speaking aloud their experiences on the lecture platform to give the lie to their detractors. Frederick Douglass, William Wells Brown and Henry Bibb traveled the lecture circuit with their harrowing stories for some time before committing them to paper. Gustavus Vassa, among others, not only wrote but also published his own autobiography. The ingenious methods of escape used by Henry "Box"

Brown and William and Ellen Craft were so highly publicized by their well-documented narratives that Douglass admonished them for having given away such valuable secrets to the enemy.

Highly respected and well intentioned abolitionists have helped to cloud the issue then and now by confusing fact with their own fiction. It seems fairly certain now that Josiah Henson, for example, became "the original Uncle Tom" after the fact. There is no real evidence that he and Mrs. Stowe met before the initial publication of *Uncle Tom's Cabin* in 1852, yet some time after 1858 she passed the mantle to Henson and he graciously donned it:

> It is difficult to determine precisely when Henson met Mrs. Stowe. Charles Edward and Lyman B. Stowe assert that the author of *Uncle Tom's Cabin* met the ex-slave in Boston in 1850. Forrest Wilson, no doubt following their lead, reiterates this statement—for which, apparently, there is not a shred of evidence. It was not until 1853 when she wrote the *Key* that Mrs. Stowe wrote the preface to the 1858 edition of Henson's autobiography. But nowhere in this book does Henson mention Mrs. Stowe! [Nichols, *Many Thousand Gone*]

A limited edition of Josiah Henson's 1849 *Narrative* was published in 1965 at "Uncle Tom's Cabin and Museum" in Dresden, Ontario, Canada. The foreword to this new edition contains the following paragraph:

> The original book narrated by Josiah Henson, is in effect, an autobiography, but it was upon facts related therein that Mrs. Harriet Beecher Stowe based her famous novel *Uncle Tom's Cabin,* first produced in 1852, and since that time, reproduced in many languages and editions, so that it is universally known.

Henson's narrative has special interest because he did not become a Running Man until he had spent thirty-five or forty years in slavery. Because of his preferential status and his extreme loyalty to his master (to the extent that he did *not* escape to freedom the first time he had the opportunity), Henson does in a sense deserve the now pejorative appelation "Uncle Tom." He did, in fact, bask in the acclaim which the new name gave him and which undoubtedly helped to increase the sale of his autobiography.

Sale of the narratives, however, was not a problem. What is extraordinary is not only the proliferation of the form but its continued popularity with the public. Charles Nichols gives the following sample statistics:

> Gustavus Vassa's *Narrative*—ten editions by 1837.

> Charles Ball's narrative—at least six editions issued between 1836 and 1859.

> Josiah Henson's narrative—sold 6,000 copies in 1852.

> "Stowe Edition" (1888)—100,000 copies.

> William Wells Brown's *Narrative* (1848)—8,000 copies by 1849.

> Frederick Douglass' narrative (1845)—seven editions by 1849.

Arna Bontemps considers the vogue of the slave narrative in the nineteenth century much like that of the Western in the twentieth:

> The narratives evoked the setting and conditions of slavery, to be sure, but they also created a parable of the human condition, the fetters of mankind and the yearning for freedom. The perils of escape and the long journey toward the North Star did not grow stale with repetition until times changed and a new parable, or myth, the Western, replaced the earlier one. [Bontemps, "The Negro Contribution"]

Yet the description of long and perilous journeys is more closely analogous to the experience of the restless frontiersman delineated during this same period by Fenimore Cooper than it is to the Pop Art Westerns conceived by the Zane Grays and disgorged onto the screen (movie and television) by generations of Hollywood hack writers. That Cooper created this authentic legend out of purely American materials is now a truism of literary history, but the fact that these two genres, related in a more than peripheral way, had a concomitant development during the early part of the same century has not, to my knowledge, been previously discussed.

The Westerner and the slave who chose to escape his condition were both outsiders. Neither wished to be part of the dominant culture, although the Westerner's lot was not forcibly inflicted upon him. He could stay and adapt to the settlement without necessarily suffering from physical deprivation, fear or anxiety. The slave's life, on the other hand, was often in imminent danger, certainly if he made a move toward freedom. He and the Westerner hungered for freedom, but while to the former it was a matter of life or death, to the/latter it meant life in a sense qualitatively different from that which he knew in the settlement. The Westerner was in most cases a solitary individual by inclination, one who preferred the company of nature to that of society; the slave was a solitary by necessity. Loneliness was a fact of his daily existence, for lasting attachments were difficult for him to retain; even familial ties were tenous and at the mercy of the slave system. The child born into slavery was forced to be on his own at an incredibly early age. His mother may have been allowed to nurse him in the fields, but, once weaned, he was watched over by brothers and sisters or a grandmother usually too ancient to pick her portion in the fields. If his mother or grandmother was a cook in the big house, he was in a highly favorable position because she was often able to "appropriate" enough food to keep him from constant hunger. If not, he became an independent scrounger, staving off hunger any way he could—it was a skill put to use later when he took to the road. Frederick Douglass was raised by his grandmother and mentions seeing his mother only once or twice in seven years, so that, although he felt certain loss when she died, it was not as though he were being separated from someone who had been close to him. Slavery, he affirms, destroyed filial ties and alienated the individual, especially the mulatto child from family and from the emotions of affection, reciprocal love and loyalty.

The process of alienation also developed many personalities characterized by hatred and aggression. Not all slaves who attempted escape were independent and resourceful like the Westerner. Many were impelled by a sudden reaction to brutality which they either witnessed or experienced; others responded to an act of extreme ingratitude. Henson, a model slave, was horror-struck to find that his master was covertly planning to sell him South. A generally well-adjusted, calm man, he suddenly found himself with murderous intentions. On impulse, James Williams took to the road in the middle of the day after being forced by the overseer to ready himself for his own torture. Some escapes, however, were premeditated and ingeniously executed by resourceful individuals. William and Ellen Craft planned their escape with phenomenal patience. They secreted the money to buy supplies in order to make a convincing suit of male clothes for Ellen, who was almost white, and who traveled North disguised as a southern gentleman with "his" man William. Wearing a sailor's uniform, Frederick Douglass escaped by carrying forged papers and "eluding Maryland patrols to ship, Melville-like on a whaling vessel from New Bedford." [Nichols, *Many Thousand Gone*] Henry "Box" Brown injured his finger with vitriol in order to free himself from work so that he could dream up an escape plan. His was one of the most ingenious and most difficult to execute because he not only had to fold himself into a box (3 feet 1 inch long, 2 feet wide, 2 feet 6 inches high), he had to stay in it for twenty-seven hours while it was shipped by freight from Richmond to Philadelphia. His ordeal was somewhat mitigated by prayer, for the escaped slave, like Cooper's Westerner, was usually a religious man.

Leatherstocking had a highly individual relationship to God; he characteristically worshipped alone as he did most other things. The slave generally worshipped the way his master decreed. However, some, like Nat Turner, were lone worshippers who reportedly had mystical experiences. Henry "Box" Brown insisted that God had answered his prayers and told him, "Go and get a box, and put yourself into it." [Henry Box Brown, *Narrative of the Life of Henry Box Brown, Written by Himself*] There were other "God-intoxicated ones: "Solomon Bayley—schooled in the Bible, a nineteenth century John Bunyan, prostrate before the Almighty and Sojourner Truth—a wizened black Sybil, seeking in every Tabernacle the heavenly city." [Nichols, *Many Thousand Gone*] Gustavus Vassa's favorite book was the Bible; it was the book most likely to be available in the master's house and it was the one which enlightened mistresses kept at hand to teach special servants. Many ex-slave narrators could not read. We know James Williams could neither read nor write and that he told his story to Whittier. William and Ellen Craft were taught to spell and write their names by a Quaker family, the first whites to befriend them. Douglass was an exception. Nothing could stop him from learning even though his master showed his mistress the folly of teaching slaves—"keep 'em ignorant," he said and she then obeyed. Douglass was also a deeply religious man, although he hated the hypocrisy of the church, especially that of Christian slaveholders—surely an oxymoron. William Wells Brown was also aware of the duplicity of Christian slaveholders: "Master was so religious, that he induced some others to join him in hiring a preacher to preach to the slaves." [*Narrative of William Wells Brown, An American Slave, Written by Himself*] Douglass was also an extraordinarily intelligent man, although not all narrators were. Williams, "Box" Brown, Moses Grandy were, like Natty Bumppo, men who had a high degree of moral and physical courage and a certain amount of innate intelligence. Alone on unknown terrain or in the forest, they faced many kinds of terror and deprivation. The Westerner was skilled in the ways of wood and stream, the slave very often was not. When he "lit out" his only compass was the North Star. Moses Grandy explained the slaves' plight:

> They suffer many privations in their attempt to reach the free states. They hide themselves, during the day, in the woods and swamps; at night, they travel, crossing rivers by swimming or by boats they may chance to meet with, and passing over hills and meadows which they do not know: In these dangerous journeys they are guided by the North Star, for they only know that the land of freedom is in the north. They subsist only on such wild fruits as they can gather, and as they are often long on their way, they reach the free states almost like skeletons. [Moses Grandy, *Narrative of the Life of Moses Grandy. Late a Slave in the United States of America*]

There is a "driven" quality to the experience of all running men: the escape from Europe to America, from law in the settlements, or from the inexorable movement of civilization westward. The most significant difference between the Westerner and the ex-slave, however, is the matter of choice; it is that difference which has been the most deleterious to the black man in his experience in America. Not having chosen of his own volition to come to this country, he has continued in the position of having only negative alternatives. The desire for a better life with *more* freedom is different from the compulsion to grasp for freedom of any kind. In addition, we have the question of inevitable penalties. The decision to move from the settlement to the plains did not always carry with it the imminent danger of death; that risk was always implicit, however, in the Negro's attempt to escape from slavery to freedom. The slave was faced then with the inevitability of retribution, should he be recaptured, or the finality of death, which was under certain circumstances, preferable. Nonetheless, we can see a kind of formula in the slave narrative which has some features in common with the story of the Westerner and which readers apparently came to expect. The ex-slave usually gave some background of his life in bondage, often naming names and places in spite of the risk of recapture. Some, of course, invented such details in order to protect themselves. In some cases, this part of the narrative (life in bondage) was sectioned off from the escape. Henry "Box" Brown's narrative is run together in the form of an abolitionist exhortation. Frederick Douglass wrote of his bondage and then of his freedom, omitting the details of his escape. Most narrators, however, included the escape plan and its execution, which was as suspenseful as any Western. The story of William and Ellen Craft's trip of a thousand miles from Macon to Philadelphia is a concatenation of harrowing events sprinkled with irony. For example, a slavetrader riding with them aboard a steamer bound for Charleston, gives William's master (Ellen disguised) some "good" advice: "I would never let no man, I don't care who he is, take a nigger into the North and bring him back here, filled to the brim as he is sure to be, with d—d abolition vices, to taint all quiet niggers with the hellish spirit of running away." [William Craft, *Running a Thousand Miles for Freedom: or The Escape of William and Ellen Craft from Slavery*] When William Wells Brown was forced to become an expatriate, he also remarked with bitter irony: "An American citizen was fleeing from a Democratic, Republican, Christian government, to receive protection under the monarchy of Great Britain." Irony is perhaps not a device used consciously by these early writers, but it is a heritage of the Negro experience that is artistically developed by such contemporary writers as Ellison, Kelley, Baldwin and Williams. This is not surprising because, as John Oliver Killens recently wrote, "Tragedy and irony and paradox have been the core of our existence, slaves and pariahs, in the homeland of the brave and the free." [The Confessions of Willie Styron," *William Styron's Nat Turner: Ten Black Writers Respond*]

William Craft included a post-escape section which gives some interesting details of northern life and its inconsistent attitude toward Negroes, a phenomenon which we are more apt to place in the twentieth century than in the nineteenth. After the Fugitive Slave Act was passed, the Crafts were advised by abolitionist friends to leave the country, particularly since their old masters wrote President Filmore, who then gave instructions for military forces to be sent to Boston to assist in their apprehension. William and Ellen Craft were among the first Negro expatriates in Europe, and their escape from America was a recapitulation, in small, of their escape from the South. It prompted William to write: "In short, it is well known in England, if not all over the world, that the Americans, as a people, are notoriously mean and cruel towards all coloured persons, whether they are bond or free." Solomon Northup, born a freeman in New York, found this particularly true since he was kidnapped and sold into slavery at the age of thirty. His papers were stolen from him in Washington, and he was sold into slavery because he was unable to prove that he was a freeman: "So we passed, hand-cuffed and in silence, through the streets of Washington—through the Capital of a nation, whose theory of government, we are told, rests on the

foundation of man's inalienable right to life, LIBERTY and the pursuit of happiness! Hail! Columbia, happyland, indeed!" [Solomon Northup, *Twelve Years as a Slave; Narrative of Solomon Northup, a Citizen of New York, Kidnapped in Washington City in 1841 and Rescued in 1853*] Northup's story, a strange narrative of twelve years of enforced slavery, follows the narrative pattern in reverse.

Most of the narratives, however, follow the general pattern of bondage—escape—freedom or bondage—escape—recapture—freedom. It is the escape—recapture—freedom pattern that recalls the artful suspense of the Western, especially such blood and thunder excitement as we find in *The Last of the Mohicans*. As Spiller has noted: "For many—and this represents one real level in the book—*The Last of the Mohicans* is a breathless unrelenting chase, unbroken save when Alice and Cora are captured by Magua, and Leatherstocking, Uncas, and Duncan Hayward, thus far pursued, become the pursuers." [Robert E. Spiller, et al., *Literary History of the United States*] Most slave narratives contain the pursuit theme, usually with the addition of bloodhounds—that much of Mrs. Stowe has real basis in fact. Henry Bibb, who escaped and was recaptured several times, continued his forays into the South in an attempt to rescue his wife and child, always pursued with the constant threat of betrayal hovering over him. Many ex-slaves became conductors on the Underground Railroad and, like Harriet Tubman and Sojourner Truth, stole slaves out of bondage. Their route was often by water, which became a symbol of freedom for the black Running Man, as it was for Twain and Melville, and often for Cooper's protagonists who made more than one daring escape by water. For water easily swallowed up the trail of the Running Man. Nat Turner's plan had been to have his men strike their blow for vengeance and run to the swamps where their trail would be obscured. James Williams escaped his master's bloodhounds by taking to the water, a method dramatized in one of Huddie Ledbetter's songs, "Old Riley."

Introduction

Now this is Riley. They had bloodhounds in them times . . . The overseer in them times had a Negro named Riley. And Old Riley was one of the best there was and Old Riley was trying to make his way to freedom. And while Riley was goin', they couldn't catch up with him, and they got the bloodhounds put on his tracks and they commenced talkin' about it.

Song:

Old Riley walked the water.

Old Riley walked the water.

On them long, hot summer days.

Riley walked the water,

Here, Rattler—Here.

[*The Leadbelly Songbook*]

Harriet Tubman led her charges to freedom by water, and many of the spirituals she sang carried her message of freedom to the slave through the covert image of water: "I looked over Jordan, and what did I see, Deep River."

In addition to the suspenseful excitement of the pursuit, the Western and the slave narrative share another characteristic. There is always some kind of violence and death in both. Cooper not only describes various kinds of torture and death peculiar to Indian culture, but also the kind of violence perpetrated by the white man when he was outside the law of the settlement. One of the most vivid chapters in *The Prairie* is devoted to the Old Testament sentence and execution of Abiram White by his brother-in-law, Ishmael Bush. The slave narrators describe in excruciating detail their often terrible lives of intermittent violence, violence committed either against themselves or their fellow slaves. The overseer, a special breed of sadist, was usually the perpetrator of violence. William Wells Brown writes of having seen his mother flogged by the overseer Cook. Frederick Douglass, with some objectivity, describes the brutality and murder (sometimes accidental) which he witnessed, but says that such actions were *not* confined to overseers. He saw some masters and mistresses run amok, proving to him that slavery corrupts and erodes the honest emotions of white and black. Moses Grandy reports that widowed slaveowners often hired professional whippers to keep their slaves in line. Henry "Box" Brown, a slave in Virginia near Richmond, reports having seen slaves cut down, whipped, hanged or half-hung, apparently in retaliation after the revolt of Nat Turner. James Williams, who was a driver under a white overseer (Huckstep) on his master's plantation in Alabama, was witness to floggings of men and women who were unable to keep up during the cotton picking season. His most horrifying description is of a pregnant woman who was tied to a tree face forward and beaten by Huckstep until she was delivered of a dead infant at the foot of the tree.

Violence and death were permanent partners in the slave system. Their threat bred surface docility but engendered repressed fear and hatred which often erupted into real aggression. Slaves, in their impotent fury, struck out at each other and at themselves when they could not escape or retaliate against their oppressors. Solomon Northup, continually harassed and threatened by his master, turned on him and whipped him with his own whip. In a state of uncontrollable anger, Douglass struck an overseer. The psychology of the slave system bred an atmosphere of incipient violence. "Everybody in the South," Douglass wrote "wants the privilege of whipping someone else. The whip is all in all." [Douglass, *My Bondage*] Some slaves refused to be flogged and they became special challenges to the overseer. Both Grandy and Williams record the stand of two heroic slaves who could be (and were) killed but not subdued by the whip. Rare was the happy, contented slave if he ever, in fact, existed. The singing, shuffling "darky" was a masquerade staged for "massa." Behind that mask was very likely a man ready to run and kill, if necessary, for his freedom.

The Running Man of the slave narrative is a heroic figure in Negro literature and an illustrious part of Negro tradition, although unfortunately not yet a part of the mainstream of American tradition. He proves, if proof were needed, that the spirit of freedom never deserted the black man even though he lived under the most appalling conditions of servitude. The hardships he faced as a slave, and later as fugitive, have been documented by some impressive observers, including Charles Lyell, Frederick Law Olmsted, Harriett Martineau and Charles Dickens; however, his own record offers us more insight into the complexity of the Running Man and his psyche than we can get from reams of objective evidence. For men they were. They ran from slavery because under that system, they were not recognized as men; they had, in fact, no identity, sometimes not even a name. William Wells Brown was forced to relinquish his Christian name because the master's son was also named William. After his final escape, having been recaptured once, he wrote, "I was not only hunting for my liberty, but also hunting for a name." [William Brown, *Narrative*] An old Quaker who helped him when he reached Ohio told him, "Since thee has got out of slavery, thee has become a man, and men always have two names." Hence, he became William Wells Brown, the man Arna Bontemps calls "the first creative prose writer of importance produced by the Negro race in America." [Bontemps, "The Negro Contribution"]

We are not here attempting to evaluate the slave narrative as an art form. It is autobiography, written with the professed purpose of influencing the reader, and has all the drawbacks of that genre, especially the problem of veracity. In addition, the narrators were, for the most part, men completely devoid of literary pretensions, although Brown later became a professional writer and Douglass a speaker, writer and influencial leader. The best read, men like Douglass, reflect some of the prevailing taste for melodrama, romance, sentimentality (e.g., Douglass: "They would thank me for dropping a tear on this page" [Douglass, *My Bondage*]). Admittedly, the subject matter lent itself to this kind of treatment. Most narratives, however, reflect the ingenuousness of the writer, his sincerity and his dedication to freedom.

Herbert F. Smith

SOURCE: "Exotics, Fantasics, and Cowboys," in *The Popular American Novel: 1865-1920*, Twayne Publishers, 1980, pp. 78-95.

[*In the following essay, Smith describes escapist fiction available in the United States during the nineteenth century, notably the light fantasies of Frank R. Stockton and cowboy novels set in the "wild west."*]

While the mainstream of American fiction bubbled merrily along from the psychological romance of Hawthorne and Melville to the psychological realism of Howells and James, and the underground current splashed from the sentimentalists to the gossip of social satire and the novel of manners, another tradition persisted among a small group of writers but an enormous audience of readers. American literary critics and historians have never been at ease among the writers of fantasy and exotic romance, perhaps because such literature is so far from the mainstream, perhaps because its enormous popularity makes it suspect. The genre persisted into a contemporary respectability not unrelated to the fact that its most important modern practitioners are academics of flawless repute. In the period 1865-1920 it remained mostly underground, in the dime novels of the House of Beadle and its followers, and periodicals typically hidden in the corn-crib. It surfaced into respectability only occasionally during the period, notably in the works of Frank R. Stockton (1834-1902), in a spate of utopian novels in the 1890s, and in the perfection of the myth of the cowboy and the wild west. Writers in the genre are consistently underestimated by most critics, partly because their defenders so consistently overestimate them.

I. FRANK R. STOCKTON AND THE ROMANCE OF FANTASY

The quality most outstanding in the writings of Frank R. Stockton is a kind of boyishness, an untrammeled enthusiasm possible only for someone who, in maturity, never lost the easy expectations of youth. It is no surprise, then, to read in a lightly fictionalized biographical story which he never managed to place with a publisher that he had from the first an easy-going attitude toward life and literature that was never to leave him. He wrote in "What Can I Do for an Old Gentleman," while still in his teens, that he

> wished to enjoy life as he worked, not after his work was done, and he was by no means a fool—so he tried Literature. Everyone knows there are two ways by which a man can make money by the joint labor of his brain and pen. One, is to learn the business as you would a trade, and become a journalist, employed by those who will harness your Pegasus, but will at the same time provide him with oats—the other is to write what one pleases, as one pleases, and endeavour to find someone who will also be pleased with it—and pay for it.

It is both Stockton's strength and his weakness that he never had to revise those attitudes. Although he seems to have drifted into writing by accompanying his engravings with texts, the truth is that he wrote prolifically from his adolescence, and managed to publish almost everything he wrote later, after he became popular. Thus his mature production seems uneven because his earliest stories were published simultaneously with some of his latest and best work.

There can be no doubt, however, about the success of the longer adult fiction of his mature years. Beginning with the loosely novelistic frame of the stories collected in *Rudder Grange* (1879) and its sequels, *The Rudder Grangers Abroad* (1891) and *Pomona's Travels* (1894)—all published serially much earlier than their copyright dates—Stockton gave free rein to an imagination that always threatened to run off with him, but never failed to delight a constantly growing readership. Imagination is the key word to describe his writing. Either outrageous and farcical settings or actions are accepted with complete aplomb, or his characters turn the humdrum into the exotic by their extraordinary behavior or perceptions. *The Casting Away of Mrs. Lecks and Mrs. Aleshine* (1886), probably his best novel of this type, illustrates the technique perfectly. In the face of shipwreck and the threat of drowning, the two mature ladies draw from their treasury of middle-class skills what is necessary to survive, using brooms as paddles, breaking out sausages and cheese in the middle of the ocean—preserved, one assumes, for just such an occasion—and paying their board religiously to the absentee landlords on their desert isle—after deducting a proper amount for their housekeeping. At the other end of the scale, when they return to Mrs. Aleshine's very ordinary Pennsylvania farm with three entranced sailors in tow, the sailors determine, as a gesture of appreciation, to paint the farm in the stripes and colors of shipping companies all over the world, "until an observer might have supposed that a commercial navy had been sunk beneath Mrs. Aleshine's house grounds, leaving nothing but its smoke-stacks visible." The art of understatement, dead-pan comedy in prose, found its highest development in Stockton's works.

In spite of his febrile imagination, Stockton was not immune to the dicta of literary fashions, but as one might expect, his efforts toward literary realism are somewhat halting and tentative. His best work in that vein is *The Hundredth Man* (1887). Verisimilitude in that novel is created by the scenes describing the events in a New York restaurant, done very much in the style of Daniel Defoe in places (for whom, along with Charles Dickens, Stockton always professed admiration). But truth to detail about the preparation and serving of food at Vatoldi's is counterpointed by some of the wildest and most comic flights of his imagination in the story of the strike of the restaurant's waiters, who want to wear dress coats instead of aprons and jackets. It is an industrial strike as seen by Hollywood casting offices. Picketers carry signs with biblical overtones like "Eat not at the house of the oppressor!" A renegade scab is placarded, while dining:

> YESTERDAY THE BOYCOTTERS GIVE ME
>   TWO DOLLARS
> TO PLAY SHAM, AND TO-DAY I AM PAID
>   THREE DOLLARS
> TO EAT, DRINK, AND BE MERRY.

Interwoven with the scenes of the restaurant is the main plot of the novel, from which it gets its title. Horace Stratford is a wealthy modern Diogenes looking for the "hundredth man," whose humane qualities distinguish him from the other ninety-nine. His fantasy leads him to interfere with an engagement, which in turn entangles him with the novel's heroine, Gay Armatt. His redemptive manipulation of her toward a more suitable mate, Arthur Thorne, earns him the role of the "hundredth man" in his own and the reader's mind. It is all very gently comic, full of social *savoir faire,* and ripe with the kind of imaginative detail one expects from Stockton. The concerns of the late nineteenth century are all present—industrial strife, the unease of the wealthy in the face of their social obligations, the strain of the newly rich when they have no tradition to channel their ideas of *noblesse oblige.* But the concerns are transmuted in the crucible of Stockton's imagination to the farcical strike, Stratford's redemptive quest, and the final determination of J. Weatherby Stull, the secret owner of Vatoldi's, to create a "law hospital" with the earnings he has gained from his restaurant's marvelous oyster stew.

Stull's "law hospital" is typical of Stockton's prescience, more often remarked by critics in his technologically futuristic novels, like *The Great War Syndicate* (1889) and *The Great Stone of Sardis* (1898). The law hospital is an act of extrapolation of present "technology" into the future no less than the others. Philanthropists had long been founding hospitals and endowing universities; Stull, with something of his creator's imagination, joins the two matrices of philanthropy as usually practiced toward the ill with his recognition of the legal plight of the poor, to invent a concept only now gaining acceptance in American society, legal "clinics" available to those who suffer most from the necessary imbalance of a capitalist economy. It is the mark of Stockton's rich imaginary powers that he virtually throws away this truly remarkable insight in *The Hundredth Man.* His invention of "negative gravity" backpacks, from which the Buck Rogers creation and the modern real thing descend, dates from 1884, but is more striking than the "law hospitals" only because of our intense preoccupation with the more flamboyant qualities of technological advance in comparison with more meaningful progress in social matters.

The Great War Syndicate, like "negative gravity," captures our imagination because of the technological fascination of inventions like the "Repeller," an ironclad ship with a long-range cannon which fires with deadly accuracy because of a computer-like aiming device. What ought to impress us about the novel is the creation of a military-industrial complex in the "War Syndicate" which is more powerful than the governments of the states in which it thrives, and which forces a *pax Americana* upon an accepting world. *The Great Stone of Sardis* is filled with technological miracles—a submarine under the North Pole icecap connected to New York by an umbilical telegraph cable, a ray for seeing through successive strata of the earth's surface—but its sociological savvy is no less striking: the hero, having discovered an enormous diamond at the North Pole, buries it to save the world from the economic disruption it would create. Comparison with F. Scott Fitzgerald's "Diamond as big as the Ritz" is inevitable; where Fitzgerald's vision is apocalyptic, Stockton's is hopeful. The good sense of Mrs. Lecks and Mrs. Aleshine persists into what for Stockton was undoubtedly a future filled with as many possibilities as dangers. It is hard not to love such a writer, however one feels about the tough-mindedness of his vision.

Stockton has been called the "principal humorist of the genteel tradition" and accused of "letting his lively fancy go its happy way in many books, some of them dictated while he lay at ease in a hammock . . . in the midst of all the crowding issues of [the eighties]." Those issues are not absent from his writing, as we have seen, but they are seen in a larger, happier context as a result of that "lively fancy." Undoubtedly Stockton's reputation has suffered simply because of the time in which he happened to be writing. Now that the pendulum is swinging back from the excesses of dogmatic realism, now that writers like Jorge Luis Borges, John Barth, and Vladimir Nabokov are the fixed points of light of our firmament (not to mention J. R. R. Tolkien, C.S. Lewis, and T.H. White), perhaps it is time for a Stockton revival. Surely the author of "The Lady or the Tiger?" cannot be considered psychologically naive, however fantastic his creation. The same is true for the sociology of *The Great War Syndicate* and the economics of *The Great Stone of Sardis.* Undoubtedly he wrote for an audience that appreciated him for the wrong, escapist, reasons, and he fell into a decline when those reasons had become suspect; now that the assumptions of both the "genteel tradition" and the "age of realism" are no longer current, Stockton deserves a rereading and reappreciation.

II. JOHN AMES MITCHELL AND THE ROMANCE OF THE APOCALYPSE

If Stockton's happy situation allowed him to invoke and smooth over a vision of the future into purest fantasy, John Ames Mitchell's brought him closer to those who felt and feel that the American dream is nightmare. As Stockton began his career by using his talents as an engraver, Mitchell began as an artist, at Phillips Exeter Academy and Harvard and at the Ecole des Beaux Arts in Paris. Mitchell chose to "harness his Pegasus" as a journalist, however, and that rein on his fancy led him into darker valleys than any Stockton imagined. Mitchell was the founder and first publisher of *Life,* a satiric weekly which during Mitchell's tenure was more like the *Harvard Lampoon* than the slick weekly it became after it was bought in 1936 by Time, Incorporated. As a satiric publication, it was a rather scattershot affair, concerning itself as much with unburning issues like women's dress fads as with the great social problems of the Age of Transition. But Mitchell did not turn his back on the larger issues of the Gilded Age; his attacks on the giants of capital brought his magazine repeated libel suits and even the threat of physical violence toward himself. His social conscience during these years was raised to a far higher level than Stockton ever reached.

At about the age of forty-five, ripened by many years of life in New York and proximity to the centers of political and economic power, Mitchell turned more and more to fiction. His early efforts were incredibly crude, but showed from the first what direction he would take. *The Last American* (1889) is a novelette which a modern high-school sophomore might be proud to have written, but hardly anyone of greater sophistication. It is written as a fragment from the journal of Khan-Li, a prince of "dimph-yoo-chur" and admiral in the Persian navy. Khan-Li is in charge of an expedition in the year 2951 which rediscovers America. His helmsman is named "Grip-til-lah" and among his companions are "Nofuhl," "Ad-el-pate," and "Bhoz-ja-khaz." Most of the humor, alas, comes from these funny names, which is perhaps the kindest thing one can say about the work. The expedition arrives in a deserted, ruined New York, and, after some rather pointless tomfoolery based on linguistic interpretation of broken inscriptions, gets down to some satire on manners, mores, and politics. American women are accused of going about too much in the world, blushing too little, and managing their own lives. Irish politicians come in for their share with the discovery of a half dollar minted in 1937, during the reign of Dennis Murphy, the last of the Hibernian dictators. Yellow journalism is scathed for providing scandal in place of responsible reporting, and the American reading public for tolerating the situation. It is all farfetched and almost embarrassing in its naiveté.

Then the ship, the *Zlohtuhb,* sets sail for Washington, where the last American is encountered. A father and his daughter create an "international incident" by serving their guests raw whiskey and then misinterpreting a courteous kiss by one of the Persians. In the ensuing struggle, the American fights gamely, but is overwhelmed. If satire is intended, it is hard to say what it is directed upon, beyond the anachronistic assumption that these Persians persist after an ultimate oil crisis.

Such senescent juvenilia are interesting only as a preparation for Mitchell's more important works, of which the best are *Dr. Thorne's Idea* (1897), a study of deviant behavior based ultimately, like Frank Norris's *McTeague,* on Lombrosso's ideas about heredity, and *The Silent War* (1906). The apocalyptic vision of *The Silent War* makes the novel kin to the savage utopias of writers like Ignatius Donnelly, while Mitchell's obvious sympathy for "good" capitalists, like his hero, Billy Chapman, shows that he is not far from the Christian socialism of Howells and H. G. Wells. The central idea behind the silent war is simply a bad guess about the future of industrial relations in America. Instead of a rapprochement between big business and big labor, a single organization of workingmen called the People's League is approaching the numbers necessary to elect its own president and congress, and threatening to create an income tax, "to tax the millionaire for the benefit of the working man, instead of taxing the working man for the benefit of the millionaire," as the system of tariffs did when the novel was written. Such reform is only what Billy Chapman himself had argued for among his plutocratic colleagues. But the League has fallen into the hands of a sinister Committee of Seven who, not content with their approaching victory at the polls, are attempting to hurry up the process by a particularly cold-blooded scheme of extortion. They have a list of millionaires whom they approach for a "donation" of $200,000 for the League. Those who refuse are murdered. After a few murders, the word gets around, and the treasury is filled.

The murders themselves are interesting, rather like the reputed Mau-Mau terrorists in Kenya. Each millionaire is "set up" by his own servants, but slain by someone else's. Billy Chapman, as a scrupulous millionaire, is, of course, in a terrible bind; sympathetic as he is to the ends of the People's League, he can not tolerate their methods, and so refuses to pay. He is preserved by the most unlikely of coincidences, but one can hardly accuse Mitchell of manufacturing a happy ending. There is every indication that in spite of Billy's specific fate, the People's League will prevail and the Committee of Seven, with its extraordinary fund-raising capacities, will become the power behind the American government. One thinks of the news stories of the junctures among the Mafia, the CIA, and the Teamster's Union and shudders. Certainly no writer presents such a chilling picture of the relations between crime, business, and labor until Ira Wolfert's *Tucker's People* in 1940.

Mitchell's radical vision is the more striking for his obvious sympathy for capitalism. Although he does caricature the greedy industrialist, banker, and Solid Citizen as foils, most of the wealthy characters in the novel (all who are given names) are quite sympathetic. They argue with the caricatures about the morality of their positions and espouse socialistic (or at least paternalistic) views. Above all, they themselves illustrate, and they urge upon the others, an avoidance of conspicuous consumption. As one of them says,

> I would suggest . . . that being recognized as gamblers, you make yourself less conspicuous. Try to travel without private cars. Avoid getting the best of everything by extravagant fees. Give people of moderate means a chance to get what they pay for.

On the other hand, Mitchell does not make the Committee of Seven terrifying. They are described as definitely "not anarchists in appearance." Rather, they have the air of "prosperous workingmen—or skilled mechanics," which, of course, makes their cold-blooded extortion and murder scheme the more horrendous. And their arguments, as Mitchell presents them, are unanswerable, even by his sympathetic spokesman for capital, Billy Chapman.

> "The working people of this country, Mr. Chapman, are on the ragged edge of revolt. You rich men, here in the East, have no conception of the bitterness—the deep resentment—at the conditions that result in this unequal distribution of wealth. Those who work the hardest get the least."

> "If you can believe that American workmen are worse off than those of other countries, you can believe anything."

> "That is not the question. In a country like this, there is plenty for all; plenty of food, clothing, space and fuel, more than enough for everybody. Why should a few have not only the best of it all, but a thousand times more than they can use, while

all the others, those who work the hardest, live in attics and cellars, eat the meanest food and never enough? And all in a land of plenty. You will admit there is something radically wrong when a few are amassing fabulous fortunes and many, however industrious, can barely live."

Moreover, Mitchell again and again makes the point that extortion and murder as political weapons are merely an extension of business principles. A spokesman for the Committee of Seven makes the exact point to Billy: "We are merely meeting you capitalists on your own ground and with your own weapons. You hold us up with your trusts, your tariffs, your irresponsible and somewhat peculiar management of the people's savings. Is it not better that a dozen or more millionaires should quietly disappear, especially if they prefer death to parting with a fraction of their fortunes, *than that mobs should rule?*" [italics added] The managerial quality of the last clause carries real terror in it. Both sides decry anarchy; each sees the means as justifying the end. Apocalypse is rarely so orderly and reasoned. It is a "silent war" indeed, and the more frightening for that.

Mitchell's later novels decline in their quality and their ferocity, but *Drowsy* (1917) deserves some discussion as a fantastic romance in the science-fiction vein à la Frank R. Stockton. Cyrus Alton gets the nickname "Drowsy" from his tendency toward fantasizing, but he hitches that sin to the wagon of a sound technological education at Harvard and M.I.T. and develops a new "electro kinetic" force which he uses to power a spaceship. A trip to the moon yields the discovery of a long-dead civilization and, more practically, a 3000-carat diamond, which he just happens to pick up among the rubble on the moon. With his newly acquired wealth and a promise not to flood the market with more stones, he continues to dabble in science, including thought-telegraphy and the first trip to Mars. His thought-telegraph works with his beloved, and his spaceship fails, the two phenomena joining to provide a happy ending with no hint of future disruption of the diamond market or the orderly growth of technology. The novel is interesting primarily as a corrective to the reader who might have misunderstood the lesson of *The Silent War:* Mitchell's vision of the ideal future is a benign capitalism based upon the combination, typically American, of inventiveness and the laws of the marketplace as described by Adam Smith.

The two novels by Mitchell define rather neatly the two kinds of futuristic romance spawned at the end of the nineteenth century by the success of Bellamy's *Looking Backward* (1888). Like *Drowsy*, Albert Chavannes' *The Future Commonwealth* (1892) and Solomon Schindler's *Young West* (1894) are more concerned with technological marvels than with sociological problems; like *The Silent War*, Henry Olerich's *A Cityless and Countryless World* (1893) and Costello N. Holford's *Aristopia* (1895) center on the organizational and sociological changes created by new societies evolving out of the inequities of the rampant capitalism of the late nineteenth century.

Of the dozens of romances of technology produced before 1920, the best were produced by a hackwriter writing anonymously for a dime novel series called The Frank Reade Library. Luis P. Senarens (1865-1939) wrote under the pseudonym "Noname" an incredible series of adventure novels for boys which anticipated the science-fiction boom of the twentieth century. He orbited one of the first space satellites in *Lost in a Comet's Tale* (1895), invented the helicopter in *Frank Reade, Jr., and His Airship* (1884), and designed the first robot in *Frank Reade and His Steam Man* (1876). His inventiveness was doubtless spurred by the formidable competition of the writers of other juveniles like the Tom Edison, Jr. series published by Street and Smith and equivalents in the Beadle series. Works for more mature readers were not lacking in predictions of airplanes, automobiles, and space travel. The journey to Mars had become almost a commonplace by the time Drowsy blasted off, while labor-saving devices in works like Chauncey Thomas's *The Crystal Button* (1891) were reducing the workday to four hours.

Technological advances could create dystopias like Donnelly's *Caesar's Column* (1890) and Twain's *Connecticut Yankee in King Arthur's Court* (1889) and a few lesser works, but more frequently were combined with social advances to produce true utopias. C. N. Holford's *Aristopia* (1895) set limits on ownership of private property which effectively did away with greed. Albert Chavannes' *Brighter Climes* (1895) combined the best of socialism in production and individualism in distribution for his "Socioland" in Africa. Henry Olerich's *A Cityless and Countryless World* (1893) described a Fourieristic world of ideal communities of one thousand members each. And so, to use a phrase made current by a much later utopian, it goes. The literary value of these works is virtually nil, and their historic and sociological value is generally restricted to those who are interested in the lunatic fringe of social change. No student of nineteenth-century history and culture can afford not to read the best writers in the genre—Bellamy, Howells's *A Traveler from Altruria,* Twain's *Connecticut Yankee.* But research beyond the next level, Stockton and Mitchell, is better left to the specialist and the enthusiast for utopias, science fiction, and juveniles.

III.   TOWARDS THE COWBOY: THOMAS A. JANVIER AND MARY HALLOCK FOOTE

Writers of the period did not have to go as far as Mars to find the exotic, of course. The West, with its blend of the Garden and the Desert, its possibilities for untold wealth in gold or sudden and cruel death at the hands of savage Indians, provided an *exotica Americana* as suitable to romance and fantasy as the most esoteric utopia. The mythos of the Western novel had already been set with Cooper's Leatherstocking tales; all that the writers of the period 1865-1920 added were refinements to the genre. Nevertheless, these refinements define the transition from the romantic age to the modern age for the novel of western adventure no less well than the equivalent works of New England, the South, or the utopians.

Cooper's novels are all based upon a sophisticated vision of the contrast between nature and culture. That sophistication is continued in the writings of Thomas Allibone Janvier, particularly in his remarkably successful Western novel, *The Aztec Treasure House* (1890). Janvier's life and works divide into three neat segments: Western travels, bohemian life in New York's Greenwich Village, and travels and studies in Provence. For the purposes of this chapter, only his Western travels are directly significant, but the evidence of his good-humored appreciation of bohemianism in his first book, *Color Studies* (1885), and his later association with Mistral and the *Societé de la Félibrige* in Provence suggest the breadth of his range and his eye for the telling detail.

The immediate inspiration for *The Aztec Treasure House* was undoubtedly H. Rider Haggard, especially *King Solomon's Mines* (1885) and *She* (1887). In the characters gathered together to make up the expedition—an anthropologist, an heroic priest, a competent metallurgist, an ex-railway shipping clerk from Massachusetts, an Indian boy and his burro, El Sabio, "the wise one"—in the succession of dangers and mysteries, from savage Indians to mysteriously sunken cities, the style is pure Rider Haggard. But Janvier did more than merely transplant African adventure to the Southwest. His narrator, Professor Thomas Palgrave, Ph.D. (Leipsic), is a wonderful creation, doubtless drawn to some extent from Janvier himself. In the midst of whatever excitement occupies the foreground of the book, the Professor is as often as not bemused by some linguistic or anthropological aside. Indians are about to try to take his life; he muses that the expression is "an imperfectly expressed . . . concept for life can be taken only in the limited sense of depriving another of it; it cannot be taken in the full sense of deprivation and acquisition combined". In the midst of a bloody retreat, he apologizes for the brevity of his account:

> I cannot tell very clearly how our retreat to the Citadel was managed, nor even of my own part in it; for fighting is but rough, wild work, which defies all attempts at scientific accuracy in describing it— and for the reason, I fancy, that it engenders a wholly unscientific frame of mind. Reduced to its lowest terms, fighting is mere barbarity; a most illogical method of settling some disputed question by brute force instead of by the refined reasoning processes of the intelligent human mind; and by the anger that it inevitably begets, the habit of accurate description, is hopelessly confused. Therefore I can say only that foot by foot we yielded the ground to the enemy that pressed upon us.

And, whenever he reaches the limit of fantastic description the reader is likely to swallow, he refers him to his soon-to-be-published magnum opus, *Pre-Columbian Conditions on the Continent of North America*.

The other characters on the expedition are hardly less well realized. The heroic priest, Fray Antonio, has a streak of pedantry that delights the narrator; moreover,

his heroism itself is suspect with its almost pathological search for martyrdom. The incredibly competent engineer, Rayburn, and the comic low character, Young, are stock creations, but they succeed in surprising the reader from time to time, Young on the social structure of the Aztec society they encounter, Rayburn with some shrewd and arch comments on human nature.

The novel includes surprisingly little "local color" of the Southwest which is at all specific. The adventures with the latter-day Aztecs are located in a never-never land which is only generally remarkable as sub-tropical. There is a good deal of social comment of a vague utopian sort in the description of the Aztec society. It seems the ancient Aztecs under the wise king Chaltzantzin practiced a kind of eugenic breeding system: all persons who, on coming to maturity, were judged weaklings or cripples, were to be killed. As soon as the law was in effect the weak-kneed liberals began tinkering with it, changing it after Chaltzantzin's reign to create a class called "Tlahuicos," who were to be permanent slaves and the pool from which the human sacrifices were drawn. One would think the Tlahuicos as a breeding pool would create an inferior society, but that was not the case. Developing over the centuries as a separate caste, yet reinfused with each generation of cripples and weaklings, the Tlahuicos had become a proletariat bubbling with revolutionary fervor, and with a natural connection to a "liberal" wing of the ruling class—the relatives of each generation's weaklings and cripples. The revolt turns out to be abortive, however, since the army remains loyal to the despotic priest-captain. All of this is interesting in itself, but it is made more so by the comments of Young and Rayburn, likening this rather exotic society to standard American politics. The priest-captain "goes in for Boss management and machine politics . . . as straight as if he was a New York alderman or the chairman of a state campaign committee in Ohio. . . . Where our chance comes in is in having the respectable element, the solid men who pay taxes and have an interest in decent government. . . . They may not pay taxes here, but that's the kind I mean," says Rayburn. It is likely that Janvier intends some sort of political comment with the Tlahuicos, perhaps alluding to the situation of the blacks in America, perhaps directing some satire toward liberal reformers. If that is the case, he has not succeeded in making any point very well, since everyone seems to lose in the end except the intrepid foursome.

It is too easy to poke fun at this novel, and it is unfair and unwise to do so. For all its faults, it succeeds admirably as a romance of adventure and develops some thought-provoking ideas about ancient Indian culture and the clash of that culture with the modern ethos. The blend of archaeology, sociology, and derring-do that Janvier managed with this novel was not to be seen again in the genre until Willa Cather's *Death Comes to the Archbishop,* where, to be sure, it was done much better. *The Aztec Treasure House* is valuable as a pioneering work, and remains well worth reading.

At the opposite extreme from Janvier's adventure novel is Mary Hallock Foote's sensitive study of Western life in the mining camps, *The Led Horse Claim* (1883). Where Janvier's writing is all mystery, suspense, and violent action, Mary Hallock Foote retells the Romeo and Juliet story in a setting remarkably apt for it—rival mines on opposite banks of Led Horse Gulch, Colorado. The plot itself is fatuous, in large part through no fault of Mrs. Foote. Her original story had the lovers separating at the end, but a happy ending was forced on her by her editor. The setting is authentic and extremely well realized. Mrs. Foote had been living in Leadville, Colorado, where her husband was a mine manager, for years. And if as a woman she could perhaps not observe, let alone write about, those segments of crude Western society which provided the staple for Joaquin Miller or Bret Harte, her astute observation and recording of the problems of genteel living in such raw surroundings is the more interesting.

The two novels together represent the parameters of Western fiction. Janvier's writing involves myth, action, esoterica; Mrs. Foote's precise observation, manners, the exoteric made interesting by its curious setting. The two possibilities of technique were to be continued in Western novels through the period to 1920, with only the occasional writer able to combine them effectively, as Owen Wister did in *The Virginian* (1902), and Eugene Manlove Rhodes did in a series of novels. Favoring either a mythic quest or local color, the "cowboy novel" developed into a distinct genre between these two antithetical directions. And, while the foremost practitioners of the genre have been well studied in this series, several noteworthy writers somewhat below the level of Wister and Rhodes demand our attention.

IV. PIONEERS OF THE COWBOY MYTH

In spite of precursors like Cooper's *The Prairie* (1827) and Washington Irving's *Adventures of Captain Bonneville* (1837), the "cowboy novel" as developed in the twentieth century was essentially fixed as a genre in the 1890s and 1900s. Its earliest manifestations are not novels, but histories of the brief epoch during which the cowboy of myth and movie came closest to existing: the years 1865-1880, when all the "events" of the cowboy novel were briefly present: the Great Cattle Drive, the extermination of the buffalo and the Indian, the great popular expansion westward and the subsequent closing of the range. The cowboy figures in all aspects of this period. Although he is most prominent in the cattle drive and the closing of the range, he lends his type to the hunting of the buffalo and the genocide of the Indian.

It is almost impossible to discover the inventor of a cliché like the cowboy; there are too many parts to the production-line model added by too many different hands to allow the historian to determine specific origins. Therefore it is probable that Emerson Hough (1857-1923) added little to the archetype of the cowboy, even though his *The Story of the Cowboy* (1897) is the first

and among the best of the early descriptions of the cowboy type, and he certainly did not allow mere facts to interfere with his mythic creation. *The Story of the Cowboy* is hackwork from beginning to end, totally dependent upon secondary sources and extremely uncritical in its handling of those sources. Hough's purpose is clear from the very first words of his introduction—to raise a monument to the type of the cowboy which would persist into an age when he was no longer present:

> The story of the West is a story of the time of heroes. Of all those who appear large upon the fading page of that day, none may claim greater stature than the chief figure of the cattle range. Cowboy, cattle man, cow-puncher, it matters not what name others have given him, he has remained—himself. From the half-tropic to the half-arctic country he has ridden, his type, his costume, his characteristics practically unchanged, one of the most dominant and self-sufficient figures in the history of the land. He never dreamed he was a hero, therefore perhaps he was one. He would scoff at monuments or record, therefore perhaps he deserves them.

It is precisely such a figure that Hough presents to the reader—and proceeds to alabasterize permanently: "the virile figure of a mounted man. He stood straight in the stirrups of his heavy saddle, but lightly and well poised. . . . a loose belt swung a revolver low down upon his hip. A wide hat blew up and back a bit with the air of his travelling, and a deep kerchief fluttered at his neck". Such writing hardly even pretends to be anything more than fiction, and throughout *The Story of the Cowboy* Hough's eye is on the epic, the heroic, the archetypal. His consideration of "Society in the Cow Country" is a brief for a Warner Brothers set, introducing each type with statements like, "there was always a sheriff in a cow town, and he was always the same sort of man—quiet, courageous, just, and much respected by his fellow-men," repeating the same kind of guff about the newspaper editor, the lawyer, the saloon-keeper, the gambler, and all the other clichés of the Western. Had he individualized his characters at all, his "history" would have been a full-fledged novel.

Not that *The Story of the Cowboy* is completely without historic relevance. Hough's description of the cattle drives is generally accurate, as are his comments on the range wars of the eighties, including a history of Billy the Kid which is remarkably unromanticized. But no effort toward historical accuracy can possibly counter-balance Hough's obvious intentions toward the picturesque in such paragraphs as this one:

> It is high and glaring noon in the little town, but it still sleeps. In their cabins some of the men have not yet thrown off their blankets. Along the one long, straggling street there are few persons moving, and those not hastily. Far out on the plain is a trail of dust winding along, where a big ranch wagon is coming in. Upon the opposite side of the town a second and more rapid trail tells where a

buckboard is coming, drawn by a pair of trotting ponies. At the end of the street, just coming up from the *arroyo,* is the figure of a horseman—a tall, slim, young man—who sits straight up on his trotting pony, his gloved hand held high and daintily, his bright kerchief just lopping up and down a bit at his neck as he sits the jogging horse, his big hat pushed back a little over his forehead. All these low buildings, not one of them above a single story, are the colour of the earth. They hold to the earth therefore as though they belonged there. This rider is also in his garb the colour of the earth, and he fits into this scene with perfect right. He also belongs there, this strong, erect, and self-sufficient figure. The environment has produced its man.

Was ever a writer more self-consciously engaged in archetypal creation? Does not such writing constitute a kind of fiction, however disguised as history? And, of course, the work was incredibly successful, reprinted many times in the twentieth century and plagiarized in general and in detail by hundreds of writers, including Hough himself in later novels like *The Covered Wagon* (1922).

If *The Story of the Cowboy* is mythic creation posing as history, Andy Adams's *The Log of a Cowboy* is the same thing as autobiography. Adams (1859-1935) gives a name to his persona, Thomas Moore Quirk, but no commentators on *The Log of a Cowboy* have been fooled into thinking that the narrator was anyone other than Andy Adams, whose experiences of trail drives exactly correspond to those of the *Log.* What no critics have noticed is that Adams uses the same archetypal techniques as Hough, except that his Tom Quirk and colleagues are individualized to the point of having names and escaping the "earth-colour" implications so patent in Hough's description. They are nonetheless complete archetypes, romantic versions of what such revisionist histories as Frantz and Choate's *American Cowboy Myth and the Reality* (1955) have shown to be entirely the creation of nostalgic and romantic imaginations. Tom Quirk is no more Andy Adams than Ishmael is Herman Melville— which is to say, of course, that he is something more. Through Tom, through the other characters in the *Log* and the stories they tell around the campfires, myths, not history, come into being. The *Log* is filled with details about a specific trail drive from the Mexican border through Texas and the plains to Montana—but so is Faulkner's *The Bear* about a specific hunt. The *Log* records faithfully virtually every kind of event possible on such a drive, river crossings, stampedes, debauches in towns along the trail, information about the handling of cattle specific enough to generate a textbook on the subject—but so does *Moby-Dick* on whaling. When all the details and trifles are added together with the epic setting and underplayed but heroic style, it becomes clear that the purpose of the book is not to detail a historical phenomenon but to generate a continuing myth. Instead of a stuffed carcass in a museum, Hough and Adams give us live wings for our imagination. Ours and central casting's.

And therein lies the difficulty. If Oedipus is a myth, so is Mickey Mouse, and, somewhere in between, Rip van Winkle. There are Mickey Mouse cowboys, a plethora of them. Frank H. Spearman (1859-1937) created a true archetype with *Whispering Smith* (1906), whose title character speaks so softly that he is given this soubriquet despite his accomplishments with a six-shooter. Alas, throughout the novel all he does is whisper and shoot villains until the reader could hardly care less. So much for Mickey Mouse. The Oedipuses of cowboy fiction are to be found in works by writers like Zane Grey, Eugene Rhodes, and Walter van Tilburg Clark, and are therefore outside the limits of this study. But several other writers have managed to create characters of considerable mythic dimensions who are nevertheless largely forgotten.

Stewart Edward White (1873-1946) was something more than a hackwriter, though the fifty or so books released under his name would seem to argue to the contrary. His Western fiction has a definite sense of place in spite of the fact that his travels in the West were limited. But in characterization he worked well within the Emerson Hough tradition of the man produced by his environment. In particular, his first three novels, *The Westerners* (1901), *The Claim Jumpers* (1901), and especially *The Blazed Trail* (1902), present the archetypal Western hero—a man thoroughly schooled in his craft, self-reliant in the Emersonian tradition, always quietly confident of his ability to cope with the unexpected, and answerable only to his own conscience in moral matters—that is, willing to take the law in his own hands, usually by way of a Colt. 45. The variations on this theme are endless, in White's novels of the West and in the genre as a whole, but the main characteristics of the Western hero remain constant from Natty Bumppo to Shane and Destry, and White was not the one to experiment rashly in this field. A later trilogy based on California history, *Gold* (1913), *The Grey Dawn* (1915), and *The Rose Dawn* (1920), shifts the emphasis from the Western archetype to the influence of place upon character, but these are perhaps not properly cowboy novels. White also wrote adventure novels about Africa and works on spiritualism, but his Western books are the basis of his reputation, and they are eminently readable.

Two otherwise quite minor novels illustrate how the cowboy hero's willingness to stand outside the law marks the major area of influence of this genre upon modern literature. Charles C. Park's *A Plaything of the Gods* (1912) is based upon the real life of Joaquin Murieta, the California bandit. The novel traces Murieta's life from his early days as a devout Catholic to his conversion to a bloodthirsty bandit intent upon revenging the wrongs done him and his Spanish colleagues by the American invaders of California. The emphasis in the novel is always on the factors justifying Murieta's behavior and the quality of fairness that he presents as he administers his own brand of justice. In one sense, the novel harks back to the old Robin Hood ballads, but in tone it is much closer to the modern cult of the anti-hero that is best illustrated in the movie *Bonnie and Clyde.* In the growth of that genre the cowboy novel is central, marking the line of descent from Emerson's comment that he would prefer to be "the devil's child" than submit to moral judgment other than his own, through Twain's Colonel Sherburn, to Berger's Little Big Man, to mention only the most "western" of the modern examples. Self-reliance and transcendentalism may mark the beginning of the tradition, but it is the American frontier and the cowboy myth that allowed it to develop.

Roger Pocock's *Curly* (1905) illustrates the other value to be derived from the cowboy myth. This novel is virtually a Populist tract in its insistence that the large landowners, the banks, and the politicians are leagued against the poor farmer-cowboy, who must turn outlaw in order to survive. The satire is not subtle here, but the technique is pure. Through the innocence of the cowboy and his innocent eye, the hypocrisy of society can be laid bare most effectively, and the cowboy's resort to extralegal practices seen only as his marching to a different drummer. Thus the genre has enriched the modern complex novel with its expansion of the transcendental paradoxes first proposed early in the nineteenth century.

Dick Harrison

SOURCE: "Popular Fiction of the Canadian Prairies: Autopsy on a Small Corpus," in *Journal of Popular Culture*, Vol. XIV, No. 2, Fall, 1980, pp. 326-32.

[*In the following essay, Harrison addresses the prairie novel, a once-popular form of literature in Canada during the late nineteenth and early twentieth centuries.*]

It may seem strange to some that in the northern half of this continent, after three and a half centuries of writing and a century of nationhood, the reading of Canadian literature must still be promoted as a virtuous act, like temperance or churchgoing. Apologists give various explanations, frequently based on cultural domination by the United States, but one reason they rarely mention is that Canada has failed to sustain a tradition of indigenous popular literature. Canadians are not spontaneously drawn to their national literature, rich though it may be, because it does not seem to turn an amiable face toward them. It has not diverted them in idle moments, and now, they fear, it means to improve them.

This was not always the case. In the closing years of the nineteenth century and the early years of the twentieth, Canadian popular literature commanded a respectable share of the domestic market. Books such as Gilbert Parker's *The Seats of the Mighty,* Ralph Connor's *The Sky Pilot,* Lucy Maud Montgomery's *Anne of Green Gables* and the verses of Robert Service (if we can include this travelling Englishman) held the place of a genuine popular literature in the sense that they were read by enough Canadians to constitute a shared literary experience. The same was true of Stephen Leacock's humorous sketches, Frank L. Packard's adventure stories and,

later, Mazo de la Roche's family sagas of the Whiteoaks of Jalna. Turning more particularly to fiction of the prairie West, Ralph Connor created "popular" fiction in another important sense of the term. Not only did he sell over five million copies of his novels, but he created for the people of Canada a romantic vision of the West in keeping with their national values and aspirations. And he was not alone; the stories of Nellie McClung and Robert J. C. Stead occupied a similar though less prominent position in the literature of the times. The Canadian West was also a favourite setting for British adventure writers such as H.R.A. Pocock, Harold Bindloss and Ridgwell Cullum and for American writers such as James Oliver Curwood.

While such popular writing has never entirely vanished from the Canadian West, it clearly has not survived as a connected tradition, and the circumstances of its death may be instructive. A careful examination of the body of popular fiction of the prairies, like any good autopsy, should yield some clues to the time and causes of death.

The record of book publication would suggest that the decade of the 1930s saw a fatal decline in popular fiction about the prairies. This was not, as might first be assumed, because the depression economy curtailed publishing. At least fifty-one book-length fictions about the prairies appeared during the 1930s, slightly more than the long-term average of five books per year. Rather, the type of fiction and the circumstances of authorship and publication reflect the state of the popular fiction industry. Most conspicuous is the disappearance of major figures such as Connor, McClung, Stead and Arthur Stringer. Connor's last prairie fiction was *To Him that Hath* in 1921; Stead's last was *Grain* in 1926. While Stringer did publish *The Mud Lark* in 1932, his popular "prairie trilogy" ended in 1922, and though Nellie McClung was still publishing books of homilies, vignettes and sketches relating to the prairies as late as 1937, she had moved to Vancouver Island and her popular prairie novels such as *Sowing Seeds in Danny* were all behind her. As these figures faded, no one emerged to take their places. The usual record for western writers became one or two titles with one-line publishing histories. Their work has not survived in the minds of Canadian readers.

I must pause at this point to acknowledge the perils of drawing conclusions from the bare facts of publication. Precise estimates of the relative popularity of the books considered here will have to await massive researches into the records of publishing houses (many now defunct) to determine numbers of printings, size of press runs and ultimate sales. My findings cannot be any more than tentative, but there are certain gross features of the history of publishing which are unmistakable. Connor, McClung, Stead and Stringer, for example, sold a succession of novels, some of which made the "bestseller" lists. Their books were commonly published in Canada and the United States and/or Britain and often went into multiple editions over the years. Beyond the work of such popular authors, "popular fiction" is admittedly not an easily defined category, but it is possible to identify types of fiction which became undeniably popular in the hands of writers like Connor and McClung. Adventure stories were obviously intended for a popular audience, both the pure adventures of international writers such as Harold Bindloss and the local variant practiced by Ralph Connor—adventures which promoted British ideals of empire and a kind of "muscular Christianity." Romances of several types are also a safe choice: romances of pioneering like Stead's, sentimental romances concentrating on personalities, like Stringer's, and sentimental domestic romances with a strong homiletic bent like those of Nellie McClung. The common thread which made the bulk of this popular writing distinctively Canadian was probably composed of the moral, political and religious convictions implied in this description. As I have said elsewhere, the fiction was dominated by a hazy identification of the human order of empire with the natural order and ultimately a divine order.

When "popular fiction" is loosely defined as included in these types of adventure story and romance, the records of publication reveal some ominous trends. In the years from the turn of the century to 1929 a preponderance of the fiction falls into the categories of romance or adventure story. Of some 151 titles now located, 110 or about 73% clearly belong to these popular genres. Adventure stories make up the majority of these, numbering 85 of the 110. This category is, in a sense, inflated by the work of international writers such as Harold Bindloss (17 titles) and Ridgwell Cullum (9 titles), but many of the works were published in Canada. The count also includes Ralph Connor and a host of other Canadian writers such as W.A. Fraser who produced one, two or three adventure stories in this period. There are some ambiguous figures such as William Lacey Amy, a Medicine Hat journalist whose "Blue Pete" stories were essentially American westerns set in the Canadian West and written primarily for a British audience. Most of the 25 romances appearing in the same period were written by Canadians, including McClung, Stead and Stringer, and published in Canada. The remaining 41 titles include everything from fictionalized reminiscences and thinly disguised sermons to serious novels such as Frederick Philip Grove's *Settlers of the Marsh.*

The record of publishing in the 1930s does not at first appear to reflect any dramatic changes. Amy is still there with four new titles; Harold Bindloss has four ending in 1935 with *Sweetwater Ranch.* The proportion of sentimental romances has dropped from 17% to 12% and the adventure stories from 56% to 45%. The greatest change is in the "other" category, steadily growing from 27% to 43%, mainly through the publication of realistic fiction.

But the main Canadian popular writers were fading in this decade, and a close look at the list of adventure stories reveals another trend. Mounted Police stories in the 1930s constitute three-quarters of that category, while in previous decades they had made up less than half. More significantly, 22 of the 35 Mounted Police stories

appearing between 1900 and 1929 had been published in Canada. Of the 17 appearing in the 1930s none was published in Canada. The bulk of the adventure story market, then, had been expatriated from the Canadian popular fiction industry.

The publishing record of the 1940s confirms that what we observe in the decade of the 1930s are not aberrations but settled trends. In the 1940s the sentimental romance virtually disappears. The adventure story drops from 23 to 17, maintaining its proportion (46%) only by virtue of the Mounted Police stories (14), most of which were again published outside Canada. The three with Canadian imprints had special claims: *The Flaming Hour* (1947) was written primarily for a juvenile audience by Edward McCourt, an established writer of serious fiction; *To Effect an Arrest* (1947) was written by Harwood Steele, son of the greatest of Mountie heroes, Sam Steele; the third was the celebrated *Mrs. Mike* (1947) by the American couple Benedict and Nancy Freedman. In the 1940s the "other" category grows from its original 27% to 54%, mainly through an increase in what we think of as "serious" fiction.

It may seem strange to be discussing ominous trends in a decade which produced Paul Hiebert's *Sarah Binks,* Edward McCourt's *Music at the Close,* W. O. Mitchell's *Who Has Seen the Wind,* Frederick Niven's *Mine Inheritance,* Sinclair Ross's *As For Me and My House,* and Christine Van der Mark's *In Due Season.* No other decade has yielded such richness and variety of accomplished fictions about the prairies, and the fate of sentimental romances and adventure stories must be seen in that light. Probably because of the war effort, publishing did decline in the 1940s, from 51 titles in the previous decade to 37 titles. Significantly, the decline was almost entirely in the popular genres we have been tracing. The "Other" category dropped only from 22 titles to 20.

To avoid exaggerating this trend, it is necessary to recognize that the quoted figures in part reflect only incidental changes in literary fashion. The rise of prairie realism, beginning with the work of Frederick Philip Grove in the mid-1920s, affected much of the writing published in the 1930s. Even novels such as H.T. Reynold's *The Unquenched Flax* (1931) which do not deserve attention as "serious" fiction are fraught with dark psychological implications, and stories which might have been romances of pioneering in an earlier decade take on sombre tones that inhibit any sentimental view of prairie life. The urge to realism was often a deliberate reaction against earlier fashions, and the vogue of the sentimental romance was passing in the wider world beyond the prairies. Furthermore, in the work of writers such as W.O. Mitchell and Ross Annett published in the 1940s, a new form of sentimental comedy was appearing to supplant the sentimental romance in the popular taste. The disappearance of the sentimental romance, then, cannot be taken entirely as a decline in popular fiction.

The expatriation of the adventure story is a more serious symptom. The Mounted Police story in particular had shown unique possibilities as a popular genre which could dramatize the nationally distinctive qualities of the Canadian West. In the stories of Ralph Connor, the Mountie was a fit champion of an anti-revolutionary, conservative, hierarchical society. That his potential was never fully developed by the Canadian popular fiction industry may be due in part to the very success of the force and the glamour which attached to its name abroad.

By the 1930s Hollywood had discovered the Mountie; he had become a property of the international entertainment industry. The distinctively Canadian view of the Mountie was giving way to the Hollywood Mountie, a democratic, individualistic hero to be distinguished from a U.S. marshal only by his red tunic. The power of the silver screen was hotting up the image of Canada's national police force to an embarrassing degree, and in an era of realism in fiction, most Canadian writers and publishers would have nothing to do with a glamourous policeman. It is, of course, another distinctive national trait that Canadians are suspicious of heroes in their own fiction, but the role of motion pictures should not be underestimated. They must have had a devastating effect on popular fiction in general. Canadian publishers, always cautious and always operating in a market of marginal dimensions, may have found the challenge too great.

Hollywood also helped to effect a broader cultural shift in which western fiction for Canadians became the fiction of the American West. To understand this shift it is necessary to look not only at what Canadians were publishing but at what they were reading. The prairie people of the 1930s were avid readers. Some were known to drive twenty miles by horse and sleigh in sub-zero weather to exchange library books, and like all Canadians their reading tastes were distinctly cosmopolitan rather than national. They read Robert Service and Zane Grey, L. M. Montgomery, Gene Stratton Porter and Nellie McClung. If they came from Ontario, they probably still read Ralph Connor. If their taste was for romantic adventure they read James Oliver Curwood's Mounted Police stories. If they could afford more literary pretensions they read Shakespeare, Browning and Longfellow. If they were interested in serious Canadian writing they might read Martha Ostenso's *Wild Geese* or a novel by Frederick Philip Grove. The majority of the books about the prairie published during the 1930s would have been unknown to them.

Books were prized partly because they were scarce, and readers relied on magazines for much of their fiction. The prairie people brought American magazines such as *Liberty, Saturday Evening Post, Lady's Home Journal, Argosy* and *National Geographic*. From this brief list it should be apparent that their reading habits differed little from those of their American neighbours. They also read Canadian magazines—*Macleans, Star Weekly, Country Guide,* the *Family Herald*—and stories in such papers as the *Winnipeg Free Press* and *Free Press Prairie Farmer*. These might have been expected to expose them to native Canadian fiction, but they did not necessarily do that.

A sampling of the fiction in representative periodicals turns up very little Canadian content. *The Family Herald and Weekly Star,* for example, was published in Montreal but styled itself "Canada's National Farm Magazine" and was widely read by rural westerners; *The Winnipeg Free Press* served one of the largest urban readerships on the prairies. By 1935 the *Free Press* had stopped publishing fiction entirely (they carried a regular "movieland" page), but the loss to Canadian popular writers could not have been great. A typical week in the *Free Press* of the 1920s had provided the readers with daily serialization of *Baree, Son of Kazan, A Love Epic of the Far North* by American adventure writer James Oliver Curwood. The Saturday "Magazine of the Story Section," some 16 pages of the paper's total 70, included a chapter from *The Gates of Doom* by Rafael Sabatini, a column by Ring Lardner, Caesar Dunn's "The Four Flusher," billed as "Broadway's current success," several stories set in the American East and one in the American West. Going back to 1915, we find the *Free Press* had no magazine section but serialized similar types of popular American novel, including Emerson Hough's *The Broken Coin*. The choice is not surprising, since Hough's books sometimes made the Canadian bestseller list and this one is said to have been showing at several theatres in Winnipeg at the time.

The *Family Herald and Weekly Star* had only a slightly better average for Canadian fiction. Among the articles on "Sheep Breeders of Vancouver Island" and "Truck Crops for Deep Muck Soils," they usually printed at least two pieces of fiction. In mid-1935 these consisted of chapters from *Cattle Kingdom,* a tale of the American West by Allan Le May, plus a less strenuous romantic fiction, usually about well-bred New England girls meeting austere but sensitive engineers; stories written by people with such names as Phyllis Moore Gallagher, Miriam Green Ellis, Charlotte Wilima Fox and B. Janeith Knight, which sound suspiciously like pen-names for one prolific hack. Frequently the *Herald* added a humorous story by P.G. Wodehouse, and infrequently it carried a Canadian author. On June 19th, 1935 they printed "What Aunt Marcella Would Have Called It," by L. M. Montgomery, O.B.E. It is not clear whether they made this exception because of the popularity of Montgomery's Anne stories or because of the O.B.E. I have found two other easily identified exceptions. In 1925 the *Herald* serialized *The Imposter, A Mystery Tale of the Sea* by Canadian writer Frank L. Packard. To date my survey of these journals amounts to little more than sampling, but after closely checking the fiction in about three years of publication of each paper spread over three decades I have turned up only one story set in the Canadian West. On April 22, 1925 the *Herald* printed "Then the Mountain Stepped In" by Wilfrid Eggleston, a murder mystery with a love triangle set at the time of the Frank slide. Note that even this is set in the mountains and not on the prairies.

This brief survey would suggest that the periodical press did little to sustain indigenous popular fiction of the

West, and the underlying cause is again economic. Magazines and newspapers could reprint popular American writers more cheaply than they could buy the original work of Canadian writers who were not as well known. For their part, the writers would not offer a story to a Canadian magazine for fifty dollars when it might bring five hundred from the *Saturday Evening Post.* Ross Annett, for example, sold his popular "Babe" stories to the *Post* during the 1930s and '40s. They were sentimental comedies set in southern Alberta, but most of his countrymen were unaware that Annett was an Alberta writer. For similar reasons, the work of such Alberta writers as W. G. Hardy, John Patrick Gillese, Kerry Wood and Harold Cruickshank did not contribute to an identifiable tradition of popular writing in the West.

Like the rising popularity of motion pictures, the reading habits of the prairie people and the publishing policies of Canadian journals were well suited to an acceptance of the American West as the habitation of popular heroic fantasies. Canadians could graduate from the West of Zane Grey to that of Ernest Haycox, Max Brand, Louis L'Amour or Metro-Goldwyn-Mayer without marking the disappearance of Ralph Connor or Gilbert Parker.

But the root cause of death of popular prairie fiction may have lain deeper than economics, in the place that the West has occupied in the Canadian consciousness. In early America—a revolutionary culture seeking its independence from European domination—the settlement of the West could acquire immense popular significance as the experience through which a new people ceased to be Europeans and became Americans, an experience which would define and mature the national character. Eastern Canadians—anti-revolutionary and conservative—had no interest in any such experience. In their minds the West could become at worst a set of colonies to supply raw materials and markets, at best a purified model of central Canadian society. Stories of the West could obviously never claim the same cultural importance in Canada they enjoyed in the United States. From a purely literary point of view, these attitudes also meant that stories of the Canadian West inherently lacked the dramatic appeal of the American frontier. American popular fiction of the West could therefore supplant the domestic product because of its superior vitality.

The literary consequences of such a shift are serious but minor compared to the broader cultural implications. These implications extend beyond fiction to all the media of popular culture. If, as John Cawelti argues in *The Six-Gun Mystique,* a nation's popular entertainments serve to articulate and reaffirm its basic cultural values, then a nation which imports its fiction, movies and television programs is inviting a confusion of values and a blurring of its cultural identity. To take a present-day example, an American child sitting down in front of his television set will have his basic values constantly reinforced, while a Canadian child—unless he harbours an unlikely taste for C.B.C. documentaries—will have his nationally distinctive values obscured. Western Canadians in particular are inclined to grow up with a fuzzy sense that they inhabit a quieter northern extension of the Wild West they are so accustomed to in books, films and television series.

A growing suspicion that this situation is incongruous if not unhealthy has led to recent efforts at reviving popular literature of the Canadian prairies. I might include the Winnipeg-based Harlequin Romances which come out at a rate of twelve per month, but their connection with the prairie setting is doubtful. If there are signs of a resurrection they are to be found in scattered and sometimes unexpected places. Rudy Wiebe's *The Temptations of Big Bear,* a serious and demanding novel which won the Governor General's Award for 1973, enjoyed a period on the bestseller's list. In 1978 Edmonton author Aritha van Herk won a $50,000 publisher's prize for her first novel, *Judith.* Novelists, including Wiebe, Ken Mitchell and W. O. Mitchell, are writing plays to satisfy a growing demand for regional drama. In little over a year, three works of prairie fiction were turned into films: Max Braithwaite's *Why Shoot the Teacher,* Herbert Harker's *Goldenrod* and W. O. Mitchell's classic *Who Has Seen the Wind.* Increasingly the encouragement for writing popular fiction of the prairies is there, and the example of W. O. Mitchell is probably the most potent. Much of Mitchell's popularity has come from work in radio and television drama, but his first novel, *Who Has Seen the Wind* (1947) remains a popular favourite as well as a critically respected work. It is the culmination of a minor strain of sentimental comedy which has somehow survived on the prairies. It has survived because Mitchell's comedy sustains a serious perception of the prairie West, and at the same time shows Canadian readers that their national literature can turn an amiable face toward them. We can only hope that Mitchell's example will encourage talented writers to develop a new popular fiction of the prairies embodying values appropriate to their place and time. Clearly we have no further use for Ralph Connor's British imperial ideals or muscular Christianity, but something distinctive has surely descended from those beginnings.

M. J. Birch

SOURCE: "The Popular Fiction Industry: Market, Formula, Ideology," in *Journal of Popular Culture,* Vol. XXI, No. 1, Winter, 1987, pp. 79-99.

[*In the following essay, Birch outlines the growth of mass-market publishing in Great Britain and delineates the relationships between ideology and genre and non-genre literature.*]

> The dominant motive in the firm's endeavour is to provide good reading. . . . For those who lack an habitual appetite for reading, Penguins have nothing to offer: they do not deal in those products which aim to excite and contaminate the mind with sensation and which could be more aptly listed in a register of poisons than in a library. But for each civilized and balanced person there are Penguins to suit each mood. [*The Penguin Story*]

Now that scholars in the field of popular culture have managed to shed much of the snobbery and elitism that characterized debates on "high" and "popular" culture it is a shock to see the same attitudes entrenched in the philosophy of a company which was itself a mass-marketing phenomenon. The Penguin philosophy of "avoiding vulgarity" and "products which aim to excite and contaminate the mind" is inscribed now as an undeniable achievement of the paperback "revolution" of the mid-thirties, a revolution associated almost entirely with Penguin books. It is time for this serious distortion to be revised. Penguins were, in fact, only the last state in a *series* of "revolutions" in the publishing and marketing of fiction and other literature which had been going on since the late 1880's and has never been sufficiently understood. This article makes a preliminary survey of the history of the popular publishing industry in Britain and suggests some guidelines for further research on the relationship between the structure of publishing industries and the forms and contents of fictions themselves in the study of ideology.

Much work in the field of mass-marketed literature is extremely inadequate, an inadequacy which can be explained simply in terms of lack of evidence, particularly on the reprinting of works, either in boards or in paperback. Copyright libraries did not as a rule take cheap reprints of works. Much of the mass of material needed for adequate study of cheap fictions was pulped in the first World War and the small amount that survived left to the mercy of paper-drives in the second. Much of it has failed to survive simply because of shoddy manufacture. Serious study of a large part of the market is only possible by the discovery of private collections (which made Louis James' *Fiction for the Working Man* possible, for instance) but collectors as a rule will only collect cheap reprints as a last resort. The results of this serious lack of information can be seen in articles like Schmoller's "The Paperback Revolution" which skips over the period from 1900 to 1935 in a few words, with the assumption that the "first" paperback revolution in America had ceased by 1900. To give an idea of the magnitude of the market in cheap literature even before the first World War one need only mention that in Britain, the firm of John Long was producing 51 titles in 6d. paperback form in 1904, the "Daily Mail" series of copyright novels had 137 titles by 1906, Cassells were publishing 102 titles in paperback in 1911, and Pearson's 179 in 1908-9. Most histories of publishing companies provide no evidence of the marketing strategies they were pursuing or the relationship between different sections of their publishing enterprise. This article concentrates on the marketing and publication of fictions in Great Britain through examination of the fictions themselves. There are obvious methodological problems in this approach, but close scrutiny of publishers' lists, often bound in at the end of their products, can provide good information about the entire range of their product, the nature of their production and marketing expectations, and the nature of the product itself.

It is now increasingly acceptable to point out that books, films or other cultural artifacts are forms of *cultural pro-duction* and that their analysis must involve approaching cultural production as an industry. This article concentrates on the relationship between the possibilities created by technological change, degrees of penetration by cultural products in the market, and the role of "star" and "formula" in the selling of fictions. Raymond Williams has recently pointed to confusions in work on "genre" or "sub-genre" in academic work—a confusion between classification by literary form, by subject matter and by intended readership "the last a developing type in terms of specialized market sectors". [Williams, *Marxism and Literature*] He grudgingly allows the last category to point to "practical differences in real production". It is upon this last category and upon "sub-genre" or "formula" that I shall be concentrating.

Until the 1880's the dominance of public libraries and the expense of "three-decker" novels meant a rigid separation between novels first produced at 38 shillings and six pence, or 21 shillings, and a range of cheaper reprints at the still relatively expensive rate of 2 shillings. "Shilling shockers" usually of a "sensational" type, a few titles with guaranteed sales produced in a large quarto format at 6d., or "bloods" like the Jack Harkaway series, at 6d. or 1 shilling, were all that supervened between these productions and tales of moral uplift produced under the aegis of the Religious Tract Society. This is to simplify a complex picture which needs more study. In the 1880's, for instance, Cassell's *National Library* was producing cheap reprints of classic works like Sir John Maundeville's *Travels*. The following decade, though, was characterized by two technological developments which led to an enormous increase in the quantity of novels produced and an enormous drop in their price. Cheaper paper and binding made the private consumption of books possible and away from the control of public libraries. Competition among publishers, and authors now known to readers by name, rather than as the anonymous author of another work, corresponded to increased variety in fiction. It also supports the sociological view that increased innovation in cultural production is related to decreased concentration of culture industries in the market-place. In the 1890's the novel, at six shillings each, were first tested by magazine and newspaper publications and came to dominate the market. The association between hard-back and magazine divisions in a publisher's marketing strategies meant that the rigid separation of the market into products available at certain price-levels diminished. Pearson's, for instance, produced magazines at 6d., at 2d., and at 1d., and a serial like George Griffith's *Romance of Golden Star* which appeared first in the penny magazine *Short Stories,* in 1895, was not, therefore, debarred from an appearance at six shillings.

The 1890's may be simply defined as a period of free capitalist competition, predicated upon a relatively small run of a product that could still make a profit. This made possible the "Key-notes" series of John Lane as well as Heinemann's "Pioneer" series, among others. "Belles" Lettres' in the 'nineties were possible because a work like Wilde's *Salome* which cost only £156 to produce, could make a profit of £432. Small runs of work at a less "artistic" level than those of Wilde, or Stephen Crane, meant that authors and publishers had two choices. Men like George R. Sims became classic literary "hacks" who wrote journalism, short stories, social criticism, doggerel verse and advertisements for hair oil. The majority, continued to be "rigid" in including three-decker novel into specific formulas.

Many authors, like Conan Doyle, wrote in several formulas,—the newly invented "consulting detective" formula of Sherlock Holmes, as well as the "historical" formula of the *White Company,* and felt trapped by the requirements of the market. Conan Doyle's attempt to kill off Sherlock Holmes is the classic example of this since he wanted his reputation to rest upon his historical novels. George Griffith, however, worked almost entirely within the new "formula" which one could call "science fiction" or "lost-race" fiction. The novel of trips to other worlds, like Griffith's *Honeymoon in Space,* however, had existed prior to the "nineties" in single examples. A novel like E. About's *Man With the Broken Ear* (N.Y. 1867) had featured the rejuvenation of a man apparently dead, but it took the developments of the "nineties" to fit themes of this kind into "formula" categories. "Formulas" simply guide consumers of popular fiction well before they buy a given work. The publisher can raise his proportion of successes by providing already-tested products. At the same time, the fact that works could make a profit even on relatively small runs had a significant effect on the range of product outside the tested formula categories. Put simply, publishers could afford to make mistakes. One finds among novels in the nineties an enormous phantasmagoria of the weird and the wonderful. A man wakes up in the southern states of America to discover that he has become black (Ignatius Donnelly, *Dr. Huguet*). Fantasies of magical powers derived from Tibet, (H.S. Burland, *Dakobra, or the White Priests of Ahriman*) or any of the other strange places of the world, or novels of demonic possession, or hypnotic powers (George Griffith, *The White Witch of Mayfair*) jostle for a place in the market with Morrison's *Tales of Mean Streets,* or Zangwill's *Children of the Ghetto* and other works of serious social observation. Authors working inside formulas were not trapped entirely by the formula. Israel Zangwill who wrote *Children* could also write a classic "locked-room" detective story, *The Big Bow Mystery.* Guy Boothby could write novels both about the evil "Dr. Nikola", and adventures of the South Seas.

Some indication of the glorious variety of the cultural production of the 'nineties at the popular level may be gained from a look at some of the items in Pearson's *Short Stories* for 1895-6. A man dies by a bite from a blue beetle created from "electric fluid". A man is saved from death in the jungle by a walking tree (December 14, 1895). The greatest sculptor in Spain is commissioned to make a sculpture of Jesus on the cross, and nails his wife's lover, alive, to the cross (December 14, 1895):

> The crucifix of the master was miraculous in its reality, with its shrivelled skin and clotted blood staining the decomposing flesh. . . . And one day, during the service . . . the half-decayed body of Don Jose Santabalzo fell from the cross in the midst of the kneeling worshippers.

A man is murdered after being presented with the head of his mistress (October 19, 1895):

> a black hairy, ball . . . a bloodless face, with cold, blue lips, and eyes from which the light of life had forever fled.

Most of these stories end in deaths of some kind. In the January 18, 1895 issue, a widow trains her dog to rip out the throat of her husband's murderer, and in the issue for January 25, 1896, a trapeze artist, hearing the voice of the lover who had abandoned her, falls "straight", like an arrow, into the open space beneath her, and lay, a mangled, quivering mass at her lover's feet. In an interesting variant (April 11, 1896), though, a man's enthusiasm for life is rekindled by a visit to "Euthanasia Villa", where a tour through the Asphyxia Chamber, the Experimental Chamber (where people offer themselves as subjects for medical experiments) the Stake Chamber (where people's limbs are pulled off) and the Decapitation Chamber, convinces him that there are worse things than staying alive. In many ways the cheapest forms of literary production are more inventive than the formula stories further up the market.

After 1900 publishers, while maintaining the connection between their six shilling novels and their cheap periodicals, added another string to their bow, again as a result of technological innovation. Increasing sophistication in colour printing meant that it was possible to reprint successful novels in attractive paperback form for the railway bookstall trade. The first paperback issues of 1902-4 tend as a rule to be typographically designed, like Boothby's *Countess Londa* (1903) or designed in very stark and simple terms, like Cutliffe-Hyne's *Filibusters* (1903), or Swan Sonnenshein's *Basilisk* (1902). A study of successive titles from the Ward Lock range reveals the speed with which these early paperbacks developed into magnificently decorative products at a sixpenny price. The design of *The World's Finger* or the *Adventures of Romney Pringle* (1903) is chaste and simple in two colours. By 1909 with *The Albert Gate Affair* and *When I was Czar* (1903) the sophistication of printing techniques developed is quite obvious. A design like that of Leroux' *Phantom of the Opera* (1908-9) anticipates the development most closely associated with paperback colour printing as a selling device—the dustwrapper. Although the flowering of dust-wrapper design was to be a feature of the "twenties" rather than the period before the first World War, all publishers in this period were attempting to keep up their profit margins on a lower-priced commodity by lowering the cost of production. An inexpensive case and a dustwrapper were an obvious solution to this price cutting problem. Nelson and others produced well-made cheap reprints in hard-back which made a profit at sevenpence.

The marketing results of making a larger volume of product at a lower return per volume are immediate and significant for the history of cheap publishing after the War, especially in marketing cheap reprints. Although Pearsons could claim in all their paperbacks that "the aim of the publishers has been to cater as far as possible for all tastes"; a glance at the works reprinted makes one wonder how far this was true. Of the 51 novels reprinted in paperback by John Long in March 1906, nearly half were in the formulas that one might call "crime and detection" (Fergus Hume, Richard Marsh, William le Queux, Dick Donovan, J. S. Fletcher). In 1908-9 the Pearson paperback relied heavily upon M. McD. Bodkin, Richard Marsh, M.P. Shiel, George Griffith and other authors of crime or fantastic fiction. At lower unit returns of a product, the glorious variety of the 1890's, was transformed into paperback reprints for the product to be sold. Publishers had to reprint formula stories from their "stars" in order to maximize their returns. Slightly earlier, in the 1890's, Ward Lock had attempted cheap reprints of their bestsellers in the "Ward Lock 2 shilling Copyright series" and F.V. White has reverted to the Railway Library-style "yellowback", both in pictorial boards, and the same rigidification of formula had appeared. The Ward Lock series, for instance was heavily dependent upon Arthur Morrison's "Martin Hewitt" detective stories. This formulaic tendency before the first World War was a harbinger of the future of the industry; although, in this period it applied mainly to cheap editions and paperback reprints. Developments after the war were to make this style of marketing standard for fiction industries.

The period of the First World War is confusing for the student of popular literature since so much has disappeared. It is a period well worth further investigation, especially since because of war-time paper shortages many novels first appeared in what earlier would have been cheap form, but for the moment one needs only remember that the winners in the free-enterprise publishing battles of the period from 1890 to 1914 could fairly be said to be Ward Lock, Newnes, and John Long. After the war, rigidification of formula in the market was to add a new front-runner—Hodder and Stoughton. Simply put, rather than being a market organized in terms of wide range and small runs, Hodder and Stoughton were to reorganize it in terms of huge runs and narrow range. The second "revolution" in cheap publishing was on its way.

This change in market strategy was dependent upon a further development in the cheap binding of books, the automatic case-binding machine, and the full exploitation of the coloured dustwrapper first developed for paperbacks. Until about 1923 all major publishers produced 2 shillings or 2s 6d novels for the reprint end of the market in coloured wrappers of increasing sophistication. In 1923, though, Hodder and Stoughton changed the nature of the 2 shilling product. Instead of reprints, Hodder customers could buy cheap copies of *new* books. Furthermore they could buy books in bold yellow wrappers

while other companies had not realized the importance of designing the spine of their product as well as its front cover. Each book was clearly identified for a particular author by a slogan ("Horler for Excitement" or "You Will Never Fail to be Thrilled by Edgar Wallace") and with a symbol (a crimson circle for Wallace, a green triangle for E. P. Oppenheim). Hodder had made three key strategies in the monopoly marketing of books—new books across an entire price range from 7s 6d, to 3s 6d, to 2 shillings, product identification, and rigid formularization in cheap fictions. He had his "star" in Edgar Wallace, in Westerns (Clarence Mulford, William McLeod Raine, Henry Oyen) in novels of the New York underworld (Frank L. Packard), and those "stars" wrote for him under contract to produce a specific product. When Edgar Wallace wrote titles which were outside the "crime" range, like *Penelope of the Polyantha* or *The Day of Uniting,* they were never published at 7s 6d or 3s 6d but only in the cheapest form.

The case of Edgar Wallace provides a perfect example of the transition of "authors" from relatively free producers in the period before the War to mere "author-functions" producing a rigidly codified product at high speed. Wallace was assisted in this by a further technological development—the dictaphone—but the important feature of this monopoly stage is the emergence of much more rigid formulas. If the "classical" detective story of Sherlock Holmes was an invention of the first "revolution" in publishing, writers of the 'nineties were able to take "the detective" as a figure and produce variations upon it. At this second "revolution" Agatha Christie set the pattern of the "country-house" detective story in an unbreakable mould, Wallace created the classical "thriller" and so on. Not only did fiction become identifiable consumer product set inside definite limits but also the authors themselves came to be owned by their publishers. Before the war Wallace had been published by Arrowsmith, the Tallis Press, Goulden and Sons, Ward Lock and others. After the war other publishers bought some of his product except that Hodder had the lion's share. The number of new Wallace titles produced by different publishers and presented in figure one demonstrates clearly the rise of Hodder and the decline of the pre-war leaders, like Ward Lock, in the market-place.

A few points should be noted in the marketing pattern of these figures. The 12 Newnes titles of 1914-17 are war-related (*General Sir John French, The Standard History of the War*) or stories of trench humour and army life (*Nobby, Smithy, Smithy and the Hun*). The eight Newnes titles of 1927-29 are each 6d paperbacks, but containing short stories culled from magazines and, strictly speaking, are not new works. The Hutchinson titles from 1931 onwards were all ghost-written by Wallace's secretary, Robert Curtis, and can hardly be said to be by Wallace at all. The "Reader's Library" category of 1927-28 will be discussed later in this essay. Although both John Long and Ward Lock attempted to cash in on the market for Wallace most of their production consisted of reissues of Wallace's work produced years earlier. In reply to

Hodder's first major success with a Wallace title (*The Crimson Circle,* in 1923) Ward Lock could only reply with a reissue of the *Daffodil Mystery* (first published in 1920) or *The Secret House* (first published in 1917). Hodder, though, was to discover in 1931 that a dependence upon the "star" in selling fictions, had a serious built-in flaw. As Pan books discovered with the death of Ian Fleming, the "star" has to stay producing. With the death of their "star" the Hodder formula approach was to be in crisis throughout the 'thirties as one can see from their eternal search for a "new" Edgar Wallace.

An alternative marketing approach which was to be developed by Penguin Books in the mid-'thirties and which was to lift all publishers from the doldrums had been anticipated by a third, almost unnoticed "revolution" in the selling of cheap literature. "Reader's Library" producing books at 6d rather than 2s could combine the wide product range characteristic of the period from 1890-1914, with the massive sales of the Hodder monopoly approach. For the same price as a Ward Lock paperback reprint from their backlist "Reader's Library" customers could buy Wilkie Collins' *Woman in White,* or Dumas, or George Eliot. The reprinting of "classics" in their early days is remarkably similar to the Penguin policy of "avoiding vulgarity" or even T. Fisher Unwin's desire in the 1890's to produce "good" books at reasonable prices. As they proceeded the publishing policy of Reader's Library became more "vulgar", insofar as a large part of the profits came from novelizations of silent movies which could be on the bookstalls as fast as the films appeared. Consumers could read John Willard's *Cat and the Canary,* Thea von Harbou's *Metropolis,* or novelizations of Douglas Fairbanks' *The Sea Beast,* Valentino's *Eagle* or *Cobra,* Mary Pickford's *My Best Girl.* All Readers Library product was characterized by perhaps the ultimate development of the coloured dustwrapper. They could only be read a few times before they disintegrated, but through a solid list of dependable classics, and even some classics that had been filmed like Jules Verne's *Michael Strogoff,* of Victor Hugo's *Les Miserables* and by instant and aggressive response to short-term market demand, Readers Library had a wide product range—nearly 600 in all—and large sales of individual units of product. Penguin books, and other paperback publishers since, have followed this same principle, particularly with tie-ins from other media, and the Penguin "Specials" of the war years can be seen as a development of quick response to temporary market demand. From the monopoly marketing techniques of Hodder, Penguin took the idea of colour-coding product for instant identification into the areas of "Crime", "Biography", "Travel" or "Belles Lettres". The paperback "revolution" used techniques and marketing strategies already exploited by others and directly related to the return on each unit of product.

Given that one can see these developments in the marketing of cheap fictions by formula, large questions then arise about the nature and significance of the forms and contents of formula fictions which can only be discussed briefly here. Most writers on "formula" in fictions seem to share the assumption that "high" art is subversive, while "popular" or "formula" art corresponds to dominant social values and that popular texts do not violate conventions or create new forms. If there is to be any serious validity in the study of formulas it is simply, in this view, that the understanding of the conventions of "sub-literary" genres will enable a better appreciation of the uses of those same conventions in "great" art. These views would be more respectable if many writers on popular fictions knew more about their subject. A statement on the popular literature of the 1890's that

> one can account for most of the best-sellers of the period—Marie Corelli, Hall Caine, M. E. Braddon—on grounds of their vulgarity and sensationalism [Colley, *The Singular Anomaly: Women Novelists in the Nineteenth Century*]

is not only calculated to make the first two authors spin rapidly in their graves but is now being undermined by approaches to popular fictions with more fruitful implications.

T. F. Boyle and Winifred Hughes' study of the "sensation novel" of the 1860's and 1870's reveals that the "popular" works of Charles Reade or Mrs. Braddon deeply subvert the melodramatic conventions that they deploy, and that they attack, in fact, conventional ideas of status, property, rationality and even romance itself. Knoepflmacher has seen the same subversion in Wilkie Collins, and Briggs has seen ghost stories as revealing "something of the variety and abundance of different responses to the crisis of faith" in the late nineteenth century. Showalter has seen the "sensation" novel as responding to the deepest anxieties of Victorian women;

> For the Victorian woman secrecy was simply a way of life. The sensationalists made crime and violence domestic, modern and suburban; but their secrets were not simply solutions to mysteries and crimes: they were the secrets of women's dislike of their roles as daughters, wives and mothers. [Showalter, *A Literature of Their Own*]

A view of popular novels as "shared fantasies of protest and escape" means that they have to be taken more seriously than mere reinforcements of "dominant social values".

Some recent work has attempted to deal with the nature of popular fictions by taking two contradictory positions simultaneously. Thus, in Cawelti's version, Westerns focus on the "resolution of tensions between conflicting interests" *at the same time* as they affirm existing attitudes. A recent, rather reductionist, work offers, however, a more fruitful initial exploration into the role of formula fictions than the bland statement "existing attitudes" by asking simply how one defines an "existing attitude". Jerry Palmer's *Thrillers* examines the nature of popular fictions, in terms of the "field of ideology in which the text is situated". His definition of the "thriller" formula as involving only a "possessively individualist" hero, and a conspiracy of some sort, needs serious redefinition since it conflates formulas like the American "hard-boiled" thriller and the classical "country-house" detective novel but offers the important initial insight that formula fictions involve the coding of ideologies within the general ideological system which operates in society. Much empirical work on specific formulas needs to be done in this context and only a few general guidelines can be suggested here. The first two important points to realize are that "ruling ideology" is not a monolithic entity but a complex system to which consumers of cultural products have access at different levels whether penny magazines, six shilling novels or two shilling reprints.

The second important consideration is to be clear about a rough definition of ideology. The "field of ideology" in any given society can be seen as a complex and historically specific social language. Within that language a society literally "speaks" about itself through the connections, relationships, and frictions between key elements. Some elements like "work", "family" or "law" are more densely connected with other elements throughout the field than others under capitalism, in the same way that "nobility," "honour," or "patronage" can be seen to specify possible relationships between people in aristocratic societies. Importantly for the study of fictions this field is never static and never free from contradictions, and specific connections are constructed or separated in the course of history. "Discourse" theorists like Foucault have followed up this insight in specific cases, like "madness" but still have not located these particular connections well enough inside the entire field. Fictions can play a key role in locating such ideological connections in two ways. Fictional plots are only possible as representations which "solve" inherent contradictions within the field (like that between "marriage" and "career" in discourses centered on women). At the same time fictions, in resolving contradictions, albeit magically, can be said to become "actively constitutive" of ideology.

All formula fictions foreground a relatively small number of ideological elements to the exclusion of others and many writers in the field of popular culture have noted some of the elements operating in popular texts. Thus Fowler has noticed the old distinction between town and country that existed in most melodrama, and a concentration on "work", "money" and "sex-roles" as central to women's magazine fiction. A more systematic analysis comparing a wider range of formulas is required. I would suggest a general key more widely applicable than a distinction between "the individual" and "sociality" in a wide range of formulas. Westerns, thrills, detective or romantic novels, are all based upon the resolution of relationships of power and dominance between protagonists, focussed upon a relatively small range of "common-sense" assumptions in dominant ideology but not necessarily "reflecting" them. All formulas are "concrete articulations of a more abstract ruling ideology" [Hill, "Ideology, Economy, and the British Cinema"] which work

> not of course, directly or crudely, but in complex and contradictory ways whose specific potencies

and inflections have to be analyzed in particular and concrete ways.

A preliminary caveat has to be made in discussing the form and content of popular fictions, insofar as it is easy to read content into texts where only form is involved. The classic thriller of Edgar Wallace relies upon an overall mystery, usually one of identity, and a series of lesser confrontations between the "unknown" and the hero. This is to reduce some very complicated plotting to oversimple terms, but one has to remember always that serial production places definite constraints upon popular fiction forms, and that something like the Wallace formula results almost inevitably from the way in which the fictions were produced. In the same way, the sudden effervescence of the short story in the 1890's resulted from the magazine base of many publishers' marketing strategies. Despite this, one can still discern similar ideological elements operating throughout texts produced in different ways. As an initial approach the analysis of "formula" as "ideology" one might take the "cricketing cracksman" or "gentleman crook" represented by E. W. Hornung's A. J. Raffles, by American variants like E. P. Train's *Social Highwayman,* and even by second cousins like Leslie Charteris's "Saint". All stretch prevailing "commonsense" assumptions prevalent in "dominant ideology". I can only make a few observations here but further work on formula fiction must follow this approach. I am assuming here that readers are familiar with the bare bones, at least, of the "Raffles" figure. One can isolate in these stories a range of ambivalent attitudes to legitimate and illegitimate wealth, class, and status, which are built into the stories on at least two levels—that of Raffles' relationship with his often ineffectual and guilt-ridden helper, Bunny Manders, and that of the metaphors "sport", "game" and "art". Raffles, because he is "a dangerous bat, a brilliant field and perhaps the very finest slow bowler of his generation", is a man who plays for the "Gentlemen". His success as a burglar rests upon the assumption that being a brilliant player of a game associated with aristocratic culture renders him above suspicion. At the same time, "crime" and "cricket" for Raffles are not inconsistent.

> "Cricket," cried Raffles, "is a good enough sport until you discover a better."

This may not sound a matter of ideology. One must remember, however, the historical specificity of ideology. Victorian upper-class minds made a very clear distinction between "games" which were played by gentlemen and for fun, and "sports" which were played by professionals for money. When Raffles mentions "the affinity" between "crime" and "cricket" as "sport" he represents a conflation of two characteristically upper and lower class activities as professionalism. Most of the misunderstandings that his helper, Bunny, has about the nature of his activity results from the fact that Bunny still sees it as "game" rather than as "sport". Another characteristic distinction in Victorian minds, that between "art for art's sake" and "useful knowledge", which were thought to be characteristic of upper and lower class activities, also emerges as an organizing principle in the Raffles texts. Speaking of Crawshay, a professional burglar whom Raffles defeats in the *Amateur Cracksman,* Bunny remarks:

> "He is certainly a sportsman", said I.
>
> "He's more", said Raffles, "he's an artist".

In another story in the same collection Raffles, in burgling a loud, vulgar, Jewish representative of "new" money (actually acquired in Illicit Diamond Buying) states explicitly that he can not dispose of his spoil, but commits the robbery "for art's sake". Raffles, a combination of "athlete of the first water" and "minor poet" is a divisive force in a society in which assumptions about "sport", "art", and "status" determine possible relationships between people. In "Gentlemen and Players" Bunny is delighted, although terrified, to be chosen for the "gentlemen" rather than for the "players". As a comedy of assumptions about class and status one can read a similarly disturbing message in the initial encounter between Raffles and Bunny, who assumes that because Raffles has "status" he also has wealth. He is quickly disabused:

> "Do you think that because a fellow has rooms in this place and belongs to a club or two, and plays a little cricket, he must necessarily have a balance at the bank?"

Many readers of the Raffles' saga would have started with the same initial assumption about the automatic connection between status and wealth. The initial encounter, however, strains more of the "common-sense" connections of late Victorian society than this. Bunny also assumes that Raffles' position as his superior at their public school makes his nature the weaker, and Raffles the stronger. But in attempting to commit suicide "for the despicable satisfaction of involving another in one's own destruction", Raffles reacts with wonder and admiration: "I had no idea that you were a chap of that sort".

On a third level one can discern elements on the "Raffles" saga which cut across these ambivalent attitudes and more directly express dominant ideology. It is important to note that this occurs much more in the later books, but the relationship between Bunny and his fiancée (who leaves him at the discovery of his association with Raffles) is used as a hope of regeneration for Bunny. On hearing that she has returned Bunny's few presents there was in Raffles "still, with the magic mischief of his smile . . . that touch of sadness that I was yet to read aright". Raffles is an outsider, and sad, despite the apparent joy with which he steals in the earlier books. At the same time, in a development which was to kill many aristocratic youths in the first World War, the Raffles figure is also used to produce a representation of "War", as well as "Crime" as "Sport".

A study of formula variants at different levels in the market place will often demonstrate the kinds of varia-tions found here within the Raffles texts themselves. One can demonstrate significant differences in relative proportions of "dominant" and "subversive" elements, even using the same formula. The implications of this for a sophisticated analysis of the "field of ideology" can not be pursued here, but in a Raffles pastiche produced in a pulp magazine, *The Story-teller,* one can see Raffles in significant transformation: "Baffles" had been caught, and his friend the "Rabbit" attempts to bribe the successful detective:

> "He is a contemptible thief", growled Mr. Beck, "that sneaks as a guest into the house that he means to rob". The Rabbit was shocked.
>
> "He plays the game fairly", he retorted, "it is his proudest boast that he has never been guilty of a breach of hospitality. He never steals from his host!"
>
> . . . For once Mr. Beck was thoroughly aroused. There was a look of fierce anger and loathing that few had ever seen on that kindly face. "Get out of my room!" he cried to the frightened Rabbit, "out before I throw you through the window, you mean, whining jackal, that feeds on the leavings of this human wolf. I have brought many a vile criminal to justice in my time, but never a viler one than this hero of yours—Baffles".

Formula variations between the British and American use of the same formula is another fruitful avenue through which to study the relationship between "formula" and "ideology". The American "Raffles" in E. P. Train's *Social Highwayman,* Courtice Jeffrey, is a purer Robin Hood figure who "never robbed a being who could not afford to lose what he had taken and . . . two thirds, at least, of his ill-gotten gains have gone to the relief of the poor and destitute". There is, naturally, no cricket, but also no visible thefts, and the book concentrates on the relationship between Jeffrey's fiancee and the fact of crime. The nearer equivalent to the "Amateur Cracksman" figure in the American context are immoral and successful con-men like George Randolph Chester's "Wallingford", or shyster lawyers as in Arthur Train's *Confessions of Artemas Quibble.* Both these American variants are dependent on a new understanding of "aristocracy" in an American ideology.

The serious study of formulas in fictions is still in its infancy. So far, most scholars seem to have been most concerned with the kind of narratology associated with the name of Propp, or with attempts to apply psychoanalytic categories to fictions. One can see novels of the "underworld" quite easily in terms of psychology, but an approach in terms of ideology makes more sense in many cases. In Frank Packard's New York, for instance, there are a large class of criminals living secret lives. One of their dens is:

> the resort, not only of the most depraved Chinese element, but of the worst "white" thugs that made New York their headquarters—here, in the succession

of cellars, roughly partitioned off to make a dozen rooms on either side of the passage, dope fiends sucked at the drug and Chinese gamblers spent the greater part of their lives; here murder was hatched and played too often to its hellish end; here the scum of the underworld sought refuge from the police.

The important ideological consideration here is the construction of a discourse which connects "criminality", "race" and "drugs" and the same connection can be seen in many other formulas. Further work must follow in specifying why certain formulas should appear at the times that they do, and working out the role of formulas at different levels in the marketplace. We may then acquire a better knowledge of that complex phenomenon that Palmer has called the "ideological field" and that is better described as the historical growth, rigidification and deformation of ideologies in societies.

FURTHER READING

Anthology

McQuade, Donald and Robert Atwan, eds. *Popular Writing in America: The Interaction of Style and Audience.* New York: Oxford University Press, 1974, 647 p.
> Includes selections from popular advertising copy, newspaper journalism, magazine articles, best sellers, and classics of fiction and nonfiction.

Secondary Sources

Austin, James C. and Donald A. Koch, eds. *Popular Literature in America: A Symposium in Honor of Lyon N. Richardson.* Bowling Green, Oh.: Bowling Green University Popular Press, 1972, 205 p.
> Sets out to correct cultural assumptions about popular literature by presenting "a kind of cross-section of literary scholarship on the popular literature of the past and present."

Cawelti, John G. *Adventure, Mystery, and Romance: Formula Stories as Art and Popular Culture.* Chicago: University of Chicago Press, 1976, 336 p.
> Examines and defines the characteristics of popular formula fiction, including its artistic qualities, typical patterns, and cultural functions.

Heffernan, Thomas J, ed. *The Popular Literature of Medieval England.* Knoxville: University of Tennessee Press, 1985, 330 p.
> Collection of essays on popular medieval writings not ordinarily seen as the suitable subjects of literary scholarship, such as folklore, romance, and comic tales.

Hicken, Mandy and Ray Prytherch. *Now Read On: A Guide to Contemporary Popular Fiction.* Brookfield, Vt.: Gower Publishing Co., 1990, 328 p.
> Contains entries on nineteen different popular subgenres of the novel—adventure stories, fantasies, gothic romances, thrillers, etc.—with basic information on the authors of each.

Holsinger, M. Paul and Mary Anne Schofield, eds. *Visions of War: World War II in Popular Literature and Culture.* Bowling Green, Oh.: Bowling Green University Popular Press, 1992, 203 p.
> Broad selection of essays on the literature of World War II seen from the perspective of the battlefield and of the women and children back home.

Inge, M. Thomas. *Handbook of American Popular Literature.* New York: Greenwood Press, 1988, 408 p.
> Essays on the various subgenres of popular fiction—including detective novels, fantasy, westerns, science fiction, and others—intended "to provide access to the body of existing commentary and scholarship on several of the main forms of popular literature."

Irons, Glenwood, ed. *Gender, Language, and Myth: Essays on Popular Narrative.* Toronto: University of Toronto Press, 1992, 318 p.
> A range of contemporary essays collected to redefine the artificial division between what is commonly considered to be great literature and popular literature.

Klein, Marcus. *Easterns, Westerns, and Private Eyes: American Matters, 1870-1900.* Madison: University of Wisconsin Press, 1994, 216 p.
> Discusses the prevalence and development of the rags-to-riches tale, the western, and the detective story in late nineteenth-century America, and the historical and cultural significance of the rise of these popular fictional forms.

Minor, Lucian W. *The Militant Hackwriter: French Popular Literature 1800-1848—Its Influence, Artistic and Political.* Bowling Green, Oh.: Bowling Green University Popular Press, 1975, 177 p.
> Reevaluates the influences of the popular novel and the melodrama on the development of French literature in the nineteenth century, maintaining that works in these genres had a profound effect on literary culture, as well as French social and political life.

Palmer, Jerry. *Potboilers: Methods, Concepts, and Case Studies in Popular Fiction.* London: Routledge, 1991, 219 p.
> "Introduces and summarizes two decades of debate about mass-produced fictions and their position within popular culture," arguing that the literary distinctions between high and low culture be forgotten.

Peek, George S. "Folklore Concepts and Popular Literature: A Strategy for Combining Folklore and Literary Studies."

Tennessee Folklore Society Bulletin XLIV, No. 1 (March 1978): 25-29.
Applies the popular literature concepts of Axel Olrik's essay "Epic Laws of Folk Narrative" to the Chester cycle plays, contending that the laws are excellent tools for better understanding medieval drama.

Radway, Janice A. "Phenomenology, Linguistics, and Popular Literature." *Journal of Popular Culture* XII, No. 1 (Summer 1978): 88-98.
Employs a phenomenological method of inquiry in order "to make positive assertions about the difference between elite artistic expression and popular culture."

——. "The Utopian Impulse in Popular Literature: Gothic Romances and 'Feminist' Protest." *American Quarterly* 33, No. 2 (Summer 1981): 140-62.
Argues that popular literature, specifically the contemporary Gothic romance, while "essentially conservative in its recommendations of conventional gender behavior" nonetheless "permits the reader first to give form to unrealized disaffection before it reassures her that such discontent is unwarranted."

Richetti, John J. *Popular Fiction Before Richardson: Narrative Patterns 1700-1739.* Oxford: Oxford University Press, 1969, 274 p.
Investigates the tropes and types of the earliest forms of the novel.

Server, Lee. *Over My Dead Body, The Sensational Age of the American Paperback: 1945-1955.* San Francisco: Chronicle Books, 1994, 108 p.
Survey of the popular escapist fiction—often sensationalistic, lurid, even "sleazy" paperbacks—from the decade 1945-1955, "a brief but gloriously subversive era in the history of American publishing."

Sturgin, Michael. "Innocence and Suffering in the Middle Ages: An Essay about Popular Taste and Popular Literature." *Journal of Popular Culture* 14, No. 1 (Summer 1980): 141-48.
Comments on the highly affective nature of most popular medieval spiritual texts, and the historical and cultural significance of this fact.

Yanarella, Ernest J. and Lee Sigelman, eds. *Political Mythology and Popular Fiction.* New York: Greenwood Press, 1988, 200 p.
Comprises essays by contemporary political scientists who "render political readings of themes from several popular genres populating today's mass fiction market."

Twentieth-Century Literary Criticism

Cumulative Indexes
Volumes 1-70

How to Use This Index

The main references

list all author entries in the following Gale Literary Criticism series:

BLC = *Black Literature Criticism*
CLC = *Contemporary Literary Criticism*
CLR = *Children's Literature Review*
CMLC = *Classical and Medieval Literature Criticism*
DA = *DISCovering Authors*
DC = *Drama Criticism*
HLC = *Hispanic Literature Criticism*
LC = *Literature Criticism from 1400 to 1800*
NCLC = *Nineteenth-Century Literature Criticism*
PC = *Poetry Criticism*
SSC = *Short Story Criticism*
TCLC = *Twentieth-Century Literary Criticism*
WLC = *World Literature Criticism, 1500 to the Present*

The cross-references

list all author entries in the following Gale biographical and literary sources:

AAYA = *Authors & Artists for Young Adults*
AITN = *Authors in the News*
BEST = *Bestsellers*
BW = *Black Writers*
CA = *Contemporary Authors*
CAAS = *Contemporary Authors Autobiography Series*
CABS = *Contemporary Authors Bibliographical Series*
CANR = *Contemporary Authors New Revision Series*
CAP = *Contemporary Authors Permanent Series*
CDALB = *Concise Dictionary of American Literary Biography*
CDBLB = *Concise Dictionary of British Literary Biography*
DLB = *Dictionary of Literary Biography*
DLBD = *Dictionary of Literary Biography Documentary Series*
DLBY = *Dictionary of Literary Biography Yearbook*
HW = *Hispanic Writers*
JRDA = *Junior DISCovering Authors*
MAICYA = *Major Authors and Illustrators for Children and Young Adults*
MTCW = *Major 20th-Century Writers*
NNAL = *Native North American Literature*
SAAS = *Something about the Author Autobiography Series*
SATA = *Something about the Author*
YABC = *Yesterday's Authors of Books for Children*

Literary Criticism Series
Cumulative Author Index

Anderson, Robert (Woodruff)
1917- . . . . **CLC 23; DAM DRAM**
See also AITN 1; CA 21-24R; CANR 32;
DLB 7

Anderson, Sherwood
1876-1941 . . . . **TCLC 1, 10, 24; DA;**
DAB; DAC; DAM MST, NOV; SSC 1;
WLC
See also CA 104; 121; CDALB 1917-1929;
DLB 4, 9, 86; DLBD 1; MTCW

Andier, Pierre
See Desnos, Robert

Andouard
See Giraudoux, (Hippolyte) Jean

Andrade, Carlos Drummond de . . . . . . **CLC 18**
See also Drummond de Andrade, Carlos

Andrade, Mario de 1893-1945 . . . . . **TCLC 43**

Andreae, Johann V(alentin)
1586-1654 . . . . **LC 32**
See also DLB 164

Andreas-Salome, Lou 1861-1937 . . . **TCLC 56**
See also DLB 66

Andrewes, Lancelot 1555-1626 . . . . **LC 5**
See also DLB 151, 172

Andrews, Cicily Fairfield
See West, Rebecca

Andrews, Elton V.
See Pohl, Frederik

Andreyev, Leonid (Nikolaevich)
1871-1919 . . . . **TCLC 3**
See also CA 104

Andric, Ivo 1892-1975 . . . . **CLC 8**
See also CA 81-84; 57-60; CANR 43;
DLB 147; MTCW

Angelique, Pierre
See Bataille, Georges

Angell, Roger 1920- . . . . **CLC 26**
See also CA 57-60; CANR 13, 44; DLB 171

Angelou, Maya
1928- . . . . **CLC 12, 35, 64, 77; BLC; DA;**
DAB; DAC; DAM MST, MULT, POET,
POP
See also AAYA 7, 20; BW 2; CA 65-68;
CANR 19, 42; DLB 38; MTCW;
SATA 49

Annensky, Innokenty (Fyodorovich)
1856-1909 . . . . **TCLC 14**
See also CA 110; 155

Annunzio, Gabriele d'
See D'Annunzio, Gabriele

Anon, Charles Robert
See Pessoa, Fernando (Antonio Nogueira)

Anouilh, Jean (Marie Lucien Pierre)
1910-1987 . . . . . . **CLC 1, 3, 8, 13, 40, 50;**
DAM DRAM
See also CA 17-20R; 123; CANR 32;
MTCW

Anthony, Florence
See Ai

Anthony, John
See Ciardi, John (Anthony)

Anthony, Peter
See Shaffer, Anthony (Joshua); Shaffer,
Peter (Levin)

Anthony, Piers 1934- . . **CLC 35; DAM POP**
See also AAYA 11; CA 21-24R; CANR 28,
56; DLB 8; MTCW; SAAS 22; SATA 84

Antoine, Marc
See Proust, (Valentin-Louis-George-Eugene-)
Marcel

Antoninus, Brother
See Everson, William (Oliver)

Antonioni, Michelangelo 1912- . . . . . **CLC 20**
See also CA 73-76; CANR 45

Antschel, Paul 1920-1970
See Celan, Paul
See also CA 85-88; CANR 33; MTCW

Anwar, Chairil 1922-1949 . . . . **TCLC 22**
See also CA 121

Apollinaire, Guillaume
1880-1918 . . . . **TCLC 3, 8, 51;**
DAM POET; PC 7
See also Kostrowitzki, Wilhelm Apollinaris
de
See also CA 152

Appelfeld, Aharon 1932- . . . . **CLC 23, 47**
See also CA 112; 133

Apple, Max (Isaac) 1941- . . . . **CLC 9, 33**
See also CA 81-84; CANR 19, 54; DLB 130

Appleman, Philip (Dean) 1926- . . . . . **CLC 51**
See also CA 13-16R; CAAS 18; CANR 6,
29, 56

Appleton, Lawrence
See Lovecraft, H(oward) P(hillips)

Apteryx
See Eliot, T(homas) S(tearns)

Apuleius, (Lucius Madaurensis)
125(?)-175(?) . . . . **CMLC 1**

Aquin, Hubert 1929-1977 . . . . **CLC 15**
See also CA 105; DLB 53

Aragon, Louis
1897-1982 . . . . . **CLC 3, 22; DAM NOV,**
POET
See also CA 69-72; 108; CANR 28;
DLB 72; MTCW

Arany, Janos 1817-1882 . . . . **NCLC 34**

Arbuthnot, John 1667-1735 . . . . **LC 1**
See also DLB 101

Archer, Herbert Winslow
See Mencken, H(enry) L(ouis)

Archer, Jeffrey (Howard)
1940- . . . . **CLC 28; DAM POP**
See also AAYA 16; BEST 89:3; CA 77-80;
CANR 22, 52; INT CANR-22

Archer, Jules 1915- . . . . **CLC 12**
See also CA 9-12R; CANR 6; SAAS 5;
SATA 4, 85

Archer, Lee
See Ellison, Harlan (Jay)

Arden, John
1930- . . . . . **CLC 6, 13, 15; DAM DRAM**
See also CA 13-16R; CAAS 4; CANR 31;
DLB 13; MTCW

Arenas, Reinaldo
1943-1990 . . . . . . **CLC 41; DAM MULT;**
HLC
See also CA 124; 128; 133; DLB 145; HW

Arendt, Hannah 1906-1975 . . . . . **CLC 66, 98**
See also CA 17-20R; 61-64; CANR 26;
MTCW

Aretino, Pietro 1492-1556 . . . . **LC 12**

Arghezi, Tudor . . . . **CLC 80**
See also Theodorescu, Ion N.

Arguedas, Jose Maria
1911-1969 . . . . **CLC 10, 18**
See also CA 89-92; DLB 113; HW

Argueta, Manlio 1936- . . . . **CLC 31**
See also CA 131; DLB 145; HW

Ariosto, Ludovico 1474-1533 . . . . **LC 6**

Aristides
See Epstein, Joseph

Aristophanes
450B.C.-385B.C. . . . . **CMLC 4; DA;**
DAB; DAC; DAM DRAM, MST; DC 2
See also DLB 176

Arlt, Roberto (Godofredo Christophersen)
1900-1942 . . . . . **TCLC 29; DAM MULT;**
HLC
See also CA 123; 131; HW

Armah, Ayi Kwei
1939- . . . . **CLC 5, 33; BLC;**
DAM MULT, POET
See also BW 1; CA 61-64; CANR 21;
DLB 117; MTCW

Armatrading, Joan 1950- . . . . **CLC 17**
See also CA 114

Arnette, Robert
See Silverberg, Robert

Arnim, Achim von (Ludwig Joachim von
Arnim) 1781-1831 . . . . **NCLC 5**
See also DLB 90

Arnim, Bettina von 1785-1859 . . . . **NCLC 38**
See also DLB 90

Arnold, Matthew
1822-1888 . . . . . **NCLC 6, 29; DA; DAB;**
DAC; DAM MST, POET; PC 5; WLC
See also CDBLB 1832-1890; DLB 32, 57

Arnold, Thomas 1795-1842 . . . . . . **NCLC 18**
See also DLB 55

Arnow, Harriette (Louisa) Simpson
1908-1986 . . . . **CLC 2, 7, 18**
See also CA 9-12R; 118; CANR 14; DLB 6;
MTCW; SATA 42; SATA-Obit 47

Arp, Hans
See Arp, Jean

Arp, Jean 1887-1966 . . . . **CLC 5**
See also CA 81-84; 25-28R; CANR 42

Arrabal
See Arrabal, Fernando

Arrabal, Fernando 1932- . . . **CLC 2, 9, 18, 58**
See also CA 9-12R; CANR 15

Arrick, Fran . . . . **CLC 30**
See also Gaberman, Judie Angell

Artaud, Antonin (Marie Joseph)
1896-1948 . . . **TCLC 3, 36; DAM DRAM**
See also CA 104; 149

Arthur, Ruth M(abel) 1905-1979 . . . . **CLC 12**
See also CA 9-12R; 85-88; CANR 4;
SATA 7, 26

Artsybashev, Mikhail (Petrovich)
1878-1927 . . . . **TCLC 31**

Arundel, Honor (Morfydd)
1919-1973 .... CLC 17
See also CA 21-22; 41-44R; CAP 2;
CLR 35; SATA 4; SATA-Obit 24

Arzner, Dorothy 1897-1979 .... CLC 98

Asch, Sholem 1880-1957 .... TCLC 3
See also CA 105

Ash, Shalom
See Asch, Sholem

Ashbery, John (Lawrence)
1927- ...... CLC 2, 3, 4, 6, 9, 13, 15, 25,
41, 77; DAM POET
See also CA 5-8R; CANR 9, 37; DLB 5,
165; DLBY 81; INT CANR-9; MTCW

Ashdown, Clifford
See Freeman, R(ichard) Austin

Ashe, Gordon
See Creasey, John

Ashton-Warner, Sylvia (Constance)
1908-1984 .... CLC 19
See also CA 69-72; 112; CANR 29; MTCW

Asimov, Isaac
1920-1992 ...... CLC 1, 3, 9, 19, 26, 76,
92; DAM POP
See also AAYA 13; BEST 90:2; CA 1-4R;
137; CANR 2, 19, 36; CLR 12; DLB 8;
DLBY 92; INT CANR-19; JRDA;
MAICYA; MTCW; SATA 1, 26, 74

Assis, Joaquim Maria Machado de
See Machado de Assis, Joaquim Maria

Astley, Thea (Beatrice May)
1925- .... CLC 41
See also CA 65-68; CANR 11, 43

Aston, James
See White, T(erence) H(anbury)

Asturias, Miguel Angel
1899-1974 .... CLC 3, 8, 13;
DAM MULT, NOV; HLC
See also CA 25-28; 49-52; CANR 32;
CAP 2; DLB 113; HW; MTCW

Atares, Carlos Saura
See Saura (Atares), Carlos

Atheling, William
See Pound, Ezra (Weston Loomis)

Atheling, William, Jr.
See Blish, James (Benjamin)

Atherton, Gertrude (Franklin Horn)
1857-1948 .... TCLC 2
See also CA 104; 155; DLB 9, 78

Atherton, Lucius
See Masters, Edgar Lee

Atkins, Jack
See Harris, Mark

Atkinson, Kate. .... CLC 99

Attaway, William (Alexander)
1911-1986 .... CLC 92; BLC;
DAM MULT
See also BW 2; CA 143; DLB 76

Atticus
See Fleming, Ian (Lancaster)

Atwood, Margaret (Eleanor)
1939- ..... CLC 2, 3, 4, 8, 13, 15, 25, 44,
84; DA; DAB; DAC; DAM MST, NOV,
POET; PC 8; SSC 2; WLC
See also AAYA 12; BEST 89:2; CA 49-52;
CANR 3, 24, 33; DLB 53;
INT CANR-24; MTCW; SATA 50

Aubigny, Pierre d'
See Mencken, H(enry) L(ouis)

Aubin, Penelope 1685-1731(?) .... LC 9
See also DLB 39

Auchincloss, Louis (Stanton)
1917- .... CLC 4, 6, 9, 18, 45;
DAM NOV; SSC 22
See also CA 1-4R; CANR 6, 29, 55; DLB 2;
DLBY 80; INT CANR-29; MTCW

Auden, W(ystan) H(ugh)
1907-1973 ...... CLC 1, 2, 3, 4, 6, 9, 11,
14, 43; DA; DAB; DAC; DAM DRAM,
MST, POET; PC 1; WLC
See also AAYA 18; CA 9-12R; 45-48;
CANR 5; CDBLB 1914-1945; DLB 10,
20; MTCW

Audiberti, Jacques
1900-1965 ...... CLC 38; DAM DRAM
See also CA 25-28R

Audubon, John James
1785-1851 .... NCLC 47

Auel, Jean M(arie)
1936- .... CLC 31; DAM POP
See also AAYA 7; BEST 90:4; CA 103;
CANR 21; INT CANR-21; SATA 91

Auerbach, Erich 1892-1957 .... TCLC 43
See also CA 118; 155

Augier, Emile 1820-1889 .... NCLC 31

August, John
See De Voto, Bernard (Augustine)

Augustine, St. 354-430 ...... CMLC 6; DAB

Aurelius
See Bourne, Randolph S(illiman)

Aurobindo, Sri 1872-1950 .... TCLC 63

Austen, Jane
1775-1817 ..... NCLC 1, 13, 19, 33, 51;
DA; DAB; DAC; DAM MST, NOV;
WLC
See also AAYA 19; CDBLB 1789-1832;
DLB 116

Auster, Paul 1947- .... CLC 47
See also CA 69-72; CANR 23, 52

Austin, Frank
See Faust, Frederick (Schiller)

Austin, Mary (Hunter)
1868-1934 .... TCLC 25
See also CA 109; DLB 9, 78

Autran Dourado, Waldomiro
See Dourado, (Waldomiro Freitas) Autran

Averroes 1126-1198 .... CMLC 7
See also DLB 115

Avicenna 980-1037 .... CMLC 16
See also DLB 115

Avison, Margaret
1918- .... CLC 2, 4, 97; DAC;
DAM POET
See also CA 17-20R; DLB 53; MTCW

Axton, David
See Koontz, Dean R(ay)

Ayckbourn, Alan
1939- ...... CLC 5, 8, 18, 33, 74; DAB;
DAM DRAM
See also CA 21-24R; CANR 31; DLB 13;
MTCW

Aydy, Catherine
See Tennant, Emma (Christina)

Ayme, Marcel (Andre) 1902-1967... CLC 11
See also CA 89-92; CLR 25; DLB 72;
SATA 91

Ayrton, Michael 1921-1975 .... CLC 7
See also CA 5-8R; 61-64; CANR 9, 21

Azorin. .... CLC 11
See also Martinez Ruiz, Jose

Azuela, Mariano
1873-1952 ..... TCLC 3; DAM MULT;
HLC
See also CA 104; 131; HW; MTCW

Baastad, Babbis Friis
See Friis-Baastad, Babbis Ellinor

Bab
See Gilbert, W(illiam) S(chwenck)

Babbis, Eleanor
See Friis-Baastad, Babbis Ellinor

Babel, Isaac
See Babel, Isaak (Emmanuilovich)

Babel, Isaak (Emmanuilovich)
1894-1941(?) ...... TCLC 2, 13; SSC 16
See also CA 104; 155

Babits, Mihaly 1883-1941 .... TCLC 14
See also CA 114

Babur 1483-1530. .... LC 18

Bacchelli, Riccardo 1891-1985 ..... CLC 19
See also CA 29-32R; 117

Bach, Richard (David)
1936- ...... CLC 14; DAM NOV, POP
See also AITN 1; BEST 89:2; CA 9-12R;
CANR 18; MTCW; SATA 13

Bachman, Richard
See King, Stephen (Edwin)

Bachmann, Ingeborg 1926-1973..... CLC 69
See also CA 93-96; 45-48; DLB 85

Bacon, Francis 1561-1626 .... LC 18, 32
See also CDBLB Before 1660; DLB 151

Bacon, Roger 1214(?)-1292 ...... CMLC 14
See also DLB 115

Bacovia, George. .... TCLC 24
See also Vasiliu, Gheorghe

Badanes, Jerome 1937-............ CLC 59

Bagehot, Walter 1826-1877 ...... NCLC 10
See also DLB 55

Bagnold, Enid
1889-1981 ...... CLC 25; DAM DRAM
See also CA 5-8R; 103; CANR 5, 40;
DLB 13, 160; MAICYA; SATA 1, 25

Bagritsky, Eduard 1895-1934 ..... TCLC 60

Bagrjana, Elisaveta
See Belcheva, Elisaveta

Bagryana, Elisaveta. .... CLC 10
See also Belcheva, Elisaveta
See also DLB 147

Bailey, Paul   1937- . . . . CLC 45
See also CA 21-24R; CANR 16; DLB 14

Baillie, Joanna   1762-1851 . . . . NCLC 2
See also DLB 93

Bainbridge, Beryl (Margaret)
1933- . . . . CLC 4, 5, 8, 10, 14, 18, 22, 62;
DAM NOV
See also CA 21-24R; CANR 24, 55;
DLB 14; MTCW

Baker, Elliott   1922- . . . . CLC 8
See also CA 45-48; CANR 2

Baker, Jean H. . . . . TCLC 3, 10
See also Russell, George William

Baker, Nicholson
1957- . . . . CLC 61; DAM POP
See also CA 135

Baker, Ray Stannard   1870-1946 . . . TCLC 47
See also CA 118

Baker, Russell (Wayne)   1925- . . . . . . CLC 31
See also BEST 89:4; CA 57-60; CANR 11,
41; MTCW

Bakhtin, M.
See Bakhtin, Mikhail Mikhailovich

Bakhtin, M. M.
See Bakhtin, Mikhail Mikhailovich

Bakhtin, Mikhail
See Bakhtin, Mikhail Mikhailovich

Bakhtin, Mikhail Mikhailovich
1895-1975 . . . . CLC 83
See also CA 128; 113

Bakshi, Ralph   1938(?)- . . . . CLC 26
See also CA 112; 138

Bakunin, Mikhail (Alexandrovich)
1814-1876 . . . . NCLC 25, 58

Baldwin, James (Arthur)
1924-1987 . . . . . . CLC 1, 2, 3, 4, 5, 8, 13,
15, 17, 42, 50, 67, 90; BLC; DA; DAB;
DAC; DAM MST, MULT, NOV, POP;
DC 1; SSC 10; WLC
See also AAYA 4; BW 1; CA 1-4R; 124;
CABS 1; CANR 3, 24;
CDALB 1941-1968; DLB 2, 7, 33;
DLBY 87; MTCW; SATA 9;
SATA-Obit 54

Ballard, J(ames) G(raham)
1930- . . . . CLC 3, 6, 14, 36; DAM NOV,
POP; SSC 1
See also AAYA 3; CA 5-8R; CANR 15, 39;
DLB 14; MTCW

Balmont, Konstantin (Dmitriyevich)
1867-1943 . . . . TCLC 11
See also CA 109; 155

Balzac, Honore de
1799-1850 . . . . NCLC 5, 35, 53; DA;
DAB; DAC; DAM MST, NOV; SSC 5;
WLC
See also DLB 119

Bambara, Toni Cade
1939-1995 . . . . . . CLC 19, 88; BLC; DA;
DAC; DAM MST, MULT
See also AAYA 5; BW 2; CA 29-32R; 150;
CANR 24, 49; DLB 38; MTCW

Bamdad, A.
See Shamlu, Ahmad

Banat, D. R.
See Bradbury, Ray (Douglas)

Bancroft, Laura
See Baum, L(yman) Frank

Banim, John   1798-1842 . . . . NCLC 13
See also DLB 116, 158, 159

Banim, Michael   1796-1874 . . . . . . NCLC 13
See also DLB 158, 159

Banjo, The
See Paterson, A(ndrew) B(arton)

Banks, Iain
See Banks, Iain M(enzies)

Banks, Iain M(enzies)   1954- . . . . CLC 34
See also CA 123; 128; INT 128

Banks, Lynne Reid . . . . CLC 23
See also Reid Banks, Lynne
See also AAYA 6

Banks, Russell   1940- . . . . CLC 37, 72
See also CA 65-68; CAAS 15; CANR 19,
52; DLB 130

Banville, John   1945- . . . . CLC 46
See also CA 117; 128; DLB 14; INT 128

Banville, Theodore (Faullain) de
1832-1891 . . . . NCLC 9

Baraka, Amiri
1934- . . . . CLC 1, 2, 3, 5, 10, 14, 33;
BLC; DA; DAC; DAM MST, MULT,
POET, POP; DC 6; PC 4
See also Jones, LeRoi
See also BW 2; CA 21-24R; CABS 3;
CANR 27, 38; CDALB 1941-1968;
DLB 5, 7, 16, 38; DLBD 8; MTCW

Barbauld, Anna Laetitia
1743-1825 . . . . NCLC 50
See also DLB 107, 109, 142, 158

Barbellion, W. N. P. . . . . TCLC 24
See also Cummings, Bruce F(rederick)

Barbera, Jack (Vincent)   1945- . . . . . . CLC 44
See also CA 110; CANR 45

Barbey d'Aurevilly, Jules Amedee
1808-1889 . . . . NCLC 1; SSC 17
See also DLB 119

Barbusse, Henri   1873-1935 . . . . TCLC 5
See also CA 105; 154; DLB 65

Barclay, Bill
See Moorcock, Michael (John)

Barclay, William Ewert
See Moorcock, Michael (John)

Barea, Arturo   1897-1957 . . . . TCLC 14
See also CA 111

Barfoot, Joan   1946- . . . . CLC 18
See also CA 105

Baring, Maurice   1874-1945 . . . . TCLC 8
See also CA 105; DLB 34

Barker, Clive   1952- . . . CLC 52; DAM POP
See also AAYA 10; BEST 90:3; CA 121;
129; INT 129; MTCW

Barker, George Granville
1913-1991 . . . . . CLC 8, 48; DAM POET
See also CA 9-12R; 135; CANR 7, 38;
DLB 20; MTCW

Barker, Harley Granville
See Granville-Barker, Harley
See also DLB 10

Barker, Howard   1946- . . . . CLC 37
See also CA 102; DLB 13

Barker, Pat(ricia)   1943- . . . . CLC 32, 94
See also CA 117; 122; CANR 50; INT 122

Barlow, Joel   1754-1812 . . . . NCLC 23
See also DLB 37

Barnard, Mary (Ethel)   1909- . . . . CLC 48
See also CA 21-22; CAP 2

Barnes, Djuna
1892-1982 . . . CLC 3, 4, 8, 11, 29; SSC 3
See also CA 9-12R; 107; CANR 16, 55;
DLB 4, 9, 45; MTCW

Barnes, Julian (Patrick)
1946- . . . . CLC 42; DAB
See also CA 102; CANR 19, 54; DLBY 93

Barnes, Peter   1931- . . . . CLC 5, 56
See also CA 65-68; CAAS 12; CANR 33,
34; DLB 13; MTCW

Baroja (y Nessi), Pio
1872-1956 . . . . TCLC 8; HLC
See also CA 104

Baron, David
See Pinter, Harold

Baron Corvo
See Rolfe, Frederick (William Serafino
Austin Lewis Mary)

Barondess, Sue K(aufman)
1926-1977 . . . . CLC 8
See also Kaufman, Sue
See also CA 1-4R; 69-72; CANR 1

Baron de Teive
See Pessoa, Fernando (Antonio Nogueira)

Barres, Maurice   1862-1923 . . . . TCLC 47
See also DLB 123

Barreto, Afonso Henrique de Lima
See Lima Barreto, Afonso Henrique de

Barrett, (Roger) Syd   1946- . . . . CLC 35

Barrett, William (Christopher)
1913-1992 . . . . CLC 27
See also CA 13-16R; 139; CANR 11;
INT CANR-11

Barrie, J(ames) M(atthew)
1860-1937 . . . . TCLC 2; DAB;
DAM DRAM
See also CA 104; 136; CDBLB 1890-1914;
CLR 16; DLB 10, 141, 156; MAICYA;
YABC 1

Barrington, Michael
See Moorcock, Michael (John)

Barrol, Grady
See Bograd, Larry

Barry, Mike
See Malzberg, Barry N(athaniel)

Barry, Philip   1896-1949 . . . . TCLC 11
See also CA 109; DLB 7

Bart, Andre Schwarz
See Schwarz-Bart, Andre

Barth, John (Simmons)
1930- . . . . . . CLC 1, 2, 3, 5, 7, 9, 10, 14,
27, 51, 89; DAM NOV; SSC 10
See also AITN 1, 2; CA 1-4R; CABS 1;
CANR 5, 23, 49; DLB 2; MTCW

Belloc, (Joseph) Hilaire (Pierre Sebastien
    Rene Swanton)
    1870-1953 ... **TCLC 7, 18; DAM POET**
    See also CA 106; 152; DLB 19, 100, 141,
    174; YABC 1

Belloc, Joseph Peter Rene Hilaire
    See Belloc, (Joseph) Hilaire (Pierre Sebastien
    Rene Swanton)

Belloc, Joseph Pierre Hilaire
    See Belloc, (Joseph) Hilaire (Pierre Sebastien
    Rene Swanton)

Belloc, M. A.
    See Lowndes, Marie Adelaide (Belloc)

Bellow, Saul
    1915- ...... **CLC 1, 2, 3, 6, 8, 10, 13, 15,**
        25, 33, 34, 63, 79; DA; DAB; DAC;
        DAM MST, NOV, POP; SSC 14; WLC
    See also AITN 2; BEST 89:3; CA 5-8R;
        CABS 1; CANR 29, 53;
        CDALB 1941-1968; DLB 2, 28; DLBD 3;
        DLBY 82; MTCW

Belser, Reimond Karel Maria de   1929-
    See Ruyslinck, Ward
    See also CA 152

Bely, Andrey .... **TCLC 7; PC 11**
    See also Bugayev, Boris Nikolayevich

Benary, Margot
    See Benary-Isbert, Margot

Benary-Isbert, Margot   1889-1979... **CLC 12**
    See also CA 5-8R; 89-92; CANR 4;
        CLR 12; MAICYA; SATA 2;
        SATA-Obit 21

Benavente (y Martinez), Jacinto
    1866-1954 ..... **TCLC 3; DAM DRAM,**
                                                        MULT
    See also CA 106; 131; HW; MTCW

Benchley, Peter (Bradford)
    1940- ..... **CLC 4, 8; DAM NOV, POP**
    See also AAYA 14; AITN 2; CA 17-20R;
        CANR 12, 35; MTCW; SATA 3, 89

Benchley, Robert (Charles)
    1889-1945 .... **TCLC 1, 55**
    See also CA 105; 153; DLB 11

Benda, Julien   1867-1956 .... **TCLC 60**
    See also CA 120; 154

Benedict, Ruth   1887-1948 .... **TCLC 60**

Benedikt, Michael   1935- .... **CLC 4, 14**
    See also CA 13-16R; CANR 7; DLB 5

Benet, Juan   1927- .... **CLC 28**
    See also CA 143

Benet, Stephen Vincent
    1898-1943 ...... **TCLC 7; DAM POET;**
                                                        SSC 10
    See also CA 104; 152; DLB 4, 48, 102;
        YABC 1

Benet, William Rose
    1886-1950 ...... **TCLC 28; DAM POET**
    See also CA 118; 152; DLB 45

Benford, Gregory (Albert)   1941-.... **CLC 52**
    See also CA 69-72; CANR 12, 24, 49;
        DLBY 82

Bengtsson, Frans (Gunnar)
    1894-1954 .... **TCLC 48**

Benjamin, David
    See Slavitt, David R(ytman)

Benjamin, Lois
    See Gould, Lois

Benjamin, Walter   1892-1940 ...... **TCLC 39**

Benn, Gottfried   1886-1956........ **TCLC 3**
    See also CA 106; 153; DLB 56

Bennett, Alan
    1934- ... **CLC 45, 77; DAB; DAM MST**
    See also CA 103; CANR 35, 55; MTCW

Bennett, (Enoch) Arnold
    1867-1931 .... **TCLC 5, 20**
    See also CA 106; 155; CDBLB 1890-1914;
        DLB 10, 34, 98, 135

Bennett, Elizabeth
    See Mitchell, Margaret (Munnerlyn)

Bennett, George Harold   1930-
    See Bennett, Hal
    See also BW 1; CA 97-100

Bennett, Hal .... **CLC 5**
    See also Bennett, George Harold
    See also DLB 33

Bennett, Jay   1912- .... **CLC 35**
    See also AAYA 10; CA 69-72; CANR 11,
        42; JRDA; SAAS 4; SATA 41, 87;
        SATA-Brief 27

Bennett, Louise (Simone)
    1919- ..... **CLC 28; BLC; DAM MULT**
    See also BW 2; CA 151; DLB 117

Benson, E(dward) F(rederic)
    1867-1940 .... **TCLC 27**
    See also CA 114; DLB 135, 153

Benson, Jackson J.   1930-.......... **CLC 34**
    See also CA 25-28R; DLB 111

Benson, Sally   1900-1972 .... **CLC 17**
    See also CA 19-20; 37-40R; CAP 1;
        SATA 1, 35; SATA-Obit 27

Benson, Stella   1892-1933........ **TCLC 17**
    See also CA 117; 155; DLB 36, 162

Bentham, Jeremy   1748-1832 ..... **NCLC 38**
    See also DLB 107, 158

Bentley, E(dmund) C(lerihew)
    1875-1956 .... **TCLC 12**
    See also CA 108; DLB 70

Bentley, Eric (Russell)   1916-....... **CLC 24**
    See also CA 5-8R; CANR 6; INT CANR-6

Beranger, Pierre Jean de
    1780-1857 .... **NCLC 34**

Berdyaev, Nicolas
    See Berdyaev, Nikolai (Aleksandrovich)

Berdyaev, Nikolai (Aleksandrovich)
    1874-1948 .... **TCLC 67**
    See also CA 120

Berendt, John (Lawrence)   1939-.... **CLC 86**
    See also CA 146

Berger, Colonel
    See Malraux, (Georges-)Andre

Berger, John (Peter)   1926- ...... **CLC 2, 19**
    See also CA 81-84; CANR 51; DLB 14

Berger, Melvin H.   1927- .... **CLC 12**
    See also CA 5-8R; CANR 4; CLR 32;
        SAAS 2; SATA 5, 88

Berger, Thomas (Louis)
    1924- .... **CLC 3, 5, 8, 11, 18, 38;**
                                                        DAM NOV
    See also CA 1-4R; CANR 5, 28, 51; DLB 2;
        DLBY 80; INT CANR-28; MTCW

Bergman, (Ernst) Ingmar
    1918- .... **CLC 16, 72**
    See also CA 81-84; CANR 33

Bergson, Henri   1859-1941........ **TCLC 32**

Bergstein, Eleanor   1938-........... **CLC 4**
    See also CA 53-56; CANR 5

Berkoff, Steven   1937-............. **CLC 56**
    See also CA 104

Bermant, Chaim (Icyk)   1929- ...... **CLC 40**
    See also CA 57-60; CANR 6, 31, 57

Bern, Victoria
    See Fisher, M(ary) F(rances) K(ennedy)

Bernanos, (Paul Louis) Georges
    1888-1948 .... **TCLC 3**
    See also CA 104; 130; DLB 72

Bernard, April   1956- .... **CLC 59**
    See also CA 131

Berne, Victoria
    See Fisher, M(ary) F(rances) K(ennedy)

Bernhard, Thomas
    1931-1989 .... **CLC 3, 32, 61**
    See also CA 85-88; 127; CANR 32, 57;
        DLB 85, 124; MTCW

Berriault, Gina   1926-............. **CLC 54**
    See also CA 116; 129; DLB 130

Berrigan, Daniel   1921-............. **CLC 4**
    See also CA 33-36R; CAAS 1; CANR 11,
        43; DLB 5

Berrigan, Edmund Joseph Michael, Jr.
    1934-1983
    See Berrigan, Ted
    See also CA 61-64; 110; CANR 14

Berrigan, Ted..................... **CLC 37**
    See also Berrigan, Edmund Joseph Michael,
        Jr.
    See also DLB 5, 169

Berry, Charles Edward Anderson   1931-
    See Berry, Chuck
    See also CA 115

Berry, Chuck..................... **CLC 17**
    See also Berry, Charles Edward Anderson

Berry, Jonas
    See Ashbery, John (Lawrence)

Berry, Wendell (Erdman)
    1934- .... **CLC 4, 6, 8, 27, 46;**
                                                        DAM POET
    See also AITN 1; CA 73-76; CANR 50;
        DLB 5, 6

Berryman, John
    1914-1972 ...... **CLC 1, 2, 3, 4, 6, 8, 10,**
                                    13, 25, 62; DAM POET
    See also CA 13-16; 33-36R; CABS 2;
        CANR 35; CAP 1; CDALB 1941-1968;
        DLB 48; MTCW

Bertolucci, Bernardo   1940- .... **CLC 16**
    See also CA 106

Bertrand, Aloysius   1807-1841 .... **NCLC 31**

Bertran de Born   c. 1140-1215 ..... **CMLC 5**

Besant, Annie (Wood)   1847-1933 ... **TCLC 9**
    See also CA 105

Bodker, Cecil 1927- .... **CLC 21**
  See also CA 73-76; CANR 13, 44; CLR 23;
  MAICYA; SATA 14

Boell, Heinrich (Theodor)
  1917-1985 .... **CLC 2, 3, 6, 9, 11, 15, 27,
    32, 72; DA; DAB; DAC; DAM MST,
    NOV; SSC 23; WLC**
  See also CA 21-24R; 116; CANR 24;
  DLB 69; DLBY 85; MTCW

Boerne, Alfred
  See Doeblin, Alfred

Boethius 480(?)-524(?) .... **CMLC 15**
  See also DLB 115

Bogan, Louise
  1897-1970 .... **CLC 4, 39, 46, 93;
    DAM POET; PC 12**
  See also CA 73-76; 25-28R; CANR 33;
  DLB 45, 169; MTCW

Bogarde, Dirk .... **CLC 19**
  See also Van Den Bogarde, Derek Jules
    Gaspard Ulric Niven
  See also DLB 14

Bogosian, Eric 1953- .... **CLC 45**
  See also CA 138

Bograd, Larry 1953-............... **CLC 35**
  See also CA 93-96; CANR 57; SAAS 21;
  SATA 33, 89

Boiardo, Matteo Maria 1441-1494 .... **LC 6**

Boileau-Despreaux, Nicolas
  1636-1711 .... **LC 3**

Bojer, Johan 1872-1959 .... **TCLC 64**

Boland, Eavan (Aisling)
  1944- .... **CLC 40, 67; DAM POET**
  See also CA 143; DLB 40

Bolt, Lee
  See Faust, Frederick (Schiller)

Bolt, Robert (Oxton)
  1924-1995 ...... **CLC 14; DAM DRAM**
  See also CA 17-20R; 147; CANR 35;
  DLB 13; MTCW

Bombet, Louis-Alexandre-Cesar
  See Stendhal

Bomkauf
  See Kaufman, Bob (Garnell)

Bonaventura................... **NCLC 35**
  See also DLB 90

Bond, Edward
  1934- ... **CLC 4, 6, 13, 23; DAM DRAM**
  See also CA 25-28R; CANR 38; DLB 13;
  MTCW

Bonham, Frank 1914-1989........ **CLC 12**
  See also AAYA 1; CA 9-12R; CANR 4, 36;
  JRDA; MAICYA; SAAS 3; SATA 1, 49;
  SATA-Obit 62

Bonnefoy, Yves
  1923- ...... **CLC 9, 15, 58; DAM MST,
    POET**
  See also CA 85-88; CANR 33; MTCW

Bontemps, Arna(ud Wendell)
  1902-1973 .... **CLC 1, 18; BLC;
    DAM MULT, NOV, POET**
  See also BW 1; CA 1-4R; 41-44R; CANR 4,
  35; CLR 6; DLB 48, 51; JRDA;
  MAICYA; MTCW; SATA 2, 44;
  SATA-Obit 24

Booth, Martin 1944-............. **CLC 13**
  See also CA 93-96; CAAS 2

Booth, Philip 1925-............... **CLC 23**
  See also CA 5-8R; CANR 5; DLBY 82

Booth, Wayne C(layson) 1921- ..... **CLC 24**
  See also CA 1-4R; CAAS 5; CANR 3, 43;
  DLB 67

Borchert, Wolfgang 1921-1947 ..... **TCLC 5**
  See also CA 104; DLB 69, 124

Borel, Petrus 1809-1859........ **NCLC 41**

Borges, Jorge Luis
  1899-1986 ... **CLC 1, 2, 3, 4, 6, 8, 9, 10,
    13, 19, 44, 48, 83; DA; DAB; DAC;
    DAM MST, MULT; HLC; SSC 4; WLC**
  See also AAYA 19; CA 21-24R; CANR 19,
  33; DLB 113; DLBY 86; HW; MTCW

Borowski, Tadeusz 1922-1951 ...... **TCLC 9**
  See also CA 106; 154

Borrow, George (Henry)
  1803-1881 .... **NCLC 9**
  See also DLB 21, 55, 166

Bosman, Herman Charles
  1905-1951 .... **TCLC 49**

Bosschere, Jean de 1878(?)-1953... **TCLC 19**
  See also CA 115

Boswell, James
  1740-1795 ..... **LC 4; DA; DAB; DAC;
    DAM MST; WLC**
  See also CDBLB 1660-1789; DLB 104, 142

Bottoms, David 1949-............ **CLC 53**
  See also CA 105; CANR 22; DLB 120;
  DLBY 83

Boucicault, Dion 1820-1890...... **NCLC 41**

Boucolon, Maryse 1937(?)-
  See Conde, Maryse
  See also CA 110; CANR 30, 53

Bourget, Paul (Charles Joseph)
  1852-1935 .... **TCLC 12**
  See also CA 107; DLB 123

Bourjaily, Vance (Nye) 1922- .... **CLC 8, 62**
  See also CA 1-4R; CAAS 1; CANR 2;
  DLB 2, 143

Bourne, Randolph S(illiman)
  1886-1918 .... **TCLC 16**
  See also CA 117; 155; DLB 63

Bova, Ben(jamin William) 1932-.... **CLC 45**
  See also AAYA 16; CA 5-8R; CAAS 18;
  CANR 11, 56; CLR 3; DLBY 81;
  INT CANR-11; MAICYA; MTCW;
  SATA 6, 68

Bowen, Elizabeth (Dorothea Cole)
  1899-1973 ...... **CLC 1, 3, 6, 11, 15, 22;
    DAM NOV; SSC 3**
  See also CA 17-18; 41-44R; CANR 35;
  CAP 2; CDBLB 1945-1960; DLB 15, 162;
  MTCW

Bowering, George 1935-........ **CLC 15, 47**
  See also CA 21-24R; CAAS 16; CANR 10;
  DLB 53

Bowering, Marilyn R(uthe) 1949-... **CLC 32**
  See also CA 101; CANR 49

Bowers, Edgar 1924- .... **CLC 9**
  See also CA 5-8R; CANR 24; DLB 5

Bowie, David .... **CLC 17**
  See also Jones, David Robert

Bowles, Jane (Sydney)
  1917-1973 .... **CLC 3, 68**
  See also CA 19-20; 41-44R; CAP 2

Bowles, Paul (Frederick)
  1910- .... **CLC 1, 2, 19, 53; SSC 3**
  See also CA 1-4R; CAAS 1; CANR 1, 19,
  50; DLB 5, 6; MTCW

Box, Edgar
  See Vidal, Gore

Boyd, Nancy
  See Millay, Edna St. Vincent

Boyd, William 1952-........ **CLC 28, 53, 70**
  See also CA 114; 120; CANR 51

Boyle, Kay
  1902-1992 ..... **CLC 1, 5, 19, 58; SSC 5**
  See also CA 13-16R; 140; CAAS 1;
  CANR 29; DLB 4, 9, 48, 86; DLBY 93;
  MTCW

Boyle, Mark
  See Kienzle, William X(avier)

Boyle, Patrick 1905-1982......... **CLC 19**
  See also CA 127

Boyle, T. C. 1948-
  See Boyle, T(homas) Coraghessan

Boyle, T(homas) Coraghessan
  1948- ..... **CLC 36, 55, 90; DAM POP;
    SSC 16**
  See also BEST 90:4; CA 120; CANR 44;
  DLBY 86

Boz
  See Dickens, Charles (John Huffam)

Brackenridge, Hugh Henry
  1748-1816 .... **NCLC 7**
  See also DLB 11, 37

Bradbury, Edward P.
  See Moorcock, Michael (John)

Bradbury, Malcolm (Stanley)
  1932- .... **CLC 32, 61; DAM NOV**
  See also CA 1-4R; CANR 1, 33; DLB 14;
  MTCW

Bradbury, Ray (Douglas)
  1920- ..... **CLC 1, 3, 10, 15, 42, 98; DA;
    DAB; DAC; DAM MST, NOV, POP;
    WLC**
  See also AAYA 15; AITN 1, 2; CA 1-4R;
  CANR 2, 30; CDALB 1968-1988; DLB 2,
  8; INT CANR-30; MTCW; SATA 11, 64

Bradford, Gamaliel 1863-1932..... **TCLC 36**
  See also DLB 17

Bradley, David (Henry, Jr.)
  1950- ..... **CLC 23; BLC; DAM MULT**
  See also BW 1; CA 104; CANR 26; DLB 33

Bradley, John Ed(mund, Jr.)
  1958- .... **CLC 55**
  See also CA 139

Bradley, Marion Zimmer
  1930- .... **CLC 30; DAM POP**
  See also AAYA 9; CA 57-60; CAAS 10;
  CANR 7, 31, 51; DLB 8; MTCW;
  SATA 90

Bradstreet, Anne
  1612(?)-1672 ...... **LC 4, 30; DA; DAC;
    DAM MST, POET; PC 10**
  See also CDALB 1640-1865; DLB 24

Brady, Joan 1939- .... **CLC 86**
  See also CA 141

Broumas, Olga 1949- .... **CLC 10, 73**
See also CA 85-88; CANR 20

Brown, Alan 1951- .... **CLC 99**

Brown, Charles Brockden
1771-1810 .... **NCLC 22**
See also CDALB 1640-1865; DLB 37, 59, 73

Brown, Christy 1932-1981 .... **CLC 63**
See also CA 105; 104; DLB 14

Brown, Claude
1937- ..... **CLC 30; BLC; DAM MULT**
See also AAYA 7; BW 1; CA 73-76

Brown, Dee (Alexander)
1908- .... **CLC 18, 47; DAM POP**
See also CA 13-16R; CAAS 6; CANR 11, 45; DLBY 80; MTCW; SATA 5

Brown, George
See Wertmueller, Lina

Brown, George Douglas
1869-1902 .... **TCLC 28**

Brown, George Mackay
1921-1996 .... **CLC 5, 48, 100**
See also CA 21-24R; 151; CAAS 6; CANR 12, 37; DLB 14, 27, 139; MTCW; SATA 35

Brown, (William) Larry 1951- ...... **CLC 73**
See also CA 130; 134; INT 133

Brown, Moses
See Barrett, William (Christopher)

Brown, Rita Mae
1944- ..... **CLC 18, 43, 79; DAM NOV, POP**
See also CA 45-48; CANR 2, 11, 35; INT CANR-11; MTCW

Brown, Roderick (Langmere) Haig-
See Haig-Brown, Roderick (Langmere)

Brown, Rosellen 1939- .... **CLC 32**
See also CA 77-80; CAAS 10; CANR 14, 44

Brown, Sterling Allen
1901-1989 .... **CLC 1, 23, 59; BLC; DAM MULT, POET**
See also BW 1; CA 85-88; 127; CANR 26; DLB 48, 51, 63; MTCW

Brown, Will
See Ainsworth, William Harrison

Brown, William Wells
1813-1884 .... **NCLC 2; BLC; DAM MULT; DC 1**
See also DLB 3, 50

Browne, (Clyde) Jackson 1948(?)- ... **CLC 21**
See also CA 120

Browning, Elizabeth Barrett
1806-1861 .... **NCLC 1, 16, 61; DA; DAB; DAC; DAM MST, POET; PC 6; WLC**
See also CDBLB 1832-1890; DLB 32

Browning, Robert
1812-1889 .... **NCLC 19; DA; DAB; DAC; DAM MST, POET; PC 2**
See also CDBLB 1832-1890; DLB 32, 163; YABC 1

Browning, Tod 1882-1962 .... **CLC 16**
See also CA 141; 117

Brownson, Orestes (Augustus)
1803-1876 .... **NCLC 50**

Bruccoli, Matthew J(oseph) 1931- ... **CLC 34**
See also CA 9-12R; CANR 7; DLB 103

Bruce, Lenny .... **CLC 21**
See also Schneider, Leonard Alfred

Bruin, John
See Brutus, Dennis

Brulard, Henri
See Stendhal

Brulls, Christian
See Simenon, Georges (Jacques Christian)

Brunner, John (Kilian Houston)
1934-1995 ...... **CLC 8, 10; DAM POP**
See also CA 1-4R; 149; CAAS 8; CANR 2, 37; MTCW

Bruno, Giordano 1548-1600 .... **LC 27**

Brutus, Dennis
1924- ..... **CLC 43; BLC; DAM MULT, POET**
See also BW 2; CA 49-52; CAAS 14; CANR 2, 27, 42; DLB 117

Bryan, C(ourtlandt) D(ixon) B(arnes)
1936- .... **CLC 29**
See also CA 73-76; CANR 13; INT CANR-13

Bryan, Michael
See Moore, Brian

Bryant, William Cullen
1794-1878 ..... **NCLC 6, 46; DA; DAB; DAC; DAM MST, POET**
See also CDALB 1640-1865; DLB 3, 43, 59

Bryusov, Valery Yakovlevich
1873-1924 .... **TCLC 10**
See also CA 107; 155

Buchan, John
1875-1940 .... **TCLC 41; DAB; DAM POP**
See also CA 108; 145; DLB 34, 70, 156; YABC 2

Buchanan, George 1506-1582 .... **LC 4**

Buchheim, Lothar-Guenther 1918- ... **CLC 6**
See also CA 85-88

Buchner, (Karl) Georg
1813-1837 .... **NCLC 26**

Buchwald, Art(hur) 1925- .... **CLC 33**
See also AITN 1; CA 5-8R; CANR 21; MTCW; SATA 10

Buck, Pearl S(ydenstricker)
1892-1973 .... **CLC 7, 11, 18; DA; DAB; DAC; DAM MST, NOV**
See also AITN 1; CA 1-4R; 41-44R; CANR 1, 34; DLB 9, 102; MTCW; SATA 1, 25

Buckler, Ernest
1908-1984 .. **CLC 13; DAC; DAM MST**
See also CA 11-12; 114; CAP 1; DLB 68; SATA 47

Buckley, Vincent (Thomas)
1925-1988 .... **CLC 57**
See also CA 101

Buckley, William F(rank), Jr.
1925- .... **CLC 7, 18, 37; DAM POP**
See also AITN 1; CA 1-4R; CANR 1, 24, 53; DLB 137; DLBY 80; INT CANR-24; MTCW

Buechner, (Carl) Frederick
1926- ...... **CLC 2, 4, 6, 9; DAM NOV**
See also CA 13-16R; CANR 11, 39; DLBY 80; INT CANR-11; MTCW

Buell, John (Edward) 1927- .... **CLC 10**
See also CA 1-4R; DLB 53

Buero Vallejo, Antonio 1916- ... **CLC 15, 46**
See also CA 106; CANR 24, 49; HW; MTCW

Bufalino, Gesualdo 1920(?)- .... **CLC 74**

Bugayev, Boris Nikolayevich 1880-1934
See Bely, Andrey
See also CA 104

Bukowski, Charles
1920-1994 .... **CLC 2, 5, 9, 41, 82; DAM NOV, POET**
See also CA 17-20R; 144; CANR 40; DLB 5, 130, 169; MTCW

Bulgakov, Mikhail (Afanas'evich)
1891-1940 .... **TCLC 2, 16; DAM DRAM, NOV; SSC 18**
See also CA 105; 152

Bulgya, Alexander Alexandrovich
1901-1956 .... **TCLC 53**
See also Fadeyev, Alexander
See also CA 117

Bullins, Ed
1935- .... **CLC 1, 5, 7; BLC; DAM DRAM, MULT; DC 6**
See also BW 2; CA 49-52; CAAS 16; CANR 24, 46; DLB 7, 38; MTCW

Bulwer-Lytton, Edward (George Earle Lytton)
1803-1873 .... **NCLC 1, 45**
See also DLB 21

Bunin, Ivan Alexeyevich
1870-1953 .... **TCLC 6; SSC 5**
See also CA 104

Bunting, Basil
1900-1985 .... **CLC 10, 39, 47; DAM POET**
See also CA 53-56; 115; CANR 7; DLB 20

Bunuel, Luis
1900-1983 .... **CLC 16, 80; DAM MULT; HLC**
See also CA 101; 110; CANR 32; HW

Bunyan, John
1628-1688 ...... **LC 4; DA; DAB; DAC; DAM MST; WLC**
See also CDBLB 1660-1789; DLB 39

Burckhardt, Jacob (Christoph)
1818-1897 .... **NCLC 49**

Burford, Eleanor
See Hibbert, Eleanor Alice Burford

Burgess, Anthony
CLC 1, 2, 4, 5, 8, 10, 13, 15, 22, 40, 62, 81, 94; DAB
See also Wilson, John (Anthony) Burgess
See also AITN 1; CDBLB 1960 to Present; DLB 14

Burke, Edmund
1729(?)-1797 ...... **LC 7, 36; DA; DAB; DAC; DAM MST; WLC**
See also DLB 104

Burke, Kenneth (Duva)
1897-1993 . . . . **CLC 2, 24**
See also CA 5-8R; 143; CANR 39; DLB 45,
63; MTCW

Burke, Leda
See Garnett, David

Burke, Ralph
See Silverberg, Robert

Burke, Thomas 1886-1945 . . . . **TCLC 63**
See also CA 113; 155

Burney, Fanny 1752-1840 . . . . **NCLC 12, 54**
See also DLB 39

Burns, Robert 1759-1796 . . . . **PC 6**
See also CDBLB 1789-1832; DA; DAB;
DAC; DAM MST, POET; DLB 109;
WLC

Burns, Tex
See L'Amour, Louis (Dearborn)

Burnshaw, Stanley 1906- . . . . . **CLC 3, 13, 44**
See also CA 9-12R; DLB 48

Burr, Anne 1937- . . . . **CLC 6**
See also CA 25-28R

Burroughs, Edgar Rice
1875-1950 . . . . **TCLC 2, 32; DAM NOV**
See also AAYA 11; CA 104; 132; DLB 8;
MTCW; SATA 41

Burroughs, William S(eward)
1914- . . . . **CLC 1, 2, 5, 15, 22, 42, 75;**
DA; DAB; DAC; DAM MST, NOV,
POP; WLC
See also AITN 2; CA 9-12R; CANR 20, 52;
DLB 2, 8, 16, 152; DLBY 81; MTCW

Burton, Richard F. 1821-1890 . . . . **NCLC 42**
See also DLB 55

Busch, Frederick 1941- . . . **CLC 7, 10, 18, 47**
See also CA 33-36R; CAAS 1; CANR 45;
DLB 6

Bush, Ronald 1946- . . . . **CLC 34**
See also CA 136

Bustos, F(rancisco)
See Borges, Jorge Luis

Bustos Domecq, H(onorio)
See Bioy Casares, Adolfo; Borges, Jorge
Luis

Butler, Octavia E(stelle)
1947- . . . . . **CLC 38; DAM MULT, POP**
See also AAYA 18; BW 2; CA 73-76;
CANR 12, 24, 38; DLB 33; MTCW;
SATA 84

Butler, Robert Olen (Jr.)
1945- . . . . **CLC 81; DAM POP**
See also CA 112; DLB 173; INT 112

Butler, Samuel 1612-1680 . . . . **LC 16**
See also DLB 101, 126

Butler, Samuel
1835-1902 . . . . . . **TCLC 1, 33; DA; DAB;**
DAC; DAM MST, NOV; WLC
See also CA 143; CDBLB 1890-1914;
DLB 18, 57, 174

Butler, Walter C.
See Faust, Frederick (Schiller)

Butor, Michel (Marie Francois)
1926- . . . . **CLC 1, 3, 8, 11, 15**
See also CA 9-12R; CANR 33; DLB 83;
MTCW

Buzo, Alexander (John) 1944- . . . . . . **CLC 61**
See also CA 97-100; CANR 17, 39

Buzzati, Dino 1906-1972 . . . . **CLC 36**
See also CA 33-36R; DLB 177

Byars, Betsy (Cromer) 1928- . . . . **CLC 35**
See also AAYA 19; CA 33-36R; CANR 18,
36, 57; CLR 1, 16; DLB 52;
INT CANR-18; JRDA; MAICYA;
MTCW; SAAS 1; SATA 4, 46, 80

Byatt, A(ntonia) S(usan Drabble)
1936- . . . **CLC 19, 65; DAM NOV, POP**
See also CA 13-16R; CANR 13, 33, 50;
DLB 14; MTCW

Byrne, David 1952- . . . . **CLC 26**
See also CA 127

Byrne, John Keyes 1926-
See Leonard, Hugh
See also CA 102; INT 102

Byron, George Gordon (Noel)
1788-1824 . . . . . **NCLC 2, 12; DA; DAB;**
DAC; DAM MST, POET; PC 16; WLC
See also CDBLB 1789-1832; DLB 96, 110

Byron, Robert 1905-1941 . . . . **TCLC 67**

C. 3. 3.
See Wilde, Oscar (Fingal O'Flahertie Wills)

Caballero, Fernan 1796-1877 . . . . . **NCLC 10**

Cabell, Branch
See Cabell, James Branch

Cabell, James Branch 1879-1958 . . . **TCLC 6**
See also CA 105; 152; DLB 9, 78

Cable, George Washington
1844-1925 . . . . **TCLC 4; SSC 4**
See also CA 104; 155; DLB 12, 74;
DLBD 13

Cabral de Melo Neto, Joao
1920- . . . . **CLC 76; DAM MULT**
See also CA 151

Cabrera Infante, G(uillermo)
1929- . . . . . **CLC 5, 25, 45; DAM MULT;**
HLC
See also CA 85-88; CANR 29; DLB 113;
HW; MTCW

Cade, Toni
See Bambara, Toni Cade

Cadmus and Harmonia
See Buchan, John

Caedmon fl. 658-680 . . . . **CMLC 7**
See also DLB 146

Caeiro, Alberto
See Pessoa, Fernando (Antonio Nogueira)

Cage, John (Milton, Jr.) 1912- . . . . . **CLC 41**
See also CA 13-16R; CANR 9;
INT CANR-9

Cain, G.
See Cabrera Infante, G(uillermo)

Cain, Guillermo
See Cabrera Infante, G(uillermo)

Cain, James M(allahan)
1892-1977 . . . . **CLC 3, 11, 28**
See also AITN 1; CA 17-20R; 73-76;
CANR 8, 34; MTCW

Caine, Mark
See Raphael, Frederic (Michael)

Calasso, Roberto 1941- . . . . **CLC 81**
See also CA 143

Calderon de la Barca, Pedro
1600-1681 . . . . **LC 23; DC 3**

Caldwell, Erskine (Preston)
1903-1987 . . . . **CLC 1, 8, 14, 50, 60;**
DAM NOV; SSC 19
See also AITN 1; CA 1-4R; 121; CAAS 1;
CANR 2, 33; DLB 9, 86; MTCW

Caldwell, (Janet Miriam) Taylor (Holland)
1900-1985 . . . . **CLC 2, 28, 39;**
DAM NOV, POP
See also CA 5-8R; 116; CANR 5

Calhoun, John Caldwell
1782-1850 . . . . **NCLC 15**
See also DLB 3

Calisher, Hortense
1911- . . . . . **CLC 2, 4, 8, 38; DAM NOV;**
SSC 15
See also CA 1-4R; CANR 1, 22; DLB 2;
INT CANR-22; MTCW

Callaghan, Morley Edward
1903-1990 . . . . . **CLC 3, 14, 41, 65; DAC;**
DAM MST
See also CA 9-12R; 132; CANR 33;
DLB 68; MTCW

Callimachus
c. 305B.C.-c. 240B.C. . . . . **CMLC 18**
See also DLB 176

Calvin, John 1509-1564 . . . . **LC 37**

Calvino, Italo
1923-1985 . . . . . **CLC 5, 8, 11, 22, 33, 39,**
73; DAM NOV; SSC 3
See also CA 85-88; 116; CANR 23; MTCW

Cameron, Carey 1952- . . . . **CLC 59**
See also CA 135

Cameron, Peter 1959- . . . . **CLC 44**
See also CA 125; CANR 50

Campana, Dino 1885-1932 . . . . **TCLC 20**
See also CA 117; DLB 114

Campanella, Tommaso 1568-1639 . . . . **LC 32**

Campbell, John W(ood, Jr.)
1910-1971 . . . . **CLC 32**
See also CA 21-22; 29-32R; CANR 34;
CAP 2; DLB 8; MTCW

Campbell, Joseph 1904-1987 . . . . **CLC 69**
See also AAYA 3; BEST 89:2; CA 1-4R;
124; CANR 3, 28; MTCW

Campbell, Maria 1940- . . . . **CLC 85; DAC**
See also CA 102; CANR 54; NNAL

Campbell, (John) Ramsey
1946- . . . . **CLC 42; SSC 19**
See also CA 57-60; CANR 7; INT CANR-7

Campbell, (Ignatius) Roy (Dunnachie)
1901-1957 . . . . **TCLC 5**
See also CA 104; 155; DLB 20

Campbell, Thomas 1777-1844 . . . . **NCLC 19**
See also DLB 93; 144

Campbell, Wilfred . . . . **TCLC 9**
See also Campbell, William

Campbell, William 1858(?)-1918
See Campbell, Wilfred
See also CA 106; DLB 92

Campion, Jane . . . . **CLC 95**
See also CA 138

Campos, Alvaro de
See Pessoa, Fernando (Antonio Nogueira)

Camus, Albert
1913-1960 .... **CLC 1, 2, 4, 9, 11, 14, 32, 63, 69; DA; DAB; DAC; DAM DRAM, MST, NOV; DC 2; SSC 9; WLC**
See also CA 89-92; DLB 72; MTCW

Canby, Vincent 1924- .... **CLC 13**
See also CA 81-84

Cancale
See Desnos, Robert

Canetti, Elias
1905-1994 .... **CLC 3, 14, 25, 75, 86**
See also CA 21-24R; 146; CANR 23; DLB 85, 124; MTCW

Canin, Ethan 1960- .... **CLC 55**
See also CA 131; 135

Cannon, Curt
See Hunter, Evan

Cape, Judith
See Page, P(atricia) K(athleen)

Capek, Karel
1890-1938 ...... **TCLC 6, 37; DA; DAB; DAC; DAM DRAM, MST, NOV; DC 1; WLC**
See also CA 104; 140

Capote, Truman
1924-1984 ...... **CLC 1, 3, 8, 13, 19, 34, 38, 58; DA; DAB; DAC; DAM MST, NOV, POP; SSC 2; WLC**
See also CA 5-8R; 113; CANR 18; CDALB 1941-1968; DLB 2; DLBY 80, 84; MTCW; SATA 91

Capra, Frank 1897-1991.......... **CLC 16**
See also CA 61-64; 135

Caputo, Philip 1941- .... **CLC 32**
See also CA 73-76; CANR 40

Card, Orson Scott
1951- ...... **CLC 44, 47, 50; DAM POP**
See also AAYA 11; CA 102; CANR 27, 47; INT CANR-27; MTCW; SATA 83

Cardenal, Ernesto
1925- .... **CLC 31; DAM MULT, POET; HLC**
See also CA 49-52; CANR 2, 32; HW; MTCW

Cardozo, Benjamin N(athan)
1870-1938 .... **TCLC 65**
See also CA 117

Carducci, Giosue 1835-1907....... **TCLC 32**

Carew, Thomas 1595(?)-1640....... **LC 13**
See also DLB 126

Carey, Ernestine Gilbreth 1908- .... **CLC 17**
See also CA 5-8R; SATA 2

Carey, Peter 1943- .... **CLC 40, 55, 96**
See also CA 123; 127; CANR 53; INT 127; MTCW

Carleton, William 1794-1869...... **NCLC 3**
See also DLB 159

Carlisle, Henry (Coffin) 1926- ...... **CLC 33**
See also CA 13-16R; CANR 15

Carlsen, Chris
See Holdstock, Robert P.

Carlson, Ron(ald F.) 1947-......... **CLC 54**
See also CA 105; CANR 27

Carlyle, Thomas
1795-1881 ...... **NCLC 22; DA; DAB; DAC; DAM MST**
See also CDBLB 1789-1832; DLB 55; 144

Carman, (William) Bliss
1861-1929 .... **TCLC 7; DAC**
See also CA 104; 152; DLB 92

Carnegie, Dale 1888-1955 .... **TCLC 53**

Carossa, Hans 1878-1956........ **TCLC 48**
See also DLB 66

Carpenter, Don(ald Richard)
1931-1995 .... **CLC 41**
See also CA 45-48; 149; CANR 1

Carpentier (y Valmont), Alejo
1904-1980 .... **CLC 8, 11, 38; DAM MULT; HLC**
See also CA 65-68; 97-100; CANR 11; DLB 113; HW

Carr, Caleb 1955(?)-.............. **CLC 86**
See also CA 147

Carr, Emily 1871-1945.......... **TCLC 32**
See also DLB 68

Carr, John Dickson 1906-1977 ...... **CLC 3**
See also CA 49-52; 69-72; CANR 3, 33; MTCW

Carr, Philippa
See Hibbert, Eleanor Alice Burford

Carr, Virginia Spencer 1929-....... **CLC 34**
See also CA 61-64; DLB 111

Carrere, Emmanuel 1957- .... **CLC 89**

Carrier, Roch
1937- ... **CLC 13, 78; DAC; DAM MST**
See also CA 130; DLB 53

Carroll, James P. 1943(?)-......... **CLC 38**
See also CA 81-84

Carroll, Jim 1951- .... **CLC 35**
See also AAYA 17; CA 45-48; CANR 42

Carroll, Lewis .... **NCLC 2, 53; WLC**
See also Dodgson, Charles Lutwidge
See also CDBLB 1832-1890; CLR 2, 18; DLB 18, 163; JRDA

Carroll, Paul Vincent 1900-1968.... **CLC 10**
See also CA 9-12R; 25-28R; DLB 10

Carruth, Hayden
1921- ...... **CLC 4, 7, 10, 18, 84; PC 10**
See also CA 9-12R; CANR 4, 38; DLB 5, 165; INT CANR-4; MTCW; SATA 47

Carson, Rachel Louise
1907-1964 .... **CLC 71; DAM POP**
See also CA 77-80; CANR 35; MTCW; SATA 23

Carter, Angela (Olive)
1940-1992 ...... **CLC 5, 41, 76; SSC 13**
See also CA 53-56; 136; CANR 12, 36; DLB 14; MTCW; SATA 66; SATA-Obit 70

Carter, Nick
See Smith, Martin Cruz

Carver, Raymond
1938-1988 .... **CLC 22, 36, 53, 55; DAM NOV; SSC 8**
See also CA 33-36R; 126; CANR 17, 34; DLB 130; DLBY 84, 88; MTCW

Cary, Elizabeth, Lady Falkland
1585-1639 .... **LC 30**

Cary, (Arthur) Joyce (Lunel)
1888-1957 .... **TCLC 1, 29**
See also CA 104; CDBLB 1914-1945; DLB 15, 100

Casanova de Seingalt, Giovanni Jacopo
1725-1798 .... **LC 13**

Casares, Adolfo Bioy
See Bioy Casares, Adolfo

Casely-Hayford, J(oseph) E(phraim)
1866-1930 .... **TCLC 24; BLC; DAM MULT**
See also BW 2; CA 123; 152

Casey, John (Dudley) 1939-........ **CLC 59**
See also BEST 90:2; CA 69-72; CANR 23

Casey, Michael 1947-............. **CLC 2**
See also CA 65-68; DLB 5

Casey, Patrick
See Thurman, Wallace (Henry)

Casey, Warren (Peter) 1935-1988 ... **CLC 12**
See also CA 101; 127; INT 101

Casona, Alejandro................. **CLC 49**
See also Alvarez, Alejandro Rodriguez

Cassavetes, John 1929-1989....... **CLC 20**
See also CA 85-88; 127

Cassian, Nina 1924-.............. **PC 17**

Cassill, R(onald) V(erlin) 1919-... **CLC 4, 23**
See also CA 9-12R; CAAS 1; CANR 7, 45; DLB 6

Cassirer, Ernst 1874-1945 .... **TCLC 61**

Cassity, (Allen) Turner 1929- .... **CLC 6, 42**
See also CA 17-20R; CAAS 8; CANR 11; DLB 105

Castaneda, Carlos 1931(?)-......... **CLC 12**
See also CA 25-28R; CANR 32; HW; MTCW

Castedo, Elena 1937-............. **CLC 65**
See also CA 132

Castedo-Ellerman, Elena
See Castedo, Elena

Castellanos, Rosario
1925-1974 ...... **CLC 66; DAM MULT; HLC**
See also CA 131; 53-56; DLB 113; HW

Castelvetro, Lodovico 1505-1571..... **LC 12**

Castiglione, Baldassare 1478-1529 ... **LC 12**

Castle, Robert
See Hamilton, Edmond

Castro, Guillen de 1569-1631........ **LC 19**

Castro, Rosalia de
1837-1885 ...... **NCLC 3; DAM MULT**

Cather, Willa
See Cather, Willa Sibert

Cather, Willa Sibert
1873-1947 .... **TCLC 1, 11, 31; DA; DAB; DAC; DAM MST, NOV; SSC 2; WLC**
See also CA 104; 128; CDALB 1865-1917; DLB 9, 54, 78; DLBD 1; MTCW; SATA 30

Cato, Marcus Porcius
234B.C.-149B.C.............. **CMLC 21**

Chesnutt, Charles W(addell)
　1858-1932 .... **TCLC 5, 39; BLC;**
　　　　　　　　　DAM MULT; SSC 7
　See also BW 1; CA 106; 125; DLB 12, 50,
　　78; MTCW

Chester, Alfred　1929(?)-1971 ...... **CLC 49**
　See also CA 33-36R; DLB 130

Chesterton, G(ilbert) K(eith)
　1874-1936 .... **TCLC 1, 6, 64;**
　　　　　　　　DAM NOV, POET; SSC 1
　See also CA 104; 132; CDBLB 1914-1945;
　　DLB 10, 19, 34, 70, 98, 149; MTCW;
　　SATA 27

Chiang Pin-chin　1904-1986
　See Ding Ling
　See also CA 118

Ch'ien Chung-shu　1910- .... **CLC 22**
　See also CA 130; MTCW

Child, L. Maria
　See Child, Lydia Maria

Child, Lydia Maria　1802-1880 .... **NCLC 6**
　See also DLB 1, 74; SATA 67

Child, Mrs.
　See Child, Lydia Maria

Child, Philip　1898-1978 .... **CLC 19, 68**
　See also CA 13-14; CAP 1; SATA 47

Childers, (Robert) Erskine
　1870-1922 .... **TCLC 65**
　See also CA 113; 153; DLB 70

Childress, Alice
　1920-1994 .... **CLC 12, 15, 86, 96; BLC;**
　　　　　　DAM DRAM, MULT, NOV; DC 4
　See also AAYA 8; BW 2; CA 45-48; 146;
　　CANR 3, 27, 50; CLR 14; DLB 7, 38;
　　JRDA; MAICYA; MTCW; SATA 7, 48,
　　81

Chin, Frank (Chew, Jr.)　1940- .... **DC 7**
　See also CA 33-36R; DAM MULT

Chislett, (Margaret) Anne　1943- .... **CLC 34**
　See also CA 151

Chitty, Thomas Willes　1926- .... **CLC 11**
　See also Hinde, Thomas
　See also CA 5-8R

Chivers, Thomas Holley
　1809-1858 .... **NCLC 49**
　See also DLB 3

Chomette, Rene Lucien　1898-1981
　See Clair, Rene
　See also CA 103

Chopin, Kate
　........ **TCLC 5, 14; DA; DAB; SSC 8**
　See also Chopin, Katherine
　See also CDALB 1865-1917; DLB 12, 78

Chopin, Katherine　1851-1904
　See Chopin, Kate
　See also CA 104; 122; DAC; DAM MST,
　　NOV

Chretien de Troyes
　c. 12th cent. - .... **CMLC 10**

Christie
　See Ichikawa, Kon

Christie, Agatha (Mary Clarissa)
　1890-1976 ..... **CLC 1, 6, 8, 12, 39, 48;**
　　　　　　　　DAB; DAC; DAM NOV
　See also AAYA 9; AITN 1, 2; CA 17-20R;
　　61-64; CANR 10, 37; CDBLB 1914-1945;
　　DLB 13, 77; MTCW; SATA 36

Christie, (Ann) Philippa
　See Pearce, Philippa
　See also CA 5-8R; CANR 4

Christine de Pizan　1365(?)-1431(?) .... **LC 9**

Chubb, Elmer
　See Masters, Edgar Lee

Chulkov, Mikhail Dmitrievich
　1743-1792 .... **LC 2**
　See also DLB 150

Churchill, Caryl　1938- .... **CLC 31, 55; DC 5**
　See also CA 102; CANR 22, 46; DLB 13;
　　MTCW

Churchill, Charles　1731-1764 .... **LC 3**
　See also DLB 109

Chute, Carolyn　1947- .... **CLC 39**
　See also CA 123

Ciardi, John (Anthony)
　1916-1986 .... **CLC 10, 40, 44;**
　　　　　　　　　　　　　DAM POET
　See also CA 5-8R; 118; CAAS 2; CANR 5,
　　33; CLR 19; DLB 5; DLBY 86;
　　INT CANR-5; MAICYA; MTCW;
　　SATA 1, 65; SATA-Obit 46

Cicero, Marcus Tullius
　106B.C.-43B.C. .... **CMLC 3**

Cimino, Michael　1943- .... **CLC 16**
　See also CA 105

Cioran, E(mil) M.　1911-1995 .... **CLC 64**
　See also CA 25-28R; 149

Cisneros, Sandra
　1954- ..... **CLC 69; DAM MULT; HLC**
　See also AAYA 9; CA 131; DLB 122, 152;
　　HW

Cixous, Helene　1937- .... **CLC 92**
　See also CA 126; CANR 55; DLB 83;
　　MTCW

Clair, Rene .... **CLC 20**
　See also Chomette, Rene Lucien

Clampitt, Amy　1920-1994 .... **CLC 32**
　See also CA 110; 146; CANR 29; DLB 105

Clancy, Thomas L., Jr.　1947-
　See Clancy, Tom
　See also CA 125; 131; INT 131; MTCW

Clancy, Tom ..... **CLC 45; DAM NOV, POP**
　See also Clancy, Thomas L., Jr.
　See also AAYA 9; BEST 89:1, 90:1

Clare, John
　1793-1864 .... **NCLC 9; DAB;**
　　　　　　　　　　　　　DAM POET
　See also DLB 55, 96

Clarin
　See Alas (y Urena), Leopoldo (Enrique
　　Garcia)

Clark, Al C.
　See Goines, Donald

Clark, (Robert) Brian　1932- .... **CLC 29**
　See also CA 41-44R

Clark, Curt
　See Westlake, Donald E(dwin)

Clark, Eleanor　1913-1996 .... **CLC 5, 19**
　See also CA 9-12R; 151; CANR 41; DLB 6

Clark, J. P.
　See Clark, John Pepper
　See also DLB 117

Clark, John Pepper
　1935- .... **CLC 38; BLC; DAM DRAM,**
　　　　　　　　　　MULT; DC 5
　See also Clark, J. P.
　See also BW 1; CA 65-68; CANR 16

Clark, M. R.
　See Clark, Mavis Thorpe

Clark, Mavis Thorpe　1909- .... **CLC 12**
　See also CA 57-60; CANR 8, 37; CLR 30;
　　MAICYA; SAAS 5; SATA 8, 74

Clark, Walter Van Tilburg
　1909-1971 .... **CLC 28**
　See also CA 9-12R; 33-36R; DLB 9;
　　SATA 8

Clarke, Arthur C(harles)
　1917- .... **CLC 1, 4, 13, 18, 35;**
　　　　　　　　　　DAM POP; SSC 3
　See also AAYA 4; CA 1-4R; CANR 2, 28,
　　55; JRDA; MAICYA; MTCW; SATA 13,
　　70

Clarke, Austin
　1896-1974 ...... **CLC 6, 9; DAM POET**
　See also CA 29-32; 49-52; CAP 2; DLB 10,
　　20

Clarke, Austin C(hesterfield)
　1934- .... **CLC 8, 53; BLC; DAC;**
　　　　　　　　　　　　DAM MULT
　See also BW 1; CA 25-28R; CAAS 16;
　　CANR 14, 32; DLB 53, 125

Clarke, Gillian　1937- .... **CLC 61**
　See also CA 106; DLB 40

Clarke, Marcus (Andrew Hislop)
　1846-1881 .... **NCLC 19**

Clarke, Shirley　1925- .... **CLC 16**

Clash, The
　See Headon, (Nicky) Topper; Jones, Mick;
　　Simonon, Paul; Strummer, Joe

Claudel, Paul (Louis Charles Marie)
　1868-1955 .... **TCLC 2, 10**
　See also CA 104

Clavell, James (duMaresq)
　1925-1994 .... **CLC 6, 25, 87;**
　　　　　　　　　　DAM NOV, POP
　See also CA 25-28R; 146; CANR 26, 48;
　　MTCW

Cleaver, (Leroy) Eldridge
　1935- ..... **CLC 30; BLC; DAM MULT**
　See also BW 1; CA 21-24R; CANR 16

Cleese, John (Marwood)　1939- ..... **CLC 21**
　See also Monty Python
　See also CA 112; 116; CANR 35; MTCW

Cleishbotham, Jebediah
　See Scott, Walter

Cleland, John　1710-1789 .... **LC 2**
　See also DLB 39

Clemens, Samuel Langhorne　1835-1910
　See Twain, Mark
　See also CA 104; 135; CDALB 1865-1917;
　　DA; DAB; DAC; DAM MST, NOV;
　　DLB 11, 12, 23, 64, 74; JRDA;
　　MAICYA; YABC 2

Cleophil
See Congreve, William

Clerihew, E.
See Bentley, E(dmund) C(lerihew)

Clerk, N. W.
See Lewis, C(live) S(taples)

Cliff, Jimmy . . . . **CLC 21**
See also Chambers, James

Clifton, (Thelma) Lucille
1936- . . . . **CLC 19, 66; BLC;**
DAM MULT, POET; PC 17
See also BW 2; CA 49-52; CANR 2, 24, 42;
CLR 5; DLB 5, 41; MAICYA; MTCW;
SATA 20, 69

Clinton, Dirk
See Silverberg, Robert

Clough, Arthur Hugh   1819-1861 . . **NCLC 27**
See also DLB 32

Clutha, Janet Paterson Frame   1924-
See Frame, Janet
See also CA 1-4R; CANR 2, 36; MTCW

Clyne, Terence
See Blatty, William Peter

Cobalt, Martin
See Mayne, William (James Carter)

Cobbett, William   1763-1835 . . . . . **NCLC 49**
See also DLB 43, 107, 158

Coburn, D(onald) L(ee)   1938- . . . . . . **CLC 10**
See also CA 89-92

Cocteau, Jean (Maurice Eugene Clement)
1889-1963 . . . . **CLC 1, 8, 15, 16, 43; DA;**
DAB; DAC; DAM DRAM, MST, NOV;
WLC
See also CA 25-28; CANR 40; CAP 2;
DLB 65; MTCW

Codrescu, Andrei
1946- . . . . **CLC 46; DAM POET**
See also CA 33-36R; CAAS 19; CANR 13,
34, 53

Coe, Max
See Bourne, Randolph S(illiman)

Coe, Tucker
See Westlake, Donald E(dwin)

Coetzee, J(ohn) M(ichael)
1940- . . . . . . **CLC 23, 33, 66; DAM NOV**
See also CA 77-80; CANR 41, 54; MTCW

Coffey, Brian
See Koontz, Dean R(ay)

Cohan, George M.   1878-1942 . . . . . **TCLC 60**

Cohen, Arthur A(llen)
1928-1986 . . . . **CLC 7, 31**
See also CA 1-4R; 120; CANR 1, 17, 42;
DLB 28

Cohen, Leonard (Norman)
1934- . . . . **CLC 3, 38; DAC; DAM MST**
See also CA 21-24R; CANR 14; DLB 53;
MTCW

Cohen, Matt   1942- . . . . **CLC 19; DAC**
See also CA 61-64; CAAS 18; CANR 40;
DLB 53

Cohen-Solal, Annie   19(?)- . . . . **CLC 50**

Colegate, Isabel   1931- . . . . **CLC 36**
See also CA 17-20R; CANR 8, 22; DLB 14;
INT CANR-22; MTCW

Coleman, Emmett
See Reed, Ishmael

Coleridge, Samuel Taylor
1772-1834 . . . . . **NCLC 9, 54; DA; DAB;**
DAC; DAM MST, POET; PC 11; WLC
See also CDBLB 1789-1832; DLB 93, 107

Coleridge, Sara   1802-1852 . . . . **NCLC 31**

Coles, Don   1928- . . . . **CLC 46**
See also CA 115; CANR 38

Colette, (Sidonie-Gabrielle)
1873-1954 . . . . **TCLC 1, 5, 16;**
DAM NOV; SSC 10
See also CA 104; 131; DLB 65; MTCW

Collett, (Jacobine) Camilla (Wergeland)
1813-1895 . . . . **NCLC 22**

Collier, Christopher   1930- . . . . **CLC 30**
See also AAYA 13; CA 33-36R; CANR 13,
33; JRDA; MAICYA; SATA 16, 70

Collier, James L(incoln)
1928- . . . . **CLC 30; DAM POP**
See also AAYA 13; CA 9-12R; CANR 4,
33; CLR 3; JRDA; MAICYA; SAAS 21;
SATA 8, 70

Collier, Jeremy   1650-1726 . . . . **LC 6**

Collier, John   1901-1980 . . . . **SSC 19**
See also CA 65-68; 97-100; CANR 10;
DLB 77

Collingwood, R(obin) G(eorge)
1889(?)-1943 . . . . **TCLC 67**
See also CA 117; 155

Collins, Hunt
See Hunter, Evan

Collins, Linda   1931- . . . . **CLC 44**
See also CA 125

Collins, (William) Wilkie
1824-1889 . . . . **NCLC 1, 18**
See also CDBLB 1832-1890; DLB 18, 70,
159

Collins, William
1721-1759 . . . . **LC 4; DAM POET**
See also DLB 109

Collodi, Carlo   1826-1890 . . . . **NCLC 54**
See also Lorenzini, Carlo
See also CLR 5

Colman, George
See Glassco, John

Colt, Winchester Remington
See Hubbard, L(afayette) Ron(ald)

Colter, Cyrus   1910- . . . . **CLC 58**
See also BW 1; CA 65-68; CANR 10;
DLB 33

Colton, James
See Hansen, Joseph

Colum, Padraic   1881-1972 . . . . **CLC 28**
See also CA 73-76; 33-36R; CANR 35;
CLR 36; MAICYA; MTCW; SATA 15

Colvin, James
See Moorcock, Michael (John)

Colwin, Laurie (E.)
1944-1992 . . . . **CLC 5, 13, 23, 84**
See also CA 89-92; 139; CANR 20, 46;
DLBY 80; MTCW

Comfort, Alex(ander)
1920- . . . . **CLC 7; DAM POP**
See also CA 1-4R; CANR 1, 45

Comfort, Montgomery
See Campbell, (John) Ramsey

Compton-Burnett, I(vy)
1884(?)-1969 . . . . . . **CLC 1, 3, 10, 15, 34;**
DAM NOV
See also CA 1-4R; 25-28R; CANR 4;
DLB 36; MTCW

Comstock, Anthony   1844-1915 . . . . **TCLC 13**
See also CA 110

Comte, Auguste   1798-1857 . . . . **NCLC 54**

Conan Doyle, Arthur
See Doyle, Arthur Conan

Conde, Maryse
1937- . . . . **CLC 52, 92; DAM MULT**
See also Boucolon, Maryse
See also BW 2

Condillac, Etienne Bonnot de
1714-1780 . . . . **LC 26**

Condon, Richard (Thomas)
1915-1996 . . . . . **CLC 4, 6, 8, 10, 45, 100;**
DAM NOV
See also BEST 90:3; CA 1-4R; 151;
CAAS 1; CANR 2, 23; INT CANR-23;
MTCW

Confucius
551B.C.-479B.C. . . . . **CMLC 19; DA;**
DAB; DAC; DAM MST

Congreve, William
1670-1729 . . . . **LC 5, 21; DA; DAB;**
DAC; DAM DRAM, MST, POET;
DC 2; WLC
See also CDBLB 1660-1789; DLB 39, 84

Connell, Evan S(helby), Jr.
1924- . . . . **CLC 4, 6, 45; DAM NOV**
See also AAYA 7; CA 1-4R; CAAS 2;
CANR 2, 39; DLB 2; DLBY 81; MTCW

Connelly, Marc(us Cook)
1890-1980 . . . . **CLC 7**
See also CA 85-88; 102; CANR 30; DLB 7;
DLBY 80; SATA-Obit 25

Connor, Ralph . . . . **TCLC 31**
See also Gordon, Charles William
See also DLB 92

Conrad, Joseph
1857-1924 . . . . **TCLC 1, 6, 13, 25, 43, 57;**
DA; DAB; DAC; DAM MST, NOV;
SSC 9; WLC
See also CA 104; 131; CDBLB 1890-1914;
DLB 10, 34, 98, 156; MTCW; SATA 27

Conrad, Robert Arnold
See Hart, Moss

Conroy, Donald Pat(rick)
1945- . . . **CLC 30, 74; DAM NOV, POP**
See also AAYA 8; AITN 1; CA 85-88;
CANR 24, 53; DLB 6; MTCW

Constant (de Rebecque), (Henri) Benjamin
1767-1830 . . . . **NCLC 6**
See also DLB 119

Conybeare, Charles Augustus
See Eliot, T(homas) S(tearns)

Cook, Michael   1933- . . . . **CLC 58**
See also CA 93-96; DLB 53

Cook, Robin   1940- . . . . **CLC 14; DAM POP**
See also BEST 90:2; CA 108; 111;
CANR 41; INT 111

Cook, Roy
    See Silverberg, Robert

Cooke, Elizabeth   1948- .... **CLC 55**
    See also CA 129

Cooke, John Esten   1830-1886 ..... **NCLC 5**
    See also DLB 3

Cooke, John Estes
    See Baum, L(yman) Frank

Cooke, M. E.
    See Creasey, John

Cooke, Margaret
    See Creasey, John

Cook-Lynn, Elizabeth
    1930- .... **CLC 93; DAM MULT**
    See also CA 133; DLB 175; NNAL

Cooney, Ray .... **CLC 62**

Cooper, Douglas   1960- .... **CLC 86**

Cooper, Henry St. John
    See Creasey, John

Cooper, J(oan) California
    .... **CLC 56; DAM MULT**
    See also AAYA 12; BW 1; CA 125;
    CANR 55

Cooper, James Fenimore
    1789-1851 .... **NCLC 1, 27, 54**
    See also CDALB 1640-1865; DLB 3;
    SATA 19

Coover, Robert (Lowell)
    1932- .... **CLC 3, 7, 15, 32, 46, 87;
                                DAM NOV; SSC 15**
    See also CA 45-48; CANR 3, 37; DLB 2;
    DLBY 81; MTCW

Copeland, Stewart (Armstrong)
    1952- .... **CLC 26**

Coppard, A(lfred) E(dgar)
    1878-1957 .... **TCLC 5; SSC 21**
    See also CA 114; DLB 162; YABC 1

Coppee, Francois   1842-1908 ...... **TCLC 25**

Coppola, Francis Ford   1939- .... **CLC 16**
    See also CA 77-80; CANR 40; DLB 44

Corbiere, Tristan   1845-1875 ..... **NCLC 43**

Corcoran, Barbara   1911- .... **CLC 17**
    See also AAYA 14; CA 21-24R; CAAS 2;
    CANR 11, 28, 48; DLB 52; JRDA;
    SAAS 20; SATA 3, 77

Cordelier, Maurice
    See Giraudoux, (Hippolyte) Jean

Corelli, Marie   1855-1924 .... **TCLC 51**
    See also Mackay, Mary
    See also DLB 34, 156

Corman, Cid .... **CLC 9**
    See also Corman, Sidney
    See also CAAS 2; DLB 5

Corman, Sidney   1924-
    See Corman, Cid
    See also CA 85-88; CANR 44; DAM POET

Cormier, Robert (Edmund)
    1925- .... **CLC 12, 30; DA; DAB; DAC;
                                DAM MST, NOV**
    See also AAYA 3, 19; CA 1-4R; CANR 5,
    23; CDALB 1968-1988; CLR 12; DLB 52;
    INT CANR-23; JRDA; MAICYA;
    MTCW; SATA 10, 45, 83

Corn, Alfred (DeWitt III)   1943- .... **CLC 33**
    See also CA 104; CAAS 25; CANR 44;
    DLB 120; DLBY 80

Corneille, Pierre
    1606-1684 .... **LC 28; DAB; DAM MST**

Cornwell, David (John Moore)
    1931- .... **CLC 9, 15; DAM POP**
    See also le Carre, John
    See also CA 5-8R; CANR 13, 33; MTCW

Corso, (Nunzio) Gregory   1930- ... **CLC 1, 11**
    See also CA 5-8R; CANR 41; DLB 5, 16;
    MTCW

Cortazar, Julio
    1914-1984 ...... **CLC 2, 3, 5, 10, 13, 15,
            33, 34, 92; DAM MULT, NOV; HLC;
                                              SSC 7**
    See also CA 21-24R; CANR 12, 32;
    DLB 113; HW; MTCW

CORTES, HERNAN   1484-1547 ..... **LC 31**

Corwin, Cecil
    See Kornbluth, C(yril) M.

Cosic, Dobrica   1921- .... **CLC 14**
    See also CA 122; 138

Costain, Thomas B(ertram)
    1885-1965 .... **CLC 30**
    See also CA 5-8R; 25-28R; DLB 9

Costantini, Humberto
    1924(?)-1987 .... **CLC 49**
    See also CA 131; 122; HW

Costello, Elvis   1955- .... **CLC 21**

Cotter, Joseph Seamon Sr.
    1861-1949 .... **TCLC 28; BLC;
                                        DAM MULT**
    See also BW 1; CA 124; DLB 50

Couch, Arthur Thomas Quiller
    See Quiller-Couch, Arthur Thomas

Coulton, James
    See Hansen, Joseph

Couperus, Louis (Marie Anne)
    1863-1923 .... **TCLC 15**
    See also CA 115

Coupland, Douglas
    1961- .... **CLC 85; DAC; DAM POP**
    See also CA 142; CANR 57

Court, Wesli
    See Turco, Lewis (Putnam)

Courtenay, Bryce   1933- .... **CLC 59**
    See also CA 138

Courtney, Robert
    See Ellison, Harlan (Jay)

Cousteau, Jacques-Yves   1910- ...... **CLC 30**
    See also CA 65-68; CANR 15; MTCW;
    SATA 38

Coward, Noel (Peirce)
    1899-1973 .... **CLC 1, 9, 29, 51;
                                        DAM DRAM**
    See also AITN 1; CA 17-18; 41-44R;
    CANR 35; CAP 2; CDBLB 1914-1945;
    DLB 10; MTCW

Cowley, Malcolm   1898-1989 .... **CLC 39**
    See also CA 5-8R; 128; CANR 3, 55;
    DLB 4, 48; DLBY 81, 89; MTCW

Cowper, William
    1731-1800 ...... **NCLC 8; DAM POET**
    See also DLB 104, 109

Cox, William Trevor
    1928- .... **CLC 9, 14, 71; DAM NOV**
    See also Trevor, William
    See also CA 9-12R; CANR 4, 37, 55;
    DLB 14; INT CANR-37; MTCW

Coyne, P. J.
    See Masters, Hilary

Cozzens, James Gould
    1903-1978 .... **CLC 1, 4, 11, 92**
    See also CA 9-12R; 81-84; CANR 19;
    CDALB 1941-1968; DLB 9; DLBD 2;
    DLBY 84; MTCW

Crabbe, George   1754-1832 .... **NCLC 26**
    See also DLB 93

Craddock, Charles Egbert
    See Murfree, Mary Noailles

Craig, A. A.
    See Anderson, Poul (William)

Craik, Dinah Maria (Mulock)
    1826-1887 .... **NCLC 38**
    See also DLB 35, 163; MAICYA; SATA 34

Cram, Ralph Adams   1863-1942 .... **TCLC 45**

Crane, (Harold) Hart
    1899-1932 .... **TCLC 2, 5; DA; DAB;
            DAC; DAM MST, POET; PC 3; WLC**
    See also CA 104; 127; CDALB 1917-1929;
    DLB 4, 48; MTCW

Crane, R(onald) S(almon)
    1886-1967 .... **CLC 27**
    See also CA 85-88; DLB 63

Crane, Stephen (Townley)
    1871-1900 .... **TCLC 11, 17, 32; DA;
            DAB; DAC; DAM MST, NOV, POET;
                                        SSC 7; WLC**
    See also AAYA 21; CA 109; 140;
    CDALB 1865-1917; DLB 12, 54, 78;
    YABC 2

Crase, Douglas   1944- .... **CLC 58**
    See also CA 106

Crashaw, Richard   1612(?)-1649 ...... **LC 24**
    See also DLB 126

Craven, Margaret
    1901-1980 .... **CLC 17; DAC**
    See also CA 103

Crawford, F(rancis) Marion
    1854-1909 .... **TCLC 10**
    See also CA 107; DLB 71

Crawford, Isabella Valancy
    1850-1887 .... **NCLC 12**
    See also DLB 92

Crayon, Geoffrey
    See Irving, Washington

Creasey, John   1908-1973 .... **CLC 11**
    See also CA 5-8R; 41-44R; CANR 8;
    DLB 77; MTCW

Crebillon, Claude Prosper Jolyot de (fils)
    1707-1777 .... **LC 28**

Credo
    See Creasey, John

Creeley, Robert (White)
    1926- ..... **CLC 1, 2, 4, 8, 11, 15, 36, 78;
                                        DAM POET**
    See also CA 1-4R; CAAS 10; CANR 23, 43;
    DLB 5, 16, 169; MTCW

Daudet, (Louis Marie) Alphonse
1840-1897 . . . . **NCLC 1**
See also DLB 123

Daumal, Rene 1908-1944 . . . . **TCLC 14**
See also CA 114

Davenport, Guy (Mattison, Jr.)
1927- . . . . **CLC 6, 14, 38; SSC 16**
See also CA 33-36R; CANR 23; DLB 130

Davidson, Avram 1923-
See Queen, Ellery
See also CA 101; CANR 26; DLB 8

Davidson, Donald (Grady)
1893-1968 . . . . **CLC 2, 13, 19**
See also CA 5-8R; 25-28R; CANR 4;
DLB 45

Davidson, Hugh
See Hamilton, Edmond

Davidson, John 1857-1909 . . . . **TCLC 24**
See also CA 118; DLB 19

Davidson, Sara 1943- . . . . **CLC 9**
See also CA 81-84; CANR 44

Davie, Donald (Alfred)
1922-1995 . . . . **CLC 5, 8, 10, 31**
See also CA 1-4R; 149; CAAS 3; CANR 1,
44; DLB 27; MTCW

Davies, Ray(mond Douglas) 1944- . . **CLC 21**
See also CA 116; 146

Davies, Rhys 1903-1978 . . . . **CLC 23**
See also CA 9-12R; 81-84; CANR 4;
DLB 139

Davies, (William) Robertson
1913-1995 . . . . . **CLC 2, 7, 13, 25, 42, 75,
91; DA; DAB; DAC; DAM MST, NOV,
POP; WLC**
See also BEST 89:2; CA 33-36R; 150;
CANR 17, 42; DLB 68; INT CANR-17;
MTCW

Davies, W(illiam) H(enry)
1871-1940 . . . . **TCLC 5**
See also CA 104; DLB 19, 174

Davies, Walter C.
See Kornbluth, C(yril) M.

Davis, Angela (Yvonne)
1944- . . . . **CLC 77; DAM MULT**
See also BW 2; CA 57-60; CANR 10

Davis, B. Lynch
See Bioy Casares, Adolfo; Borges, Jorge
Luis

Davis, Gordon
See Hunt, E(verette) Howard, (Jr.)

Davis, Harold Lenoir 1896-1960 . . . . **CLC 49**
See also CA 89-92; DLB 9

Davis, Rebecca (Blaine) Harding
1831-1910 . . . . **TCLC 6**
See also CA 104; DLB 74

Davis, Richard Harding
1864-1916 . . . . **TCLC 24**
See also CA 114; DLB 12, 23, 78, 79;
DLBD 13

Davison, Frank Dalby 1893-1970 . . . **CLC 15**
See also CA 116

Davison, Lawrence H.
See Lawrence, D(avid) H(erbert Richards)

Davison, Peter (Hubert) 1928- . . . . . **CLC 28**
See also CA 9-12R; CAAS 4; CANR 3, 43;
DLB 5

Davys, Mary 1674-1732 . . . . **LC 1**
See also DLB 39

Dawson, Fielding 1930- . . . . **CLC 6**
See also CA 85-88; DLB 130

Dawson, Peter
See Faust, Frederick (Schiller)

Day, Clarence (Shepard, Jr.)
1874-1935 . . . . **TCLC 25**
See also CA 108; DLB 11

Day, Thomas 1748-1789 . . . . **LC 1**
See also DLB 39; YABC 1

Day Lewis, C(ecil)
1904-1972 . . . . **CLC 1, 6, 10;
DAM POET; PC 11**
See also Blake, Nicholas
See also CA 13-16; 33-36R; CANR 34;
CAP 1; DLB 15, 20; MTCW

Dazai, Osamu . . . . **TCLC 11**
See also Tsushima, Shuji

de Andrade, Carlos Drummond
See Drummond de Andrade, Carlos

Deane, Norman
See Creasey, John

**de Beauvoir, Simone (Lucie Ernestine Marie
Bertrand)**
See Beauvoir, Simone (Lucie Ernestine
Marie Bertrand) de

de Brissac, Malcolm
See Dickinson, Peter (Malcolm)

de Chardin, Pierre Teilhard
See Teilhard de Chardin, (Marie Joseph)
Pierre

Dee, John 1527-1608 . . . . **LC 20**

Deer, Sandra 1940- . . . . **CLC 45**

De Ferrari, Gabriella 1941- . . . . **CLC 65**
See also CA 146

Defoe, Daniel
1660(?)-1731 . . . . **LC 1; DA; DAB; DAC;
DAM MST, NOV; WLC**
See also CDBLB 1660-1789; DLB 39, 95,
101; JRDA; MAICYA; SATA 22

de Gourmont, Remy(-Marie-Charles)
See Gourmont, Remy (-Marie-Charles) de

de Hartog, Jan 1914- . . . . **CLC 19**
See also CA 1-4R; CANR 1

de Hostos, E. M.
See Hostos (y Bonilla), Eugenio Maria de

de Hostos, Eugenio M.
See Hostos (y Bonilla), Eugenio Maria de

Deighton, Len . . . . **CLC 4, 7, 22, 46**
See also Deighton, Leonard Cyril
See also AAYA 6; BEST 89:2;
CDBLB 1960 to Present; DLB 87

Deighton, Leonard Cyril 1929-
See Deighton, Len
See also CA 9-12R; CANR 19, 33;
DAM NOV, POP; MTCW

Dekker, Thomas
1572(?)-1632 . . . . . **LC 22; DAM DRAM**
See also CDBLB Before 1660; DLB 62, 172

Delafield, E. M. 1890-1943 . . . . **TCLC 61**
See also Dashwood, Edmee Elizabeth
Monica de la Pasture
See also DLB 34

de la Mare, Walter (John)
1873-1956 . . . . **TCLC 4, 53; DAB; DAC;
DAM MST, POET; SSC 14; WLC**
See also CDBLB 1914-1945; CLR 23;
DLB 162; SATA 16

Delaney, Franey
See O'Hara, John (Henry)

Delaney, Shelagh
1939- . . . . **CLC 29; DAM DRAM**
See also CA 17-20R; CANR 30;
CDBLB 1960 to Present; DLB 13;
MTCW

Delany, Mary (Granville Pendarves)
1700-1788 . . . . **LC 12**

Delany, Samuel R(ay, Jr.)
1942- . . . . **CLC 8, 14, 38; BLC;
DAM MULT**
See also BW 2; CA 81-84; CANR 27, 43;
DLB 8, 33; MTCW

De La Ramee, (Marie) Louise 1839-1908
See Ouida
See also SATA 20

de la Roche, Mazo 1879-1961 . . . . . . **CLC 14**
See also CA 85-88; CANR 30; DLB 68;
SATA 64

Delbanco, Nicholas (Franklin)
1942- . . . . **CLC 6, 13**
See also CA 17-20R; CAAS 2; CANR 29,
55; DLB 6

del Castillo, Michel 1933- . . . . **CLC 38**
See also CA 109

Deledda, Grazia (Cosima)
1875(?)-1936 . . . . **TCLC 23**
See also CA 123

Delibes, Miguel . . . . **CLC 8, 18**
See also Delibes Setien, Miguel

Delibes Setien, Miguel 1920-
See Delibes, Miguel
See also CA 45-48; CANR 1, 32; HW;
MTCW

DeLillo, Don
1936- . . . . . **CLC 8, 10, 13, 27, 39, 54, 76;
DAM NOV, POP**
See also BEST 89:1; CA 81-84; CANR 21;
DLB 6, 173; MTCW

de Lisser, H. G.
See De Lisser, H(erbert) G(eorge)
See also DLB 117

De Lisser, H(erbert) G(eorge)
1878-1944 . . . . **TCLC 12**
See also de Lisser, H. G.
See also BW 2; CA 109; 152

Deloria, Vine (Victor), Jr.
1933- . . . . **CLC 21; DAM MULT**
See also CA 53-56; CANR 5, 20, 48;
DLB 175; MTCW; NNAL; SATA 21

Del Vecchio, John M(ichael)
1947- . . . . **CLC 29**
See also CA 110; DLBD 9

de Man, Paul (Adolph Michel)
1919-1983 . . . . **CLC 55**
See also CA 128; 111; DLB 67; MTCW

De Marinis, Rick 1934-.......... **CLC 54**
See also CA 57-60; CAAS 24; CANR 9, 25, 50

Dembry, R. Emmet
See Murfree, Mary Noailles

Demby, William
1922- ..... **CLC 53; BLC; DAM MULT**
See also BW 1; CA 81-84; DLB 33

de Menton, Francisco
See Chin, Frank (Chew, Jr.)

Demijohn, Thom
See Disch, Thomas M(ichael)

de Montherlant, Henry (Milon)
See Montherlant, Henry (Milon) de

Demosthenes 384B.C.-322B.C. ... **CMLC 13**
See also DLB 176

de Natale, Francine
See Malzberg, Barry N(athaniel)

Denby, Edwin (Orr) 1903-1983..... **CLC 48**
See also CA 138; 110

Denis, Julio
See Cortazar, Julio

Denmark, Harrison
See Zelazny, Roger (Joseph)

Dennis, John 1658-1734........... **LC 11**
See also DLB 101

Dennis, Nigel (Forbes) 1912-1989.... **CLC 8**
See also CA 25-28R; 129; DLB 13, 15;
MTCW

De Palma, Brian (Russell) 1940-.... **CLC 20**
See also CA 109

De Quincey, Thomas 1785-1859 ... **NCLC 4**
See also CDBLB 1789-1832; DLB 110; 144

Deren, Eleanora 1908(?)-1961
See Deren, Maya
See also CA 111

Deren, Maya .... **CLC 16**
See also Deren, Eleanora

Derleth, August (William)
1909-1971 .... **CLC 31**
See also CA 1-4R; 29-32R; CANR 4;
DLB 9; SATA 5

Der Nister 1884-1950........... **TCLC 56**

de Routisie, Albert
See Aragon, Louis

Derrida, Jacques 1930-........ **CLC 24, 87**
See also CA 124; 127

Derry Down Derry
See Lear, Edward

Dersonnes, Jacques
See Simenon, Georges (Jacques Christian)

Desai, Anita
1937- .... **CLC 19, 37, 97; DAB;
DAM NOV**
See also CA 81-84; CANR 33, 53; MTCW;
SATA 63

de Saint-Luc, Jean
See Glassco, John

de Saint Roman, Arnaud
See Aragon, Louis

Descartes, Rene 1596-1650 ...... **LC 20, 35**

De Sica, Vittorio 1901(?)-1974 ..... **CLC 20**
See also CA 117

Desnos, Robert 1900-1945....... **TCLC 22**
See also CA 121; 151

Destouches, Louis-Ferdinand
1894-1961 .... **CLC 9, 15**
See also Celine, Louis-Ferdinand
See also CA 85-88; CANR 28; MTCW

de Tolignac, Gaston
See Griffith, D(avid Lewelyn) W(ark)

Deutsch, Babette 1895-1982 .... **CLC 18**
See also CA 1-4R; 108; CANR 4; DLB 45;
SATA 1; SATA-Obit 33

Devenant, William 1606-1649 ...... **LC 13**

Devkota, Laxmiprasad
1909-1959 .... **TCLC 23**
See also CA 123

De Voto, Bernard (Augustine)
1897-1955 .... **TCLC 29**
See also CA 113; DLB 9

De Vries, Peter
1910-1993 .... **CLC 1, 2, 3, 7, 10, 28, 46;
DAM NOV**
See also CA 17-20R; 142; CANR 41;
DLB 6; DLBY 82; MTCW

Dexter, John
See Bradley, Marion Zimmer

Dexter, Martin
See Faust, Frederick (Schiller)

Dexter, Pete
1943- .... **CLC 34, 55; DAM POP**
See also BEST 89:2; CA 127; 131; INT 131;
MTCW

Diamano, Silmang
See Senghor, Leopold Sedar

Diamond, Neil 1941- .... **CLC 30**
See also CA 108

Diaz del Castillo, Bernal 1496-1584.. **LC 31**

di Bassetto, Corno
See Shaw, George Bernard

Dick, Philip K(indred)
1928-1982 .... **CLC 10, 30, 72;
DAM NOV, POP**
See also CA 49-52; 106; CANR 2, 16;
DLB 8; MTCW

Dickens, Charles (John Huffam)
1812-1870 ...... **NCLC 3, 8, 18, 26, 37,
50; DA; DAB; DAC; DAM MST, NOV;
SSC 17; WLC**
See also CDBLB 1832-1890; DLB 21, 55,
70, 159, 166; JRDA; MAICYA; SATA 15

Dickey, James (Lafayette)
1923-1997 .... **CLC 1, 2, 4, 7, 10, 15, 47;
DAM NOV, POET, POP**
See also AITN 1, 2; CA 9-12R; 156;
CABS 2; CANR 10, 48;
CDALB 1968-1988; DLB 5; DLBD 7;
DLBY 82, 93; INT CANR-10; MTCW

Dickey, William 1928-1994...... **CLC 3, 28**
See also CA 9-12R; 145; CANR 24; DLB 5

Dickinson, Charles 1951-.......... **CLC 49**
See also CA 128

Dickinson, Emily (Elizabeth)
1830-1886 .... **NCLC 21; DA; DAB;
DAC; DAM MST, POET; PC 1; WLC**
See also CDALB 1865-1917; DLB 1;
SATA 29

Dickinson, Peter (Malcolm)
1927-.................... **CLC 12, 35**
See also AAYA 9; CA 41-44R; CANR 31;
CLR 29; DLB 87, 161; JRDA; MAICYA;
SATA 5, 62

Dickson, Carr
See Carr, John Dickson

Dickson, Carter
See Carr, John Dickson

Diderot, Denis 1713-1784 .... **LC 26**

Didion, Joan
1934- .. **CLC 1, 3, 8, 14, 32; DAM NOV**
See also AITN 1; CA 5-8R; CANR 14, 52;
CDALB 1968-1988; DLB 2, 173;
DLBY 81, 86; MTCW

Dietrich, Robert
See Hunt, E(verette) Howard, (Jr.)

Dillard, Annie
1945- .... **CLC 9, 60; DAM NOV**
See also AAYA 6; CA 49-52; CANR 3, 43;
DLBY 80; MTCW; SATA 10

Dillard, R(ichard) H(enry) W(ilde)
1937- .... **CLC 5**
See also CA 21-24R; CAAS 7; CANR 10;
DLB 5

Dillon, Eilis 1920-1994........... **CLC 17**
See also CA 9-12R; 147; CAAS 3; CANR 4,
38; CLR 26; MAICYA; SATA 2, 74;
SATA-Obit 83

Dimont, Penelope
See Mortimer, Penelope (Ruth)

Dinesen, Isak........ CLC 10, 29, 95; SSC 7
See also Blixen, Karen (Christentze
Dinesen)

Ding Ling....................... CLC 68
See also Chiang Pin-chin

Disch, Thomas M(ichael) 1940-... **CLC 7, 36**
See also AAYA 17; CA 21-24R; CAAS 4;
CANR 17, 36, 54; CLR 18; DLB 8;
MAICYA; MTCW; SAAS 15; SATA 92

Disch, Tom
See Disch, Thomas M(ichael)

d'Isly, Georges
See Simenon, Georges (Jacques Christian)

Disraeli, Benjamin 1804-1881 .. **NCLC 2, 39**
See also DLB 21, 55

Ditcum, Steve
See Crumb, R(obert)

Dixon, Paige
See Corcoran, Barbara

Dixon, Stephen 1936-..... **CLC 52; SSC 16**
See also CA 89-92; CANR 17, 40, 54;
DLB 130

Dobell, Sydney Thompson
1824-1874 .... **NCLC 43**
See also DLB 32

Doblin, Alfred .... TCLC 13
See also Doeblin, Alfred

Dobrolyubov, Nikolai Alexandrovich
1836-1861 .... **NCLC 5**

Dobyns, Stephen 1941-........... **CLC 37**
See also CA 45-48; CANR 2, 18

Doctorow, E(dgar) L(aurence)
　　1931- ..... **CLC 6, 11, 15, 18, 37, 44, 65;**
　　　　　　　　　　　　　　　　DAM NOV, POP
　　See also AITN 2; BEST 89:3; CA 45-48;
　　　CANR 2, 33, 51; CDALB 1968-1988;
　　　DLB 2, 28, 173; DLBY 80; MTCW

Dodgson, Charles Lutwidge　1832-1898
　　See Carroll, Lewis
　　See also CLR 2; DA; DAB; DAC;
　　　DAM MST, NOV, POET; MAICYA;
　　　YABC 2

Dodson, Owen (Vincent)
　　1914-1983 .... **CLC 79; BLC;**
　　　　　　　　　　　　　　　　DAM MULT
　　See also BW 1; CA 65-68; 110; CANR 24;
　　　DLB 76

Doeblin, Alfred　1878-1957 .... **TCLC 13**
　　See also Doblin, Alfred
　　See also CA 110; 141; DLB 66

Doerr, Harriet　1910- .... **CLC 34**
　　See also CA 117; 122; CANR 47; INT 122

Domecq, H(onorio) Bustos
　　See Bioy Casares, Adolfo; Borges, Jorge
　　　Luis

Domini, Rey
　　See Lorde, Audre (Geraldine)

Dominique
　　See Proust, (Valentin-Louis-George-Eugene-)
　　　Marcel

Don, A
　　See Stephen, Leslie

Donaldson, Stephen R.
　　1947- .... **CLC 46; DAM POP**
　　See also CA 89-92; CANR 13, 55;
　　　INT CANR-13

Donleavy, J(ames) P(atrick)
　　1926- .... **CLC 1, 4, 6, 10, 45**
　　See also AITN 2; CA 9-12R; CANR 24, 49;
　　　DLB 6, 173; INT CANR-24; MTCW

Donne, John
　　1572-1631 .... **LC 10, 24; DA; DAB;**
　　　　　　　　　DAC; DAM MST, POET; PC 1
　　See also CDBLB Before 1660; DLB 121,
　　　151

Donnell, David　1939(?)- .... **CLC 34**

Donoghue, P. S.
　　See Hunt, E(verette) Howard, (Jr.)

Donoso (Yanez), Jose
　　1924-1996 .... **CLC 4, 8, 11, 32, 99;**
　　　　　　　　　　　　　　DAM MULT; HLC
　　See also CA 81-84; 155; CANR 32;
　　　DLB 113; HW; MTCW

Donovan, John　1928-1992 .... **CLC 35**
　　See also AAYA 20; CA 97-100; 137;
　　　CLR 3; MAICYA; SATA 72;
　　　SATA-Brief 29

Don Roberto
　　See Cunninghame Graham, R(obert)
　　　B(ontine)

Doolittle, Hilda
　　1886-1961 ..... **CLC 3, 8, 14, 31, 34, 73;**
　　　　　　　　DA; DAC; DAM MST, POET; PC 5;
　　　　　　　　　　　　　　　　　　WLC
　　See also H. D.
　　See also CA 97-100; CANR 35; DLB 4, 45;
　　　MTCW

Dorfman, Ariel
　　1942- .... **CLC 48, 77; DAM MULT;**
　　　　　　　　　　　　　　　　　　HLC
　　See also CA 124; 130; HW; INT 130

Dorn, Edward (Merton)　1929-... **CLC 10, 18**
　　See also CA 93-96; CANR 42; DLB 5;
　　　INT 93-96

Dorsan, Luc
　　See Simenon, Georges (Jacques Christian)

Dorsange, Jean
　　See Simenon, Georges (Jacques Christian)

Dos Passos, John (Roderigo)
　　1896-1970 ..... **CLC 1, 4, 8, 11, 15, 25,**
　　　　　　　34, 82; DA; DAB; DAC; DAM MST,
　　　　　　　　　　　　　　　　NOV; WLC
　　See also CA 1-4R; 29-32R; CANR 3;
　　　CDALB 1929-1941; DLB 4, 9; DLBD 1;
　　　MTCW

Dossage, Jean
　　See Simenon, Georges (Jacques Christian)

Dostoevsky, Fedor Mikhailovich
　　1821-1881 ..... **NCLC 2, 7, 21, 33, 43;**
　　　　　　　DA; DAB; DAC; DAM MST, NOV;
　　　　　　　　　　　　　　　SSC 2; WLC

Doughty, Charles M(ontagu)
　　1843-1926 .... **TCLC 27**
　　See also CA 115; DLB 19, 57, 174

Douglas, Ellen .... **CLC 73**
　　See also Haxton, Josephine Ayres;
　　　Williamson, Ellen Douglas

Douglas, Gavin　1475(?)-1522 ...... **LC 20**

Douglas, Keith　1920-1944 .... **TCLC 40**
　　See also DLB 27

Douglas, Leonard
　　See Bradbury, Ray (Douglas)

Douglas, Michael
　　See Crichton, (John) Michael

Douglas, Norman　1868-1952 ...... **TCLC 68**

Douglass, Frederick
　　1817(?)-1895 .... **NCLC 7, 55; BLC; DA;**
　　　　　　　　DAC; DAM MST, MULT; WLC
　　See also CDALB 1640-1865; DLB 1, 43, 50,
　　　79; SATA 29

Dourado, (Waldomiro Freitas) Autran
　　1926- .... **CLC 23, 60**
　　See also CA 25-28R; CANR 34

Dourado, Waldomiro Autran
　　See Dourado, (Waldomiro Freitas) Autran

Dove, Rita (Frances)
　　1952- .... **CLC 50, 81; DAM MULT,**
　　　　　　　　　　　　　　　　POET; PC 6
　　See also BW 2; CA 109; CAAS 19;
　　　CANR 27, 42; DLB 120

Dowell, Coleman　1925-1985 .... **CLC 60**
　　See also CA 25-28R; 117; CANR 10;
　　　DLB 130

Dowson, Ernest (Christopher)
　　1867-1900 .... **TCLC 4**
　　See also CA 105; 150; DLB 19, 135

Doyle, A. Conan
　　See Doyle, Arthur Conan

Doyle, Arthur Conan
　　1859-1930 .... **TCLC 7; DA; DAB;**
　　　　　　　DAC; DAM MST, NOV; SSC 12; WLC
　　See also AAYA 14; CA 104; 122;
　　　CDBLB 1890-1914; DLB 18, 70, 156;
　　　MTCW; SATA 24

Doyle, Conan
　　See Doyle, Arthur Conan

Doyle, John
　　See Graves, Robert (von Ranke)

Doyle, Roddy　1958(?)- .... **CLC 81**
　　See also AAYA 14; CA 143

Doyle, Sir A. Conan
　　See Doyle, Arthur Conan

Doyle, Sir Arthur Conan
　　See Doyle, Arthur Conan

Dr. A
　　See Asimov, Isaac; Silverstein, Alvin

Drabble, Margaret
　　1939- .... **CLC 2, 3, 5, 8, 10, 22, 53;**
　　　　　　　DAB; DAC; DAM MST, NOV, POP
　　See also CA 13-16R; CANR 18, 35;
　　　CDBLB 1960 to Present; DLB 14, 155;
　　　MTCW; SATA 48

Drapier, M. B.
　　See Swift, Jonathan

Drayham, James
　　See Mencken, H(enry) L(ouis)

Drayton, Michael　1563-1631 .... **LC 8**

Dreadstone, Carl
　　See Campbell, (John) Ramsey

Dreiser, Theodore (Herman Albert)
　　1871-1945 .... **TCLC 10, 18, 35; DA;**
　　　　　　　DAC; DAM MST, NOV; WLC
　　See also CA 106; 132; CDALB 1865-1917;
　　　DLB 9, 12, 102, 137; DLBD 1; MTCW

Drexler, Rosalyn　1926- .... **CLC 2, 6**
　　See also CA 81-84

Dreyer, Carl Theodor　1889-1968.... **CLC 16**
　　See also CA 116

Drieu la Rochelle, Pierre(-Eugene)
　　1893-1945 .... **TCLC 21**
　　See also CA 117; DLB 72

Drinkwater, John　1882-1937 ...... **TCLC 57**
　　See also CA 109; 149; DLB 10, 19, 149

Drop Shot
　　See Cable, George Washington

Droste-Hulshoff, Annette Freiin von
　　1797-1848 .... **NCLC 3**
　　See also DLB 133

Drummond, Walter
　　See Silverberg, Robert

Drummond, William Henry
　　1854-1907 .... **TCLC 25**
　　See also DLB 92

Drummond de Andrade, Carlos
　　1902-1987 .... **CLC 18**
　　See also Andrade, Carlos Drummond de
　　See also CA 132; 123

Drury, Allen (Stuart)　1918-........ **CLC 37**
　　See also CA 57-60; CANR 18, 52;
　　　INT CANR-18

Dryden, John
     1631-1700 . . . . **LC 3, 21; DA; DAB;**
     DAC; DAM DRAM, MST, POET;
     DC 3; WLC
     See also CDBLB 1660-1789; DLB 80, 101,
     131

Duberman, Martin 1930- . . . . **CLC 8**
     See also CA 1-4R; CANR 2

Dubie, Norman (Evans) 1945- . . . . . . **CLC 36**
     See also CA 69-72; CANR 12; DLB 120

Du Bois, W(illiam) E(dward) B(urghardt)
     1868-1963 . . . . **CLC 1, 2, 13, 64, 96;**
     BLC; DA; DAC; DAM MST, MULT,
     NOV; WLC
     See also BW 1; CA 85-88; CANR 34;
     CDALB 1865-1917; DLB 47, 50, 91;
     MTCW; SATA 42

Dubus, Andre
     1936- . . . . **CLC 13, 36, 97; SSC 15**
     See also CA 21-24R; CANR 17; DLB 130;
     INT CANR-17

Duca Minimo
     See D'Annunzio, Gabriele

Ducharme, Rejean 1941- . . . . **CLC 74**
     See also DLB 60

Duclos, Charles Pinot 1704-1772 . . . . . **LC 1**

Dudek, Louis 1918- . . . . **CLC 11, 19**
     See also CA 45-48; CAAS 14; CANR 1;
     DLB 88

Duerrenmatt, Friedrich
     1921-1990 . . . . . . **CLC 1, 4, 8, 11, 15, 43;**
     DAM DRAM
     See also CA 17-20R; CANR 33; DLB 69,
     124; MTCW

Duffy, Bruce (?)- . . . . **CLC 50**

Duffy, Maureen 1933- . . . . **CLC 37**
     See also CA 25-28R; CANR 33; DLB 14;
     MTCW

Dugan, Alan 1923- . . . . **CLC 2, 6**
     See also CA 81-84; DLB 5

du Gard, Roger Martin
     See Martin du Gard, Roger

Duhamel, Georges 1884-1966 . . . . **CLC 8**
     See also CA 81-84; 25-28R; CANR 35;
     DLB 65; MTCW

Dujardin, Edouard (Emile Louis)
     1861-1949 . . . . **TCLC 13**
     See also CA 109; DLB 123

Dumas, Alexandre (Davy de la Pailleterie)
     1802-1870 . . . . **NCLC 11; DA; DAB;**
     DAC; DAM MST, NOV; WLC
     See also DLB 119; SATA 18

Dumas, Alexandre
     1824-1895 . . . . **NCLC 9; DC 1**

Dumas, Claudine
     See Malzberg, Barry N(athaniel)

Dumas, Henry L. 1934-1968 . . . . . **CLC 6, 62**
     See also BW 1; CA 85-88; DLB 41

du Maurier, Daphne
     1907-1989 . . . . **CLC 6, 11, 59; DAB;**
     DAC; DAM MST, POP; SSC 18
     See also CA 5-8R; 128; CANR 6, 55;
     MTCW; SATA 27; SATA-Obit 60

Dunbar, Paul Laurence
     1872-1906 . . . . . . **TCLC 2, 12; BLC; DA;**
     DAC; DAM MST, MULT, POET; PC 5;
     SSC 8; WLC
     See also BW 1; CA 104; 124;
     CDALB 1865-1917; DLB 50, 54, 78;
     SATA 34

Dunbar, William 1460(?)-1530(?) . . . . **LC 20**
     See also DLB 132, 146

Duncan, Dora Angela
     See Duncan, Isadora

Duncan, Isadora 1877(?)-1927 . . . . . **TCLC 68**
     See also CA 118; 149

Duncan, Lois 1934- . . . . **CLC 26**
     See also AAYA 4; CA 1-4R; CANR 2, 23,
     36; CLR 29; JRDA; MAICYA; SAAS 2;
     SATA 1, 36, 75

Duncan, Robert (Edward)
     1919-1988 . . . . **CLC 1, 2, 4, 7, 15, 41, 55;**
     DAM POET; PC 2
     See also CA 9-12R; 124; CANR 28; DLB 5,
     16; MTCW

Duncan, Sara Jeannette
     1861-1922 . . . . **TCLC 60**
     See also DLB 92

Dunlap, William 1766-1839 . . . . **NCLC 2**
     See also DLB 30, 37, 59

Dunn, Douglas (Eaglesham)
     1942- . . . . **CLC 6, 40**
     See also CA 45-48; CANR 2, 33; DLB 40;
     MTCW

Dunn, Katherine (Karen) 1945- . . . . . **CLC 71**
     See also CA 33-36R

Dunn, Stephen 1939- . . . . **CLC 36**
     See also CA 33-36R; CANR 12, 48, 53;
     DLB 105

Dunne, Finley Peter 1867-1936 . . . . **TCLC 28**
     See also CA 108; DLB 11, 23

Dunne, John Gregory 1932- . . . . **CLC 28**
     See also CA 25-28R; CANR 14, 50;
     DLBY 80

Dunsany, Edward John Moreton Drax
     Plunkett 1878-1957
     See Dunsany, Lord
     See also CA 104; 148; DLB 10

Dunsany, Lord . . . . **TCLC 2, 59**
     See also Dunsany, Edward John Moreton
     Drax Plunkett
     See also DLB 77, 153, 156

du Perry, Jean
     See Simenon, Georges (Jacques Christian)

Durang, Christopher (Ferdinand)
     1949- . . . . **CLC 27, 38**
     See also CA 105; CANR 50

Duras, Marguerite
     1914-1996 . . . . . **CLC 3, 6, 11, 20, 34, 40,**
     68, 100
     See also CA 25-28R; 151; CANR 50;
     DLB 83; MTCW

Durban, (Rosa) Pam 1947- . . . . **CLC 39**
     See also CA 123

Durcan, Paul
     1944- . . . . **CLC 43, 70; DAM POET**
     See also CA 134

Durkheim, Emile 1858-1917 . . . . . . **TCLC 55**

Durrell, Lawrence (George)
     1912-1990 . . . . **CLC 1, 4, 6, 8, 13, 27, 41;**
     DAM NOV
     See also CA 9-12R; 132; CANR 40;
     CDBLB 1945-1960; DLB 15, 27;
     DLBY 90; MTCW

Durrenmatt, Friedrich
     See Duerrenmatt, Friedrich

Dutt, Toru 1856-1877 . . . . **NCLC 29**

Dwight, Timothy 1752-1817 . . . . . . **NCLC 13**
     See also DLB 37

Dworkin, Andrea 1946- . . . . **CLC 43**
     See also CA 77-80; CAAS 21; CANR 16,
     39; INT CANR-16; MTCW

Dwyer, Deanna
     See Koontz, Dean R(ay)

Dwyer, K. R.
     See Koontz, Dean R(ay)

Dylan, Bob 1941- . . . . . . **CLC 3, 4, 6, 12, 77**
     See also CA 41-44R; DLB 16

Eagleton, Terence (Francis) 1943-
     See Eagleton, Terry
     See also CA 57-60; CANR 7, 23; MTCW

Eagleton, Terry . . . . **CLC 63**
     See also Eagleton, Terence (Francis)

Early, Jack
     See Scoppettone, Sandra

East, Michael
     See West, Morris L(anglo)

Eastaway, Edward
     See Thomas, (Philip) Edward

Eastlake, William (Derry) 1917- . . . . . **CLC 8**
     See also CA 5-8R; CAAS 1; CANR 5;
     DLB 6; INT CANR-5

Eastman, Charles A(lexander)
     1858-1939 . . . . . **TCLC 55; DAM MULT**
     See also DLB 175; NNAL; YABC 1

Eberhart, Richard (Ghormley)
     1904- . . **CLC 3, 11, 19, 56; DAM POET**
     See also CA 1-4R; CANR 2;
     CDALB 1941-1968; DLB 48; MTCW

Eberstadt, Fernanda 1960- . . . . **CLC 39**
     See also CA 136

Echegaray (y Eizaguirre), Jose (Maria Waldo)
     1832-1916 . . . . **TCLC 4**
     See also CA 104; CANR 32; HW; MTCW

Echeverria, (Jose) Esteban (Antonino)
     1805-1851 . . . . **NCLC 18**

Echo
     See Proust, (Valentin-Louis-George-Eugene-)
     Marcel

Eckert, Allan W. 1931- . . . . **CLC 17**
     See also AAYA 18; CA 13-16R; CANR 14,
     45; INT CANR-14; SAAS 21; SATA 29,
     91; SATA-Brief 27

Eckhart, Meister 1260(?)-1328(?) . . **CMLC 9**
     See also DLB 115

Eckmar, F. R.
     See de Hartog, Jan

Eco, Umberto
     1932- . . . **CLC 28, 60; DAM NOV, POP**
     See also BEST 90:1; CA 77-80; CANR 12,
     33, 55; MTCW

Eddison, E(ric) R(ucker)
1882-1945 . . . . **TCLC 15**
See also CA 109; 156

Edel, (Joseph) Leon 1907- . . . . . . **CLC 29, 34**
See also CA 1-4R; CANR 1, 22; DLB 103;
INT CANR-22

Eden, Emily 1797-1869 . . . . **NCLC 10**

Edgar, David
1948- . . . . **CLC 42; DAM DRAM**
See also CA 57-60; CANR 12; DLB 13;
MTCW

Edgerton, Clyde (Carlyle) 1944- . . . . **CLC 39**
See also AAYA 17; CA 118; 134; INT 134

Edgeworth, Maria 1768-1849 . . . **NCLC 1, 51**
See also DLB 116, 159, 163; SATA 21

Edmonds, Paul
See Kuttner, Henry

Edmonds, Walter D(umaux) 1903- . . **CLC 35**
See also CA 5-8R; CANR 2; DLB 9;
MAICYA; SAAS 4; SATA 1, 27

Edmondson, Wallace
See Ellison, Harlan (Jay)

Edson, Russell . . . . **CLC 13**
See also CA 33-36R

Edwards, Bronwen Elizabeth
See Rose, Wendy

Edwards, G(erald) B(asil)
1899-1976 . . . . **CLC 25**
See also CA 110

Edwards, Gus 1939- . . . . **CLC 43**
See also CA 108; INT 108

Edwards, Jonathan
1703-1758 . . . . **LC 7; DA; DAC;**
DAM MST
See also DLB 24

Efron, Marina Ivanovna Tsvetaeva
See Tsvetaeva (Efron), Marina (Ivanovna)

Ehle, John (Marsden, Jr.) 1925- . . . . **CLC 27**
See also CA 9-12R

Ehrenbourg, Ilya (Grigoryevich)
See Ehrenburg, Ilya (Grigoryevich)

Ehrenburg, Ilya (Grigoryevich)
1891-1967 . . . . **CLC 18, 34, 62**
See also CA 102; 25-28R

Ehrenburg, Ilyo (Grigoryevich)
See Ehrenburg, Ilya (Grigoryevich)

Eich, Guenter 1907-1972 . . . . **CLC 15**
See also CA 111; 93-96; DLB 69, 124

Eichendorff, Joseph Freiherr von
1788-1857 . . . . **NCLC 8**
See also DLB 90

Eigner, Larry . . . . **CLC 9**
See also Eigner, Laurence (Joel)
See also CAAS 23; DLB 5

Eigner, Laurence (Joel) 1927-1996
See Eigner, Larry
See also CA 9-12R; 151; CANR 6

Einstein, Albert 1879-1955 . . . . **TCLC 65**
See also CA 121; 133; MTCW

Eiseley, Loren Corey 1907-1977 . . . . . **CLC 7**
See also AAYA 5; CA 1-4R; 73-76;
CANR 6

Eisenstadt, Jill 1963- . . . . **CLC 50**
See also CA 140

Eisenstein, Sergei (Mikhailovich)
1898-1948 . . . . **TCLC 57**
See also CA 114; 149

Eisner, Simon
See Kornbluth, C(yril) M.

Ekeloef, (Bengt) Gunnar
1907-1968 . . . . **CLC 27; DAM POET**
See also CA 123; 25-28R

Ekelof, (Bengt) Gunnar
See Ekeloef, (Bengt) Gunnar

Ekwensi, C. O. D.
See Ekwensi, Cyprian (Odiatu Duaka)

Ekwensi, Cyprian (Odiatu Duaka)
1921- . . . . . . **CLC 4; BLC; DAM MULT**
See also BW 2; CA 29-32R; CANR 18, 42;
DLB 117; MTCW; SATA 66

Elaine . . . . **TCLC 18**
See also Leverson, Ada

El Crummo
See Crumb, R(obert)

Elia
See Lamb, Charles

Eliade, Mircea 1907-1986 . . . . **CLC 19**
See also CA 65-68; 119; CANR 30; MTCW

Eliot, A. D.
See Jewett, (Theodora) Sarah Orne

Eliot, Alice
See Jewett, (Theodora) Sarah Orne

Eliot, Dan
See Silverberg, Robert

Eliot, George
1819-1880 . . . . . **NCLC 4, 13, 23, 41, 49;**
DA; DAB; DAC; DAM MST, NOV;
WLC
See also CDBLB 1832-1890; DLB 21, 35, 55

Eliot, John 1604-1690 . . . . **LC 5**
See also DLB 24

Eliot, T(homas) S(tearns)
1888-1965 . . . . . **CLC 1, 2, 3, 6, 9, 10, 13,**
15, 24, 34, 41, 55, 57; DA; DAB; DAC;
DAM DRAM, MST, POET; PC 5;
WLC 2
See also CA 5-8R; 25-28R; CANR 41;
CDALB 1929-1941; DLB 7, 10, 45, 63;
DLBY 88; MTCW

Elizabeth 1866-1941 . . . . **TCLC 41**

Elkin, Stanley L(awrence)
1930-1995 . . . . . . **CLC 4, 6, 9, 14, 27, 51,**
91; DAM NOV, POP; SSC 12
See also CA 9-12R; 148; CANR 8, 46;
DLB 2, 28; DLBY 80; INT CANR-8;
MTCW

Elledge, Scott . . . . **CLC 34**

Elliot, Don
See Silverberg, Robert

Elliott, Don
See Silverberg, Robert

Elliott, George P(aul) 1918-1980 . . . . . **CLC 2**
See also CA 1-4R; 97-100; CANR 2

Elliott, Janice 1931- . . . . **CLC 47**
See also CA 13-16R; CANR 8, 29; DLB 14

Elliott, Sumner Locke 1917-1991 . . . **CLC 38**
See also CA 5-8R; 134; CANR 2, 21

Elliott, William
See Bradbury, Ray (Douglas)

Ellis, A. E. . . . . **CLC 7**

Ellis, Alice Thomas . . . . **CLC 40**
See also Haycraft, Anna

Ellis, Bret Easton
1964- . . . . **CLC 39, 71; DAM POP**
See also AAYA 2; CA 118; 123; CANR 51;
INT 123

Ellis, (Henry) Havelock
1859-1939 . . . . **TCLC 14**
See also CA 109

Ellis, Landon
See Ellison, Harlan (Jay)

Ellis, Trey 1962- . . . . **CLC 55**
See also CA 146

Ellison, Harlan (Jay)
1934- . . . . . . **CLC 1, 13, 42; DAM POP;**
SSC 14
See also CA 5-8R; CANR 5, 46; DLB 8;
INT CANR-5; MTCW

Ellison, Ralph (Waldo)
1914-1994 . . . . **CLC 1, 3, 11, 54, 86;**
BLC; DA; DAB; DAC; DAM MST,
MULT, NOV; WLC
See also AAYA 19; BW 1; CA 9-12R; 145;
CANR 24, 53; CDALB 1941-1968;
DLB 2, 76; DLBY 94; MTCW

Ellmann, Lucy (Elizabeth) 1956- . . . . **CLC 61**
See also CA 128

Ellmann, Richard (David)
1918-1987 . . . . **CLC 50**
See also BEST 89:2; CA 1-4R; 122;
CANR 2, 28; DLB 103; DLBY 87;
MTCW

Elman, Richard 1934- . . . . **CLC 19**
See also CA 17-20R; CAAS 3; CANR 47

Elron
See Hubbard, L(afayette) Ron(ald)

Eluard, Paul . . . . **TCLC 7, 41**
See also Grindel, Eugene

Elyot, Sir Thomas 1490(?)-1546 . . . . . **LC 11**

Elytis, Odysseus
1911-1996 . . . . **CLC 15, 49, 100;**
DAM POET
See also CA 102; 151; MTCW

Emecheta, (Florence Onye) Buchi
1944- . . **CLC 14, 48; BLC; DAM MULT**
See also BW 2; CA 81-84; CANR 27;
DLB 117; MTCW; SATA 66

Emerson, Ralph Waldo
1803-1882 . . . . . **NCLC 1, 38; DA; DAB;**
DAC; DAM MST, POET; WLC
See also CDALB 1640-1865; DLB 1, 59, 73

Eminescu, Mihail 1850-1889 . . . . . **NCLC 33**

Empson, William
1906-1984 . . . . **CLC 3, 8, 19, 33, 34**
See also CA 17-20R; 112; CANR 31;
DLB 20; MTCW

Enchi Fumiko (Ueda) 1905-1986 . . . . **CLC 31**
See also CA 129; 121

Farren, Richard M.
See Betjeman, John

Fassbinder, Rainer Werner
1946-1982 . . . . CLC 20
See also CA 93-96; 106; CANR 31

Fast, Howard (Melvin)
1914- . . . . CLC 23; DAM NOV
See also AAYA 16; CA 1-4R; CAAS 18;
CANR 1, 33, 54; DLB 9; INT CANR-33;
SATA 7

Faulcon, Robert
See Holdstock, Robert P.

Faulkner, William (Cuthbert)
1897-1962 . . . . . CLC 1, 3, 6, 8, 9, 11, 14,
18, 28, 52, 68; DA; DAB; DAC;
DAM MST, NOV; SSC 1; WLC
See also AAYA 7; CA 81-84; CANR 33;
CDALB 1929-1941; DLB 9, 11, 44, 102;
DLBD 2; DLBY 86; MTCW

Fauset, Jessie Redmon
1884(?)-1961 . . . . CLC 19, 54; BLC;
DAM MULT
See also BW 1; CA 109; DLB 51

Faust, Frederick (Schiller)
1892-1944(?) . . . . . TCLC 49; DAM POP
See also CA 108; 152

Faust, Irvin   1924- . . . . CLC 8
See also CA 33-36R; CANR 28; DLB 2, 28;
DLBY 80

Fawkes, Guy
See Benchley, Robert (Charles)

Fearing, Kenneth (Flexner)
1902-1961 . . . . CLC 51
See also CA 93-96; DLB 9

Fecamps, Elise
See Creasey, John

Federman, Raymond   1928- . . . . . . CLC 6, 47
See also CA 17-20R; CAAS 8; CANR 10,
43; DLBY 80

Federspiel, J(uerg) F.   1931- . . . . CLC 42
See also CA 146

Feiffer, Jules (Ralph)
1929- . . . . . . CLC 2, 8, 64; DAM DRAM
See also AAYA 3; CA 17-20R; CANR 30;
DLB 7, 44; INT CANR-30; MTCW;
SATA 8, 61

Feige, Hermann Albert Otto Maximilian
See Traven, B.

Feinberg, David B.   1956-1994 . . . . . CLC 59
See also CA 135; 147

Feinstein, Elaine   1930- . . . . CLC 36
See also CA 69-72; CAAS 1; CANR 31;
DLB 14, 40; MTCW

Feldman, Irving (Mordecai)   1928- . . . . CLC 7
See also CA 1-4R; CANR 1; DLB 169

Fellini, Federico   1920-1993 . . . . . CLC 16, 85
See also CA 65-68; 143; CANR 33

Felsen, Henry Gregor   1916- . . . . CLC 17
See also CA 1-4R; CANR 1; SAAS 2;
SATA 1

Fenton, James Martin   1949- . . . . CLC 32
See also CA 102; DLB 40

Ferber, Edna   1887-1968 . . . . CLC 18, 93
See also AITN 1; CA 5-8R; 25-28R; DLB 9,
28, 86; MTCW; SATA 7

Ferguson, Helen
See Kavan, Anna

Ferguson, Samuel   1810-1886 . . . . . NCLC 33
See also DLB 32

Fergusson, Robert   1750-1774 . . . . LC 29
See also DLB 109

Ferling, Lawrence
See Ferlinghetti, Lawrence (Monsanto)

Ferlinghetti, Lawrence (Monsanto)
1919(?)- . . . . CLC 2, 6, 10, 27;
DAM POET; PC 1
See also CA 5-8R; CANR 3, 41;
CDALB 1941-1968; DLB 5, 16; MTCW

Fernandez, Vicente Garcia Huidobro
See Huidobro Fernandez, Vicente Garcia

Ferrer, Gabriel (Francisco Victor) Miro
See Miro (Ferrer), Gabriel (Francisco
Victor)

Ferrier, Susan (Edmonstone)
1782-1854 . . . . NCLC 8
See also DLB 116

Ferrigno, Robert   1948(?)- . . . . CLC 65
See also CA 140

Ferron, Jacques   1921-1985 . . . CLC 94; DAC
See also CA 117; 129; DLB 60

Feuchtwanger, Lion   1884-1958 . . . . . TCLC 3
See also CA 104; DLB 66

Feuillet, Octave   1821-1890 . . . . . . NCLC 45

Feydeau, Georges (Leon Jules Marie)
1862-1921 . . . . . TCLC 22; DAM DRAM
See also CA 113; 152

Ficino, Marsilio   1433-1499 . . . . LC 12

Fiedeler, Hans
See Doeblin, Alfred

Fiedler, Leslie A(aron)
1917- . . . . CLC 4, 13, 24
See also CA 9-12R; CANR 7; DLB 28, 67;
MTCW

Field, Andrew   1938- . . . . CLC 44
See also CA 97-100; CANR 25

Field, Eugene   1850-1895 . . . . NCLC 3
See also DLB 23, 42, 140; DLBD 13;
MAICYA; SATA 16

Field, Gans T.
See Wellman, Manly Wade

Field, Michael . . . . TCLC 43

Field, Peter
See Hobson, Laura Z(ametkin)

Fielding, Henry
1707-1754 . . . . . . LC 1; DA; DAB; DAC;
DAM DRAM, MST, NOV; WLC
See also CDBLB 1660-1789; DLB 39, 84,
101

Fielding, Sarah   1710-1768 . . . . LC 1
See also DLB 39

Fierstein, Harvey (Forbes)
1954- . . . . . CLC 33; DAM DRAM, POP
See also CA 123; 129

Figes, Eva   1932- . . . . CLC 31
See also CA 53-56; CANR 4, 44; DLB 14

Finch, Robert (Duer Claydon)
1900- . . . . CLC 18
See also CA 57-60; CANR 9, 24, 49;
DLB 88

Findley, Timothy
1930- . . . . . . CLC 27; DAC; DAM MST
See also CA 25-28R; CANR 12, 42;
DLB 53

Fink, William
See Mencken, H(enry) L(ouis)

Firbank, Louis   1942-
See Reed, Lou
See also CA 117

Firbank, (Arthur Annesley) Ronald
1886-1926 . . . . TCLC 1
See also CA 104; DLB 36

Fisher, M(ary) F(rances) K(ennedy)
1908-1992 . . . . CLC 76, 87
See also CA 77-80; 138; CANR 44

Fisher, Roy   1930- . . . . CLC 25
See also CA 81-84; CAAS 10; CANR 16;
DLB 40

Fisher, Rudolph
1897-1934 . . . . TCLC 11; BLC;
DAM MULT; SSC 25
See also BW 1; CA 107; 124; DLB 51, 102

Fisher, Vardis (Alvero)   1895-1968 . . . . CLC 7
See also CA 5-8R; 25-28R; DLB 9

Fiske, Tarleton
See Bloch, Robert (Albert)

Fitch, Clarke
See Sinclair, Upton (Beall)

Fitch, John IV
See Cormier, Robert (Edmund)

Fitzgerald, Captain Hugh
See Baum, L(yman) Frank

FitzGerald, Edward   1809-1883 . . . . NCLC 9
See also DLB 32

Fitzgerald, F(rancis) Scott (Key)
1896-1940 . . . . TCLC 1, 6, 14, 28, 55;
DA; DAB; DAC; DAM MST, NOV;
SSC 6; WLC
See also AITN 1; CA 110; 123;
CDALB 1917-1929; DLB 4, 9, 86;
DLBD 1; DLBY 81; MTCW

Fitzgerald, Penelope   1916- . . . CLC 19, 51, 61
See also CA 85-88; CAAS 10; CANR 56;
DLB 14

Fitzgerald, Robert (Stuart)
1910-1985 . . . . CLC 39
See also CA 1-4R; 114; CANR 1; DLBY 80

FitzGerald, Robert D(avid)
1902-1987 . . . . CLC 19
See also CA 17-20R

Fitzgerald, Zelda (Sayre)
1900-1948 . . . . TCLC 52
See also CA 117; 126; DLBY 84

Flanagan, Thomas (James Bonner)
1923- . . . . CLC 25, 52
See also CA 108; CANR 55; DLBY 80;
INT 108; MTCW

Flaubert, Gustave
1821-1880 . . . . NCLC 2, 10, 19; DA;
DAB; DAC; DAM MST, NOV; SSC 11;
WLC
See also DLB 119

Flecker, Herman Elroy
See Flecker, (Herman) James Elroy

Fredro, Aleksander 1793-1876. . . . . NCLC 8

Freeling, Nicolas 1927- . . . . CLC 38
See also CA 49-52; CAAS 12; CANR 1, 17, 50; DLB 87

Freeman, Douglas Southall
1886-1953 . . . . TCLC 11
See also CA 109; DLB 17

Freeman, Judith 1946- . . . . CLC 55
See also CA 148

Freeman, Mary Eleanor Wilkins
1852-1930 . . . . TCLC 9; SSC 1
See also CA 106; DLB 12, 78

Freeman, R(ichard) Austin
1862-1943 . . . . TCLC 21
See also CA 113; DLB 70

French, Albert 1943- . . . . CLC 86

French, Marilyn
1929- . . . . CLC 10, 18, 60;
DAM DRAM, NOV, POP
See also CA 69-72; CANR 3, 31; INT CANR-31; MTCW

French, Paul
See Asimov, Isaac

Freneau, Philip Morin 1752-1832. . NCLC 1
See also DLB 37, 43

Freud, Sigmund 1856-1939 . . . . TCLC 52
See also CA 115; 133; MTCW

Friedan, Betty (Naomi) 1921- . . . . . . CLC 74
See also CA 65-68; CANR 18, 45; MTCW

Friedlander, Saul 1932- . . . . CLC 90
See also CA 117; 130

Friedman, B(ernard) H(arper)
1926- . . . . CLC 7
See also CA 1-4R; CANR 3, 48

Friedman, Bruce Jay 1930- . . . . CLC 3, 5, 56
See also CA 9-12R; CANR 25, 52; DLB 2, 28; INT CANR-25

Friel, Brian 1929- . . . . CLC 5, 42, 59
See also CA 21-24R; CANR 33; DLB 13; MTCW

Friis-Baastad, Babbis Ellinor
1921-1970 . . . . CLC 12
See also CA 17-20R; 134; SATA 7

Frisch, Max (Rudolf)
1911-1991 . . . . . CLC 3, 9, 14, 18, 32, 44;
DAM DRAM, NOV
See also CA 85-88; 134; CANR 32; DLB 69, 124; MTCW

Fromentin, Eugene (Samuel Auguste)
1820-1876 . . . . NCLC 10
See also DLB 123

Frost, Frederick
See Faust, Frederick (Schiller)

Frost, Robert (Lee)
1874-1963 . . . . CLC 1, 3, 4, 9, 10, 13, 15,
26, 34, 44; DA; DAB; DAC; DAM MST,
POET; PC 1; WLC
See also AAYA 21; CA 89-92; CANR 33; CDALB 1917-1929; DLB 54; DLBD 7; MTCW; SATA 14

Froude, James Anthony
1818-1894 . . . . NCLC 43
See also DLB 18, 57, 144

Froy, Herald
See Waterhouse, Keith (Spencer)

Fry, Christopher
1907- . . . . . CLC 2, 10, 14; DAM DRAM
See also CA 17-20R; CAAS 23; CANR 9, 30; DLB 13; MTCW; SATA 66

Frye, (Herman) Northrop
1912-1991 . . . . CLC 24, 70
See also CA 5-8R; 133; CANR 8, 37; DLB 67, 68; MTCW

Fuchs, Daniel 1909-1993 . . . . CLC 8, 22
See also CA 81-84; 142; CAAS 5; CANR 40; DLB 9, 26, 28; DLBY 93

Fuchs, Daniel 1934- . . . . CLC 34
See also CA 37-40R; CANR 14, 48

Fuentes, Carlos
1928- . . . . . . CLC 3, 8, 10, 13, 22, 41, 60;
DA; DAB; DAC; DAM MST, MULT,
NOV; HLC; SSC 24; WLC
See also AAYA 4; AITN 2; CA 69-72; CANR 10, 32; DLB 113; HW; MTCW

Fuentes, Gregorio Lopez y
See Lopez y Fuentes, Gregorio

Fugard, (Harold) Athol
1932- . . . . CLC 5, 9, 14, 25, 40, 80;
DAM DRAM; DC 3
See also AAYA 17; CA 85-88; CANR 32, 54; MTCW

Fugard, Sheila 1932- . . . . CLC 48
See also CA 125

Fuller, Charles (H., Jr.)
1939- . . . . CLC 25; BLC; DAM DRAM,
MULT; DC 1
See also BW 2; CA 108; 112; DLB 38; INT 112; MTCW

Fuller, John (Leopold) 1937- . . . . CLC 62
See also CA 21-24R; CANR 9, 44; DLB 40

Fuller, Margaret . . . . NCLC 5, 50
See also Ossoli, Sarah Margaret (Fuller marchesa d')

Fuller, Roy (Broadbent)
1912-1991 . . . . CLC 4, 28
See also CA 5-8R; 135; CAAS 10; CANR 53; DLB 15, 20; SATA 87

Fulton, Alice 1952- . . . . CLC 52
See also CA 116; CANR 57

Furphy, Joseph 1843-1912 . . . . TCLC 25

Fussell, Paul 1924- . . . . CLC 74
See also BEST 90:1; CA 17-20R; CANR 8, 21, 35; INT CANR-21; MTCW

Futabatei, Shimei 1864-1909 . . . . . TCLC 44

Futrelle, Jacques 1875-1912 . . . . . . TCLC 19
See also CA 113; 155

Gaboriau, Emile 1835-1873 . . . . . . NCLC 14

Gadda, Carlo Emilio 1893-1973 . . . . CLC 11
See also CA 89-92; DLB 177

Gaddis, William
1922- . . . . . CLC 1, 3, 6, 8, 10, 19, 43, 86
See also CA 17-20R; CANR 21, 48; DLB 2; MTCW

Gage, Walter
See Inge, William (Motter)

Gaines, Ernest J(ames)
1933- . . . . CLC 3, 11, 18, 86; BLC;
DAM MULT
See also AAYA 18; AITN 1; BW 2; CA 9-12R; CANR 6, 24, 42; CDALB 1968-1988; DLB 2, 33, 152; DLBY 80; MTCW; SATA 86

Gaitskill, Mary 1954- . . . . CLC 69
See also CA 128

Galdos, Benito Perez
See Perez Galdos, Benito

Gale, Zona
1874-1938 . . . . . . TCLC 7; DAM DRAM
See also CA 105; 153; DLB 9, 78

Galeano, Eduardo (Hughes) 1940- . . . CLC 72
See also CA 29-32R; CANR 13, 32; HW

Galiano, Juan Valera y Alcala
See Valera y Alcala-Galiano, Juan

Gallagher, Tess
1943- . . CLC 18, 63; DAM POET; PC 9
See also CA 106; DLB 120

Gallant, Mavis
1922- . . . . CLC 7, 18, 38; DAC;
DAM MST; SSC 5
See also CA 69-72; CANR 29; DLB 53; MTCW

Gallant, Roy A(rthur) 1924- . . . . CLC 17
See also CA 5-8R; CANR 4, 29, 54; CLR 30; MAICYA; SATA 4, 68

Gallico, Paul (William) 1897-1976 . . . CLC 2
See also AITN 1; CA 5-8R; 69-72; CANR 23; DLB 9, 171; MAICYA; SATA 13

Gallo, Max Louis 1932- . . . . CLC 95
See also CA 85-88

Gallois, Lucien
See Desnos, Robert

Gallup, Ralph
See Whitemore, Hugh (John)

Galsworthy, John
1867-1933 . . . . . . TCLC 1, 45; DA; DAB;
DAC; DAM DRAM, MST, NOV;
SSC 22; WLC 2
See also CA 104; 141; CDBLB 1890-1914; DLB 10, 34, 98, 162

Galt, John 1779-1839 . . . . NCLC 1
See also DLB 99, 116, 159

Galvin, James 1951- . . . . CLC 38
See also CA 108; CANR 26

Gamboa, Federico 1864-1939 . . . . . TCLC 36

Gandhi, M. K.
See Gandhi, Mohandas Karamchand

Gandhi, Mahatma
See Gandhi, Mohandas Karamchand

Gandhi, Mohandas Karamchand
1869-1948 . . . . . TCLC 59; DAM MULT
See also CA 121; 132; MTCW

Gann, Ernest Kellogg 1910-1991 . . . . CLC 23
See also AITN 1; CA 1-4R; 136; CANR 1

Garcia, Cristina 1958- . . . . CLC 76
See also CA 141

Garcia Lorca, Federico
1898-1936 ... **TCLC 1, 7, 49; DA; DAB; DAC; DAM DRAM, MST, MULT, POET; DC 2; HLC; PC 3; WLC**
See also CA 104; 131; DLB 108; HW; MTCW

Garcia Marquez, Gabriel (Jose)
1928- .... **CLC 2, 3, 8, 10, 15, 27, 47, 55, 68; DA; DAB; DAC; DAM MST, MULT, NOV, POP; HLC; SSC 8; WLC**
See also AAYA 3; BEST 89:1, 90:4; CA 33-36R; CANR 10, 28, 50; DLB 113; HW; MTCW

Gard, Janice
See Latham, Jean Lee

Gard, Roger Martin du
See Martin du Gard, Roger

Gardam, Jane 1928- .... **CLC 43**
See also CA 49-52; CANR 2, 18, 33, 54; CLR 12; DLB 14, 161; MAICYA; MTCW; SAAS 9; SATA 39, 76; SATA-Brief 28

Gardner, Herb(ert) 1934- .... **CLC 44**
See also CA 149

Gardner, John (Champlin), Jr.
1933-1982 ..... **CLC 2, 3, 5, 7, 8, 10, 18, 28, 34; DAM NOV, POP; SSC 7**
See also AITN 1; CA 65-68; 107; CANR 33; DLB 2; DLBY 82; MTCW; SATA 40; SATA-Obit 31

Gardner, John (Edmund)
1926- .... **CLC 30; DAM POP**
See also CA 103; CANR 15; MTCW

Gardner, Miriam
See Bradley, Marion Zimmer

Gardner, Noel
See Kuttner, Henry

Gardons, S. S.
See Snodgrass, W(illiam) D(e Witt)

Garfield, Leon 1921-1996 .... **CLC 12**
See also AAYA 8; CA 17-20R; 152; CANR 38, 41; CLR 21; DLB 161; JRDA; MAICYA; SATA 1, 32, 76; SATA-Obit 90

Garland, (Hannibal) Hamlin
1860-1940 .... **TCLC 3; SSC 18**
See also CA 104; DLB 12, 71, 78

Garneau, (Hector de) Saint-Denys
1912-1943 .... **TCLC 13**
See also CA 111; DLB 88

Garner, Alan
1934- .... **CLC 17; DAB; DAM POP**
See also AAYA 18; CA 73-76; CANR 15; CLR 20; DLB 161; MAICYA; MTCW; SATA 18, 69

Garner, Hugh 1913-1979 .... **CLC 13**
See also CA 69-72; CANR 31; DLB 68

Garnett, David 1892-1981 .... **CLC 3**
See also CA 5-8R; 103; CANR 17; DLB 34

Garos, Stephanie
See Katz, Steve

Garrett, George (Palmer)
1929- .... **CLC 3, 11, 51**
See also CA 1-4R; CAAS 5; CANR 1, 42; DLB 2, 5, 130, 152; DLBY 83

Garrick, David
1717-1779 ...... **LC 15; DAM DRAM**
See also DLB 84

Garrigue, Jean 1914-1972 .... **CLC 2, 8**
See also CA 5-8R; 37-40R; CANR 20

Garrison, Frederick
See Sinclair, Upton (Beall)

Garth, Will
See Hamilton, Edmond; Kuttner, Henry

Garvey, Marcus (Moziah, Jr.)
1887-1940 .... **TCLC 41; BLC; DAM MULT**
See also BW 1; CA 120; 124

Gary, Romain .... **CLC 25**
See also Kacew, Romain
See also DLB 83

Gascar, Pierre .... **CLC 11**
See also Fournier, Pierre

Gascoyne, David (Emery) 1916- .... **CLC 45**
See also CA 65-68; CANR 10, 28, 54; DLB 20; MTCW

Gaskell, Elizabeth Cleghorn
1810-1865 .... **NCLC 5; DAB; DAM MST; SSC 25**
See also CDBLB 1832-1890; DLB 21, 144, 159

Gass, William H(oward)
1924- ... **CLC 1, 2, 8, 11, 15, 39; SSC 12**
See also CA 17-20R; CANR 30; DLB 2; MTCW

Gasset, Jose Ortega y
See Ortega y Gasset, Jose

Gates, Henry Louis, Jr.
1950- .... **CLC 65; DAM MULT**
See also BW 2; CA 109; CANR 25, 53; DLB 67

Gautier, Theophile
1811-1872 .... **NCLC 1, 59; DAM POET; SSC 20**
See also DLB 119

Gawsworth, John
See Bates, H(erbert) E(rnest)

Gay, Oliver
See Gogarty, Oliver St. John

Gaye, Marvin (Penze) 1939-1984 ... **CLC 26**
See also CA 112

Gebler, Carlo (Ernest) 1954- .... **CLC 39**
See also CA 119; 133

Gee, Maggie (Mary) 1948- .... **CLC 57**
See also CA 130

Gee, Maurice (Gough) 1931- .... **CLC 29**
See also CA 97-100; SATA 46

Gelbart, Larry (Simon) 1923- ... **CLC 21, 61**
See also CA 73-76; CANR 45

Gelber, Jack 1932- .... **CLC 1, 6, 14, 79**
See also CA 1-4R; CANR 2; DLB 7

Gellhorn, Martha (Ellis) 1908- .. **CLC 14, 60**
See also CA 77-80; CANR 44; DLBY 82

Genet, Jean
1910-1986 ...... **CLC 1, 2, 5, 10, 14, 44, 46; DAM DRAM**
See also CA 13-16R; CANR 18; DLB 72; DLBY 86; MTCW

Gent, Peter 1942- .... **CLC 29**
See also AITN 1; CA 89-92; DLBY 82

Gentlewoman in New England, A
See Bradstreet, Anne

Gentlewoman in Those Parts, A
See Bradstreet, Anne

George, Jean Craighead 1919- ...... **CLC 35**
See also AAYA 8; CA 5-8R; CANR 25; CLR 1; DLB 52; JRDA; MAICYA; SATA 2, 68

George, Stefan (Anton)
1868-1933 .... **TCLC 2, 14**
See also CA 104

Georges, Georges Martin
See Simenon, Georges (Jacques Christian)

Gerhardi, William Alexander
See Gerhardie, William Alexander

Gerhardie, William Alexander
1895-1977 .... **CLC 5**
See also CA 25-28R; 73-76; CANR 18; DLB 36

Gerstler, Amy 1956- .... **CLC 70**
See also CA 146

Gertler, T. .... **CLC 34**
See also CA 116; 121; INT 121

gfgg .... **CLC XvXzc**

Ghalib .... **NCLC 39**
See also Ghalib, Hsadullah Khan

Ghalib, Hsadullah Khan 1797-1869
See Ghalib
See also DAM POET

Ghelderode, Michel de
1898-1962 .... **CLC 6, 11; DAM DRAM**
See also CA 85-88; CANR 40

Ghiselin, Brewster 1903- .... **CLC 23**
See also CA 13-16R; CAAS 10; CANR 13

Ghose, Zulfikar 1935- .... **CLC 42**
See also CA 65-68

Ghosh, Amitav 1956- .... **CLC 44**
See also CA 147

Giacosa, Giuseppe 1847-1906 ...... **TCLC 7**
See also CA 104

Gibb, Lee
See Waterhouse, Keith (Spencer)

Gibbon, Lewis Grassic .... **TCLC 4**
See also Mitchell, James Leslie

Gibbons, Kaye
1960- .... **CLC 50, 88; DAM POP**
See also CA 151

Gibran, Kahlil
1883-1931 .... **TCLC 1, 9; DAM POET, POP; PC 9**
See also CA 104; 150

Gibran, Khalil
See Gibran, Kahlil

Gibson, William
1914- .... **CLC 23; DA; DAB; DAC; DAM DRAM, MST**
See also CA 9-12R; CANR 9, 42; DLB 7; SATA 66

Gibson, William (Ford)
1948- .... **CLC 39, 63; DAM POP**
See also AAYA 12; CA 126; 133; CANR 52

Green, Julian (Hartridge) 1900-
See Green, Julien
See also CA 21-24R; CANR 33; DLB 4, 72;
MTCW

Green, Julien . . . . **CLC 3, 11, 77**
See also Green, Julian (Hartridge)

Green, Paul (Eliot)
1894-1981 . . . . . . **CLC 25; DAM DRAM**
See also AITN 1; CA 5-8R; 103; CANR 3;
DLB 7, 9; DLBY 81

Greenberg, Ivan 1908-1973
See Rahv, Philip
See also CA 85-88

Greenberg, Joanne (Goldenberg)
1932- . . . . **CLC 7, 30**
See also AAYA 12; CA 5-8R; CANR 14,
32; SATA 25

Greenberg, Richard 1959(?)- . . . . **CLC 57**
See also CA 138

Greene, Bette 1934- . . . . **CLC 30**
See also AAYA 7; CA 53-56; CANR 4;
CLR 2; JRDA; MAICYA; SAAS 16;
SATA 8

Greene, Gael . . . . **CLC 8**
See also CA 13-16R; CANR 10

Greene, Graham
1904-1991 . . . . **CLC 1, 3, 6, 9, 14, 18, 27,
37, 70, 72; DA; DAB; DAC; DAM MST,
NOV; WLC**
See also AITN 2; CA 13-16R; 133;
CANR 35; CDBLB 1945-1960; DLB 13,
15, 77, 100, 162; DLBY 91; MTCW;
SATA 20

Greer, Richard
See Silverberg, Robert

Gregor, Arthur 1923- . . . . **CLC 9**
See also CA 25-28R; CAAS 10; CANR 11;
SATA 36

Gregor, Lee
See Pohl, Frederik

Gregory, Isabella Augusta (Persse)
1852-1932 . . . . **TCLC 1**
See also CA 104; DLB 10

Gregory, J. Dennis
See Williams, John A(lfred)

Grendon, Stephen
See Derleth, August (William)

Grenville, Kate 1950- . . . . **CLC 61**
See also CA 118; CANR 53

Grenville, Pelham
See Wodehouse, P(elham) G(renville)

Greve, Felix Paul (Berthold Friedrich)
1879-1948
See Grove, Frederick Philip
See also CA 104; 141; DAC; DAM MST

Grey, Zane
1872-1939 . . . . **TCLC 6; DAM POP**
See also CA 104; 132; DLB 9; MTCW

Grieg, (Johan) Nordahl (Brun)
1902-1943 . . . . **TCLC 10**
See also CA 107

Grieve, C(hristopher) M(urray)
1892-1978 . . . . **CLC 11, 19; DAM POET**
See also MacDiarmid, Hugh; Pteleon
See also CA 5-8R; 85-88; CANR 33;
MTCW

Griffin, Gerald 1803-1840 . . . . **NCLC 7**
See also DLB 159

Griffin, John Howard 1920-1980 . . . . **CLC 68**
See also AITN 1; CA 1-4R; 101; CANR 2

Griffin, Peter 1942- . . . . **CLC 39**
See also CA 136

Griffith, D(avid Lewelyn) W(ark)
1875(?)-1948 . . . . **TCLC 68**
See also CA 119; 150

Griffith, Lawrence
See Griffith, D(avid Lewelyn) W(ark)

Griffiths, Trevor 1935- . . . . **CLC 13, 52**
See also CA 97-100; CANR 45; DLB 13

Grigson, Geoffrey (Edward Harvey)
1905-1985 . . . . **CLC 7, 39**
See also CA 25-28R; 118; CANR 20, 33;
DLB 27; MTCW

Grillparzer, Franz 1791-1872 . . . . . **NCLC 1**
See also DLB 133

Grimble, Reverend Charles James
See Eliot, T(homas) S(tearns)

Grimke, Charlotte L(ottie) Forten
1837(?)-1914
See Forten, Charlotte L.
See also BW 1; CA 117; 124; DAM MULT,
POET

Grimm, Jacob Ludwig Karl
1785-1863 . . . . **NCLC 3**
See also DLB 90; MAICYA; SATA 22

Grimm, Wilhelm Karl 1786-1859 . . **NCLC 3**
See also DLB 90; MAICYA; SATA 22

**Grimmelshausen, Johann Jakob Christoffel
von** 1621-1676 . . . . **LC 6**
See also DLB 168

Grindel, Eugene 1895-1952
See Eluard, Paul
See also CA 104

Grisham, John 1955- . . **CLC 84; DAM POP**
See also AAYA 14; CA 138; CANR 47

Grossman, David 1954- . . . . **CLC 67**
See also CA 138

Grossman, Vasily (Semenovich)
1905-1964 . . . . **CLC 41**
See also CA 124; 130; MTCW

Grove, Frederick Philip . . . . **TCLC 4**
See also Greve, Felix Paul (Berthold
Friedrich)
See also DLB 92

Grubb
See Crumb, R(obert)

Grumbach, Doris (Isaac)
1918- . . . . **CLC 13, 22, 64**
See also CA 5-8R; CAAS 2; CANR 9, 42;
INT CANR-9

Grundtvig, Nicolai Frederik Severin
1783-1872 . . . . **NCLC 1**

Grunge
See Crumb, R(obert)

Grunwald, Lisa 1959- . . . . **CLC 44**
See also CA 120

Guare, John
1938- . . . . **CLC 8, 14, 29, 67;
DAM DRAM**
See also CA 73-76; CANR 21; DLB 7;
MTCW

Gudjonsson, Halldor Kiljan 1902-
See Laxness, Halldor
See also CA 103

Guenter, Erich
See Eich, Guenter

Guest, Barbara 1920- . . . . **CLC 34**
See also CA 25-28R; CANR 11, 44; DLB 5

Guest, Judith (Ann)
1936- . . . . **CLC 8, 30; DAM NOV, POP**
See also AAYA 7; CA 77-80; CANR 15;
INT CANR-15; MTCW

Guevara, Che . . . . **CLC 87; HLC**
See also Guevara (Serna), Ernesto

Guevara (Serna), Ernesto 1928-1967
See Guevara, Che
See also CA 127; 111; CANR 56;
DAM MULT; HW

Guild, Nicholas M. 1944- . . . . **CLC 33**
See also CA 93-96

Guillemin, Jacques
See Sartre, Jean-Paul

Guillen, Jorge
1893-1984 . . . . . . **CLC 11; DAM MULT,
POET**
See also CA 89-92; 112; DLB 108; HW

Guillen, Nicolas (Cristobal)
1902-1989 . . . . **CLC 48, 79; BLC;
DAM MST, MULT, POET; HLC**
See also BW 2; CA 116; 125; 129; HW

Guillevic, (Eugene) 1907- . . . . **CLC 33**
See also CA 93-96

Guillois
See Desnos, Robert

Guillois, Valentin
See Desnos, Robert

Guiney, Louise Imogen
1861-1920 . . . . **TCLC 41**
See also DLB 54

Guiraldes, Ricardo (Guillermo)
1886-1927 . . . . **TCLC 39**
See also CA 131; HW; MTCW

Gumilev, Nikolai Stephanovich
1886-1921 . . . . **TCLC 60**

Gunesekera, Romesh . . . . **CLC 91**

Gunn, Bill . . . . **CLC 5**
See also Gunn, William Harrison
See also DLB 38

Gunn, Thom(son William)
1929- . . . . **CLC 3, 6, 18, 32, 81;
DAM POET**
See also CA 17-20R; CANR 9, 33;
CDBLB 1960 to Present; DLB 27;
INT CANR-33; MTCW

Gunn, William Harrison 1934(?)-1989
See Gunn, Bill
See also AITN 1; BW 1; CA 13-16R; 128;
CANR 12, 25

Gunnars, Kristjana 1948- . . . . **CLC 69**
See also CA 113; DLB 60

Gurganus, Allan
1947- . . . . **CLC 70; DAM POP**
See also BEST 90:1; CA 135

Gurney, A(lbert) R(amsdell), Jr.
1930- . . . . **CLC 32, 50, 54; DAM DRAM**
See also CA 77-80; CANR 32

Harling, Robert 1951(?)- .... **CLC 53**
See also CA 147

Harmon, William (Ruth) 1938- ..... **CLC 38**
See also CA 33-36R; CANR 14, 32, 35;
SATA 65

Harper, F. E. W.
See Harper, Frances Ellen Watkins

Harper, Frances E. W.
See Harper, Frances Ellen Watkins

Harper, Frances E. Watkins
See Harper, Frances Ellen Watkins

Harper, Frances Ellen
See Harper, Frances Ellen Watkins

Harper, Frances Ellen Watkins
1825-1911 .... **TCLC 14; BLC;**
DAM MULT, POET
See also BW 1; CA 111; 125; DLB 50

Harper, Michael S(teven) 1938- .. **CLC 7, 22**
See also BW 1; CA 33-36R; CANR 24;
DLB 41

Harper, Mrs. F. E. W.
See Harper, Frances Ellen Watkins

Harris, Christie (Lucy) Irwin
1907- .... **CLC 12**
See also CA 5-8R; CANR 6; DLB 88;
JRDA; MAICYA; SAAS 10; SATA 6, 74

Harris, Frank 1856-1931 .... **TCLC 24**
See also CA 109; 150; DLB 156

Harris, George Washington
1814-1869 .... **NCLC 23**
See also DLB 3, 11

Harris, Joel Chandler
1848-1908 .... **TCLC 2; SSC 19**
See also CA 104; 137; DLB 11, 23, 42, 78,
91; MAICYA; YABC 1

Harris, John (Wyndham Parkes Lucas)
Beynon 1903-1969
See Wyndham, John
See also CA 102; 89-92

Harris, MacDonald .... **CLC 9**
See also Heiney, Donald (William)

Harris, Mark 1922- .... **CLC 19**
See also CA 5-8R; CAAS 3; CANR 2, 55;
DLB 2; DLBY 80

Harris, (Theodore) Wilson 1921- .... **CLC 25**
See also BW 2; CA 65-68; CAAS 16;
CANR 11, 27; DLB 117; MTCW

Harrison, Elizabeth Cavanna 1909-
See Cavanna, Betty
See also CA 9-12R; CANR 6, 27

Harrison, Harry (Max) 1925- ...... **CLC 42**
See also CA 1-4R; CANR 5, 21; DLB 8;
SATA 4

Harrison, James (Thomas)
1937- ...... **CLC 6, 14, 33, 66; SSC 19**
See also CA 13-16R; CANR 8, 51;
DLBY 82; INT CANR-8

Harrison, Jim
See Harrison, James (Thomas)

Harrison, Kathryn 1961- .... **CLC 70**
See also CA 144

Harrison, Tony 1937- .... **CLC 43**
See also CA 65-68; CANR 44; DLB 40;
MTCW

Harriss, Will(ard Irvin) 1922- ...... **CLC 34**
See also CA 111

Harson, Sley
See Ellison, Harlan (Jay)

Hart, Ellis
See Ellison, Harlan (Jay)

Hart, Josephine
1942(?)- .... **CLC 70; DAM POP**
See also CA 138

Hart, Moss
1904-1961 ...... **CLC 66; DAM DRAM**
See also CA 109; 89-92; DLB 7

Harte, (Francis) Bret(t)
1836(?)-1902 .... **TCLC 1, 25; DA; DAC;**
DAM MST; SSC 8; WLC
See also CA 104; 140; CDALB 1865-1917;
DLB 12, 64, 74, 79; SATA 26

Hartley, L(eslie) P(oles)
1895-1972 .... **CLC 2, 22**
See also CA 45-48; 37-40R; CANR 33;
DLB 15, 139; MTCW

Hartman, Geoffrey H. 1929- .... **CLC 27**
See also CA 117; 125; DLB 67

Hartmann von Aue
c. 1160-c. 1205 .... **CMLC 15**
See also DLB 138

Hartmann von Aue 1170-1210.... **CMLC 15**

Haruf, Kent 1943- .... **CLC 34**
See also CA 149

Harwood, Ronald
1934- .... **CLC 32; DAM DRAM, MST**
See also CA 1-4R; CANR 4, 55; DLB 13

Hasek, Jaroslav (Matej Frantisek)
1883-1923 .... **TCLC 4**
See also CA 104; 129; MTCW

Hass, Robert
1941- .... **CLC 18, 39, 99; PC 16**
See also CA 111; CANR 30, 50; DLB 105

Hastings, Hudson
See Kuttner, Henry

Hastings, Selina .... **CLC 44**

Hathorne, John 1641-1717......... **LC 38**

Hatteras, Amelia
See Mencken, H(enry) L(ouis)

Hatteras, Owen .... **TCLC 18**
See also Mencken, H(enry) L(ouis); Nathan,
George Jean

Hauptmann, Gerhart (Johann Robert)
1862-1946 ...... **TCLC 4; DAM DRAM**
See also CA 104; 153; DLB 66, 118

Havel, Vaclav
1936- .... **CLC 25, 58, 65;**
DAM DRAM; DC 6
See also CA 104; CANR 36; MTCW

Haviaras, Stratis .... **CLC 33**
See also Chaviaras, Strates

Hawes, Stephen 1475(?)-1523(?) ..... **LC 17**

Hawkes, John (Clendennin Burne, Jr.)
1925- ...... **CLC 1, 2, 3, 4, 7, 9, 14, 15,**
27, 49
See also CA 1-4R; CANR 2, 47; DLB 2, 7;
DLBY 80; MTCW

Hawking, S. W.
See Hawking, Stephen W(illiam)

Hawking, Stephen W(illiam)
1942- .... **CLC 63**
See also AAYA 13; BEST 89:1; CA 126;
129; CANR 48

Hawthorne, Julian 1846-1934 ..... **TCLC 25**

Hawthorne, Nathaniel
1804-1864 .... **NCLC 39; DA; DAB;**
DAC; DAM MST, NOV; SSC 3; WLC
See also AAYA 18; CDALB 1640-1865;
DLB 1, 74; YABC 2

Haxton, Josephine Ayres 1921-
See Douglas, Ellen
See also CA 115; CANR 41

Hayaseca y Eizaguirre, Jorge
See Echegaray (y Eizaguirre), Jose (Maria
Waldo)

Hayashi Fumiko 1904-1951....... **TCLC 27**

Haycraft, Anna
See Ellis, Alice Thomas
See also CA 122

Hayden, Robert E(arl)
1913-1980 ...... **CLC 5, 9, 14, 37; BLC;**
DA; DAC; DAM MST, MULT, POET;
PC 6
See also BW 1; CA 69-72; 97-100; CABS 2;
CANR 24; CDALB 1941-1968; DLB 5,
76; MTCW; SATA 19; SATA-Obit 26

Hayford, J(oseph) E(phraim) Casely
See Casely-Hayford, J(oseph) E(phraim)

Hayman, Ronald 1932-........... **CLC 44**
See also CA 25-28R; CANR 18, 50;
DLB 155

Haywood, Eliza (Fowler)
1693(?)-1756 .... **LC 1**

Hazlitt, William 1778-1830...... **NCLC 29**
See also DLB 110, 158

Hazzard, Shirley 1931- .... **CLC 18**
See also CA 9-12R; CANR 4; DLBY 82;
MTCW

Head, Bessie
1937-1986 .... **CLC 25, 67; BLC;**
DAM MULT
See also BW 2; CA 29-32R; 119; CANR 25;
DLB 117; MTCW

Headon, (Nicky) Topper 1956(?)- ... **CLC 30**

Heaney, Seamus (Justin)
1939- ...... **CLC 5, 7, 14, 25, 37, 74, 91;**
DAB; DAM POET
See also CA 85-88; CANR 25, 48;
CDBLB 1960 to Present; DLB 40;
DLBY 95; MTCW

Hearn, (Patricio) Lafcadio (Tessima Carlos)
1850-1904 .... **TCLC 9**
See also CA 105; DLB 12, 78

Hearne, Vicki 1946- .... **CLC 56**
See also CA 139

Hearon, Shelby 1931-............. **CLC 63**
See also AITN 2; CA 25-28R; CANR 18,
48

Heat-Moon, William Least......... CLC 29
See also Trogdon, William (Lewis)
See also AAYA 9

Hebbel, Friedrich
1813-1863 .... **NCLC 43; DAM DRAM**
See also DLB 129

Hebert, Anne
　　1916- . . . . CLC 4, 13, 29; DAC;
　　　　　　　　　　　　DAM MST, POET
　　See also CA 85-88; DLB 68; MTCW

Hecht, Anthony (Evan)
　　1923- . . . . . . CLC 8, 13, 19; DAM POET
　　See also CA 9-12R; CANR 6; DLB 5, 169

Hecht, Ben　1894-1964 . . . . CLC 8
　　See also CA 85-88; DLB 7, 9, 25, 26, 28, 86

Hedayat, Sadeq　1903-1951 . . . . TCLC 21
　　See also CA 120

Hegel, Georg Wilhelm Friedrich
　　1770-1831 . . . . NCLC 46
　　See also DLB 90

Heidegger, Martin　1889-1976 . . . . . . CLC 24
　　See also CA 81-84; 65-68; CANR 34;
　　　MTCW

Heidenstam, (Carl Gustaf) Verner von
　　1859-1940 . . . . TCLC 5
　　See also CA 104

Heifner, Jack　1946- . . . . CLC 11
　　See also CA 105; CANR 47

Heijermans, Herman　1864-1924 . . . TCLC 24
　　See also CA 123

Heilbrun, Carolyn G(old)　1926- . . . . . CLC 25
　　See also CA 45-48; CANR 1, 28

Heine, Heinrich　1797-1856 . . . . NCLC 4, 54
　　See also DLB 90

Heinemann, Larry (Curtiss)　1944- . . CLC 50
　　See also CA 110; CAAS 21; CANR 31;
　　　DLBD 9; INT CANR-31

Heiney, Donald (William)　1921-1993
　　See Harris, MacDonald
　　See also CA 1-4R; 142; CANR 3

Heinlein, Robert A(nson)
　　1907-1988 . . . . . . CLC 1, 3, 8, 14, 26, 55;
　　　　　　　　　　　　　　　DAM POP
　　See also AAYA 17; CA 1-4R; 125;
　　　CANR 1, 20, 53; DLB 8; JRDA;
　　　MAICYA; MTCW; SATA 9, 69;
　　　SATA-Obit 56

Helforth, John
　　See Doolittle, Hilda

Hellenhofferu, Vojtech Kapristian z
　　See Hasek, Jaroslav (Matej Frantisek)

Heller, Joseph
　　1923- . . . . CLC 1, 3, 5, 8, 11, 36, 63; DA;
　　　DAB; DAC; DAM MST, NOV, POP;
　　　　　　　　　　　　　　　WLC
　　See also AITN 1; CA 5-8R; CABS 1;
　　　CANR 8, 42; DLB 2, 28; DLBY 80;
　　　INT CANR-8; MTCW

Hellman, Lillian (Florence)
　　1906-1984 . . . . . . CLC 2, 4, 8, 14, 18, 34,
　　　　　　　　　　44, 52; DAM DRAM; DC 1
　　See also AITN 1, 2; CA 13-16R; 112;
　　　CANR 33; DLB 7; DLBY 84; MTCW

Helprin, Mark
　　1947- . . . . CLC 7, 10, 22, 32;
　　　　　　　　　　　　　DAM NOV, POP
　　See also CA 81-84; CANR 47; DLBY 85;
　　　MTCW

Helvetius, Claude-Adrien
　　1715-1771 . . . . LC 26

Helyar, Jane Penelope Josephine　1933-
　　See Poole, Josephine
　　See also CA 21-24R; CANR 10, 26;
　　　SATA 82

Hemans, Felicia　1793-1835 . . . . . . NCLC 29
　　See also DLB 96

Hemingway, Ernest (Miller)
　　1899-1961 . . . . CLC 1, 3, 6, 8, 10, 13, 19,
　　　30, 34, 39, 41, 44, 50, 61, 80; DA; DAB;
　　　DAC; DAM MST, NOV; SSC 25; WLC
　　See also AAYA 19; CA 77-80; CANR 34;
　　　CDALB 1917-1929; DLB 4, 9, 102;
　　　DLBD 1; DLBY 81, 87; MTCW

Hempel, Amy　1951- . . . . CLC 39
　　See also CA 118; 137

Henderson, F. C.
　　See Mencken, H(enry) L(ouis)

Henderson, Sylvia
　　See Ashton-Warner, Sylvia (Constance)

Henley, Beth . . . . CLC 23; DC 6
　　See also Henley, Elizabeth Becker
　　See also CABS 3; DLBY 86

Henley, Elizabeth Becker　1952-
　　See Henley, Beth
　　See also CA 107; CANR 32; DAM DRAM,
　　　MST; MTCW

Henley, William Ernest
　　1849-1903 . . . . TCLC 8
　　See also CA 105; DLB 19

Hennissart, Martha
　　See Lathen, Emma
　　See also CA 85-88

Henry, O. . . . . TCLC 1, 19; SSC 5; WLC
　　See also Porter, William Sydney

Henry, Patrick　1736-1799 . . . . LC 25

Henryson, Robert　1430(?)-1506(?) . . . . LC 20
　　See also DLB 146

Henry VIII　1491-1547 . . . . LC 10

Henschke, Alfred
　　See Klabund

Hentoff, Nat(han Irving)　1925- . . . . . CLC 26
　　See also AAYA 4; CA 1-4R; CAAS 6;
　　　CANR 5, 25; CLR 1; INT CANR-25;
　　　JRDA; MAICYA; SATA 42, 69;
　　　SATA-Brief 27

Heppenstall, (John) Rayner
　　1911-1981 . . . . CLC 10
　　See also CA 1-4R; 103; CANR 29

Heraclitus
　　c. 540B.C.-c. 450B.C. . . . . CMLC 22
　　See also DLB 176

Herbert, Frank (Patrick)
　　1920-1986 . . . . . CLC 12, 23, 35, 44, 85;
　　　　　　　　　　　　　　　DAM POP
　　See also AAYA 21; CA 53-56; 118;
　　　CANR 5, 43; DLB 8; INT CANR-5;
　　　MTCW; SATA 9, 37; SATA-Obit 47

Herbert, George
　　1593-1633 . . . . LC 24; DAB;
　　　　　　　　　　　　　DAM POET; PC 4
　　See also CDBLB Before 1660; DLB 126

Herbert, Zbigniew
　　1924- . . . . CLC 9, 43; DAM POET
　　See also CA 89-92; CANR 36; MTCW

Herbst, Josephine (Frey)
　　1897-1969 . . . . CLC 34
　　See also CA 5-8R; 25-28R; DLB 9

Hergesheimer, Joseph
　　1880-1954 . . . . TCLC 11
　　See also CA 109; DLB 102, 9

Herlihy, James Leo　1927-1993 . . . . . . CLC 6
　　See also CA 1-4R; 143; CANR 2

Hermogenes　fl. c. 175- . . . . CMLC 6

Hernandez, Jose　1834-1886 . . . . . NCLC 17

Herodotus　c. 484B.C.-429B.C. . . . . . CMLC 17
　　See also DLB 176

Herrick, Robert
　　1591-1674 . . . . . LC 13; DA; DAB; DAC;
　　　　　　　　　　　DAM MST, POP; PC 9
　　See also DLB 126

Herring, Guilles
　　See Somerville, Edith

Herriot, James
　　1916-1995 . . . . CLC 12; DAM POP
　　See also Wight, James Alfred
　　See also AAYA 1; CA 148; CANR 40;
　　　SATA 86

Herrmann, Dorothy　1941- . . . . CLC 44
　　See also CA 107

Herrmann, Taffy
　　See Herrmann, Dorothy

Hersey, John (Richard)
　　1914-1993 . . . . CLC 1, 2, 7, 9, 40, 81, 97;
　　　　　　　　　　　　　　　DAM POP
　　See also CA 17-20R; 140; CANR 33;
　　　DLB 6; MTCW; SATA 25;
　　　SATA-Obit 76

Herzen, Aleksandr Ivanovich
　　1812-1870 . . . . NCLC 10, 61

Herzl, Theodor　1860-1904 . . . . TCLC 36

Herzog, Werner　1942- . . . . CLC 16
　　See also CA 89-92

Hesiod　c. 8th cent. B.C.- . . . . CMLC 5
　　See also DLB 176

Hesse, Hermann
　　1877-1962 . . . . CLC 1, 2, 3, 6, 11, 17, 25,
　　　69; DA; DAB; DAC; DAM MST, NOV;
　　　　　　　　　　　　　　SSC 9; WLC
　　See also CA 17-18; CAP 2; DLB 66;
　　　MTCW; SATA 50

Hewes, Cady
　　See De Voto, Bernard (Augustine)

Heyen, William　1940- . . . . CLC 13, 18
　　See also CA 33-36R; CAAS 9; DLB 5

Heyerdahl, Thor　1914- . . . . CLC 26
　　See also CA 5-8R; CANR 5, 22; MTCW;
　　　SATA 2, 52

Heym, Georg (Theodor Franz Arthur)
　　1887-1912 . . . . TCLC 9
　　See also CA 106

Heym, Stefan　1913- . . . . CLC 41
　　See also CA 9-12R; CANR 4; DLB 69

Heyse, Paul (Johann Ludwig von)
　　1830-1914 . . . . TCLC 8
　　See also CA 104; DLB 129

Heyward, (Edwin) DuBose
　　1885-1940 . . . . TCLC 59
　　See also CA 108; DLB 7, 9, 45; SATA 21

Hibbert, Eleanor Alice Burford
    1906-1993 . . . . **CLC 7; DAM POP**
    See also BEST 90:4; CA 17-20R; 140;
    CANR 9, 28; SATA 2; SATA-Obit 74

Hichens, Robert S. 1864-1950 . . . . . **TCLC 64**
    See also DLB 153

Higgins, George V(incent)
    1939- . . . . **CLC 4, 7, 10, 18**
    See also CA 77-80; CAAS 5; CANR 17, 51;
    DLB 2; DLBY 81; INT CANR-17;
    MTCW

Higginson, Thomas Wentworth
    1823-1911 . . . . **TCLC 36**
    See also DLB 1, 64

Highet, Helen
    See MacInnes, Helen (Clark)

Highsmith, (Mary) Patricia
    1921-1995 . . . . **CLC 2, 4, 14, 42;
                                    DAM NOV, POP**
    See also CA 1-4R; 147; CANR 1, 20, 48;
    MTCW

Highwater, Jamake (Mamake)
    1942(?)- . . . . **CLC 12**
    See also AAYA 7; CA 65-68; CAAS 7;
    CANR 10, 34; CLR 17; DLB 52;
    DLBY 85; JRDA; MAICYA; SATA 32,
    69; SATA-Brief 30

Highway, Tomson
    1951- . . . . . **CLC 92; DAC; DAM MULT**
    See also CA 151; NNAL

Higuchi, Ichiyo 1872-1896 . . . . **NCLC 49**

Hijuelos, Oscar
    1951- . . . . **CLC 65; DAM MULT, POP;
                                    HLC**
    See also BEST 90:1; CA 123; CANR 50;
    DLB 145; HW

Hikmet, Nazim 1902(?)-1963 . . . . . . **CLC 40**
    See also CA 141; 93-96

Hildegard von Bingen
    1098-1179 . . . . **CMLC 20**
    See also DLB 148

Hildesheimer, Wolfgang
    1916-1991 . . . . **CLC 49**
    See also CA 101; 135; DLB 69, 124

Hill, Geoffrey (William)
    1932- . . . **CLC 5, 8, 18, 45; DAM POET**
    See also CA 81-84; CANR 21;
    CDBLB 1960 to Present; DLB 40;
    MTCW

Hill, George Roy 1921- . . . . **CLC 26**
    See also CA 110; 122

Hill, John
    See Koontz, Dean R(ay)

Hill, Susan (Elizabeth)
    1942- . . **CLC 4; DAB; DAM MST, NOV**
    See also CA 33-36R; CANR 29; DLB 14,
    139; MTCW

Hillerman, Tony
    1925- . . . . **CLC 62; DAM POP**
    See also AAYA 6; BEST 89:1; CA 29-32R;
    CANR 21, 42; SATA 6

Hillesum, Etty 1914-1943 . . . . **TCLC 49**
    See also CA 137

Hilliard, Noel (Harvey) 1929- . . . . . **CLC 15**
    See also CA 9-12R; CANR 7

Hillis, Rick 1956- . . . . **CLC 66**
    See also CA 134

Hilton, James 1900-1954 . . . . **TCLC 21**
    See also CA 108; DLB 34, 77; SATA 34

Himes, Chester (Bomar)
    1909-1984 . . . . **CLC 2, 4, 7, 18, 58; BLC;
                                    DAM MULT**
    See also BW 2; CA 25-28R; 114; CANR 22;
    DLB 2, 76, 143; MTCW

Hinde, Thomas . . . . **CLC 6, 11**
    See also Chitty, Thomas Willes

Hindin, Nathan
    See Bloch, Robert (Albert)

Hine, (William) Daryl 1936- . . . . **CLC 15**
    See also CA 1-4R; CAAS 15; CANR 1, 20;
    DLB 60

Hinkson, Katharine Tynan
    See Tynan, Katharine

Hinton, S(usan) E(loise)
    1950- . . . . **CLC 30; DA; DAB; DAC;
                                    DAM MST, NOV**
    See also AAYA 2; CA 81-84; CANR 32;
    CLR 3, 23; JRDA; MAICYA; MTCW;
    SATA 19, 58

Hippius, Zinaida . . . . **TCLC 9**
    See also Gippius, Zinaida (Nikolayevna)

Hiraoka, Kimitake 1925-1970
    See Mishima, Yukio
    See also CA 97-100; 29-32R; DAM DRAM;
    MTCW

Hirsch, E(ric) D(onald), Jr. 1928- . . . **CLC 79**
    See also CA 25-28R; CANR 27, 51;
    DLB 67; INT CANR-27; MTCW

Hirsch, Edward 1950- . . . . **CLC 31, 50**
    See also CA 104; CANR 20, 42; DLB 120

Hitchcock, Alfred (Joseph)
    1899-1980 . . . . **CLC 16**
    See also CA 97-100; SATA 27;
    SATA-Obit 24

Hitler, Adolf 1889-1945 . . . . **TCLC 53**
    See also CA 117; 147

Hoagland, Edward 1932- . . . . **CLC 28**
    See also CA 1-4R; CANR 2, 31, 57; DLB 6;
    SATA 51

Hoban, Russell (Conwell)
    1925- . . . . **CLC 7, 25; DAM NOV**
    See also CA 5-8R; CANR 23, 37; CLR 3;
    DLB 52; MAICYA; MTCW; SATA 1,
    40, 78

Hobbes, Thomas 1588-1679 . . . . **LC 36**
    See also DLB 151

Hobbs, Perry
    See Blackmur, R(ichard) P(almer)

Hobson, Laura Z(ametkin)
    1900-1986 . . . . **CLC 7, 25**
    See also CA 17-20R; 118; CANR 55;
    DLB 28; SATA 52

Hochhuth, Rolf
    1931- . . . . . **CLC 4, 11, 18; DAM DRAM**
    See also CA 5-8R; CANR 33; DLB 124;
    MTCW

Hochman, Sandra 1936- . . . . **CLC 3, 8**
    See also CA 5-8R; DLB 5

Hochwaelder, Fritz
    1911-1986 . . . . . . **CLC 36; DAM DRAM**
    See also CA 29-32R; 120; CANR 42;
    MTCW

Hochwalder, Fritz
    See Hochwaelder, Fritz

Hocking, Mary (Eunice) 1921- . . . . . **CLC 13**
    See also CA 101; CANR 18, 40

Hodgins, Jack 1938- . . . . **CLC 23**
    See also CA 93-96; DLB 60

Hodgson, William Hope
    1877(?)-1918 . . . . **TCLC 13**
    See also CA 111; DLB 70, 153, 156

Hoeg, Peter 1957- . . . . **CLC 95**
    See also CA 151

Hoffman, Alice
    1952- . . . . **CLC 51; DAM NOV**
    See also CA 77-80; CANR 34; MTCW

Hoffman, Daniel (Gerard)
    1923- . . . . **CLC 6, 13, 23**
    See also CA 1-4R; CANR 4; DLB 5

Hoffman, Stanley 1944- . . . . **CLC 5**
    See also CA 77-80

Hoffman, William M(oses) 1939- . . . **CLC 40**
    See also CA 57-60; CANR 11

Hoffmann, E(rnst) T(heodor) A(madeus)
    1776-1822 . . . . **NCLC 2; SSC 13**
    See also DLB 90; SATA 27

Hofmann, Gert 1931- . . . . **CLC 54**
    See also CA 128

Hofmannsthal, Hugo von
    1874-1929 . . . . **TCLC 11; DAM DRAM;
                                    DC 4**
    See also CA 106; 153; DLB 81, 118

Hogan, Linda
    1947- . . . . **CLC 73; DAM MULT**
    See also CA 120; CANR 45; DLB 175;
    NNAL

Hogarth, Charles
    See Creasey, John

Hogarth, Emmett
    See Polonsky, Abraham (Lincoln)

Hogg, James 1770-1835 . . . . **NCLC 4**
    See also DLB 93, 116, 159

Holbach, Paul Henri Thiry Baron
    1723-1789 . . . . **LC 14**

Holberg, Ludvig 1684-1754 . . . . **LC 6**

Holden, Ursula 1921- . . . . **CLC 18**
    See also CA 101; CAAS 8; CANR 22

Holderlin, (Johann Christian) Friedrich
    1770-1843 . . . . **NCLC 16; PC 4**

Holdstock, Robert
    See Holdstock, Robert P.

Holdstock, Robert P. 1948- . . . . **CLC 39**
    See also CA 131

Holland, Isabelle 1920- . . . . **CLC 21**
    See also AAYA 11; CA 21-24R; CANR 10,
    25, 47; JRDA; MAICYA; SATA 8, 70

Holland, Marcus
    See Caldwell, (Janet Miriam) Taylor
    (Holland)

Hollander, John 1929- . . . . . . **CLC 2, 5, 8, 14**
    See also CA 1-4R; CANR 1, 52; DLB 5;
    SATA 13

Hollander, Paul
    See Silverberg, Robert

Holleran, Andrew 1943(?)-........ CLC 38
    See also CA 144

Hollinghurst, Alan 1954-....... CLC 55, 91
    See also CA 114

Hollis, Jim
    See Summers, Hollis (Spurgeon, Jr.)

Holly, Buddy 1936-1959 .... TCLC 65

Holmes, John
    See Souster, (Holmes) Raymond

Holmes, John Clellon 1926-1988.... CLC 56
    See also CA 9-12R; 125; CANR 4; DLB 16

Holmes, Oliver Wendell
        1809-1894 .... NCLC 14
    See also CDALB 1640-1865; DLB 1;
        SATA 34

Holmes, Raymond
    See Souster, (Holmes) Raymond

Holt, Victoria
    See Hibbert, Eleanor Alice Burford

Holub, Miroslav 1923-............ CLC 4
    See also CA 21-24R; CANR 10

Homer
        c. 8th cent. B.C.-.... CMLC 1, 16; DA;
            DAB; DAC; DAM MST, POET
    See also DLB 176

Honig, Edwin 1919-............. CLC 33
    See also CA 5-8R; CAAS 8; CANR 4, 45;
        DLB 5

Hood, Hugh (John Blagdon)
        1928- .... CLC 15, 28
    See also CA 49-52; CAAS 17; CANR 1, 33;
        DLB 53

Hood, Thomas 1799-1845........ NCLC 16
    See also DLB 96

Hooker, (Peter) Jeremy 1941-...... CLC 43
    See also CA 77-80; CANR 22; DLB 40

hooks, bell .... CLC 94
    See also Watkins, Gloria

Hope, A(lec) D(erwent) 1907-.... CLC 3, 51
    See also CA 21-24R; CANR 33; MTCW

Hope, Brian
    See Creasey, John

Hope, Christopher (David Tully)
        1944- .... CLC 52
    See also CA 106; CANR 47; SATA 62

Hopkins, Gerard Manley
        1844-1889 .... NCLC 17; DA; DAB;
            DAC; DAM MST, POET; PC 15; WLC
    See also CDBLB 1890-1914; DLB 35, 57

Hopkins, John (Richard) 1931-...... CLC 4
    See also CA 85-88

Hopkins, Pauline Elizabeth
        1859-1930 .... TCLC 28; BLC;
            DAM MULT
    See also BW 2; CA 141; DLB 50

Hopkinson, Francis 1737-1791 ...... LC 25
    See also DLB 31

Hopley-Woolrich, Cornell George 1903-1968
    See Woolrich, Cornell
    See also CA 13-14; CAP 1

Horatio
    See Proust, (Valentin-Louis-George-Eugene-)
        Marcel

Horgan, Paul (George Vincent O'Shaughnessy)
        1903-1995 ...... CLC 9, 53; DAM NOV
    See also CA 13-16R; 147; CANR 9, 35;
        DLB 102; DLBY 85; INT CANR-9;
        MTCW; SATA 13; SATA-Obit 84

Horn, Peter
    See Kuttner, Henry

Hornem, Horace Esq.
    See Byron, George Gordon (Noel)

Hornung, E(rnest) W(illiam)
        1866-1921 .... TCLC 59
    See also CA 108; DLB 70

Horovitz, Israel (Arthur)
        1939- .... CLC 56; DAM DRAM
    See also CA 33-36R; CANR 46; DLB 7

Horvath, Odon von
    See Horvath, Oedoen von
    See also DLB 85, 124

Horvath, Oedoen von 1901-1938... TCLC 45
    See also Horvath, Odon von
    See also CA 118

Horwitz, Julius 1920-1986........ CLC 14
    See also CA 9-12R; 119; CANR 12

Hospital, Janette Turner 1942-..... CLC 42
    See also CA 108; CANR 48

Hostos, E. M. de
    See Hostos (y Bonilla), Eugenio Maria de

Hostos, Eugenio M. de
    See Hostos (y Bonilla), Eugenio Maria de

Hostos, Eugenio Maria
    See Hostos (y Bonilla), Eugenio Maria de

Hostos (y Bonilla), Eugenio Maria de
        1839-1903 .... TCLC 24
    See also CA 123; 131; HW

Houdini
    See Lovecraft, H(oward) P(hillips)

Hougan, Carolyn 1943- .... CLC 34
    See also CA 139

Household, Geoffrey (Edward West)
        1900-1988 .... CLC 11
    See also CA 77-80; 126; DLB 87; SATA 14;
        SATA-Obit 59

Housman, A(lfred) E(dward)
        1859-1936 ...... TCLC 1, 10; DA; DAB;
            DAC; DAM MST, POET; PC 2
    See also CA 104; 125; DLB 19; MTCW

Housman, Laurence 1865-1959 ..... TCLC 7
    See also CA 106; 155; DLB 10; SATA 25

Howard, Elizabeth Jane 1923- ... CLC 7, 29
    See also CA 5-8R; CANR 8

Howard, Maureen 1930- ..... CLC 5, 14, 46
    See also CA 53-56; CANR 31; DLBY 83;
        INT CANR-31; MTCW

Howard, Richard 1929- ...... CLC 7, 10, 47
    See also AITN 1; CA 85-88; CANR 25;
        DLB 5; INT CANR-25

Howard, Robert Ervin 1906-1936... TCLC 8
    See also CA 105

Howard, Warren F.
    See Pohl, Frederik

Howe, Fanny 1940- .... CLC 47
    See also CA 117; SATA-Brief 52

Howe, Irving 1920-1993.......... CLC 85
    See also CA 9-12R; 141; CANR 21, 50;
        DLB 67; MTCW

Howe, Julia Ward 1819-1910 ..... TCLC 21
    See also CA 117; DLB 1

Howe, Susan 1937-.............. CLC 72
    See also DLB 120

Howe, Tina 1937-................ CLC 48
    See also CA 109

Howell, James 1594(?)-1666 .... LC 13
    See also DLB 151

Howells, W. D.
    See Howells, William Dean

Howells, William D.
    See Howells, William Dean

Howells, William Dean
        1837-1920 .... TCLC 7, 17, 41
    See also CA 104; 134; CDALB 1865-1917;
        DLB 12, 64, 74, 79

Howes, Barbara 1914-1996 .... CLC 15
    See also CA 9-12R; 151; CAAS 3;
        CANR 53; SATA 5

Hrabal, Bohumil 1914-1997..... CLC 13, 67
    See also CA 106; 156; CAAS 12; CANR 57

Hsun, Lu
    See Lu Hsun

Hubbard, L(afayette) Ron(ald)
        1911-1986 .... CLC 43; DAM POP
    See also CA 77-80; 118; CANR 52

Huch, Ricarda (Octavia)
        1864-1947 .... TCLC 13
    See also CA 111; DLB 66

Huddle, David 1942- .... CLC 49
    See also CA 57-60; CAAS 20; DLB 130

Hudson, Jeffrey
    See Crichton, (John) Michael

Hudson, W(illiam) H(enry)
        1841-1922 .... TCLC 29
    See also CA 115; DLB 98, 153, 174;
        SATA 35

Hueffer, Ford Madox
    See Ford, Ford Madox

Hughart, Barry 1934-............. CLC 39
    See also CA 137

Hughes, Colin
    See Creasey, John

Hughes, David (John) 1930- .... CLC 48
    See also CA 116; 129; DLB 14

Hughes, Edward James
    See Hughes, Ted
    See also DAM MST, POET

Hughes, (James) Langston
        1902-1967 ..... CLC 1, 5, 10, 15, 35, 44;
            BLC; DA; DAB; DAC; DAM DRAM,
            MST, MULT, POET; DC 3; PC 1;
            SSC 6; WLC
    See also AAYA 12; BW 1; CA 1-4R;
        25-28R; CANR 1, 34; CDALB 1929-1941;
        CLR 17; DLB 4, 7, 48, 51, 86; JRDA;
        MAICYA; MTCW; SATA 4, 33

Hughes, Richard (Arthur Warren)
1900-1976 ..... **CLC 1, 11; DAM NOV**
See also CA 5-8R; 65-68; CANR 4;
DLB 15, 161; MTCW; SATA 8;
SATA-Obit 25

Hughes, Ted
1930- .... **CLC 2, 4, 9, 14, 37; DAB;
DAC; PC 7**
See also Hughes, Edward James
See also CA 1-4R; CANR 1, 33; CLR 3;
DLB 40, 161; MAICYA; MTCW;
SATA 49; SATA-Brief 27

Hugo, Richard F(ranklin)
1923-1982 .... **CLC 6, 18, 32;
DAM POET**
See also CA 49-52; 108; CANR 3; DLB 5

Hugo, Victor (Marie)
1802-1885 .... **NCLC 3, 10, 21; DA;
DAB; DAC; DAM DRAM, MST, NOV,
POET; PC 17; WLC**
See also DLB 119; SATA 47

Huidobro, Vicente
See Huidobro Fernandez, Vicente Garcia

Huidobro Fernandez, Vicente Garcia
1893-1948 .... **TCLC 31**
See also CA 131; HW

Hulme, Keri 1947- .... **CLC 39**
See also CA 125; INT 125

Hulme, T(homas) E(rnest)
1883-1917 .... **TCLC 21**
See also CA 117; DLB 19

Hume, David 1711-1776............. **LC 7**
See also DLB 104

Humphrey, William 1924-......... **CLC 45**
See also CA 77-80; DLB 6

Humphreys, Emyr Owen 1919-.... **CLC 47**
See also CA 5-8R; CANR 3, 24; DLB 15

Humphreys, Josephine 1945-.... **CLC 34, 57**
See also CA 121; 127; INT 127

Huneker, James Gibbons
1857-1921 .... **TCLC 65**
See also DLB 71

Hungerford, Pixie
See Brinsmead, H(esba) F(ay)

Hunt, E(verette) Howard, (Jr.)
1918- .... **CLC 3**
See also AITN 1; CA 45-48; CANR 2, 47

Hunt, Kyle
See Creasey, John

Hunt, (James Henry) Leigh
1784-1859 ..... **NCLC 1; DAM POET**

Hunt, Marsha 1946-.............. **CLC 70**
See also BW 2; CA 143

Hunt, Violet 1866-1942 .... **TCLC 53**
See also DLB 162

Hunter, E. Waldo
See Sturgeon, Theodore (Hamilton)

Hunter, Evan
1926- .... **CLC 11, 31; DAM POP**
See also CA 5-8R; CANR 5, 38; DLBY 82;
INT CANR-5; MTCW; SATA 25

Hunter, Kristin (Eggleston) 1931-... **CLC 35**
See also AITN 1; BW 1; CA 13-16R;
CANR 13; CLR 3; DLB 33;
INT CANR-13; MAICYA; SAAS 10;
SATA 12

Hunter, Mollie 1922-............. **CLC 21**
See also McIlwraith, Maureen Mollie
Hunter
See also AAYA 13; CANR 37; CLR 25;
DLB 161; JRDA; MAICYA; SAAS 7;
SATA 54

Hunter, Robert (?)-1734............ **LC 7**

Hurston, Zora Neale
1903-1960 .... **CLC 7, 30, 61; BLC; DA;
DAC; DAM MST, MULT, NOV; SSC 4**
See also AAYA 15; BW 1; CA 85-88;
DLB 51, 86; MTCW

Huston, John (Marcellus)
1906-1987 .... **CLC 20**
See also CA 73-76; 123; CANR 34; DLB 26

Hustvedt, Siri 1955-.............. **CLC 76**
See also CA 137

Hutten, Ulrich von 1488-1523....... **LC 16**

Huxley, Aldous (Leonard)
1894-1963 ..... **CLC 1, 3, 4, 5, 8, 11, 18,
35, 79; DA; DAB; DAC; DAM MST,
NOV; WLC**
See also AAYA 11; CA 85-88; CANR 44;
CDBLB 1914-1945; DLB 36, 100, 162;
MTCW; SATA 63

Huysmans, Charles Marie Georges
1848-1907
See Huysmans, Joris-Karl
See also CA 104

Huysmans, Joris-Karl........... TCLC 7, 69
See also Huysmans, Charles Marie Georges
See also DLB 123

Hwang, David Henry
1957-.... **CLC 55; DAM DRAM; DC 4**
See also CA 127; 132; INT 132

Hyde, Anthony 1946-............. **CLC 42**
See also CA 136

Hyde, Margaret O(ldroyd) 1917-... **CLC 21**
See also CA 1-4R; CANR 1, 36; CLR 23;
JRDA; MAICYA; SAAS 8; SATA 1, 42,
76

Hynes, James 1956(?)-............. **CLC 65**

Ian, Janis 1951-................ **CLC 21**
See also CA 105

Ibanez, Vicente Blasco
See Blasco Ibanez, Vicente

Ibarguengoitia, Jorge 1928-1983.... **CLC 37**
See also CA 124; 113; HW

Ibsen, Henrik (Johan)
1828-1906 .... **TCLC 2, 8, 16, 37, 52;
DA; DAB; DAC; DAM DRAM, MST;
DC 2; WLC**
See also CA 104; 141

Ibuse Masuji 1898-1993........... **CLC 22**
See also CA 127; 141

Ichikawa, Kon 1915-............. **CLC 20**
See also CA 121

Idle, Eric 1943-................. **CLC 21**
See also Monty Python
See also CA 116; CANR 35

Ignatow, David 1914-...... **CLC 4, 7, 14, 40**
See also CA 9-12R; CAAS 3; CANR 31, 57;
DLB 5

Ihimaera, Witi 1944- .... **CLC 46**
See also CA 77-80

Ilf, Ilya........................ TCLC 21
See also Fainzilberg, Ilya Arnoldovich

Illyes, Gyula 1902-1983............ **PC 16**
See also CA 114; 109

Immermann, Karl (Lebrecht)
1796-1840 .... **NCLC 4, 49**
See also DLB 133

Inclan, Ramon (Maria) del Valle
See Valle-Inclan, Ramon (Maria) del

Infante, G(uillermo) Cabrera
See Cabrera Infante, G(uillermo)

Ingalls, Rachel (Holmes) 1940-..... **CLC 42**
See also CA 123; 127

Ingamells, Rex 1913-1955 .... **TCLC 35**

Inge, William (Motter)
1913-1973 .. **CLC 1, 8, 19; DAM DRAM**
See also CA 9-12R; CDALB 1941-1968;
DLB 7; MTCW

Ingelow, Jean 1820-1897 .... **NCLC 39**
See also DLB 35, 163; SATA 33

Ingram, Willis J.
See Harris, Mark

Innaurato, Albert (F.) 1948(?)- .. **CLC 21, 60**
See also CA 115; 122; INT 122

Innes, Michael
See Stewart, J(ohn) I(nnes) M(ackintosh)

Ionesco, Eugene
1909-1994 .... **CLC 1, 4, 6, 9, 11, 15, 41,
86; DA; DAB; DAC; DAM DRAM,
MST; WLC**
See also CA 9-12R; 144; CANR 55;
MTCW; SATA 7; SATA-Obit 79

Iqbal, Muhammad 1873-1938 ..... **TCLC 28**

Ireland, Patrick
See O'Doherty, Brian

Iron, Ralph
See Schreiner, Olive (Emilie Albertina)

Irving, John (Winslow)
1942-..... **CLC 13, 23, 38; DAM NOV,
POP**
See also AAYA 8; BEST 89:3; CA 25-28R;
CANR 28; DLB 6; DLBY 82; MTCW

Irving, Washington
1783-1859 ..... **NCLC 2, 19; DA; DAB;
DAM MST; SSC 2; WLC**
See also CDALB 1640-1865; DLB 3, 11, 30,
59, 73, 74; YABC 2

Irwin, P. K.
See Page, P(atricia) K(athleen)

Isaacs, Susan 1943- ... **CLC 32; DAM POP**
See also BEST 89:1; CA 89-92; CANR 20,
41; INT CANR-20; MTCW

Isherwood, Christopher (William Bradshaw)
1904-1986 .... **CLC 1, 9, 11, 14, 44;
DAM DRAM, NOV**
See also CA 13-16R; 117; CANR 35;
DLB 15; DLBY 86; MTCW

Jimenez Mantecon, Juan
See Jimenez (Mantecon), Juan Ramon

Joel, Billy . . . . **CLC 26**
See also Joel, William Martin

Joel, William Martin 1949-
See Joel, Billy
See also CA 108

John of the Cross, St. 1542-1591 . . . . **LC 18**

Johnson, B(ryan) S(tanley William)
1933-1973 . . . . **CLC 6, 9**
See also CA 9-12R; 53-56; CANR 9;
DLB 14, 40

Johnson, Benj. F. of Boo
See Riley, James Whitcomb

Johnson, Benjamin F. of Boo
See Riley, James Whitcomb

Johnson, Charles (Richard)
1948- . . . . **CLC 7, 51, 65; BLC;**
DAM MULT
See also BW 2; CA 116; CAAS 18;
CANR 42; DLB 33

Johnson, Denis 1949- . . . . **CLC 52**
See also CA 117; 121; DLB 120

Johnson, Diane 1934- . . . . **CLC 5, 13, 48**
See also CA 41-44R; CANR 17, 40;
DLBY 80; INT CANR-17; MTCW

Johnson, Eyvind (Olof Verner)
1900-1976 . . . . **CLC 14**
See also CA 73-76; 69-72; CANR 34

Johnson, J. R.
See James, C(yril) L(ionel) R(obert)

Johnson, James Weldon
1871-1938 . . . . **TCLC 3, 19; BLC;**
DAM MULT, POET
See also BW 1; CA 104; 125;
CDALB 1917-1929; CLR 32; DLB 51;
MTCW; SATA 31

Johnson, Joyce 1935- . . . . **CLC 58**
See also CA 125; 129

Johnson, Lionel (Pigot)
1867-1902 . . . . **TCLC 19**
See also CA 117; DLB 19

Johnson, Mel
See Malzberg, Barry N(athaniel)

Johnson, Pamela Hansford
1912-1981 . . . . **CLC 1, 7, 27**
See also CA 1-4R; 104; CANR 2, 28;
DLB 15; MTCW

Johnson, Robert 1911(?)-1938 . . . . . **TCLC 69**

Johnson, Samuel
1709-1784 . . . . . **LC 15; DA; DAB; DAC;**
DAM MST; WLC
See also CDBLB 1660-1789; DLB 39, 95,
104, 142

Johnson, Uwe
1934-1984 . . . . **CLC 5, 10, 15, 40**
See also CA 1-4R; 112; CANR 1, 39;
DLB 75; MTCW

Johnston, George (Benson) 1913- . . . **CLC 51**
See also CA 1-4R; CANR 5, 20; DLB 88

Johnston, Jennifer 1930- . . . . **CLC 7**
See also CA 85-88; DLB 14

Jolley, (Monica) Elizabeth
1923- . . . . **CLC 46; SSC 19**
See also CA 127; CAAS 13

Jones, Arthur Llewellyn 1863-1947
See Machen, Arthur
See also CA 104

Jones, D(ouglas) G(ordon) 1929- . . . . **CLC 10**
See also CA 29-32R; CANR 13; DLB 53

Jones, David (Michael)
1895-1974 . . . . **CLC 2, 4, 7, 13, 42**
See also CA 9-12R; 53-56; CANR 28;
CDBLB 1945-1960; DLB 20, 100; MTCW

Jones, David Robert 1947-
See Bowie, David
See also CA 103

Jones, Diana Wynne 1934- . . . . **CLC 26**
See also AAYA 12; CA 49-52; CANR 4,
26, 56; CLR 23; DLB 161; JRDA;
MAICYA; SAAS 7; SATA 9, 70

Jones, Edward P. 1950- . . . . **CLC 76**
See also BW 2; CA 142

Jones, Gayl
1949- . . . . **CLC 6, 9; BLC; DAM MULT**
See also BW 2; CA 77-80; CANR 27;
DLB 33; MTCW

Jones, James 1921-1977 . . . . **CLC 1, 3, 10, 39**
See also AITN 1, 2; CA 1-4R; 69-72;
CANR 6; DLB 2, 143; MTCW

Jones, John J.
See Lovecraft, H(oward) P(hillips)

Jones, LeRoi . . . . **CLC 1, 2, 3, 5, 10, 14**
See also Baraka, Amiri

Jones, Louis B. . . . . **CLC 65**
See also CA 141

Jones, Madison (Percy, Jr.) 1925- . . . **CLC 4**
See also CA 13-16R; CAAS 11; CANR 7,
54; DLB 152

Jones, Mervyn 1922- . . . . **CLC 10, 52**
See also CA 45-48; CAAS 5; CANR 1;
MTCW

Jones, Mick 1956(?)- . . . . **CLC 30**

Jones, Nettie (Pearl) 1941- . . . . **CLC 34**
See also BW 2; CA 137; CAAS 20

Jones, Preston 1936-1979 . . . . **CLC 10**
See also CA 73-76; 89-92; DLB 7

Jones, Robert F(rancis) 1934- . . . . . . **CLC 7**
See also CA 49-52; CANR 2

Jones, Rod 1953- . . . . **CLC 50**
See also CA 128

Jones, Terence Graham Parry
1942- . . . . **CLC 21**
See also Jones, Terry; Monty Python
See also CA 112; 116; CANR 35; INT 116

Jones, Terry
See Jones, Terence Graham Parry
See also SATA 67; SATA-Brief 51

Jones, Thom 1945(?)- . . . . **CLC 81**

Jong, Erica
1942- . . . . **CLC 4, 6, 8, 18, 83;**
DAM NOV, POP
See also AITN 1; BEST 90:2; CA 73-76;
CANR 26, 52; DLB 2, 5, 28, 152;
INT CANR-26; MTCW

Jonson, Ben(jamin)
1572(?)-1637 . . . . . . **LC 6, 33; DA; DAB;**
DAC; DAM DRAM, MST, POET;
DC 4; PC 17; WLC
See also CDBLB Before 1660; DLB 62, 121

Jordan, June
1936- . . . . . **CLC 5, 11, 23; DAM MULT,**
POET
See also AAYA 2; BW 2; CA 33-36R;
CANR 25; CLR 10; DLB 38; MAICYA;
MTCW; SATA 4

Jordan, Pat(rick M.) 1941- . . . . **CLC 37**
See also CA 33-36R

Jorgensen, Ivar
See Ellison, Harlan (Jay)

Jorgenson, Ivar
See Silverberg, Robert

Josephus, Flavius c. 37-100 . . . . . . **CMLC 13**

Josipovici, Gabriel 1940- . . . . **CLC 6, 43**
See also CA 37-40R; CAAS 8; CANR 47;
DLB 14

Joubert, Joseph 1754-1824 . . . . **NCLC 9**

Jouve, Pierre Jean 1887-1976 . . . . . . **CLC 47**
See also CA 65-68

Joyce, James (Augustine Aloysius)
1882-1941 . . . . **TCLC 3, 8, 16, 35, 52;**
DA; DAB; DAC; DAM MST, NOV,
POET; SSC 3; WLC
See also CA 104; 126; CDBLB 1914-1945;
DLB 10, 19, 36, 162; MTCW

Jozsef, Attila 1905-1937 . . . . **TCLC 22**
See also CA 116

Juana Ines de la Cruz 1651(?)-1695 . . . **LC 5**

Judd, Cyril
See Kornbluth, C(yril) M.; Pohl, Frederik

Julian of Norwich 1342(?)-1416(?) . . . . **LC 6**
See also DLB 146

Juniper, Alex
See Hospital, Janette Turner

Junius
See Luxemburg, Rosa

Just, Ward (Swift) 1935- . . . . **CLC 4, 27**
See also CA 25-28R; CANR 32;
INT CANR-32

Justice, Donald (Rodney)
1925- . . . . **CLC 6, 19; DAM POET**
See also CA 5-8R; CANR 26, 54;
DLBY 83; INT CANR-26

Juvenal c. 55-c. 127 . . . . **CMLC 8**

Juvenis
See Bourne, Randolph S(illiman)

Kacew, Romain 1914-1980
See Gary, Romain
See also CA 108; 102

Kadare, Ismail 1936- . . . . **CLC 52**

Kadohata, Cynthia . . . . **CLC 59**
See also CA 140

Kafka, Franz
1883-1924 . . . . **TCLC 2, 6, 13, 29, 47, 53;**
DA; DAB; DAC; DAM MST, NOV;
SSC 5; WLC
See also CA 105; 126; DLB 81; MTCW

Kahanovitsch, Pinkhes
See Der Nister

Kahn, Roger 1927- . . . . **CLC 30**
See also CA 25-28R; CANR 44; DLB 171;
SATA 37

Kain, Saul
See Sassoon, Siegfried (Lorraine)

Kaiser, Georg 1878-1945 . . . . **TCLC 9**
See also CA 106; DLB 124

Kaletski, Alexander 1946- . . . . **CLC 39**
See also CA 118; 143

Kalidasa fl. c. 400- . . . . **CMLC 9**

Kallman, Chester (Simon)
1921-1975 . . . . **CLC 2**
See also CA 45-48; 53-56; CANR 3

Kaminsky, Melvin 1926-
See Brooks, Mel
See also CA 65-68; CANR 16

Kaminsky, Stuart M(elvin) 1934- . . . **CLC 59**
See also CA 73-76; CANR 29, 53

Kane, Francis
See Robbins, Harold

Kane, Paul
See Simon, Paul (Frederick)

Kane, Wilson
See Bloch, Robert (Albert)

Kanin, Garson 1912- . . . . **CLC 22**
See also AITN 1; CA 5-8R; CANR 7;
DLB 7

Kaniuk, Yoram 1930- . . . . **CLC 19**
See also CA 134

Kant, Immanuel 1724-1804 . . . . . . **NCLC 27**
See also DLB 94

Kantor, MacKinlay 1904-1977 . . . . . . **CLC 7**
See also CA 61-64; 73-76; DLB 9, 102

Kaplan, David Michael 1946- . . . . . . **CLC 50**

Kaplan, James 1951- . . . . **CLC 59**
See also CA 135

Karageorge, Michael
See Anderson, Poul (William)

Karamzin, Nikolai Mikhailovich
1766-1826 . . . . **NCLC 3**
See also DLB 150

Karapanou, Margarita 1946- . . . . **CLC 13**
See also CA 101

Karinthy, Frigyes 1887-1938 . . . . . **TCLC 47**

Karl, Frederick R(obert) 1927- . . . . . **CLC 34**
See also CA 5-8R; CANR 3, 44

Kastel, Warren
See Silverberg, Robert

Kataev, Evgeny Petrovich 1903-1942
See Petrov, Evgeny
See also CA 120

Kataphusin
See Ruskin, John

Katz, Steve 1935- . . . . **CLC 47**
See also CA 25-28R; CAAS 14; CANR 12;
DLBY 83

Kauffman, Janet 1945- . . . . **CLC 42**
See also CA 117; CANR 43; DLBY 86

Kaufman, Bob (Garnell)
1925-1986 . . . . **CLC 49**
See also BW 1; CA 41-44R; 118; CANR 22;
DLB 16, 41

Kaufman, George S.
1889-1961 . . . . . . **CLC 38; DAM DRAM**
See also CA 108; 93-96; DLB 7; INT 108

Kaufman, Sue . . . . **CLC 3, 8**
See also Barondess, Sue K(aufman)

Kavafis, Konstantinos Petrou 1863-1933
See Cavafy, C(onstantine) P(eter)
See also CA 104

Kavan, Anna 1901-1968 . . . . . . **CLC 5, 13, 82**
See also CA 5-8R; CANR 6, 57; MTCW

Kavanagh, Dan
See Barnes, Julian (Patrick)

Kavanagh, Patrick (Joseph)
1904-1967 . . . . **CLC 22**
See also CA 123; 25-28R; DLB 15, 20;
MTCW

Kawabata, Yasunari
1899-1972 . . . . **CLC 2, 5, 9, 18;**
DAM MULT; SSC 17
See also CA 93-96; 33-36R

Kaye, M(ary) M(argaret) 1909- . . . . . **CLC 28**
See also CA 89-92; CANR 24; MTCW;
SATA 62

Kaye, Mollie
See Kaye, M(ary) M(argaret)

Kaye-Smith, Sheila 1887-1956 . . . . . **TCLC 20**
See also CA 118; DLB 36

Kaymor, Patrice Maguilene
See Senghor, Leopold Sedar

Kazan, Elia 1909- . . . . **CLC 6, 16, 63**
See also CA 21-24R; CANR 32

Kazantzakis, Nikos
1883(?)-1957 . . . . **TCLC 2, 5, 33**
See also CA 105; 132; MTCW

Kazin, Alfred 1915- . . . . **CLC 34, 38**
See also CA 1-4R; CAAS 7; CANR 1, 45;
DLB 67

Keane, Mary Nesta (Skrine) 1904-1996
See Keane, Molly
See also CA 108; 114; 151

Keane, Molly . . . . **CLC 31**
See also Keane, Mary Nesta (Skrine)
See also INT 114

Keates, Jonathan 19(?)- . . . . **CLC 34**

Keaton, Buster 1895-1966 . . . . **CLC 20**

Keats, John
1795-1821 . . . . **NCLC 8; DA; DAB;**
DAC; DAM MST, POET; PC 1; WLC
See also CDBLB 1789-1832; DLB 96, 110

Keene, Donald 1922- . . . . **CLC 34**
See also CA 1-4R; CANR 5

Keillor, Garrison . . . . **CLC 40**
See also Keillor, Gary (Edward)
See also AAYA 2; BEST 89:3; DLBY 87;
SATA 58

Keillor, Gary (Edward) 1942-
See Keillor, Garrison
See also CA 111; 117; CANR 36;
DAM POP; MTCW

Keith, Michael
See Hubbard, L(afayette) Ron(ald)

Keller, Gottfried 1819-1890 . . . . **NCLC 2**
See also DLB 129

Kellerman, Jonathan
1949- . . . . **CLC 44; DAM POP**
See also BEST 90:1; CA 106; CANR 29, 51;
INT CANR-29

Kelley, William Melvin 1937- . . . . . . **CLC 22**
See also BW 1; CA 77-80; CANR 27;
DLB 33

Kellogg, Marjorie 1922- . . . . **CLC 2**
See also CA 81-84

Kellow, Kathleen
See Hibbert, Eleanor Alice Burford

Kelly, M(ilton) T(erry) 1947- . . . . . . **CLC 55**
See also CA 97-100; CAAS 22; CANR 19,
43

Kelman, James 1946- . . . . **CLC 58, 86**
See also CA 148

Kemal, Yashar 1923- . . . . **CLC 14, 29**
See also CA 89-92; CANR 44

Kemble, Fanny 1809-1893 . . . . **NCLC 18**
See also DLB 32

Kemelman, Harry 1908-1996 . . . . **CLC 2**
See also AITN 1; CA 9-12R; 155; CANR 6;
DLB 28

Kempe, Margery 1373(?)-1440(?) . . . . . **LC 6**
See also DLB 146

Kempis, Thomas a 1380-1471 . . . . **LC 11**

Kendall, Henry 1839-1882 . . . . . . **NCLC 12**

Keneally, Thomas (Michael)
1935- . . . . . . **CLC 5, 8, 10, 14, 19, 27, 43;**
DAM NOV
See also CA 85-88; CANR 10, 50; MTCW

Kennedy, Adrienne (Lita)
1931- . . . . . **CLC 66; BLC; DAM MULT;**
DC 5
See also BW 2; CA 103; CAAS 20; CABS 3;
CANR 26, 53; DLB 38

Kennedy, John Pendleton
1795-1870 . . . . **NCLC 2**
See also DLB 3

Kennedy, Joseph Charles 1929-
See Kennedy, X. J.
See also CA 1-4R; CANR 4, 30, 40;
SATA 14, 86

Kennedy, William
1928- . . . **CLC 6, 28, 34, 53; DAM NOV**
See also AAYA 1; CA 85-88; CANR 14,
31; DLB 143; DLBY 85; INT CANR-31;
MTCW; SATA 57

Kennedy, X. J. . . . . **CLC 8, 42**
See also Kennedy, Joseph Charles
See also CAAS 9; CLR 27; DLB 5;
SAAS 22

Kenny, Maurice (Francis)
1929- . . . . **CLC 87; DAM MULT**
See also CA 144; CAAS 22; DLB 175;
NNAL

Kent, Kelvin
See Kuttner, Henry

Kenton, Maxwell
See Southern, Terry

Kenyon, Robert O.
See Kuttner, Henry

Kerouac, Jack . . . . . **CLC 1, 2, 3, 5, 14, 29, 61**
See also Kerouac, Jean-Louis Lebris de
See also CDALB 1941-1968; DLB 2, 16;
DLBD 3; DLBY 95

Kerouac, Jean-Louis Lebris de 1922-1969
See Kerouac, Jack
See also AITN 1; CA 5-8R; 25-28R;
CANR 26, 54; DA; DAB; DAC;
DAM MST, NOV, POET, POP; MTCW;
WLC

Kerr, Jean 1923-................ **CLC 22**
See also CA 5-8R; CANR 7; INT CANR-7

Kerr, M. E. .... **CLC 12, 35**
See also Meaker, Marijane (Agnes)
See also AAYA 2; CLR 29; SAAS 1

Kerr, Robert .... **CLC 55**

Kerrigan, (Thomas) Anthony
1918-..................... **CLC 4, 6**
See also CA 49-52; CAAS 11; CANR 4

Kerry, Lois
See Duncan, Lois

Kesey, Ken (Elton)
1935-...... **CLC 1, 3, 6, 11, 46, 64; DA;**
DAB; DAC; DAM MST, NOV, POP;
WLC
See also CA 1-4R; CANR 22, 38;
CDALB 1968-1988; DLB 2, 16; MTCW;
SATA 66

Kesselring, Joseph (Otto)
1902-1967 ..... **CLC 45; DAM DRAM,**
MST
See also CA 150

Kessler, Jascha (Frederick) 1929-.... **CLC 4**
See also CA 17-20R; CANR 8, 48

Kettelkamp, Larry (Dale) 1933- .... **CLC 12**
See also CA 29-32R; CANR 16; SAAS 3;
SATA 2

Key, Ellen 1849-1926........... **TCLC 65**

Keyber, Conny
See Fielding, Henry

Keyes, Daniel
1927-............ **CLC 80; DA; DAC;**
DAM MST, NOV
See also CA 17-20R; CANR 10, 26, 54;
SATA 37

Keynes, John Maynard
1883-1946 .... **TCLC 64**
See also CA 114; DLBD 10

Khanshendel, Chiron
See Rose, Wendy

Khayyam, Omar
1048-1131 .... **CMLC 11; DAM POET;**
PC 8

Kherdian, David 1931-........... **CLC 6, 9**
See also CA 21-24R; CAAS 2; CANR 39;
CLR 24; JRDA; MAICYA; SATA 16, 74

Khlebnikov, Velimir .... **TCLC 20**
See also Khlebnikov, Viktor Vladimirovich

Khlebnikov, Viktor Vladimirovich 1885-1922
See Khlebnikov, Velimir
See also CA 117

Khodasevich, Vladislav (Felitsianovich)
1886-1939................... **TCLC 15**
See also CA 115

Kielland, Alexander Lange
1849-1906 .... **TCLC 5**
See also CA 104

Kiely, Benedict 1919-......... **CLC 23, 43**
See also CA 1-4R; CANR 2; DLB 15

Kienzle, William X(avier)
1928-............ **CLC 25; DAM POP**
See also CA 93-96; CAAS 1; CANR 9, 31;
INT CANR-31; MTCW

Kierkegaard, Soren 1813-1855.... **NCLC 34**

Killens, John Oliver 1916-1987..... **CLC 10**
See also BW 2; CA 77-80; 123; CAAS 2;
CANR 26; DLB 33

Killigrew, Anne 1660-1685........... **LC 4**
See also DLB 131

Kim
See Simenon, Georges (Jacques Christian)

Kincaid, Jamaica
1949-............. **CLC 43, 68; BLC;**
DAM MULT, NOV
See also AAYA 13; BW 2; CA 125;
CANR 47; DLB 157

King, Francis (Henry)
1923-.......... **CLC 8, 53; DAM NOV**
See also CA 1-4R; CANR 1, 33; DLB 15,
139; MTCW

King, Martin Luther, Jr.
1929-1968 .... **CLC 83; BLC; DA; DAB;**
DAC; DAM MST, MULT
See also BW 2; CA 25-28; CANR 27, 44;
CAP 2; MTCW; SATA 14

King, Stephen (Edwin)
1947-............ **CLC 12, 26, 37, 61;**
DAM NOV, POP; SSC 17
See also AAYA 1, 17; BEST 90:1;
CA 61-64; CANR 1, 30, 52; DLB 143;
DLBY 80; JRDA; MTCW; SATA 9, 55

King, Steve
See King, Stephen (Edwin)

King, Thomas
1943- ..... **CLC 89; DAC; DAM MULT**
See also CA 144; DLB 175; NNAL

Kingman, Lee................ **CLC 17**
See also Natti, (Mary) Lee
See also SAAS 3; SATA 1, 67

Kingsley, Charles 1819-1875..... **NCLC 35**
See also DLB 21, 32, 163; YABC 2

Kingsley, Sidney 1906-1995...... **CLC 44**
See also CA 85-88; 147; DLB 7

Kingsolver, Barbara
1955-......... **CLC 55, 81; DAM POP**
See also AAYA 15; CA 129; 134; INT 134

Kingston, Maxine (Ting Ting) Hong
1940- .... **CLC 12, 19, 58; DAM MULT,**
NOV
See also AAYA 8; CA 69-72; CANR 13,
38; DLB 173; DLBY 80; INT CANR-13;
MTCW; SATA 53

Kinnell, Galway
1927-........ **CLC 1, 2, 3, 5, 13, 29**
See also CA 9-12R; CANR 10, 34; DLB 5;
DLBY 87; INT CANR-34; MTCW

Kinsella, Thomas 1928-......... **CLC 4, 19**
See also CA 17-20R; CANR 15; DLB 27;
MTCW

Kinsella, W(illiam) P(atrick)
1935-............. **CLC 27, 43; DAC;**
DAM NOV, POP
See also AAYA 7; CA 97-100; CAAS 7;
CANR 21, 35; INT CANR-21; MTCW

Kipling, (Joseph) Rudyard
1865-1936 ...... **TCLC 8, 17; DA; DAB;**
DAC; DAM MST, POET; PC 3; SSC 5;
WLC
See also CA 105; 120; CANR 33;
CDBLB 1890-1914; CLR 39; DLB 19, 34,
141, 156; MAICYA; MTCW; YABC 2

Kirkup, James 1918- .... **CLC 1**
See also CA 1-4R; CAAS 4; CANR 2;
DLB 27; SATA 12

Kirkwood, James 1930(?)-1989 ...... **CLC 9**
See also AITN 2; CA 1-4R; 128; CANR 6,
40

Kirshner, Sidney
See Kingsley, Sidney

Kis, Danilo 1935-1989 .... **CLC 57**
See also CA 109; 118; 129; MTCW

Kivi, Aleksis 1834-1872......... **NCLC 30**

Kizer, Carolyn (Ashley)
1925- ..... **CLC 15, 39, 80; DAM POET**
See also CA 65-68; CAAS 5; CANR 24;
DLB 5, 169

Klabund 1890-1928.............. **TCLC 44**
See also DLB 66

Klappert, Peter 1942-............. **CLC 57**
See also CA 33-36R; DLB 5

Klein, A(braham) M(oses)
1909-1972 .... **CLC 19; DAB; DAC;**
DAM MST
See also CA 101; 37-40R; DLB 68

Klein, Norma 1938-1989 .... **CLC 30**
See also AAYA 2; CA 41-44R; 128;
CANR 15, 37; CLR 2, 19;
INT CANR-15; JRDA; MAICYA;
SAAS 1; SATA 7, 57

Klein, T(heodore) E(ibon) D(onald)
1947-..................... **CLC 34**
See also CA 119; CANR 44

Kleist, Heinrich von
1777-1811 .... **NCLC 2, 37;**
DAM DRAM; SSC 22
See also DLB 90

Klima, Ivan 1931-..... **CLC 56; DAM NOV**
See also CA 25-28R; CANR 17, 50

Klimentov, Andrei Platonovich 1899-1951
See Platonov, Andrei
See also CA 108

Klinger, Friedrich Maximilian von
1752-1831 .... **NCLC 1**
See also DLB 94

Klopstock, Friedrich Gottlieb
1724-1803 .... **NCLC 11**
See also DLB 97

Knapp, Caroline 1959-............ **CLC 99**
See also CA 154

Knebel, Fletcher 1911-1993........ **CLC 14**
See also AITN 1; CA 1-4R; 140; CAAS 3;
CANR 1, 36; SATA 36; SATA-Obit 75

Knickerbocker, Diedrich
See Irving, Washington

Knight, Etheridge
1931-1991 .... **CLC 40; BLC;**
DAM POET; PC 14
See also BW 1; CA 21-24R; 133; CANR 23;
DLB 41

Knight, Sarah Kemble 1666-1727 ..... **LC 7**
See also DLB 24

Knister, Raymond 1899-1932...... **TCLC 56**
See also DLB 68

Kyprianos, Iossif
See Samarakis, Antonis

La Bruyere, Jean de 1645-1696...... **LC 17**

Lacan, Jacques (Marie Emile)
1901-1981 .... **CLC 75**
See also CA 121; 104

**Laclos, Pierre Ambroise Francois Choderlos
de** 1741-1803 .... **NCLC 4**

La Colere, Francois
See Aragon, Louis

Lacolere, Francois
See Aragon, Louis

La Deshabilleuse
See Simenon, Georges (Jacques Christian)

Lady Gregory
See Gregory, Isabella Augusta (Persse)

Lady of Quality, A
See Bagnold, Enid

**La Fayette, Marie (Madelaine Pioche de la
Vergne Comtes** 1634-1693...... **LC 2**

Lafayette, Rene
See Hubbard, L(afayette) Ron(ald)

Laforgue, Jules
1860-1887 .... **NCLC 5, 53; PC 14;
SSC 20**

Lagerkvist, Paer (Fabian)
1891-1974 .... **CLC 7, 10, 13, 54;
DAM DRAM, NOV**
See also Lagerkvist, Par
See also CA 85-88; 49-52; MTCW

Lagerkvist, Par .... **SSC 12**
See also Lagerkvist, Paer (Fabian)

Lagerloef, Selma (Ottiliana Lovisa)
1858-1940 .... **TCLC 4, 36**
See also Lagerlof, Selma (Ottiliana Lovisa)
See also CA 108; SATA 15

Lagerlof, Selma (Ottiliana Lovisa)
See Lagerloef, Selma (Ottiliana Lovisa)
See also CLR 7; SATA 15

La Guma, (Justin) Alex(ander)
1925-1985 .... **CLC 19; DAM NOV**
See also BW 1; CA 49-52; 118; CANR 25;
DLB 117; MTCW

Laidlaw, A. K.
See Grieve, C(hristopher) M(urray)

Lainez, Manuel Mujica
See Mujica Lainez, Manuel
See also HW

Laing, R(onald) D(avid)
1927-1989 .... **CLC 95**
See also CA 107; 129; CANR 34; MTCW

Lamartine, Alphonse (Marie Louis Prat) de
1790-1869 ..... **NCLC 11; DAM POET;
PC 16**

Lamb, Charles
1775-1834 ...... **NCLC 10; DA; DAB;
DAC; DAM MST; WLC**
See also CDBLB 1789-1832; DLB 93, 107,
163; SATA 17

Lamb, Lady Caroline 1785-1828.. **NCLC 38**
See also DLB 116

Lamming, George (William)
1927- .... **CLC 2, 4, 66; BLC;
DAM MULT**
See also BW 2; CA 85-88; CANR 26;
DLB 125; MTCW

L'Amour, Louis (Dearborn)
1908-1988 .... **CLC 25, 55; DAM NOV,
POP**
See also AAYA 16; AITN 2; BEST 89:2;
CA 1-4R; 125; CANR 3, 25, 40;
DLBY 80; MTCW

Lampedusa, Giuseppe (Tomasi) di
1896-1957 .... **TCLC 13**
See also Tomasi di Lampedusa, Giuseppe
See also DLB 177

Lampman, Archibald 1861-1899 .. **NCLC 25**
See also DLB 92

Lancaster, Bruce 1896-1963........ **CLC 36**
See also CA 9-10; CAP 1; SATA 9

Lanchester, John .... **CLC 99**

Landau, Mark Alexandrovich
See Aldanov, Mark (Alexandrovich)

Landau-Aldanov, Mark Alexandrovich
See Aldanov, Mark (Alexandrovich)

Landis, Jerry
See Simon, Paul (Frederick)

Landis, John 1950-................ **CLC 26**
See also CA 112; 122

Landolfi, Tommaso 1908-1979... **CLC 11, 49**
See also CA 127; 117; DLB 177

Landon, Letitia Elizabeth
1802-1838 .... **NCLC 15**
See also DLB 96

Landor, Walter Savage
1775-1864 .... **NCLC 14**
See also DLB 93, 107

Landwirth, Heinz 1927-
See Lind, Jakov
See also CA 9-12R; CANR 7

Lane, Patrick
1939- .... **CLC 25; DAM POET**
See also CA 97-100; CANR 54; DLB 53;
INT 97-100

Lang, Andrew 1844-1912........ **TCLC 16**
See also CA 114; 137; DLB 98, 141;
MAICYA; SATA 16

Lang, Fritz 1890-1976 .... **CLC 20**
See also CA 77-80; 69-72; CANR 30

Lange, John
See Crichton, (John) Michael

Langer, Elinor 1939- .... **CLC 34**
See also CA 121

Langland, William
1330(?)-1400(?) ..... **LC 19; DA; DAB;
DAC; DAM MST, POET**
See also DLB 146

Langstaff, Launcelot
See Irving, Washington

Lanier, Sidney
1842-1881 ...... **NCLC 6; DAM POET**
See also DLB 64; DLBD 13; MAICYA;
SATA 18

Lanyer, Aemilia 1569-1645 ..... **LC 10, 30**
See also DLB 121

Lao Tzu .... **CMLC 7**

Lapine, James (Elliot) 1949-....... **CLC 39**
See also CA 123; 130; CANR 54; INT 130

Larbaud, Valery (Nicolas)
1881-1957 .... **TCLC 9**
See also CA 106; 152

Lardner, Ring
See Lardner, Ring(gold) W(ilmer)

Lardner, Ring W., Jr.
See Lardner, Ring(gold) W(ilmer)

Lardner, Ring(gold) W(ilmer)
1885-1933 .... **TCLC 2, 14**
See also CA 104; 131; CDALB 1917-1929;
DLB 11, 25, 86; MTCW

Laredo, Betty
See Codrescu, Andrei

Larkin, Maia
See Wojciechowska, Maia (Teresa)

Larkin, Philip (Arthur)
1922-1985 .... **CLC 3, 5, 8, 9, 13, 18, 33,
39, 64; DAB; DAM MST, POET**
See also CA 5-8R; 117; CANR 24;
CDBLB 1960 to Present; DLB 27;
MTCW

Larra (y Sanchez de Castro), Mariano Jose de
1809-1837 .... **NCLC 17**

Larsen, Eric 1941-............... **CLC 55**
See also CA 132

Larsen, Nella
1891-1964 .... **CLC 37; BLC;
DAM MULT**
See also BW 1; CA 125; DLB 51

Larson, Charles R(aymond) 1938-... **CLC 31**
See also CA 53-56; CANR 4

Larson, Jonathan 1961(?)-1996..... **CLC 99**

Las Casas, Bartolome de 1474-1566.. **LC 31**

Lasker-Schueler, Else 1869-1945 .. **TCLC 57**
See also DLB 66, 124

Latham, Jean Lee 1902-........... **CLC 12**
See also AITN 1; CA 5-8R; CANR 7;
MAICYA; SATA 2, 68

Latham, Mavis
See Clark, Mavis Thorpe

Lathen, Emma .... **CLC 2**
See also Hennissart, Martha; Latsis, Mary
J(ane)

Lathrop, Francis
See Leiber, Fritz (Reuter, Jr.)

Latsis, Mary J(ane)
See Lathen, Emma
See also CA 85-88

Lattimore, Richmond (Alexander)
1906-1984 .... **CLC 3**
See also CA 1-4R; 112; CANR 1

Laughlin, James 1914-........... **CLC 49**
See also CA 21-24R; CAAS 22; CANR 9,
47; DLB 48

Laurence, (Jean) Margaret (Wemyss)
1926-1987 .... **CLC 3, 6, 13, 50, 62;
DAC; DAM MST; SSC 7**
See also CA 5-8R; 121; CANR 33; DLB 53;
MTCW; SATA-Obit 50

Laurent, Antoine 1952-.......... **CLC 50**

Lauscher, Hermann
See Hesse, Hermann

Lemann, Nancy 1956-............ **CLC 39**
See also CA 118; 136

Lemonnier, (Antoine Louis) Camille
1844-1913 .... **TCLC 22**
See also CA 121

Lenau, Nikolaus 1802-1850 ..... **NCLC 16**

L'Engle, Madeleine (Camp Franklin)
1918- .... **CLC 12; DAM POP**
See also AAYA 1; AITN 2; CA 1-4R;
CANR 3, 21, 39; CLR 1, 14; DLB 52;
JRDA; MAICYA; MTCW; SAAS 15;
SATA 1, 27, 75

Lengyel, Jozsef 1896-1975......... **CLC 7**
See also CA 85-88; 57-60

Lenin 1870-1924
See Lenin, V. I.
See also CA 121

Lenin, V. I. .... **TCLC 67**
See also Lenin

Lennon, John (Ono)
1940-1980 .... **CLC 12, 35**
See also CA 102

Lennox, Charlotte Ramsay
1729(?)-1804 .... **NCLC 23**
See also DLB 39

Lentricchia, Frank (Jr.) 1940-...... **CLC 34**
See also CA 25-28R; CANR 19

Lenz, Siegfried 1926-............ **CLC 27**
See also CA 89-92; DLB 75

Leonard, Elmore (John, Jr.)
1925- ...... **CLC 28, 34, 71; DAM POP**
See also AITN 1; BEST 89:1, 90:4;
CA 81-84; CANR 12, 28, 53; DLB 173;
INT CANR-28; MTCW

Leonard, Hugh .... **CLC 19**
See also Byrne, John Keyes
See also DLB 13

Leonov, Leonid (Maximovich)
1899-1994 .... **CLC 92; DAM NOV**
See also CA 129; MTCW

Leopardi, (Conte) Giacomo
1798-1837 .... **NCLC 22**

Le Reveler
See Artaud, Antonin (Marie Joseph)

Lerman, Eleanor 1952-............ **CLC 9**
See also CA 85-88

Lerman, Rhoda 1936-............ **CLC 56**
See also CA 49-52

Lermontov, Mikhail Yuryevich
1814-1841 .... **NCLC 47**

Leroux, Gaston 1868-1927....... **TCLC 25**
See also CA 108; 136; SATA 65

Lesage, Alain-Rene 1668-1747...... **LC 28**

Leskov, Nikolai (Semyonovich)
1831-1895 .... **NCLC 25**

Lessing, Doris (May)
1919- ..... **CLC 1, 2, 3, 6, 10, 15, 22, 40,**
94; DA; DAB; DAC; DAM MST, NOV;
SSC 6
See also CA 9-12R; CAAS 14; CANR 33,
54; CDBLB 1960 to Present; DLB 15,
139; DLBY 85; MTCW

Lessing, Gotthold Ephraim
1729-1781 .... **LC 8**
See also DLB 97

Lester, Richard 1932-............ **CLC 20**

Lever, Charles (James)
1806-1872 .... **NCLC 23**
See also DLB 21

Leverson, Ada 1865(?)-1936(?) .... **TCLC 18**
See also Elaine
See also CA 117; DLB 153

Levertov, Denise
1923- ...... **CLC 1, 2, 3, 5, 8, 15, 28, 66;**
DAM POET; PC 11
See also CA 1-4R; CAAS 19; CANR 3, 29,
50; DLB 5, 165; INT CANR-29; MTCW

Levi, Jonathan................... **CLC 76**

Levi, Peter (Chad Tigar) 1931-..... **CLC 41**
See also CA 5-8R; CANR 34; DLB 40

Levi, Primo
1919-1987 .... **CLC 37, 50; SSC 12**
See also CA 13-16R; 122; CANR 12, 33;
DLB 177; MTCW

Levin, Ira 1929- ..... **CLC 3, 6; DAM POP**
See also CA 21-24R; CANR 17, 44;
MTCW; SATA 66

Levin, Meyer
1905-1981 .... **CLC 7; DAM POP**
See also AITN 1; CA 9-12R; 104;
CANR 15; DLB 9, 28; DLBY 81;
SATA 21; SATA-Obit 27

Levine, Norman 1924- .... **CLC 54**
See also CA 73-76; CAAS 23; CANR 14;
DLB 88

Levine, Philip
1928- .... **CLC 2, 4, 5, 9, 14, 33;**
DAM POET
See also CA 9-12R; CANR 9, 37, 52;
DLB 5

Levinson, Deirdre 1931-.......... **CLC 49**
See also CA 73-76

Levi-Strauss, Claude 1908- .... **CLC 38**
See also CA 1-4R; CANR 6, 32, 57; MTCW

Levitin, Sonia (Wolff) 1934- .... **CLC 17**
See also AAYA 13; CA 29-32R; CANR 14,
32; JRDA; MAICYA; SAAS 2; SATA 4,
68

Levon, O. U.
See Kesey, Ken (Elton)

Levy, Amy 1861-1889.......... **NCLC 59**
See also DLB 156

Lewes, George Henry
1817-1878 .... **NCLC 25**
See also DLB 55, 144

Lewis, Alun 1915-1944........... **TCLC 3**
See also CA 104; DLB 20, 162

Lewis, C. Day
See Day Lewis, C(ecil)

Lewis, C(live) S(taples)
1898-1963 ..... **CLC 1, 3, 6, 14, 27; DA;**
DAB; DAC; DAM MST, NOV, POP;
WLC
See also AAYA 3; CA 81-84; CANR 33;
CDBLB 1945-1960; CLR 3, 27; DLB 15,
100, 160; JRDA; MAICYA; MTCW;
SATA 13

Lewis, Janet 1899-.............. **CLC 41**
See also Winters, Janet Lewis
See also CA 9-12R; CANR 29; CAP 1;
DLBY 87

Lewis, Matthew Gregory
1775-1818 .... **NCLC 11**
See also DLB 39, 158

Lewis, (Harry) Sinclair
1885-1951 ..... **TCLC 4, 13, 23, 39; DA;**
DAB; DAC; DAM MST, NOV; WLC
See also CA 104; 133; CDALB 1917-1929;
DLB 9, 102; DLBD 1; MTCW

Lewis, (Percy) Wyndham
1884(?)-1957............. **TCLC 2, 9**
See also CA 104; DLB 15

Lewisohn, Ludwig 1883-1955...... **TCLC 19**
See also CA 107; DLB 4, 9, 28, 102

Leyner, Mark 1956-............ **CLC 92**
See also CA 110; CANR 28, 53

Lezama Lima, Jose
1910-1976 ..... **CLC 4, 10; DAM MULT**
See also CA 77-80; DLB 113; HW

L'Heureux, John (Clarke) 1934-.... **CLC 52**
See also CA 13-16R; CANR 23, 45

Liddell, C. H.
See Kuttner, Henry

Lie, Jonas (Lauritz Idemil)
1833-1908(?) .... **TCLC 5**
See also CA 115

Lieber, Joel 1937-1971............. **CLC 6**
See also CA 73-76; 29-32R

Lieber, Stanley Martin
See Lee, Stan

Lieberman, Laurence (James)
1935- .... **CLC 4, 36**
See also CA 17-20R; CANR 8, 36

Lieksman, Anders
See Haavikko, Paavo Juhani

Li Fei-kan 1904-
See Pa Chin
See also CA 105

Lifton, Robert Jay 1926-.......... **CLC 67**
See also CA 17-20R; CANR 27;
INT CANR-27; SATA 66

Lightfoot, Gordon 1938-.......... **CLC 26**
See also CA 109

Lightman, Alan P. 1948- .... **CLC 81**
See also CA 141

Ligotti, Thomas (Robert)
1953- .... **CLC 44; SSC 16**
See also CA 123; CANR 49

Li Ho 791-817.................... **PC 13**

Liliencron, (Friedrich Adolf Axel) Detlev von
1844-1909 .... **TCLC 18**
See also CA 117

Lilly, William 1602-1681.......... **LC 27**

Lima, Jose Lezama
See Lezama Lima, Jose

Lima Barreto, Afonso Henrique de
1881-1922 .... **TCLC 23**
See also CA 117

Limonov, Edward 1944-.......... **CLC 67**
See also CA 137

Lin, Frank
See Atherton, Gertrude (Franklin Horn)

Lincoln, Abraham 1809-1865..... **NCLC 18**

Lind, Jakov . . . . CLC 1, 2, 4, 27, 82
See also Landwirth, Heinz
See also CAAS 4

Lindbergh, Anne (Spencer) Morrow
1906- . . . . CLC 82; DAM NOV
See also CA 17-20R; CANR 16; MTCW;
SATA 33

Lindsay, David 1878-1945 . . . . TCLC 15
See also CA 113

Lindsay, (Nicholas) Vachel
1879-1931 . . . . TCLC 17; DA; DAC;
DAM MST, POET; WLC
See also CA 114; 135; CDALB 1865-1917;
DLB 54; SATA 40

Linke-Poot
See Doeblin, Alfred

Linney, Romulus 1930- . . . . CLC 51
See also CA 1-4R; CANR 40, 44

Linton, Eliza Lynn 1822-1898 . . . . NCLC 41
See also DLB 18

Li Po 701-763 . . . . CMLC 2

Lipsius, Justus 1547-1606 . . . . LC 16

Lipsyte, Robert (Michael)
1938- . . . . CLC 21; DA; DAC;
DAM MST, NOV
See also AAYA 7; CA 17-20R; CANR 8,
57; CLR 23; JRDA; MAICYA; SATA 5,
68

Lish, Gordon (Jay) 1934- . . CLC 45; SSC 18
See also CA 113; 117; DLB 130; INT 117

Lispector, Clarice 1925-1977 . . . . . . CLC 43
See also CA 139; 116; DLB 113

Littell, Robert 1935(?)- . . . . CLC 42
See also CA 109; 112

Little, Malcolm 1925-1965
See Malcolm X
See also BW 1; CA 125; 111; DA; DAB;
DAC; DAM MST, MULT; MTCW

Littlewit, Humphrey Gent.
See Lovecraft, H(oward) P(hillips)

Litwos
See Sienkiewicz, Henryk (Adam Alexander
Pius)

Liu E 1857-1909 . . . . TCLC 15
See also CA 115

Lively, Penelope (Margaret)
1933- . . . . CLC 32, 50; DAM NOV
See also CA 41-44R; CANR 29; CLR 7;
DLB 14, 161; JRDA; MAICYA; MTCW;
SATA 7, 60

Livesay, Dorothy (Kathleen)
1909- . . . . CLC 4, 15, 79; DAC;
DAM MST, POET
See also AITN 2; CA 25-28R; CAAS 8;
CANR 36; DLB 68; MTCW

Livy c. 59B.C.-c. 17 . . . . CMLC 11

Lizardi, Jose Joaquin Fernandez de
1776-1827 . . . . NCLC 30

Llewellyn, Richard
See Llewellyn Lloyd, Richard Dafydd
Vivian
See also DLB 15

Llewellyn Lloyd, Richard Dafydd Vivian
1906-1983 . . . . CLC 7, 80
See also Llewellyn, Richard
See also CA 53-56; 111; CANR 7;
SATA 11; SATA-Obit 37

Llosa, (Jorge) Mario (Pedro) Vargas
See Vargas Llosa, (Jorge) Mario (Pedro)

Lloyd Webber, Andrew 1948-
See Webber, Andrew Lloyd
See also AAYA 1; CA 116; 149;
DAM DRAM; SATA 56

Llull, Ramon c. 1235-c. 1316 . . . . . CMLC 12

Locke, Alain (Le Roy)
1886-1954 . . . . TCLC 43
See also BW 1; CA 106; 124; DLB 51

Locke, John 1632-1704 . . . . LC 7, 35
See also DLB 101

Locke-Elliott, Sumner
See Elliott, Sumner Locke

Lockhart, John Gibson
1794-1854 . . . . NCLC 6
See also DLB 110, 116, 144

Lodge, David (John)
1935- . . . . CLC 36; DAM POP
See also BEST 90:1; CA 17-20R; CANR 19,
53; DLB 14; INT CANR-19; MTCW

Loennbohm, Armas Eino Leopold 1878-1926
See Leino, Eino
See also CA 123

Loewinsohn, Ron(ald William)
1937- . . . . CLC 52
See also CA 25-28R

Logan, Jake
See Smith, Martin Cruz

Logan, John (Burton) 1923-1987 . . . . . CLC 5
See also CA 77-80; 124; CANR 45; DLB 5

Lo Kuan-chung 1330(?)-1400(?) . . . . . . LC 12

Lombard, Nap
See Johnson, Pamela Hansford

London, Jack . . TCLC 9, 15, 39; SSC 4; WLC
See also London, John Griffith
See also AAYA 13; AITN 2;
CDALB 1865-1917; DLB 8, 12, 78;
SATA 18

London, John Griffith 1876-1916
See London, Jack
See also CA 110; 119; DA; DAB; DAC;
DAM MST, NOV; JRDA; MAICYA;
MTCW

Long, Emmett
See Leonard, Elmore (John, Jr.)

Longbaugh, Harry
See Goldman, William (W.)

Longfellow, Henry Wadsworth
1807-1882 . . . . . NCLC 2, 45; DA; DAB;
DAC; DAM MST, POET
See also CDALB 1640-1865; DLB 1, 59;
SATA 19

Longley, Michael 1939- . . . . CLC 29
See also CA 102; DLB 40

Longus fl. c. 2nd cent. - . . . . CMLC 7

Longway, A. Hugh
See Lang, Andrew

Lonnrot, Elias 1802-1884 . . . . NCLC 53

Lopate, Phillip 1943- . . . . CLC 29
See also CA 97-100; DLBY 80; INT 97-100

Lopez Portillo (y Pacheco), Jose
1920- . . . . CLC 46
See also CA 129; HW

Lopez y Fuentes, Gregorio
1897(?)-1966 . . . . CLC 32
See also CA 131; HW

Lorca, Federico Garcia
See Garcia Lorca, Federico

Lord, Bette Bao 1938- . . . . CLC 23
See also BEST 90:3; CA 107; CANR 41;
INT 107; SATA 58

Lord Auch
See Bataille, Georges

Lord Byron
See Byron, George Gordon (Noel)

Lorde, Audre (Geraldine)
1934-1992 . . . . CLC 18, 71; BLC;
DAM MULT, POET; PC 12
See also BW 1; CA 25-28R; 142; CANR 16,
26, 46; DLB 41; MTCW

Lord Houghton
See Milnes, Richard Monckton

Lord Jeffrey
See Jeffrey, Francis

Lorenzini, Carlo 1826-1890
See Collodi, Carlo
See also MAICYA; SATA 29

Lorenzo, Heberto Padilla
See Padilla (Lorenzo), Heberto

Loris
See Hofmannsthal, Hugo von

Loti, Pierre . . . . TCLC 11
See also Viaud, (Louis Marie) Julien
See also DLB 123

Louie, David Wong 1954- . . . . CLC 70
See also CA 139

Louis, Father M.
See Merton, Thomas

Lovecraft, H(oward) P(hillips)
1890-1937 . . . . TCLC 4, 22; DAM POP;
SSC 3
See also AAYA 14; CA 104; 133; MTCW

Lovelace, Earl 1935- . . . . CLC 51
See also BW 2; CA 77-80; CANR 41;
DLB 125; MTCW

Lovelace, Richard 1618-1657 . . . . LC 24
See also DLB 131

Lowell, Amy
1874-1925 . . . . TCLC 1, 8; DAM POET;
PC 13
See also CA 104; 151; DLB 54, 140

Lowell, James Russell 1819-1891 . . NCLC 2
See also CDALB 1640-1865; DLB 1, 11, 64,
79

Lowell, Robert (Traill Spence, Jr.)
1917-1977 . . . CLC 1, 2, 3, 4, 5, 8, 9, 11,
15, 37; DA; DAB; DAC; DAM MST,
NOV; PC 3; WLC
See also CA 9-12R; 73-76; CABS 2;
CANR 26; DLB 5, 169; MTCW

Lowndes, Marie Adelaide (Belloc)
1868-1947 . . . . TCLC 12
See also CA 107; DLB 70

Lowry, (Clarence) Malcolm
1909-1957 . . . . **TCLC 6, 40**
See also CA 105; 131; CDBLB 1945-1960;
DLB 15; MTCW

Lowry, Mina Gertrude 1882-1966
See Loy, Mina
See also CA 113

Loxsmith, John
See Brunner, John (Kilian Houston)

Loy, Mina . . . . **CLC 28; DAM POET; PC 16**
See also Lowry, Mina Gertrude
See also DLB 4, 54

Loyson-Bridet
See Schwob, (Mayer Andre) Marcel

Lucas, Craig 1951- . . . . **CLC 64**
See also CA 137

Lucas, George 1944- . . . . **CLC 16**
See also AAYA 1; CA 77-80; CANR 30;
SATA 56

Lucas, Hans
See Godard, Jean-Luc

Lucas, Victoria
See Plath, Sylvia

Ludlam, Charles 1943-1987 . . . . . **CLC 46, 50**
See also CA 85-88; 122

Ludlum, Robert
1927- . . . **CLC 22, 43; DAM NOV, POP**
See also AAYA 10; BEST 89:1, 90:3;
CA 33-36R; CANR 25, 41; DLBY 82;
MTCW

Ludwig, Ken . . . . **CLC 60**

Ludwig, Otto 1813-1865 . . . . **NCLC 4**
See also DLB 129

Lugones, Leopoldo 1874-1938 . . . . . **TCLC 15**
See also CA 116; 131; HW

Lu Hsun 1881-1936 . . . . . . **TCLC 3; SSC 20**
See also Shu-Jen, Chou

Lukacs, George . . . . **CLC 24**
See also Lukacs, Gyorgy (Szegeny von)

Lukacs, Gyorgy (Szegeny von) 1885-1971
See Lukacs, George
See also CA 101; 29-32R

Luke, Peter (Ambrose Cyprian)
1919-1995 . . . . **CLC 38**
See also CA 81-84; 147; DLB 13

Lunar, Dennis
See Mungo, Raymond

Lurie, Alison 1926- . . . . **CLC 4, 5, 18, 39**
See also CA 1-4R; CANR 2, 17, 50; DLB 2;
MTCW; SATA 46

Lustig, Arnost 1926- . . . . **CLC 56**
See also AAYA 3; CA 69-72; CANR 47;
SATA 56

Luther, Martin 1483-1546 . . . . **LC 9, 37**

Luxemburg, Rosa 1870(?)-1919 . . . . **TCLC 63**
See also CA 118

Luzi, Mario 1914- . . . . **CLC 13**
See also CA 61-64; CANR 9; DLB 128

Lyly, John 1554(?)-1606 . . . . **DC 7**
See also DAM DRAM; DLB 62, 167

L'Ymagier
See Gourmont, Remy (-Marie-Charles) de

Lynch, B. Suarez
See Bioy Casares, Adolfo; Borges, Jorge
Luis

Lynch, David (K.) 1946- . . . . **CLC 66**
See also CA 124; 129

Lynch, James
See Andreyev, Leonid (Nikolaevich)

Lynch Davis, B.
See Bioy Casares, Adolfo; Borges, Jorge
Luis

Lyndsay, Sir David 1490-1555 . . . . . . **LC 20**

Lynn, Kenneth S(chuyler) 1923- . . . . **CLC 50**
See also CA 1-4R; CANR 3, 27

Lynx
See West, Rebecca

Lyons, Marcus
See Blish, James (Benjamin)

Lyre, Pinchbeck
See Sassoon, Siegfried (Lorraine)

Lytle, Andrew (Nelson) 1902-1995 . . **CLC 22**
See also CA 9-12R; 150; DLB 6; DLBY 95

Lyttelton, George 1709-1773 . . . . **LC 10**

Maas, Peter 1929- . . . . **CLC 29**
See also CA 93-96; INT 93-96

Macaulay, Rose 1881-1958 . . . . . **TCLC 7, 44**
See also CA 104; DLB 36

Macaulay, Thomas Babington
1800-1859 . . . . **NCLC 42**
See also CDBLB 1832-1890; DLB 32, 55

MacBeth, George (Mann)
1932-1992 . . . . **CLC 2, 5, 9**
See also CA 25-28R; 136; DLB 40; MTCW;
SATA 4; SATA-Obit 70

MacCaig, Norman (Alexander)
1910- . . . . . **CLC 36; DAB; DAM POET**
See also CA 9-12R; CANR 3, 34; DLB 27

MacCarthy, (Sir Charles Otto) Desmond
1877-1952 . . . . **TCLC 36**

MacDiarmid, Hugh
. . . . **CLC 2, 4, 11, 19, 63; PC 9**
See also Grieve, C(hristopher) M(urray)
See also CDBLB 1945-1960; DLB 20

MacDonald, Anson
See Heinlein, Robert A(nson)

Macdonald, Cynthia 1928- . . . . . . **CLC 13, 19**
See also CA 49-52; CANR 4, 44; DLB 105

MacDonald, George 1824-1905 . . . . . **TCLC 9**
See also CA 106; 137; DLB 18, 163;
MAICYA; SATA 33

Macdonald, John
See Millar, Kenneth

MacDonald, John D(ann)
1916-1986 . . . . **CLC 3, 27, 44;**
DAM NOV, POP
See also CA 1-4R; 121; CANR 1, 19;
DLB 8; DLBY 86; MTCW

Macdonald, John Ross
See Millar, Kenneth

Macdonald, Ross . . . . . **CLC 1, 2, 3, 14, 34, 41**
See also Millar, Kenneth
See also DLBD 6

MacDougal, John
See Blish, James (Benjamin)

MacEwen, Gwendolyn (Margaret)
1941-1987 . . . . **CLC 13, 55**
See also CA 9-12R; 124; CANR 7, 22;
DLB 53; SATA 50; SATA-Obit 55

Macha, Karel Hynek 1810-1846 . . **NCLC 46**

Machado (y Ruiz), Antonio
1875-1939 . . . . **TCLC 3**
See also CA 104; DLB 108

Machado de Assis, Joaquim Maria
1839-1908 . . . . . **TCLC 10; BLC; SSC 24**
See also CA 107; 153

Machen, Arthur . . . . **TCLC 4; SSC 20**
See also Jones, Arthur Llewellyn
See also DLB 36, 156

Machiavelli, Niccolo
1469-1527 . . . . **LC 8, 36; DA; DAB;**
DAC; DAM MST

MacInnes, Colin 1914-1976 . . . . . . **CLC 4, 23**
See also CA 69-72; 65-68; CANR 21;
DLB 14; MTCW

MacInnes, Helen (Clark)
1907-1985 . . . . . **CLC 27, 39; DAM POP**
See also CA 1-4R; 117; CANR 1, 28;
DLB 87; MTCW; SATA 22;
SATA-Obit 44

Mackay, Mary 1855-1924
See Corelli, Marie
See also CA 118

Mackenzie, Compton (Edward Montague)
1883-1972 . . . . **CLC 18**
See also CA 21-22; 37-40R; CAP 2;
DLB 34, 100

Mackenzie, Henry 1745-1831 . . . . **NCLC 41**
See also DLB 39

Mackintosh, Elizabeth 1896(?)-1952
See Tey, Josephine
See also CA 110

MacLaren, James
See Grieve, C(hristopher) M(urray)

Mac Laverty, Bernard 1942- . . . . **CLC 31**
See also CA 116; 118; CANR 43; INT 118

MacLean, Alistair (Stuart)
1922-1987 . . . . **CLC 3, 13, 50, 63;**
DAM POP
See also CA 57-60; 121; CANR 28; MTCW;
SATA 23; SATA-Obit 50

Maclean, Norman (Fitzroy)
1902-1990 . . . . **CLC 78; DAM POP;**
SSC 13
See also CA 102; 132; CANR 49

MacLeish, Archibald
1892-1982 . . . . **CLC 3, 8, 14, 68;**
DAM POET
See also CA 9-12R; 106; CANR 33; DLB 4,
7, 45; DLBY 82; MTCW

MacLennan, (John) Hugh
1907-1990 . . . . **CLC 2, 14, 92; DAC;**
DAM MST
See also CA 5-8R; 142; CANR 33; DLB 68;
MTCW

MacLeod, Alistair
1936- . . . . . . **CLC 56; DAC; DAM MST**
See also CA 123; DLB 60

Marat, Jean Paul 1743-1793 . . . . **LC 10**

Marcel, Gabriel Honore
1889-1973 . . . . **CLC 15**
See also CA 102; 45-48; MTCW

Marchbanks, Samuel
See Davies, (William) Robertson

Marchi, Giacomo
See Bassani, Giorgio

Margulies, Donald . . . . **CLC 76**

Marie de France c. 12th cent. - . . . . **CMLC 8**

Marie de l'Incarnation 1599-1672 . . . . **LC 10**

Marier, Captain Victor
See Griffith, D(avid Lewelyn) W(ark)

Mariner, Scott
See Pohl, Frederik

Marinetti, Filippo Tommaso
1876-1944 . . . . **TCLC 10**
See also CA 107; DLB 114

Marivaux, Pierre Carlet de Chamblain de
1688-1763 . . . . **LC 4; DC 7**

Markandaya, Kamala . . . . **CLC 8, 38**
See also Taylor, Kamala (Purnaiya)

Markfield, Wallace 1926- . . . . **CLC 8**
See also CA 69-72; CAAS 3; DLB 2, 28

Markham, Edwin 1852-1940 . . . . . . **TCLC 47**
See also DLB 54

Markham, Robert
See Amis, Kingsley (William)

Marks, J
See Highwater, Jamake (Mamake)

Marks-Highwater, J
See Highwater, Jamake (Mamake)

Markson, David M(errill) 1927- . . . . **CLC 67**
See also CA 49-52; CANR 1

Marley, Bob . . . . **CLC 17**
See also Marley, Robert Nesta

Marley, Robert Nesta 1945-1981
See Marley, Bob
See also CA 107; 103

Marlowe, Christopher
1564-1593 . . . . . **LC 22; DA; DAB; DAC;**
DAM DRAM, MST; DC 1; WLC
See also CDBLB Before 1660; DLB 62

Marlowe, Stephen 1928-
See Queen, Ellery
See also CA 13-16R; CANR 6, 55

Marmontel, Jean-Francois
1723-1799 . . . . **LC 2**

Marquand, John P(hillips)
1893-1960 . . . . **CLC 2, 10**
See also CA 85-88; DLB 9, 102

Marques, Rene
1919-1979 . . . . . . **CLC 96; DAM MULT;**
HLC
See also CA 97-100; 85-88; DLB 113; HW

Marquez, Gabriel (Jose) Garcia
See Garcia Marquez, Gabriel (Jose)

Marquis, Don(ald Robert Perry)
1878-1937 . . . . **TCLC 7**
See also CA 104; DLB 11, 25

Marric, J. J.
See Creasey, John

Marrow, Bernard
See Moore, Brian

Marryat, Frederick 1792-1848 . . . . **NCLC 3**
See also DLB 21, 163

Marsden, James
See Creasey, John

Marsh, (Edith) Ngaio
1899-1982 . . . . . . **CLC 7, 53; DAM POP**
See also CA 9-12R; CANR 6; DLB 77;
MTCW

Marshall, Garry 1934- . . . . **CLC 17**
See also AAYA 3; CA 111; SATA 60

Marshall, Paule
1929- . . . . **CLC 27, 72; BLC;**
DAM MULT; SSC 3
See also BW 2; CA 77-80; CANR 25;
DLB 157; MTCW

Marsten, Richard
See Hunter, Evan

Marston, John
1576-1634 . . . . **LC 33; DAM DRAM**
See also DLB 58, 172

Martha, Henry
See Harris, Mark

Martial c. 40-c. 104 . . . . **PC 10**

Martin, Ken
See Hubbard, L(afayette) Ron(ald)

Martin, Richard
See Creasey, John

Martin, Steve 1945- . . . . **CLC 30**
See also CA 97-100; CANR 30; MTCW

Martin, Valerie 1948- . . . . **CLC 89**
See also BEST 90:2; CA 85-88; CANR 49

Martin, Violet Florence
1862-1915 . . . . **TCLC 51**

Martin, Webber
See Silverberg, Robert

Martindale, Patrick Victor
See White, Patrick (Victor Martindale)

Martin du Gard, Roger
1881-1958 . . . . **TCLC 24**
See also CA 118; DLB 65

Martineau, Harriet 1802-1876 . . . . **NCLC 26**
See also DLB 21, 55, 159, 163, 166;
YABC 2

Martines, Julia
See O'Faolain, Julia

Martinez, Jacinto Benavente y
See Benavente (y Martinez), Jacinto

Martinez Ruiz, Jose 1873-1967
See Azorin; Ruiz, Jose Martinez
See also CA 93-96; HW

Martinez Sierra, Gregorio
1881-1947 . . . . **TCLC 6**
See also CA 115

Martinez Sierra, Maria (de la O'LeJarraga)
1874-1974 . . . . **TCLC 6**
See also CA 115

Martinsen, Martin
See Follett, Ken(neth Martin)

Martinson, Harry (Edmund)
1904-1978 . . . . **CLC 14**
See also CA 77-80; CANR 34

Marut, Ret
See Traven, B.

Marut, Robert
See Traven, B.

Marvell, Andrew
1621-1678 . . . . . . **LC 4; DA; DAB; DAC;**
DAM MST, POET; PC 10; WLC
See also CDBLB 1660-1789; DLB 131

Marx, Karl (Heinrich)
1818-1883 . . . . **NCLC 17**
See also DLB 129

Masaoka Shiki . . . . **TCLC 18**
See also Masaoka Tsunenori

Masaoka Tsunenori 1867-1902
See Masaoka Shiki
See also CA 117

Masefield, John (Edward)
1878-1967 . . . . **CLC 11, 47; DAM POET**
See also CA 19-20; 25-28R; CANR 33;
CAP 2; CDBLB 1890-1914; DLB 10, 19,
153, 160; MTCW; SATA 19

Maso, Carole 19(?)- . . . . **CLC 44**

Mason, Bobbie Ann
1940- . . . . **CLC 28, 43, 82; SSC 4**
See also AAYA 5; CA 53-56; CANR 11,
31; DLB 173; DLBY 87; INT CANR-31;
MTCW

Mason, Ernst
See Pohl, Frederik

Mason, Lee W.
See Malzberg, Barry N(athaniel)

Mason, Nick 1945- . . . . **CLC 35**

Mason, Tally
See Derleth, August (William)

Mass, William
See Gibson, William

Masters, Edgar Lee
1868-1950 . . . . . . **TCLC 2, 25; DA; DAC;**
DAM MST, POET; PC 1
See also CA 104; 133; CDALB 1865-1917;
DLB 54; MTCW

Masters, Hilary 1928- . . . . **CLC 48**
See also CA 25-28R; CANR 13, 47

Mastrosimone, William 19(?)- . . . . . . **CLC 36**

Mathe, Albert
See Camus, Albert

Mather, Cotton 1663-1728 . . . . **LC 38**
See also CDALB 1640-1865; DLB 24, 30,
140

Mather, Increase 1639-1723 . . . . **LC 38**
See also DLB 24

Matheson, Richard Burton 1926- . . . **CLC 37**
See also CA 97-100; DLB 8, 44; INT 97-100

Mathews, Harry 1930- . . . . **CLC 6, 52**
See also CA 21-24R; CAAS 6; CANR 18,
40

Mathews, John Joseph
1894-1979 . . . . . . **CLC 84; DAM MULT**
See also CA 19-20; 142; CANR 45; CAP 2;
DLB 175; NNAL

Mathias, Roland (Glyn) 1915- . . . . . . **CLC 45**
See also CA 97-100; CANR 19, 41; DLB 27

Matsuo Basho 1644-1694 . . . . **PC 3**
See also DAM POET

Mattheson, Rodney
See Creasey, John

Matthews, Greg 1949- .... **CLC 45**
See also CA 135

Matthews, William 1942-......... **CLC 40**
See also CA 29-32R; CAAS 18; CANR 12,
57; DLB 5

Matthias, John (Edward) 1941-...... **CLC 9**
See also CA 33-36R; CANR 56

Matthiessen, Peter
1927- .... **CLC 5, 7, 11, 32, 64;**
DAM NOV
See also AAYA 6; BEST 90:4; CA 9-12R;
CANR 21, 50; DLB 6, 173; MTCW;
SATA 27

Maturin, Charles Robert
1780(?)-1824 .... **NCLC 6**

Matute (Ausejo), Ana Maria
1925- .... **CLC 11**
See also CA 89-92; MTCW

Maugham, W. S.
See Maugham, W(illiam) Somerset

Maugham, W(illiam) Somerset
1874-1965 .... **CLC 1, 11, 15, 67, 93;**
DA; DAB; DAC; DAM DRAM, MST,
NOV; SSC 8; WLC
See also CA 5-8R; 25-28R; CANR 40;
CDBLB 1914-1945; DLB 10, 36, 77, 100,
162; MTCW; SATA 54

Maugham, William Somerset
See Maugham, W(illiam) Somerset

Maupassant, (Henri Rene Albert) Guy de
1850-1893 ..... **NCLC 1, 42; DA; DAB;**
DAC; DAM MST; SSC 1; WLC
See also DLB 123

Maupin, Armistead
1944- .... **CLC 95; DAM POP**
See also CA 125; 130; INT 130

Maurhut, Richard
See Traven, B.

Mauriac, Claude 1914-1996........ **CLC 9**
See also CA 89-92; 152; DLB 83

Mauriac, Francois (Charles)
1885-1970 .... **CLC 4, 9, 56; SSC 24**
See also CA 25-28; CAP 2; DLB 65;
MTCW

Mavor, Osborne Henry 1888-1951
See Bridie, James
See also CA 104

Maxwell, William (Keepers, Jr.)
1908- .... **CLC 19**
See also CA 93-96; CANR 54; DLBY 80;
INT 93-96

May, Elaine 1932- .... **CLC 16**
See also CA 124; 142; DLB 44

Mayakovski, Vladimir (Vladimirovich)
1893-1930 .... **TCLC 4, 18**
See also CA 104

Mayhew, Henry 1812-1887 ...... **NCLC 31**
See also DLB 18, 55

Mayle, Peter 1939(?)-............. **CLC 89**
See also CA 139

Maynard, Joyce 1953- .... **CLC 23**
See also CA 111; 129

Mayne, William (James Carter)
1928- .... **CLC 12**
See also AAYA 20; CA 9-12R; CANR 37;
CLR 25; JRDA; MAICYA; SAAS 11;
SATA 6, 68

Mayo, Jim
See L'Amour, Louis (Dearborn)

Maysles, Albert 1926- .... **CLC 16**
See also CA 29-32R

Maysles, David 1932-............. **CLC 16**

Mazer, Norma Fox 1931- .... **CLC 26**
See also AAYA 5; CA 69-72; CANR 12,
32; CLR 23; JRDA; MAICYA; SAAS 1;
SATA 24, 67

Mazzini, Guiseppe 1805-1872 .... **NCLC 34**

McAuley, James Phillip
1917-1976 .... **CLC 45**
See also CA 97-100

McBain, Ed
See Hunter, Evan

McBrien, William Augustine
1930- .... **CLC 44**
See also CA 107

McCaffrey, Anne (Inez)
1926- ...... **CLC 17; DAM NOV, POP**
See also AAYA 6; AITN 2; BEST 89:2;
CA 25-28R; CANR 15, 35, 55; DLB 8;
JRDA; MAICYA; MTCW; SAAS 11;
SATA 8, 70

McCall, Nathan 1955(?)-.......... **CLC 86**
See also CA 146

McCann, Arthur
See Campbell, John W(ood, Jr.)

McCann, Edson
See Pohl, Frederik

McCarthy, Charles, Jr. 1933-
See McCarthy, Cormac
See also CANR 42; DAM POP

McCarthy, Cormac 1933-..... **CLC 4, 57, 59**
See also McCarthy, Charles, Jr.
See also DLB 6, 143

McCarthy, Mary (Therese)
1912-1989 ...... **CLC 1, 3, 5, 14, 24, 39,**
59; SSC 24
See also CA 5-8R; 129; CANR 16, 50;
DLB 2; DLBY 81; INT CANR-16;
MTCW

McCartney, (James) Paul
1942- .... **CLC 12, 35**
See also CA 146

McCauley, Stephen (D.) 1955- ..... **CLC 50**
See also CA 141

McClure, Michael (Thomas)
1932- .... **CLC 6, 10**
See also CA 21-24R; CANR 17, 46;
DLB 16

McCorkle, Jill (Collins) 1958-...... **CLC 51**
See also CA 121; DLBY 87

McCourt, James 1941-............. **CLC 5**
See also CA 57-60

McCoy, Horace (Stanley)
1897-1955 .... **TCLC 28**
See also CA 108; 155; DLB 9

McCrae, John 1872-1918........ **TCLC 12**
See also CA 109; DLB 92

McCreigh, James
See Pohl, Frederik

McCullers, (Lula) Carson (Smith)
1917-1967 .... **CLC 1, 4, 10, 12, 48, 100;**
DA; DAB; DAC; DAM MST, NOV;
SSC 9, 24; WLC
See also AAYA 21; CA 5-8R; 25-28R;
CABS 1, 3; CANR 18;
CDALB 1941-1968; DLB 2, 7, 173;
MTCW; SATA 27

McCulloch, John Tyler
See Burroughs, Edgar Rice

McCullough, Colleen
1938(?)- .... **CLC 27; DAM NOV, POP**
See also CA 81-84; CANR 17, 46; MTCW

McDermott, Alice 1953- .... **CLC 90**
See also CA 109; CANR 40

McElroy, Joseph 1930- .... **CLC 5, 47**
See also CA 17-20R

McEwan, Ian (Russell)
1948- .... **CLC 13, 66; DAM NOV**
See also BEST 90:4; CA 61-64; CANR 14,
41; DLB 14; MTCW

McFadden, David 1940-.......... **CLC 48**
See also CA 104; DLB 60; INT 104

McFarland, Dennis 1950- .... **CLC 65**

McGahern, John
1934- .... **CLC 5, 9, 48; SSC 17**
See also CA 17-20R; CANR 29; DLB 14;
MTCW

McGinley, Patrick (Anthony)
1937- .... **CLC 41**
See also CA 120; 127; CANR 56; INT 127

McGinley, Phyllis 1905-1978 ...... **CLC 14**
See also CA 9-12R; 77-80; CANR 19;
DLB 11, 48; SATA 2, 44; SATA-Obit 24

McGinniss, Joe 1942-............. **CLC 32**
See also AITN 2; BEST 89:2; CA 25-28R;
CANR 26; INT CANR-26

McGivern, Maureen Daly
See Daly, Maureen

McGrath, Patrick 1950-.......... **CLC 55**
See also CA 136

McGrath, Thomas (Matthew)
1916-1990 .... **CLC 28, 59; DAM POET**
See also CA 9-12R; 132; CANR 6, 33;
MTCW; SATA 41; SATA-Obit 66

McGuane, Thomas (Francis III)
1939- .... **CLC 3, 7, 18, 45**
See also AITN 2; CA 49-52; CANR 5, 24,
49; DLB 2; DLBY 80; INT CANR-24;
MTCW

McGuckian, Medbh
1950- .... **CLC 48; DAM POET**
See also CA 143; DLB 40

McHale, Tom 1942(?)-1982....... **CLC 3, 5**
See also AITN 1; CA 77-80; 106

McIlvanney, William 1936-........ **CLC 42**
See also CA 25-28R; DLB 14

McIlwraith, Maureen Mollie Hunter
See Hunter, Mollie
See also SATA 2

McInerney, Jay
1955- . . . . **CLC 34; DAM POP**
See also AAYA 18; CA 116; 123;
CANR 45; INT 123

McIntyre, Vonda N(eel) 1948- . . . . . **CLC 18**
See also CA 81-84; CANR 17, 34; MTCW

McKay, Claude
. . . . **TCLC 7, 41; BLC; DAB; PC 2**
See also McKay, Festus Claudius
See also DLB 4, 45, 51, 117

McKay, Festus Claudius 1889-1948
See McKay, Claude
See also BW 1; CA 104; 124; DA; DAC;
DAM MST, MULT, NOV, POET;
MTCW; WLC

McKuen, Rod 1933- . . . . **CLC 1, 3**
See also AITN 1; CA 41-44R; CANR 40

McLoughlin, R. B.
See Mencken, H(enry) L(ouis)

McLuhan, (Herbert) Marshall
1911-1980 . . . . **CLC 37, 83**
See also CA 9-12R; 102; CANR 12, 34;
DLB 88; INT CANR-12; MTCW

McMillan, Terry (L.)
1951- . . . . **CLC 50, 61; DAM MULT,
NOV, POP**
See also AAYA 21; BW 2; CA 140

McMurtry, Larry (Jeff)
1936- . . . . **CLC 2, 3, 7, 11, 27, 44;
DAM NOV, POP**
See also AAYA 15; AITN 2; BEST 89:2;
CA 5-8R; CANR 19, 43;
CDALB 1968-1988; DLB 2, 143;
DLBY 80, 87; MTCW

McNally, T. M. 1961- . . . . **CLC 82**

McNally, Terrence
1939- . . . **CLC 4, 7, 41, 91; DAM DRAM**
See also CA 45-48; CANR 2, 56; DLB 7

McNamer, Deirdre 1950- . . . . **CLC 70**

McNeile, Herman Cyril 1888-1937
See Sapper
See also DLB 77

McNickle, (William) D'Arcy
1904-1977 . . . . . . **CLC 89; DAM MULT**
See also CA 9-12R; 85-88; CANR 5, 45;
DLB 175; NNAL; SATA-Obit 22

McPhee, John (Angus) 1931- . . . . . . **CLC 36**
See also BEST 90:1; CA 65-68; CANR 20,
46; MTCW

McPherson, James Alan
1943- . . . . **CLC 19, 77**
See also BW 1; CA 25-28R; CAAS 17;
CANR 24; DLB 38; MTCW

McPherson, William (Alexander)
1933- . . . . **CLC 34**
See also CA 69-72; CANR 28;
INT CANR-28

Mead, Margaret 1901-1978 . . . . **CLC 37**
See also AITN 1; CA 1-4R; 81-84;
CANR 4; MTCW; SATA-Obit 20

Meaker, Marijane (Agnes) 1927-
See Kerr, M. E.
See also CA 107; CANR 37; INT 107;
JRDA; MAICYA; MTCW; SATA 20, 61

Medoff, Mark (Howard)
1940- . . . . **CLC 6, 23; DAM DRAM**
See also AITN 1; CA 53-56; CANR 5;
DLB 7; INT CANR-5

Medvedev, P. N.
See Bakhtin, Mikhail Mikhailovich

Meged, Aharon
See Megged, Aharon

Meged, Aron
See Megged, Aharon

Megged, Aharon 1920- . . . . **CLC 9**
See also CA 49-52; CAAS 13; CANR 1

Mehta, Ved (Parkash) 1934- . . . . **CLC 37**
See also CA 1-4R; CANR 2, 23; MTCW

Melanter
See Blackmore, R(ichard) D(oddridge)

Melikow, Loris
See Hofmannsthal, Hugo von

Melmoth, Sebastian
See Wilde, Oscar (Fingal O'Flahertie Wills)

Meltzer, Milton 1915- . . . . **CLC 26**
See also AAYA 8; CA 13-16R; CANR 38;
CLR 13; DLB 61; JRDA; MAICYA;
SAAS 1; SATA 1, 50, 80

Melville, Herman
1819-1891 . . . . . **NCLC 3, 12, 29, 45, 49;
DA; DAB; DAC; DAM MST, NOV;
SSC 1, 17; WLC**
See also CDALB 1640-1865; DLB 3, 74;
SATA 59

Menander
c. 342B.C.-c. 292B.C. . . . . **CMLC 9;
DAM DRAM; DC 3**
See also DLB 176

Mencken, H(enry) L(ouis)
1880-1956 . . . . **TCLC 13**
See also CA 105; 125; CDALB 1917-1929;
DLB 11, 29, 63, 137; MTCW

Mendelsohn, Jane 1965(?)- . . . . **CLC 99**
See also CA 154

Mercer, David
1928-1980 . . . . **CLC 5; DAM DRAM**
See also CA 9-12R; 102; CANR 23;
DLB 13; MTCW

Merchant, Paul
See Ellison, Harlan (Jay)

Meredith, George
1828-1909 . . **TCLC 17, 43; DAM POET**
See also CA 117; 153; CDBLB 1832-1890;
DLB 18, 35, 57, 159

Meredith, William (Morris)
1919- . . **CLC 4, 13, 22, 55; DAM POET**
See also CA 9-12R; CAAS 14; CANR 6, 40;
DLB 5

Merezhkovsky, Dmitry Sergeyevich
1865-1941 . . . . **TCLC 29**

Merimee, Prosper
1803-1870 . . . . **NCLC 6; SSC 7**
See also DLB 119

Merkin, Daphne 1954- . . . . **CLC 44**
See also CA 123

Merlin, Arthur
See Blish, James (Benjamin)

Merrill, James (Ingram)
1926-1995 . . . . **CLC 2, 3, 6, 8, 13, 18, 34,
91; DAM POET**
See also CA 13-16R; 147; CANR 10, 49;
DLB 5, 165; DLBY 85; INT CANR-10;
MTCW

Merriman, Alex
See Silverberg, Robert

Merritt, E. B.
See Waddington, Miriam

Merton, Thomas
1915-1968 . . **CLC 1, 3, 11, 34, 83; PC 10**
See also CA 5-8R; 25-28R; CANR 22, 53;
DLB 48; DLBY 81; MTCW

Merwin, W(illiam) S(tanley)
1927- . . . . . . **CLC 1, 2, 3, 5, 8, 13, 18, 45,
88; DAM POET**
See also CA 13-16R; CANR 15, 51; DLB 5,
169; INT CANR-15; MTCW

Metcalf, John 1938- . . . . **CLC 37**
See also CA 113; DLB 60

Metcalf, Suzanne
See Baum, L(yman) Frank

Mew, Charlotte (Mary)
1870-1928 . . . . **TCLC 8**
See also CA 105; DLB 19, 135

Mewshaw, Michael 1943- . . . . **CLC 9**
See also CA 53-56; CANR 7, 47; DLBY 80

Meyer, June
See Jordan, June

Meyer, Lynn
See Slavitt, David R(ytman)

Meyer-Meyrink, Gustav 1868-1932
See Meyrink, Gustav
See also CA 117

Meyers, Jeffrey 1939- . . . . **CLC 39**
See also CA 73-76; CANR 54; DLB 111

Meynell, Alice (Christina Gertrude Thompson)
1847-1922 . . . . **TCLC 6**
See also CA 104; DLB 19, 98

Meyrink, Gustav . . . . **TCLC 21**
See also Meyer-Meyrink, Gustav
See also DLB 81

Michaels, Leonard
1933- . . . . **CLC 6, 25; SSC 16**
See also CA 61-64; CANR 21; DLB 130;
MTCW

Michaux, Henri 1899-1984 . . . . . . **CLC 8, 19**
See also CA 85-88; 114

Michelangelo 1475-1564 . . . . **LC 12**

Michelet, Jules 1798-1874 . . . . **NCLC 31**

Michener, James A(lbert)
1907(?)- . . . . **CLC 1, 5, 11, 29, 60;
DAM NOV, POP**
See also AITN 1; BEST 90:1; CA 5-8R;
CANR 21, 45; DLB 6; MTCW

Mickiewicz, Adam 1798-1855 . . . . . **NCLC 3**

Middleton, Christopher 1926- . . . . . . **CLC 13**
See also CA 13-16R; CANR 29, 54;
DLB 40

Middleton, Richard (Barham)
1882-1911 . . . . **TCLC 56**
See also DLB 156

Montesquieu, Charles-Louis de Secondat
1689-1755 . . . . **LC 7**

Montgomery, (Robert) Bruce 1921-1978
See Crispin, Edmund
See also CA 104

Montgomery, L(ucy) M(aud)
1874-1942 . . . . **TCLC 51; DAC;**
DAM MST
See also AAYA 12; CA 108; 137; CLR 8;
DLB 92; DLBD 14; JRDA; MAICYA;
YABC 1

Montgomery, Marion H., Jr. 1925- . . **CLC 7**
See also AITN 1; CA 1-4R; CANR 3, 48;
DLB 6

Montgomery, Max
See Davenport, Guy (Mattison, Jr.)

Montherlant, Henry (Milon) de
1896-1972 . . . . **CLC 8, 19; DAM DRAM**
See also CA 85-88; 37-40R; DLB 72;
MTCW

Monty Python
See Chapman, Graham; Cleese, John
(Marwood); Gilliam, Terry (Vance); Idle,
Eric; Jones, Terence Graham Parry; Palin,
Michael (Edward)
See also AAYA 7

Moodie, Susanna (Strickland)
1803-1885 . . . . **NCLC 14**
See also DLB 99

Mooney, Edward 1951-
See Mooney, Ted
See also CA 130

Mooney, Ted . . . . **CLC 25**
See also Mooney, Edward

Moorcock, Michael (John)
1939- . . . . **CLC 5, 27, 58**
See also CA 45-48; CAAS 5; CANR 2, 17,
38; DLB 14; MTCW

Moore, Brian
1921- . . . . . . **CLC 1, 3, 5, 7, 8, 19, 32, 90;**
DAB; DAC; DAM MST
See also CA 1-4R; CANR 1, 25, 42; MTCW

Moore, Edward
See Muir, Edwin

Moore, George Augustus
1852-1933 . . . . **TCLC 7; SSC 19**
See also CA 104; DLB 10, 18, 57, 135

Moore, Lorrie . . . . **CLC 39, 45, 68**
See also Moore, Marie Lorena

Moore, Marianne (Craig)
1887-1972 . . . . **CLC 1, 2, 4, 8, 10, 13, 19,**
47; DA; DAB; DAC; DAM MST, POET;
PC 4
See also CA 1-4R; 33-36R; CANR 3;
CDALB 1929-1941; DLB 45; DLBD 7;
MTCW; SATA 20

Moore, Marie Lorena 1957-
See Moore, Lorrie
See also CA 116; CANR 39

Moore, Thomas 1779-1852 . . . . **NCLC 6**
See also DLB 96, 144

Morand, Paul 1888-1976 . . **CLC 41; SSC 22**
See also CA 69-72; DLB 65

Morante, Elsa 1918-1985 . . . . **CLC 8, 47**
See also CA 85-88; 117; CANR 35;
DLB 177; MTCW

Moravia, Alberto
1907-1990 . . . . **CLC 2, 7, 11, 27, 46**
See also Pincherle, Alberto
See also DLB 177

More, Hannah 1745-1833 . . . . **NCLC 27**
See also DLB 107, 109, 116, 158

More, Henry 1614-1687 . . . . **LC 9**
See also DLB 126

More, Sir Thomas 1478-1535 . . . . **LC 10, 32**

Moreas, Jean . . . . **TCLC 18**
See also Papadiamantopoulos, Johannes

Morgan, Berry 1919- . . . . **CLC 6**
See also CA 49-52; DLB 6

Morgan, Claire
See Highsmith, (Mary) Patricia

Morgan, Edwin (George) 1920- . . . . . **CLC 31**
See also CA 5-8R; CANR 3, 43; DLB 27

Morgan, (George) Frederick
1922- . . . . **CLC 23**
See also CA 17-20R; CANR 21

Morgan, Harriet
See Mencken, H(enry) L(ouis)

Morgan, Jane
See Cooper, James Fenimore

Morgan, Janet 1945- . . . . **CLC 39**
See also CA 65-68

Morgan, Lady 1776(?)-1859 . . . . . . **NCLC 29**
See also DLB 116, 158

Morgan, Robin 1941- . . . . **CLC 2**
See also CA 69-72; CANR 29; MTCW;
SATA 80

Morgan, Scott
See Kuttner, Henry

Morgan, Seth 1949(?)-1990 . . . . **CLC 65**
See also CA 132

Morgenstern, Christian
1871-1914 . . . . **TCLC 8**
See also CA 105

Morgenstern, S.
See Goldman, William (W.)

Moricz, Zsigmond 1879-1942 . . . . . **TCLC 33**

Morike, Eduard (Friedrich)
1804-1875 . . . . **NCLC 10**
See also DLB 133

Mori Ogai . . . . **TCLC 14**
See also Mori Rintaro

Mori Rintaro 1862-1922
See Mori Ogai
See also CA 110

Moritz, Karl Philipp 1756-1793 . . . . . . **LC 2**
See also DLB 94

Morland, Peter Henry
See Faust, Frederick (Schiller)

Morren, Theophil
See Hofmannsthal, Hugo von

Morris, Bill 1952- . . . . **CLC 76**

Morris, Julian
See West, Morris L(anglo)

Morris, Steveland Judkins 1950(?)-
See Wonder, Stevie
See also CA 111

Morris, William 1834-1896 . . . . **NCLC 4**
See also CDBLB 1832-1890; DLB 18, 35,
57, 156

Morris, Wright 1910- . . . **CLC 1, 3, 7, 18, 37**
See also CA 9-12R; CANR 21; DLB 2;
DLBY 81; MTCW

Morrison, Chloe Anthony Wofford
See Morrison, Toni

Morrison, James Douglas 1943-1971
See Morrison, Jim
See also CA 73-76; CANR 40

Morrison, Jim . . . . **CLC 17**
See also Morrison, James Douglas

Morrison, Toni
1931- . . . . **CLC 4, 10, 22, 55, 81, 87;**
BLC; DA; DAB; DAC; DAM MST,
MULT, NOV, POP
See also AAYA 1; BW 2; CA 29-32R;
CANR 27, 42; CDALB 1968-1988;
DLB 6, 33, 143; DLBY 81; MTCW;
SATA 57

Morrison, Van 1945- . . . . **CLC 21**
See also CA 116

Morrissy, Mary 1958- . . . . **CLC 99**

Mortimer, John (Clifford)
1923- . . . . . . **CLC 28, 43; DAM DRAM,**
POP
See also CA 13-16R; CANR 21;
CDBLB 1960 to Present; DLB 13;
INT CANR-21; MTCW

Mortimer, Penelope (Ruth) 1918- . . . . **CLC 5**
See also CA 57-60; CANR 45

Morton, Anthony
See Creasey, John

Mosher, Howard Frank 1943- . . . . . . **CLC 62**
See also CA 139

Mosley, Nicholas 1923- . . . . **CLC 43, 70**
See also CA 69-72; CANR 41; DLB 14

Mosley, Walter
1952- . . . . . **CLC 97; DAM MULT, POP**
See also AAYA 17; BW 2; CA 142;
CANR 57

Moss, Howard
1922-1987 . . . . **CLC 7, 14, 45, 50;**
DAM POET
See also CA 1-4R; 123; CANR 1, 44;
DLB 5

Mossgiel, Rab
See Burns, Robert

Motion, Andrew (Peter) 1952- . . . . . . **CLC 47**
See also CA 146; DLB 40

Motley, Willard (Francis)
1909-1965 . . . . **CLC 18**
See also BW 1; CA 117; 106; DLB 76, 143

Motoori, Norinaga 1730-1801 . . . . **NCLC 45**

Mott, Michael (Charles Alston)
1930- . . . . **CLC 15, 34**
See also CA 5-8R; CAAS 7; CANR 7, 29

Mountain Wolf Woman
1884-1960 . . . . **CLC 92**
See also CA 144; NNAL

Moure, Erin 1955- . . . . **CLC 88**
See also CA 113; DLB 60

Mowat, Farley (McGill)
    1921- . . . . . . **CLC 26; DAC; DAM MST**
    See also AAYA 1; CA 1-4R; CANR 4, 24,
    42; CLR 20; DLB 68; INT CANAR-24;
    JRDA; MAICYA; MTCW; SATA 3, 55

Moyers, Bill 1934- . . . . **CLC 74**
    See also AITN 2; CA 61-64; CANR 31, 52

Mphahlele, Es'kia
    See Mphahlele, Ezekiel
    See also DLB 125

Mphahlele, Ezekiel
    1919- . . . . . **CLC 25; BLC; DAM MULT**
    See also Mphahlele, Es'kia
    See also BW 2; CA 81-84; CANR 26

Mqhayi, S(amuel) E(dward) K(rune Loliwe)
    1875-1945 . . . . **TCLC 25; BLC;**
                                              DAM MULT
    See also CA 153

Mrozek, Slawomir 1930- . . . . **CLC 3, 13**
    See also CA 13-16R; CAAS 10; CANR 29;
    MTCW

Mrs. Belloc-Lowndes
    See Lowndes, Marie Adelaide (Belloc)

Mtwa, Percy (?)- . . . . **CLC 47**

Mueller, Lisel 1924- . . . . **CLC 13, 51**
    See also CA 93-96; DLB 105

Muir, Edwin 1887-1959 . . . . **TCLC 2**
    See also CA 104; DLB 20, 100

Muir, John 1838-1914 . . . . **TCLC 28**

Mujica Lainez, Manuel
    1910-1984 . . . . **CLC 31**
    See also Lainez, Manuel Mujica
    See also CA 81-84; 112; CANR 32; HW

Mukherjee, Bharati
    1940- . . . . **CLC 53; DAM NOV**
    See also BEST 89:2; CA 107; CANR 45;
    DLB 60; MTCW

Muldoon, Paul
    1951- . . . . **CLC 32, 72; DAM POET**
    See also CA 113; 129; CANR 52; DLB 40;
    INT 129

Mulisch, Harry 1927- . . . . **CLC 42**
    See also CA 9-12R; CANR 6, 26, 56

Mull, Martin 1943- . . . . **CLC 17**
    See also CA 105

Mulock, Dinah Maria
    See Craik, Dinah Maria (Mulock)

Munford, Robert 1737(?)-1783 . . . . **LC 5**
    See also DLB 31

Mungo, Raymond 1946- . . . . **CLC 72**
    See also CA 49-52; CANR 2

Munro, Alice
    1931- . . . . . . **CLC 6, 10, 19, 50, 95; DAC;**
                              DAM MST, NOV; SSC 3
    See also AITN 2; CA 33-36R; CANR 33,
    53; DLB 53; MTCW; SATA 29

Munro, H(ector) H(ugh) 1870-1916
    See Saki
    See also CA 104; 130; CDBLB 1890-1914;
    DA; DAB; DAC; DAM MST, NOV;
    DLB 34, 162; MTCW; WLC

Murasaki, Lady . . . . **CMLC 1**

Murdoch, (Jean) Iris
    1919- . . . . . . **CLC 1, 2, 3, 4, 6, 8, 11, 15,**
        22, 31, 51; DAB; DAC; DAM MST,
                                                     NOV
    See also CA 13-16R; CANR 8, 43;
    CDBLB 1960 to Present; DLB 14;
    INT CANR-8; MTCW

Murfree, Mary Noailles
    1850-1922 . . . . **SSC 22**
    See also CA 122; DLB 12, 74

Murnau, Friedrich Wilhelm
    See Plumpe, Friedrich Wilhelm

Murphy, Richard 1927- . . . . **CLC 41**
    See also CA 29-32R; DLB 40

Murphy, Sylvia 1937- . . . . **CLC 34**
    See also CA 121

Murphy, Thomas (Bernard) 1935- . . . **CLC 51**
    See also CA 101

Murray, Albert L. 1916- . . . . **CLC 73**
    See also BW 2; CA 49-52; CANR 26, 52;
    DLB 38

Murray, Les(lie) A(llan)
    1938- . . . . **CLC 40; DAM POET**
    See also CA 21-24R; CANR 11, 27, 56

Murry, J. Middleton
    See Murry, John Middleton

Murry, John Middleton
    1889-1957 . . . . **TCLC 16**
    See also CA 118; DLB 149

Musgrave, Susan 1951- . . . . **CLC 13, 54**
    See also CA 69-72; CANR 45

Musil, Robert (Edler von)
    1880-1942 . . . . **TCLC 12, 68; SSC 18**
    See also CA 109; CANR 55; DLB 81, 124

Muske, Carol 1945- . . . . **CLC 90**
    See also Muske-Dukes, Carol (Anne)

Muske-Dukes, Carol (Anne) 1945-
    See Muske, Carol
    See also CA 65-68; CANR 32

Musset, (Louis Charles) Alfred de
    1810-1857 . . . . **NCLC 7**

My Brother's Brother
    See Chekhov, Anton (Pavlovich)

Myers, L. H. 1881-1944 . . . . **TCLC 59**
    See also DLB 15

Myers, Walter Dean
    1937- . . . . . **CLC 35; BLC; DAM MULT,**
                                                     NOV
    See also AAYA 4; BW 2; CA 33-36R;
    CANR 20, 42; CLR 4, 16, 35; DLB 33;
    INT CANR-20; JRDA; MAICYA;
    SAAS 2; SATA 41, 71; SATA-Brief 27

Myers, Walter M.
    See Myers, Walter Dean

Myles, Symon
    See Follett, Ken(neth Martin)

Nabokov, Vladimir (Vladimirovich)
    1899-1977 . . . . . **CLC 1, 2, 3, 6, 8, 11, 15,**
        23, 44, 46, 64; DA; DAB; DAC;
        DAM MST, NOV; SSC 11; WLC
    See also CA 5-8R; 69-72; CANR 20;
    CDALB 1941-1968; DLB 2; DLBD 3;
    DLBY 80, 91; MTCW

Nagai Kafu . . . . **TCLC 51**
    See also Nagai Sokichi

Nagai Sokichi 1879-1959
    See Nagai Kafu
    See also CA 117

Nagy, Laszlo 1925-1978 . . . . **CLC 7**
    See also CA 129; 112

Naipaul, Shiva(dhar Srinivasa)
    1945-1985 . . . . . **CLC 32, 39; DAM NOV**
    See also CA 110; 112; 116; CANR 33;
    DLB 157; DLBY 85; MTCW

Naipaul, V(idiadhar) S(urajprasad)
    1932- . . . . **CLC 4, 7, 9, 13, 18, 37; DAB;**
                              DAC; DAM MST, NOV
    See also CA 1-4R; CANR 1, 33, 51;
    CDBLB 1960 to Present; DLB 125;
    DLBY 85; MTCW

Nakos, Lilika 1899(?)- . . . . **CLC 29**

Narayan, R(asipuram) K(rishnaswami)
    1906- . . . . . . **CLC 7, 28, 47; DAM NOV;**
                                                     SSC 25
    See also CA 81-84; CANR 33; MTCW;
    SATA 62

Nash, (Frediric) Ogden
    1902-1971 . . . . **CLC 23; DAM POET**
    See also CA 13-14; 29-32R; CANR 34;
    CAP 1; DLB 11; MAICYA; MTCW;
    SATA 2, 46

Nathan, Daniel
    See Dannay, Frederic

Nathan, George Jean 1882-1958 . . . **TCLC 18**
    See also Hatteras, Owen
    See also CA 114; DLB 137

Natsume, Kinnosuke 1867-1916
    See Natsume, Soseki
    See also CA 104

Natsume, Soseki . . . . **TCLC 2, 10**
    See also Natsume, Kinnosuke

Natti, (Mary) Lee 1919-
    See Kingman, Lee
    See also CA 5-8R; CANR 2

Naylor, Gloria
    1950- . . . . . **CLC 28, 52; BLC; DA; DAC;**
                      DAM MST, MULT, NOV, POP
    See also AAYA 6; BW 2; CA 107;
    CANR 27, 51; DLB 173; MTCW

Neihardt, John Gneisenau
    1881-1973 . . . . **CLC 32**
    See also CA 13-14; CAP 1; DLB 9, 54

Nekrasov, Nikolai Alekseevich
    1821-1878 . . . . **NCLC 11**

Nelligan, Emile 1879-1941 . . . . **TCLC 14**
    See also CA 114; DLB 92

Nelson, Willie 1933- . . . . **CLC 17**
    See also CA 107

Nemerov, Howard (Stanley)
    1920-1991 . . . . **CLC 2, 6, 9, 36;**
                                              DAM POET
    See also CA 1-4R; 134; CABS 2; CANR 1,
    27, 53; DLB 5, 6; DLBY 83;
    INT CANR-27; MTCW

Neruda, Pablo
    1904-1973 . . . . . **CLC 1, 2, 5, 7, 9, 28, 62;**
        DA; DAB; DAC; DAM MST, MULT,
                      POET; HLC; PC 4; WLC
    See also CA 19-20; 45-48; CAP 2; HW;
    MTCW

Nerval, Gerard de
1808-1855 ..... **NCLC 1; PC 13; SSC 18**

Nervo, (Jose) Amado (Ruiz de)
1870-1919 .... **TCLC 11**
See also CA 109; 131; HW

Nessi, Pio Baroja y
See Baroja (y Nessi), Pio

Nestroy, Johann 1801-1862...... **NCLC 42**
See also DLB 133

Neufeld, John (Arthur) 1938- ...... **CLC 17**
See also AAYA 11; CA 25-28R; CANR 11, 37, 56; MAICYA; SAAS 3; SATA 6, 81

Neville, Emily Cheney 1919-....... **CLC 12**
See also CA 5-8R; CANR 3, 37; JRDA; MAICYA; SAAS 2; SATA 1

Newbound, Bernard Slade 1930-
See Slade, Bernard
See also CA 81-84; CANR 49;
DAM DRAM

Newby, P(ercy) H(oward)
1918- .... **CLC 2, 13; DAM NOV**
See also CA 5-8R; CANR 32; DLB 15;
MTCW

Newlove, Donald 1928- .... **CLC 6**
See also CA 29-32R; CANR 25

Newlove, John (Herbert) 1938-..... **CLC 14**
See also CA 21-24R; CANR 9, 25

Newman, Charles 1938-.......... **CLC 2, 8**
See also CA 21-24R

Newman, Edwin (Harold) 1919- .... **CLC 14**
See also AITN 1; CA 69-72; CANR 5

Newman, John Henry
1801-1890 .... **NCLC 38**
See also DLB 18, 32, 55

Newton, Suzanne 1936- .... **CLC 35**
See also CA 41-44R; CANR 14; JRDA;
SATA 5, 77

Nexo, Martin Andersen
1869-1954 .... **TCLC 43**

Nezval, Vitezslav 1900-1958 ...... **TCLC 44**
See also CA 123

Ng, Fae Myenne 1957(?)-.......... **CLC 81**
See also CA 146

Ngema, Mbongeni 1955- .... **CLC 57**
See also BW 2; CA 143

Ngugi, James T(hiong'o)........ **CLC 3, 7, 13**
See also Ngugi wa Thiong'o

Ngugi wa Thiong'o
1938- ..... **CLC 36; BLC; DAM MULT,**
NOV
See also Ngugi, James T(hiong'o)
See also BW 2; CA 81-84; CANR 27;
DLB 125; MTCW

Nichol, B(arrie) P(hillip)
1944-1988 .... **CLC 18**
See also CA 53-56; DLB 53; SATA 66

Nichols, John (Treadwell) 1940- .... **CLC 38**
See also CA 9-12R; CAAS 2; CANR 6;
DLBY 82

Nichols, Leigh
See Koontz, Dean R(ay)

Nichols, Peter (Richard)
1927- .... **CLC 5, 36, 65**
See also CA 104; CANR 33; DLB 13;
MTCW

Nicolas, F. R. E.
See Freeling, Nicolas

Niedecker, Lorine
1903-1970 .... **CLC 10, 42; DAM POET**
See also CA 25-28; CAP 2; DLB 48

Nietzsche, Friedrich (Wilhelm)
1844-1900 .... **TCLC 10, 18, 55**
See also CA 107; 121; DLB 129

Nievo, Ippolito 1831-1861 .... **NCLC 22**

Nightingale, Anne Redmon 1943-
See Redmon, Anne
See also CA 103

Nik. T. O.
See Annensky, Innokenty (Fyodorovich)

Nin, Anais
1903-1977 ...... **CLC 1, 4, 8, 11, 14, 60;**
DAM NOV, POP; SSC 10
See also AITN 2; CA 13-16R; 69-72;
CANR 22, 53; DLB 2, 4, 152; MTCW

Nishiwaki, Junzaburo 1894-1982 .... **PC 15**
See also CA 107

Nissenson, Hugh 1933-.......... **CLC 4, 9**
See also CA 17-20R; CANR 27; DLB 28

Niven, Larry .... **CLC 8**
See also Niven, Laurence Van Cott
See also DLB 8

Niven, Laurence Van Cott 1938-
See Niven, Larry
See also CA 21-24R; CAAS 12; CANR 14,
44; DAM POP; MTCW

Nixon, Agnes Eckhardt 1927-...... **CLC 21**
See also CA 110

Nizan, Paul 1905-1940.......... **TCLC 40**
See also DLB 72

Nkosi, Lewis
1936- ..... **CLC 45; BLC; DAM MULT**
See also BW 1; CA 65-68; CANR 27;
DLB 157

Nodier, (Jean) Charles (Emmanuel)
1780-1844 .... **NCLC 19**
See also DLB 119

Nolan, Christopher 1965-.......... **CLC 58**
See also CA 111

Noon, Jeff 1957-................. **CLC 91**
See also CA 148

Norden, Charles
See Durrell, Lawrence (George)

Nordhoff, Charles (Bernard)
1887-1947 .... **TCLC 23**
See also CA 108; DLB 9; SATA 23

Norfolk, Lawrence 1963-.......... **CLC 76**
See also CA 144

Norman, Marsha
1947- .... **CLC 28; DAM DRAM**
See also CA 105; CABS 3; CANR 41;
DLBY 84

Norris, Benjamin Franklin, Jr.
1870-1902 .... **TCLC 24**
See also Norris, Frank
See also CA 110

Norris, Frank
See Norris, Benjamin Franklin, Jr.
See also CDALB 1865-1917; DLB 12, 71

Norris, Leslie 1921-.............. **CLC 14**
See also CA 11-12; CANR 14; CAP 1;
DLB 27

North, Andrew
See Norton, Andre

North, Anthony
See Koontz, Dean R(ay)

North, Captain George
See Stevenson, Robert Louis (Balfour)

North, Milou
See Erdrich, Louise

Northrup, B. A.
See Hubbard, L(afayette) Ron(ald)

North Staffs
See Hulme, T(homas) E(rnest)

Norton, Alice Mary
See Norton, Andre
See also MAICYA; SATA 1, 43

Norton, Andre 1912- .... **CLC 12**
See also Norton, Alice Mary
See also AAYA 14; CA 1-4R; CANR 2, 31;
DLB 8, 52; JRDA; MTCW; SATA 91

Norton, Caroline 1808-1877...... **NCLC 47**
See also DLB 21, 159

Norway, Nevil Shute 1899-1960
See Shute, Nevil
See also CA 102; 93-96

Norwid, Cyprian Kamil
1821-1883 .... **NCLC 17**

Nosille, Nabrah
See Ellison, Harlan (Jay)

Nossack, Hans Erich 1901-1978..... **CLC 6**
See also CA 93-96; 85-88; DLB 69

Nostradamus 1503-1566............ **LC 27**

Nosu, Chuji
See Ozu, Yasujiro

Notenburg, Eleanora (Genrikhovna) von
See Guro, Elena

Nova, Craig 1945-.............. **CLC 7, 31**
See also CA 45-48; CANR 2, 53

Novak, Joseph
See Kosinski, Jerzy (Nikodem)

Novalis 1772-1801 .... **NCLC 13**
See also DLB 90

Nowlan, Alden (Albert)
1933-1983 .. **CLC 15; DAC; DAM MST**
See also CA 9-12R; CANR 5; DLB 53

Noyes, Alfred 1880-1958 .... **TCLC 7**
See also CA 104; DLB 20

Nunn, Kem 19(?)-................. **CLC 34**

Nye, Robert
1939- .... **CLC 13, 42; DAM NOV**
See also CA 33-36R; CANR 29; DLB 14;
MTCW; SATA 6

Nyro, Laura 1947- .... **CLC 17**

Oates, Joyce Carol
1938- ...... **CLC 1, 2, 3, 6, 9, 11, 15, 19,**
33, 52; DA; DAB; DAC; DAM MST,
NOV, POP; SSC 6; WLC
See also AAYA 15; AITN 1; BEST 89:2;
CA 5-8R; CANR 25, 45;
CDALB 1968-1988; DLB 2, 5, 130;
DLBY 81; INT CANR-25; MTCW

Orwell, George
..... TCLC 2, 6, 15, 31, 51; DAB; WLC
See also Blair, Eric (Arthur)
See also CDBLB 1945-1960; DLB 15, 98

Osborne, David
See Silverberg, Robert

Osborne, George
See Silverberg, Robert

Osborne, John (James)
1929-1994 ..... CLC 1, 2, 5, 11, 45; DA;
DAB; DAC; DAM DRAM, MST; WLC
See also CA 13-16R; 147; CANR 21, 56;
CDBLB 1945-1960; DLB 13; MTCW

Osborne, Lawrence 1958- .... CLC 50

Oshima, Nagisa 1932- .... CLC 20
See also CA 116; 121

Oskison, John Milton
1874-1947 ..... TCLC 35; DAM MULT
See also CA 144; DLB 175; NNAL

Ossoli, Sarah Margaret (Fuller marchesa d')
1810-1850
See Fuller, Margaret
See also SATA 25

Ostrovsky, Alexander
1823-1886 .... NCLC 30, 57

Otero, Blas de 1916-1979......... CLC 11
See also CA 89-92; DLB 134

Otto, Whitney 1955-............. CLC 70
See also CA 140

Ouida .... TCLC 43
See also De La Ramee, (Marie) Louise
See also DLB 18, 156

Ousmane, Sembene 1923- .... CLC 66; BLC
See also BW 1; CA 117; 125; MTCW

Ovid
43B.C.-18(?) ... CMLC 7; DAM POET;
PC 2

Owen, Hugh
See Faust, Frederick (Schiller)

Owen, Wilfred (Edward Salter)
1893-1918 ...... TCLC 5, 27; DA; DAB;
DAC; DAM MST, POET; WLC
See also CA 104; 141; CDBLB 1914-1945;
DLB 20

Owens, Rochelle 1936-............ CLC 8
See also CA 17-20R; CAAS 2; CANR 39

Oz, Amos
1939- .... CLC 5, 8, 11, 27, 33, 54;
DAM NOV
See also CA 53-56; CANR 27, 47; MTCW

Ozick, Cynthia
1928- .... CLC 3, 7, 28, 62; DAM NOV,
POP; SSC 15
See also BEST 90:1; CA 17-20R; CANR 23;
DLB 28, 152; DLBY 82; INT CANR-23;
MTCW

Ozu, Yasujiro 1903-1963 .... CLC 16
See also CA 112

Pacheco, C.
See Pessoa, Fernando (Antonio Nogueira)

Pa Chin .... CLC 18
See also Li Fei-kan

Pack, Robert 1929-............. CLC 13
See also CA 1-4R; CANR 3, 44; DLB 5

Padgett, Lewis
See Kuttner, Henry

Padilla (Lorenzo), Heberto 1932-... CLC 38
See also AITN 1; CA 123; 131; HW

Page, Jimmy 1944-................ CLC 12

Page, Louise 1955-............... CLC 40
See also CA 140

Page, P(atricia) K(athleen)
1916- .... CLC 7, 18; DAC; DAM MST;
PC 12
See also CA 53-56; CANR 4, 22; DLB 68;
MTCW

Page, Thomas Nelson 1853-1922.... SSC 23
See also CA 118; DLB 12, 78; DLBD 13

Paget, Violet 1856-1935
See Lee, Vernon
See also CA 104

Paget-Lowe, Henry
See Lovecraft, H(oward) P(hillips)

Paglia, Camille (Anna) 1947-....... CLC 68
See also CA 140

Paige, Richard
See Koontz, Dean R(ay)

Pakenham, Antonia
See Fraser, (Lady) Antonia (Pakenham)

Palamas, Kostes 1859-1943 .... TCLC 5
See also CA 105

Palazzeschi, Aldo 1885-1974....... CLC 11
See also CA 89-92; 53-56; DLB 114

Paley, Grace
1922- .... CLC 4, 6, 37; DAM POP;
SSC 8
See also CA 25-28R; CANR 13, 46;
DLB 28; INT CANR-13; MTCW

Palin, Michael (Edward) 1943- ..... CLC 21
See also Monty Python
See also CA 107; CANR 35; SATA 67

Palliser, Charles 1947-............ CLC 65
See also CA 136

Palma, Ricardo 1833-1919........ TCLC 29

Pancake, Breece Dexter 1952-1979
See Pancake, Breece D'J
See also CA 123; 109

Pancake, Breece D'J.............. CLC 29
See also Pancake, Breece Dexter
See also DLB 130

Panko, Rudy
See Gogol, Nikolai (Vasilyevich)

Papadiamantis, Alexandros
1851-1911 .... TCLC 29

Papadiamantopoulos, Johannes 1856-1910
See Moreas, Jean
See also CA 117

Papini, Giovanni 1881-1956....... TCLC 22
See also CA 121

Paracelsus 1493-1541.............. LC 14

Parasol, Peter
See Stevens, Wallace

Pareto, Vilfredo 1848-1923 .... TCLC 69

Parfenie, Maria
See Codrescu, Andrei

Parini, Jay (Lee) 1948- .... CLC 54
See also CA 97-100; CAAS 16; CANR 32

Park, Jordan
See Kornbluth, C(yril) M.; Pohl, Frederik

Parker, Bert
See Ellison, Harlan (Jay)

Parker, Dorothy (Rothschild)
1893-1967 .... CLC 15, 68;
DAM POET; SSC 2
See also CA 19-20; 25-28R; CAP 2;
DLB 11, 45, 86; MTCW

Parker, Robert B(rown)
1932- ...... CLC 27; DAM NOV, POP
See also BEST 89:4; CA 49-52; CANR 1,
26, 52; INT CANR-26; MTCW

Parkin, Frank 1940-.............. CLC 43
See also CA 147

Parkman, Francis, Jr.
1823-1893 .... NCLC 12
See also DLB 1, 30

Parks, Gordon (Alexander Buchanan)
1912- ... CLC 1, 16; BLC; DAM MULT
See also AITN 2; BW 2; CA 41-44R;
CANR 26; DLB 33; SATA 8

Parmenides
c. 515B.C.-c. 450B.C......... CMLC 22
See also DLB 176

Parnell, Thomas 1679-1718 .... LC 3
See also DLB 94

Parra, Nicanor
1914- ...... CLC 2; DAM MULT; HLC
See also CA 85-88; CANR 32; HW; MTCW

Parrish, Mary Frances
See Fisher, M(ary) F(rances) K(ennedy)

Parson
See Coleridge, Samuel Taylor

Parson Lot
See Kingsley, Charles

Partridge, Anthony
See Oppenheim, E(dward) Phillips

Pascal, Blaise 1623-1662 .... LC 35

Pascoli, Giovanni 1855-1912 ...... TCLC 45

Pasolini, Pier Paolo
1922-1975 .... CLC 20, 37; PC 17
See also CA 93-96; 61-64; DLB 128, 177;
MTCW

Pasquini
See Silone, Ignazio

Pastan, Linda (Olenik)
1932- .... CLC 27; DAM POET
See also CA 61-64; CANR 18, 40; DLB 5

Pasternak, Boris (Leonidovich)
1890-1960 ...... CLC 7, 10, 18, 63; DA;
DAB; DAC; DAM MST, NOV, POET;
PC 6; WLC
See also CA 127; 116; MTCW

Patchen, Kenneth
1911-1972 ... CLC 1, 2, 18; DAM POET
See also CA 1-4R; 33-36R; CANR 3, 35;
DLB 16, 48; MTCW

Pater, Walter (Horatio)
1839-1894 .... NCLC 7
See also CDBLB 1832-1890; DLB 57, 156

Paterson, A(ndrew) B(arton)
1864-1941 .... TCLC 32
See also CA 155

Rivera, Jose Eustasio 1889-1928... **TCLC 35**
See also HW

Rivers, Conrad Kent 1933-1968...... **CLC 1**
See also BW 1; CA 85-88; DLB 41

Rivers, Elfrida
See Bradley, Marion Zimmer

Riverside, John
See Heinlein, Robert A(nson)

Rizal, Jose 1861-1896.......... **NCLC 27**

Roa Bastos, Augusto (Antonio)
1917- ..... **CLC 45; DAM MULT; HLC**
See also CA 131; DLB 113; HW

Robbe-Grillet, Alain
1922- ...... **CLC 1, 2, 4, 6, 8, 10, 14, 43**
See also CA 9-12R; CANR 33; DLB 83;
MTCW

Robbins, Harold
1916- .... **CLC 5; DAM NOV**
See also CA 73-76; CANR 26, 54; MTCW

Robbins, Thomas Eugene 1936-
See Robbins, Tom
See also CA 81-84; CANR 29; DAM NOV,
POP; MTCW

Robbins, Tom................. **CLC 9, 32, 64**
See also Robbins, Thomas Eugene
See also BEST 90:3; DLBY 80

Robbins, Trina 1938- .... **CLC 21**
See also CA 128

Roberts, Charles G(eorge) D(ouglas)
1860-1943 .... **TCLC 8**
See also CA 105; CLR 33; DLB 92;
SATA 88; SATA-Brief 29

Roberts, Elizabeth Madox
1886-1941 .... **TCLC 68**
See also CA 111; DLB 9, 54, 102;
SATA 33; SATA-Brief 27

Roberts, Kate 1891-1985 .... **CLC 15**
See also CA 107; 116

Roberts, Keith (John Kingston)
1935- .... **CLC 14**
See also CA 25-28R; CANR 46

Roberts, Kenneth (Lewis)
1885-1957 .... **TCLC 23**
See also CA 109; DLB 9

Roberts, Michele (B.) 1949-........ **CLC 48**
See also CA 115

Robertson, Ellis
See Ellison, Harlan (Jay); Silverberg, Robert

Robertson, Thomas William
1829-1871 .... **NCLC 35; DAM DRAM**

Robinson, Edwin Arlington
1869-1935 .... **TCLC 5; DA; DAC;**
DAM MST, POET; PC 1
See also CA 104; 133; CDALB 1865-1917;
DLB 54; MTCW

Robinson, Henry Crabb
1775-1867 .... **NCLC 15**
See also DLB 107

Robinson, Jill 1936-.............. **CLC 10**
See also CA 102; INT 102

Robinson, Kim Stanley 1952- ...... **CLC 34**
See also CA 126

Robinson, Lloyd
See Silverberg, Robert

Robinson, Marilynne 1944-........ **CLC 25**
See also CA 116

Robinson, Smokey................. **CLC 21**
See also Robinson, William, Jr.

Robinson, William, Jr. 1940-
See Robinson, Smokey
See also CA 116

Robison, Mary 1949-......... **CLC 42, 98**
See also CA 113; 116; DLB 130; INT 116

Rod, Edouard 1857-1910 .... **TCLC 52**

Roddenberry, Eugene Wesley 1921-1991
See Roddenberry, Gene
See also CA 110; 135; CANR 37; SATA 45;
SATA-Obit 69

Roddenberry, Gene .... **CLC 17**
See also Roddenberry, Eugene Wesley
See also AAYA 5; SATA-Obit 69

Rodgers, Mary 1931-............. **CLC 12**
See also CA 49-52; CANR 8, 55; CLR 20;
INT CANR-8; JRDA; MAICYA;
SATA 8

Rodgers, W(illiam) R(obert)
1909-1969 .... **CLC 7**
See also CA 85-88; DLB 20

Rodman, Eric
See Silverberg, Robert

Rodman, Howard 1920(?)-1985..... **CLC 65**
See also CA 118

Rodman, Maia
See Wojciechowska, Maia (Teresa)

Rodriguez, Claudio 1934-......... **CLC 10**
See also DLB 134

Roelvaag, O(le) E(dvart)
1876-1931 .... **TCLC 17**
See also CA 117; DLB 9

Roethke, Theodore (Huebner)
1908-1963 ...... **CLC 1, 3, 8, 11, 19, 46;**
DAM POET; PC 15
See also CA 81-84; CABS 2;
CDALB 1941-1968; DLB 5; MTCW

Rogers, Thomas Hunton 1927- ..... **CLC 57**
See also CA 89-92; INT 89-92

Rogers, Will(iam Penn Adair)
1879-1935 ...... **TCLC 8; DAM MULT**
See also CA 105; 144; DLB 11; NNAL

Rogin, Gilbert 1929-............. **CLC 18**
See also CA 65-68; CANR 15

Rohan, Koda .... **TCLC 22**
See also Koda Shigeyuki

Rohmer, Eric.................... **CLC 16**
See also Scherer, Jean-Marie Maurice

Rohmer, Sax .... **TCLC 28**
See also Ward, Arthur Henry Sarsfield
See also DLB 70

Roiphe, Anne (Richardson)
1935- .... **CLC 3, 9**
See also CA 89-92; CANR 45; DLBY 80;
INT 89-92

Rojas, Fernando de 1465-1541 ..... **LC 23**

Rolfe, Frederick (William Serafino Austin
Lewis Mary) 1860-1913...... **TCLC 12**
See also CA 107; DLB 34, 156

Rolland, Romain 1866-1944....... **TCLC 23**
See also CA 118; DLB 65

Rolle, Richard c. 1300-c. 1349 ... **CMLC 21**
See also DLB 146

Rolvaag, O(le) E(dvart)
See Roelvaag, O(le) E(dvart)

Romain Arnaud, Saint
See Aragon, Louis

Romains, Jules 1885-1972 .... **CLC 7**
See also CA 85-88; CANR 34; DLB 65;
MTCW

Romero, Jose Ruben 1890-1952 ... **TCLC 14**
See also CA 114; 131; HW

Ronsard, Pierre de
1524-1585 .... **LC 6; PC 11**

Rooke, Leon
1934- .... **CLC 25, 34; DAM POP**
See also CA 25-28R; CANR 23, 53

Roosevelt, Theodore 1858-1919.... **TCLC 69**
See also CA 115; DLB 47

Roper, William 1498-1578.......... **LC 10**

Roquelaure, A. N.
See Rice, Anne

Rosa, Joao Guimaraes 1908-1967... **CLC 23**
See also CA 89-92; DLB 113

Rose, Wendy
1948- .... **CLC 85; DAM MULT; PC 13**
See also CA 53-56; CANR 5, 51; DLB 175;
NNAL; SATA 12

Rosen, Richard (Dean) 1949-....... **CLC 39**
See also CA 77-80; INT CANR-30

Rosenberg, Isaac 1890-1918....... **TCLC 12**
See also CA 107; DLB 20

Rosenblatt, Joe .... **CLC 15**
See also Rosenblatt, Joseph

Rosenblatt, Joseph 1933-
See Rosenblatt, Joe
See also CA 89-92; INT 89-92

Rosenfeld, Samuel 1896-1963
See Tzara, Tristan
See also CA 89-92

Rosenstock, Sami
See Tzara, Tristan

Rosenstock, Samuel
See Tzara, Tristan

Rosenthal, M(acha) L(ouis)
1917-1996 .... **CLC 28**
See also CA 1-4R; 152; CAAS 6; CANR 4,
51; DLB 5; SATA 59

Ross, Barnaby
See Dannay, Frederic

Ross, Bernard L.
See Follett, Ken(neth Martin)

Ross, J. H.
See Lawrence, T(homas) E(dward)

Ross, Martin
See Martin, Violet Florence
See also DLB 135

Ross, (James) Sinclair
1908- ...... **CLC 13; DAC; DAM MST;**
SSC 24
See also CA 73-76; DLB 88

Rossetti, Christina (Georgina)
1830-1894 ..... **NCLC 2, 50; DA; DAB;**
DAC; DAM MST, POET; PC 7; WLC
See also DLB 35, 163; MAICYA; SATA 20

Saintsbury, George (Edward Bateman)
1845-1933 . . . . **TCLC 31**
See also DLB 57, 149

Sait Faik . . . . **TCLC 23**
See also Abasiyanik, Sait Faik

Saki . . . . **TCLC 3; SSC 12**
See also Munro, H(ector) H(ugh)

Sala, George Augustus . . . . **NCLC 46**

Salama, Hannu 1936- . . . . **CLC 18**

Salamanca, J(ack) R(ichard)
1922- . . . . **CLC 4, 15**
See also CA 25-28R

Sale, J. Kirkpatrick
See Sale, Kirkpatrick

Sale, Kirkpatrick 1937- . . . . **CLC 68**
See also CA 13-16R; CANR 10

Salinas, Luis Omar
1937- . . . . . **CLC 90; DAM MULT; HLC**
See also CA 131; DLB 82; HW

Salinas (y Serrano), Pedro
1891(?)-1951 . . . . **TCLC 17**
See also CA 117; DLB 134

Salinger, J(erome) D(avid)
1919- . . . . . . **CLC 1, 3, 8, 12, 55, 56; DA;
DAB; DAC; DAM MST, NOV, POP;
SSC 2; WLC**
See also AAYA 2; CA 5-8R; CANR 39;
CDALB 1941-1968; CLR 18; DLB 2, 102,
173; MAICYA; MTCW; SATA 67

Salisbury, John
See Caute, David

Salter, James 1925- . . . . **CLC 7, 52, 59**
See also CA 73-76; DLB 130

Saltus, Edgar (Everton)
1855-1921 . . . . **TCLC 8**
See also CA 105

Saltykov, Mikhail Evgrafovich
1826-1889 . . . . **NCLC 16**

Samarakis, Antonis 1919- . . . . **CLC 5**
See also CA 25-28R; CAAS 16; CANR 36

Sanchez, Florencio 1875-1910 . . . . . **TCLC 37**
See also CA 153; HW

Sanchez, Luis Rafael 1936- . . . . **CLC 23**
See also CA 128; DLB 145; HW

Sanchez, Sonia
1934- . . . . . . **CLC 5; BLC; DAM MULT;
PC 9**
See also BW 2; CA 33-36R; CANR 24, 49;
CLR 18; DLB 41; DLBD 8; MAICYA;
MTCW; SATA 22

Sand, George
1804-1876 . . . . **NCLC 2, 42, 57; DA;
DAB; DAC; DAM MST, NOV; WLC**
See also DLB 119

Sandburg, Carl (August)
1878-1967 . . . . **CLC 1, 4, 10, 15, 35; DA;
DAB; DAC; DAM MST, POET; PC 2;
WLC**
See also CA 5-8R; 25-28R; CANR 35;
CDALB 1865-1917; DLB 17, 54;
MAICYA; MTCW; SATA 8

Sandburg, Charles
See Sandburg, Carl (August)

Sandburg, Charles A.
See Sandburg, Carl (August)

Sanders, (James) Ed(ward) 1939- . . . **CLC 53**
See also CA 13-16R; CAAS 21; CANR 13,
44; DLB 16

Sanders, Lawrence
1920- . . . . **CLC 41; DAM POP**
See also BEST 89:4; CA 81-84; CANR 33;
MTCW

Sanders, Noah
See Blount, Roy (Alton), Jr.

Sanders, Winston P.
See Anderson, Poul (William)

Sandoz, Mari(e Susette)
1896-1966 . . . . **CLC 28**
See also CA 1-4R; 25-28R; CANR 17;
DLB 9; MTCW; SATA 5

Saner, Reg(inald Anthony) 1931- . . . . **CLC 9**
See also CA 65-68

Sannazaro, Jacopo 1456(?)-1530 . . . . . . **LC 8**

Sansom, William
1912-1976 . . . . . . **CLC 2, 6; DAM NOV;
SSC 21**
See also CA 5-8R; 65-68; CANR 42;
DLB 139; MTCW

Santayana, George 1863-1952 . . . . . **TCLC 40**
See also CA 115; DLB 54, 71; DLBD 13

Santiago, Danny . . . . **CLC 33**
See also James, Daniel (Lewis)
See also DLB 122

Santmyer, Helen Hoover
1895-1986 . . . . **CLC 33**
See also CA 1-4R; 118; CANR 15, 33;
DLBY 84; MTCW

Santos, Bienvenido N(uqui)
1911-1996 . . . . . . **CLC 22; DAM MULT**
See also CA 101; 151; CANR 19, 46

Sapper . . . . **TCLC 44**
See also McNeile, Herman Cyril

Sapphire 1950- . . . . **CLC 99**

Sappho
fl. 6th cent. B.C.- . . . . **CMLC 3;
DAM POET; PC 5**
See also DLB 176

Sarduy, Severo 1937-1993 . . . . **CLC 6, 97**
See also CA 89-92; 142; DLB 113; HW

Sargeson, Frank 1903-1982 . . . . **CLC 31**
See also CA 25-28R; 106; CANR 38

Sarmiento, Felix Ruben Garcia
See Dario, Ruben

Saroyan, William
1908-1981 . . . . . **CLC 1, 8, 10, 29, 34, 56;
DA; DAB; DAC; DAM DRAM, MST,
NOV; SSC 21; WLC**
See also CA 5-8R; 103; CANR 30; DLB 7,
9, 86; DLBY 81; MTCW; SATA 23;
SATA-Obit 24

Sarraute, Nathalie
1900- . . . . **CLC 1, 2, 4, 8, 10, 31, 80**
See also CA 9-12R; CANR 23; DLB 83;
MTCW

Sarton, (Eleanor) May
1912-1995 . . . . **CLC 4, 14, 49, 91;
DAM POET**
See also CA 1-4R; 149; CANR 1, 34, 55;
DLB 48; DLBY 81; INT CANR-34;
MTCW; SATA 36; SATA-Obit 86

Sartre, Jean-Paul
1905-1980 . . . . **CLC 1, 4, 7, 9, 13, 18, 24,
44, 50, 52; DA; DAB; DAC;
DAM DRAM, MST, NOV; DC 3; WLC**
See also CA 9-12R; 97-100; CANR 21;
DLB 72; MTCW

Sassoon, Siegfried (Lorraine)
1886-1967 . . . . **CLC 36; DAB;
DAM MST, NOV, POET; PC 12**
See also CA 104; 25-28R; CANR 36;
DLB 20; MTCW

Satterfield, Charles
See Pohl, Frederik

Saul, John (W. III)
1942- . . . . . . **CLC 46; DAM NOV, POP**
See also AAYA 10; BEST 90:4; CA 81-84;
CANR 16, 40

Saunders, Caleb
See Heinlein, Robert A(nson)

Saura (Atares), Carlos 1932- . . . . **CLC 20**
See also CA 114; 131; HW

Sauser-Hall, Frederic 1887-1961 . . . . **CLC 18**
See also Cendrars, Blaise
See also CA 102; 93-96; CANR 36; MTCW

Saussure, Ferdinand de
1857-1913 . . . . **TCLC 49**

Savage, Catharine
See Brosman, Catharine Savage

Savage, Thomas 1915- . . . . **CLC 40**
See also CA 126; 132; CAAS 15; INT 132

Savan, Glenn 19(?)- . . . . **CLC 50**

Sayers, Dorothy L(eigh)
1893-1957 . . . . . **TCLC 2, 15; DAM POP**
See also CA 104; 119; CDBLB 1914-1945;
DLB 10, 36, 77, 100; MTCW

Sayers, Valerie 1952- . . . . **CLC 50**
See also CA 134

Sayles, John (Thomas)
1950- . . . . **CLC 7, 10, 14**
See also CA 57-60; CANR 41; DLB 44

Scammell, Michael 1935- . . . . **CLC 34**
See also CA 156

Scannell, Vernon 1922- . . . . **CLC 49**
See also CA 5-8R; CANR 8, 24, 57;
DLB 27; SATA 59

Scarlett, Susan
See Streatfeild, (Mary) Noel

Schaeffer, Susan Fromberg
1941- . . . . **CLC 6, 11, 22**
See also CA 49-52; CANR 18; DLB 28;
MTCW; SATA 22

Schary, Jill
See Robinson, Jill

Schell, Jonathan 1943- . . . . **CLC 35**
See also CA 73-76; CANR 12

Schelling, Friedrich Wilhelm Joseph von
1775-1854 . . . . **NCLC 30**
See also DLB 90

Schendel, Arthur van 1874-1946 . . . **TCLC 56**

Scherer, Jean-Marie Maurice 1920-
See Rohmer, Eric
See also CA 110

Schevill, James (Erwin) 1920- . . . . **CLC 7**
See also CA 5-8R; CAAS 12

Serna, Ramon Gomez de la
See Gomez de la Serna, Ramon

Serpieres
See Guillevic, (Eugene)

Service, Robert
See Service, Robert W(illiam)
See also DAB; DLB 92

Service, Robert W(illiam)
1874(?)-1958 ...... **TCLC 15; DA; DAC; DAM MST, POET; WLC**
See also Service, Robert
See also CA 115; 140; SATA 20

Seth, Vikram
1952- .... **CLC 43, 90; DAM MULT**
See also CA 121; 127; CANR 50; DLB 120; INT 127

Seton, Cynthia Propper
1926-1982 .... **CLC 27**
See also CA 5-8R; 108; CANR 7

Seton, Ernest (Evan) Thompson
1860-1946 .... **TCLC 31**
See also CA 109; DLB 92; DLBD 13; JRDA; SATA 18

Seton-Thompson, Ernest
See Seton, Ernest (Evan) Thompson

Settle, Mary Lee 1918- .... **CLC 19, 61**
See also CA 89-92; CAAS 1; CANR 44; DLB 6; INT 89-92

Seuphor, Michel
See Arp, Jean

Sevigne, Marie (de Rabutin-Chantal) Marquise de 1626-1696 .... **LC 11**

Sewall, Samuel 1652-1730 .... **LC 38**
See also DLB 24

Sexton, Anne (Harvey)
1928-1974 .... **CLC 2, 4, 6, 8, 10, 15, 53; DA; DAB; DAC; DAM MST, POET; PC 2; WLC**
See also CA 1-4R; 53-56; CABS 2; CANR 3, 36; CDALB 1941-1968; DLB 5, 169; MTCW; SATA 10

Shaara, Michael (Joseph, Jr.)
1929-1988 .... **CLC 15; DAM POP**
See also AITN 1; CA 102; 125; CANR 52; DLBY 83

Shackleton, C. C.
See Aldiss, Brian W(ilson)

Shacochis, Bob .... **CLC 39**
See also Shacochis, Robert G.

Shacochis, Robert G. 1951-
See Shacochis, Bob
See also CA 119; 124; INT 124

Shaffer, Anthony (Joshua)
1926- .... **CLC 19; DAM DRAM**
See also CA 110; 116; DLB 13

Shaffer, Peter (Levin)
1926- ...... **CLC 5, 14, 18, 37, 60; DAB; DAM DRAM, MST; DC 7**
See also CA 25-28R; CANR 25, 47; CDBLB 1960 to Present; DLB 13; MTCW

Shakey, Bernard
See Young, Neil

Shalamov, Varlam (Tikhonovich)
1907(?)-1982 .... **CLC 18**
See also CA 129; 105

Shamlu, Ahmad 1925- .... **CLC 10**

Shammas, Anton 1951-........... **CLC 55**

Shange, Ntozake
1948- .... **CLC 8, 25, 38, 74; BLC; DAM DRAM, MULT; DC 3**
See also AAYA 9; BW 2; CA 85-88; CABS 3; CANR 27, 48; DLB 38; MTCW

Shanley, John Patrick 1950-....... **CLC 75**
See also CA 128; 133

Shapcott, Thomas W(illiam) 1935-.. **CLC 38**
See also CA 69-72; CANR 49

Shapiro, Jane.................... **CLC 76**

Shapiro, Karl (Jay) 1913-.. **CLC 4, 8, 15, 53**
See also CA 1-4R; CAAS 6; CANR 1, 36; DLB 48; MTCW

Sharp, William 1855-1905 .... **TCLC 39**
See also DLB 156

Sharpe, Thomas Ridley 1928-
See Sharpe, Tom
See also CA 114; 122; INT 122

Sharpe, Tom..................... **CLC 36**
See also Sharpe, Thomas Ridley
See also DLB 14

Shaw, Bernard................... **TCLC 45**
See also Shaw, George Bernard
See also BW 1

Shaw, G. Bernard
See Shaw, George Bernard

Shaw, George Bernard
1856-1950 ... **TCLC 3, 9, 21; DA; DAB; DAC; DAM DRAM, MST; WLC**
See also Shaw, Bernard
See also CA 104; 128; CDBLB 1914-1945; DLB 10, 57; MTCW

Shaw, Henry Wheeler
1818-1885 .... **NCLC 15**
See also DLB 11

Shaw, Irwin
1913-1984 .... **CLC 7, 23, 34; DAM DRAM, POP**
See also AITN 1; CA 13-16R; 112; CANR 21; CDALB 1941-1968; DLB 6, 102; DLBY 84; MTCW

Shaw, Robert 1927-1978 .... **CLC 5**
See also AITN 1; CA 1-4R; 81-84; CANR 4; DLB 13, 14

Shaw, T. E.
See Lawrence, T(homas) E(dward)

Shawn, Wallace 1943- .... **CLC 41**
See also CA 112

Shea, Lisa 1953-................. **CLC 86**
See also CA 147

Sheed, Wilfrid (John Joseph)
1930- .... **CLC 2, 4, 10, 53**
See also CA 65-68; CANR 30; DLB 6; MTCW

Sheldon, Alice Hastings Bradley
1915(?)-1987
See Tiptree, James, Jr.
See also CA 108; 122; CANR 34; INT 108; MTCW

Sheldon, John
See Bloch, Robert (Albert)

Shelley, Mary Wollstonecraft (Godwin)
1797-1851 .... **NCLC 14, 59; DA; DAB; DAC; DAM MST, NOV; WLC**
See also AAYA 20; CDBLB 1789-1832; DLB 110, 116, 159; SATA 29

Shelley, Percy Bysshe
1792-1822 .... **NCLC 18; DA; DAB; DAC; DAM MST, POET; PC 14; WLC**
See also CDBLB 1789-1832; DLB 96, 110, 158

Shepard, Jim 1956-.............. **CLC 36**
See also CA 137; SATA 90

Shepard, Lucius 1947- .... **CLC 34**
See also CA 128; 141

Shepard, Sam
1943- .... **CLC 4, 6, 17, 34, 41, 44; DAM DRAM; DC 5**
See also AAYA 1; CA 69-72; CABS 3; CANR 22; DLB 7; MTCW

Shepherd, Michael
See Ludlum, Robert

Sherburne, Zoa (Morin) 1912-...... **CLC 30**
See also AAYA 13; CA 1-4R; CANR 3, 37; MAICYA; SAAS 18; SATA 3

Sheridan, Frances 1724-1766........ **LC 7**
See also DLB 39, 84

Sheridan, Richard Brinsley
1751-1816 .... **NCLC 5; DA; DAB; DAC; DAM DRAM, MST; DC 1; WLC**
See also CDBLB 1660-1789; DLB 89

Sherman, Jonathan Marc.......... **CLC 55**

Sherman, Martin 1941(?)-......... **CLC 19**
See also CA 116; 123

Sherwin, Judith Johnson 1936-... **CLC 7, 15**
See also CA 25-28R; CANR 34

Sherwood, Frances 1940-......... **CLC 81**
See also CA 146

Sherwood, Robert E(mmet)
1896-1955 ...... **TCLC 3; DAM DRAM**
See also CA 104; 153; DLB 7, 26

Shestov, Lev 1866-1938 .... **TCLC 56**

Shevchenko, Taras 1814-1861 .... **NCLC 54**

Shiel, M(atthew) P(hipps)
1865-1947 .... **TCLC 8**
See also CA 106; DLB 153

Shields, Carol 1935-......... **CLC 91; DAC**
See also CA 81-84; CANR 51

Shields, David 1956-.............. **CLC 97**
See also CA 124; CANR 48

Shiga, Naoya 1883-1971... **CLC 33; SSC 23**
See also CA 101; 33-36R

Shilts, Randy 1951-1994 .... **CLC 85**
See also AAYA 19; CA 115; 127; 144; CANR 45; INT 127

Shimazaki, Haruki 1872-1943
See Shimazaki Toson
See also CA 105; 134

Shimazaki Toson................. **TCLC 5**
See also Shimazaki, Haruki

Sholokhov, Mikhail (Aleksandrovich)
1905-1984 .... **CLC 7, 15**
See also CA 101; 112; MTCW; SATA-Obit 36

Sjowall, Maj
See Sjoewall, Maj

Skelton, Robin 1925- . . . . **CLC 13**
See also AITN 2; CA 5-8R; CAAS 5;
CANR 28; DLB 27, 53

Skolimowski, Jerzy 1938- . . . . **CLC 20**
See also CA 128

Skram, Amalie (Bertha)
1847-1905 . . . . **TCLC 25**

Skvorecky, Josef (Vaclav)
1924- . . . . **CLC 15, 39, 69; DAC;**
DAM NOV
See also CA 61-64; CAAS 1; CANR 10, 34;
MTCW

Slade, Bernard. . . . . **CLC 11, 46**
See also Newbound, Bernard Slade
See also CAAS 9; DLB 53

Slaughter, Carolyn 1946- . . . . **CLC 56**
See also CA 85-88

Slaughter, Frank G(ill) 1908- . . . . . . **CLC 29**
See also AITN 2; CA 5-8R; CANR 5;
INT CANR-5

Slavitt, David R(ytman) 1935- . . . . **CLC 5, 14**
See also CA 21-24R; CAAS 3; CANR 41;
DLB 5, 6

Slesinger, Tess 1905-1945 . . . . **TCLC 10**
See also CA 107; DLB 102

Slessor, Kenneth 1901-1971. . . . . . . **CLC 14**
See also CA 102; 89-92

Slowacki, Juliusz 1809-1849 . . . . . **NCLC 15**

Smart, Christopher
1722-1771 . . . **LC 3; DAM POET; PC 13**
See also DLB 109

Smart, Elizabeth 1913-1986. . . . . . . **CLC 54**
See also CA 81-84; 118; DLB 88

Smiley, Jane (Graves)
1949- . . . . **CLC 53, 76; DAM POP**
See also CA 104; CANR 30, 50;
INT CANR-30

Smith, A(rthur) J(ames) M(arshall)
1902-1980 . . . . **CLC 15; DAC**
See also CA 1-4R; 102; CANR 4; DLB 88

Smith, Adam 1723-1790. . . . . **LC 36**
See also DLB 104

Smith, Alexander 1829-1867 . . . . . **NCLC 59**
See also DLB 32, 55

Smith, Anna Deavere 1950- . . . . **CLC 86**
See also CA 133

Smith, Betty (Wehner) 1896-1972. . . **CLC 19**
See also CA 5-8R; 33-36R; DLBY 82;
SATA 6

Smith, Charlotte (Turner)
1749-1806 . . . . **NCLC 23**
See also DLB 39, 109

Smith, Clark Ashton 1893-1961 . . . . **CLC 43**
See also CA 143

Smith, Dave. . . . . **CLC 22, 42**
See also Smith, David (Jeddie)
See also CAAS 7; DLB 5

Smith, David (Jeddie) 1942-
See Smith, Dave
See also CA 49-52; CANR 1; DAM POET

Smith, Florence Margaret 1902-1971
See Smith, Stevie
See also CA 17-18; 29-32R; CANR 35;
CAP 2; DAM POET; MTCW

Smith, Iain Crichton 1928- . . . . **CLC 64**
See also CA 21-24R; DLB 40, 139

Smith, John 1580(?)-1631 . . . . **LC 9**

Smith, Johnston
See Crane, Stephen (Townley)

Smith, Joseph, Jr. 1805-1844 . . . . **NCLC 53**

Smith, Lee 1944-. . . . . **CLC 25, 73**
See also CA 114; 119; CANR 46; DLB 143;
DLBY 83; INT 119

Smith, Martin
See Smith, Martin Cruz

Smith, Martin Cruz
1942- . . . . . **CLC 25; DAM MULT, POP**
See also BEST 89:4; CA 85-88; CANR 6,
23, 43; INT CANR-23; NNAL

Smith, Mary-Ann Tirone 1944-. . . . . **CLC 39**
See also CA 118; 136

Smith, Patti 1946- . . . . **CLC 12**
See also CA 93-96

Smith, Pauline (Urmson)
1882-1959 . . . . **TCLC 25**

Smith, Rosamond
See Oates, Joyce Carol

Smith, Sheila Kaye
See Kaye-Smith, Sheila

Smith, Stevie . . . . **CLC 3, 8, 25, 44; PC 12**
See also Smith, Florence Margaret
See also DLB 20

Smith, Wilbur (Addison) 1933-. . . . . **CLC 33**
See also CA 13-16R; CANR 7, 46; MTCW

Smith, William Jay 1918- . . . . **CLC 6**
See also CA 5-8R; CANR 44; DLB 5;
MAICYA; SAAS 22; SATA 2, 68

Smith, Woodrow Wilson
See Kuttner, Henry

Smolenskin, Peretz 1842-1885. . . . **NCLC 30**

Smollett, Tobias (George) 1721-1771 . . **LC 2**
See also CDBLB 1660-1789; DLB 39, 104

Snodgrass, W(illiam) D(e Witt)
1926- . . . . **CLC 2, 6, 10, 18, 68;**
DAM POET
See also CA 1-4R; CANR 6, 36; DLB 5;
MTCW

Snow, C(harles) P(ercy)
1905-1980 . . . . **CLC 1, 4, 6, 9, 13, 19;**
DAM NOV
See also CA 5-8R; 101; CANR 28;
CDBLB 1945-1960; DLB 15, 77; MTCW

Snow, Frances Compton
See Adams, Henry (Brooks)

Snyder, Gary (Sherman)
1930- . . **CLC 1, 2, 5, 9, 32; DAM POET**
See also CA 17-20R; CANR 30; DLB 5, 16,
165

Snyder, Zilpha Keatley 1927- . . . . . . **CLC 17**
See also AAYA 15; CA 9-12R; CANR 38;
CLR 31; JRDA; MAICYA; SAAS 2;
SATA 1, 28, 75

Soares, Bernardo
See Pessoa, Fernando (Antonio Nogueira)

Sobh, A.
See Shamlu, Ahmad

Sobol, Joshua. . . . . **CLC 60**

Soderberg, Hjalmar 1869-1941 . . . . **TCLC 39**

Sodergran, Edith (Irene)
See Soedergran, Edith (Irene)

Soedergran, Edith (Irene)
1892-1923 . . . . **TCLC 31**

Softly, Edgar
See Lovecraft, H(oward) P(hillips)

Softly, Edward
See Lovecraft, H(oward) P(hillips)

Sokolov, Raymond 1941-. . . . . **CLC 7**
See also CA 85-88

Solo, Jay
See Ellison, Harlan (Jay)

Sologub, Fyodor . . . . **TCLC 9**
See also Teternikov, Fyodor Kuzmich

Solomons, Ikey Esquir
See Thackeray, William Makepeace

Solomos, Dionysios 1798-1857 . . . **NCLC 15**

Solwoska, Mara
See French, Marilyn

Solzhenitsyn, Aleksandr I(sayevich)
1918- . . . . . . **CLC 1, 2, 4, 7, 9, 10, 18, 26,**
34, 78; DA; DAB; DAC; DAM MST,
NOV; WLC
See also AITN 1; CA 69-72; CANR 40;
MTCW

Somers, Jane
See Lessing, Doris (May)

Somerville, Edith 1858-1949 . . . . . . **TCLC 51**
See also DLB 135

Somerville & Ross
See Martin, Violet Florence; Somerville,
Edith

Sommer, Scott 1951- . . . . **CLC 25**
See also CA 106

Sondheim, Stephen (Joshua)
1930- . . . . **CLC 30, 39; DAM DRAM**
See also AAYA 11; CA 103; CANR 47

Sontag, Susan
1933- . . . . **CLC 1, 2, 10, 13, 31;**
DAM POP
See also CA 17-20R; CANR 25, 51; DLB 2,
67; MTCW

Sophocles
496(?)B.C.-406(?)B.C.. . . . . **CMLC 2; DA;**
DAB; DAC; DAM DRAM, MST; DC 1
See also DLB 176

Sordello 1189-1269. . . . . **CMLC 15**

Sorel, Julia
See Drexler, Rosalyn

Sorrentino, Gilbert
1929- . . . . **CLC 3, 7, 14, 22, 40**
See also CA 77-80; CANR 14, 33; DLB 5,
173; DLBY 80; INT CANR-14

Soto, Gary
1952- . . . . **CLC 32, 80; DAM MULT;**
HLC
See also AAYA 10; CA 119; 125;
CANR 50; CLR 38; DLB 82; HW;
INT 125; JRDA; SATA 80

Taylor, Mildred D. . . . . **CLC 21**
    See also AAYA 10; BW 1; CA 85-88;
    CANR 25; CLR 9; DLB 52; JRDA;
    MAICYA; SAAS 5; SATA 15, 70

Taylor, Peter (Hillsman)
    1917-1994 . . . . . **CLC 1, 4, 18, 37, 44, 50,**
                                            71; SSC 10
    See also CA 13-16R; 147; CANR 9, 50;
    DLBY 81, 94; INT CANR-9; MTCW

Taylor, Robert Lewis 1912- . . . . **CLC 14**
    See also CA 1-4R; CANR 3; SATA 10

Tchekhov, Anton
    See Chekhov, Anton (Pavlovich)

Teasdale, Sara 1884-1933. . . . . **TCLC 4**
    See also CA 104; DLB 45; SATA 32

Tegner, Esaias 1782-1846. . . . . **NCLC 2**

Teilhard de Chardin, (Marie Joseph) Pierre
    1881-1955 . . . . **TCLC 9**
    See also CA 105

Temple, Ann
    See Mortimer, Penelope (Ruth)

Tennant, Emma (Christina)
    1937- . . . . **CLC 13, 52**
    See also CA 65-68; CAAS 9; CANR 10, 38;
    DLB 14

Tenneshaw, S. M.
    See Silverberg, Robert

Tennyson, Alfred
    1809-1892 . . . . **NCLC 30; DA; DAB;**
        DAC; DAM MST, POET; PC 6; WLC
    See also CDBLB 1832-1890; DLB 32

Teran, Lisa St. Aubin de . . . . **CLC 36**
    See also St. Aubin de Teran, Lisa

Terence
    195(?)B.C.-159B.C. . . . . **CMLC 14; DC 7**

Teresa de Jesus, St. 1515-1582 . . . . . . **LC 18**

Terkel, Louis 1912-
    See Terkel, Studs
    See also CA 57-60; CANR 18, 45; MTCW

Terkel, Studs . . . . **CLC 38**
    See also Terkel, Louis
    See also AITN 1

Terry, C. V.
    See Slaughter, Frank G(ill)

Terry, Megan 1932- . . . . **CLC 19**
    See also CA 77-80; CABS 3; CANR 43;
    DLB 7

Tertz, Abram
    See Sinyavsky, Andrei (Donatevich)

Tesich, Steve 1943(?)-1996. . . . . . **CLC 40, 69**
    See also CA 105; 152; DLBY 83

Teternikov, Fyodor Kuzmich 1863-1927
    See Sologub, Fyodor
    See also CA 104

Tevis, Walter 1928-1984 . . . . **CLC 42**
    See also CA 113

Tey, Josephine. . . . . **TCLC 14**
    See also Mackintosh, Elizabeth
    See also DLB 77

Thackeray, William Makepeace
    1811-1863 . . . . **NCLC 5, 14, 22, 43; DA;**
        DAB; DAC; DAM MST, NOV; WLC
    See also CDBLB 1832-1890; DLB 21, 55,
    159, 163; SATA 23

Thakura, Ravindranatha
    See Tagore, Rabindranath

Tharoor, Shashi 1956- . . . . **CLC 70**
    See also CA 141

Thelwell, Michael Miles 1939- . . . . . **CLC 22**
    See also BW 2; CA 101

Theobald, Lewis, Jr.
    See Lovecraft, H(oward) P(hillips)

Theodorescu, Ion N. 1880-1967
    See Arghezi, Tudor
    See also CA 116

Theriault, Yves
    1915-1983 . . **CLC 79; DAC; DAM MST**
    See also CA 102; DLB 88

Theroux, Alexander (Louis)
    1939- . . . . **CLC 2, 25**
    See also CA 85-88; CANR 20

Theroux, Paul (Edward)
    1941- . . . . **CLC 5, 8, 11, 15, 28, 46;**
                                            DAM POP
    See also BEST 89:4; CA 33-36R; CANR 20,
    45; DLB 2; MTCW; SATA 44

Thesen, Sharon 1946- . . . . **CLC 56**

Thevenin, Denis
    See Duhamel, Georges

Thibault, Jacques Anatole Francois
    1844-1924
    See France, Anatole
    See also CA 106; 127; DAM NOV; MTCW

Thiele, Colin (Milton) 1920- . . . . **CLC 17**
    See also CA 29-32R; CANR 12, 28, 53;
    CLR 27; MAICYA; SAAS 2; SATA 14,
    72

Thomas, Audrey (Callahan)
    1935- . . . . **CLC 7, 13, 37; SSC 20**
    See also AITN 2; CA 21-24R; CAAS 19;
    CANR 36; DLB 60; MTCW

Thomas, D(onald) M(ichael)
    1935- . . . . **CLC 13, 22, 31**
    See also CA 61-64; CAAS 11; CANR 17,
    45; CDBLB 1960 to Present; DLB 40;
    INT CANR-17; MTCW

Thomas, Dylan (Marlais)
    1914-1953 . . . **TCLC 1, 8, 45; DA; DAB;**
        DAC; DAM DRAM, MST, POET;
                                    PC 2; SSC 3; WLC
    See also CA 104; 120; CDBLB 1945-1960;
    DLB 13, 20, 139; MTCW; SATA 60

Thomas, (Philip) Edward
    1878-1917 . . . . . . **TCLC 10; DAM POET**
    See also CA 106; 153; DLB 19

Thomas, Joyce Carol 1938- . . . . **CLC 35**
    See also AAYA 12; BW 2; CA 113; 116;
    CANR 48; CLR 19; DLB 33; INT 116;
    JRDA; MAICYA; MTCW; SAAS 7;
    SATA 40, 78

Thomas, Lewis 1913-1993 . . . . **CLC 35**
    See also CA 85-88; 143; CANR 38; MTCW

Thomas, Paul
    See Mann, (Paul) Thomas

Thomas, Piri 1928- . . . . **CLC 17**
    See also CA 73-76; HW

Thomas, R(onald) S(tuart)
    1913- . . . . **CLC 6, 13, 48; DAB;**
                                            DAM POET
    See also CA 89-92; CAAS 4; CANR 30;
    CDBLB 1960 to Present; DLB 27;
    MTCW

Thomas, Ross (Elmore) 1926-1995 . . **CLC 39**
    See also CA 33-36R; 150; CANR 22

Thompson, Francis Clegg
    See Mencken, H(enry) L(ouis)

Thompson, Francis Joseph
    1859-1907 . . . . **TCLC 4**
    See also CA 104; CDBLB 1890-1914;
    DLB 19

Thompson, Hunter S(tockton)
    1939- . . . . **CLC 9, 17, 40; DAM POP**
    See also BEST 89:1; CA 17-20R; CANR 23,
    46; MTCW

Thompson, James Myers
    See Thompson, Jim (Myers)

Thompson, Jim (Myers)
    1906-1977(?) . . . . **CLC 69**
    See also CA 140

Thompson, Judith . . . . **CLC 39**

Thomson, James
    1700-1748 . . . . . **LC 16, 29; DAM POET**
    See also DLB 95

Thomson, James
    1834-1882 . . . . . **NCLC 18; DAM POET**
    See also DLB 35

Thoreau, Henry David
    1817-1862 . . . . **NCLC 7, 21, 61; DA;**
                            DAB; DAC; DAM MST; WLC
    See also CDALB 1640-1865; DLB 1

Thornton, Hall
    See Silverberg, Robert

Thucydides c. 455B.C.-399B.C. . . . . **CMLC 17**
    See also DLB 176

Thurber, James (Grover)
    1894-1961 . . . . **CLC 5, 11, 25; DA; DAB;**
        DAC; DAM DRAM, MST, NOV; SSC 1
    See also CA 73-76; CANR 17, 39;
    CDALB 1929-1941; DLB 4, 11, 22, 102;
    MAICYA; MTCW; SATA 13

Thurman, Wallace (Henry)
    1902-1934 . . . . **TCLC 6; BLC;**
                                            DAM MULT
    See also BW 1; CA 104; 124; DLB 51

Ticheburn, Cheviot
    See Ainsworth, William Harrison

Tieck, (Johann) Ludwig
    1773-1853 . . . . **NCLC 5, 46**
    See also DLB 90

Tiger, Derry
    See Ellison, Harlan (Jay)

Tilghman, Christopher 1948(?)- . . . . . **CLC 65**

Tillinghast, Richard (Williford)
    1940- . . . . **CLC 29**
    See also CA 29-32R; CAAS 23; CANR 26,
    51

Timrod, Henry 1828-1867 . . . . **NCLC 25**
    See also DLB 3

Tindall, Gillian 1938- . . . . **CLC 7**
    See also CA 21-24R; CANR 11

Tiptree, James, Jr. .... **CLC 48, 50**
See also Sheldon, Alice Hastings Bradley
See also DLB 8

Titmarsh, Michael Angelo
See Thackeray, William Makepeace

Tocqueville, Alexis (Charles Henri Maurice Clerel Comte) 1805-1859..... **NCLC 7**

Tolkien, J(ohn) R(onald) R(euel)
1892-1973 .... **CLC 1, 2, 3, 8, 12, 38;
DA; DAB; DAC; DAM MST, NOV,
POP; WLC**
See also AAYA 10; AITN 1; CA 17-18;
45-48; CANR 36; CAP 2;
CDBLB 1914-1945; DLB 15, 160; JRDA;
MAICYA; MTCW; SATA 2, 32;
SATA-Obit 24

Toller, Ernst 1893-1939......... **TCLC 10**
See also CA 107; DLB 124

Tolson, M. B.
See Tolson, Melvin B(eaunorus)

Tolson, Melvin B(eaunorus)
1898(?)-1966 .... **CLC 36; BLC;
DAM MULT, POET**
See also BW 1; CA 124; 89-92; DLB 48, 76

Tolstoi, Aleksei Nikolaevich
See Tolstoy, Alexey Nikolaevich

Tolstoy, Alexey Nikolaevich
1882-1945 .... **TCLC 18**
See also CA 107

Tolstoy, Count Leo
See Tolstoy, Leo (Nikolaevich)

Tolstoy, Leo (Nikolaevich)
1828-1910 ...... **TCLC 4, 11, 17, 28, 44;
DA; DAB; DAC; DAM MST, NOV;
SSC 9; WLC**
See also CA 104; 123; SATA 26

Tomasi di Lampedusa, Giuseppe 1896-1957
See Lampedusa, Giuseppe (Tomasi) di
See also CA 111

Tomlin, Lily .... **CLC 17**
See also Tomlin, Mary Jean

Tomlin, Mary Jean 1939(?)-
See Tomlin, Lily
See also CA 117

Tomlinson, (Alfred) Charles
1927- .... **CLC 2, 4, 6, 13, 45;
DAM POET; PC 17**
See also CA 5-8R; CANR 33; DLB 40

Tonson, Jacob
See Bennett, (Enoch) Arnold

Toole, John Kennedy
1937-1969 .... **CLC 19, 64**
See also CA 104; DLBY 81

Toomer, Jean
1894-1967 ...... **CLC 1, 4, 13, 22; BLC;
DAM MULT; PC 7; SSC 1**
See also BW 1; CA 85-88;
CDALB 1917-1929; DLB 45, 51; MTCW

Torley, Luke
See Blish, James (Benjamin)

Tornimparte, Alessandra
See Ginzburg, Natalia

Torre, Raoul della
See Mencken, H(enry) L(ouis)

Torrey, E(dwin) Fuller 1937-....... **CLC 34**
See also CA 119

Torsvan, Ben Traven
See Traven, B.

Torsvan, Benno Traven
See Traven, B.

Torsvan, Berick Traven
See Traven, B.

Torsvan, Berwick Traven
See Traven, B.

Torsvan, Bruno Traven
See Traven, B.

Torsvan, Traven
See Traven, B.

Tournier, Michel (Edouard)
1924- .... **CLC 6, 23, 36, 95**
See also CA 49-52; CANR 3, 36; DLB 83;
MTCW; SATA 23

Tournimparte, Alessandra
See Ginzburg, Natalia

Towers, Ivar
See Kornbluth, C(yril) M.

Towne, Robert (Burton) 1936(?)-.... **CLC 87**
See also CA 108; DLB 44

Townsend, Sue 1946- .. **CLC 61; DAB; DAC**
See also CA 119; 127; INT 127; MTCW;
SATA 55; SATA-Brief 48

Townshend, Peter (Dennis Blandford)
1945- .... **CLC 17, 42**
See also CA 107

Tozzi, Federigo 1883-1920....... **TCLC 31**

Traill, Catharine Parr
1802-1899 .... **NCLC 31**
See also DLB 99

Trakl, Georg 1887-1914.......... **TCLC 5**
See also CA 104

Transtroemer, Tomas (Goesta)
1931- .... **CLC 52, 65; DAM POET**
See also CA 117; 129; CAAS 17

Transtromer, Tomas Gosta
See Transtroemer, Tomas (Goesta)

Traven, B. (?)-1969............. **CLC 8, 11**
See also CA 19-20; 25-28R; CAP 2; DLB 9,
56; MTCW

Treitel, Jonathan 1959- .... **CLC 70**

Tremain, Rose 1943-............... **CLC 42**
See also CA 97-100; CANR 44; DLB 14

Tremblay, Michel
1942- ...... **CLC 29; DAC; DAM MST**
See also CA 116; 128; DLB 60; MTCW

Trevanian .... **CLC 29**
See also Whitaker, Rod(ney)

Trevor, Glen
See Hilton, James

Trevor, William
1928- ..... **CLC 7, 9, 14, 25, 71; SSC 21**
See also Cox, William Trevor
See also DLB 14, 139

Trifonov, Yuri (Valentinovich)
1925-1981 .... **CLC 45**
See also CA 126; 103; MTCW

Trilling, Lionel 1905-1975 .... **CLC 9, 11, 24**
See also CA 9-12R; 61-64; CANR 10;
DLB 28, 63; INT CANR-10; MTCW

Trimball, W. H.
See Mencken, H(enry) L(ouis)

Tristan
See Gomez de la Serna, Ramon

Tristram
See Housman, A(lfred) E(dward)

Trogdon, William (Lewis) 1939-
See Heat-Moon, William Least
See also CA 115; 119; CANR 47; INT 119

Trollope, Anthony
1815-1882 ..... **NCLC 6, 33; DA; DAB;
DAC; DAM MST, NOV; WLC**
See also CDBLB 1832-1890; DLB 21, 57,
159; SATA 22

Trollope, Frances 1779-1863 ..... **NCLC 30**
See also DLB 21, 166

Trotsky, Leon 1879-1940........ **TCLC 22**
See also CA 118

Trotter (Cockburn), Catharine
1679-1749 .... **LC 8**
See also DLB 84

Trout, Kilgore
See Farmer, Philip Jose

Trow, George W. S. 1943-........ **CLC 52**
See also CA 126

Troyat, Henri 1911-.............. **CLC 23**
See also CA 45-48; CANR 2, 33; MTCW

Trudeau, G(arretson) B(eekman) 1948-
See Trudeau, Garry B.
See also CA 81-84; CANR 31; SATA 35

Trudeau, Garry B. .... **CLC 12**
See also Trudeau, G(arretson) B(eekman)
See also AAYA 10; AITN 2

Truffaut, Francois 1932-1984....... **CLC 20**
See also CA 81-84; 113; CANR 34

Trumbo, Dalton 1905-1976 .... **CLC 19**
See also CA 21-24R; 69-72; CANR 10;
DLB 26

Trumbull, John 1750-1831....... **NCLC 30**
See also DLB 31

Trundlett, Helen B.
See Eliot, T(homas) S(tearns)

Tryon, Thomas
1926-1991 ...... **CLC 3, 11; DAM POP**
See also AITN 1; CA 29-32R; 135;
CANR 32; MTCW

Tryon, Tom
See Tryon, Thomas

Ts'ao Hsueh-ch'in 1715(?)-1763....... **LC 1**

Tsushima, Shuji 1909-1948
See Dazai, Osamu
See also CA 107

Tsvetaeva (Efron), Marina (Ivanovna)
1892-1941 .... **TCLC 7, 35; PC 14**
See also CA 104; 128; MTCW

Tuck, Lily 1938-................. **CLC 70**
See also CA 139

Tu Fu 712-770.................... **PC 9**
See also DAM MULT

Tunis, John R(oberts) 1889-1975 ... **CLC 12**
See also CA 61-64; DLB 22, 171; JRDA;
MAICYA; SATA 37; SATA-Brief 30

Tuohy, Frank.................... CLC 37
See also Tuohy, John Francis
See also DLB 14, 139

Tuohy, John Francis 1925-
See Tuohy, Frank
See also CA 5-8R; CANR 3, 47

Turco, Lewis (Putnam) 1934- ... CLC 11, 63
See also CA 13-16R; CAAS 22; CANR 24,
51; DLBY 84

Turgenev, Ivan
1818-1883 .... NCLC 21; DA; DAB;
DAC; DAM MST, NOV; DC 7; SSC 7;
WLC

Turgot, Anne-Robert-Jacques
1727-1781 .... LC 26

Turner, Frederick 1943-.......... CLC 48
See also CA 73-76; CAAS 10; CANR 12,
30, 56; DLB 40

Tutu, Desmond M(pilo)
1931- ..... CLC 80; BLC; DAM MULT
See also BW 1; CA 125

Tutuola, Amos
1920- .... CLC 5, 14, 29; BLC;
DAM MULT
See also BW 2; CA 9-12R; CANR 27;
DLB 125; MTCW

Twain, Mark
..... TCLC 6, 12, 19, 36, 48, 59; SSC 6;
WLC
See also Clemens, Samuel Langhorne
See also AAYA 20; DLB 11, 12, 23, 64, 74

Tyler, Anne
1941-........ CLC 7, 11, 18, 28, 44, 59;
DAM NOV, POP
See also AAYA 18; BEST 89:1; CA 9-12R;
CANR 11, 33, 53; DLB 6, 143; DLBY 82;
MTCW; SATA 7, 90

Tyler, Royall 1757-1826......... NCLC 3
See also DLB 37

Tynan, Katharine 1861-1931 .... TCLC 3
See also CA 104; DLB 153

Tyutchev, Fyodor 1803-1873 ..... NCLC 34

Tzara, Tristan
1896-1963 .... CLC 47; DAM POET
See also Rosenfeld, Samuel; Rosenstock,
Sami; Rosenstock, Samuel
See also CA 153

Uhry, Alfred
1936- ..... CLC 55; DAM DRAM, POP
See also CA 127; 133; INT 133

Ulf, Haerved
See Strindberg, (Johan) August

Ulf, Harved
See Strindberg, (Johan) August

Ulibarri, Sabine R(eyes)
1919- .... CLC 83; DAM MULT
See also CA 131; DLB 82; HW

Unamuno (y Jugo), Miguel de
1864-1936 ... TCLC 2, 9; DAM MULT,
NOV; HLC; SSC 11
See also CA 104; 131; DLB 108; HW;
MTCW

Undercliffe, Errol
See Campbell, (John) Ramsey

Underwood, Miles
See Glassco, John

Undset, Sigrid
1882-1949 .... TCLC 3; DA; DAB;
DAC; DAM MST, NOV; WLC
See also CA 104; 129; MTCW

Ungaretti, Giuseppe
1888-1970 .... CLC 7, 11, 15
See also CA 19-20; 25-28R; CAP 2;
DLB 114

Unger, Douglas 1952-............ CLC 34
See also CA 130

Unsworth, Barry (Forster) 1930-.... CLC 76
See also CA 25-28R; CANR 30, 54

Updike, John (Hoyer)
1932- ...... CLC 1, 2, 3, 5, 7, 9, 13, 15,
23, 34, 43, 70; DA; DAB; DAC;
DAM MST, NOV, POET, POP;
SSC 13; WLC
See also CA 1-4R; CABS 1; CANR 4, 33,
51; CDALB 1968-1988; DLB 2, 5, 143;
DLBD 3; DLBY 80, 82; MTCW

Upshaw, Margaret Mitchell
See Mitchell, Margaret (Munnerlyn)

Upton, Mark
See Sanders, Lawrence

Urdang, Constance (Henriette)
1922-..................... CLC 47
See also CA 21-24R; CANR 9, 24

Uriel, Henry
See Faust, Frederick (Schiller)

Uris, Leon (Marcus)
1924- .... CLC 7, 32; DAM NOV, POP
See also AITN 1, 2; BEST 89:2; CA 1-4R;
CANR 1, 40; MTCW; SATA 49

Urmuz
See Codrescu, Andrei

Urquhart, Jane 1949-........ CLC 90; DAC
See also CA 113; CANR 32

Ustinov, Peter (Alexander) 1921-.... CLC 1
See also AITN 1; CA 13-16R; CANR 25,
51; DLB 13

Vaculik, Ludvik 1926-.......... CLC 7
See also CA 53-56

Valdez, Luis (Miguel)
1940- ..... CLC 84; DAM MULT; HLC
See also CA 101; CANR 32; DLB 122; HW

Valenzuela, Luisa
1938- ... CLC 31; DAM MULT; SSC 14
See also CA 101; CANR 32; DLB 113; HW

Valera y Alcala-Galiano, Juan
1824-1905 .... TCLC 10
See also CA 106

Valery, (Ambroise) Paul (Toussaint Jules)
1871-1945 .... TCLC 4, 15;
DAM POET; PC 9
See also CA 104; 122; MTCW

Valle-Inclan, Ramon (Maria) del
1866-1936 ..... TCLC 5; DAM MULT;
HLC
See also CA 106; 153; DLB 134

Vallejo, Antonio Buero
See Buero Vallejo, Antonio

Vallejo, Cesar (Abraham)
1892-1938 .... TCLC 3, 56;
DAM MULT; HLC
See also CA 105; 153; HW

Vallette, Marguerite Eymery
See Rachilde

Valle Y Pena, Ramon del
See Valle-Inclan, Ramon (Maria) del

Van Ash, Cay 1918-............. CLC 34

Vanbrugh, Sir John
1664-1726 .... LC 21; DAM DRAM
See also DLB 80

Van Campen, Karl
See Campbell, John W(ood, Jr.)

Vance, Gerald
See Silverberg, Robert

Vance, Jack..................... CLC 35
See also Vance, John Holbrook
See also DLB 8

Vance, John Holbrook 1916-
See Queen, Ellery; Vance, Jack
See also CA 29-32R; CANR 17; MTCW

Van Den Bogarde, Derek Jules Gaspard Ulric
Niven 1921-
See Bogarde, Dirk
See also CA 77-80

Vandenburgh, Jane .... CLC 59

Vanderhaeghe, Guy 1951- .... CLC 41
See also CA 113

van der Post, Laurens (Jan)
1906-1996 .... CLC 5
See also CA 5-8R; 155; CANR 35

van de Wetering, Janwillem 1931- .. CLC 47
See also CA 49-52; CANR 4

Van Dine, S. S. .... TCLC 23
See also Wright, Willard Huntington

Van Doren, Carl (Clinton)
1885-1950 .... TCLC 18
See also CA 111

Van Doren, Mark 1894-1972..... CLC 6, 10
See also CA 1-4R; 37-40R; CANR 3;
DLB 45; MTCW

Van Druten, John (William)
1901-1957 .... TCLC 2
See also CA 104; DLB 10

Van Duyn, Mona (Jane)
1921- .... CLC 3, 7, 63; DAM POET
See also CA 9-12R; CANR 7, 38; DLB 5

Van Dyne, Edith
See Baum, L(yman) Frank

van Itallie, Jean-Claude 1936-....... CLC 3
See also CA 45-48; CAAS 2; CANR 1, 48;
DLB 7

van Ostaijen, Paul 1896-1928 ..... TCLC 33

Van Peebles, Melvin
1932-........ CLC 2, 20; DAM MULT
See also BW 2; CA 85-88; CANR 27

Vansittart, Peter 1920-............ CLC 42
See also CA 1-4R; CANR 3, 49

Van Vechten, Carl 1880-1964 ...... CLC 33
See also CA 89-92; DLB 4, 9, 51

Van Vogt, A(lfred) E(lton) 1912-..... CLC 1
See also CA 21-24R; CANR 28; DLB 8;
SATA 14

Varda, Agnes 1928- .... CLC 16
See also CA 116; 122

Wakoski, Diane
1937- . . . . CLC 2, 4, 7, 9, 11, 40;
DAM POET; PC 15
See also CA 13-16R; CAAS 1; CANR 9;
DLB 5; INT CANR-9

Wakoski-Sherbell, Diane
See Wakoski, Diane

Walcott, Derek (Alton)
1930- . . . . CLC 2, 4, 9, 14, 25, 42, 67, 76;
BLC; DAB; DAC; DAM MST, MULT,
POET; DC 7
See also BW 2; CA 89-92; CANR 26, 47;
DLB 117; DLBY 81; MTCW

Waldman, Anne 1945- . . . . CLC 7
See also CA 37-40R; CAAS 17; CANR 34;
DLB 16

Waldo, E. Hunter
See Sturgeon, Theodore (Hamilton)

Waldo, Edward Hamilton
See Sturgeon, Theodore (Hamilton)

Walker, Alice (Malsenior)
1944- . . . . CLC 5, 6, 9, 19, 27, 46, 58;
BLC; DA; DAB; DAC; DAM MST,
MULT, NOV, POET, POP; SSC 5
See also AAYA 3; BEST 89:4; BW 2;
CA 37-40R; CANR 9, 27, 49;
CDALB 1968-1988; DLB 6, 33, 143;
INT CANR-27; MTCW; SATA 31

Walker, David Harry 1911-1992. . . . CLC 14
See also CA 1-4R; 137; CANR 1; SATA 8;
SATA-Obit 71

Walker, Edward Joseph 1934-
See Walker, Ted
See also CA 21-24R; CANR 12, 28, 53

Walker, George F.
1947- . . . . CLC 44, 61; DAB; DAC;
DAM MST
See also CA 103; CANR 21, 43; DLB 60

Walker, Joseph A.
1935- . . . . CLC 19; DAM DRAM, MST
See also BW 1; CA 89-92; CANR 26;
DLB 38

Walker, Margaret (Abigail)
1915- . . . . CLC 1, 6; BLC; DAM MULT
See also BW 2; CA 73-76; CANR 26, 54;
DLB 76, 152; MTCW

Walker, Ted . . . . CLC 13
See also Walker, Edward Joseph
See also DLB 40

Wallace, David Foster 1962- . . . . CLC 50
See also CA 132

Wallace, Dexter
See Masters, Edgar Lee

Wallace, (Richard Horatio) Edgar
1875-1932 . . . . TCLC 57
See also CA 115; DLB 70

Wallace, Irving
1916-1990 . . . . . CLC 7, 13; DAM NOV,
POP
See also AITN 1; CA 1-4R; 132; CAAS 1;
CANR 1, 27; INT CANR-27; MTCW

Wallant, Edward Lewis
1926-1962 . . . . CLC 5, 10
See also CA 1-4R; CANR 22; DLB 2, 28,
143; MTCW

Walley, Byron
See Card, Orson Scott

Walpole, Horace 1717-1797. . . . . LC 2
See also DLB 39, 104

Walpole, Hugh (Seymour)
1884-1941 . . . . TCLC 5
See also CA 104; DLB 34

Walser, Martin 1927- . . . . CLC 27
See also CA 57-60; CANR 8, 46; DLB 75,
124

Walser, Robert
1878-1956 . . . . TCLC 18; SSC 20
See also CA 118; DLB 66

Walsh, Jill Paton. . . . . CLC 35
See also Paton Walsh, Gillian
See also AAYA 11; CLR 2; DLB 161;
SAAS 3

Walter, Villiam Christian
See Andersen, Hans Christian

Wambaugh, Joseph (Aloysius, Jr.)
1937- . . . . CLC 3, 18; DAM NOV, POP
See also AITN 1; BEST 89:3; CA 33-36R;
CANR 42; DLB 6; DLBY 83; MTCW

Ward, Arthur Henry Sarsfield 1883-1959
See Rohmer, Sax
See also CA 108

Ward, Douglas Turner 1930-. . . . . . . CLC 19
See also BW 1; CA 81-84; CANR 27;
DLB 7, 38

Ward, Mary Augusta
See Ward, Mrs. Humphry

Ward, Mrs. Humphry
1851-1920 . . . . TCLC 55
See also DLB 18

Ward, Peter
See Faust, Frederick (Schiller)

Warhol, Andy 1928(?)-1987. . . . . . . CLC 20
See also AAYA 12; BEST 89:4; CA 89-92;
121; CANR 34

Warner, Francis (Robert le Plastrier)
1937- . . . . CLC 14
See also CA 53-56; CANR 11

Warner, Marina 1946-. . . . . CLC 59
See also CA 65-68; CANR 21, 55

Warner, Rex (Ernest) 1905-1986. . . . CLC 45
See also CA 89-92; 119; DLB 15

Warner, Susan (Bogert)
1819-1885 . . . . NCLC 31
See also DLB 3, 42

Warner, Sylvia (Constance) Ashton
See Ashton-Warner, Sylvia (Constance)

Warner, Sylvia Townsend
1893-1978 . . . . CLC 7, 19; SSC 23
See also CA 61-64; 77-80; CANR 16;
DLB 34, 139; MTCW

Warren, Mercy Otis 1728-1814. . . NCLC 13
See also DLB 31

Warren, Robert Penn
1905-1989 . . . . CLC 1, 4, 6, 8, 10, 13, 18,
39, 53, 59; DA; DAB; DAC; DAM MST,
NOV, POET; SSC 4; WLC
See also AITN 1; CA 13-16R; 129;
CANR 10, 47; CDALB 1968-1988;
DLB 2, 48, 152; DLBY 80, 89;
INT CANR-10; MTCW; SATA 46;
SATA-Obit 63

Warshofsky, Isaac
See Singer, Isaac Bashevis

Warton, Thomas
1728-1790 . . . . LC 15; DAM POET
See also DLB 104, 109

Waruk, Kona
See Harris, (Theodore) Wilson

Warung, Price 1855-1911. . . . . TCLC 45

Warwick, Jarvis
See Garner, Hugh

Washington, Alex
See Harris, Mark

Washington, Booker T(aliaferro)
1856-1915 . . . . TCLC 10; BLC;
DAM MULT
See also BW 1; CA 114; 125; SATA 28

Washington, George 1732-1799. . . . . . LC 25
See also DLB 31

Wassermann, (Karl) Jakob
1873-1934 . . . . TCLC 6
See also CA 104; DLB 66

Wasserstein, Wendy
1950- . . . . CLC 32, 59, 90;
DAM DRAM; DC 4
See also CA 121; 129; CABS 3; CANR 53;
INT 129

Waterhouse, Keith (Spencer)
1929- . . . . CLC 47
See also CA 5-8R; CANR 38; DLB 13, 15;
MTCW

Waters, Frank (Joseph)
1902-1995 . . . . CLC 88
See also CA 5-8R; 149; CAAS 13; CANR 3,
18; DLBY 86

Waters, Roger 1944-. . . . . CLC 35

Watkins, Frances Ellen
See Harper, Frances Ellen Watkins

Watkins, Gerrold
See Malzberg, Barry N(athaniel)

Watkins, Gloria 1955(?)-
See hooks, bell
See also BW 2; CA 143

Watkins, Paul 1964-. . . . . CLC 55
See also CA 132

Watkins, Vernon Phillips
1906-1967 . . . . CLC 43
See also CA 9-10; 25-28R; CAP 1; DLB 20

Watson, Irving S.
See Mencken, H(enry) L(ouis)

Watson, John H.
See Farmer, Philip Jose

Watson, Richard F.
See Silverberg, Robert

Waugh, Auberon (Alexander) 1939-. . CLC 7
See also CA 45-48; CANR 6, 22; DLB 14

Wharton, James
See Mencken, H(enry) L(ouis)

Wharton, William (a pseudonym)
.... **CLC 18, 37**
See also CA 93-96; DLBY 80; INT 93-96

Wheatley (Peters), Phillis
1754(?)-1784 .... **LC 3; BLC; DA; DAC; DAM MST, MULT, POET; PC 3; WLC**
See also CDALB 1640-1865; DLB 31, 50

Wheelock, John Hall 1886-1978 .... **CLC 14**
See also CA 13-16R; 77-80; CANR 14; DLB 45

White, E(lwyn) B(rooks)
1899-1985 .. **CLC 10, 34, 39; DAM POP**
See also AITN 2; CA 13-16R; 116; CANR 16, 37; CLR 1, 21; DLB 11, 22; MAICYA; MTCW; SATA 2, 29; SATA-Obit 44

White, Edmund (Valentine III)
1940- .... **CLC 27; DAM POP**
See also AAYA 7; CA 45-48; CANR 3, 19, 36; MTCW

White, Patrick (Victor Martindale)
1912-1990 .. **CLC 3, 4, 5, 7, 9, 18, 65, 69**
See also CA 81-84; 132; CANR 43; MTCW

White, Phyllis Dorothy James 1920-
See James, P. D.
See also CA 21-24R; CANR 17, 43; DAM POP; MTCW

White, T(erence) H(anbury)
1906-1964 .... **CLC 30**
See also CA 73-76; CANR 37; DLB 160; JRDA; MAICYA; SATA 12

White, Terence de Vere
1912-1994 .... **CLC 49**
See also CA 49-52; 145; CANR 3

White, Walter F(rancis)
1893-1955 .... **TCLC 15**
See also White, Walter
See also BW 1; CA 115; 124; DLB 51

White, William Hale 1831-1913
See Rutherford, Mark
See also CA 121

Whitehead, E(dward) A(nthony)
1933- .... **CLC 5**
See also CA 65-68

Whitemore, Hugh (John) 1936- .... **CLC 37**
See also CA 132; INT 132

Whitman, Sarah Helen (Power)
1803-1878 .... **NCLC 19**
See also DLB 1

Whitman, Walt(er)
1819-1892 ..... **NCLC 4, 31; DA; DAB; DAC; DAM MST, POET; PC 3; WLC**
See also CDALB 1640-1865; DLB 3, 64; SATA 20

Whitney, Phyllis A(yame)
1903- .... **CLC 42; DAM POP**
See also AITN 2; BEST 90:3; CA 1-4R; CANR 3, 25, 38; JRDA; MAICYA; SATA 1, 30

Whittemore, (Edward) Reed (Jr.)
1919- .... **CLC 4**
See also CA 9-12R; CAAS 8; CANR 4; DLB 5

Whittier, John Greenleaf
1807-1892 .... **NCLC 8, 59**
See also DLB 1

Whittlebot, Hernia
See Coward, Noel (Peirce)

Wicker, Thomas Grey 1926-
See Wicker, Tom
See also CA 65-68; CANR 21, 46

Wicker, Tom .... **CLC 7**
See also Wicker, Thomas Grey

Wideman, John Edgar
1941- .... **CLC 5, 34, 36, 67; BLC; DAM MULT**
See also BW 2; CA 85-88; CANR 14, 42; DLB 33, 143

Wiebe, Rudy (Henry)
1934- .... **CLC 6, 11, 14; DAC; DAM MST**
See also CA 37-40R; CANR 42; DLB 60

Wieland, Christoph Martin
1733-1813 .... **NCLC 17**
See also DLB 97

Wiene, Robert 1881-1938 .... **TCLC 56**

Wieners, John 1934- .... **CLC 7**
See also CA 13-16R; DLB 16

Wiesel, Elie(zer)
1928- ...... **CLC 3, 5, 11, 37; DA; DAB; DAC; DAM MST, NOV**
See also AAYA 7; AITN 1; CA 5-8R; CAAS 4; CANR 8, 40; DLB 83; DLBY 87; INT CANR-8; MTCW; SATA 56

Wiggins, Marianne 1947- .... **CLC 57**
See also BEST 89:3; CA 130

Wight, James Alfred 1916-
See Herriot, James
See also CA 77-80; SATA 55; SATA-Brief 44

Wilbur, Richard (Purdy)
1921- ... **CLC 3, 6, 9, 14, 53; DA; DAB; DAC; DAM MST, POET**
See also CA 1-4R; CABS 2; CANR 2, 29; DLB 5, 169; INT CANR-29; MTCW; SATA 9

Wild, Peter 1940- .... **CLC 14**
See also CA 37-40R; DLB 5

Wilde, Oscar (Fingal O'Flahertie Wills)
1854(?)-1900 .... **TCLC 1, 8, 23, 41; DA; DAB; DAC; DAM DRAM, MST, NOV; SSC 11; WLC**
See also CA 104; 119; CDBLB 1890-1914; DLB 10, 19, 34, 57, 141, 156; SATA 24

Wilder, Billy .... **CLC 20**
See also Wilder, Samuel
See also DLB 26

Wilder, Samuel 1906-
See Wilder, Billy
See also CA 89-92

Wilder, Thornton (Niven)
1897-1975 ...... **CLC 1, 5, 6, 10, 15, 35, 82; DA; DAB; DAC; DAM DRAM, MST, NOV; DC 1; WLC**
See also AITN 2; CA 13-16R; 61-64; CANR 40; DLB 4, 7, 9; MTCW

Wilding, Michael 1942- .... **CLC 73**
See also CA 104; CANR 24, 49

Wiley, Richard 1944- .... **CLC 44**
See also CA 121; 129

Wilhelm, Kate .... **CLC 7**
See also Wilhelm, Katie Gertrude
See also AAYA 20; CAAS 5; DLB 8; INT CANR-17

Wilhelm, Katie Gertrude 1928-
See Wilhelm, Kate
See also CA 37-40R; CANR 17, 36; MTCW

Wilkins, Mary
See Freeman, Mary Eleanor Wilkins

Willard, Nancy 1936- .... **CLC 7, 37**
See also CA 89-92; CANR 10, 39; CLR 5; DLB 5, 52; MAICYA; MTCW; SATA 37, 71; SATA-Brief 30

Williams, C(harles) K(enneth)
1936- .... **CLC 33, 56; DAM POET**
See also CA 37-40R; CAAS 26; CANR 57; DLB 5

Williams, Charles
See Collier, James L(incoln)

Williams, Charles (Walter Stansby)
1886-1945 .... **TCLC 1, 11**
See also CA 104; DLB 100, 153

Williams, (George) Emlyn
1905-1987 ...... **CLC 15; DAM DRAM**
See also CA 104; 123; CANR 36; DLB 10, 77; MTCW

Williams, Hugo 1942- .... **CLC 42**
See also CA 17-20R; CANR 45; DLB 40

Williams, J. Walker
See Wodehouse, P(elham) G(renville)

Williams, John A(lfred)
1925- ... **CLC 5, 13; BLC; DAM MULT**
See also BW 2; CA 53-56; CAAS 3; CANR 6, 26, 51; DLB 2, 33; INT CANR-6

Williams, Jonathan (Chamberlain)
1929- .... **CLC 13**
See also CA 9-12R; CAAS 12; CANR 8; DLB 5

Williams, Joy 1944- .... **CLC 31**
See also CA 41-44R; CANR 22, 48

Williams, Norman 1952- .... **CLC 39**
See also CA 118

Williams, Sherley Anne
1944- ..... **CLC 89; BLC; DAM MULT, POET**
See also BW 2; CA 73-76; CANR 25; DLB 41; INT CANR-25; SATA 78

Williams, Shirley
See Williams, Sherley Anne

Williams, Tennessee
1911-1983 ..... **CLC 1, 2, 5, 7, 8, 11, 15, 19, 30, 39, 45, 71; DA; DAB; DAC; DAM DRAM, MST; DC 4; WLC**
See also AITN 1, 2; CA 5-8R; 108; CABS 3; CANR 31; CDALB 1941-1968; DLB 7; DLBD 4; DLBY 83; MTCW

Williams, Thomas (Alonzo)
1926-1990 .... **CLC 14**
See also CA 1-4R; 132; CANR 2

Williams, William C.
See Williams, William Carlos

Wouk, Herman
    1915- .. **CLC 1, 9, 38; DAM NOV, POP**
See also CA 5-8R; CANR 6, 33; DLBY 82;
INT CANR-6; MTCW

Wright, Charles (Penzel, Jr.)
    1935- .... **CLC 6, 13, 28**
See also CA 29-32R; CAAS 7; CANR 23,
36; DLB 165; DLBY 82; MTCW

Wright, Charles Stevenson
    1932- .... **CLC 49; BLC 3;**
           DAM MULT, POET
See also BW 1; CA 9-12R; CANR 26;
DLB 33

Wright, Jack R.
See Harris, Mark

Wright, James (Arlington)
    1927-1980 .... **CLC 3, 5, 10, 28;**
           DAM POET
See also AITN 2; CA 49-52; 97-100;
CANR 4, 34; DLB 5, 169; MTCW

Wright, Judith (Arandell)
    1915- .... **CLC 11, 53; PC 14**
See also CA 13-16R; CANR 31; MTCW;
SATA 14

Wright, L(aurali) R. 1939-........ **CLC 44**
See also CA 138

Wright, Richard (Nathaniel)
    1908-1960 .... **CLC 1, 3, 4, 9, 14, 21, 48,**
    74; BLC; DA; DAB; DAC; DAM MST,
    MULT, NOV; SSC 2; WLC
See also AAYA 5; BW 1; CA 108;
CDALB 1929-1941; DLB 76, 102;
DLBD 2; MTCW

Wright, Richard B(ruce) 1937-...... **CLC 6**
See also CA 85-88; DLB 53

Wright, Rick 1945-............... **CLC 35**

Wright, Rowland
See Wells, Carolyn

Wright, Stephen Caldwell 1946-.... **CLC 33**
See also BW 2

Wright, Willard Huntington 1888-1939
See Van Dine, S. S.
See also CA 115

Wright, William 1930-............ **CLC 44**
See also CA 53-56; CANR 7, 23

Wroth, LadyMary 1587-1653(?) ..... **LC 30**
See also DLB 121

Wu Ch'eng-en 1500(?)-1582(?)........ **LC 7**

Wu Ching-tzu 1701-1754 .... **LC 2**

Wurlitzer, Rudolph 1938(?)- ... **CLC 2, 4, 15**
See also CA 85-88; DLB 173

Wycherley, William
    1641-1715 ..... **LC 8, 21; DAM DRAM**
See also CDBLB 1660-1789; DLB 80

Wylie, Elinor (Morton Hoyt)
    1885-1928 .... **TCLC 8**
See also CA 105; DLB 9, 45

Wylie, Philip (Gordon) 1902-1971... **CLC 43**
See also CA 21-22; 33-36R; CAP 2; DLB 9

Wyndham, John................... **CLC 19**
See also Harris, John (Wyndham Parkes
Lucas) Beynon

Wyss, Johann David Von
    1743-1818 .... **NCLC 10**
See also JRDA; MAICYA; SATA 29;
SATA-Brief 27

Xenophon
    c. 430B.C.-c. 354B.C........ **CMLC 17**
See also DLB 176

Yakumo Koizumi
See Hearn, (Patricio) Lafcadio (Tessima
Carlos)

Yanez, Jose Donoso
See Donoso (Yanez), Jose

Yanovsky, Basile S.
See Yanovsky, V(assily) S(emenovich)

Yanovsky, V(assily) S(emenovich)
    1906-1989 .... **CLC 2, 18**
See also CA 97-100; 129

Yates, Richard 1926-1992 ..... **CLC 7, 8, 23**
See also CA 5-8R; 139; CANR 10, 43;
DLB 2; DLBY 81, 92; INT CANR-10

Yeats, W. B.
See Yeats, William Butler

Yeats, William Butler
    1865-1939 ..... **TCLC 1, 11, 18, 31; DA;**
    DAB; DAC; DAM DRAM, MST,
    POET; WLC
See also CA 104; 127; CANR 45;
CDBLB 1890-1914; DLB 10, 19, 98, 156;
MTCW

Yehoshua, A(braham) B.
    1936- .... **CLC 13, 31**
See also CA 33-36R; CANR 43

Yep, Laurence Michael 1948-...... **CLC 35**
See also AAYA 5; CA 49-52; CANR 1, 46;
CLR 3, 17; DLB 52; JRDA; MAICYA;
SATA 7, 69

Yerby, Frank G(arvin)
    1916-1991 .... **CLC 1, 7, 22; BLC;**
    DAM MULT
See also BW 1; CA 9-12R; 136; CANR 16,
52; DLB 76; INT CANR-16; MTCW

Yesenin, Sergei Alexandrovich
See Esenin, Sergei (Alexandrovich)

Yevtushenko, Yevgeny (Alexandrovich)
    1933- .... **CLC 1, 3, 13, 26, 51;**
    DAM POET
See also CA 81-84; CANR 33, 54; MTCW

Yezierska, Anzia 1885(?)-1970 ..... **CLC 46**
See also CA 126; 89-92; DLB 28; MTCW

Yglesias, Helen 1915-........... **CLC 7, 22**
See also CA 37-40R; CAAS 20; CANR 15;
INT CANR-15; MTCW

Yokomitsu Riichi 1898-1947 ...... **TCLC 47**

Yonge, Charlotte (Mary)
    1823-1901 .... **TCLC 48**
See also CA 109; DLB 18, 163; SATA 17

York, Jeremy
See Creasey, John

York, Simon
See Heinlein, Robert A(nson)

Yorke, Henry Vincent 1905-1974 ... **CLC 13**
See also Green, Henry
See also CA 85-88; 49-52

Yosano Akiko 1878-1942 .. **TCLC 59; PC 11**

Yoshimoto, Banana .... **CLC 84**
See also Yoshimoto, Mahoko

Yoshimoto, Mahoko 1964-
See Yoshimoto, Banana
See also CA 144

Young, Al(bert James)
    1939- ..... **CLC 19; BLC; DAM MULT**
See also BW 2; CA 29-32R; CANR 26;
DLB 33

Young, Andrew (John) 1885-1971.... **CLC 5**
See also CA 5-8R; CANR 7, 29

Young, Collier
See Bloch, Robert (Albert)

Young, Edward 1683-1765.......... **LC 3**
See also DLB 95

Young, Marguerite (Vivian)
    1909-1995 .... **CLC 82**
See also CA 13-16; 150; CAP 1

Young, Neil 1945-............... **CLC 17**
See also CA 110

Young Bear, Ray A.
    1950- .... **CLC 94; DAM MULT**
See also CA 146; DLB 175; NNAL

Yourcenar, Marguerite
    1903-1987 .... **CLC 19, 38, 50, 87;**
    DAM NOV
See also CA 69-72; CANR 23; DLB 72;
DLBY 88; MTCW

Yurick, Sol 1925-................ **CLC 6**
See also CA 13-16R; CANR 25

Zabolotskii, Nikolai Alekseevich
    1903-1958 .... **TCLC 52**
See also CA 116

Zamiatin, Yevgenii
See Zamyatin, Evgeny Ivanovich

Zamora, Bernice (B. Ortiz)
    1938- ..... **CLC 89; DAM MULT; HLC**
See also CA 151; DLB 82; HW

Zamyatin, Evgeny Ivanovich
    1884-1937 .... **TCLC 8, 37**
See also CA 105

Zangwill, Israel 1864-1926....... **TCLC 16**
See also CA 109; DLB 10, 135

Zappa, Francis Vincent, Jr. 1940-1993
See Zappa, Frank
See also CA 108; 143; CANR 57

Zappa, Frank.................... **CLC 17**
See also Zappa, Francis Vincent, Jr.

Zaturenska, Marya 1902-1982.... **CLC 6, 11**
See also CA 13-16R; 105; CANR 22

Zeami 1363-1443................... **DC 7**

Zelazny, Roger (Joseph)
    1937-1995 .... **CLC 21**
See also AAYA 7; CA 21-24R; 148;
CANR 26; DLB 8; MTCW; SATA 57;
SATA-Brief 39

Zhdanov, Andrei A(lexandrovich)
    1896-1948 .... **TCLC 18**
See also CA 117

Zhukovsky, Vasily 1783-1852 .... **NCLC 35**

Ziegenhagen, Eric .... **CLC 55**

Zimmer, Jill Schary
See Robinson, Jill

Zimmerman, Robert
  See Dylan, Bob

Zindel, Paul
      1936- ..... **CLC 6, 26; DA; DAB; DAC;
            DAM DRAM, MST, NOV; DC 5**
  See also AAYA 2; CA 73-76; CANR 31;
    CLR 3, 45; DLB 7, 52; JRDA; MAICYA;
    MTCW; SATA 16, 58

Zinov'Ev, A. A.
  See Zinoviev, Alexander (Aleksandrovich)

Zinoviev, Alexander (Aleksandrovich)
      1922- .... **CLC 19**
  See also CA 116; 133; CAAS 10

Zoilus
  See Lovecraft, H(oward) P(hillips)

Zola, Emile (Edouard Charles Antoine)
      1840-1902 ...... **TCLC 1, 6, 21, 41; DA;
        DAB; DAC; DAM MST, NOV; WLC**
  See also CA 104; 138; DLB 123

Zoline, Pamela   1941- .... **CLC 62**

Zorrilla y Moral, Jose   1817-1893.. **NCLC 6**

Zoshchenko, Mikhail (Mikhailovich)
      1895-1958 .... **TCLC 15; SSC 15**
  See also CA 115

Zuckmayer, Carl   1896-1977....... **CLC 18**
  See also CA 69-72; DLB 56, 124

Zuk, Georges
  See Skelton, Robin

Zukofsky, Louis
      1904-1978 .... **CLC 1, 2, 4, 7, 11, 18;
               DAM POET; PC 11**
  See also CA 9-12R; 77-80; CANR 39;
    DLB 5, 165; MTCW

Zweig, Paul   1935-1984........ **CLC 34, 42**
  See also CA 85-88; 113

Zweig, Stefan   1881-1942 .... **TCLC 17**
  See also CA 112; DLB 81, 118

Zwingli, Huldreich   1484-1531....... **LC 37**

Literary Criticism Series
Cumulative Topic Index

This index lists all topic entries in Gale's *Classical and Medieval Literature Criticism, Contemporary Literary Criticism, Literature Criticism from 1400 to 1800, Nineteenth-Century Literature Criticism,* and *Twentieth-Century Literary Criticism.*

Age of Johnson LC 15: 1-87
   Johnson's London, 3-15
   aesthetics of neoclassicism, 15-36
   "age of prose and reason," 36-45
   clubmen and bluestockings, 45-56
   printing technology, 56-62
   periodicals: "a map of busy life," 62-74
   transition, 74-86

AIDS in Literature CLC 81: 365-416

Alcohol and Literature TCLC 70: 1-58
   overview, 2-8
   fiction, 8-48
   poetry and drama, 48-58

American Abolitionism NCLC 44: 1-73
   overviews, 2-26
   abolitionist ideals, 26-46
   the literature of abolitionism, 46-72

American Black Humor Fiction TCLC 54: 1-85
   characteristics of black humor, 2-13
   origins and development, 13-38
   black humor distinguished from related literary trends, 38-60
   black humor and society, 60-75
   black humor reconsidered, 75-83

American Civil War in Literature NCLC 32: 1-109
   overviews, 2-20
   regional perspectives, 20-54
   fiction popular during the war, 54-79
   the historical novel, 79-108

American Frontier in Literature NCLC 28: 1-103
   definitions, 2-12
   development, 12-17
   nonfiction writing about the frontier, 17-30
   frontier fiction, 30-45
   frontier protagonists, 45-66
   portrayals of Native Americans, 66-86
   feminist readings, 86-98
   twentieth-century reaction against frontier literature, 98-100

American Humor Writing NCLC 52: 1-59
   overviews, 2-12
   the Old Southwest, 12-42
   broader impacts, 42-5
   women humorists, 45-58

American Popular Song, Golden Age of TCLC 42: 1-49
   background and major figures, 2-34
   the lyrics of popular songs, 34-47

American Proletarian Literature TCLC 54: 86-175
   overviews, 87-95
   American proletarian literature and the American Communist Party, 95-111
   ideology and literary merit, 111-7
   novels, 117-36
   Gastonia, 136-48
   drama, 148-54
   journalism, 154-9
   proletarian literature in the United States, 159-74

American Romanticism NCLC 44: 74-138
   overviews, 74-84
   sociopolitical influences, 84-104
   Romanticism and the American frontier, 104-15
   thematic concerns, 115-37

American Western Literature TCLC 46: 1-100
   definition and development of American Western literature, 2-7
   characteristics of the Western novel, 8-23
   Westerns as history and fiction, 23-34
   critical reception of American Western literature, 34-41
   the Western hero, 41-73
   women in Western fiction, 73-91
   later Western fiction, 91-9

Art and Literature TCLC 54: 176-248
   overviews, 176-93
   definitions, 193-219
   influence of visual arts on literature, 219-31
   spatial form in literature, 231-47

Arthurian Literature CMLC 10: 1-127
   historical context and literary beginnings, 2-27
   development of the legend through Malory, 27-64
   development of the legend from Malory to the Victorian Age, 65-81
   themes and motifs, 81-95
   principal characters, 95-125

Arthurian Revival NCLC 36: 1-77
   overviews, 2-12
   Tennyson and his influence, 12-43
   other leading figures, 43-73
   the Arthurian legend in the visual arts, 73-6

Australian Literature TCLC 50: 1-94
   origins and development, 2-21
   characteristics of Australian literature, 21-33
   historical and critical perspectives, 33-41
   poetry, 41-58
   fiction, 58-76
   drama, 76-82
   Aboriginal literature, 82-91

Topic Index

Topic Index

Topic Index

Cumulative Nationality Index

Kazantzakis, Nikos **2, 5, 33**
Palamas, Kostes **5**
Papadiamantis, Alexandros **29**
Sikelianos, Angelos **39**

HAITIAN
Roumain, Jacques (Jean Baptiste) **19**

HUNGARIAN
Ady, Endre **11**
Babits, Mihaly **14**
Csath, Geza **13**
Herzl, Theodor **36**
Horvath, Oedoen von **45**
Jozsef, Attila **22**
Karinthy, Frigyes **47**
Mikszath, Kalman **31**
Molnar, Ferenc **20**
Moricz, Zsigmond **33**
Radnoti, Miklos **16**

ICELANDIC
Sigurjonsson, Johann **27**

INDIAN
Aurobindo, Sri **63**
Chatterji, Saratchandra **13**
Gandhi, Mohandas Karamchand **59**
Iqbal, Muhammad **28**
Premchand **21**
Tagore, Rabindranath **3, 53**

INDONESIAN
Anwar, Chairil **22**

IRANIAN
Hedayat, Sadeq **21**

IRISH
Cary, (Arthur) Joyce (Lunel) **1, 29**
Dunsany, Lord **2, 59**
Gogarty, Oliver St. John **15**
Gregory, Isabella Augusta (Persse) **1**
Harris, Frank **24**
Joyce, James (Augustine Aloysius) **3, 8, 16, 35, 52**
Ledwidge, Francis **23**
Martin, Violet Florence **51**
Moore, George Augustus **7**
O'Grady, Standish (James) **5**
Riddell, J. H. **40**
Shaw, Bernard **45**
Shaw, George Bernard **3, 9, 21**
Somerville, Edith **51**
Stephens, James **4**
Stoker, Bram **8**
Synge, (Edmund) J(ohn) M(illington) **6, 37**
Tynan, Katharine **3**
Wilde, Oscar (Fingal O'Flahertie Wills) **1, 8, 23, 41**
Yeats, William Butler **1, 11, 18, 31**

ITALIAN
Alvaro, Corrado **60**
Betti, Ugo **5**
Brancati, Vitaliano **12**
Campana, Dino **20**
Carducci, Giosue **32**
Croce, Benedetto **37**
D'Annunzio, Gabriele **6, 40**
Deledda, Grazia (Cosima) **23**
Giacosa, Giuseppe **7**

Lampedusa, Giuseppe (Tomasi) di **13**
Malaparte, Curzio **52**
Marinetti, Filippo Tommaso **10**
Papini, Giovanni **22**
Pareto, Vilfredo **69**
Pascoli, Giovanni **45**
Pavese, Cesare **3**
Pirandello, Luigi **4, 29**
Saba, Umberto **33**
Svevo, Italo **2, 35**
Tozzi, Federigo **31**
Verga, Giovanni (Carmelo) **3**

JAMAICAN
De Lisser, H(erbert) G(eorge) **12**
Garvey, Marcus (Moziah Jr.) **41**
Mais, Roger **8**
McKay, Claude **7, 41**
Redcam, Tom **25**

JAPANESE
Akutagawa, Ryunosuke **16**
Dazai, Osamu **11**
Futabatei, Shimei **44**
Hagiwara Sakutaro **60**
Hayashi Fumiko **27**
Ishikawa, Takuboku **15**
Masaoka Shiki **18**
Miyamoto, Yuriko **37**
Mori Ogai **14**
Nagai Kafu **51**
Natsume, Soseki **2, 10**
Rohan, Koda **22**
Shimazaki Toson **5**
Yokomitsu Riichi **47**
Yosano Akiko **59**

LATVIAN
Rainis, Janis **29**

LEBANESE
Gibran, Kahlil **1, 9**

LESOTHAN
Mofolo, Thomas (Mokopu) **22**

LITHUANIAN
Kreve (Mickevicius), Vincas **27**

MEXICAN
Azuela, Mariano **3**
Gamboa, Federico **36**
Nervo, (Jose) Amado (Ruiz de) **11**
Reyes, Alfonso **33**
Romero, Jose Ruben **14**

NEPALI
Devkota, Laxmiprasad **23**

NEW ZEALANDER
Mander, (Mary) Jane **31**
Mansfield, Katherine **2, 8, 39**

NICARAGUAN
Dario, Ruben **4**

NORWEGIAN
Bjornson, Bjornstjerne (Martinius) **7, 37**
Bojer, Johan **64**
Grieg, (Johan) Nordahl (Brun) **10**
Hamsun, Knut **2, 14, 49**
Ibsen, Henrik (Johan) **2, 8, 16, 37, 52**

Kielland, Alexander Lange **5**
Lie, Jonas (Lauritz Idemil) **5**
Obstfelder, Sigbjoern **23**
Skram, Amalie (Bertha) **25**
Undset, Sigrid **3**

PAKISTANI
Iqbal, Muhammad **28**

PERUVIAN
Palma, Ricardo **29**
Vallejo, Cesar (Abraham) **3, 56**

POLISH
Asch, Sholem **3**
Borowski, Tadeusz **9**
Conrad, Joseph **1, 6, 13, 25, 43, 57**
Peretz, Isaac Loeb **16**
Prus, Boleslaw **48**
Przybyszewski, Stanislaw **36**
Reymont, Wladyslaw (Stanislaw) **5**
Schulz, Bruno **5, 51**
Sienkiewicz, Henryk (Adam Alexander Pius) **3**
Singer, Israel Joshua **33**
Witkiewicz, Stanislaw Ignacy **8**

PORTUGUESE
Pessoa, Fernando (Antonio Nogueira) **27**

PUERTO RICAN
Hostos (y Bonilla), Eugenio Maria de **24**

ROMANIAN
Bacovia, George **24**
Rebreanu, Liviu **28**

RUSSIAN
Aldanov, Mark (Alexandrovich) **23**
Andreyev, Leonid (Nikolaevich) **3**
Annensky, Innokenty (Fyodorovich) **14**
Artsybashev, Mikhail (Petrovich) **31**
Babel, Isaak (Emmanuilovich) **2, 13**
Bagritsky, Eduard **60**
Balmont, Konstantin (Dmitriyevich) **11**
Bely, Andrey **7**
Berdyaev, Nikolai (Aleksandrovich) **67**
Blok, Alexander (Alexandrovich) **5**
Bryusov, Valery Yakovlevich **10**
Bulgakov, Mikhail (Afanas'evich) **2, 16**
Bulgya, Alexander Alexandrovich **53**
Bunin, Ivan Alexeyevich **6**
Chekhov, Anton (Pavlovich) **3, 10, 31, 55**
Der Nister **56**
Eisenstein, Sergei (Mikhailovich) **57**
Esenin, Sergei (Alexandrovich) **4**
Fadeyev, Alexander **53**
Gladkov, Fyodor (Vasilyevich) **27**
Gorky, Maxim **8**
Gumilev, Nikolai Stephanovich **60**
Guro, Elena **56**
Hippius, Zinaida **9**
Ilf, Ilya **21**
Ivanov, Vyacheslav Ivanovich **33**
Khlebnikov, Velimir **20**
Khodasevich, Vladislav (Felitsianovich) **15**
Korolenko, Vladimir Galaktionovich **22**
Kropotkin, Peter (Aleksieevich) **36**
Kuprin, Aleksandr Ivanovich **5**
Kuzmin, Mikhail **40**
Lenin, V. I. **67**
Mandelstam, Osip (Emilievich) **2, 6**

Nationality Index

ISBN 0-7876-1170-0

90000

9 780787 611705